6/99

Bestseller Index

For J.E. Strange,
who gave me the opportunity
to turn a writing hobby
into a journalism career.
Twice.

Bestseller Index

*All Books, by Author, on
the Lists of Publishers Weekly
and The New York Times
Through 1990*

KEITH L. JUSTICE

McFarland & Company, Inc., Publishers
Jefferson, North Carolina, and London

The author gratefully acknowledges the permission granted by the R.R. Bowker Company for the use of data from their various bestseller lists apearing in *Publishers Weekly*; © copyright R.R. Bowker Company, each year 1919 through 1990. All rights reserved.

The author also gratefully acknowledges the permission granted by the New York Times Company for the use of data from their several bestseller lists appearing in *The New York Times*; © copyright 1935, 1936, 1937, 1938, 1939, 1940, 1941, 1943, 1944, 1945, 1946, 1947, 1948, 1949, 1950, 1951, 1952, 1953, 1954, 1955, 1956, 1957, 1958, 1959, 1960, 1961, 1962, 1963, 1964, 1965, 1966, 1967, 1968, 1969, 1970, 1971, 1972, 1973, 1974, 1975, 1976, 1977, 1978, 1979, 1980, 1981, 1982, 1983, 1984, 1985, 1986, 1987, 1988, 1989, 1990 The New York Times Company. All rights reserved.

Publisher's Note: Every reasonable step has been taken, in the ten years of developing this reference book, to insure the accuracy of transcribed, corrected, revised, and augmented author, title, and list-appearance data and in the proofreading of same. Having exercised their best efforts, author and publisher are not responsible for the consequences of any error that may remain.

British Library Cataloguing-in-Publication data are available

Library of Congress Cataloguing-in-Publication Data

Justice, Keith L.
    Bestseller index : all books, by author, on the lists of Publishers weekly and the New York times through 1990 / Keith Justice.
      p. cm.
    Includes index.
    ISBN 0-7864-0422-1 (library binding : 50# alkaline paper) ∞
    1. Best sellers—United States—Bibliography. I. Title.
Z1033.B3J87   1998
016.028'9'0973—dc21   97-31639
                                            CIP

Manufactured in the United States of America

McFarland & Company, Inc., Publishers
Box 611, Jefferson, North Carolina 28640

CONTENTS

PREFACE

Recent American popular culture has thrived on lists of every description: the ten best-dressed women, the ten sexiest male movie stars, the best states or cities to live in, the best vacation destinations, the top-grossing movies of the past week, the 40 most popular songs. The love of lists has become so epidemic that now there are books devoted exclusively to lists—the books by Wallace and Wallechinsky, for example, or David Letterman's book of various (humorous) lists.

Lists, however, can be dangerous. By design, lists place items in a certain order, occasionally implying—and often declaring outright—that some things are better than others by virtue of their positions on a list. This attribute of lists is not a problem when the criteria for inclusion are relatively objective or when the intended audience is likely to be well aware of the limitations of lists. After all, if an Elvis Presley record or a Beatles song stayed on the top of the pop charts longer than any other record, that fact speaks for itself.

This index of the *New York Times Book Review* and *Publishers Weekly* bestseller lists was intended to present information that speaks for itself. If a par-

ticular author had 25 books on the charts during his or her writing career, that is a fact. If a particular book spent 500 weeks on the bestseller lists, that is a fact. A fact can be proved, but an interpretation of that fact's significance may be open to question. To determine the validity of an interpretation, it is necessary to understand how and why the factual information was gathered and documented.

This book draws together all the *New York Times Book Review* and *Publishers Weekly* bestseller lists through 1990, presenting researchers with the information necessary to reconstruct the general chart activity of each book. Obtaining information about books and their chart activity was the basic motivation of the compiler, who about 20 years ago became interested in the fact that most everything else, from movies to popular songs, is regularly rated according to how much money each has grossed at the box office or how many weeks each has spent on the pop charts. Books, on the other hand, have been largely neglected in this arena.

The limited information available on the performance of bestselling books tends to focus on the number of copies

printed. Such information is an important indicator of the popularity of books
that have sold in massive numbers in
the past few decades of publishing. But
copies-printed figures leave some aspects
of popular culture obscured. It may be
of interest to some researchers, for
example, that one of the most popular
science fiction novels of the twentieth
century, *Stranger in a Strange Land* by
Robert A. Heinlein, has gone through
more than 50 printings but has not
spent a single week on any of the bestseller lists. (In the last years of his
career, Heinlein did place six novels on
the lists, although these are not considered to be his "best" novels.) A copies-
printed index cannot provide the access
to information about books and chart
appearances provided by a bestseller list
index.

The goal of the *Bestseller Index* was
to provide documented information
reliable and comprehensive enough for
research purposes, but interesting enough
that a curious reader might browse
through the index just to find out interesting tidbits about a favorite author's
books. The index itself is not intended
to provide any judgments on the relative merits of a particular book. A fact,
per se, is neutral, assuming positive or
negative value only when it is used to
draw a conclusion or make a comparison.

Statistics routinely are used to cloud
and confuse issues. A minuscule and
meaningless difference measured in
hundredths or thousandths of a unit
may separate two figures, but because
one number is larger or smaller—by
however slim a margin—that difference
may translate into a list in which the
numbers are ranked. One of the numbers then becomes "bigger" (i.e., "better") or "smaller" (i.e., "worse") than the
other, depending on the ranking and
the purpose of the list.

In the same way, the fact that book
A spent 136 weeks on the bestseller lists
while book B spent 135 weeks may be
interesting, but the information is relative. The researcher (or browser, as the
case may be) should keep the overall
value of lists in perspective. The bestseller lists are not indicators of absolute
literary value. On the one hand, literary figures such as William Faulkner
and Ernest Hemingway have placed
numerous volumes on the lists; on the
other hand, many books with no re-
deeming literary or social value, such as
collections of pornographic jokes, have
spent weeks, and even months, as listed
bestsellers.

The bestseller lists are simply one
indicator of public opinion and popular
tastes during a given period. Popular
tastes generally cannot indicate what is
best about American publishing, culture, society and civilization—but neither do they always indicate what is
worst. It may be interesting to note that
between 1919 and 1990, five books by
F. Scott Fitzgerald reached the American
bestseller lists, and that during the same
71-year period, 27 volumes of Garfield
cartoons appeared on the charts. These
figures suggest that Garfield cartoon
books are far more popular than works
by F. Scott Fitzgerald and regularly out-
sell works by that esteemed author, but
such lopsided representation on the
bestseller lists does not mean Garfield
cartoons have more "value" than works
by Fitzgerald. With chart statistics, less
is not more, and more is not less. No
one is going to reach any useful conclusions about the respective qualities
of Fitzgerald and Garfield simply on
the basis of bestseller list performance.

Both Fitzgerald and Garfield (and
Hemingway and *Star Trek*, and Faulkner and Danielle Steel, and so forth)
unquestionably have had an impact on
popular culture. That impact can be

evaluated in many ways. But the number of weeks a particular book spent on the bestseller lists is only one measure of social or commercial significance, and chart longevity bears little or no relationship to overall social or commercial value.

Paperback cover blurbs often tout the number of weeks a book spent on the bestseller lists in previous editions. Other books may be advertised as bestsellers simply on the basis of a single week's appearance on one list. Obviously, if a book spends only one week on a bestseller list it can be designated a "bestseller." But until now there has been no simple means of checking a book's chart performance on the *New York Times Book Review* and *Publishers Weekly* bestseller lists to find out just what the numbers are. Exactly what they mean must remain for the reader to interpret.

In a past edition of *The Guinness Book of World Records* it is stated as a matter of record that as of January 10, 1985, *A Light in the Attic* by Shel Silverstein had appeared on the *New York Times Book Review* bestseller list for 112 weeks and therefore (supposedly) had spent more weeks on the list than any other book. This is patently wrong, and was as untrue in 1985 as it is now. On October 17, 1982, *The Joy of Sex* by Alex Comfort accumulated its 437th week on the *New York Times Book Review* list.

The 1997 edition of *Guinness* lists *The Road Less Traveled* by M. Scott Peck as the current titleholder for greatest number of weeks on the *New York Times Book Review* bestsellers list, with 598 weeks as of 4/14/95. This is probably correct, although complete information has been tabulated only to 1990. It may be another two to three years before the *Road Less Traveled* information can be confirmed.

It is hoped that this book will fill a niche, providing information that may be of interest to those who would like to find out how many books a particular author placed or how many weeks a favorite book spent on the bestseller lists. Remember, this volume is not intended to be an arbiter of cultural or literary values. If a book titled *The Destruction of the Earth's Ecology* spends only one week on the charts and another titled *Shanna, Nude Priestess of the Brain-Eating Warrior Women of Planet Xantoros* spends 30, these chart performances are simply facts. If conclusions are to be drawn from those facts, readers will need to do that for themselves—and they also must take responsibility for the value of those conclusions.

ACKNOWLEDGMENTS

A project like this involves contributions by more people than I can remember, much less list here. The idea for this index germinated over 20 years ago and then was left to lie more or less dormant for about 12 years. Once I decided to begin the index in earnest, I grossly underestimated the time it would take to finish the project—underestimated not just once, but several times. In the beginning I believed the compilation might be accomplished in a year or two, but I soon—and often—had ample opportunity to see just how erroneous one's estimates can be. I worked on the index in my "spare time," writing the information by hand on file cards in the evenings. At the end of five years, I had a couple of dozen boxes filled with file cards to show for my efforts, and finally realized it would take more than a work-on-it-when-I-can commitment to the index to move it out of the amorphous phase and shape it into something vaguely resembling a useful reference. So I bought a computer and tried to take the project a bit more seriously.

Because of the long-term nature of the project, it is my wife, Virginia, who has put up with it the longest. My children have a passing familiarity with the index, but little more; they are grown up, married, and have careers and children of their own now. Virginia, on the other hand, has been with the project every step of the way. She has accompanied me to libraries to do research; she has spent countless hours pushing coins into photocopying machines to help me obtain copies of every bestseller list indexed herein; and she has never once complained about the time, money, travel, and sheer effort that have been poured into the project. To her go the greatest thanks for the assistance and the patience she generously lavished upon me and the index.

Library staffs who have been very helpful to us include those of the Meridian Community College Library, the Meridian Public Library and the library at the University of Alabama at Tuscaloosa. One person who deserves special thanks is Dr. Scott R. Johnson at the Meridian Community College Library. Dr. Johnson seemed to take a special interest in the project while I was in the final stages, trying to reconcile stubbornly errant bits of information. There were books for which no publisher was specified; authors identified by last name for whom I had no first names; and multitudes of incorrect and suspect items that required correction or verification in some way. When this list had been whittled down to several hundred items, I carried it to various libraries in my efforts to locate the information, and occasionally ran into the problem of requiring access to "professional resources" to find what I needed. To my surprise and dismay, that access was often denied.

Then, just when it looked as if some of the very resources I needed to finish the book were going to be unavailable to me, Dr. Johnson requested a copy of my final-correction printout and used the professional resources at his disposal to complete the identifications, find the names, fill in the blanks and otherwise provide some of the information I needed. There is no adequate means to thank him for this unexpected assistance. At the very least, his efforts trimmed weeks, perhaps months, from the amount of time required to finish the project. My thanks for the time and effort Dr. Johnson expended to assist me.

When a research project is accomplished over a period of years, the compiler's interest in it will ebb and flow somewhat. When a project turns out to be much bigger, more difficult and far more time-consuming than the brash, overconfident researcher initially realized, inevitably there will be times when compiling a large volume of very specialized information can become a test of wills. Though the compiler may have believed, at first, that he was the directed force, the running water that would shape the stubborn stone of the project to his will, there were times when he was forced to wonder if things were the other way around. When such uncertainty arises, a project can stall, and the frustration quotient increases. At these times, one of the best ways to maintain interest in the project is for someone else to demonstrate a genuine interest in it. My friend Fred Brewer and I spent many weekends working together at the wire desk of the daily newspaper where we were employed, and we often used general discussions of my bestseller index as a springboard to lengthy conversations about books and authors. Now that we both have moved on and no longer work together, I miss those conversations. Thanks, Fred.

Whenever it is necessary for someone to process a large amount of information, inevitably there will be mistakes. I have done my best to minimize these, but have no doubt that some errors still are to be found stubbornly camouflaged among the facts. Although this volume could not have been issued without the assistance of many who diverted streams, rivulets or even torrents of information in my direction, it was my responsibility to separate the facts from the mistakes, preserving the former and discarding the latter. If I have failed to do this properly, I apologize. There is nothing so useless as a shopping list of excuses for failure, so I offer none. Instead—and despite the fact that as intellectual currency, a pound of promises has about as much purchasing power as sixteen ounces of excuses—I simply state if this volume contains errors that are brought to my attention, they will be corrected in any future editions.

INTRODUCTION

Bestseller lists, in one form or another, have been published throughout the twentieth century, and some few lists were compiled on a regular basis even in the nineteenth century. When the criteria for this compilation were being developed, the decision was made to limit the index to two lists in the twentieth century. This was done to provide representative information for the modern publishing age and to limit the amount of time required to assemble the index. The *New York Times Book Review* and *Publishers Weekly* lists were selected because they are two of the most popular, widely disseminated, readily available and authoritative lists currently in publication. The *NYTBR* list, especially, is used in the marketplace as a rough indicator of a book's commercial appeal. The number of weeks a particular book spent on the *NYTBR* lists often is used in advertisements for books and on the jacket copy of reprinted editions of popular books.

Indexing for *PW* begins in 1919, the year in which the magazine published its first list based on the reports of booksellers. The *New York Times* list is indexed from 1935, when it first appeared as a monthly feature. (For more about how these lists began and how they have changed over the years, see "A Brief History of the Bestseller Lists," beginning on page 4.)

The year 1990 was chosen as the closing date; in early 1991, the compiler finally acquired the last photocopies of all the bestseller lists up through the end of the previous year. Once the week-by-week activity for each title was in the process of being tabulated on 5 × 8 file cards, attempting to admit additional years into the index would have kept the project in a state of constant turmoil. Few libraries are able to keep up-to-the-minute on their microfilm purchases; the periodicals are sometimes months behind in their wait for a trip to the bindery; and loose collections of periodicals often are missing some individual numbers. Once the raw data (photocopies) are obtained, then the processing of the information must follow. If 1991 had been added, it could have taken until the end of 1992 to do so. Then the year 1992 would be over, so the search for all the 1992 materials could begin, but that might not be completed until the end of 1993, and so on. As with any index of something that is ongoing, an arbitrary stopping point must be desig-

1

nated or the project will never end. For this index, the collection of raw information was called to a halt after the lists for 1990 were acquired. The time since 1990 has been used to process and format the information, mostly by hand. Computerized processing of the massive amount of raw data would have required customized programming. At the very end, after the chart data had been tabulated, a computer was used to store and print out the information. As far as the compiler of this volume is aware, there still is no comprehensive non-customized programming that will allow machine processing of the data.

During the early years of the modern bestseller lists, often there was no month-to-month or week-to-week consistency in the titles of the charts, the number of books listed on the charts, or even the appearance of the charts. Occasionally a bestseller list would disappear altogether for one month, only to reappear without explanation the next. But as publishing moved into the 1950s, these lapses and arbitrary changes became less frequent until they disappeared altogether. The lists were shaped into standard formats and became stable features that could be counted on to appear in each issue of their respective publications. Adjustments were sometimes made to accommodate changes in the publishing world—such as the addition of how-to and reference, paperback, and audio book categories—but these adjustments were not capricious.

Because these lists were sometimes published weekly and sometimes monthly, the compiler established one rule for the sake of consistency: A book was given credit for four weeks each time it appeared on a monthly chart. If a book spent six months on the chart, that was converted to 24 weeks. Such conversions presented a slight problem when a book spent many months on a monthly list, since figuring four weeks per month gives only 48 weeks for a year. It might have been possible to determine the exact number of weeks each individual book spent on the charts when the bestseller lists were published monthly, but this would have involved comparing chart publication dates, the dates a book appeared on the lists, eternal calendars, and possibly several other items. That would have taken an additional, indeterminate, but undoubtedly lengthy period of time, and would not have been feasible for a part-time compiler trying to finish this index within the scope of one lifetime.

In any case, even if all the extra work had been done, the result would not have differed materially from what appears in this volume. The books that have exhibited truly phenomenal chart activity have done so in the years of weekly list publication, and the loss of one week's credit for appearance on monthly bestseller lists would not have changed any rankings that might be developed from the chart information in this index. For example, the book that has spent the most weeks on the juvenile lists is *Charlotte's Web* by E.B. White; the book that has spent the most weeks on the adult nonfiction lists is *The Joy of Sex* by Alex Comfort. The beloved *Charlotte's Web* spent 489 weeks on the *NYTBR* and *PW* bestseller lists, while *Joy of Sex* spent 753 weeks on the two lists. An error of one or two weeks— or 10 or 20, or even 100 weeks—in figuring the totals for any books still would not have placed any others in close contention for the record number of weeks on the charts.

Every book that appeared on the charts has been listed, including many titles that appeared for a single week on the lower fringes of the lists and then were lost in the horde of new titles forever leap-frogging over each other on their way up. All chart appearances were separated—that is, if a chart was called "nonfiction" one week and "general" the next, those listings are credited separately in a book's entry. In some few cases, books (reports by commissions, for example) were issued by more than one publisher, and in some cases, book series (especially juvenile book series) were listed as such rather than as individual titles. When information about these unusual circumstances was supplied on the list, that information is included in the index entry. The name of the publisher of each book is also included.

The researcher, or even the casual browser, should keep in mind that an index examining the bestseller lists represents an opportunity to look back over 71 years of publishing history. When the lists began, no thought was given to making things precise, consistent, and therefore easy to interpret seven decades later. Many aspects of the *PW* and *NYTBR* bestseller lists can be puzzling or confusing. A book may appear on the charts of one publication, for example, but not the other. This circumstance can occur for several reasons. For example, the *NYTBR* added a paperback list in 1965, but *PW* had no such list until 1976; so for more than a decade, a paperback book listed in the *NYTBR* had no place for a listing in *PW*. Even today, the list categories do not always match up; for example, the *NYTBR* "Advice, How-to and Miscellaneous" list does not have a direct counterpart

in *PW*. Also, the reporting methods may differ at different times in the publications' histories.

There is another category of differences between bestseller lists that, for want of a better title, might be called the "Who Knows?" difference. Some books will appear on one set of bestseller lists and not the other for reasons no one can explain. Any "explanations" would be guesses. Part of the fun of seeing 71 years of publishing history alphabetically indexed and the pertinent numbers calculated for easy reference and comparison is the little inconsistencies and incongruities that become apparent. Inconsistencies can be difficult to deal with at times, but they also remind us that we are human and, therefore, imperfect. They also tell us that things have changed in many ways in the last 71 years, and that someone somewhere made changes to adapt the lists to new trends and conditions. In other words, someone was doing the best he or she could do—not plotting how to make things more difficult (or easier) for researchers 50 years hence.

Absolute, unwavering consistency over a period of many decades can be a one-way trip down a dead-end road. As the world changes, so must we. Inconsistencies, and the changes they indicate, may keep us from cruising down a superhighway to any final (and probably mythical) goal, but if they also help us steer clear of wasting too much time trapped in dead-ends, perhaps that is enough.

A BRIEF HISTORY OF
THE BESTSELLER LISTS

Publishers Weekly

The indexing in this volume for *Publishers Weekly* begins with a list published on May 13, 1919, and titled "A New Record of Best Sellers." Various other lists appeared in *Publishers Weekly* before 1919, but these were taken from other sources (e.g. the "Atlantic's Bookshelf" list or the "Books in Demand at the Library" list) or were ancillary or one-shot auxiliary lists such as the list of best-selling war-related books published on 6/6/18. The "New Record of Best Sellers" was selected as the starting point for indexing here because it represents a directed effort to gauge the popularity of best-selling books according to national sales figures. The brief introduction to the first list states:

H.S. Browne & Co. are starting with the May number of their "Books of the Month" a new series of records of best sellers in the book field. The figures are based on the reports from 62 booksellers: 21 from the Eastern states, 16 from the Middle West, 13 from the Southern states, 12 from the far West.

The list includes 16 titles, 10 under the heading "Best Selling Fiction" and 6 under the heading "Best-Selling General Books." The first books to appear at the top of these lists were *The Four Horsemen of the Apocalypse* by Blasco Ibanez (fiction) and *A Minstrel in France* by Harry Lauder (general). The positions were not numbered.

"A New Record of Best Sellers," as a listing, underwent minor changes over the next two years. By the issue of 6/7/19, the chart or list positions—still 10 for fiction and 6 for the general category—were numbered, and the number of bookstores contributing figures for the development of the lists often changed. On 8/2/19, for example, 55 bookstores in 43 cities contributed information for the lists, but the following month, 9/6/19, the rankings were determined with the help of 60 bookstores in 53 cities.

The first major change occurred on 3/27/20, when the "general" category was expanded from six to eight titles, and three months later, on 6/12/20, was expanded again to include 10 titles. But two months later, on 8/14/20, the "general list" was reduced once again to the original six titles.

A change in the listing format appeared in the 9/25/20 issue of *PW*. The heading "Books of the Month" was placed in a circle; another heading in large script read "Best Sellers Last Month"; and the previous explanation of information-gathering methods was replaced with, "Compiled and arranged in the order of their popularity from exclusive reports of leading booksellers in every section of the country." The entries were not numbered.

Although new graphics had been adopted to give the list a more distinctive appearance, there continued to be minor fluctuations in the number of titles included in the list. The first lists with the new graphic look (8/25/20) had 10 fiction and 10 general titles. By the issue of 6/11/21, the lists were reduced to six fiction and six general titles. In the 1/7/22 issue of *PW* the new circle logo was dropped. It was reinstated in the 5/13/22 issue, and the lists were expanded again, this time to 12 fiction titles and 12 nonfiction titles.

There was never any problem choosing a name for the fiction list— fiction is fiction—but apparently the magazine was having trouble settling on a title for the other list. Sometimes it was called the "general" list, sometimes the "nonfiction" list, and sometimes the "general literature" list. Even correct spelling appeared to present a problem. In the 4/18/25 edition, the general literature list was titled "General Liturature." This heading remained the same in the next edition but was "corrected," on 6/20/25, to "General Literarure." In the July issue, published 7/18/25, the recalcitrant heading was at last properly identified.

Whether to number the entries also seems to have been a persistent question during the early years of the list, for the listings would go numberless for months only to have the numbers appear for a few weeks and then disappear once again. Other occasional format changes include listing the book title first, listing the author first, listing the author by last name only, and listing the author by full name. A one-column format was used during the first 10 years of the list (the magazine as a whole utilized a two-column page format) but the single-column list was expanded to two columns in the issue dated 8/10/29. The next month the list was reduced back to single-column format.

The first true innovation in the *PW* bestseller lists occurred on 2/15/30, when the magazine added a juvenile list. In this issue, the three lists—fiction, nonfiction and juvenile—contained 10 titles each, and the entries were unnumbered.

Two years later, the magazine experimented not only with a change of format, but with a change in attitude toward the lists. For the first 13 years of their existence, the *PW* bestseller lists, notwithstanding minor adjustments in graphic appearance, took a no-nonsense approach to information presentation. Suddenly, in the issue dated 4/23/32, a horse-racing motif was adopted, and the lists were presented in horse-racing terms whenever possible.

In the first appearance of this motif, the juvenile list was separated from the fiction and nonfiction lists, and the latter were neatly grouped in a single column on the left side of the page. On the right were general brief comments about each book's appearance, performance or track record (e.g., "A veteran racer in the rental libraries" or "Westchester [N.Y.] bookies report that it bogged down on their tracks"). By the next month, the juvenile list was discontinued, and would not reappear in *PW* for nearly 60 years.

The fiction and nonfiction lists were retitled the "P.W. Form-Sheet" and subtitled "Neck and Neck." For the issue dated 11/12/32 the horse-racing motif was scratched briefly and an election motif adopted: "P.W.s Election Extra; The Winning Ticket." The horse-racing metaphor was trotted out again in December, but by March 1933 the theme was on its way out to pasture. In April, the overall chart heading was changed to "Market News," and this heading remained stable until 6/15/35, when the "Market News" heading was dropped and the monthly subtitle ("The January Best Sellers," "The February Best Sellers," etc.) became the main heading.

Occasional changes also occurred in the description of the process for determining bestseller status. By 5/9/36, the identifying legend had changed to "Compiled on a percentage basis from the reports of 94 booksellers." The list evolved into a columnar format and included a percentage number for each book on the list for the current month and for the two previous months, plus an indication of the number of months each book had spent on the list. The entries, listed in a grid format with lines between the titles, were numbered.

Changes were few and minor for nearly six years. Then, on 8/8/42, *PW* introduced a new system. The monthly list, complete with percentage numbers and other information, was retained, but the first weekly list was added to the magazine. The first such list contained seven fiction and seven nonfiction titles, although that number would fluctuate from five to nine in successive issues over the next several years. The headings for the two lists became "National Bestsellers" (the monthly list) and "Best Sellers of the Week." The weekly and monthly lists were retained, with only minor modifications, until 5/19/58,

when a modernized layout was adopted for bestseller list page. A small photo of the number one title on each list was printed in the left margin, and the fiction and nonfiction lists contained 10 titles each.

The book jacket photos, which represented one of the most dramatic graphic changes in the bestseller list format, survived only until 1961, when they disappeared. With the issue of 1/2/67, the monthly lists' percentage information for the current and two previous months plus the number of months each title had remained on the list was dropped, to be replaced with each book's position on the list the previous month, the position for the current month, the total number of months spent on the list to date, the date of publication (month/year) and the number of copies in print. The weekly list format was revamped to present only the basic information about each book: title, author, publisher and price. There were 12 titles on each of the two lists, and the procedural description was changed to "Compiled from selected large-city bookstores and from best seller lists in newspapers across the United States."

The dual weekly/monthly list format was retained until the last issue of 1973. The last separate "monthly" list appeared in the issue of 12/17/73, and beginning with the first issue of 1974 *PW* adopted a true weekly list.

One of the magazine's most important changes occurred in 1976 when *PW* adopted two paperback bestseller lists, one for mass market titles and one for trade. The mass market list contained 10 titles and the trade paper list five, although this would change quickly. By the issue of 3/29/76, the mass market list was expanded to include 15 titles. The next year, with the issue of 10/10/77, the trade paperback list was expanded to 10 titles. The two hard-cover lists, fiction and nonfiction, were expanded from 10 to 15 titles each.

The lists were reasonably stable for a decade thereafter. The next major change occurred with the issue of 1/10/86, when the simple listings which had been used for 10 years were augmented with two additional items of information for each title: each book's position on the list the previous week and the number of weeks each had spent on the list. The format also was changed again, this time from a simple two-column listing with no separation between titles to a gridded one-column format with lines between each title. The 15 fiction titles were arranged to take up the entire left-hand column on the hardcover list page, and the 15 nonfiction titles were arranged likewise on the right. On the paperback page, the 15 mass market titles were presented in the left column and the 10 trade titles on the right. The description of compilation procedure had changed to "Compiled from data received from large-city, university and chain bookstores, book wholesalers and independent distributors nationwide."

This format was utilized for more than four years. With the issue of 8/31/90 the list numbers were placed in black boxes, a change that would herald a virtual explosion of changes to follow. In August, a monthly list of children's bestsellers was incorporated into the magazine, adding five separate bestseller categories: Picture Books (ten titles), Younger Readers (five titles), Middle Readers (five titles), Young Adults (five titles) and Nonfiction (five titles).

In October 1990, two more monthly divisions were added with two separate lists in each: A Religious Bestsellers list, separated into hardcover and paperback, and an Audio Bestsellers list, divided into fiction and nonfiction. The two Religious Bestsellers listings contained 15 titles each in October and 20 each in November. The Religious Bestseller lists did not appear in any December issues of *PW*. The monthly Audio Bestseller lists first appeared in October, and also were published in November and December of that year.

New York Times Book Review

The first monthly bestseller list in the *New York Times Book Review* appeared in undramatic fashion in the issue dated 10/6/35. The list was rudimentary and functional, with 10 numbered entries in each of two lists, one for fiction and one for nonfiction. Information included title, author name, date of publication, publisher and price. The lists, which appeared to be little more than an afterthought, were presented in a 4¼" wide by 3½" deep line box labeled "Monthly List of Best-Selling Books." A brief introduction in the first list explained: "For the period Aug. 19 to Sept. 17, ranked according to the Baker & Taylor Company's sales to retailers throughout the country. The date is that of publication."

Titles to seize the number one positions on the first lists were *Vein of Iron* by Ellen Glasgow (fiction) and *North to the Orient* by Anne Morrow Lindbergh (nonfiction).

On February 6, 1938, the fiction and nonfiction lists were expanded to 15 titles each, and from that point the length of the lists alternated between 10 and 15 titles per month. Apart from this variation, the lists and their format remained reasonably stable, although the editorial department of the magazine remained uncertain about what to call them. As with *Publishers Weekly*, apparently there was no question about the title for the fiction list, but the other title underwent almost constant change. For the first several years of its existence, the monthly *NYTBR* bestseller list changed at least once each year from "general" to "nonfiction" or from "nonfiction" to "general," and in some years the switch occurred more than once. In 1938 alone, the title of the list was changed at least four times.

After the issue dated 1/7/40, the bestseller list disappeared from the *NYTBR* for more than two years. When a list reappeared in the magazine in the issue dated 8/9/42, it was presented weekly, in a two-column format with a bold border. There were two unnumbered lists, fiction (17 titles) and nonfiction (16 titles). The box was headlined "The Best Selling Books, Here and Elsewhere." A grid pattern showed the relative positions of each book in 14 major cities: New York, Boston, Philadelphia, Washington, Baltimore, Atlanta, Cleveland, Detroit, Chicago, St. Louis, New Orleans, Dallas, San Francisco and Los Angeles.

A paragraph explaining the general reasoning behind the compilation of the list states: "This chart is based upon reports from booksellers in fourteen cities which appear each Monday on the book page of *The New York Times*. The order in which the titles are listed is based upon the number of cities which report them as among the bestsellers. The numerals indicate their relative standing."

While the format stayed the same for many years after the bestseller lists' reappearance in 1942, the number of titles included in each list remained fluid for three years. During this period, individual charts contained 12 to 27 titles, probably averaging 15. One suspects that the lists were used primarily as space filler and were shortened as needed to accommodate other copy.

In the issue dated 9/9/45 (the first weekly list in which the titles were numbered), the "city grid" portion of the listings was dropped and replaced with information showing each book's position on the lists for each of the preceding three weeks. The information about each book was limited to the title and the author's last name, and the length of the two lists was standardized at 16 titles each. The heading was changed from "The Best Selling Books, Here and Elsewhere" to "The Best Sellers." The explanatory legend was changed to "An analysis based on reports from leading booksellers in 22 cities, showing the sales rating of 16 leading fiction and general titles, and their relative standing over the past 3 weeks."

Changes were few and minor for the next 17 years (for example, in the issue dated 9/7/52 the list heading was changed from "The Best Sellers" to "Best Seller List"). The next major landmark was a 15-week publishing hiatus caused by a printer's strike. After the issue dated 12/16/62, the strike prevented the publication of another list until the 4/7/63 issue. The basic format remained the same, but the number of titles in each of the two lists was reduced to 10.

In the issue dated 11/29/64, the blocky line box surrounding the bestseller lists—a feature which made them easy to locate in each issue—was dropped and replaced with a much less distinctive line box. The fiction and general lists within the new format contained 12 titles each. The information on each title included the book title, author's last name, the book's chart position for the previous two weeks, and the number of weeks each title had spent on the lists to date.

The next year, in the issue dated 12/5/65, a paperback list was added. The paperback list began as a monthly listing, usually published in the month's first issue. By the issue of 5/14/67, the heading "The New York Times Book Review," in old English script, was placed above the list headings, and though the list heading "Paperbacks" was retained, the heading for the hardcover lists was changed from "Best Sellers" to "Current Best Sellers."

At five titles each, the two paperback lists, titled "fiction" and "general," were very short. There were occasional cosmetic changes, and in the issue dated 5/7/67 the information provided for each title was reduced slightly. The information about previous list positioning for the past two weeks on the chart was reduced to the position for the previous week and the number of weeks each book had spent on the chart.

In the earliest years of the paperback list, the *New York Times* apparently perceived a need for this information despite the fact that paperback publishing had not yet achieved generally recognized importance. Like the story papers, dime novels and pulp magazines of other publishing eras, the paperback book was born to serve a market that did not suggest immediate respectability, and even though paperback sales continued to increase—and therefore continued to prove the medium's viability and ever more powerful commercial influence—the lists providing information on paperback sales were yet to be considered fully legitimate.

In fact, after six years of publication, the *NYTBR* paperback lists were demoted to the bottom of the page. The "Recommended New Titles" feature was moved to the top of the page, and the lists followed it. In the issue dated 2/10/74, the lists were changed from an abbreviated one-column format to a two-column feature with the fiction category on the left, the general category on the right, and each category

containing 10 titles. The information for each title included the full author name, title, publisher, price, and a brief descriptive one-liner for each title— e.g., the descriptive phrase for *Burr* by Gore Vidal: "A wicked entertainment about the conventional textbook villain."

After this round of changes, *Burr* was the top title in the fiction list; *The Joy of Sex*, by Alex Comfort, occupied the top position on the general list.

In the issue of 3/10/74, the paperback list was revamped again and made a more prominent feature. The fiction and general categories were discarded and replaced with "mass market" and "trade" lists. The chart positions were unnumbered, and each chart contained 10 titles, although otherwise the previous format was retained. The next month—with the issue dated 4/14/74— the list was numbered again. The next year, in the issue dated 1/12/75, the trade paperback list was reduced to five titles, and the monthly publication schedule for the paperback list was changed. The paperback list appeared twice in January and went into full weekly publication in March.

In the issue dated 4/3/77, the mass market paperback list was expanded to 15 titles, although the trade list remained at five titles. The chart heading "Paperback" was changed to "Paperback Best Sellers." In the same issue there was a minor change made also in the hardcover lists—the perennial dilemma of "general" versus "nonfiction" apparently reared its head once again, and this time "nonfiction" won out.

Five months later, in the issue dated 9/11/77, the five-title trade paperback list was expanded to 15 titles and the fiction and nonfiction hardcover lists went from 10 to 15 titles each. Stability was the order of the day for the next six years, until in the issue dated

1/1/84 the paperback nonfiction list was divided into a "General" list and an "Advice, How-To and Miscellaneous" list. The first how-to list had 11 titles, and the general list had only 4. The paperback fiction list remained at 15 titles. The two nonfiction lists—general and how-to—would fluctuate from week to week, sometimes dropping as low as 3 titles and sometimes rising as high as 12; but the number of titles in the two paperback nonfiction lists added together usually totaled 15.

In the issue of 1/1/84 there also appeared a major change in the hardcover lists. The hardcover fiction and nonfiction lists remained at 15 titles each, but a new hardcover "Advice, How-To and Miscellaneous" list was added. The first such list contained five titles, and all paperback and hardcover lists remained relatively unchanged from 1984 to 1990.

The *NYTBR* juvenile/children's list has appeared intermittently in the magazine. A list of five juvenile titles was included in the larger list's third appearance (December 1, 1935) but was immediately withdrawn. The next juve-nile list was published in the issue dated 11/16/52, titled "Children's Best Sellers," and it contained 16 titles. A sentence explained that the list represented "an analysis based on reports from leading booksellers in 30 cities, showing the year's sales rating of 16 leading children's books published during the first 10 months of 1952."

The *NYTBR* children's list was published annually in November from 1952 through 1958, then in 1959 the list appeared twice, in May and November. Twice-yearly publication became the standard until 1973, although in 1963 the list was reduced from 16 to 10 titles. But after 1973, the list was suspended for four years.

When the children's list reappeared in the issue dated 11/13/77, it was divided into "Hardcover Best Sellers" and "Paperback Best Sellers," each list containing 15 titles. A juvenile list in the same general format was published the next year in the issue dated 4/30/78, but from that year to 1990 a children's or juvenile bestseller's list did not reappear in *The New York Times Book Review*.

Bestseller Index

AN EXPLANATION OF THE FORMAT

1. Steel, Danielle

Crossings (Delacorte) PW hc fic 9/24/82 (#12), pk 10/15/82 (#4, 2 wk), 22 wk; NYT fic 9/26/82 (#10), pk 10/17/82 (#5, 3 wk), 24 wk; (Dell) NYT pb fic 3/11/84 (#2, 5 wk), 27 wk; PW mm pb 3/16/84 (#3), pk 3/23/84 (#2, 5 wk), 21 wk; tot 94 wk.

The format of this reference work was designed to be as simple as possible while allowing the researcher to reconstruct a book's performance on all the *New York Times* and *Publishers Weekly* bestseller lists on which it appeared. The main listing is alphabetical by author. Under each author listing the book title entries are arranged chronologically, and within the title entries the information on chart activity is also chronological, i.e., the first bestseller list upon which the book appeared is presented first, and so on.

The main body of the above title listing is read as follows: Danielle Steel's *Crossings* was first published by Delacorte (hardcover edition), and it first appeared on the *Publishers Weekly* hardcover fiction list on 9/24/82 at position #12. It reached its peak position on 10/15/82 at #4, and remained at its peak position on that chart for two weeks, spending a total of 22 weeks on that list. On the *NYT* fiction list, the book debuted on 9/26/82 at the #10 position, peaked on 10/17/82 at the #5 position, spent a total of three weeks in the #5 position on that list, and remained on the list for a total of 24 weeks. The paperback edition was published by Dell. The paper edition debuted on the *New York Times* paperback fiction list on 3/11/84 at the #2 position. Because the debut position is the same as the final peak position, the position and weeks-at-peak-position indicators are followed by the total weeks on the chart with no separate peak position date. The paper edition of *Crossings* debuted on the *Publishers Weekly* mass market paperback list on 3/16/84 at #3, peaked on 3/23/84 at the #2 position, remained in its peak position for five weeks and spent a total of 21 weeks on the list. The last indicator in the *Crossings* entry shows that the book spent a total of 94 weeks on the *NYT* and *PW* lists combined.

11

In some instances, there may be additional information included, such as the fact that both an original and a revised edition appeared on the chart, or "adult" and "juvenile" editions were published. Under such special circumstances, the chart performances of the different editions are listed separately, but the overall chart performance figures (total weeks on all charts) are combined.

Anyone researching the chart performance of a book should be aware that to provide every possible item of information about each book and its chart appearances would have been impossible. Novels often reach the charts shortly after publication and disappear, only to reappear on the charts when a film or TV miniseries based on the book is released or some other significant milestone is achieved. *Gone with the Wind* is an excellent example. It made its first chart appearance in 1936; 31 years later, in 1967, a paperback edition appeared briefly on the charts, and after an additional two decades, in 1986, a fiftieth anniversary facsimile edition placed the book on the charts for a third run.

Thus the total number of weeks spent on a chart does not necessarily refer to consecutive weeks; nor does the number indicating weeks at peak position. Chart position is a quickly changing reflection of a book's impact on the commercial marketplace. As new books are released, a title with an established run on the charts may be forced to a lower position (or forced off the charts altogether), only to reappear at a later date when the demands of the marketplace shift attention from a newer volume with less commercial appeal to an older book with more appeal.

Authors are listed under real names rather than pseudonyms whenever real names could be determined. Thus a reader looking for "Twain, Mark" or "Dr. Seuss" will find a cross-reference to "Clemens, Samuel" or "Geisel, Theodor." If all of an author's listed books were published under the same pseudonym, that pseudonym is given in brackets following the author's name. Otherwise the pseudonym follows the book title. When an author's name is known to be a pseudonym but the real name is not readily available, the name is marked "[pseud.]."

There are no separate listings for books *written* and books *edited* by the same individual. All the individual's books are arranged chronologically in one entry, and his or her relationship to each book is indicated. If an individual served as editor for a title listed under his or her name, the abbreviation "[ed.]" will appear after the title. More complicated descriptors or explanations are spelled out as necessary, e.g., "[consulting editor]," "[project manager]," "[characters created by Smith, story written by Jones]."

ABBREVIATIONS USED

aud fic	Audio Fiction List
aud nf	Audio Nonfiction List
ch bst	Children's Bestseller List
ch fic	Children's Fiction List
ch hc	Children's Hardcover List
ch nf	Children's Nonfiction List
ch pb	Children's Paperback List
fic	Fiction List
gen	General List
gen lit	General Literature List
hc fic	Hardcover Fiction List
hc nf	Hardcover Nonfiction List
hc rel	Hardcover Religious List
juv	Juvenile List
mm pb	Mass Market Paperback List
msc	Advice, How-To and Misc. List
msc pb	Advice, How-To and Misc. Paperback List
nf	Nonfiction List
NYT	*New York Times*
NYTBR	*New York Times Book Review*
pb fic	Paperback Fiction List
pb gen	Paperback General List
pb nf	Paperback Nonfiction List
pb rel	Paperback Religious List
pk	peak position
PW	*Publishers Weekly*
td pb	Trade Paperback List

THE INDEX
(BY AUTHOR)

Accoce, Pierre, and Pierre Quet
A Man Called Lucy (Coward) NYT gen 6/11/67 (#7, 1 wk).

Acheson, Dean Gooderham
The Pattern of Responsibility [ed. McGeorge Bundy] (Houghton) NYT gen 1/27/52 (#16, 1 wk).
A Democrat Looks at His Party (Harper) NYT gen 12/4/55 (#14), pk 12/18/55 (#8, 1 wk), 11 wk.
Power and Diplomacy (Harvard Univ.) NYT gen 2/9/58 (#9, 1 wk), 6 wk.
Sketches from Life (Harper) NYT gen 6/11/61 (#13), pk 7/16/61 (#9, 1 wk), 11 wk.
Present at the Creation: My Years at the State Department (Norton) PW nf 10/27/69 (#10), pk 12/8/69 (#1, 1 wk), 23 wk; NYT gen 11/2/69 (#4), pk 11/16/69 (#3, 12 wk), 17 wk; tot 40 wk.

Ackerman, Diane
A Natural History of the Senses (Random) NYT nf 8/5/90 (#13), pk 8/26/90 (#9, 1 wk), 8 wk; PW hc nf 8/31/90 (#15), pk 9/7/90 (#14, 1 wk), 3 wk; tot 11 wk.

Adamic, Louis
The Native's Return (Harper) PW nf 3/10/34 (#3), pk 4/14/34 (#2, 4 wk), 20 wk.
My America (Harper) NYT gen 7/3/38 (#2, 4 wk), 12 wk; PW nf 7/9/38 (#4, 4 wk), 8 wk; tot 20 wk.
From Many Lands (Harper) PW nf 1/11/41 (#9, 4 wk).
My Native Land (Harper) NYT gen 12/12/43 (#25), pk 1/23/44 (#16, 1 wk), 4 wk.
Nation of Nations (Harper) NYT gen 12/9/45 (#14, 1 wk).
Dinner at the White House (Harper) NYT gen 11/3/46 (#14, 1 wk).

Adams, Adrienne
See Hans Christian Andersen

Adams, Alice
Superior Women (Knopf) NYT fic 10/21/84 (#12), pk 11/11/84 (#10, 1 wk), 7 wk; PW hc fic 10/26/84 (#14, 2 wk), 4 wk; (Fawcett) PW mm pb 8/30/85 (#10), pk 9/13/85 (#4, 2 wk), 11 wk; NYT pb fic 9/1/85 (#10), pk 9/22/85 (#4, 1 wk), 11 wk; tot 33 wk.

Adams, Ansel Easton
Born Free and Equal (U.S. Camera) NYT gen 3/25/45 (#17), pk 4/8/45 (#14, 1 wk), 3 wk.

_____, with Mary Street Alinder
Ansel Adams: An Autobiography (New York Graphic Society/Little Brown) NYT nf 12/8/85 (#9), pk 12/15/85 (#8, 3 wk), 6 wk; PW hc nf 12/13/85 (#13), pk 1/3/86 (#10, 1 wk), 5 wk; tot 11 wk.

Adams, Charles T.
Contract Bridge at Sight (Bruce Roberts) PW nf 2/21/31 (#9), pk 3/21/31 (#8, 4 wk), 12 wk.

Adams, Douglas
The Restaurant at the End of the Universe (Pocket) PW mm pb 10/22/82 (#15), pk 1/14/83 (#5, 1 wk), 12 wk; NYT mm pb 11/21/82 (#15), pk 12/26/82 (#3, 2 wk), 12 wk; tot 24 wk.
Life, the Universe and Everything: The Cosmic Conclusion to the Hitchhiker Trilogy (Harmony) NYT fic 10/31/82 (#14), pk 1/23/83 (#7, 3 wk), 21 wk; PW hc fic 11/5/82 (#11), pk 2/4/83 (#6, 1 wk), 19 wk; (Pocket) PW mm pb 10/21/83 (#11), pk 11/4/83 (#4, 1 wk), 6 wk; NYT mm pb 10/23/83 (#5, 1 wk), 6 wk; tot 52 wk.
The Hitchhiker's Guide to the Galaxy (Pocket) PW mm pb 12/3/82 (#11), pk 1/7/83 (#5, 1 wk), 10 wk; NYT mm pb 12/26/82 (#15), pk 1/16/83 (#7, 3 wk), 8 wk; tot 18 wk.
So Long, and Thanks for All the Fish (Harcourt) PW hc fic 12/14/84 (#13), pk 1/25/85 (#3, 2 wk), 21 wk; NYT fic 12/16/84 (#6), pk 1/20/85 (#3, 2 wk), 15 wk; (Pocket) NYT pb fic 11/17/85 (#8), pk 12/1/85 (#7, 1 wk), 9 wk; PW mm pb 11/22/85 (#5, 3 wk), 8 wk; tot 53 wk.
Dirk Gently's Holistic Detective Agency (Simon & Schuster) NYT fic 6/28/87 (#13), pk 7/26/87 (#5, 5 wk), 14 wk; PW hc fic 7/10/87 (#14), pk 7/17/87 (#5, 4 wk), 12 wk; (Pocket) PW mm pb 5/13/88 (#11), pk 6/10/88 (#3, 1 wk), 10 wk; NYT pb fic 5/15/88 (#5, 3 wk), 8 wk; tot 44 wk.
The Long Dark Tea-Time of the Soul (Simon & Schuster) PW hc fic 3/10/89 (#13), pk 3/24/89 (#6, 3 wk), 11 wk; NYT fic 3/12/89 (#13), pk 4/2/89 (#6, 3 wk), 10 wk; (Pocket) NYT pb fic 1/14/90 (#5, 2 wk), 6 wk; PW mm pb 1/19/90 (#7), pk 1/26/90 (#4, 2 wk), 5 wk; tot 32 wk.

Adams, Franklin Pierce
Innocent Merriment [ed.] (McGraw) NYT nf 11/29/42 (#18, 1 wk).

Adams, Henry
The Education of Henry Adams (Houghton) PW gen 5/3/19 (#3, 4 wk), 28 wk.
Letters of Henry Adams (Houghton) PW nf 11/22/30 (#9, 4 wk).

Adams, James Truslow
The Adams Family (Little Brown) PW nf 7/12/30 (#5), pk 8/23/30 (#3, 4 wk), 24 wk.
The Epic of America (Little Brown) PW nf 11/14/31 (#3), pk 1/16/32 (#1, 16 wk), 68 wk.
The March of Democracy (Scribner) PW nf 11/12/32 (#1, 8 wk), 24 wk.

The March of Democracy Vol. 2 (Scribner) PW nf 4/15/33 (#1, 4 wk), 16 wk.

America's Tragedy (Scribner) PW nf 11/10/34 (#8), pk 12/15/34 (#5, 8 wk), 16 wk.

The Living Jefferson (Scribner) PW nf 5/9/36 (#7, 4 wk), 8 wk.

_____, et al.

Album of American History [eds.] (Scribner) NYT gen 4/30/44 (#12, 1 wk).

Adams, Ramon Frederick

Western Words (Univ. of Oxford) NYT gen 12/24/44 (#19, 1 wk).

The Book of the American West [ed. Jay Monaghan] (Messner) NYT gen 12/8/63 (#10, 1 wk).

Adams, Richard

Watership Down (Macmillan) PW fic 3/25/74 (#7), pk 4/15/74 (#1, 15 wk), 39 wk; NYT fic 4/14/74 (#4), pk 5/5/74 (#1, 13 wk), 33 wk; (Avon) NYT mm pb 4/20/75 (#5), pk 5/18/75 (#3, 1 wk), 14 wk; PW mm pb 12/25/78 (#15), pk 1/22/79 (#8, 1 wk), 9 wk; tot 95 wk.

Shardik (Simon & Schuster) NYT fic 5/18/75 (#7), pk 7/6/75 (#2, 3 wk), 19 wk; PW fic 5/19/75 (#8), pk 6/9/75 (#3, 2 wk), 17 wk; (Avon) PW mm pb 2/16/76 (#6), pk 2/23/76 (#3, 1 wk), 9 wk; NYT mm pb 2/22/76 (#7), pk 2/29/76 (#6, 1 wk), 3 wk; tot 48 wk.

The Tyger Voyage (Knopf) NYT ch hc 11/13/77 (#13, 46 wk).

The Plague Dogs (Knopf) PW nc fic 3/20/78 (#15), pk 4/10/78 (#10, 2 wk), 12 wk; NYT fic 4/2/78 (#10), pk 4/9/78 (#7, 2 wk), 12 wk; (Fawcett/Crest) PW mm pb 3/19/79 (#14, 1 wk); NYT mm pb 3/25/79 (#13, 2 wk), 3 wk; tot 28 wk.

The Girl in a Swing (Knopf) PW hc fic 6/13/80 (#13, 2 wk), 5 wk; PW mm pb 3/20/81 (#7), pk 3/27/81 (#4, 2 wk), 9 wk; NYT mm pb 3/22/81 (#15), pk 3/29/81 (#6, 2 wk), 9 wk; tot 23 wk.

Maia (NAL) NYT pb fic 2/9/86 (#15), pk 3/2/86 (#13, 1 wk), 2 wk.

Adams, Samuel Hopkins

Revelry (Boni & Liveright) PW fic 2/19/27 (#5, 8 wk), 16 wk.

A. Woollcott: His Life and His World (Reynal & Hitchcock) NYT gen 6/24/45 (#9), pk 7/1/45 (#3, 3 wk), 18 wk; PW nf 6/30/45 (#4), pk 7/7/45 (#2, 1 wk), 11 wk; tot 29 wk.

Sunrise to Sunset (Random) NYT fic 8/6/50 (#16, 1 wk).

Grandfather Stories (Random) NYT fic 8/14/55 (#14), pk 9/11/55 (#7, 1 wk), 13 wk; PW nf 9/17/55 (#8, 3 wk); tot 16 wk.

Tenderloin (Random) NYT fic 2/15/59 (#14), pk 3/22/59 (#9, 1 wk), 6 wk; PW fic 3/16/59 (#9, 1 wk), 2 wk; tot 8 wk.

Adams, Sherman

Firsthand Report (Harper) NYT gen 7/16/61 (#8), pk 7/23/61 (#7, 1 wk), 12 wk; PW nf 7/17/61 (#10), pk 7/24/61 (#9, 3 wk), 5 wk; tot 17 wk.

Adamski, George

Inside the Space Ships (Abelard Schuman) NYT gen 8/21/55 (#13), pk 9/25/55 (#11, 1 wk), 3 wk.

See also Desmond Leslie and_____

Adamson, Joy

Born Free (Pantheon) NYT gen 5/15/60 (#10), pk 8/7/60 (#1, 13 wk), 48 wk; PW nf 5/30/60 (#6), pk 8/1/60 (#1, 11 wk), 42 wk; tot 90 wk.

Living Free (Harcourt) NYT gen 11/5/61 (#7), pk 12/24/61 (#2, 2 wk), 22 wk; PW nf 11/13/61 (#7), pk 1/22/62 (#1, 1 wk), 17 wk; tot 39 wk.

Forever Free (Harper) NYT gen 5/19/63 (#9, 2 wk); PW nf 5/20/63 (#8, 1 wk); tot 3 wk.

Adler, Bill

The Kennedy Wit [ed.] (Citadel) NYT gen 8/9/64 (#10), pk 11/8/64 (#4, 3 wk), 25 wk; PW nf 9/7/64 (#7), pk 10/19/64 (#3, 2 wk), 27 wk; tot 52 wk.

See also Bess Myerson and_____

_____, and Thomas Chastain

Who Killed the Robins Family? [created by Adler, written by Chastain] (Morrow) NYT fic 9/4/83 (#12), pk 1/29/84 (#1, 1 wk), 36 wk; PW hc fic 9/9/83 (#10), pk 2/3/84 (#2, 6 wk), 35 wk; (Warner) PW mm pb 9/14/84 (#13, 1 wk); NYT pb fic 9/23/84 (#10, 1 wk); tot 73 wk.

Revenge of the Robins Family [created by Adler, written by Chastain] (Morrow) PW hc fic 8/17/84 (#11, 2 wk), 8 wk; NYT fic 8/26/84 (#15), pk 9/9/84 (#13, 1 wk), 4 wk; tot 12 wk.

Adler, Mortimer J.

How to Read a Book (Simon & Schuster) PW nf 4/13/40 (#2), pk 5/11/40 (#1, 8 wk), 24 wk.

How to Think About War and Peace (Simon & Schuster) NYT gen 3/19/44 (#17), pk 3/26/44 (#13, 1 wk), 2 wk.

See also Louis O. Kelso and_____

Adler, Polly

A House Is Not a Home (Rinehart) NYT gen 6/21/53 (#16), pk 8/2/53 (#2, 11 wk), 27 wk; PW nf 7/18/53 (#4), pk 8/22/53 (#2, 6 wk), 20 wk; tot 47 wk.

Agar, Herbert
A Time for Greatness (Little Brown) NYT nf 11/1/42 (#11), pk 12/20/42 (#10, 1 wk), 12 wk.

Agee, James
A Death in the Family (Grosset & Dunlap) NYT fic 12/29/57 (#16), pk 3/2/58 (#9, 1 wk), 16 wk.

Agee, Philip
Inside the Company: CIA Diary (Stonehill/Braziller) NYT gen 8/31/75 (#10, 2 wk); PW nf 9/15/75 (#10, 1 wk); tot 3 wk.

Agnew, Spiro T.
The Canfield Decision (Playboy) PW hc fic 6/21/76 (#8), pk 7/12/76 (#6, 1 wk), 6 wk; NYT fic 6/27/76 (#10, 6 wk); tot 12 wk.

Agutter, Jenny
See Sidney Sheldon

Ahlberg, Janet, and Allan Ahlberg
Starting School (Puffin) PW ch pic 9/28/90 (#6, 4 wk).

Aiken, Joan
The Wolves of Willoughby Chase (Doubleday) NYT ch bst 5/10/64 (#8, 19 wk).

Albert, Dora
You're Better Than You Think (Prentice Hall) NYT gen 8/10/58 (#14, 1 wk).

Albom, Mitch
See Bo Schembechler and_____

Albrand, Martha
No Surrender (World Almanac) NYT fic 11/8/42 (#20, 1 wk).

Alcott, Carroll
My War with Japan (Holt) NYT gen 7/11/43 (#19, 1 wk).

Aldington, Richard
All Men Are Enemies (Doubleday) PW fic 9/16/33 (#5, 4 wk).
The Duke (Viking) NYT gen 12/12/43 (#15, 2 wk), 4 wk.

Aldis, Dorothy
7 to 7 (Minton Balch) PW juv 4/18/31 (#10, 4 wk).

Aldrich, Bess Streeter
A White Bird Flying (Appleton) PW fic 9/19/31 (#2, 12 wk), 28 wk.
Miss Bishop (Appleton) PW fic 10/14/33 (#4, 4 wk), 16 wk.
Spring Came on Forever (Appleton) NYT fic 11/3/35 (#4, 4 wk), 8 wk; PW fic 11/9/35 (#7), pk 1/11/36 (#4, 4 wk), 16 wk; tot 24 wk.
Song of Years (Appleton) NYT fic 2/5/39 (#4, 4 wk), 12 wk; PW fic 2/11/39 (#7), pk 3/11/39 (#5, 4 wk), 16 wk; tot 28 wk.

The Lieutenant's Lady (Appleton) NYT fic 10/25/42 (#14), pk 1/3/43 (#12, 2 wk), 9 wk; PW fic 11/14/42 (#10, 1 wk); tot 10 wk.

Aldrich, Richard
Gertrude Lawrence as Mrs. A (Greystone) NYT gen 1/16/55 (#14), pk 2/20/55 (#2, 7 wk), 33 wk; PW nf 2/5/55 (#4), pk 3/5/55 (#1, 3 wk), 23 wk; tot 56 wk.

Aldridge, James
Signed with Their Honour (Little Brown) NYT fic 10/4/42 (#10), pk 10/25/42 (#5, 1 wk), 13 wk; PW fic 10/10/42 (#8), pk 10/17/42 (#4, 1 wk), 4 wk; tot 17 wk.
The Diplomat (Little Brown) NYT fic 3/19/50 (#12, 1 wk), 3 wk.

Aleichem, Sholom [pseud.]
The Old Country (Crown) NYT fic 7/28/46 (#14), pk 8/11/46 (#8, 1 wk), 8 wk.

Alexander, Dan Dale
Arthritis and Common Sense (Witkower) NYT gen 4/15/56 (#14), pk 7/15/56 (#1, 2 wk), 44 wk; PW nf 5/14/56 (#6), pk 7/9/56 (#1, 3 wk), 33 wk; tot 77 wk.

Alexander, Grand Duke
Once a Grand Duke (Farrar) PW nf 3/19/32 (#10), pk 5/14/32 (#5, 8 wk), 24 wk.
Always a Grand Duke (Farrar) PW nf 6/10/33 (#6, 4 wk), 8 wk.

Alexander, Lloyd
The High King (Dell) NYT ch bst 5/4/69 (#10, 19 wk).

Alexander, Roy
The Cruise of the Raider "Wolf" (Yale Univ.) NYT gen 1/7/40 (#15, 1 wk).

Alexander, Shana
Nutcracker: Money, Madness, Murder—A Family Album (Doubleday) NYT nf 7/7/85 (#14), pk 7/28/85 (#6, 2 wk), 11 wk; PW hc nf 7/12/85 (#12), pk 8/16/85 (#6, 1 wk), 10 wk; (Dell) NYT pb nf 1/19/86 (#3, 2 wk), 8 wk; PW mm pb 1/31/86 (#13, 1 wk); tot 30 wk.

Algren, Nelson
The Man with the Golden Arm (Doubleday) NYT fic 10/2/49 (#12), pk 10/23/49 (#7, 3 wk), 22 wk.
A Walk on the Wild Side (Farrar) NYT fic 6/10/56 (#12), pk 6/24/56 (#8, 3 wk), 15 wk.

Alinder, Mary Street
See Ansel Adams and_____

Aline, Countess of Romanones
See Aline Griffith

Alinsky, Saul David
Reveille for Radicals (Random) NYT gen 2/17/46 (#12), pk 3/3/46 (#10, 1 wk), 8 wk.

Allee, Marjorie
Jane's Island (Houghton) PW juv 7/18/31 (#8, 4 wk).

Alleg, Henri
The Question (Braziller) NYT gen 7/6/58 (#12), pk 7/13/58 (#8, 1 wk), 3 wk.

Allen, C.M.
How to Wheel and Deal in Gold and Silver (Allen Advertising) NYT td pb 7/14/74 (#10, 4 wk).

Allen, Charlotte Vale
Destinies (Berkley) NYT mm pb 3/21/82 (#14, 1 wk); PW mm pb 4/9/82 (#14, 1 wk); tot 2 wk.

Allen, Fred
Treadmill to Oblivion (Little Brown) NYT gen 12/26/54 (#14), pk 2/6/55 (#6, 2 wk), 18 wk; PW nf 2/5/55 (#5, 2 wk), 6 wk; tot 24 wk.
Much Ado About Me (Little Brown) NYT gen 12/9/56 (#11), pk 1/20/57 (#3, 1 wk), 20 wk; PW nf 12/17/56 (#7), pk 1/21/57 (#3, 2 wk), 15 wk; tot 35 wk.
Fred Allen's Letters [ed. Joe McCarthy] (Doubleday) NYT gen 6/6/65 (#8, 1 wk); PW nf 6/14/65 (#7, 1 wk); tot 2 wk.

Allen, Frederick Lewis
Only Yesterday (Harper) PW nf 1/16/32 (#4), pk 4/23/32 (#1, 20 wk), 44 wk.
Since Yesterday (Harper) PW nf 3/9/40 (#7), pk 4/13/40 (#4, 8 wk), 16 wk.
The Great Pierpont Morgan (Harper) NYT gen 4/24/49 (#15), pk 5/15/49 (#8, 2 wk), 8 wk.
The Big Change (Harper) NYT gen 11/23/52 (#13), pk 1/4/53 (#7, 3 wk), 16 wk; PW nf 12/13/52 (#10), pk 1/17/53 (#7, 1 wk), 4 wk; tot 20 wk.
See also Agnes Rogers and_____

Allen, George Edward
Presidents Who Have Known Me (Simon & Schuster) NYT gen 11/5/50 (#16), pk 11/12/50 (#10, 3 wk), 8 wk.

Allen, Hervey
Anthony Adverse (Farrar) PW fic 8/12/33 (#1, 44 wk), 84 wk.
Action at Aquila (Farrar) NYT fic 4/3/38 (#1, 4 wk), 8 wk; PW fic 4/9/38 (#2, 8 wk), 16 wk; tot 24 wk.
The Forest and the Fort (Farrar) NYT fic 4/18/43 (#5), pk 5/9/43 (#4, 2 wk), 24 wk; PW fic 4/24/43 (#5), pk 5/1/43 (#3, 3 wk), 17 wk; tot 41 wk.
Bedford Village (Farrar) NYT fic 4/9/44 (#9), pk 5/7/44 (#5, 3 wk), 13 wk; PW fic 4/29/44 (#5), pk 4/22/44 (#3, 3 wk), 9 wk; tot 22 wk.

Toward the Morning (Rinehart) NYT fic 9/12/48 (#11), pk 10/17/48 (#3, 2 wk), 15 wk; PW fic 9/25/48 (#5), pk 10/30/48 (#1, 1 wk), 8 wk; tot 23 wk.

Allen, Ida Cogswell Bailey
Pressure Cooking (Garden City) NYT gen 5/11/47 (#13, 1 wk).

Allen, Robert G.
Nothing Down: How to Buy Real Estate with Little or No Money (Simon & Schuster) PW hc 4/18/80 (#14), pk 5/10/85 (#2, 1 wk), 134 wk; NYT nf 4/27/80 (#13), pk 9/7/80 (#7, 4 wk), 58 wk; NYT msc 1/29/84 (#2), pk 2/19/84 (#1, 10 wk), 71 wk; tot 263 wk.
Creating Wealth (Simon & Schuster) NYT nf 5/29/83 (#4, 14 wk), 28 wk; PW hc nf 6/3/83 (#4, 12 wk), 40 wk; NYT msc 1/1/84 (#3), pk 2/5/81 (#1, 2 wk), 13 wk; tot 81 wk.

Allen, Col. Robert Sharon
Our Fair City [ed.] (Vanguard) NYT gen 3/23/47 (#13), pk 3/30/47 (#6, 1 wk), 9 wk; PW nf 5/17/47 (#10, 1 wk); tot 10 wk.
Lucky Forward (Vanguard) NYT gen 10/19/47 (#7, 3 wk), 9 wk; PW nf 11/15/47 (#10, 1 wk); tot 10 wk.
Truman Merry-Go-Round (Vanguard) NYT gen 10/15/50 (#10), pk 11/5/50 (#9, 2 wk), 9 wk.
See also Drew Pearson and_____

Allen, Woody
Without Feathers (Random) PW nf 7/21/75 (#10), pk 8/4/75 (#5, 6 wk), 13 wk; NYT gen 8/10/75 (#7), pk 8/31/75 (#5, 6 wk), 12 wk; (Warner) PW mm pb 6/14/76 (#6, 2 wk), 6 wk; tot 31 wk.
Side Effects (Random) NYT nf 10/19/80 (#3), pk 1/25/81 (#2, 1 wk), 21 wk; PW hc nf 10/24/80 (#7), pk 10/31/80 (#3, 7 wk), 19 wk; (Ballantine) PW mm pb 10/2/81 (#10), pk 10/9/81 (#8, 1 wk), 3 wk; tot 43 wk.

Allende, Isabel
The House of the Spirits (Knopf) NYT fic 6/16/85 (#15), pk 7/14/85 (#9, 1 wk), 2 wk; (Bantam) NYT pb fic 8/10/86 (#14, 2 wk), tot 4 wk.

Alliluyeva, Svetlana
Twenty Letters to a Friend (Harper) NYT gen 10/22/67 (#5), pk 11/19/67 (#4, 2 wk), 9 wk; PW nf 10/23/67 (#8), pk 11/20/67 (#2, 1 wk), 20 wk; tot 29 wk.

Allison, Linda
Blood and Guts (Little Brown) NYT ch pb 11/13/77 (#13, 46 wk).

Alsberg, Henry Garfield
The American Guide [ed.] (Hastings) NYT gen 10/2/49 (#14, 1 wk).

Alsop, Joseph W., Jr. and Robert Kinter
American White Paper (Simon & Schuster) PW nf 6/8/40 (#2), pk 7/13/40 (#1, 4 wk), 16 wk.

Alsop, Stewart
The Center: People and Power in Political Washington (Harper) NYT gen 5/19/68 (#9), pk 6/30/68 (#6, 1 wk), 9 wk; PW nf 7/8/68 (#10), pk 7/22/68 (#8, 1 wk), 3 wk; tot 12 wk.

_____, and Thomas Braden
Sub Rosa: The O.S.S. and American Espionage (Harcourt) NYT gen 3/31/46 (#12, 1 wk).

Alther, Lisa
Kinflicks (Knopf) NYT fic 4/18/76 (#10), pk 5/16/76 (#8, 2 wk), 7 wk; PW hc fic 4/12/76 (#9), pk 5/17/76 (#6, 1 wk), 9 wk; (NAL/Signet) NYT mm pb 3/20/77 (#9), pk 3/27/77 (#3, 5 wk), 14 wk; PW mm pb 3/21/77 (#3, 4 wk), 14 wk; tot 44 wk.
Original Sins (NAL/Signet) PW mm pb 4/16/82 (#11), pk 5/7/82 (#10, 1 wk), 5 wk; NYT mm pb 4/18/82 (#14), pk 5/9/82 (#12, 1 wk), 5 wk; tot 10 wk.
Other Women (NAL) NYT pb fic 8/18/85 (#9, 2 wk), 9 wk; PW mm pb 8/23/85 (#12, 2 wk), 5 wk; tot 14 wk.

Alvarez, Alfred
The Savage God (Random) NYT gen 6/11/72 (#10), pk 6/25/72 (#9, 2 wk), 4 wk.

Alvin, Julius
Gross Jokes (Zebra) NYT mm pb 12/18/83 (#15), pk 12/25/83 (#9, 1 wk), 2 wk; NYT msc pb 1/1/84 (#3), pk 1/8/84 (#2, 1 wk), 7 wk; PW mm pb 1/6/84 (#12), pk 1/13/84 (#9, 1 wk), 2 wk; tot 11 wk.
Totally Gross Jokes (Zebra) NYT msc pb 1/1/84 (#8, 1 wk), 2 wk.
Utterly Gross Jokes (Zebra) NYT msc pb 2/26/84 (#4, 2 wk), 9 wk.

Amado, Jorge
Gabriela, Clove and Cinnamon (Knopf) NYT fic 10/14/62 (#16), pk 11/4/62 (#14, 2 wk), 6 wk.

Ambler, Eric
Judgment of Deltchev (Knopf) NYT fic 5/13/51 (#15, 1 wk).
The Schirmer Inheritance (Knopf) NYT fic 8/16/53 (#11, 1 wk), 4 wk.
The Light of Day (Knopf) PW fic 4/1/63 (#7), pk 4/8/63 (#6, 1 wk), 6 wk.
A Kind of Anger (Atheneum) PW fic 11/30/64 (#12, 3 wk).
The Levanter (Atheneum) NYT fic 7/23/72 (#9), pk 9/3/72 (#7, 1 wk), 10 wk; PW fic

7/24/72 (#9), pk 8/7/72 (#7, 3 wk), 11 wk; tot 21 wk.

Ames, Louise Bates
See Frances Lillian Ilg and_____

Amis, Martin
London Fields (Crown) PW hc fic 4/6/90 (#15), pk 4/20/90 (#10, 1 wk), 4 wk; NYT fic 4/8/90 (#12, 1 wk); tot 5 wk.

Amory, Cleveland
The Proper Bostonians (Dutton) NYT gen 11/9/47 (#9), pk 12/28/47 (#6, 1 wk), 32 wk; PW nf 1/3/48 (#5, 2 wk), 7 wk; tot 39 wk.
Home Town (Harper) NYT fic 1/29/50 (#15), pk 2/5/50 (#12, 1 wk), 6 wk.
The Last Resorts (Harper) NYT gen 11/30/52 (#7), pk 12/14/52 (#4, 2 wk), 23 wk; PW nf 12/13/52 (#5, 1 wk), 6 wk; tot 29 wk.
Who Killed Society? (Harper) NYT gen 1/1/61 (#10), pk 2/19/61 (#2, 7 wk), 22 wk; PW nf 1/9/61 (#9), pk 2/20/61 (#2, 7 wk), 21 wk; tot 43 wk.
The Cat Who Came for Christmas (Little Brown) NYT nf 11/29/87 (#8), pk 1/24/88 (#2, 2 wk), 20 wk; PW hc nf 12/4/87 (#12), pk 2/5/88 (#3, 1 wk), 15 wk; (Penguin) PW td pb 10/28/88 (#9), pk 12/2/88 (#1, 5 wk), 16 wk; NYT pb nf 10/30/88 (#3), pk 11/20/88 (#1, 8 wk), 25 wk; tot 76 wk.
The Cat and the Curmudgeon (Little Brown) NYT nf 10/21/90 (#9), pk 11/4/90 (#6, 4 wk), 11 wk; PW hc nf 11/2/90 (#12), pk 12/14/90 (#9, 1 wk), 4 wk; tot 15 wk.

_____, and Frederick Bradlee
Vanity Fair [eds.] (Viking) NYT gen 12/4/60 (#16), pk 1/7/61 (#6, 1 wk), 12 wk; PW nf 12/26/60 (#6), pk 1/9/61 (#5, 1 wk), 8 wk; tot 20 wk.

Andersen, Hans Christian
Thumbelina [illus. Adrienne Adams] (Scribner) NYT ch bst 11/11/62 (#10, 26 wk).

Anderson, Dave
See John Madden and_____

Anderson, Erica, and Eugene Exman
The World of Albert Schweitzer (Harper) NYT gen 2/6/55 (#15), pk 2/27/55 (#9, 1 wk), 6 wk; PW nf 3/12/55 (#9, 1 wk); tot 7 wk.

Anderson, Jack
See Drew Pearson and_____

Anderson, Louis
Dear Dad: Letters from an Adult Child (Viking) PW hc nf 2/16/90 (#14, 1 wk); NYT nf 4/1/90 (#13, 1 wk); tot 2 wk.

Anderson, Peggy
Nurse (St. Martin's) PW hc nf 12/25/78 (#13), pk 3/5/79 (#8, 1 wk), 17 wk; NYT nf

1/21/79 (#12), pk 3/4/79 (#8, 3 wk), 17 wk; (Berkley) PW mm pb 10/8/79 (#11), pk 10/29/79 (#1, 1 wk), 13 wk; NYT mm pb 10/21/79 (#7), pk 11/4/79 (#2, 1 wk), 16 wk; tot 63 wk.
Children's Hospital (Bantam) NYT pb nf 5/18/86 (#6, 1 wk), 3 wk.

Anderson, Sparky, with Dan Ewald
Bless You Boys (Contemporary) NYT mm pb 11/11/84 (#7, 1 wk).

Anderson, Cmdr. William R., and Clair Blay, Jr.
Nautilus 90 North (World) NYT gen 1/18/59 (#16), pk 3/1/59 (#5, 3 wk), 16 wk; PW nf 2/2/59 (#8), pk 2/23/59 (#6, 4 wk), 12 wk; tot 28 wk.

Andrews, Bert
Washington Witchhunt (Random) NYT gen 8/22/48 (#13, 1 wk).

Andrews, Lynn V.
Jaguar Woman (Harper) NYT nf 9/29/85 (#13, 1 wk), 2 wk.
Star Woman (Warner) NYT nf 10/19/86 (#13, 1 wk), 2 wk.
Crystal Woman (Warner) NYT nf 10/18/87 (#13, 1 wk), 2 wk.

Andrews, M.P.
Social Planning by Frontier Thinkers (R.R. Smith) NYT gen 5/28/44 (#12, 1 wk), 2 wk.

Andrews, Robert Hardy
Burning Gold (Doubleday) NYT fic 9/9/45 (#10, 1 wk), 4 wk.

Andrews, Roy Chapman
Nature's Ways: How Nature Takes Care of Its Own (Crown) NYT gen 7/15/51 (#16), pk 7/29/51 (#10, 1 wk), 7 wk.
All About Dinosaurs (Random) NYT ch bst 11/14/54 (#12, 40 wk).

Andrews, V.C.
Flowers in the Attic (Pocket) PW mm pb 11/19/79 (#5), pk 12/24/79 (#4, 1 wk), 20 wk; NYT mm pb 11/25/79 (#12), pk 1/6/80 (#4, 1 wk), 15 wk; NYT pb fic 12/20/87 (#15), pk 1/3/88 (#11, 3 wk), 6 wk; tot 41 wk.
Petals on the Wind (Pocket) PW mm pb 6/13/80 (#5), pk 7/11/80 (#1, 1 wk), 17 wk; NYT mm pb 6/15/80 (#6), pk 6/22/80 (#1, 4 wk), 19 wk; tot 36 wk.
If There Be Thorns (Pocket) PW mm pb 6/12/81 (#3), pk 6/26/81 (#1, 7 wk), 16 wk; NYT mm pb 6/14/81 (#2), pk 6/21/81 (#1, 8 wk), 20 wk; tot 36 wk.
My Sweet Audrina (Pocket) NYT mm pb 4/10/83 (#10), pk 4/17/83 (#2, 4 wk), 15 wk; PW mm pb 4/15/83 (#6), pk 5/6/83 (#1, 1 wk), 15 wk; tot 30 wk.
Seeds of Yesterday (Pocket) NYT pb fic

3/11/84 (#1, 6 wk), 17 wk; PW mm pb 3/16/84 (#2), pk 3/23/84 (#1, 5 wk), 15 wk; tot 32 wk.
Heaven (Pocket) NYT pb fic 10/6/85 (#8), pk 10/20/85 (#1, 3 wk), 17 wk; PW mm pb 10/11/85 (#7), pk 10/18/85 (#2, 3 wk), 13 wk; tot 30 wk.
Dark Angel (Pocket) NYT pb fic 11/9/86 (#5), pk 11/16/86 (#1, 2 wk), 14 wk; PW mm pb 11/14/86 (#9), pk 11/21/86 (#1, 1 wk), 12 wk; tot 26 wk.
Garden of Shadows (Pocket) NYT pb fic 11/8/87 (#3), pk 11/15/87 (#1, 2 wk), 17 wk; PW mm pb 11/13/87 (#9), pk 12/11/87 (#1, 4 wk), 17 wk; tot 34 wk.
Fallen Hearts (Pocket) NYT pb fic 8/7/88 (#4), pk 8/14/88 (#1, 7 wk), 12 wk; PW mm pb 8/12/88 (#10), pk 8/19/88 (#1, 5 wk), 10 wk; tot 22 wk.
Gates of Paradise (Pocket) NYT pb fic 6/4/89 (#3), pk 6/11/89 (#1, 4 wk), 10 wk; PW mm pb 6/9/89 (#1, 5 wk), 10 wk; tot 20 wk.
Dawn (Pocket) NYT pb fic 11/4/90 (#3), pk 11/11/90 (#1, 5 wk), 9 wk; PW mm pb 11/9/90 (#2), pk 11/16/90 (#1, 4 wk), 7 wk; tot 16 wk.
Web of Dreams (Pocket) NYT pb fic 2/4/90 (#1, 3 wk), 12 wk; PW mm pb 2/9/90 (#2), pk 2/23/90 (#1, 1 wk), 10 wk; tot 22 wk.

Andrezel, Pierre
The Angelic Avengers (Random) NYT fic 2/2/47 (#11), pk 2/23/47 (#8, 2 wk), 6 wk; PW fic 2/15/47 (#10, 1 wk); tot 7 wk.

Angas, Lawrence
The Coming American Boom (Simon & Schuster) PW nf 10/13/34 (#6, 4 wk).

Angell, Roger
The Summer Game (Viking) NYT gen 7/30/72 (#10), pk 9/10/72 (#4, 1 wk), 5 wk; PW nf 8/7/72 (#9, 4 wk), 5 wk; tot 10 wk.
Five Seasons: A Baseball Companion (Simon & Schuster) PW hc nf 7/25/77 (#10), pk 8/8/77 (#5, 1 wk), 3 wk.
Late Innings (Simon & Schuster) NYT nf 6/27/82 (#12), pk 7/18/82 (#11, 1 wk), 6 wk.

Angelou, Maya
I Know Why the Caged Bird Sings (Random) NYT gen 4/19/70 (#8), pk 5/10/70 (#7, 1 wk), 6 wk; PW nf 5/11/70 (#8, 3 wk), 5 wk; tot 11 wk.
All God's Children Need Traveling Shoes (Random) NYT nf 5/25/86 (#13), pk 6/1/86 (#11, 1 wk), 5 wk.

Anger, Kenneth
Hollywood Babylon (Dell/Delta) NYT td pb 4/4/76 (#5, 3 wk), 3 wk; PW td pb 4/5/76 (#5), pk 4/12/76 (#4, 1 wk), 2 wk; tot 5 wk.

Angle, Paul M.
The Lincoln Reader [ed.] (Rutgers Univ.)
NYT gen 3/2/47 (#7), pk 3/16/47 (#3, 2 wk),
14 wk; PW nf 3/15/47 (#5), pk 3/29/47 (#3,
2 wk), 7 wk; tot 21 wk.

Anglund, Joan Walsh
A Friend Is Someone Who Likes You (Harcourt) NYT ch bst 11/2/58 (#11), pk 5/14/61
(#1, 20 wk), 174 wk.
The Brave Cowboy (Harcourt) NYT ch bst
5/10/59 (#9), pk 11/1/59 (#6, 25 wk), 44 wk.
Love Is a Special Way of Feeling (Harcourt)
NYT ch bst 5/8/60 (#1, 63 wk), 142 wk.
Cowboy and His Friend (Harcourt) NYT ch
bst 11/12/61 (#8, 26 wk).
In a Pumpkin Shell (Harcourt) NYT ch bst
5/14/61 (#10), pk 11/12/61 (#2, 26 wk), 46 wk.
Christmas Is a Time of Giving (Harcourt)
NYT ch bst 11/11/62 (#4, 26 wk).
Spring Is a New Beginning (Harcourt) NYT
ch bst 5/12/63 (#1, 19 wk), 45 wk.
A Pocketful of Proverbs (Harcourt) NYT ch
bst 5/10/64 (#3), pk 11/1/64 (#2, 25 wk), 44
wk.
Childhood Is a Time of Innocence (Harcourt)
NYT ch bst 11/1/64 (#5, 25 wk), 51 wk.
A Book of Good Tidings from the Bible (Harcourt) NYT ch bst 11/6/66 (#8, 26 wk).
What Color Is Love? (Harcourt) NYT ch
bst 5/8/66 (#5), pk 11/6/66 (#1, 26 wk), 45
wk.
A Is for Always (Harcourt) NYT ch bst
5/5/68 (#10, 19 wk).
Morning Is a Little Child (Harcourt) NYT
ch bst 11/9/69 (#10, 26 wk).

Angly, Edward
See Jesse H. Jones and_____

Anno, Mitsumasa
Anno's Counting Book (Crowell) NYT ch
hc 11/13/77 (#11, 46 wk).

Anonymous
The Adventures of Mickey Mouse (McKay)
PW juv 6/20/31 (#6), pk 7/18/31 (#1, 4 wk),
40 wk.
AAA North American Road Atlas 1985
(American Automobile Association/Random) NYT msc pb 2/17/85 (#7, 3 wk), 11 wk.
AAF: Official Guide to the Army Air Forces
(Bonanza) NYT gen 7/30/44 (#13, 1 wk).
The Baby (Simon & Schuster) NYT gen
3/5/50 (#8), pk 3/26/50 (#2, 5 wk), 11 wk;
PW nf 3/18/50 (#10), pk 3/25/50 (#2, 6 wk),
9 wk; tot 20 wk.
Behind the Mirrors (Putnam) PW gen lit
9/16/22 (#10, 4 wk).
The Best from Yank: An Anthology (World)
NYT gen 5/20/45 (#18), pk 6/17/45 (#4, 2

wk), 15 wk; PW nf 6/16/45 (#9), pk 6/23/45
(#4, 1 wk), 4 wk; tot 19 wk.
Better Homes and Gardens Garden Book
(Meredith) NYT gen 4/22/51 (#11), pk 5/27/
51 (#5, 7 wk), 24 wk; PW nf 6/9/51 (#7), pk
6/16/51 (#5, 3 wk), 5 wk; tot 29 wk.
Better Homes and Gardens Handyman's Book
(Meredith) NYT gen 10/14/51 (#12), pk
10/28/51 (#9, 1 wk), 14 wk.
Better Homes and Gardens New Cookbook
(Meredith) NYT msc 12/28/86 (#4), pk 1/3/
88 (#2, 2 wk), 12 wk.
Betty Crocker's Cookbook (Golden/Western)
NYT msc 12/21/86 (#5), pk 1/11/87 (#4, 4
wk), 8 wk.
Betty Crocker's International Cookbook (Random) NYT nf 11/16/80 (#14), pk 2/1/81 (#2,
3 wk), 28 wk; PW hc nf 1/9/81 (#14), pk 2/6/
81 (#6, 1 wk), 13 wk; tot 41 wk.
Betty Crocker's Picture Cook Book (McGraw) PW nf 11/18/50 (#9), pk 12/16/50 (#6,
1 wk), 3 wk; NYT gen 7/1/51 (#15, 2 wk), 3
wk; tot 6 wk.
The Children's Bible (Golden) NYT ch bst
11/7/65 (#9), pk 5/8/66 (#7, 19 wk), 64 wk.
Consumer Reports Buying Guide 1984 (Doubleday) NYT msc pb 2/19/84 (#10, 1 wk).
*Diane...: The Twin Peaks Tapes of Agent
Cooper* [read by Kyle MacLachlan] (Simon
& Schuster) PW aud fic 11/2/90 (#1, 8 wk).
Eyewitness Juniors Series (Knopf) PW ch
nf 8/31/90 (#4, 8 wk), 16 wk.
First Prayers [illus. Tasha Tudor] (Oxford
Univ.) NYT ch bst 11/16/52 (#16, 40 wk).
The Glass of Fashion (Putnam) PW gen lit
11/12/21 (#5, 4 wk).
Grease: The Fotonovel (Fotonovel Publications) PW mm pb 10/30/78 (#13), pk 11/27/
78 (#8, 2 wk), 15 wk; NYT mm pb 11/12/78
(#13), pk 12/3/78 (#8, 2 wk), 13 wk; tot 28 wk.
Holy Bible: Revised Standard Version (Nelson) NYT gen 10/19/52 (#7), pk 2/15/53 (#1,
1 wk), 64 wk.
Information, Please (Dan Golenpaul Assoc.)
NYT gen 6/11/39 (#9, 4 wk), 12 wk.
Information Please Almanac 1947 (Garden
City) NYT gen 2/9/47 (#14), pk 3/2/47 (#2,
10 wk), 27 wk; PW nf 2/15/47 (#10), pk
3/29/47 (#1, 1 wk), 17 wk; tot 44 wk.
Information Please Almanac 1948 (Garden
City) NYT gen 1/25/48 (#15), pk 3/7/48 (#2,
3 wk), 26 wk; PW nf 2/14/48 (#5), pk 3/13/
48 (#2, 2 wk), 17 wk; tot 43 wk.
Information Please Almanac 1949 (Farrar)
NYT gen 2/6/49 (#9), pk 2/20/49 (#5, 1
wk), 7 wk; PW nf 2/12/49 (#8), pk 2/19/49
(#6, 1 wk), 3 wk; tot 10 wk.
Information Please Almanac 1950 (Macmillan) PW nf 2/11/50 (#10, 1 wk).

Information Please Almanac 1951 (Dan Golenpaul Assoc.) NYT gen 2/4/51 (#9, 1 wk), 4 wk.

Information Please Almanac 1987 (Houghton) NYT msc pb 1/18/87 (#10, 1 wk).

Information Please Almanac 1989 (Houghton) NYT msc pb 1/22/89 (#5, 1 wk); PW td pb 2/3/89 (#8, 1 wk); tot 2 wk.

Information Please Almanac 1990 (Houghton) NYT msc pb 1/7/90 (#4, 2 wk); PW td pb 1/19/90 (#10), pk 1/26/90 (#8, 2 wk), 4 wk; tot 6 wk.

Life's Picture History of World War II (Simon & Schuster) NYT gen 12/17/50 (#16), pk 1/14/51 (#10, 1 wk), 5 wk; PW nf 1/13/51 (#9, 1 wk); tot 6 wk.

Living Spanish (Crown) PW aud nf 10/5/90 (#9), pk 11/2/90 (#6, 4 wk), 8 wk.

Macmillan Dictionary for Children (Macmillan) NYT ch hc 4/30/78 (#1, 24 wk).

Madame Solario (Viking) NYT fic 9/16/56 (#14), pk 9/30/56 (#10, 1 wk), 3 wk.

The Magic of Michael Jackson (Sharon/NAL) NYT pb nf 3/18/84 (#6, 3 wk), 5 wk; PW td pb 3/23/84 (#6), pk 3/30/84 (#5, 2 wk), 7 wk; tot 12 wk.

Mary Poppins [chart performance includes combined sales of at least three titles, including "Mary Poppins" and "Mary Poppins Comes Back" and a Walt Disney adaptation] (Golden) NYT ch bst 11/1/64 (#1, 44 wk), 63 wk.

Meet the New Kids on the Block (NAL/Signet) NYT pb nf 6/3/90 (#9), pk 6/17/90 (#7, 1 wk), 2 wk.

Mickey Mouse Movie Stories (McKay) PW juv 4/23/32 (#7, 4 wk).

The Mirrors of Downing Street (Putnam) PW gen lit 4/23/21 (#9), pk 1/7/22 (#3, 8 wk), 28 wk; PW nf 5/13/22 (#12, 4 wk); tot 32 wk.

Mirrors of 1932 (Brewer Warren & Putnam) PW nf 9/19/31 (#4, 8 wk), 12 wk.

Mirrors of Washington (Putnam) PW gen lit 11/12/21 (#1, 8 wk), 16 wk; PW nf 4/1/22 (#2, 4 wk), 8 wk; tot 24 wk.

Mobil Travel Guide: California and the West (Rand McNally) NYT msc pb 8/24/86 (#5, 1 wk).

The Mother Goose Treasury [illus. Raymond Briggs] (Coward McCann) NYT ch bst 11/5/67 (#9, 26 wk).

The Muppet Movie (Bantam/Peacock) NYT td pb 11/4/79 (#15, 1 wk).

The New English Bible (Oxford Univ.) NYT gen 4/5/70 (#6), pk 5/3/70 (#3, 3 wk), 20 wk.

The New English Bible: The New Testament (Cambridge Univ./Oxford Univ.) NYT gen 4/2/61 (#8), pk 5/28/61 (#1, 1 wk), 71 wk; PW

nf 4/3/61 (#8), pk 5/15/61 (#1, 2 wk), 85 wk; tot 156 wk.

The New Testament: Revised Standard Version (Nelson) NYT gen 3/24/46 (#10, 1 wk), 6 wk; PW nf 5/11/46 (#8, 1 wk), 3 wk; tot 9 wk.

The New Women's Survival Catalogue (Berkley) NYT td pb 3/10/74 (#7, 4 wk).

The New York Public Library Desk Reference (Stonesong/Webster's/Prentice Hall) PW hc nf 12/22/89 (#12), pk 1/5/90 (#11, 1 wk), 4 wk.

The New Yorker 1950-1955 Album (Harper) NYT gen 10/30/55 (#16), pk 12/4/55 (#8, 2 wk), 15 wk; PW nf 1/21/56 (#7, 1 wk); tot 16 wk.

The New Yorker Album of Drawings 1925-1975 (Viking) PW nf 12/15/75 (#10), pk 1/5/76 (#8, 3 wk), 6 wk; NYT gen 12/28/75 (#9), pk 1/11/76 (#5, 1 wk), 7 wk; tot 13 wk.

The New Yorker Book of Cat Cartoons (Knopf) PW hc nf 12/21/90 (#15, 1 wk).

The New Yorker 25th Anniversary Album (Harper) NYT gen 11/4/51 (#12), pk 12/9/51 (#2, 11 wk), 24 wk; PW nf 12/1/51 (#4), pk 12/22/51 (#1, 2 wk), 14 wk; tot 38 wk.

The New Yorker War Album (Random) NYT nf 1/3/43 (#10, 1 wk).

1986 Buying Guide Issue (Consumer's Union) NYT msc pb 2/16/86 (#6, 1 wk).

Official New Kids on the Block Eight Book Covers (Golden) PW ch nf 9/28/90 (#5, 4 wk).

The Official System of Contract Bridge (Winston) PW nf 11/14/31 (#6, 4 wk), 8 wk.

The Old Farmer's Almanac 1974 [ed. Robert B. Thomas] (Yankee) NYT td pb 12/8/74 (#7), pk 1/26/75 (#3, 1 wk), 6 wk.

The Old Farmer's Almanac 1984 [ed. Robert B. Thomas] (Yankee) NYT msc pb 1/22/84 (#8, 1 wk), 2 wk.

The Old Farmer's Almanac 1985 [ed. Judson Hale] (Yankee) NYT msc pb 11/25/84 (#4), pk 12/9/84 (#2, 2 wk), 11 wk; PW td pb 2/1/85 (#8, 1 wk); tot 12 wk.

The Old Farmer's Almanac 1986 [ed. Robert B. Thomas] (Yankee) NYT msc pb 11/3/85 (#4), pk 11/10/85 (#3, 3 wk), 14 wk; PW td pb 11/15/85 (#7), pk 12/6/85 (#5, 2 wk), 8 wk; tot 22 wk.

The Old Farmer's Almanac 1987 [ed. Robert B. Thomas] (Yankee) NYT msc pb 11/2/86 (#7, 2 wk), 10 wk; PW td pb 11/21/86 (#9, 1 wk), 2 wk; tot 12 wk.

The Old Farmer's Almanac 1990 (Yankee) PW td pb 11/3/89 (#9), pk 11/24/89 (#5, 1 wk), 12 wk; NYT msc pb 11/5/89 (#5), pk 11/19/89 (#4, 5 wk), 8 wk; tot 20 wk.

The Old Farmer's Almanac 1991 (Yankee)

NYT msc pb 10/14/90 (#4), pk 11/4/90 (#2, 1 wk), 4 wk; PW td pb 10/19/90 (#8), pk 11/9/90 (#6, 1 wk), 8 wk; tot 4 wk.

Painted Windows (Putnam) PW nf 5/13/ 22 (#4, 4 wk), 8 wk; PW gen lit 6/17/22 (#5, 4 wk), 8 wk; tot 16 wk.

Philadelphia Scrapple (Dietz) NYT gen 2/24/57 (#16, 1 wk).

The Presidential Transcripts (Dell) NYT mm pb 6/9/74 (#2), pk 7/14/74 (#1, 4 wk), 8 wk.

The Price Waterhouse Guide to the New Tax Law (Bantam) NYT msc pb 11/16/86 (#8), pk 12/7/86 (#2, 4 wk), 16 wk; PW mm pb 11/21/86 (#11), pk 12/12/86 (#6, 1 wk), 14 wk; tot 30 wk.

Rand McNally '74 Road Atlas (Rand McNally) NYT td pb 6/9/74 (#9), pk 7/14/ 74 (#4, 4 wk), 16 wk.

Rand McNally '75 Road Atlas (Rand McNally) NYT td pb 3/2/75 (#4), pk 4/6/75 (#3, 1 wk), 21 wk.

Rand McNally U.S. Road Atlas 1976 (Rand McNally) PW td pb 6/14/76 (#5), pk 9/20/ 76 (#1, 1 wk), 22 wk.

Rand McNally Road Atlas 1977 (Rand McNally) PW td pb 2/28/77 (#5), pk 3/21/ 77 (#1, 1 wk), 33 wk.

Rand McNally Road Atlas 1978 (Rand McNally) PW td pb 3/13/78 (#4), pk 4/10/78 (#1, 16 wk), 37 wk.

Rand McNally Road Atlas 1979 (Rand McNally) PW td pb 12/11/78 (#10), pk 5/7/ 79 (#2, 4 wk), 30 wk.

Rand McNally Road Atlas 1980 (Rand McNally) PW td pb 2/8/80 (#10), pk 4/25/ 80 (#2, 5 wk), 34 wk.

Rand McNally Road Atlas 1981 (Rand McNally) PW td pb 2/6/81 (#10), pk 2/20/81 (#3, 1 wk), 33 wk.

Rand McNally Road Atlas 1982 [ed. John Leverenz] (Rand McNally) PW td pb 7/30/ 82 (#8, 4 wk), 6 wk.

Rand McNally Road Atlas 1984 (Rand McNally) NYT msc pb 3/18/84 (#5), pk 7/ 15/84 (#1, 8 wk), 35 wk; PW td pb 8/31/84 (#7), pk 9/14/84 (#4, 1 wk), 3 wk; tot 38 wk.

Rand McNally Road Atlas 1985 [ed. John Leverenz] (Rand McNally) NYT msc pb 3/10/85 (#7), pk 7/21/85 (#1, 7 wk), 35 wk; PW td pb 3/22/85 (#6), pk 8/30/85 (#2, 1 wk), 20 wk; tot 55 wk.

Rand McNally Road Atlas 1986 (Rand McNally) NYT msc pb 11/17/85 (#5), pk 5/11/86 (#1, 5 wk), 51 wk; PW td pb 11/29/85 (#3), pk 7/11/86 (#1, 1 wk), 45 wk; tot 96 wk.

Rand McNally Road Atlas 1987 (Rand McNally) NYT msc pb 11/16/86 (#10), pk 8/23/87 (#2, 1 wk), 37 wk; PW td pb 11/21/86

(#10), pk 12/12/86 (#2, 1 wk), 47 wk; tot 84 wk.

Rand McNally Road Atlas 1988 (Rand McNally) NYT msc pb 1/31/88 (#4), pk 3/ 20/88 (#2, 8 wk), 34 wk; PW td pb 3/18/88 (#10), pk 3/25/88 (#8, 1 wk), 4 wk; tot 38 wk.

Rand McNally Road Atlas 1989 (Rand McNally) PW td pb 11/11/88 (#10), pk 8/25/ 89 (#8, 1 wk), 8 wk; NYT msc pb 12/11/88 (#5), pk 1/29/89 (#2, 1 wk), 38 wk; tot 46 wk.

Rand McNally Road Atlas 1990 (Rand McNally) PW td pb 11/24/89 (#10), pk 7/30/ 90 (#5, 1 wk), 13 wk; NYT msc pb 12/3/89 (#4), pk 7/15/90 (#1, 8 wk), 33 wk; tot 46 wk.

Random House Collegiate Dictionary (Random) NYT msc 6/3/84 (#3, 5 wk), 6 wk.

Random House Dictionary of the English Language (Random) PW nf 11/7/66 (#12), pk 1/23/67 (#2, 1 wk), 14 wk; NYT gen 11/13/66 (#9), pk 12/25/66 (#5, 1 wk), 13 wk; tot 27 wk.

The Real Mother Goose [illus. Blanche Fisher Wright] (Rand McNally) NYT ch bst 11/6/66 (#6, 52 wk), 102 wk.

Revised Standard Version of the Holy Bible (Nelson) PW nf 10/25/52 (#4), pk 1/24/53 (#1, 1 wk), 40 wk.

Royal Canadian Air Force Exercise Plans for Physical Fitness (Simon & Schuster) NYT td pb 4/10/77 (#5, 1 wk).

The Scout Jamboree Book (Putnam) PW juv 3/15/30 (#5), pk 4/12/30 (#4, 8 wk), 16 wk.

Shirley Temple's Storybook (Random) NYT ch bst 5/10/59 (#4), pk 11/1/59 (#1, 25 wk), 44 wk.

Star Wars Album (Ballantine) PW td pb 5/1/78 (#10, 1 wk).

The Strange Death of Adolph Hitler (Citadel) NYT gen 4/9/39 (#14, 4 wk).

Target: Germany—The Army Air Force's Official Story (Simon & Schuster) NYT gen 1/9/44 (#21), pk 1/23/44 (#6, 1 wk), 5 wk; PW nf 1/29/44 (#4, 1 wk), 2 wk; tot 7 wk.

Teenage Mutant Ninja Turtles Totally Awesome Activity Book (Random) PW ch nf 9/28/90 (#3, 4 wk), 8 wk.

Walt Disney's Lady and the Tramp (Simon & Schuster) NYT ch bst 11/13/55 (#1, 40 wk).

Walt Disney's Story Book of Peter Pan (Simon & Schuster) NYT ch bst 11/16/52 (#12, 80 wk).

A War Atlas for Americans (Simon & Schuster) NYT gen 6/25/44 (#15), pk 7/9/44 (#7, 3 wk), 10 wk; PW nf 7/15/44 (#8), pk 7/29/44 (#5, 1 wk), 3 wk; tot 13 wk.

War Birds (Doran) PW nf 3/19/27 (#5, 4 wk), 8 wk.

The Way Things Work: An Illustrated Encyclopedia of Technology (Simon & Schuster)

PW nf 1/8/68 (#11), pk 2/5/68 (#7, 6 wk), 17 wk; NYT gen 3/3/68 (#10), pk 3/24/68 (#7, 7 wk), 10 wk; tot 27 wk.

Webster's New World Dictionary, Second College Edition (Simon & Schuster) NYT msc 1/1/84 (#2, 3 wk), 54 wk.

Webster's New World Dictionary, Third College Edition (Prentice Hall/Simon & Schuster) NYT msc 1/1/89 (#5), pk 2/19/89 (#3, 2 wk), 23 wk.

Webster's Ninth New Collegiate Dictionary (Merriam Webster) NYT msc 2/19/84 (#4), pk 6/2/84 (#1, 20 wk), 193 wk; PW hc nf 6/12/87 (#11), pk 6/19/87 (#7, 3 wk), 9 wk; tot 202 wk.

Weight Watcher's Fast and Fabulous Cookbook (NAL) NYT msc 2/19/84 (#5), pk 3/25/84 (#1, 1 wk), 9 wk; PW hc nf 3/2/84 (#12), pk 3/16/84 (#9, 1 wk), 12 wk; tot 21 wk.

Weight Watcher's Quick and Easy Menu Cookbook (NAL) NYT msc 2/21/88 (#4), pk 3/6/88 (#3, 5 wk), 8 wk.

Weight Watcher's 365-Day Menu Cookbook (NAL) PW hc nf 2/19/82 (#13), pk 3/12/82 (#8, 2 wk), 17 wk; NYT nf 2/28/82 (#11), pk 4/4/82 (#7, 1 wk), 27 wk; tot 44 wk.

The White House Transcripts (Bantam) NYT mm pb 6/9/74 (#1, 8 wk).

Whole Earth Epilogue (Point/Penguin) NYT td pb 11/10/74 (#5), pk 12/8/74 (#2, 5 wk), 12 wk.

The World Almanac (New York World Telegram) PW nf 3/19/49 (#9, 1 wk).

The World Almanac and Book of Facts 1979 (Newspaper Enterprise Assn./Grosset & Dunlap) PW td pb 1/29/79 (#6, 2 wk), 4 wk.

The World Almanac and Book of Facts 1980 [ed. George E. Delury] (Newspaper Enterprise Assn./Grosset & Dunlap) PW td pb 2/1/80 (#4, 1 wk), 3 wk.

The World Almanac and Book of Facts 1984 [ed. Hana Umlauf Lane] (Newspaper Enterprise Assn./World Almanac) NYT msc pb 1/1/84 (#11), pk 1/22/84 (#4, 3 wk), 11 wk; PW td pb 1/20/84 (#7), pk 2/3/84 (#3, 1 wk), 9 wk; tot 20 wk.

The World Almanac and Book of Facts 1985 [ed. Hana Umlauf Lane] (Newspaper Enterprise Assn./World Almanac) NYT msc pb 12/23/84 (#1, 5 wk), 12 wk; PW mm pb 1/11/85 (#3), pk 1/18/85 (#2, 3 wk), 10 wk; tot 22 wk.

The World Almanac and Book of Facts 1986 [ed. Hana Umlauf Lane] (Newspaper Enterprise Assn./World Almanac) NYT msc pb 12/22/85 (#1, 3 wk), 15 wk; PW td pb 1/3/86 (#4), pk 1/10/86 (#2, 2 wk), 17 wk; tot 32 wk.

The World Almanac and Book of Facts 1987 [ed. Mark S. Hoffman] (World Almanac/

Pharos) NYT msc pb 12/14/86 (#12), pk 1/4/87 (#2, 1 wk), 8 wk; PW td pb 12/26/86 (#4), pk 1/23/87 (#1, 3 wk), 11 wk; tot 19 wk.

The World Almanac and Book of Facts 1988 [ed. Mark S. Hoffman] (World Almanac/ Pharos) NYT msc pb 12/20/87 (#5), pk 1/17/88 (#1, 3 wk), 9 wk; PW td pb 12/25/87 (#10), pk 1/29/88 (#1, 3 wk), 12 wk; tot 21 wk.

The World Almanac and Book of Facts 1989 [ed. Mark S. Hoffman] (World Almanac/ Pharos) NYT msc pb 12/25/88 (#3), pk 1/15/89 (#1, 4 wk), 9 wk; PW td pb 1/6/89 (#6), pk 2/3/89 (#1, 1 wk), 9 wk; tot 18 wk.

The World Almanac and Book of Facts 1990 [ed. Mark S. Hoffman] (World Almanac/ Pharos) PW td pb 12/8/89 (#10), pk 2/2/90 (#2, 1 wk), 13 wk; NYT msc pb 12/10/89 (#5), pk 1/21/90 (#1, 2 wk), 11 wk; tot 24 wk.

The World Almanac and Book of Facts 1991 [ed. Mark S. Hoffman] (World Almanac/ Pharos) PW td pb 12/14/90 (#8), pk 12/21/90 (#5, 1 wk), 2 wk; NYT msc pb 12/23/90 (#4), pk 12/30/90 (#3, 1 wk), 2 wk; tot 4 wk.

The World Almanac for 1947 [ed. E. Eastman Levine] (New York World Telegram) NYT gen 3/16/47 (#13), pk 4/6/47 (#10, 1 wk), 4 wk.

Year: Mid-Century Edition, 1900–1950 (Year) NYT gen 1/14/51 (#12, 1 wk).

Anson, Jay
The Amityville Horror: A True Story (Prentice Hall) NYT nf 10/9/77 (#15), pk 11/27/77 (#2, 1 wk), 41 wk; PW hc nf 10/17/77 (#12), pk 11/21/77 (#4, 7 wk), 43 wk; (Bantam) PW mm pb 8/14/78 (#14), pk 8/21/78 (#2, 3 wk), 38 wk; NYT mm pb 11/12/78 (#7), pk 9/2/79 (#2, 1 wk), 39 wk; tot 161 wk.

666 (Pocket) PW mm pb 4/23/82 (#12, 1 wk), 2 wk; NYT mm pb 4/25/82 (#9, 1 wk), 3 wk; tot 5 wk.

Anthony, Katharine
Queen Elizabeth (Knopf) PW nf 11/9/29 (#6), pk 12/14/29 (#5, 4 wk), 8 wk.

Anthony, Piers
Ogre, Ogre (Ballantine/Del Rey) NYT mm pb 10/10/82 (#11, 1 wk), 3 wk; PW mm pb 10/15/82 (#15), pk 10/22/82 (#9, 1 wk), 5 wk; tot 8 wk.

Night Mare (Ballantine/Del Rey) NYT mm pb 1/9/83 (#12, 1 wk), 2 wk; PW mm pb 1/14/83 (#13), pk 1/21/83 (#8, 1 wk), 4 wk; tot 6 wk.

Juxtaposition (Ballantine/Del Rey) NYT mm pb 5/8/83 (#13), pk 5/15/83 (#10, 1 wk), 2 wk; PW mm pb 5/13/83 (#15), pk 5/20/83 (#10, 1 wk), 4 wk; tot 6 wk.

Dragon on a Pedestal (Ballantine/Del Rey) NYT mm pb 10/9/83 (#10), pk 10/16/83 (#9,

1 wk), 5 wk; PW mm pb 10/14/83 (#11), pk 10/21/83 (#7, 1 wk), 4 wk; tot 9 wk.

On a Pale Horse (Ballantine/Del Rey) NYT pb fic 8/19/84 (#15), pk 9/9/84 (#14, 1 wk), 2 wk; PW mm pb 8/24/84 (#10, 1 wk); tot 3 wk.

Race Against Time (Tor) PW mm pb 9/20/85 (#15), pk 9/27/85 (#14, 1 wk), 3 wk.

Crewel Lye (Ballantine/Del Rey) NYT pb fic 1/6/85 (#9), pk 1/20/85 (#6, 1 wk), 6 wk; PW mm pb 1/18/85 (#9), pk 1/25/85 (#4, 1 wk), 5 wk; tot 11 wk.

Bearing an Hourglass (Ballantine/Del Rey) NYT pb fic 10/13/85 (#12), pk 10/20/85 (#11, 1 wk), 3 wk.

Bearing an Hourglass #2 (Ballantine/Del Rey) PW mm pb 10/18/85 (#10), pk 10/25/85 (#8, 1 wk), 4 wk.

Bio of a Space Tyrant, Vol. 3: Politician (Avon) PW mm pb 5/3/85 (#12), pk 5/10/85 (#11, 1 wk), 2 wk.

Golem in the Gears (Ballantine/Del Rey) NYT pb fic 2/2/86 (#14), pk 2/9/86 (#7, 1 wk), 6 wk; PW mm pb 2/21/86 (#14), pk 2/28/86 (#9, 1 wk), 4 wk; tot 10 wk.

With a Tangled Skein: Book Three of the Incarnations of Immortality (Ballantine/Del Rey) NYT pb fic 10/12/86 (#13, 2 wk), 3 wk; PW mm pb 10/17/86 (#14), pk 10/24/86 (#12, 1 wk), 4 wk; tot 7 wk.

Vale of the Vole (Avon) NYT pb fic 10/4/87 (#9), pk 10/11/87 (#6, 1 wk), 7 wk; PW mm pb 10/9/87 (#7, 3 wk), 6 wk; tot 13 wk.

Wielding a Red Sword (Ballantine/Del Rey) NYT pb fic 12/13/87 (#14, 1 wk); PW mm pb 12/18/87 (#7, 1 wk), 2 wk; tot 3 wk.

Out of Phaze (Ace) PW mm pb 4/8/88 (#15), pk 4/15/88 (#10, 1 wk), 5 wk; NYT pb fic 4/10/88 (#8, 3 wk), 5 wk; tot 10 wk.

Heaven Cent: Xanth #11 (Avon) NYT pb fic 10/9/88 (#3, 1 wk), 6 wk; PW mm pb 10/21/88 (#4, 1 wk), 7 wk; tot 13 wk.

Being a Green Mother: Book Five of Incarnations of Immortality (Ballantine/Del Rey) NYT pb fic 10/9/88 (#14, 1 wk); PW mm pb 10/28/88 (#14, 1 wk), 2 wk; tot 3 wk.

Robot Adept (Ace) NYT pb fic 3/19/89 (#14), pk 4/2/89 (#12, 1 wk), 4 wk.

Man from Mundania (Avon) NYT pb fic 10/8/89 (#7, 2 wk), 5 wk; PW mm pb 10/13/89 (#8), pk 10/20/89 (#6, 1 wk), 6 wk; tot 11 wk.

For Love of Evil (Avon) NYT pb fic 2/11/90 (#18), pk 2/18/90 (#13, 1 wk), 2 wk.

Unicorn Point (Ace) NYT pb fic 1/14/90 (#7, 1 wk), 3 wk; PW mm pb 1/26/90 (#14), pk 2/2/90 (#9, 1 wk), 2 wk; tot 5 wk.

And Eternity (Morrow) PW hc fic 1/26/90 (#14, 1 wk).

Isle of View (Avon) NYT pb fic 9/30/90 (#13), pk 10/7/90 (#4, 1 wk), 5 wk; PW mm pb 10/12/90 (#4, 1 wk), 3 wk; tot 8 wk.

Arcalli, Franco
See Bernardo Bertolucci and_____

Arce, Hector
The Secret Life of Tyrone Power (Morrow) PW hc nf 6/25/79 (#15), pk 7/9/79 (#12, 1 wk), 5 wk.

Archambault, John
See Bill Martin, Jr., and_____

Archbold, Rick
See Robert D. Ballard and_____

Archer, Jeffrey
Shall We Tell the President? (Viking) NYT fic 12/25/77 (#15, 1 wk).

Kane & Abel (Simon & Schuster) PW hc fic 4/18/80 (#11), pk 8/22/80 (#6, 1 wk), 29 wk; NYT fic 4/20/80 (#13), pk 6/22/80 (#4, 1 wk), 29 wk; (Fawcett/Crest) PW mm pb 2/27/81 (#5), pk 4/3/81 (#1, 2 wk), 31 wk; NYT mm pb 3/8/81 (#3), pk 4/5/81 (#1, 2 wk), 26 wk; NYT pb fic 12/1/85 (#13, 2 wk); tot 117 wk.

The Prodigal Daughter (Linden/Simon & Schuster) PW hc fic 6/4/82 (#11), pk 8/13/82 (#1, 4 wk), 22 wk; NYT fic 6/6/82 (#15), pk 7/4/82 (#1, 5 wk), 23 wk; (Pocket) NYT mm pb 6/5/83 (#6), pk 6/19/83 (#2, 4 wk), 15 wk; PW mm pb 6/10/83 (#5), pk 7/8/83 (#1, 3 wk), 14 wk; tot 74 wk.

First Among Equals (Linden/Simon & Schuster) NYT fic 8/5/84 (#15), pk 8/26/84 (#1, 3 wk), 18 wk; PW hc fic 8/17/84 (#7), pk 8/31/84 (#1, 2 wk), 16 wk; (Pocket) NYT pb fic 8/11/85 (#4), pk 8/18/85 (#1, 2 wk), 10 wk; PW mm pb 8/16/85 (#2), pk 8/23/85 (#1, 3 wk), 11 wk; tot 55 wk.

A Matter of Honor (Linden/Simon & Schuster) NYT fic 7/6/86 (#15), pk 7/13/86 (#2, 3 wk), 17 wk; PW hc fic 7/11/86 (#12), pk 8/1/86 (#2, 1 wk), 18 wk; (Pocket) NYT pb fic 7/12/87 (#5, 3 wk), 9 wk; PW mm pb 7/17/87 (#7), pk 7/24/87 (#5, 4 wk), 8 wk; tot 52 wk.

A Twist in the Tale (Simon & Schuster) NYT fic 1/29/89 (#15), pk 2/12/89 (#9, 1 wk), 4 wk; PW hc fic 2/3/89 (#12), pk 2/10/89 (#8, 1 wk), 7 wk; (Pocket) PW mm pb 12/22/89 (#14), pk 1/12/90 (#9, 1 wk), 3 wk; NYT pb fic 12/24/89 (#12, 1 wk), 3 wk; tot 17 wk.

Archibald, Norman
Heaven High, Hell Deep (Boni) PW nf 3/16/35 (#8, 4 wk).

Arden, Leslie
Love and Honor (Jove) NYT mm pb 8/31/

80 (#1, 1 wk), 2 wk; PW mm pb 9/5/80 (#14, 1 wk); tot 3 wk.

Ardmore, Jane Kesner
See Edith Head and____
See Eddie Cantor and____

Ardrey, Robert
The Territorial Imperative (Atheneum) NYT gen 10/23/66 (#9, 2 wk), 3 wk; PW nf 10/24/66 (#11), pk 10/31/66 (#9, 2 wk), 7 wk; tot 10 wk.

Aricha, Amos, and Eli Landau
Phoenix (NAL/Signet) PW mm pb 6/25/79 (#14), pk 7/9/79 (#12, 1 wk), 4 wk.

Arkell, Reginald
Old Herbaceous (Harcourt) NYT fic 3/11/51 (#14), pk 4/29/51 (#10, 1 wk), 24 wk; PW fic 6/9/51 (#10), pk 7/14/51 (#9, 1 wk), 2 wk; tot 26 wk.

Arkwright, Frank
The ABC of Technocracy (Harper) PW nf 2/11/33 (#6, 4 wk).

Arlen, Michael
The Green Hat (Doran) PW fic 4/18/25 (#6, 4 wk), 12 wk.
May Fair (Doran) PW fic 7/18/25 (#5, 4 wk).
Young Men in Love (Doran) PW fic 6/25/27 (#4, 4 wk), 8 wk.

Armbrister, Trevor
See Donald Riegle and____

Armer, Laura A.
Waterless Mountain (Longmans Green) PW juv 10/17/31 (#6), pk 1/16/32 (#4, 4 wk), 16 wk.

Armitage, Flora
The Desert and the Stars (Holt) NYT gen 9/18/55 (#11, 1 wk).

Armour, Tommy
How to Play Your Best Golf All the Time (Simon & Schuster) NYT gen 5/17/53 (#16), pk 7/12/53 (#3, 3 wk), 25 wk; PW nf 6/27/53 (#4), pk 7/18/53 (#3, 3 wk), 15 wk; tot 40 wk.

Armstrong, Hamilton Fish
We or They: Two Worlds in Conflict (Macmillan) NYT nf 3/7/37 (#8), pk 5/9/37 (#7, 4 wk), 8 wk; PW nf 5/8/37 (#8, 4 wk); tot 12 wk.
When There Is No Peace (Macmillan) NYT gen 3/5/39 (#8, 4 wk).
Tito and Goliath (Macmillan) NYT gen 3/4/51 (#15, 1 wk).

Armstrong, Margaret
Fanny Kemble (Macmillan) NYT gen 7/31/38 (#3, 4 wk), 8 wk; PW nf 8/13/38 (#3), pk 9/10/38 (#2, 4 wk), 16 wk; tot 24 wk.

Trelawny (Macmillan) PW nf 12/14/40 (#5), pk 1/11/41 (#3, 4 wk), 12 wk.

Armstrong, Scott
See Bob Woodward and____

Arnall, Ellis Gibbs
The Shore Dimly Seen (Lippincott) NYT gen 2/9/47 (#13, 1 wk), 4 wk.

Arnhym, Albert A.
See Gen. Thomas S. Power and____

Arno, Peter
Peter Arno's Hullabaloo (Liveright) PW nf 2/21/31 (#10, 4 wk).
Man in the Shower (Simon & Schuster) NYT gen 11/12/44 (#16, 1 wk), 3 wk.

Arnold, Elliott
The Commandos (Duell Sloan & Pearce) NYT fic 8/9/42 (#12), pk 9/13/42 (#9, 1 wk), 8 wk.
Tomorrow Will Sing (Duell Sloan & Pearce) NYT fic 3/11/45 (#10, 1 wk).
Everybody Slept Here (Duell Sloan & Pearce) NYT fic 5/16/48 (#15), pk 5/30/48 (#9, 1 wk), 6 wk.
A Night of Watching (Scribner) NYT fic 7/30/67 (#10), pk 9/10/67 (#4, 1 wk), 20 wk; PW fic 7/31/67 (#6), pk 9/4/67 (#1, 1 wk), 21 wk; tot 41 wk.

Arnold, Henry Harley
Global Mission (Harper) NYT gen 10/16/49 (#16, 2 wk).

Arnold, Thurman W.
The Folklore of Capitalism (Yale Univ.) NYT gen 2/6/38 (#11), pk 4/3/38 (#6, 4 wk), 12 wk; PW nf 2/12/38 (#10), pk 4/9/38 (#5, 4 wk), 12 wk; tot 24 wk.

Arnow, Harriette Louisa Simpson
Hunter's Horn (Macmillan) NYT fic 6/19/49 (#15), pk 8/14/49 (#13, 1 wk), 5 wk.
The Dollmaker (Macmillan) NYT fic 5/16/54 (#13), pk 6/27/54 (#4, 1 wk), 31 wk; PW fic 5/29/54 (#5), pk 6/26/54 (#4, 1 wk), 18 wk; tot 49 wk.

Aronson, Harvey
See F. Lee Bailey and____

Arpel, Adrien, with Ronnie Sue Ebenstein
Adrien Arpel's Three-Week Crash Makeover/Shapeover Beauty Program (Atheneum) NYT nf 4/2/78 (#14), pk 5/14/78 (#4, 1 wk), 20 wk; PW hc nf 4/3/78 (#11), pk 5/8/78 (#4, 1 wk), 20 wk; (Pocket/Wallaby) PW td pb 3/26/79 (#7), pk 5/7/79 (#3, 1 wk), 12 wk; NYT td pb 4/8/79 (#12), pk 4/29/79 (#1, 1 wk), 15 wk; tot 67 wk.
How to Look Ten Years Younger (Rawson

Wade/Atheneum) PW hc nf 6/20/80 (#15, 1 wk).

Arquette, Cliff
Charley Weaver's Letters from Mamma (Winston) NYT gen 5/4/59 (#14), pk 7/5/59 (#10, 1 wk), 21 wk; PW nf 7/20/59 (#8, 1 wk), 2 wk; tot 23 wk.

Arthur Young & Co. [all titles ed. Peter W. Bernstein]
The Arthur Young Tax Guide 1985 (Ballantine) NYT msc pb 2/3/85 (#4), pk 3/3/85 (#2, 2 wk), 13 wk; PW td pb 2/8/85 (#4), pk 3/1/85 (#1, 4 wk), 11 wk; tot 24 wk.
The Arthur Young Tax Guide 1986 (Ballantine) NYT msc pb 1/19/86 (#7), pk 2/2/86 (#1, 7 wk), 16 wk; PW td pb 1/31/86 (#8), pk 2/7/86 (#2, 4 wk), 15 wk; tot 31 wk.
The Arthur Young Tax Guide 1987 (Ballantine) NYT msc pb 1/25/87 (#10), pk 2/15/87 (#3, 1 wk), 11 wk; PW td pb 1/30/87 (#3), pk 2/27/87 (#1, 2 wk), 10 wk; tot 21 wk.
The Arthur Young Tax Guide 1988 (Ballantine) PW td pb 1/22/88 (#10), pk 2/19/88 (#1, 2 wk), 12 wk; NYT msc pb 2/7/88 (#1, 6 wk), 7 wk; tot 19 wk.
The Arthur Young Tax Guide 1989 (Ballantine) PW td pb 1/27/89 (#7), pk 2/24/89 (#1, 1 wk), 12 wk; NYT msc pb 2/5/89 (#3), pk 2/12/89 (#2, 3 wk), 6 wk; tot 18 wk.
The Arthur Young Tax Guide 1990 (Ballantine) PW td pb 1/26/90 (#9), pk 3/2/90 (#4, 1 wk), 8 wk; NYT msc pb 2/4/90 (#5, 3 wk); tot 11 wk.

Asbell, Bernard
When F.D.R. Died (Holt) NYT gen 5/7/61 (#16, 1 wk).

Asbury, Herbert
The Barbary Coast (Knopf) PW nf 9/16/33 (#9), pk 10/14/33 (#8, 8 wk), 12 wk.

Asch, Sholem
The Nazarene (Putnam) NYT fic 12/10/39 (#3, 8 wk); PW fic 12/16/39 (#4), pk 1/13/40 (#1, 4 wk), 28 wk; tot 36 wk.
The Apostle (Putnam) PW fic 10/9/43 (#6), pk 12/25/43 (#1, 1 wk), 32 wk; NYT fic 10/10/43 (#6), pk 11/28/43 (#3, 5 wk), 44 wk; tot 76 wk.
East River (Putnam) NYT fic 11/10/46 (#7), pk 11/24/46 (#1, 1 wk), 28 wk; PW fic 11/23/46 (#3), pk 11/30/46 (#1, 2 wk), 21 wk; tot 49 wk.
Mary (Putnam) NYT fic 10/23/49 (#9), pk 11/27/49 (#2, 9 wk), 29 wk; PW fic 11/5/49 (#3), pk 12/3/49 (#2, 9 wk), 19 wk; tot 48 wk.
Moses (Putnam) NYT fic 10/14/51 (#9), pk 12/30/51 (#4, 1 wk), 26 wk; PW fic 11/10/51 (#4, 7 wk), 14 wk; tot 40 wk.
A Passage in the Night (Putnam) NYT fic 11/29/53 (#16), pk 1/3/54 (#15, 1 wk), 6 wk.
The Prophet (Putnam) NYT fic 12/4/55 (#12, 1 wk), 9 wk.

Ash, Mary Kay
Mary Kay on People Management (Warner) NYT msc 10/7/84 (#4), pk 10/14/84 (#3, 1 wk), 7 wk; PW hc nf 10/12/84 (#12), pk 10/26/84 (#6, 1 wk), 9 wk; tot 16 wk.
See also Beauty Experts at Mary Kay Cosmetics

Ashe, Penelope
Naked Came the Stranger (Stuart) NYT fic 8/31/69 (#7), pk 11/2/69 (#3, 1 wk), 13 wk; PW fic 9/1/69 (#8), pk 9/15/69 (#5, 2 wk), 14 wk; NYT pb fic 5/3/70 (#4, 4 wk); tot 31 wk.

Asher, Cash
See Chief William Red Fox and_____

Ashford, Daisy
The Young Visiters (Doran) PW fic 11/1/19 (#3), pk 1/31/20 (#2, 4 wk), 12 wk.

Ashmore, Harry S.
An Epitaph for Dixie (Norton) NYT gen 2/16/58 (#13, 1 wk).

Ashton, Helen
The Half-Crown House (Dodd) NYT fic 8/19/56 (#16, 1 wk).

Ashton-Warner, Sylvia
Spinster (Simon & Schuster) NYT fic 4/12/59 (#14), pk 5/17/59 (#12, 2 wk), 8 wk.

Asimov, Isaac
Foundation's Edge (Doubleday) PW hc fic 10/15/82 (#11), pk 11/26/82 (#3, 1 wk), 24 wk; NYT fic 10/17/82 (#13), pk 12/5/82 (#3, 1 wk), 25 wk; (Ballantine/Del Rey) NYT mm pb 11/6/83 (#9), pk 11/13/83 (#3, 2 wk), 12 wk; PW mm pb 11/11/83 (#4), pk 11/18/83 (#3, 2 wk), 11 wk; tot 72 wk.
Foundation and Earth (Doubleday) NYT fic 10/19/86 (#12), pk 11/2/86 (#7, 4 wk), 15 wk; PW hc fic 10/24/86 (#7), pk 10/31/86 (#5, 2 wk), 13 wk; (Ballantine/Del Rey) NYT pb fic 10/11/87 (#5), pk 10/25/87 (#3, 1 wk), 8 wk; PW mm pb 10/16/87 (#6), pk 10/30/87 (#4, 3 wk), 8 wk; tot 44 wk.
Prelude to Foundation (Doubleday/Foundation) PW hc fic 5/13/88 (#12), pk 6/24/88 (#9, 1 wk), 8 wk; NYT fic 5/22/88 (#13), pk 6/19/88 (#10, 1 wk), 9 wk; (Bantam) NYT pb fic 4/9/89 (#11), pk 4/16/89 (#6, 1 wk), 6 wk; PW mm pb 4/14/89 (#5, 2 wk), 5 wk; tot 28 wk.
The Robots of Dawn (Doubleday) PW hc

fic 11/11/83 (#11), pk 1/6/84 (#6, 1 wk), 17 wk;
NYT fic 11/20/83 (#7), pk 11/27/83 (#6, 5
wk), 13 wk; (Ballantine/Del Rey) NYT pb fic
11/4/84 (#7), pk 11/11/84 (#4, 3 wk), 10 wk;
PW mm pb 11/9/84 (#9), pk 11/23/84 (#4, 1
wk), 8 wk; tot 48 wk.
   Robots and Empire (Doubleday) PW hc fic
10/11/85 (#12), pk 10/18/85 (#10, 1 wk), 7 wk;
(Ballantine/Del Rey) NYT pb fic 11/9/86
(#14), pk 11/23/86 (#9, 2 wk), 4 wk; PW mm
pb 11/14/86 (#8), pk 11/28/86 (#7, 1 wk), 4
wk; tot 15 wk.
   Nemesis (Doubleday/Foundation) PW hc
fic 10/27/89 (#10, 1 wk), 4 wk; (Bantam) PW
mm pb 9/28/90 (#15), pk 10/5/90 (#11, 1 wk),
3 wk; NYT pb fic 9/30/90 (#14), pk 10/7/90
(#9, 1 wk), 5 wk; tot 12 wk.

**Asprin, Robert Lynn, and Lynn
Abbey**
   Wings of Omen [ed.] (Ace) NYT pb fic
11/11/84 (#10, 1 wk).

Asquith, Margot
   The Autobiography of Margot Asquith
(Doran) PW gen lit 1/8/21 (#4), pk 2/26/21
(#1, 4 wk), 16 wk.

Astaire, Fred
   Steps in Time (Harper) NYT gen 7/5/59
(#14), pk 7/26/59 (#13, 1 wk), 2 wk.

Astor, Mary
   My Story (Doubleday) NYT gen 2/1/59
(#13), pk 3/1/59 (#10, 1 wk), 7 wk.

Atherton, Gertrude Franklin Horn
   The Sisters-In-Law (Stokes) PW fic
3/26/21 (#4, 12 wk).
   Black Oxen (Boni & Liveright) PW fic
3/17/23 (#3), pk 4/14/23 (#1, 16 wk), 28 wk.
   The Immortal Marriage (Boni & Liveright)
PW fic 6/25/27 (#10), pk 7/30/27 (#6, 4 wk),
12 wk.
   The Sophisticates (Liveright) PW fic 4/18/
31 (#6, 4 wk).
   The Horn of Life (Appleton) NYT fic 11/
8/42 (#14), pk 12/6/42 (#13, 1 wk), 4 wk.
   My San Francisco (Bobbs Merrill) NYT
gen 1/5/47 (#16), pk 1/19/47 (#12, 1 wk), 2
wk.

Athos, Anthony G.
   See Richard Tanner Pascale and_____

Atkins, Dr. Robert C.
   Dr. Atkins' Diet Revolution (McKay) PW
nf 11/27/72 (#4), pk 2/26/73 (#1, 20 wk), 47
wk; NYT gen 12/3/72 (#8), pk 2/18/73 (#1,
28 wk), 49 wk; NYT pb gen 11/11/73 (#2),
pk 12/9/73 (#1, 4 wk), 12 wk; NYT mm pb
7/14/74 (#10, 4 wk); tot 112 wk.
   Dr. Atkins' Nutrition Breakthrough (Mor-

row) NYT nf 4/26/81 (#14), pk 6/7/81 (#5, 1
wk), 17 wk; PW hc nf 5/22/81 (#13), pk
5/29/81 (#11, 1 wk), 5 wk; tot 22 wk.

_____, **and Shirley Motter Linde**
   Dr. Atkins' Superenergy Diet (Crown) PW
hc nf 4/18/77 (#10), pk 4/25/77 (#9, 2 wk),
3 wk.

Atkinson, Oriana Torrey
   Over at Uncle Joe's (Bobbs Merrill) NYT
gen 6/29/47 (#15, 2 wk).

Atkinson, Rick
   The Long Gray Line (Houghton) NYT nf
11/19/89 (#14), pk 11/26/89 (#13, 2 wk), 3 wk;
PW hc nf 12/1/89 (#14, 1 wk); tot 4 wk.

Attenborough, David
   Life on Earth (Little Brown) PW hc nf
2/12/82 (#15), pk 2/19/82 (#10, 1 wk), 8 wk;
NYT nf 3/28/82 (#11), pk 4/25/82 (#8, 1 wk),
8 wk; tot 16 wk.
   The Living Planet (Little Brown) NYT nf
3/3/85 (#15), pk 3/17/85 (#7, 1 wk), 7 wk;
PW hc nf 3/22/85 (#15, 1 wk); tot 8 wk.

Atwood, Margaret
   The Handmaid's Tale (Houghton) PW hc
fic 2/28/86 (#12), pk 3/28/86 (#5, 2 wk), 15
wk; NYT fic 3/2/86 (#6), pk 3/16/86 (#5, 2
wk), 15 wk; (Fawcett) NYT pb fic 1/25/87
(#9), pk 2/8/87 (#2, 3 wk), 27 wk; PW mm
pb 1/30/87 (#8), pk 2/20/87 (#2, 2 wk), 18
wk; tot 75 wk.
   Cat's Eye (Doubleday) NYT fic 2/19/89
(#9), pk 3/5/89 (#5, 2 wk), 15 wk; PW hc fic
2/24/89 (#9), pk 3/3/89 (#5, 2 wk), 12 wk;
(Bantam) NYT pb fic 12/3/89 (#13), pk 12/
31/89 (#6, 2 wk), 10 wk; PW mm pb 12/8/89
(#12), pk 1/19/90 (#9, 1 wk), 6 wk; tot 43 wk.

Auchincloss, Louis
   Sybil (Houghton) NYT fic 2/3/52 (#15, 1
wk).
   The House of Five Talents (Houghton)
NYT fic 10/2/60 (#10), pk 10/23/60 (#7, 1
wk), 12 wk; PW fic 10/24/60 (#9), pk 10/31/
60 (#8, 1 wk), 6 wk; tot 18 wk.
   Portrait in Brownstone (Houghton) NYT
fic 7/29/62 (#15), pk 9/16/62 (#7, 2 wk), 14
wk; PW fic 8/6/62 (#12), pk 8/13/62 (#7, 3
wk), 12 wk; tot 26 wk.
   Powers of Attorney (Houghton) NYT fic
9/22/63 (#10, 3 wk); PW fic 9/30/63 (#6, 1
wk), 3 wk; tot 6 wk.
   The Rector of Justin (Houghton) NYT fic
8/2/64 (#6), pk 10/4/64 (#1, 1 wk), 35 wk;
PW fic 8/17/64 (#7), pk 10/5/64 (#1, 3 wk),
36 wk; tot 71 wk.
   The Embezzler (Houghton) NYT fic
2/20/66 (#7), pk 3/27/66 (#2, 3 wk), 27 wk;
PW fic 2/28/66 (#6), pk 4/4/66 (#1, 2 wk),

31 wk; NYT pb fic 4/2/67 (#5, 4 wk); tot 62 wk.

Tales of Manhattan (Houghton) PW fic 4/10/67 (#7), pk 5/29/67 (#3, 1 wk), 21 wk; NYT fic 4/16/67 (#9), pk 5/14/67 (#4, 2 wk), 18 wk; tot 39 wk.

A World of Profit (Houghton) NYT fic 12/29/68 (#9), pk 2/16/69 (#6, 2 wk), 13 wk; PW fic 1/6/69 (#6), pk 2/24/69 (#5, 2 wk), 16 wk; tot 29 wk.

I Come as a Thief (Houghton) PW fic 9/11/72 (#9, 3 wk), 5 wk; NYT fic 10/8/72 (#10, 1 wk); tot 6 wk.

The Partners (Houghton) PW fic 3/18/74 (#10), pk 4/1/74 (#4, 1 wk), 15 wk; NYT fic 3/24/74 (#7), pk 4/7/74 (#5, 4 wk), 15 wk; tot 30 wk.

The Dark Lady (Houghton) NYT fic 9/11/77 (#14, 1 wk).

Audubon, John James
The Birds of America (Macmillan) PW nf 12/11/37 (#4, 4 wk), 12 wk.

Auel, Jean M.
Clan of the Cave Bear (Crown) NYT fic 10/12/80 (#11), pk 1/11/81 (#8, 2 wk), 18 wk; PW hc fic 11/7/80 (#11, 1 wk), 12 wk; (Bantam) PW mm pb 8/14/81 (#9), pk 2/7/86 (#4, 1 wk), 41 wk; NYT mm pb 8/16/81 (#11), pk 10/11/81 (#6, 1 wk), 25 wk; NYT pb fic 1/1/84 (#7), pk 2/2/86 (#4, 1 wk), 37 wk; tot 133 wk.

The Valley of Horses (Crown) PW hc fic 9/3/82 (#10), pk 10/1/82 (#2, 1 wk), 45 wk; NYT fic 9/5/82 (#11), pk 9/19/82 (#2, 2 wk), 47 wk; (Bantam) NYT mm pb 9/4/83 (#2), pk 9/11/83 (#1, 6 wk), 22 wk; PW mm pb 9/9/83 (#2), pk 9/23/83 (#1, 5 wk), 26 wk; NYT pb fic 1/12/84 (#15), pk 1/26/86 (#9, 1 wk), 19 wk; tot 159 wk.

The Mammoth Hunters (Crown) NYT fic 11/24/85 (#1, 11 wk), 47 wk; PW hc fic 11/29/85 (#1, 12 wk), 46 wk; (Bantam) NYT pb fic 11/30/86 (#1, 8 wk), 16 wk; PW mm pb 12/5/86 (#1, 5 wk), 10 wk; tot 119 wk.

The Plains of Passage (Crown) PW hc fic 10/26/90 (#1, 9 wk); NYT fic 10/28/90 (#1, 10 wk); tot 19 wk.

Auletta, Ken
Greed and Glory on Wall Street: The Fall of the House of Lehman (Random) NYT nf 2/9/86 (#15), pk 3/9/86 (#6, 1 wk), 13 wk; PW hc nf 3/21/86 (#14), pk 4/4/86 (#12, 1 wk), 6 wk; tot 19 wk.

Auslander, Joseph, and Audrey Wurdemann
My Uncle Jan (Longmans) NYT fic 5/23/48 (#14, 1 wk), 2 wk.

Austin, Margot
Churchmouse Stories (Dutton) NYT ch bst 11/17/57 (#5, 40 wk).

Austin, Nancy K.
See Thomas J. Peters and_____

Ausubel, Nathan
A Treasury of Jewish Folklore [ed.] (Crown) NYT gen 8/22/48 (#16), pk 10/3/48 (#13, 2 wk), 8 wk.

Author of "Elizabeth and Her German Garden"
See Mary Annette Beauchamp Russell

Averbuch, Bernard
See John W. Noble and_____

Awlinson, Richard
Waterdeep (TSR) NYT pb fic 11/5/89 (#15, 1 wk).

Aydelotte, Dora
Trumpets Calling (Appleton) NYT fic 3/6/38 (#7, 4 wk).

Ayer, Margaret Hubbard, and Isabella Taves
The Three Lives of Harriet Hubbard Ayer (Lippincott) NYT gen 7/21/57 (#16, 1 wk).

Aynesworth, Hugh
See Stephen G. Michaud and_____

Ayres, Ruby Mildred
Afterglow (Doubleday) NYT fic 5/3/36 (#6, 4 wk).

Too Much Together (Doubleday) NYT fic 7/5/36 (#7, 4 wk).

The Tree Drops a Leaf (Doubleday) NYT fic 2/6/38 (#14, 4 wk).

Bacall, Lauren
Lauren Bacall by Myself (Knopf) PW hc nf 1/22/79 (#11), pk 2/5/79 (#1, 7 wk), 29 wk; NYT nf 2/4/79 (#2), pk 2/11/79 (#1, 7 wk), 31 wk; (Ballantine) PW mm pb 1/18/80 (#2), pk 1/25/80 (#1, 2 wk), 12 wk; NYT mm pb 1/20/80 (#2), pk 1/27/80 (#1, 2 wk), 14 wk; tot 86 wk.

Bach, Richard
Jonathan Livingston Seagull (Macmillan) PW nf 2/21/72 (#10), pk 6/19/72 (#1, 3 wk), 15 wk; NYT fic 4/30/72 (#10), pk 7/2/72 (#1, 38 wk), 70 wk; PW fic 7/24/72 (#1, 32 wk), 61 wk; NYT pb fic 2/11/73 (#2), pk 3/11/73 (#1, 16 wk), 32 wk; tot 178 wk.

Illusions: The Adventures of a Reluctant Messiah (Friede/Delacorte) PW hc fic 6/13/77 (#8), pk 8/15/77 (#2, 1 wk), 86 wk; NYT fic 6/19/77 (#9), pk 9/11/77 (#2, 3 wk), 81 wk; (Dell) NYT mm pb 7/8/79 (#8, 2 wk), 8 wk; PW mm pb 7/9/79 (#9, 1 wk), 5 wk; tot 180 wk.

There's No Such Place as Far Away (Friede/

Delacorte) PW hc fic 6/4/79 (#15), pk 7/30/
79 (#7, 1 wk), 27 wk; NYT fic 6/24/79 (#11),
pk 7/29/79 (#6, 1 wk), 25 wk; tot 52 wk.
  The Bridge Across Forever (Morrow) NYT
nf 9/9/84 (#10), pk 10/7/84 (#2, 3 wk), 54
wk; PW hc nf 9/21/84 (#14), pk 10/19/84 (#3,
3 wk), 31 wk; (Dell) NYT pb nf 2/2/86 (#4),
pk 2/9/86 (#2, 6 wk), 34 wk; PW mm pb 2/
7/86 (#10), pk 2/28/86 (#5, 1 wk), 9 wk; tot
128 wk.
  One (Silver Arrow/Morrow) PW hc fic 11/
4/88 (#11), pk 11/25/88 (#4, 9 wk), 16 wk;
NYT fic 11/6/88 (#7), pk 12/11/88 (#3, 2 wk),
16 wk; (Dell) NYT pb fic 11/12/89 (#13), pk
11/19/89 (#8, 2 wk), 4 wk; PW mm pb 11/17/
89 (#11, 1 wk), 2 wk; tot 38 wk.

Bach, Steven
  *Final Cut: Dreams and Disasters in the
Making of Heaven's Gate* (Morrow) PW hc nf
8/30/85 (#13, 2 wk), 3 wk; NYT nf 9/8/85
(#12), pk 9/15/85 (#9, 1 wk), 4 wk; tot 7 wk.

Bacheller, Irving
  A Man for the Ages (Bobbs Merrill) PW fic
1/31/20 (#4), pk 3/27/20 (#3, 8 wk), 20 wk.
  In the Days of Poor Richard (Bobbs Merrill) PW fic 9/16/22 (#10, 4 wk), 8 wk.
  Dawn (Macmillan) PW fic 5/21/27 (#8, 4
wk).

Bacher, June Masters
  Love's Enduring Hope (Harvest) PW pb rel
10/5/90 (#14, 4 wk).

Bachman, Richard
  See Stephen King

Baez, Joan
  And a Voice to Sing With (Summit) NYT
nf 8/2/87 (#13), pk 8/30/87 (#10, 1 wk), 5
wk.

Bagni, Gwen and Paul Dubov
  Backstairs at the White House (Bantam) PW
mm pb 2/19/79 (#12), pk 3/5/79 (#10, 1 wk),
6 wk; NYT mm pb 3/11/79 (#13), pk 3/25/79
(#12, 1 wk), 2 wk; tot 8 wk.

Bagnold, Enid
  National Velvet (Morrow) PW fic 6/15/35
(#6), pk 7/13/35 (#5, 4 wk; 16 wk.
  The Loved and Envied (Doubleday) NYT
fic 1/28/51 (#6, 1 wk), 9 wk.

**Baigent, Michael, Richard Leigh and
  Henry Lincoln**
  Holy Blood, Holy Grail (Delacorte) PW hc
nf 3/26/82 (#15), pk 4/9/82 (#4, 1 wk), 12
wk; NYT nf 4/4/82 (#15), pk 4/25/82 (#7, 1
wk), 13 wk; tot 25 wk.

Bailey, Charles Waldo, III
  See Fletcher Knebel and_____

Bailey, Covert
  Fit or Fat? (Houghton) NYT td pb 4/24/
83 (#15), pk 5/29/83 (#9, 1 wk), 23 wk; NYT
msc pb 6/10/84 (#7), pk 8/19/84 (#6, 1 wk),
10 wk; tot 33 wk.
  The Fit or Fat Target Diet (Houghton) PW
td pb 6/15/84 (#8, 3 wk), 6 wk; NYT msc pb
6/17/84 (#6, 2 wk), 8 wk; tot 14 wk.

Bailey, F. Lee
  Secrets (Stein & Day) NYT fic 2/11/79
(#14), pk 3/11/79 (#13, 1 wk), 2 wk; PW hc
fic 2/19/79 (#15), pk 3/5/79 (#14, 1 wk), 4 wk;
tot 6 wk.

_____, with Harvey Aronson
  The Defense Never Rests (Stein & Day)
NYT gen 1/16/72 (#10), pk 4/16/72 (#2, 1
wk), 22 wk; PW nf 1/31/72 (#7), pk 4/10/72
(#2, 2 wk), 19 wk; NYT pb gen 10/8/72 (#5,
4 wk); tot 45 wk.

Bailey, Henry Christopher
  Black Land, White Land (Doubleday) NYT
fic 3/7/37 (#9, 4 wk).

Bailey, Temple
  The Tin Soldier (Penn) PW fic 5/3/19 (#7),
pk 6/7/19 (#5, 4 wk), 20 wk.
  The Trumpeter Swan (Penn) PW fic 11/27/
20 (#4, 8 wk), 12 wk.
  The Dim Lantern (Penn) PW fic 3/17/23
(#2, 8 wk), 20 wk.
  The Blue Window (Penn) PW fic 4/17/26
(#4), pk 5/15/26 (#3, 4 wk), 20 wk.
  Wallflowers (Penn) PW fic 10/22/27 (#7, 8
wk).
  Silver Slippers (Penn) PW fic 11/24/28
(#9), pk 12/22/28 (#3, 4 wk), 16 wk.
  Wild Wind (Penn) PW fic 10/18/30 (#5, 4
wk), 8 wk.
  Burning Beauty (Penn) PW fic 1/11/30 (#7,
4 wk).
  Little Girl Lost (Penn) PW fic 9/10/32 (#5,
4 wk).
  Enchanted Ground (Penn) PW fic 9/16/33
(#6, 4 wk).
  Fair as the Moon (Grosset & Dunlap)
NYT fic 10/6/35 (#3, 4 wk).
  Tomorrow's Promise (Grosset & Dunlap)
NYT fic 10/9/38 (#10, 4 wk).
  The Pink Camellia (Houghton) NYT fic
9/20/42 (#15), pk 10/4/42 (#12, 1 wk), 3 wk.

Bainbridge, John
  Garbo (Doubleday) NYT gen 4/24/55
(#14), pk 5/22/55 (#13, 1 wk), 6 wk.

Bainton, Roland Herbert
  Here I Stand: A Life of Martin Luther
(Abingdon Cokesbury) NYT gen 4/1/51
(#16, 1 wk).

Bair, Dierdre
Simone de Beauvoir (Summit) NYT nf 5/20/90 (#15, 2 wk).

Baker, Bobby, with Larry L. King
Wheeling and Dealing: Confessions of a Capitol Hill Operator (Norton) PW hc nf 7/17/78 (#13), pk 8/7/78 (#12, 1 wk), 4 wk.

Baker, Carlos
Ernest Hemingway: A Life Story (Scribner) PW nf 4/28/69 (#9), pk 6/16/69 (#1, 1 wk), 25 wk; NYT gen 5/4/69 (#6), pk 5/25/69 (#2, 6 wk), 20 wk; tot 45 wk.

Baker, Dorothy Dodds
Young Man with a Horn (Houghton) NYT fic 7/3/38 (#12, 4 wk).
Trio (Houghton) NYT fic 8/15/43 (#10, 3 wk), 11 wk.

Baker, Sgt. George
The Sad Sack (Simon & Schuster) NYT fic 3/18/45 (#17, 1 wk).

Baker, Louise Maxwell
Party Line (McGraw) NYT fic 4/15/45 (#11, 1 wk).
Out on a Limb (Whittlesey/McGraw) NYT gen 11/17/46 (#15), pk 12/8/46 (#12, 1 wk), 8 wk.

Baker, Mark
Nam (Berkley) PW mm pb 4/8/83 (#12, 1 wk).
Cops: Their Lives in Their Own Words (Pocket) NYT pb nf 5/18/86 (#2), pk 6/1/86 (#1, 2 wk), 10 wk; PW mm pb 5/23/86 (#14), pk 6/6/86 (#10, 1 wk), 3 wk; tot 13 wk.

Baker, Ray Stannard
American Chronicle (Scribner) NYT gen 5/6/45 (#16, 1 wk).

Baker, Russell
Growing Up (Congdon & Weed) NYT nf 11/14/82 (#13), pk 12/26/82 (#3, 2 wk), 43 wk; PW hc nf 11/26/82 (#11), pk 12/24/82 (#4, 1 wk), 32 wk; (NAL/Plume) NYT td pb 10/23/83 (#10), pk 12/11/83 (#2, 1 wk), 10 wk; PW td pb 10/28/83 (#8), pk 11/11/83 (#2, 7 wk), 24 wk; NYT pb nf 1/1/84 (#2), pk 1/15/84 (#1, 2 wk), 17 wk; PW mm pb 12/21/84 (#15), pk 1/11/85 (#10, 1 wk), 4 wk; tot 130 wk.
The Good Times (Morrow) PW hc nf 6/9/89 (#15), pk 7/28/89 (#2, 1 wk), 16 wk; NYT nf 6/11/89 (#8), pk 7/16/89 (#2, 2 wk), 18 wk; tot 34 wk.

Baker, Samm Sinclair
See Herman Tarnower M.D. and_____
See Dr. Irwin Maxwell Stillman and_____

Baker, Trudy, and Rachel Jones

Coffee, Tea or Me? (Taplinger) PW nf 1/29/68 (#13, 1 wk); NYT pb gen 12/1/68 (#2, 4 wk), 16 wk; tot 17 wk.

Baldrige, Letitia
Of Diamonds and Diplomats (Houghton) NYT gen 10/13/68 (#8), pk 11/10/68 (#5, 1 wk), 13 wk; PW nf 10/28/68 (#9), pk 11/25/68 (#3, 1 wk), 10 wk; tot 23 wk.

Baldwin, Faith
Babs (Dodd) PW juv 3/21/31 (#9, 4 wk).
The Moon's Our Home (Farrar) NYT fic 2/2/36 (#5, 4 wk).
Men Are Such Fools (Farrar) NYT fic 10/4/36 (#9, 4 wk).
That Man Is Mine (Grosset & Dunlap) NYT fic 1/31/37 (#10, 4 wk).
The Heart Has Wings (Collier) NYT fic 6/6/37 (#7, 4 wk).
Twenty-Four Hours a Day (Collier) NYT fic 10/10/37 (#8, 4 wk).
Rich Girl, Poor Girl (Collier) NYT fic 7/3/38 (#10, 4 wk).
Hotel Hostess (Collier) NYT fic 11/6/38 (#14, 4 wk).
Enchanted Oasis (Collier) NYT fic 3/6/38 (#8, 4 wk).
White Magic (Collier) NYT fic 10/8/39 (#5, 4 wk).
The High Road (Collier) NYT fic 2/5/39 (#11, 4 wk).
Career by Proxy (Farrar) NYT fic 6/11/39 (#3, 4 wk).

Baldwin, Hanson
Sea Fights and Shipwrecks (Hanover) NYT gen 10/23/55 (#14), pk 11/13/55 (#10, 1 wk), 2 wk; PW nf 11/19/55 (#10, 1 wk); tot 3 wk.

Baldwin, Hanson Weightman, et al.
We Saw It Happen (Simon & Schuster) NYT gen 2/5/39 (#12, 4 wk), 8 wk.

Baldwin, James
Nobody Knows My Name (Dial) NYT gen 8/27/61 (#13), pk 9/17/61 (#9, 1 wk), 9 wk.
Another Country (Dial) NYT fic 7/8/62 (#14), pk 9/2/62 (#6, 4 wk), 24 wk; PW fic 7/30/62 (#6), pk 9/10/62 (#4, 2 wk), 17 wk; tot 41 wk.
The Fire Next Time (Dial) PW nf 3/4/63 (#4), pk 7/1/63 (#1, 12 wk), 43 wk; NYT gen 4/7/63 (#3), pk 7/7/63 (#1, 12 wk), 35 wk; tot 78 wk.
Tell Me How Long the Train's Been Gone (Dial) NYT fic 7/7/68 (#7, 1 wk), 2 wk; NYT pb fic 9/7/69 (#5, 4 wk); tot 6 wk.
If Beale Street Could Talk (Dial) PW fic 6/24/74 (#8), pk 7/29/74 (#7, 1 wk), 10 wk; NYT fic 7/7/74 (#9), pk 8/18/74 (#7, 1 wk), 7 wk; tot 17 wk.

Baldwin, Monica
I Leap Over the Wall (Rinehart) NYT gen 2/19/50 (#14), pk 4/2/50 (#4, 1 wk), 24 wk; PW nf 3/25/50 (#3, 2 wk), 5 wk; tot 29 wk.

Ball, Walter S.
Carmella Commands (Harper) PW juv 2/15/30 (#8, 4 wk).

Ballantine, Betty
See Frank Frazetta and_____

Ballard, J.G.
Empire of the Sun (Pocket) PW mm pb 1/29/88 (#12, 1 wk).

Ballard, Robert D., with Rick Archbold
The Discovery of the Titanic (Madison Press/Warner) NYT nf 11/1/87 (#15), pk 11/15/87 (#9, 2 wk), 10 wk; PW hc nf 11/20/87 (#11), pk 11/27/87 (#9, 1 wk), 3 wk; tot 13 wk.
The Discovery of the Bismarck (Warner) NYT nf 12/23/90 (#14, 1 wk).

Balsan, Consuelo Vanderbilt
The Glitter and the Gold (Harper) NYT gen 10/5/52 (#12), pk 11/2/52 (#4, 5 wk), 20 wk; PW nf 10/18/52 (#4), pk 11/8/52 (#3, 4 wk), 12 wk; tot 32 wk.

Balsiger, David, and Charles E. Sellier, Jr.
The Lincoln Conspiracy (Sunn/NAL) PW mm pb 10/17/77 (#15), pk 10/31/77 (#2, 1 wk), 10 wk; NYT mm pb 10/23/77 (#7), pk 10/30/77 (#2, 1 wk), 11 wk; tot 21 wk.

Bamford, James
The Puzzle Palace: A Report on America's Most Secret Agency (Houghton) NYT nf 11/7/82 (#11, 2 wk); PW hc nf 11/12/82 (#13, 2 wk), 4 wk; tot 6 wk.

Bandy, Way
Designing Your Face: An Illustrated Guide for Using Cosmetics (Random) PW hc nf 11/14/77 (#10, 1 wk), 10 wk; NYT nf 12/4/77 (#8, 1 wk), 22 wk; tot 32 wk.

Bankhead, Tallulah
Tallulah (Harper) NYT gen 10/19/52 (#2), pk 10/26/52 (#1, 16 wk), 27 wk; PW nf 10/25/52 (#2), pk 11/1/52 (#1, 12 wk), 18 wk; tot 45 wk.

Banks, Ernest, and Jim Enright
Mr. Cub (Follett) NYT gen 5/30/71 (#10), pk 6/27/71 (#9, 2 wk), 4 wk.

Banks, Lynne Reid
The Secret of the Indian (Avon/Camelot) PW ch md rd 11/30/90 (#5), pk 12/21/90 (#2, 4 wk), 8 wk.

Banner, Angela
Ant and Bee and the ABC (Price Stern Sloan) NYT ch bst 11/5/67 (#8, 26 wk).

Banning, Margaret Culking
The Iron Will (Grosset & Dunlap) NYT fic 5/3/36 (#9, 4 wk).

Barber, Rowland
See Harpo Marx and_____

Barbour, Thomas
Naturalist at Large (Little Brown) NYT gen 11/7/43 (#12, 1 wk), 2 wk.

Bard, Mary
The Doctor Wears Three Faces (Lippincott) NYT gen 5/15/49 (#15), pk 6/5/49 (#11, 2 wk), 10 wk.

Barker, Clive
The Damnation Game (Putnam/Ace) PW hc fic 5/29/87 (#15), pk 6/5/87 (#10, 1 wk), 5 wk; NYT fic 5/31/87 (#15, 1 wk), 2 wk; (Charter) NYT pb fic 7/10/88 (#15), pk 7/17/88 (#12, 1 wk), 3 wk; PW mm pb 7/15/88 (#10, 1 wk), 3 wk; tot 13 wk.
The Great and Secret Show (Harper) PW hc fic 2/9/90 (#15), pk 3/16/90 (#7, 1 wk), 7 wk; NYT fic 2/18/90 (#15), pk 3/11/90 (#14, 1 wk), 3 wk; (HarperCollins) PW mm pb 11/9/90 (#14), pk 11/16/90 (#10, 1 wk), 6 wk; NYT pb fic 11/18/90 (#7), pk 11/25/90 (#6, 1 wk), 3 wk; tot 19 wk.

Barker, Shirley
Rivers Parting (Crown) NYT fic 1/21/51 (#11), pk 2/25/51 (#10, 1 wk), 6 wk; PW fic 2/17/51 (#10), pk 3/17/51 (#9, 1 wk), 2 wk; tot 8 wk.

Barley, Lynn
See Frank Miller, et al.

Barmine, Alexandre
One Who Survived (Putnam) NYT gen 8/5/45 (#14), pk 8/26/45 (#13, 1 wk), 2 wk.

Barnes, Clare, Jr.
White Collar Zoo (Doubleday) NYT gen 7/24/49 (#11), pk 9/4/49 (#1, 18 wk), 37 wk; PW nf 8/13/49 (#8), pk 9/10/49 (#1, 19 wk), 33 wk; tot 70 wk.
Home Sweet Zoo (Doubleday) NYT gen 12/18/49 (#7), pk 1/29/50 (#2, 1 wk), 17 wk; PW nf 12/31/49 (#5), pk 1/14/50 (#2, 6 wk), 14 wk; tot 31 wk.

Barnes, Joanna
Pastora (Avon) PW mm pb 11/27/81 (#10), pk 12/18/81 (#5, 1 wk), 6 wk; NYT mm pb 11/29/81 (#11), pk 12/27/81 (#6, 1 wk), 9 wk; tot 15 wk.

Barnes, Margaret Ayer
Years of Grace (Houghton) PW fic 9/20/30 (#3, 12 wk), 32 wk.

Westward Passage (Houghton) PW fic 1/16/
32 (#3), pk 2/13/32 (#2, 4 wk), 12 wk.
Within This Present (Houghton) PW fic
12/9/33 (#3), pk 1/13/34 (#2, 8 wk), 32 wk.
Edna His Wife (Houghton) NYT fic 12/1/
35 (#2, 4 wk), 8 wk; PW fic 12/14/35 (#3),
pk 1/11/36 (#1, 4 wk), 16 wk; tot 24 wk.
Wisdom's Gate (Houghton) NYT fic 12/4/
38 (#4, 4 wk); PW fic 12/10/38 (#6, 4 wk),
12 wk; tot 16 wk.

Barnes, Margaret Campbell
With All My Heart (Macrae Smith) NYT
fic 10/7/51 (#16, 1 wk).

Barnett, Lincoln Kinnear
The Universe and Dr. Einstein (Sloane)
NYT gen 3/6/49 (#11, 1 wk), 6 wk.

Barnhart, Clarence L.
*The Thorndike-Barnhart Comprehensive
Desk Dictionary* [ed.] (Doubleday) PW nf
3/17/51 (#10), pk 3/24/51 (#7, 1 wk), 2 wk;
NYT gen 4/22/51 (#16, 1 wk); tot 3 wk.

Barr, Pat
Jade (Warner) NYT mm pb 9/4/83 (#12),
pk 9/25/83 (#9, 1 wk), 5 wk; PW mm pb
9/16/83 (#11, 1 wk), 3 wk; tot 8 wk.

Barr, Roseanne
Roseanne: My Life as a Woman (Harper)
NYT nf 10/15/89 (#7), pk 10/22/89 (#2, 3
wk), 17 wk; PW hc nf 10/20/89 (#8), pk
10/27/89 (#1, 1 wk), 16 wk; NYT pb nf 10/21/
90 (#9, 1 wk); tot 34 wk.

Barr, Stringfellow
Purely Academic (Simon & Schuster) NYT
fic 2/9/58 (#11, 1 wk), 4 wk.

Barrett, Monte
Sun in Their Eyes (Bobbs Merrill) NYT fic
10/8/44 (#12, 5 wk), 9 wk.

Barrett, William E.
The Left Hand of God (Doubleday) NYT
fic 2/18/51 (#11), pk 4/15/51 (#8, 1 wk), 16 wk;
PW fic 5/12/51 (#10, 1 wk); tot 17 wk.
Shadows of the Images (Doubleday) NYT
fic 11/22/53 (#16), pk 12/20/53 (#10, 2 wk),
11 wk; PW fic 1/2/54 (#6, 1 wk); tot 12 wk.

Barrington, E. [pseud.]
Glorious Apollo (Dodd) PW fic 9/26/25
(#3), pk 10/24/25 (#2, 4 wk), 16 wk.
The Exquisite Perdita (Dodd) PW fic 9/18/
26 (#6, 4 wk).
The Thunderer (Dodd) PW fic 10/22/27
(#4, 4 wk).
The Empress of Hearts (Dodd) PW fic
12/22/28 (#10, 4 wk).
The Laughing Queen (Dodd) PW fic 9/14/
29 (#10, 4 wk).

Barris, Chuck
You and Me, Babe (Harper's Magazine)
PW fic 4/29/74 (#9), pk 5/27/74 (#6, 1 wk),
8 wk; NYT fic 5/5/74 (#7, 2 wk), 7 wk; tot
15 wk.

Barron, Robert
See Jim Fisk and_____

**Barrows, Sydney Biddle, and William
  Novak**
*Mayflower Madam: The Secret Life of Syd-
ney Biddle Barrows* (Arbor House) NYT nf
9/21/86 (#14), pk 10/5/86 (#3, 3 wk), 8 wk;
PW hc nf 10/3/86 (#10), pk 10/10/86 (#5, 3
wk), 7 wk; (Ivy/Ballantine) NYT pb nf 6/28/
87 (#6), pk 7/19/87 (#1, 4 wk), 20 wk; PW
mm pb 7/3/87 (#12), pk 7/10/87 (#7, 1 wk),
9 wk; tot 44 wk.

Barry, Dave
*Dave Barry Slept Here: A Sort of History of
the United States* (Random) NYT nf 7/2/89
(#14), pk 7/16/89 (#9, 4 wk), 11 wk; PW hc
nf 7/28/89 (#15, 1 wk), (Fawcett/Columbine)
PW td pb 6/22/90 (#9, 1 wk); tot 13 wk.
Dave Barry Turns 40 (Crown) PW hc nf
6/1/90 (#13), pk 6/22/90 (#2, 8 wk), 21 wk;
NYT nf 6/3/90 (#7), pk 6/10/90 (#2, 10 wk),
20 wk; tot 41 wk.

Barry, Stephen P.
Royal Service (Macmillan) NYT nf 4/24/
83 (#15, 1 wk).

**Barrymore, Diana, and Gerold
  Frank**
Too Much, Too Soon (Holt) NYT gen 4/28/
57 (#12), pk 5/19/57 (#6, 3 wk), 22 wk; PW
nf 5/13/57 (#5), pk 5/27/57 (#4, 1 wk), 11 wk;
tot 33 wk.

Barrymore, Drew, with Todd Gold
Little Girl Lost (Pocket) NYT nf 3/4/90
(#14, 1 wk).

Barrymore, Ethel
Memories (Harper) NYT gen 5/8/55 (#6,
1 wk), 12 wk; PW nf 6/4/55 (#7, 3 wk), 5 wk;
tot 17 wk.

**Barrymore, Lionel, and Cameron
  Shipp**
We Barrymores (Appleton) NYT gen 6/3/
51 (#13), pk 6/24/51 (#7, 2 wk), 12 wk; PW
nf 6/30/51 (#5, 1 wk), 3 wk; tot 15 wk.

Barsocchini, Peter
See Merv Griffin and_____

Barth, Alan
The Loyalty of Free Men (Archon) NYT
gen 2/25/51 (#12), pk 3/4/51 (#11, 1 wk), 3
wk.

Barth, John
Giles Goat-Boy (Doubleday) NYT fic 8/28/66 (#8), pk 9/11/66 (#4, 3 wk), 12 wk; PW fic 9/5/66 (#8), pk 10/3/66 (#4, 1 wk), 14 wk; NYT pb fic 9/3/67 (#4, 4 wk), 8 wk; tot 34 wk.

Bartley, William Warren, III
Werner Erhard—The Transformation of a Man: The Founding of EST (Potter/Crown) PW hc nf 11/6/78 (#15), pk 11/13/78 (#11, 1 wk), 4 wk; NYT nf 11/26/78 (#15, 1 wk); tot 5 wk.

Barton, Bruce
The Man Nobody Knows (Bobbs Merrill) PW gen lit 7/18/25 (#5), pk 9/26/25 (#4, 4 wk), 8 wk; PW nf 10/24/25 (#3), pk 3/20/25 (#1, 20 wk), 72 wk; tot 80 wk.
The Book Nobody Knows (Bobbs Merrill) PW nf 8/14/26 (#1, 8 wk), 36 wk.
What Can a Man Believe? (Bobbs Merrill) PW nf 10/22/27 (#6), pk 11/26/27 (#5, 4 wk), 12 wk.

Barton, William Eleazar
The Life of Abraham Lincoln (Bobbs Merrill) PW gen lit 4/18/25 (#4, 4 wk).

Baruch, Bernard Mannes
A Philosophy for Our Time (Simon & Schuster) NYT gen 9/19/54 (#14), pk 9/26/54 (#12, 3 wk), 6 wk.
Baruch: My Own Story (Holt) NYT gen 9/8/57 (#3), pk 9/22/57 (#1, 19 wk), 43 wk; PW nf 9/9/57 (#3), pk 9/16/57 (#1, 15 wk), 38 wk; tot 81 wk.
Baruch: The Public Years (Holt) NYT gen 10/30/60 (#13), pk 12/11/60 (#4, 3 wk), 18 wk; PW nf 11/7/60 (#8), pk 11/28/60 (#4, 2 wk), 15 wk; tot 33 wk.

Barzini, Luigi
The Italians (Atheneum) NYT gen 9/20/64 (#10), pk 1/10/65 (#3, 4 wk), 38 wk; PW nf 9/28/64 (#7), pk 11/30/64 (#3, 3 wk), 36 wk; NYT pb gen 12/5/65 (#4, 4 wk); tot 78 wk.

Barzun, Jacques
The House of Intellect (Harper) NYT gen 6/7/59 (#15), pk 7/5/59 (#7, 2 wk), 21 wk; PW nf 6/22/59 (#9), pk 7/27/59 (#6, 1 wk), 13 wk; tot 34 wk.

Base, Graeme
The Eleventh Hour: A Curious Mystery (Abrams) NYT fic 12/3/89 (#13), pk 12/10/89 (#7, 1 wk), 8 wk; PW hc fic 1/5/90 (#12), pk 1/12/90 (#11, 1 wk), 2 wk; PW ch pic 8/31/90 (#5, 8 wk); tot 18 wk.

Bass, Jules
See J.R.R. Tolkien

Basso, Hamilton
The View from Pompey's Head (Doubleday) NYT fic 11/7/54 (#14), pk 1/2/55 (#1, 14 wk), 40 wk; PW fic 11/27/54 (#3), pk 1/1/55 (#1, 10 wk), 28 wk; tot 68 wk.
The Light Infantry Ball (Doubleday) NYT fic 6/21/59 (#15), pk 7/5/59 (#8, 3 wk), 13 wk; PW fic 7/13/59 (#8, 2 wk), 7 wk; tot 20 wk.

Bates, Ernest Sutherland
The Bible [ed.] (Simon & Schuster) PW nf 1/16/37 (#3, 4 wk), 16 wk; NYT gen 1/31/37 (#3, 4 wk), 12 wk; tot 28 wk.

Bates, Herbert Ernest
Spella Ho (Little Brown) NYT fic 12/4/38 (#12, 4 wk).
Fair Stood the Wind for France (Little Brown) NYT fic 7/2/44 (#11), pk 7/16/44 (#8, 1 wk), 10 wk.
The Purple Plain (Little Brown) NYT fic 1/18/48 (#16), pk 2/1/48 (#12, 1 wk), 5 wk.
Love for Lydia (Little Brown) NYT fic 2/8/53 (#12, 1 wk), 3 wk.

Batra, Ravi
The Great Depression of 1990 (Simon & Schuster) NYT nf 7/12/87 (#13), pk 11/15/87 (#1, 2 wk), 37 wk; PW hc nf 7/17/87 (#9), pk 11/20/87 (#1, 1 wk), 34 wk; (Dell) NYT pb nf 6/12/88 (#7), pk 6/19/88 (#2, 1 wk), 14 wk; PW mm pb 6/24/88 (#9), pk 7/1/88 (#8, 1 wk), 3 wk; tot 88 wk.
Surviving the Great Depression of 1990 (Simon & Schuster) NYT nf 10/16/88 (#5, 1 wk), 7 wk; PW hc nf 10/21/88 (#10), pk 11/18/88 (#9, 1 wk), 6 wk; tot 13 wk.

Batson, Sallie
See Callan Pinckney and_____

Baty, Eban Neal
Citizen Abroad (Viking) NYT gen 8/14/60 (#16, 1 wk).

Baudelaire, Charles
Flowers of Evil [trans. Edna St. Vincent Millay and George Dillon] (Harper) NYT nf 5/3/36 (#10, 4 wk).

Baum, Lyman Frank
The New Wizard of Oz [as by L. Frank Baum] (Grosset & Dunlap) NYT gen 10/8/39 (#7, 4 wk).

Baum, Vicki
Grand Motel (Doubleday) PW fic 3/21/31 (#2), pk 4/18/31 (#1, 8 wk), 20 wk.
And Life Goes On (Doubleday) PW fic 4/23/32 (#8, 4 wk).
Tale of Bali (Literary Guild) NYT fic 2/6/38 (#5, 4 wk).
The Weeping Wood (Doubleday) NYT fic 1/2/44 (#8, 1 wk), 5 wk.

Hotel Berlin '43 (Doubleday) NYT fic 4/30/44 (#7, 1 wk), 7 wk; PW fic 6/10/44 (#8, 1 wk), 2 wk; tot 9 wk.

Theme for Ballet (Doubleday) NYT fic 8/3/58 (#15, 1 wk).

Baxter, Walter
Look Down in Mercy (Heineman/Putnam) NYT fic 4/27/52 (#16), pk 5/11/52 (#14, 1 wk), 2 wk.

Bayer, William
Switch (NAL/Signet) PW mm pb 6/21/85 (#14), pk 6/28/85 (#12, 3 wk), 4 wk; NYT pb fic 6/23/85 (#15), pk 7/7/85 (#10, 1 wk), 3 wk; tot 7 wk.

Pattern Crimes (NAL/Signet) NYT pb fic 4/24/88 (#16, 1 wk).

Bayliss, Marguerite F.
The Bolinvars (Holt) NYT fic 12/31/44 (#9), pk 1/14/45 (#8, 3 wk), 6 wk.

Beach, Cmdr. Edward L.
Submarine! (Holt) NYT fic 7/20/52 (#12), pk 8/3/52 (#7, 4 wk), 14 wk; PW nf 8/16/52 (#8), pk 9/6/52 (#4, 1 wk), 7 wk; tot 21 wk.

Run Silent, Run Deep (Holt) NYT fic 4/24/55 (#8), pk 5/8/55 (#6, 3 wk), 19 wk; PW fic 5/14/55 (#7, 5 wk), 10 wk; tot 29 wk.

Beach, Rex
Flowing Gold (Harper) PW fic 1/27/23 (#11, 4 wk).

Beadle, Muriel
These Ruins Are Inhabited (Doubleday) NYT gen 7/9/61 (#12, 2 wk), 8 wk.

Beal, John Robinson
John Foster Dulles (Harper) NYT gen 5/5/57 (#14), pk 5/19/57 (#12, 1 wk), 3 wk.

Beals, Carleton
Dawn Over the Amazon (Duell Sloan & Pearce) NYT fic 7/25/43 (#17), pk 8/29/43 (#10, 1 wk), 2 wk.

Beard, Charles Austin
Whither Mankind [ed.] (Longmans) PW nf 12/22/28 (#6), pk 2/16/29 (#3, 4 wk), 16 wk.

The Republic (Viking) NYT gen 10/31/43 (#14), pk 2/13/44 (#9, 1 wk), 9 wk; PW nf 4/15/44 (#9, 1 wk); tot 10 wk.

President Roosevelt and the Coming of the War, 1941 (Yale Univ.) NYT gen 5/2/48 (#9), pk 5/30/48 (#5, 1 wk), 11 wk; PW nf 5/15/48 (#9), pk 5/22/48 (#5, 1 wk), 3 wk; tot 14 wk.

_____, **and Mary R. Beard**
The Rise of American Civilization (Macmillan) PW nf 3/15/30 (#2, 4 wk), 12 wk.

America in Midpassage (Macmillan) NYT gen 6/11/39 (#12), pk 7/9/39 (#6, 4 wk), 12 wk; PW nf 7/15/39 (#5, 4 wk), 12 wk; tot 24 wk.

A Basic History of the United States (Blakiston) NYT gen 9/10/44 (#11), pk 9/24/44 (#5, 2 wk), 8 wk; PW nf 9/30/44 (#5, 3 wk), 5 wk; tot 13 wk.

Beard, Henry
Miss Piggy's Guide to Life [as by Miss Piggy, as told to Henry Beard] (Muppet Press/Knopf) PW hc nf 6/19/81 (#7), pk 7/24/81 (#4, 8 wk), 28 wk; NYT nf 6/28/81 (#7), pk 7/5/81 (#4, 9 wk), 30 wk; tot 58 wk.

_____, **and Roy McKie**
Sailing (Workman) NYT td pb 9/27/81 (#13), pk 10/25/81 (#10, 5 wk), 16 wk.

Gardening (Workman) NYT td pb 7/4/82 (#15), pk 7/11/82 (#14, 1 wk), 2 wk.

Beard, James
The New James Beard (Knopf) NYT nf 1/17/82 (#15), pk 1/24/82 (#12, 1 wk), 2 wk.

Beasley, Norman
Knudsen: A Biography (Whittlesey/McGraw) NYT gen 7/6/47 (#15, 1 wk), 2 wk.

The Cross and the Crown (Duell Sloan & Pearce) NYT gen 11/30/52 (#16), pk 2/1/53 (#14, 1 wk), 6 wk.

Beasley, Ruth
See June M. Reinisch and_____

Beattie, Ann
Falling in Place (Random) PW hc fic 6/6/80 (#13), pk 6/13/80 (#10, 1 wk), 3 wk.

Love Always (Vintage) PW td pb 8/22/86 (#10, 1 wk).

Beattie, Melody
Codependent No More: How to Stop Controlling Others and Start Caring for Yourself (Harper/Hazelden) PW td pb 4/1/88 (#10), pk 2/10/89 (#1, 27 wk), 136 wk; NYT msc pb 5/29/88 (#5), pk 2/12/89 (#1, 17 wk), 116 wk; (Metacom) PW aud nf 10/5/90 (#2, 4 wk), 8 wk; tot 260 wk.

Beyond Codependency and Getting Better All the Time (Harper/Hazelden) PW td pb 6/2/89 (#8), pk 8/4/89 (#3, 2 wk), 23 wk; NYT msc pb 6/11/89 (#4), pk 8/20/89 (#2, 3 wk), 21 wk; tot 44 wk.

Codependents' Guide to the Twelve Steps (Simon & Schuster) PW aud nf 12/7/90 (#9, 4 wk).

The Language of Letting Go (Perennial) PW td pb 8/17/90 (#8), pk 8/24/90 (#2, 1 wk), 10 wk; (Metacom) PW aud nf 12/7/90 (#6, 4 wk); tot 14 wk.

Beatts, Anne, and John Head
Saturday Night Live [eds.] (Avon) PW td pb 11/21/77 (#6), pk 12/26/77 (#1, 3 wk), 15

wk; NYT td pb 12/18/77 (#12), pk 1/8/78 (#4, 2 wk), 15 wk; tot 30 wk.

Beaty, David
The Four Winds (Morrow) NYT fic 2/13/55 (#16, 1 wk).

Beauman, Sally
Destiny (Bantam) PW hc fic 3/27/87 (#14), pk 5/1/87 (#3, 1 wk), 13 wk; NYT fic 3/29/87 (#6), pk 4/12/87 (#4, 2 wk), 14 wk; NYT pb fic 2/7/88 (#4), pk 2/14/88 (#1, 4 wk), 13 wk; PW mm pb 2/12/88 (#9), pk 3/4/88 (#1, 2 wk), 13 wk; tot 53 wk.
Dark Angel (Bantam) PW hc fic 8/3/90 (#15, 2 wk); NYT fic 8/19/90 (#15, 1 wk); tot 3 wk.

Beauty Experts at Mary Kay Cosmetics
The Mary Kay Guide to Beauty [introduction by Mary Kay Ash] (Addison Wesley) NYT nf 10/16/83 (#5), pk 10/23/83 (#3, 1 wk), 12 wk; PW hc nf 10/21/83 (#8), pk 11/11/83 (#5, 1 wk), 10 wk; tot 22 wk.

Beck, L. Adams
The Story of Oriental Philosophy (Cosmopolitan) PW nf 10/27/28 (#9, 4 wk).

Beck, Pamela, and Patti Massman
Fling (Evans/Dutton) PW hc fic 5/18/84 (#14, 1 wk); (Dell) NYT PB fic 5/19/85 (#15), pk 6/2/85 (#12, 1 wk), 2 wk; PW mm pb 5/24/85 (#15), pk 6/7/85 (#12, 1 wk), 3 wk; tot 6 wk.

Beck, Simone
See Julia Child and_____

Becker, Marion
See Irma S. Rombauer and_____

Becker, Stephen
A Covenant with Death (Atheneum) NYT fic 2/7/65 (#10), pk 3/7/65 (#6, 1 wk), 10 wk; PW fic 2/8/65 (#11), pk 2/15/65 (#7, 4 wk), 11 wk; tot 21 wk.

Becker, Suzy
All I Need to Know I Learned from My Cat (Workman) NYT msc pb 12/2/90 (#2), pk 12/23/90 (#1, 1 wk), 5 wk; PW td pb 12/7/90 (#1, 3 wk), tot 8 wk.

Bedford, Sybille
A Legacy (Simon & Schuster) NYT fic 3/3/57 (#15), pk 4/14/57 (#8, 1 wk), 16 wk; PW fic 5/20/57 (#10, 1 wk); tot 17 wk.

Beebe, Charles William
Jungle Days (Putnam) PW nf 9/26/25 (#6, 8 wk).
The Arcturus Adventure (Putnam) PW nf 7/17/26 (#4, 4 wk).

Nonsuch (Brewer Warren & Putnam) PW nf 5/14/32 (#7, 4 wk).
Half Mile Down (Harcourt) PW nf 1/12/35 (#6, 4 wk), 8 wk.
High Jungle (Duell Sloan & Pearce) NYT gen 6/26/49 (#12, 1 wk), 2 wk.

Beebe, Elswyth Thane [all titles as by Elswyth Thane]
Ever After (Duell Sloan & Pearce) NYT fic 11/11/45 (#15, 1 wk).
The Light Heart (Duell Sloan & Pearce) NYT fic 3/23/47 (#16, 1 wk).
Kissing Kin (Duell Sloan & Pearce) NYT fic 12/19/48 (#11, 2 wk), 5 wk.

Beebe, Lucius Morris
Mixed Train Daily (Howell North) NYT gen 10/19/47 (#13, 1 wk).
The Big Spenders (Doubleday) PW nf 5/30/66 (#10), pk 7/25/66 (#7, 4 wk), 13 wk; NYT gen 6/12/66 (#10), pk 8/28/66 (#7, 1 wk), 8 wk; tot 21 wk.

_____, **and Charles C. Clegg**
U.S. West (Dutton) NYT gen 10/23/49 (#13, 1 wk).
Cable Car Carnival (G. Hardy) NYT gen 7/1/51 (#12, 1 wk), 4 wk.
The American West (Dutton) NYT gen 10/30/55 (#13, 3 wk), 5 wk.
The Age of Steam (Rinehart) NYT gen 10/6/57 (#16), pk 10/13/57 (#12, 1 wk), 2 wk.

Beecher, Elizabeth
Walt Disney's Davy Crockett (Simon & Schuster) NYT ch bst 11/13/55 (#2, 40 wk).
Walt Disney's 20,000 Leagues Under the Sea (Simon & Schuster) NYT ch bst 11/13/55 (#8, 40 wk).

Beer, Thomas
The Mauve Decade (Knopf) PW nf 6/19/26 (#10), pk 7/17/26 (#7, 12 wk), 20 wk.

Bego, Mark
Michael! (Pinnacle) PW mm pb 3/2/84 (#13), pk 3/23/84 (#9, 3 wk), 6 wk; NYT pb nf 3/11/84 (#5), pk 3/25/84 (#4, 2 wk), 6 wk; tot 12 wk.

Behan, Brendan
Borstal Boy (Knopf) NYT gen 3/29/59 (#16, 1 wk).

Behn, Noel
The Kremlin Letter (Simon & Schuster) NYT fic 7/24/66 (#10), pk 7/31/66 (#9, 4 wk), 7 wk; PW fic 8/1/66 (#11), pk 9/5/66 (#5, 1 wk), 10 wk; tot 17 wk.

Behrman, Samuel Nathaniel
Duveen (Random) NYT gen 4/13/52 (#12), pk 5/18/52 (#7, 1 wk), 9 wk.

Portrait of Max (Random) NYT gen 1/8/61 (#11, 1 wk).

Beith, Janet
No Second Spring (Stokes) PW fic 10/14/33 (#7, 8 wk).

Belbenoit, Rene
Dry Guillotine (Dutton) NYT nf 4/3/38 (#5, 4 wk), 20 wk; PW nf 5/14/38 (#6, 8 wk), 16 wk; tot 36 wk.

Belden, Jack
Retreat with Stilwell (Knopf) NYT gen 4/4/43 (#12, 1 wk), 3 wk.

Belfrage, Cedric
Away from It All (Simon & Schuster) NYT nf 5/9/37 (#10, 4 wk).

Bell, Cmdr. Frederick G.
Condition Red (Longmans Green) NYT gen 12/19/43 (#19), pk 1/23/44 (#10, 1 wk), 4 wk.

Bell, Jack
The Splendid Misery (Doubleday) NYT gen 3/27/60 (#16, 1 wk).

Bell, Quentin
Virginia Woolf (Harvest House) NYT gen 2/25/73 (#10, 1 wk); NYT td pb 7/14/74 (#8, 4 wk), 8 wk; tot 9 wk.

Bell, Thelma
Black Face (Doubleday) PW juv 5/16/31 (#8, 4 wk), 8 wk.

Bell, Vereen
Two of a Kind (Little Brown) NYT fic 1/31/43 (#18), pk 2/14/43 (#12, 1 wk), 3 wk.

Bellamann, Henry
King's Row (Simon & Schuster) PW fic 6/8/40 (#7), pk 7/13/40 (#4, 12 wk), 31 wk; NYT fic 8/9/42 (#5, 3 wk), 20 wk; tot 51 wk.
The Floods of Spring (Simon & Schuster) NYT fic 8/9/42 (#17), pk 9/13/42 (#10, 1 wk), 2 wk.
Victoria Grandolet (Simon & Schuster) NYT fic 1/23/44 (#10), pk 1/30/44 (#8, 1 wk), 9 wk; PW fic 2/12/44 (#9, 2 wk); tot 11 wk.

_____, **and Katherine Bellamann**
Parris Mitchell of King's Row (Simon & Schuster) NYT fic 5/9/48 (#10), pk 5/30/48 (#3, 1 wk), 12 wk; PW fic 6/12/48 (#5, 1 wk), 3 wk; tot 15 wk.

Belliveau, Fred, and Lin Richter
Understanding Human Sexual Inadequacy (Little Brown) NYT pb gen 10/4/70 (#5, 4 wk).

Belloc, Hilaire
Richelieu (Lippincott) PW nf 1/11/30 (#10, 4 wk).

Bellow, Saul
The Adventures of Augie March (Viking) NYT fic 10/11/53 (#8, 5 wk), 9 wk.
Henderson the Rain King (Viking) NYT fic 3/15/59 (#16), pk 3/29/59 (#12, 1 wk), 3 wk.
Herzog (Viking) NYT fic 10/11/64 (#10), pk 10/25/64 (#1, 29 wk), 42 wk; PW fic 10/12/64 (#9), pk 11/9/64 (#1, 25 wk), 44 wk; NYT pb fic 12/5/65 (#1, 4 wk), 20 wk; tot 106 wk.
Mr. Sammler's Planet (Viking) NYT fic 2/22/70 (#5), pk 3/15/70 (#4, 2 wk), 14 wk; PW fic 3/2/70 (#4, 3 wk), 14 wk; NYT pb fic 3/7/71 (#5, 8 wk); tot 36 wk.
Humboldt's Gift (Viking) NYT fic 9/7/75 (#10), pk 11/23/75 (#2, 1 wk), 24 wk; PW fic 9/15/75 (#9), pk 9/29/75 (#5, 6 wk), 19 wk; PW hc fic 2/2/76 (#7, 1 wk), 2 wk; (Avon) PW mm pb 9/27/76 (#8), pk 10/4/76 (#4, 2 wk), 18 wk; NYT mm pb 10/24/76 (#10), pk 11/21/76 (#6, 1 wk), 4 wk; tot 67 wk.
To Jerusalem and Back: A Personal Account (Viking) PW hc nf 11/15/76 (#10), pk 12/27/76 (#7, 1 wk), 10 wk; NYT gen 11/21/76 (#9, 7 wk), 11 wk; tot 21 wk.
The Dean's December (Harper) PW hc fic 1/29/82 (#11), pk 2/26/82 (#4, 2 wk), 14 wk; NYT fic 2/7/82 (#6), pk 3/7/82 (#3, 1 wk), 12 wk; (Pocket) NYT mm pb 1/23/83 (#14, 2 wk), 3 wk; PW mm pb 1/28/83 (#8, 1 wk), 5 wk; tot 34 wk.
Him with His Foot in His Mouth and Other Stories (Harper) NYT fic 6/17/84 (#12, 3 wk), 8 wk; PW hc fic 7/6/84 (#12), pk 7/27/84 (#11, 1 wk), 5 wk; tot 13 wk.
More Die of Heartbreak (Morrow) NYT fic 6/14/87 (#14), pk 7/19/87 (#5, 1 wk), 13 wk; PW hc fic 6/19/87 (#13), pk 7/17/87 (#10, 2 wk), 9 wk; tot 22 wk.

Bemelmans, Ludwig
The Donkey Inside (Viking) PW nf 3/15/41 (#8, 4 wk).
I Love You, I Love You, I Love You (Viking) NYT nf 10/11/42 (#9, 1 wk), 2 wk.
Now I Lay Me Down to Sleep (Viking) NYT fic 3/12/44 (#9, 1 wk), 5 wk; PW fic 4/15/44 (#10, 1 wk); tot 6 wk.
The Blue Danube (Viking) NYT fic 5/6/45 (#11, 1 wk), 3 wk.
Dirty Eddie (Viking) NYT fic 9/7/47 (#12), pk 10/12/47 (#4, 1 wk), 12 wk; PW fic 10/11/47 (#5, 2 wk), 3 wk; tot 15 wk.
The Eye of God (Viking) NYT fic 12/4/49 (#15), pk 12/11/49 (#14, 1 wk), 3 wk.
Father, Dear Father (Viking) NYT gen 9/13/53 (#11), pk 9/20/53 (#9, 2 wk), 7 wk.
Madeline's Rescue (Viking) NYT ch bst 11/15/53 (#2, 40 wk).

To the One I Love the Best (Viking) NYT gen 3/13/55 (#8), pk 4/10/55 (#4, 1 wk), 13 wk; PW nf 3/26/55 (#5), pk 4/2/55 (#4, 3 wk), 8 wk; tot 21 wk.

The Woman of My Life (Viking) NYT fic 11/10/57 (#14), pk 11/17/57 (#13, 1 wk), 2 wk.

Madeline and the Red Hat (Viking) NYT ch bst 11/17/57 (#4, 40 wk).

Benchley, Nathaniel Goddard
The Off Islanders (McGraw) NYT fic 8/27/61 (#15), pk 9/17/61 (#13, 1 wk), 3 wk.

Benchley, Peter Bradford
Jaws (Doubleday) PW fic 3/4/74 (#10), pk 4/8/74 (#1, 1 wk), 43 wk; NYT fic 3/10/74 (#10), pk 3/31/74 (#2, 13 wk), 45 wk; (Bantam) NYT mm pb 2/9/75 (#3), pk 2/23/75 (#1, 24 wk), 39 wk; tot 127 wk.

The Deep (Doubleday) PW hc fic 5/24/76 (#8), pk 6/21/76 (#2, 6 wk), 22 wk; NYT fic 5/30/76 (#10), pk 6/27/76 (#2, 6 wk), 24 wk; (Bantam) NYT mm pb 4/24/77 (#10), pk 6/5/77 (#1, 6 wk), 20 wk; PW mm pb 4/25/77 (#7), pk 5/30/77 (#1, 6 wk), 19 wk; tot 85 wk.

The Island (Doubleday) NYT fic 5/27/79 (#15), pk 7/8/79 (#4, 2 wk), 18 wk; PW hc fic 5/28/79 (#8), pk 7/30/79 (#4, 1 wk), 17 wk; (Bantam) PW mm pb 3/28/80 (#9), pk 4/4/80 (#5, 1 wk), 8 wk; NYT mm pb 3/30/80 (#10), pk 4/6/80 (#2, 1 wk), 17 wk; tot 60 wk.

Q Clearance (Random) NYT fic 7/27/86 (#15, 2 wk); (Charter) NYT pb fic 9/20/87 (#16, 1 wk); tot 3 wk.

Benchley, Robert Charles
My Ten Years in a Quandary and How They Grew (Harper) NYT gen 7/5/36 (#9), pk 8/2/36 (#5, 4 wk), 12 wk; PW nf 7/11/36 (#10), pk 8/15/36 (#8, 4 wk), 12 wk; tot 24 wk.

After 1903—What? (Harper) NYT gen 2/6/38 (#6, 4 wk), 8 wk.

Benchley Beside Himself (Harper) NYT gen 9/19/43 (#19), pk 9/26/43 (#14, 1 wk), 2 wk

Chips Off the Old Benchley (Harper) NYT gen 11/20/49 (#16, 1 wk).

Bender, Marilyn
The Beautiful People (Coward McCann) PW nf 10/30/67 (#11), pk 11/6/67 (#9, 1 wk), 4 wk; NYT gen 11/19/67 (#8, 1 wk), 2 wk; tot 6 wk.

Bendiner, Robert
The Riddle of the State Department (Farrar) NYT nf 9/20/42 (#14, 2 wk), 4 wk.

Benefield, Barry
Valiant Is the Word for Carrie (Reynal & Hitchcock) NYT fic 12/1/35 (#9, 4 wk); PW fic 1/11/36 (#7, 4 wk), 8 wk; tot 12 wk.

April Was When It Began (Reynal & Hitchcock) PW fic 9/16/39 (#9, 4 wk).

Benet, Stephen Vincent
John Brown's Body (Doubleday) PW nf 10/27/28 (#7), pk 11/24/28 (#2, 12 wk), 32 wk.

James Shore's Daughter (Doubleday) PW fic 6/9/34 (#6, 4 wk).

Western Star (Farrar) NYT gen 7/25/43 (#10), pk 8/1/43 (#7, 2 wk), 6 wk.

America (Farrar) NYT gen 7/2/44 (#12, 1 wk).

Bengtsson, Frans Gunnar
The Long Ships (Knopf) NYT fic 10/3/54 (#12), pk 10/10/54 (#10, 2 wk), 6 wk.

Benjamin, Ancel, and Margaret Keys
Eat Well and Stay Well (Doubleday) NYT gen 5/3/59 (#9, 1 wk), 8 wk.

Bennett, Arnold
Imperial Palace (Doubleday) PW fic 2/21/31 (#8), pk 3/21/31 (#5, 4 wk), 16 wk.

Bennett, Lerone, Jr.
See John H. Johnson and_____

Benney, Mark
See Henry Ernest Degras

Benson, Edward Frederic
Queen Victoria (Longmans Green) PW nf 6/15/35 (#6, 4 wk), 8 wk.

Queen Victoria's Daughters (Appleton) NYT nf 1/8/39 (#8, 4 wk).

Benson, Herbert, M.D., with Miriam Z. Klipper
The Relaxation Response (Morrow) PW nf 10/27/75 (#7), pk 12/8/75 (#1, 4 wk), 24 wk; NYT gen 11/9/75 (#9), pk 12/21/75 (#1, 1 wk), 24 wk; (Avon) PW mm pb 9/6/76 (#13, 1 wk), 3 wk; tot 51 wk.

Benson, Sally
Meet Me in St. Louis (Random) NYT fic 8/23/42 (#12, 1 wk).

Bentley, Phyllis Eleanor
Inheritance (Macmillan) PW fic 10/15/32 (#8), pk 1/14/33 (#2, 4 wk), 20 wk.

A Modern Tragedy (Macmillan) PW fic 3/10/34 (#4, 8 wk), 12 wk.

Sleep in Peace (Macmillan) NYT fic 6/5/38 (#3, 4 wk).

Berenson, Bernard
Sketch for a Self-Portrait (Indiana Univ.) NYT gen 5/15/49 (#11), pk 5/29/49 (#10, 1 wk), 3 wk.

Berenstain, Stan and Jan Berenstain
The Berenstain Bears and the Prize Pumpkin (Random) PW ch yn rd 10/26/90 (#1, 8 wk).

The Berenstain Bears and the Slumber Party (Random) PW ch yn rd 8/31/90 (#1, 8 wk).

The Berenstain Bears Trick or Treat (Random) PW ch yn rd 9/28/90 (#3), pk 10/26/90 (#2, 8 wk), 12 wk.

The Berenstain Bears' Trouble with Pets (Random) PW ch yn rd 11/30/90 (#3), pk 12/21/90 (#1, 4 wk), 8 wk.

Berg, A. Scott
Max Perkins: Editor of Genius (Congdon/Dutton) PW hc nf 8/21/78 (#12, 1 wk), 3 wk.

Goldwyn (Knopf) NYT nf 4/30/89 (#12), pk 5/7/89 (#10, 1 wk), 7 wk; PW hc nf 5/5/89 (#14, 2 wk); tot 9 wk.

Berge, Wendell
Cartels: Challenge to a Free World (Public Affairs Press) NYT gen 3/25/45 (#20, 1 wk).

Bergen, Candice
Knock Wood (Simon & Schuster) PW hc nf 4/27/84 (#14), pk 5/25/84 (#10, 1 wk), 7 wk; NYT nf 4/29/84 (#15), pk 5/20/84 (#9, 1 wk), 7 wk; (Ballantine) NYT pb nf 3/10/85 (#6), pk 3/17/85 (#2, 3 wk), 8 wk; PW mm pb 4/5/85 (#14, 1 wk); tot 23 wk.

Berger, Meyer
The Story of the New York Times (Simon & Schuster) NYT gen 10/7/51 (#11), pk 10/21/51 (#9, 1 wk), 6 wk.

Meyer Berger's New York (Random) NYT gen 4/10/60 (#13), pk 5/1/60 (#11, 2 wk), 8 wk.

See also James Keller and_____

Berger, Dr. Stuart M.
Dr. Berger's Immune Power Diet (NAL/Signet) NYT msc 6/16/85 (#1, 15 wk), 22 wk; PW hc nf 6/21/85 (#4), pk 7/19/85 (#2, 1 wk), 23 wk; NYT msc pb 4/13/86 (#6), pk 4/20/86 (#1, 3 wk), 8 wk; PW mm pb 4/25/86 (#12, 2 wk), 4 wk; tot 57 wk.

How to Be Your Own Nutritionist (Morrow) NYT msc 3/29/87 (#5), pk 4/19/87 (#2, 1 wk), 8 wk; PW hc nf 4/3/87 (#15), pk 4/24/87 (#5, 1 wk), 7 wk; tot 15 wk.

What Your Doctor Didn't Learn in Medical School ... and What You Can Do About It! (Morrow) NYT msc 6/19/88 (#5), pk 7/3/88 (#4, 1 wk), 6 wk; PW hc nf 6/24/88 (#12, 2 wk); tot 8 wk.

Berger, Thomas
Neighbors (Lawrence/Delacorte) PW hc fic 5/9/80 (#15, 1 wk).

Bergman, Ingrid, and Alan Burgess
Ingrid Bergman: My Story (Delacorte) PW hc nf 9/26/80 (#10), pk 11/14/80 (#5, 3 wk), 17 wk; NYT nf 9/28/80 (#12), pk 11/2/80 (#3, 1 wk), 19 wk; (Dell) PW mm pb 10/16/81 (#15), pk 10/23/81 (#14, 1 wk), 2 wk; NYT mm pb 10/18/81 (#9, 1 wk), 3 wk; tot 41 wk.

Berkowitz, Bernard
See Mildred Newman and_____
See Mildred Newman, et al.

Berlin, Ellen
Land I Have Chosen (Doubleday) NYT fic 7/16/44 (#11, 1 wk), 2 wk; PW fic 8/12/44 (#10, 1 wk); tot 3 wk.

Lace Curtain (Doubleday) NYT fic 8/8/48 (#13), pk 9/12/48 (#7, 1 wk), 11 wk.

Silver Platter (Doubleday) NYT gen 6/9/57 (#12), pk 8/25/57 (#5, 2 wk), 22 wk; PW nf 7/8/57 (#8), pk 8/12/57 (#5, 2 wk), 13 wk; tot 35 wk.

Berlitz, Charles with J. Manson Valentine
The Bermuda Triangle (Doubleday) NYT gen 11/17/74 (#10), pk 2/2/75 (#1, 18 wk), 40 wk; PW nf 12/2/74 (#5), pk 1/13/75 (#1, 14 wk), 35 wk; (Avon) NYT mm pb 9/28/75 (#7), pk 10/12/75 (#2, 1 wk), 7 wk; tot 82 wk.

Berne, Eric
The Mind in Action (Simon & Schuster) NYT gen 4/4/48 (#14, 1 wk), 2 wk.

Games People Play: The Psychology of Human Relationships (Grove) NYT gen 7/25/65 (#8), pk 9/4/66 (#2, 8 wk), 107 wk; PW nf 8/23/65 (#10), pk 10/10/66 (#1, 2 wk), 109 wk; NYT pb gen 10/1/67 (#1, 24 wk), 24 wk; tot 240 wk.

What Do You Say After You Say Hello? (Grove) PW nf 10/2/72 (#10, 1 wk); NYT pb gen 6/10/73 (#4, 4 wk); tot 5 wk.

Bernstein, Carl
See Bob Woodward and_____

Bernstein, Carl, and Bob Woodward
All the President's Men (Simon & Schuster) PW nf 5/27/74 (#9), pk 6/17/74 (#1, 16 wk), 31 wk; NYT gen 6/2/74 (#9), pk 6/30/74 (#1, 20 wk), 34 wk; (Warner) mm pb 1/12/75 (#3), pk 5/9/76 (#1, 7 wk), 30 wk; PW mm pb 4/12/76 (#9), pk 5/3/76 (#1, 8 wk), 22 wk; tot 117 wk.

Bernstein, Leonard
The Joy of Music (Simon & Schuster) NYT gen 12/27/59 (#12), pk 3/6/60 (#5, 2 wk), 26 wk; PW nf 1/4/60 (#9), pk 2/15/60 (#4, 1 wk), 18 wk; tot 44 wk.

Bernstein, Morey
The Search for Bridey Murphy (Doubleday) NYT gen 1/22/56 (#14), pk 3/4/56 (#1, 12 wk), 27 wk; PW nf 2/11/56 (#5), pk 3/3/56 (#1, 11 wk), 20 wk; tot 47 wk.

Bernstein, Peter W.
See Arthur Young Co. and_____

Berra, Yogi, with Tom Horton
Yogi: It Ain't Over... (McGraw) NYT nf 5/21/89 (#13, 2 wk), 3 wk.

Bertolucci, Bernardo, and Franco Arcalli
Last Tango in Paris (Delacorte) NYT pb fic 6/10/73 (#5), pk 7/8/73 (#4, 4 wk), 8 wk.

Bettelheim, Bruno
The Uses of Enchantment: The Meaning and Importance of Fairy Tales (Vintage) PW td pb 6/27/77 (#5), pk 7/4/77 (#4, 1 wk), 3 wk.

Bettger, Frank
How I Raised Myself from Failure to Success in Selling (Prentice Hall) NYT gen 5/7/50 (#15), pk 6/11/50 (#10, 1 wk), 9 wk; PW nf 6/17/50 (#9, 1 wk); tot 10 wk.

Beuchner, Frederick
A Long Day's Dying (Knopf) NYT fic 1/29/50 (#11), pk 2/26/50 (#10, 2 wk), 8 wk.

Beveridge, Albert J.
Abraham Lincoln, 1809–1858 (Houghton) PW nf 11/24/28 (#6), pk 12/22/28 (#5, 4 wk), 8 wk.

Beveridge, Sir William Henry
Social Insurance and Allied Services (Macmillan) NYT nf 1/24/43 (#12), pk 2/7/43 (#7, 1 wk), 3 wk.
Full Employment in a Free Society (Norton) NYT gen 3/25/45 (#13, 1 wk).

Biancolli, Louis
See Mary Garden and_____

Bibby, Geoffrey
The Testimony of the Spade (Knopf) NYT gen 1/20/57 (#16), pk 1/27/57 (#14, 1 wk), 2 wk.

Biddle, Cordelia Drexel, as told to Kyle Crichton
My Philadelphia Father (Doubleday) NYT gen 5/29/55 (#13), pk 6/5/55 (#9, 1 wk), 9 wk.

Biddle, Francis
Mr. Justice Holmes (Scribner) NYT nf 2/28/43 (#19, 1 wk).

Biddle, Livingston
Main Line (Messner) NYT fic 6/4/50 (#14), pk 6/11/50 (#13, 1 wk), 3 wk.

Biggers, Earl Derr
Behind That Curtain (Bobbs Merrill) PW fic 6/30/28 (#9, 4 wk).
The Black Camel (Bobbs Merrill) PW fic 8/10/29 (#4, 4 wk), 8 wk.
Keeper of the Keys (Bobbs Merrill) PW fic 9/10/32 (#9, 4 wk).

Bigham, Madge A.
Sonny Elephant (Little Brown) PW juv 12/20/30 (#10, 4 wk).

Billings, Robert W.
See Dick Butkus and_____

Binchy, Maeve
Light a Penny Candle (Dell) NYT pb fic 4/15/84 (#12), pk 4/29/84 (#8, 1 wk), 9 wk; PW mm pb 4/20/84 (#11), pk 5/11/84 (#9, 2 wk), 10 wk; tot 19 wk.
Echoes (Dell) NYT pb fic 1/18/87 (#15, 3 wk).
Firefly Summer (Dell) NYT pb fic 8/6/89 (#9), pk 8/20/89 (#5, 1 wk), 9 wk; PW mm pb 8/11/89 (#9), pk 9/8/89 (#7, 1 wk), 8 wk; tot 17 wk.
Silver Wedding (Dell) NYT pb fic 12/9/90 (#15), pk 12/16/90 (#10, 1 wk), 3 wk.

Bing, Sir Rudolf
5,000 Nights at the Opera (Doubleday) NYT gen 12/3/72 (#9, 1 wk), 2 wk; PW nf 12/11/72 (#10), pk 1/1/73 (#7, 1 wk), 3 wk; tot 5 wk.

Bingay, Malcolm W.
Detroit Is My Own Home Town (Bobbs Merrill) NYT gen 4/21/46 (#13), pk 9/29/46 (#10, 1 wk), 22 wk.

Bingham, M.T.
See Emily Dickinson, et al.

Binns, Archie
The Land Is Bright (Scribner) NYT fic 4/9/39 (#12, 4 wk).

Binstock, Louis
The Power of Faith (Prentice Hall) NYT gen 4/20/52 (#14, 2 wk), 3 wk.

Bird, Christopher
See Peter Tompkins and_____

Bird, Larry, with Bob Ryan
Drive: The Story of My Life (Doubleday) NYT nf 11/12/89 (#14), pk 12/10/89 (#5, 3 wk), 15 wk; PW hc nf 12/1/89 (#15), pk 12/15/89 (#8, 3 wk), 7 wk; tot 22 wk.

Birmingham, Stephen
"Our Crowd": The Great Jewish Families of New York (Harper) NYT gen 7/16/67 (#10), pk 9/10/67 (#1, 22 wk), 47 wk; PW nf 7/24/67 (#9), pk 10/9/67 (#1, 13 wk), 49 wk; NYT pb gen 9/1/68 (#2), pk 10/6/68 (#1, 4 wk), 24 wk; tot 120 wk.
The Right People (Little Brown) NYT gen 5/19/68 (#8), pk 6/16/68 (#3, 1 wk), 21 wk; PW nf 5/27/68 (#9), pk 7/1/68 (#2, 1 wk), 23 wk; tot 44 wk.
The Grandees (Harper) PW nf 4/5/71 (#6), pk 6/7/71 (#3, 1 wk), 14 wk; NYT gen 4/18/71 (#8), pk 5/2/71 (#7, 4 wk), 11 wk; tot 25 wk.

Real Lace (Harper) NYT gen 12/2/73 (#10), pk 1/20/74 (#9, 1 wk), 7 wk; PW nf 12/31/73 (#9), pk 1/14/74 (#8, 1 wk), 2 wk; tot 9 wk.
The Grandes Dames (Simon & Schuster) NYT nf 7/25/82 (#15, 1 wk).
The Auerbach Will (Little Brown) NYT fic 9/25/83 (#12), pk 11/13/83 (#6, 1 wk), 21 wk; PW hc fic 10/7/83 (#13), pk 11/4/83 (#6, 1 wk), 16 wk; (Berkley) NYT pb fic 9/9/84 (#7), 9/23/84 (#1, 5 wk), 14 wk; PW mm pb 9/14/84 (#4), pk 10/12/84 (#1, 1 wk), 14 wk; tot 65 wk.
The Rest of Us: The Rise of America's Eastern European Jews (Little Brown) NYT nf 9/2/84 (#14), pk 9/23/84 (#4, 1 wk), 12 wk; PW hc nf 9/14/84 (#11), pk 10/12/84 (#9, 2 wk), 10 wk; tot 22 wk.
The LeBaron Secret (Little Brown) NYT fic 2/9/86 (#12), pk 2/16/86 (#7, 2 wk), 8 wk; PW hc fic 2/28/86 (#14), pk 3/7/86 (#12, 1 wk), 5 wk; (Berkley) NYT pb fic 3/8/87 (#13), pk 3/22/87 (#6, 1 wk), 5 wk; tot 18 wk.

Birnbach, Lisa
The Official Preppy Handbook [ed.] (Workman) NYT td pb 12/7/80 (#15), pk 12/28/80 (#1, 17 wk), 65 wk; PW td pb 12/12/80 (#3), pk 12/26/80 (#1, 17 wk), 50 wk; tot 115 wk.
Lisa Birnbach's College Book (Ballantine) PW td pb 10/12/84 (#8, 4 wk).

Birnbaum, Stephen
Steve Birnbaum Brings You the Best of Walt Disney World (Houghton) PW td pb 4/4/86 (#9, 1 wk).
Walt Disney World 1990: Official Guide [ed.] (Avon) NYT msc pb 3/4/90 (#3, 1 wk), 2 wk; PW td pb 3/23/90 (#8), pk 4/13/90 (#6, 2 wk), 7 wk; tot 9 wk.

Bishop, Jim
The Glass Crutch (Doubleday) NYT fic 12/9/45 (#16, 1 wk).
The Day Lincoln Was Shot (Harper) NYT gen 2/20/55 (#13), pk 3/20/55 (#5, 4 wk), 19 wk; PW nf 3/12/55 (#7), pk 3/19/55 (#5, 2 wk), 8 wk; tot 27 wk.
The Day Christ Died (Harper) NYT gen 5/26/57 (#15), pk 6/23/57 (#1, 7 wk), 34 wk; PW nf 6/10/57 (#3), pk 7/1/57 (#1, 6 wk), 23 wk; tot 57 wk.
The Day Christ Was Born (Harper) NYT gen 1/15/61 (#13, 1 wk).
A Day in the Life of President Kennedy (Random) NYT fic 3/15/64 (#3), pk 4/19/64 (#2, 6 wk), 23 wk; PW nf 3/16/64 (#6), pk 4/20/64 (#2, 5 wk), 24 wk; tot 47 wk.
The Day Kennedy Was Shot (Funk & Wagnalls) NYT gen 12/22/68 (#6), pk 2/16/69

(#4, 2 wk), 13 wk; PW nf 12/30/68 (#10), pk 2/10/69 (#5, 2 wk), 13 wk; tot 26 wk.

Bishop, Joseph Bucklin
See Theodore Roosevelt and_____

Bissell, Richard
Say, Darling (Little Brown) NYT fic 4/14/57 (#15), pk 4/28/57 (#7, 2 wk), 14 wk; PW fic 4/29/57 (#6, 1 wk), 4 wk; tot 18 wk.
You Can Always Tell a Harvard Man (McGraw) NYT gen 12/9/62 (#11, 1 wk).

Bissinger, H.G.
Friday Night Lights (Addison Wesley) NYT nf 10/7/90 (#13), pk 11/4/90 (#7, 2 wk), 13 wk; PW hc nf 10/26/90 (#9), pk 11/9/90 (#8, 1 wk), 8 wk; tot 21 wk.

Bjorn, Thyra Ferre
Papa's Wife (Rinehart) NYT fic 10/16/55 (#11, 2 wk), 8 wk.

Black, Campbell
Raiders of the Lost Ark (Ballantine) PW mm pb 7/10/81 (#13), pk 7/24/81 (#9, 1 wk), 5 wk; NYT mm pb 7/19/81 (#12, 1 wk); tot 6 wk.

Black, Shirley Temple
Child Star: An Autobiography (McGraw) NYT nf 11/13/88 (#5), pk 11/27/88 (#3, 3 wk), 20 wk; PW hc nf 11/18/88 (#7), pk 12/16/88 (#2, 1 wk), 16 wk; (Warner) NYT pb nf 10/1/89 (#3), pk 10/8/89 (#2, 3 wk), 9 wk; PW mm pb 10/20/89 (#13, 2 wk), 3 wk; tot 48 wk.

Blair, Alan
See Par Lagerkvist

Blair, Clay
See James R. Shepley and_____

Blair, Gwenda
Almost Golden: Jessica Savitch and the Selling of Network News (Simon & Schuster) NYT nf 8/7/88 (#9), pk 8/28/88 (#8, 1 wk), 9 wk; PW hc nf 9/2/88 (#12, 2 wk), 5 wk; (Avon) NYT pb nf 2/5/89 (#5), pk 2/19/89 (#2, 1 wk), 13 wk; tot 27 wk.

Blair, Jesse
I Ain't Much Baby—But I'm All I've Got (Doubleday) NYT td pb 4/14/74 (#8), pk 6/9/74 (#4, 4 wk), 24 wk.

Blair, Leona
Privilege (Bantam) NYT pb fic 1/24/88 (#10, 1 wk), 2 wk.

Blake, Jennifer
Love's Wild Desire (Popular) NYT mm pb 6/19/77 (#12), pk 9/4/77 (#11, 1 wk), 2 wk; PW mm pb 7/18/77 (#11, 1 wk); tot 3 wk.
Tender Betrayal (Popular) NYT mm pb 7/22/79 (#14, 1 wk).

Embrace and Conquer (Fawcett/Colum-
bine) NYT td pb 11/15/81 (#8), pk 11/22/81
(#7, 1 wk), 5 wk; PW td pb 11/20/81 (#9), pk
11/27/81 (#7, 2 wk), 4 wk; tot 9 wk.

Royal Seduction (Fawcett/Columbine)
NYT td pb 8/14/83 (#11), pk 8/28/83 (#7, 3
wk), 8 wk; PW td pb 8/26/83 (#8), pk 9/2/83
(#7, 2 wk), 6 wk; tot 14 wk.

Surrender in Moonlight (Fawcett/Colum-
bine) PW td pb 6/1/84 (#10, 2 wk).

Fierce Eden (Fawcett/Columbine) PW td
pb 7/26/85 (#3), pk 8/2/85 (#2, 1 wk), 3 wk.

Blake, Michael
Dances with Wolves (Fawcett) NYT pb fic
12/16/90 (#14), pk 12/30/90 (#1, 1 wk), 3 wk;
PW mm pb 12/21/90 (#11, 1 wk); tot 4 wk.

Blake, Robert
Disraeli (St. Martin's) NYT gen 4/16/67
(#10), pk 5/28/67 (#7, 2 wk), 8 wk; PW nf
5/1/67 (#9), pk 6/5/67 (#7, 2 wk), 10 wk; tot
18 wk.

Blake, Stephanie
Daughter of Destiny (Playboy) PW mm pb
10/31/77 (#15, 1 wk).

**Blakely, Pat, with Barbara Haislet and
Judith Hentges**
Free Stuff for Kids (Meadowbrook Press)
PW td pb 7/30/79 (#10), pk 8/6/79 (#8, 4
wk), 5 wk; NYT td pb 9/23/79 (#9, 1 wk), 15
wk; tot 20 wk.

Blakeslee, Sandra
See Judith S. Wallerstein and_____

Blanch, Lesley
The Wilder Shores of Love (Simon &
Schuster) NYT gen 10/10/54 (#15, 1 wk).
See also Harriet Wilson and_____

**Blanchard, Kenneth, and Patricia
Zigarmi**
Leadership and the One Minute Manager
(Morrow) PW hc nf 3/15/85 (#14), pk 4/12/
85 (#12, 1 wk), 7 wk.

_____, **and Robert Lorber**
Putting the One Minute Manager to Work
(Morrow) PW hc nf 3/2/84 (#13), pk 4/6/84
(#6, 1 wk), 14 wk; NYT msc 3/25/84 (#2, 2
wk), 10 wk; tot 24 wk.

419. _____, **and Spencer Johnson**
The One Minute Manager (Morrow) NYT
nf 10/3/82 (#11), pk 6/12/83 (#2, 6 wk), 59
wk; PW hc nf 10/8/82 (#14), pk 11/12/82 (#3,
29 wk), 55 wk; (Berkley) NYT td pb 10/16/
83 (#2), pk 11/6/83 (#1, 8 wk), 11 wk; PW td
pb 10/21/83 (#4), pk 11/4/83 (#1, 17 wk), 117
wk; NYT msc pb 1/1/84 (#2), pk 1/22/84 (#1,
20 wk), 102 wk; tot 344 wk.

Blanding, Don
Pilot Bails Out (Dodd) NYT gen 9/12/43
(#18, 1 wk), 2 wk.

Blanshard, Paul
American Freedom and Catholic Power
(Beacon) NYT gen 6/26/49 (#16), pk 9/18/
49 (#6, 1 wk), 39 wk; PW nf 9/17/49 (#9),
pk 9/24/49 (#5, 1 wk), 7 wk; tot 46 wk.

Communism, Democracy and Catholic Power
(Beacon) PW nf 7/14/51 (#6, 1 wk), 2 wk;
NYT gen 6/10/51 (#16), pk 7/1/51 (#8, 2 wk),
17 wk; tot 19 wk.

Blanton, Smiley
Love or Perish (Simon & Schuster) NYT
gen 2/19/56 (#11), pk 6/24/56 (#3, 5 wk), 43
wk; PW nf 3/10/56 (#7), pk 6/25/56 (#4, 5
wk), 29 wk; tot 72 wk.
See also Norman Vincent Peale and_____

Blatty, William Peter
The Exorcist (Harper) NYT fic 6/20/71
(#9), pk 7/25/71 (#1, 12 wk), 55 wk; PW fic
6/28/71 (#7), pk 8/2/71 (#1, 12 wk), 54 wk;
(Bantam) NYT pb fic 7/9/72 (#1, 20 wk), 52
wk; tot 161 wk.

Legion (Simon & Schuster) PW hc fic
7/15/83 (#12), pk 8/12/83 (#9, 1 wk), 9 wk;
NYT fic 9/4/83 (#15, 1 wk); (Pocket) NYT
pb fic 5/13/84 (#4, 1 wk), 4 wk; tot 14 wk.

Blay, Clair, Jr.
See Cmdr. William R. Anderson and_____

Blech, William James
The World Is Mine (Simon & Schuster)
NYT fic 9/4/38 (#9, 4 wk).

Bledsoe, Jerry
*Bitter Blood: The True Story of Southern
Family Pride, Madness and Multiple Murder*
(NAL/Onyx) NYT pb nf 4/9/89 (#11), pk 4/
16/89 (#1, 11 wk), 26 wk; PW mm pb 4/21/89
(#11), pk 5/26/89 (#7, 1 wk), 14 wk; tot 40 wk.

**Blixen, Karen [all titles as by Isak Dine-
sen]**
Seven Gothic Tales (Smith & Haas) PW fic
5/12/34 (#7), pk 6/9/34 (#4, 4 wk), 16 wk.

Out of Africa (Random) NYT nf 4/3/38
(#7, 4 wk), 8 wk; PW nf 5/14/38 (#10, 8 wk);
tot 16 wk.

Winter's Tales (Random) NYT fic 6/6/43
(#12), pk 7/11/43 (#9, 1 wk), 10 wk.

Last Tales (Random) NYT fic 11/24/57
(#12), pk 12/15/57 (#9, 1 wk), 9 wk.

Shadows on the Grass (Random) NYT gen
1/29/61 (#10), pk 2/5/61 (#7, 1 wk), 9 wk; PW
nf 2/13/61 (#10), pk 3/6/61 (#8, 1 wk), 3 wk;
tot 12 wk.

Ehrengard (Random) PW fic 7/22/63 (#10,
1 wk).

Out of Africa and Shadows on the Grass (Random/Vintage) NYT pb nf 1/5/86 (#1, 18 wk), 35 wk; PW td pb 1/17/86 (#2), pk 1/24/86 (#1, 17 wk), 31 wk; tot 66 wk.

Bloch, Arthur
Murphy's Law, and Other Reasons Why Things Go Wrong (Price Stern Sloan) NYT td pb 7/23/78 (#10), pk 4/15/79 (#3, 2 wk), 80 wk; PW td pb 8/7/78 (#6), pk 4/9/79 (#4, 2 wk), 32 wk; tot 112 wk.
Murphy's Law Book Two: More Reasons Why Things Go Wrong (Price Stern Sloan) NYT td pb 3/2/80 (#13), pk 4/20/80 (#4, 1 wk), 33 wk; PW td pb 3/21/80 (#10), pk 4/4/80 (#4, 1 wk), 16 wk; tot 49 wk.

Bloch, Robert
Psycho II (Warner) NYT mm pb 9/26/82 (#12, 1 wk).

Blochman, Lawrence G.
See Cecil St. Laurent

Block, Herbert
The Herblock Book (Simon & Schuster) NYT gen 11/2/52 (#16), pk 12/21/52 (#10, 2 wk), 17 wk.
Herblock's Here and Now (Simon & Schuster) NYT gen 1/1/56 (#14), pk 1/15/56 (#10, 1 wk), 12 wk.
Herblock's Special for Today (Simon & Schuster) NYT gen 11/16/58 (#15), pk 2/1/59 (#10, 2 wk), 12 wk.

Block, Jeff
See Malcolm Forbes and_____

Block, Libbie
The Hills of Beverly (Doubleday) NYT fic 9/8/57 (#16, 1 wk).

Bloom, Allan
The Closing of the American Mind: How Higher Education Has Failed Democracy and Impoverished the Souls of Today's Students (Simon & Schuster/Touchstone) NYT nf 5/3/87 (#11), pk 6/7/87 (#1, 10 wk), 45 wk; PW hc nf 5/15/87 (#14), pk 6/19/87 (#1, 9 wk), 39 wk; NYT mm pb 5/8/88 (#3), pk 5/22/88 (#1, 2 wk), 33 wk; PW td pb 5/13/88 (#8), pk 5/27/88 (#2, 3 wk), 19 wk; tot 136 wk.

Bloom, Harold
The Book of J [interpreted by Bloom; trans. David Rosenberg] (Grove/Weidenfeld & Nicolson) NYT nf 11/4/90 (#12, 2 wk), 4 wk; PW hc nf 11/30/90 (#14, 1 wk), 2 wk; tot 6 wk.

Bloom, Murray Teigh
The Trouble with Lawyers (Simon & Schuster) NYT gen 3/9/69 (#10), pk 4/27/69 (#5, 2 wk), 14 wk; PW nf 3/31/69 (#10), pk 5/5/69 (#6, 1 wk), 12 wk; tot 26 wk.

Bloomfield, Harold H., M.D., Michael Peter Cain, Dennis T. Jaffe and Robert B. Kory
TM: Discovering Inner Energy and Overcoming Stress (Delacorte) NYT gen 6/1/75 (#9), pk 7/27/75 (#2, 8 wk), 27 wk; PW nf 6/9/75 (#9), pk 7/14/75 (#2, 10 wk), 25 wk; (Dell) NYT mm pb 11/23/75 (#7), pk 12/7/75 (#3, 3 wk), 12 wk; PW mm pb 2/2/76 (#7, 1 wk); tot 65 wk.

Blum, Howard
Wanted! (Quadrangle/New York Times) NYT nf 5/1/77 (#10, 1 wk).

Blume, Judy
Tales of a Fourth Grade Nothing (Dell) NYT ch pb 11/13/77 (#4), pk 4/30/78 (#2, 24 wk), 70 wk.
Wifey (Putnam) PW hc fic 11/6/78 (#12, 2 wk), 5 wk; NYT fic 11/12/78 (#14), pk 12/3/78 (#10, 1 wk), 8 wk; (Pocket) PW mm pb 7/2/79 (#11), pk 8/6/79 (#2, 4 wk), 21 wk; NYT mm pb 7/8/79 (#9), pk 7/22/79 (#1, 2 wk), 20 wk; tot 54 wk.
Are You There God? It's Me, Margaret (Dell/Yearling) NYT ch pb 4/30/78 (#12, 24 wk).
Smart Women (Putnam) NYT fic 2/12/84 (#10), pk 3/4/84 (#2, 3 wk), 18 wk; PW hc fic 2/17/84 (#8), pk 3/16/84 (#2, 4 wk), 18 wk; (Pocket) NYT pb fic 3/10/85 (#6), pk 3/24/85 (#2, 3 wk), 12 wk; PW mm pb 3/15/85 (#8), pk 3/29/85 (#2, 4 wk), 11 wk; tot 59 wk.
Fudge-A-Mania (Dutton) PW ch mid rd 10/26/90 (#5), pk 11/30/90 (#4, 8 wk), 12 wk.

Blunt, Betty B.
Bet It's a Boy (Stephen Daye) PW nf 9/14/40 (#5), pk 10/12/40 (#3, 12 wk), 16 wk.

Bly, Robert
Iron John: A Book About Men (Addison Wesley) NYT nf 11/25/90 (#12), pk 12/2/90 (#5, 2 wk), 6 wk; PW hc nf 11/30/90 (#12), pk 12/7/90 (#11, 1 wk), 3 wk; tot 9 wk.

Blythe, LeGette
Bold Galilean (Grosset & Dunlap) NYT fic 3/13/49 (#16, 1 wk).

Bocca, Geoffrey
Elizabeth and Philip (Holt) NYT gen 5/31/53 (#15), pk 6/14/53 (#15, 1 wk), 3 wk.
See also Hugh C. McDonald and_____

Boe, Eugene
The Official Cambridge Diet Book (Bantam) NYT td pb 4/10/83 (#10), pk 4/17/83 (#5, 1 wk), 9 wk; PW td pb 4/22/83 (#7), pk 5/13/83 (#5, 1 wk), 6 wk; tot 15 wk.

Bogner, Norman
Seventh Avenue (Coward McCann) PW fic 4/3/67 (#10, 1 wk); (Dell) PW mm pb

2/28/77 (#11), pk 3/7/77 (#9, 1 wk), 3 wk; NYT mm pb 3/6/77 (#7, 1 wk), 2 wk; tot 6 wk.

Boileau, Ethel

Clansmen (Dutton) NYT fic 7/5/36 (#3, 4 wk); PW fic 7/11/36 (#5, 4 wk), 12 wk; tot 16 wk.

Ballade in G-Minor (Dutton) NYT fic 4/3/38 (#9, 4 wk); PW fic 4/9/38 (#9, 4 wk); tot 8 wk.

Bok, Curtis

I Too, Nicodemus (Knopf) NYT gen 10/13/46 (#6), pk 11/17/46 (#4, 1 wk), 6 wk.

Bok, Edward W.

The Americanization of Edward Bok (Scribner) PW gen lit 1/8/21 (#10), pk 6/17/22 (#4, 8 wk), 84 wk; nf 4/1/22 (#5), pk 11/24/23 (#4, 4 wk), 16 wk; tot 100 wk.

A Man from Maine (Scribner) PW gen lit 5/26/23 (#6), pk 7/21/23 (#3, 8 wk), 16 wk.

Twice Thirty (Scribner) PW gen lit 4/18/25 (#3, 4 wk), 12 wk.

Boleslavski, Richard, and Helen Woodward

Way of the Lancer (Bobbs Merrill) PW nf 4/23/32 (#8, 4 wk), 8 wk.

Bolitho, Hector

King Edward VIII (Lippincott) NYT nf 6/6/37 (#3, 4 wk), 8 wk; PW nf 6/12/37 (#8, 4 wk), 12 wk; tot 20 wk.

Bolles, Blair

How to Get Rich in Washington (Norton) NYT gen 3/23/52 (#11, 2 wk), 5 wk.

Bolles, Richard Nelson

What Color Is Your Parachute? [1978] (Ten Speed) PW td pb 5/29/78 (#8), pk 9/18/78 (#7, 2 wk), 16 wk.

What Color Is Your Parachute? [1979] (Ten Speed) NYT td pb 2/4/79 (#10), pk 5/13/79 (#2, 4 wk), 46 wk; PW td pb 3/5/79 (#7), pk 8/20/79 (#2, 1 wk), 40 wk; tot 86 wk.

What Color Is Your Parachute? [1980] (Ten Speed) NYT td pb 1/27/80 (#6), pk 3/23/80 (#4, 11 wk), 49 wk; PW td pb 2/29/80 (#8), pk 6/13/80 (#3, 4 wk), 41 wk; tot 90 wk.

What Color Is Your Parachute? [1981] (Ten Speed) PW td pb 1/23/81 (#9), pk 2/13/81 (#5, 1 wk), 24 wk; NYT td pb 1/25/81 (#13), pk 2/22/81 (#5, 5 wk), 45 wk; tot 69 wk.

What Color Is Your Parachute? [1982] (Ten Speed) NYT td pb 1/24/82 (#14), pk 6/6/82 (#4, 2 wk), 43 wk; PW td pb 6/11/82 (#8), pk 7/2/82 (#6, 3 wk), 23 wk; tot 66 wk.

What Color Is Your Parachute? [1983] (Ten Speed) NYT td pb 1/23/83 (#15), pk 5/1/83 (#7, 6 wk), 44 wk; PW td pb 5/6/83 (#10), pk 6/10/83 (#6, 1 wk), 15 wk; tot 59 wk.

What Color Is Your Parachute? [1985] (Ten Speed) NYT msc pb 7/7/85 (#8), pk 9/8/85 (#5, 2 wk), 18 wk.

What Color Is Your Parachute? [1986] (Ten Speed) NYT msc pb 3/23/86 (#5), pk 5/18/86 (#2, 2 wk), 31 wk; PW td pb 4/18/86 (#8), pk 6/6/86 (#4, 2 wk), 28 wk; tot 59 wk.

What Color Is Your Parachute? [1987] (Ten Speed) NYT msc pb 3/22/87 (#6), pk 4/12/87 (#5, 1 wk), 6 wk; PW td pb 4/10/87 (#8), pk 4/17/87 (#7, 2 wk), 3 wk; tot 9 wk.

What Color Is Your Parachute? [1988] (Ten Speed) PW td pb 3/25/88 (#10), pk 4/15/88 (#7, 1 wk), 4 wk.

What Color Is Your Parachute? [1989] (Ten Speed) PW td pb 2/24/89 (#10), pk 3/10/89 (#3, 2 wk), 7 wk; NYT msc pb 3/5/89 (#4), pk 3/19/89 (#3, 1 wk), 4 wk; tot 11 wk.

What Color Is Your Parachute? The 20th Anniversary Edition (Ten Speed) PW td pb 3/16/90 (#6, 2 wk), 5 wk.

Bolton, Isabel

Do I Wake or Sleep? (Scribners) NYT fic 12/22/46 (#16, 1 wk).

Bombeck, Erma

The Grass Is Always Greener Over the Septic Tank (McGraw) PW hc nf 10/4/76 (#8), pk 11/15/76 (#4, 8 wk), 46 wk; NYT gen 10/24/76 (#8), pk 11/28/76 (#4, 7 wk), 48 wk; (Fawcett/Crest) PW mm pb 9/19/77 (#6), pk 10/17/77 (#2, 1 wk), 17 wk; NYT mm pb 9/25/77 (#7), pk 10/9/77 (#3, 2 wk), 34 wk; tot 145 wk.

If Life Is a Bowl of Cherries—What Am I Doing in the Pits? (McGraw) PW hc nf 4/10/78 (#9), pk 5/22/78 (#1, 18 wk), 51 wk; NYT nf 4/16/78 (#7), pk 5/28/78 (#1, 14 wk), 40 wk; (Fawcett/Crest) PW mm pb 4/2/79 (#4), pk 4/9/79 (#1, 2 wk), 13 wk; NYT mm pb 4/8/79 (#2), pk 4/15/79 (#1, 2 wk), 16 wk; tot 120 wk.

Aunt Erma's Cope Book (McGraw) PW hc nf 10/8/79 (#7), 11/26/79 (#1, 3 wk), 27 wk; NYT nf 10/14/79 (#6), pk 10/28/79 (#1, 10 wk), 39 wk; (Fawcett Crest) PW mm pb 10/3/80 (#9), pk 10/10/80 (#5, 1 wk), 6 wk; NYT mm pb 10/5/80 (#10), pk 1/18/81 (#5, 1 wk), 13 wk; tot 85 wk.

Motherhood: The Second-Oldest Profession (McGraw) PW hc nf 9/23/83 (#12), pk 11/11/83 (#1, 13 wk), 51 wk; NYT nf 9/25/83 (#10), pk 10/23/83 (#1, 21 wk), 52 wk; (Dell) NYT pb nf 10/7/84 (#3), pk 10/21/84 (#1, 7 wk), 17 wk; PW mm pb 10/12/84 (#5), pk 11/2/84 (#1, 1 wk), 14 wk; tot 134 wk.

Family: The Ties That Bind ... and Gag! (McGraw) NYT nf 9/13/87 (#11), pk 12/13/87 (#2, 4 wk), 25 wk; PW hc nf 9/18/87

(#12), pk 12/18/87 (#3, 4 wk), 20 wk; (Fawcett/Crest) NYT pb nf 11/27/88 (#4), pk 12/4/88 (#3, 7 wk), 13 wk; PW mm pb 12/9/88 (#8), pk 1/13/89 (#6, 1 wk), 8 wk; tot 66 wk.

I Want to Grow Hair, I Want to Grow Up, I Want to Go to Boise (Harper) NYT nf 10/15/89 (#6, 2 wk), 12 wk; PW hc nf 10/20/89 (#7, 2 wk), 5 wk; NYT pb nf 9/2/90 (#9), pk 9/16/90 (#2, 1 wk), 8 wk; tot 25 wk.

Bonanno, Margaret Wander
Dwellers in the Crucible (Pocket) NYT pb fic 9/15/85 (#12, 1 wk), PW mm pb 9/27/85 (#10, 1 wk), 3 wk; tot 4 wk.

Strangers from the Sky (Pocket) NYT pb fic 7/12/87 (#6, 1 wk), 6 wk; PW mm pb 7/17/87 (#12), pk 7/31/87 (#9, 1 wk), 4 wk; tot 10 wk.

Bond, Larry
Red Phoenix (Warner) PW hc fic 6/2/89 (#14), pk 7/21/89 (#2, 1 wk), 19 wk; NYT fic 6/4/89 (#14), pk 7/2/89 (#4, 3 wk), 15 wk; NYT pb fic 5/6/90 (#3), pk 5/20/90 (#2, 2 wk), 8 wk; PW mm pb 5/11/90 (#2, 4 wk), 8 wk; tot 50 wk.

Bond, Simon
101 Uses for a Dead Cat (Potter) PW td pb 5/15/81 (#8), pk 7/17/81 (#1, 13 wk), 46 wk; NYT td pb 5/24/81 (#13), pk 7/5/81 (#1, 10 wk), 51 wk; tot 97 wk.

Unspeakable Acts (Potter) NYT td pb 1/10/82 (#13), pk 1/17/82 (#12, 1 wk), 10 wk.

Bonham, Barbara
Passion's Price (Playboy) NYT mm pb 8/21/77 (#14, 1 wk).

Boni, Margaret B.
The Fireside Book of Favorite American Songs [ed.] (Simon & Schuster) NYT gen 12/14/52 (#16, 2 wk).

The Fireside Book of Folk Songs [ed.] (Simon & Schuster) NYT gen 11/9/47 (#12), pk 12/14/47 (#7, 1 wk), 12 wk; PW nf 1/17/48 (#10, 1 wk); tot 13 wk.

Bonner, Paul Hyde
SPQR (Scribner) NYT fic 4/13/52 (#11), pk 5/25/52 (#7, 1 wk), 18 wk.

Hotel Talleyrand (Scribner) NYT fic 4/26/53 (#16), pk 5/31/53 (#5, 1 wk), 13 wk; PW fic 5/16/53 (#9), pk 5/23/53 (#5, 1 wk), 3 wk; tot 16 wk.

Excelsior! (Scribner) NYT fic 7/10/55 (#9), pk 8/14/55 (#5, 1 wk), 13 wk; PW fic 7/30/55 (#6), pk 8/20/55 (#5, 1 wk), 6 wk; tot 19 wk.

With Both Eyes Open (Scribner) NYT fic 5/27/56 (#14), pk 6/3/56 (#10, 1 wk), 2 wk.

The Art of Llewellyn Jones (Scribner) NYT fic 8/2/59 (#15), pk 10/11/59 (#7, 2 wk), 16 wk; PW fic 8/24/59 (#7), pk 10/12/59 (#6, 1 wk), 7 wk; tot 23 wk.

Bonnet, Theodore
The Mudlark (Doubleday) NYT fic 9/4/49 (#10), pk 10/9/49 (#6, 2 wk), 21 wk; PW fic 10/15/49 (#9), pk 11/5/49 (#5, 1 wk), 6 wk; tot 27 wk.

Dutch (Doubleday) NYT fic 5/1/55 (#16), pk 5/15/55 (#11, 4 wk), 11 wk.

Bonsal, Stephen J.
Unfinished Business (Doubleday) NYT gen 3/19/44 (#13), pk 3/26/44 (#6, 1 wk), 8 wk.

Bonventure, Peter
See Howard Cosell and_____

Boone, Pat
'Twixt Twelve and Twenty (Prentice Hall) NYT gen 1/4/59 (#6), pk 2/8/59 (#2, 7 wk), 39 wk; PW nf 1/12/59 (#6), pk 3/16/59 (#1, 1 wk), 29 wk; tot 68 wk.

Boorstin, Daniel J.
The Discoverers (Random) PW hc nf 12/23/83 (#15), pk 2/10/84 (#5, 1 wk), 16 wk; NYT nf 1/8/84 (#13), pk 2/12/84 (#3, 1 wk), 24 wk; tot 40 wk.

Booth, Pat
Palm Beach (Ballantine) NYT pb fic 8/10/86 (#8), pk 8/24/86 (#5, 1 wk), 8 wk; PW mm pb 8/15/86 (#13), pk 8/29/86 (#6, 1 wk), 6 wk; tot 14 wk.

The Sisters (Ballantine) NYT pb fic 5/8/88 (#10), pk 5/22/88 (#5, 1 wk), 7 wk; PW mm pb 5/13/88 (#10), pk 6/3/88 (#4, 1 wk), 6 wk; tot 13 wk.

Beverly Hills (Ballantine) NYT pb fic 8/5/90 (#16), pk 8/19/90 (#8, 2 wk), 6 wk; PW mm pb 8/17/90 (#15), pk 8/24/90 (#9, 1 wk), 3 wk; tot 9 wk.

Boothe, Clare
Europe in the Spring (Knopf) PW nf 11/16/40 (#8, 8 wk).

Borden, Mary
Strange Week-End (Harper) NYT fic 3/6/38 (#14, 4 wk).

Passport for a Girl (Harper) NYT fic 7/9/39 (#6, 4 wk).

Bork, Robert H.
The Tempting of America (Free Press) PW hc nf 12/8/89 (#11), pk 2/2/90 (#4, 1 wk), 14 wk; NYT nf 12/17/89 (#13), pk 1/21/90 (#4, 2 wk), 16 wk; tot 30 wk.

Borkin, Joseph, and Charles A. Welsh
Germany's Master Plan (Duell Sloan & Pearce) NYT nf 2/28/43 (#15), pk 3/14/43 (#10, 1 wk), 4 wk.

Borland, Hal
When the Legends Die (Lippincott) NYT

fic 7/7/63 (#10, 2 wk); PW fic 7/8/63 (#9, 2 wk), 4 wk; tot 6 wk.

Borysenko, Joan, and Larry Roth-stein
Minding the Body, Mending the Mind (Addison Wesley) NYT msc 10/11/87 (#5, 1 wk).

Bosco, Dominick
See Ronald Markham and_____

Bosse, Malcolm
The Warlord (Simon & Schuster) NYT fic 6/19/83 (#15), pk 7/31/83 (#11, 1 wk), 6 wk; PW hc fic 7/8/83 (#13, 1 wk), 2 wk; (Bantam) NYT pb fic 6/10/84 (#7), pk 6/24/84 (#6, 1 wk), 7 wk; PW mm pb 6/15/84 (#14), pk 7/6/84 (#6, 1 wk), 6 wk; tot 21 wk.

Bossert, Patrick
You Can Do the Cube (Penguin) PW td pb 10/16/81 (#8), pk 11/6/81 (#1, 4 wk), 21 wk; NYT td pb 10/18/81 (#8), pk 1/24/82 (#1, 2 wk), 25 wk; tot 46 wk.

Boston Women's Health Book Collective
Our Bodies, Our Selves (Simon & Schuster/Touchstone) NYT td pb 3/10/74 (#4), pk 6/6/76 (#2, 4 wk), 140 wk; PW td pb 5/3/76 (#2), pk 7/12/76 (#1, 2 wk), 69 wk; tot 209 wk.
Ourselves and Our Children (Random) NYT td pb 12/24/78 (#14), pk 2/4/79 (#11, 1 wk), 10 wk; PW td pb 1/22/79 (#10), pk 1/29/79 (#3, 1 wk), 6 wk; tot 16 wk.
The New Our Bodies, Our Selves (Touchstone/Simon & Schuster) PW td pb 2/22/85 (#10, 2 wk).

Boswell, James
Boswell's London Journal, 1762-1763 [ed. Frederick A. Pottle] (McGraw) NYT gen 11/26/50 (#6), pk 12/31/50 (#2, 7 wk), 27 wk; PW nf 12/2/50 (#5), pk 12/23/50 (#2, 8 wk), 17 wk; tot 44 wk.
Boswell in Holland [ed. Frederick A. Pottle] (McGraw) NYT gen 5/11/52 (#16), pk 5/25/52 (#7, 2 wk), 12 wk; PW nf 5/31/52 (#5, 1 wk), 3 wk; tot 15 wk.
Boswell on the Grand Tour [ed. Frank Brady and Frederick A. Pottle] (McGraw) NYT gen 6/12/55 (#9), pk 7/3/55 (#8, 1 wk), 9 wk.
Boswell's Life of Johnson (Simon & Schuster) NYT ch bst 11/2/58 (#14, 40 wk).

Boswell, John, with Patty Brown and Will Elder
Chuck & Di Have a Baby (Fireside) NYT td pb 7/18/82 (#15, 1 wk).
See also Jim Fitzgerald, et al.

Bosworth, Brian, with Rich Reilly
The Boz: Confessions of a Modern Anti-Hero

(Doubleday) NYT nf 9/4/88 (#7), pk 9/25/88 (#2, 1 wk), 10 wk; PW hc nf 9/9/88 (#9), pk 9/30/88 (#4, 2 wk), 9 wk; tot 19 wk.

Bosworth, Patricia
Diane Arbus (Knopf) NYT nf 9/2/84 (#15, 1 wk).

Botkin, Benjamin Albert
A Treasury of American Folklore (Crown) NYT gen 6/4/44 (#13), pk 6/25/44 (#7, 1 wk), 20 wk; PW nf 7/1/44 (#5, 1 wk), 4 wk; tot 24 wk.
A Treasury of New England Folklore [ed.] (Bonanza/Crown) NYT gen 12/21/47 (#15), pk 1/4/48 (#9, 1 wk), 7 wk.
A Treasury of Western Folklore [ed.] (Bonanza/Crown) NYT gen 12/23/51 (#16, 1 wk).

Bottome, Phyllis
Private Worlds (Houghton) PW fic 5/12/34 (#2, 8 wk), 20 wk.
The Mortal Storm (Little Brown) NYT fic 5/1/38 (#3, 4 wk), 24 wk; PW fic 5/14/38 (#6), pk 7/9/38 (#3, 12 wk), 28 wk; tot 52 wk.
Danger Signal (Little Brown) NYT fic 3/5/39 (#4, 4 wk); PW fic 3/11/39 (#9, 4 wk); tot 8 wk.
Survival (Little Brown) NYT gen 10/24/43 (#9), pk 11/14/43 (#8, 1 wk), 2 wk; PW fic 11/13/43 (#9, 1 wk); tot 3 wk.
The Life Line (Little Brown) NYT fic 4/7/46 (#16, 1 wk).

Boulton, Agnes
Part of a Long Story (Doubleday) NYT gen 9/7/58 (#16, 1 wk).

Bourke-White, Margaret
Portrait of Myself (Simon & Schuster) NYT gen 7/28/63 (#9, 3 wk); PW nf 8/12/63 (#11, 1 wk); tot 4 wk.

Bourne, Peter
Drums of Destiny (Putnam) NYT fic 10/12/47 (#10), pk 11/9/47 (#5, 1 wk), 15 wk; PW fic 11/15/47 (#6, 1 wk), 2 wk; tot 17 wk.
Flames of Empire (Putnam) NYT fic 11/13/49 (#16, 1 wk).
The Golden Road (Putnam) NYT fic 8/26/51 (#16, 1 wk).

Bouton, Jim
Ball Four [ed. Leonard Shecter] (World) NYT gen 7/12/70 (#9), pk 8/9/70 (#3, 1 wk), 17 wk; PW nf 8/3/70 (#5), pk 8/24/70 (#4, 3 wk), 17 wk; NYT pb gen 4/4/71 (#4, 8 wk); tot 42 wk.

Bowen, Catherine Drinker
Yankee from Olympus (Little Brown) NYT gen 5/7/44 (#13), pk 6/18/44 (#1, 7 wk), 52 wk; PW nf 5/27/44 (#2), pk 6/17/44 (#1, 7 wk), 40 wk; tot 92 wk.

John Adams and the American Revolution (Little Brown) NYT gen 7/9/50 (#8), pk 7/30/50 (#5, 1 wk), 15 wk; PW nf 7/15/50 (#8), pk 7/22/50 (#2, 1 wk), 10 wk; tot 25 wk.

The Lion and the Throne (Little Brown) NYT gen 4/7/57 (#11), pk 4/14/57 (#10, 3 wk), 8 wk; PW nf 4/15/57 (#8, 1 wk); tot 9 wk.

Francis Bacon (Atlantic Little Brown) PW nf 8/19/63 (#10, 1 wk); NYT gen 9/1/63 (#9, 1 wk); tot 2 wk.

See also Barbara von Meck and_____

Bowen, Elizabeth
The House in Paris (Knopf) NYT fic 4/5/36 (#6, 4 wk).

Death of the Heart (Knopf) NYT fic 3/5/39 (#9, 4 wk).

The Heat of the Day (Knopf) NYT fic 3/13/49 (#14), pk 3/20/49 (#7, 1 wk), 8 wk.

A World of Love (Knopf) NYT fic 2/6/55 (#12), pk 2/27/55 (#10, 1 wk), 5 wk.

A Time in Rome (Knopf) NYT gen 3/13/60 (#16), pk 4/17/60 (#14, 1 wk), 4 wk.

Eva Trout (Knopf) PW fic 11/25/68 (#8, 1 wk), 2 wk.

Bowers, Claude G.
Jefferson and Hamilton (Houghton) PW nf 3/20/26 (#9, 8 wk), 12 wk.

The Tragic Era (Houghton) PW nf 10/12/29 (#4), pk 12/14/29 (#1, 4 wk), 24 wk.

Beveridge and the Progressive Era (Houghton) PW nf 10/15/32 (#9, 4 wk).

Jefferson in Power (Houghton) PW nf 10/10/36 (#6, 4 wk), 12 wk.

The Young Jefferson (Houghton) NYT gen 4/15/45 (#15), pk 4/22/45 (#12, 1 wk), 5 wk.

Bowles, Chester
Ambassador's Report (Harper) NYT gen 1/24/54 (#13), pk 3/21/54 (#6, 1 wk), 17 wk; PW nf 3/20/54 (#5, 1 wk), 2 wk; tot 19 wk.

Bowles, Paul Frederic
The Sheltering Sky (New Directions) NYT fic 1/1/50 (#15), pk 1/15/50 (#9, 2 wk), 11 wk.

Let It Come Down (Random) NYT fic 3/16/52 (#16), pk 3/30/52 (#9, 2 wk), 5 wk.

Boyar, Jane and Burt Boyar
See Sammy Davis, Jr. and_____

Boyd, James
Drums (Scribner) PW fic 7/18/25 (#8, 4 wk), 8 wk.

Marching On (Scribner) PW fic 6/25/27 (#3, 8 wk), 16 wk.

Bitter Creek (Scribner) NYT fic 5/7/39 (#12, 4 wk).

Boyd, Martin
Lucinda Brayford (Dutton) NYT fic 3/21/

48 (#9), pk 3/28/48 (#6, 2 wk), 8 wk; PW fic 4/17/48 (#8), pk 4/24/48 (#4, 1 wk), 2 wk; tot 10 wk.

Boyington, Pappy
Baa Baa Black Sheep (Putnam) NYT gen 8/17/58 (#10), pk 10/12/58 (#3, 10 wk), 35 wk; PW nf 9/8/58 (#5), pk 10/27/58 (#3, 9 wk), 27 wk; tot 62 wk.

Boyle, Kay
Avalanche (Simon & Schuster) NYT fic 1/30/44 (#12), pk 2/20/44 (#7, 4 wk), 24 wk.

Boyne, Walter J., and Steven C. Thompson
The Wild Blue: The Novel of the U.S. Air Force (Crown) PW hc fic 10/31/86 (#11, 1 wk), 6 wk; NYT fic 10/19/86 (#15, 2 wk); (Ivy) PW mm pb 8/7/87 (#15), pk 8/14/87 (#13, 2 wk), 3 wk; NYT pb fic 8/9/87 (#14), pk 8/16/87 (#12, 2 wk), 4 wk; tot 15 wk.

Boynton, Sandra
Chocolate: The Consuming Passion (Workman) NYT td pb 6/13/82 (#15), pk 7/18/82 (#3, 1 wk), 24 wk; PW td pb 6/25/82 (#9), pk 7/9/82 (#5, 4 wk), 21 wk; tot 45 wk.

Bozell, L. Brent
See William F. Buckley, Jr. and_____

Brace, Gerald Warner
The Islands (Putnam) NYT fic 7/5/36 (#8, 4 wk).

The Garretson Chronicle (Norton) NYT fic 9/28/47 (#16), pk 1/25/48 (#5, 1 wk), 25 wk; PW fic 11/15/47 (#10), pk 1/31/48 (#4, 1 wk), 9 wk; tot 34 wk.

The Spire (Norton) NYT fic 9/21/52 (#14, 1 wk), 2 wk.

Bracken, Peg
The I Hate to Cook Book (Harcourt) NYT pb gen 1/2/66 (#2), pk 3/6/66 (#1, 4 wk), 24 wk.

Bradbury, Ray
The Stories of Ray Bradbury (Knopf) NYT fic 12/28/80 (#14, 1 wk), 2 wk.

Braden, Thomas
See Stewart Alsop and_____

Bradford, Barbara Taylor
A Woman of Substance (Doubleday) PW hc fic 7/23/79 (#15), pk 8/27/79 (#12, 1 wk), 8 wk; NYT fic 8/19/79 (#14), pk 9/16/79 (#10, 1 wk), 7 wk; (Avon) PW mm pb 6/13/80 (#8), pk 7/18/80 (#1, 1 wk), 41 wk; NYT mm pb 6/15/80 (#9), pk 7/20/80 (#1, 1 wk), 44 wk; NYT pb fic 11/18/84 (#14), pk 12/16/84 (#12, 1 wk), 4 wk; tot 104 wk.

Voice of the Heart (Doubleday) NYT fic

4/3/83 (#4, 6 wk), 23 wk; PW hc fic 4/8/83 (#5), pk 4/15/83 (#2, 1 wk), 20 wk; (Bantam) NYT pb fic 3/4/84 (#8), pk 3/11/84 (#3, 4 wk), 10 wk; PW mm pb 3/9/84 (#6), pk 3/16/84 (#1, 1 wk), 10 wk; tot 63 wk.
Hold the Dream (Doubleday) PW hc fic 5/17/85 (#13), pk 6/7/85 (#1, 2 wk), 19 wk; NYT fic 5/19/85 (#8), pk 6/9/85 (#1, 1 wk), 19 wk; (Bantam) NYT pb fic 4/6/86 (#8), pk 4/27/86 (#1, 4 wk), 13 wk; PW mm pb 4/11/86 (#11), pk 4/18/86 (#1, 6 wk), 13 wk; tot 64 wk.
Act of Will (Doubleday) NYT fic 6/22/86 (#16), pk 7/6/86 (#3, 2 wk), 16 wk; PW hc fic 6/27/86 (#13), pk 7/18/86 (#2, 1 wk), 15 wk; (Bantam) NYT pb fic 6/7/87 (#4), pk 6/14/87 (#1, 4 wk), 12 wk; PW mm pb 6/12/87 (#2), pk 6/19/87 (#1, 4 wk), 9 wk; tot 52 wk.
To Be the Best (Doubleday) NYT fic 7/10/88 (#4), pk 7/17/88 (#2, 3 wk), 13 wk; PW hc fic 7/15/88 (#5), pk 7/22/88 (#2, 3 wk), 14 wk; (Bantam) NYT pb fic 5/7/89 (#6), pk 5/14/89 (#1, 3 wk), 9 wk; PW mm pb 5/12/89 (#4), pk 5/19/89 (#1, 3 wk), 9 wk; tot 45 wk.
The Women in His Life (Random) NYT fic 8/12/90 (#5), pk 8/26/90 (#2, 1 wk), 11 wk; PW hc fic 8/24/90 (#5), pk 8/31/90 (#3, 3 wk), 9 wk; [read by Lynn Redgrave] PW aud fic 10/5/90 (#9), pk 11/2/90 (#7, 4 wk), 8 wk; tot 28 wk.

Bradford, Gamaliel
Damaged Souls (Houghton) PW gen lit 9/15/23 (#7, 4 wk); PW nf 11/24/23 (#12, 4 wk); tot 8 wk.

Bradford, Richard
Red Sky at Morning (Lippincott) NYT fic 6/30/68 (#8), pk 9/8/68 (#5, 2 wk), 15 wk; PW fic 7/8/68 (#7), pk 9/2/68 (#5, 3 wk), 16 wk; NYT pb fic 7/6/69 (#4, 4 wk); tot 35 wk.

Bradlee, Benjamin C.
Conversations with Kennedy (Norton) NYT gen 5/25/75 (#8), pk 7/6/75 (#2, 1 wk), 17 wk; PW nf 5/26/75 (#10), pk 6/16/75 (#3, 2 wk), 14 wk; (Pocket) PW mm pb 6/7/76 (#14, 1 wk); tot 32 wk.

Bradlee, Frederick
See Cleveland Amory and_____

Bradley, David Vernard
No Place to Hide (Little Brown) NYT gen 1/2/49 (#12), pk 1/30/49 (#10, 1 wk), 7 wk.

Bradley, Marion Zimmer
The Mists of Avalon (Knopf) NYT fic 2/20/83 (#12), pk 3/20/83 (#7, 1 wk), 13 wk; PW hc fic 2/25/83 (#13), pk 3/18/83 (#8, 2 wk), 10 wk; (Ballantine) PW td pb 5/18/84 (#8), pk 6/15/84 (#3, 2 wk), 10 wk; tot 33 wk.

Bradley, Omar N.
A Soldier's Story (Holt) NYT gen 7/1/51 (#11), pk 8/5/51 (#3, 1 wk), 18 wk; PW nf 7/14/51 (#5), pk 8/4/51 (#3, 3 wk), 12 wk; tot 30 wk.

Bradshaw, Bernard
See Ellen Terry and_____

Bradshaw, John
Homecoming: Reclaiming and Championing Your Inner Child (Bantam) NYT msc 7/22/90 (#5), pk 8/12/90 (#1, 12 wk), 21 wk; PW hc nf 8/3/90 (#9), pk 9/14/90 (#1, 4 wk), 20 wk; tot 41 wk.
Healing the Shame That Binds You (Health Communications) PW td pb 2/9/90 (#10), pk 3/16/90 (#5, 2 wk), 9 wk; NYT msc pb 2/4/90 (#6), pk 2/11/90 (#5, 1 wk), 3 wk; PW aid nf 10/5/90 (#5), pk 11/2/90 (#1, 8 wk), 12 wk; tot 24 wk.
Bradshaw On: The Family (Health Communications) PW aud nf 10/5/90 (#4, 4 wk), 12 wk.

Brady, Frank
See James Boswell

Bragg, Melvyn
Richard Burton: A Life (Little Brown) NYT nf 3/5/89 (#16), pk 3/19/89 (#8, 1 wk), 6 wk; PW hc nf 3/17/89 (#12, 1 wk); tot 7 wk.

Braggiotti, Gloria
Born in a Crowd (Crowell) NYT gen 3/24/57 (#16, 1 wk).

Braine, John
Room at the Top (Houghton) NYT fic 12/8/57 (#15, 1 wk).

Branch, Taylor
Parting the Waters: America in the King Years (Simon & Schuster) NYT nf 1/15/89 (#13), pk 2/5/89 (#6, 2 wk), 12 wk; PW hc nf 1/20/89 (#13), pk 2/24/89 (#8, 1 wk), 11 wk; tot 23 wk.
See also Bill Russell and_____

Brand, Millen
The Outward Room (Simon & Schuster) NYT fic 6/6/37 (#2, 4 wk), 12 wk; PW fic 6/12/37 (#6), pk 7/10/37 (#3, 4 wk), 12 wk; tot 24 wk.
The Heroes (Simon & Schuster) NYT fic 6/11/39 (#6, 4 wk).

Brand, Stewart
The Last Whole Earth Catalog [ed.] (Random) PW nf 10/25/71 (#10), pk 12/27/71 (#6, 4 wk), 13 wk; NYT gen 11/7/71 (#9), pk 1/16/71 (#6, 2 wk), 18 wk; NYT pb gen 7/9/72 (#3, 4 wk); tot 35 wk.
The Updated Last Whole Earth Catalog

[ed.] (Random) NYT td pb 1/12/75 (#2, 1 wk), 4 wk.

The Next Whole Earth Catalog [ed.] (Point/Random) PW td pb 12/12/80 (#8), pk 1/16/81 (#3, 6 wk), 17 wk; NYT td pb 12/21/80 (#14), pk 12/28/80 (#4, 2 wk), 18 wk; tot 35 wk.

Brande, Dorothea
Wake Up and Live! (Simon & Schuster) NYT nf 5/3/36 (#1, 4 wk); PW nf 5/9/36 (#5), pk 7/11/36 (#1, 4 wk), 44 wk; NYT gen 7/5/36 (#1, 4 wk), 20 wk; tot 68 wk.

Branden, Barbara
The Passion of Ayn Rand (Doubleday) NYT nf 8/10/86 (#16), pk 8/24/86 (#13, 5 wk), 6 wk.

Brandewyne, Rebecca
And Gold Was Ours (Warner) NYT pb fic 12/2/84 (#12), pk 12/9/84 (#11, 1 wk), 3 wk.

The Outlaw Hearts (Warner) NYT pb fic 5/4/86 (#14), pk 5/18/86 (#11, 1 wk), 2 wk; PW mm pb 5/16/86 (#10, 1 wk), 2 wk; tot 4 wk.

Desire in Disguise (Warner) NYT pb fic 4/5/87 (#10, 1 wk), 2 wk; PW mm pb 4/24/87 (#13, 1 wk); tot 3 wk.

Passion Moon Rising (Pocket) NYT pb fic 2/14/88 (#16, 1 wk).

Brannon, J.B.
See Joe Weil and_____

Braun, Lilian Jackson
The Cat Who Went Underground (Jove) PW mm pb 9/22/89 (#9, 1 wk), 3 wk.

The Cat Who Lived High (Putnam) PW hc fic 9/7/90 (#15, 1 wk).

The Cat Who Sniffed Glue (Jove) PW mm pb 3/31/89 (#15), pk 4/7/89 (#14, 1 wk), 2 wk.

The Cat Who Talked to Ghosts (Jove) NYT pb fic 9/9/90 (#10, 1 wk), 5 wk; PW mm pb 9/14/90 (#9), pk 9/21/90 (#3, 1 wk), 7 wk; tot 12 wk.

Breasted, James H., and James Harvey Robinson
The Human Adventure (Harper) PW nf 12/18/26 (#7, 4 wk).

Breathed, Berke
Bloom County: Loose Tails (Little Brown) PW td pb 11/4/83 (#10), pk 11/11/83 (#9, 2 wk), 3 wk.

Bloom County: American Tails (Little Brown) PW td pb 6/3/83 (#6), pk 6/10/83 (#4, 2 wk), 21 wk; NYT td pb 6/5/83 (#11), pk 8/21/83 (#5, 4 wk), 32 wk; tot 53 wk.

'Toons for Our Times: A Bloom County Book (Little Brown) NYT msc pb 4/22/84 (#3), pk 4/29/84 (#2, 6 wk), 20 wk; PW td pb

4/27/84 (#4), pk 5/11/84 (#2, 7 wk), 23 wk; tot 43 wk.

Penguin Dreams and Stranger Things (Little Brown) PW td pb 4/19/85 (#2), pk 4/26/85 (#1, 13 wk), 30 wk; NYT msc pb 4/21/85 (#1, 12 wk), 37 wk; tot 67 wk.

Bloom County Babylon: Five Years of Basic Naughtiness (Little Brown) NYT msc pb 8/31/86 (#4), pk 9/14/86 (#2, 10 wk), 22 wk; PW td pb 9/5/86 (#5), pk 9/19/86 (#1, 6 wk), 21 wk; tot 43 wk.

Billy and the Boingers Bootleg (Little Brown) NYT msc pb 8/30/87 (#1, 9 wk), 21 wk; PW td pb 9/4/87 (#2), pk 9/11/87 (#1, 8 wk), 22 wk; tot 43 wk.

Tales Too Ticklish to Tell (Little Brown) NYT msc pb 9/18/88 (#5), pk 9/25/88 (#1, 2 wk), 17 wk; PW td pb 9/23/88 (#4), pk 10/14/88 (#2, 1 wk), 17 wk; tot 34 wk.

The Night of the Mary Kay Commandos: Featuring Smell-O-Toons (Little Brown) NYT msc pb 9/10/89 (#1, 5 wk), 13 wk; PW td pb 9/15/89 (#1, 3 wk), 17 wk; tot 30 wk.

Happy Trails (Little Brown) NYT msc pb 3/25/90 (#4), pk 4/1/90 (#3, 4 wk), 7 wk; PW td pb 3/30/90 (#10), pk 4/20/90 (#3, 2 wk), 15 wk; tot 22 wk.

Classics of Western Literature (Little Brown) NYT msc pb 9/16/90 (#5, 1 wk); PW td pb 9/21/90 (#10), pk 9/28/90 (#2, 1 wk), 8 wk; tot 9 wk.

Breger, Dave
Private Breger (Rand McNally) NYT nf 8/9/42 (#10, 1 wk), 4 wk.

Brennan, Ray
See Roget Touhy and_____

Breskin, David, with Cheryl McCall and Robert Hilburn
We Are the World (Perigee) NYT msc pb 5/12/85 (#10), pk 5/19/85 (#8, 1 wk), 2 wk.

Breslin, Catherine
Unholy Child (NAL/Signet) NYT mm pb 11/16/80 (#13), pk 11/23/80 (#4, 4 wk), 12 wk; PW mm pb 11/21/80 (#5), pk 12/12/80 (#3, 1 wk), 8 wk; tot 20 wk.

Breslin, Howard
The Tamarack Tree (Macmillan) NYT fic 1/4/48 (#13, 1 wk).

Breslin, Jimmy
The Gang That Couldn't Shoot Straight (Viking) PW fic 1/5/70 (#8), pk 3/16/70 (#3, 1 wk), 28 wk; NYT fic 1/18/70 (#9), pk 3/1/70 (#5, 3 wk), 26 wk; NYT pb fic 5/2/71 (#5, 4 wk); tot 58 wk.

World Without End, Amen (Viking) NYT fic 9/16/73 (#10), pk 10/14/73 (#4, 4 wk), 17

wk; PW fic 9/24/73 (#7), pk 10/29/73 (#4, 1 wk), 14 wk; tot 31 wk.

How the Good Guys Finally Won: Notes from an Impeachment Summer (Viking) PW nf 6/2/75 (#6), pk 6/30/75 (#4, 1 wk), 17 wk; NYT gen 6/8/75 (#10), pk 7/13/75 (#3, 1 wk), 18 wk; (Ballantine) PW mm pb 4/19/76 (#14, 1 wk), 2 wk; tot 37 wk.

Table Money (Ticknor & Fields) NYT fic 8/10/86 (#14, 1 wk).

Brett, Jan
The Wild Christmas Reindeer (Putnam) PW ch pic 11/30/90 (#3), pk 12/21/90 (#1, 4 wk), 8 wk; NYT fic 12/16/90 (#10, 1 wk), 3 wk; tot 11 wk.

Brewer-Giorgio, Gail
Is Elvis Alive? (Tudor) NYT pb nf 8/14/88 (#10), pk 8/28/88 (#6, 2 wk), 4 wk.

Brickhill, Paul
Reach for the Sky (Norton) NYT gen 8/29/54 (#15), pk 9/5/54 (#13, 1 wk), 7 wk; PW nf 10/16/54 (#10, 1 wk); tot 8 wk.

Bridenbaugh, Carl, and Jessica Bridenbaugh
Rebels and Gentlemen: Philadelphia in the Age of Franklin (Reynal & Hitchcock) NYT nf 11/8/42 (#18, 1 wk).

Bridge, Ann
See Mary Dolling Sanders O'Malley

Briffault, Robert
Europa (Scribner) NYT fic 10/6/35 (#5), pk 11/3/35 (#3, 4 wk), 12 wk; PW fic 10/12/35 (#3), pk 11/9/35 (#2, 4 wk), 20 wk; tot 32 wk.

Europa in Limbo (Scribner) NYT fic 11/7/37 (#9, 4 wk).

Briggs, Raymond
See Anonymous (The Mother Goose Treasury)

Brill, Steven
The Teamsters (Simon & Schuster) PW hc nf 10/23/78 (#12), pk 10/30/78 (#11, 1 wk), 4 wk; NYT nf 12/10/78 (#15, 1 wk); tot 5 wk.

Brin, David
The Uplift War (Bantam) NYT pb fic 6/28/87 (#14), pk 7/5/87 (#13, 1 wk), 2 wk.

Brinig, Myron
The Sisters (Farrar) NYT fic 3/7/37 (#10, 4 wk); PW fic 3/13/37 (#9, 12 wk), 16 wk; tot 20 wk.

May Flavin (Farrar) NYT fic 7/31/38 (#2, 4 wk).

Anne Minton's Life (Farrar) NYT fic 7/9/39 (#5, 4 wk).

You and I (Farrar) NYT fic 12/16/45 (#15, 1 wk).

Brink, Carol
Buffalo Coat (Macmillan) NYT fic 1/14/45 (#13, 1 wk).

Brinkley, Christie
Christie Brinkley's Outdoor Beauty & Fitness Book (Simon & Schuster) PW hc nf 8/19/83 (#15, 1 wk).

Brinkley, David
Washington Goes to War (Knopf) NYT nf 4/24/88 (#6), pk 5/1/88 (#4, 2 wk), 16 wk; PW hc nf 4/29/88 (#7, 4 wk), 12 wk; (Ballantine) NYT pb nf 7/23/89 (#2, 3 wk), 13 wk; PW mm pb 7/28/89 (#13), pk 8/11/89 (#7, 1 wk), 5 wk; tot 46 wk.

Brinkley, William
Don't Go Near the Water (Random) NYT fic 7/22/56 (#13), pk 8/12/56 (#1, 15 wk), 39 wk; PW fic 8/6/56 (#4), pk 8/13/56 (#1, 13 wk), 32 wk; tot 71 wk.

The Lost Ship (Ballantine) PW td pb 3/10/89 (#8, 1 wk).

Briskin, Jacqueline
Paloverde (McGraw) NYT fic 2/18/79 (#13, 1 wk); (Warner) NYT mm pb 2/17/80 (#13), pk 3/9/80 (#7, 3 wk), 10 wk; PW mm pb 2/22/80 (#9), pk 3/14/80 (#5, 1 wk), 7 wk; tot 18 wk.

The Onyx (Dell) NYT mm pb 5/8/83 (#14), pk 5/22/83 (#8, 1 wk), 7 wk; PW mm pb 5/27/83 (#13), pk 6/3/83 (#10, 1 wk), 4 wk; tot 11 wk.

Everything and More (Putnam) NYT fic 9/25/83 (#14), pk 10/30/83 (#9, 1 wk), 8 wk; PW hc fic 10/7/83 (#15), pk 10/28/83 (#10, 1 wk), 8 wk; (Berkley) NYT pb fic 6/10/84 (#4, 3 wk), 9 wk; PW mm pb 6/15/84 (#5), pk 7/6/84 (#2, 1 wk), 9 wk; tot 34 wk.

Too Much Too Soon (Putnam) NYT fic 8/25/85 (#13), pk 9/15/85 (#8, 1 wk), 7 wk; PW hc fic 8/30/85 (#12), pk 9/13/85 (#7, 1 wk), 6 wk; (Berkley) NYT pb fic 6/1/86 (#16), pk 6/15/86 (#4, 3 wk), 9 wk; PW mm pb 6/6/86 (#6), pk 6/13/86 (#4, 2 wk), 9 wk; tot 31 wk.

Dreams Are Not Enough (Putnam) PW hc fic 2/20/87 (#14), pk 3/13/87 (#8, 2 wk), 8 wk; NYT fic 2/22/87 (#15), pk 3/1/5/87 (#8, 1 wk), 5 wk; (Berkley) NYT pb fic 10/4/87 (#12), pk 10/25/87 (#8, 1 wk), 6 wk; PW mm pb 10/9/87 (#11, 1 wk), 5 wk; tot 24 wk.

The Naked Heart (Delacorte) PW hc nf 5/12/89 (#12, 2 wk), 5 wk; NYT fic 5/21/89 (#13), pk 5/28/89 (#12, 1 wk), 3 wk; (Dell) NYT pb fic 4/15/90 (#10), pk 4/22/90 (#9, 1 wk), 4 wk; PW mm pb 4/20/90 (#12, 1 wk), 2 wk; tot 14 wk.

Bristol, Claude M.
TNT: The Power Within You (Prentice

Hall) NYT gen 7/18/54 (#13), pk 10/17/54 (#5, 3 wk), 24 wk; PW nf 8/14/54 (#9), pk 10/23/54 (#5, 5 wk), 12 wk; tot 36 wk.

Bristow, Gwen
The Handsome Road (Crowell) NYT fic 6/5/38 (#5, 4 wk), 8 wk; PW fic 6/11/38 (#8, 8 wk), 16 wk; tot 24 wk.
This Side of Glory (Crowell) PW fic 5/11/40 (#8, 4 wk), 8 wk.
Jubilee Trail (Crowell) NYT fic 2/26/50 (#11), pk 5/7/50 (#3, 7 wk), 46 wk; PW fic 3/18/50 (#6), pk 7/15/50 (#2, 1 wk), 33 wk; tot 79 wk.
Celia Garth (Crowell) NYT fic 5/24/59 (#9), pk 6/28/59 (#6, 9 wk), 21 wk; PW fic 6/22/59 (#7), pk 7/6/59 (#6, 9 wk), 15 wk; tot 36 wk.
Calico Palace (Crowell) NYT fic 5/17/70 (#10), pk 6/28/70 (#5, 4 wk), 30 wk; PW fic 6/1/70 (#10), pk 10/19/70 (#3, 1 wk), 24 wk; NYT pb fic 7/11/71 (#4), pk 8/8/71 (#2, 4 wk), 16 wk; tot 70 wk.

Brittain, Vera
Testament of Youth (Macmillan) PW nf 12/9/33 (#6), pk 1/13/34 (#3, 4 wk), 20 wk.
Honourable Estate (Macmillan) PW fic 1/16/37 (#10, 4 wk).

Britten, Benjamin, and Imogen Holst
The Wonderful World of Music (Garden City) NYT ch bst 11/1/59 (#8, 25 wk).

Britton, Nan
The President's Daughter (Elizabeth Ann Guild) PW nf 12/31/27 (#10, 4 wk).

Brodie, Fawn M.
The Devil Drives (Norton) PW nf 7/31/67 (#11, 1 wk).
Thomas Jefferson (Norton) NYT gen 5/5/74 (#9), pk 6/16/74 (#2, 1 wk), 16 wk; PW nf 5/6/74 (#9), pk 6/3/74 (#6, 1 wk), 13 wk; tot 29 wk.

Brody, Ilse
Gone with the Windsors (Winston) NYT gen 10/11/53 (#9), pk 11/15/53 (#3, 1 wk), 17 wk; PW nf 10/24/53 (#5), pk 11/21/53 (#3, 1 wk), 10 wk; tot 27 wk.

Brody, Jane
Jane Brody's Nutrition Book (Norton) NYT nf 7/5/81 (#14), pk 10/18/81 (#7, 1 wk), 20 wk; PW hc nf 8/28/81 (#14, 2 wk), 4 wk; tot 24 wk.
Jane Brody's Good Food Book: Living the High Carbohydrate Way (Norton) PW hc nf 11/15/85 (#9, 1 wk), 12 wk; NYT msc 12/8/85 (#5), pk 12/15/85 (#3, 2 wk), 9 wk; tot 21 wk.

Brogan, Denis William
Politics in America (Harper) NYT gen 2/13/55 (#14, 2 wk), 3 wk.

Bromfield, Louis
Early Autumn (Stokes) PW fic 12/18/26 (#9, 4 wk).
A Good Woman (Stokes) PW fic 9/24/27 (#1, 8 wk), 16 wk.
The Strange Case of Miss Annie Spragg (Stokes) PW fic 10/27/28 (#9), pk 11/24/28 (#2, 4 wk), 16 wk.
Twenty-Four Hours (Stokes) PW fic 10/18/30 (#3), pk 11/22/30 (#1, 4 wk), 12 wk.
A Modern Hero (Stokes) PW fic 6/11/32 (#2, 4 wk), 12 wk.
The Farm (Harper) PW fic 9/16/33 (#4), pk 10/14/33 (#2, 4 wk), 12 wk.
The Rains Came (Harper) PW fic 11/13/37 (#10), pk 12/11/37 (#3, 20 wk), 40 wk; NYT fic 12/12/37 (#1, 4 wk), 28 wk; tot 68 wk.
It Takes All Kinds (Harper) NYT fic 11/5/39 (#7, 4 wk).
Night in Bombay (Harper) PW fic 6/8/40 (#6), pk 7/13/40 (#3, 8 wk), 16 wk.
Wild Is the River (Harper) PW fic 12/13/41 (#5), pk 1/17/42 (#4, 4 wk), 12 wk.
Until the Day Break (Harper) PW fic 7/11/42 (#5, 4 wk), 7 wk; NYT fic 8/9/42 (#6, 1 wk), 5 wk; tot 12 wk.
Mrs. Parkington (Harper) PW fic 1/23/43 (#5), pk 2/6/43 (#2, 7 wk), 20 wk; NYT fic 1/24/43 (#8), pk 3/14/43 (#1, 1 wk), 24 wk; tot 44 wk.
What Became of Anna Bolton (Harper) NYT fic 4/23/44 (#12, 1 wk), 3 wk; PW fic 5/13/44 (#9, 2 wk); tot 5 wk.
Pleasant Valley (Harper) NYT gen 4/29/45 (#14), pk 12/2/45 (#3, 2 wk), 52 wk; PW nf 6/9/45 (#5), pk 8/18/45 (#3, 7 wk), 35 wk; tot 87 wk.
A Few Brass Tacks (Harper) NYT gen 7/21/46 (#15, 1 wk).
Malabar Farm (Harper) NYT gen 5/23/48 (#12), pk 8/1/48 (#4, 1 wk), 21 wk; PW nf 6/5/48 (#5), pk 7/10/48 (#3, 1 wk), 16 wk; tot 37 wk.
Mr. Smith (Harper) NYT fic 9/9/51 (#16), pk 9/23/51 (#7, 1 wk), 12 wk; PW fic 10/13/51 (#7, 1 wk), 2 wk; tot 14 wk.
From My Experience (Harper) NYT gen 7/3/55 (#12), pk 7/31/55 (#10, 2 wk), 9 wk.

Bronowski, Jacob
The Ascent of Man (Little Brown) PW nf 3/3/75 (#8), pk 5/5/75 (#2, 5 wk), 37 wk; NYT gen 3/9/75 (#9), pk 5/4/75 (#2, 3 wk), tot 34 wk; PW hc nf 2/2/76 (#8, 1 wk); td pb 10/4/76 (#5), pk 11/29/76 (#3, 3 wk), 10 wk; NYT td pb 10/31/76 (#4, 3 wk), 5 wk; tot 87 wk.

Bronson, Jill Ireland
Life Wish (Little Brown) PW hc nf 2/27/87 (#12), pk 3/6/87 (#9, 1 wk), 6 wk; NYT nf 3/8/87 (#15), pk 3/15/87 (#12, 2 wk), 4 wk; tot 10 wk.

Bronson, William
How to Kill a Golden State (Knopf) PW nf 7/29/68 (#9, 1 wk).

Brookhouser, Frank
Our Philadelphia (Doubleday) NYT gen 12/1/57 (#14), pk 12/8/57 (#10, 2 wk), 6 wk.

Brookner, Anita
Hotel Du Lac (Pantheon) NYT fic 3/17/85 (#14), pk 4/21/85 (#10, 1 wk), 9 wk; PW hc fic 4/19/85 (#12, 3 wk), 5 wk; tot 14 wk.

Brooks, C. Harry
The Practice of Autosuggestion (Dodd) PW gen lit 9/16/22 (#12), pk 12/23/22 (#5, 8 wk), 28 wk.

Brooks, John
The Go-Go Years (Weybright & Talley) PW nf 11/5/73 (#8, 1 wk).

Brooks, John Nixon
The Big Wheel (Harper) NYT fic 9/18/49 (#13), pk 9/25/49 (#12, 1 wk), 3 wk.

Brooks, Leslie Leonard
Johnny Crow's New Garden (Warne) NYT juv 12/1/35 (#3, 4 wk).

Brooks, Richard
The Brick Foxhole (Harper) NYT fic 8/5/45 (#11, 1 wk), 2 wk.

Brooks, Terry
The Sword of Shannara (Ballantine/Del Rey) NYT td pb 5/1/77 (#5), pk 5/22/77 (#2, 14 wk), 28 wk; PW td pb 5/9/77 (#2, 10 wk), 21 wk; NYT mm pb 7/23/78 (#11, 1 wk); tot 50 wk.
The Elfstones of Shannara (Ballantine/Del Rey) NYT td pb 8/8/82 (#6), pk 8/15/82 (#3, 4 wk), 16 wk; PW td pb 8/13/82 (#4), pk 8/20/82 (#3, 4 wk), 15 wk; NYT pb fic 1/8/84 (#13, 1 wk); PW mm pb 1/27/84 (#15, 2 wk); tot 34 wk.
The Wishsong of Shannara (Ballantine/Del Rey) NYT pb fic 5/5/85 (#9), pk 5/12/85 (#7, 2 wk), 8 wk; PW td pb 5/10/85 (#2), pk 5/17/85 (#1, 1 wk), 14 wk; tot 22 wk.
Magic Kingdom for Sale— Sold! (Ballantine/Del Rey) PW hc fic 4/25/86 (#15), pk 5/16/86 (#9, 2 wk), 5 wk; NYT fic 5/11/86 (#12, 1 wk), 2 wk; NYT pb fic 4/5/87 (#11), pk 4/26/87 (#6, 1 wk), 9 wk; PW mm pb 4/10/87 (#14), pk 4/24/87 (#5, 1 wk), 7 wk; tot 23 wk.
The Black Unicorn (Ballantine/Del Rey)

PW mm pb 9/9/88 (#12, 1 wk), 3 wk; NYT pb fic 9/11/88 (#11, 1 wk), 2 wk; tot 5 wk.
Wizard at Large (Ballantine/Del Rey) NYT pb fic 8/6/89 (#16), pk 8/20/89 (#9, 1 wk), 5 wk; PW mm pb 8/18/89 (#15), pk 8/25/89 (#9, 1 wk), 3 wk; tot 8 wk.
The Scions of Shannara: Book One of the Heritage of Shannara (Ballantine/Del Rey) NYT fic 3/11/90 (#4, 1 wk), 9 wk; PW hc fic 3/16/90 (#8), pk 4/20/90 (#4, 1 wk), 10 wk; tot 19 wk.

Brooks, Van Wyck
The Flowering of New England (Dutton) NYT gen 10/4/36 (#9), pk 7/4/37 (#4, 4 wk), 16 wk; PW nf 11/14/36 (#10), pk 1/16/37 (#8, 12 wk), 28 wk; tot 44 wk.
New England: Indian Summer (Dutton) PW nf 9/14/40 (#3), pk 10/12/40 (#2, 4 wk), 20 wk.
The World of Washington Irving (Dutton) NYT gen 10/15/44 (#21), pk 1/21/45 (#2, 1 wk), 26 wk; PW nf 10/28/44 (#5), pk 12/2/44 (#3, 1 wk), 16 wk; tot 42 wk.
The Times of Melville and Whitman (Dutton) NYT gen 12/21/47 (#14, 1 wk).
The Confident Years 1885–1915 (Dutton) NYT gen 1/27/52 (#14), pk 2/3/52 (#13, 1 wk), 5 wk.

Brooks, Win
The Shining Tides (Morrow) NYT fic 8/3/52 (#11), pk 8/24/52 (#10, 1 wk), 5 wk.

Brosnan, Jim
The Long Season (Harper) NYT gen 10/2/60 (#14, 1 wk).

Brothers, Dr. Joyce
How to Get Everything You Want Out of Life (Simon & Schuster) PW hc nf 3/12/79 (#12), pk 5/7/79 (#9, 1 wk), 10 wk; NYT nf 4/8/79 (#15), pk 5/6/79 (#10, 2 wk), 10 wk; tot 20 wk.
What Every Woman Should Know About Men (Simon & Schuster) PW hc nf 2/26/82 (#15), pk 3/26/82 (#10, 2 wk), 11 wk; NYT nf 3/28/82 (#8, 1 wk), 10 wk; tot 21 wk.

Brough, James
See Elliott Roosevelt and____
See Hedda Hopper and____

Brousson, Jean Jacques
Anatole France Himself (Lippincott) PW nf 9/26/25 (#5, 4 wk), 12 wk.

Brown, Anthony Cave
Bodyguard of Lies (Harper) PW nf 1/19/76 (#10, 1 wk); NYT gen 2/1/76 (#9, 1 wk); PW hc nf 2/16/76 (#10, 1 wk); tot 3 wk.

Brown, Cecil
Suez to Singapore (Random) NYT nf 11/15/

42 (#5), pk 11/22/42 (#2, 7 wk), 27 wk; PW nf 11/21/42 (#2, 6 wk), 19 wk; tot 46 wk.

Brown, Christy
Down All the Days (Stein & Day) NYT fic 7/12/70 (#9, 1 wk).

Brown, Claude
Manchild in the Promised Land (Macmillan) PW nf 9/6/65 (#10), pk 10/25/65 (#6, 1 wk), 12 wk; NYT gen 9/12/65 (#9, 3 wk), 5 wk; NYT pb gen 1/1/67 (#3, 4 wk); tot 21 wk.

Brown, Constantine
See Drew Pearson and_____

Brown, Dale
Flight of the Old Dog (Fine) PW hc fic 7/31/87 (#13, 1 wk), 4 wk; (Berkley) NYT pb fic 5/1/88 (#8), pk 5/8/88 (#4, 3 wk), 9 wk; PW mm pb 5/6/88 (#5), pk 5/13/88 (#2, 1 wk), 9 wk; tot 22 wk.

Silver Tower (Berkley) NYT pb fic 4/2/89 (#10), pk 4/23/89 (#7, 1 wk), 5 wk; PW mm pb 4/7/89 (#11), pk 4/21/89 (#8, 1 wk), 5 wk; tot 10 wk.

Day of the Cheetah (Fine) PW hc fic 6/23/89 (#11), pk 7/28/89 (#5, 1 wk), 12 wk; NYT fic 7/2/89 (#10), pk 7/30/89 (#8, 1 wk), 9 wk; (Berkley) PW mm pb 6/1/90 (#8), pk 6/29/90 (#4, 1 wk), 7 wk; NYT pb fic 6/3/90 (#7), pk 6/10/90 (#5, 3 wk), 5 wk; tot 33 wk.

Hammerheads (Fine) NYT fic 8/5/90 (#14), pk 8/19/90 (#10, 1 wk), 6 wk; PW hc fic 8/10/90 (#12), pk 8/31/90 (#8, 2 wk), 6 wk; tot 12 wk.

Brown, Dee
Bury My Heart at Wounded Knee (Holt) NYT gen 3/14/71 (#10), pk 5/30/71 (#1, 24 wk), 57 wk; PW nf 3/29/71 (#7), pk 5/17/71 (#1, 23 wk), 55 wk; NYT pb gen 5/14/72 (#1, 16 wk), 20 wk; tot 132 wk.

Creek Mary's Blood (Holt) PW hc fic 4/4/80 (#14), pk 4/11/80 (#10, 2 wk), 10 wk; NYT fic 4/6/80 (#14), pk 4/27/80 (#9, 1 wk), 11 wk; tot 21 wk.

Brown, Dennis
The Complete Indoor Gardener [consulting ed.] (Random) NYT td pb 6/15/75 (#5, 2 wk).

Brown, Eve
Champagne Cholly (Dutton) NYT gen 6/8/47 (#15, 1 wk).

Brown, Harriet C.
Grandmother Brown's Hundred Years (Little Brown) PW nf 12/14/29 (#8), pk 1/11/30 (#6, 4 wk), 16 wk.

Brown, Harry
A Walk in the Sun (Knopf) NYT fic 7/23/44 (#12), pk 9/10/44 (#8, 1 wk), 7 wk.

Brown, Helen Gurley
Sex and the Single Girl (Geis) NYT gen 7/1/62 (#11), pk 9/23/62 (#5, 2 wk), 25 wk; PW nf 7/23/62 (#9), pk 9/24/62 (#6, 3 wk), 24 wk; tot 49 wk.

Having It All: Love, Success, Sex, Money (Linden/Simon & Schuster) PW hc nf 11/12/82 (#14), pk 11/26/82 (#9, 2 wk), 17 wk; NYT nf 11/21/82 (#11), pk 11/28/82 (#10, 2 wk), 16 wk; (Pocket) NYT mm pb 11/20/83 (#13, 1 wk), 2 wk; PW mm pb 12/2/83 (#15, 1 wk); tot 36 wk.

Brown, Jim, and Steve Delsohn
Out of Bounds (Zebra) NYT nf 10/8/89 (#9), pk 10/15/89 (#8, 1 wk), 4 wk; PW hc nf 10/13/89 (#10, 2 wk), 3 wk; tot 7 wk.

Brown, Joe Evan
Your Kids and Mine (Doubleday) NYT gen 11/26/44 (#17), pk 12/17/44 (#8, 1 wk), 15 wk.

Brown, Lt. John Mason
To All Hands (Whittlesey) NYT gen 12/5/43 (#18), pk 1/2/44 (#5, 1 wk), 12 wk; PW nf 1/15/44 (#10, 1 wk); tot 13 wk.

Many a Watchful Night (Whittlesey/McGraw) NYT gen 1/14/45 (#17, 1 wk), 2 wk.

Brown, Marcia
Once a Mouse... (Scribner) NYT ch bst 5/13/62 (#8), pk 11/11/62 (#7, 26 wk), 45 wk.

Brown, Margaret Wise
Three Little Animals (Harper) NYT ch bst 11/18/56 (#13), pk 11/17/57 (#9, 40 wk), 80 wk.

Goodnight Moon (Harper) NYT ch bst 11/4/73 (#10), pk 4/30/78 (#7, 24 wk), 50 wk; NYT ch pb 4/30/78 (#13, 24 wk); tot 74 wk.

Brown, Palmer
Cheerful (Harper) NYT ch bst 11/17/57 (#13, 40 wk).

Brown, Patty
See John Boswell, et al.

Brown, Peter, and Steven Gaines
The Love You Make: An Insider's Story of the Beatles (McGraw) NYT nf 5/1/83 (#12), pk 5/22/83 (#6, 2 wk), 16 wk; PW hc nf 5/13/83 (#7), pk 6/10/83 (#5, 2 wk), 19 wk; NYT pb nf 3/18/84 (#7, 2 wk); tot 37 wk.

Brown, Richard
See Earl Schenck Miers and_____

Brown, Rita Mae
Southern Discomfort (Harper) NYT fic 5/16/82 (#15, 1 wk).

Sudden Death (Bantam) NYT fic 5/29/83 (#14), pk 6/26/83 (#12, 1 wk), 4 wk; PW hc fic 6/10/83 (#12, 1 wk), 3 wk; tot 7 wk.

High Hearts (Bantam) NYT fic 5/18/86 (#12, 1 wk), 5 wk.

Brown, Sandra
Mirror Image (Warner) NYT pb fic 6/3/90 (#8, 1 wk), 5 wk; PW mm pb 6/22/90 (#13, 2 wk); tot 7 wk.

Brown, Warren
The Chicago Cubs (Putnam) NYT gen 9/8/46 (#16), pk 9/29/46 (#9, 2 wk), 8 wk.

Browne, Douglas G., and E.V. Tullet
The Scalpel of Scotland Yard: The Life of Sir Bernard Spilsbury (Dutton) NYT gen 3/2/52 (#16, 1 wk).

Browne, Gerald A.
11 Harrowhouse (Arbor House) PW fic 5/8/72 (#10), pk 6/5/72 (#8, 2 wk), 7 wk.
19 Purchase Street (Arbor House) PW hc fic 9/3/82 (#15), pk 10/29/82 (#13, 1 wk), 6 wk; NYT fic 9/5/82 (#15), pk 10/10/82 (#10, 1 wk), 7 wk; (Berkley) NYT mm pb 9/8/83 (#9), pk 10/16/83 (#6, 1 wk), 4 wk; PW mm pb 9/23/83 (#14), pk 9/30/83 (#8, 1 wk), 6 wk; tot 23 wk.
Stone 588 (Arbor House) NYT fic 2/9/86 (#11), pk 2/23/86 (#9, 2 wk), 10 wk; PW hc fic 2/21/86 (#15), pk 2/28/86 (#7, 2 wk), 7 wk; (Berkley) NYT pb fic 4/5/87 (#7), pk 4/19/87 (#3, 2 wk), 10 wk; PW mm pb 4/10/87 (#9), pk 5/8/87 (#3, 1 wk), 9 wk; tot 36 wk.
Hot Siberian (Avon) NYT pb fic 11/12/89 (#14, 1 wk); PW mm pb 11/17/89 (#12, 1 wk); tot 2 wk.

Browne, Harry
How You Can Profit from the Coming Devaluation (Arlington) NYT gen 11/1/70 (#10, 2 wk).
How I Found Freedom in an Unfree World (Macmillan) PW nf 4/30/73 (#8, 1 wk).
You Can Profit from a Monetary Crisis (Macmillan) PW nf 2/4/74 (#5), pk 4/29/74 (#1, 3 wk), 40 wk; NYT gen 2/24/74 (#10), pk 4/28/74 (#1, 1 wk), 39 wk; (Bantam) NYT mm pb 2/2/75 (#4, 1 wk), 2 wk; tot 81 wk.
New Profits from the Monetary Crisis (Morrow) PW hc nf 12/11/78 (#15, 4 wk); NYT nf 1/28/79 (#13, 1 wk), 3 wk; tot 7 wk.

Browne, Lewis
This Believing World (Macmillan) PW nf 11/20/26 (#6), pk 2/19/27 (#5, 4 wk), 20 wk.
See What I Mean? (World Almanac) NYT fic 11/7/43 (#13), pk 12/5/43 (#8, 1 wk), 3 wk.

Brownmiller, Susan
Against Our Will: Men, Women and Rape (Simon & Schuster) PW nf 11/17/75 (#10),

pk 12/1/75 (#6, 1 wk), 5 wk; NYT gen 11/30/75 (#8, 1 wk), 2 wk; tot 7 wk.

Bruce, John Roberts
Gaudy Century (Random) NYT gen 12/26/48 (#14), pk 1/30/49 (#13, 1 wk), 5 wk.

Bruck, Connie
The Predators' Ball (American Lawyer/Simon & Schuster) NYT nf 9/18/88 (#15, 1 wk).

Bruckberger, Raymond-Leopold
Image of America (Viking) NYT gen 8/2/59 (#16), pk 8/23/59 (#13, 1 wk), 8 wk.

Bruff, Nancy
The Manatee (Dutton) NYT fic 11/11/45 (#14), pk 11/25/45 (#7, 1 wk), 10 wk; PW fic 12/15/45 (#9, 1 wk); tot 11 wk.

Brullers, Jean
You Shall Know Them [as by Vercours] (Little Brown) NYT fic 7/26/53 (#15), pk 8/30/53 (#10, 1 wk), 6 wk.

Brundy, Clyde M.
High Empire (Avon) NYT mm pb 8/11/74 (#9, 4 wk).

Brush, Katharine
Young Man of Manhattan (Farrar) PW fic 2/15/30 (#5), pk 3/15/30 (#1, 4 wk), 16 wk.
Red Headed Woman (Farrar) PW fic 11/14/31 (#8, 4 wk).
Out of My Mind (Doubleday) NYT gen 11/7/43 (#18), pk 11/14/43 (#15, 1 wk), 3 wk.

Brush, Stephanie
Men: An Owner's Manual (Linden/Simon & Schuster) NYT nf 9/23/84 (#13, 1 wk), 2 wk.

Bryan, C.D.B.
The National Geographic Society: 100 Years of Adventure and Discovery (Abrams) NYT nf 12/27/87 (#14), pk 1/10/88 (#9, 1 wk), 3 wk; PW hc nf 1/8/88 (#11), pk 1/15/88 (#8, 1 wk), 2 wk; tot 5 wk.

Bryan, Dorothy
Johnny Penguin (Doubleday) PW juv 8/15/31 (#9, 4 wk).

Bryan, Lt. Cmdr. J., III
See Fleet Adm. William F. Halsey and
_____

_____ **and Charles J.V. Murphy**
The Windsor Story (Morrow) NYT nf 1/13/80 (#14), pk 2/17/80 (#12, 1 wk), 5 wk; PW hc nf 2/1/80 (#13, 1 wk), 4 wk; tot 9 wk.

Bryant, Sir Arthur
The Turn of the Tide (Doubleday) NYT gen 6/2/57 (#16), pk 7/7/57 (#3, 2 wk), 17 wk; PW nf 6/24/57 (#4), pk 7/22/57 (#2, 1 wk), 11 wk; tot 28 wk.

Triumph in the West (Doubleday) NYT gen 12/20/59 (#12, 2 wk).

Bryson, Bill
Mother Tongue (Morrow) PW hc nf 9/7/90 (#15, 1 wk).

Brzezinski, Zbigniew
Grand Failure: Communism's Terminal Crisis (Scribner) PW hc nf 4/7/89 (#10, 2 wk).

Buchan, John
Pilgrim's Way (Houghton) PW nf 10/12/40 (#6), pk 1/11/41 (#2, 4 wk), 20 wk.
Mountain Meadow (Houghton) PW fic 4/12/41 (#8, 8 wk).

Buchanan, Lamont
A Pictorial History of the Confederacy (Crown) NYT gen 12/30/51 (#16, 1 wk).

Buchheim, Lothar-Gunther
The Boat (Knopf) PW fic 6/30/75 (#10), pk 8/4/75 (#9, 2 wk), 5 wk; NYT fic 7/27/75 (#10), pk 8/24/75 (#9, 1 wk), 4 wk; (Bantam) PW mm pb 5/10/76 (#10), pk 6/7/76 (#5, 1 wk), 7 wk; NYT mm pb 5/23/76 (#9, 5 wk), 5 wk; tot 21 wk.

Buchwald, Ann
See Marjabelle Young Stewart and _____

Buchwald, Art
Down the Seine and Up the Potomac with Art Buchwald (Putnam) NYT nf 12/18/77 (#9), pk 1/8/78 (#8, 1 wk), 7 wk; PW hc nf 1/2/78 (#15), pk 1/16/78 (#10, 1 wk), 3 wk; tot 10 wk.
The Buchwald Stops Here (Putnam) NYT nf 12/17/78 (#15), pk 1/21/79 (#11, 1 wk), 5 wk.
Laid Back in Washington (Putnam) PW hc nf 12/18/81 (#14), pk 1/15/82 (#6, 1 wk), 10 wk; NYT nf 12/27/81 (#10), pk 1/10/82 (#6, 2 wk), 14 wk; tot 24 wk.
While Reagan Slept (Putnam) NYT nf 11/27/83 (#15), pk 12/18/83 (#4, 3 wk), 14 wk; PW hc nf 12/9/83 (#12), pk 1/6/84 (#4, 1 wk), 13 wk; tot 27 wk.
You Can Fool All of the People All of the Time (Putnam) NYT nf 12/22/85 (#11), pk 1/5/86 (#8, 1 wk), 7 wk; PW hc nf 1/3/86 (#12), pk 1/10/86 (#11, 1 wk), 4 wk; tot 11 wk.
I Think I Don't Remember (Putnam) NYT nf 12/20/87 (#9), pk 12/27/87 (#8, 1 wk), 4 wk; PW hc nf 1/8/88 (#12), pk 1/15/88 (#7, 1 wk), 2 wk; tot 6 wk.

Buck, Craig
See Dr. Susan Forward and _____

Buck, Pearl S.
The Good Earth (John Day) PW fic 4/18/31 (#7), pk 8/15/31 (#1, 16 wk), 84 wk.
Sons (John Day) PW fic 11/12/32 (#1, 8 wk), 16 wk.

The First Wife (John Day) PW fic 8/12/33 (#7, 4 wk).
The Mother (John Day) PW fic 2/10/34 (#7, 4 wk), 8 wk.
A House Divided (Reynal & Hitchcock) PW fic 2/9/35 (#9), pk 3/16/35 (#5, 4 wk), 16 wk.
The Exile (Reynal & Hitchcock) NYT fic 4/5/36 (#9, 4 wk); PW fic 4/11/36 (#5, 4 wk), 8 wk; tot 12 wk.
This Proud Heart (Reynal & Hitchcock) NYT fic 3/6/38 (#3, 4 wk), 8 wk; PW fic 3/12/38 (#7), pk 4/9/38 (#6, 4 wk), 12 wk; tot 20 wk.
The Patriot (John Day) PW fic 4/8/39 (#6, 8 wk), 12 wk; NYT fic 4/9/39 (#1, 4 wk), 8 wk; tot 20 wk.
Dragon Seed (John Day) PW fic 3/14/42 (#1, 4 wk), 20 wk; NYT fic 8/30/42 (#9, 1 wk), 3 wk; tot 23 wk.
The Promise (John Day) NYT fic 11/28/43 (#10), pk 12/12/43 (#8, 1 wk), 6 wk.
Portrait of a Marriage (John Day) NYT fic 12/30/45 (#11, 1 wk), 3 wk.
Pavilion of Women (John Day) NYT fic 12/15/46 (#15), pk 12/29/46 (#4, 4 wk), 18 wk; PW fic 1/4/47 (#4, 5 wk), 11 wk; tot 29 wk.
Peony (John Day) NYT fic 6/6/48 (#10), pk 7/18/48 (#3, 1 wk), 14 wk; PW fic 6/19/48 (#9), pk 6/26/48 (#4, 3 wk), 9 wk; tot 23 wk.
Kinfolk (John Day) NYT fic 5/15/49 (#7), pk 6/19/49 (#6, 2 wk), 13 wk; PW fic 6/4/49 (#5, 1 wk), 2 wk; tot 15 wk.
God's Men (John Day) NYT fic 4/29/51 (#11), pk 5/13/51 (#8, 4 wk), 15 wk; PW fic 6/9/51 (#9, 1 wk), 2 wk; tot 17 wk.
The Hidden Flower (John Day) NYT fic 6/8/52 (#14), pk 7/6/52 (#6, 2 wk), 17 wk; PW fic 6/28/52 (#5), pk 7/26/52 (#4, 1 wk), 7 wk; tot 24 wk.
Come, My Beloved (John Day) NYT fic 8/30/53 (#11), pk 9/6/53 (#7, 1 wk), 11 wk; PW fic 10/17/53 (#8, 1 wk), tot 12 wk.
My Several Worlds (John Day) NYT gen 11/28/54 (#12), pk 3/20/55 (#3, 2 wk), 27 wk; PW nf 12/18/54 (#6), pk 2/19/55 (#3, 2 wk), 19 wk; tot 46 wk.
Imperial Woman (John Day) NYT fic 4/15/56 (#15), pk 5/13/56 (#2, 4 wk), 24 wk; PW fic 4/28/56 (#3), pk 5/7/56 (#2, 5 wk), 17 wk; tot 41 wk.
Letter from Peking (John Day) NYT fic 7/28/57 (#12), pk 8/18/57 (#2, 3 wk), 18 wk; PW fic 8/5/57 (#8), pk 8/26/57 (#3, 2 wk), 13 wk; tot 31 wk.
Command the Morning (John Day) NYT fic 6/7/59 (#14, 2 wk), 3 wk.
A Bridge for Passing (John Day) NYT gen

4/29/62 (#15), pk 6/10/62 (#10, 1 wk) 9 wk;
PW nf 7/23/62 (#10, 1 wk); tot 10 wk.

The Living Reed (John Day) NYT fic
10/13/63 (#8), pk 10/27/63 (#4, 8 wk), 22 wk;
PW fic 10/28/63 (#6), pk 11/4/63 (#4, 4 wk),
20 wk; tot 42 wk.

The Time Is Noon (John Day) NYT fic
4/9/67 (#10, 2 wk); PW fic 4/17/67 (#10), pk
5/8/67 (#9, 1 wk), 4 wk; tot 6 wk.

The Three Daughters of Madame Liang
(John Day) NYT fic 8/31/69 (#9, 1 wk), 2
wk.

Buckley, Christopher
The White House Mess (Knopf) NYT fic
4/20/86 (#14, 2 wk), 3 wk.

Buckley, William Frank, Jr.
God and Man at Yale (Regnery) NYT gen
11/25/51 (#16, 1 wk).

The Unmaking of a Mayor (Viking) NYT
pb gen 1/7/68 (#2, 4 wk).

Saving the Queen (Doubleday) PW hc fic
2/2/76 (#9), pk 3/15/76 (#2, 1 wk), 15 wk;
NYT fic 2/8/76 (#10), pk 3/21/76 (#3, 3 wk),
15 wk; tot 30 wk.

Stained Glass (Doubleday) PW hc fic 5/15/
78 (#15), pk 7/3/78 (#3, 1 wk), 17 wk; NYT
fic 5/28/78 (#8), pk 7/2/78 (#4, 3 wk), 12 wk;
tot 29 wk.

Who's on First (Doubleday) PW hc fic 3/7/
80 (#12), pk 4/25/80 (#4, 1 wk), 15 wk; NYT
fic 3/23/80 (#6, 6 wk), 13 wk; (Avon) PW
mm pb 2/27/81 (#6), pk 3/6/81 (#5, 1 wk), 5
wk; NYT mm pb 3/1/81 (#14), pk 3/22/81
(#9, 1 wk), 4 wk; tot 37 wk.

Marco Polo, If You Can (Doubleday) PW
hc fic 1/29/82 (#12), pk 2/12/82 (#3, 4 wk),
14 wk; NYT fic 1/31/82 (#12), pk 2/21/82 (#2,
3 wk), 14 wk; tot 28 wk.

Atlantic High: A Celebration (Doubleday)
PW hc nf 10/1/82 (#14), pk 10/15/82 (#8, 2
wk), 13 wk; NYT nf 10/10/82 (#10), pk 10/17/
82 (#8, 1 wk), 14 wk; tot 27 wk.

The Story of Henri Tod (Doubleday) PW hc
fic 1/27/84 (#12), pk 3/2/84 (#4, 1 wk), 12 wk;
NYT fic 1/29/84 (#10), pk 2/5/84 (#6, 3 wk),
10 wk; tot 22 wk.

See You Later, Alligator (Doubleday) NYT
fic 2/24/85 (#11), pk 3/17/85 (#6, 2 wk), 11
wk; PW hc fic 3/1/85 (#13), pk 3/22/85 (#5,
1 wk), 9 wk; tot 20 wk.

High Jinx (Doubleday) PW hc fic 4/11/86
(#15), pk 4/25/86 (#11, 1 wk), 6 wk; NYT fic
4/13/86 (#15), pk 4/20/86 (#10, 1 wk), 4 wk;
tot 10 wk.

Mongoose: R.I.P. (Random) PW hc fic
1/15/88 (#14), pk 2/12/88 (#10, 3 wk), 10 wk;
NYT fic 1/24/88 (#12), pk 2/14/88 (#9, 1 wk),
8 wk; tot 18 wk.

_____, and L. Brent Bozell
McCarthy and His Enemies (Regnery)
NYT gen 4/18/54 (#11), pk 5/23/54 (#7, 3
wk), 13 wk; PW nf 5/29/54 (#5, 1 wk), 2 wk;
tot 15 wk.

Budd, Lillian
April Snow (Lipincott) NYT fic 6/17/51
(#12), pk 7/29/51 (#9, 1 wk), 16 wk.

Budenz, Louis Francis
This Is My Story (Whittlesey/McGraw)
NYT gen 4/6/47 (#14), pk 5/11/47 (#11, 1
wk), 6 wk.

Budoff, Dr. Penny Wise
No More Hot Flashes and Other Good News
(Putnam) PW hc nf 10/21/83 (#14), pk 11/25/
83 (#13, 3 wk), 6 wk; NYT nf 11/20/83 (#10,
1 wk), 4 wk; tot 10 wk.

Buffet, Jimmy
*Tales from Margaritaville: Fictional Facts
and Factual Fictions* (Harcourt) NYT fic 10/
15/89 (#17), pk 11/12/89 (#4, 1 wk), 27 wk;
PW hc fic 10/20/89 (#11), pk 1/5/90 (#6, 3
wk), 25 wk; tot 52 wk.

Bugliosi, Vincent, with Curt Gentry
Helter Skelter (Norton) NYT gen 12/22/74
(#10), pk 3/16/75 (#2, 7 wk), 27 wk; PW nf
1/20/75 (#9), pk 3/17/75 (#2, 4 wk), 25 wk;
(Bantam) NYT mm pb 11/2/75 (#7), pk 11/9/
75 (#1, 16 wk), 33 wk; PW mm pb 2/2/76 (#1,
5 wk), 23 wk; tot 108 wk.

_____, with Ken Hurwitz
Till Death Us Do Part (Norton) PW hc nf
7/17/78 (#11), pk 7/24/78 (#8, 3 wk), 15 wk;
(Bantam) NYT mm pb 6/17/79 (#10), pk 6/
24/79 (#7, 2 wk), 7 wk; PW mm pb 6/18/79
(#8, 1 wk), 5 wk; tot 27 wk.

The Shadow of Cain (Bantam) NYT mm
pb 8/22/82 (#10, 1 wk).

Bull, John, and John Farrand, Jr.
*The Audubon Society Field Guide to North
American Birds: Eastern Region* (KPF) NYT
td pb 10/23/77 (#15), pk 11/13/77 (#1, 4 wk),
43 wk; PW td pb 11/28/77 (#9), pk 5/1/78
(#2, 1 wk), 35 wk; tot 78 wk.

Bullitt, William C.
The Great Globe Itself (Scribner) NYT gen
8/11/46 (#5), pk 8/25/46 (#4, 8 wk), 12 wk;
PW nf 8/17/46 (#10), pk 8/24/46 (#4, 6 wk),
9 wk; tot 21 wk.

Bundy, McGeorge
See Dean G. Acheson and_____
See Henry L. Stimson and_____

Buranelli, Prosper
Cross-Word Puzzles (Simon & Schuster)
PW gen lit 4/18/25 (#8, 4 wk).

The Cross-Word Puzzle Book: Sixteenth Series (Simon & Schuster) PW nf 8/23/30 (#10, 4 wk).

_____, et al.
Cross-Word Puzzle Book: Series 39 (Simon & Schuster) NYT gen 10/4/36 (#7, 4 wk).

Burdick, Eugene
The Ninth Wave (Houghton) NYT fic 6/24/56 (#16), pk 9/2/56 (#8, 3 wk), 20 wk; PW fic 8/20/56 (#10), pk 10/15/56 (#9, 1 wk), 3 wk; tot 23 wk.
The Blue of Capricorn (Houghton) NYT gen 1/21/62 (#15, 2 wk).
The 480 (McGraw) NYT fic 7/12/64 (#10), pk 8/9/64 (#7, 3 wk), 13 wk; PW fic 7/27/64 (#9), pk 8/24/64 (#6, 2 wk), 12 wk; tot 25 wk.
Nina's Book (Houghton) NYT pb fic 2/6/66 (#5, 4 wk).
See also William J. Lederer and_____

_____ and Harvey Wheeler
Fail-Safe (McGraw) NYT fic 11/4/62 (#13), pk 12/16/62 (#2, 1 wk), 16 wk; PW fic 11/5/62 (#11), pk 1/7/63 (#1, 3 wk), 31 wk; tot 47 wk.

Burford, Lolah
Alyx (NAL) NYT mm pb 10/30/77 (#15, 1 wk).

Burger, Neal R.
See George E. Simpson and_____

Burgess, Alan
See Ingrid Bergman and_____

Burgess, Anthony
A Clockwork Orange (Norton) NYT pb fic 3/12/72 (#5), pk 4/9/72 (#4, 4 wk), 8 wk.
Earthly Powers (Simon & Schuster) PW hc fic 2/13/81 (#13), pk 2/27/81 (#12, 1 wk), 4 wk.

Burgess, Thornton W.
The Burgess Seashore Book for Children (Little Brown) PW juv 2/15/30 (#6), pk 8/23/30 (#3, 4 wk), 28 wk.

Burke, Billie, and Cameron Shipp
With a Feather on My Nose (Appleton) NYT gen 6/19/49 (#9), pk 7/24/49 (#6, 1 wk), 16 wk; PW nf 8/13/49 (#7, 1 wk), 2 wk; tot 18 wk.

Burke, James
Connections (Little Brown) NYT nf 12/16/79 (#14), pk 1/6/80 (#8, 1 wk), 6 wk; PW hc nf 12/24/79 (#15), pk 1/25/80 (#10, 1 wk), 5 wk; tot 11 wk.

Burkett, Larry
Business by the Book (Nelson) PW hc rel 10/5/90 (#14, 4 wk).

Burman, Ben Lucien
Rooster Crows for Day (Dutton) NYT fic 10/14/45 (#16, 1 wk).

Burnett, Carol
One More Time (Random) NYT nf 11/2/86 (#6), pk 11/19/86 (#3, 1 wk), 11 wk; PW hc nf 11/7/86 (#9), pk 11/14/86 (#6, 1 wk), 9 wk; (Avon) NYT pb nf 10/18/87 (#8), pk 11/1/87 (#7, 2 wk), 5 wk; tot 25 wk.

Burnett, Frances Hodgson
Robin (Stokes) PW fic 8/26/22 (#5), pk 9/16/22 (#2, 4 wk), 12 wk.
Head of the House of Coombe (Stokes) PW fic 4/1/22 (#4), pk 5/13/22 (#2, 4 wk), 20 wk.
The Secret Garden [illus. Tasha Tudor] (Lippincott) NYT ch bst 11/10/63 (#10, 26 wk).

Burnett, Whit
This Is My Best [ed.] (Halcyon House) NYT nf 12/6/42 (#10), pk 1/17/43 (#8, 1 wk), 5 wk.

Burnett, William Riley
The Dark Command (Knopf) NYT fic 5/1/38 (#13, 4 wk).

Burnford, Sheila
The Incredible Journey (Atlantic Little Brown) NYT fic 5/7/61 (#13), pk 9/10/61 (#9, 1 wk), 39 wk; PW fic 7/10/61 (#11), pk 1/1/62 (#8, 1 wk), 5 wk; tot 44 wk.

Burnham, James
The Struggle for the World (John Day) NYT gen 4/20/47 (#11), pk 4/27/47 (#9, 1 wk), 6 wk.

Burns, David, M.D.
Feeling Good (NAL/Signet) NYT msc pb 4/10/88 (#2, 1 wk), 11 wk; PW mm pb 4/15/88 (#15), pk 4/29/88 (#8, 3 wk), 9 wk; tot 20 wk.

Burns, Esther, and Eloise Wilkin
Mrs. Peregrine at the Fair (Messner) NYT gen 8/6/39 (#12, 4 wk).

Burns, George
How to Live to Be 100—or More: The Ultimate Diet, Sex and Exercise Book (Putnam) NYT nf 6/5/83 (#15), pk 7/3/83 (#4, 1 wk), 16 wk; PW hc nf 6/17/83 (#13), pk 7/15/83 (#6, 3 wk), 14 wk; (NAL/Signet) PW td pb 2/24/84 (#10, 3 wk); tot 33 wk.
Dr. Burns' Prescription for Happiness (Putnam) NYT nf 11/4/84 (#14), pk 11/25/84 (#5, 1 wk), 18 wk; PW hc nf 11/23/84 (#14), 12/21/84 (#6, 1 wk), 9 wk; tot 27 wk.
Gracie: A Love Story (Putnam) NYT nf 11/20/88 (#10), pk 12/4/88 (#1, 4 wk), 22 wk; PW hc nf 11/25/88 (#10), pk 12/9/88 (#1, 4 wk), 20 wk; (Penguin) NYT pb nf 11/19/89 (#3, 1 wk), 10 wk; PW td pb 12/1/89 (#9), pk 12/8/89 (#7, 1 wk), 3 wk; tot 55 wk.

_____, and David Fisher
All My Best Friends (Putnam) NYT nf
11/26/89 (#8), pk 12/3/89 (#5, 1 wk), 12 wk;
PW hc nf 12/8/89 (#8), pk 12/15/89 (#6, 2
wk), 8 wk; tot 20 wk.

Burns, James MacGregor
Roosevelt: The Lion and the Fox (Harcourt)
NYT gen 9/2/56 (#8), pk 9/23/56 (#5, 1 wk),
11 wk; PW nf 9/10/56 (#6), pk 9/24/56 (#4,
2 wk), 4 wk; tot 15 wk.
The Deadlock of Democracy (Prentice Hall)
PW nf 4/1/63 (#8, 1 wk).

Burns, John Horne
The Gallery (Harper) NYT fic 8/10/47
(#15), pk 9/21/47 (#13, 1 wk), 2 wk.
Lucifer with a Book (Harper) NYT fic 4/
17/49 (#12), pk 5/1/49 (#9, 1 wk), 8 wk.

Burns, Ric and Ken Burns
See Geoffrey C. Ward and_____

Burros, Marian
Pure and Simple (Morrow) PW hc nf 10/
23/78 (#13), pk 10/30/78 (#12, 1 wk), 3 wk;
NYT nf 11/12/78 (#15), pk 11/19/78 (#10, 1
wk), 3 wk; tot 6 wk.
Keep It Simple (Morrow) PW hc nf 7/24/
81 (#14, 2 wk), 6 wk; NYT nf 8/23/81 (#14),
pk 9/20/81 (#4, 1 wk), 9 wk; tot 15 wk.

Burrough, Bryan and John Helyar
*Barbarians at the Gate; The Fall of R.J.R.
Nabisco* (Harper) NYT nf 1/28/90 (#8), pk
3/11/90 (#1, 1 wk), 38 wk; PW hc nf 2/2/90
(#13), pk 3/9/90 (#1, 1 wk), 36 wk; tot 74 wk.

Burroughs, Edgar Rice
Jungle Tales of Tarzan (McClurg) PW fic
7/5/19 (#7, 4 wk).
Tarzan, the Untamed (McClurg) PW fic
7/3/20 (#6, 4 wk), 12 wk.

Burrows, Millar
The Dead Sea Scrolls (Viking) NYT gen
4/1/56 (#16), pk 5/6/56 (#14, 1 wk), 3 wk.

Burstein, Nancy
Thirty Days to a Flatter Stomach for Women
(Bantam) NYT td pb 2/20/83 (#14), pk 3/13/
83 (#12, 2 wk), 5 wk.
See also Roy Matthews and_____

Burt, Katharine Newlin
The Branding Iron (Houghton) PW fic
10/25/19 (#10), pk 11/1/19 (#6, 8 wk), 12 wk.
Hidden Creek (Houghton) PW fic 10/23/
20 (#6, 4 wk).

Burt, Maxwell Struthers
Interpreter's House (Scribner) PW fic 6/21/
24 (#7, 4 wk).
The Delectable Mountains (Scribner) PW
fic 3/19/27 (#8, 4 wk), 8 wk.

Festival (Scribner) PW fic 3/21/31 (#3, 4
wk), 8 wk.
Along These Streets (Scribner) PW fic 3/14/
42 (#9, 4 wk), 8 wk.
Philadelphia: Holy Experiment (Doubleday) NYT gen 4/15/45 (#11), pk 7/8/45 (#7,
1 wk), 23 wk.

Burt, Nathaniel
The Perennial Philadelphians (Little Brown)
NYT gen 11/10/63 (#10, 1 wk).

Burton, Jean
See Jan Fortune and_____

Busbee, Shirlee
Gypsy Lady (Avon) PW mm pb 1/9/78
(#14), pk 1/16/78 (#13, 1 wk), 3 wk.
Lady Vixen (Avon) PW mm pb 4/11/80
(#13, 1 wk); NYT mm pb 4/27/80 (#14, 1 wk);
tot 2 wk.
Deceive Not My Heart (Avon) NYT pb fic
2/5/84 (#14), pk 2/12/84 (#5, 1 wk), 5 wk;
PW mm pb 2/17/84 (#10), pk 2/24/84 (#8, 1
wk), 4 wk; tot 9 wk.
The Tiger Lily (Avon) NYT pb fic 1/27/85
(#10), pk 2/17/85 (#5, 1 wk), 6 wk; PW mm
pb 2/8/85 (#8), pk 2/22/85 (#7, 1 wk), 4 wk;
tot 10 wk.
The Spanish Rose (Avon) NYT pb fic 5/11/
86 (#9), pk 5/18/86 (#6, 1 wk), 4 wk; PW mm
pb 5/16/86 (#5, 1 wk), 4 wk; tot 8 wk.
Midnight Masquerade (Avon) NYT pb fic
8/7/88 (#14, 2 wk).

Buscaglia, Leo
Personhood (Fawcett/Columbine) NYT td
pb 4/11/82 (#13), pk 5/23/82 (#4, 2 wk), 52
wk; PW td pb 4/30/82 (#9), pk 5/14/82 (#4,
2 wk), 17 wk; NYT td pb 8/7/83 (#14, 1 wk),
2 wk; tot 71 wk.
Living, Loving & Learning (Slack/Holt)
PW hc nf 4/9/82 (#13), pk 5/21/82 (#2, 14
wk), 55 wk; NYT nf 4/25/82 (#14), pk 6/6/
82 (#1, 1 wk), 54 wk; (Fawcett/Columbine)
NYT td pb 4/24/83 (#1, 9 wk), 36 wk; PW
td pb 4/29/83 (#2), pk 5/6/83 (#1, 9 wk), 73
wk; (Fawcett) NYT pb nf 1/1/84 (#4), pk
1/8/84 (#3, 4 wk), 57 wk; tot 275 wk.
Love (Fawcett) PW mm pb 5/21/82 (#13),
pk 1/7/83 (#8, 2 wk), 15 wk; NYT mm pb
5/30/82 (#14), pk 1/9/83 (#2, 1 wk), 27 wk;
NYT pb nf 8/19/84 (#9), pk 3/2/86 (#7, 1
wk), 4 wk; tot 46 wk.
The Fall of Freddie the Leaf (Slack/Holt)
NYT nf 11/21/82 (#9), pk 2/27/83 (#8, 1 wk),
27 wk; PW hc nf 12/17/82 (#14), pk 12/24/82
(#12, 3 wk), 10 wk; tot 37 wk.
The Way of the Bull (Fawcett/Crest) PW
mm pb 3/11/83 (#12), pk 3/18/83 (#11, 1 wk),
3 wk.

Loving Each Other (Slack/Holt) NYT nf 9/2/84 (#2), pk 9/9/84 (#1, 8 wk), 58 wk; PW hc nf 9/7/84 (#10), pk 9/28/84 (#1, 7 wk), 49 wk; (Fawcett) NYT pb nf 4/13/86 (#7), pk 6/1/86 (#3, 2 wk), 22 wk; (Fawcett/Columbine) PW td pb 4/18/86 (#7), pk 5/23/86 (#1, 5 wk), 27 wk; tot 156 wk.

Bus 9 to Paradise (Slack/Morrow) NYT nf 2/16/86 (#3), pk 2/23/86 (#1, 4 wk), 27 wk; PW hc nf 2/21/86 (#9), pk 3/14/86 (#2, 3 wk), 19 wk; (Fawcett/Columbine) td pb 6/19/87 (#9, 2 wk); NYT pb nf 6/21/87 (#11), pk 8/2/87 (#8, 1 wk), 6 wk; tot 54 wk.

Seven Stories of Christmas Love (Slack/Morrow) NYT nf 11/29/87 (#15), pk 12/20/87 (#3, 2 wk), 13 wk; PW hc nf 12/11/87 (#10), pk 1/8/88 (#2, 1 wk), 11 wk; tot 24 wk.

Papa, My Father: A Celebration of Dads (Slack/Morrow) NYT nf 6/25/89 (#11), pk 7/2/89 (#7, 1 wk), 5 wk; PW hc nf 6/30/89 (#10, 2 wk); tot 7 wk.

Busch, Niven
Duel in the Sun (Morrow) NYT fic 2/6/44 (#13), pk 2/20/44 (#11, 1 wk), 6 wk.

They Dream of Home (Appleton) NYT fic 1/7/45 (#14, 1 wk).

California Street (Simon & Schuster) PW fic 7/27/59 (#10), pk 8/3/59 (#8, 4 wk), 9 wk; NYT fic 6/28/59 (#13), pk 8/2/59 (#7, 3 wk), 19 wk; tot 28 wk.

Busch, Niven
The San Franciscans (Simon & Schuster) PW fic 6/4/62 (#10, 1 wk); NYT fic 6/10/62 (#11, 1 wk), 5 wk; tot 6 wk.

Busch, Noel Fairchild
Adlai E. Stevenson of Illinois (Farrar) NYT gen 8/17/52 (#10), pk 9/28/52 (#5, 1 wk), 13 wk.

Bush, Barbara
Millie's Book [as Dictated to Barbara Bush] (Morrow) NYT nf 9/30/90 (#1, 1 wk), 14 wk; PW hc nf 10/5/90 (#2, 3 wk), 12 wk; tot 26 wk.

Bush, Mildred Kerr
See Bush, Barbara

Bush, Vannevar
Modern Arms and Free Men (Simon & Schuster) NYT gen 12/11/49 (#16), pk 1/15/50 (#6, 4 wk), 14 wk; PW nf 1/14/50 (#7), pk 1/21/50 (#6, 1 wk), 3 wk; tot 17 wk.

Butcher, Capt. Harry C.
My Three Years with Eisenhower (Simon & Schuster) NYT gen 5/12/46 (#14), pk 5/26/46 (#3, 4 wk), 16 wk; PW nf 6/1/46 (#5), pk 6/15/46 (#4, 2 wk), 6 wk; tot 22 wk.

Butkus, Dick, with Robert W. Billings
Stop-Action (Dutton) PW nf 1/1/73 (#10, 1 wk).

Butler, George
See Charles Gaines and_____

Butterfield, Roger P.
The American Past (Simon & Schuster) PW nf 11/15/47 (#8), pk 1/10/48 (#1, 1 wk), 14 wk; NYT gen 11/16/47 (#6), pk 12/21/47 (#3, 6 wk), 21 wk; tot 35 wk.

The Saturday Evening Post Treasury [ed.] (Simon & Schuster) NYT gen 11/21/54 (#10), pk 12/26/54 (#4, 5 wk), 16 wk; PW nf 12/4/54 (#5), pk 12/18/54 (#4, 5 wk), 11 wk; tot 27 wk.

Byars, Betsy
The Summer of the Swans (Viking) NYT ch bst 5/2/71 (#8, 19 wk).

Byas, Hugh
The Japanese Enemy (Knopf) PW nf 4/11/42 (#9, 4 wk).

Government by Assassination (Knopf) NYT nf 1/31/43 (#18, 1 wk).

Byatt, A.S.
Possession: A Romance (Random) PW hc fic 11/16/90 (#15), pk 12/21/90 (#9, 1 wk), 3 wk; NYT fic 12/23/90 (#15, 2 wk); tot 5 wk.

Byers, Margaretta, and Consuelo Kamholz
Designing Women (Simon & Schuster) NYT gen 10/9/38 (#6, 4 wk), 8 wk; PW nf 10/15/38 (#10, 4 wk); tot 12 wk.

Byrd, Adm. Richard Evelyn
Skyward (Putnam) PW nf 5/26/28 (#5, 4 wk), 8 wk.

Little America (Putnam) PW nf 2/21/31 (#2, 4 wk), 12 wk.

Discovery (Putnam) PW nf 1/11/36 (#5, 4 wk), 8 wk.

Alone (Putnam) NYT gen 12/4/38 (#4), pk 1/8/39 (#3, 8 wk), 24 wk; PW nf 12/10/38 (#5), pk 3/11/39 (#2, 4 wk), 24 wk; tot 48 wk.

Byrne, Donn
Hangman's House (Century) PW fic 6/19/26 (#3, 4 wk), 16 wk.

Brother Saul (Century) PW fic 6/25/27 (#7, 4 wk), 8 wk.

Destiny Bay (Appleton) PW fic 11/24/28 (#8, 4 wk).

Crusade (Little Brown) PW fic 4/28/28 (#9), pk 5/26/28 (#8, 4 wk), 8 wk.

Field of Honor (Century) PW fic 11/9/29 (#8, 4 wk), 12 wk.

Byrnes, James F.
Speaking Frankly (Harper) NYT gen 11/2/

47 (#6), pk 11/16/47 (#1, 8 wk), 25 wk; PW nf 11/8/47 (#5), pk 11/22/47 (#1, 8 wk), 20 wk; tot 45 wk.

Cabell, James Branch
The Silver Stallion (McBride) PW fic 6/19/26 (#8, 8 wk).

Caen, Herbert Eugene
Baghdad-by-the-Bay (Doubleday) NYT gen 11/6/49 (#12, 1 wk), 10 wk.
Baghdad 1951 (Doubleday) NYT gen 12/17/50 (#15), pk 1/7/51 (#13, 1 wk), 5 wk.
Don't Call It Frisco (Doubleday) NYT gen 11/22/53 (#14, 1 wk), 2 wk.
Herb Caen's Guide to San Francisco (Doubleday) NYT gen 3/10/57 (#14), pk 4/7/57 (#12, 1 wk), 5 wk.
Herb Caen's New Guide to San Francisco (Doubleday) NYT gen 5/25/58 (#15), pk 6/1/58 (#10, 2 wk), 5 wk.
Only in San Francisco (Doubleday) PW nf 1/16/61 (#10, 1 wk).
San Francisco: City on the Golden Hills [illus. Dong Kingman] (Doubleday) PW nf 10/30/67 (#9), pk 11/13/67 (#8, 1 wk), 7 wk.

Cagney, James
Cagney by Cagney (Doubleday) NYT gen 3/21/76 (#10, 1 wk).

Cahn, Robert
See Perle Mesta and_____

Cain, James Mallahan
The Postman Always Rings Twice (Knopf) PW fic 4/14/34 (#9, 4 wk).
Serenade (Knopf) NYT fic 1/9/38 (#7, 4 wk), 8 wk; PW fic 2/12/38 (#10, 4 wk); tot 12 wk.
Past All Dishonor (Knopf) NYT fic 6/16/46 (#9, 2 wk), 7 wk.
The Butterfly (Knopf) NYT fic 2/16/47 (#16), pk 3/16/47 (#12, 1 wk), 4 wk.
The Moth (Knopf) NYT fic 8/1/48 (#16), pk 8/15/48 (#11, 1 wk), 6 wk.

Cain, Michael Peter
See Harold H. Bloomfield, M.D., et al.

Caine, Hall
The Master of Man (Lippincott) PW fic 11/12/21 (#5, 4 wk).

Caine, Lynn
Widow (Morrow) NYT gen 8/11/74 (#10, 1 wk); PW nf 9/9/74 (#9, 1 wk); tot 2 wk.

Calder, Nigel
Einstein's Universe (Viking) PW hc nf 4/2/79 (#15), pk 4/16/79 (#9, 2 wk), 5 wk.

Caldwell, Erskine
Georgia Boy (Duell Sloan & Pearce) NYT fic 5/16/43 (#8, 1 wk), 2 wk.

Caldwell, Taylor
Dynasty of Death (Scribners) NYT fic 11/6/38 (#6, 4 wk); PW fic 11/12/38 (#5, 4 wk), 12 wk; tot 16 wk.
The Arm and the Darkness (Scribner) NYT fic 4/11/43 (#12, 1 wk).
The Final Hour (Scribner) NYT fic 4/30/44 (#17, 1 wk); (Fawcett) NYT mm pb 6/9/74 (#9), pk 7/14/74 (#6, 4 wk), 8 wk; tot 9 wk.
The Wide House (Scribner) NYT fic 5/13/45 (#8), pk 7/8/45 (#5, 2 wk), 20 wk; PW fic 6/30/45 (#5, 1 wk), 2 wk; tot 22 wk.
This Side of Innocence (Scribner) NYT fic 4/28/46 (#5), pk 5/12/46 (#1, 9 wk), 41 wk; PW fic 5/4/46 (#4), pk 5/25/46 (#1, 12 wk), 33 wk; tot 74 wk.
There Was a Time (Scribner) NYT fic 5/25/47 (#9), pk 6/8/47 (#3, 1 wk), 14 wk; PW fic 6/14/47 (#7), pk 6/21/47 (#3, 1 wk), 8 wk; tot 22 wk.
Melissa (Scribner) NYT fic 7/11/48 (#7), pk 8/1/48 (#3, 3 wk), 17 wk; PW fic 7/24/48 (#2, 1 wk), 10 wk; tot 27 wk.
Let Love Come Last (Scribner) NYT fic 8/21/49 (#6), pk 9/18/49 (#2, 2 wk), 22 wk; PW fic 8/27/49 (#4), pk 9/10/49 (#1, 1 wk), 18 wk; tot 40 wk.
The Balance Wheel (Scribners) NYT fic 1/21/51 (#12), pk 3/4/51 (#3, 2 wk), 18 wk; PW fic 2/17/51 (#6), pk 2/24/51 (#4, 5 wk), 7 wk; tot 25 wk.
The Devil's Advocate (Crown) NYT fic 5/18/52 (#16), pk 6/1/52 (#7, 1 wk), 13 wk; PW fic 6/14/52 (#10), pk 3/21/60 (#4, 1 wk), 30 wk.
Never Victorious, Never Defeated (McGraw) NYT fic 5/16/54 (#11), pk 6/27/54 (#2, 2 wk), 29 wk; PW fic 5/29/54 (#6), pk 6/19/54 (#2, 2 wk), 20 wk; tot 49 wk.
Tender Victory (McGraw) NYT fic 1/22/56 (#13), pk 2/26/56 (#10, 1 wk), 14 wk.
The Sound of Thunder (Doubleday) NYT fic 10/27/57 (#14), pk 12/15/57 (#6, 5 wk), 21 wk; PW fic 12/2/57 (#7), pk 12/16/57 (#5, 2 wk), 7 wk; tot 28 wk.
Dear and Glorious Physician (Doubleday) NYT fic 4/5/59 (#7), pk 11/15/59 (#3, 7 wk), 64 wk; PW fic 4/6/59 (#5), pk 12/28/59 (#2, 1 wk), 59 wk; tot 123 wk.
The Listener (Doubleday) NYT fic 10/9/60 (#15), pk 12/18/60 (#9, 2 wk), 24 wk; PW fic 10/17/60 (#9), pk 11/21/60 (#7, 1 wk), 12 wk; tot 36 wk.
A Prologue to Love (Doubleday) NYT fic 12/3/61 (#14), pk 2/25/62 (#3, 4 wk), 30 wk; PW fic 1/1/62 (#7), pk 2/12/62 (#3, 5 wk), 23 wk; tot 53 wk.
Grandmother and the Priests (Doubleday)

PW fic 3/25/63 (#10), pk 6/10/63 (#3, 3 wk), 27 wk; NYT fic 4/14/63 (#9), pk 6/16/63 (#3, 1 wk), 22 wk; tot 49 wk.

A Pillar of Iron (Doubleday) NYT fic 5/23/ 65 (#9), pk 6/6/65 (#8, 2 wk), 12 wk; PW fic 6/7/65 (#6, 1 wk), 14 wk; tot 26 wk.

No One Hears But Him (Doubleday) NYT fic 4/24/66 (#10, 1 wk).

Testimony of Two Men (Doubleday) PW fic 5/27/68 (#11), pk 10/21/68 (#2, 1 wk), 38 wk; NYT fic 5/12/68 (#8), pk 7/7/68 (#3, 12 wk), 42 wk; NYT pb fic 8/3/69 (#5), pk 10/5/69 (#3, 20 wk), 28 wk; (Fawcett) NYT mm pb 5/22/77 (#14), pk 6/19/77 (#3, 1 wk), 9 wk; PW mm pb 5/23/77 (#10), pk 6/20/77 (#4, 1 wk), 8 wk; tot 125 wk.

Great Lion of God (Doubleday) NYT fic 5/ 3/70 (#9), pk 7/19/70 (#2, 2 wk), 34 wk; PW fic 5/18/70 (#8), pk 8/17/70 (#2, 1 wk), 33 wk; NYT pb fic 6/6/71 (#2), pk 7/11/71 (#1, 8 wk), 16 wk; tot 83 wk.

Captains and the Kings (Doubleday) NYT fic 4/30/72 (#5), pk 8/27/72 (#2, 1 wk), 31 wk; PW fic 5/1/72 (#9), pk 6/12/72 (#2, 2 wk), 33 wk; NYT pb fic 6/10/73 (#2, 24 wk), 32 wk; (Fawcett/Crest) PW mm pb 10/4/76 (#11), pk 10/18/76 (#1, 1 wk), 16 wk; NYT mm pb 10/10/76 (#8), pk 10/31/76 (#1, 1 wk), 15 wk; tot 127 wk.

Glory and the Lightning (Doubleday) NYT fic 12/1/74 (#8, 1 wk), 3 wk; PW fic 2/17/75 (#9, 1 wk); (Fawcett) NYT mm pb 10/26/75 (#9), pk 11/2/75 (#5, 1 wk), 5 wk; tot 9 wk.

The Romance of Atlantis (Fawcett) PW mm pb 4/5/76 (#14, 1 wk).

Ceremony of the Innocent (Doubleday) PW hc fic 11/8/76 (#8), pk 12/13/76 (#5, 1 wk), 16 wk; NYT fic 11/21/76 (#10), pk 1/2/77 (#6, 2 wk), 13 wk; (Fawcett/Crest) PW mm pb 10/24/77 (#7), pk 11/7/77 (#2, 2 wk), 9 wk; NYT mm pb 10/30/77 (#8), pk 11/6/77 (#5, 1 wk), 13 wk; tot 51 wk.

Bright Flows the River (Doubleday) PW hc fic 11/6/78 (#13), pk 11/13/78 (#10, 1 wk), 13 wk; NYT fic 11/12/78 (#11), pk 12/17/78 (#5, 1 wk), 19 wk; (Fawcett/Crest) PW mm pb 11/26/79 (#8), pk 12/24/79 (#1, 3 wk), 12 wk; NYT mm pb 12/9/79 (#4), pk 12/23/79 (#1, 1 wk), 15 wk; tot 59 wk.

Answer as a Man (Putnam) PW hc fic 12/12/80 (#11), pk 1/30/81 (#2, 8 wk), 22 wk; NYT fic 12/28/80 (#8), pk 2/1/81 (#2, 4 wk), 20 wk; (Fawcett/Crest) PW mm pb 12/11/81 (#6), pk 1/22/82 (#1, 1 wk), 14 wk; NYT mm pb 12/13/81 (#5), pk 12/20/81 (#2, 5 wk), 16 wk; tot 72 wk.

Callahan, Steven
   Adrift: Seventy-Six Days Lost at Sea

(Houghton) NYT nf 3/2/86 (#5, 2 wk), 15 wk; PW hc nf 3/7/86 (#11, 2 wk), 8 wk; (Ballantine) NYT pb nf 5/10/87 (#6), pk 5/24/87 (#5, 2 wk), 14 wk; tot 37 wk.

Calmenson, Stephanie
   See Joanna Cole and_____

Calmer, Ned
   The Strange Land (Scribner) NYT fic 2/ 26/50 (#15), pk 3/12/50 (#10, 1 wk), 7 wk.

Cameron, Margaret
   The Seven Purposes (Harper) PW gen 9/6/ 19 (#3), pk 10/25/19 (#2, 8 wk), 16 wk.

Camp, William Martin
   Retreat, Hell (Appleton) NYT fic 12/12/43 (#10, 1 wk), 3 wk.

Campbell, Joseph
   Hero with a Thousand Faces (Princeton Univ.) NYT pb nf 7/17/88 (#7), pk 7/24/88 (#6, 2 wk), 27 wk; PW td pb 7/22/88 (#10), pk 8/12/88 (#8, 1 wk), 7 wk; tot 34 wk.

   Transformations of Myth Through Time (Harper/Perennial) NYT pb nf 3/11/90 (#10, 1 wk).

_____, with Bill Moyers
   The Power of Myth (Doubleday) NYT pb nf 6/19/88 (#7), pk 7/31/88 (#1, 1 wk), 78 wk; PW td pb 6/24/88 (#5), pk 9/16/88 (#2, 2 wk), 31 wk; (Mystic Fire/Parabola) PW aud nf 12/7/90 (#10, 4 wk); tot 113 wk.

Campolo, Tony
   The Kingdom of God Is a Party (Word) PW hc rel 10/5/90 (#8, 4 wk), 8 wk.

Camus, Albert
   The Plague (Knopf) NYT fic 8/22/48 (#11), pk 8/29/48 (#8, 2 wk), 9 wk.

   The Fall (Knopf) NYT fic 3/10/57 (#16), pk 4/7/57 (#7, 3 wk), 15 wk; PW fic 4/8/57 (#7, 2 wk); tot 17 wk.

   Exile and the Kingdom (Knopf) NYT fic 3/30/58 (#15), pk 5/4/58 (#12, 1 wk), 9 wk.

   Resistance, Rebellion and Death (Knopf) NYT gen 3/19/61 (#15), pk 4/2/61 (#13, 2 wk), 6 wk.

   Notebooks 1935–1942 (Knopf) NYT gen 9/1/63 (#8, 1 wk).

   A Happy Death [trans. Richard Howard] (Knopf) NYT fic 7/9/72 (#9, 1 wk), 2 wk.

Canby, Henry Seidel
   Thoreau (Houghton) NYT gen 11/5/39 (#9, 4 wk); PW nf 11/11/39 (#10, 8 wk); tot 12 wk.

Caner, George Colket
   It's How You Take It (Coward McCann) NYT gen 6/16/46 (16, 2 wk).

Canfield, Dorothy
The Brimming Cup (Harcourt) PW fic
4/23/21 (#6), pk 6/11/21 (#2, 12 wk), 16 wk.
Rough-Hewn (Harcourt) PW fic 12/23/22
(#5, 4 wk), 16 wk.
Her Son's Wife (Harcourt) PW fic 10/16/26
(#10), pk 11/20/26 (#6, 4 wk), 8 wk.
The Deepening Stream (Harcourt) PW fic
11/22/30 (#7), pk 2/21/31 (#3, 4 wk), 16 wk.
Bonfire (Harcourt) PW fic 11/11/33 (#9),
pk 12/9/33 (#6, 4 wk), 12 wk.
Seasoned Timber (Harcourt) PW fic 4/8/39
(#9, 4 wk); NYT fic 4/9/39 (#6, 4 wk), 8 wk;
tot 12 wk.

Caniff, Milton
Male Call (Grosset & Dunlap) NYT gen
8/26/45 (#18), pk 9/16/45 (#10, 1 wk), 7 wk.

Canin, Ethan
Emperor of the Air (Houghton) NYT fic
3/20/88 (#16), pk 5/1/88 (#12, 1 wk), 7 wk;
PW hc fic 4/15/88 (#11, 1 wk); tot 8 wk.

Cannon, Cornelia James
Red Rust (Little Brown) PW fic 4/28/28
(#3, 4 wk), 8 wk.

Cannon, LeGrand, Jr.
Look to the Mountain (Holt) NYT fic
11/22/42 (#8), pk 1/3/43 (#5, 1 wk), 19 wk;
PW fic 12/12/42 (#6), pk 12/26/42 (#5, 3 wk),
6 wk; tot 25 wk.

Cantor, Eddie
Caught Short (Simon & Schuster) PW nf
1/11/30 (#9, 4 wk), 8 wk.

_____, and Jane Ardmore
Take My Life (Doubleday) NYT gen 6/23/
57 (#14), pk 8/11/57 (#9, 1 wk), 13 wk; PW
nf 8/19/57 (#9, 1 wk); tot 14 wk.

Capa, Robert
See John Steinbeck and_____

Capote, Truman
Other Voices, Other Rooms (Random) NYT
fic 2/15/48 (#9), pk 2/22/48 (#7, 1 wk), 9 wk;
PW fic 3/13/48 (#10, 1 wk); tot 10 wk.
The Grass Harp (Random) NYT fic 11/4/51
(#16, 1 wk).
Breakfast at Tiffany's (Random) NYT fic
12/7/58 (#15), pk 1/18/59 (#12, 1 wk), 10 wk.
In Cold Blood (Random) NYT gen 1/23/66
(#6), pk 2/6/66 (#1, 14 wk), 37 wk; PW nf
1/24/66 (#9), pk 2/14/66 (#1, 14 wk), 41 wk;
NYT pb gen 2/5/67 (#1, 12 wk), 32 wk; tot
110 wk.
Music for Chameleons (Random) PW hc nf
8/22/80 (#15), pk 9/12/80 (#2, 1 wk), 13 wk;
NYT nf 8/31/80 (#13), pk 9/28/80 (#3, 4
wk), 16 wk; (NAL) NYT mm pb 6/28/81
(#15), pk 7/5/81 (#13, 1 wk), 2 wk; tot 31 wk.

Capp, Al
The Life and Times of the Shmoo (Simon &
Schuster) NYT gen 1/9/49 (#16), pk 2/6/49
(#14, 1 wk), 4 wk.

Caputo, Philip
A Rumor of War (Holt) PW hc nf 8/8/77
(#10, 1 wk); NYT nf 10/16/77 (#14, 1 wk); tot
2 wk.
Horn of Africa (Holt) NYT fic 1/11/81 (#15,
1 wk).

Carey, Diane
Dreadnought! (Pocket) NYT pb fic 5/18/86
(#10, 1 wk), 2 wk; PW mm pb 5/30/86 (#15),
pk 6/6/86 (#14, 1 wk), 3 wk; tot 5 wk.
Battlestations! (Pocket) NYT pb fic 11/16/
86 (#14), pk 11/23/86 (#11, 1 wk), 2 wk; PW
mm pb 12/5/86 (#13, 1 wk), 2 wk; tot 4 wk.
Ghost Ship (Pocket) NYT pb fic 7/17/88
(#14, 1 wk); PW mm pb 7/22/88 (#14, 1 wk);
tot 2 wk.
Final Frontier (Pocket) NYT pb fic 1/10/
88 (#14), pk 1/17/88 (#5, 1 wk), 5 wk; PW
mm pb 1/22/88 (#6, 1 wk), 3 wk; tot 8 wk.

Carey, Ernestine Gilbreth
Jumping Jupiter (Crowell) NYT gen 3/9/
52 (#15, 1 wk).
See also Frank B. Gilbreth, Jr., and_____

Carey, Mary
The Gremlins Storybook (Golden) NYT fic
7/15/84 (#14), pk 8/5/84 (#10, 2 wk), 6 wk.

Carfrae, Elizabeth
The Past Was Asleep (Putnam) NYT fic
8/6/39 (#14, 4 wk).

Cariou, Len
See Scott Turow

Carle, Eric
The Very Quiet Cricket (Philomel) PW ch
pic 12/21/90 (#6, 4 wk).

Carleton, Jetta
The Moonflower Vine (Simon & Schuster)
PW fic 3/11/63 (#6), pk 4/1/63 (#5, 1 wk), 17
wk; NYT fic 4/7/63 (#6), pk 4/21/63 (#5, 1
wk), 11 wk; tot 28 wk.

Carleton, Marjorie Chalmer
The Swan Sang Once (Morrow) NYT fic
2/16/47 (#15, 1 wk).

Carlinsky, Dan
See Edwin Goodgold and_____

Carlson, John Roy [pseud.]
Under Cover (Dutton) PW nf 8/7/43 (#5),
pk 9/4/43 (#1, 25 wk), 44 wk; NYT gen
8/8/43 (#13), pk 9/12/43 (#1, 28 wk), 48 wk;
tot 92 wk.
The Plotters (Dutton) NYT gen 12/8/46
(#5), pk 12/22/46 (#3, 2 wk), 19 wk; PW nf

12/21/46 (#6), pk 1/4/47 (#3, 1 wk), 14 wk; tot 33 wk.
Cairo to Damascus (Knopf) NYT gen 11/18/51 (#16, 1 wk).

Carlson, Randy
See Kevin Leman and_____

Carmer, Carl
Stars Fell on Alabama (Farrar) PW nf 8/11/34 (#2, 12 wk), 20 wk.
Listen for a Lonesome Drum (Farrar) NYT gen 8/2/36 (#3, 4 wk), 8 wk; PW nf 8/15/36 (#6), pk 9/12/36 (#5, 4 wk), 12 wk; tot 20 wk.
The Hudson (Farrar) NYT gen 8/6/39 (#3, 4 wk); PW nf 9/16/39 (#10, 4 wk); tot 8 wk.
Genesee Fever (Farrar) PW fic 2/14/42 (#9, 4 wk).

Carnegie, Dale
How to Win Friends and Influence People (Simon & Schuster) NYT gen 1/31/37 (#6), pk 3/7/37 (#1, 44 wk), 92 wk; PW nf 2/6/37 (#2), pk 3/13/37 (#1, 36 wk), 80 wk; tot 172 wk.
How to Stop Worrying and Start Living (Simon & Schuster) NYT gen 6/27/48 (#6), pk 8/1/48 (#1, 14 wk), 60 wk; PW nf 7/10/48 (#4), pk 8/14/48 (#1, 13 wk), 44 wk; tot 104 wk.

Carney, Otis
When the Bough Breaks (Houghton) NYT fic 11/17/57 (#15), pk 12/8/57 (#14, 1 wk), 3 wk.
See also Charles F. Spaulding and_____

Caro, Robert A.
The Power Broker (Vintage) NYT td pb 8/24/75 (#5, 1 wk).
The Path to Power: Volume 1 of the Years of Lyndon Johnson (Knopf) PW hc nf 12/17/82 (#11), pk 1/14/83 (#5, 2 wk), 16 wk; NYT nf 12/19/82 (#14), pk 1/16/83 (#7, 2 wk), 13 wk; tot 29 wk.
Means of Ascent (Knopf) NYT nf 3/25/90 (#5), pk 4/8/90 (#1, 2 wk), 16 wk; PW hc nf 3/30/90 (#5), pk 4/13/90 (#1, 3 wk), 13 wk; tot 29 wk.

Carpenter, Frank George
Carp's Washington (McGraw) NYT gen 5/29/60 (#12), pk 6/26/60 (#9, 1 wk), 9 wk.

Carpenter, Liz
Ruffles and Flourishes (Doubleday) NYT gen 2/15/70 (#9), pk 3/29/70 (#4, 1 wk), 10 wk; PW nf 3/23/70 (#10), pk 4/6/70 (#4, 1 wk), 6 wk; tot 16 wk.

Carpenter, Margaret
Experiment Perilous (Little Brown) NYT fic 4/25/43 (#12, 2 wk); PW fic 5/15/43 (#8, 1 wk); tot 3 wk.

Carpenter, Teresa
Missing Beauty (Zebra) NYT pb nf 9/3/89 (#8), pk 9/24/89 (#2, 1 wk), 8 wk; PW mm pb 9/29/89 (#12, 1 wk); tot 9 wk.

Carr, John Dickson
The Problem of the Green Capsule (Harper) NYT fic 7/9/39 (#12, 4 wk).
The Life of Sir Arthur Conan Doyle (Harper) NYT gen 3/13/49 (#12), pk 3/20/49 (#11, 2 wk), 6 wk.

Carr, Roy and Tony Tyler
The Beatles (Harmony/Crown) NYT td pb 6/1/75 (#4), pk 6/29/75 (#3, 4 wk), 8 wk.

Carrel, Alexis
Man, the Unknown (Harper) NYT nf 11/3/35 (#9), pk 11/8/36 (#3, 4 wk), 44 wk; PW nf 11/9/35 (#7), pk 10/10/36 (#2, 4 wk), 68 wk; tot 112 wk.

Carrick, Helen
See Ruth Hoffman and_____

Carrighar, Sally
Icebound Summer (Knopf) NYT gen 9/6/53 (#14, 1 wk).

Carrol, Shana
Raven (Harcourt/Jove) PW mm pb 3/13/78 (#14, 1 wk).

Carroll, Arthur Gray
I Can Go Home Again (Univ. of North California) NYT gen 12/12/43 (#13, 1 wk), 4 wk.

Carroll, Gladys Hasty
As the Earth Turns (Macmillan) PW fic 6/10/33 (#1, 8 wk), 28 wk.
A Few Foolish Ones (Macmillan) PW fic 6/15/35 (#7, 4 wk), 8 wk.
Neighbor to the Sky (Macmillan) NYT fic 6/6/37 (#6, 4 wk); PW fic 7/10/37 (#7, 4 wk); tot 8 wk.
West of the Hill (Macmillan) NYT fic 10/9/49 (#14), pk 10/30/49 (#10, 1 wk), 7 wk.

Carroll, James
Mortal Friends (Little Brown) PW hc fic 6/26/78 (#15), pk 7/17/78 (#10, 1 wk), 11 wk; NYT fic 7/2/78 (#12), pk 7/16/78 (#9, 1 wk), 7 wk; (Dell) PW mm pb 5/21/79 (#8), pk 6/11/79 (#4, 2 wk), 13 wk; NYT mm pb 5/27/79 (#7), pk 6/24/79 (#4, 2 wk), 13 wk; tot 44 wk.
Family Trade (Little Brown) PW hc fic 7/9/82 (#12), pk 7/16/82 (#11, 1 wk), 5 wk; (NAL/Signet) NYT mm pb 6/12/83 (#13), pk 6/19/83 (#5, 1 wk), 8 wk; PW mm pb 6/17/83 (#10), pk 6/24/83 (#6, 2 wk), 7 wk; tot 20 wk.
Prince of Peace (NAL/Signet) PW mm pb 10/25/85 (#12, 1 wk), 2 wk; NYT pb fic 10/27/85 (#14, 1 wk); tot 3 wk.

Carroll, Joy
Proud Blood (Dell) PW mm pb 2/6/78 (#13, 1 wk).

Carroll, Leone Rutledge
Pressure Cookery (Barrows) NYT gen 3/16/47 (#15), pk 4/20/47 (#9, 1 wk), 7 wk.

Carson, Rachel L.
The Sea Around Us (Oxford Univ.) PW nf 8/4/51 (#5), pk 9/1/51 (#1, 41 wk), 67 wk; NYT gen 7/22/51 (#5), pk 9/9/51 (#1, 39 wk), 81 wk; [juvenile edition illus. Anne Terry White] (Golden) NYT ch bst 11/1/59 (#14, 25 wk); tot 173 wk.
Under the Sea-Wind (Oxford Univ.) NYT gen 4/27/52 (#10), pk 6/1/52 (#4, 2 wk), 19 wk; PW nf 5/10/52 (#5), pk 6/21/52 (#3, 1 wk), 12 wk; tot 31 wk.
The Edge of the Sea (Houghton) NYT gen 11/20/55 (#8), pk 12/18/55 (#3, 5 wk), 23 wk; PW nf 12/3/55 (#4), pk 12/24/55 (#3, 4 wk), 13 wk; tot 36 wk.
Silent Spring (Houghton) NYT gen 10/7/62 (#11), pk 10/28/62 (#1, 6 wk), 16 wk; PW nf 10/8/62 (#12), pk 11/5/62 (#1, 7 wk), 32 wk; tot 48 wk.
The Sense of Wonder (Harper) PW nf 11/1/65 (#12), pk 12/6/65 (#10, 1 wk), 4 wk.

Carson, Robert
The Magic Lantern (Holt) NYT fic 12/28/52 (#15), pk 1/18/53 (#10, 1 wk), 8 wk.

Carson, Rubin
National Love, Sex & Marriage Test (Doubleday/Dolphin) PW td pb 3/13/78 (#10, 1 wk).

Carter, Anne
See Zoe Oldenbourg

Carter, Boake
Black Shirt, Black Skin (Telegraph Press) NYT nf 11/3/35 (#5, 4 wk).

Carter, Carmen
Dreams of the Raven (Pocket) NYT pb fic 6/7/87 (#10), pk 6/14/87 (#7, 1 wk), 4 wk.

Carter, Carmen, with Peter David, Michael Jan Friedman and Robert Greenberger
Doomsday World (Pocket) NYT pb fic 7/15/90 (#10, 1 wk), 3 wk.

Carter, Jimmy
Keeping Faith: Memoirs of a President (Bantam) NYT nf 11/7/82 (#13), pk 12/12/82 (#3, 1 wk), 11 wk; PW hc nf 11/12/82 (#9), pk 12/24/82 (#6, 2 wk), 11 wk; tot 22 wk.
The Blood of Abraham: Insights into the Middle East (Houghton) NYT nf 4/21/85 (#14), pk 5/5/85 (#7, 1 wk), 6 wk; PW hc nf 5/10/85 (#15), pk 5/17/85 (#13, 1 wk), 4 wk; tot 10 wk.

An Outdoor Journal (Bantam) NYT nf 7/31/88 (#14, 1 wk).

_____, and Rosalynn Carter
Everything to Gain: Making the Most of the Rest of Your Life (Random) NYT nf 6/21/87 (#10), pk 6/28/87 (#4, 1 wk), 10 wk; PW hc nf 6/26/87 (#13), pk 7/3/87 (#3, 2 wk), 7 wk; tot 17 wk.

Carter, Rosalynn
First Lady from Plains (Houghton) NYT nf 5/13/84 (#10), pk 6/17/84 (#1, 1 wk), 18 wk; PW hc nf 5/18/84 (#12), pk 6/1/84 (#3, 1 wk), 18 wk; (Fawcett/Gold Medal) NYT mm pb 5/5/85 (#5), pk 5/19/85 (#4, 5 wk), 8 wk; PW mm pb 5/10/85 (#14, 1 wk); tot 45 wk.

Carter, Steven, and Julia Sokol
Men Who Can't Love (Evans) NYT msc 8/2/87 (#5), pk 8/9/87 (#4, 3 wk), 4 wk; PW hc nf 8/7/87 (#11), pk 8/21/87 (#10, 1 wk), 6 wk; tot 10 wk.

Caruso, Dorothy
Enrico Caruso: His Life and Death (Simon & Schuster) NYT gen 6/10/45 (#18), pk 7/8/45 (#8, 2 wk), 10 wk.

Cary, Joyce
To Be a Pilgrim (Harper) NYT fic 5/8/49 (#16, 1 wk).
The Horse's Mouth (Harper) NYT fic 2/12/50 (#12), pk 3/12/50 (#4, 1 wk), 19 wk; PW fic 3/4/50 (#5, 3 wk), 6 wk; tot 25 wk.
A Fearful Joy (Harper) NYT fic 10/29/50 (#11, 1 wk), 4 wk.
Prisoner of Grace (Harper) NYT fic 11/2/52 (#11), pk 11/9/52 (#9, 1 wk), 6 wk.
Not Honour More (Harper) NYT fic 6/19/55 (#13, 1 wk), 2 wk.

Casey, Douglas R.
Crisis Investing: Opportunities and Profits in the Coming Great Depression (Stratford/Harper) PW hc nf 8/15/80 (#11), pk 9/26/80 (#1, 10 wk), 34 wk; NYT nf 9/7/80 (#2), pk 9/21/80 (#1, 10 wk), 34 wk; (Pocket) NYT mm pb 7/19/81 (#10), pk 7/26/81 (#6, 1 wk) 3 wk; tot 71 wk.
Strategic Investing (Simon & Schuster) NYT nf 5/30/82 (#15), pk 6/6/82 (#8, 1 wk), 6 wk; PW hc nf 6/11/82 (#14), pk 7/9/82 (#10, 1 wk), 5 wk; tot 11 wk.

Casey, John
Spartina (Avon) PW td pb 7/20/90 (#5, 2 wk), 3 wk.

Casey, Robert Joseph
Torpedo Junction (Bobbs Merrill) NYT nf 1/10/43 (#11), pk 2/28/43 (#8, 1 wk), 12 wk.
Such Interesting People (Bobbs Merrill) NYT gen 1/30/44 (#16, 1 wk), 2 wk.

This Is Where I Came In (Bobbs Merrill) NYT gen 8/19/45 (#19), pk 9/16/45 (#13, 1 wk), 3 wk.

Battle Below (Bobbs Merrill) NYT gen 8/19/45 (#9), pk 9/9/45 (#8, 1 wk), 9 wk.

More Interesting People (Bobbs Merrill) NYT gen 11/2/47 (#12, 1 wk).

Casserly, Jack
See Barry M. Goldwater and_____

Cassidy, Henry Clarence
Moscow Dateline (Houghton) NYT gen 6/20/43 (#15), pk 7/4/43 (#8, 2 wk), 9 wk.

Cassill, R.V.
Doctor Cobb's Game (Geis) PW fic 1/4/71 (#10), pk 2/8/71 (#7, 2 wk), 7 wk; NYT fic 1/24/71 (#10), pk 2/14/71 (#9, 1 wk), 4 wk; tot 11 wk.

Cassini, Igor
Pay the Price (Zebra) PW mm pb 7/22/83 (#15), pk 7/29/83 (#12, 1 wk), 3 wk.

Cassini, Countess Marguerite
Never a Dull Moment (Harper) NYT gen 5/13/56 (#14, 1 wk).

Castagnetta, Grace
See Hendrik W. van Loon and_____

Castaneda, Carlos
Journey to Ixtlan: The Lessons of Don Juan (Simon & Schuster) NYT gen 11/26/72 (#10), pk 1/28/73 (#7, 6 wk), 25 wk; PW nf 11/27/72 (#10), pk 2/26/73 (#4, 1 wk), 21 wk; tot 46 wk.

Tales of Power (Simon & Schuster) NYT gen 11/10/74 (#10), pk 12/22/74 (#2, 1 wk), 19 wk; PW nf 11/11/74 (#6), pk 11/25/74 (#2, 4 wk), 15 wk; (Simon & Schuster/Touchstone) NYT td pb 10/12/75 (#2, 2 wk), 5 wk; tot 39 wk.

The Second Ring of Power (Simon & Schuster) NYT nf 12/18/77 (#13), pk 2/19/78 (#2, 1 wk), 21 wk; PW hc nf 12/26/77 (#10), pk 2/20/78 (#2, 2 wk), 20 wk; PW td pb 4/16/79 (#4), pk 4/23/79 (#3, 1 wk), 10 wk; NYT td pb 5/6/79 (#11), pk 5/27/79 (#4, 1 wk), 12 wk; tot 63 wk.

The Eagle's Gift (Simon & Schuster) PW hc nf 5/15/81 (#14), pk 5/29/81 (#4, 8 wk), 23 wk; NYT nf 5/17/81 (#10), pk 6/28/81 (#4, 1 wk), 24 wk; (Pocket) PW mm pb 5/28/82 (#14), pk 6/4/82 (#13, 1 wk), 2 wk; tot 49 wk.

The Fire from Within (Simon & Schuster) NYT nf 5/20/84 (#12), pk 6/17/84 (#2, 1 wk), 22 wk; PW hc nf 6/15/84 (#11), pk 7/27/84 (#8, 2 wk), 13 wk; (Pocket) NYT pb nf 9/22/85 (#5, 1 wk), 6 wk; tot 41 wk.

Castelot, Andre
Queen of France (Harper) NYT gen 8/11/57 (#14), pk 8/25/57 (#13, 1 wk), 3 wk.

Castle, E.W.
Billions, Blunders and Baloney (Devin Adair) NYT gen 3/27/55 (#16, 1 wk).

Castle, Marian
Deborah (Morrow) NYT fic 6/16/46 (#16), pk 6/30/46 (#13, 1 wk), 5 wk.

Catalano, Grace
New Kids on the Block (Bantam) NYT pb nf 12/17/89 (#8), pk 1/28/90 (#2, 6 wk), 23 wk; PW mm pb 2/23/90 (#10), pk 4/13/90 (#8, 1 wk), 10 wk; tot 33 wk.

New Kids on the Block Scrapbook (NAL/Signet) NYT pb nf 4/22/90 (#4), pk 4/29/90 (#3, 2 wk), 6 wk; PW td pb 5/11/90 (#9), pk 5/18/90 (#7, 2 wk), 4 wk; tot 10 wk.

Cather, Willa
One of Ours (Knopf) PW fic 11/18/22 (#7), pk 12/23/22 (#6, 8 wk), 28 wk.

A Lost Lady (Knopf) PW fic 11/24/23 (#6, 4 wk).

The Professor's House (Knopf) PW fic 10/24/25 (#7), pk 11/21/25 (#6, 8 wk), 12 wk.

Death Comes for the Archbishop (Knopf) PW fic 10/22/27 (#3, 8 wk), 12 wk.

Shadows on the Rock (Knopf) PW fic 9/19/31 (#1, 12 wk), 24 wk.

Obscure Destinies (Knopf) PW fic 9/10/32 (#2, 4 wk), 8 wk.

Lucy Gayheart (Knopf) PW fic 9/14/35 (#1, 4 wk), 12 wk; NYT fic 10/6/35 (#10, 4 wk); tot 16 wk.

Sapphira and the Slave Girl (Knopf) PW fic 1/11/41 (#4), pk 2/8/41 (#3, 4 wk), 16 wk.

The Old Beauty and Others (Knopf) NYT fic 10/3/48 (#16), pk 10/24/48 (#8, 2 wk), 9 wk.

Catlin, A.W.
With the Help of God and a Few Marines (Doubleday) PW gen 5/3/19 (#4, 4 wk), 8 wk.

Cato, Nancy
All the Rivers Run (NAL/Signet) NYT pb fic 2/5/84 (#13), pk 2/19/84 (#10, 1 wk), 4 wk; PW mm pb 2/24/84 (#11, 1 wk); tot 5 wk.

Catton, Bruce
A Stillness at Appomattox (Doubleday) NYT gen 1/17/54 (#16), pk 3/7/54 (#12, 2 wk), 10 wk; PW nf 7/17/54 (#10, 1 wk); tot 11 wk.

This Hallowed Ground (Doubleday) NYT gen 11/18/56 (#9), pk 12/2/56 (#2, 9 wk), 28 wk; PW nf 12/3/56 (#4), pk 12/17/56 (#2, 6 wk), 21 wk; tot 49 wk.

Grant Moves South (Little Brown) NYT gen 2/28/60 (#9), pk 4/17/60 (#4, 1 wk), 21 wk; PW nf 3/7/60 (#6), pk 4/25/60 (#4, 1 wk), 16 wk; tot 37 wk.

The Coming Fury (Doubleday) NYT gen 11/19/61 (#11), pk 1/14/62 (#7, 1 wk), 18 wk; PW nf 12/4/61 (#9), pk 1/8/62 (#7, 4 wk), 12 wk; tot 30 wk.

Terrible Swift Sword: The Centennial History of the Civil War Vol. 2 (Doubleday) PW nf 5/27/63 (#10), pk 9/2/63 (#4, 1 wk), 18 wk; NYT gen 6/23/63 (#6), pk 7/28/63 (#4, 2 wk), 12 wk; tot 30 wk.

Never Call Retreat (Doubleday) PW nf 9/27/65 (#10), pk 10/4/65 (#8, 1 wk), 5 wk; NYT gen 10/24/65 (#8, 1 wk); tot 6 wk.

Grant Takes Command (Little Brown) NYT gen 4/20/69 (#10), pk 5/11/69 (#9, 1 wk), 2 wk; PW nf 5/12/69 (#8, 2 wk); tot 4 wk.

_____, et al.

The American Heritage Picture History of the Civil War (Doubleday) NYT gen 11/13/60 (#16), pk 1/8/61 (#3, 1 wk), 19 wk; pb gen 12/5/60 (#7), pk 12/12/60 (#4, 2 wk), 12 wk; tot 31 wk.

Caunitz, William J.

One Police Plaza (Crown) PW hc fic 4/6/84 (#15, 2 wk); (Bantam) NYT pb fic 2/10/85 (#9), pk 2/17/85 (#2, 3 wk), 10 wk; PW mm pb 2/15/85 (#5), pk 3/1/85 (#2, 2 wk), 9 wk; tot 21 wk.

Suspects (Crown) PW hc fic 8/15/86 (#14), pk 9/12/86 (#6, 1 wk), 10 wk; NYT fic 8/17/86 (#14), pk 9/7/86 (#8, 2 wk), 10 wk; (Bantam) NYT pb fic 8/30/87 (#10), pk 9/6/87 (#7, 2 wk), 7 wk; PW mm pb 9/4/87 (#8), pk 9/11/87 (#6, 1 wk), 6 wk; tot 33 wk.

Black Sand (Crown) NYT fic 3/19/89 (#13), pk 4/2/89 (#12, 1 wk), 4 wk; PW hc fic 4/7/89 (#15, 1 wk); (Bantam) NYT pb fic 2/11/90 (#9), pk 2/18/90 (#5, 5 wk), 6 wk; PW mm pb 2/16/90 (#15), pk 2/23/90 (#7, 1 wk), 4 wk; tot 15 wk.

Cavanah, Frances

Family Reading Festival (Prentice Hall) NYT ch bst 11/2/58 (#16, 40 wk).

Cave, Hugh B.

Long Were the Nights (Dodd) NYT gen 12/19/43 (#22), pk 2/6/44 (#11, 1 wk), 11 wk.

Cavett, Dick, and Christopher Porterfield

Cavett (Harcourt) PW nf 9/23/74 (#10), pk 10/21/74 (#6, 2 wk), 10 wk; NYT gen 10/20/74 (#10), pk 11/10/74 (#7, 2 wk), 7 wk; tot 17 wk.

Cecil, Lord David

The Young Melbourne (Bobbs Merrill) NYT gen 10/8/39 (#10, 4 wk), 8 wk.

Two Quiet Lives (Bobbs Merrill) NYT gen 3/21/48 (#16, 2 wk).

Melbourne (Bobbs Merrill) NYT gen 10/10/54 (#14), pk 11/7/54 (#7, 2 wk), 18 wk.

Ceram, C.W.

Gods, Graves and Scholars (Knopf) NYT gen 12/2/51 (#12), pk 3/30/52 (#7, 1 wk), 31 wk; PW nf 3/15/52 (#7), pk 4/19/52 (#6, 1 wk), 5 wk; tot 36 wk.

The Secret of the Hittites (Knopf) NYT gen 1/29/56 (#16), pk 3/4/56 (#7, 2 wk), 19 wk; PW nf 2/25/56 (#7, 1 wk), 2 wk; tot 21 wk.

The March of Archaeology (Knopf) NYT gen 11/9/58 (#13, 1 wk), 2 wk.

Cerf, Bennett

Try and Stop Me! (Simon & Schuster) NYT gen 12/3/44 (#17), pk 2/11/45 (#2, 3 wk), 66 wk; PW nf 12/16/44 (#10), pk 2/3/45 (#2, 2 wk), 40 wk; tot 106 wk.

Laughing Stock (Grosset & Dunlap) NYT gen 11/4/45 (#16, 1 wk).

Shake Well Before Using (Simon & Schuster) NYT gen 12/19/48 (#12), pk 1/2/49 (#5, 2 wk), 17 wk; PW nf 2/12/49 (#9), pk 2/26/49 (#7, 1 wk), 3 wk; tot 20 wk.

Good for a Laugh (Hanover House) NYT gen 12/21/52 (#14, 1 wk).

An Encyclopedia of Modern American Humor [ed.] (Hanover House) NYT gen 12/19/54 (#12), pk 2/13/55 (#9, 2 wk), 14 wk; PW nf 1/15/55 (#5, 1 wk), 2 wk; tot 16 wk.

The Life of the Party (Hanover) NYT gen 12/2/56 (#15), pk 1/27/57 (#9, 1 wk), 13 wk; PW nf 1/21/57 (#9), pk 2/18/57 (#7, 1 wk), 5 wk; tot 18 wk.

Reading for Pleasure [ed.] (Harper) NYT gen 1/5/58 (#12, 1 wk), 3 wk; PW nf 1/20/58 (#8, 1 wk), 2 wk; tot 5 wk.

At Random: Reminiscences of Bennett Cerf [ed. Phyllis Cerf Wagner and Albert Erskine] (Random) NYT nf 10/30/77 (#13), pk 11/13/77 (#12, 1 wk), 4 wk; PW hc nf 11/7/77 (#11, 1 wk); tot 5 wk.

Cerf, Christopher

See Marlo Thomas, et al.
See Tony Hendra, et al.

Chabon, Michael

The Mysteries of Pittsburgh (Morrow) NYT fic 5/1/88 (#13), pk 5/8/88 (#12, 2 wk), 6 wk; PW hc fic 5/6/88 (#9, 2 wk), 7 wk; tot 13 wk.

Chamales, Tom T.

Never So Few (Scribner) NYT fic 4/14/57 (#16, 1 wk).

Chamberlain, G.A.

White Man (Bobbs Merrill) PW fic 5/3/19 (#8, 4 wk), 8 wk.

Chamberlain, John
See Charles Andrew Willoughby and
_____

Chamberlain, Neville
In Search of Peace (Putnam) NYT gen 8/6/39 (#11, 4 wk).

Chamberlain, Samuel
Six New England Villages (Hastings) NYT gen 8/15/48 (#13, 1 wk).

Chambers, Oswald
My Utmost for His Highest (Barbour/Discovery) PW pb rel 10/5/90 (#3, 4 wk), 8 wk; PW hc rel 10/5/90 (#12), pk 11/9/90 (#5, 4 wk), 8 wk; tot 16 wk.

Chambers, Robert W.
In Secret (Doran) PW fic 9/6/19 (#3, 4 wk), 8 wk.

Chambers, Whittaker
Witness (Random) NYT gen 6/1/52 (#13), pk 6/22/52 (#1, 13 wk), 26 wk; PW nf 6/14/52 (#6), pk 6/21/52 (#1, 11 wk), 20 wk; tot 46 wk.

Chancellor, John
Peril and Promise: A Commentary on America (Harper) PW hc nf 6/15/90 (#13), pk 7/13/90 (#9, 1 wk), 8 wk; NYT nf 6/24/90 (#9), pk 7/8/90 (#7, 1 wk), 6 wk; tot 14 wk.

Chandler, Raymond
The Little Sister (Hamilton) NYT fic 10/23/49 (#15, 1 wk).

_____, and Robert B. Parker
Poodle Springs (Putnam) NYT fic 10/29/89 (#10), pk 11/5/89 (#9, 2 wk), 4 wk; PW hc fic 11/3/89 (#11), pk 11/10/89 (#10, 1 wk), 4 wk; (Berkley) PW mm pb 11/16/90 (#15), pk 11/30/90 (#14, 1 wk), 2 wk; NYT pb fic 11/25/90 (#15, 1 wk); tot 11 wk.

Chanler, Mrs. Winthrop
Roman Spring (Little Brown) PW nf 10/13/34 (#10, 4 wk).

Chaplin, Charles
My Autobiography (Simon & Schuster) PW nf 10/5/64 (#8), pk 11/23/64 (#1, 1 wk), 23 wk; NYT gen 10/11/64 (#10), pk 11/1/64 (#2, 5 wk), 21 wk; tot 44 wk.

Chapman, Frederick Spencer
The Jungle Is Neutral (Norton) NYT gen 9/25/49 (#16, 1 wk).

Chappell, Geroge Shepard [all titles as by Walter E. Traprock]
The Cruise of the Kawa (Putnam) PW gen lit 1/7/22 (#5, 4 wk); PW nf 4/1/22 (#6, 4 wk); tot 8 wk.
My Northern Exposure (Putnam) PW gen lit 11/18/22 (#12, 4 wk).

Charlton, Moyra
Tally Ho (Putnam) PW juv 4/18/31 (#8, 4 wk).

Charrel, Ralph
How I Turned Ordinary Complaints into Thousands of Dollars (Stein & Day) PW nf 4/1/74 (#10, 2 wk).

Charriere, Henri
Papillon (Morrow) NYT gen 10/4/70 (#9), pk 11/1/70 (#5, 2 wk), 10 wk; PW nf 10/5/70 (#6), pk 10/26/70 (#4, 2 wk), 12 wk; (Pocket) NYT pb gen 11/14/71 (#5), pk 2/13/72 (#4, 4 wk), 16 wk; NYT mm pb 3/10/74 (#5, 4 wk); tot 42 wk.

Charteris, Leslie
Prelude for War (Hodder & Stoughton) NYT fic 7/31/38 (#12, 4 wk).
The Happy Highwayman (Triangle) NYT fic 7/9/39 (#13, 4 wk).

Chase, Alan
Falange (Putnam) NYT gen 8/8/43 (#16, 1 wk).

Chase, Chris
See Rosalind Russell and _____
See Betty Ford and _____

Chase, Ilka
Past Imperfect (Doubleday) PW nf 5/9/42 (#4), pk 6/13/42 (#3, 4 wk), 16 wk; NYT nf 8/9/42 (#8), pk 8/23/42 (#6, 1 wk), 16 wk; tot 32 wk.
In Bed We Cry (Doubleday) PW fic 11/27/43 (#5), pk 1/1/44 (#4, 1 wk), 15 wk; NYT fic 11/28/43 (#8), pk 12/5/43 (#5, 15 wk), 24 wk; tot 39 wk.
I Love Miss Tilli Bean (Doubleday) NYT fic 3/17/46 (#13), pk 3/31/46 (#10, 1 wk), 4 wk.
Free Admission (Doubleday) NYT gen 5/16/48 (#14), pk 5/30/48 (#12, 1 wk), 3 wk.
New York 22 (Doubleday) NYT fic 4/1/51 (#12), pk 4/22/51 (#5, 1 wk), 13 wk; PW fic 4/28/51 (#4, 1 wk), 3 wk; tot 16 wk.

Chase, Mary Ellen
A Goodly Fellowship (Macmillan) NYT gen 12/10/39 (#12), pk 1/7/40 (#8, 4 wk), 8 wk; PW nf 1/13/40 (#10, 8 wk); tot 16 wk.
Mary Peters (Macmillan) PW fic 11/10/34 (#2, 4 wk), 16 wk.
Silas Crockett (Macmillan) NYT fic 12/1/35 (#4, 4 wk); PW fic 12/14/35 (#7), pk 1/11/36 (#3, 4 wk), 16 wk; tot 20 wk.
Dawn in Lyonesse (Macmillan) NYT fic 4/3/38 (#13), pk 5/1/38 (#5, 4 wk), 12 wk; PW fic 5/14/38 (#7, 4 wk), 8 wk; tot 20 wk.
Windswept (Macmillan) PW fic 12/13/41 (#4), pk 2/14/42 (#1, 4 wk), 28 wk; NYT fic 9/6/42 (#11, 1 wk); tot 29 wk.

The White Gate (Norton) NYT gen 12/26/54 (#12), pk 1/2/55 (#10, 1 wk), 8 wk; PW nf 1/15/55 (#10, 1 wk); tot 9 wk.

The Edge of Darkness (Norton) NYT fic 11/24/57 (#10), pk 1/19/58 (#5, 2 wk), 15 wk; PW fic 12/16/57 (#8), pk 1/20/58 (#4, 2 wk), 9 wk; tot 24 wk.

The Lovely Ambition (Norton) NYT fic 7/3/60 (#13), pk 12/25/60 (#4, 1 wk), 36 wk; PW fic 7/18/60 (#8), pk 11/21/60 (#3, 3 wk), 32 wk; tot 68 wk.

Chase, Sarah Leah
See Julee Rosso, et al.

Chase, Stuart
Men and Machines (Macmillan) PW nf 9/14/29 (#10, 4 wk).

Mexico (Macmillan) PW nf 9/19/31 (#3, 12 wk), 24 wk.

A New Deal (Macmillan) PW nf 10/15/32 (#5), pk 12/17/32 (#3, 4 wk), 28 wk.

Technocracy, An Interpretation (John Day) PW nf 2/11/33 (#10, 4 wk).

The Economy of Abundance (Macmillan) PW nf 5/12/34 (#9, 4 wk).

Rich Land, Poor Land (Whittlesey/McGraw) NYT nf 11/8/36 (#10, 4 wk).

The Tyranny of Words (Harcourt) NYT fic 3/6/38 (#4, 4 wk), 8 wk; PW nf 3/12/38 (#7, 4 wk); tot 12 wk.

The Road We Are Traveling (Twentieth Century Fund) PW nf 6/13/42 (#10, 4 wk); NYT nf 9/6/42 (#16, 1 wk); tot 5 wk.

Where's the Money Coming From? (Greenwood) NYT gen 1/30/44 (#19), pk 2/6/44 (#16, 1 wk), 2 wk.

Democracy Under Pressure (Twentieth Century Fund) NYT gen 2/4/45 (#14, 1 wk), 2 wk.

The Proper Study of Mankind (Harper) NYT gen 11/28/48 (#13, 1 wk).

_____, and F.J. Schlink
Your Money's Worth (Macmillan) PW nf 9/24/27 (#7, 4 wk), 8 wk.

Chase, Truddi
When Rabbit Howls (Jove) NYT pb nf 6/10/90 (#1, 4 wk), 17 wk; PW mm pb 6/15/90 (#6, 1 wk), 12 wk; tot 29 wk.

Chase-Riboud, Barbara
Sally Hemings (Avon) PW mm pb 7/11/80 (#14), pk 7/18/80 (#13, 1 wk), 3 wk.

Chastain, Thomas
See Bill Adler and_____

Chater, Arthur D.
See Sigrid Undset

Chatterton, Ruth
Homeward Borne (Simon & Schuster)

NYT fic 5/28/50 (#12), pk 6/25/50 (#5, 3 wk), 23 wk; PW fic 6/17/50 (#9), pk 7/8/50 (#3, 2 wk), 10 wk; tot 33 wk.

Chatwin, Bruce
On the Black Hill (Viking) PW hc fic 2/18/83 (#13, 1 wk), 2 wk.

The Songlines (Sifton/Viking) NYT fic 8/30/87 (#14), pk 9/20/87 (#11, 1 wk), 5 wk.

What Am I Doing Here (Viking) NYT nf 10/8/89 (#12, 1 wk).

Chaucer, Geoffrey
Canterbury Tales [illus. Rockwell Kent] (Covici Friede) PW nf 1/12/35 (#9, 4 wk).

Chanticleer and the Fox [illus. Barbara Cooney] (Crowell) NYT ch bst 5/10/59 (#7, 19 wk).

Cheetham, Erika
See Nostradamus

Cheever, John
The Wapshot Chronicle (Harper) NYT fic 4/14/57 (#14), pk 5/12/57 (#8, 1 wk), 13 wk; PW fic 5/20/57 (#8, 2 wk); tot 15 wk.

The Wapshot Scandal (Harper) NYT fic 1/26/64 (#8), pk 3/8/64 (#4, 8 wk), 23 wk; PW fic 1/27/64 (#9), pk 3/16/64 (#3, 5 wk), 23 wk; tot 46 wk.

The Brigadier and the Golf Widow (Harper) PW fic 12/14/64 (#11), pk 1/4/65 (#10, 1 wk), 4 wk.

Bullet Park (Knopf) PW fic 5/12/69 (#9), pk 5/26/69 (#5, 2 wk), 11 wk; NYT fic 5/18/69 (#10), pk 6/15/69 (#8, 1 wk), 8 wk; tot 19 wk.

The World of Apples (Knopf) NYT fic 6/17/73 (#8, 1 wk); PW fic 6/25/73 (#8, 1 wk); tot 2 wk.

Falconer (Knopf) PW hc fic 3/28/77 (#5), pk 5/2/77 (#1, 5 wk), 22 wk; NYT fic 4/3/77 (#5), pk 5/22/77 (#1, 3 wk), 25 wk; (Ballantine) PW mm pb 2/13/78 (#9, 2 wk), 8 wk; NYT mm pb 2/19/78 (#12), pk 3/12/78 (#9, 2 wk), 7 wk; tot 62 wk.

The Stories of John Cheever (Knopf) PW hc fic 11/27/78 (#15), pk 1/8/79 (#4, 6 wk), 29 wk; NYT fic 12/24/78 (#12), pk 1/28/79 (#3, 1 wk), 26 wk; (Ballantine) PW mm pb 3/14/80 (#13), pk 3/21/80 (#12, 1 wk), 5 wk; tot 60 wk.

Oh What a Paradise It Seems (Knopf) PW hc fic 4/2/82 (#14), pk 4/9/82 (#11, 1 wk), 3 wk.

Chellis, Marcia
Living with the Kennedys: The Joan Kennedy Story (Simon & Schuster) NYT nf 10/6/85 (#14), pk 10/27/85 (#7, 1 wk), 6 wk; PW hc nf 10/11/85 (#14), pk 10/18/85 (#9, 1 wk), 5 wk; (Jove) NYT pb nf 7/13/86 (#3, 3

wk), 7 wk; PW mm pb 8/1/86 (#13, 1 wk), 2 wk; tot 20 wk.

Cheng, Nien
Life and Death in Shanghai (Grove) NYT nf 6/28/87 (#14), pk 7/12/87 (#8, 3 wk), 13 wk; PW hc nf 7/10/87 (#11), pk 7/31/87 (#7, 1 wk), 9 wk; (Penguin) NYT pb nf 5/22/88 (#6, 2 wk), 6 wk; PW td pb 6/3/88 (#9), pk 6/10/88 (#8, 1 wk), 2 wk; tot 30 wk.

Chennault, Anna
A Thousand Springs (Eriksson) NYT gen 7/22/62 (#14), pk 8/26/62 (#13, 3 wk), 7 wk; PW nf 9/3/62 (#15), pk 10/1/62 (#12, 1 wk), 4 wk; tot 11 wk.

Chennault, Claire Lee
The Way of a Fighter (Putnam) NYT gen 3/6/49 (#16, 1 wk).

Cherne, Leo M.
M-Day (Simon & Schuster) PW nf 9/14/40 (#9, 4 wk).
The Rest of Your Life (Doubleday) NYT gen 7/23/44 (#17), pk 10/1/44 (#14, 1 wk), 4 wk.

Cherry, Lynn
The Great Kapok Tree (Gulliver/Harcourt) PW ch pic 8/31/90 (#10, 4 wk).

Chessman, Carl
Cell 2455, Death Row (Prentice Hall) NYT gen 5/30/54 (#12), pk 6/27/54 (#8, 1 wk), 20 wk; PW nf 7/17/54 (#9, 1 wk), 2 wk; tot 22 wk.

Chester, Lewis L., Godfrey H. Hodgson and Bruce P. Page
An American Melodrama: The Presidential Campaign of 1968 (Viking) NYT gen 6/15/69 (#9, 1 wk).

Chevalier, Elizabeth Pickett
Drivin' Woman (Macmillan) PW fic 8/8/42 (#3), pk 8/29/42 (#1, 1 wk), 19 wk; NYT fic 8/9/42 (#3), pk 9/6/42 (#1, 1 wk), 29 wk; tot 48 wk.

Chichester, Sir Francis Charles
Gypsy Moth Circles the World (Coward McCann) NYT gen 3/17/68 (#9), pk 4/21/68 (#3, 1 wk), 14 wk; PW nf 3/25/68 (#9), pk 4/15/68 (#4, 2 wk), 12 wk; tot 26 wk.

Child, Julia
The French Chef Cookbook (Knopf) PW nf 5/6/68 (#9), pk 6/3/68 (#4, 1 wk), 12 wk; NYT gen 5/12/68 (#9), pk 5/26/68 (#3, 1 wk), 12 wk; tot 24 wk.
Julia Child & Company (Knopf) PW td pb 10/30/78 (#8), pk 12/4/78 (#1, 2 wk), 21 wk; NYT td pb 11/12/78 (#1), pk 1/28/79 (#1, 3 wk), 30 wk; NYT nf 12/24/78 (#11), pk 12/31/78 (#9, 1 wk), 4 wk; tot 55 wk.

Julia Child & More Company (Knopf) NYT td pb 1/27/80 (#5), pk 2/3/80 (#4, 4 wk), 26 wk; PW td pb 2/15/80 (#10, 3 wk); tot 29 wk.
The Way to Cook (Knopf) PW hc nf 11/3/89 (#13), pk 1/26/90 (#9, 1 wk), 12 wk; NYT msc 11/26/89 (#5), pk 12/31/89 (#2, 2 wk), 10 wk; tot 22 wk.

_____, and Simone Beck
Mastering the Art of French Cooking Vol. 2 (Knopf) PW nf 1/11/71 (#9, 1 wk).

Child Study Association of America
Read to Yourself Storybook [illus. Leonard Shortall] (Crowell) NYT ch bst 11/13/55 (#4, 40 wk).

Childers, James
See James Street and_____

Children's Television Workshop and the Producers of Sesame Street
The Sesame Street Book of Numbers, and The Sesame Street Book of Letters (Preschool Press/Time Life) NYT ch bst 11/8/70 (#3, 24 wk).

Childs, Marquis William
Sweden: The Middle Way (Yale Univ.) NYT nf 4/5/36 (#9, 4 wk); NYT gen 8/2/36 (#7), pk 9/13/36 (#6, 4 wk), 8 wk; tot 12 wk.
Eisenhower: Captive Hero (Harcourt) NYT gen 9/7/58 (#15), pk 10/12/58 (#8, 1 wk), 10 wk.
The Peacemakers (Harcourt) NYT fic 11/12/61 (#15), pk 12/24/61 (#13, 1 wk), 5 wk.

Cho, Emily, and Linda Grover
Looking Terrific (Ballantine) NYT td pb 10/28/79 (#12, 1 wk), 3 wk.

Choate, Pat
Agents of Influence (Knopf) PW hc nf 11/23/90 (#15, 1 wk).

Christie, Agatha
Peril at End House (Dodd) PW fic 4/23/32 (#5, 4 wk).
The Boomerang Clue (Dodd) NYT fic 11/3/35 (#6, 4 wk).
Cards on the Table (Dodd) NYT fic 3/7/37 (#6, 4 wk).
Death on the Nile (Dodd) NYT fic 3/6/38 (#11, 4 wk).
Appointment with Death (Grosset & Dunlap) NYT fic 10/9/38 (#14, 4 wk).
Murder for Christmas (Books Inc.) NYT fic 3/5/39 (#15, 4 wk).
Absent in the Spring [as by Mary Westmacott] (Farrar) NYT fic 10/29/44 (#14), pk 11/12/44 (#13, 1 wk), 3 wk.
Endless Night (Dodd) PW fic 4/22/68 (#10, 1 wk).

By the Pricking of My Thumbs (Dodd) NYT fic 2/2/69 (#8, 1 wk); PW fic 3/24/69 (#10, 1 wk); tot 2 wk.

Passenger to Frankfurt (Dodd) NYT fic 12/6/70 (#10), pk 12/27/70 (#3, 3 wk), 25 wk; PW fic 12/14/70 (#8), pk 3/15/71 (#3, 1 wk), 25 wk; NYT pb fic 2/13/72 (#3, 3 wk), 8 wk; tot 58 wk.

Nemesis (Dodd) NYT fic 12/26/71 (#9), pk 1/2/72 (#8, 2 wk), 11 wk; PW fic 1/10/72 (#9), pk 2/28/72 (#5, 1 wk), 12 wk; tot 23 wk.

Postern of Fate (Dodd) NYT fic 12/23/73 (#9), pk 2/10/74 (#4, 4 wk), 14 wk; PW fic 12/31/73 (#10), pk 1/28/74 (#5, 1 wk), 9 wk; (Bantam) NYT mm pb 11/10/74 (#9), pk 12/8/74 (#8, 4 wk), 8 wk; tot 31 wk.

Elephants Can Remember (Dodd) PW fic 1/1/73 (#7, 2 wk), 12 wk; NYT fic 1/21/73 (#10), pk 2/25/73 (#7, 1 wk), 10 wk; NYT pb fic 1/6/74 (#1, 4 wk); tot 26 wk.

Curtain (Dodd) NYT fic 10/5/75 (#9), pk 11/30/75 (#1, 19 wk), 33 wk; PW fic 10/6/75 (#6), pk 11/24/75 (#1, 9 wk), 16 wk; PW hc fic 2/2/76 (#1, 7 wk), 15 wk; (Pocket) PW mm pb 10/18/76 (#12), pk 11/8/76 (#2, 1 wk), 15 wk; NYT mm pb 10/24/76 (#9), pk 10/31/76 (#4, 7 wk), 13 wk; tot 92 wk.

Sleeping Murder (Dodd) NYT fic 9/26/76 (#8), pk 11/7/76 (#1, 7 wk), 26 wk; PW hc fic 9/27/76 (#5), pk 10/11/76 (#1, 10 wk), 22 wk; (Bantam) PW mm pb 9/19/77 (#8), pk 9/26/77 (#5, 3 wk), 9 wk; NYT mm pb 10/2/77 (#8), pk 10/9/77 (#6, 1 wk), 8 wk; tot 62 wk.

An Autobiography (Dodd) PW hc nf 12/26/77 (#15) pk 1/2/78 (#13, 1 wk), 3 wk.

Churchill, Randolph S.

Winston S. Churchill: Youth, 1874–1900 (Houghton) NYT gen 12/11/66 (#9), pk 1/1/67 (#6, 4 wk), 10 wk; PW nf 1/9/67 (#10), pk 1/23/67 (#4, 2 wk), 8 wk; tot 18 wk.

Churchill, Sir Winston S.

Blood, Sweat and Tears (Putnam) PW nf 5/10/41 (#3), pk 6/14/41 (#1, 4 wk), 20 wk.

The Gathering Storm (Little Brown) NYT gen 7/4/48 (#8), pk 8/8/48 (#1, 5 wk), 42 wk; PW nf 7/17/48 (#4), pk 7/24/48 (#1, 7 wk), 22 wk; tot 64 wk.

Their Finest Hour (Houghton) PW nf 4/16/49 (#10), pk 5/14/49 (#2, 1 wk), 13 wk; NYT gen 4/17/49 (#4, 5 wk), 17 wk; tot 30 wk.

The Hinge of Fate (Houghton) NYT gen 12/17/50 (#5), pk 12/24/50 (#4, 3 wk), 13 wk; PW nf 12/23/50 (#5), pk 1/6/51 (#3, 2 wk), 8 wk; tot 21 wk.

The Grand Alliance (Houghton) PW nf 5/13/50 (#4), pk 6/3/50 (#1, 3 wk), 11 wk; NYT gen 5/14/50 (#3, 7 wk), 14 wk; tot 25 wk.

Closing the Ring (Houghton) NYT gen 12/9/51 (#8), pk 1/27/52 (#4, 1 wk), 15 wk; PW nf 12/15/51 (#6), pk 12/22/51 (#3, 2 wk), 7 wk; tot 22 wk.

Triumph and Tragedy (Houghton) NYT gen 12/20/53 (#4), pk 12/27/53 (#3, 7 wk), 14 wk; PW nf 1/2/54 (#4), pk 1/30/54 (#2, 1 wk), 9 wk; tot 23 wk.

The New World (Dodd) NYT gen 12/2/56 (#12), pk 12/23/56 (#4, 1 wk), 15 wk; PW nf 12/17/56 (#4), pk 1/7/57 (#3, 1 wk), 9 wk; tot 24 wk.

The Birth of Britain (Dodd) NYT gen 4/29/56 (#12), pk 5/27/56 (#1, 8 wk), 24 wk; PW nf 5/14/56 (#3), pk 5/28/56 (#1, 7 wk), 18 wk; tot 42 wk.

The Age of Revolution (Dodd) NYT gen 10/27/57 (#6), pk 11/3/57 (#5, 5 wk), 13 wk; PW nf 11/4/57 (#5), pk 12/16/57 (#4, 1 wk), 8 wk; tot 21 wk.

The Great Democracies (Dodd) NYT gen 3/23/58 (#16), pk 4/20/58 (#4, 1 wk), 13 wk; PW nf 4/14/58 (#7), pk 4/28/58 (#4, 1 wk), 7 wk; tot 20 wk.

Chute, Beatrice Joy

Greenwillow (Dutton) NYT fic 8/5/56 (#15, 1 wk).

The Moon and the Thorn (Dutton) NYT fic 10/29/61 (#14, 1 wk).

Chute, Carolyn

The Beans of Egypt, Maine (Ticknor & Fields) PW td pb 3/22/85 (#10), pk 4/26/85 (#7, 1 wk), 11 wk; NYT pb fic 5/5/85 (#15, 1 wk); tot 12 wk.

Chute, Marchette Gaylord

Shakespeare of London (Dutton) NYT gen 4/30/50 (#15), pk 5/7/50 (#13, 1 wk), 2 wk.

Ciano, Count Galeazzo

The Ciano Diaries 1939–1943 [ed. Hugh Gibson] (Doubleday) NYT gen 2/3/46 (#4), pk 2/17/46 (#2, 3 wk), 14 wk; PW nf 2/16/46 (#4), pk 2/23/46 (#2, 1 wk), 8 wk; tot 22 wk.

Ciardi, John

I Met a Man (Houghton) NYT ch bst 11/12/61 (#4, 26 wk).

Ciechanowski, Jan

Defeat in Victory (Doubleday) NYT gen 3/2/47 (#9), pk 3/9/47 (#7, 2 wk), 6 wk.

Clad, Noel

Love and Money (Random) NYT fic 7/5/59 (#14, 1 wk).

Claiborne, Craig, and Pierre Franey

Craig Claiborne's Gourmet Diet (Times Books) PW hc fic 7/18/80 (#9), pk 9/26/80 (#5, 3 wk), 37 wk; NYT nf 7/20/80 (#15), pk 8/31/80 (#4, 3 wk), 40 wk; tot 77 wk.

Clancy, Tom

The Hunt for Red October (Naval Institute) PW hc fic 3/22/85 (#15), pk 5/3/85 (#2, 9 wk), 31 wk; NYT fic 3/24/85 (#10), pk 7/7/85 (#2, 2 wk), 29 wk; (Berkley) NYT pb fic 10/6/85 (#3), pk 10/13/85 (#1, 4 wk), 112 wk; PW mm pb 10/11/85 (#2), pk 10/18/85 (#1, 7 wk), 83 wk; [read by Richard Crenna] (Audio Partners/Publishers Group West) PW aud fic 10/5/90 (#10, 4 wk); tot 259 wk.

Red Storm Rising (Putnam) NYT fic 8/3/86 (#2), pk 8/17/86 (#1, 6 wk), 50 wk; PW hc fic 8/8/86 (#9), pk 8/22/86 (#1, 7 wk), 50 wk; (Berkley) NYT pb fic 7/19/87 (#3), pk 8/16/87 (#1, 2 wk), 41 wk; PW mm pb 7/24/87 (#2), pk 7/31/87 (#1, 5 wk), 31 wk; tot 172 wk.

Patriot Games (Putnam) NYT fic 8/2/87 (#1, 5 wk), 38 wk; PW hc fic 8/7/87 (#3), pk 8/14/87 (#1, 4 wk), 39 wk; (Berkley) NYT pb fic 7/17/88 (#1, 4 wk), 27 wk; PW mm pb 7/22/88 (#1, 4 wk), 19 wk; tot 123 wk.

The Cardinal of the Kremlin (Putnam) NYT fic 8/7/88 (#1, 12 wk), 41 wk; PW hc fic 8/12/88 (#1, 12 wk), 39 wk; (Berkley) NYT pb fic 7/16/89 (#2), pk 7/23/89 (#1, 5 wk), 26 wk; PW mm pb 7/21/89 (#2), pk 7/28/89 (#1, 6 wk), 19 wk; tot 125 wk.

Clear and Present Danger (Putnam) NYT fic 9/3/89 (#1, 9 wk), 45 wk; PW hc fic 9/8/89 (#1, 10 wk), 44 wk; (Berkley) NYT pb fic 7/22/90 (#1, 3 wk), 15 wk; PW mm pb 7/27/90 (#1, 4 wk), 15 wk; [read by David Ogden Stiers] (Simon & Schuster) PW aud fic 10/5/90 (#4, 4 wk), 8 wk; tot 127 wk.

Clapesattle, Helen

The Doctors Mayo (Univ. of Minnesota) PW nf 2/14/42 (#5, 4 wk), 12 wk.

Clapper, Olive Ewing

Washington Tapestry (Whittlesey/McGraw) NYT gen 2/24/46 (#16), pk 3/24/46 (#5, 1 wk), 10 wk.

Clapper, Raymond

Watching the World (Whittlesey/McGraw) NYT gen 8/13/44 (#13, 1 wk).

Clark, Blake

Robinson Crusoe, U.S.N. (Whittlesey) NYT gen 5/20/45 (#16, 1 wk), 3 wk.

Clark, Kenneth

Civilisation (Harper) NYT gen 8/2/70 (#10), pk 1/10/70 (#1, 1 wk), 32 wk; PW nf 11/30/70 (#9), pk 1/4/71 (#2, 5 wk), 26 wk; NYT pb gen 4/9/72 (#4, 4 wk); tot 62 wk.

Another Part of the Wood: A Self-Portrait (Harper) NYT gen 5/4/75 (#9, 1 wk).

Clark, Mark Wayne

Calculated Risk (Harper) NYT gen 11/12/50 (#16), pk 11/19/50 (#10, 1 wk), 5 wk.

Clark, Mary Higgins

Where Are the Children? (Dell) PW mm pb 5/24/76 (#14), pk 8/16/76 (#4, 2 wk), 27 wk; NYT mm pb 6/13/76 (#10), pk 9/5/76 (#4, 3 wk), 18 wk; tot 45 wk.

A Stranger Is Watching (Simon & Schuster) PW hc fic 3/20/78 (#12), pk 5/1/78 (#7, 3 wk), 13 wk; NYT fic 3/26/78 (#12), pk 5/14/78 (#8, 2 wk), 13 wk; (Dell) PW mm pb 3/26/79 (#10), pk 4/16/79 (#6, 2 wk), 10 wk; NYT mm pb 4/1/79 (#11), pk 4/15/79 (#4, 2 wk), 12 wk; tot 48 wk.

The Cradle Will Fall (Simon & Schuster) PW hc fic 7/11/80 (#15), pk 7/18/80 (#14, 4 wk), 7 wk; NYT fic 7/27/80 (#13), pk 8/10/80 (#10, 1 wk), 6 wk; (Dell) PW mm pb 6/12/81 (#10), pk 6/26/81 (#3, 4 wk), 15 wk; NYT mm pb 6/14/81 (#7), pk 7/5/81 (#3, 1 wk), 15 wk; tot 43 wk.

A Cry in the Night (Dell) NYT mm pb 10/9/83 (#12), pk 10/23/83 (#1, 1 wk), 10 wk; PW mm pb 10/14/83 (#12), pk 10/28/83 (#1, 1 wk), 10 wk; tot 20 wk.

Stillwatch (Simon & Schuster) NYT fic 10/28/84 (#10), pk 11/25/84 (#4, 1 wk), 11 wk; PW hc fic 11/2/84 (#12), pk 11/23/84 (#5, 1 wk), 15 wk; (Dell) NYT pb fic 3/30/86 (#9), pk 4/13/86 (#1, 2 wk), 12 wk; PW mm pb 4/4/86 (#9), pk 4/11/86 (#2, 3 wk), 11 wk; tot 49 wk.

Weep No More, My Lady (Simon & Schuster) NYT fic 7/5/87 (#13), pk 7/19/87 (#3, 2 wk), 17 wk; PW hc fic 7/10/87 (#12), pk 7/24/87 (#3, 2 wk), 14 wk; (Dell) NYT pb fic 7/10/88 (#4), pk 7/17/88 (#2, 4 wk), 12 wk; PW mm pb 7/15/88 (#4), pk 7/22/88 (#2, 4 wk), 12 wk; tot 55 wk.

While My Pretty One Sleeps (Simon & Schuster) NYT fic 5/14/89 (#8), pk 5/28/89 (#1, 2 wk), 21 wk; PW hc fic 5/26/89 (#3), pk 6/2/89 (#1, 2 wk), 20 wk; (Pocket) NYT pb fic 7/1/90 (#3), pk 7/8/90 (#1, 2 wk), 11 wk; PW mm pb 7/6/90 (#3), pk 7/13/90 (#1, 2 wk), 12 wk; tot 64 wk.

Terror Stalks the Class Reunion (Simon & Schuster) PW aud fic 10/5/90 (#5, 4 wk).

Clark, Ramsey

Crime in America (Simon & Schuster) NYT gen 12/13/70 (#10), pk 2/28/71 (#6, 1 wk), 14 wk; PW nf 1/4/71 (#10), pk 1/25/71 (#7, 2 wk), 13 wk; NYT pb gen 6/6/71 (#5, 4 wk); tot 31 wk.

Clark, Walter Van Tilburg

The City of Trembling Leaves (Random) NYT fic 7/15/45 (#20), pk 8/12/45 (#12, 1 wk), 3 wk.

The Track of the Cat (Random) NYT fic

6/26/49 (#12), pk 7/31/49 (#7, 3 wk), 9 wk; PW fic 8/13/49 (#7, 1 wk); tot 10 wk.

Clarke, Arthur C.
Imperial Earth (Ballantine) PW mm pb 12/6/76 (#14, 1 wk), 2 wk.

2010: Odyssey Two (Ballantine/Del Rey) NYT fic 11/14/82 (#5), pk 12/12/82 (#2, 7 wk), 24 wk; PW hc fic 11/19/82 (#14), pk 1/21/83 (#1, 1 wk), 22 wk; NYT pb fic 2/5/84 (#4), pk 2/12/84 (#2, 2 wk), 13 wk; PW mm pb 2/10/84 (#6), pk 2/17/84 (#5, 2 wk), 10 wk; tot 69 wk.

The Songs of Distant Earth (Ballantine/Del Rey) NYT fic 5/4/86 (#11, 1 wk), 4 wk; PW hc fic 5/9/86 (#15), pk 5/23/86 (#7, 2 wk), 6 wk; PW mm pb 5/15/87 (#10), pk 6/5/87 (#5, 1 wk), 7 wk; NYT pb fic 5/10/87 (#7), pk 5/24/87 (#4, 1 wk), 7 wk; tot 24 wk.

2061: Odyssey Three (Ballantine/Del Rey) NYT fic 12/6/87 (#13), pk 3/13/88 (#4, 1 wk), 19 wk; PW hc fic 12/11/87 (#10), pk 2/12/88 (#3, 1 wk), 19 wk; NYT pb fic 5/7/89 (#11), pk 5/21/89 (#4, 1 wk), 6 wk; PW mm pb 5/12/89 (#5), pk 6/2/89 (#2, 1 wk), 7 wk; tot 51 wk.

_____, **and Gentry Lee**
Cradle (Warner) NYT pb fic 7/9/89 (#15), pk 7/30/89 (#12, 1 wk), 3 wk; PW hc fic 8/26/88 (#15, 1 wk); tot 4 wk.

Rama II (Bantam/Spectra) NYT pb fic 12/2/90 (#10, 1 wk), 4 wk; PW mm pb 12/7/90 (#8, 1 wk), 3 wk; tot 7 wk.

Clarke, Covington
Desert Wings (Reilly & Lee) PW juv 8/23/30 (#8, 4 wk), 8 wk.

Clarke, Gerald
Capote (Simon & Schuster) NYT nf 6/12/88 (#15), pk 7/10/88 (#6, 2 wk), 13 wk; PW hc nf 7/8/88 (#15), pk 8/5/88 (#8, 1 wk), 10 wk; tot 23 wk.

Clarke, Venable
Sky Caravan (Reilly & Lee) PW juv 8/15/31 (#10, 4 wk).

Clavell, James
King Rat (Little Brown) NYT fic 9/23/62 (#13, 1 wk).

Tai-Pan (Atheneum) NYT fic 6/12/66 (#9), pk 10/2/66 (#2, 1 wk), 44 wk; PW fic 6/13/66 (#8), pk 9/5/66 (#1, 2 wk), 40 wk; NYT pb fic 5/7/67 (#4), pk 6/4/67 (#1, 4 wk), 12 wk; tot 96 wk.

Shogun (Atheneum) PW fic 7/14/75 (#6), pk 8/18/75 (#3, 6 wk), 31 wk; NYT fic 7/20/75 (#7), pk 8/24/75 (#3, 5 wk), 32 wk; (Dell) PW mm pb 6/14/76 (#5), pk 6/28/76 (#1, 7 wk), 29 wk; NYT mm pb 6/27/76 (#4), pk 10/5/80 (#1, 5 wk), 29 wk; tot 121 wk.

Noble House (Delacorte) PW hc fic 5/1/81 (#15), pk 5/15/81 (#1, 15 wk), 47 wk; NYT fic 5/10/81 (#1, 15 wk), 47 wk; (Dell) PW mm pb 4/23/82 (#2), pk 4/30/82 (#1, 4 wk), 15 wk; NYT mm pb 4/25/82 (#1, 4 wk), 13 wk; NYT pb fic 3/13/88 (#10, 1 wk); tot 123 wk.

Whirlwind (Morton) NYT fic 11/9/86 (#4), pk 11/23/86 (#1, 4 wk), 22 wk; PW hc fic 11/14/86 (#4), pk 11/21/86 (#1, 5 wk), 20 wk; (Avon) NYT pb fic 11/1/87 (#7), pk 11/8/87 (#1, 1 wk), 11 wk; PW mm pb 11/6/87 (#6), pk 11/13/87 (#1, 1 wk), 11 wk; tot 64 wk.

Clay, Lucius Du Bignon
Decision in Germany (Doubleday) NYT gen 2/26/50 (#8), pk 3/5/50 (#7, 1 wk), 8 wk.

Clayre, Alasdair
The Heart of the Dragon (Houghton) NYT nf 6/9/85 (#15), pk 6/16/85 (#9, 2 wk), 8 wk.

Cleary, Beverly
Muggie Maggie (Morrow) PW ch yn rd 8/31/90 (#4), pk 10/26/90 (#3, 4 wk), 12 wk.

Cleaveland, Agnes Morley
No Life for a Lady (Houghton) PW nf 10/11/41 (#10, 4 wk).

Cleaver, Eldridge
Soul on Ice (McGraw) PW nf 6/10/68 (#10), pk 11/4/68 (#8, 1 wk), 7 wk; NYT gen 8/18/68 (#10), pk 10/27/68 (#8, 1 wk), 4 wk; NYT pb gen 3/2/69 (#2), pk 5/4/69 (#1, 24 wk), 56 wk; tot 67 wk.

Clegg, Charles C.
See Lucius M. Beebe and_____

Cleland, John
Memoirs of a Woman of Pleasure (Putnam) PW fic 8/5/63 (#9, 1 wk).

Clemenceau, Georges
Grandeur and Misery of Victory (Harcourt) PW nf 5/17/30 (#2, 4 wk), 8 wk.

Clemens, Samuel [all titles as by Mark Twain]
Tom Sawyer (Grosset & Dunlap) PW juv 2/15/30 (#7), pk 5/17/30 (#1, 4 wk), 76 wk; (Harper) PW juv 6/20/31 (#4, 4 wk), 16 wk; tot 92 wk.

Letters from the Earth [ed. Bernard de Voto] (Harper) NYT gen 10/21/62 (#16), pk 12/9/62 (#5, 2 wk), 9 wk; PW nf 11/5/62 (#9), pk 2/4/63 (#3, 1 wk), 20 wk; tot 29 wk.

Clements, Florence Ryerson, and Colin Clements
Harriet (Scribners) NYT gen 9/19/43 (#20), pk 10/17/43 (#13, 2 wk), 6 wk.

Cleveland, June
See Dana Lamb and_____

Clift, Charmian, and George John-ston
High Valley (Bobbs Merrill) NYT fic 6/25/50 (#14), pk 9/3/50 (#12, 1 wk), 10 wk.

Clive, John
See J.D. Gilman and_____

Cloete, Stuart
The Turning Wheels (Houghton) PW fic 12/11/37 (#5), pk 1/15/38 (#4, 8 wk), 20 wk; NYT fic 12/12/37 (#3, 4 wk), 8 wk; tot 28 wk.
Watch for the Dawn (Houghton) NYT fic 10/8/39 (#4, 4 wk), 8 wk; PW fic 10/14/39 (#4, 8 wk); tot 16 wk.
Congo Song (Houghton) NYT fic 3/14/43 (#18), pk 4/4/43 (#6, 1 wk), 11 wk; PW fic 4/10/43 (#9), pk 4/24/43 (#7, 1 wk), 2 wk; tot 13 wk.
Against These Three (Houghton) NYT gen 8/12/45 (#8), pk 9/9/45 (#7, 1 wk), 8 wk.
The African Giant (Harper) NYT gen 10/2/55 (#14), pk 11/6/55 (#8, 1 wk), 11 wk.

Close, Upton
See Josef Washington Hall

Clowes, Carolyn
The Pandora Principle (Pocket) NYT pb fic 4/8/90 (#12), pk 4/15/90 (#7, 1 wk), 4 wk; PW mm pb 4/27/90 (#15), pk 5/4/90 (#14, 1 wk), 2 wk; tot 6 wk.

Coakley, Mary Lewis
Mister Music Maker, Lawrence Welk (Doubleday) NYT gen 7/6/58 (#11), pk 8/10/58 (#8, 1 wk), 11 wk; PW nf 7/21/58 (#9), pk 8/11/58 (#8, 2 wk), 4 wk; tot 15 wk.

Coatsworth, Elizabeth
The Cat Who Went to Heaven (Macmillan) PW juv 7/18/31 (#6), pk 8/15/31 (#1, 20 wk), 40 wk.

Cobb, Humphrey
Paths of Glory (Viking) PW fic 7/13/35 (#7), pk 8/10/35 (#5, 4 wk), 12 wk.

Cobb, Irvin S.
Exit Laughing (Bobbs Merrill) PW nf 4/12/41 (#10), pk 5/10/41 (#4, 8 wk), 20 wk.

Cobbs, Price M.
See William H. Grier and_____

Cobleigh, Ira U.
Happiness Is a Stock That Doubles in a Year (Geis/Random) NYT gen 10/1/67 (#10), pk 10/8/67 (#9, 5 wk), 6 wk.

Coburn, Andrew
Babysitter (Pocket) PW mm pb 5/30/80 (#13, 1 wk), 2 wk.

Cochran, Molly
See Warren Murphy and_____

Coco, James, and Marion Paone
The James Coco Diet (Bantam) NYT msc 2/12/84 (#5), pk 2/26/84 (#1, 2 wk), 12 wk; PW hc nf 2/24/84 (#9), pk 3/2/84 (#4, 2 wk), 13 wk; NYT msc pb 2/24/85 (#9, 2 wk); tot 27 wk.

Coàn, Robert Peter Tristram
Kennebec: Cradle of Americans (Farrar) NYT gen 8/8/37 (#9, 4 wk).
Missouri Compromise (Little Brown) NYT gen 6/15/47 (#12, 1 wk).
Not to the Swift (Norton) NYT fic 4/30/61 (#14, 1 wk).

Cohen, Barbara
Molly's Pilgrim [illus. Michael J. Deraney] (Bantam/Skylark) PW ch yn rd 12/21/90 (#3, 4 wk).

Cohen, David
Christmas in America [ed.] (Collins) NYT nf 12/11/88 (#14), pk 1/8/89 (#5, 1 wk), 7 wk; PW hc nf 12/23/88 (#13, 2 wk), 5 wk; tot 12 wk.
See also Rick Smolan and_____

Cohen, Herb
You Can Negotiate Anything (Stuart) PW hc nf 12/5/80 (#13), pk 3/27/81 (#6, 4 wk), 41 wk; NYT nf 3/1/81 (#11), pk 4/19/81 (#4, 1 wk), 35 wk; (Bantam) NYT mm pb 3/7/82 (#15, 1 wk); tot 77 wk.

Cohen, Jerry S.
See Morton Mintz and_____

Cohn, David Lewis
Combustion on Wheels (Houghton) NYT gen 1/14/45 (#13, 1 wk).

Cohn, Lester
Coming Home (Viking) NYT fic 6/10/45 (#9), pk 7/22/45 (#7, 1 wk), 12 wk.

Coit, Margaret L.
Mr. Baruch (Houghton) NYT gen 12/29/57 (#14), pk 1/12/58 (#10, 1 wk), 7 wk.

Cole, Joanna
The Magic School Bus Inside the Human Body [illus. Bruce Degen] (Scholastic) PW ch nf 11/30/90 (#3, 4 wk), 8 wk.
The Magic School Bus Lost in the Solar System [illus. Bruce Degen] (Scholastic) PW ch nf 10/26/90 (#2), pk 11/30/90 (#1, 4 wk), 12 wk.

_____, and Stephanie Calmenson
Ready ... Set ... Read! [comp.] (Doubleday) PW ch yn rd 12/21/90 (#5, 4 wk).

Cole, Marley
Jehovah's Witnesses (Vanguard) NYT gen 7/17/55 (#13), pk 8/7/55 (#8, 4 wk), 9 wk; PW nf 8/13/55 (#8, 1 wk), 2 wk; tot 11 wk.

Coleman, Jonathan
At Mother's Request (Atheneum) NYT nf 8/25/85 (#15, 1 wk); (Pocket) pb nf 2/9/86 (#7), pk 1/25/87 (#5, 1 wk), 2 wk; PW mm pb 1/30/87 (#10, 1 wk); tot 4 wk.
Exit the Rainmaker (Dell) NYT pb nf 10/ 7/90 (#9), pk 10/14/90 (#8, 2 wk), 5 wk.

Coleman, Lonnie
Beulah Land (Doubleday) NYT fic 12/16/ 73 (#9), pk 1/27/74 (#7, 1 wk), 9 wk; (Dell) mm pb 10/13/74 (#5), pk 11/10/74 (#2, 4 wk), 9 wk; tot 18 wk.

Colette, Sidonie Gabrielle Claudine
Earthly Paradise: Colette's Autobiography Drawn from Her Lifetime Writings [ed. Robert Phelps] (Farrar) NYT gen 6/5/66 (#10), pk 6/19/66 (#9, 3 wk), 6 wk; PW nf 6/20/66 (#10), pk 7/4/66 (#8, 1 wk), 5 wk; tot 11 wk.

Coley, Christopher M.
See Sidney M. Wolfe, M.D., et al.

Collier, Peter, and David Horowitz
The Rockefellers: An American Dynasty (Holt) NYT gen 5/2/76 (#7), pk 5/23/76 (#6, 4 wk), 16 wk; PW hc nf 5/24/76 (#8), pk 6/7/76 (#6, 2 wk), 12 wk; tot 28 wk.
The Kennedys: An American Drama (Summit/Simon & Schuster) NYT nf 7/1/84 (#14), pk 7/22/84 (#1, 7 wk), 25 wk; PW hc nf 7/6/84 (#14), pk 8/3/84 (#1, 2 wk), 23 wk; (Warner) NYT pb nf 7/14/85 (#1, 2 wk), 9 wk; PW mm pb 7/26/85 (#15, 1 wk); tot 58 wk.

Collins, Frederick Lewis
The F.B.I. in Peace and War (Putnam) NYT gen 11/7/43 (#19, 1 wk).

Collins, Jackie
Chances (Geis/Warner) NYT fic 10/4/81 (#15, 1 wk); PW hc fic 10/16/81 (#14, 2 wk); PW mm pb 8/13/82 (#6), pk 9/10/82 (#2, 1 wk), 17 wk; NYT mm pb 8/15/82 (#6), pk 9/ 12/82 (#1, 1 wk), 18 wk; tot 38 wk.
Hollywood Wives (Simon & Schuster) NYT fic 8/7/83 (#8), pk 8/21/83 (#4, 8 wk), 28 wk; PW hc fic 8/12/83 (#7), pk 8/26/83 (#2, 1 wk), 29 wk; (Pocket) NYT pb fic 7/8/ 84 (#2), 7/15/84 (#1, 3 wk), 18 wk; PW mm pb 7/13/84 (#1, 5 wk), 18 wk; tot 93 wk.
The World Is Full of Married Men (Pocket) NYT pb fic 12/23/84 (#9, 1 wk).
Sinners (Pocket) NYT pb fic 10/14/84 (#14), pk 10/28/84 (#4, 1 wk), 10 wk; PW mm pb 10/26/84 (#5), pk 11/2/84 (#4, 3 wk), 8 wk; tot 18 wk.
The Bitch (Pocket) NYT pb fic 8/19/84 (#14), pk 9/2/84 (#11, 3 wk), 5 wk; PW mm pb 9/7/84 (#13), pk 9/14/84 (#10, 1 wk), 3 wk; tot 8 wk.

Lucky (Simon & Schuster) NYT fic 8/25/ 85 (#4), pk 9/1/85 (#1, 2 wk), 23 wk; PW hc fic 8/30/85 (#4), pk 9/6/85 (#1, 2 wk), 19 wk; (Pocket) NYT pb fic 7/6/86 (#8), pk 7/13/86 (#1, 3 wk), 12 wk; PW mm pb 7/11/86 (#12), pk 7/25/86 (#1, 2 wk), 10 wk; tot 64 wk.
Hollywood Husbands (Simon & Schuster) NYT fic 10/19/86 (#3, 4 wk), 17 wk; PW hc fic 10/24/86 (#3, 4 wk), 15 wk; (Pocket) NYT pb fic 8/19/87 (#8), pk 8/16/87 (#3, 3 wk), 9 wk; PW mm pb 8/14/87 (#8), pk 8/21/87 (#3, 2 wk), 9 wk; tot 50 wk.
Rock Star (Simon & Schuster) NYT fic 4/24/88 (#3), pk 5/1/88 (#2, 1 wk), 17 wk; PW hc fic 4/29/88 (#4), pk 5/6/88 (#2, 2 wk), 16 wk; (Pocket) NYT pb fic 12/25/88 (#9), pk 1/15/89 (#2, 3 wk), 11 wk; PW mm pb 1/6/89 (#4), pk 1/13/89 (#2, 2 wk), 7 wk; tot 51 wk.
Lady Boss (Simon & Schuster) NYT fic 10/7/90 (#9), pk 10/28/90 (#2, 2 wk), 13 wk; PW hc fic 10/12/90 (#7), pk 10/26/90 (#2, 2 wk), 11 wk; tot 24 wk.

Collins, Joan
Past Imperfect (Simon & Schuster) NYT nf 4/29/84 (#9), pk 5/20/84 (#2, 2 wk), 15 wk; PW hc nf 5/4/84 (#8), pk 6/15/84 (#2, 1 wk), 14 wk; (Berkley) NYT pb nf 4/7/85 (#1, 8 wk), 11 wk; PW mm pb 4/12/85 (#9), pk 4/19/85 (#6, 1 wk), 6 wk; tot 46 wk.
Prime Time (Simon & Schuster) NYT fic 10/9/88 (#11), pk 10/30/88 (#8, 1 wk), 6 wk; PW hc fic 10/14/88 (#10), pk 10/21/88 (#7, 3 wk), 6 wk; (Pocket) NYT pb fic 9/17/89 (#15), pk 9/24/89 (#14, 1 wk), 2 wk; PW mm pb 10/6/89 (#15, 1 wk); tot 15 wk.

Collins, Larry
Fall from Grace (Simon & Schuster) NYT fic 7/21/85 (#12), pk 7/28/85 (#9, 1 wk), 9 wk; PW hc fic 7/26/85 (#11), pk 8/9/85 (#10, 1 wk), 4 wk; (NAL/Signet) NYT pb fic 8/10/ 86 (#11, 2 wk), 3 wk; tot 16 wk.
Maze (Simon & Schuster) NYT fic 7/9/89 (#14, 2 wk).

_____, and Dominique Lapierre
Is Paris Burning? (Simon & Schuster) NYT gen 6/27/65 (#7), pk 7/25/65 (#2, 6 wk), 36 wk; PW nf 6/28/65 (#7), pk 8/16/65 (#1, 1 wk), 39 wk; NYT pb gen 6/5/66 (#2, 8 wk), 36 wk; tot 111 wk.
Or I'll Dress You in Mourning (Simon & Schuster) NYT gen 6/23/68 (#9), pk 7/7/68 (#6, 4 wk), 14 wk; PW nf 7/1/68 (#9), pk 7/ 29/68 (#3, 2 wk), 15 wk; tot 29 wk.
O Jerusalem! (Simon & Schuster) PW nf 6/5/72 (#8), pk 7/24/72 (#1, 6 wk), 27 wk; NYT gen 6/11/72 (#7), pk 7/23/72 (#1, 4

wk), 25 wk; NYT pb gen 6/10/73 (#2, 8 wk), 16 wk; tot 68 wk.

Freedom at Midnight (Simon & Schuster) NYT gen 11/30/75 (#10), pk 12/14/75 (#8, 2 wk), 3 wk; PW nf 12/8/75 (#8, 1 wk), 2 wk; tot 5 wk.

The Fifth Horseman (Simon & Schuster) PW hc fic 9/5/80 (#7), pk 9/26/80 (#2, 2 wk), 28 wk; NYT fic 9/14/80 (#11), pk 9/28/80 (#3, 5 wk), 28 wk; (Avon) PW mm pb 8/21/81 (#14), pk 9/4/81 (#4, 2 wk), 9 wk; NYT mm pb 8/23/81 (#11), pk 9/20/81 (#7, 1 wk), 8 wk; tot 73 wk.

Collins, Norman
Dulcimer Street (Duell Sloan & Pearce) NYT fic 2/9/47 (#9), pk 2/16/47 (#6, 2 wk), 17 wk; PW fic 3/15/47 (#9, 1 wk), 2 wk; tot 19 wk.

Colson, Charles W.
Born Again (Chosen Books/Revell) PW hc nf 5/3/76 (#9), pk 6/7/76 (#7, 1 wk), 9 wk; NYT gen 5/30/76 (#10, 1 wk); tot 10 wk.

Colum, Mary
Life and the Dream (Doubleday) NYT gen 4/20/47 (#13, 2 wk), 3 wk.

Colver, Ann
Mr. Lincoln's Wife (Farrar) NYT fic 6/20/43 (#12, 2 wk), 3 wk.

Colville, Sir John
The Fringes of Power (Norton) NYT nf 2/16/86 (#12), pk 2/23/86 (#9, 2 wk), 7 wk; PW hc nf 3/7/86 (#12, 1 wk), 4 wk; tot 11 wk.

Comandini, Adele
Doctor Kate: Angel on Snowshoes (Rinehart) NYT gen 4/8/56 (#13, 1 wk), 6 wk.

Comfort, Alex
The Joy of Sex (Crown) NYT gen 12/3/72 (#7), pk 8/5/73 (#1, 11 wk), 73 wk; PW nf 12/4/72 (#5), pk 6/4/73 (#1, 19 wk), 69 wk; (Simon & Schuster/Fireside) NYT td pb 3/10/74 (#1, 54 wk), 364 wk; PW td pb 2/2/76 (#5), pk 6/14/76 (#1, 15 wk), 247 wk; tot 753 wk.

More Joy of Sex [illus. Charles Raymond and Christopher Foss] (Crown) PW nf 8/19/74 (#7), pk 9/30/74 (#6, 1 wk), 16 wk; NYT gen 9/15/74 (#9), pk 10/6/74 (#6, 2 wk), 12 wk; (Simon & Schuster/Fireside) NYT td pb 10/26/75 (#1, 2 wk), 25 wk; PW td pb 9/13/76 (#5), pk 9/20/76 (#4, 2 wk), 4 wk; tot 57 wk.

Commager, Henry Steele
The St. Nicholas Anthology [ed.] (Random) NYT gen 12/5/48 (#14), pk 1/9/49 (#9, 1 wk), 8 wk; PW nf 1/15/49 (#10, 1 wk); tot 9 wk.

Compton-Burnett, Ivy
Two Worlds and Their Ways (Knopf) NYT fic 6/26/49 (#16, 2 wk).

Comstock, Nan
See Joan Wychoff

Conant, James Bryant
Science and Common Sense (Yale Univ.) NYT gen 3/11/51 (#16, 1 wk).

The American High School Today (McGraw) NYT gen 3/1/59 (#14), pk 4/5/59 (#6, 1 wk), 11 wk; PW nf 3/9/59 (#10), pk 4/20/59 (#5, 1 wk), 6 wk; tot 17 wk.

The Education of American Teachers (McGraw) NYT gen 10/13/63 (#8), pk 11/10/63 (#7, 2 wk), 9 wk; PW nf 11/11/63 (#7, 1 wk), 5 wk; tot 14 wk.

Condon, Richard
The Manchurian Candidate (McGraw) NYT fic 7/26/59 (#15, 1 wk).

An Infinity of Mirrors (Random) PW fic 10/26/64 (#10, 1 wk), 8 wk.

Winter Kills (Dial) NYT fic 7/7/74 (#8), pk 8/25/74 (#7, 1 wk), 8 wk; PW fic 7/15/74 (#8), pk 8/12/74 (#6, 4 wk), 8 wk; (Dell) NYT mm pb 8/10/75 (#9, 1 wk); tot 17 wk.

Conn, Charles Paul
The Possible Dream: A Candid Look at Amway (Revell) NYT nf 9/11/77 (#11), pk 11/13/77 (#7, 1 wk), 11 wk; PW hc nf 10/3/77 (#10), pk 10/31/77 (#8, 1 wk), 7 wk; tot 18 wk.

The Winner's Circle (Revell) PW hc nf 5/28/79 (#9, 1 wk), 8 wk; NYT nf 6/24/79 (#10, 1 wk); tot 9 wk.

An Uncommon Freedom (Revell) PW hc nf 6/11/82 (#10, 1 wk), 3 wk.

Conn, Phoebe
Captive Heart (Zebra) NYT pb fic 3/31/85 (#10, 1 wk), 2 wk.

Connell, Evan Shelby, Jr.
Mrs. Bridge (Viking) NYT fic 2/8/59 (#15), pk 3/29/59 (#8, 1 wk), 13 wk; PW fic 3/30/59 (#6, 1 wk), 4 wk; tot 17 wk.

Son of the Morning Star (North Point) NYT nf 12/16/84 (#14), pk 2/24/85 (#4, 2 wk), 25 wk; PW hc nf 1/18/85 (#15), pk 3/1/85 (#8, 1 wk), 13 wk; (Harper) PW td pb 10/11/85 (#10), pk 11/15/85 (#8, 1 wk), 8 wk; NYT pb nf 10/20/85 (#5), pk 1/5/86 (#3, 1 wk), 8 wk; tot 54 wk.

Connelly, Marcus Cook
The Green Pastures (Holt) PW nf 7/12/30 (#4, 4 wk), 20 wk.

Connor, Ralph
The Sky Pilot of No Man's Land (Doran) PW fic 5/3/19 (#3), pk 6/7/19 (#2, 4 wk), 16 wk.

Conrad, Barnaby

Matador (Houghton) NYT fic 7/13/52 (#9), pk 8/3/52 (#3, 2 wk), 21 wk; PW fic 8/2/52 (#5), pk 8/9/52 (#4, 4 wk), 13 wk; tot 34 wk.

Death of Manolete (Houghton) NYT gen 8/10/58 (#10, 2 wk), 6 wk.

Conrad, Joseph

The Arrow of Gold (Doubleday) PW fic 6/7/19 (#9), pk 7/5/19 (#2, 8 wk), 20 wk.

The Rescue (Doubleday) PW fic 8/14/20 (#5, 4 wk), 8 wk.

The Rover (Doubleday) PW fic 4/19/24 (#7, 4 wk).

Conran, Shirley

Lace (Simon & Schuster) PW hc fic 8/20/82 (#12), pk 9/24/82 (#4, 2 wk), 14 wk; NYT fic 8/29/82 (#15), pk 9/26/82 (#6, 2 wk), 13 wk; (Pocket) NYT mm pb 7/10/83 (#9), pk 7/24/83 (#2, 1 wk), 19 wk; PW mm pb 7/15/83 (#10), pk 7/22/83 (#3, 3 wk), 18 wk; tot 64 wk.

Lace II (Pocket) NYT pb fic 3/17/85 (#7, 3 wk), 6 wk; PW mm pb 3/22/85 (#9), pk 3/29/85 (#6, 1 wk), 6 wk; tot 12 wk.

Savages (Pocket) NYT pb fic 7/17/88 (#11), pk 7/24/88 (#9, 1 wk), 6 wk; PW mm pb 7/22/88 (#11, 2 wk), 6 wk; tot 12 wk.

Conroy, Pat

The Lords of Discipline (Bantam) PW mm pb 2/5/82 (#11, 1 wk), 2 wk; NYT mm pb 2/14/82 (#15, 2 wk); tot 4 wk.

The Prince of Tides (Houghton) NYT fic 10/5/86 (#10), pk 10/26/86 (#4, 2 wk), 51 wk; PW hc fic 10/10/86 (#15), pk 11/7/86 (#5, 2 wk), 42 wk; (Bantam) NYT pb fic 12/6/87 (#6), pk 12/13/87 (#3, 6 wk), 29 wk; PW mm pb 12/11/87 (#10), pk 1/29/88 (#3, 1 wk), 40 wk; tot 162 wk.

Considine, Robert [Bob]

It's the Irish (Doubleday) NYT gen 10/15/61 (#15, 1 wk).

See also Babe Ruth and_____

See also Jack Dempsey, et al.

See also Gen. Jonathan Mayhew Wainwright and_____

Conway, James

Napa (Todd/Houghton) NYT nf 11/4/90 (#17, 1 wk).

Conway, Jill Ker

The Road from Coorain (Vintage) NYT pb nf 9/16/90 (#7), pk 12/2/90 (#2, 1 wk), 16 wk.

Cook, Fannie

Mrs. Palmer's Honey (Doubleday) NYT fic 3/3/46 (#15, 3 wk), 6 wk.

Cook, Robin

Coma: A Novel (Little Brown) PW hc fic 7/11/77 (#10), pk 9/19/77 (#6, 1 wk), 16 wk; NYT fic 7/24/77 (#9), pk 9/11/77 (#6, 3 wk), 13 wk; (NAL/Signet) NYT mm pb 12/18/77 (#14), pk 1/1/78 (#1, 14 wk), 25 wk; PW mm pb 12/12/77 (#6), pk 1/23/78 (#1, 12 wk), 23 wk; tot 77 wk.

Sphinx (Putnam) PW hc fic 6/11/79 (#15), pk 7/9/79 (#9, 1 wk), 10 wk; NYT fic 7/1/79 (#13), pk 7/8/79 (#8, 1 wk), 7 wk; (NAL/Signet) PW mm pb 5/16/80 (#8), pk 5/30/80 (#6, 2 wk), 9 wk; NYT mm pb 5/18/80 (#12), pk 6/1/80 (#5, 1 wk), 9 wk; tot 35 wk.

Brain (Putnam) PW hc fic 2/13/81 (#7), pk 3/27/81 (#2, 3 wk), 18 wk; NYT fic 2/15/81 (#11), pk 3/22/81 (#2, 2 wk), 14 wk; (NAL/Signet) mm pb 1/10/82 (#13), pk 1/17/82 (#3, 1 wk), 10 wk; PW mm pb 1/15/82 (#3, 1 wk), 8 wk; tot 50 wk.

Fever (Putnam) PW hc fic 2/19/82 (#7), pk 3/26/82 (#3, 3 wk), 15 wk; NYT fic 2/28/82 (#13), pk 4/11/82 (#7, 2 wk), 11 wk; (NAL/Signet) NYT mm pb 1/2/83 (#14), pk 1/23/83 (#1, 1 wk), 10 wk; PW mm pb 1/7/83 (#14), pk 1/21/83 (#2, 2 wk), 10 wk; tot 46 wk.

Godplayer (Putnam) PW hc fic 7/8/83 (#14), pk 8/5/83 (#5, 3 wk), 13 wk; NYT fic 7/10/83 (#15), pk 7/31/83 (#4, 3 wk), 11 wk; (NAL/Signet) NYT pb fic 6/3/84 (#9), pk 6/10/84 (#2, 1 wk), 9 wk; PW mm pb 6/8/84 (#8), pk 6/22/84 (#2, 2 wk), 9 wk; tot 42 wk.

Mindbend (Putnam) PW hc fic 3/15/85 (#14), pk 3/29/85 (#5, 1 wk), 9 wk; NYT fic 3/17/85 (#9, 3 wk), 8 wk; (NAL/Signet) NYT pb fic 1/5/86 (#11), pk 1/19/86 (#8, 3 wk), 7 wk; PW mm pb 1/17/86 (#6), pk 1/31/86 (#5, 1 wk), 5 wk; tot 29 wk.

Outbreak (Putnam) PW hc fic 2/20/87 (#12), pk 3/13/87 (#5, 1 wk), 10 wk; NYT fic 2/22/87 (#11), pk 3/15/87 (#4, 4 wk), 9 wk; (Berkley) NYT pb fic 1/31/88 (#5), pk 2/7/88 (#2, 3 wk), 9 wk; PW mm pb 2/5/88 (#8), pk 2/12/88 (#3, 3 wk), 8 wk; tot 36 wk.

Mortal Fear (Putnam) PW hc fic 1/29/88 (#11), pk 2/19/88 (#6, 1 wk), 11 wk; NYT fic 1/31/88 (#14), pk 2/28/88 (#10, 1 wk), 9 wk; (Berkley) NYT pb fic 1/29/89 (#11), pk 2/19/89 (#3, 1 wk), 7 wk; PW mm pb 2/3/89 (#10), pk 2/10/89 (#2, 1 wk), 8 wk; tot 35 wk.

Mutation (Putnam) PW hc fic 1/27/89 (#11), pk 2/10/89 (#5, 2 wk), 10 wk; NYT fic 1/29/89 (#12), pk 2/5/89 (#6, 3 wk), 9 wk; (Berkley) NYT pb fic 1/28/90 (#12), pk 2/11/90 (#2, 2 wk), 9 wk; PW mm pb 2/2/90 (#13), pk 2/9/90 (#3, 3 wk), 8 wk; tot 36 wk.

Harmful Intent (Putnam) NYT fic 1/14/90 (#15), pk 1/28/90 (#4, 1 wk), 8 wk; PW hc fic

1/19/90 (#8), pk 2/9/90 (#4, 1 wk), 9 wk; tot 17 wk.

Cooke, Alistair
A Generation on Trial: USA vs. Alger Hiss (Knopf) NYT gen 10/22/50 (#16, 1 wk).
One Man's America (Knopf) NYT gen 6/8/52 (#16), pk 7/27/52 (#15, 1 wk), 4 wk.
Alistair Cooke's America (Knopf) PW nf 11/12/73 (#6), pk 12/10/73 (#1, 4 wk), 24 wk; NYT gen 11/18/73 (#7), pk 12/9/73 (#1, 9 wk), 27 wk; tot 51 wk.
Six Men (Knopf) PW hc nf 10/10/77 (#10), pk 11/7/77 (#4, 2 wk), 17 wk; NYT nf 10/16/77 (#13), pk 11/27/77 (#3, 1 wk), 15 wk; tot 32 wk.
The Americans: 50 Talks on Our Life and Times (Knopf) NYT nf 12/23/79 (#10), pk 1/6/80 (#6, 2 wk), 12 wk; PW hc nf 12/24/79 (#14), pk 1/18/80 (#9, 1 wk), 7 wk; tot 19 wk.

Coolidge, Calvin
The Autobiography of Calvin Coolidge (Cosmopolitan) PW nf 12/14/29 (#9), pk 1/11/30 (#8, 4 wk), 8 wk.

Coon, Carleton Stevens
The Story of Man (Knopf) NYT gen 12/5/54 (#11, 1 wk), 2 wk.

Cooney, Barbara
See Geoffrey Chaucer

Coonts, Stephen
Flight of the Intruder (Naval Institute Press) PW hc fic 10/24/86 (#13), pk 1/9/87 (#4, 3 wk), 28 wk; NYT fic 11/2/86 (#12), pk 11/30/86 (#7, 9 wk), 28 wk; (Pocket) NYT pb fic 10/18/87 (#5), pk 11/1/87 (#3, 1 wk), 9 wk; PW mm pb 10/23/87 (#8), pk 11/6/87 (#5, 1 wk), 8 wk; tot 73 wk.
Final Flight (Doubleday) NYT fic 10/16/88 (#11), pk 10/23/88 (#4, 2 wk), 16 wk; PW hc fic 10/21/88 (#9), pk 11/4/88 (#4, 3 wk), 14 wk; (Dell) NYT pb fic 10/8/89 (#10, 10/29/89 (#3, 2 wk), 8 wk; PW mm pb 10/13/89 (#7), pk 10/27/89 (#1, 1 wk), 8 wk; tot 46 wk.
The Minotaur (Doubleday) PW hc fic 10/13/89 (#14), pk 10/27/89 (#6, 3 wk), 9 wk; NYT fic 10/15/89 (#12), pk 10/22/89 (#7, 1 wk), 6 wk; (Dell) NYT pb fic 10/7/90 (#13), pk 10/28/90 (#3, 1 wk), 8 wk; PW mm pb 10/19/90 (#7), pk 11/2/90 (#5, 2 wk), 7 wk; tot 30 wk.
Under Siege (Pocket) NYT fic 10/21/90 (#17), pk 11/25/90 (#8, 1 wk), 7 wk; PW hc fic 10/26/90 (#12), pk 11/23/90 (#7, 1 wk), 9 wk; tot 16 wk.

Cooper, Courtney Ryley
Designs in Scarlet (Little Brown) NYT gen 5/7/39 (#8, 4 wk); PW nf 5/13/39 (#7, 8 wk), 12 wk; tot 16 wk.

Cooper, Dr. Kenneth H.
Aerobics (Evans/Lippincott) NYT pb gen 5/5/68 (#2), pk 7/7/68 (#1, 4 wk), 28 wk.
Controlling Cholesterol: Dr. Kenneth H. Cooper's Preventative Medicine Program (Bantam) NYT msc 4/10/88 (#4), pk 5/8/88 (#3, 2 wk), 18 wk; PW hc nf 4/22/88 (#7, 1 wk), 7 wk; NYT msc pb 2/12/89 (#5), pk 2/19/89 (#4, 2 wk), 4 wk; tot 29 wk.

Cooper, Madison A.
Sironia, Texas (Houghton) NYT fic 11/23/52 (#9), pk 11/30/52 (#7, 1 wk), 10 wk.

Cooper, Morton
The King (Geis/NAL) NYT pb fic 2/4/68 (#5), pk 3/3/68 (#3, 4 wk), 12 wk.

Coover, Robert
The Public Burning (Viking) NYT fic 10/2/77 (#15, 1 wk).

Copeland, Miles
The Game of Nations (Simon & Schuster) NYT gen 6/28/70 (#10, 1 wk).

Coppel, Alfred
Thirty-Four East (Harcourt) NYT fic 6/9/74 (#10, 1 wk); (Popular) NYT mm pb 5/25/75 (#9, 1 wk), 2 wk; tot 3 wk.

Corbett, Elizabeth Frances
Mrs. Meigs and Mr. Cunningham (Appleton) NYT fic 10/4/36 (#5, 4 wk).
She Was Carrie Eaton (Appleton) NYT fic 10/9/38 (#7, 4 wk).
Light of Other Days (Appleton) NYT fic 4/3/38 (#4, 4 wk).
Charley Manning (Appleton) NYT fic 10/8/39 (#10, 4 wk).
The Red-Haired Lady (Doubleday) NYT fic 6/24/45 (#15), pk 7/1/45 (#13, 1 wk), 2 wk.

Corbett, James Edward
Man-Eaters of Kumaon (Oxford Univ.) NYT gen 4/28/46 (#11), pk 5/5/46 (#9, 1 wk), 7 wk.

Cordell, Alexander
The Rape of the Fair Country (Doubleday) NYT fic 6/14/59 (#12, 1 wk).

Corle, Edwin
Coarse Gold (Dutton) NYT fic 11/15/42 (#18), pk 12/27/42 (#17, 1 wk), 2 wk.

Corman, Avery
Kramer Versus Kramer (NAL/Signet) PW mm pb 11/13/78 (#12), pk 1/18/80 (#6, 1 wk), 13 wk; NYT mm pb 11/19/78 (#11), pk 11/26/78 (#8, 1 wk), 13 wk; tot 26 wk.
The Old Neighborhood (Linden/Simon & Schuster) NYT fic 11/9/80 (#14, 3 wk), 4 wk; PW mm pb 9/25/81 (#15, 1 wk); tot 5 wk.

Cornell, Katharine, as told to Ruth Woodbury Sedgwick
I Wanted to Be an Actress (Random) NYT gen 5/7/39 (#6, 4 wk).

Corwin, Norman
On a Note of Triumph (Simon & Schuster) NYT fic 6/10/45 (#5, 1 wk), 8 wk.

Coryn, Marjorie
Good-Bye My Son (Appleton) NYT fic 4/11/43 (#16, 1 wk).

Cosby, Bill
Fatherhood (Doubleday/Dolphin) NYT nf 5/11/86 (#9), pk 5/25/86 (#1, 26 wk), 55 wk; PW hc nf 5/16/86 (#13), pk 6/6/86 (#1, 22 wk), 53 wk; (Berkley) NYT pb nf 5/3/87 (#2), pk 5/10/87 (#1, 14 wk), 50 wk; PW td pb 5/8/87 (#3), pk 5/15/87 (#1, 8 wk), 40 wk; tot 198 wk.

Time Flies (Doubleday/Dolphin) NYT nf 10/4/87 (#5), pk 12/6/87 (#1, 6 wk), 22 wk; PW hc nf 10/9/87 (#6), pk 12/11/87 (#1, 5 wk), 20 wk; (Bantam) NYT pb nf 12/4/88 (#4), pk 12/11/88 (#2, 7 wk), 11 wk; PW mm pb 12/16/88 (#8), pk 12/23/88 (#4, 1 wk), 7 wk; tot 60 wk.

Love and Marriage (Doubleday) NYT nf 4/30/89 (#2, 3 wk), 18 wk; PW hc nf 5/5/89 (#9), pk 5/12/89 (#4, 4 wk), 16 wk; (Bantam) NYT pb nf 5/13/90 (#2), pk 5/20/90 (#1, 2 wk), 10 wk; PW mm pb 5/18/90 (#14), pk 5/25/90 (#9, 1 wk), 5 wk; tot 49 wk.

Coscarelli, Kate
Fame and Fortune (NAL/Signet) NYT pb fic 3/17/85 (#9), pk 3/24/85 (#8, 2 wk), 4 wk; PW mm pb 3/22/85 (#11, 2 wk), 5 wk; tot 9 wk.

Perfect Order (NAL/Onyx) NYT pb fic 8/24/86 (#14, 1 wk).

Cosell, Howard
Cosell (Playboy) NYT gen 10/14/73 (#10), pk 12/30/73 (#5, 2 wk), 21 wk; PW nf 10/29/73 (#10), pk 11/12/73 (#5, 1 wk), 16 wk; (Pocket) NYT mm pb 8/11/74 (#7, 4 wk); tot 41 wk.

_____, **with Peter Bonventure**
I Never Played the Game (Morrow) NYT nf 10/20/85 (#14), pk 12/15/85 (#3, 6 wk), 21 wk; PW hc nf 11/1/85 (#7), 1/3/86 (#3, 3 wk), 16 wk; tot 37 wk.

Costain, Thomas Bertram
For My Great Folly (Putnam) NYT fic 9/6/42 (#13), pk 9/20/42 (#9, 1 wk), 3 wk.

Ride with Me (Doubleday) NYT fic 9/10/44 (#13), pk 9/24/44 (#12, 1 wk), 3 wk.

The Black Rose (Doubleday) NYT fic 9/16/45 (#7), pk 10/7/45 (#1, 17 wk), 39 wk; PW

fic 9/22/45 (#5), pk 10/6/45 (#1, 18 wk), 34 wk; tot 73 wk.

The Moneyman (Doubleday) NYT fic 8/3/47 (#4), pk 8/17/47 (#1, 12 wk), 31 wk; PW fic 8/9/47 (#4), pk 8/23/47 (#1, 13 wk), 27 wk; tot 58 wk.

The Conquerors (Doubleday) NYT gen 11/13/49 (#14), pk 11/27/49 (#10, 1 wk), 5 wk.

High Towers (Doubleday) NYT fic 1/23/49 (#6), pk 2/13/49 (#3, 6 wk), 18 wk; PW fic 2/5/49 (#3, 8 wk), 11 wk; tot 29 wk.

Son of a Hundred Kings (Doubleday) NYT fic 11/12/50 (#6), pk 12/17/50 (#2, 1 wk), 19 wk; PW fic 11/18/50 (#9), pk 12/2/50 (#1, 1 wk), 14 wk; tot 33 wk.

The Magnificent Century (Doubleday) NYT gen 10/7/51 (#16), pk 11/11/51 (#4, 1 wk), 10 wk; PW nf 10/27/51 (#5), pk 11/3/51 (#4, 1 wk), 3 wk; tot 13 wk.

The Silver Chalice (Doubleday) NYT fic 8/3/52 (#14), pk 9/7/52 (#1, 15 wk), 68 wk; PW fic 8/16/52 (#9), pk 9/6/52 (#1, 17 wk), 53 wk; tot 121 wk.

The White and the Gold (Doubleday) NYT gen 10/24/54 (#15), pk 11/28/54 (#14, 1 wk), 3 wk.

The Tontine (Doubleday) NYT fic 10/9/55 (#15), pk 11/6/55 (#3, 2 wk), 23 wk; PW fic 10/29/55 (#3, 2 wk), 13 wk; tot 36 wk.

Below the Salt (Doubleday) NYT fic 10/13/57 (#7), pk 11/17/57 (#3, 11 wk), 26 wk; PW fic 10/28/57 (#6), pk 12/2/57 (#2, 6 wk), 21 wk; tot 47 wk.

The Three Edwards (Doubleday) NYT gen 11/9/58 (#15), pk 1/11/59 (#7, 2 wk), 13 wk; PW nf 12/1/58 (#7), pk 2/9/59 (#3, 1 wk), 5 wk; tot 18 wk.

The Darkness and the Dawn (Doubleday) NYT fic 11/1/59 (#13), pk 11/29/59 (#4, 1 wk), 19 wk; PW fic 11/16/59 (#9), pk 12/7/59 (#2, 1 wk), 14 wk; tot 33 wk.

The Last Plantagenets (Doubleday) NYT gen 2/18/62 (#14), pk 3/11/62 (#5, 1 wk), 19 wk; PW nf 3/5/62 (#9), pk 3/19/62 (#4, 1 wk), 15 wk; tot 34 wk.

Costello, John
See Edwin T. Layton, et al.

Costello, William
The Facts About Nixon (Viking) NYT gen 2/7/60 (#12), pk 2/14/60 (#11, 1 wk), 4 wk.

Coulson, Maj. Thomas
Mata Hari (Harper) PW nf 7/12/30 (#9, 4 wk).

Coulter, Catherine
Moonspun Magic (NAL/Onyx) NYT pb fic 8/14/88 (#13, 1 wk).

Night Shadow (Avon) NYT pb fic 8/6/89

(#7, 1 wk), 3 wk; PW mm pb 8/11/89 (#11, 1 wk); tot 4 wk.

Night Fire (Avon) NYT pb fic 2/5/89 (#14, 2 wk); PW mm pb 2/17/89 (#14), pk 2/24/89 (#13, 1 wk), 3 wk; tot 5 wk.

False Pretenses (NAL/Onyx) NYT pb fic 5/21/89 (#14, 1 wk).

Night Storm (Avon) NYT pb fic 2/4/90 (#15), pk 2/11/90 (#7, 1 wk), 4 wk; PW mm pb 2/23/90 (#9), pk 3/2/90 (#7, 1 wk), 2 wk; tot 6 wk.

Earth Song (NAL/Onyx) NYT pb fic 9/16/90 (#7, 1 wk), 2 wk.

Courter, Gay

The Midwife (Houghton) NYT fic 4/26/81 (#15), pk 5/3/81 (#14, 1 wk), 4 wk; (NAL/Signet) PW mm pb 5/14/82 (#5), pk 7/2/82 (#3, 1 wk), 12 wk; NYT mm pb 5/16/82 (#6), pk 7/4/82 (#5, 1 wk), 13 wk; tot 29 wk.

River of Dreams (NAL/Signet) NYT pb fic 4/14/85 (#10, 2 wk), 4 wk; PW mm pb 4/19/85 (#13), pk 4/26/85 (#9, 1 wk), 3 wk; tot 7 wk.

Code Ezra (NAL/Signet) NYT pb fic 8/23/87 (#14, 1 wk).

Courtney, Marguerite Taylor

Laurette (Rinehart) NYT gen 5/22/55 (#12), pk 6/5/55 (#11, 2 wk), 11 wk.

Cousins, Norman

Modern Man Is Obsolete (Viking) NYT gen 11/25/45 (#15), pk 12/2/45 (#14, 1 wk), 2 wk.

Dr. Schweitzer of Lambarene (Harper) NYT gen 7/24/60 (#16), pk 8/7/60 (#15, 1 wk), 2 wk.

Anatomy of an Illness as Perceived by the Patient (Norton) NYT nf 11/25/79 (#11), pk 3/16/80 (#2, 1 wk), 47 wk; PW hc nf 12/10/79 (#12), pk 3/7/79 (#3, 2 wk), 40 wk; (Bantam) td pb 4/24/81 (#9), pk 5/1/81 (#8, 1 wk), 2 wk; NYT td pb 4/26/81 (#8), pk 5/10/81 (#4, 1 wk), 12 wk; tot 101 wk.

Head First: The Biology of Hope (Dutton) NYT nf 11/19/89 (#13), pk 5/6/90 (#3, 1 wk), 24 wk; PW hc nf 11/24/89 (#15), pk 5/11/90 (#9, 2 wk), 6 wk; tot 30 wk.

Cousteau, Jacques Y., and Frederic Dumas

The Silent World (Harper) NYT gen 2/22/53 (#8), pk 3/29/53 (#3, 13 wk), 39 wk; PW nf 3/7/53 (#5), pk 3/21/53 (#3, 14 wk), 28 wk; tot 67 wk.

Cove, Emile

Self-Mastery Through Conscious Autosuggestion (American Library Service) PW gen lit 9/16/22 (#11), pk 3/3/23 (#1, 8 wk), 32 wk.

Covey, Stephen R.

The Seven Habits of Highly Effective People

(Simon & Schuster) PW hc nf 2/23/90 (#14), pk 4/20/90 (#12, 4 wk), 16 wk; PW aud nf 10/5/90 (#6), pk 11/2/90 (#2, 8 wk), 12 wk; (Simon & Schuster/Fireside) NYT msc pb 10/21/90 (#3, 2 wk), 5 wk; PW td pb 11/9/90 (#8), pk 11/23/90 (#7, 1 wk), 4 wk; tot 37 wk.

Cowan, Dr. Connell, and Dr. Melvyn Kinder

Smart Women, Foolish Choices: Finding the Right Men and Avoiding the Wrong Ones (Potter) NYT nf 4/7/85 (#9), pk 5/12/85 (#2, 3 wk), 39 wk; PW hc nf 4/14/85 (#10), pk 5/17/85 (#2, 1 wk), 31 wk; (NAL) NYT pb nf 3/16/86 (#5), pk 4/6/86 (#1, 1 wk), 36 wk; PW mm pb 3/21/86 (#11), pk 4/11/86 (#5, 1 wk), 8 wk; tot 114 wk.

Women Men Love, Women Men Leave (Potter/Crown) PW hc nf 6/5/87 (#15), pk 7/3/87 (#5, 1 wk), 10 wk; NYT msc 6/7/87 (#4), pk 7/19/87 (#1, 1 wk), 12 wk; (NAL/Signet) PW mm pb 5/27/88 (#14, 1 wk); NYT msc pb 6/5/88 (#4, 1 wk), 2 wk; tot 25 wk.

Coward, Noel

Present Indicative (Doubleday) PW nf 5/8/37 (#4), pk 7/10/37 (#2, 4 wk), 24 wk; NYT gen 5/9/37 (#2, 4 wk), 20 wk; tot 44 wk.

To Step Aside (Doubleday) NYT fic 1/7/40 (#15, 4 wk).

Future Indefinite (Doubleday) NYT gen 8/8/54 (#16), pk 8/22/54 (#12, 2 wk), 6 wk.

Pomp and Circumstance (Doubleday) NYT fic 12/4/60 (#15), pk 3/5/61 (#7, 1 wk), 28 wk; PW fic 1/2/61 (#10), pk 2/13/61 (#7, 2 wk), 14 wk; tot 42 wk.

Cowles, Virginia

Looking for Trouble (Harper) PW nf 9/13/41 (#6), pk 10/11/41 (#5, 4 wk), 8 wk.

Cox, Deborah, and Juliet Davis

30 Days to a More Beautiful Bottom (Bantam) PW td pb 9/10/82 (#8), pk 10/22/82 (#7, 3 wk), 13 wk; NYT td pb 9/26/82 (#9), pk 11/14/82 (#6, 1 wk), 10 wk; tot 23 wk.

Cox, Harvey G.

The Secular City (Macmillan) NYT pb gen 5/1/66 (#4, 16 wk).

Coyle, Harold

Team Yankee: A Novel of World War III (Presidio) NYT fic 9/20/87 (#15), pk 10/11/87 (#12, 1 wk), 3 wk; PW hc fic 9/25/87 (#10, 1 wk), 10 wk; (Berkley) PW mm pb 9/2/88 (#10), pk 9/23/88 (#1, 3 wk), 10 wk; NYT pb fic 9/4/88 (#8), pk 9/25/88 (#2, 1 wk), 8 wk; tot 31 wk.

Sword Point (Simon & Schuster) PW hc fic 10/7/88 (#15), pk 10/21/88 (#12, 1 wk), 4 wk; NYT fic 10/16/88 (#12, 1 wk); (Pocket) NYT pb fic 8/13/89 (#8), pk 8/20/89 (#7, 2 wk), 5 wk; PW mm pb 8/18/89 (#9, 2 wk), 4 wk; tot 14 wk.

Bright Star (Simon & Schuster) NYT fic 4/22/90 (#12), pk 5/13/90 (#9, 1 wk), 5 wk; PW hc fic 4/27/90 (#10), pk 5/4/90 (#8, 2 wk), 8 wk; tot 13 wk.

Coyne, John
The Legacy (Berkley) PW mm pb 5/21/79 (#10), pk 6/11/79 (#7, 1 wk), 6 wk; NYT mm pb 5/27/79 (#13), pk 6/10/79 (#12, 1 wk), 3 wk; tot 9 wk.

The Piercing (Berkley) NYT mm pb 8/3/80 (#13, 1 wk), 2 wk.

Cozzens, James Gould
The Last Adam (Harcourt) PW fic 2/11/33 (#5), pk 3/11/33 (#3, 4 wk), 12 wk.

Men and Brethren (Harcourt) NYT fic 2/2/36 (#8, 4 wk).

The Just and the Unjust (Harcourt) NYT fic 8/9/42 (#16), pk 9/20/42 (#8, 1 wk), 9 wk; PW fic 9/12/42 (#8, 1 wk); tot 10 wk.

Guard of Honor (Harcourt) NYT fic 1/16/49 (#14), pk 5/29/49 (#13, 2 wk), 5 wk.

By Love Possessed (Harcourt) NYT fic 9/8/57 (#14), pk 9/22/57 (#1, 24 wk), 41 wk; PW fic 9/16/57 (#4), pk 9/30/57 (#1, 22 wk), 35 wk; tot 76 wk.

Children and Others (Harcourt) PW fic 9/28/64 (#11, 1 wk).

Crabb, Larry
Inside Out (NavPress) PW hc rel 11/9/90 (#16, 4 wk).

Craig, John D.
Danger Is My Business (Simon & Schuster) NYT nf 4/3/38 (#9, 4 wk); PW nf 5/14/38 (#9, 4 wk); tot 8 wk.

Craig, Marjorie
Miss Craig's 21-Day Shape-Up Program for Men and Women (Random) NYT gen 1/5/69 (#10), pk 3/23/69 (#3, 4 wk), 32 wk; PW nf 3/10/69 (#8), pk 4/7/69 (#4, 7 wk), 30 wk; tot 62 wk.

Craig, William
The Fall of Japan (Dial) PW nf 10/2/67 (#10, 3 wk), 4 wk.

Cran, William
See Robert McCrum, et al.

Crane, Aimee
A Gallery of Great Paintings [ed.] (Crown) NYT gen 12/3/44 (#14, 1 wk).

Crane, Cheryl, with Cliff Jahr
Detour: A Hollywood Story (Belvedere/Arbor House/Morrow) NYT nf 1/31/88 (#15), pk 2/21/88 (#8, 2 wk), 10 wk; PW hc

nf 2/5/88 (#14), pk 2/19/88 (#7, 2 wk), 7 wk; (Avon) NYT pb nf 1/29/89 (#10, 1 wk); tot 18 wk.

Crankshaw, Edward
Cracks in the Kremlin Wall (Viking) NYT gen 9/9/51 (#15, 1 wk), 2 wk.

Craven, Margaret
I Heard the Owl Call My Name (Doubleday) PW fic 2/11/74 (#9), pk 4/15/74 (#6, 2 wk), 18 wk; NYT fic 3/3/74 (#9), pk 5/26/74 (#6, 1 wk), 20 wk; (Dell) NYT mm pb 1/12/75 (#8, 1 wk); tot 39 wk.

Craven, Thomas
Men of Art (Simon & Schuster) PW nf 5/16/31 (#7, 4 wk).

Modern Art (Simon & Schuster) PW nf 7/14/34 (#8, 8 wk), 12 wk.

A Treasury of Art Masterpieces [ed.] (Simon & Schuster) NYT gen 11/5/39 (#1, 4 wk), 12 wk; PW nf 11/11/39 (#4), pk 12/16/39 (#2, 8 wk), 16 wk; tot 28 wk.

Crawford, Christina
Mommie Dearest (Morrow) PW hc nf 11/6/78 (#11), pk 1/15/79 (#1, 3 wk), 45 wk; NYT nf 11/19/78 (#5), pk 11/26/78 (#1, 10 wk), 42 wk; (Berkley) PW mm pb 11/5/79 (#3), pk 11/19/79 (#1, 4 wk), 19 wk; NYT mm pb 11/11/79 (#2), pk 11/18/79 (#1, 3 wk), 15 wk; tot 121 wk.

Crawford, Marion
The Little Princesses (Harcourt) NYT gen 7/30/50 (#16), pk 9/3/50 (#1, 2 wk), 22 wk; PW nf 8/12/50 (#6), pk 8/19/50 (#1, 4 wk), 11 wk; tot 33 wk.

Mother and Queen (Prentice Hall) NYT gen 2/3/52 (#15, 1 wk).

Elizabeth the Queen (Prentice Hall) NYT gen 4/6/52 (#14), pk 5/4/52 (#5, 1 wk), 14 wk; PW nf 5/17/52 (#7), pk 6/14/52 (#5, 1 wk), 2 wk; tot 16 wk.

Creasey, John
The Man in the Blue Mask [as by Anthony Morton] NYT fic 3/7/37 (#5, 4 wk).

Creel, George
The War, the World and Wilson (Harper) PW gen lit 9/25/20 (#9), pk 10/23/20 (#7, 8 wk), 12 wk.

Crenna, Richard
See Tom Clancy

Crews, Frederick C.
The Pooh Perplex (Dutton) PW nf 1/20/64 (#9, 1 wk).

Crichton, Kyle Samuel
The Marx Brothers (Doubleday) NYT gen 7/16/50 (#12, 2 wk), 3 wk.

See also Cordelia Drexel Biddle and_____

Crichton, Michael
The Andromeda Strain (Knopf) NYT fic 6/29/69 (#8), pk 10/5/69 (#3, 3 wk), 30 wk; PW fic 7/7/69 (#7), pk 9/29/69 (#2, 2 wk), 26 wk; NYT pb fic 7/5/70 (#2, 8 wk), 32 wk; tot 88 wk.

The Terminal Man (Knopf) NYT fic 5/21/72 (#8), pk 8/6/72 (#5, 1 wk), 19 wk; PW fic 5/29/72 (#5), pk 7/10/72 (#4, 2 wk), 16 wk; NYT pb fic 5/13/73 (#2, 4 wk), 8 wk; tot 43 wk.

The Great Train Robbery (Knopf) PW fic 6/23/75 (#10), pk 7/14/75 (#3, 3 wk), 24 wk; NYT fic 6/29/75 (#9), pk 8/3/75 (#3, 5 wk), 23 wk; (Bantam) PW mm pb 6/21/76 (#7), pk 7/12/76 (#2, 1 wk), 11 wk; NYT mm pb 6/27/76 (#7), pk 7/11/76 (#6, 2 wk), 6 wk; tot 64 wk.

Congo (Knopf) PW hc fic 12/5/80 (#13, 1 wk), 4 wk; NYT fic 12/28/80 (#13), pk 2/15/81 (#6, 1 wk), 12 wk; (Avon) NYT mm pb 10/25/81 (#9), pk 11/15/81 (#2, 1 wk), 12 wk; PW mm pb 10/30/81 (#7), pk 11/6/81 (#3, 3 wk), 10 wk; tot 38 wk.

Sphere (Ballantine) NYT fic 6/21/87 (#13), pk 8/9/87 (#6, 1 wk), 13 wk; PW hc fic 6/26/87 (#12), pk 8/14/87 (#7, 1 wk), 14 wk; NYT pb fic 7/31/88 (#14), pk 8/21/88 (#3, 2 wk), 11 wk; PW mm pb 8/12/88 (#3, 5 wk), 10 wk; tot 48 wk.

Jurassic Park (Knopf) PW hc fic 11/30/90 (#11), pk 12/14/90 (#6, 2 wk), 4 wk; NYT fic 12/2/90 (#12), pk 12/16/90 (#8, 3 wk), 5 wk; tot 9 wk.

Crichton, Robert
The Great Imposter (Random) NYT gen 8/9/59 (#16), pk 9/27/59 (#8, 2 wk), 16 wk; PW nf 10/19/59 (#8, 1 wk); tot 17 wk.

The Secret of Santa Vittoria (Simon & Schuster) PW fic 9/5/66 (#10), pk 11/7/66 (#1, 20 wk), 47 wk; NYT fic 9/18/66 (#8), pk 11/20/66 (#1, 18 wk), 47 wk; NYT pb fic 11/5/67 (#3), pk 1/7/68 (#2, 8 wk), 20 wk; tot 114 wk.

The Camerons (Knopf) NYT fic 11/26/72 (#10), pk 12/17/72 (#5, 5 wk), 21 wk; PW fic 11/27/72 (#10), pk 1/15/73 (#4, 2 wk), 19 wk; (Warner) NYT mm pb 3/10/74 (#4, 4 wk), 8 wk; tot 48 wk.

Crispin, A.C.
Yesterday's Son (Pocket) NYT mm pb 8/14/83 (#14, 1 wk).

V. (Pinnacle) NYT pb fic 4/29/84 (#9), pk 5/27/84 (#2, 1 wk), 6 wk; PW mm pb 5/11/84 (#12), pk 6/1/84 (#4, 1 wk), 5 wk; tot 11 wk.

Time for Yesterday (Pocket) NYT pb fic 4/10/88 (#13), pk 4/17/88 (#6, 1 wk), 4 wk; PW mm pb 4/22/88 (#12), pk 4/29/88 (#7, 1 wk), 3 wk; tot 7 wk.

The Eyes of the Beholders (Pocket) NYT pb fic 9/16/90 (#9, 1 wk), 2 wk.

Crittenden, Louise
See Rose Jeanne Slifer and_____

Crockett, James Underwood
Crockett's Victory Garden (Little Brown) PW td pb 6/20/77 (#4), pk 6/19/78 (#1, 1 wk), 37 wk; NYT td pb 7/3/77 (#4), pk 7/9/78 (#1, 1 wk), 77 wk; tot 114 wk.

Crockett's Indoor Garden (Little Brown) NYT td pb 11/12/78 (#13), pk 1/7/79 (#4, 2 wk), 15 wk; PW td pb 11/20/78 (#10), pk 1/15/79 (#4, 1 wk), 8 wk; tot 23 wk.

Crockett, Lucy Herndon
The Magnificent Bastards (Farrar) NYT fic 5/9/54 (#15, 1 wk).

Cromie, Robert Allen
The Great Chicago Fire (McGraw) NYT gen 11/2/58 (#15), pk 11/9/58 (#11, 1 wk), 10 wk.

Cronin, A.J.
Hatter's Castle (Little Brown) PW fic 9/19/31 (#4, 4 wk), 12 wk.

Three Loves (Little Brown) PW fic 5/14/32 (#2, 4 wk), 12 wk.

Grand Canary (Little Brown) PW fic 6/10/33 (#3, 4 wk), 12 wk.

The Stars Look Down (Little Brown) NYT fic 11/3/35 (#1, 4 wk); PW fic 11/9/35 (#3, 4 wk), 12 wk; tot 16 wk.

The Citadel (Little Brown) PW fic 10/9/37 (#3), pk 12/11/37 (#1, 28 wk), 64 wk; NYT fic 10/10/37 (#1, 16 wk), 64 wk; tot 128 wk.

The Keys of the Kingdom (Little Brown) PW fic 8/16/41 (#3), pk 9/13/41 (#1, 20 wk), 40 wk.

The Green Years (Little Brown) NYT fic 12/3/44 (#9), pk 12/17/44 (#1, 18 wk), 33 wk; PW fic 12/9/44 (#2), pk 12/23/44 (#1, 15 wk), 27 wk; tot 60 wk.

Shannon's Way (Little Brown) NYT fic 8/8/48 (#6), pk 9/5/48 (#1, 3 wk), 23 wk; PW fic 8/14/48 (#8), pk 9/11/48 (#1, 3 wk), 15 wk; tot 38 wk.

The Spanish Gardener (Little Brown) NYT fic 9/17/50 (#8), pk 10/1/50 (#4, 3 wk), 17 wk; PW fic 9/23/50 (#4), pk 9/30/50 (#3, 2 wk), 10 wk; tot 27 wk.

Adventures in Two Worlds (McGraw) NYT gen 3/16/52 (#12), pk 3/30/52 (#5, 4 wk), 23 wk; PW nf 3/29/52 (#4), pk 5/24/52 (#3, 1 wk), 12 wk; tot 35 wk.

Beyond This Place (Little Brown) NYT fic 8/2/53 (#16), pk 10/11/53 (#1, 6 wk), 34 wk; PW fic 8/22/53 (#4), pk 9/26/53 (#1, 9 wk), 27 wk; tot 61 wk.

A Thing of Beauty (Little Brown) NYT fic

6/10/56 (#9), pk 7/22/56 (#2, 2 wk), 21 wk; PW fic 7/2/56 (#5), pk 7/30/56 (#2, 2 wk), 16 wk; tot 37 wk.

The Northern Light (Little Brown) NYT fic 6/15/58 (#11), pk 7/6/58 (#5, 1 wk), 14 wk; PW fic 7/7/58 (#7), pk 7/28/58 (#5, 2 wk), 6 wk; tot 20 wk.

The Judas Tree (Little Brown) NYT fic 11/12/61 (#12), pk 12/31/61 (#8, 1 wk), 15 wk; PW fic 12/25/61 (#9, 1 wk); tot 16 wk.

A Song of Sixpence (Little Brown) PW fic 11/9/64 (#11), pk 1/4/65 (#5, 1 wk), 10 wk; NYT fic 11/22/64 (#10, 3 wk); tot 13 wk.

Crosby, Bing, and Pete Martin
Call Me Lucky (Simon & Schuster) NYT gen 7/19/53 (#15), pk 8/16/53 (#6, 3 wk), 15 wk; PW nf 8/15/53 (#10), pk 8/22/53 (#3, 1 wk), 5 wk; tot 20 wk.

Crosby, David, and Carl Gottlieb
Long Time Gone (Doubleday) NYT nf 12/4/88 (#14, 1 wk).

Crossman, Richard Howard Stafford
See Arthur Koestler, et al.

Crouse, Lindsay
See Anne Rice

Crow, Carl
400 Million Customers (Harper) PW nf 10/9/37 (#10), pk 11/13/37 (#6, 4 wk), 12 wk; NYT gen 11/7/37 (#8, 4 wk); tot 16 wk.

Master Kung (Harper) NYT gen 7/3/38 (#7, 4 wk); PW nf 7/9/38 (#8, 4 wk), tot 8 wk.

Crowder, Herbert
Ambush at Osirak (Jove) PW mm pb 2/24/89 (#12), pk 3/3/89 (#11, 1 wk), 3 wk; NYT pb fic 3/5/89 (#12, 1 wk); tot 4 wk.

Crowther, Bosley
The Lion's Share (Dutton) NYT gen 5/19/57 (#13, 1 wk).

Hollywood Rajah (Holt) PW nf 4/11/60 (#10), pk 5/23/60 (#7, 1 wk), 7 wk; NYT gen 4/17/60 (#9), pk 5/22/60 (#7, 1 wk), 12 wk; tot 19 wk.

Croy, Homer
Country Cured (Harper) NYT gen 11/28/43 (#24, 1 wk).

Crum, Bartley C.
Behind the Silken Curtain (Simon & Schuster) NYT gen 5/4/47 (#14), pk 6/15/47 (#6, 1 wk), 19 wk; PW nf 6/14/47 (#9, 1 wk); tot 20 wk.

Culbertson, Ely
Contract Bridge Blue Book (Bridge World) PW nf 3/21/31 (#6), pk 5/16/31 (#4, 4 wk), 28 wk.

Culbertson's Summary (Bridge World) PW nf 7/18/31 (#9), pk 8/15/31 (#2, 20 wk), 56 wk.

Contract Bridge for Auction Players (Garden City) PW nf 5/14/32 (#9, 4 wk).

Contract Bridge Blue Book of 1933 (Bridge World) PW nf 3/11/33 (#1, 4 wk), 12 wk.

Culbertson's Summary of 1933 (Bridge World) PW nf 5/13/33 (#9), pk 6/10/33 (#7, 4 wk), 12 wk.

Culbertson's Own Contract Bridge Self-Teacher (Bridge World) PW nf 4/14/34 (#10, 4 wk); NYT nf 10/6/35 (#6, 4 wk), 8 wk; tot 12 wk.

Culbertson's New Summary of Contract Bridge (Bridge World) PW nf 5/11/35 (#5, 4 wk), 16 wk.

Culbertson's New Summary of Bidding and Play (Bridge World) NYT nf 10/6/35 (#7), pk 11/3/35 (#6, 4 wk), 8 wk.

Contract Bridge Complete (Winston) NYT nf 4/3/38 (#14, 4 wk).

Culbertson's Own New Contract Bridge Self-Teacher (Bridge World) NYT nf 4/3/38 (#10, 4 wk).

Five-Suit Bridge [ed.] (Simon & Schuster) NYT gen 5/1/38 (#7, 4 wk).

Cullman, Marguerite
Ninety Dozen Glasses (Norton) NYT gen 5/8/60 (#16, 1 wk).

Cummings, Bob
Stay Young and Vital (Prentice Hall) NYT gen 2/26/61 (#13, 2 wk), 6 wk.

Cunningham, Mary, with Fran Schumer
Powerplay: What Really Happened at Bendix (Linden/Simon & Schuster) NYT nf 6/17/84 (#13), pk 7/22/84 (#10, 2 wk), 10 wk; PW hc nf 6/22/84 (#7), pk 7/6/84 (#3, 1 wk), 10 wk; tot 20 wk.

Cuppy, Will
The Decline and Fall of Practically Everybody (Holt) NYT gen 12/10/50 (#16), pk 1/14/51 (#6, 3 wk), 18 wk; PW nf 1/13/51 (#7), pk 2/17/51 (#5, 1 wk), 3 wk; tot 21 wk.

Curie, Eve
Madame Curie (Doubleday) NYT gen 1/9/38 (#5), pk 5/7/39 (#2, 1 wk), 12 wk; PW nf 1/15/38 (#2), pk 2/12/38 (#1, 4 wk), 40 wk; tot 52 wk.

Journey Among Warriors (Doubleday) PW nf 5/29/43 (#3), pk 6/19/43 (#2, 10 wk), 26 wk; NYT gen 5/30/43 (#5), pk 6/13/43 (#2, 14 wk), 36 wk; tot 62 wk.

Curley, James Michael
I'd Do It Again (Prentice Hall) NYT gen 6/30/57 (#13, 1 wk), 2 wk.

Curtis, Charles P., Jr., and Ferris Greenslet
The Practical Cogitator [eds.] (Houghton) NYT gen 11/18/45 (#14), pk 2/3/46 (#7, 2 wk), 19 wk; PW nf 2/9/46 (#10), pk 3/9/46 (#6, 1 wk), 3 wk; tot 22 wk.

Curvers, Alexis Theophile
Tempo di Roma (McGraw) NYT fic 7/5/59 (#16, 2 wk).

Curwood, James Oliver
The Valley of Silent Men (Cosmopolitan) PW fic 10/23/20 (#1, 12 wk), 24 wk.
The River's End (Cosmopolitan) PW fic 1/3/20 (#4, 8 wk), 20 wk.
Flaming Forest (Cosmopolitan) PW fic 11/12/21 (#3, 4 wk), 8 wk.
The Country Beyond (Cosmopolitan) PW fic 9/16/22 (#3, 4 wk), 28 wk.
The Alaskan (Cosmopolitan) PW fic 9/15/23 (#2, 8 wk).
The Ancient Highway (Cosmopolitan) PW fic 9/26/25 (#8, 4 wk).
The Black Hunter (Cosmopolitan) PW fic 9/18/26 (#4, 4 wk), 8 wk.
The Plains of Abraham (Doubleday) PW fic 6/30/28 (#7, 4 wk).

Cushing, Harvey
The Life of Sir William Osler (Oxford Univ.) PW gen lit 7/18/25 (#9, 4 wk); PW nf 9/26/25 (#9), pk 10/24/25 (#8, 4 wk), 8 wk; tot 12 wk.
From a Surgeon's Journal (Little Brown) PW nf 6/13/36 (#9), pk 7/11/36 (#7, 4 wk), 12 wk.

Cussler, Clive
Raise the Titanic! (Viking) PW hc fic 11/29/76 (#7), pk 1/31/77 (#2, 7 wk), 21 wk; NYT fic 12/5/76 (#9), pk 2/6/77 (#2, 6 wk), 22 wk; (Bantam) PW mm pb 10/17/77 (#11), pk 10/31/77 (#4, 1 wk), 12 wk; NYT mm pb 10/23/77 (#6), pk 11/6/77 (#2, 1 wk), 15 wk; tot 70 wk.
Vixen 03 (Viking) PW hc fic 11/13/78 (#14), pk 11/20/78 (#12, 1 wk), 2 wk; (Bantam) NYT mm pb 10/14/79 (#15, 3 wk); PW mm pb 10/15/79 (#10), pk 10/29/79 (#9, 1 wk), 3 wk; tot 8 wk.
Night Probe! (Bantam) PW hc fic 8/14/81 (#15), pk 8/28/81 (#10, 3 wk), 11 wk; NYT fic 8/23/81 (#15), pk 10/4/81 (#8, 1 wk), 13 wk; PW mm pb 4/16/82 (#10), pk 4/30/82 (#4, 2 wk), 6 wk; NYT mm pb 4/18/82 (#9), pk 4/25/82 (#4, 3 wk), 7 wk; tot 37 wk.
Pacific Vortex! (Bantam) NYT mm pb 12/26/82 (#5), pk 1/2/83 (#2, 1 wk), 9 wk; PW mm pb 1/7/83 (#2, 2 wk), 7 wk; tot 16 wk.
Deep Six (Simon & Schuster) NYT fic 6/

3/84 (#9), pk 7/29/84 (#5, 1 wk), 15 wk; PW hc fic 6/8/84 (#10), pk 7/20/84 (#5, 3 wk), 14 wk; (Pocket) NYT pb fic 6/9/85 (#10), pk 6/16/85 (#4, 1 wk), 9 wk; PW mm pb 6/14/85 (#11), pk 7/12/85 (#4, 1 wk), 8 wk; tot 46 wk.
Cyclops (Simon & Schuster) PW hc fic 1/14/86 (#12), pk 2/7/86 (#4, 5 wk), 14 wk; NYT fic 1/26/86 (#6), pk 2/2/86 (#4, 5 wk), 14 wk; (Pocket) NYT pb fic 12/7/86 (#11), pk 12/21/86 (#5, 3 wk), 9 wk; PW mm pb 12/12/86 (#9), pk 12/26/86 (#4, 2 wk), 7 wk; tot 44 wk.
Treasure (Simon & Schuster) NYT fic 3/20/88 (#4), pk 4/10/88 (#3, 2 wk), 18 wk; PW hc fic 3/25/88 (#5), pk 4/15/88 (#3, 3 wk), 18 wk; (Pocket) NYT pb fic 11/6/88 (#7), pk 11/13/88 (#3, 3 wk), 11 wk; PW mm pb 11/11/88 (#3), pk 11/18/88 (#2, 1 wk), 11 wk; PW td pb 11/18/88 (#2, 1 wk); tot 59 wk.
Dragon (Simon & Schuster) NYT fic 5/13/90 (#10), pk 6/3/90 (#3, 1 wk), 17 wk; PW hc fic 5/25/90 (#6), pk 6/1/90 (#3, 3 wk), 15 wk; tot 32 wk.

Cutler, Ann, and Rudolph McShane
The Trachtenberg Speed System of Basic Mathematics [eds.] (Doubleday) PW nf 3/19/62 (#10), pk 4/2/62 (#9, 1 wk), 4 wk.

Dacey, Norman F.
How to Avoid Probate (Crown) NYT gen 4/17/66 (#8), pk 7/17/66 (#1, 17 wk), 48 wk; PW nf 5/2/66 (#8), pk 7/18/66 (#1, 15 wk), 45 wk; tot 93 wk.
How to Avoid Probate—Updated! (Crown) PW td pb 8/15/80 (#10), pk 9/5/80 (#7, 1 wk), 5 wk; NYT td pb 8/17/80 (#14), pk 9/28/80 (#9, 1 wk), 7 wk; tot 12 wk.

Dahl, Francis Wellington, and Charles W. Morton
Dahl's Boston (Little Brown) NYT gen 12/8/46 (#10), pk 1/5/47 (#8, 1 wk), 6 wk.

Dahl, Roald
Kiss Kiss (Knopf) NYT fic 2/28/60 (#14), pk 3/13/60 (#10, 3 wk), 12 wk; PW fic 3/7/60 (#9, 4 wk), 5 wk; tot 17 wk.
Charlie and the Chocolate Factory (Knopf) NYT ch bst 11/7/65 (#5), pk 11/7/71 (#1, 26 wk), 296 wk.
James and the Giant Peach (Knopf) NYT ch bst 11/8/70 (#10, 24 wk).
Charlie and the Great Glass Elevator (Knopf) NYT ch bst 11/5/72 (#2, 45 wk), 71 wk.
Matilda (Puffin) PW ch md rd 8/31/90 (#2), pk 9/28/90 (#1, 8 wk), 20 wk.

Dailey, Janet
Touch the Wind (Pocket) PW mm pb 5/28/

79 (#15), pk 6/4/79 (#13, 1 wk), 2 wk; NYT mm pb 6/3/79 (#11, 1 wk), 2 wk; tot 4 wk.

The Rogue (Pocket) NYT mm pb 2/17/80 (#12, 1 wk).

Ride the Thunder (Pocket) PW mm pb 7/18/80 (#14), pk 7/25/80 (#9, 1 wk), 4 wk; NYT mm pb 7/20/80 (#15), pk 8/3/80 (#9, 1 wk), 5 wk; tot 9 wk.

Night Way (Pocket) NYT mm pb 1/18/81 (#9), pk 2/1/81 (#5, 1 wk), 7 wk; PW mm pb 1/23/81 (#4, 1 wk), 5 wk; tot 12 wk.

This Calder Sky (Pocket) NYT td pb 8/9/81 (#4), pk 8/16/81 (#1, 2 wk), 11 wk; PW td pb 8/14/81 (#5), pk 8/21/81 (#2, 1 wk), 7 wk; PW mm pb 2/19/82 (#12, 1 wk), 2 wk; tot 20 wk.

This Calder Range (Pocket) NYT td pb 4/18/82 (#3, 4 wk), 11 wk; PW td pb 4/23/82 (#4), pk 5/7/82 (#3, 2 wk), 8 wk; tot 19 wk.

Stands a Calder Man (Pocket) NYT td pb 1/16/83 (#3, 2 wk), 10 wk; PW td pb 1/21/83 (#8), pk 1/28/83 (#5, 2 wk), 6 wk; tot 16 wk.

Calder Born, Calder Bred (Pocket) NYT td pb 10/16/83 (#4), pk 10/23/83 (#3, 1 wk), 9 wk; PW td pb 10/21/83 (#6), pk 10/28/83 (#4, 1 wk), 6 wk; tot 15 wk.

Silver Wings, Santiago Blue (Simon & Schuster/Poseidon) PW hc fic 8/17/84 (#13), pk 8/24/84 (#8, 2 wk), 8 wk; NYT fic 8/19/84 (#9, 1 wk), 7 wk; (Pocket) NYT pb fic 7/14/85 (#5), pk 7/21/85 (#4, 1 wk), 5 wk; PW mm pb 7/19/85 (#5, 1 wk), 4 wk; tot 24 wk.

The Pride of Hannah Wade (Pocket) NYT pb fic 2/17/85 (#6), pk 2/24/85 (#4, 1 wk), 5 wk; PW td pb 2/22/85 (#2, 2 wk), 5 wk; tot 10 wk.

The Great Alone (Simon & Schuster/Poseidon) PW hc fic 6/13/86 (#11, 1 wk), 4 wk; (Pocket) NYT pb fic 4/12/87 (#6), pk 4/19/87 (#4, 4 wk), 8 wk; PW mm pb 4/17/87 (#5), pk 4/24/87 (#2, 2 wk), 8 wk; tot 20 wk.

The Glory Game (Pocket) NYT pb fic 4/13/86 (#9), pk 5/4/86 (#8, 1 wk), 5 wk; PW mm pb 4/25/86 (#9, 2 wk), 3 wk; tot 8 wk.

Heiress (Little Brown) NYT fic 5/17/87 (#13), pk 6/7/87 (#4, 1 wk), 16 wk; PW hc fic 5/29/87 (#12), pk 6/26/87 (#4, 1 wk), 12 wk; (Fawcett/Crest) NYT pb fic 6/26/88 (#6), pk 7/3/88 (#4, 3 wk), 11 wk; PW mm pb 7/1/88 (#12), pk 7/15/88 (#2, 1 wk), 10 wk; tot 49 wk.

Rivals (Little Brown) NYT fic 1/22/89 (#10), pk 2/5/89 (#3, 3 wk), 11 wk; PW hc fic 1/27/89 (#8), pk 2/24/89 (#3, 2 wk), 9 wk; (Fawcett/Gold Medal) NYT pb fic 3/25/90 (#16), pk 4/1/90 (#3, 3 wk), 10 wk; PW mm pb 4/6/90 (#5), pk 4/13/90 (#3, 3 wk), 7 wk; tot 37 wk.

Masquerade (Little Brown) NYT fic 4/8/

90 (#11), pk 4/22/90 (#4, 1 wk), 10 wk; PW hc fic 4/13/90 (#8), pk 4/27/90 (#4, 2 wk), 10 wk; tot 20 wk.

Dakin, Edwin F.
See Edward R. Dewey and_____

Daley, Robert
Year of the Dragon (NAL/Signet) NYT mm pb 10/10/82 (#12), pk 10/17/82 (#10, 2 wk), 4 wk; PW mm pb 10/15/82 (#8, 2 wk), 4 wk; tot 8 wk.

Hands of a Stranger (NAL/Signet) NYT pb fic 10/26/86 (#14), pk 11/2/86 (#12, 1 wk), 2 wk; PW mm pb 10/31/86 (#15), pk 11/7/86 (#12, 1 wk), 3 wk; tot 5 wk.

Dalgliesh, Alice
The Thanksgiving Story (Scribner) NYT ch bst 11/13/55 (#15, 40 wk).

Dali, Salvador
The Secret Life of Salvador Dali (Dial) NYT nf 1/24/43 (#17, 1 wk).

Dallin, David J.
The Big Three (Yale Univ.) NYT gen 9/23/45 (#14, 1 wk).

Damon, Bertha
Grandma Called It Carnal (Simon & Schuster) PW nf 2/11/39 (#8, 4 wk), 12 wk; NYT gen 12/4/38 (#8), pk 3/5/39 (#7, 4 wk), 12 wk; tot 24 wk.

A Sense of Humus (Simon & Schuster) NYT gen 7/25/43 (#17), pk 9/5/43 (#13, 1 wk), 3 wk.

Damore, Leo
Senatorial Privilege: The Chappaquiddick Cover-Up (Regnery/Gateway) NYT nf 8/14/88 (#13), pk 10/16/88 (#6, 3 wk), 19 wk; PW hc nf 8/19/88 (#15), pk 10/28/88 (#8, 1 wk), 15 wk; (Dell) NYT pb nf 7/2/89 (#9), pk 7/9/89 (#1, 6 wk), 13 wk; PW mm pb 7/14/89 (#15), pk 8/4/89 (#4, 1 wk), 10 wk; tot 57 wk.

Dane, Clemence
Broome Stages (Doubleday) PW fic 12/19/31 (#9, 4 wk).

The Moon Is Feminine (Doubleday) NYT fic 10/9/38 (#15, 4 wk).

The Flower Girls (Norton) NYT fic 7/10/55 (#13), pk 7/31/55 (#4, 4 wk), 17 wk; PW fic 7/23/55 (#4, 4 wk), 10 wk; tot 27 wk.

Daniel, Clifton
Chronicle of the 20th Century [ed.] (Chronicle/American Booksellers) NYT nf 11/22/87 (#14), pk 1/3/88 (#9, 2 wk), 17 wk; PW hc nf 11/27/87 (#14), pk 1/15/88 (#6, 1 wk), 8 wk; tot 25 wk.

Chronicle of America [ed.] (ECAM/Prentice Hall) NYT nf 12/24/89 (#15), pk 1/7/90 (#9, 1 wk), 4 wk.

Daniel, Hawthorne
Judge Medina (Funk & Wagnalls) NYT gen 9/14/52 (#16, 1 wk).

Daniels, Jonathan
A Southerner Discovers the South (Macmillan) NYT gen 9/4/38 (#5, 4 wk), 8 wk; PW nf 9/10/38 (#5, 4 wk), 8 wk; tot 16 wk.
A Southerner Discovers New England (Macmillan) PW nf 7/13/40 (#10, 4 wk).
The Man of Independence (Lippincott) NYT gen 10/15/50 (#12), pk 10/29/50 (#9, 1 wk), 5 wk.
The Time Between the Wars (Doubleday) PW nf 9/12/66 (#11), pk 9/26/66 (#9, 2 wk), 5 wk; NYT gen 9/18/66 (#10, 2 wk); tot 7 wk.

Daniels, Josephus
The Life of Woodrow Wilson 1856–1924 (Winston) PW nf 6/21/24 (#7, 4 wk).

Daninos, Pierre
The Notebooks of Major Thompson (Knopf) NYT gen 10/9/55 (#16), pk 11/13/55 (#9, 1 wk), 7 wk.

Dannen, Frederick
Hit Men: Power Brokers and Fast Money Inside the Music Business (Times/Random) PW hc nf 8/24/90 (#15), pk 9/7/90 (#9, 1 wk), 6 wk; NYT nf 9/9/90 (#15), pk 9/30/90 (#13, 1 wk), 3 wk; tot 9 wk.

Darrow, Clarence
The Story of My Life (Scribner) PW nf 3/19/32 (#6), pk 5/14/32 (#4, 8 wk), 16 wk.

_____, and Arthur Weinberg
Attorney for the Damned: Clarence Darrow (Simon & Schuster) PW nf 2/17/58 (#8), pk 3/31/58 (#5, 1 wk), 7 wk; NYT gen 1/12/58 (#15), pk 3/23/58 (#6, 1 wk), 20 wk; tot 27 wk.

Darrow, Whitney, Jr.
You're Sitting on My Eyelashes (Random) NYT gen 1/16/44 (#20, 1 wk).

Dart, Iris Rainer
Beaches (Bantam) NYT pb fic 7/6/86 (#15), pk 8/10/86 (#6, 1 wk), 8 wk; PW mm pb 7/18/86 (#9), pk 8/1/86 (#6, 1 wk), 7 wk; tot 15 wk.

Darvas, Nicolas
How I Made $2,000,000 in the Stock Market (Citadel) NYT gen 7/3/60 (#10), pk 9/4/60 (#2, 8 wk), 27 wk; PW nf 7/18/60 (#9), pk 9/5/60 (#1, 1 wk), 20 wk; tot 47 wk.

Dashwood, Edmee Elizabeth Monica de la Pasture [all titles as by E.M. Delafield]
The Provincial Lady in London (Harper) PW fic 3/11/33 (#10, 4 wk).

The Provincial Lady in America (Harper) PW fic 7/14/34 (#7, 4 wk), 8 wk.
Faster! Faster! (Harper) PW fic 4/11/36 (#10, 4 wk).
Nothing Is Safe (Harper) NYT fic 9/12/37 (#5, 4 wk).
Late and Soon (Harper) NYT fic 8/1/43 (#10, 2 wk), 3 wk.

Daugherty, Harry M., and Thomas Dixon
The Inside Story of the Harding Tragedy (Churchill) PW nf 3/19/32 (#9, 4 wk).

Davenport, Marcia
Of Lena Geyer (Scribner) PW fic 11/14/36 (#9), pk 1/16/37 (#7, 4 wk), 20 wk.
The Valley of Decision (Scribner) NYT fic 11/15/42 (#9), pk 12/20/42 (#2, 17 wk), 79 wk; PW fic 11/21/42 (#4), pk 12/19/42 (#2, 14 wk), 56 wk; tot 135 wk.
East Side, West Side (Scribner) NYT fic 11/9/47 (#7), pk 2/8/48 (#1, 2 wk), 28 wk; PW fic 11/22/47 (#3), pk 11/29/47 (#1, 2 wk), 20 wk; tot 48 wk.
My Brother's Keeper (Scribner) NYT fic 11/14/54 (#11), pk 12/19/54 (#6, 4 wk), 20 wk; PW fic 12/18/54 (#8), pk 2/19/55 (#5, 1 wk), 7 wk; tot 27 wk.
The Constant Image (Scribners) NYT fic 2/14/60 (#9), pk 3/13/60 (#3, 11 wk), 29 wk; PW fic 2/22/60 (#7), pk 3/7/60 (#3, 13 wk), 23 wk; tot 52 wk.
Too Strong for Fantasy (Scribner) NYT gen 11/26/67 (#8, 1 wk); PW nf 11/27/67 (#12), pk 12/11/67 (#7, 1 wk), 7 wk; tot 8 wk.

David, Peter
A Rock and a Hard Place (Pocket) NYT pb fic 1/14/90 (#13, 1 wk).
See also Carmen Carter, et al.

Davidson, David Albert
The Steeper Cliff (Random) NYT fic 8/24/47 (#11, 1 wk), 2 wk.
The Hour of Truth (Random) NYT fic 2/20/49 (#16, 1 wk).

Davidson, Marshall B.
Life in America (Houghton) NYT gen 11/4/51 (#10, 1 wk), 2 wk; PW nf 11/17/51 (#10, 1 wk); tot 3 wk.

Davidson, Sara
Loose Change: Three Women of the Sixties (Pocket) PW mm pb 2/20/78 (#14), pk 3/20/78 (#4, 1 wk), 7 wk; NYT mm pb 3/26/78 (#12), pk 4/2/78 (#8, 1 wk), 3 wk; tot 10 wk.
See also Rock Hudson and_____

Davies, Hunter
The Beatles—The Authorized Biography

(McGraw) NYT gen 10/6/68 (#10, 2 wk), 2 wk; PW nf 11/25/68 (#8, 1 wk); tot 3 wk.

Davies, Joseph E.
Mission to Moscow (Simon & Schuster) PW nf 2/14/42 (#3), pk 3/14/42 (#1, 8 wk), 25 wk.

Davies, Robertson
Fifth Business (Viking) NYT fic 3/28/71 (#10, 2 wk).
What's Bred in the Bone (Sifton/Viking) NYT fic 12/8/85 (#15), pk 1/19/86 (#10, 2 wk), 10 wk; PW hc fic 1/3/86 (#15), pk 2/7/86 (#11, 2 wk), 9 wk; tot 19 wk.
Lyre of Orpheus (Viking) NYT fic 1/15/89 (#12), pk 2/12/89 (#8, 2 wk), 9 wk; PW hc fic 1/20/89 (#13), pk 2/17/89 (#9, 1 wk), 7 wk; tot 16 wk.

Davis, Adelle
Let's Eat Right to Keep Fit (Harcourt) NYT pb gen 1/3/71 (#5, 8 wk).
Let's Get Well (Harcourt) NYT pb gen 1/14/73 (#5, 4 wk).

Davis, Bette, with Michael Herskowitz
This 'n' That (Putnam) NYT nf 4/19/87 (#8), pk 5/3/87 (#4, 1 wk), 15 wk; PW hc nf 4/24/87 (#9), pk 5/1/87 (#3, 2 wk), 10 wk; (Berkley) NYT pb nf 3/6/88 (#3, 5 wk), 11 wk; PW mm pb 3/18/88 (#12), pk 3/25/88 (#11, 2 wk), 3 wk; tot 39 wk.

Davis, Burke
They Called Him Stonewall (Holt) NYT gen 11/7/54 (#12, 1 wk).
Gray Fox: Robert E. Lee and the Civil War (Rinehart) NYT gen 5/20/56 (#13), pk 6/17/56 (#11, 1 wk), 13 wk.

Davis, Clyde Brion
The Great American Novel (Farrar) NYT fic 7/3/38 (#8, 4 wk).
Nebraska Coast (Farrar) NYT fic 8/6/39 (#7, 4 wk).

Davis, Elmer
But We Were Born Free (Bobbs Merrill) NYT gen 3/7/54 (#8), pk 4/18/54 (#1, 2 wk), 37 wk; PW nf 3/13/54 (#6), pk 4/3/54 (#1, 2 wk), 33 wk; tot 70 wk.
Two Minutes Till Midnight (Bobbs Merrill) NYT gen 3/13/55 (#16), pk 4/3/55 (#6, 1 wk), 12 wk; PW nf 4/9/55 (#10), pk 4/23/55 (#6, 1 wk), 2 wk; tot 14 wk.

Davis, Fitzroy
Quicksilver (Harcourt) NYT fic 10/11/42 (#15, 1 wk), 4 wk.

Davis, Forrest
See Ernest Lindley and_____

Davis, Gwen
The Pretenders (World) NYT fic 7/20/69 (#6), pk 10/19/69 (#4, 1 wk), 18 wk; PW fic 8/4/69 (#7), pk 10/20/69 (#3, 1 wk), 18 wk; NYT pb fic 5/3/70 (#3, 8 wk); tot 44 wk.
Silk Lady (Warner) NYT pb fic 7/12/87 (#15), pk 7/19/87 (#14, 1 wk), 3 wk.

Davis, Harold Lenoir
Honey in the Horn (Harper) NYT fic 10/6/35 (#2, 4 wk), 8 wk; PW fic 10/12/35 (#4, 4 wk), 12 wk; tot 20 wk.
Winds of Morning (Morrow) NYT fic 1/27/52 (#15), pk 2/10/52 (#7, 1 wk), 10 wk.

Davis, Jim
Garfield at Large (Ballantine) NYT td pb 4/20/80 (#14), pk 4/27/80 (#1, 11 wk), 144 wk; PW td pb 4/25/80 (#7), pk 6/20/80 (#1, 2 wk), 71 wk; tot 215 wk.
Garfield Bigger Than Life (Ballantine) NYT td pb 11/8/81 (#13), pk 11/15/81 (#1, 11 wk), 63 wk; PW td pb 11/13/81 (#4), pk 11/20/81 (#1, 8 wk), 30 wk; tot 93 wk.
Garfield Gains Weight (Ballantine) NYT td pb 3/22/81 (#6), pk 4/26/81 (#1, 2 wk), 96 wk; PW td pb 3/27/81 (#5), pk 4/17/81 (#1, 3 wk), 56 wk; tot 152 wk.
The Garfield Treasury (Ballantine) NYT td pb 11/21/82 (#13), pk 12/19/82 (#3, 1 wk), 16 wk; PW td pb 11/26/82 (#10), pk 12/17/82 (#4, 3 wk), 13 wk; tot 29 wk.
Garfield Weighs In (Ballantine) PW td pb 3/26/82 (#3), pk 4/2/82 (#1, 10 wk), 34 wk; NYT td pb 3/28/82 (#1, 11 wk), 50 wk; tot 84 wk.
Garfield Takes the Cake (Ballantine) PW td pb 10/8/82 (#3), pk 10/22/82 (#1, 6 wk), 21 wk; NYT td pb 10/10/82 (#1, 6 wk), 33 wk; tot 54 wk.
Here Comes Garfield (Ballantine) NYT td pb 10/24/82 (#5), pk 10/31/82 (#4, 4 wk), 20 wk; PW td pb 10/29/82 (#6), pk 11/5/82 (#3, 3 wk), 10 wk; tot 16 wk.
Garfield Sits Around the House (Ballantine) NYT td pb 10/9/83 (#5), pk 10/16/83 (#1, 3 wk), 17 wk; PW td pb 10/14/83 (#3), 10/21/83 (#1, 2 wk), 16 wk; tot 33 wk.
The Second Garfield Treasury (Ballantine) PW td pb 12/9/83 (#10), pk 12/23/83 (#4, 1 wk), 9 wk; NYT td pb 12/11/83 (#8), pk 12/25/83 (#4, 1 wk), 3 wk; NYT msc pb 1/1/84 (#7, 2 wk), 3 wk; tot 15 wk.
Garfield Eats His Heart Out (Ballantine) PW td pb 3/18/83 (#10), pk 3/25/83 (#1, 6 wk), 26 wk; NYT td pb 3/20/83 (#1, 5 wk), 29 wk; tot 55 wk.
Garfield: His 9 Lives (Ballantine) PW td pb 12/14/84 (#7, 1 wk), 3 wk; NYT msc pb 12/30/84 (#9, 2 wk); tot 5 wk.

Garfield Tips the Scales (Ballantine) NYT msc pb 3/18/84 (#6), pk 3/25/84 (#1, 2 wk), 13 wk; PW td pb 3/23/84 (#8), pk 4/20/84 (#2, 2 wk), 12 wk; tot 25 wk.

Garfield in the Rough (Ballantine) PW td pb 11/16/84 (#9), pk 11/23/84 (#8, 2 wk), 3 wk; NYT msc pb 11/25/84 (#5, 1 wk), 2 wk; tot 5 wk.

Garfield Loses His Feet (Ballantine) NYT msc pb 10/7/84 (#1, 8 wk), 16 wk; PW td pb 10/12/84 (#4), pk 10/19/84 (#1, 6 wk), 15 wk; tot 31 wk.

The Third Garfield Treasury (Ballantine) PW td pb 12/13/85 (#8), pk 1/3/86 (#7, 1 wk), 5 wk; NYT msc pb 12/22/85 (#6, 1 wk), 5 wk; tot 10 wk.

Garfield Rolls On (Ballantine) NYT msc pb 10/6/85 (#3), pk 10/20/85 (#1, 8 wk), 16 wk; PW td pb 10/18/85 (#2, 5 wk), 12 wk; tot 28 wk.

Garfield Makes It Big (Ballantine) NYT msc pb 3/24/85 (#2, 6 wk), 18 wk; PW td pb 3/29/85 (#1, 4 wk), 15 wk; tot 33 wk.

Garfield Out to Lunch (Ballantine) NYT msc pb 3/23/86 (#1, 4 wk), 15 wk; PW td pb 3/28/86 (#4), pk 4/11/86 (#2, 3 wk), 17 wk; tot 32 wk.

Garfield in Paradise (Ballantine) PW td pb 5/30/86 (#10), pk 6/20/86 (#3, 1 wk), 7 wk; NYT msc pb 6/1/86 (#7), pk 6/8/86 (#5, 2 wk), 7 wk; tot 14 wk.

Garfield Swallows His Pride (Ballantine) PW td pb 10/30/87 (#4), pk 11/6/87 (#3, 2 wk), 11 wk; NYT msc pb 11/8/87 (#3, 1 wk), 5 wk; tot 16 wk.

Garfield: Food for Thought (Ballantine) NYT msc pb 3/15/87 (#8), pk 3/22/87 (#3, 1 wk), 7 wk; PW td pb 3/20/87 (#6), pk 4/3/87 (#1, 4 wk), 9 wk; tot 16 wk.

Garfield Worldwide (Ballantine) PW td pb 3/4/88 (#7), pk 3/18/88 (#1, 3 wk), 10 wk; NYT msc pb 3/13/88 (#5), pk 4/17/88 (#2, 1 wk), 5 wk; tot 15 wk.

Garfield Rounds Out (Ballantine) PW td pb 10/28/88 (#8, 1 wk), 2 wk; NYT msc pb 11/6/88 (#8, 1 wk); tot 3 wk.

Garfield Chews the Fat (Ballantine) NYT msc pb 3/12/89 (#5), pk 4/2/89 (#4, 2 wk), 4 wk; PW td pb 3/17/89 (#2, 3 wk), 10 wk; tot 14 wk.

Garfield Goes to Waist (Ballantine) PW td pb 3/16/90 (#7), pk 3/23/90 (#5, 1 wk), 6 wk.

Garfield Hangs Out (Ballantine) PW td pb 11/2/90 (#6, 1 wk).

_____, and Lorenzo Music

Garfield on the Town (Ballantine) NYT td pb 10/30/83 (#9), pk 11/13/83 (#6, 2 wk), 9 wk; PW td pb 11/18/83 (#7), pk 12/2/83 (#6, 1 wk), 6 wk; tot 15 wk.

Davis, John H.

The Kennedys: Dynasty and Disaster (McGraw) NYT pb nf 5/5/85 (#4, 3 wk), 6 wk.

Davis, Juliet

See Deborah Cox and_____

Davis, Kathryn Lynn

Too Deep for Tears (Pocket) NYT pb fic 1/14/90 (#11), pk 2/11/90 (#5, 1 wk), 7 wk; PW mm pb 1/26/90 (#9), pk 2/23/90 (#6, 1 wk), 7 wk; tot 14 wk.

Davis, Kenneth

Soldier of Democracy (Doubleday) NYT gen 12/23/45 (#12), pk 2/3/46 (#3, 1 wk), 15 wk; PW nf 1/5/46 (#4), pk 1/19/46 (#3, 2 wk), 8 wk; tot 23 wk.

Davis, Miles, with Quincy Troupe

Miles (Bantam) NYT nf 11/5/89 (#16, 1 wk).

Davis, Patti, and Maureen Strange Foster

Home Front (Crown) PW hc fic 3/21/86 (#12), pk 4/18/86 (#6, 1 wk), 10 wk; NYT fic 3/30/86 (#9), pk 4/6/86 (#6, 2 wk), 9 wk; tot 19 wk.

Davis, Richard Glen Michael

See Mary Jane Frances Meara, et al.

Davis, Sammy, Jr., with Jane Boyar and Burt Boyar

Yes I Can (Farrar) PW nf 10/25/65 (#7), pk 11/29/65 (#4, 3 wk), 25 wk; NYT gen 10/31/65 (#7), pk 12/5/65 (#4, 1 wk), 21 wk; NYT pb gen 11/6/66 (#1, 4 wk), 12 wk; tot 58 wk.

Why Me? (Warner) NYT pb nf 6/10/90 (#7, 1 wk), 4 wk.

Davis, Stephen

Hammer of the Gods: The Led Zeppelin Saga (Morrow) NYT nf 8/11/85 (#14), pk 9/8/85 (#8, 4 wk), 10 wk; PW hc nf 8/23/85 (#12), pk 9/13/85 (#10, 1 wk), 8 wk; tot 18 wk.

See also Mick Fleetwood and_____

Dawson, Coningsby

Living Bayonets (Lane) PW gen 5/3/19 (#2, 4 wk), 8 wk.

The Kingdom Round the Corner (Cosmopolitan) PW fic 8/6/21 (#3, 4 wk), 8 wk.

The Vanishing Point (Cosmopolitan) PW fic 5/13/22 (#12), pk 6/17/22 (#11, 4 wk), 8 wk.

The Coast of Folly (Cosmopolitan) PW fic 4/19/24 (#3, 4 wk).

Day, Alexandra

Carl's Christmas (Farrar) PW ch pic 11/30/90 (#7), pk 12/21/90 (#2, 4 wk), 8 wk; NYT fic 12/16/90 (#4, 1 wk), 3 wk; tot 11 wk.

Day, A rthur G.
See James A. Michener and_____

Day, Clarence
Life with Father (Knopf) PW nf 9/14/35 (#3), pk 3/14/36 (#2, 4 wk), 44 wk; NYT nf 10/6/35 (#4), pk 11/3/35 (#3, 4 wk), 24 wk; tot 68 wk.
After All (Knopf) NYT gen 10/4/36 (#4, 4 wk); PW nf 10/10/36 (#9, 4 wk); tot 8 wk.
Life with Mother (Knopf) PW nf 10/9/37 (#2, 4 wk), 12 wk; NYT gen 10/10/37 (#1, 4 wk), 12 wk; tot 24 wk.

Day, Donald
See Will Rogers

_____, **and Beth Feagles Day**
Will Rogers (McKay) NYT gen 9/30/62 (#13), pk 10/21/62 (#11, 1 wk), 8 wk.

Day, Gerry
See Alan Dean Foster, et al.

Dayan, Yael
New Face in the Mirror (World Almanac) NYT fic 10/18/59 (#15, 1 wk).

Dean, John W., III
Blind Ambition: The White House Years (Simon & Schuster) PW hc nf 11/1/76 (#9), pk 1/3/77 (#3, 3 wk) 22 wk; NYT gen 11/7/76 (#8), pk 1/2/77 (#3, 4 wk), 23 wk; (Pocket) PW mm pb 8/22/77 (#9, 3 wk), 5 wk; NYT mm pb 8/28/77 (#10, 2 wk), 7 wk; tot 57 wk.

Dean, Maureen
Washington Wives (Charter) NYT pb fic 10/30/88 (#11, 1 wk), 3 wk; PW mm pb 11/25/88 (#15, 1 wk); tot 4 wk.

Dean, Gen. William Frishe, as told to William L. Worden
General Dean's Story (Viking) NYT gen 7/11/54 (#15, 1 wk).

Deane, John R.
The Strange Alliance (Viking) NYT gen 2/2/47 (#10), pk 2/23/47 (#6, 1 wk), 10 wk; PW nf 4/19/47 (#10, 1 wk); tot 11 wk.

De Angeli, Marguerite
Book of Nursery and Mother Goose Rhymes (Doubleday) NYT ch bst 11/14/54 (#3, 40 wk).

DeAngelis, Barbara
Secrets About Men Every Woman Should Know (Delacorte) PW hc nf 3/2/90 (#13), pk 3/30/90 (#1, 1 wk), 19 wk; NYT msc 3/4/90 (#1, 5 wk), 13 wk; tot 32 wk.

DeBakey, Michael E., Antonio M. Gotto, Jr., Lynne W. Scott and John P. Foreyt
The Living Heart Diet (Raven/Simon & Schuster) NYT msc 6/2/85 (#3, 1 wk), 2 wk;

PW hc nf 6/14/85 (#12, 1 wk), 4 wk; tot 6 wk.

De Barbin, Lucy, and Dary Matera
Are You Lonesome Tonight? (Villard) NYT nf 6/28/87 (#16, 1 wk); (Charter) pb nf 9/4/88 (#10, 1 wk); tot 2 wk.

De Beauvoir, Simone
The Second Sex (Knopf) NYT gen 3/15/53 (#15), pk 3/22/53 (#9, 1 wk), 5 wk; PW mm pb 11/12/79 (#9), pk 11/19/79 (#7, 2 wk), 5 wk; tot 10 wk.
The Mandarins (World) NYT fic 6/10/56 (#13), pk 7/8/56 (#3, 9 wk), 24 wk; PW fic 6/25/56 (#4), pk 7/9/56 (#2, 1 wk), 22 wk; tot 46 wk.
The Coming of Age [trans. Patrick O'Brian] (Putnam) NYT gen 7/9/72 (#10), pk 7/23/72 (#9, 1 wk), 2 wk.

De Bell, Garrett
The Environmental Handbook [comp.] (Ballantine) NYT pb gen 5/3/70 (#4, 8 wk).

De Blasis, Celeste
Wild Swan (Bantam) NYT pb fic 7/14/85 (#12, 2 wk), 3 wk.
Swan's Chance (Bantam) NYT pb fic 9/14/86 (#14), pk 9/21/86 (#11, 1 wk), 4 wk.
A Season of Swans (Bantam) NYT pb fic 11/4/90 (#14, 1 wk).

De Borchgrave, Arnaud
See Robert Moss and_____

_____, **and Robert Moss**
The Spike (Crown) PW hc fic 5/30/80 (#11), pk 8/22/80 (#2, 2 wk), 27 wk; NYT fic 6/15/80 (#11), pk 8/17/80 (#2, 2 wk), 21 wk; (Avon) NYT mm pb 5/24/81 (#6), pk 5/31/81 (#5, 2 wk), 11 wk; PW mm pb 5/29/81 (#6), pk 6/5/81 (#4, 1 wk), 11 wk; tot 70 wk.

De Brunhoff, Laurent
Babar Comes to America (Random) NYT ch bst 11/6/66 (#10, 26 wk).

De Capite, Michael
Maria (Longmans) NYT fic 2/14/43 (#17, 1 wk).

De Chavez, Estafania D.
An Easy Way to Spanish Fluency (Casa Colina) NYT gen 10/1/44 (#18), pk 10/22/44 (#13, 1 wk), 2 wk.

Decter, Moshe
See James Rorty and_____

Dedmon, Emmett
Fabulous Chicago (Random) NYT gen 11/22/53 (#12), pk 11/29/53 (#11, 3 wk), 10 wk.

Deeping, Warwick
Sorrell and Son (Knopf) PW fic 7/17/26 (#9), pk 12/18/26 (#4, 8 wk), 44 wk.

Kitty (Knopf) PW fic 11/26/27 (#2, 8 wk), 12 wk.

Doomsday (Knopf) PW fic 3/19/27 (#4), pk 4/23/27 (#3, 8 wk), 24 wk.

Old Pybus (Knopf) PW fic 10/27/28 (#3), pk 11/24/28 (#1, 8 wk), 20 wk.

Roper's Row (Knopf) PW fic 9/14/29 (#2, 8 wk), 20 wk.

Exile (Knopf) PW fic 4/12/30 (#2, 4 wk), 12 wk.

The Ten Commandments (Knopf) PW fic 10/17/31 (#5), pk 11/14/31 (#3, 4 wk), 16 wk.

Bridge of Desire (McBride) PW fic 4/18/31 (#2, 8 wk) 20 wk.

Smith (Knopf) PW fic 11/12/32 (#8, 4 wk), 8 wk.

Old Wine and New (Knopf) PW fic 5/14/ 32 (#9), pk 6/11/32 (#3, 4 wk), 16 wk.

The Challenge of Love (McBride) PW fic 4/23/32 (#7, 4 wk).

Seven Men Came Back (Knopf) PW fic 7/ 14/34 (#10, 4 wk).

The Golden Cord (Knopf) NYT fic 10/6/35 (#7, 4 wk).

No Hero-This (Knopf) NYT fic 11/8/36 (#8, 4 wk).

Marriage by Conquest (McBride) NYT fic 4/5/36 (#7, 4 wk).

The Woman at the Door (Knopf) NYT fic 12/12/37 (#8, 4 wk).

Blind Man's Year (Knopf) NYT fic 7/4/37 (#2, 4 wk).

Malice of Men (Knopf) NYT fic 10/9/38 (#8, 4 wk).

Folly Island (Knopf) NYT fic 12/10/39 (#15, 4 wk).

Bluewater (Knopf) NYT fic 5/7/39 (#14, 4 wk).

DeFelitta, Frank

Audrey Rose (Putnam) NYT fic 3/7/76 (#8, 2 wk); PW hc fic 3/8/76 (#10, 1 wk); (Warner) mm pb 11/8/76 (#7), pk 11/29/76 (#1, 5 wk), 15 wk; NYT mm pb 11/14/76 (#5), pk 11/21/76 (#1, 10 wk), 19 wk; tot 37 wk.

The Entity (Warner) PW mm pb 9/17/79 (#12), pk 10/1/79 (#7, 2 wk), 8 wk; NYT mm pb 9/23/79 (#12), pk 10/28/79 (#8, 1 wk), 8 wk; tot 16 wk.

Sea Trial (Avon) PW td pb 9/19/80 (#3), pk 10/10/80 (#2, 1 wk), 7 wk; NYT td pb 9/21/80 (#5, 2 wk), 9 wk; tot 16 wk.

For the Love of Audrey Rose (Warner) NYT mm pb 7/11/82 (#14), pk 8/1/82 (#10, 1 wk), 4 wk; PW mm pb 8/6/82 (#15, 1 wk); tot 5 wk.

De Gasztold, Carmen Bernos

Prayers from the Ark [trans. Rumer Godden] (Viking) NYT ch bst 11/10/63 (#9, 26 wk).

Degen, Bruce

See Joanna Cole

De Graaf, Kasper, and Malcolm Garrett

Duran Duran (Cherry Lane Books) NYT pb nf 7/22/84 (#8, 1 wk).

Degras, Henry Ernest

Angels in Undress [as by Mark Benney] (Random) NYT nf 5/9/37 (#3, 4 wk).

De Hartog, Jan

The Distant Shore (Harper) NYT fic 9/14/ 52 (#9), pk 9/28/52 (#8, 2 wk), 8 wk; PW fic 10/11/52 (#10, 1 wk); tot 9 wk.

The Spiral Road (Harper) NYT fic 5/12/57 (#14, 1 wk), 2 wk.

The Inspector (Atheneum) NYT fic 8/7/60 (#16, 1 wk).

The Captain (Atheneum) NYT fic 1/1/67 (#9), pk 3/5/67 (#4, 1 wk), 18 wk; PW fic 1/16/67 (#8), pk 2/27/67 (#3, 2 wk), 22 wk; tot 40 wk.

De Havilland, Olivia

Every Frenchman Has One (Random) NYT gen 6/24/62 (#13, 1 wk), 5 wk.

Deighton, Len

Funeral in Berlin (Putnam) NYT fic 1/31/ 65 (#10), pk 3/7/65 (#3, 5 wk), 20 wk; PW fic 2/8/65 (#10), pk 4/5/65 (#2, 1 wk), 18 wk; NYT pb fic 12/5/65 (#5, 4 wk); tot 42 wk.

The Billion Dollar Brain (Putnam) PW fic 1/24/66 (#11), pk 2/28/66 (#5, 3 wk), 18 wk; NYT fic 1/30/66 (#8), pk 2/6/66 (#7, 2 wk), 13 wk; tot 31 wk.

Horse Under Water (Putnam) PW fic 1/22/68 (#9, 1 wk), 3 wk.

Yesterday's Spy (Warner) PW mm pb 7/19/76 (#13, 1 wk).

SS-GB (Knopf) PW hc fic 3/12/79 (#13), pk 3/26/79 (#3, 2 wk), 16 wk; NYT fic 3/25/ 79 (#5), pk 4/29/79 (#3, 1 wk), 16 wk; (Ballantine) PW mm pb 3/14/80 (#8), pk 3/28/ 80 (#2, 1 wk), 10 wk; NYT mm pb 3/23/80 (#6), pk 3/30/80 (#3, 1 wk), 8 wk; tot 50 wk.

XPD (Knopf) PW hc fic 5/8/81 (#13), pk 6/19/81 (#8, 1 wk), 14 wk; NYT fic 5/17/81 (#14), pk 6/14/81 (#6, 1 wk), 13 wk; (Ballantine) PW mm pb 5/14/82 (#4), pk 5/28/82 (#3, 1 wk), 9 wk; NYT mm pb 5/16/82 (#5, 2 wk), 9 wk; tot 45 wk.

Goodbye, Mickey Mouse (Knopf) PW hc fic 12/17/82 (#14), pk 1/21/83 (#9, 3 wk), 12 wk; NYT fic 12/19/82 (#13), pk 2/13/83 (#9, 1 wk), 13 wk; (Ballantine) NYT mm pb 10/9/ 83 (#15), pk 10/23/83 (#7, 1 wk), 5 wk; PW mm pb 10/14/83 (#9), pk 10/21/83 (#8, 2 wk), 6 wk; tot 36 wk.

Berlin Game (Knopf) PW hc fic 12/23/83

(#14), pk 2/3/83 (#4, 2 wk), 14 wk; NYT fic 12/25/83 (#14), pk 1/15/84 (#4, 1 wk), 14 wk; (Ballantine) pb fic 1/13/85 (#10), pk 1/20/85 (#3, 2 wk), 9 wk; PW mm pb 1/18/85 (#10), pk 2/1/85 (#4, 2 wk), 9 wk; tot 46 wk.

London Match (Knopf) NYT fic 12/15/85 (#15), pk 1/26/86 (#9, 1 wk), 10 wk; PW hc fic 12/20/85 (#14), pk 1/24/86 (#10, 3 wk), 9 wk; (Ballantine) NYT pb fic 1/11/87 (#15), pk 1/18/87 (#9, 1 wk), 5 wk; PW mm pb 1/16/87 (#11, 1 wk), 4 wk; tot 28 wk.

Mexico Set (Knopf) NYT fic 3/3/85 (#14), pk 3/17/85 (#8, 3 wk), 8 wk; PW hc fic 3/15/85 (#12, 3 wk), 6 wk; (Ballantine) PW mm pb 1/17/86 (#13), pk 1/24/86 (#10, 1 wk), 4 wk; NYT pb fic 1/19/86 (#15), pk 1/26/86 (#12, 2 wk), 4 wk; tot 22 wk.

Only When I Laugh (Mysterious/Ballantine) PW hc fic 4/3/87 (#15, 1 wk).

Winter: A Novel of a Berlin Family (Knopf) NYT fic 1/3/88 (#16), pk 1/31/88 (#8, 1 wk), 11 wk; PW hc fic 1/8/88 (#15), pk 1/22/88 (#8, 1 wk), 11 wk; (Ballantine) NYT pb fic 1/8/89 (#15), pk 1/29/89 (#5, 1 wk), 6 wk; PW mm pb 1/13/89 (#9), pk 1/20/89 (#7, 2 wk), 5 wk; tot 33 wk.

Spy Hook (Knopf) NYT fic 12/25/88 (#13), pk 1/15/89 (#7, 1 wk), 10 wk; PW hc fic 1/6/89 (#9), pk 1/20/89 (#7, 1 wk), 7 wk; (Ballantine) NYT pb fic 1/7/90 (#9), pk 1/21/90 (#4, 2 wk), 6 wk; PW mm pb 1/12/90 (#15), pk 1/19/90 (#6, 2 wk), 5 wk; tot 28 wk.

Spy Line (Knopf) PW hc fic 12/15/89 (#14), pk 12/22/89 (#12, 1 wk), 4 wk; NYT fic 1/7/90 (#15), pk 1/14/90 (#12, 2 wk), 4 wk; tot 8 wk.

Spy Sinker (Bessie/HarperCollins) PW hc fic 9/14/90 (#13), pk 9/28/90 (#4, 1 wk), 6 wk; NYT fic 9/16/90 (#9), pk 9/23/90 (#5, 1 wk), 6 wk; tot 12 wk.

De Jong, Meindert
The Wheel on the School (Harper) NYT ch bst 11/13/55 (#3, 40 wk).

De Kruif, Paul
Microbe Hunters (Harcourt) PW nf 10/16/26 (#9, 4 wk), 8 wk.
Hunger Fighters (Harcourt) PW nf 11/24/28 (#8, 4 wk).
Men Against Death (Harcourt) PW nf 12/17/32 (#9), pk 1/14/33 (#7, 8 wk), 12 wk.
The Fight for Life (Harcourt) NYT gen 6/5/38 (#1, 4 wk); PW nf 6/11/38 (#8, 4 wk), 8 wk; tot 12 wk.
The Male Hormone (Garden City) NYT gen 6/17/45 (#19), pk 7/1/45 (#15, 1 wk), 6 wk.

Delafield, E.M.
See Edmee Elizabeth Monica de la Pasture Dashwood

Deland, Margaret Wade Campbell
The Vehement Flame (Harper) PW fic 7/29/22 (#3), pk 8/26/22 (#2, 4 wk), 12 wk.
Captain Archer's Daughter (Harper) PW fic 6/11/32 (#7, 4 wk).

Delaplane, Stanton Hill
Postcards from Delaplane (Doubleday) NYT gen 4/12/53 (#14), pk 5/17/53 (#11, 2 wk), 8 wk.
The Little World of Stanton Delaplane (Coward McCann) NYT gen 6/21/59 (#15), pk 6/28/59 (#12, 2 wk), 6 wk.

De la Roche, Mazo
Jalna (Little Brown) PW fic 11/26/27 (#1, 8 wk), 12 wk.
Whiteoaks of Jalna (Little Brown) PW fic 10/12/29 (#5), pk 11/9/29 (#2, 4 wk), 20 wk.
Finch's Fortune (Little Brown) PW fic 10/17/31 (#3, 4 wk), 16 wk.
Lark Ascending (Little Brown) PW fic 9/10/32 (#8, 4 wk), 8 wk.
The Master of Jalna (Little Brown) PW fic 10/14/33 (#3, 8 wk), 12 wk.
Young Renny (Little Brown) PW fic 6/15/35 (#5), pk 7/13/35 (#2, 4 wk), 16 wk.
Whiteoak Harvest (Little Brown) NYT fic 11/8/36 (#3, 4 wk); PW fic 11/14/36 (#4, 4 wk), 12 wk; tot 16 wk.
Growth of a Man (Little Brown) NYT fic 10/9/38 (#6, 4 wk), 8 wk; PW fic 10/15/38 (#10, 4 wk); tot 12 wk.
Whiteoak Heritage (Little Brown) PW fic 10/12/40 (#9, 4 wk).
The Building of Jalna (Little Brown) NYT fic 11/12/44 (#17), pk 11/26/44 (#9, 1 wk), 7 wk; PW fic 12/16/44 (#10, 2 wk); tot 9 wk.
Return to Jalna (Little Brown) NYT fic 11/24/46 (#16, 3 wk).
Mary Wakefield (Little Brown) NYT fic 1/30/49 (#9), pk 2/20/49 (#7, 4 wk), 10 wk; PW fic 2/12/49 (#9), pk 3/5/49 (#6, 1 wk), 4 wk; tot 14 wk.
Renny's Daughter (Little Brown) NYT fic 11/4/51 (#14, 1 wk).

Delderfield, Ronald Frederick
God Is an Englishman (Simon & Schuster) NYT fic 9/13/70 (#10), pk 10/18/70 (#4, 3 wk), 24 wk; PW fic 9/21/70 (#8), pk 10/26/70 (#3, 1 wk), 24 wk; NYT pb fic 9/12/71 (#2), pk 10/10/71 (#1, 16 wk), 24 wk; tot 72 wk.
Theirs Was the Kingdom (Simon & Schuster) NYT fic 9/26/71 (#9), pk 10/31/71 (#5, 3 wk), 13 wk; PW fic 9/27/71 (#9), pk 10/25/71 (#4, 1 wk), 14 wk; tot 27 wk.
To Serve Them All My Days (Simon & Schuster) NYT fic 10/1/72 (#9), pk 10/29/72 (#7, 2 wk), 11 wk; PW fic 10/30/72 (#10), pk 11/20/72 (#6, 1 wk), 9 wk; tot 20 wk.

Diana (Putnam) NYT pb fic 4/9/72 (#5, 4 wk).

Give Us This Day (Simon & Schuster) PW fic 1/21/74 (#9, 1 wk); (Pocket) NYT mm pb 2/2/75 (#6, 1 wk); tot 2 wk.

Del Dotto, Dave
How to Make Nothing But Money (Simon & Schuster) PW hc nf 2/23/90 (#15), pk 3/2/90 (#10, 1 wk), 2 wk.

DeLillo, Don
Libra (Viking) NYT fic 8/14/88 (#13), pk 9/11/88 (#9, 1 wk), 5 wk; PW hc fic 8/19/88 (#14, 3 wk), 5 wk; tot 10 wk.

Dell, Ethel M.
The Lamp in the Desert (Putnam) PW fic 11/1/19 (#8), pk 1/3/20 (#2, 4 wk), 16 wk.

The Top of the World (Putnam) PW fic 10/23/20 (#4), pk 11/27/20 (#2, 4 wk), 20 wk.

Charles Rex (Putnam) PW fic 11/18/22 (#12, 4 wk).

A Man Under Authority (Putnam) PW fic 3/20/26 (#9, 4 wk).

The Black Knight (Putnam) PW fic 3/19/27 (#9, 4 wk).

Storm Drift (Putnam) PW fic 5/16/31 (#10, 4 wk).

Honeyball Farm (Knopf) NYT fic 4/4/37 (#9, 4 wk).

The Juice of the Pomegranate (Chivers) NYT fic 3/6/38 (#15, 4 wk).

Dell, Floyd
Moon-Calf (Knopf) PW fic 4/23/21 (#9, 4 wk).

Delmar, Vina
Bad Girl (Harcourt) PW fic 5/26/28 (#9), pk 6/30/28 (#4, 4 wk), 12 wk.

Beloved (Harcourt) NYT fic 4/22/56 (#15), pk 4/29/56 (#14, 3 wk), 6 wk.

DeLorean, John Z., with Ted Schwarz
DeLorean (Zondervan) NYT nf 10/20/85 (#13, 1 wk), 3 wk.

Delsohn, Steve
See Jim Brown and_____

Delury, George E.
See Anonymous (World Almanac)

Del Vecchio, John M.
The 13th Valley (Bantam) PW hc fic 8/13/82 (#13), pk 9/24/82 (#10, 1 wk), 11 wk; NYT fic 9/26/82 (#13, 1 wk), 4 wk; NYT mm pb 10/2/83 (#7), pk 10/23/83 (#6, 1 wk), 7 wk; PW mm pb 10/7/83 (#7), pk 10/14/83 (#3, 1 wk), 8 wk; tot 30 wk.

DeLyser, Femmy
Jane Fonda's Workout Book for Pregnancy,

Birth and Recovery (Simon & Schuster) PW hc nf 10/8/82 (#15), pk 10/29/82 (#8, 1 wk), 13 wk; NYT nf 10/17/82 (#10), pk 10/31/82 (#6, 1 wk), 23 wk; tot 36 wk.

De Madariaga, Salvador
The Heart of Jade (Creative Age) NYT fic 4/16/44 (#17, 1 wk).

Demarest, Phyllis Gordon
The Naked Risk (Doubleday) NYT fic 2/28/54 (#16, 1 wk).

Demaris, Ovid
Captive City (Lyle Stuart) NYT gen 8/17/69 (#8), pk 8/31/69 (#7, 6 wk), 9 wk; PW nf 9/29/69 (#9), pk 10/13/69 (#7, 1 wk), 3 wk; tot 12 wk.

The Last Mafioso: The Treacherous World of Jimmy Fratianno (Times) PW hc nf 2/6/81 (#13), pk 3/13/81 (#3, 4 wk), 17 wk; NYT nf 2/8/81 (#11), pk 3/8/81 (#3, 3 wk), 14 wk; (Bantam) PW mm pb 11/6/81 (#8), pk 12/11/81 (#5, 1 wk), 10 wk; NYT mm pb 11/8/81 (#8), pk 11/29/81 (#4, 2 wk), 10 wk; tot 51 wk.

The Vegas Legacy (Dell) NYT pb fic 2/12/84 (#15), pk 2/19/84 (#14, 1 wk), 2 wk; PW mm pb 2/24/84 (#15, 1 wk); tot 3 wk.

See also Ed Reid and_____

De Mille, Agnes
Dance to the Piper (Little Brown) NYT gen 2/3/52 (#9), pk 3/2/52 (#3, 1 wk), 12 wk; PW nf 3/15/52 (#10, 2 wk); tot 14 wk.

DeMille, Nelson
Word of Honor (Warner) NYT pb fic 3/15/87 (#13), pk 3/29/87 (#10, 1 wk), 5 wk.

The Charm School (Warner) NYT fic 6/12/88 (#15), pk 7/3/88 (#14, 1 wk), 2 wk; pb fic 2/5/89 (#11), pk 2/12/89 (#6, 3 wk), 9 wk; PW mm pb 2/10/89 (#8), pk 2/24/89 (#4, 1 wk), 8 wk; tot 19 wk.

The Gold Coast (Warner) NYT fic 4/29/90 (#14), pk 5/6/90 (#9, 1 wk), 11 wk; PW hc fic 5/4/90 (#9, 1 wk), 10 wk; tot 21 wk.

Dempsey, Jack, with Bob Considine and Bill Slocum
Dempsey (Simon & Schuster) NYT gen 6/19/60 (#11, 2 wk).

Dennis, Geoffrey Pomeroy
Coronation Commentary (Dodd) NYT gen 6/6/37 (#1, 4 wk), 12 wk; PW fic 6/12/37 (#2, 4 wk), 8 wk; tot 20 wk.

Dennis, Nigel Forbes
Cards of Identity (Vanguard) NYT fic 11/6/55 (#11, 2 wk).

Dennis, Patrick
Auntie Mame (Vanguard) NYT fic 2/20/55 (#16), pk 8/28/55 (#1, 5 wk), 112 wk; PW fic

4/23/55 (#7), pk 9/3/55 (#1, 3 wk), 82 wk; tot 194 wk.
Around the World with Auntie Mame (Harcourt) NYT fic 8/31/58 (#9), pk 10/5/58 (#2, 5 wk), 29 wk; PW fic 9/18/58 (#4), pk 9/29/58 (#1, 2 wk), 28 wk; tot 57 wk.
Little Me (Dutton) NYT fic 11/5/61 (#16), pk 12/24/61 (#4, 6 wk), 25 wk; PW fic 11/27/61 (#6), pk 1/1/62 (#4, 1 wk), 17 wk; tot 42 wk.
Genius (Harcourt) NYT fic 11/18/62 (#12), pk 12/16/62 (#6, 1 wk), 5 wk; PW fic 12/3/62 (#10), pk 1/7/63 (#4, 1 wk), 10 wk; tot 15 wk.
The Joyous Season (Harcourt) PW fic 2/22/65 (#8, 1 wk), 6 wk.
See also Dorothy Erskine and_____
See also Barbara Hooton and_____

Denniston, Denise, and Peter McWilliams
The TM Book (Price Stern Sloan) NYT td pb 8/3/75 (#4), pk 9/7/75 (#1, 3 wk), 15 wk; (Warner) NYT mm pb 11/30/75 (#10), pk 12/7/75 (#8, 2 wk), 4 wk; tot 19 wk.

De Ovies, Raimundo
Somewhere to Be Had (Morehouse Gorham) NYT nf 2/28/43 (#16, 1 wk).

Depew, Chauncey M.
My Memories of Eighty Years (Scribner) PW nf 5/13/22 (#9, 4 wk); PW gen lit 6/17/22 (#8, 8 wk); tot 12 wk.

De Poncins, Gontran
Kabloona (Reynal & Hitchcock) PW nf 4/12/41 (#9), pk 5/10/41 (#5, 4 wk), 12 wk.

De Quille, Dan
See William Wright

Deraney, Michael J.
See Barbara Cohen

De Regniers, Beatrice Schenk
A Little House of Your Own (Harcourt) NYT ch bst 11/13/55 (#13, 40 wk).
May I Bring a Friend? (Atheneum) NYT ch bst 5/9/65 (#5), pk 11/7/65 (#4, 26 wk), 45 wk.

Deriabin, Peter
The Secret World (Doubleday) NYT gen 11/29/59 (#14, 1 wk).

Dermout, Maria
Yesterday (Simon & Schuster) NYT fic 10/4/59 (#15, 1 wk).

De Roussy de Sales, Raoul
The Making of Tomorrow (Reynal & Hitchcock) PW nf 6/13/42 (#7, 4 wk), 8 wk; NYT nf 8/9/42 (#13, 1 wk); tot 9 wk.

Dershowitz, Alan M.
The Best Defense (Random) PW hc nf 6/25/82 (#13, 1 wk), 2 wk.

De Saint-Exupery, Antoine
Wind, Sand and Stars (Reynal & Hitchcock) NYT gen 8/6/39 (#2, 4 wk), 20 wk; PW nf 8/12/39 (#5), pk 2/10/40 (#2, 4 wk), 40 wk; tot 60 wk.
Flight to Arras (Reynal & Hitchcock) PW nf 3/14/42 (#9), pk 4/11/42 (#2, 4 wk), 20 wk; NYT nf 8/9/42 (#12), pk 8/16/42 (#11, 1 wk), 3 wk; tot 23 wk.
The Little Prince (Reynal & Hitchcock) NYT fic 5/23/43 (#10, 1 wk), 2 wk; NYT ch bst 5/7/67 (#9), pk 5/24/70 (#3, 21 wk), 289 wk; tot 291 wk.

De St. Mery, Moreau
Moreau de St. Mery's American Journey [trans. Kenneth Roberts and Anna M. Roberts] (Doubleday) NYT gen 6/22/47 (#14), pk 7/20/47 (#5, 7 wk), 15 wk; PW nf 7/26/47 (#5, 5 wk), 7 wk; tot 22 wk.

De Seversky, Maj. Alexander Procofieff
Victory through Air Power (Simon & Schuster) PW nf 6/13/42 (#5), pk 8/8/42 (#1, 6 wk), 20 wk; NYT nf 8/9/42 (#2), pk 8/16/42 (#1, 4 wk), 18 wk; tot 38 wk.
America—Too Young to Die! (McGraw) NYT gen 8/6/61 (#12, 3 wk), 7 wk.

De Toledano, Ralph, and Victor Lansky
Seeds of Treason (Funk & Wagnalls) NYT gen 4/23/50 (#12), pk 5/21/50 (#4, 5 wk), 21 wk; PW nf 5/13/50 (#7), pk 6/3/50 (#3, 1 wk), 8 wk; tot 29 wk.

De Trevino, Elizabeth Borton
I, Juan de Pareja (Farrar) NYT ch bst 5/8/66 (#9, 19 wk).

Des Barres, Pamela
I'm with the Band (Jove) NYT pb nf 9/18/88 (#10), pk 10/2/88 (#7, 5 wk), 9 wk.

Deveraux, Jude
Velvet Song (Pocket) NYT mm pb 2/13/83 (#14, 1 wk); PW mm pb 2/18/83 (#15, 1 wk); tot 2 wk.
Counterfeit Lady (Pocket) NYT pb fic 12/9/84 (#12), pk 1/6/85 (#8, 1 wk), 4 wk.
Twin of Fire (Pocket) NYT pb fic 8/11/85 (#10), pk 8/25/85 (#9, 1 wk), 4 wk; PW mm pb 8/16/85 (#12), pk 8/30/85 (#8, 1 wk), 3 wk; tot 7 wk.
Twin of Ice (Pocket) PW mm pb 6/21/85 (#13, 2 wk), 3 wk.
Lost Lady (Pocket) NYT pb fic 4/14/85 (#12, 1 wk), 2 wk.
River Lady (Pocket) NYT pb fic 12/15/85 (#15), pk 12/22/85 (#13, 1 wk), 2 wk; PW mm pb 12/20/85 (#12, 2 wk), 3 wk; tot 5 wk.
The Temptress (Pocket) NYT pb fic 8/17/

86 (#13, 1 wk); PW mm pb 8/29/86 (#13, 1 wk); tot 2 wk.

The Raider (Pocket) NYT pb fic 6/7/87 (#9), pk 6/14/87 (#6, 2 wk), 5 wk; PW mm pb 6/19/87 (#6, 1 wk), 3 wk; tot 8 wk.

The Princess (Pocket) NYT pb fic 11/15/87 (#7), pk 11/22/87 (#5, 2 wk), 5 wk; PW mm pb 11/20/87 (#15), pk 12/4/87 (#7, 2 wk), 4 wk; tot 9 wk.

The Maiden (Pocket) NYT pb fic 10/16/88 (#5, 1 wk), 4 wk; PW mm pb 10/28/88 (#6, 1 wk), 3 wk; tot 7 wk.

The Awakening (Pocket) NYT pb fic 6/5/88 (#11), pk 6/19/88 (#4, 1 wk), 6 wk; PW mm pb 6/10/88 (#10), pk 7/1/88 (#5, 1 wk), 6 wk; tot 12 wk.

Wishes (Pocket) NYT pb fic 11/12/89 (#3, 1 wk), 4 wk; PW mm pb 11/17/89 (#9), pk 12/1/89 (#6, 1 wk), 4 wk; tot 8 wk.

The Taming (Pocket) NYT pb fic 5/7/89 (#15), pk 5/14/89 (#3, 1 wk), 5 wk; PW mm pb 5/19/89 (#5, 1 wk), 3 wk; tot 8 wk.

A Knight in Shining Armor (Pocket) NYT fic 8/13/89 (#9), pk 8/27/89 (#5, 1 wk), 10 wk; PW hc fic 8/25/89 (#7, 2 wk), 8 wk; NYT pb fic 6/10/90 (#11), pk 6/24/90 (#4, 1 wk), 6 wk; PW mm pb 6/29/90 (#3, 1 wk), 4 wk; tot 28 wk.

Mountain Laurel (Pocket) NYT fic 7/15/90 (#11), pk 7/22/90 (#10, 2 wk), 4 wk; PW hc fic 7/20/90 (#15), pk 8/10/90 (#10, 2 wk), 5 wk; tot 9 wk.

Devorkin, David
Timetrap (Pocket) NYT pb fic 6/5/88 (#12), pk 6/12/88 (#5, 1 wk), 5 wk; PW mm pb 6/17/88 (#15), pk 6/24/88 (#13, 1 wk), 2 wk; tot 7 wk.

De Voto, Bernard Augustine
The Year of Decision: 1846 (Little Brown) NYT gen 5/9/43 (#19, 1 wk).

Across the Wide Missouri (Houghton) NYT gen 11/30/47 (#15), pk 1/11/48 (#11, 1 wk), 2 wk.

Mountain Time (Little Brown) NYT fic 3/2/47 (#12, 1 wk).

See also Samuel Clemens

DeVries, Peter
The Tunnel of Love (Little Brown) NYT fic 6/20/54 (#14), pk 7/4/54 (#12, 1 wk), 8 wk.

Comfort Me with Apples (Little Brown) NYT fic 5/20/56 (#10), pk 6/10/56 (#7, 1 wk), 13 wk; PW fic 6/18/56 (#10, 1 wk); tot 14 wk.

The Mackeral Plaza (Little Brown) NYT fic 4/20/58 (#12), pk 6/1/58 (#8, 1 wk), 11 wk.

The Tents of Wickedness (Little Brown) NYT fic 8/9/59 (#13), pk 8/16/59 (#7, 2 wk), 8 wk; PW fic 8/24/59 (#8, 1 wk), 3 wk; tot 11 wk.

Through the Fields of Clover (Little Brown) NYT fic 3/19/61 (#14, 1 wk), 2 wk.

Reuben, Reuben (Little Brown) PW fic 3/9/64 (#8, 1 wk), 2 wk; NYT fic 3/22/64 (#9, 3 wk), 5 wk; tot 7 wk.

The Vale of Laughter (Little Brown) PW fic 11/27/67 (#9), pk 1/22/68 (#7, 1 wk), 6 wk.

DeWeese, Gene
Chain of Attack (Pocket) NYT pb fic 2/15/87 (#12), pk 2/22/87 (#9, 1 wk), 3 wk; PW mm pb 2/27/87 (#14), pk 3/6/87 (#13, 1 wk), 2 wk; tot 5 wk.

The Final Nexus (Pocket) NYT pb fic 12/11/88 (#12), pk 12/18/88 (#8, 1 wk), 4 wk; PW mm pb 12/16/88 (#10, 2 wk), 4 wk; tot 8 wk.

Dewey, Edward R., and Edwin F. Dakin
Cycles (Holt) NYT gen 5/18/47 (#13), pk 8/17/47 (#10, 2 wk), 16 wk; PW nf 6/14/47 (#10), pk 8/16/47 (#8, 1 wk), 4 wk; tot 20 wk.

Dewey, Thomas E.
Journey to the Far Pacific (Doubleday) NYT gen 8/3/52 (#10), pk 8/17/52 (#7, 2 wk), 10 wk; PW nf 9/13/52 (#9), pk 9/20/52 (#7, 1 wk), 2 wk; tot 12 wk.

Dewlen, Al
Twilight of Honor (McGraw) NYT fic 2/11/62 (#13), pk 3/11/62 (#12, 1 wk), 9 wk.

Dexter, Peter
Paris Trout (Penguin) PW td pb 8/11/89 (#8), pk 8/25/89 (#5, 2 wk), 11 wk.

Diamant, Gertrude
The Days of Ofelia (Houghton) NYT nf 9/20/42 (#15), pk 9/27/42 (#8, 1 wk), 3 wk.

Diamond, Harvey, and Marilyn Diamond
Fit for Life (Warner) PW hc nf 7/12/85 (#14), pk 11/22/85 (#1, 22 wk), 73 wk; NYT msc 8/11/85 (#5), pk 9/29/85 (#1, 40 wk), 67 wk; NYT msc pb 2/1/87 (#3), pk 2/8/87 (#2, 12 wk), 19 wk; PW mm pb 2/6/87 (#11), pk 3/20/87 (#4, 1 wk), 25 wk; tot 184 wk.

Dibner, Martin
The Deep Six (Doubleday) NYT fic 9/6/53 (#16), pk 9/13/53 (#14, 3 wk), 6 wk.

Dickens, Charles
The Life of Our Lord (Simon & Schuster) PW nf 6/9/34 (#1, 4 wk), 12 wk.

Dickens, Monica
The Happy Prisoner (Lippincott) NYT fic 9/7/47 (#16), pk 9/28/47 (#15, 1 wk), 3 wk.

Dickey, James
Deliverance (Houghton) NYT fic 4/12/70 (#7), pk 4/26/70 (#3, 9 wk), 26 wk; PW fic

4/27/70 (#5), pk 6/1/70 (#2, 5 wk), 28 wk; NYT pb fic 5/2/71 (#3, 12 wk), 16 wk; tot 70 wk.

Dickinson, Emily
Bolts of Melody: New Poems of Emily Dickinson [ed. H.L. Todd and M.T. Bingham] (Harper) NYT gen 5/6/45 (#14, 1 wk).

Didion, Joan
Play It as It Lays (Farrar) PW fic 8/31/70 (#7), pk 9/14/70 (#6, 1 wk), 6 wk; NYT fic 9/6/70 (#10, 1 wk); tot 7 wk.
A Book of Common Prayer (Simon & Schuster) PW hc fic 4/18/77 (#9), pk 5/16/77 (#4, 1 wk), 12 wk; NYT fic 4/24/77 (#10), pk 5/15/77 (#8, 5 wk), 15 wk; (Pocket) PW mm pb 2/20/78 (#15), pk 3/13/78 (#10, 1 wk), 5 wk; NYT mm pb 3/5/78 (#13, 1 wk), 3 wk; tot 35 wk.
The White Album (Simon & Schuster) PW hc nf 7/2/79 (#10), pk 7/30/79 (#7, 1 wk), 17 wk; NYT nf 7/22/79 (#13), pk 9/9/79 (#7, 1 wk), 13 wk; tot 30 wk.
Salvador (Simon & Schuster) NYT nf 4/10/83 (#12), pk 4/17/83 (#8, 1 wk), 8 wk; PW hc nf 4/22/83 (#9), pk 5/20/83 (#8, 1 wk), 9 wk; tot 17 wk.
Democracy (Simon & Schuster) NYT fic 5/20/84 (#13), pk 6/3/84 (#12, 1 wk), 4 wk.

Di Donato, Pietro
Christ in Concrete (Bobbs Merrill) NYT fic 10/8/39 (#3, 4 wk), 12 wk; PW fic 10/14/39 (#8), pk 11/11/39 (#5, 4 wk), 12 wk; tot 24 wk.

Diehl, William
Chameleon (Random) PW hc fic 2/26/82 (#15, 1 wk); (Ballantine) NYT mm pb 11/7/82 (#11), pk 12/12/82 (#2, 1 wk), 12 wk; PW mm pb 11/19/82 (#6), pk 12/17/82 (#2, 1 wk), 7 wk; tot 20 wk.
Hooligans (Villard) NYT fic 7/22/84 (#14, 1 wk); (Ballantine) NYT pb fic 5/12/85 (#15), pk 5/19/85 (#10, 3 wk), 4 wk; PW mm pb 5/17/85 (#10, 1 wk), 4 wk; tot 9 wk.
Thai Horse (Villard) PW hc fic 2/12/88 (#14), pk 2/19/88 (#13, 1 wk), 3 wk; NYT fic 2/21/88 (#14), pk 3/6/88 (#13, 1 wk), 2 wk; (Ballantine) NYT pb fic 2/12/89 (#13), pk 2/19/89 (#9, 2 wk), 4 wk; PW mm pb 2/17/89 (#11), pk 2/24/89 (#7, 1 wk), 4 wk; tot 13 wk.

Di Lampedusa, Guiseppe
The Leopard (Pantheon) NYT fic 5/15/60 (#15), pk 7/10/60 (#2, 1 wk), 38 wk; PW fic 5/30/60 (#4), pk 7/11/60 (#1, 1 wk), 35 wk; tot 73 wk.

Dilenschneider, Robert
Power and Influence (Prentice Hall) PW hc nf 6/15/90 (#12, 1 wk).

Dillard, Annie
An American Childhood (Harper) NYT nf 10/4/87 (#14), pk 10/11/87 (#13, 1 wk), 5 wk.
The Writing Life (Harper) NYT nf 9/17/89 (#11), pk 9/24/89 (#9, 3 wk), 9 wk.

Dillard, J.M.
Demons (Pocket) NYT pb fic 7/13/86 (#13, 1 wk), 2 wk; PW mm pb 7/25/86 (#15, 2 wk); tot 4 wk.
Bloodthirst (Pocket) NYT pb fic 12/13/87 (#10, 1 wk), 2 wk; PW mm pb 12/18/87 (#9, 1 wk), 3 wk; tot 5 wk.
The Final Frontier (Pocket) NYT pb fic 6/18/89 (#9), pk 6/25/89 (#3, 1 wk), 4 wk; PW mm pb 6/23/89 (#9, 2 wk), 4 wk; tot 8 wk.
The Lost Years (Pocket) NYT fic 10/8/89 (#12), pk 10/15/89 (#6, 2 wk), 7 wk; PW hc fic 10/13/89 (#9), pk 10/27/89 (#5, 1 wk), 9 wk; NYT pb fic 8/19/90 (#13, 1 wk); tot 17 wk.

Dilliard, Irving
See Learned Hand and_____

Dillon, Edward J.
The Inside Story of the Peace Conference (Harper) PW gen 6/12/20 (#4, 4 wk), 12 wk.

Dillon, George
See Charles Baudelaire

Dillon, Katherine V.
See Gordon W. Prange, et al.

Dillon, Leo, and Diane Dillon
See Leontyne Price and_____

Dillon, Richard H.
Meriwether Lewis (Coward McCann) NYT gen 4/18/65 (#9, 2 wk); PW nf 4/26/65 (#8, 2 wk), 6 wk; tot 8 wk.

Dills, Lanie
The Official CB Slanguage Dictionary (Martin) NYT td pb 4/18/76 (#3), pk 6/13/76 (#1, 8 wk), 25 wk; PW td pb 4/19/76 (#4), pk 6/21/76 (#1, 4 wk), 18 wk; tot 43 wk.

Dimnet, Ernest
The Art of Thinking (Simon & Schuster) PW nf 2/16/29 (#7), pk 4/13/29 (#1, 4 wk), 60 wk.
What We Live By (Simon & Schuster) PW nf 8/13/32 (#3, 8 wk), 16 wk.

DiMona, Joseph
See Dr. Thomas T. Noguchi and_____
See H.R. Haldeman and_____

Dineen, Joseph Francis
The Purple Shamrock (Norton) NYT gen 10/2/49 (#16), pk 10/23/49 (#10, 1 wk), 6 wk.

Dinesen, Isak
See Karen Blixen

Diver, Maud
A Wild Bird (Houghton) PW fic 8/10/29 (#9, 4 wk).
Ships of Youth (Houghton) PW fic 7/18/31 (#6), pk 8/15/31 (#5, 4 wk), 8 wk.

Dixon, Franklin W.
The Jungle Pyramid (Grosset & Dunlap) NYT ch hc 11/13/77 (#3, 46 wk).

Dixon, Jeane, with Rene Noorber-gen
My Life and Prophecies (Morrow) NYT gen 9/28/69 (#6), pk 10/26/69 (#4, 1 wk), 12 wk; PW nf 10/6/69 (#9), pk 11/17/69 (#2, 1 wk), 12 wk; tot 24 wk.

Dixon, Thomas
See Harry M. Daugherty and_____

Djilas, Milovan
The New Class (Praeger) NYT gen 9/1/57 (#9), pk 9/15/57 (#3, 11 wk), 33 wk; PW nf 9/9/57 (#7), pk 10/14/57 (#2, 1 wk), 21 wk; tot 54 wk.
Land Without Justice (Harcourt) NYT gen 5/25/58 (#14), pk 6/8/58 (#9, 1 wk), 3 wk.
Conversations with Stalin (Harcourt) NYT gen 6/3/62 (#15), pk 7/8/62 (#6, 1 wk), 14 wk; PW nf 6/11/62 (#8), pk 7/30/62 (#5, 1 wk), 12 wk; tot 26 wk.

Dmitri, Ivan
See Levon West

Dobie, James Frank
A Texan in England (Little Brown) NYT gen 5/27/45 (#12, 2 wk), 9 wk.

Dobkin, Marjorie Housepian
A Houseful of Love (Random) NYT fic 7/21/57 (#14), pk 8/25/57 (#13, 1 wk), 4 wk.

Dobson, James
Preparing for Adolescence (Regal/Gospel Light) PW pb rel 10/5/90 (#11, 4 wk).
Love for a Lifetime (Multnomah) PW hc rel 10/5/90 (#6, 8 wk).
Love Must Be Tough (Word) PW hc rel 11/9/90 (#14, 4 wk).

Dobson, Kenneth
Away All Boats (Little Brown) NYT fic 3/21/54 (#14), pk 4/18/54 (#3, 2 wk), 30 wk; PW fic 4/10/54 (#6), pk 5/8/54 (#2, 1 wk), 14 wk; tot 44 wk.

Dr. Seuss
See Theodor Geisel

Doctor X [pseud.]
Intern (Harper) NYT gen 7/25/65 (#7), pk 9/5/65 (#2, 4 wk), 18 wk; PW nf 7/26/65 (#7), pk 9/20/65 (#2, 8 wk), 28 wk; NYT pb gen 7/3/66 (#3), pk 8/7/66 (#1, 4 wk), 16 wk; tot 62 wk.

Doctorow, E.L.
Ragtime (Random) PW fic 7/28/75 (#3), pk 8/11/75 (#1, 15 wk), 38 wk; NYT fic 8/3/75 (#7), pk 8/24/75 (#1, 13 wk), 39 wk; (Bantam) PW mm pb 7/19/76 (#4), pk 7/26/76 (#1, 2 wk), 13 wk; NYT mm pb 7/25/76 (#5), pk 8/15/76 (#2, 1 wk), 10 wk; tot 100 wk.
Loon Lake (Random) PW hc fic 10/3/80 (#13), pk 10/17/80 (#6, 5 wk), 22 wk; NYT fic 10/5/80 (#15), pk 10/26/80 (#4, 6 wk), 25 wk; (Bantam) PW mm pb 12/11/81 (#13), pk 12/18/81 (#12, 1 wk), 6 wk; tot 53 wk.
World's Fair (Random) NYT fic 11/17/85 (#13), pk 12/8/85 (#7, 1 wk), 13 wk; PW hc fic 11/22/85 (#15), pk 12/6/85 (#9, 2 wk), 9 wk; tot 22 wk.
Billy Bathgate (Random) PW hc fic 2/24/89 (#12), pk 3/31/89 (#4, 3 wk), 14 wk; NYT fic 3/5/89 (#8), pk 3/12/89 (#4, 3 wk), 12 wk; (HarperPaperbacks) PW mm pb 2/2/90 (#14) 2/16/90 (#5, 2 wk), 11 wk; NYT pb fic 2/4/90 (#8), pk 2/18/90 (#4, 1 wk), 10 wk; tot 47 wk.

Dodd, Martha
Through Embassy Eyes (Harcourt) PW nf 4/8/39 (#8), pk 5/13/39 (#6, 4 wk), 12 wk; NYT gen 4/9/39 (#11), pk 5/7/39 (#7, 4 wk), 12 wk; tot 24 wk.

Dodd, William E.
Ambassador Dodd's Diary [ed. William E. Dodd, Jr., and Martha Dodd] (Harcourt) PW nf 4/12/41 (#7, 8 wk).

Dodge, David
How Green Was My Father (Simon & Schuster) NYT gen 7/13/47 (#16, 1 wk).
The Poor Man's Guide to Europe (Random) NYT gen 5/3/53 (#10), pk 6/7/53 (#8, 2 wk), 15 wk; PW nf 6/13/53 (#10), pk 6/27/53 (#6, 1 wk), 2 wk; tot 17 wk.

Dody, Sandford
See Helen Hayes and_____

Donahue, Phil
Donahue: My Own Story (Simon & Schuster) PW hc nf 2/8/80 (#15), pk 3/21/80 (#2, 2 wk), 22 wk; NYT nf 2/17/80 (#7), pk 3/23/80 (#1, 2 wk), 28 wk; (Fawcett/Crest) PW mm pb 12/12/80 (#6), pk 1/16/81 (#2, 1 wk), 6 wk; NYT mm pb 12/14/80 (#14), pk 12/28/80 (#2, 4 wk), 9 wk; tot 65 wk.
The Human Animal (Simon & Schuster) NYT nf 10/6/85 (#15, 1 wk).

Donald, David Herbert
Lincoln's Herndon (Knopf) NYT gen 11/14/48 (#12, 1 wk).
Divided We Fought (Macmillan) NYT gen 1/11/53 (#16, 1 wk).

Donaldson, Sam
  Hold On, Mr. President! (Random) NYT nf 4/12/87 (#12), pk 5/10/87 (#2, 1 wk), 16 wk; PW hc nf 4/17/87 (#14), pk 5/15/87 (#3, 1 wk), 14 wk; (Fawcett) NYT pb nf 2/28/88 (#7), pk 3/20/88 (#6, 3 wk), 10 wk; tot 40 wk.

Donaldson, Stephen R.
  The Wounded Land (Ballantine/Del Rey) PW mm pb 5/15/81 (#7, 1 wk), 5 wk; NYT mm pb 5/17/81 (#15, 1 wk); tot 6 wk.
  The One Tree (Ballantine/Del Rey) PW hc fic 4/30/82 (#5), pk 5/21/82 (#2, 1 wk), 22 wk; NYT fic 5/2/82 (#3), pk 5/9/82 (#2, 3 wk), 21 wk; NYT mm pb 4/10/83 (#5, 2 wk), 5 wk; PW mm pb 4/15/83 (#8), pk 4/22/83 (#5, 1 wk), 5 wk; tot 53 wk.
  White Gold Wielder: Book Three of the Second Chronicles of Thomas Covenant (Ballantine/Del Rey) NYT fic 4/10/83 (#2, 2 wk), 29 wk; PW hc fic 4/15/83 (#4), pk 4/22/83 (#3, 4 wk), 26 wk; PW mm pb 4/23/84 (#7), pk 4/20/84 (#5, 1 wk), 5 wk; tot 60 wk.
  The Mirror of Her Dreams (Ballantine/Del Rey) NYT fic 11/23/86 (#15), pk 11/30/86 (#14, 1 wk), 4 wk; PW hc fic 11/28/86 (#14), pk 12/19/86 (#9, 1 wk), 8 wk; tot 12 wk.
  A Man Rides Through: Mordant's Need, Vol. II (Ballantine/Del Rey) NYT fic 12/6/87 (#12, 1 wk), 3 wk; PW hc fic 12/11/87 (#11), pk 12/18/87 (#9, 1 wk), 6 wk; PW mm pb 11/11/88 (#13), pk 11/18/88 (#7, 1 wk), 5 wk; NYT pb fic 11/20/88 (#14), pk 11/27/88 (#13, 1 wk), 2 wk; tot 16 wk.

Donleavy, B.J.P.
  The Beastly Beatitudes of Balthazar (Lawrence/Delacorte) NYT fic NYT fic 1/19/69 (#9, 1 wk); PW fic 1/27/69 (#10), pk 2/3/69 (#7, 2 wk), 4 wk; tot 5 wk.

Donleavy, James Patrick
  The Ginger Man (McDowell Oblensky) NYT fic 7/20/58 (#16, 1 wk).

Donoghue, William E., with Thomas Tilling
  William E. Donoghue's Complete Money Market Guide (Harper) PW hc nf 3/13/81 (#14), pk 5/1/81 (#8, 1 wk), 15 wk; NYT nf 3/29/81 (#3, 1 wk), 18 wk; tot 33 wk.
  William E. Donoghue's No-Load Mutual Fund Guide: How to Take Advantage of the Investment Opportunity of the 80s (Harper) PW hc nf 3/25/83 (#9, 2 wk), 11 wk.

Donovan, Robert J.
  Eisenhower: The Inside Story (Harper) NYT gen 7/15/56 (#13), pk 8/5/56 (#1, 11 wk), 22 wk; PW nf 7/30/56 (#3), pk 8/13/56 (#1, 8 wk), 17 wk; tot 39 wk.

PT 109: John F. Kennedy in World War II (McGraw) NYT gen 12/24/61 (#16), pk 1/21/61 (#12, 1 wk), 9 wk.
  See also Joseph William Martin and_____

Doohan, James
  See Judith and Garfield Reeves-Stevens

Dooley, Dr. Thomas A.
  The Night They Burned the Mountain (Farrar) NYT gen 5/8/60 (#12), pk 7/3/60 (#5, 4 wk), 21 wk; PW nf 5/30/60 (#7), pk 7/18/60 (#4, 1 wk), 13 wk; tot 34 wk.
  Dr. Tom Dooley's Three Great Books: Deliver Us from Evil, The Edge of Tomorrow and The Night They Burned the Mountain (Farrar) NYT gen 3/12/61 (#12, 2 wk), 6 wk.

Dorris, Michael
  The Broken Cord (Harper) NYT nf 5/6/90 (#14, 1 wk), 2 wk.

Dorsey, George
  Christopher of San Francisco (Macmillan) NYT gen 6/17/62 (#12, 1 wk).

Dorsey, George Amos
  Why We Behave Like Human Beings (Harper) PW nf 3/20/26 (#3), pk 7/17/26 (#2, 16 wk), 64 wk.
  Hows and Whys of Human Behavior (Harper) PW nf 2/16/29 (#8), pk 3/9/29 (#5, 4 wk), 16 wk.
  Man's Own Show: Civilization (Harper) PW nf 10/17/31 (#8, 4 wk), 12 wk.

Dos Passos, John
  The Big Money (Harcourt) PW fic 9/12/36 (#8), pk 10/10/36 (#4, 4 wk), 12 wk; NYT fic 9/13/36 (#5, 4 wk); tot 16 wk.
  Adventures of a Young Man (Harcourt) NYT fic 7/9/39 (#4, 4 wk).
  Number One (Houghton) NYT fic 3/28/43 (#19), pk 4/18/43 (#6, 1 wk), 8 wk; PW fic 5/15/43 (#10, 1 wk); tot 9 wk.
  The Men Who Made the Nation (Doubleday) NYT gen 3/10/57 (#16, 3 wk).
  Tour of Duty (Houghton) NYT gen 9/29/46 (#12, 1 wk).
  The Grand Design (Houghton) NYT fic 1/30/49 (#11), pk 2/6/49 (#8, 1 wk), 5 wk.
  Chosen Country (Houghton) NYT fic 1/13/52 (#14, 1 wk), 2 wk.
  Midcentury (Houghton) NYT fic 3/19/61 (#12), pk 5/28/61 (#5, 1 wk), 16 wk; PW fic 3/27/61 (#6), pk 4/24/61 (#4, 1 wk), 11 wk; tot 27 wk.

Douglas, Jack
  My Brother Was an Only Child (Dutton) NYT gen 4/26/59 (#12), pk 6/7/59 (#6, 8 wk), 23 wk; PW nf 5/11/59 (#9), pk 6/1/59 (#6, 5 wk), 14 wk; tot 37 wk.

Never Trust a Naked Bus Driver (Dutton) NYT gen 5/1/60 (#13, 1 wk), 3 wk.

Douglas, Kirk
The Ragman's Son (Simon & Schuster) PW hc nf 8/26/88 (#11), pk 10/14/88 (#3, 1 wk), 13 wk; NYT nf 8/28/88 (#9), pk 9/18/88 (#2, 4 wk), 17 wk; (Pocket) NYT pb fic 7/9/89 (#9), pk 8/27/89 (#1, 2 wk), 15 wk; PW mm pb 7/21/89 (#14), pk 9/1/89 (#11, 1 wk), 4 wk; tot 49 wk.
Dance with the Devil (Random) NYT fic 8/5/90 (#15, 1 wk).

Douglas, Lloyd Cassel
The Magnificent Obsession (Willett) PW fic 6/11/32 (#8), pk 4/15/33 (#5, 4 wk), 36 wk; NYT fic 2/2/36 (#10, 8 wk); tot 44 wk.
Forgive Us Our Trespasses (Houghton) PW fic 12/17/32 (#5), pk 2/11/33 (#2, 12 wk), 24 wk.
Green Light (Houghton) PW fic 4/13/35 (#1, 20 wk), 52 wk.
White Banners (Houghton) NYT fic 11/8/36 (#2, 4 wk), 8 wk; PW fic 11/14/36 (#2, 8 wk), 20 wk; tot 28 wk.
Home for Christmas (Houghton) NYT fic 1/9/38 (#3, 4 wk), 8 wk; PW fic 1/15/38 (#5, 4 wk); tot 12 wk.
Disputed Passage (Houghton) NYT fic 2/5/39 (#2, 4 wk), 16 wk; PW fic 2/11/39 (#3, 12 wk), 20 wk; tot 36 wk.
Doctor Hudson's Secret Journal (Houghton) NYT fic 12/10/39 (#5, 4 wk), 8 wk; PW fic 12/16/39 (#8), pk 1/13/40 (#7, 4 wk), 12 wk; tot 20 wk.
Invitation to Live (Houghton) PW fic 12/14/40 (#8), pk 1/11/41 (#7, 4 wk), 12 wk.
The Robe (Houghton) NYT fic 11/1/42 (#14), pk 11/22/42 (#1, 46 wk), 176 wk; PW fic 11/7/42 (#5), pk 11/21/42 (#1, 47 wk), 116 wk; tot 292 wk.
The Big Fisherman (Houghton) NYT fic 11/28/48 (#7), pk 12/19/48 (#1, 16 wk), 61 wk; PW fic 12/11/48 (#5), pk 12/18/48 (#1, 19 wk), 43 wk; tot 104 wk.
Time to Remember (Houghton) NYT gen 11/11/51 (#16), pk 11/25/51 (#15, 1 wk), 2 wk.

Douglas, William Orville
Of Men and Mountains (Harper) NYT gen 5/7/50 (#16), pk 6/11/50 (#13, 2 wk), 5 wk.
Strange Lands and Friendly People (Harper) NYT gen 11/25/51 (#10), pk 12/9/51 (#7, 1 wk), 17 wk; PW nf 1/12/52 (#8), pk 2/16/52 (#5, 1 wk), 3 wk; tot 20 wk.
Beyond the High Himalayas (Doubleday) NYT gen 10/19/52 (#9), pk 1/11/52 (#8, 1 wk), 18 wk; PW nf 11/15/52 (#9), pk 12/13/52 (#7, 1 wk), 2 wk; tot 20 wk.
North from Malaya (Doubleday) NYT gen 6/21/53 (#11), pk 8/2/53 (#6, 2 wk), 13 wk;

PW nf 7/18/53 (#5), pk 8/8/53 (#4, 1 wk), 4 wk; tot 17 wk.
An Almanac of Liberty (Doubleday) NYT gen 12/19/54 (#13, 3 wk), 7 wk.
My Wilderness (Doubleday) NYT gen 12/25/60 (#13), pk 1/8/61 (#10, 1 wk), 5 wk.
Points of Rebellion (Random) NYT gen 3/15/70 (#10), pk 5/3/70 (#7, 2 wk), 7 wk; NYT pb gen 5/3/70 (#5), pk 7/5/70 (#2, 8 wk), 16 wk; PW nf 5/18/70 (#8, 1 wk), 4 wk; tot 27 wk.
Go East, Young Man (Random) NYT gen 5/12/74 (#10), pk 6/2/74 (#8, 2 wk), 6 wk; PW nf 5/20/74 (#8), pk 6/10/74 (#7, 1 wk), 6 wk; tot 12 wk.
The Court Years, 1939–1975: The Autobiography of William O. Douglas (Random) PW hc nf 10/31/80 (#15), pk 1/16/81 (#12, 1 wk), 5 wk; NYT nf 12/28/80 (#15, 1 wk); tot 6 wk.

Dowdey, Clifford
The Land They Fought For (Doubleday) NYT gen 7/10/55 (#11, 1 wk), 3 wk.
Death of a Nation (Knopf) NYT gen 7/27/58 (#11, 2 wk).

Dowling, Colette
The Cinderella Complex: Women's Hidden Fear of Independence (Summit) NYT nf 7/26/81 (#11), pk 10/4/81 (#4, 3 wk), 26 wk; PW hc nf 7/31/81 (#12), pk 9/18/81 (#4, 4 wk), 21 wk; (Pocket) mm pb 6/25/82 (#10), pk 7/9/82 (#5, 1 wk), 15 wk; NYT mm pb 6/27/82 (#3, 1 wk), 13 wk; tot 75 wk.

Downing, J. Hyatt
A Prayer for Tomorrow (Putnam) NYT fic 5/1/38 (#15, 4 wk).

Doyle, Arthur Conan
The Vital Message (Doran) PW gen 3/27/20 (#8, 4 wk).

Doyle, Richard
Imperial 109 (Bantam) PW mm pb 7/24/78 (#10, 1 wk), 3 wk.

Dravecky, Dave, with Tim Stafford
Comeback (Zondervan/HarperSanFrancisco) PW hc rel 10/5/90 (#7, 8 wk).

Dreiser, Theodore
The Bulwark (Doubleday) NYT fic 4/14/46 (#8), pk 4/21/46 (#5, 1 wk), 9 wk.

Drew, Wayland
Willow (Ballantine/Del Rey) NYT pb fic 6/19/88 (#13, 1 wk).

Drewry, J.E.
Post Biographies of Famous Journalists (Saturday Evening Post) NYT nf 2/7/43 (#12, 1 wk).

Drimmer, Frederick
Very Special People (Bantam) PW mm pb
5/3/76 (#15, 1 wk).

Drinkwater, John
Abraham Lincoln (Houghton) PW gen 3/
27/20 (#2, 4 wk), 20 wk; gen lit 3/26/21 (#6,
4 wk), 8 wk; tot 28 wk.
The Outline of Literature, Vol. 1 (Putnam)
PW gen lit 8/18/23 (#12), pk 9/15/23 (#8, 4
wk), 8 wk; PW nf 11/24/23 (#11, 4 wk); tot
12 wk.

Driscoll, Charles Benedict
The Life of O.O. McIntyre (Greystone)
NYT gen 9/4/38 (#12, 4 wk).

Droban, Leonard
Come with Me to Macedonia (Knopf) NYT
fic 9/29/57 (#16, 1 wk).

Drosnin, Michael
Citizen Hughes (Holt) NYT nf 2/10/85
(#3, 5 wk), 13 wk; PW hc nf 2/15/85 (#8), pk
3/8/85 (#2, 2 wk), 13 wk; (Bantam) NYT
mm pb 3/16/86 (#6), pk 3/23/86 (#4, 2 wk),
5 wk; tot 31 wk.

Drucker, Peter F.
The Age of Discontinuity (Harper) NYT
gen 4/27/69 (#10) pk 5/18/69 (#9, 1 wk), 2 wk.
Management (Harper) PW nf 3/11/74
(#9), pk 4/15/74 (#3, 1 wk), 19 wk; NYT gen
3/17/74 (#8), pk 4/14/74 (#4, 4 wk), 17 wk;
tot 36 wk.
Managing in Turbulent Times (Harper)
PW hc nf 6/13/80 (#14), pk 7/4/80 (#12, 1
wk), 7 wk; NYT nf 8/31/80 (#11, 1 wk); tot
8 wk.

Drury, Allen
Advise and Consent (Doubleday) NYT fic
8/16/59 (#12), pk 10/4/59 (#1, 27 wk), 102
wk; PW fic 8/24/59 (#10), pk 10/5/59 (#1, 36
wk), 94 wk; tot 196 wk.
A Shade of Difference (Doubleday) PW fic
10/1/62 (#13), pk 11/5/62 (#1, 6 wk), 24 wk;
NYT fic 10/7/62 (#9), pk 10/28/62 (#1, 4
wk), 12 wk; tot 36 wk.
Capable of Honor (Doubleday) NYT fic
10/2/66 (#10), pk 12/18/66 (#2, 13 wk), 41 wk;
PW fic 10/10/66 (#7), pk 10/31/66 (#1, 1 wk),
40 wk; NYT pb fic 3/3/68 (#2, 4 wk), 8 wk;
tot 89 wk.
Preserve and Protect (Doubleday) PW fic
9/23/68 (#7), pk 11/25/68 (#2, 2 wk), 30 wk;
NYT fic 9/29/68 (#5), pk 10/13/68 (#2, 4
wk), 28 wk; NYT pb fic 11/2/69 (#5, 8 wk);
tot 66 wk.
The Throne of Saturn (Doubleday) NYT
fic 3/7/71 (#6), pk 3/21/71 (#2, 2 wk), 17 wk;
PW fic 3/8/71 (#7), pk 3/29/71 (#3, 3 wk),
20 wk; tot 37 wk.

Come Nineveh, Come Tyre (Doubleday)
NYT fic 11/25/73 (#8), pk 2/3/73 (#2, 8 wk),
26 wk; PW fic 11/26/73 (#5), pk 1/14/74 (#2,
8 wk), 24 wk; (Avon) NYT mm pb 11/10/74
(#8), pk 12/8/74 (#5, 4 wk), 8 wk; tot 58 wk.
The Promise of Joy (Doubleday) PW fic
3/24/75 (#10), pk 6/16/75 (#3, 2 wk), 20 wk;
NYT fic 3/30/75 (#7), pk 4/27/75 (#3, 6 wk),
19 wk; (Avon) PW mm pb 3/8/76 (#9, 2 wk),
3 wk; tot 42 wk.
Return to Thebes (Doubleday) PW hc fic
3/21/77 (#7, 1 wk).
Decision (Doubleday) PW hc fic 9/2/83
(#13, 1 wk), 3 wk.

Druyan, Ann
See Carl Sagan and_____

Dryer, Bernard V.
The Image Makers (Harper) NYT fic 7/6/
58 (#13), pk 8/31/58 (#4, 2 wk), 20 wk; PW
fic 7/7/58 (#6), pk 8/11/58 (#4, 2 wk), 12 wk;
tot 32 wk.

Duane, Diane
Spock's World (Pocket) NYT fic 9/11/88
(#6), pk 9/18/88 (#4, 2 wk), 8 wk; PW hc fic
9/16/88 (#5), pk 9/30/88 (#3, 1 wk), 11 wk;
NYT pb fic 8/13/89 (#13, 1 wk), 2 wk; tot 21
wk.
Doctor's Orders (Pocket) NYT pb fic 6/10/
90 (#13, 3 wk).

_____, and Peter Morwood
The Romulan Way (Pocket) NYT pb fic
8/9/87 (#16), pk 8/16/87 (#9, 1 wk), 3 wk;
PW mm pb 8/21/87 (#12), pk 8/28/87 (#11,
1 wk), 3 wk; tot 6 wk.

Du Bois, William Pene
See Edward Lear

Dubov, Paul
See Gwen Bagni and_____

Duchess of Windsor
See Windsor, Duchess of

Dudintsov, Vladimir
Not by Bread Alone (Dutton) NYT fic
11/17/57 (#11, 2 wk), 7 wk.

Duerrenmatt, Friedrich
The Pledge (Knopf) NYT fic 4/19/59 (#13,
1 wk).

Duffield, E.S.
See James Forrestal, et al.

Dufty, William
See Billie Holiday and_____

Dugan, James
The Great Iron Ship (Harper) NYT gen
2/28/54 (#13, 1 wk), 4 wk.

Duguid, Julian
Green Hell (Century) PW nf 6/20/31 (#4, 12 wk), 16 wk.

Duhe, Camille
See Vidal Sassoon, et al.

Du Jardin, Rosamond Neal
Double Date (Lippincott) NYT ch bst 11/16/52 (#11, 40 wk).
Boy Trouble (Lippincott) NYT ch bst 11/15/53 (#8, 40 wk).
A Man for Marcy (Lippincott) NYT ch bst 11/14/54 (#11, 40 wk).
Double Feature (Lippincott) NYT ch bst 11/14/54 (#7, 40 wk).
Showboat Summer (Lippincott) NYT ch bst 11/18/56 (#9, 40 wk).
Wedding in the Family (Lippincott) NYT ch bst 11/1/59 (#16, 25 wk).

Dukakis, Kitty, and Jane Scovell
Now You Know (Simon & Schuster) NYT nf 9/23/90 (#12), pk 9/30/90 (#7, 2 wk), 5 wk; PW hc nf 9/28/90 (#13), pk 10/5/90 (#5, 1 wk), 5 wk; tot 10 wk.

Duke, Patty, and Kenneth Turan
Call Me Anna: The Autobiography of Patty Duke (Bantam) NYT nf 8/9/87 (#6, 5 wk), 10 wk; PW hc nf 8/14/87 (#5, 5 wk), 9 wk; NYT pb nf 6/5/88 (#9), pk 6/19/88 (#4, 4 wk), 9 wk; PW mm pb 6/17/88 (#12), pk 7/1/88 (#7, 1 wk), 5 wk; tot 33 wk.

Duke of Windsor
See Windsor, Duke of

Dulles, John Foster
War or Peace (Macmillan) NYT gen 5/14/50 (#13), pk 5/28/50 (#11, 1 wk), 5 wk.

Dumas, Frederic
See Jacques Y. Cousteau and_____

Du Maurier, Dame Daphne
Jamaica Inn (Doubleday) PW fic 6/13/36 (#6, 4 wk), 8 wk; NYT fic 7/5/36 (#10, 4 wk); tot 12 wk.
The Du Mauriers (Doubleday) NYT nf 6/6/37 (#7, 4 wk).
Rebecca (Doubleday) NYT fic 11/6/38 (#1, 4 wk), 24 wk; PW fic 11/12/38 (#3), pk 12/10/38 (#1, 4 wk), 40 wk; tot 64 wk.
Come Wind, Come Weather (Doubleday) PW nf 4/12/41 (#5, 4 wk), 12 wk.
Frenchman's Creek (Doubleday) PW fic 3/14/42 (#2, 4 wk), 12 wk; NYT fic 9/6/42 (#14, 1 wk); tot 13 wk.
Hungry Hill (Doubleday) PW fic 6/26/43 (#5), pk 7/24/43 (#2, 4 wk), 18 wk; NYT fic 6/27/43 (#15), pk 8/1/43 (#2, 4 wk), 23 wk; tot 41 wk.
The King's General (Doubleday) NYT fic

1/20/46 (#9), pk 2/3/46 (#1, 6 wk), 28 wk; PW fic 2/2/46 (#2), pk 2/16/46 (#1, 6 wk), 20 wk; tot 48 wk.
The Parasites (Doubleday) NYT fic 1/15/50 (#11), pk 2/19/50 (#1, 5 wk), 21 wk; PW fic 1/28/50 (#3), pk 2/18/50 (#1, 6 wk), 14 wk; tot 35 wk.
My Cousin Rachel (Doubleday) NYT fic 2/17/52 (#11), pk 3/30/52 (#1, 8 wk), 36 wk; PW fic 3/1/52 (#4), pk 3/29/52 (#1, 9 wk), 29 wk; tot 65 wk.
Kiss Me Again, Stranger (Doubleday) NYT fic 3/29/53 (#11), pk 5/10/53 (#4, 4 wk), 24 wk; PW fic 4/25/53 (#4, 6 wk), 12 wk; tot 36 wk.
Mary Anne (Doubleday) NYT fic 6/20/54 (#11), pk 8/1/54 (#1, 11 wk), 34 wk; PW fic 7/3/54 (#4), pk 7/31/54 (#1, 11 wk), 25 wk; tot 59 wk.
The Scapegoat (Doubleday) NYT fic 3/3/57 (#13), pk 3/24/57 (#1, 14 wk), 31 wk; PW fic 3/11/57 (#7), pk 3/25/57 (#1, 12 wk), 26 wk; tot 57 wk.
The Breaking Point (Doubleday) NYT fic 11/22/59 (#14), pk 11/29/59 (#13, 2 wk), 7 wk.
The Glass-Blowers (Doubleday) PW fic 4/1/63 (#4), pk 5/20/63 (#1, 6 wk), 27 wk; NYT fic 4/14/63 (#4), pk 5/19/63 (#1, 6 wk), 23 wk; tot 50 wk.
The Flight of the Falcon (Doubleday) NYT fic 5/9/65 (#9), pk 5/30/65 (#6, 2 wk), 14 wk; PW fic 5/17/65 (#9), pk 5/31/65 (#6, 4 wk), 14 wk; tot 28 wk.
The House on the Strand (Doubleday) NYT fic 10/12/69 (#8), pk 11/9/69 (#2, 7 wk), 30 wk; PW fic 10/20/69 (#9), pk 11/17/69 (#2, 6 wk), 28 wk; NYT pb fic 1/3/71 (#4), pk 2/7/71 (#3, 4 wk), 8 wk; tot 66 wk.
Rule Britannia (Doubleday) NYT fic 2/18/73 (#9, 1 wk).
See also Sir Arthur Thomas Quiller-Couch and_____

Duncan, David Douglas
The Private World of Pablo Picasso (Harper) NYT gen 4/6/58 (#16), pk 6/22/58 (#9, 1 wk), 12 wk.
Picasso's Picassos (Harper) NYT gen 12/24/61 (#15), pk 1/14/62 (#13, 2 wk), 3 wk.

Duncan, Isadora
My Life (Boni & Liveright) PW nf 4/28/28 (#9, 4 wk), 12 wk.

Duncan, Lois
Don't Look Behind You (Dell/Laurel Leaf) PW ch yn ad 9/28/90 (#4, 4 wk), 8 wk.

Duncan, Robert L.
Dragons at the Gate (NAL/Signet) PW mm pb 5/31/76 (#11, 1 wk), 2 wk.

Duncan, Thomas W.
Gus the Great (Lippincott) NYT fic 10/12/47 (#13), pk 10/26/47 (#4, 1 wk), 17 wk; PW fic 11/1/47 (#5), pk 11/8/47 (#4, 1 wk), 7 wk; tot 24 wk.

Duncan Hines
Lodging for a Night (Adventures in Good Eating) NYT gen 6/11/39 (#11, 4 wk).
Adventures in Good Eating (Adventures in Good Eating) NYT gen 7/9/39 (#10), pk 8/6/39 (#9, 4 wk), 8 wk; PW nf 8/12/39 (#9, 8 wk); tot 16 wk.

Dundy, Elaine
The Dud Avocado (Dutton) NYT fic 8/17/58 (#13), pk 8/24/58 (#11, 3 wk), 6 wk; PW fic 9/1/58 (#8, 1 wk), 2 wk; tot 8 wk.

Dunham, Barrows
Man Against Myth (Little Brown) NYT gen 5/25/47 (#14, 2 wk).

Dunleavy, Steve
See Red West, et al.

Dunn, Judy
Little Duck (Random) NYT ch pb 11/13/77 (#1, 46 wk), 70 wk.
Little Lamb (Random) NYT ch pb 11/13/77 (#2, 46 wk), 70 wk.

Dunne, Dominick
The Two Mrs. Grenvilles (Crown) PW hc fic 8/16/85 (#12), pk 10/4/85 (#5, 3 wk), 18 wk; NYT fic 8/18/85 (#11), pk 8/25/85 (#5, 5 wk), 16 wk; (Bantam) NYT pb fic 6/1/86 (#5), pk 6/15/86 (#2, 3 wk), 16 wk; PW mm pb 6/6/86 (#5), pk 6/13/86 (#2, 2 wk), 15 wk; tot 65 wk.
People Like Us (Crown) PW hc fic 5/13/88 (#15), pk 6/24/88 (#3, 1 wk), 14 wk; NYT fic 5/15/88 (#12), pk 6/12/88 (#4, 1 wk), 14 wk; (Bantam) PW mm pb 4/14/89 (#6), pk 5/5/89 (#3, 1 wk), 8 wk; NYT pb fic 4/16/89 (#5, 2 wk), 5 wk; tot 41 wk.
An Inconvenient Woman (Crown) NYT fic 5/13/90 (#13), pk 6/10/90 (#6, 2 wk), 18 wk; PW hc fic 5/18/90 (#8), pk 7/13/90 (#3, 1 wk), 17 wk; tot 35 wk.

Dunne, John Gregory
True Confessions: A Novel (Robbins/Dutton) PW hc fic 11/28/77 (#14, 1 wk); NYT fic 12/4/77 (#15), pk 12/11/77 (#14, 1 wk), 2 wk; tot 3 wk.
Dutch Shea, Jr. (Linden) NYT fic 5/23/82 (#14), pk 6/6/82 (#13, 1 wk), 3 wk.
The Red White and Blue (Simon & Schuster) NYT fic 3/22/87 (#13, 1 wk), 3 wk; PW hc fic 3/27/87 (#10, 1 wk), 2 wk; tot 5 wk.

Du Nouy, Pierre Lecomte
Human Destiny (Longmans Green) NYT gen 3/23/47 (#8), pk 5/11/47 (#2, 4 wk), 57 wk; PW nf 4/12/47 (#4), pk 5/10/47 (#2, 3 wk), 38 wk; tot 95 wk.

Dunphy, Eamon
Unforgettable Fire: Past, Present and Future— The Definitive Biography of U2 (Warner) NYT nf 4/3/88 (#13), pk 4/17/88 (#10, 1 wk), 4 wk; PW hc nf 4/15/88 (#12, 2 wk); tot 6 wk.

Du Pont, Diane
French Passion (Fawcett) NYT mm pb 11/6/77 (#12, 1 wk), 2 wk.

Durand, Loup
Daddy (Warner) NYT pb fic 3/11/90 (#15), pk 3/18/90 (#11, 1 wk), 3 wk; PW mm pb 3/30/90 (#15, 1 wk); tot 4 wk.

Durant, William James
The Mansions of Philosophy (Simon & Schuster) PW nf 8/10/29 (#5, 8 wk), 16 wk.
Caesar and Christ: The Story of Civilization Vol. 3 (Simon & Schuster) NYT gen 12/10/44 (#19), pk 1/21/45 (#6, 1 wk), 7 wk; PW nf 1/13/45 (#10, 1 wk); tot 8 wk.
The Story of Philosophy (Simon & Schuster) PW nf 8/14/26 (#9), pk 10/16/26 (#1, 24 wk), 64 wk; (Garden City) PW nf 4/12/30 (#7), pk 5/17/30 (#5, 4 wk), 28 wk; tot 92 wk.
Transition (Simon & Schuster) PW nf 11/26/27 (#10, 4 wk).
The Story of Civilization (Simon & Schuster) PW nf 9/14/35 (#5, 4 wk), 12 wk.
The Renaissance: The Story of Civilization Vol. 5 (Simon & Schuster) NYT gen 10/25/53 (#11, 1 wk), 5 wk.
The Reformation: The Story of Civilization Vol. 6 (Simon & Schuster) NYT gen 10/13/57 (#15), pk 10/27/57 (#5, 1 wk), 13 wk; PW nf 10/28/57 (#5, 1 wk), 8 wk; tot 21 wk.

_____, and Ariel Durant
The Age of Reason Begins: The Story of Civilization Vol. 8 (Simon & Schuster) NYT gen 9/24/61 (#15), pk 10/29/61 (#8, 2 wk), 16 wk; PW nf 10/2/61 (#9), pk 10/30/61 (#7, 1 wk), 8 wk; tot 24 wk.
The Age of Napoleon: The Story of Civilization Vol. 9 (Simon & Schuster) NYT gen 12/14/75 (#9), pk 1/4/76 (#6, 1 wk), 7 wk; PW nf 1/5/76 (#7, 2 wk), 4 wk; hc nf 2/2/76 (#10), pk 2/16/76 (#9, 1 wk), 3 wk; tot 14 wk.

Duranty, Walter
I Write as I Please (Simon & Schuster) PW nf 1/11/36 (#6), pk 2/15/36 (#4, 4 wk), 20 wk; NYT gen 2/2/36 (#5, 4 wk), 8 wk; tot 28 wk.
One Life, One Kopec (Literary Guild) NYT fic 9/12/37 (#6, 4 wk).
U.S.S.R. (Lippincott) NYT gen 4/30/44 (#8, 1 wk), 2 wk.

Duras, Marguerite
The Lover (Pantheon) NYT fic 7/21/85 (#13), pk 8/4/85 (#9, 3 wk), 9 wk; PW hc fic 8/9/85 (#14), pk 8/23/85 (#11, 1 wk), 5 wk; (Harper/Perennial) PW td pb 6/27/86 (#9), pk 7/25/86 (#6, 1 wk), 5 wk; tot 19 wk.

Durham, Marilyn
The Man Who Loved Cat Dancing (Harcourt) PW fic 10/16/72 (#9, 1 wk), 2 wk; NYT fic 11/12/72 (#9, 1 wk); NYT pb fic 8/12/73 (#5), pk 9/9/73 (#4, 4 wk), 12 wk; tot 15 wk.

Durocher, Leo, and Ed Linn
Nice Guys Finish Last (Simon & Schuster) NYT gen 7/27/75 (#9, 1 wk).

Durrell, Ann and Marilyn Sachs
The Big Book for Peace [eds.] (Dutton) PW ch mid rd 12/21/90 (#5, 4 wk).

Durrell, Gerald
Rosy Is My Relative (Viking) PW fic 7/8/ 68 (#9, 1 wk), 2 wk.

Durrell, Lawrence
Justine (Dutton) NYT fic 10/20/57 (#15, 1 wk).
Mountolive (Dutton) NYT fic 4/19/59 (#15), pk 5/10/59 (#11, 1 wk), 4 wk.
Clea (Dutton) NYT fic 4/10/60 (#16), pk 5/8/60 (#7, 1 wk), 13 wk; PW fic 4/25/60 (#10), pk 5/9/60 (#6, 1 wk), 7 wk; tot 20 wk.
The Black Book (Dutton) NYT fic 10/9/60 (#11, 1 wk), 6 wk.
Tunc (Dutton) PW fic 4/29/68 (#8), pk 6/3/68 (#7, 1 wk), 10 wk; NYT fic 5/5/68 (#8), pk 7/21/68 (#7, 1 wk), 10 wk; tot 20 wk.

D'Usseau, Armand
See James Gow and_____

Dvorkin, David
Timetrap (Pocket) 6/5/88 #12), pk 6/12/88 (#5, 1 wk), 5 wk.

_____, and Daniel Dvorkin
The Captain's Honor (Pocket) NYT pb fic 9/17/89 (#11, 2 wk).

Dyer, Dr. Wayne W.
Your Erroneous Zones (Funk & Wagnalls) PW hc nf 8/16/76 (#8), pk 4/11/77 (#1, 11 wk), 64 wk; NYT gen 8/29/76 (#8), pk 10/3/ 76 (#2, 7 wk), 31 wk; NYT nf 4/3/77 (#2), pk 5/8/77 (#1, 14 wk), 33 wk; (Avon) PW mm pb 10/10/77 (#3), pk 10/17/77 (#1, 12 wk), 49 wk; NYT mm pb 10/16/77 (#2), pk 10/23/77 (#1, 9 wk), 50 wk; tot 227 wk.
Pulling Your Own Strings (Crowell) PW hc nf 5/8/78 (#8), pk 6/19/78 (#3, 3 wk), 31 wk; NYT nf 5/14/78 (#9), pk 6/18/78 (#2, 1

wk), 20 wk; (Avon) PW mm pb 9/17/79 (#11), pk 10/15/79 (#1, 1 wk), 13 wk; NYT mm pb 9/23/79 (#6), pk 10/7/79 (#5, 4 wk), 13 wk; tot 77 wk.
The Sky's the Limit (Simon & Schuster) NYT nf 10/5/80 (#6), pk 10/26/80 (#2, 2 wk), 28 wk; PW hc nf 10/17/80 (#5), pk 10/24/80 (#2, 5 wk), 25 wk; (Pocket) PW mm pb 10/23/81 (#9, 1 wk), 3 wk; NYT mm pb 10/25/81 (#10, 1 wk), 3 wk; tot 59 wk.
You'll See It When You Believe It (Morrow) PW hc nf 10/6/89 (#10), pk 10/13/89 (#8, 1 wk), 6 wk; NYT msc 10/29/89 (#5, 1 wk); tot 7 wk.

Dylan, Bob
Tarantula (Macmillan) NYT gen 6/13/71 (#10, 1 wk).

Eareckson, Joni, and Joe Musser
Joni (Worldwide) NYT td pb 4/17/77 (#3), pk 4/24/77 (#2, 1 wk), 7 wk.

Earhart, Amelia
Last Flight (Harcourt) NYT gen 1/9/38 (#4), pk 2/6/38 (#3, 4 wk), 12 wk; PW nf 1/15/38 (#9, 4 wk); tot 16 wk.

Earley, Pete
Family of Spies (Bantam) NYT pb nf 2/25/ 90 (#9, 1 wk).

Earthworks Group
50 Simple Things You Can Do to Save the Earth (Earthworks/Publishers Group West) NYT msc pb 2/11/90 (#1, 17 wk), 31 wk; PW td pb 2/16/90 (#2), pk 3/2/90 (#1, 12 wk), 31 wk; tot 62 wk.
50 Simple Things Kids Can Do to Save the Earth (Andrews & McMeel) NYT msc pb 4/29/90 (#3), pk 5/13/90 (#2, 1 wk), 8 wk; PW td pb 5/4/90 (#3), pk 5/18/90 (#2, 1 wk), 12 wk; PW ch nf 8/31/90 (#1, 8 wk), 16 wk; tot 36 wk.

Eastman, P.D.
Are You My Mother? (Random) NYT ch bst 11/12/61 (#15, 26 wk).
The Cat in the Hat Beginner Book Dictionary (Random) NYT ch bst 11/1/64 (#6), pk 11/7/65 (#1, 26 wk), 89 wk.

Eaton, Evelyn
Quietly My Captain Waits (Harper) PW fic 7/13/40 (#7), pk 8/10/40 (#5, 4 wk), 16 wk.
Restless Are the Sails (Harper) PW fic 8/16/ 41 (#10, 4 wk).
The Sea Is So Wide (Harper) NYT fic 3/28/ 43 (#17), pk 5/16/43 (#9, 1 wk), 3 wk.

Eban, Abba
My People (Behrman/Random) NYT gen 2/2/69 (#10, 1 wk); PW nf 2/10/69 (#10), pk 2/24/69 (#9, 2 wk), 3 wk; tot 4 wk.

Heritage: Civilization and the Jews (Summit/Simon & Schuster) NYT nf 10/21/84 (#5), pk 11/4/84 (#4, 1 wk), 17 wk; PW hc nf 11/2/84 (#9), pk 12/14/84 (#6, 1 wk), 14 wk; tot 31 wk.

Ebenstein, Ronnie Sue
See Adrien Arpel and_____

Eberhart, Mignon G.
The Pattern (Doubleday) NYT fic 7/4/37 (#5, 4 wk).
Hasty Wedding (Triangle) NYT fic 7/3/38 (#7, 4 wk).
The Glass Slipper (Doubleday) NYT fic 12/4/38 (#15, 4 wk).
The Chiffon Scarf (Popular Library) NYT fic 10/8/39 (#9, 4 wk).

Ebert, Alan, with Janice Rotchstein
Traditions (Bantam) NYT mm pb 1/16/83 (#11), pk 1/23/83 (#8, 1 wk), 4 wk; PW mm pb 1/21/83 (#9, 2 wk), 4 wk; tot 8 wk.

Echard, Margaret
Born in Wedlock (Doubleday) NYT fic 12/16/56 (#15, 1 wk), 2 wk.

Ecklar, Julia
The Kobayashi Maru (Pocket) NYT pb fic 12/17/89 (#10, 1 wk), 3 wk; PW mm pb 1/5/90 (#14, 1 wk); tot 4 wk.

Eco, Umberto
The Name of the Rose (Wolff/Harcourt) NYT fic 6/26/83 (#10), pk 8/7/83 (#1, 5 wk), 47 wk; PW hc fic 7/1/83 (#11), pk 8/12/83 (#1, 5 wk), 43 wk; (Warner) PW mm pb 6/1/84 (#8), pk 6/8/84 (#1, 5 wk), 18 wk; NYT pb fic 6/3/84 (#1, 6 wk), 16 wk; tot 124 wk.
Foucault's Pendulum (Wolff/Harcourt) NYT fic 10/22/89 (#11), pk 11/5/89 (#3, 2 wk), 17 wk; PW hc fic 10/27/89 (#12), pk 11/10/89 (#2, 1 wk), 16 wk; (Ballantine) NYT pb fic 12/9/90 (#8), pk 12/30/90 (#4, 1 wk), 4 wk; PW mm pb 12/14/90 (#10), pk 12/21/90 (#5, 1 wk), 2 wk; tot 39 wk.

Eddings, David
Enchanters' End Game (Ballantine/Del Rey) NYT pb fic 12/2/84 (#8), pk 12/16/84 (#7, 1 wk), 5 wk; PW mm pb 12/14/84 (#8, 2 wk), 4 wk; tot 9 wk.
Castle of Wizardry: Book Four of the Belgriad (Ballantine/Del Rey) NYT pb fic 5/6/84 (#13, 1 wk), 2 wk; PW mm pb 5/18/84 (#12, 1 wk), 2 wk; tot 4 wk.
Guardians of the West (Ballantine/Del Rey) NYT fic 5/3/87 (#12, 3 wk), 5 wk; PW hc fic 5/8/87 (#12), pk 5/15/87 (#11, 3 wk), 6 wk; NYT pb fic 3/6/88 (#15), pk 3/13/88 (#11, 1

wk), 6 wk; PW mm pb 3/25/88 (#14), pk 4/1/88 (#12, 1 wk), 3 wk; tot 20 wk.
King of the Murgos (Ballantine/Del Rey) NYT fic 4/10/88 (#9), pk 4/17/88 (#6, 1 wk), 6 wk; PW hc fic 4/15/88 (#12), pk 4/22/88 (#6, 2 wk), 8 wk; PW mm pb 3/10/89 (#12, 1 wk), 4 wk; NYT pb fic 3/12/89 (#12), pk 3/19/89 (#10, 1 wk), 4 wk; tot 22 wk.
Demon Lord of Karanda (Ballantine/Del Rey) NYT fic 8/28/88 (#11), pk 9/11/88 (#7, 1 wk), 7 wk; PW hc fic 9/2/88 (#11), pk 9/30/88 (#5, 1 wk), 8 wk; NYT pb fic 11/12/89 (#12), pk 11/26/89 (#9, 1 wk), 4 wk; PW mm pb 11/17/89 (#8, 1 wk), 3 wk; tot 22 wk.
Sorceress of Darshiva (Ballantine/Del Rey) NYT fic 12/3/89 (#7, 1 wk), 5 wk; PW hc fic 12/15/89 (#7, 1 wk), 6 wk; NYT pb fic 11/4/90 (#15), pk 11/11/90 (#6, 2 wk), 5 wk; PW mm pb 11/16/90 (#14), pk 11/23/90 (#6, 1 wk), 4 wk; tot 20 wk.
The Diamond Throne: Book I of the Elenium (Ballantine/Del Rey) NYT fic 5/7/89 (#9, 1 wk), 5 wk; PW hc fic 5/12/89 (#8, 2 wk), 6 wk; NYT pb fic 7/8/90 (#13, 1 wk), 2 wk; tot 13 wk.
The Ruby Knight (Ballantine/Del Rey) NYT fic 11/18/90 (#7, 3 wk), 5 wk; PW hc fic 11/30/90 (#9), pk 12/7/90 (#7, 1 wk), 4 wk; tot 9 wk.

Edelstein, Barbara, M.D.
The Woman Doctor's Diet for Women (Prentice Hall) NYT nf 7/23/78 (#14), pk 11/12/78 (#7, 1 wk), 5 wk; PW hc nf 9/11/78 (#12, 1 wk), 6 wk; NYT mm pb 6/17/79 (#12, 1 wk); tot 12 wk.

Eden, Anthony
Full Circle (Houghton) NYT gen 3/27/60 (#15), pk 4/3/60 (#13, 1 wk), 2 wk.

Eden, Dorothy
The Vines of Yarrabee (Coward McCann) NYT fic 3/16/69 (#10), pk 4/6/69 (#5, 1 wk), 16 wk; PW fic 4/7/69 (#8), pk 4/21/69 (#6, 1 wk), 11 wk; tot 27 wk.
Melbury Square (Coward) PW fic 2/22/71 (#10, 1 wk).
The Millionaire's Daughter (Fawcett) NYT mm pb 6/29/75 (#9), pk 7/6/75 (#8, 2 wk), 4 wk.
The Time of the Dragon (Fawcett/Crest) NYT mm pb 1/30/77 (#10, 1 wk); PW mm pb 2/7/77 (#15, 2 wk); tot 3 wk.
The Salamanca Drum (Fawcett/Crest) PW mm pb 6/5/78 (#12, 2 wk), 3 wk.

Eden, Emily
The Semi-Attached Couple (Houghton) NYT fic 8/17/47 (#13), pk 8/31/47 (#9, 1 wk), 3 wk.

Editors of Boys' Life
Boys' Life Treasury (Simon & Schuster)
NYT ch bst 11/2/58 (#13, 40 wk).

Editors of Consumer Guide
How to Win at Pac-Man (Pocket) PW mm
pb 4/16/82 (#14, 1 wk), 2 wk.

Editors of Eastman Kodak Co.
The Joy of Photography (Addison Wesley)
NYT td pb 12/23/79 (#4, 1 wk), 16 wk; PW
td pb 1/11/80 (#7), pk 1/25/80 (#4, 1 wk), 4
wk; tot 20 wk.

Editors of Life
The World We Live In (Simon & Schuster)
NYT gen 12/11/55 (#16), pk 1/1/56 (#13, 2
wk), 5 wk; [juvenile edition] NYT ch bst
11/18/56 (#8, 40 wk), 59 wk; tot 64 wk.
Life: The First Fifty Years, 1936-1986 (Little Brown) NYT nf 11/30/86 (#16), pk 12/21/
86 (#6, 1 wk), 6 wk; PW hc nf 12/5/86 (#14),
pk 12/12/86 (#5, 3 wk), 5 wk; NYT pb nf
12/27/87 (#10), pk 1/10/88 (#4, 1 wk), 3 wk;
tot 14 wk.

Editors of Runner's World Maga-
   zine
The Complete Runner (Avon) PW td pb 4/
17/78 (#8), pk 6/12/78 (#1, 1 wk), 25 wk;
NYT td pb 5/7/78 (#8), pk 6/4/78 (#1, 7 wk),
16 wk; tot 41 wk.

Editors of Spy Magazine
Separated at Birth? (Doubleday/Dolphin)
PW td pb 11/18/88 (#10), pk 12/9/88 (#4, 5
wk), 13 wk; NYT msc pb 12/4/88 (#5), pk
12/11/88 (#3, 2 wk), 7 wk; tot 20 wk.

Editors of Sunset Books and Sunset
   Magazine
Gold Rush Country (Lane) NYT gen 4/21/
57 (#16), pk 5/12/57 (#13, 1 wk), 4 wk.

Edman, Irwin
Philosopher's Holiday (Viking) NYT gen
2/5/39 (#15, 4 wk); PW nf 2/11/39 (#9, 4 wk);
tot 8 wk.
Philosopher's Quest (Viking/Macmillan)
NYT gen 4/13/47 (#12, 2 wk), 3 wk.

Edmonds, Walter Dumax
Rome Haul (Little Brown) PW fic 4/13/29
(#8, 4 wk).
Drums Along the Mohawk (Little Brown)
PW fic 9/12/36 (#4), pk 10/10/36 (#2, 20 wk),
52 wk; NYT fic 9/13/36 (#2, 8 wk), 24 wk;
tot 76 wk.
Chad Hanna (Little Brown) PW fic 5/11/
40 (#4, 4 wk), 12 wk.
In the Hands of the Senecas (Grosset &
Dunlap) NYT fic 2/23/47 (#16), pk 3/2/47
(#11, 1 wk), 2 wk.

Edward VIII
See Windsor, Duke of

Edwards, Alexander
A Star Is Born (Warner) NYT mm pb 1/
30/77 (#9), pk 2/20/77 (#5, 1 wk), 5 wk; PW
mm pb 2/14/77 (#12), pk 2/21/77 (#11, 2 wk),
6 wk; tot 11 wk.

Edwards, Anne
Vivien Leigh: A Biography (Simon &
Schuster) NYT nf 7/24/77 (#6), pk 8/21/77
(#5, 2 wk), 19 wk; PW hc nf 7/11/77 (#7), pk
7/25/77 (#5, 3 wk), 20 wk; (Pocket) PW mm
pb 6/19/78 (#13), pk 7/3/78 (#10, 2 wk), 5
wk; tot 44 wk.
A Remarkable Woman (Morrow) NYT nf
2/9/86 (#14, 1 wk).

Edwards, Betty
Drawing on the Right Side of the Brain
(Tarcher/St. Martin's) NYT td pb 3/23/80
(#13), pk 5/18/80 (#6, 2 wk), 61 wk; PW td
pb 3/28/80 (#10), pk 6/6/80 (#5, 1 wk), 26
wk; tot 87 wk.

Edwards, Frank
Flying Saucers—Serious Business (Stuart)
PW nf 8/1/66 (#11), pk 10/3/66 (#6, 2 wk),
15 wk; NYT gen 8/7/66 (#9), pk 9/25/66 (#5,
1 wk), 16 wk; NYT pb gen 11/6/66 (#4), pk
12/4/66 (#1, 8 wk), 20 wk; tot 51 wk.

Edwards, Julie Andrews
Mandy (Harper) NYT ch bst 5/7/72 (#10,
19 wk).

Edwards, Michael
Priscilla, Elvis and Me (St. Martin's) NYT
pb nf 9/24/89 (#6, 1 wk), 2 wk.

Edwards, N.E.S.
Treasures of Tutankhamun (Ballantine) NYT
td pb 8/21/77 (#5), pk 2/19/78 (#1, 1 wk), 42
wk; PW td pb 10/31/77 (#9), pk 3/6/78 (#6,
2 wk), 18 wk; tot 60 wk.

Egginton, Joyce
From Cradle to Grave (Jove) NYT pb nf
5/13/90 (#4, 3 wk), 7 wk; PW mm pb 5/25/
90 (#8, 1 wk), 2 wk; tot 9 wk.

Ehlert, Lois
See Bill Martin, Jr., and John Archambault

Ehrenburg, Ilya
The Fall of Paris (Knopf) NYT fic 8/22/43
(#14), pk 8/29/43 (#9, 1 wk), 2 wk.

Ehrenreich, Barbara
The Worst Years of Our Lives (Pantheon)
NYT nf 7/15/90 (#14, 1 wk).

Ehrlich, Max
The Reincarnation of Peter Proud (Bantam)
NYT mm pb 5/4/75 (#10), pk 5/18/75 (#7,
2 wk), 8 wk.

Ehrlich, Paul R.
The Population Bomb (Ballantine) NYT pb gen 3/1/70 (#2, 16 wk), 28 wk.

Ehrlichman, John Daniel
The Company (Pocket) NYT mm pb 5/22/77 (#15, 1 wk).
Washington Behind Closed Doors (Pocket) PW mm pb 9/26/77 (#11), pk 10/3/77 (#10, 1 wk), 3 wk.
Witness to Power (Simon & Schuster) PW hc nf 2/12/82 (#9), pk 2/26/82 (#3, 1 wk), 10 wk; NYT nf 2/14/82 (#13), pk 2/28/82 (#4, 3 wk), 9 wk; tot 19 wk.

Einstein, Albert, and Leopold In-feld
The Evolution of Physics (Simon & Schuster) NYT gen 5/1/38 (#8), pk 6/5/38 (#4, 4 wk), 12 wk; PW nf 5/14/38 (#4), pk 6/11/38 (#3, 8 wk), 16 wk; tot 28 wk.

Eisenberg, Arlene, Heidi E. Murkoff and Sandee E. Hathaway
What to Expect When You're Expecting (Workman) PW td pb 8/11/89 (#10), pk 9/7/90 (#4, 2 wk), 11 wk; NYT msc pb 9/2/90 (#6), pk 9/23/90 (#4, 1 wk), 3 wk; tot 14 wk.

Eisenhower, David
Eisenhower: At War, 1943–1945 (Random) NYT nf 10/5/86 (#11, 2 wk), 6 wk; PW hc nf 10/24/86 (#15), pk 10/31/86 (#14, 1 wk), 2 wk; tot 8 wk.

Eisenhower, Dwight David
Eisenhower's Own Story of the War (Arco) NYT gen 7/28/46 (#10, 1 wk), 5 wk.
Crusade in Europe (Doubleday) NYT gen 11/28/48 (#16), pk 12/26/48 (#1, 11 wk), 27 wk; PW nf 12/18/48 (#3), pk 12/25/48 (#1, 11 wk), 20 wk; tot 47 wk.
The White House Years: Mandate for Change, 1953–1956 (Doubleday) NYT gen 11/17/63 (#9), pk 12/8/63 (#2, 12 wk), 20 wk; PW nf 11/25/63 (#7), pk 12/30/63 (#1, 4 wk), 20 wk; tot 40 wk.
The White House Years: Waging Peace, 1956–1961 (Doubleday) NYT gen 11/21/65 (#9, 1 wk); PW nf 11/29/65 (#10, 1 wk); tot 2 wk.
At Ease: Stories I Tell to Friends (Doubleday) PW nf 7/3/67 (#10), pk 8/14/67 (#3, 1 wk), 38 wk; NYT gen 7/23/67 (#6), pk 8/27/67 (#3, 1 wk), 29 wk; tot 67 wk.

Eisenhower, John S.D.
The Bitter Woods (Putnam) NYT gen 2/16/69 (#9, 1 wk); PW nf 3/17/69 (#10, 1 wk); tot 2 wk.

Eisenhower, Julie Nixon
Pat Nixon: The Untold Story (Simon & Schuster) NYT nf 11/30/86 (#11), pk 12/7/86

(#4, 1 wk), 10 wk; PW hc nf 12/12/86 (#10), pk 12/19/86 (#8, 2 wk), 4 wk; (Zebra) NYT pb nf 11/8/87 (#6, 1 wk), 5 wk; tot 19 wk.

Eisenhower, Milton
The Wine Is Bitter (Doubleday) NYT gen 8/25/63 (#9), pk 9/22/63 (#5, 1 wk), 12 wk; PW nf 9/23/63 (#9), pk 9/30/63 (#6, 1 wk), 9 wk; tot 21 wk.

Eisenschiml, Otto
Without Fame (Alliance) NYT nf 11/22/42 (#21), pk 12/6/42 (#12, 1 wk), 5 wk.

Ekert-Rotholz, Alice
The Time of the Dragons (Viking) NYT fic 7/13/58 (#14), pk 8/17/58 (#5, 2 wk), 16 wk; PW fic 8/4/58 (#10), pk 8/25/58 (#5, 1 wk), 10 wk; tot 26 wk.

Elbert, Joyce
The Crazy Ladies (NAL) NYT pb fic 3/1/70 (#4), pk 4/5/70 (#3, 4 wk), 8 wk.

Elbling, Peter
See Tony Hendra, et al.

Elder, Will
See John Boswell, et al.

Elegant, Robert S.
Dynasty (McGraw) PW hc fic 8/15/77 (#7), pk 9/19/77 (#2, 1 wk), 25 wk; NYT fic 8/21/77 (#10), pk 9/18/77 (#3, 1 wk), 30 wk; (Fawcett/Crest) PW mm pb 9/25/78 (#6), pk 10/9/78 (#5, 2 wk), 12 wk; NYT mm pb 11/12/78 (#11, 1 wk), 9 wk; tot 76 wk.
Manchu (McGraw) NYT fic 11/30/80 (#13), pk 12/21/80 (#11, 3 wk), 10 wk; PW hc fic 12/26/80 (#14, 3 wk), 4 wk; (Fawcett/Crest) PW mm pb 2/5/82 (#9, 1 wk), 3 wk; NYT mm pb 2/14/82 (#10, 1 wk), 4 wk; tot 21 wk.
Mandarin (Simon & Schuster) PW hc fic 11/25/83 (#15, 1 wk); NYT pb fic 10/21/84 (#12, 1 wk), 2 wk; tot 3 wk.

Eliot, Thomas Stearns [all titles as by T. S. Eliot]
Notes Towards the Definition of Culture (Harcourt) NYT gen 4/10/49 (#15, 1 wk).
The Cocktail Party (Harcourt) NYT gen 3/26/50 (#16), pk 5/7/50 (#3, 1 wk), 24 wk; PW nf 5/6/50 (#5), pk 5/20/50 (#4, 1 wk), 6 wk; tot 30 wk.
The Confidential Clerk (Harcourt) NYT gen 3/28/54 (#16, 1 wk).

Elizabeth
See Mary Annette Beauchamp Russell

Ellerbee, Linda
And So It Goes: Adventures in Television (Putnam) PW hc nf 6/13/86 (#13), pk 8/29/86 (#3, 1 wk), 19 wk; NYT nf 6/15/86 (#15),

pk 8/17/86 (#3, 2 wk), 18 wk; (Berkley) pb
nf 5/31/87 (#7), pk 6/21/87 (#2, 1 wk), 15 wk;
PW mm pb 6/5/87 (#15), pk 6/19/87 (#11, 2
wk), 6 wk; tot 58 wk.

Ellis, Amanda Mae
  Elizabeth the Woman (Dutton) NYT fic
9/30/51 (#16, 1 wk).

Ellis, Bret Easton
  Less Than Zero (Simon & Schuster) PW
hc fic 8/9/85 (#15), pk 8/23/85 (#9, 1 wk), 8
wk; NYT fic 9/15/85 (#13), pk 9/22/85 (#12,
1 wk), 3 wk; (Penguin) PW td pb 6/13/86
(#10), pk 7/25/86 (#3, 1 wk), 13 wk; tot 24
wk.

Ellis, Havelock
  Dance of Life (Houghton) PW gen lit 9/15/
23 (#12), pk 11/24/23 (#9, 8 wk), 12 wk.

Ellis, William Donohue
  The Bounty Lands (World Almanac) NYT
fic 12/28/52 (#13, 2 wk), 3 wk.
  Jonathan Blair (World Almanac) NYT fic
12/12/54 (#15), pk 1/23/55 (#13, 1 wk), 4 wk.

Ellison, Ralph
  The Invisible Man (Random) NYT fic
5/4/52 (#14), pk 6/22/52 (#8, 1 wk), 13 wk.

Ellmann, Richard
  Oscar Wilde (Knopf) NYT nf 2/21/88
(#15), pk 3/20/88 (#7, 1 wk), 10 wk; PW hc
nf 3/4/88 (#15), pk 3/25/88 (#9, 1 wk), 7 wk;
tot 17 wk.

Ellroy, James
  Black Dahlia (Mysterious) NYT pb fic
9/18/88 (#13, 1 wk); PW mm pb 10/14/88
(#15, 1 wk); tot 2 wk.

Ellsberg, Cmdr. Edward
  On the Bottom (Dodd) PW nf 6/8/29 (#7,
4 wk), 8 wk.
  Hell on Ice (Doubleday) NYT fic 3/6/38
(#10, 4 wk); PW nf 3/12/38 (#9), pk 4/9/38
(#4, 4 wk), 12 wk; tot 16 wk.
  Captain Paul (Dodd) PW fic 7/12/41 (#5,
4 wk), 8 wk.

Elon, Amos
  The Israelis: Founders and Sons (Holt) PW
nf 6/7/71 (#7, 1 wk), 2 wk.

Elting, Mary
  The Answer Book (Grosset & Dunlap)
NYT ch bst 5/8/60 (#7, 19 wk), 66 wk.

Elward, James
  See Helen Van Slyke and_____

Emberley, Barbara
  Drummer Hoff (Prentice Hall) NYT ch bst
5/5/68 (#8, 19 wk).

Emett, Frederick Rowland
  New World for Nellie (Harcourt) NYT ch
bst 11/16/52 (#5, 40 wk).

Ende, Michael
  The Neverending Story [trans. Ralph Man-
heim] (Doubleday) PW hc fic 12/2/83 (#15),
pk 1/27/84 (#10, 2 wk), 10 wk; NYT fic
12/4/83 (#13), pk 1/22/84 (#9, 1 wk), 12 wk;
(Penguin) PW td pb 8/17/84 (#10), pk 8/24/
84 (#8, 1 wk), 3 wk; tot 25 wk.

Endore, Guy
  King of Paris (Simon & Schuster) NYT fic
10/21/56 (#10), pk 10/28/56 (#6, 4 wk), 18
wk; PW fic 11/5/56 (#7), pk 12/3/56 (#6, 2
wk), 10 wk; tot 28 wk.

**Engelbrecht, H.C., and F.C. Hani-
ghen**
  Merchants of Death (Dodd) PW nf 6/9/34
(#10, 4 wk).

Engstrand, Stuart David
  The Sling and the Arrow (Creative Age)
NYT fic 6/8/47 (#13), pk 8/17/47 (#9, 1 wk),
10 wk.

Enright, Jim
  See Ernest Banks and_____

Enters, Agnes
  Silly Girl (Houghton) NYT gen 4/2/44
(#15, 3 wk), 5 wk.

Ephron, Delia
  *How to Eat Like a Child and Other Lessons
in Not Being a Grown-Up* (Ballantine) PW
td pb 12/3/79 (#7), pk 1/18/80 (#4, 1 wk), 9
wk; NYT td pb 12/16/79 (#13), pk 1/20/80
(#3, 1 wk), 32 wk; tot 41 wk.
  Teenage Romance (Viking) PW hc nf 10/
30/81 (#12, 1 wk), 5 wk; NYT nf 11/29/81
(#14), pk 12/6/81 (#12, 3 wk), 7 wk; tot 12
wk.

Ephron, Nora
  Crazy Salad (Knopf) PW nf 9/1/75 (#9, 1
wk), 3 wk; NYT gen 9/28/75 (#10, 1 wk); tot
4 wk.
  Scribble Scrabble (Knopf) NYT nf 7/9/78
(#15, 1 wk).
  Heartburn (Knopf) NYT fic 5/1/83 (#9),
pk 6/5/83 (#3, 1 wk), 29 wk; PW hc fic 5/6/
83 (#10), pk 6/17/83 (#3, 1 wk), 25 wk;
(Pocket) NYT pb fic 4/8/84 (#15), pk 4/22/
84 (#4, 1 wk), 8 wk; PW mm pb 4/20/84
(#7), pk 5/4/84 (#5, 2 wk), 6 wk; tot 68 wk.

Erdman, Paul E.
  The Billion Dollar Sure Thing (Scribner)
NYT fic 8/5/73 (#7), pk 9/30/73 (#3, 7 wk),
23 wk; PW fic 8/6/73 (#6), pk 9/10/73 (#1,
1 wk), 20 wk; tot 43 wk.
  The Silver Bears (Scribner) NYT fic 8/25/

74 (#8, 1 wk), 2 wk; PW fic 9/2/74 (#8, 1 wk), 6 wk; tot 8 wk.

The Crash of '79 (Simon & Schuster) NYT fic 12/12/76 (#8), pk 3/20/77 (#2, 9 wk), 45 wk; PW hc fic 12/27/76 (#10), pk 7/18/77 (#2, 8 wk), 45 wk; (Pocket) PW mm pb 11/14/77 (#11), pk 11/28/77 (#3, 4 wk), 15 wk; NYT mm pb 11/20/77 (#13), pk 12/18/77 (#2, 1 wk), 18 wk; tot 123 wk.

The Last Days of America (Simon & Schuster) PW hc fic 8/28/81 (#11), pk 10/2/81 (#6, 1 wk), 14 wk; NYT fic 8/30/81 (#12), pk 9/13/81 (#6, 2 wk), 17 wk; (Pocket) PW mm pb 7/23/82 (#14), pk 7/30/82 (#11, 1 wk), 3 wk; NYT mm pb 7/25/82 (#13), pk 8/1/82 (#7, 1 wk), 2 wk; tot 36 wk.

The Panic of '89 (Doubleday) PW hc fic 1/23/87 (#13), pk 3/20/87 (#5, 1 wk), 15 wk; NYT fic 1/25/87 (#13), pk 2/15/87 (#6, 5 wk), 13 wk; (Charter) NYT pb fic 2/7/88 (#12), pk 2/21/88 (#9, 2 wk), 5 wk; PW mm pb 2/12/88 (#12), pk 3/11/88 (#11, 1 wk), 5 wk; tot 38 wk.

What's Next? How to Prepare Yourself for the Crash of '89 and Profit in the 1990s (Doubleday) PW hc nf 4/22/88 (#13), pk 5/6/88 (#12, 1 wk), 3 wk; NYT msc 5/8/88 (#4, 1 wk), 2 wk; tot 5 wk.

The Palace (Doubleday) PW hc fic 2/19/88 (#15), pk 3/4/88 (#12, 1 wk), 4 wk; NYT fic 3/13/88 (#15, 1 wk); tot 5 wk.

Erdrich, Louise
The Beet Queen (Holt) NYT fic 9/28/86 (#15), pk 10/12/86 (#8, 3 wk), 15 wk; PW hc fic 10/3/86 (#14), pk 10/31/86 (#9, 1 wk), 10 wk; (Bantam) NYT pb fic 10/18/87 (#14, 1 wk); tot 26 wk.

Tracks (Holt) NYT fic 10/9/88 (#12, 1 wk), 4 wk.

Ernst, Morris Leopold
The Best Is Yet (Harper) NYT gen 5/20/45 #14), pk 6/17/45 (#6, 1 wk), 8 wk.

The First Freedom (Macmillan) NYT gen 4/14/46 (#16, 1 wk).

Erskine, Albert
See Bennett Cerf, et al.

Erskine, Dorothy, and Patrick Dennis
The Pink Hotel (Putnam) NYT fic 8/4/57 (#12), pk 8/25/57 (#6, 1 wk), 13 wk; PW fic 8/12/57 (#8), pk 8/26/57 (#6, 1 wk), 8 wk; tot 21 wk.

Erskine, John
The Private Life of Helen of Troy (Bobbs Merrill) PW fic 3/20/26 (#2), pk 4/17/26 (#1, 4 wk), 28 wk.

Galahad (Bobbs Merrill) PW fic 12/18/26 (#2), pk 2/19/27 (#1, 4 wk), 16 wk.

Adam and Eve (Bobbs Merrill) PW fic 12/31/27 (#6, 4 wk).

Sincerity (Bobbs Merrill) PW fic 12/14/29 (#8, 12 wk).

The Start of the Road (Stokes) NYT fic 12/4/38 (#13, 4 wk).

Erskine, Rosalind
The Passion Flower Hotel (Simon & Schuster) NYT fic 12/9/62 (#16), pk 12/16/62 (#13, 1 wk), 2 wk; PW fic 1/7/63 (#8, 1 wk); tot 3 wk.

Ertz, Susan
After Noon (Appleton) PW fic 6/19/26 (#4), pk 8/14/26 (#2, 4 wk), 16 wk.

Now East Now West (Appleton) PW fic 10/22/27 (#10, 4 wk).

The Galaxy (Appleton) PW fic 9/14/29 (#4), pk 10/12/29 (#3, 4 wk), 16 wk.

The Story of Julian (Appleton) PW fic 10/17/31 (#6, 4 wk).

No Hearts to Break (Appleton) NYT fic 11/7/37 (#5, 4 wk).

One Fight More (Appleton) NYT fic 12/10/39 (#9, 4 wk).

The Prodigal Heart (Harper) NYT fic 10/15/50 (#15, 1 wk).

Charmed Circle (Harper) NYT fic 7/15/56 (#12), pk 7/29/56 (#8, 3 wk), 11 wk; PW fic 10/15/56 (#10, 1 wk); tot 12 wk.

Ervin, Sam
See National Advisory Commission on Civil Disorder

Erwin, Annabel
Liliane (Warner) NYT mm pb 12/26/76 (#10), pk 1/23/77 (#5, 1 wk), 8 wk; PW mm pb 12/27/76 (#10), pk 1/24/77 (#5, 1 wk), 10 wk; tot 18 wk.

Esty, Lucien
See Julian Spafford and_____

Etnier, Elizabeth
On Gilbert Head (Little Brown) NYT fic 10/10/37 (#3, 4 wk).

Evans, Bergen
A Dictionary of Contemporary American Usage (Random) NYT gen 9/29/57 (#16, 1 wk).

Evans, Linda
Linda Evans' Beauty and Exercise Book (Simon & Schuster/Wallaby) NYT td pb 8/14/83 (#7, 4 wk), 10 wk; PW td pb 8/26/83 (#7, 1 wk), 8 wk; tot 18 wk.

Everroad, Jim
How to Flatten Your Stomach (Price Stern Sloan) NYT td pb 6/25/78 (#14), pk 2/18/79

(#1, 20 wk), 103 wk; PW td pb 7/17/78 (#8), pk 9/18/78 (#1, 19 wk), 84 wk; tot 187 wk.

_____, and Lonna Moscow
How to Trim Your Hips and Shape Your Thighs (Price Stern Sloan) NYT td pb 8/12/79 (#13), pk 9/30/79 (#5, 2 wk), 19 wk; PW td pb 8/13/79 (#9), pk 10/15/79 (#4, 1 wk), 15 wk; tot 34 wk.

Ewald, Dan
See Sparky Anderson and_____

Exman, Eugene
See Erica Anderson and_____

Eyre, Katherine Wigmore
The Lute and the Glove (Appleton) NYT fic 11/20/55 (#14), pk 11/27/55 (#13, 1 wk), 2 wk.
The Chinese Box (Appleton) NYT fic 5/17/59 (#15), pk 6/7/59 (#10, 5 wk), 15 wk.
The Doomed Oasis (Knopf) NYT fic 1/1/61 (#13, 1 wk), 5 wk.

Eyster, Warren
Far from the Customary Skies (Random) NYT fic 4/26/53 (#15), pk 5/3/53 (#12, 1 wk), 3 wk.

Eyton, Audrey
The F-Plan Diet (Crown) NYT nf 4/3/83 (#12), pk 5/1/83 (#6, 3 wk), 20 wk; PW hc nf 4/8/83 (#11), pk 5/6/83 (#6, 3 wk), 15 wk; (Bantam) NYT msc pb 2/12/84 (#6), pk 2/19/84 (#4, 1 wk), 3 wk; tot 38 wk.

Faber, Adele, and Elaine Mazlish
Siblings Without Rivalry: How to Help Your Children Live Together So You Can Live Too (Norton) NYT msc 6/21/87 (#5), pk 7/26/87 (#1, 2 wk), 10 wk; PW hc nf 6/26/87 (#15), pk 7/31/87 (#10, 2 wk), 7 wk; tot 17 wk.

Faber, Harold
The Kennedy Years [ed.] (Viking) NYT gen 12/13/64 (#9), pk 12/20/64 (#4, 1 wk), 12 wk; PW nf 1/4/65 (#9), pk 1/18/65 (#3, 1 wk), 8 wk; tot 20 wk.

Fabian, Warner
Flaming Youth (Boni & Liveright) PW fic 4/14/23 (#8), pk 7/21/23 (#4, 4 wk), 20 wk.

Fabricius, Johan
The Son of Marietta (Little Brown) PW fic 2/15/36 (#6), pk 3/14/36 (#5, 4 wk), 12 wk.

Fadiman, Clifton
I Believe [ed.] (Simon & Schuster) NYT gen 10/8/39 (#13, 4 wk).
Reading I've Liked [ed.] (Simon & Schuster) PW nf 11/15/41 (#2, 4 wk), 20 wk.
Party of One: The Selected Writings of Clifton Fadiman (World) NYT gen 5/22/55 (#11, 2 wk), 4 wk.

The Lifetime Reading Plan (World Almanac) NYT gen 4/24/60 (#15), pk 5/8/60 (#11, 1 wk), 4 wk.

Fairbairn, Ann
Five Smooth Stones (Crown) PW fic 4/3/67 (#8, 1 wk), 2 wk; NYT pb fic 8/4/68 (#4), pk 9/1/68 (#2, 4 wk), 24 wk; tot 26 wk.

Fairbairn, William Ewart
Get Tough! (Paladin) NYT nf 9/6/42 (#11, 1 wk), 4 wk.

Fairbank, Janet Ayer
Rich Man Poor Man (Houghton) PW fic 1/16/37 (#9), pk 2/6/37 (#5, 4 wk), 12 wk.

Falkner, John Meade
Moonfleet (Grosset & Dunlap) NYT fic 9/16/51 (#15), pk 9/23/51 (#14, 1 wk), 2 wk.

Fallaci, Oriana
A Man (Simon & Schuster) PW hc fic 12/26/80 (#10), pk 1/16/81 (#8, 3 wk), 14 wk; NYT fic 12/28/80 (#15), pk 1/11/81 (#14, 1 wk), 4 wk; tot 18 wk.

Fallada, Hans
Little Man, What Now? (Simon & Schuster) PW fic 7/15/33 (#4), pk 8/12/33 (#3, 8 wk), 16 wk.

Fallows, James M.
See Mark J. Green, et al.

Falstaff, Jake
Come Back to Wayne County (Houghton) NYT fic 11/8/42 (#21), pk 1/17/43 (#14, 1 wk), 5 wk.

Falstein, Louis
Face of a Hero (Harcourt) NYT fic 10/8/50 (#16, 1 wk).

Farago, Ladislas
Patton: Ordeal and Triumph (Obolensky) NYT gen 11/29/64 (#9), pk 12/13/64 (#6, 1 wk), 3 wk; PW nf 12/7/64 (#13), pk 1/4/65 (#5, 1 wk), 8 wk; tot 11 wk.
The Game of the Foxes (McKay) NYT gen 2/6/72 (#8), pk 3/19/72 (#1, 10 wk), 29 wk; PW nf 2/14/72 (#5), pk 3/6/72 (#1, 11 wk), 30 wk; NYT pb 3/11/73 (#3, 4 wk); tot 63 wk.

Farley, James A.
Jim Farley's Story (Whittlesey) NYT gen 3/21/48 (#10), pk 4/11/48 (#2, 7 wk), 20 wk; PW nf 4/3/48 (#3), pk 4/24/48 (#1, 2 wk), 15 wk; tot 35 wk.

Farley, Walter
The Black Stallion's Filly (Random) NYT ch bst 11/16/52 (#1, 40 wk).

The Black Stallion Revolts (Random) NYT ch bst 11/15/53 (#1, 40 wk).

The Black Stallion's Sulky Colt (Random) NYT ch bst 11/14/54 (#4, 40 wk).

The Island Stallion Races (Random) NYT ch bst 11/18/56 (#4, 40 wk).

The Black Stallion's Courage (Random) NYT ch bst 11/17/57 (#8, 40 wk).

The Black Stallion and Flame (Random) NYT ch bst 11/13/60 (#9, 27 wk).

Farmer, Fannie M.

Boston Cooking School Book (Little Brown) PW gen lit 5/26/23 (#12), pk 7/18/25 (#1, 4 wk), 32 wk; nf 6/21/24 (#3, 8 wk), 56 wk; tot 88 wk.

Farnham, Marynia L. Foot

See Ferdinand Lundberg and_____

Farnol, Jeffery

Sir John Dering (Little Brown) PW fic 11/24/23 (#11, 4 wk).

The Loring Mystery (Little Brown) PW fic 4/18/25 (#7, 4 wk).

High Adventure (Little Brown) PW fic 5/15/26 (#7, 4 wk), 8 wk.

Guyfford of Weare (Little Brown) PW fic 11/24/28 (#10, 4 wk).

Farrand, John, Jr.

See John Bull and_____

Farrar, Geraldine

Such Sweet Compulsion (Greystone) NYT gen 12/4/38 (#6, 4 wk).

Farrell, James Thomas

No Star Is Lost (Vanguard) NYT fic 11/6/38 (#7, 4 wk).

Bernard Clare (Vanguard) NYT fic 6/9/46 (#16), pk 7/7/46 (#13, 1 wk), 3 wk.

Farris, John

The Fury (Fawcett/Popular Library) PW mm pb 4/24/78 (#13), pk 5/1/78 (#12, 1 wk), 2 wk.

Farson, Negley

The Way of a Transgressor (Harcourt) PW nf 3/14/36 (#6), pk 4/11/36 (#1, 12 wk), 36 wk; NYT nf 4/5/36 (#3, 8 wk), 12 wk; NYT gen 8/2/36 (#6, 4 wk), 8 wk; tot 56 wk.

Transgressor in the Tropics (Harcourt) NYT gen 2/6/38 (#9, 4 wk), 8 wk.

Behind God's Back (Harcourt) PW nf 4/12/41 (#3, 4 wk), 8 wk.

Fast, Howard

Citizen Tom Paine (Duell Sloan & Pearce) NYT gen 5/30/43 (#13), pk 6/20/43 (#5, 1 wk), 15 wk.

Freedom Road (Duell Sloan & Pearce) NYT fic 9/10/44 (#9), pk 9/24/44 (#8, 2 wk), 7 wk.

The American (Duell Sloan & Pearce) NYT fic 8/11/46 (#12), pk 8/25/46 (#4, 1 wk), 8 wk.

Body Language (Evans) NYT gen 8/9/70 (#7), pk 8/16/70 (#6, 12 wk), 22 wk; PW nf 9/7/70 (#10), pk 10/19/70 (#4, 2 wk), 18 wk; NYT pb gen 6/6/71 (#3, 8 wk), 8 wk; tot 48 wk.

The Immigrants (Houghton) PW hc fic 10/10/77 (#13), pk 2/27/78 (#8, 1 wk), 20 wk; NYT fic 10/16/77 (#13), pk 11/6/77 (#5, 1 wk); (Dell) PW mm pb 9/18/78 (#11), pk 10/16/78 (#1, 2 wk), 21 wk; NYT mm pb 11/12/78 (#4), pk 12/17/79 (#3, 4 wk), 16 wk; tot 79 wk.

Second Generation (Houghton) PW hc fic 10/2/78 (#11), pk 1/1/79 (#3, 2 wk), 27 wk; NYT fic 11/12/78 (#5), pk 12/24/78 (#3, 3 wk), 20 wk; (Dell) PW mm pb 9/10/79 (#10), pk 10/8/79 (#1, 1 wk), 14 wk; NYT mm pb 9/16/79 (#11), pk 9/23/79 (#2, 5 wk), 17 wk; tot 78 wk.

The Establishment (Houghton) PW hc fic 10/1/79 (#15), pk 11/5/79 (#2, 5 wk), 21 wk; NYT fic 10/14/79 (#8), pk 10/28/79 (#1, 5 wk), 26 wk; (Dell) PW mm pb 10/10/80 (#10), pk 10/17/80 (#2, 1 wk), 9 wk; NYT mm pb 10/12/80 (#4), pk 10/19/80 (#3, 4 wk), 14 wk; tot 70 wk.

The Legacy (Houghton) PW hc fic 9/25/81 (#9), pk 10/23/81 (#5, 3 wk), 15 wk; NYT fic 9/27/81 (#13), pk 11/8/81 (#4, 1 wk), 17 wk; (Dell) NYT mm pb 10/31/82 (#8), pk 11/14/82 (#2, 3 wk), 11 wk; PW mm pb 11/5/82 (#6), pk 11/26/82 (#1, 2 wk), 8 wk; tot 51 wk.

Max (Houghton) NYT fic 10/3/82 (#15), pk 10/17/82 (#8, 2 wk), 12 wk; PW hc fic 10/8/82 (#13), pk 10/22/82 (#11, 1 wk), 5 wk; (Dell) NYT mm pb 9/11/83 (#8), pk 10/2/83 (#5, 1 wk), 7 wk; PW mm pb 9/16/83 (#10), pk 10/7/83 (#4, 1 wk), 6 wk; tot 30 wk.

The Outsider (Houghton) NYT fic 9/16/84 (#13), pk 9/23/84 (#11, 1 wk), 5 wk; PW hc fic 10/19/84 (#15, 1 wk); (Dell) NYT pb fic 7/28/85 (#14), pk 8/11/85 (#7, 2 wk), 9 wk; PW mm pb 8/2/85 (#14), pk 8/9/85 (#8, 1 wk), 5 wk; tot 20 wk.

The Immigrant's Daughter (Houghton) PW hc fic 10/4/85 (#12, 3 wk), 5 wk; NYT nf 10/6/85 (#12), pk 10/20/85 (#11, 3 wk), 8 wk; (Dell) NYT pb fic 2/1/87 (#12), pk 2/15/87 (#3, 1 wk), 9 wk; PW mm pb 2/6/87 (#13), pk 2/20/87 (#11, 1 wk), 6 wk; tot 28 wk.

The Dinner Party (Houghton) NYT fic 3/1/87 (#14), pk 3/15/87 (#13, 1 wk), 4 wk; (Dell) PW mm pb 12/4/87 (#14), pk 12/25/87 (#6, 1 wk), 6 wk; NYT pb fic 12/6/87 (#9), pk 12/20/87 (#7, 1 wk), 6 wk; tot 16 wk.

Faulkner, William
Light in August (Smith & Haas) PW fic 11/12/32 (#9, 4 wk).
The Wild Palms (Random) NYT fic 3/5/39 (#8, 4 wk).
Requiem for a Nun (Random) NYT fic 10/14/51 (#14), pk 10/21/51 (#10, 2 wk), 7 wk.
A Fable (Random) NYT fic 8/22/54 (#6), pk 9/12/54 (#4, 2 wk), 15 wk; PW fic 8/28/54 (#6), pk 9/18/54 (#5, 3 wk), 9 wk; tot 24 wk.
The Town (Random) NYT fic 5/19/57 (#14), pk 5/26/57 (#6, 3 wk), 12 wk; PW fic 6/3/57 (#8), pk 6/24/57 (#5, 1 wk), 7 wk; tot 19 wk.
The Mansion (Random) NYT fic 11/29/59 (#15), pk 12/6/59 (#10, 7 wk), 13 wk.
The Reivers (Random) NYT fic 6/24/62 (#10), pk 8/5/62 (#4, 5 wk), 25 wk; PW fic 7/2/62 (#9), pk 8/27/62 (#3, 4 wk), 23 wk; tot 48 wk.

Faust, Joan Lee
The New York Times Book of House Plants (A&W) NYT td pb 5/25/75 (#5), pk 6/15/75 (#3, 1 wk), 3 wk.

Fay, Bernard
Franklin, The Apostle of Modern Times (Little Brown) PW nf 1/11/30 (#1, 4 wk), 12 wk.

Fay, Paul B., Jr.
The Pleasure of His Company (Harper) PW nf 9/26/66 (#11), pk 10/10/66 (#7, 1 wk), 6 wk.

Fedoroff, Alexander
This Side of the Angels (Obolensky) NYT fic 12/25/60 (#16, 1 wk).

Fedorova, Nina
The Family (Little Brown) PW fic 11/16/40 (#4, 8 wk), 20 wk.

Feiner, Ruth
Yesterday's Dreams (Lippincott) NYT fic 8/6/39 (#11, 4 wk).

Feingold, Ben F., M.D. and Helene S. Feingold
The Feingold Cookbook for Hyperactive Children (Random) PW td pb 5/7/79 (#5), pk 5/14/79 (#3, 1 wk), 9 wk; NYT td pb 5/20/79 (#11), pk 6/24/79 (#4, 1 wk), 12 wk; tot 21 wk.

Feinstein, John
A Season on the Brink (Macmillan) NYT nf 1/4/87 (#13), pk 2/1/87 (#1, 14 wk), 25 wk; PW hc nf 1/16/87 (#9), pk 2/20/87 (#1, 14 wk), 23 wk; (Pocket/Fireside) NYT pb nf 12/13/87 (#3), pk 12/20/87 (#2, 5 wk), 11 wk; PW mm pb 1/8/88 (#11), pk 1/15/88 (#9, 1 wk), 3 wk; tot 62 wk.

Feirstein, Bruce
Real Men Don't Eat Quiche [illus. Lee Lorenz] (Pocket) PW td pb 5/28/82 (#8), pk 6/25/82 (#1, 16 wk), 45 wk; NYT td pb 6/6/82 (#7), pk 6/27/82 (#1, 10 wk), 47 wk; tot 72 wk.
See also Scott Redman and_____

Feist, Raymond E.
A Darkness at Sethanon (Bantam/Spectra) NYT pb fic 2/1/87 (#15), pk 2/8/87 (#13, 2 wk), 3 wk; PW mm pb 2/6/87 (#12, 1 wk), 2 wk; tot 5 wk.
Prince of the Blood (Doubleday/Foundation) NYT fic 8/20/89 (#15, 1 wk); (Bantam/Spectra) NYT pb fic 5/27/90 (#11, 1 wk), 3 wk; PW mm pb 6/1/90 (#6, 1 wk), 2 wk; tot 6 wk.

Feldman, David
Why Do Clocks Run Clockwise? And Other Imponderables (Harper/Perennial) PW td pb 12/23/88 (#9), pk 1/6/89 (#8, 2 wk), 4 wk.

Feller, Robert William Andrew
Strikeout Story (Grosset & Dunlap) NYT gen 6/1/47 (#11), pk 7/6/47 (#10, 2 wk), 11 wk.

Femina, Jerry Della
From Those Wonderful Folks Who Gave You Pearl Harbor (Simon & Schuster) PW nf 7/6/70 (#7), pk 7/13/70 (#6, 1 wk), 4 wk; NYT gen 7/26/70 (#10, 1 wk); NYT pb gen 3/7/71 (#5, 4 wk); tot 9 wk.

Ferber, Edna
So Big (Doubleday) PW fic 4/19/24 (#1, 8 wk), 16 wk.
Show Boat (Doubleday) PW fic 9/18/26 (#5), pk 10/16/26 (#1, 12 wk), 20 wk.
Cimarron (Doubleday) PW fic 4/12/30 (#10), pk 5/17/30 (#1, 8 wk), 40 wk.
American Beauty (Doubleday) PW fic 11/14/31 (#5), pk 12/19/31 (#3, 4 wk), 16 wk.
They Brought Their Women (Doubleday) PW fic 7/15/33 (#9, 4 wk).
Come and Get It (Doubleday) PW fic 3/16/35 (#8), pk 4/13/35 (#2, 4 wk), 24 wk.
A Peculiar Treasure (Doubleday) NYT gen 3/5/39 (#1, 4 wk), 12 wk; PW nf 3/11/39 (#4), pk 4/8/39 (#3, 4 wk), 24 wk; tot 36 wk.
Saratoga Trunk (Doubleday) PW fic 12/13/41 (#2, 8 wk), 20 wk.
Great Son (Doubleday) NYT fic 2/18/45 (#9), pk 3/25/45 (#2, 2 wk), 17 wk; PW fic 2/24/45 (#4), pk 3/3/45 (#1, 3 wk), 13 wk; tot 30 wk.
Giant (Doubleday) NYT fic 10/12/52 (#12), pk 11/16/52 (#2, 3 wk), 27 wk; PW fic 10/25/52 (#4), pk 11/15/52 (#2, 4 wk), 17 wk; tot 44 wk.

Ice Palace (Doubleday) NYT fic 3/30/58 (#14), pk 6/1/58 (#2, 5 wk), 28 wk; PW fic 4/14/58 (#6), pk 5/26/58 (#2, 5 wk), 26 wk; tot 54 wk.
A Kind of Magic (Doubleday) NYT gen 10/13/63 (#10, 1 wk).

Ferguson, Charles Wright
Naked to Mine Enemies (Little Brown) NYT gen 2/16/58 (#8, 1 wk), 9 wk.

Ferguson, Sybil
The Diet Center Program: Lose Weight Fast and Keep It Off Forever (Little Brown) NYT nf 5/8/83 (#14), pk 5/22/83 (#7, 1 wk), 15 wk; PW hc nf 5/13/83 (#13), pk 5/27/83 (#9, 3 wk), 11 wk; tot 26 wk.

Fermi, Laura
Atoms in the Family (Univ. of Chicago) NYT gen 11/21/54 (#12, 1 wk), 7 wk.

Ferraro, Geraldine A.
Ferraro: My Story (Bantam) NYT nf 11/3/85 (#15), pk 11/17/85 (#9, 1 wk), 10 wk.

Ferril, Helen, and Anne Folsom
Indoor Bird Watcher's Manual (Duell Sloan & Pearce) NYT gen 4/30/50 (#14, 1 wk).

Ferris, Theodore Parker
This Created World (Harper) NYT gen 4/2/44 (#16, 1 wk).

Feuchtwanger, Lion
The Ugly Duchess (Viking) PW fic 4/28/28 (#8, 4 wk).
The Oppermanns (Viking) PW fic 5/12/34 (#5, 4 wk), 8 wk.
Simone (Viking) NYT fic 8/27/44 (#9, 1 wk), 3 wk.
Proud Destiny (Viking) NYT fic 10/5/47 (#13), pk 11/16/47 (#3, 1 wk), 18 wk; PW fic 10/25/47 (#4, 4 wk), 8 wk; tot 26 wk.
This Is the Hour (Viking) NYT fic 6/10/51 (#8), pk 7/15/51 (#7, 1 wk), 13 wk; PW fic 7/14/51 (#7, 1 wk), 2 wk; tot 15 wk.
'Tis Folly to Be Wise (Messner) NYT fic 6/7/53 (#16, 1 wk).

Feynman, Richard P.
"Surely You're Joking, Mr. Feynman!": The Adventures of a Curious Character (Norton) NYT nf 3/17/85 (#8), pk 3/31/85 (#5, 1 wk), 15 wk; PW hc nf 4/12/85 (#15), pk 4/19/85 (#13, 2 wk), 4 wk; (Bantam) NYT pb nf 2/16/86 (#7), pk 3/2/86 (#6, 3 wk), 14 wk; tot 33 wk.

_____, with Ralph Leighton
"What Do You Care What Other People Think?": Further Adventures of a Curious Character (Norton) NYT nf 12/4/88 (#11), pk 2/19/89 (#6, 1 wk), 20 wk; PW hc nf 12/16/88 (#14), pk 3/10/89 (#12, 1 wk), 6 wk; (Bantam)

NYT pb nf 12/3/89 (#9, 1 wk), 3 wk; tot 29 wk.

Field, Bradda
Bride of Glory (Greystone) PW fic 4/11/42 (#8, 4 wk).

Field, Marshall
Freedom Is More Than a Word (Univ. of California) NYT gen 5/20/45 (#19), pk 6/17/45 (#18, 1 wk), 5 wk.

Field, Rachel
Hitty: Her First Hundred Years (Macmillan) PW juv 2/15/30 (#2), pk 7/12/30 (#1, 28 wk), 88 wk.
Calico Bush (Macmillan) PW juv 1/16/32 (#5, 4 wk), 12 wk.
Time Out of Mind (Macmillan) PW fic 5/11/35 (#4), pk 8/10/35 (#2, 4 wk), 24 wk.
All This, and Heaven Too (Macmillan) NYT fic 12/4/38 (#2), pk 1/8/39 (#1, 12 wk), 36 wk; PW fic 12/10/38 (#2), pk 1/14/38 (#1, 20 wk), 40 wk; tot 76 wk.
And Now Tomorrow (Macmillan) PW fic 7/11/42 (#1, 5 wk), 16 wk; NYT fic 8/9/42 (#1, 1 wk), 18 wk; tot 34 wk.

Fielding, Joy
Kiss Mommy Goodbye (NAL) NYT mm pb 6/20/82 (#15, 1 wk).
The Other Woman (NAL/Signet) NYT mm pb 11/13/83 (#15), pk 11/20/83 (#9, 1 wk), 3 wk; PW mm pb 12/2/83 (#14, 1 wk); tot 4 wk.

Finch, Christopher
The Art of Walt Disney (NAL/Abrams) NYT td pb 4/20/75 (#3, 1 wk), 4 wk.
Rainbow (Grosset & Dunlap) NYT td pb 11/16/75 (#5, 2 wk).

Finch, Percy
See Holland McTyeire Smith and_____

Fink, David Harold, M.D.
Release from Nervous Tension (Simon & Schuster) NYT gen 9/19/43 (#11, 1 wk).

Finletter, Gretchen
From the Top of the Stairs (Little Brown) NYT gen 10/6/46 (#8), pk 10/13/46 (#7, 1 wk) 16 wk; PW nf 1/18/47 (#9, 1 wk); tot 17 wk.
The Dinner Party (Harper) NYT fic 5/22/55 (#14), pk 7/17/55 (#6, 1 wk), 18 wk; PW fic 6/25/55 (#8), pk 7/2/55 (#7, 1 wk), 6 wk; tot 24 wk.

Finletter, Thomas Knight
Power and Policy (Harcourt) NYT gen 11/14/54 (#16, 1 wk).

Fiore, Quentin
See Marshall McLuhan and_____

Fireman, Judy
The Cat Catalog: The Ultimate Cat Book
[ed.] (Workman) NYT td pb 12/26/76 (#2,
1 wk), 5 wk; PW td pb 12/27/76 (#4), pk
1/3/77 (#3, 2 wk), 4 wk; tot 9 wk.

**Fischer, Bobby, Stuart Margulies and
Donn Mosenfelder**
Bobby Fischer Teaches Chess (Bantam) NYT
pb gen 10/8/72 (#2, 4 wk).

Fischer, Louis
Men and Politics (Duell Sloan & Pearce)
PW nf 7/12/41 (#9, 4 wk).

Fisher, Anne
Live with a Man and Love It (Dodd) NYT
gen 10/10/37 (#10, 4 wk).

Fisher, Carrie
Postcards from the Edge (Simon & Schuster) PW hc fic 9/11/87 (#9, 1 wk), 7 wk; NYT
fic 9/20/87 (#16), pk 9/27/87 (#13, 1 wk), 2
wk; (Pocket) PW mm pb 9/28/90 (#14), pk
10/12/90 (#3, 4 wk), 10 wk; NYT pb fic
9/30/90 (#7), pk 10/7/90 (#3, 2 wk), 8 wk;
tot 27 wk.
Surrender the Pink (Simon & Schuster)
PW hc fic 9/28/90 (#14), pk 10/12/90 (#6, 2
wk), 9 wk; NYT fic 9/30/90 (#14), pk 10/7/90
(#6, 1 wk), 6 wk; tot 15 wk.

Fisher, Charles
The Columnists (Howell & Soskin) NYT
gen 5/7/44 (#18, 1 wk).

Fisher, David
See George Burns and_____
See Ron Luciano and_____

Fisher, James Maxwell
The Wonderful World (Hanover) NYT ch
bst 11/14/54 (#8, 40 wk).
The Wonderful World of the Sea (Garden
City) NYT ch bst 11/17/57 (#6, 40 wk).
See also Roger Tory Peterson and_____

**Fisher, James Tucker, and Lowell S.
Hawley**
A Few Buttons Missing (Lippincott) NYT
gen 9/23/51 (#13, 1 wk).

Fisher, Philip A.
Common Stocks and Uncommon Profits (Harper) NYT gen 8/17/58 (#16, 1 wk).

Fisher, Roger, and William Ury
*Getting to Yes: Negotiating Agreement With-
out Giving In* (Penguin) PW td pb 3/11/83
(#6), pk 4/22/83 (#4, 1 wk), 14 wk; NYT td
pb 3/20/83 (#11), pk 5/15/83 (#10, 1 wk), 12
wk; tot 26 wk.

Fisher, Vardis
Children of God (Harper) NYT fic 10/8/39

(#2, 4 wk), 8 wk; PW fic 10/14/39 (#2, 4 wk),
12 wk; tot 20 wk.
Pemmican (Doubleday) NYT fic 7/22/56
(#15, 3 wk), 4 wk.

Fishman, Jack
My Darling Clementine (McKay) NYT
gen 7/14/63 (#7), pk 8/18/63 (#3, 7 wk), 26
wk; PW nf 7/15/63 (#8), pk 9/2/63 (#1, 1 wk),
26 wk; tot 52 wk.

Fisk, Jim, and Robert Barron
The Official M.B.A. Handbook (Simon &
Schuster/Wallaby) PW td pb 8/13/82 (#5),
pk 9/24/82 (#3, 2 wk), 16 wk; NYT td pb
8/15/82 (#15), pk 9/26/82 (#4, 1 wk), 16 wk;
tot 32 wk.

Fitzgerald, F. Scott
This Side of Paradise (Scribner) PW fic
9/25/20 (#4, 4 wk), 8 wk.
The Beautiful and the Damned (Scribner)
PW fic 5/13/22 (#6, 4 wk), 8 wk.
Tender Is the Night (Scribner) PW fic
5/12/34 (#10, 8 wk).
The Letters of F. Scott Fitzgerald [ed.
Andrew Turnbull] (Scribner) PW nf 12/9/63
(#9, 1 wk).
The Great Gatsby (Scribner) NYT td pb
4/14/74 (#2, 4 wk), 12 wk; (Bantam) NYT
mm pb 4/14/74 (#8), pk 5/12/74 (#1, 4 wk),
16 wk; tot 28 wk.

FitzGerald, Frances
Fire in the Lake (Atlantic Little Brown)
NYT gen 9/24/72 (#10), pk 10/1/72 (#7, 4
wk), 13 wk; PW nf 10/16/72 (#10), pk 11/27/
72 (#6, 1 wk), 8 wk; NYT pb gen 10/14/73
(#3, 4 wk); tot 25 wk.

Fitzgerald, Jim, and John Boswell
First Family Paper Dolls & Cut-Outs Book
[illus. Al Kilgore] (Dell) PW td pb 12/11/81
(#7, 1 wk), 7 wk; NYT td pb 12/27/81 (#10,
1 wk), 4 wk; tot 11 wk.

Fixx, James F.
The Complete Book of Running (Random)
NYT nf 11/27/77 (#12), pk 2/26/78 (#1, 11
wk), 85 wk; PW hc nf 11/28/77 (#10), pk
2/20/78 (#1, 14 wk), 74 wk; tot 159 wk.
Jim Fixx's Second Book of Running (Random) NYT nf 4/27/80 (#11), pk 7/6/80 (#4,
1 wk), 22 wk; PW hc nf 5/2/80 (#9), pk
5/16/80 (#7, 4 wk), 16 wk; tot 38 wk.

Flack, Marjorie
Angus and the Cat (Doubleday) PW juv
12/19/31 (#7), 3/19/32 (#4, 4 wk), 20 wk.
Angus and the Ducks (Doubleday) PW juv
10/18/30 (#4, 12 wk), 28 wk.

Flanagan, John Theodore
America Is West [ed.] (Univ. of Minnesota) NYT gen 1/6/46 (#11, 1 wk).

Flanagan, Thomas
The Year of the French (Pocket) PW mm pb 11/14/80 (#15, 1 wk).
The Tenants of Time (Abrams/Dutton) NYT fic 1/24/88 (#14), pk 3/6/88 (#4, 1 wk), 10 wk; PW hc fic 1/29/88 (#13), pk 2/5/88 (#8, 2 wk), 8 wk; (Warner) PW mm pb 3/17/89 (#12), pk 3/24/89 (#11, 1 wk), 3 wk; NYT pb fic 3/19/89 (#15), pk 3/26/89 (#13, 1 wk), 3 wk; tot 24 wk.

Flanner, Jamet
Paris Was Yesterday (Viking) NYT gen 9/10/72 (#10), pk 10/8/72 (#6, 2 wk), 9 wk; PW nf 9/11/72 (#9), pk 10/2/72 (#7, 1 wk), 11 wk; tot 20 wk.

Flannery, Harry W.
Assignment to Berlin (Knopf) PW nf 8/8/42 (#7, 1 wk), 2 wk; NYT nf 8/9/42 (#7, 3 wk), 11 wk; tot 13 wk.

Flato, Charles
The Golden Book of the Civil War (Golden) NYT ch bst 5/13/62 (#12), pk 11/11/62 (#9, 26 wk), 45 wk.

Flavin, Martin
Journey in the Dark (Harper) NYT fic 11/21/43 (#7), pk 11/28/43 (#6, 1 wk), 4 wk; PW fic 12/18/43 (#8, 1 wk), 2 wk; tot 6 wk.

Fleetwood, Mick, and Stephen Davis
Fleetwood (Morrow) NYT nf 10/28/90 (#15), pk 11/18/90 (#9, 1 wk), 7 wk; PW hc nf 11/2/90 (#9), pk 11/30/90 (#7, 1 wk), 6 wk; tot 13 wk.

Fleischer, Leonore
Agnes of God [screenplay by John Piel-meier] (NAL/Signet) PW mm pb 11/8/85 (#13, 1 wk).
See also George Vecsey and____

Fleming, Berry
Colonel Effingham's Raid (Duell Sloan & Pearce) NYT fic 3/28/43 (#18), pk 4/4/43 (#14, 1 wk), 2 wk.
The Fortune Tellers (Lippincott) NYT fic 12/9/51 (#16, 1 wk).

Fleming, Ian
On Her Majesty's Secret Service (NAL) NYT fic 9/15/63 (#9), pk 10/27/63 (#7, 11 wk), 25 wk; PW fic 9/23/63 (#9), pk 10/21/63 (#5, 3 wk), 25 wk; tot 50 wk.
You Only Live Twice (NAL) NYT fic 9/6/64 (#7), pk 12/20/64 (#5, 2 wk), 23 wk; PW fic 9/14/64 (#7), pk 11/2/64 (#4, 1 wk), 21 wk; tot 44 wk.

The Man with the Golden Gun (NAL) NYT fic 8/22/65 (#9), pk 9/19/65 (#5, 1 wk), 12 wk; PW fic 8/23/65 (#10), pk 10/4/65 (#2, 1 wk), 17 wk; NYT pb fic 9/4/66 (#5, 4 wk); tot 33 wk.
Chitty-Chitty-Bang-Bang (Random) NYT ch bst 5/9/65 (#3), pk 11/7/65 (#2, 26 wk), 90 wk.

Fleming, Peter
Brazilian Adventure (Scribner) PW nf 2/10/34 (#3), pk 3/10/34 (#2, 4 wk), 16 wk.
Operation Sea Lion (Simon & Schuster) NYT gen 8/11/57 (#11), pk 8/18/57 (#7, 1 wk), 9 wk; PW nf 8/26/57 (#8, 1 wk); tot 10 wk.

Fleming, Thomas
The Officers' Wives (Doubleday) NYT fic 5/3/81 (#15, 3 wk); (Warner) NYT mm pb 3/14/82 (#8), pk 4/4/82 (#7, 1 wk), 11 wk; PW mm pb 3/19/82 (#11), pk 4/16/82 (#4, 1 wk), 9 wk; tot 23 wk.
Time and Tide (Bantam) PW mm pb 1/20/89 (#15, 2 wk); NYT pb fic 1/22/89 (#11, 1 wk), 2 wk; tot 4 wk.

Flesch, Rudolf
Why Johnny Can't Read (Harper) NYT gen 4/10/55 (#12), pk 6/19/55 (#3, 1 wk), 37 wk; PW nf 4/23/55 (#9), pk 8/13/55 (#3, 1 wk), 27 wk; tot 64 wk.

Fletcher, Inglis
Raleigh's Eden (Bobbs Merrill) PW fic 11/16/40 (#10, 4 wk).
Lusty Wind for Carolina (Blakiston) NYT fic 12/17/44 (#13), pk 12/24/44 (#11, 2 wk), 3 wk.
Toil of the Brave (Bobbs Merrill) NYT fic 12/8/46 (#14), pk 12/22/46 (#11, 3 wk), 10 wk; PW fic 1/18/47 (#7, 1 wk), 2 wk; tot 12 wk.
Roanoke Hundred (Bobbs Merrill) NYT fic 11/14/48 (#12), pk 12/26/48 (#8, 3 wk), 13 wk; PW fic 1/15/49 (#8, 1 wk); tot 14 wk.
Bennett's Welcome (Bobbs Merrill) NYT fic 11/5/50 (#10), pk 12/17/50 (#7, 3 wk), 13 wk; PW fic 12/16/50 (#6, 1 wk), 2 wk; tot 15 wk.
Queen's Gift (Bobbs Merrill) NYT fic 11/9/52 (#16), pk 11/16/52 (#8, 2 wk), 15 wk; PW fic 12/13/52 (#7, 1 wk), 3 wk; tot 18 wk.
The Scotswoman (Bobbs Merrill) NYT fic 5/1/55 (#12), pk 5/15/55 (#10, 7 wk), 14 wk; PW fic 6/11/55 (#7, 1 wk), 2 wk; tot 16 wk.
The Wind in the Forest (Bobbs Merrill) PW fic 1/20/58 (#10, 1 wk).

Fletcher, Steffi, and Jane Werner Watson
Walt Disney's Treasury (Simon & Schuster) NYT ch bst 11/14/54 (#16, 40 wk).

Fleury, Comte
Memoirs of the Empress Eugenie (Appleton)
PW gen lit 10/23/20 (#6), pk 11/27/20 (#4,
4 wk), 12 wk.

Flexner, James Thomas
Washington: The Indispensible Man (NAL/
Signet) NYT pb nf 4/29/84 (#7, 1 wk); PW
mm pb 5/4/84 (#13, 1 wk); tot 2 wk.

Flint, Emily
See Edward Weeks and_____

Flood, Charles Bracelen
Love Is a Bridge (Houghton) NYT fic 10/
25/53 (#15), pk 3/21/54 (#9, 1 wk), 23 wk.

Flynn, Edward Joseph
You're the Boss (Viking) NYT gen 10/5/47
(#12, 1 wk), 4 wk.

Flynn, Errol
My Wicked, Wicked Ways (Putnam) NYT
gen 1/24/60 (#10), pk 2/28/60 (#4, 6 wk), 22
wk; PW nf 2/1/60 (#7), pk 2/29/60 (#3, 1
wk), 17 wk; tot 39 wk.

Flynn, John Thomas
A Country Squire in the White House (Doubleday) PW nf 8/10/40 (#6), pk 9/14/40 (#1,
12 wk), 20 wk.
The Roosevelt Myth (Devin Adair) NYT
gen 9/19/48 (#16), pk 11/14/48 (#2, 1 wk), 24
wk; PW nf 10/16/48 (#8), pk 11/20/48 (#3, 1
wk), 12 wk; tot 36 wk.
The Road Ahead (Devin Adair) NYT gen
11/13/49 (#15), pk 3/12/50 (#9, 2 wk), 12 wk;
PW nf 3/18/50 (#7, 1 wk); tot 13 wk.
While You Slept (Devin Adair) NYT gen
2/17/52 (#15, 3 wk), 4 wk.
The Lattimore Story (Devin Adair) NYT
gen 6/7/53 (#16, 1 wk).

Foldes, Jolan
The Street of the Fishing Cat (Farrar) NYT
fic 1/31/37 (#6, 4 wk), 8 wk; PW fic 2/6/37
(#7), pk 3/13/37 (#6, 4 wk), 8 wk; tot 16 wk.
I'm Getting Married (Farrar) NYT fic 2/6/
38 (#9, 4 wk).

Follett, Ken
Eye of the Needle (Arbor House) PW hc fic
7/3/78 (#10), pk 8/14/78 (#2, 4 wk), 27 wk;
NYT fic 7/9/78 (#13), pk 8/13/78 (#4, 1 wk),
18 wk; (NAL/Signet) PW mm pb 7/2/79
(#4), pk 7/16/79 (#2, 2 wk), 20 wk; NYT mm
pb 7/8/79 (#3), pk 8/19/79 (#2, 1 wk), 26 wk;
tot 91 wk.
Triple (Arbor House) PW hc fic 9/3/79
(#12), pk 12/10/79 (#2, 2 wk), 33 wk; NYT
fic 9/9/79 (#13), pk 12/9/79 (#1, 2 wk), 34
wk; (NAL/Signet) PW mm pb 10/17/80
(#4), pk 10/31/80 (#1, 2 wk), 18 wk; NYT mm

pb 10/19/80 (#4), pk 11/2/80 (#1, 3 wk), 15
wk; tot 100 wk.
The Key to Rebecca (Morrow) PW hc fic
9/26/80 (#12), pk 10/24/80 (#1, 2 wk), 30 wk;
NYT fic 9/28/80 (#8), pk 10/19/80 (#1, 2
wk), 30 wk; (NAL/Signet) PW mm pb 9/4/
81 (#7), pk 9/11/81 (#1, 7 wk), 15 wk; NYT
mm pb 9/6/81 (#5), pk 9/13/81 (#1, 6 wk), 17
wk; tot 92 wk.
The Man from St. Petersburg (Morrow) PW
hc fic 5/7/82 (#13), pk 5/28/82 (#2, 7 wk),
24 wk; NYT fic 5/16/82 (#5), pk 6/6/82 (#1,
1 wk), 23 wk; (NAL/Signet) NYT mm pb
5/8/83 (#1, 5 wk), 17 wk; PW mm pb 5/13/83
(#2), pk 5/20/83 (#1, 5 wk), 18 wk; tot 82 wk.
On Wings of Eagles (Morrow) PW hc nf
9/2/83 (#12), pk 9/30/83 (#2, 4 wk), 34 wk;
NYT nf 9/4/83 (#14), pk 10/2/83 (#2, 1 wk),
36 wk; (NAL/Signet) NYT pb nf 9/2/84
(#2), pk 9/9/84 (#1, 6 wk), 18 wk; PW mm
pb 9/7/84 (#4), pk 9/14/84 (#1, 6 wk), 18 wk;
tot 106 wk.
The Modigliani Scandal (NAL/Signet) PW
mm pb 5/24/85 (#9), pk 5/31/85 (#4, 1 wk),
13 wk; NYT pb fic 6/2/85 (#8, 1 wk), 7 wk;
tot 20 wk.
Lie Down with Lions (Morrow) PW hc fic
1/31/86 (#7), pk 3/7/86 (#1, 2 wk), 23 wk;
NYT fic 2/2/86 (#3), pk 2/16/86 (#1, 2 wk),
24 wk; (NAL/Signet) NYT pb fic 12/7/86
(#3), pk 1/25/87 (#1, 1 wk), 19 wk; PW mm
pb 12/12/86 (#5), pk 1/16/87 (#1, 3 wk), 17
wk; tot 83 wk.
Paper Money (NAL/Signet) PW mm pb
10/23/87 (#11), pk 11/27/87 (#5, 2 wk), 10 wk;
NYT pb fic 10/25/87 (#13), pk 11/22/87 (#7,
2 wk), 7 wk; tot 17 wk.
The Pillars of the Earth (Morrow) NYT fic
9/17/89 (#13), pk 9/24/89 (#2, 6 wk), 18 wk;
PW hc fic 9/22/89 (#4), pk 9/29/89 (#2, 6
wk), 18 wk; (NAL/Signet) NYT pb fic 7/29/
90 (#4), pk 8/5/90 (#3, 6 wk), 13 wk; PW
mm pb 8/3/90 (#10), pk 9/7/90 (#2, 2 wk),
13 wk; tot 66 wk.

Folsom, Anne
See Helen Ferril and_____

**Fonda, Henry, as told to Howard Teich-
man**
Fonda: My Life (NAL) NYT nf 12/20/81
(#10, 1 wk); PW hc nf 1/15/82 (#11, 1 wk);
(NAL/Signet) PW mm pb 9/24/82 (#15), pk
10/8/82 (#14, 1 wk), 3 wk; tot 5 wk.

Fonda, Jane
Jane Fonda's Workout Book (Simon &
Schuster) PW hc nf 1/22/82 (#15), pk 3/5/82
(#1, 28 wk), 89 wk; NYT nf 1/24/82 (#8), pk
3/14/82 (#1, 34 wk), 92 wk; NYT msc 1/8/84
(#4), pk 1/22/84 (#3, 1 wk), 3 wk; PW td pb

2/3/84 (#9), pk 2/10/84 (#3, 4 wk), 19 wk; NYT msc pb 2/5/84 (#5), pk 2/19/84 (#3, 3 wk), 15 wk; tot 218 wk.

Jane Fonda's New Workout & Weight-Loss Program (Simon & Schuster) PW hc nf 7/18/86 (#12, 1 wk), 4 wk; NYT msc 8/10/86 (#4, 2 wk); tot 6 wk.

_____, and Mignon McCarthy
Women Coming of Age (Simon & Schuster) NYT msc 12/9/84 (#3), pk 2/10/85 (#1, 4 wk), 17 wk; PW hc nf 12/21/84 (#14), pk 2/15/85 (#2, 2 wk), 16 wk; tot 33 wk.

Fontaine, Joan
No Bed of Roses (Morrow) PW hc nf 10/9/78 (#15, 1 wk).

Fontaine, Robert Louis
The Happy Time (Simon & Schuster) NYT fic 7/22/45 (#17), pk 9/2/45 (#9, 1 wk), 4 wk.

Fontana, D.C.
Vulcan's Glory (Pocket) NYT pb fic 2/5/89 (#16), pk 2/12/89 (#11, 1 wk), 5 wk; PW mm pb 2/17/89 (#13, 1 wk), 2 wk; tot 7 wk.

Fonteyn, Margot
Margot Fonteyn: An Autobiography (Knopf) NYT gen 6/6/76 (#10), pk 6/27/76 (#7, 1 wk), 5 wk; PW hc nf 6/14/76 (#10), pk 6/28/76 (#8, 1 wk), 5 wk; tot 10 wk.

Footner, Hulbert
Rivers of the Eastern Shore (Farrar) NYT gen 11/19/44 (#8, 1 wk), 11 wk.

Forbes, Esther
Paradise (Harcourt) NYT fic 4/4/37 (#5, 4 wk), 8 wk; PW fic 4/10/37 (#5, 8 wk), 12 wk; tot 20 wk.

The General's Lady (Harcourt) NYT fic 11/6/38 (#10, 4 wk); PW fic 11/12/38 (#9, 4 wk); tot 8 wk.

Paul Revere and the World He Lived In (Houghton) PW nf 8/8/42 (#6, 1 wk), 3 wk; NYT nf 8/9/42 (#6, 2 wk), 16 wk; tot 19 wk.

The Running of the Tide (Houghton) NYT fic 10/17/48 (#13), pk 11/28/48 (#4, 1 wk), 22 wk; PW fic 11/13/48 (#7), pk 11/20/48 (#4, 3 wk), 9 wk; tot 31 wk.

Rainbow on the Road (Houghton) NYT fic 2/21/54 (#13), pk 3/7/54 (#6, 3 wk), 11 wk; PW fic 3/13/54 (#4, 1 wk), 5 wk; tot 16 wk.

Forbes, Kathryn Alen
See Kathryn Anderson McLean

Forbes, Malcolm, with Jeff Block
They Went That-A-Way: How the Famous, the Infamous and the Great Died (Simon & Schuster) PW hc nf 9/30/88 (#14), pk 10/28/88 (#13, 1 wk), 4 wk; NYT nf 10/2/88 (#10, 3 wk), 4 wk; tot 8 wk.

Ford, Betty with Chris Chase
Betty: A Glad Awakening (Doubleday) NYT nf 3/22/87 (#7, 1 wk), 6 wk; PW hc fic 3/27/87 (#9, 1 wk), 3 wk; tot 9 wk.

Ford, Corey
Salt Water Taffy (Putnam) PW nf 8/10/29 (#4, 4 wk), 16 wk.

Ford, Gerald R.
A Time to Heal (Reader's Digest/Harper) NYT nf 7/1/79 (#14), pk 7/8/79 (#12, 1 wk), 4 wk.

Ford, John M.
How Much for Just the Planet? (Pocket) NYT pb fic 10/25/87 (#11, 1 wk); PW mm pb 10/30/87 (#12, 1 wk); tot 2 wk.

Ford, Peter
See Michael Howell and_____

Forester, Cecil Scott [all titles as by C.S. Forester]
Captain Horatio Hornblower (Little Brown) NYT fic 6/11/39 (#4, 4 wk), 8 wk; PW fic 7/15/39 (#8), pk 9/16/39 (#6, 4 wk), 28 wk; tot 36 wk.

To the Indies (Little Brown) PW fic 9/14/40 (#4, 4 wk), 8 wk.

The Captain from Connecticut (Little Brown) PW fic 7/12/41 (#6), pk 8/16/41 (#4, 4 wk), 12 wk.

The Ship (Little Brown) NYT fic 6/6/43 (#11), pk 7/25/43 (#5, 1 wk), 16 wk; PW fic 7/10/43 (#8), pk 7/17/43 (#5, 2 wk), 8 wk; tot 24 wk.

Commodore Hornblower (Little Brown) NYT fic 6/10/45 (#13), pk 6/17/45 (#2, 2 wk), 18 wk; PW fic 6/23/45 (#2, 4 wk), 10 wk; tot 28 wk.

Lord Hornblower (Little Brown) NYT fic 10/20/46 (#13), pk 10/27/46 (#5, 1 wk), 6 wk.

The Sky and the Forest (Little Brown) NYT fic 9/5/48 (#13), pk 9/12/48 (#10, 1 wk), 3 wk.

Mr. Midshipman Hornblower (Little Brown) NYT fic 4/2/50 (#16), pk 4/16/50 (#8, 1 wk), 8 wk; PW fic 5/13/50 (#8, 1 wk); tot 9 wk.

Lieutenant Hornblower (Little Brown) NYT fic 4/20/52 (#8), pk 5/11/52 (#5, 1 wk), 13 wk; PW fic 5/10/52 (#5, 2 wk), 4 wk; tot 17 wk.

Hornblower and the Atropos (Little Brown) NYT fic 10/11/53 (#13, 1 wk).

The Good Shepherd (Little Brown) NYT fic 4/10/55 (#16), pk 5/8/55 (#4, 5 wk), 18 wk; PW fic 4/23/55 (#5), pk 4/30/55 (#3, 2 wk), 14 wk; tot 32 wk.

The Age of Fighting Sail (Doubleday) NYT gen 8/5/56 (#13), pk 8/26/56 (#10, 1 wk), 9 wk.

Admiral Hornblower in the West Indies (Little Brown) NYT fic 10/5/58 (#12, 1 wk).

Hornblower and the Hotspur (Little Brown)
NYT fic 9/2/62 (#13), pk 9/23/62 (#6, 1 wk),
9 wk; PW fic 9/10/62 (#11), pk 10/1/62 (#8,
1 wk), 5 wk; tot 14 wk.

Foreyt, John P.
See Michael E. DeBakey, et al.

Forman, Harrison
Report from Red China (Holt) NYT gen
5/27/45 (#19, 1 wk).

Forrestal, James Vincent
The Forrestal Diaries [ed. Walter Millis
and E.S. Duffield] (Viking) NYT gen 10/28/
51 (#7), pk 11/11/51 (#2, 4 wk), 20 wk; PW
nf 11/10/51 (#2, 5 wk), 12 wk; tot 32 wk.

Forster, E.M.
Maurice (Norton) NYT fic 10/31/71 (#9, 1
wk), 2 wk; PW fic 11/8/71 (#6, 1 wk); tot 3
wk.
A Passage to India (Harcourt) PW pb fic
2/24/85 (#12), pk 3/3/85 (#5, 1 wk), 7 wk;
PW td pb 3/1/85 (#6), pk 3/15/85 (#3, 1 wk),
8 wk; tot 15 wk.

Forsyth, Frederick
The Day of the Jackal (Viking) PW fic
8/30/71 (#7), pk 10/18/71 (#1, 8 wk), 39 wk;
NYT fic 9/5/71 (#8), pk 10/17/71 (#1, 7 wk),
36 wk; NYT pb fic 10/8/72 (#1, 20 wk), 36
wk; tot 111 wk.
The Odessa File (Viking) NYT fic 11/5/72
(#8), pk 3/25/73 (#1, 6 wk), 48 wk; PW fic
11/6/72 (#5), pk 2/5/73 (#1, 8 wk), 42 wk;
NYT mm pb 3/10/74 (#6, 4 wk), 8 wk; tot
98 wk.
The Dogs of War (Viking) PW fic 7/1/74
(#8), pk 8/5/74 (#2, 7 wk), 35 wk; NYT fic
7/14/74 (#6), pk 8/18/74 (#2, 7 wk), 35 wk;
(Bantam) NYT mm pb 9/7/75 (#6), pk
9/14/75 (#2, 3 wk), 7 wk; tot 77 wk.
The Negotiator (Bantam) NYT fic 4/30/89
(#5), pk 5/14/89 (#2, 3 wk), 18 wk; PW hc
fic 5/5/89 (#5), pk 5/12/89 (#2, 8 wk), 19 wk;
NYT pb fic 4/8/90 (#7), pk 4/22/90 (#1, 1
wk), 9 wk; PW mm pb 4/13/90 (#7), pk 4/27/
90 (#1, 2 wk), 8 wk; tot 54 wk.
Devil's Alternative (Viking) PW hc fic
1/25/80 (#15), pk 2/29/80 (#1, 3 wk), 30 wk;
NYT fic 2/3/80 (#2, 4 wk), 29 wk; (Bantam)
PW mm pb 1/23/81 (#2), pk 1/30/81 (#1, 3
wk), 12 wk; NYT mm pb 1/25/81 (#1, 3 wk),
13 wk; tot 84 wk.
No Comebacks (Viking) NYT fic 7/11/82
(#14, 3 wk), 4 wk; (Bantam) NYT mm pb 4/
17/83 (#14), pk 5/1/83 (#8, 1 wk), 5 wk; PW
mm pb 4/22/83 (#13), pk 5/6/83 (#11, 2 wk),
4 wk; tot 13 wk.
The Fourth Protocol (Viking) NYT fic 8/
19/84 (#14), pk 9/16/84 (#1, 6 wk), 29 wk;

PW hc fic 8/24/84 (#11), pk 9/14/84 (#1, 7
wk), 28 wk; (Bantam) NYT pb fic 9/8/85
(#9), pk 9/22/85 (#2, 2 wk), 11 wk; PW mm
pb 9/13/85 (#6), pk 9/20/85 (#2, 3 wk), 10
wk; tot 78 wk.

Fortune, Jan, and Jean Burton
Elisabet Ney (Knopf) NYT gen 5/2/43
(#22), pk 5/30/43 (#20, 1 wk), 3 wk.

**Forward, Dr. Susan, with Craig
Buck**
*Toxic Parents: Overcoming Their Hurtful
Legacy and Reclaiming Your Life* (Bantam)
PW hc nf 8/25/89 (#7), pk 10/13/89 (#3, 2
wk), 15 wk; NYT msc 9/3/89 (#3), pk 10/8/
89 (#1, 2 wk), 11 wk; NYT msc pb 9/23/90
(#5), pk 9/30/90 (#2, 3 wk), 5 wk; PW mm
pb 10/5/90 (#15), pk 10/12/90 (#11, 1 wk), 5
wk; tot 36 wk.

_____, and Joan Torres
*Men Who Hate Women & The Women Who
Love Them* (Bantam) PW hc nf 9/12/86
(#14), pk 10/3/86 (#2, 12 wk), 37 wk; NYT
msc 9/21/86 (#4), pk 9/28/86 (#1, 21 wk), 35
wk; PW mm pb 6/12/87 (#9), pk 6/26/87
(#3, 1 wk), 8 wk; NYT msc pb 6/14/87 (#1,
3 wk), 10 wk; tot 90 wk.

Fosdick, Harry Emerson
Twelve Tests of Character (Association Press)
PW gen lit 4/19/24 (#8, 4 wk).
Modern Use of the Bible (Macmillan) PW
gen lit 4/18/25 (#10, 8 wk).
As I See Religion (Harper) PW nf 7/9/32
(#10, 4 wk).
On Being a Real Person (Harper) NYT nf
3/21/43 (#23), pk 3/28/43 (#9, 1 wk), 2 wk;
PW nf 3/27/43 (#3), pk 4/17/43 (#1, 2 wk),
23 wk; NYT gen 4/4/43 (#3), pk 4/25/43
(#1, 2 wk), 28 wk; tot 53 wk.
The Man from Nazareth (Harper) NYT
gen 11/6/49 (#15, 1 wk).

Foss, Christopher
See Alex Comfort

Foster, Alan Dean
Splinter of the Mind's Eye (Ballantine/Del
Rey) PW mm pb 4/10/78 (#14), pk 5/8/78
(#5, 1 wk), 11 wk; NYT mm pb 4/23/78 (#9,
2 wk), 12 wk; tot 23 wk.
Alien (Warner) PW mm pb 6/11/79 (#10),
pk 6/18/79 (#3, 3 wk), 9 wk; NYT mm pb
6/17/79 (#7), pk 6/24/79 (#3, 2 wk), 12 wk;
tot 21 wk.
The Black Hole [screenplay by Jeb Rosebrook and Gerry Day] (Ballantine/Del Rey)
NYT mm pb 12/23/79 (#10), pk 1/6/80 (#7,
1 wk), 3 wk; PW mm pb 12/24/79 (#9), pk
1/11/80 (#8, 1 wk), 4 wk; tot 7 wk.

Starman (Warner) NYT pb fic 12/16/84 (#15, 1 wk).

The Last Starfighter (Berkley) NYT pb fic 6/10/84 (#15), pk 6/24/84 (#12, 1 wk), 4 wk; PW mm pb 6/29/84 (#13), pk 7/6/84 (#12, 1 wk), 3 wk; tot 7 wk.

Aliens (Warner) NYT pb fic 8/10/86 (#15, 1 wk).

Flinx in Flux (Ballantine/Del Rey) NYT pb fic 7/10/88 (#14, 1 wk).

Foster, Elizabeth
The Islanders (Houghton) NYT gen 3/10/46 (#14, 1 wk).

Foster, Marian Curtis
Miss Flora McFlimsey's Birthday [as by Mariana] (Lothrop Lee & Shepard) NYT ch bst 11/16/52 (#15, 40 wk).

Foster, Maureen Strange
See Patti Davis and_____

Foster, Michael
American Dream (Morrow) NYT fic 8/8/37 (#3, 4 wk), 8 wk; PW fic 8/14/37 (#6, 8 wk), 12 wk; tot 20 wk.

Fournier, Alain
The Wanderer (Houghton) PW fic 2/16/29 (#8, 4 wk).

Fowler, Gene
Timber Line (Covici Friede) PW nf 2/10/34 (#9, 4 wk), 8 wk.

Good Night, Sweet Prince (Viking) NYT gen 1/30/44 (#5), pk 3/26/44 (#1, 12 wk), 41 wk; PW nf 2/12/44 (#5), pk 3/11/44 (#1, 11 wk), 27 wk; tot 68 wk.

A Solo in Tom-Toms (Viking) NYT gen 5/12/46 (#12), pk 6/23/46 (#5, 1 wk), 18 wk; PW nf 6/8/46 (#7), pk 6/29/46 (#5, 1 wk), 6 wk; tot 24 wk.

Beau James (Viking) NYT gen 4/24/49 (#7), pk 5/1/49 (#5, 4 wk), 15 wk; PW nf 5/14/49 (#5), pk 6/4/49 (#3, 1 wk), 5 wk; tot 20 wk.

Schnozzola (Viking) NYT gen 10/14/51 (#13), pk 10/21/51 (#8, 2 wk), 8 wk; PW nf 11/17/51 (#9, 1 wk); tot 9 wk.

Minutes of the Last Meeting (Viking) NYT gen 4/25/54 (#11), pk 5/30/54 (#4, 8 wk), 23 wk; PW nf 5/15/54 (#10), pk 6/5/54 (#3, 2 wk), 14 wk; tot 37 wk.

Skyline (Viking) NYT gen 2/19/61 (#16), pk 4/23/61 (#6, 1 wk), 20 wk; PW nf 2/27/61 (#8), pk 3/13/61 (#5, 2 wk), 14 wk; tot 34 wk.

Fowler, Henry Watson, and Sir Ernest Gowers
A Dictionary of Modern English Usage, Second Edition [revised by] (Oxford Univ.) NYT

gen 6/13/65 (#9), pk 6/20/65 (#8, 2 wk), 4 wk; PW nf 6/28/65 (#9, 1 wk); tot 5 wk.

Fowles, John
The Collector (Little Brown) NYT fic 8/18/63 (#10), pk 9/1/63 (#6, 4 wk), 10 wk; PW fic 8/26/63 (#10), pk 9/9/63 (#6, 1 wk), 9 wk; tot 19 wk.

The Magus (Little Brown) PW fic 2/14/66 (#11), pk 3/21/66 (#10, 1 wk), 5 wk; NYT fic 2/20/66 (#10, 1 wk); tot 6 wk.

The French Lieutenant's Woman (Little Brown) NYT fic 11/30/69 (#5), pk 2/8/70 (#1, 12 wk), 53 wk; PW fic 12/1/69 (#4), pk 1/5/70 (#1, 14 wk), 53 wk; NYT pb fic 3/7/71 (#2, 12 wk), 24 wk; (NAL) PW mm pb 10/23/81 (#10), pk 11/13/81 (#3, 1 wk), 14 wk; NYT mm pb 11/1/81 (#10), pk 12/13/81 (#8, 3 wk), 13 wk; tot 157 wk.

The Ebony Tower (Little Brown) PW fic 12/2/74 (#9), pk 12/30/74 (#4, 8 wk), 19 wk; NYT fic 12/8/74 (#10), pk 2/9/75 (#4, 1 wk), 16 wk; (NAL/Signet) NYT mm pb 11/23/75 (#9), pk 12/28/75 (#8, 1 wk), 8 wk; tot 43 wk.

Daniel Martin (Little Brown) NYT fic 9/25/77 (#15), pk 11/6/77 (#4, 6 wk), 27 wk; PW hc fic 10/3/77 (#7), pk 10/10/77 (#4, 14 wk), 22 wk; (NAL/Signet) PW mm pb 9/25/78 (#8), pk 10/2/78 (#7, 3 wk), 8 wk; tot 57 wk.

A Maggot (Little Brown) PW hc fic 9/13/85 (#15), pk 9/27/85 (#8, 1 wk), 9 wk; NYT fic 9/15/85 (#16), pk 10/6/85 (#6, 1 wk), 9 wk; (NAL/Signet) PW mm pb 10/3/86 (#14), pk 10/10/86 (#13, 1 wk), 2 wk; NYT pb fic 10/5/86 (#12, 1 wk); tot 21 wk.

Fox, John, Jr.
Erskine Dale, Pioneer (Scribner) PW fic 11/27/20 (#8, 4 wk).

Francis, Arlene
That Certain Something (Messner) NYT gen 6/19/60 (#13, 1 wk), 2 wk.

Francis, Clare
Night Sky (Morrow) NYT fic 2/19/84 (#9), pk 3/18/84 (#8, 1 wk), 10 wk; PW hc fic 3/30/84 (#14, 1 wk); (Warner) NYT pb fic 2/10/85 (#8, 2 wk), 6 wk; PW mm pb 2/15/85 (#10, 1 wk), 2 wk; tot 19 wk.

Francis, Dick
Whip Hand (Harper) NYT fic 5/25/80 (#14), pk 6/22/80 (#13, 1 wk), 5 wk; PW hc fic 6/20/80 (#13, 1 wk), 2 wk; (Pocket) PW mm pb 3/27/81 (#15, 1 wk); tot 8 wk.

Reflex (Putnam) PW hc fic 4/10/81 (#11), pk 5/8/81 (#3, 1 wk), 13 wk; NYT fic 4/12/81 (#8), pk 4/26/81 (#5, 4 wk), 15 wk; (Fawcett) PW mm pb 5/7/82 (#7, 1 wk), 5 wk; NYT mm pb 5/16/82 (#14), pk 5/23/82 (#11, 1 wk), 4 wk; tot 37 wk.

Twice Shy (Putnam) PW hc fic 4/9/82 (#15), pk 4/16/82 (#3, 3 wk), 15 wk; NYT fic 4/18/82 (#14), pk 4/25/82 (#3, 2 wk), 16 wk; (Fawcett/Crest) PW mm pb 3/11/83 (#8, 1 wk), 6 wk; NYT mm pb 3/13/83 (#15), pk 3/20/83 (#14, 1 wk), 2 wk; tot 39 wk.

Banker (Putnam) PW hc fic 4/1/83 (#12), pk 4/22/83 (#4, 1 wk), 15 wk; NYT fic 4/3/83 (#7), pk 4/17/83 (#6, 4 wk), 16 wk; (Ballantine) pb fic 3/25/84 (#15), pk 4/8/84 (#7, 1 wk), 7 wk; PW mm pb 4/6/84 (#7), pk 4/27/84 (#4, 1 wk), 5 wk; tot 43 wk.

The Danger (Putnam) NYT fic 4/1/84 (#8), pk 4/8/84 (#2, 1 wk), 13 wk; PW hc fic 4/6/84 (#8), pk 4/20/84 (#2, 1 wk), 10 wk; (Fawcett/Crest) NYT pb fic 3/31/85 (#9), pk 4/21/85 (#5, 1 wk), 8 wk; PW mm pb 4/5/85 (#10), pk 4/12/85 (#4, 3 wk), 8 wk; tot 39 wk.

Proof (Putnam) NYT fic 3/24/85 (#9), pk 3/31/85 (#5, 1 wk), 12 wk; PW hc fic 3/29/85 (#8), pk 4/5/85 (#5, 3 wk), 10 wk; (Fawcett) NYT pb fic 3/30/86 (#6, 1 wk), 9 wk; PW mm pb 4/4/86 (#8), pk 4/25/86 (#5, 1 wk), 8 wk; tot 39 wk.

Break In (Putnam) NYT fic 3/23/86 (#9), pk 4/6/86 (#2, 3 wk), 13 wk; PW hc fic 3/28/86 (#11), pk 5/2/86 (#4, 1 wk), 12 wk; (Fawcett/Crest) NYT pb fic 3/29/87 (#6), pk 4/19/87 (#2, 2 wk), 13 wk; PW mm pb 4/3/87 (#9), pk 4/17/87 (#2, 2 wk), 9 wk; tot 47 wk.

Bolt (Putnam) NYT fic 3/15/87 (#11), pk 4/12/87 (#3, 2 wk), 13 wk; PW hc fic 3/20/87 (#9), pk 4/10/87 (#3, 1 wk), 12 wk; (Fawcett/Crest) NYT pb fic 3/27/88 (#6), pk 4/3/88 (#4, 3 wk), 8 wk; PW mm pb 4/1/88 (#5), pk 4/8/88 (#2, 1 wk), 6 wk; tot 39 wk.

Hot Money (Putnam) NYT fic 3/13/88 (#11), pk 3/20/88 (#3, 3 wk), 12 wk; PW hc fic 3/18/88 (#13), pk 3/25/88 (#3, 3 wk), 10 wk; (Fawcett/Crest) NYT pb fic 2/26/89 (#10), pk 3/5/89 (#4, 2 wk), 7 wk; PW mm pb 3/3/89 (#8), pk 3/10/89 (#4, 2 wk), 7 wk; tot 36 wk.

Straight (Putnam) NYT fic 11/26/89 (#15), pk 12/3/89 (#6, 3 wk), 10 wk; PW hc fic 12/1/89 (#9), pk 12/8/89 (#6, 3 wk), 9 wk; tot 19 wk.

The Edge (Putnam) NYT fic 2/26/89 (#9), pk 3/5/89 (#3, 4 wk), 11 wk; PW hc fic 3/3/89 (#9), pk 3/17/89 (#2, 1 wk), 11 wk; (Fawcett/Crest) NYT pb fic 3/4/90 (#4, 3 wk), 7 wk; PW mm pb 3/9/90 (#8), pk 3/23/90 (#3, 1 wk), 6 wk; tot 35 wk.

Longshot (Putnam) NYT fic 10/28/90 (#8), pk 11/18/90 (#3, 1 wk), 10 wk; PW hc fic 11/2/90 (#11), pk 11/16/90 (#2, 1 wk), 8 wk; tot 18 wk.

Franck, Harry A.
Vagabonds Through Changing Germany (Harper) PW gen lit 9/25/20 (#6, 4 wk), 8 wk.

Roaming Through the West Indies (Century) PW gen lit 11/27/20 (#5), pk 1/8/21 (#1, 4 wk), 20 wk.

Franey, Pierre
The New York Times 60-Minute Gourmet (Times) NYT nf 3/2/80 (#14), pk 7/20/80 (#13, 1 wk), 2 wk; (Fawcett) NYT td pb 8/16/81 (#15, 1 wk); tot 3 wk.
See also Craig Claiborne and_____

Frank, Anne
Anne Frank: The Diary of a Young Girl (Doubleday) NYT gen 7/6/52 (#14), pk 9/14/52 (#2, 1 wk), 23 wk; PW nf 8/2/52 (#5), pk 8/23/52 (#2, 2 wk), 14 wk; tot 37 wk.

Frank, Gerold
The Deed (Simon & Schuster) PW nf 7/29/63 (#9, 1 wk), 2 wk.
The Boston Strangler (NAL) NYT gen 11/20/66 (#10), pk 12/18/66 (#5, 1 wk), 19 wk; PW nf 11/28/66 (#3, 2 wk), 18 wk; NYT pb gen 9/3/67 (#2, 4 wk), 8 wk; tot 45 wk.
Judy (Harper) NYT gen 7/20/75 (#10, 1 wk).
See also Sheilah Graham and_____
See also Diana Barrymore and_____

Frank, Jerome
Save America First (Harper) NYT gen 7/31/38 (#12, 4 wk).

Frank, Pat
Mr. Adam (Lippincott) NYT fic 10/13/46 (#16), pk 11/17/46 (#6, 1 wk), 36 wk; PW fic 10/26/46 (#5), pk 11/23/46 (#4, 1 wk), 11 wk; tot 47 wk.
An Affair of State (Lippincott) NYT fic 11/7/48 (#14, 1 wk).
Hold Back the Night (Lippincott) NYT fic 4/6/52 (#12), pk 5/4/52 (#7, 1 wk), 9 wk.

Frank, Waldo
The Bridegroom Cometh (Doubleday) NYT fic 7/9/39 (#9, 4 wk).

Frankau, Gilbert
The Dangerous Years (Dutton) NYT fic 2/6/38 (#7, 4 wk), 8 wk; PW fic 3/12/38 (#9, 4 wk); tot 12 wk.
Royal Regiment (Dutton) NYT fic 2/5/39 (#13, 8 wk); PW fic 2/11/39 (#10, 4 wk); tot 12 wk.

Frankau, Pamela
To the Moment of Triumph (Harper) NYT fic 2/15/53 (#16), pk 3/8/53 (#10, 1 wk), 6 wk.
A Wreath for the Enemy (Harper) NYT fic 7/18/54 (#12), pk 8/1/54 (#8, 1 wk), 8 wk.

Ask Me No More (Harper) NYT fic 11/30/
58 (#16, 1 wk).

**Frankfurter, Felix, and Harlan B.
Phillips**
Felix Frankfurter Reminisces (Reynal &
Hitchcock) NYT gen 6/26/60 (#10), pk 9/18/
60 (#4, 1 wk), 30 wk; PW nf 7/11/60 (#9), pk
8/22/60 (#6, 5 wk), 13 wk; tot 43 wk.

Fraser, Antonia
Mary Queen of Scots (Delacorte) PW nf
12/8/69 (#5), pk 2/9/70 (#2, 6 wk), 37 wk;
NYT gen 12/14/69 (#9), pk 3/22/70 (#2, 4
wk), 38 wk; NYT pb gen 5/2/71 (#3), pk
6/6/71 (#2, 4 wk), 12 wk; tot 87 wk.
The Weaker Vessel (Knopf) NYT nf 10/21/
84 (#12), pk 11/4/84 (#9, 2 wk), 16 wk; PW
hc nf 11/9/84 (#15), pk 11/23/84 (#13, 1 wk),
10 wk; tot 26 wk.

Frazetta, Frank
Frank Frazetta: Book Two [ed. Betty Bal-
lantine] (Bantam/Peacock) NYT td pb 6/26/
77 (#5), pk 7/31/77 (#4, 1 wk), 3 wk.

Frazier, Ian
Great Plains (Farrar) NYT nf 7/16/89 (#10,
1 wk), 10 wk.

Fredborg, Arvid
Behind the Steel Wall (Viking) NYT gen
2/6/44 (#8), pk 2/13/44 (#6, 2 wk), 7 wk; PW
nf 3/18/44 (#10, 1 wk); tot 8 wk.

Frede, Richard
The Interns (Random) NYT fic 6/19/60
(#16), pk 7/31/60 (#14, 2 wk), 8 wk.

Frederick, Carl
Est: Playing the Game the New Way (Dell)
PW td pb 3/15/76 (#5), pk 3/29/76 (#4, 1
wk), 4 wk; NYT td pb 3/21/76 (#3), pk 3/28/
76 (#2, 2 wk), 6 wk; tot 10 wk.

Freed, Roger
T.A. for Tots (Price Stern) NYT td pb 7/14/
74 (#9, 4 wk).

Freedman, Benedict and Nancy
Mrs. Mike (Coward McCann) NYT fic
3/23/47 (#11), pk 4/6/47 (#5, 8 wk), 25 wk;
PW fic 4/5/47 (#5), pk 4/19/47 (#4, 6 wk),
13 wk; tot 38 wk.

Freeman, Cynthia
A World Full of Strangers (Bantam) PW
mm pb 9/27/76 (#11), pk 10/4/76 (#7, 1 wk),
8 wk; NYT mm pb 10/17/76 (#10), pk 11/7/
76 (#9, 1 wk), 3 wk; tot 11 wk.
Portraits (Arbor House) NYT fic 12/23/79
(#15), pk 2/24/80 (#4, 3 wk), 27 wk; PW hc
fic 12/24/79 (#15), pk 2/29/80 (#5, 4 wk), 24
wk; (Bantam) PW mm pb 10/17/80 (#8), pk
11/7/80 (#1, 1 wk), 14 wk; NYT mm pb 10/19/

80 (#8), pk 11/2/80 (#2, 5 wk), 19 wk; tot 84
wk.
The Days of Winter (Bantam) PW mm pb
4/16/79 (#14, 1 wk).
Come Pour the Wine (Arbor House) PW
hc fic 10/17/80 (#9), pk 11/7/80 (#4, 5 wk),
25 wk; NYT fic 10/19/80 (#11), pk P 12/7/80
(#3, 2 wk), 27 wk; (Bantam) PW mm pb 10/
16/81 (#11), pk 11/6/81 (#2, 2 wk), 12 wk;
NYT mm pb 10/18/81 (#5), pk 10/25/81 (#1,
2 wk), 13 wk; tot 77 wk.
No Time for Tears (Arbor House) PW hc
fic 11/13/81 (#12), pk 11/27/81 (#3, 3 wk), 18
wk; NYT fic 11/15/81 (#13), pk 11/29/81 (#3,
2 wk), 19 wk; (Bantam) NYT mm pb 11/7/82
(#2), pk 11/21/82 (#1, 2 wk), 10 wk; PW mm
pb 11/12/82 (#4), pk 11/19/82 (#2, 2 wk), 6
wk; tot 53 wk.
Illusions (Putnam) NYT fic 12/2/84 (#13),
pk 1/27/85 (#6, 2 wk), 15 wk; PW hc fic
12/7/84 (#9), pk 2/1/85 (#6, 3 wk), 13 wk;
(Berkley) NYT pb fic 2/2/86 (#5), pk
2/16/86 (#3, 1 wk), 9 wk; PW mm pb 2/7/86
(#5), pk 2/14/86 (#4, 2 wk), 9 wk; tot 46 wk.
Seasons of the Heart (Putnam) PW hc fic
3/28/86 (#12), pk 4/25/86 (#6, 1 wk), 8 wk;
NYT fic 3/30/86 (#7), pk 4/20/86 (#5, 1 wk),
9 wk; (Berkley) NYT pb fic 2/1/87 (#13), pk
2/22/87 (#3, 2 wk), 9 wk; PW mm pb 2/13/
87 (#14), pk 2/20/87 (#8, 1 wk), 5 wk; tot 31
wk.
The Last Princess (Putnam) NYT fic 4/10/
88 (#12), pk 5/1/88 (#7, 1 wk), 8 wk; PW hc
fic 4/15/88 (#13), pk 4/22/88 (#7, 1 wk), 7
wk; (Berkley) NYT pb fic 3/5/89 (#8), pk
3/26/89 (#5, 2 wk), 8 wk; PW mm pb 3/10/
89 (#13), pk 4/7/89 (#6, 1 wk), 9 wk; tot 32
wk.
Always and Forever (Putnam) PW hc fic
5/4/90 (#11, 2 wk), 4 wk; NYT fic 5/27/90
(#14, 1 wk); tot 5 wk.

Freeman, Douglas Southall
R.E. Lee (Scribner) PW nf 1/12/35 (#7), pk
3/16/35 (#2, 4 wk), 28 wk.
Lee's Lieutenants Vol. 1 (Scribner) NYT nf
11/8/42 (#9), pk 11/5/44 (#4, 2 wk), 48 wk;
PW nf 12/12/42 (#6, 4 wk), 8 wk; tot 56 wk.
Lee's Lieutenants Vol. 2 (Scribner) PW nf
4/17/43 (#5, 2 wk), 6 wk; NYT gen 5/9/43
(#5, 1 wk), 9 wk; tot 15 wk.
Lee's Lieutenants Vol. 3 (Scribner) PW nf
11/11/44 (#9), pk 11/18/44 (#5, 2 wk), 5 wk.
George Washington, Vols. 1 & 2 (Scribner)
NYT gen 11/7/48 (#12), pk 11/28/48 (#10, 3
wk), 10 wk.
George Washington, Vols. 3 & 4 (Scribner)
NYT gen 11/4/51 (#13, 1 wk).

Freeman, H.W.
Joseph and His Brethren (Holt) PW fic 2/
16/29 (#4), pk 3/9/29 (#2, 4 wk), 16 wk.

Freeman, Lucy
Fight Against Fears (Crown) NYT gen 7/
29/51 (#12), pk 9/9/51 (#7, 3 wk), 16 wk; PW
nf 10/13/51 (#9), pk 10/20/51 (#6, 1 wk), 2
wk; tot 18 wk.

Freeman, Lydia
Pet of the Met (Viking) NYT ch bst 11/15/
53 (#9, 40 wk).

Freeman, Mae Blacker
You Will Go to the Moon (Random) NYT
ch bst 11/1/59 (#5, 25 wk).

Freeman, Nancy
Joshua, Son of None (Dell) NYT mm pb 9/
8/74 (#9, 4 wk).

Frenaye, Frances
See Carlo Levi

French, Marilyn
The Women's Room (Summit/Simon &
Schuster) PW hc fic 11/28/77 (#10), pk 3/6/
78 (#4, 2 wk), 44 wk; NYT fic 12/4/77 (#13),
pk 3/19/78 (#4, 3 wk), 36 wk; (Harcourt/
Jove) PW mm pb 10/16/78 (#9), pk 10/30/78
(#1, 9 wk), 48 wk; NYT mm pb 11/12/78 (#1,
6 wk), 44 wk; tot 172 wk.
The Bleeding Heart (Summit) PW hc fic
3/14/80 (#13), pk 4/18/80 (#4, 2 wk), 15 wk;
NYT fic 3/30/80 (#15), pk 4/27/80 (#4, 2
wk), 16 wk; (Ballantine) PW mm pb 3/13/81
(#5), pk 3/20/81 (#3, 1 wk), 10 wk; NYT mm
pb 3/22/81 (#5), pk 4/5/81 (#4, 2 wk), 9 wk;
tot 50 wk.
Her Mother's Daughter (Ballantine) NYT
pb fic 10/9/88 (#13), pk 10/30/88 (#2, 1 wk),
12 wk; PW mm pb 10/14/88 (#8), pk 10/21/88
(#2, 1 wk), 11 wk; tot 23 wk.

Freuchen, Peter
Arctic Adventure (Farrar) NYT nf 5/3/36
(#8, 4 wk); PW nf 5/9/36 (#10, 4 wk); tot 8
wk.
It's All Adventure (Farrar) NYT gen 7/31/
38 (#13, 4 wk).

_____, and David Loth
Peter Freuchen's Book of the Seven Seas
(Messner) NYT gen 12/22/57 (#9), pk 3/9/
58 (#5, 2 wk), 21 wk; PW nf 12/30/57 (#6),
pk 1/6/58 (#5, 4 wk), 14 wk; tot 35 wk.

_____, and Finn S. Salomonson
The Arctic Year (Putnam) NYT gen 5/18/
58 (#15, 1 wk).

Freud, Sigmund
Moses and Monotheism (Vintage) NYT gen
8/6/39 (#10, 4 wk).

An Outline of Psychoanalysis (Norton) NYT
gen 4/10/49 (#13, 1 wk).

Frick, Grace
See Marguerite Yourcenar

**Fricke, John, Jay Scarfone and William
    Stillman**
*The Wizard of Oz: The Official 50th Anni-
versary Pictorial History* (Warner) PW hc nf
9/8/89 (#12, 2 wk).

Fricker, Mary
See Stephen Pizzo, et al.

Friday, Nancy
*My Mother/My Self: A Daughter's Search for
Identity* (Delacorte) PW hc nf 1/16/78 (#14),
pk 4/3/78 (#2, 7 wk), 41 wk; NYT nf 2/5/78
(#9), pk 4/2/78 (#3, 10 wk), 28 wk; (Dell)
PW mm pb 10/23/78 (#9), pk 11/13/78 (#1,
4 wk), 46 wk; NYT mm pb 11/12/78 (#2), pk
11/19/78 (#1, 8 wk), 41 wk; tot 156 wk.
Men in Love (Delacorte) PW hc nf 4/25/
80 (#11), pk 5/30/80 (#3, 5 wk), 22 wk; NYT
nf 5/4/80 (#7), pk 5/18/80 (#1, 1 wk), 23 wk;
(Dell) PW mm pb 3/13/81 (#8), pk 4/10/81
(#2, 1 wk), 12 wk; NYT mm pb 3/15/81 (#6),
pk 3/22/81 (#2, 1 wk), 13 wk; tot 70 wk.

Friedan, Betty
The Feminine Mystique (Norton) NYT gen
4/28/63 (#10), pk 6/23/63 (#7, 1 wk), 6 wk;
PW nf 6/17/63 (#10), pk 9/16/63 (#9, 1 wk),
5 wk; tot 11 wk.

Friedman, Bruce Jay
A Mother's Kisses (Simon & Schuster)
NYT fic 9/13/64 (#10), pk 10/4/64 (#8, 2
wk), 9 wk; PW fic 9/28/64 (#10), pk 10/5/64
(#8, 1 wk), 6 wk; tot 15 wk.

Friedman, Meyer, and Ray H. Rosenman
Type A Behavior and Your Heart (Knopf)
PW nf 5/13/74 (#9, 1 wk), 4 wk; NYT gen
5/26/74 (#10, 1 wk); tot 5 wk.

Friedman, Michael Jan
Double, Double (Pocket) NYT pb fic 4/16/
89 (#10, 1 wk), 3 wk; PW mm pb 4/21/89
(#12), pk 4/28/89 (#7, 1 wk), 2 wk; tot 5 wk.
Fortune's Light (Pocket) NYT pb fic
12/30/90 (#15, 1 wk).
See also Carmen Carter, et al.

**Friedman, Milton, and Rose Fried-
man**
Free to Choose: A Personal Statement (Harcourt) PW hc nf 2/8/80 (#11), pk 3/28/80
(#1, 10 wk), 51 wk; NYT nf 2/10/80 (#12), pk
4/6/80 (#1, 6 wk), 51 wk; (Avon) PW mm pb
1/30/81 (#6), pk 2/6/81 (#4, 3 wk), 8 wk;
NYT mm pb 2/1/81 (#13), pk 3/1/81 (#4, 1
wk), 9 wk; tot 119 wk.

Friedman, Myra
Buried Alive (Morrow) PW nf 10/1/73 (#9, 1 wk); NYT gen 10/7/73 (#9, 1 wk); tot 2 wk.

Friedman, Philip
Reasonable Doubt (Ivy) NYT pb fic 10/28/90 (#10), pk 11/18/90 (#3, 2 wk), 10 wk; PW mm pb 11/2/90 (#7), pk 11/23/90 (#3, 3 wk), 8 wk; tot 18 wk.

Friedman, Sonya
Men Are Just Desserts (Warner) NYT nf 6/19/83 (#15), pk 6/26/83 (#12, 1 wk), 3 wk; PW hc nf 7/1/83 (#15, 5 wk); tot 8 wk.

Smart Cookies Don't Crumble (Putnam) PW hc nf 7/12/85 (#15), pk 8/2/85 (#10, 1 wk), 7 wk; NYT msc 7/14/85 (#5), pk 8/11/85 (#2, 1 wk), 7 wk; (Pocket) NYT msc pb 6/15/86 (#6, 1 wk), 4 wk; tot 18 wk.

Friedman, Thomas L.
From Beirut to Jerusalem (Farrar) NYT nf 7/30/89 (#15), pk 8/27/89 (#5, 1 wk), 21 wk; PW hc nf 8/11/89 (#14), pk 8/25/89 (#6, 4 wk), 12 wk; (Doubleday/Anchor) NYT pb nf 8/19/90 (#6), pk 9/23/90 (#2, 1 wk), 20 wk; PW td pb 9/7/90 (#8), pk 9/14/90 (#4, 3 wk), 16 wk; tot 69 wk.

Friendly, Fred
Due to Circumstances Beyond Our Control (Random) PW nf 4/17/67 (#10, 3 wk), 5 wk; NYT gen 4/30/67 (#9, 2 wk); tot 7 wk.

Fromm, Bella
Blood and Banquets (Harper) NYT nf 1/3/43 (#14), pk 1/24/43 (#13, 1 wk), 2 wk.

Fromm, Erich
The Sane Society (Holt) NYT gen 9/25/55 (#15), pk 10/2/55 (#12, 1 wk), 2 wk.

Frost, David
"I Gave Them a Sword": Behind the Scenes of the Nixon Interviews (Morrow) PW hc nf 3/6/78 (#11, 1 wk), 3 wk.

_____, and **Antony Jay**
The English (Stein & Day) NYT gen 3/17/68 (#7, 2 wk), 9 wk; PW nf 3/18/68 (#10), pk 4/29/68 (#7, 2 wk), 15 wk; tot 24 wk.

Frost, Robert
A Further Range (Holt) NYT gen 7/5/36 (#3, 4 wk).
You Come Too (Holt) NYT ch bst 11/13/60 (#14, 27 wk).
In the Clearing (Holt) NYT gen 4/15/62 (#10), pk 5/27/62 (#4, 4 wk), 26 wk; PW nf 4/23/62 (#7), pk 6/18/62 (#3, 1 wk), 24 wk; tot 50 wk.

Froud, Brian
See J.J. Llewellyn and_____

Froud, Brian, and Alan Lee
Faeries [described and illustrated by] (Abrams) PW hc nf 11/13/78 (#14), pk 1/8/79 (#5, 2 wk), 12 wk; NYT nf 11/19/78 (#15), pk 1/7/79 (#5, 1 wk), 17 wk; (Bantam) NYT td pb 1/13/80 (#12, 1 wk), 2 wk; tot 31 wk.

Fry, Christopher
The Lady's Not for Burning (Oxford Univ.) NYT gen 5/21/50 (#16), pk 1/28/51 (#9, 1 wk), 13 wk.

Fuentes, Carlos
The Old Gringo (Farrar) NYT fic 12/15/85 (#14, 1 wk).

Fujikawa, Gyo
Oh, What a Busy Day! (Grosset & Dunlap) NYT ch hc 11/13/77 (#6, 46 wk).

Fulbright, Sen. William J.
The Arrogance of Power (Random) NYT gen 2/26/67 (#10), pk 3/26/67 (#9, 1 wk), 3 wk; PW nf 3/6/67 (#13), pk 4/3/67 (#8, 1 wk), 3 wk; tot 6 wk.

Fulghum, Robert
All I Really Need to Know I Learned in Kindergarten (Villard) NYT nf 11/6/88 (#11), pk 1/1/89 (#1, 34 wk), 101 wk; PW hc nf 11/11/88 (#9), pk 1/13/89 (#1, 21 wk), 77 wk; (Ivy) NYT pb nf 11/26/89 (#1, 46 wk), 58 wk; PW mm pb 12/1/89 (#11), pk 12/22/89 (#1, 8 wk), 54 wk; (Random) aud nf 10/5/90 (#8, 4 wk), 8 wk; tot 298 wk.

It Was on Fire When I Lay Down on It (Villard) PW hc nf 9/22/89 (#9), pk 1/12/90 (#1, 4 wk), 45 wk; NYT nf 9/24/89 (#5), pk 1/7/90 (#1, 3 wk), 51 wk; tot 96 wk.

Fuller, Iola
See Iola Fuller McCoy

Fuller, John G.
The Ghost of Flight 401 (Berkley) PW mm pb 1/23/78 (#9), pk 3/6/78 (#3, 3 wk), 14 wk; NYT mm pb 1/29/78 (#14), pk 3/12/78 (#3, 4 wk), 13 wk; tot 27 wk.

Fuller, Tony
See Peter Goldman and_____

Fulop-Miller, Rene
Rasputin the Holy Devil (Viking) PW nf 12/22/28 (#7), pk 2/16/29 (#5, 4 wk), 16 wk.

Funke, Lewis
See Helen Hayes and_____

Furman, Bess
Washington By-Line (Knopf) NYT gen 2/27/49 (#12, 2 wk), 4 wk.
White House Profile (Bobbs Merrill) NYT gen 1/6/52 (#13, 1 wk), 2 wk.

Fynn [pseud.]
Mister God, This Is Anna (Ballantine) PW

mm pb 11/1/76 (#11), pk 1/3/77 (#7, 1 wk), 15 wk; NYT mm pb 12/5/76 (#6, 1 wk), 3 wk; tot 18 wk.

Gabor, Mark
The Pin-Up (Universe) NYT td pb 3/10/ 74 (#6, 1 wk), 4 wk.

Ga'g, Wanda
Snippy and Snappy (Coward McCann) PW juv 11/14/31 (#4, 4 wk), 8 wk.
Gone Is Gone (Coward McCann) NYT juv 12/1/35 (#2, 4 wk).
Millions of Cats (Coward McCann) NYT ch pb 11/13/77 (#15), pk 4/30/78 (#10, 24 wk), 70 wk.

Gage, Elizabeth
A Glimpse of Stocking (Pocket) NYT pb fic 4/23/89 (#11, 1 wk), 3 wk; PW mm pb 4/28/ 89 (#13, 1 wk), 3 wk; tot 6 wk.

Gaines, Charles, and George Butler
Pumping Iron (Simon & Schuster) NYT td pb 4/20/75 (#5, 1 wk).

Gaines, Steven
See Peter Brown and_____

Gainham, Sarah
Night Falls on the City (Holt) NYT fic 8/13/67 (#9), pk 9/24/67 (#3, 2 wk), 16 wk; PW fic 8/28/67 (#5), pk 10/9/67 (#1, 2 wk), 16 wk; tot 32 wk.
A Place in the Country (Holt) NYT fic 8/31/69 (#10), pk 9/28/69 (#7, 1 wk), 9 wk; PW fic 9/8/69 (#10), pk 10/20/69 (#7, 1 wk), 9 wk; tot 18 wk.

Gaither, Frances
The Red Cock Crows (Macmillan) NYT fic 6/25/44 (#14), pk 7/23/44 (#11, 1 wk), 5 wk.
Double Muscadine (Macmillan) NYT fic 3/27/49 (#15), pk 5/1/49 (#7, 1 wk), 12 wk; PW fic 5/14/49 (#8, 1 wk); tot 13 wk.

Galbraith, John Kenneth
The Great Crash of 1929 (Houghton) NYT gen 6/5/55 (#15, 1 wk).
The Affluent Society (Houghton) NYT gen 6/22/58 (#8), pk 8/24/58 (#2, 3 wk), 28 wk; PW nf 7/7/58 (#6), pk 8/25/58 (#2, 1 wk); tot 52 wk.
The Liberal Hour (Houghton) NYT gen 9/4/60 (#10), pk 10/16/60 (#6, 2 wk), 15 wk; PW nf 9/12/60 (#9), pk 10/3/60 (#5, 1 wk), 5 wk; tot 20 wk.
The New Industrial State (Houghton) NYT gen 7/16/67 (#7), pk 7/23/67 (#1, 8 wk), 32 wk; PW nf 7/24/67 (#2), pk 7/31/67 (#1, 7 wk), 33 wk; NYT pb gen 12/1/68 (#3, 4 wk); tot 69 wk.
The Triumph (Houghton) NYT fic 5/5/68

(#10), pk 6/9/68 (#7, 1 wk), 5 wk; PW fic 5/6/ 68 (#7), pk 6/3/68 (#6, 1 wk), 5 wk; tot 10 wk.
Ambassador's Journal (Houghton) NYT gen 11/16/69 (#10), pk 11/30/69 (#4, 1 wk), 13 wk; PW nf 12/1/69 (#8), pk 12/29/69 (#5, 1 wk), 12 wk; tot 25 wk.
Economics and the Public Purpose (Houghton) PW nf 10/15/73 (#10, 1 wk).
Money (Houghton) NYT gen 10/5/75 (#9), pk 11/16/75 (#5, 1 wk), 8 wk; PW nf 10/13/75 (#10), pk 10/27/75 (#6, 2 wk), 6 wk; tot 14 wk.
The Age of Uncertainty (Houghton) NYT nf 5/1/77 (#8, 1 wk), 4 wk; PW hc nf 5/9/77 (#9, 2 wk), 4 wk; tot 8 wk.

Gale, Zona
Light Woman (Appleton) NYT fic 5/9/37 (#6, 4 wk).

Gallagher, Mary Barelli
My Life with Jacqueline Kennedy (McKay) NYT gen 9/28/69 (#5), pk 10/19/69 (#2, 3 wk), 14 wk; PW nf 10/6/69 (#6), pk 11/3/69 (#2, 3 wk), 12 wk; NYT pb gen 10/4/70 (#4, 4 wk), 8 wk; tot 34 wk.

Gallagher, Patricia
Castles in the Air (Avon) PW mm pb 5/31/ 76 (#14, 2 wk), 5 wk.
Mystic Rose (Avon) PW mm pb 10/3/77 (#9), pk 10/10/77 (#7, 1 wk), 5 wk; NYT mm pb 10/9/77 (#10, 1 wk), 2 wk; tot 7 wk.

Gallico, Paul
The Lonely (Knopf) NYT fic 10/9/49 (#15), pk 11/20/49 (#12, 1 wk), 3 wk; PW fic 12/17/49 (#9, 1 wk); tot 4 wk.
Thomasina (Doubleday) NYT fic 12/29/57 (#14), pk 1/19/58 (#8, 1 wk), 10 wk.
Too Many Ghosts (Doubleday) NYT fic 11/29/59 (#14), pk 1/10/60 (#11, 1 wk), 10 wk.
Mrs. 'Arris Goes to Paris (Doubleday) NYT fic 1/4/59 (#16), pk 3/8/59 (#6, 8 wk), 37 wk; PW fic 3/2/59 (#7), pk 5/4/59 (#5, 2 wk), 24 wk; tot 61 wk.
Mrs. 'Arris Goes to New York (Doubleday) NYT fic 4/3/60 (#14), pk 5/15/60 (#7, 1 wk), 14 wk; PW fic 5/9/60 (#10), pk 5/16/60 (#7, 1 wk), 6 wk; tot 20 wk.
The Poseidon Adventure (Coward McCann) NYT fic 8/29/69 (#10, 1 wk).

Gallwey, W. Timothy, and Robert Kriegel
Inner Skiing (Random) NYT nf 1/29/78 (#11), pk 2/19/78 (#8, 2 wk), 10 wk.

Galsworthy, John
Saint's Progress (Scribner) PW fic 9/6/19 (#4, 4 wk), 12 wk.
Tatterdemalion (Scribner) PW fic 6/12/20 (#10, 4 wk).

In Chancery (Scribner) PW fic 1/8/21 (#6, 4 wk).
The White Monkey (Scribner) PW fic 4/18/25 (#8, 4 wk).
The Silver Spoon (Scribner) PW fic 8/14/26 (#3), pk 9/18/26 (#2, 4 wk), 16 wk.
Swan Song (Scribner) PW fic 10/27/28 (#1, 4 wk), 12 wk.
On Forsyte 'Change (Scribner) PW fic 11/22/30 (#8, 8 wk).
Maid in Waiting (Scribner) PW fic 12/19/31 (#1, 12 wk), 16 wk.
Flowering Wilderness (Scribner) PW fic 12/17/32 (#2), pk 1/14/33 (#1, 8 wk), 20 wk.
One More River (Scribner) PW fic 11/11/33 (#2, 8 wk), 16 wk.

Gambrell, Anson
Anson Jones (Doubleday) NYT gen 3/21/48 (#13, 3 wk).

Gandhi, Mohandas Karamchand
Gandhi's Autobiography (Public Affairs Press) NYT gen 10/10/48 (#16, 2 wk).

Ganey, Terry
Innocent Blood (St. Martin's) NYT pb nf 7/8/90 (#12, 1 wk).

Gann, Ernest K.
The High and the Mighty (Sloane) NYT fic 5/10/53 (#14), pk 8/16/53 (#3, 8 wk), 56 wk; PW fic 6/13/53 (#9), pk 1/9/54 (#3, 2 wk), 35 wk; tot 91 wk.
Soldier of Fortune (Sloane) NYT fic 10/24/54 (#10), pk 12/19/54 (#4, 1 wk), 25 wk; PW fic 11/13/54 (#7), pk 12/25/54 (#3, 1 wk), 14 wk; tot 39 wk.
Twilight for the Gods (Sloane) NYT fic 2/10/57 (#11), pk 2/17/57 (#8, 1 wk), 11 wk; PW fic 3/18/57 (#9, 2 wk); tot 13 wk.
Fate Is the Hunter (Simon & Schuster) NYT gen 2/19/61 (#9), pk 4/2/61 (#3, 2 wk), 25 wk; PW nf 2/27/61 (#7), pk 3/27/61 (#3, 3 wk), 21 wk; tot 46 wk.
Of Good and Evil (Simon & Schuster) PW fic 11/25/63 (#9, 1 wk), 3 wk.
The Antagonists (Simon & Schuster) NYT fic 2/21/71 (#10), pk 5/2/71 (#6, 2 wk), 14 wk; PW fic 3/29/71 (#9), pk 5/24/71 (#6, 1 wk), 12 wk; tot 26 wk.
Band of Brothers (Simon & Schuster) NYT fic 2/3/74 (#10, 1 wk).
Masada (Jove) NYT mm pb 3/29/81 (#11), pk 4/26/81 (#2, 2 wk), 6 wk; PW mm pb 4/3/81 (#14), pk 4/24/81 (#2, 2 wk), 6 wk; tot 12 wk.
The Aviator (Arbor House) PW hc fic 2/27/81 (#13), pk 3/6/81 (#11, 1 wk), 9 wk; NYT fic 3/29/81 (#10, 1 wk), 4 wk; tot 13 wk.

Gannett, Lewis Stiles
Cream Hill (Viking) NYT gen 6/5/49 (#10, 2 wk), 8 wk.

Garagiola, Joe
Baseball Is a Funny Game (Lippincott) NYT gen 7/10/60 (#16), pk 9/18/60 (#11, 1 wk), 14 wk; PW nf 10/17/60 (#9, 1 wk); tot 15 wk.

Garbo, Norman, and Howard Goodkind
Confrontation (Harper) PW fic 7/4/66 (#10, 1 wk).

Garden, Mary, and Louis Biancolli
Mary Garden's Story (Simon & Schuster) NYT gen 5/13/51 (#12), pk 6/3/51 (#9, 1 wk), 7 wk.

Gardiner, Dorothy
The Golden Lady (Doubleday) NYT fic 5/3/36 (#7, 4 wk).

Gardner, Ava
Ava: My Story (Bantam) NYT nf 10/28/90 (#13), pk 11/4/90 (#10, 1 wk), 3 wk; PW hc nf 11/2/90 (#15), pk 11/9/90 (#14, 1 wk), 2 wk; tot 5 wk.

Gardner, Craig Shaw
Batman (Warner) NYT pb fic 6/4/89 (#13), pk 7/16/89 (#5, 1 wk), 11 wk; PW mm pb 6/23/89 (#8), pk 6/30/89 (#5, 2 wk), 8 wk; tot 19 wk.

Gardner, Erle Stanley
The Case of the Caretaker's Cat (World) NYT fic 11/3/35 (#8, 4 wk).
The D.A. Calls It Murder (Triangle) NYT fic 1/31/37 (#9, 4 wk).
The Case of the Lame Canary (Grosset & Dunlap) NYT fic 10/10/37 (#10, 4 wk).
The Case of the Shoplifter's Shoe (Grosset & Dunlap) NYT fic 10/9/38 (#9, 4 wk).
The Case of the Substitute Face (Grosset & Dunlap) NYT fic 5/1/38 (#8, 4 wk).
The D.A. Holds a Candle (World) NYT fic 1/8/39 (#10, 4 wk).
The Case of the Perjured Parrot (Morrow) NYT fic 4/9/39 (#9, 4 wk).
The Case of the Rolling Bones (Grosset & Dunlap) NYT fic 10/8/39 (#6, 4 wk).
The D.A. Draws a Circle (Grosset & Dunlap) NYT fic 1/7/40 (#14, 4 wk).

Gardner, Gerald
Who's in Charge Here? (Pocket) NYT gen 8/12/62 (#12), pk 9/16/62 (#5, 2 wk), 18 wk; PW nf 8/27/62 (#11), pk 10/15/62 (#5, 1 wk), 14 wk; tot 32 wk.

Gardner, John
The Sunlight Dialogues (Knopf) PW fic 2/5/73 (#8), pk 4/2/73 (#4, 1 wk), 12 wk;

NYT fic 2/11/73 (#8), pk 3/25/73 (#5, 1 wk), 15 wk; tot 27 wk.

Nickel Mountain (Knopf) PW fic 1/14/74 (#9), pk 3/4/74 (#5, 1 wk), 6 wk; NYT fic 1/20/74 (#10), pk 3/24/74 (#6, 1 wk), 10 wk; tot 16 wk.

October Light (Knopf) PW hc fic 1/24/77 (#10), pk 3/7/77 (#6, 1 wk), 10 wk; NYT fic 1/30/77 (#9), pk 3/13/77 (#6, 2 wk), 10 wk; tot 20 wk.

Freddy's Book (Knopf) PW hc fic 4/11/80 (#15), pk 4/18/80 (#13, 1 wk), 4 wk.

License Renewed (Marek) PW hc fic 5/15/81 (#13), pk 6/19/81 (#6, 1 wk), 15 wk; NYT fic 5/24/81 (#13), pk 7/5/81 (#9, 3 wk), 12 wk; (Berkley) PW mm pb 5/21/82 (#8), pk 6/4/82 (#3, 4 wk), 10 wk; NYT mm pb 5/23/82 (#10), pk 6/13/82 (#4, 1 wk), 10 wk; tot 47 wk.

For Special Services (Coward McCann) PW hc fic 5/21/82 (#9), pk 6/11/82 (#4, 1 wk), 15 wk; NYT fic 5/23/82 (#13), pk 7/4/82 (#6, 1 wk), 15 wk; (Berkley) NYT mm pb 4/10/83 (#7), pk 4/17/83 (#6, 1 wk), 6 wk; PW mm pb 4/15/83 (#7), pk 4/29/83 (#6, 1 wk), 7 wk; tot 43 wk.

Icebreaker (Putnam) NYT fic 4/17/83 (#10), pk 4/24/83 (#9, 1 wk), 11 wk; PW hc fic 4/22/83 (#10), pk 5/13/83 (#7, 1 wk), 11 wk; (Berkley) NYT pb fic 5/13/84 (#9), pk 5/27/84 (#7, 2 wk), 6 wk; PW mm pb 5/18/84 (#9), pk 5/25/84 (#3, 1 wk), 5 wk; tot 33 wk.

Role of Honor (Putnam) NYT fic 9/23/84 (#14), pk 10/21/84 (#9, 1 wk), 8 wk; PW hc fic 10/5/84 (#7), pk 10/12/84 (#6, 1 wk), 8 wk; (Berkley) PW mm pb 5/10/85 (#15), pk 5/24/85 (#3, 1 wk), 6 wk; NYT pb fic 5/12/85 (#6), pk 5/19/85 (#4, 2 wk), 5 wk; tot 27 wk.

Nobody Lives Forever (Putnam) NYT fic 6/1/86 (#12), pk 6/8/86 (#9, 1 wk), 4 wk; PW hc fic 6/6/86 (#11), pk 6/13/86 (#9, 2 wk), 5 wk; (Jove) NYT pb fic 7/12/87 (#10, 1 wk), 4 wk; PW mm pb 7/17/87 (#13), pk 7/24/87 (#9, 1 wk), 3 wk; tot 16 wk.

No Deals, Mr. Bond (Putnam) NYT fic 4/26/87 (#11), pk 5/17/87 (#9, 1 wk), 7 wk; PW hc fic 5/1/87 (#10), pk 5/15/87 (#8, 2 wk), 6 wk; (Charter) NYT pb fic 4/10/88 (#9, 1 wk), 3 wk; PW mm pb 4/22/88 (#10, 1 wk), 2 wk; tot 18 wk.

Scorpius (Putnam) PW hc fic 5/27/88 (#12), pk 6/17/88 (#7, 1 wk), 8 wk; NYT fic 5/29/88 (#13), pk 6/12/88 (#11, 1 wk), 6 wk; (Charter) NYT pb fic 1/14/90 (#12), pk 1/21/90 (#7, 1 wk), 3 wk; tot 17 wk.

Win, Lose or Die (Putnam) NYT fic 8/20/89 (#11, 1 wk), 4 wk; PW hc fic 8/25/89 (#8, 2 wk), 4 wk; tot 8 wk.

Broken Claw (Putnam) PW hc fic 8/24/90 (#11, 1 wk).

Garner, Elvira
Ezekiel (Holt) NYT gen 11/7/37 (#5, 4 wk), 12 wk.

Garnett, David
Aspects of Love (Harcourt) NYT fic 2/19/56 (#13), pk 3/11/56 (#10, 2 wk), 8 wk.

Garrett, George P.
Death of the Fox (Doubleday) NYT fic 11/7/71 (#10), pk 11/21/71 (#9, 1 wk), 2 wk.

Garrett, Malcolm
See Kasper de Graaf and_____

Garson, Barbara
MacBird (Grove) NYT pb fic 4/2/67 (#4, 4 wk).

Garth, David
Fire on the Wind (Putnam) NYT fic 6/17/51 (#15, 1 wk), 2 wk.

Garwood, Julie
Gentle Warrior (Pocket) PW mm pb 12/1/89 (#15, 1 wk).

The Bride (Pocket) NYT pb fic 7/16/89 (#15, 1 wk); PW mm pb 7/21/89 (#11, 1 wk); tot 2 wk.

Honor's Splendour (Pocket) NYT pb fic 3/18/90 (#13, 1 wk).

Rebellious Desire (Pocket) PW mm pb 1/19/90 (#15), pk 2/2/90 (#10, 1 wk), 3 wk.

Guardian Angel (Pocket) NYT pb fic 5/13/90 (#4, 2 wk), 4 wk; PW mm pb 5/18/90 (#7, 2 wk), 4 wk; tot 8 wk.

The Gift (Pocket) NYT pb fic 12/23/90 (#14), pk 12/30/90 (#6, 2 wk), 2 wk.

Gary, Romain
The Roots of Heaven (Simon & Schuster) NYT fic 2/16/58 (#15), pk 3/9/58 (#9, 2 wk), 10 wk; PW fic 3/3/58 (#8, 1 wk); tot 11 wk.

Lady L. (Simon & Schuster) NYT fic 1/25/59 (#15), pk 2/22/59 (#6, 2 wk), 17 wk; PW fic 2/9/59 (#7), pk 3/2/59 (#6, 3 wk), 12 wk; tot 29 wk.

Promise at Dawn (Harper) NYT gen 11/5/61 (#13), pk 11/19/61 (#9, 1 wk), 7 wk; PW nf 11/6/61 (#9, 1 wk), 3 wk; tot 10 wk.

Gates, Gary Paul
See Mike Wallace and_____
See Dan Rather and_____

Gavin, James M.
War and Peace in the Space Age (Harper) NYT gen 8/31/58 (#12), pk 9/21/58 (#7, 2 wk), 11 wk; PW nf 9/29/58 (#8, 1 wk); tot 12 wk.

Gay, Peter
Freud (Norton) NYT nf 6/5/88 (#12), pk 6/12/88 (#9, 1 wk), 4 wk.

Gayle, Zona
Faint Perfume (Appleton) PW fic 4/14/23 (#9), pk 5/26/23 (#6, 4 wk), 12 wk.

Geasland, Jack
See Bari Wood and_____

Gebler, Ernest
The Plymouth Adventure (Doubleday) NYT fic 5/21/50 (#12), pk 6/11/50 (#7, 4 wk), 12 wk; PW fic 6/17/50 (#5, 1 wk), 2 wk; tot 14 wk.

Gedye, George Eric Rowe
Betrayal in Central Europe (Harper) NYT gen 4/9/39 (#4, 4 wk), 8 wk.

Geer, Andrew
Mercy in Hell (McGraw) NYT gen 8/15/43 (#15, 1 wk).

Geis, Bernard
See Groucho Marx and_____

Geis, Darlene
Dinosaurs and Other Prehistoric Animals (Grosset & Dunlap) NYT ch bst 11/1/59 (#9, 25 wk).

Geisel, Theodor [all titles as by Dr. Seuss]
Scrambled Eggs Super! (Random) NYT ch bst 11/15/53 (#3, 40 wk).
Horton Hears a Who! (Random) NYT ch bst 11/14/54 (#9, 40 wk).
On Beyond Zebra (Random) NYT ch bst 11/13/55 (#16, 40 wk).
If I Ran the Circus (Random) NYT ch bst 11/18/56 (#12, 40 wk), 80 wk.
The Cat in the Hat (Random) NYT ch bst 11/17/57 (#1, 40 wk), 117 wk.
How the Grinch Stole Christmas (Random) NYT ch bst 11/2/58 (#8, 40 wk).
Yertle the Turtle and Other Stories (Random) NYT ch bst 11/2/58 (#2, 40 wk), 78 wk.
The Cat in the Hat Comes Back (Random) NYT ch bst 11/2/58 (#7), pk 5/10/59 (#1, 19 wk), 78 wk.
Happy Birthday to You! (Random) NYT ch bst 11/1/59 (#15), pk 11/13/60 (#3, 27 wk), 71 wk.
One Fish Two Fish Red Fish Blue Fish (Random) NYT ch bst 5/8/60 (#2, 46 wk), 66 wk.
Green Eggs and Ham (Random) NYT ch bst 11/13/60 (#4), pk 11/12/61 (#1, 26 wk), 92 wk.
The Sneetches and Other Stories (Random) NYT ch bst 11/12/61 (#10), pk 11/11/62 (#3, 26 wk), 71 wk.
The Sleep Book (Random) NYT ch bst 11/11/62 (#6, 26 wk), 45 wk.

Hop on Pop (Random) NYT ch bst 5/12/63 (#7), pk 11/10/63 (#1, 26 wk), 64 wk.
Dr. Seuss' ABC (Random) NYT ch bst 11/10/63 (#8, 26 wk).
Fox in Socks (Random) NYT ch bst 5/9/65 (#4), pk 11/7/65 (#3, 26 wk), 45 wk.
I Had Trouble in Getting to Solla Sollew (Random) NYT ch bst 11/6/66 (#3, 26 wk).
I Can Lick 30 Tigers Today (Random) NYT ch bst 5/24/70 (#9, 21 wk).
The Butter Battle Book (Random) NYT fic 3/18/84 (#9), pk 4/15/84 (#2, 2 wk), 39 wk; PW hc fic 4/6/84 (#7), pk 4/27/84 (#4, 3 wk), 22 wk; tot 61 wk.
You're Only Old Once! (Random) NYT nf 3/16/86 (#5), pk 3/23/86 (#1, 7 wk), 62 wk; PW hc nf 3/28/86 (#9), pk 4/11/86 (#2, 8 wk), 35 wk; tot 97 wk.
Oh, the Places You'll Go! (Random) NYT fic 2/25/90 (#3), pk 3/4/90 (#1, 1 wk), 45 wk; PW hc fic 3/2/90 (#10), pk 3/16/90 (#2, 3 wk), 37 wk; PW ch pic 8/31/90 (#1, 12 wk), 20 wk; tot 102 wk.
See also Alexander Abingdon

Gelb, Arthur, and Barbara Gelb
O'Neill (Harper) NYT gen 4/29/62 (#16), pk 5/6/62 (#11, 1 wk), 9 wk.

Gellhorn, Martha
Liana (Scribner) NYT fic 2/13/44 (#12), pk 2/20/44 (#11, 1 wk), 3 wk.

Genet, Jean
Our Lady of the Flowers (Modern Library) NYT fic 11/24/63 (#10, 1 wk).

Gent, Peter
North Dallas Forty (Morrow) PW fic 10/29/73 (#10, 3 wk); (NAL) NYT mm pb 9/8/74 (#10, 4 wk); tot 7 wk.
The Franchise (Ballantine) NYT pb fic 11/11/84 (#9), pk 11/25/84 (#6, 1 wk), 4 wk; PW mm pb 11/16/84 (#13), pk 11/30/84 (#9, 1 wk), 4 wk; tot 8 wk.

Gentry, Curt
See Vincent Bugliosi and_____

George, Jean Craighead
Julie of the Wolves (G.K. Hall) NYT ch bst 5/6/73 (#9, 19 wk).

George, Nelson
The Michael Jackson Story (Dell) NYT pb nf 3/4/84 (#4), pk 3/18/84 (#3, 4 wk), 10 wk; PW mm pb 3/9/84 (#11), pk 3/23/84 (#6, 2 wk), 7 wk; tot 17 wk.

Gerahty, Digby George [all titles as by Robert Standish]
The Three Bamboos (Macmillan) NYT fic 12/27/42 (#14), pk 1/24/43 (#11, 1 wk), 10 wk.

Bonin (Macmillan) NYT fic 6/18/44 (#12, 1 wk), 2 wk.

Elephant Walk (Macmillan) NYT fic 7/31/49 (#10), pk 8/7/49 (#8, 1 wk), 7 wk; PW fic 8/13/49 (#9, 2 wk); tot 9 wk.

Geraud, Andre
The Gravediggers of France (Firtig) NYT gen 10/15/44 (#16, 1 wk), 2 wk.

Gerber, Albert Benjamin
Bashful Billionaire (Stuart) NYT gen 12/31/67 (#9, 1 wk).

Gerrold, David
Encounter at Farpoint (Pocket) NYT pb fic 10/25/87 (#14, 1 wk).

Gesell, Arnold, Frances L. Ilg and Louise Bates Ames
Youth (Harper) NYT gen 6/3/56 (#15), pk 8/5/56 (#8, 1 wk), 18 wk; PW nf 7/2/56 (#6, 4 wk), 9 wk; tot 27 wk.

Gheerbrant, Alain
Journey to the Far Amazon (Simon & Schuster) NYT gen 7/4/54 (#16), pk 7/18/54 (#12, 2 wk), 8 wk.

Giancana, Antoinette, and Thomas C. Renner
Mafia Princess: Growing Up in Sam Giancana's Family (Morrow) NYT nf 4/1/84 (#14), pk 4/22/84 (#6, 2 wk), 9 wk; PW hc nf 4/20/84 (#13), pk 5/18/84 (#7, 1 wk), 7 wk; (Avon) NYT pb nf 2/24/85 (#2), pk 3/10/85 (#1, 4 wk), 11 wk; PW mm pb 3/1/85 (#8), pk 3/8/85 (#7, 2 wk), 6 wk; tot 33 wk.

Gibbings, Robert
Lovely Is the Lee (Dutton) NYT gen 12/30/45 (#14), pk 1/13/46 (#7, 3 wk), 15 wk.

Gibbons, Barbara
See Jean Perry Spodnik and_____

Gibbons, F.P.
And They Thought We Wouldn't Fight (Doran) PW gen 5/3/19 (#5, 4 wk).

Gibbs, Arthur Hamilton
Soundings (Little Brown) PW fic 4/18/25 (#5), pk 7/18/25 (#2, 8 wk), 28 wk.

Labels (Little Brown) PW fic 10/16/26 (#9), pk 11/20/26 (#4, 4 wk), 12 wk.

Harness (Little Brown) PW fic 11/24/28 (#6), pk 12/22/28 (#2, 4 wk), 12 wk.

Chances (Little Brown) PW fic 7/12/30 (#5), pk 8/23/30 (#1, 8 wk), 16 wk.

Undertow (Little Brown) PW fic 8/13/32 (#5, 4 wk), 8 wk.

Rivers Glide On (Little Brown) PW fic 9/15/34 (#10, 4 wk).

The Need We Have (Little Brown) NYT fic 9/13/36 (#8, 4 wk).

A Half Inch of Candle (Little Brown) NYT fic 1/7/40 (#11, 4 wk).

Gibbs, George
The Splendid Outcast (Appleton) PW fic 3/27/20 (#9, 4 wk).

The Vagrant Duke (Appleton) PW fic 3/26/21 (#10, 4 wk).

Gibbs, Sir Philip Hamilton
Now It Can Be Told (Harper) PW gen 6/12/20 (#2), pk 8/14/20 (#1, 4 wk), 12 wk; PW gen lit 9/25/20 (#1, 12 wk), 32 wk; tot 44 wk.

The Middle of the Road (Doran) PW fic 4/14/23 (#11), pk 8/18/23 (#5, 4 wk), 20 wk.

Heirs Apparent (Doran) PW fic 4/19/24 (#10), pk 6/21/24 (#2, 4 wk), 8 wk.

The Reckless Lady (Doran) PW fic 4/18/25 (#9), pk 6/20/25 (#6, 4 wk), 12 wk.

Unchanging Quest (Doran) PW fic 3/20/26 (#6, 4 wk), 12 wk.

Young Anarchy (Doran) PW fic 3/19/27 (#7, 4 wk), 8 wk.

The Hidden City (Doubleday) PW fic 3/15/30 (#8), pk 4/12/30 (#6, 4 wk), 8 wk.

The Winding Lane (Doubleday) PW fic 5/16/31 (#6, 4 wk), 8 wk.

The Golden Years (Doubleday) PW fic 4/23/32 (#4, 4 wk), 8 wk.

Ordeal in England (Doubleday) PW nf 10/9/37 (#9, 4 wk); NYT gen 10/10/37 (#7, 4 wk); tot 8 wk.

Cities of Refuge (Doubleday) PW fic 2/6/37 (#8), pk 3/13/37 (#7, 4 wk), 8 wk.

Great Argument (Doubleday) NYT fic 5/1/38 (#6, 4 wk).

Gibbs, Wolcott
More in Sorrow (Holt) NYT gen 10/12/58 (#15), pk 10/19/58 (#13, 1 wk), 4 wk.

Gibney, Frank
The Operators (Harper) NYT gen 8/14/60 (#14), pk 9/11/60 (#12, 1 wk), 3 wk.

Gibson, Hugh
The Road to Foreign Policy (Doubleday) NYT gen 8/20/44 (#16, 1 wk).
See Count Galeazzo Ciano and_____
See Herbert C. Hoover and_____

Gibson, William
A Mass for the Dead (Atheneum) NYT gen 5/5/68 (#10, 1 wk); PW nf 5/6/68 (#10, 1 wk), 2 wk; tot 3 wk.

Gilbert, Bill
See Duke Snider and_____

Gilbert, Douglas
Lost Chords (Doubleday) NYT nf 10/11/42 (#21, 1 wk).

Gilbert, Edwin
Native Stone (Doubleday) NYT fic 2/19/
56 (#15), pk 4/15/56 (#13, 1 wk), 6 wk.
Silver Spoon (Lippincott) NYT fic 5/26/57
(#11), pk 8/11/57 (#2, 1 wk), 26 wk; PW fic
6/3/57 (#6), pk 8/19/57 (#2, 1 wk), 16 wk; tot
42 wk.
The Hourglass (Lippincott) NYT fic 4/26/
59 (#16), pk 6/7/59 (#11, 3 wk), 9 wk.
The Beautiful Life (Putnam) PW fic 1/16/
67 (#11), pk 2/6/67 (#7, 1 wk), 8 wk.

Gilbert, George B.
Forty Years a Country Preacher (Harper)
PW nf 7/13/40 (#7, 4 wk).

**Gilbert, Mort, and E. Albert
Gilbert**
Life Insurance: A Legalized Racket (Farrar)
NYT gen 7/5/36 (#6, 4 wk), 8 wk.

Gilbreth, Frank Bunker, Jr.
Inside Nantucket (Crowell) NYT gen 9/5/
54 (#15), pk 10/3/54 (#13, 1 wk), 2 wk.

**_____, and Ernestine Gilbreth
Carey**
Cheaper by the Dozen (Crowell) NYT gen
1/30/49 (#11), pk 3/13/49 (#1, 22 wk), 47 wk;
PW nf 2/12/49 (#5), pk 3/12/49 (#1, 21 wk),
38 wk; tot 85 wk.
Belles on Their Toes (Crowell) NYT gen
10/22/50 (#10), pk 11/19/50 (#3, 2 wk), 17 wk;
PW nf 10/28/50 (#5), pk 11/18/50 (#3, 5 wk),
12 wk; tot 29 wk.

Gilden, K.B.
Hurry Sundown (Doubleday) PW fic 2/8/
65 (#8), pk 3/15/65 (#2, 4 wk), 19 wk; NYT
fic 2/14/65 (#7), pk 3/7/65 (#2, 4 wk), 15 wk;
tot 34 wk.

Gilder, George
Wealth and Poverty (Basic) PW hc nf 3/13/
81 (#15), pk 5/8/81 (#4, 2 wk), 22 wk; NYT
nf 4/12/81 (#14), pk 5/10/81 (#2, 1 wk), 13 wk;
tot 35 wk.

Gilfillan, Lauren
I Went to Pit College (Viking) PW nf 4/14/
34 (#9, 4 wk).

Gill, Brendan
Here at the New Yorker (Random) PW nf
3/10/75 (#8), pk 4/21/75 (#1, 3 wk), 17 wk;
NYT gen 3/16/75 (#9), pk 5/11/75 (#2, 2
wk), 17 wk; tot 34 wk.

**Giller, Dr. Robert M., and Kathy
Matthews**
*Medical Makeover: The Revolutionary, No-
Willpower Program for Lifetime Health* (Beech
Tree/Morrow) NYT msc 7/20/86 (#5), pk
8/24/86 (#4, 2 wk), 9 wk; PW hc nf 8/1/86
(#12), pk 9/26/86 (#7, 1 wk), 9 wk; tot 18 wk.

Maximum Metabolism (Putnam) PW hc nf
3/17/89 (#13, 1 wk), 2 wk.

Gilliam, Harold
San Francisco Bay (Doubleday) NYT gen
11/10/57 (#12), pk 11/17/57 (#7, 1 wk), 19 wk.
The Natural World of San Francisco (Doubleday) PW nf 3/27/67 (#9, 1 wk), 5 wk.

Gilman, J.D., and John Clive
KG 200 (Simon & Schuster) PW hc fic
11/21/77 (#15, 5 wk); NYT fic NYT fic 1/1/78
(#14), pk 2/19/78 (#13, 1 wk), 8 wk; (Avon)
NYT mm pb 11/19/78 (#10, 1 wk), 2 wk.

Gilman, Peter
Diamond Head (Coward McCann) NYT
fic 7/17/60 (#13), pk 10/16/60 (#7, 1 wk), 18
wk; PW fic 8/22/60 (#9), pk 8/29/60 (#6, 2
wk), 6 wk; tot 24 wk.

Gilot, Francoise, and Carlton Lake
Life with Picasso (McGraw) NYT gen 1/3/
65 (#9), pk 2/14/65 (#6, 1 wk), 12 wk; PW nf
1/18/65 (#7), pk 2/8/65 (#6, 2 wk), 14 wk;
NYT pb gen 12/5/65 (#5), pk 1/2/66 (#3, 4
wk), 12 wk; tot 38 wk.

Gingold, Alfred
Items from Our Catalog (Avon) NYT td pb
12/12/82 (#7), pk 1/2/83 (#1, 11 wk), 33 wk;
PW td pb 12/17/82 (#9), pk 1/7/83 (#1, 11
wk), 24 wk; tot 57 wk.
More Items from Our Catalog (Avon) NYT
td pb 10/9/83 (#13), pk 12/11/83 (#6, 3 wk),
14 wk; PW td pb 10/21/83 (#5, 1 wk), 8 wk;
tot 22 wk.

Gingrich, Arnold
The Bedside Esquire [ed.] (Grosset & Dunlap) NYT gen 10/29/44 (#23, 1 wk).

Gino, Carol
The Nurse's Story (Bantam) PW mm pb
10/21/83 (#12), pk 10/28/83 (#10, 2 wk), 4 wk.
Rusty's Story (Bantam) NYT pb nf 2/2/86
(#7, 1 wk), 4 wk.

Ginott, Dr. Haim G.
Between Parent and Child (Macmillan)
PW nf 9/18/67 (#7), pk 2/19/68 (#1, 6 wk),
59 wk; NYT gen 11/26/67 (#10), pk 2/25/68
(#1, 8 wk), 60 wk; pb gen 4/6/69 (#3), pk
7/6/69 (#2, 8 wk), 20 wk; tot 139 wk.
Between Parent and Teenager (Macmillan)
NYT gen 5/25/69 (#9), pk 7/6/69 (#2, 2 wk),
25 wk; PW nf 6/2/69 (#9), pk 7/21/69 (#1, 1
wk), 26 wk; tot 51 wk.

Ginsburg, Philip E.
Poisoned Blood (Warner) NYT pb nf 5/21/
89 (#9), pk 5/28/89 (#7, 1 wk), 6 wk.

Gipe, George
Gremlins (Avon) NYT pb fic 6/24/84

(#10), pk 7/1/84 (#2, 1 wk), 7 wk; PW mm
pb 6/29/84 (#10), pk 7/6/84 (#4, 1 wk), 5 wk;
tot 12 wk.

Gipson, Fred
   Hound-Dog Man (Harper) NYT fic 1/30/
49 (#15), pk 2/13/49 (#12, 2 wk), 8 wk; PW
fic 3/19/49 (#8, 1 wk); tot 9 wk.

Girzone, Joseph F.
   Joshua and the Children (Macmillan) NYT
fic 8/20/89 (#17), pk 9/10/89 (#6, 1 wk), 12
wk; PW hc fic 8/25/89 (#14), pk 10/13/89
(#6, 1 wk), 11 wk; PW pb rel 10/5/90 (#13),
pk 11/9/90 (#8, 4 wk), 8 wk; tot 31 wk.
   The Shepherd (Macmillan) NYT fic 11/25/
90 (#13, 1 wk), 2 wk.

Givens, Charles J.
   Wealth Without Risk: How to Develop a Personal Fortune Without Going Out on a Limb
(Simon & Schuster) PW hc nf 1/27/89 (#11),
pk 3/24/89 (#1, 2 wk), 94 wk; NYT msc
1/29/89 (#3), pk 2/26/89 (#1, 39 wk), 93 wk;
tot 187 wk.
   Financial Self-Defense (Simon & Schuster)
NYT msc 12/2/90 (#5), pk 12/30/90 (#1, 1
wk), 4 wk; PW hc nf 12/14/90 (#8), pk 12/21/
90 (#7, 1 wk), 2 wk; tot 6 wk.

Gizycka, Countess Eleanor M. Patterson
   Glass Houses (Minton Balch) PW fic 5/15/
26 (#9, 4 wk).

Glasco, Gordon
   The Days of Eternity (Bantam) NYT pb fic
9/16/84 (#6, 1 wk), 5 wk; PW mm pb 9/28/84
(#12), pk 10/5/84 (#10, 1 wk), 2 wk; tot 7 wk.

Glasgow, Ellen
   The Builders (Doubleday) PW fic 1/3/20
(#10, 4 wk).
   Barren Ground (Doubleday) PW fic 6/20/
25 (#5, 4 wk), 8 wk.
   The Romantic Comedians (Doubleday) PW
fic 11/20/26 (#9), pk 12/18/26 (#5, 4 wk), 12
wk.
   They Stooped to Folly (Doubleday) PW fic
9/14/29 (#3, 4 wk), 12 wk.
   The Sheltered Life (Doubleday) PW fic 10/
15/32 (#2, 4 wk), 16 wk.
   Vein of Iron (Harcourt) NYT fic 10/6/35
(#1, 4 wk), 8 wk; PW fic 10/12/35 (#1, 8 wk),
20 wk; tot 28 wk.
   In This Our Life (Harcourt) PW fic 5/10/41
(#3, 4 wk), 12 wk.
   The Woman Within (Harcourt) NYT gen
11/21/54 (#14, 2 wk).

Glaspell, Susan
   Ambrose Holt and Family (Stokes) PW fic
5/16/31 (#9, 4 wk), 8 wk.

Glasser, Ronald J.
   365 Days (Braziller) NYT pb gen 6/11/72
(#5, 4 wk).

Gleick, James
   Chaos: Making a New Science (Viking)
NYT nf 1/24/88 (#11), pk 2/14/88 (#7, 3 wk),
29 wk; PW hc nf 3/18/88 (#14), pk 3/25/88
(#11, 3 wk), 7 wk; (Penguin) NYT pb nf 12/
18/88 (#7), pk 3/5/89 (#4, 4 wk), 43 wk; PW
td pb 2/10/89 (#6, 5 wk), 13 wk; tot 92 wk.

Glover, Bob, and Jack Shepherd
   *The Runner's Handbook: A Complete Fitness
Guide for Men and Women on the Run* (Penguin) PW td pb 5/8/78 (#5), pk 6/5/78 (#1,
1 wk), 19 wk; NYT td pb 5/28/78 (#5), pk
6/25/78 (#4, 4 wk), 12 wk; tot 31 wk.

Gluck, Herb
   See Mickey Mantle and_____
   See Alex Karras and_____

Glut, Donald F.
   Star Wars: From the Adventures of Luke Skywalker [story by George Lucas] (Ballantine/
Del Rey) PW mm pb 6/20/77 (#7), pk 7/25/
77 (#2, 7 wk), 24 wk; NYT mm pb 7/3/77
(#7), pk 8/7/77 (#1, 3 wk), 17 wk; tot 41 wk.

_____ and George Lucas
   The Empire Strikes Back (Ballantine/Del
Rey) PW mm pb 5/16/80 (#4), pk 6/13/80
(#1, 1 wk), 17 wk; NYT mm pb 5/18/80 (#4,
1 wk), 18 wk; tot 35 wk.

Gluyas, Constance
   Rogue's Mistress (NAL/Signet) PW mm pb
7/25/77 (#10, 2 wk), 4 wk; NYT mm pb
7/31/77 (#11), pk 8/14/77 (#8, 1 wk), 6 wk;
tot 10 wk.

Goddard, Kenneth
   Balefire (Bantam) NYT pb fic 5/13/84
(#15), pk 5/27/84 (#11, 1 wk), 4 wk; PW mm
pb 5/25/84 (#13, 1 wk); tot 5 wk.

Godden, Jon
   The Seven Islands (Knopf) NYT fic 8/12/
56 (#13, 1 wk).

_____, and Rumer Godden
   Two Under the Indian Sun (Knopf) PW nf
7/4/66 (#11), pk 9/5/66 (#2, 1 wk), 15 wk;
NYT gen 7/10/66 (#10), pk 8/21/66 (#6, 2
wk), 13 wk; tot 28 wk.

Godden, Rumer
   Black Narcissus (Little Brown) PW fic
9/16/39 (#2, 4 wk), 12 wk; NYT fic 10/8/39
(#8, 4 wk), 8 wk; tot 20 wk.
   The River (Little Brown) NYT fic 11/17/46
(#13, 1 wk).
   A Candle for St. Jude (Viking) NYT fic
8/29/48 (#12, 2 wk), 4 wk.

A Breath of Air (Viking) NYT fic 2/25/51 (#11, 1 wk), 2 wk.

Kingfishers Catch Fire (Viking) NYT fic 6/14/53 (#10), pk 7/26/53 (#5, 2 wk), 17 wk; PW fic 7/11/53 (#7), pk 7/18/53 (#5, 1 wk), 3 wk; tot 20 wk.

An Episode of Sparrows (Viking) NYT fic 12/18/55 (#10), pk 1/1/56 (#8, 4 wk), 16 wk; PW fic 1/21/56 (#10, 1 wk); tot 17 wk.

The Greengage Summer (Viking) NYT fic 4/13/58 (#12), pk 6/15/58 (#5, 2 wk), 21 wk; PW fic 5/19/58 (#10), pk 6/23/58 (#4, 1 wk), 12 wk; tot 33 wk.

China Court (Viking) NYT fic 3/26/61 (#11), pk 6/11/61 (#5, 1 wk), 21 wk; PW fic 4/10/61 (#8), pk 5/1/61 (#6, 3 wk), 12 wk; tot 33 wk.

The Battle of the Villa Fiorita (Viking) PW fic 10/7/63 (#10), pk 11/18/63 (#4, 2 wk), 16 wk; NYT fic 10/20/63 (#9), pk 11/3/63 (#5, 2 wk), 14 wk; tot 30 wk.

In This House of Brede (Viking) NYT fic 10/12/69 (#10), pk 1/4/70 (#4, 1 wk), 19 wk; PW fic 11/10/69 (#10), pk 12/15/69 (#3, 1 wk), 17 wk; tot 36 wk.

See also Carmen Bernos de Gasztold
See also Jon Godden and_____

Godey, John
    The Taking of Pelham One Two Three (Putnam) PW fic 3/5/73 (#10), pk 4/2/73 (#3, 4 wk), 15 wk; NYT fic 3/18/73 (#9), pk 4/1/73 (#4, 5 wk), 15 wk; (Dell) NYT mm pb 3/10/74 (#10, 8 wk); tot 38 wk.

Godwin, Gail
    A Mother and Two Daughters (Viking) PW hc fic 2/12/82 (#13), pk 4/9/82 (#7, 1 wk), 12 wk; NYT fic 2/28/82 (#12), pk 4/25/82 (#8, 1 wk), 18 wk; (Avon) NYT mm pb 1/9/83 (#5), pk 1/30/83 (#1, 1 wk), 11 wk; PW mm pb 1/14/83 (#6), pk 2/4/83 (#1, 1 wk), 11 wk; tot 52 wk.

The Finishing School (Viking) NYT fic 2/17/85 (#14), pk 3/10/85 (#5, 2 wk), 11 wk; PW hc fic 2/22/85 (#15), pk 3/15/85 (#6, 1 wk), 8 wk; (Avon) PW mm pb 2/14/86 (#15), pk 2/21/86 (#10, 1 wk), 3 wk; NYT pb fic 2/16/86 (#9, 1 wk), 4 wk; tot 26 wk.

A Southern Family (Morrow) NYT fic 10/18/87 (#13), pk 11/1/87 (#7, 1 wk), 8 wk; PW hc fic 10/23/87 (#14), pk 11/6/87 (#9, 2 wk), 8 wk; (Avon) NYT pb fic 10/9/88 (#11), pk 10/23/88 (#4, 1 wk), 9 wk; PW mm pb 10/14/88 (#7), pk 11/4/88 (#6, 1 wk), 6 wk; tot 31 wk.

Goebbels, Joseph Paul
    The Goebbels Diaries 1942–1943 [trans. & ed. by Louis P. Lochner] (Doubleday) NYT gen 5/16/48 (#8, 2 wk), 7 wk.

Goerner, Fred
    The Search for Amelia Earhart (Doubleday) NYT gen 10/9/66 (#10), pk 10/23/66 (#7, 2 wk), 8 wk; PW nf 10/10/66 (#8), pk 11/21/66 (#5, 1 wk), 16 wk; tot 24 wk.

Goertz, Arthemise
    Give Us Our Dream (Whittlesey) NYT fic 7/27/47 (#11), pk 8/17/47 (#10, 1 wk), 6 wk.

Gold, Herbert
    Fathers (Random) NYT fic 4/16/67 (#6, 1 wk), 12 wk; PW fic 5/1/67 (#7), pk 5/8/67 (#5, 1 wk), 12 wk; tot 24 wk.

Gold, Todd
    See Drew Barrymore and_____

Goldbeck, Nikki, and David Goldbeck
    Nikki & David Goldbeck's American Wholefoods Cuisine: Over 1300 Meatless, Wholesome Recipes from Short Order to Gourmet (NAL) PW hc nf 6/3/83 (#14), pk 6/10/83 (#12, 1 wk), 2 wk.

Golden, Harry Lewis
    Only in America (World) NYT gen 8/3/58 (#14), pk 9/21/58 (#1, 25 wk), 59 wk; PW nf 8/11/58 (#7), pk 9/15/58 (#1, 23 wk), 52 wk; tot 111 wk.

For 2 Cents Plain (World) NYT gen 7/19/59 (#9), pk 9/13/59 (#1, 3 wk), 33 wk; PW nf 7/27/59 (#8), pk 10/26/59 (#1, 1 wk), 25 wk; tot 58 wk.

Enjoy, Enjoy! (World) NYT gen 7/31/60 (#14), pk 9/11/60 (#3, 5 wk), 26 wk; PW nf 8/15/60 (#9), pk 10/3/60 (#2, 1 wk), 19 wk; tot 45 wk.

Carl Sandburg (World) NYT gen 12/17/61 (#14, 1 wk).

You're Entitle (World) NYT gen 9/2/62 (#15, 2 wk), 3 wk.

Golding, Louis
    Magnolia Street (Farrar) PW fic 4/23/32 (#9), pk 7/9/32 (#3, 4 wk), 20 wk.

The Silver Daughters (Farrar) PW fic 6/9/34 (#9, 4 wk).

Mr. Emmanuel (Viking) PW fic 9/16/39 (#8, 4 wk).

Golding, William
    The Inheritors (Harcourt) PW fic 9/10/62 (#12, 1 wk).

The Spire (Harcourt) NYT fic 5/17/64 (#9), pk 6/14/64 (#3, 1 wk), 15 wk; PW fic 5/18/64 (#9), pk 6/8/64 (#6, 7 wk), 15 wk; tot 30 wk.

Lord of the Flies (Wideview/Perigee) NYT pb fic 4/15/90 (#16), pk 4/22/90 (#11, 2 wk), 4 wk; PW td pb 4/27/90 (#6, 1 wk), 2 wk; tot 6 wk.

Goldman, Albert
Elvis (McGraw) PW hc nf 11/13/81 (#11), pk 12/4/81 (#6, 1 wk), 15 wk; NYT nf 11/15/81 (#15), pk 12/13/81 (#10, 3 wk), 14 wk; (Avon) PW mm pb 11/12/82 (#8, 1 wk), 4 wk; NYT mm pb 11/14/82 (#12), pk 11/21/82 (#8, 1 wk), 4 wk; tot 37 wk.
The Lives of John Lennon (Morrow) NYT nf 9/11/88 (#2, 3 wk), 9 wk; PW hc nf 9/16/88 (#3, 4 wk), 9 wk; (Bantam) NYT pb nf 7/16/89 (#9, 1 wk); tot 19 wk.

Goldman, Eric Frederick
The Crucial Decade (Knopf) NYT gen 9/23/56 (#13, 1 wk).
The Tragedy of Lyndon B. Johnson (Knopf) NYT gen 3/9/69 (#4, 1 wk), 9 wk; PW nf 3/24/69 (#4, 1 wk), 8 wk; tot 17 wk.

Goldman, Peter, and Tony Fuller
Charlie Company (Ballantine) NYT pb nf 5/13/84 (#7), pk 5/20/84 (#4, 1 wk), 4 wk.

Goldman, William
Marathon Man (Delacorte/Dell) NYT mm pb 10/26/75 (#7, 1 wk), 2 wk; PW mm pb 11/15/76 (#10, 1 wk), 3 wk; tot 5 wk.
Magic (Dell) PW mm pb 8/22/77 (#11, 1 wk), 4 wk; NYT mm pb 8/28/77 (#14), pk 9/18/77 (#7, 1 wk), 5 wk; tot 9 wk.
Tinsel (Delacorte) PW hc fic 8/27/79 (#14), pk 9/3/79 (#10, 1 wk), 7 wk; NYT fic 9/2/79 (#10), pk 9/9/79 (#5, 1 wk), 8 wk; (Dell) NYT mm pb 7/27/80 (#6, 1 wk), 4 wk; PW mm pb 8/1/80 (#12, 1 wk), 3 wk; tot 22 wk.
The Princess Bride (Ballantine/Del Rey) PW mm pb 11/13/87 (#12, 1 wk).
Brothers (Warner) PW hc fic 3/13/87 (#14, 1 wk); NYT pb fic 3/6/88 (#9, 2 wk), 5 wk; PW mm pb 3/18/88 (#10), pk 3/25/88 (#8, 1 wk), 6 wk; tot 12 wk.

Goldsmith, Barbara
Little Gloria ... Happy at Last (Knopf) PW hc nf 7/11/80 (#12), pk 8/15/80 (#4, 1 wk), 16 wk; NYT nf 7/27/80 (#5), pk 8/24/80 (#3, 1 wk), 13 wk; (Dell) PW mm pb 7/24/81 (#12), pk 7/31/81 (#10, 1 wk), 3 wk; NYT mm pb 7/26/81 (#8), pk 8/2/81 (#6, 1 wk), 4 wk; tot 36 wk.
Johnson vs. Johnson (Knopf) NYT nf 4/5/87 (#15, 1 wk); (Dell) NYT pb nf 3/6/88 (#10, 1 wk); tot 2 wk.

Goldsmith, Lynn
New Kids on the Block (Kodak/Rizzoli) NYT pb nf 11/25/90 (#10), pk 12/30/90 (#4, 1 wk), 5 wk.

Goldstein, Donald M.
See Gordon W. Prange, et al.

Goldwater, Barry M.
The Conscience of a Conservative (Victor) NYT gen 6/26/60 (#15), pk 8/28/60 (#5, 2 wk), 31 wk; PW nf 7/25/60 (#10), pk 8/8/60 (#3, 1 wk), 19 wk; tot 50 wk.
Why Not Victory? (McGraw) NYT gen 5/27/62 (#16), pk 7/8/62 (#11, 1 wk), 12 wk.
With No Apologies: The Personal and Political Memoirs of United States Senator Barry M. Goldwater (Morrow) NYT nf 12/30/79 (#14), pk 1/6/80 (#11, 1 wk), 5 wk; PW hc nf 1/25/80 (#15, 1 wk); tot 6 wk.

_____, with Jack Casserly
Goldwater (Doubleday) NYT nf 10/30/88 (#13), pk 11/20/88 (#6, 1 wk), 17 wk; PW hc nf 11/4/88 (#7), pk 11/18/88 (#4, 1 wk), 12 wk; tot 29 wk.

Golenbock, Peter
Personal Fouls (Carroll & Graf) NYT nf 8/20/89 (#9), pk 9/3/89 (#5, 2 wk), 7 wk; PW hc nf 9/8/89 (#10, 2 wk); tot 9 wk.
See also Craig Nettles and_____
See also Sparky Lyle and_____
See also Billy Martin and_____

Golon, Sergeanne
Angelique (Lippincott) NYT fic 10/12/58 (#15), pk 11/16/58 (#7, 1 wk), 12 wk; PW fic 11/17/58 (#8, 1 wk); tot 13 wk.

Gonick, Larry
The Cartoon History of the Universe Vols. 1–7 (Doubleday) PW td pb 12/21/90 (#9, 1 wk).

Goode, Ruth
See Solomon Hurok and_____

Goodgold, Edwin, and Dan Carlinsky
Trivia (Dell) NYT pb gen 5/1/66 (#5, 4 wk).

Goodkind, Howard
See Norman Garbo and_____

Goodman, Ezra
The Fifty-Year Decline and Fall of Hollywood (Simon & Schuster) NYT gen 4/2/61 (#14, 1 wk), 2 wk.

Goodman, Linda
Linda Goodman's Sun Signs (Taplinger) NYT gen 8/24/69 (#10), pk 10/19/69 (#9, 1 wk), 4 wk; PW nf 9/22/69 (#10, 1 wk); tot 5 wk.
Linda Goodman's Love Signs (Harper) PW hc nf 1/15/79 (#12), pk 1/29/79 (#5, 3 wk), 22 wk; NYT nf 1/28/79 (#12), pk 3/11/79 (#4, 1 wk), 18 wk; (Fawcett/Columbine) PW td pb 11/21/80 (#8), pk 11/28/80 (#6, 1 wk), 5 wk; NYT td pb 11/23/80 (#15), pk 3/1/81 (#11, 1 wk), 8 wk; tot 53 wk.

Goodrich, Marcus
Delilah (Farrar) PW fic 3/15/41 (#5, 8 wk), 16 wk.

Goodwin, Archie
See Walt Simonson and_____

Goodwin, Dorothy Kearns
The Fitzgeralds and the Kennedys (Simon & Schuster) NYT nf 2/22/87 (#7), pk 3/15/87 (#2, 2 wk), 18 wk; PW hc nf 2/27/87 (#10), pk 3/27/87 (#3, 2 wk), 14 wk; (St. Martin's) NYT pb nf 2/28/88 (#8), pk 3/27/88 (#4, 1 wk), 13 wk; PW mm pb 3/16/90 (#15, 1 wk); tot 46 wk.

Gorbachev, Mikhail
Perestroika: New Thinking for Our Country and the World (Bessie/Harper) PW hc nf 12/25/87 (#15), pk 1/29/87 (#11, 1 wk), 7 wk; NYT nf 12/27/87 (#15), pk 1/24/87 (#10, 1 wk), 8 wk; tot 15 wk.

Gordon, Arthur
Reprisal (Harper) NYT fic 9/10/50 (#16), pk 10/1/50 (#13, 1 wk), 5 wk.

Gordon, Barbara
I'm Dancing as Fast as I Can (Harper) NYT nf 7/1/79 (#12), pk 9/2/79 (#10, 1 wk), 15 wk; PW hc nf 7/16/79 (#15), pk 8/6/79 (#11, 2 wk), 13 wk; (Bantam) PW mm pb 5/9/80 (#5, 2 wk), 10 wk; NYT mm pb 5/18/80 (#14), pk 6/1/80 (#8, 1 wk), 7 wk; tot 45 wk.

Gordon, Mary
Final Payments (Random) PW hc fic 6/12/78 (#15), pk 7/10/78 (#10, 1 wk), 10 wk; NYT fic 6/25/78 (#15, 5 wk); (Ballantine) PW mm pb 1/8/79 (#14), pk 3/26/79 (#3, 1 wk), 16 wk; NYT mm pb 1/21/79 (#13), pk 2/4/79 (#5, 1 wk), 11 wk; tot 42 wk.
The Company of Women (Random) PW hc fic 3/13/81 (#6), pk 4/3/81 (#5, 1 wk), 11 wk; NYT fic 3/15/81 (#14), pk 3/29/81 (#5, 4 wk), 14 wk; (Ballantine) PW mm pb 1/15/82 (#13), pk 2/5/82 (#5, 1 wk), 9 wk; NYT mm pb 1/17/82 (#8), pk 2/7/82 (#4, 1 wk), 8 wk; tot 42 wk.
Men and Angels (Random) NYT fic 5/5/85 (#12, 2 wk), 3 wk; (Ballantine) NYT pb fic 5/4/86 (#15, 1 wk); tot 4 wk.

Gordon, Noah
The Rabbi (McGraw) NYT fic 8/29/65 (#10), pk 10/24/65 (#8, 4 wk), 22 wk; PW fic 9/27/65 (#10), pk 10/4/65 (#7, 1 wk), 20 wk; NYT pb fic 9/4/66 (#2, 12 wk), 24 wk; tot 66 wk.
The Death Committee (McGraw) NYT fic 8/10/69 (#9, 1 wk), 2 wk.

Gordon, Ruth
Myself Among Others (Atheneum) PW nf

6/14/71 (#10), pk 7/26/71 (#9, 3 wk), 6 wk; NYT gen 8/1/71 (#9, 2 wk); tot 8 wk.

Gordon, Thomas
P.E.T. (NAL/Plume) NYT td pb 2/15/76 (#5), pk 11/28/76 (#4, 2 wk), 4 wk.

Goren, Charles H.
Goren's New Contract Bridge Complete (Doubleday) NYT gen 11/24/57 (#16), pk 2/2/58 (#12, 1 wk), 4 wk; PW nf 1/6/58 (#8, 1 wk); tot 5 wk.

Gorman, Herbert
The Wine of San Lorenzo (Farrar) NYT fic 6/24/45 (#13), pk 7/15/45 (#9, 1 wk), 11 wk.

Gottlieb, Carl
The Jaws Log (Dell) NYT mm pb 8/24/75 (#6, 1 wk), 5 wk.
See also David Crosby and_____

Gotto, Antonio M., Jr.
See Michael E. DeBakey, et al.

Goudge, Eileen
Garden of Lies (Viking) NYT fic 6/11/89 (#13), pk 7/9/89 (#12, 3 wk), 8 wk; PW hc fic 6/30/89 (#15, 3 wk); (NAL/Signet) NYT pb fic 6/24/90 (#12), pk 7/8/90 (#4, 1 wk), 11 wk; PW mm pb 6/29/90 (#15), pk 7/20/90 (#5, 1 wk), 10 wk; tot 32 wk.

Goudge, Elizabeth
A City of Bells (Coward McCann) PW fic 8/14/37 (#8, 4 wk), 12 wk.
Towers in the Mist (Coward McCann) NYT fic 7/3/38 (#4, 4 wk), 8 wk; PW fic 7/9/38 (#6, 4 wk), 8 wk; tot 16 wk.
The Sister of the Angels (Coward McCann) NYT fic 12/10/39 (#13, 4 wk), 8 wk.
The Middle Window (Coward McCann) NYT fic 5/7/39 (#6, 4 wk).
The Bird in the Tree (Coward McCann) PW fic 7/13/40 (#6), pk 8/10/40 (#4, 4 wk), 12 wk.
The Castle on the Hill (Coward McCann) PW fic 6/13/42 (#7, 4 wk), 8 wk.
Green Dolphin Street (Coward McCann) NYT fic 9/17/44 (#10), pk 10/15/44 (#1, 5 wk), 48 wk; PW fic 9/23/44 (#5), pk 9/30/44 (#1, 10 wk), 22 wk; tot 70 wk.
Pilgrim's Inn (Coward McCann) NYT fic 4/25/48 (#5), pk 5/9/48 (#1, 4 wk), 24 wk; PW fic 5/1/48 (#4), pk 5/8/48 (#1, 9 wk), 17 wk; tot 41 wk.
Gentian Hill (Coward McCann) NYT fic 1/15/50 (#13), pk 1/29/50 (#4, 5 wk), 16 wk; PW fic 2/4/50 (#3, 3 wk), 9 wk; tot 25 wk.
The Heart of the Family (Coward McCann) NYT fic 10/11/53 (#16), pk 10/25/53 (#12, 2 wk), 10 wk.
The Rosemary Tree (Coward McCann)

NYT fic 6/17/56 (#14), pk 7/15/56 (#9, 4 wk), 16 wk; PW fic 7/23/56 (#8, 1 wk), 2 wk; tot 18 wk.

The White Witch (Coward McCann) NYT fic 1/26/58 (#12), pk 2/16/58 (#4, 5 wk), 20 wk; PW fic 2/10/58 (#5), pk 3/10/58 (#4, 4 wk), 14 wk; tot 34 wk.

The Dean's Watch (Coward McCann) NYT fic 10/16/60 (#16), pk 12/18/60 (#3, 3 wk), 25 wk; PW fic 10/31/60 (#7), pk 12/26/60 (#3, 2 wk), 19 wk; tot 44 wk.

The Scent of Water (Coward McCann) PW fic 10/21/63 (#10), pk 12/16/63 (#9, 3 wk), 10 wk; NYT fic 1/5/64 (#10, 3 wk); tot 13 wk.

Child from the Sea (Coward McCann) NYT fic 9/20/70 (#10), pk 11/29/70 (#4, 1 wk), 26 wk; PW fic 9/21/70 (#9), pk 11/23/70 (#3, 2 wk), 25 wk; NYT pb fic 11/14/71 (#5), pk 1/9/72 (#3, 4 wk), 16 wk; tot 67 wk.

Gould, John

Farmer Takes a Wife (Morrow) NYT gen 2/24/46 (#14), pk 3/31/46 (#7, 2 wk), 13 wk; PW nf 3/9/46 (#10), pk 4/6/46 (#8, 1 wk), 3 wk; tot 16 wk.

And One to Grow On (Morrow) NYT gen 7/10/49 (#12, 1 wk), 2 wk.

Gould, Judith

Sins (NAL/Signet) PW mm pb 11/19/82 (#12), pk 12/3/82 (#5, 1 wk), 5 wk; NYT mm pb 11/21/82 (#12), pk 12/19/82 (#11, 1 wk), 4 wk; NYT pb fic 2/23/86 (#15, 1 wk); tot 10 wk.

Gould, Lois

Such Good Friends (Random) NYT fic 7/5/ 70 (#8), pk 7/12/70 (#7, 1 wk), 7 wk; PW fic 7/6/70 (#8), pk 7/13/70 (#6, 1 wk), 9 wk; tot 16 wk.

Gould, Ralph Ernest

Yankee Storekeeper (Whittlesey/McGraw) NYT gen 6/9/46 (#12), pk 8/18/46 (#9, 2 wk), 18 wk.

Gould, Stephen Jay

Wonderful Life (Norton) NYT nf 11/12/89 (#13), pk 12/3/89 (#12, 1 wk), 10 wk.

Goulden, Joseph C.

The Superlawyers (Weybright & Talley) NYT gen 6/18/72 (#9), pk 8/27/72 (#3, 1 wk), 20 wk; PW nf 6/26/72 (#8), pk 9/4/72 (#3, 1 wk), 18 wk; tot 38 wk.

Gouzenko, Igor

The Fall of a Titan (Norton) NYT fic 8/8/ 54 (#8), pk 8/15/54 (#6, 1 wk), 24 wk; PW fic 8/21/54 (#6, 2 wk), 6 wk; tot 30 wk.

Govan, Christine Noble

Jennifer's House (Houghton) NYT fic 4/8/ 45 (#12, 1 wk), 2 wk.

Gover, Robert

$100 Misunderstanding (Grove) NYT fic 12/2/62 (#15), pk 4/7/63 (#8, 1 wk), 4 wk; PW fic 12/10/62 (#11), pk 1/14/63 (#5, 1 wk), 10 wk; tot 14 wk.

Gow, James, and Armand d'Usseau

Tomorrow the World (Scribner) NYT gen 10/31/43 (#18, 1 wk), 2 wk.

Gowers, Sir Ernest

See Henry Watson Fowler and_____

Grady, Mike

See Linda Lovelace and_____

Graedon, Joe

The People's Pharmacy (Avon) PW td pb 10/17/77 (#9), pk 11/14/77 (#1, 11 wk), 39 wk; NYT td pb 10/30/77 (#10), pk 12/4/77 (#1, 11 wk), 43 wk; tot 82 wk.

The People's Pharmacy 2 (Avon) PW td pb 11/7/80 (#3), pk 11/28/80 (#1, 4 wk), 26 wk; NYT td pb 11/9/80 (#13), pk 11/23/80 (#1, 4 wk), 29 wk; tot 55 wk.

Grafton, Susan

"F" Is for Fugitive (Bantam) NYT pb fic 4/29/90 (#15), pk 5/6/90 (#9, 1 wk), 8 wk; PW mm pb 5/11/90 (#12), pk 6/8/90 (#8, 1 wk), 7 wk; tot 15 wk.

"G" Is for Gumshoe (Holt) PW hc fic 5/4/90 (#12), pk 5/11/90 (#10, 1 wk), 5 wk; NYT fic 5/6/90 (#8, 1 wk), 6 wk; tot 11 wk.

Graham, Alice Walworth

The Vows of the Peacock (Doubleday) NYT fic 5/15/55 (#16, 1 wk).

Graham, Billy

World Aflame (Doubleday) PW nf 11/1/65 (#11), pk 12/6/65 (#7, 2 wk), 13 wk; NYT gen 11/7/65 (#10), pk 1/16/66 (#6, 1 wk), 12 wk; tot 25 wk.

Angels (Doubleday) PW nf 11/3/75 (#9), pk 1/26/76 (#2, 1 wk), 12 wk; NYT gen 11/30/75 (#7), pk 1/11/76 (#3, 2 wk), 25 wk; PW hc nf 2/2/76 (#2), pk 2/9/76 (#1, 2 wk), 18 wk; tot 55 wk.

How to Be Born Again (Word) PW hc nf 10/10/77 (#15, 1 wk).

Approaching Hoofbeats: The Four Horsemen of the Apocalypse (Word) NYT nf 1/1/84 (#12), pk 2/5/84 (#7, 3 wk), 15 wk; PW hc nf 1/13/84 (#12), pk 1/20/84 (#10, 2 wk), 9 wk; tot 24 wk.

Graham, Elinor

Our Way Down East (Macmillan) NYT gen 11/7/43 (#15), pk 11/14/43 (#13, 1 wk), 4 wk.

Graham, Frank

McGraw of the Giants (Putnam) NYT gen 5/28/44 (#14), pk 7/16/44 (#13, 1 wk), 6 wk.

Graham, Gwenthalyn

Earth and High Heaven (Lippincott) NYT fic 10/29/44 (#13), pk 4/22/45 (#1, 2 wk), 40 wk; PW fic 11/11/44 (#10), pk 11/18/44 (#2, 4 wk), 32 wk; tot 72 wk.

Graham, Sheilah and Gerold Frank

Beloved Infidel (Holt) NYT gen 2/8/59 (#14), pk 3/15/59 (#9, 1 wk), 4 wk.

Grahame, Kenneth

The Wind in the Willows (Scribner) NYT ch bst 5/8/60 (#6, 19 wk), 58 wk.

Grandma Moses

See Anna Mary Robertson Moses

Grant, Dr. Toni

Being a Woman: Fulfilling Your Femininity and Finding Love (Random) PW hc nf 4/8/88 (#15, 2 wk); NYT msc 4/17/88 (#5), pk 5/22/88 (#3, 1 wk), 6 wk; tot 8 wk.

Grass, Gunter

The Tin Drum (Pantheon) PW fic 3/25/63 (#7), pk 5/6/63 (#6, 2 wk), 14 wk; NYT fic 4/14/63 (#10), pk 5/26/63 (#6, 2 wk), 9 wk; tot 23 wk.

Local Anaesthetic (Harcourt) NYT fic 5/10/70 (#9, 1 wk), 2 wk.

The Flounder (Harcourt) PW hc fic 12/11/78 (#15, 2 wk).

Graves, John Temple

The Fighting South (Putnam) NYT gen 5/16/43 (#19), pk 7/4/43 (#13, 1 wk), 4 wk.

Graves, Robert

I, Claudius (Smith & Haas) PW fic 8/11/34 (#5, 8 wk), 12 wk; (Vintage) PW td pb 12/5/77 (#8), pk 1/23/78 (#1, 10 wk), 28 wk; NYT td pb 1/22/78 (#12), pk 3/5/78 (#1, 8 wk), 23 wk; tot 63 wk.

Claudius the God (Smith & Haas) PW fic 5/11/35 (#9, 4 wk), 4 wk; (Vintage) PW td pb 1/23/78 (#9), pk 2/13/78 (#2, 1 wk), 12 wk; NYT td pb 2/26/78 (#12), pk 4/2/78 (#3, 1 wk), 10 wk; tot 26 wk.

Wife to Mr. Milton (Creative Age) NYT fic 3/18/45 (#12, 1 wk).

Gray, Austin Kayingham

Teresa: Or Her Demon Lover (Scribner) NYT gen 11/25/45 (#13, 1 wk).

Gray, Francine du Plessix

Lovers and Tyrants (Simon & Schuster) PW hc fic 11/8/76 (#10), pk 11/15/76 (#9, 3 wk), 9 wk; NYT fic 11/28/76 (#10, 2 wk); tot 11 wk.

Greeley, Andrew M.

The Cardinal Sins (Geis/Warner) PW hc fic 6/5/81 (#14), pk 10/23/81 (#4, 1 wk), 32 wk; NYT fic 6/28/81 (#9), pk 10/18/81 (#3, 1 wk), 32 wk; PW mm pb 2/5/82 (#10), pk 2/19/82 (#3, 5 wk), 22 wk; NYT mm pb 2/7/82 (#12), pk 2/21/82 (#1, 1 wk), 22 wk; tot 108 wk.

Thy Brother's Wife (Geis/Warner) PW hc fic 4/2/82 (#15), pk 4/23/82 (#6, 4 wk), 19 wk; NYT fic 4/11/82 (#14), pk 5/9/82 (#4, 1 wk), 19 wk; NYT mm pb 2/6/83 (#1, 2 wk), 10 wk; PW mm pb 2/11/83 (#3), pk 2/18/83 (#2, 1 wk), 10 wk; tot 58 wk.

Ascent into Hell (Geis/Warner) PW hc fic 6/3/83 (#12), pk 7/15/83 (#6, 1 wk), 13 wk; NYT fic 6/5/83 (#12), pk 6/26/83 (#7, 3 wk), 14 wk; pb fic 2/26/84 (#9), pk 3/4/84 (#2, 1 wk), 10 wk; PW mm pb 3/2/84 (#7), pk 3/9/84 (#2, 1 wk), 9 wk; tot 46 wk.

Lord of the Dance (Geis/Warner) NYT fic 3/11/84 (#13), pk 4/8/84 (#6, 2 wk), 12 wk; PW hc fic 3/23/84 (#7), pk 4/6/84 (#5, 1 wk), 11 wk; NYT pb fic 3/3/85 (#4), pk 3/10/85 (#2, 2 wk), 10 wk; PW mm pb 3/8/85 (#6), pk 3/22/85 (#2, 1 wk), 9 wk; tot 42 wk.

Virgin and Martyr (Geis/Warner) NYT fic 3/17/85 (#13, 1 wk), 4 wk; PW hc fic 3/22/85 (#13, 1 wk); NYT pb fic 2/2/86 (#11), pk 2/16/86 (#4, 1 wk), 8 wk; PW mm pb 2/7/86 (#9), pk 2/14/86 (#7, 2 wk), 5 wk; tot 18 wk.

Happy Are the Meek (Warner) NYT pb fic 9/8/85 (#14), pk 9/22/85 (#7, 1 wk), 6 wk; PW mm pb 9/13/85 (#15), pk 10/4/85 (#10, 1 wk), 5 wk; tot 11 wk.

Happy Are the Clean of Heart (Warner) NYT pb fic 8/10/86 (#16, 1 wk).

Angels of September (Geis/Warner) PW hc fic 2/7/86 (#9), pk 2/28/86 (#5, 1 wk), 9 wk; NYT fic 2/16/86 (#8), pk 3/2/86 (#7, 1 wk), 6 wk; pb fic 12/28/86 (#11), pk 1/25/86 (#6, 1 wk), 10 wk; PW mm pb 1/9/87 (#12, 2 wk), 4 wk; tot 29 wk.

Patience of a Saint (Geis/Warner) PW hc fic 1/30/87 (#13), pk 2/13/87 (#12, 1 wk), 5 wk; NYT fic 2/8/87 (#11, 1 wk), 6 wk; NYT pb fic 12/6/87 (#7, 2 wk), 9 wk; PW mm pb 12/18/87 (#13), pk 12/25/87 (#9, 1 wk), 6 wk; tot 26 wk.

God Game (Doherty/Tor) NYT pb fic 5/17/87 (#8, 1 wk), 3 wk.

Rite of Spring (Warner) NYT pb fic 11/13/88 (#14), pk 11/20/88 (#11, 1 wk), 3 wk.

Green, Abel, and Joe Laurie, Jr.

Show Biz (Holt) NYT gen 12/2/51 (#11), pk 3/16/52 (#3, 2 wk), 23 wk; PW nf 1/12/52 (#10), pk 3/1/52 (#2, 1 wk), 9 wk; tot 32 wk.

Green, Anne

The Selbys (Dutton) PW fic 7/12/30 (#10), pk 8/23/30 (#9, 4 wk), 8 wk.

Reader, I Married Him (Dutton) PW fic 3/21/31 (#4, 8 wk).

Just Before Dawn (Harper) NYT fic 5/2/43 (#10, 1 wk).

Green, Gerald
The Last Angry Man (Scribner) NYT fic 2/24/57 (#12), pk 6/30/57 (#4, 1 wk), 31 wk; PW fic 4/1/57 (#6), pk 5/27/57 (#3, 1 wk), 21 wk; tot 52 wk.
The Lotus Eaters (Scribner) NYT fic 10/4/59 (#12), pk 10/25/59 (#9, 1 wk), 9 wk; PW fic 10/26/59 (#7, 1 wk), 2 wk; tot 11 wk.
The Heartless Light (Scribner) NYT fic 6/4/61 (#16, 1 wk).
Holocaust (Bantam) PW mm pb 4/24/78 (#10), pk 5/8/78 (#2, 2 wk), 7 wk; NYT mm pb 4/30/78 (#11), pk 5/7/78 (#2, 3 wk), 6 wk; tot 13 wk.
The Healers (Putnam) PW hc fic 4/2/79 (#15, 1 wk); (Berkley) PW mm pb 3/28/80 (#15, 1 wk); tot 2 wk.

Green, Hannah
The Dead of the House (Doubleday) PW fic 4/24/72 (#10, 1 wk).

Green, Henry
Loving (Viking) NYT fic 11/6/49 (#13), pk 12/4/49 (#6, 2 wk), 9 wk.
Nothing (Viking) NYT fic 4/16/50 (#13), pk 4/23/50 (#9, 1 wk), 7 wk.
Doting (Viking) NYT fic 6/1/52 (#15, 2 wk).

Green, Julian
The Closed Garden (Harper) PW fic 6/30/28 (#8, 4 wk).
The Dark Journey (Harper) PW fic 11/9/29 (#9, 4 wk).
Memories of Happy Days (Harper) NYT nf 12/13/42 (#19, 2 wk).

Green, Mark J., James M. Fallows and David R. Zwick
Who Runs Congress? (Bantam) NYT pb gen 11/12/72 (#1, 4 wk), 12 wk.

Greenberg, Martin H.
The Further Adventures of Batman [ed.] (Bantam) NYT pb fic 7/23/89 (#15, 1 wk).

Greenberger, Robert
See Carmen Carter, et al.

Greenburg, Dan
How to Be a Jewish Mother (Price Stern Sloan) NYT gen 5/30/65 (#7, 4 wk), 7 wk; PW nf 6/7/65 (#8, 3 wk), 7 wk; tot 14 wk.
Love Kills (Pocket) NYT mm pb 7/15/79 (#15), pk 8/12/79 (#14, 1 wk), 2 wk.

Greene, Bob
Good Morning, Merry Sunshine: A Father's Journal of His Child's First Year (Atheneum) NYT nf 6/24/84 (#16), pk 8/26/84 (#4, 1 wk), 17 wk; PW hc nf 6/29/84 (#15), pk 9/14/84 (#5, 1 wk), 15 wk; tot 32 wk.

Be True to Your School (Atheneum) NYT nf 5/17/87 (#14, 1 wk), 2 wk.

Greene, Gael
Blue Skies, No Candy (Morrow) NYT fic 11/14/76 (#8), pk 12/5/76 (#6, 2 wk), 8 wk; PW hc fic 11/22/76 (#9), pk 1/3/77 (#8, 1 wk), 2 wk; (Warner) mm pb 1/16/78 (#8), pk 1/23/78 (#5, 1 wk), 9 wk; NYT mm pb 1/22/78 (#15), pk 3/5/78 (#9, 1 wk), 12 wk; tot 31 wk, *Dr. Love* (NAL) NYT mm pb 7/24/83 (#13, 1 wk).

Greene, Graham
The Heart of the Matter (Viking) NYT fic 8/1/48 (#15), pk 8/22/48 (#3, 2 wk), 16 wk; PW fic 8/14/48 (#9), pk 8/28/48 (#4, 3 wk), 8 wk; tot 24 wk.
The End of the Affair (Viking) NYT fic 11/11/51 (#15), pk 11/25/51 (#4, 7 wk), 26 wk; PW fic 12/8/51 (#5), pk 12/22/51 (#4, 2 wk), 10 wk; tot 36 wk.
The Quiet American (Viking) NYT fic 3/25/56 (#16), pk 4/22/56 (#4, 2 wk), 16 wk; PW fic 4/21/56 (#10), pk 4/28/56 (#2, 1 wk), 6 wk; tot 22 wk.
Our Man in Havana (Viking) NYT fic 11/16/58 (#14), pk 11/30/58 (#11, 1 wk), 5 wk.
A Burnt-Out Case (Viking) NYT fic 2/26/61 (#16), pk 4/9/61 (#3, 6 wk), 26 wk; PW fic 3/13/61 (#4), pk 4/10/61 (#1, 1 wk), 20 wk; tot 46 wk.
The Comedians (Viking) NYT fic 2/20/66 (#6), pk 3/13/66 (#5, 2 wk), 18 wk; PW fic 2/28/66 (#8), pk 4/4/66 (#4, 1 wk), 18 wk; NYT pb fic 6/4/67 (#4, 4 wk), 12 wk; tot 48 wk.
Travels with My Aunt (Viking) NYT fic 2/1/70 (#10), pk 3/29/70 (#2, 2 wk), 22 wk; PW fic 2/9/70 (#10), pk 3/30/70 (#2, 2 wk), 25 wk; tot 47 wk.
The Honorary Consul (Simon & Schuster) NYT fic 10/7/73 (#6), pk 11/25/73 (#1, 2 wk), 27 wk; PW fic 10/8/73 (#8), pk 10/29/73 (#1, 3 wk), 24 wk; tot 51 wk.
The Human Factor (Simon & Schuster) PW hc fic 3/20/78 (#11), pk 4/17/78 (#1, 3 wk), 21 wk; NYT fic 3/26/78 (#15), pk 4/16/78 (#3, 1 wk), 21 wk; (Avon) NYT mm pb 2/25/79 (#10), pk 3/18/79 (#3, 1 wk), 13 wk; PW mm pb 2/26/79 (#7), pk 3/19/79 (#3, 1 wk), 12 wk; tot 67 wk.
Doctor Fischer of Geneva or the Bomb Party (Simon & Schuster) PW hc fic 6/20/80 (#12, 1 wk), 6 wk; NYT fic 6/29/80 (#11, 1 wk), 4 wk; tot 10 wk.
Monsignor Quixote (Simon & Schuster) NYT fic 10/10/82 (#13, 1 wk); PW hc fic 10/22/82 (#13), pk 10/29/82 (#11, 1 wk), 8 wk; tot 9 wk.

Greengrass, Paul
   See Peter Wright and_____

Greenslet, Ferris
   The Lowells and Their Seven Worlds
   (Houghton) NYT gen 10/13/46 (#10), pk
   10/20/46 (#5, 1 wk), 14 wk; PW nf 10/26/46
   (#3, 1 wk), 4 wk; tot 18 wk.
   See also Charles P. Curtis, Jr., and_____

Greer, Germaine
   The Female Eunuch (McGraw) NYT gen
   5/16/71 (#9), pk 7/25/71 (#1, 1 wk), 25 wk;
   PW nf 5/17/71 (#9), pk 8/2/71 (#1, 2 wk), 24
   wk; NYT pb gen 4/9/72 (#1, 4 wk), 12 wk;
   tot 61 wk.

Greer, Howard
   Designing Male (Putnam) NYT gen 10/7/
   51 (#15, 1 wk).

Gregory, Jill
   The Wayward Heart (Ace) NTR td pb 4/4/
   82 (#14, 1 wk).

Gregory, Philippa
   Wideacre (Pocket) NYT pb fic 1/31/88
   (#14, 1 wk).

Greider, William
   *Secrets of the Temple: How the Federal
   Reserve Runs the Country* (Simon & Schuster) NYT nf 2/7/88 (#15, 2 wk); PW hc nf
   2/19/88 (#8, 2 wk), 4 wk; tot 6 wk.

Grenfell, Dr. Wilfred
   A Labrador Doctor (Houghton) PW gen
   1/3/20 (#5, 4 wk).

Gresham, William
   Nightmare Alley (Rinehart) NYT fic 10/13/
   46 (#15, 1 wk), 2 wk.

Grew, Joseph C.
   Report from Tokyo (Simon & Schuster)
   PW nf 12/19/42 (#5), pk 1/30/43 (#3, 1 wk),
   12 wk; NYT nf 12/27/42 (#8), pk 1/24/43
   (#4, 4 wk), 17 wk; tot 29 wk.
   Ten Years in Japan (Simon & Schuster)
   NYT gen 6/4/44 (#5), pk 6/25/44 (#2, 4 wk),
   23 wk; PW nf 6/10/44 (#5), pk 6/24/44 (#2,
   2 wk), 13 wk; tot 36 wk.

**Grey, Lord Edward, First Viscount Grey
   of Fallodon**
   Twenty-Five Years (Stokes) PW nf 11/21/
   25 (#1, 8 wk).

**Grey, Loren Zane [all titles as by Zane
   Grey]**
   The Desert of Wheat (Harper) PW fic 5/3/
   19 (#2, 4 wk), 16 wk.
   The Man of the Forest (Harper) PW fic 3/
   27/20 (#1, 12 wk), 20 wk.
   The Mysterious Rider (Harper) PW fic
   2/26/21 (#1, 8 wk), 20 wk.

To the Last Man (Harper) PW fic 4/1/22
(#2, 4 wk).
Wanderer of the Wasteland (Harper) PW fic
3/3/23 (#1, 8 wk), 16 wk.
The Call of the Canyon (Harper) PW fic 4/
19/24 (#5, 4 wk).
The Thundering Herd (Harper) PW fic
4/18/25 (#10, 4 wk).
The Vanishing American (Harper) PW fic
3/20/26 (#7, 4 wk).
Under the Tonto Rim (Harper) PW fic 2/
19/27 (#6, 4 wk).
Forlorn River (Harper) PW fic 12/31/27
(#8, 4 wk).
Nevada (Harper) PW fic 5/26/28 (#4, 4
wk), 8 wk.
The Shepherd of Guadaloupe (Harper) PW
fic 7/12/30 (#6, 4 wk), 8 wk.
Sunset Pass (Harper) PW fic 2/21/31 (#6,
4 wk), 8 wk.
Arizona Ames (Harper) PW fic 2/13/32
(#8, 4 wk).
The Trail Driver (Grosset & Dunlap)
NYT fic 2/2/36 (#2, 4 wk).
The Lost Wagon Train (Harper) NYT fic
11/8/36 (#10, 4 wk).
West of the Pecos (Collier) NYT fic 6/6/37
(#8, 4 wk).
Raiders of Spanish Peaks (Harper) NYT fic
6/5/38 (#9, 4 wk).
Western Union (Walter J. Black) NYT fic
12/10/39 (#11, 4 wk).
Knights of the Range (Grosset & Dunlap)
NYT fic 2/5/39 (#12, 4 wk).

Grice, Julia
   Lovefire (Avon) PW mm pb 11/7/77 (#10,
   1 wk), 4 wk; NYT mm pb 11/13/77 (#12), pk
   11/27/77 (#11, 1 wk), 5 wk; tot 9 wk.
   Emerald Fire (Avon) NYT mm pb 12/10/
   78 (#11, 1 wk); PW mm pb 12/25/78 (#11, 1
   wk), 2 wk; tot 3 wk.

**Grier, William H. and Price M.
   Cobbs**
   Black Rage (Basic) NYT gen 9/29/68 (#10,
   1 wk); PW 9/30/68 (#10) pk 10/7/68 (#7, 1
   wk), 2 wk; tot 3 wk.

Griffin, Gwyn
   Master of This Vessel (Holt) NYT fic 9/3/61
   (#11, 1 wk), 2 wk.
   An Operational Necessity (Putnam) PW fic
   8/28/67 (#9), pk 10/9/67 (#6, 1 wk), 10 wk;
   NYT fic 9/10/67 (#9), pk 10/8/67 (#8, 1 wk),
   8 wk; tot 18 wk.

Griffin, Jonathan
   See Nikos Kazantzakis

Griffin, Merv, and Peter Barsocchini
   Merv: An Autobiography (Simon & Schus-

ter) NYT nf 10/26/80 (#8, 1 wk), 3 wk; PW hc nf 10/31/80 (#14, 2 wk); tot 5 wk.

Griffin, W.E.B.

The Berets (Jove) NYT pb fic 2/17/85 (#15, 1 wk).

The Generals (Jove) NYT pb fic 3/2/86 (#14, 1 wk).

Semper Fi (Jove) NYT pb fic 11/16/86 (#13), pk 11/23/86 (#10, 1 wk), 5 wk; PW mm pb 11/28/86 (#15), pk 12/5/86 (#12, 1 wk), 3 wk; tot 8 wk.

The New Breed (Putnam) PW hc fic 9/25/87 (#9), pk 10/2/87 (#7, 1 wk), 6 wk; NYT fic 9/27/87 (#14), pk 10/4/87 (#10, 1 wk), 5 wk; (Jove) PW mm pb 7/22/88 (#8, 1 wk), 2 wk; tot 13 wk.

Call to Arms (Jove) PW mm pb 9/18/87 (#6), pk 9/25/87 (#3, 1 wk), 6 wk; NYT pb fic 9/13/87 (#6), pk 9/20/87 (#4, 1 wk), 6 wk; tot 12 wk.

The Aviators (Putnam) PW hc fic 9/2/88 (#15), pk 9/16/88 (#9, 2 wk), 8 wk; NYT fic 9/18/88 (#13, 2 wk), 4 wk; (Jove) pb fic 5/14/89 (#12), pk 5/21/89 (#8, 1 wk), 3 wk; PW mm pb 5/19/89 (#9), pk 5/26/89 (#6, 1 wk), 4 wk; tot 19 wk.

The Counterattack (Putnam) NYT fic 2/4/90 (#12), pk 2/25/90 (#5, 1 wk), 11 wk; PW hc fic 2/9/90 (#10), pk 2/16/90 (#4, 4 wk), 11 wk; (Jove) NYT pb fic 9/9/90 (#6), pk 9/23/90 (#5, 1 wk), 4 wk; PW mm pb 9/14/90 (#5, 1 wk), 4 wk; tot 30 wk.

Griffis, Stanton

Lying in State (Doubleday) NYT gen 1/11/53 (#15, 1 wk).

Griffith, Aline [all titles as by Aline, Countess of Romanones]

The Spy Wore Red: My Adventures as an Undercover Agent in World War II (Random) NYT nf 7/5/87 (#14), pk 8/2/87 (#6, 1 wk), 13 wk; PW hc nf 7/24/87 (#13, 2 wk); (Charter) NYT pb fic 6/26/88 (#8, 2 wk), 4 wk; tot 19 wk.

The Spy Went Dancing (Putnam) NYT nf 3/18/90 (#10), pk 4/8/90 (#8, 1 wk), 6 wk; PW hc nf 3/23/90 (#10, 1 wk), 4 wk; tot 10 wk.

Grimes, Martha

The Five Bells and Baldebone (Little Brown) NYT fic 9/6/87 (#8, 1 wk), 7 wk; PW hc fic 9/11/87 (#10, 1 wk), 2 wk; (Dell) NYT pb fic 9/11/88 (#16), pk 9/18/88 (#4, 2 wk), 7 wk; PW mm pb 9/16/88 (#10), pk 10/7/88 (#3, 2 wk), 7 wk; tot 23 wk.

I Am the Only Running Footman (Dell) NYT pb fic 10/11/87 (#12, 2 wk), 5 wk; PW mm pb 10/16/87 (#7, 1 wk), 7 wk; tot 12 wk.

The Old Silent (Little Brown) PW hc fic 9/1/89 (#12), pk 9/22/89 (#5, 2 wk), 8 wk; NYT fic 9/3/89 (#7), pk 9/17/89 (#5, 1 wk), 8 wk; (Dell) NYT pb fic 9/9/90 (#12), pk 9/16/90 (#5, 1 wk), 5 wk; PW mm pb 9/14/90 (#8), pk 9/21/90 (#6, 3 wk), 6 wk; tot 27 wk.

Grimm, Jacob

Snow White and the Seven Dwarfs [trans. Randall Jarrell] (Farrar) NYT ch bst 5/6/73 (#3, 19 wk), 45 wk.

Grimm, Wilhelm

Dear Mili [illus. Maurice Sendak] (di Capua/Farrar) NYT fic 11/20/88 (#11), pk 11/27/88 (#5, 3 wk), 10 wk; PW hc fic 12/2/88 (#11), pk 12/23/88 (#7, 2 wk), 7 wk; tot 17 wk.

Griswold, Francis

A Sea Island Lady (Morrow) PW fic 1/13/40 (#9, 8 wk), 12 wk.

Grizzard, Lewis

Elvis Is Dead and I Don't Feel So Good Myself (Peachtree) NYT nf 11/25/84 (#13), pk 12/23/84 (#9, 2 wk), 14 wk.

Shoot Low, Boys—They're Ridin' Shetland Ponies (Peachtree) NYT nf 12/1/85 (#15), pk 12/22/85 (#9, 3 wk), 9 wk; PW hc nf 1/10/86 (#13, 1 wk), 3 wk; tot 12 wk.

My Daddy Was a Pistol, and I'm a Son of a Gun (Villard) NYT nf 10/19/86 (#15), pk 10/26/86 (#12, 1 wk), 3 wk.

Don't Bend Over in the Garden, Granny, You Know Them Taters Got Eyes (Villard) NYT nf 11/20/88 (#9), pk 12/4/88 (#6, 5 wk), 16 wk; PW hc fic 12/9/88 (#13), pk 1/6/89 (#6, 1 wk), 7 wk; tot 23 wk.

Chili Dawgs Always Bark at Night (Villard) NYT nf 11/5/89 (#17), pk 12/24/89 (#10, 3 wk), 10 wk.

If I Ever Get Back to Georgia, I'm Gonna Nail My Feet to the Ground (Villard) NYT nf 12/23/90 (#15), pk 12/30/90 (#11, 1 wk), 2 wk.

Groden, Robert J., and Harrison Edward Livingstone

High Treason (Berkley) NYT pb nf 11/4/90 (#8), pk 12/9/90 (#2, 1 wk), 8 wk.

Groseclose, Elgin

Ararat (Carrick & Evans) NYT fic 10/8/39 (#15, 4 wk).

Gross, Joel

The Books of Rachel (NAL/Signet) PW mm pb 1/16/81 (#15, pk 1/30/81 (#4, 1 wk), 9 wk; NYT mm pb 1/25/81 (#4, 5 wk, 9 wk; tot 18.

Maura's Dream (NAL/Signet) NYT mm pb 1/24/82 (#13), pk 2/7/82 (#11, 1 wk), 3 wk; PW mm pb 1/29/82 (#15, 1 wk); tot 4 wk.

Gross, Leonard
See Laurence E. Morehouse and_____

Gross, Milt
Nize Baby (Doran) PW nf 8/14/26 (#8), pk 9/18/26 (#6, 4 wk), 8 wk.
What's This? (Simon & Schuster) NYT gen 8/2/36 (#8, 4 wk).

Grossberger, Lewis
See Vic Ziegel and_____

Grosvenor, Loelia Ponsonby, Duchess of Windsor
Grace and Favour (Reynal) NYT gen 6/3/62 (#16, 1 wk).

Grover, Linda
See Emily Cho and_____

Grubb, Davis
The Night of the Hunter (Harper) NYT fic 3/14/54 (#13), pk 4/4/54 (#5, 7 wk), 17 wk; PW fic 4/10/54 (#8), pk 5/15/54 (#6, 1 wk), 3 wk; tot 20 wk.
A Dream of Kings (Scribners) NYT fic 10/23/55 (#15, 1 wk).

Gruelle, John B.
Raggedy Ann in Cookie Land (Volland) PW juv 9/19/31 (#9), pk 4/23/32 (#1, 4 wk), 28 wk.

Guareschi, Giovanni
The Little World of Don Camillo (Pellegrini & Cudahy) NYT fic 9/10/50 (#10), pk 10/29/50 (#6, 3 wk), 27 wk; PW fic 10/14/50 (#7), pk 1/13/51 (#6, 1 wk), 5 wk; tot 32 wk.
Don Camillo and His Flock (Pellegrini & Cudahy) NYT fic 8/31/52 (#14), pk 9/28/52 (#6, 1 wk), 25 wk; PW fic 9/27/52 (#5, 2 wk), 11 wk; tot 36 wk.
Don Camillo's Dilemma (Farrar) NYT fic 7/25/54 (#12), pk 8/22/54 (#11, 1 wk), 8 wk; PW fic 8/14/54 (#9, 1 wk); tot 9 wk.

Guedalla, Philip
Wellington (Harper) PW nf 1/16/32 (#6, 4 wk), 8 wk.
The Hundred Years (Doubleday) NYT nf 3/7/37 (#3, 4 wk), 8 wk; PW nf 3/13/37 (#3, 4 wk), 8 wk; tot 16 wk.
Mr. Churchill (Reynal & Hitchcock) PW nf 3/14/42 (#4, 4 wk), 8 wk.

Guest, Edgar E.
Passing Throng (Reilly) PW gen lit 7/21/23 (#11), pk 8/18/23 (#10, 4 wk), 8 wk.
Rhymes of Childhood (Reilly & Lee) PW nf 6/21/24 (#8, 4 wk).
Poems (Reilly & Lee) PW gen lit 6/20/25 (#8, 4 wk), 8 wk.
The Light of Faith (Reilly & Lee) PW nf 5/15/26 (#9, 8 wk).

Guest, Judith
Ordinary People (Viking) PW hc fic 8/16/76 (#10), pk 10/4/76 (#3, 1 wk), 17 wk; NYT fic 8/29/76 (#8), pk 9/26/76 (#4, 2 wk), 19 wk; (Ballantine) PW mm pb 7/18/77 (#7), pk 8/1/77 (#3, 1 wk), 24 wk; NYT mm pb 7/24/77 (#7), pk 9/4/77 (#5, 1 wk), 23 wk; tot 83 wk.
Second Heaven (Viking) NYT fic 10/31/82 (#13), pk 11/14/82 (#9, 1 wk), 15 wk; PW hc fic 11/26/82 (#15, 2 wk); (NAL/Signet) NYT mm pb 10/2/83 (#8), pk 10/23/83 (#3, 1 wk), 8 wk; PW mm pb 10/7/83 (#8), pk 10/28/83 (#2, 1 wk), 10 wk; tot 35 wk.

Guild, Caroline
Rainbow in Tahiti (Doubleday) NYT gen 4/18/48 (#16), pk 4/25/48 (#13, 2 wk), 3 wk.

Guiles, Fred Lawrence
Norma Jean: The Life of Marilyn Monroe (Paragon) NYT gen 8/3/69 (#8, 1 wk).

Guinness, Alec
Blessings in Disguise (Knopf) NYT nf 3/30/86 (#15), pk 4/20/86 (#4, 1 wk), 11 wk; PW hc nf 4/18/86 (#12), pk 5/2/86 (#8, 1 wk), 6 wk; tot 17 wk.

Gulbranssen, Trygve
Beyond Sing the Woods (Putnam) PW fic 6/13/36 (#7, 8 wk), 12 wk.
The Wind from the Mountains (Putnam) NYT fic 7/4/37 (#1, 4 wk); PW fic 7/10/37 (#5), pk 8/14/37 (#4, 4 wk), 16 wk; tot 20 wk.

Gunther, John
Inside Europe (Harper) NYT nf 4/5/36 (#4), pk 5/3/36 (#2, 4 wk), 32 wk; PW nf 4/11/36 (#5), pk 5/9/36 (#4, 12 wk), 48 wk; tot 80 wk.
Inside Asia (Harper) NYT gen 7/9/39 (#2), pk 8/6/39 (#1, 4 wk), 20 wk; PW nf 7/15/39 (#1, 16 wk), 36 wk; tot 56 wk.
Inside Europe: 1940 War Edition (Harper) PW nf 3/9/40 (#3, 4 wk), 20 wk.
Inside Latin America (Harper) PW nf 12/13/41 (#2), pk 1/17/42 (#1, 8 wk), 28 wk.
D Day (Harper) NYT gen 4/2/44 (#9), pk 5/28/44 (#5, 1 wk), 17 wk; PW nf 4/8/44 (#5), pk 4/29/44 (#4, 2 wk), 6 wk; tot 23 wk.
The Troubled Midnight (Harper) NYT fic 3/25/45 (#13), pk 4/1/45 (#10, 1 wk), 2 wk.
Inside U.S.A. (Harper) NYT gen 6/15/47 (#8), pk 6/29/47 (#1, 26 wk), 59 wk; PW nf 6/28/47 (#3), pk 7/5/47 (#1, 23 wk), 47 wk; tot 106 wk.
Death Be Not Proud (Harper) NYT gen 2/27/49 (#11), pk 4/3/49 (#5, 2 wk), 13 wk; PW nf 3/26/49 (#4, 2 wk), 6 wk; tot 19 wk.
Behind the Curtain (Harper) NYT gen 7/3/49 (#6), pk 7/24/49 (#4, 3 wk), 16 wk;

PW nf 7/16/49 (#8), pk 7/23/49 (#3, 1 wk), 7 wk; tot 23 wk.

Roosevelt in Retrospect (Harper) NYT gen 6/18/50 (#8), pk 7/9/50 (#1, 5 wk), 17 wk; PW nf 7/1/50 (#2), pk 7/8/50 (#1, 5 wk), 11 wk; tot 28 wk.

The Riddle of MacArthur (Harper) NYT gen 2/25/51 (#7), pk 5/20/51 (#5, 1 wk), 18 wk; PW nf 3/17/51 (#8), pk 6/2/51 (#5, 1 wk), 5 wk; tot 23 wk.

Eisenhower (Harper) NYT gen 2/17/52 (#10), pk 2/24/52 (#8, 2 wk), 8 wk; PW nf 3/15/52 (#8, 1 wk); tot 9 wk.

Inside Africa (Harper) NYT gen 10/9/55 (#13), pk 11/6/55 (#2, 13 wk), 31 wk; PW nf 10/29/55 (#2, 13 wk), 20 wk; tot 51 wk.

Inside Russia Today (Harper) NYT gen 4/27/58 (#6), pk 7/6/58 (#1, 11 wk), 37 wk; PW nf 5/5/58 (#4), pk 5/26/58 (#1, 14 wk), 34 wk; tot 71 wk.

Taken at the Flood (Harper) NYT gen 9/18/60 (#13), pk 11/20/60 (#9, 1 wk), 23 wk; PW nf 10/3/60 (#8, 1 wk), 3 wk; tot 26 wk.

Inside Europe Today (Harper) NYT gen 7/30/61 (#12), pk 8/20/61 (#4, 12 wk), 21 wk; PW nf 8/7/61 (#7), pk 8/21/61 (#3, 2 wk), 19 wk; tot 40 wk.

The Lost City (Harper) PW fic 11/2/64 (#10), pk 11/23/64 (#7, 3 wk), 9 wk; NYT fic 11/29/64 (#10, 1 wk); tot 10 wk.

Inside South America (Harper) NYT gen 2/26/67 (#7), pk 3/12/67 (#6, 4 wk), 13 wk; PW nf 3/6/67 (#7), pk 4/10/67 (#4, 2 wk), 15 wk; tot 28 wk.

Guptill, Arthur Leighton
Norman Rockwell, Illustrator (Watson Guptill) NYT gen 1/10/71 (#7, 1 wk).

Gurganus, Allan
The Oldest Living Confederate Widow Tells All (Knopf) NYT fic 9/17/89 (#7), pk 10/1/89 (#4, 1 wk), 16 wk; PW hc fic 9/22/89 (#11), pk 10/6/89 (#5, 3 wk), 11 wk; (Ivy) NYT pb fic 9/30/90 (#10), pk 10/7/90 (#7, 4 wk), 12 wk; PW mm pb 10/5/90 (#12), pk 10/12/90 (#5, 3 wk), 12 wk; tot 51 wk.

Gutelle, Andrew
Baseball's Best: Five True Stories (Random) PW ch yr rd 9/28/90 (#5, 4 wk).

Guth, Dorothy Lobrano
See E.B. White and_____

Guthman, Edwin O.
See Robert Kennedy

Guthrie, Alfred Bertram, Jr.
The Big Sky (Sloane) NYT fic 5/25/47 (#12), pk 6/8/47 (#4, 3 wk), 21 wk; PW fic 6/14/47 (#8), pk 6/21/47 (#4, 1 wk), 7 wk; tot 28 wk.

The Way West (Sloane) NYT fic 10/30/49 (#7), pk 11/20/49 (#4, 8 wk), 19 wk; PW fic 11/12/49 (#6), pk 1/14/50 (#3, 2 wk), 14 wk; tot 33 wk.

These Thousand Hills (Houghton) NYT fic 12/16/56 (#13), pk 1/20/57 (#10, 1 wk), 9 wk.

Gwynne, Fred
A Chocolate Moose for Dinner (Dutton/Windmill) NYT ch pb 11/13/77 (#8, 46 wk).

H&R Block
H&R Block Income Tax Workbook (Macmillan/Triangle) NYT td pb 3/10/74 (#9, 4 wk).

H&R Block Income Tax Workbook [1985] (Macmillan/Collier) NYT msc pb 1/20/85 (#6), pk 2/24/85 (#5, 2 wk), 6 wk; PW td pb 2/8/85 (#6, 1 wk), 3 wk; tot 9 wk.

H&R Block Income Tax Workbook [1986] (Macmillan/Collier) NYT msc pb 2/16/86 (#5, 2 wk); PW td pb 3/7/86 (#10), pk 3/28/86 (#8, 1 wk), 5 wk; tot 7 wk.

H&R Block 1987 Income Tax Guide and Workbook (Macmillan/Collier) PW td pb 3/13/87 (#10, 1 wk).

Haas, Peter
Manhunt (Random) NYT nf 6/29/86 (#15, 1 wk); (Jove) NYT pb nf 5/3/87 (#9, 1 wk), 2 wk; tot 3 wk.

Haas, Dr. Robert
Eat to Win: The Sports Nutrition Bible (Rawson/Scribner) NYT msc 4/1/84 (#1, 28 wk), 36 wk; PW hc nf 4/6/84 (#7), pk 4/20/84 (#1, 17 wk), 39 wk; (NAL/Signet) NYT msc pb 2/3/85 (#3), pk 2/10/85 (#1, 10 wk), 43 wk; PW mm pb 2/8/85 (#15), pk 2/15/85 (#2, 2 wk), 15 wk; tot 133 wk.

Eat to Succeed: The Haas Maximum Performance Program (Rawson) NYT msc 2/23/86 (#5, 4 wk); PW hc nf 2/28/86 (#14), pk 3/14/86 (#9, 2 wk), 7 wk; tot 11 wk.

Habe, Hans
A Thousand Shall Fall (Harcourt) PW nf 10/11/41 (#8, 4 wk).

Haber, Heinz
The Walt Disney Story of Our Friend the Atom (Golden) NYT ch bst 11/17/57 (#2, 40 wk).

Haber, Joyce
The Users (Delacorte) NYT fic 12/12/76 (#5), pk 3/6/77 (#4, 2 wk), 15 wk; PW hc fic 12/13/76 (#8), pk 2/14/77 (#5, 2 wk), 14 wk; (Dell) PW mm pb 7/25/77 (#11), pk 8/8/77 (#3, 2 wk), 8 wk; NYT mm pb 7/31/77 (#10), pk 8/14/77 (#3, 1 wk), 9 wk; tot 46 wk.

Hachiya, Michihiko
Hiroshima Diary (Univ. of North Carolina)

NYT gen 8/28/55 (#11), pk 10/2/55 (#7, 1 wk), 9 wk; PW nf 10/15/55 (#9, 1 wk); tot 10 wk.

Hackett, Francis
Henry the Eighth (Liveright) PW nf 5/11/29 (#3), pk 6/8/29 (#1, 12 wk), 28 wk.
Francis the First (Doubleday) PW nf 4/13/35 (#2), pk 5/11/35 (#1, 8 wk), 24 wk.
Queen Anne Boleyn (Doubleday) NYT fic 11/5/39 (#9, 4 wk); PW fic 11/11/39 (#10, 4 wk); tot 8 wk.

Hackett, Gen. Sir John, et al.
The Third World War: August 1985 (Macmillan) PW hc fic 4/9/79 (#12), pk 6/11/79 (#2, 4 wk), 50 wk; NYT fic 5/6/79 (#15), pk 6/10/79 (#3, 4 wk), 40 wk; (Berkley) PW mm pb 4/11/80 (#2, 1 wk), 10 wk; NYT mm pb 4/13/80 (#5), pk 5/4/80 (#4, 2 wk), 9 wk; tot 109 wk.

Hackett, Pat
See Andy Warhol and_____

Hackworth, David H., and Julie Sherman
About Face: Odyssey of an American Warrior (Simon & Schuster) NYT nf 5/14/89 (#14), pk 5/28/89 (#6, 1 wk), 13 wk; PW hc nf 5/26/89 (#15), 6/16/89 (#14, 1 wk), 2 wk; tot 15 wk.

Hader, Berta and Elmer Hader
The Farmer in the Dell (Macmillan) PW juv 12/19/31 (#5, 4 wk).

Hagan, Patricia
Passion's Fury (Avon) NYT mm pb 7/26/81 (#12, 1 wk).
Love and Glory (Avon) NYT mm pb 4/25/82 (#14), pk 5/2/82 (#12, 1 wk), 2 wk; PW mm pb 5/7/82 (#15, 1 wk); tot 3 wk.

Hagedorn, Hermann
The Book of Courage (Winston) PW juv 3/15/30 (#10), pk 8/23/30 (#5, 4 wk), 32 wk.
The Roosevelt Family of Sagamore Hill (Macmillan) NYT gen 9/5/54 (#14), pk 9/26/54 (#8, 5 wk), 14 wk; PW nf 10/16/54 (#9), pk 11/13/54 (#6, 1 wk), 4 wk; tot 18 wk.

Hagopian, Richard
The Dove Brings Peace (Farrar) NYT fic 5/7/44 (#15, 1 wk).

Hahn, Emily
The Soong Sisters (Doubleday) PW nf 6/14/41 (#6, 4 wk), 8 wk; NYT gen 4/25/43 (#15, 1 wk), 2 wk; tot 10 wk.
China to Me (Doubleday) NYT fic 12/17/44 (#19), pk 3/4/45 (#4, 1 wk), 25 wk; PW nf 2/10/45 (#7, 3 wk), 4 wk; tot 29 wk.
England to Me (Doubleday) NYT gen 2/20/49 (#12, 1 wk).

Haig, Alexander M, Jr.
Caveat: Realism, Reagan and Foreign Policy (Macmillan) NYT nf 5/6/84 (#12), pk 5/20/84 (#7, 1 wk), 10 wk; PW hc nf 5/11/84 (#12), pk 6/1/84 (#6, 1 wk), 10 wk; tot 20 wk.

Hailey, Arthur
Hotel (Doubleday) NYT fic 2/28/65 (#10), pk 4/25/65 (#3, 8 wk), 44 wk; PW fic 3/15/65 (#10), pk 5/24/65 (#3, 5 wk), 50 wk; NYT pb fic 8/7/66 (#1, 16 wk), 32 wk; tot 126 wk.
Airport (Doubleday) NYT fic 3/31/68 (#7), pk 4/7/68 (#1, 30 wk), 64 wk; PW fic 4/1/68 (#7), pk 4/15/68 (#1, 28 wk), 63 wk; (Bantam) NYT pb fic 8/3/69 (#1, 24 wk), 56 wk; tot 183 wk.
Wheels (Doubleday) NYT fic 10/3/71 (#7), pk 11/7/71 (#1, 7 wk), 33 wk; PW fic 10/11/71 (#3), pk 11/15/71 (#1, 6 wk), 34 wk; NYT pb fic 2/11/73 (#3), pk 3/11/73 (#2, 4 wk), 16 wk; tot 83 wk.
The Moneychangers (Doubleday) NYT fic 3/30/75 (#5), pk 5/4/75 (#1, 14 wk), 37 wk; PW fic 3/31/75 (#6), pk 4/28/75 (#1, 12 wk), 35 wk; (Bantam) PW mm pb 2/16/76 (#3), pk 2/23/76 (#1, 3 wk), 22 wk; NYT mm pb 2/22/76 (#4), pk 3/7/76 (#1, 2 wk), 18 wk; tot 112 wk.
Overload (Doubleday) PW hc fic 1/15/79 (#14), pk 3/26/79 (#1, 2 wk), 24 wk; NYT fic 1/28/79 (#7), pk 2/25/79 (#1, 2 wk), 19 wk; (Bantam) PW mm pb 1/25/80 (#15), pk 2/8/80 (#5, 1 wk), 9 wk; NYT mm pb 1/27/80 (#7), pk 2/3/80 (#2, 2 wk), 12 wk; tot 64 wk.
Strong Medicine (Doubleday) NYT fic 9/30/84 (#10), pk 10/21/84 (#3, 2 wk), 21 wk; PW hc fic 10/12/84 (#8), pk 10/26/84 (#3, 1 wk), 17 wk; (Dell) NYT pb fic 12/29/85 (#13), pk 1/19/86 (#3, 4 wk), 14 wk; PW mm pb 1/10/86 (#8), pk 1/17/86 (#3, 5 wk), 10 wk; tot 62 wk.
The Evening News (Doubleday) PW hc fic 4/13/90 (#12), pk 5/4/90 (#5, 1 wk), 11 wk; NYT fic 4/15/90 (#9), pk 4/22/90 (#5, 1 wk), 9 wk; tot 20 wk.

Hailey, Elizabeth Forsythe
A Woman of Independent Means (Avon) PW mm pb 8/13/79 (#11), pk 11/12/79 (#10, 1 wk), 17 wk; NYT mm pb 8/26/79 (#13), pk 9/9/79 (#11, 1 wk), 9 wk; tot 26 wk.
Life Sentences (Delacorte) NYT fic 11/7/82 (#12), pk 11/21/82 (#11, 2 wk), 14 wk; PW hc fic 11/12/82 (#10, 2 wk), 14 wk; (Dell) NYT mm pb 11/13/83 (#11), pk 11/20/83 (#6, 2 wk), 7 wk; PW mm pb 11/18/83 (#7), pk 12/9/83 (#5, 1 wk), 7 wk; tot 42 wk.
Joanna's Husband and David's Wife (Delacorte) NYT fic 3/23/86 (#15), pk 4/13/86 (#7, 1 wk), 8 wk; PW hc fic 3/28/86 (#14),

pk 4/4/86 (#11, 1 wk), 6 wk; (Dell) NYT pb
fic 3/8/87 (#4), pk 4/12/87 (#2, 1 wk), 8 wk;
PW mm pb 3/13/87 (#7), pk 3/27/87 (#5, 1
wk), 9 wk; tot 31 wk.

Haines, William Wister
Command Decision (Little Brown) NYT
fic 2/2/47 (#14, 1 wk), 3 wk.

Haislet, Barbara
See Pat Blakely, et al.

Halasz, Nicholas
Captain Dreyfus (Grove) NYT gen 9/4/55
(#11, 1 wk), 3 wk.

Halberstam, David
The Best and the Brightest (Random) NYT
gen 12/3/72 (#6), pk 1/21/73 (#1, 2 wk), 36
wk; PW nf 12/11/72 (#2), pk 1/1/73 (#1, 7
wk), 32 wk; NYT pb gen 1/6/74 (#1, 4 wk);
tot 72 wk.
The Powers That Be (Knopf) PW hc nf
5/14/79 (#7), pk 5/28/79 (#2, 5 wk), 21 wk;
NYT nf 5/20/79 (#10), pk 5/27/79 (#2, 1
wk), 28 wk; tot 49 wk.
The Breaks of the Game (Knopf) NYT nf
12/27/81 (#15, 4 wk); PW hc nf 1/15/82 (#12,
1 wk), 4 wk; tot 8 wk.
The Amateurs (Morrow) NYT nf 8/18/85
(#9), pk 9/1/85 (#6, 1 wk), 9 wk; PW hc nf
9/6/85 (#14), pk 9/13/85 (#11, 1 wk), 3 wk;
tot 12 wk.
*The Reckoning: An Authoritative Examina-
tion of the Automobile Industry* (Morrow)
NYT nf 10/12/86 (#15), pk 11/2/86 (#3, 1 wk),
27 wk; PW hc nf 10/24/86 (#14), pk 11/7/86
(#5, 1 wk), 21 wk; (Avon) NYT pb nf 9/20/87
(#10), pk 11/8/87 (#8, 1 wk), 7 wk; tot 55 wk.
Summer of '49 (Morrow) NYT nf 5/28/89
(#7), pk 7/2/89 (#1, 1 wk), 19 wk; PW hc nf
6/2/89 (#12), pk 6/30/89 (#2, 2 wk), 15 wk;
(Avon) NYT pb nf 4/8/90 (#5), pk 4/22/90
(#3, 1 wk), 21 wk; tot 55 wk.

**Haldeman, H.R., with Joseph
DiMona**
The Ends of Power (Times Books) PW hc
fic 3/6/78 (#9), pk 3/13/78 (#2, 3 wk), 12 wk;
NYT nf 3/12/78 (#11), pk 3/19/78 (#1, 2 wk),
10 wk; tot 22 wk.

Hale, Bryant
See Deems Taylor, et al.

Hale, Judson
See Anonymous (Old Farmer's Almanac)

Hale, Nancy
The Prodigal Women (Scribner) PW fic
10/17/42 (#3, 5 wk), 14 wk; NYT fic 10/18/42
(#16), pk 11/8/42 (#2, 1 wk), 26 wk; tot 40 wk.
The Sign of Jonah (Scribner) NYT fic 11/12/
50 (#16), pk 11/26/50 (#13, 2 wk), 6 wk.

A New England Girlhood (Little Brown)
NYT gen 6/29/58 (#14, 2 wk), 5 wk.

Haley, Alex
Roots (Doubleday) PW hc nf 10/4/76 (#7),
pk 12/13/76 (#1, 15 wk), 39 wk; NYT gen
10/10/76 (#5), pk 11/21/76 (#1, 22 wk), 47 wk;
(Dell) PW mm pb 11/14/77 (#4), pk 11/21/77
(#2, 4 wk), 11 wk; NYT mm pb 11/20/77 (#3),
pk 11/27/77 (#1, 1 wk), 12 wk; 109 wk.
See also Malcolm Little and____

Haley, J. Evetts
George W. Littlefield: Texan (Univ. of Oklahoma) NYT gen 11/28/43 (#16), pk 12/12/43
(#12, 1 wk), 5 wk.

Hall, Douglas Kent
See Arnold Schwarzenegger and____

Hall, James Norman
Lost Island (Little Brown) NYT fic 6/25/
44 (#11, 2 wk), 3 wk.
The Far Lands (Little Brown) NYT fic 12/
31/50 (#13), pk 1/14/51 (#12, 1 wk), 3 wk.
My Island Home (Little Brown) NYT gen
1/4/53 (#13, 1 wk).
See also Charles B. Nordhoff and____

Hall, Josef Washington
Behind the Face of Japan [as by Upton
Close] (Appleton) NYT nf 11/29/42 (#21),
pk 12/13/42 (#16, 1 wk), 2 wk.

Hall, Melvin Adams
Journey to the End of an Era (Scribner)
NYT gen 4/20/47 (#14, 1 wk).

Hall, Oakley M.
Corpus of Joe Bailey (Viking) NYT fic 5/3/
53 (#15), pk 5/10/53 (#10, 1 wk), 6 wk.
Warlock (Viking) NYT fic 10/5/58 (#16, 1
wk).

Hall, Radclyffe
The Well of Loneliness (Covici Friede) PW
fic 5/11/29 (#10), pk 6/8/29 (#9, 4 wk), 8
wk.

Hall, Rich
Unexplained Sniglets of the Universe (Col-
lier/Macmillan) PW td pb 5/16/86 (#8), pk
5/30/86 (#7, 1 wk), 6 wk; NYT msc pb 5/18/
86 (#6), pk 6/1/86 (#4, 1 wk), 4 wk; tot 10
wk.

____, and Friends
Sniglets (Collier/Macmillan) NYT msc pb
6/10/84 (#6), pk 12/29/85 (#2, 1 wk), 40 wk;
PW td pb 6/15/84 (#9), pk 7/6/84 (#3, 2 wk),
33 wk; tot 73 wk.
More Sniglets (Collier/Macmillan) PW td
pb 4/26/85 (#8), pk 5/3/85 (#6, 1 wk), 13 wk;
NYT msc pb 4/28/85 (#9), pk 5/26/85 (#5,
1 wk), 18 wk; tot 31 wk.

Hall, Rubylea
The Great Tide (Duell Sloan & Pearce) NYT fic 11/2/47 (#16, 1 wk).

Halle, Louis Joseph
Spring in Washington (Atheneum) NYT gen 5/18/47 (#16, 2 wk).

Halley, H.H.
Halley's Bible Handbook (Zondervan) PW hc rel 11/9/90 (#15, 4 wk).

Halliburton, Richard
The Royal Road to Romance (Bobbs Merrill) PW nf 2/19/27 (#7), pk 4/23/27 (#5, 12 wk), 36 wk.
The Glorious Adventure (Bobbs Merrill) PW nf 7/30/27 (#2, 4 wk), 20 wk.
New Worlds to Conquer (Bobbs Merrill) PW nf 1/11/30 (#2, 4 wk), 16 wk.
The Flying Carpet (Bobbs Merrill) PW nf 1/14/33 (#3, 8 wk), 12 wk.
Seven League Boots (Bobbs Merrill) NYT gen 12/1/35 (#10, 4 wk); PW nf 1/11/36 (#9, 4 wk); tot 8 wk.
Richard Halliburton: His Story of His Life's Adventure (Bobbs Merrill) PW nf 8/10/40 (#5, 4 wk), 12 wk.

Hallinan, Nancy
Rough Winds of May (Harper) NYT fic 4/24/55 (#16, 1 wk).

Hallinan, Vincent
A Lion in Court (Putnam) PW nf 3/4/63 (#8), pk 4/8/63 (#7, 1 wk), 4 wk.

Halsey, Margaret
With Malice Toward Some (Simon & Schuster) PW nf 9/10/38 (#9), pk 10/15/38 (#1, 8 wk), 32 wk; NYT gen 10/9/38 (#1, 8 wk), 36 wk; tot 68 wk.
Some of My Best Friends Are Soldiers (Simon & Schuster) NYT fic 10/22/44 (#9, 2 wk), 4 wk.
Color Blind (McGraw) NYT gen 11/3/46 (#15), pk 11/17/46 (#11, 1 wk), 3 wk.

Halsey, Fleet Admiral William F., and Lt. Cmdr. J. Bryan III
Admiral Halsey's Story (Whittlesey) NYT gen 11/30/47 (#16), pk 12/7/47 (#14, 1 wk), 4 wk.

Halsman, Philippe
Frenchman: A Photographic Interview (Simon & Schuster) NYT gen 12/4/49 (#12), pk 12/11/49 (#9, 2 wk), 10 wk.

Halter, Marek
The Book of Abraham (Holt) NYT fic 5/18/86 (#8), pk 6/1/86 (#6, 1 wk), 6 wk; PW hc fic 5/23/86 (#11), pk 6/6/86 (#9, 1 wk), 5 wk; tot 11 wk.

Hamilton, Thomas J.
Appeasement's Child (Knopf) NYT nf 3/21/43 (#7, 1 wk), 6 wk.

Hamlin, Helen
Nine-Mile Bridge (Norton) NYT gen 7/29/45 (#13), pk 8/12/45 (#19, 1 wk), 2 wk.

Hammarskjold, Dag
Markings (Knopf) NYT gen 11/15/64 (#5), pk 12/20/64 (#1, 31 wk), 46 wk; PW nf 11/23/64 (#5), pk 1/4/65 (#1, 29 wk), 52 wk; tot 98 wk.

Hammer, Armand, and Neil Lyndon
Hammer: A Witness to History (Putnam) NYT nf 5/17/87 (#11), pk 6/21/87 (#2, 2 wk), 18 wk; PW hc nf 5/22/87 (#9), pk 5/29/87 (#2, 5 wk), 17 wk; tot 35 wk.

Hammett, Dashiell
The Thin Man (Knopf) PW fic 2/10/34 (#5, 8 wk), 12 wk.

Hammond, John Hays
The Autobiography of John Hays Hammond (Farrar) PW nf 5/11/35 (#10), pk 8/10/35 (#6, 4 wk), 16 wk.

Hancock, Ralph
Fabulous Boulevard (Funk & Wagnalls) NYT gen 10/16/49 (#15), pk 11/13/49 (#12, 1 wk), 3 wk.

Hand, Learned
The Spirit of Liberty: Papers and Addresses of Learned Hand [ed. Irving Dilliard] (Knopf) NYT gen 6/15/52 (#14), pk 7/27/52 (#12, 1 wk), 7 wk.

Handford, Martin
The Great Waldo Search (Little Brown) NYT msc 12/17/89 (#2), pk 4/29/90 (#1, 8 wk), 55 wk; PW ch pic 8/31/90 (#2, 8 wk), 20 wk; tot 75 wk.
Where's Waldo? The Ultimate Fun Book! (Little Brown) NYT msc 10/7/90 (#3), pk 12/9/90 (#2, 3 wk), 13 wk; PW ch pic 11/30/90 (#6), pk 12/21/90 (#4, 4 wk), 8 wk; NYT msc pb 12/2/90 (#5, 3 wk); tot 24 wk.
Find Waldo Now (Little Brown) PW ch pc 8/31/90 (#4, 8 wk), 12 wk; NYT msc 12/2/90 (#1, 2 wk), 4 wk; tot 16 wk.

Hannibal, Edward
Chocolate Days, Popsicle Weeks (Houghton) NYT pb fic 9/12/71 (#5, 4 wk).

Hanighen, F.C.
See H.C. Engelbrecht and_____

Hans, Marcie
The Executive Coloring Book (Funny Products Co.) NYT gen 3/4/62 (#16), pk 3/25/62 (#14, 2 wk), 5 wk.

Hanson, Lawrence, and Elisabeth Hanson
Noble Savage: The Life of Paul Gaugin (Random) NYT gen 2/27/55 (#13, 1 wk).

Harding, Bertita Leonarz
Golden Fleece (Bobbs Merrill) NYT nf 4/4/37 (#7, 4 wk); PW nf 4/10/37 (#9, 8 wk); tot 12 wk.
Farewell 'Toinette (Bobbs Merrill) NYT fic 5/1/38 (#7, 4 wk).
Imperial Twilight (Bobbs Merrill) NYT gen 11/5/39 (#7, 4 wk).
Amazon Throne (Bobbs Merrill) PW nf 7/12/41 (#8, 4 wk), 8 wk.
Lost Waltz: A Story of Exile (Bobbs Merrill) NYT gen 1/28/45 (#20), pk 4/8/45 (#18, 1 wk), 3 wk.

Hardwick, Elizabeth
Sleepless Nights (Vintage) NYT td pb 5/25/80 (#12, 1 wk), 3 wk.

Hardy, Lyndon
Secret of the Sixth Magic (Ballantine/Del Rey) NYT pb fic 9/9/84 (#13, 1 wk).

Hargrove, Marion
See Here Private Hargrove (Holt) NYT nf 8/30/42 (#14), pk 10/18/42 (#1, 15 wk), 41 wk; PW nf 9/12/42 (#10), pk 10/17/42 (#1, 14 wk), 32 wk; tot 73 wk.

Harley, Willard
His Needs, Her Needs (Revell) PW hc rel 11/9/90 (#18, 4 wk).

Harmon, Sandra
See Priscilla Beaulieu Presley with_____

Harrer, Heinrich
Seven Years in Tibet (Dutton) NYT gen 3/21/54 (#10), pk 5/2/54 (#5, 1 wk), 17 wk; PW nf 4/10/54 (#7), pk 4/24/54 (#5, 1 wk), 6 wk; tot 23 wk.

Harriman, Margaret Case
The Vicious Circle (Rinehart) NYT gen 3/25/51 (#15), pk 4/22/51 (#10, 1 wk), 7 wk.
Blessed Are the Debonair (Rinehart) NYT gen 8/26/56 (#14, 1 wk), 2 wk.
And the Price Is Right (World) NYT gen 2/9/58 (#16, 1 wk), 2 wk.

Harris, Jean
Stranger in Two Worlds (Macmillan) NYT nf 9/7/86 (#14), pk 9/21/86 (#12, 1 wk), 3 wk.

Harris, Joel Chandler
The Complete Tales of Uncle Remus (Houghton) NYT ch bst 11/18/56 (#7, 40 wk).

Harris, Laura
Aesop's Fables (Garden City) NYT ch bst 11/13/55 (#12, 40 wk).

Harris, Marilyn
Bledding Sorrow (Avon) PW mm pb 6/13/77 (#14, 1 wk).
This Other Eden (Avon) PW mm pb 4/10/78 (#15, 1 wk).

Harris, Middleton
The Black Book (Random) NYT td pb 4/14/74 (#9, 4 wk).

Harris, Ruth
Husbands and Lovers (Fawcett) NYT pb fic 5/11/86 (#14, 1 wk).
Modern Women (St. Martin's) NYT pb fic 9/9/90 (#13), pk 9/23/90 (#9, 1 wk), 3 wk.

Harris, Sydney J.
On the Contrary (Houghton) NYT gen 12/20/64 (#8, 1 wk).

Harris, Thomas
I'm OK—You're OK (Harper) PW nf 4/19/71 (#10), pk 8/21/72 (#1, 13 wk), 77 wk; NYT gen 4/16/72 (#9), pk 6/25/72 (#1, 23 wk), 70 wk; NYT pb gen 8/12/73 (#1, 16 wk), 24 wk; tot 171 wk.

Harris, Thomas
Black Sunday (Putnam) NYT fic 2/23/75 (#9), pk 4/13/75 (#6, 3 wk), 14 wk; PW fic 3/10/75 (#8), pk 3/31/75 (#4, 4 wk), 14 wk; (Bantam) mm pb 4/12/76 (#6), pk 4/19/76 (#5, 4 wk), 12 wk; NYT mm pb 4/18/76 (#5), pk 5/30/76 (#4, 1 wk), 12 wk; tot 52 wk.
Red Dragon (Putnam) NYT fic 12/20/81 (#14), pk 3/14/82 (#12, 1 wk), 9 wk; PW hc fic 1/22/82 (#14, 1 wk); (Bantam) NYT mm pb 10/10/82 (#8), pk 10/17/82 (#4, 4 wk), 9 wk; PW mm pb 10/15/82 (#10), pk 11/5/82 (#3, 1 wk), 8 wk; tot 27 wk.
The Silence of the Lambs (St. Martin's) PW hc fic 9/2/88 (#14), pk 10/14/88 (#8, 1 wk), 11 wk; NYT fic 9/11/88 (#14), pk 10/2/88 (#6, 2 wk), 8 wk; NYT pb fic 5/28/89 (#5), pk 6/11/89 (#3, 2 wk), 15 wk; PW mm pb 6/2/89 (#5), pk 7/7/89 (#2, 1 wk), 16 wk; tot 50 wk.

Harris, W.A.
The Illustrated Elvis (Grosset & Dunlap/Today Press) PW td pb 9/19/77 (#4), pk 9/26/77 (#2, 1 wk), 8 wk; NYT td pb 10/2/77 (#2), pk 10/9/77 (#1, 1 wk), 8 wk; tot 16 wk.

Harrison, Harry
A Stainless Steel Rat Is Born (Bantam) PW mm pb 10/18/85 (#12, 1 wk), 2 wk.

Harrison, Henry Sydnor
Saint Teresa (Houghton) PW fic 5/13/22 (#3), pk 6/17/22 (#2, 4 wk), 12 wk.

Harrison, Payne
Storming Intrepid (Crown) PW hc fic 2/10/89 (#15), pk 2/24/89 (#14, 3 wk), 4 wk; NYT fic 2/19/89 (#14, 3 wk); (Ivy) NYT pb fic

3/4/90 (#11), pk 3/18/90 (#8, 2 wk), 7 wk; PW mm pb 3/16/90 (#8, 1 wk), 4 wk; tot 18 wk.

Harrison, Richard E.
Look at the World (Knopf) NYT gen 7/23/44 (#10, 1 wk), 4 wk.

Hart, B.H., and Liddell Hart
See Erwin Rommel, et al.

Hart, Gary
A New Democracy: A Democratic Vision for the 1980s and Beyond (Morrow) PW td pb 4/20/84 (#9, 2 wk), 4 wk.

Hart, Hornell Norris
Autoconditioning (Prentice Hall) NYT gen 9/23/56 (#16), pk 10/7/56 (#13, 2 wk), 6 wk.

Hart, Moss
Act One (Random) NYT gen 10/4/59 (#13), pk 11/1/59 (#1, 19 wk), 41 wk; PW nf 10/5/59 (#7), pk 11/2/59 (#1, 14 wk), 36 wk; tot 77 wk.

Harte, Houston
In Our Image [illus. Guy Rowe] (Oxford Univ.) NYT gen 10/30/49 (#12, 1 wk).

Hartley, Leslie Poles
The Go-Between (Stein & Day) NYT fic 9/26/54 (#12, 1 wk), 2 wk.

Harvey, Kathryn
Butterfly (Avon) NYT pb fic 9/10/89 (#7), pk 9/24/89 (#3, 2 wk), 9 wk; PW mm pb 9/15/89 (#9), pk 10/6/89 (#2, 1 wk), 9 wk; tot 18 wk.

Harvey, Paul
Remember These Things (Heritage Foundation) NYT gen 2/22/53 (#13, 1 wk), 3 wk.
Paul Harvey's The Rest of the Story (Bantam) PW mm pb 12/25/78 (#14), pk 1/1/79 (#11, 1 wk), 3 wk.

Hatch, Alden
General Ike (Consolidated) NYT gen 8/12/45 (#17, 1 wk).

Hatch, Katherine
See Helen Hayes and_____

Hatcher, Harlan
Lake Erie (Bobbs Merrill) NYT gen 9/2/45 (#12), pk 10/7/45 (#9, 1 wk), 8 wk.
The Great Lakes (Oxford Univ.) NYT gen 1/14/45 (#20, 1 wk).

Hathaway, Katharine Butler
Little Locksmith (Coward McCann) NYT gen 11/21/43 (#20), pk 12/5/43 (#8, 1 wk), 7 wk.

Hathaway, Sandee E.
See Arlene Eisenberg, et al.

Hauck, Louise Platt
Whippoorwill House (Grosset & Dunlap) NYT fic 9/13/36 (#9, 4 wk).

Chan Osborne's Wife (Grosset & Dunlap) NYT fic 6/5/38 (#10, 4 wk).

Haugan, Randolph E.
Christmas: An American Annual of Christmas Literature and Art [1937] [ed.] (Augsburg) NYT gen 1/9/38 (#7, 4 wk).
Christmas: An American Annual of Christmas Literature and Art [1938] [ed.] (Augsburg) NYT gen 12/4/38 (#11), pk 1/8/39 (#5, 4 wk), 8 wk.
Christmas: An American Annual of Christmas Literature and Art [1939] [ed.] (Augsburg) NYT gen 12/10/39 (#3, 8 wk).

Hauman, George, and Doris Hauman
See Watty Piper

Hauser, Gayelord
Look Younger, Live Longer (Farrar) NYT gen 4/9/50 (#15), pk 10/15/50 (#1, 1 wk), 63 wk; PW nf 6/17/50 (#8), pk 10/21/50 (#2, 10 wk), 38 wk; tot 101 wk.
Mirror, Mirror on the Wall (Farrar) NYT gen 4/16/61 (#16), pk 5/21/61 (#6, 1 wk), 35 wk; PW nf 5/1/61 (#8), pk 6/19/61 (#6, 1 wk), 11 wk; tot 46 wk.

Hauser, Heinrich
The German Talks Back (Holt) NYT gen 10/21/45 (#8, 1 wk).

Havel, Vaclav
Disturbing the Peace (Knopf) PW hc nf 8/17/90 (#13, 1 wk); NYT nf 7/22/90 (#14), pk 7/29/90 (#13, 1 wk), 2 wk; tot 3 wk.

Havemann, Ernest, and Patricia Salter West
They Went to College (Harcourt) NYT gen 4/27/52 (#13, 2 wk), 5 wk.

Havighurst, Walter
The Long Ships Passing (Macmillan) NYT nf 8/9/42 (#11), pk 8/23/42 (#8, 1 wk), 18 wk.
The Heartland (Harper) NYT gen 11/25/62 (#16, 1 wk).

Haviland, Diana
The Passionate Pretenders (Fawcett) NYT mm pb 7/31/77 (#15, 1 wk).

Hawes, Elizabeth
Fashion Is Spinach (Random) NYT gen 5/1/38 (#6), pk 7/3/38 (#5, 4 wk), 16 wk; PW nf 6/11/38 (#5, 4 wk), 12 wk; tot 28 wk.
Men Can Take It (Random) NYT gen 7/9/39 (#15, 4 wk).
Why Women Cry: Or Wenches with Wrenches (Reynal & Hitchcock) NYT fic 12/19/43 (#11, 1 wk).

Hawking, Stephen W.
A Brief History of Time: From the Big Bang

to Black Holes (Bantam) NYT nf 4/24/88 (#3), pk 6/26/88 (#1, 19 wk), 112 wk; PW hc nf 4/29/88 (#8), pk 7/15/88 (#1, 16 wk), 98 wk; NYT pb nf 6/10/90 (#6), pk 7/1/90 (#3, 2 wk), 29 wk; PW td pb 6/22/90 (#1, 6 wk), 15 wk; (Dove Audio) aud nf 10/5/90 (#10), pk 11/2/90 (#4, 4 wk), 12 wk; tot 266 wk.

Hawley, Cameron
Executive Suite (Houghton) NYT fic 1/4/53 (#11), pk 2/15/53 (#10, 2 wk), 15 wk.
Cash McCall (Houghton) NYT fic 11/27/55 (#8), pk 1/8/55 (#3, 2 wk), 29 wk; PW fic 12/10/55 (#6), pk 12/24/55 (#3, 6 wk), 19 wk; tot 48 wk.
The Lincoln Lords (Little Brown) NYT fic 3/20/60 (#9), pk 5/15/60 (#4, 3 wk), 22 wk; PW fic 3/28/60 (#6), pk 5/2/60 (#4, 3 wk), 17 wk; tot 39 wk.
The Hurricane Years (Little Brown) NYT fic 10/20/68 (#8), pk 11/17/68 (#5, 8 wk), 23 wk; PW fic 10/21/68 (#10), pk 11/18/68 (#4, 2 wk), 21 wk; tot 44 wk.

Hawley, Lowell S.
See James Tucker Fisher and_____

Hawthorne, Hildegarde
California Missions: Their Romance and Beauty (Appleton) NYT gen 5/16/43 (#15, 1 wk).

Hay, Louise L.
You Can Heal Your Life (Hay House) NYT msc pb 4/24/88 (#2, 8 wk), 14 wk; PW td pb 4/29/88 (#3), pk 5/6/88 (#2, 1 wk), 16 wk; tot 30 wk.

Hayden, Naura
Everything You've Always Wanted to Know About Energy But Were Too Weak to Ask (Hawthorne) PW hc nf 5/2/77 (#9, 1 wk); NYT nf 5/15/77 (#8, 1 wk); (Pocket) PW mm pb 10/24/77 (#14, 1 wk); NYT mm pb 10/30/77 (#9, 1 wk), 4 wk; tot 7 wk.

Hayden, Nora
How to Satisfy a Woman Every Time (Bibli O'Phile/Dutton) NYT nf 6/12/83 (#15), pk 9/18/83 (#11, 1 wk), 10 wk.

Hayden, Sterling
Voyage: A Novel of 1896 (Putnam) PW hc fic 1/31/77 (#9), pk 3/14/77 (#5, 1 wk), 9 wk; NYT fic 2/6/77 (#9), pk 3/13/77 (#5, 1 wk), 10 wk; (Avon) NYT mm pb 1/29/78 (#12), pk 2/12/78 (#5, 2 wk), 9 wk; PW mm pb 1/30/78 (#6), pk 2/13/78 (#4, 1 wk), 9 wk; tot 37 wk.

Haydn, Hiram
By Nature Free (Bobbs Merrill) NYT fic 4/18/43 (#14, 1 wk).
The Time Is Noon (Crown) NYT fic 4/18/

48 (#16), pk 4/25/48 (#7, 3 wk), 11 wk; PW fic 5/15/48 (#10, 1 wk); tot 12 wk.

Haydn, Richard
The Journal of Edwin Carp (Simon & Schuster) NYT fic 10/3/54 (#15, 1 wk), 2 wk.

Hayek, Friedrich A.
The Road to Serfdom (Univ. of Chicago) NYT gen 4/1/45 (#11), pk 6/3/45 (#5, 3 wk), 16 wk; PW nf 5/12/45 (#8), pk 5/26/45 (#3, 1 wk), 3 wk; tot 19 wk.

Hayes, Alfred
The Girl on the Via Flaminia (Harper) NYT fic 4/10/49 (#16), pk 4/24/49 (#12, 1 wk), 4 wk.

Hayes, Bill, and William Hoffer
Midnight Express (Fawcett/Popular Library) PW mm pb 11/20/78 (#14), pk 12/25/78 (#4, 2 wk), 12 wk; NYT mm pb 12/3/78 (#12), pk 12/24/78 (#6, 1 wk), 14 wk; tot 26 wk.

Hayes, Helen, with Sandford Dody
On Reflection (Evans) NYT gen 11/17/68 (#6), pk 1/5/69 (#3, 1 wk), 15 wk; PW nf 12/9/68 (#8), pk 1/20/69 (#3, 1 wk), 13 wk; tot 28 wk.

_____, **with Lewis Funke**
A Gift of Joy (Evans) NYT gen 11/21/65 (#10), pk 1/2/66 (#4, 2 wk), 17 wk; PW nf 12/6/65 (#8), pk 12/27/65 (#4, 2 wk), 20 wk; NYT pb gen 11/6/66 (#3, 4 wk); tot 41 wk.

_____, **with Katherine Hatch**
My Life in Three Acts (Harcourt) PW hc nf 6/1/90 (#14), pk 6/8/90 (#13, 1 wk), 6 wk; NYT nf 6/3/90 (#9, 1 wk), 7 wk; tot 13 wk.

Hayes, Joseph A.
The Desperate Hours (Random) NYT fic 4/4/54 (#10), pk 5/9/54 (#9, 1 wk), 10 wk; PW fic 5/15/54 (#7, 1 wk); tot 11 wk.

Hayes, Marrijane
Bon Voyage (Random) NYT fic 2/24/57 (#15, 1 wk).

Hays, Arthur Garfield
City Lawyer: The Autobiography of a Law Practice (Simon & Schuster) NYT nf 9/13/42 (#12), pk 9/27/42 (#11, 1 wk), 4 wk.

Hayward, Brooke
Haywire (Knopf) PW hc nf 3/21/77 (#6), pk 5/16/77 (#3, 5 wk), 17 wk; NYT gen 3/27/77 (#10, 1 wk); NYT nf 4/3/77 (#8), pk 6/5/77 (#3, 3 wk), 16 wk; (Bantam) PW mm pb 3/20/78 (#7, 1 wk), 5 wk; NYT mm pb 4/9/78 (#14, 1 wk), 2 wk; tot 41 wk.

Hayward, Linda
The First Thanksgiving [illus. James Watling] (Random) PW ch yn rd 11/30/90 (#5), pk 12/21/90 (#2, 4 wk), 8 wk.

Hazlitt, Henry
Economics in One Lesson (Harper) NYT gen 9/22/46 (#15), pk 10/6/46 (#7, 1 wk), 3 wk.

Hazzard, Shirley
The Transit of Venus (Viking) NYT fic 5/4/80 (#14, 1 wk); (Playboy) PW mm pb 8/21/81 (#15), pk 8/28/81 (#14, 1 wk), 2 wk; tot 3 wk.

Head, Edith, and Jane Kesner Ardmore
The Dress Doctor (Little Brown) NYT gen 4/12/59 (#14), pk 5/31/59 (#11, 2 wk), 11 wk.

Head, John
See Anne Beatts and_____

Heald, Cynthia
Becoming a Woman of Excellence (NavPress) PW pb rel 11/9/90 (#5, 4 wk).

Heard, John
See Scott Turow

Hearst, Patricia Campbell
Every Secret Thing (Doubleday) NYT nf 2/28/82 (#15, 1 wk).

Heatter, Maida
Maida Heatter's Book of Great Chocolate Desserts (Knopf) NYT nf 2/15/81 (#15), pk 3/15/81 (#12, 1 wk), 4 wk.

Hebler, Dave
See Red West, et al.

Hebson, Ann
The Lattimer Legend (Macmillan) NYT fic 1/21/62 (#15, 1 wk).

Hecht, Ben
A Guide for the Bedevilled (Scribner) NYT gen 4/16/44 (#15), pk 6/11/44 (#7, 1 wk), 13 wk.
A Child of the Century (Simon & Schuster) NYT gen 7/4/54 (#12), pk 8/22/54 (#3, 6 wk), 24 wk; PW nf 7/31/54 (#5), pk 10/2/54 (#3, 1 wk), 14 wk; tot 38 wk.
Charlie (Harper) NYT gen 8/4/57 (#15), pk 9/1/57 (#13, 1 wk), 5 wk.

Hedrick, V.P.
The Land of the Crooked Tree (Oxford Univ.) NYT gen 12/26/48 (#15, 1 wk).

Heggen, Thomas
Mister Roberts (Houghton) NYT fic 9/15/46 (#13), pk 11/3/46 (#8, 2 wk), 28 wk; PW fic 11/16/46 (#9), pk 1/18/47 (#8, 1 wk), 3 wk; tot 31 wk.

Heiden, Konrad
Der Fuehrer (Houghton) NYT gen 2/20/44 (#10), pk 3/19/44 (#4, 1 wk), 8 wk; PW nf 3/11/44 (#3, 1 wk), 3 wk; tot 11 wk.

Heinlein, Robert A.
Time Enough for Love (Berkley) NYT mm pb 3/10/74 (#9, 4 wk).
The Number of the Beast (Fawcett/Columbine) PW td pb 8/8/80 (#10), pk 8/29/80 (#1, 4 wk), 15 wk; NYT td pb 8/17/80 (#10), pk 8/24/80 (#3, 3 wk), 15 wk; (Fawcett/Gold Medal) PW mm pb 7/9/82 (#13), pk 7/30/82 (#5, 1 wk), 5 wk; NYT mm pb 7/11/82 (#13), pk 7/25/82 (#9, 1 wk), 4 wk; tot 39 wk.
Friday (Holt) PW hc fic 5/14/82 (#9), pk 7/23/82 (#8, 1 wk), 15 wk; NYT fic 6/27/82 (#12), pk 7/18/82 (#8, 1 wk), 10 wk; (Ballantine/Del Rey) NYT mm pb 8/7/83 (#11), pk 8/14/83 (#5, 1 wk), 9 wk; PW mm pb 8/12/83 (#11), pk 8/26/83 (#5, 1 wk), 8 wk; tot 42 wk.
Job: A Comedy of Justice (Ballantine/Del Rey) NYT fic 9/2/84 (#14), pk 9/16/84 (#6, 1 wk), 11 wk; PW hc fic 9/7/84 (#10), pk 9/28/84 (#5, 1 wk), 13 wk; NYT pb fic 11/10/85 (#11), pk 11/17/85 (#9, 1 wk), 5 wk; PW mm pb 11/15/85 (#6, 1 wk), 6 wk; tot 35 wk.
The Cat Who Walks Through Walls (Putnam) NYT fic 11/17/85 (#14), pk 12/8/85 (#8, 1 wk), 11 wk; PW hc fic 11/22/85 (#9), pk 12/13/85 (#7, 2 wk), 10 wk; (Berkley) NYT pb fic 11/2/86 (#14), pk 11/16/86 (#3, 1 wk), 7 wk; PW mm pb 11/7/86 (#15), pk 11/21/86 (#4, 1 wk), 7 wk; tot 35 wk.
To Sail Beyond the Sunset (Putnam) PW hc fic 7/17/87 (#13), pk 7/24/87 (#9, 1 wk), 7 wk; NYT fic 7/19/87 (#13), pk 8/9/87 (#12, 1 wk), 5 wk; (Ace) NYT pb fic 6/12/88 (#10, 3 wk), 5 wk; PW mm pb 6/17/88 (#13), pk 7/8/88 (#5, 1 wk), 5 wk; tot 22 wk.

Heinrich, Willi
The Cross of Iron [trans. Richard Winston and Clara Winston] (Bobbs Merrill) NYT fic 5/20/56 (#15), pk 6/3/56 (#9, 1 wk), 7 wk.

Heiser, Victor G.
An American Doctor's Odyssey (Norton) NYT gen 10/4/36 (#2), pk 1/31/37 (#1, 4 wk), 32 wk; PW nf 10/10/36 (#5), pk 11/14/36 (#1, 16 wk), 64 wk; tot 96 wk.
You're the Doctor (Norton) PW nf 6/10/39 (#10), pk 7/15/39 (#9, 4 wk), 8 wk; NYT gen 6/11/39 (#4, 4 wk), 12 wk; tot 20 wk.

Heisler, John
See Lou Holtz and_____

Heller, Joseph
Catch-22 (Simon & Schuster) NYT pb fic 8/2/70 (#5), pk 10/4/70 (#2, 4 wk), 16 wk.
Something Happened (Knopf) PW fic 10/21/74 (#9), pk 11/4/74 (#2, 10 wk), 30 wk; NYT fic 10/27/74 (#9), pk 2/9/75 (#1, 1 wk), 29 wk; (Ballantine) NYT mm pb 9/21/75 (#4), pk 9/28/75 (#1, 4 wk), 18 wk; tot 77 wk.

Good as Gold (Simon & Schuster) PW hc fic 3/19/79 (#15), pk 4/2/79 (#2, 10 wk), 26 wk; NYT fic 3/25/79 (#14), pk 4/15/79 (#1, 2 wk), 25 wk; (Pocket) PW mm pb 1/18/80 (#3, 2 wk), 10 wk; NYT mm pb 1/20/80 (#5), pk 1/27/80 (#4, 1 wk), 9 wk; tot 70 wk.

God Knows (Knopf) NYT fic 10/7/84 (#10), pk 10/14/84 (#2, 2 wk), 16 wk; PW hc fic 10/12/84 (#10), pk 10/26/84 (#2, 1 wk), 15 wk; (Dell) PW mm pb 10/11/85 (#10), pk 10/18/85 (#9, 1 wk), 4 wk; NYT pb fic 10/13/85 (#10), pk 10/20/85 (#9, 1 wk), 4 wk; tot 39 wk.

_____, and **Speed Vogel**
No Laughing Matter (Putnam) NYT nf 3/16/86 (#10, 1 wk), 4 wk.

Hellman, Lillian
An Unfinished Woman: A Memoir (Little Brown) NYT gen 7/27/69 (#7), pk 8/31/69 (#6, 3 wk), 10 wk; PW nf 7/28/69 (#8), pk 10/6/69 (#5, 1 wk), 14 wk; tot 24 wk.

Pentimento (Little Brown) PW nf 10/8/73 (#9), pk 11/5/73 (#2, 1 wk), 17 wk; NYT gen 10/14/73 (#9), pk 11/4/73 (#3, 3 wk), 19 wk; tot 36 wk.

Scoundrel Time (Little Brown) PW hc nf 5/10/76 (#8), pk 6/7/76 (#2, 4 wk), 21 wk; NYT gen 5/16/76 (#7), pk 6/13/76 (#2, 5 wk), 23 wk; tot 44 wk.

Helm, MacKinley
Angel Mo' and Her Son Roland Hays (Little Brown) NYT nf 1/10/43 (#13, 4 wk).

Helprin, Mark
Winter's Tale (Harcourt) NYT fic 9/25/83 (#8), pk 10/16/83 (#6, 2 wk), 19 wk; PW hc fic 9/30/83 (#11), pk 10/28/83 (#9, 2 wk), 13 wk; (Pocket) NYT pb fic 8/12/84 (#13), pk 9/2/84 (#9, 2 wk), 8 wk; PW mm pb 8/17/84 (#10), pk 8/24/84 (#9, 2 wk), 8 wk; tot 48 wk.

Swan Lake (Ariel/Houghton) NYT fic 12/3/89 (#8, 1 wk), 7 wk.

Helyar, John
See Bryan Burrough and_____

Hemfelt, Robert
See Dr. Frank Minirth, et al.

_____, with **Frank Minirth** and **Paul Meier**
Love Is a Choice (Nelson) PW hc rel 10/5/90 (#4), pk 11/9/90 (#3, 4 wk), 8 wk.

Hemingway, Ernest
A Farewell to Arms (Scribner) PW fic 11/9/29 (#3), pk 12/14/29 (#2, 12 wk), 20 wk.

Death in the Afternoon (Scribner) PW nf 11/12/32 (#4, 4 wk), 12 wk.

To Have and Have Not (Scribner) NYT fic

11/7/37 (#10), pk 12/12/37 (#5, 4 wk), 8 wk; PW fic 11/13/37 (#5, 4 wk), 12 wk; tot 20 wk.

For Whom the Bell Tolls (Scribner) PW fic 11/16/40 (#3), pk 12/14/40 (#1, 8 wk), 32 wk.

Men at War [ed.] (Crown) NYT nf 11/22/42 (#18), pk 12/13/42 (#11, 1 wk), 4 wk.

Across the River and into the Trees (Scribner) NYT fic 9/24/50 (#2), pk 10/15/50 (#1, 7 wk), 21 wk; PW fic 9/30/50 (#4), pk 10/28/50 (#1, 3 wk), 15 wk; tot 36 wk.

The Old Man and the Sea (Scribner) NYT fic 9/14/52 (#13), pk 10/5/52 (#3, 1 wk), 26 wk; PW fic 10/4/52 (#4), pk 10/11/52 (#3, 2 wk), 15 wk; tot 41 wk.

Winner Take Nothing (Scribner) PW fic 12/9/33 (#9, 4 wk).

A Moveable Feast (Scribner) NYT gen 5/24/64 (#4), pk 6/14/64 (#1, 19 wk), 29 wk; PW nf 5/25/64 (#7), pk 6/22/64 (#1, 15 wk), 31 wk; NYT pb gen 12/5/65 (#1, 4 wk), 16 wk; tot 76 wk.

By-Line: Ernest Hemingway [ed. William White] (Scribner) PW nf 6/26/67 (#9), pk 7/3/67 (#7, 2 wk), 7 wk; NYT gen 6/18/67 (#9), pk 7/2/67 (#7, 1 wk), 5 wk; tot 12 wk.

Islands in the Stream (Scribner) NYT fic 10/18/70 (#6), pk 11/15/70 (#2, 10 wk), 24 wk; PW fic 10/26/70 (#4), pk 1/4/71 (#1, 1 wk), 28 wk; NYT pb fic 3/12/72 (#3, 4 wk); tot 56 wk.

The Dangerous Summer (Scribner) NYT nf 7/21/85 (#10, 1 wk), 7 wk; PW hc nf 8/9/85 (#15, 1 wk); tot 8 wk.

The Garden of Eden (Scribner) NYT fic 6/1/86 (#11), pk 6/15/86 (#5, 2 wk), 17 wk; PW hc fic 6/6/86 (#15), pk 6/20/86 (#5, 1 wk), 17 wk; tot 34 wk.

Hemon, Louis
Maria Chapdelaine (Macmillan) PW fic 5/13/22 (#5), pk 7/29/22 (#4, 4 wk), 20 wk.

Hemphill, Christopher
See Diana Vreeland, et al.

Henderson, Sir Neville
Failure of a Mission (Putnam) PW nf 5/11/40 (#8), pk 6/8/40 (#3, 4 wk), 12 wk.

Henderson, Thomas "Hollywood," and Peter Knobler
Out of Control: Confessions of an NFL Casualty (Putnam) PW hc nf 10/9/87 (#15), pk 10/16/87 (#12, 1 wk), 4 wk.

Hendra, Tony, with Christopher Cerf and Peter Elbling
The 80's: A Look Back at the Tumultuous Decade 1980–1989 [eds.] (Workman) NYT td pb 1/20/80 (#15), pk 2/10/80 (#13, 2 wk), 6 wk; PW td pb 1/25/80 (#6, 3 wk), 3 wk; tot 9 wk.

Hendrick, Burton J.
Life and Letters of Walter H. Page (Doubleday) PW gen lit 11/18/22 (#10), pk 1/27/23 (#3, 4 wk), 40 wk; PW nf 11/24/23 (#6), pk 12/19/25 (#2, 4 wk), 20 wk; tot 60 wk.

Hendrix, Harville
Getting the Love You Want: A Guide for Couples (Holt) NYT msc 8/21/88 (#4), pk 3/19/88 (#3, 1 wk), 7 wk; PW hc nf 8/26/88 (#8), pk 4/7/89 (#6, 2 wk), 12 wk; (Harper-Collins) PW td pb 10/12/90 (#10, 1 wk); tot 20 wk.

Hennessey, Joseph
See Alexander Woollcott, et al.

Hennig, Margaret, and Anne Jardim
The Managerial Woman (Doubleday/Anchor) NYT nf 8/7/77 (#10), pk 8/21/77 (#8, 2 wk), 12 wk; PW hc nf 9/19/77 (#10, 3 wk), 10 wk; tot 22 wk.

Henriques, Robert David Quixano
No Arms, No Armour (Farrar) PW fic 2/10/40 (#7, 4 wk), 8 wk.
Too Little Love (Viking) NYT fic 7/2/50 (#15), pk 7/30/50 (#8, 4 wk), 12 wk; PW fic 8/12/50 (#10), pk 8/19/50 (#5, 2 wk), 3 wk; tot 15 wk.
A Hundred Hours to Suez (Viking) NYT gen 4/28/57 (#16), pk 5/12/57 (#15, 1 wk), 2 wk.

Henry, Marguerite
Brighty of the Grand Canyon (Rand McNally) NYT ch bst 11/14/54 (#1, 40 wk).
Justin Morgan Had a Horse (Rand McNally) NYT ch bst 11/13/55 (#6, 40 wk).
Wagging Tails (Rand McNally) NYT ch bst 11/18/56 (#6, 40 wk).
Cinnabar, The One O'Clock Fox (Rand McNally) NYT ch bst 11/1/7/57 (#11, 40 wk).
Black Gold (Rand McNally) NYT ch bst 11/2/58 (#4, 40 wk).
Gaudenzia: Pride of the Palio (Rand McNally) NYT ch bst 5/14/61 (#15), pk 11/12/61 (#5, 26 wk), 46 wk.
Stormy: Misty's Foal (Rand McNally) NYT ch bst 5/10/64 (#6), pk 11/1/64 (#3, 25 wk), 44 wk.
The White Stallion of Lapizza (Rand McNally) NYT ch bst 11/7/65 (#6, 26 wk).
Mustang (Rand McNally) NYT ch bst 11/5/67 (#3, 26 wk).

Henry, Robert Selph
"First with the Most" Forrest (Bobbs Merrill) NYT gen 12/17/44 (#12), pk 1/7/45 (#18, 1 wk), 2 wk.

Hentges, Judith
See Pat Blakely, et al.

Hepburn, Katharine
The Making of "The African Queen" (Knopf) NYT nf 9/20/87 (#11), pk 10/4/87 (#7, 2 wk), 10 wk; PW hc nf 10/2/87 (#13), pk 11/6/87 (#8, 1 wk), 8 wk; tot 18 wk.

Herbert, A.P.
The Water Gipsies (Doubleday) PW fic 2/21/31 (#10, 8 wk).
Holy Deadlock (Doubleday) PW fic 9/15/34 (#6, 4 wk), 8 wk.

Herbert, Anthony B., and James T. Wooten
Soldier (Holt) NYT gen 3/4/73 (#10), pk 3/11/73 (#9, 3 wk), 6 wk; PW nf 4/16/73 (#10, 1 wk); tot 7 wk.

Herbert, Frank
Children of Dune (Putnam) PW hc fic 6/28/76 (#9, 1 wk); (Berkley) mm pb 2/21/77 (#10), pk 2/28/77 (#3, 3 wk), 12 wk; NYT mm pb 2/27/77 (#8), pk 3/13/77 (#5, 1 wk), 6 wk; tot 19 wk.
God Emperor of Dune (Putnam) PW hc fic 4/24/81 (#8), pk 6/19/81 (#3, 3 wk), 28 wk; NYT fic 4/26/81 (#14), pk 6/14/81 (#3, 3 wk), 25 wk; (Berkley) PW td pb 4/16/82 (#8), pk 4/30/82 (#4, 2 wk), 12 wk; NYT td pb 4/18/82 (#10), pk 5/9/82 (#5, 2 wk), 16 wk; NYT mm pb 5/15/83 (#14), pk 5/22/83 (#9, 1 wk), 7 wk; PW mm pb 5/20/83 (#11), pk 5/27/83 (#4, 1 wk), 7 wk; tot 95 wk.
The White Plague (Berkley) PW mm pb 12/16/83 (#7, 2 wk), 4 wk; NYT mm pb 12/18/83 (#10, 1 wk); NYT pb fic 1/1/84 (#11, 1 wk), 2 wk; tot 7 wk.
The Lazarus Effect (Berkley) PW mm pb 8/24/84 (#11, 1 wk).
Heretics of Dune (Putnam) NYT fic 4/8/84 (#13), pk 4/29/84 (#3, 1 wk), 20 wk; PW hc fic 4/13/84 (#8), pk 4/27/84 (#2, 1 wk), 19 wk; (Berkley) PW td pb 3/29/85 (#4, 1 wk), 5 wk; NYT pb fic 3/30/86 (#15), pk 4/20/86 (#11, 1 wk), 5 wk; PW mm pb 4/4/86 (#12, 1 wk), 3 wk; tot 52 wk.
Dune (Berkley) NYT pb fic 12/2/84 (#13), pk 1/6/85 (#1, 2 wk), 12 wk; PW mm pb 12/14/84 (#14), pk 1/18/85 (#1, 2 wk), 10 wk; tot 22 wk.
Dune Messiah (Berkley) NYT pb fic 1/20/85 (#15, 2 wk); PW mm pb 1/25/85 (#15, 2 wk); tot 4 wk.
Chapterhouse: Dune (Putnam) NYT FIC 4/21/85 (#14), pk 5/12/85 (#2, 2 wk), 16 wk; PW hc fic 4/26/85 (#8), pk 5/17/85 (#1, 1 wk), 16 wk; (Berkley) td pb 10/24/86 (#9, 1 wk), 2 wk; (Ace) NYT pb fic 7/12/87 (#14, 1 wk); tot 35 wk.

Herbert, Xavier
Capricornia (Appleton) NYT gen 5/23/43 (#11), pk 6/13/43 (#5, 1 wk), 19 wk; PW fic 6/5/43 (#5, 1 wk), 9 wk; tot 28 wk.

Hereford, Robert A.
Old Man River (Caxton) NYT nf 1/3/43 (#13), pk 1/10/43 (#10, 2 wk), 10 wk.

Hergesheimer, Joseph
Cytherea (Knopf) PW fic 4/1/22 (#5, 4 wk), 16 wk.
The Bright Shawl (Knopf) PW fic 12/23/22 (#12, 4 wk).
The Party Dress (Knopf) PW fic 5/17/30 (#7, 4 wk), 8 wk.
The Limestone Tree (Knopf) PW fic 2/21/31 (#7, 4 wk).

Herlihy, James Leo
All Fall Down (Dutton) NYT fic 9/11/60 (#15), pk 10/2/60 (#14, 1 wk), 2 wk.

Herman, Richard, Jr.
Force of Eagles (Fine) PW hc fic 3/30/90 (#13, 1 wk).

Herndon, William Henry
The Hidden Lincoln (Viking) NYT nf 4/3/38 (#13, 4 wk).

Herold, J. Christopher
Mistress to an Age (Bobbs Merrill) NYT gen 11/30/58 (#14, 1 wk).

Heron, Echo
Intensive Care (Ivy) NYT pb nf 7/3/88 (#10), pk 7/17/88 (#6, 1 wk), 7 wk.

Heron, Michael
See Erich von Daniken

Herr, Michael
Dispatches (Knopf) PW hc nf 1/23/78 (#15), pk 2/20/78 (#8, 1 wk), 10 wk; (Avon) PW td pb 10/16/78 (#6), pk 10/23/78 (#4, 2 wk), 4 wk; NYT td pb 11/12/78 (#11), pk 11/19/78 (#10, 2 wk), 5 wk; tot 19 wk.

Herriot, James
All Creatures Great and Small (St. Martin's) NYT gen 1/14/73 (#8), pk 3/25/73 (#5, 1 wk), 17 wk; PW nf 1/22/73 (#6, 4 wk), 18 wk; (Bantam) NYT pb gen 12/9/73 (#5), pk 1/6/74 (#3, 4 wk), 8 wk; mm pb 2/23/75 (#10), pk 3/2/75 (#8, 1 wk), 3 wk; tot 46 wk.
All Things Bright and Beautiful (St. Martin's) PW nf 10/7/74 (#7), pk 10/28/74 (#1, 10 wk), 28 wk; NYT gen 10/13/74 (#9), pk 11/17/74 (#1, 11 wk), 32 wk; (Bantam) mm pb 10/12/75 (#5), pk 10/26/75 (#1, 2 wk), 16 wk; PW mm pb 2/2/76 (#9, 1 wk), 2 wk; tot 78 wk.
All Things Wise and Wonderful (St. Martin's) PW hc nf 8/22/77 (#8), pk 9/19/77 (#1,

21 wk), 48 wk; NYT nf 9/4/77 (#8), pk 9/11/77 (#1, 24 wk), 50 wk; (Bantam) PW mm pb 9/18/78 (#5), pk 10/9/78 (#1, 1 wk), 17 wk; NYT mm pb 11/12/78 (#8), pk 12/3/78 (#3, 2 wk), 15 wk; tot 130 wk.
James Herriot's Yorkshire (St. Martin's) PW hc nf 11/12/79 (#12), pk 12/10/79 (#4, 4 wk), 20 wk; NYT nf 11/25/79 (#9), pk 12/23/79 (#3, 1 wk), 22 wk; NYT td pb 5/31/81 (#13), pk 6/28/81 (#12, 1 wk), 6 wk; tot 48 wk.
The Lord God Made Them All (St. Martin's) PW hc nf 5/8/81 (#7), pk 5/22/81 (#1, 8 wk), 45 wk; NYT nf 5/10/81 (#4), pk 5/17/81 (#1, 9 wk), 48 wk; (Bantam) PW mm pb 5/14/82 (#3), pk 5/28/82 (#1, 2 wk), 10 wk; NYT mm pb 5/16/82 (#2), pk 5/23/82 (#1, 2 wk), 12 wk; tot 115 wk.
The Best of James Herriot (St. Martin's) NYT nf 9/18/83 (#15), pk 12/11/83 (#2, 5 wk), 32 wk; PW hc nf 9/23/83 (#11), pk 12/9/83 (#3, 5 wk), 27 wk; tot 59 wk.
Moses and the Kitten (St. Martin's) NYT nf 10/14/84 (#15), pk 10/28/84 (#3, 3 wk), 30 wk; PW hc nf 11/2/84 (#13), pk 1/11/85 (#6, 1 wk), 14 wk; tot 44 wk.
Only One Woof (St. Martin's) NYT nf 11/17/85 (#14), pk 12/1/85 (#8, 2 wk), 15 wk; PW hc nf 12/20/85 (#14), pk 1/3/86 (#13, 1 wk), 3 wk; tot 18 wk.
James Herriot's Dog Stories (St. Martin's) NYT nf 5/18/86 (#16), pk 6/22/86 (#3, 8 wk), 43 wk; PW hc nf 5/30/86 (#13), pk 7/4/86 (#4, 2 wk), 29 wk; NYT pb nf 5/3/87 (#1, 1 wk), 24 wk; PW mm pb 5/8/87 (#12), pk 5/29/87 (#3, 1 wk), 8 wk; tot 104 wk.
The Christmas Day Kitten (St. Martin's) NYT nf 12/7/86 (#14), pk 12/14/86 (#6, 1 wk), 7 wk; PW hc nf 12/26/86 (#14), pk 1/9/87 (#12, 1 wk), 3 wk; tot 10 wk.

Hersey, John
Into the Valley (Knopf) NYT nf 3/7/43 (#11), pk 4/11/43 (#6, 1 wk), 9 wk.
A Bell for Adano (Knopf) NYT fic 3/5/44 (#10), pk 3/26/44 (#3, 2 wk), 33 wk; PW fic 3/11/44 (#4), pk 4/1/44 (#3, 2 wk), 20 wk; tot 53 wk.
Hiroshima (Knopf) NYT gen 12/1/46 (#15), pk 12/22/46 (#13, 1 wk), 5 wk.
The Wall (Knopf) NYT fic 3/12/50 (#9), pk 3/26/50 (#1, 5 wk), 34 wk; PW fic 3/25/50 (#4), pk 4/1/50 (#1, 4 wk), 22 wk; tot 56 wk.
A Single Pebble (Knopf) NYT fic 6/24/56 (#12), pk 8/12/56 (#4, 2 wk), 23 wk; PW fic 7/9/56 (#7), pk 8/20/56 (#4, 2 wk), 16 wk; tot 39 wk.
The War Lover (Knopf) NYT fic 10/25/59 (#11), pk 11/29/59 (#2, 1 wk), 22 wk; PW fic

11/2/59 (#7), pk 1/4/60 (#3, 1 wk), 14 wk; tot 36 wk.

The Child Buyer (Knopf) NYT fic 10/23/60 (#14), pk 11/13/60 (#8, 1 wk), 11 wk; PW fic 11/7/60 (#9), pk 11/14/60 (#5, 1 wk), 6 wk; tot 17 wk.

Under the Eye of the Storm (Knopf) PW fic 4/10/67 (#6, 1 wk), 8 wk; NYT fic 4/16/67 (#7, 1 wk), 6 wk; tot 14 wk.

The Algiers Motel Incident (Knopf) NYT pb gen 8/4/68 (#2), pk 9/1/68 (#1, 4 wk), 16 wk.

Blues (Knopf) NYT fic 7/19/87 (#12, 1 wk), 2 wk.

Hersh, Seymour M.
The Price of Power (Summit/Simon & Schuster) NYT nf 6/26/83 (#13), pk 7/17/83 (#5, 5 wk), 11 wk; PW hc nf 7/1/83 (#9), pk 7/8/83 (#4, 5 wk), 14 wk; tot 25 wk.

Hershiser, Orel, with Jerry B. Jenkins
Out of the Blue (Wolgemuth & Hyatt) NYT nf 4/23/89 (#5, 1 wk), 8 wk.

Herskowitz, Mickey
See Bette Davis and_____
See Dan Rather and_____

Hertzler, Arthur E.
The Horse and Buggy Doctor (Harper) NYT gen 9/4/38 (#1, 4 wk), 28 wk; PW nf 9/10/38 (#3), pk 10/15/38 (#2, 4 wk), 32 wk; tot 60 wk.

Hervey, Harry
School for Eternity (Putnam) PW fic 10/11/41 (#10, 4 wk).

Herwig, Ron
128 House Plants You Can Grow (Macmillan) NYT td pb 10/13/74 (#10, 4 wk).
128 More House Plants You Can Grow (Macmillan) NYT td pb 10/13/74 (#5, 4 wk).

Herzog, Maurice
Annapurna (Dutton) NYT gen 1/25/53 (#14), pk 2/22/53 (#1, 12 wk), 40 wk; PW nf 2/14/53 (#8), pk 2/28/53 (#1, 11 wk), 33 wk; tot 73 wk.

Hesburgh, Theodore M., with Jerry Reedy
God, Country, Notre Dame (Doubleday) NYT nf 12/30/90 (#13, 1 wk).

Hesse, Hermann
Narcissus and Goldmund (Farrar) NYT pb fic 3/2/69 (#5), pk 4/6/69 (#4, 4 wk), 8 wk.

Heyer, Georgette
Penhallow (Doubleday) NYT gen 10/24/43 (#10), pk 10/31/43 (#9, 1 wk), 2 wk.

Heyerdahl, Thor
Kon-Tiki (Rand McNally) NYT gen 9/17/

50 (#16), pk 10/8/50 (#1, 34 wk), 81 wk; PW nf 10/7/50 (#1, 38 wk), 65 wk; (young reader's edition) NYT ch bst 11/12/61 (#14, 26 wk); tot 172 wk.

Aku-Aku (Rand McNally) NYT gen 9/21/58 (#12), pk 10/19/58 (#1, 2 wk), 28 wk; PW nf 9/29/58 (#7), pk 10/13/58 (#1, 7 wk), 26 wk; tot 54 wk.

The Ra Expeditions (Doubleday) NYT gen 9/5/71 (#10), pk 10/10/71 (#5, 2 wk), 12 wk; PW nf 9/13/71 (#10), pk 10/25/71 (#5, 1 wk), 10 wk; tot 22 wk.

Heym, Stefan
Hostages (Putnam) NYT nf 11/8/42 (#19), pk 11/15/42 (#7, 1 wk), 13 wk.
The Crusaders (Little Brown) NYT fic 10/3/48 (#10), pk 10/17/48 (#6, 2 wk), 10 wk; PW fic 11/13/48 (#8, 1 wk); tot 11 wk.

Heymann, C. David
Poor Little Rich Girl (Pocket) NYT pb nf 11/29/87 (#11), pk 12/6/87 (#3, 1 wk), 3 wk.
A Woman Named Jackie (Stuart/Carol) NYT nf 5/14/89 (#9), pk 5/21/89 (#1, 7 wk), 23 wk; PW hc nf 5/19/89 (#7), pk 5/26/89 (#1, 8 wk), 21 wk; (NAL/Signet) NYT pb nf 5/27/90 (#4), pk 6/17/90 (#2, 2 wk), 15 wk; PW mm pb 6/1/90 (#7), pk 6/22/90 (#5, 1 wk), 9 wk; tot 68 wk.

Heyward, Du Bose
Mamba's Daughters (Doubleday) PW fic 3/9/29 (#3), pk 4/13/29 (#2, 4 wk), 16 wk.
Lost Morning (Farrar) NYT fic 10/4/36 (#6, 4 wk).

Heywood, Joseph
The Berkut (Dell) PW mm pb 12/16/88 (#15), pk 12/23/88 (#12, 1 wk), 2 wk.

Hichens, Robert Smythe
The Pyramid (Doubleday) NYT fic 5/3/36 (#10, 4 wk).
Secret Information (Doubleday) NYT fic 6/5/38 (#14, 4 wk).

Hickel, Walter J.
Who Owns America? (G.K. Hall) NYT gen 11/14/71 (#9, 1 wk).

Hickman, Tracy
See Margaret Weis and_____

Hickok, Eliza Merrill
The Quiz Kids (Houghton) NYT gen 3/30/47 (#15, 1 wk).

Hicks, Granville
Only One Storm (Macmillan) PW fic 5/9/42 (#5, 4 wk), 8 wk.

Higginbotham, Pearl
See Mary Ellen Pinkham and_____

Higgins, George V.
The Friends of Eddie Coyle (Knopf) NYT fic 3/12/72 (#8), pk 5/7/72 (#5, 1 wk), 12 wk; PW fic 4/3/72 (#10), pk 4/24/72 (#8, 2 wk), 10 wk; tot 22 wk.
Digger's Game (Knopf) PW fic 4/9/73 (#6, 2 wk), 6 wk; NYT fic 4/15/73 (#10, 2 wk); tot 8 wk.
Gogan's Trade (Knopf) NYT fic 4/28/74 (#10, 1 wk).

Higgins, Jack
The Eagle Has Landed (Holt) PW fic 8/4/75 (#8), pk 1/12/76 (#5, 2 wk), 33 wk; NYT fic 8/10/75 (#9), pk 9/7/75 (#6, 7 wk), 32 wk; (Bantam) PW mm pb 8/9/76 (#5), pk 8/23/76 (#3, 3 wk), 12 wk; NYT mm pb 8/15/76 (#5), pk 8/29/76 (#2, 2 wk), 10 wk; tot 87 wk.
Storm Warning (Holt) NYT fic 10/3/76 (#10), pk 11/14/76 (#3, 12 wk), 25 wk; PW hc fic 10/4/76 (#8), pk 11/8/76 (#3, 9 wk), 23 wk; (Bantam) PW mm pb 7/18/77 (#9), pk 7/25/77 (#7, 1 wk), 7 wk; NYT mm pb 7/24/77 (#15), pk 7/31/77 (#9, 2 wk), 4 wk; tot 59 wk.
Day of Judgment (Holt) PW hc fic 4/16/79 (#11, 1 wk), 3 wk.
Solo (Stein & Day) PW hc fic 6/20/80 (#14), pk 8/15/80 (#6, 1 wk), 13 wk; NYT fic 7/13/80 (#15), pk 8/17/80 (#9, 1 wk), 7 wk; (Dell) NYT mm pb 10/18/81 (#12), pk 10/25/81 (#6, 3 wk), 7 wk; PW mm pb 10/23/81 (#8), pk 10/30/81 (#5, 1 wk), 9 wk; tot 36 wk.
Luciano's Luck (Stein & Day) PW hc fic 8/28/81 (#15), pk 10/2/81 (#13, 1 wk), 2 wk; NYT fic 8/30/81 (#13), pk 9/13/81 (#8, 1 wk), 9 wk; (Dell) PW mm pb 9/17/82 (#10), pk 10/1/82 (#7, 2 wk), 7 wk; NYT mm pb 9/19/82 (#14), pk 9/26/82 (#10, 2 wk), 7 wk; tot 25 wk.
Touch the Devil (Stein & Day) PW hc fic 7/30/82 (#14), pk 8/13/82 (#7, 3 wk), 8 wk; NYT fic 8/15/82 (#8, 1 wk), 8 wk; (NAL/Signet) NYT mm pb 9/4/83 (#9), pk 9/8/83 (#5, 3 wk), 8 wk; PW mm pb 9/9/83 (#7), pk 9/23/83 (#5, 2 wk), 6 wk; tot 30 wk.
Exocet (Stein & Day) PW hc fic 8/19/83 (#14), pk 8/26/83 (#13, 1 wk), 3 wk; NYT fic 8/28/83 (#15), pk 9/11/83 (#14, 1 wk), 2 wk; (NAL/Signet) NYT pb fic 7/8/84 (#5, 1 wk), 9 wk; PW mm pb 7/13/84 (#8), pk 7/27/84 (#6, 1 wk), 6 wk; tot 20 wk.
Confessional (Stein & Day) PW hc fic 6/7/85 (#14), pk 7/5/85 (#13, 1 wk), 5 wk; NYT fic 7/7/85 (#15, 1 wk); (NAL/Signet) NYT pb fic 7/13/86 (#9), pk 7/20/86 (#8, 1 wk), 5 wk; PW mm pb 7/18/86 (#14), pk 7/25/86 (#8, 1 wk), 4 wk; tot 15 wk.

Night of the Fox (Simon & Schuster) PW hc fic 1/16/87 (#11), pk 2/6/87 (#4, 6 wk), 15 wk; NYT fic 1/18/87 (#11), pk 2/15/87 (#4, 3 wk), 14 wk; (Pocket) NYT pb fic 12/6/87 (#14), pk 12/20/87 (#5, 3 wk), 9 wk; PW mm pb 12/18/87 (#8), pk 12/25/87 (#5, 1 wk), 7 wk; tot 45 wk.
A Season in Hell (Simon & Schuster) PW hc fic 1/20/89 (#9), pk 2/3/89 (#3, 3 wk), 11 wk; NYT fic 1/22/89 (#9), pk 2/19/89 (#4, 1 wk), 10 wk; (Pocket) NYT pb fic 12/10/89 (#9), pk 12/17/89 (#4, 1 wk), 6 wk; PW mm pb 12/15/89 (#9), pk 12/22/89 (#7, 2 wk), 5 wk; tot 32 wk.
Cold Harbour (Simon & Schuster) NYT fic 1/21/90 (#15), pk 2/11/90 (#4, 1 wk), 12 wk; PW hc fic 2/2/90 (#11), pk 2/16/90 (#5, 2 wk), 8 wk; (Pocket) NYT pb fic 10/14/90 (#14), pk 11/4/90 (#13, 1 wk), 4 wk; PW mm pb 11/2/90 (#11, 1 wk), 2 wk; tot 26 wk.

Higgins, Marguerite
War in Korea (Doubleday) NYT gen 5/6/51 (#16), pk 5/27/51 (#12, 2 wk), 6 wk.

High, Monique
The Four Winds of Heaven (Dell) PW mm pb 1/30/81 (#14, 1 wk), 2 wk.

Higham, Charles
Kate: The Life of Katharine Hepburn (Norton) NYT gen 6/1/75 (#10), pk 6/8/75 (#9, 4 wk), 9 wk; PW nf 6/16/75 (#9, 1 wk), 3 wk; tot 12 wk.
Errol Flynn: The Untold Story (Doubleday) PW hc nf 4/18/80 (#13, 2 wk), 3 wk.
The Duchess of Windsor (McGraw) PW hc nf 7/22/88 (#8), pk 8/5/88 (#5, 2 wk), 13 wk; NYT nf 7/24/88 (#15), pk 9/11/88 (#3, 1 wk), 20 wk; (Charter) NYT pb nf 8/13/89 (#6), pk 9/3/89 (#5, 1 wk), 7 wk; tot 40 wk.

_____, and Roy Moseley
Cary Grant: The Lonely Heart (Harcourt) PW hc nf 4/21/89 (#14), pk 4/28/89 (#11, 1 wk), 2 wk; NYT nf 4/23/89 (#15, 1 wk); tot 3 wk.

Highet, Gilbert
People, Places and Books (Oxford Univ.) NYT gen 5/31/53 (#14), pk 6/14/53 (#13, 1 wk), 4 wk.

Hijuelos, Oscar
The Mambo Kings Play Songs of Love (HarperCollins/Perennial) PW td pb 8/31/90 (#9), pk 10/12/90 (#6, 1 wk), 9 wk; NYT pb fic 9/2/90 (#15, 1 wk); tot 10 wk.

Hilburn, Robert
See David Breskin, et al.

Hildebrandt, Greg, Tim Hildebrandt and Jerry Nichols
Urshurak [as by The Hildebrandt Brothers

and Jerry Nichols] (Bantam) NYT td pb 10/28/79 (#13, 1 wk), 3 wk.

Hill, Eric
Where's Spot? (Putnam) PW ch pic 8/31/90 (#9, 8 wk).

Hill, Grace Livingston
The Strange Proposal (Grosset & Dunlap) NYT fic 12/1/35 (#8, 4 wk).
Mystery Flowers (Grosset & Dunlap) NYT fic 8/2/36 (#7, 4 wk).
April Gold (Grosset & Dunlap) NYT fic 5/3/36 (#5, 4 wk).
Daphne Dean (Grosset & Dunlap) NYT fic 8/8/37 (#5, 4 wk).
Homing (Grosset & Dunlap) NYT fic 7/31/38 (#9, 4 wk).
Marigold (Grosset & Dunlap) NYT fic 4/3/38 (#15, 4 wk).
The Seventh Hour (Grosset & Dunlap) NYT fic 4/9/39 (#14, 4 wk).
Patricia (Grosset & Dunlap) NYT fic 6/6/39 (#5, 4 wk).

Hill, Max
Exchange Ship (Farrar) NYT nf 2/7/43 (#13, 1 wk).

Hill, Ruth Beebe
Hanta Yo: An American Saga (Doubleday) NYT fic 3/4/79 (#6), pk 5/20/79 (#3, 3 wk), 30 wk; PW hc fic 3/5/79 (#9), pk 5/14/79 (#4, 2 wk), 26 wk; (Warner) PW mm pb 3/14/80 (#6), pk 4/4/80 (#2, 1 wk), 12 wk; NYT mm pb 3/16/80 (#10), pk 4/6/80 (#7, 1 wk), 10 wk; tot 78 wk.

Hill, Weldon [pseud.]
Onionhead (McKay) NYT fic 3/31/57 (#16), pk 4/28/57 (#14, 1 wk), 4 wk.

Hillerman, Tony
A Thief of Time (Harper) NYT fic 7/17/88 (#8), pk 7/24/88 (#7, 2 wk), 10 wk; PW hc fic 7/22/88 (#10), pk 8/5/88 (#8, 2 wk), 8 wk; (HarperPaperbacks) PW mm pb 12/22/89 (#13), pk 1/19/90 (#4, 1 wk), 11 wk; NYT pb fic 12/24/89 (#5), pk 1/14/90 (#3, 3 wk), 12 wk; tot 41 wk.
Talking God (Harper) NYT fic 6/4/89 (#11), pk 7/2/89 (#2, 2 wk), 15 wk; PW hc fic 6/9/89 (#9), pk 7/7/89 (#6, 4 wk), 13 wk; NYT pb fic 12/30/90 (#13, 1 wk); tot 29 wk.
Coyote Waits (HarperCollins) NYT fic 7/8/90 (#11), pk 7/15/90 (#3, 5 wk), 13 wk; PW hc fic 7/13/90 (#8), pk 8/17/90 (#2, 1 wk), 12 wk; PW aud fic 10/5/90 (#2, 4 wk), 8 wk; tot 33 wk.

Hillis, Marjorie
Live Alone and Like It (Bobbs Merrill) PW nf 9/12/36 (#7), pk 11/14/36 (#2, 12 wk), 32 wk; NYT gen 9/13/36 (#2), pk 10/4/36 (#1, 8 wk), 24 wk; tot 56 wk.
Orchids on Your Budget (Bobbs Merrill) NYT gen 7/4/37 (#3), pk 8/8/37 (#2, 4 wk), 16 wk; PW nf 7/10/37 (#6), pk 8/14/37 (#2, 8 wk), 20 wk; tot 36 wk.

Hillman, William
Mr. President (Farrar) NYT gen 4/6/52 (#3), pk 4/20/52 (#1, 1 wk), 14 wk; PW nf 4/12/52 (#4), pk 4/26/52 (#1, 2 wk), 8 wk; tot 22 wk.

Hillyer, B.B.
Teenage Mutant Ninja Turtles (Dell/Yearling) NYT pb fic 4/15/90 (#15), pk 4/29/90 (#5, 1 wk), 7 wk.

Hillyer, Elinor
Madamoiselle's Home Planning Scrapbook (Macmillan) NYT gen 3/17/46 (#16), pk 4/7/46 (#15, 1 wk), 3 wk.

Hillyer, Virgel Mores
A Child's Geography of the World (Century) PW juv 2/15/30 (#1, 12 wk), 60 wk.
A Child's History of the World (Century) PW juv 3/15/30 (#4), pk 4/12/30 (#3, 4 wk), 64 wk.

Hilton, Conrad
Be My Guest (Prentice Hall) NYT gen 2/23/58 (#11, 2 wk), 5 wk; PW nf 3/3/58 (#7, 1 wk); tot 6 wk.

Hilton, James
Lost Horizon (Morrow) PW fic 12/15/34 (#4), pk 3/16/35 (#3, 4 wk), 28 wk.
Good-Bye, Mr. Chips (Little Brown) PW fic 8/11/34 (#7), pk 1/12/35 (#1, 4 wk), 52 wk.
We Are Not Alone (Little Brown) NYT fic 4/4/37 (#2, 4 wk), 8 wk; PW fic 4/10/37 (#6), pk 5/8/37 (#3, 4 wk), 16 wk; tot 24 wk.
Random Harvest (Little Brown) PW fic 2/8/41 (#6), pk 3/15/41 (#1, 16 wk), 40 wk.
The Story of Dr. Wassell (Little Brown) NYT gen 5/16/43 (#11), pk 6/6/43 (#8, 1 wk), 14 wk; PW fic 6/12/43 (#9, 1 wk); tot 15 wk.
So Well Remembered (Little Brown) NYT fic 8/12/45 (#14), pk 9/23/45 (#1, 2 wk), 25 wk; PW fic 8/25/45 (#3), pk 9/1/45 (#1, 4 wk), 16 wk; tot 41 wk.
Nothing So Strange (Little Brown) NYT fic 11/9/47 (#11), pk 11/23/47 (#4, 1 wk), 13 wk; PW fic 11/15/47 (#9), pk 11/29/47 (#5, 3 wk), 7 wk; tot 20 wk.
Morning Journey (Little Brown) NYT fic 3/11/51 (#8), pk 3/25/51 (#4, 5 wk), 13 wk; PW fic 3/31/51 (#4, 4 wk), 6 wk; tot 19 wk.
Time and Time Again (Little Brown) NYT fic 9/6/53 (#9), pk 11/8/53 (#2, 2 wk), 27 wk; PW fic 9/19/53 (#7), pk 11/14/53 (#1, 1 wk), 21 wk; tot 48 wk.

Hindus, Maurice Gerschon
Red Bread (Cape & Smith) PW nf 6/20/31 (#10), pk 7/18/31 (#6, 8 wk), 16 wk.
Humanity Uprooted (Cape & Smith) PW nf 2/21/31 (#5, 4 wk), 16 wk.
We Shall Live Again (Doubleday) NYT gen 6/11/39 (#15), pk 7/9/39 (#13, 4 wk), 8 wk.
Mother Russia (Doubleday) NYT gen 7/18/43 (#15), pk 7/25/43 (#9, 1 wk), 2 wk.

Hinshaw, David
The Home Front (Putnam) NYT gen 9/19/43 (#17, 1 wk).

Hirdt, Steve, and Peter Hirdt
See Seymour Siwoff, et al.

Hirsch, E.D., Jr.
Cultural Literacy: What Every American Needs to Know (Houghton) NYT nf 6/7/87 (#2, 4 wk), 23 wk; PW hc nf 6/19/87 (#12), pk 8/7/87 (#2, 1 wk), 21 wk; (Vintage) NYT pb nf 5/22/88 (#10), pk 6/12/88 (#3, 1 wk), 19 wk; PW td pb 6/3/88 (#6), pk 6/17/88 (#5, 1 wk), 7 wk; tot 70 wk.

_____, with Joseph F. Kett and James Trefil
The Dictionary of Cultural Literacy (Houghton) NYT msc 11/20/88 (#3), pk 12/25/88 (#1, 4 wk), 17 wk; PW hc nf 11/25/88 (#8), pk 1/13/89 (#4, 1 wk), 18 wk; tot 35 wk.

Hirschfeld, Burt
Secrets (Pocket) PW mm pb 5/10/76 (#14), pk 5/24/76 (#13, 1 wk), 3 wk.
Aspen (Bantam) NYT mm pb 2/1/76 (#5), pk 2/8/76 (#4, 3 wk), 12 wk; PW mm pb 2/2/76 (#5), pk 2/9/76 (#4, 2 wk), 7 wk; tot 19 wk.

Hirschfield, Tom
How to Master Video Games (Bantam) PW mm pb 1/15/82 (#12), pk 1/29/82 (#10, 1 wk), 9 wk; NYT mm pb 1/31/82 (#15), pk 3/7/82 (#14, 1 wk), 3 wk; tot 12 wk.

Hirshberg, Al
See James A. Piersall and_____

Hiss, Alger
In the Court of Public Opinion (Knopf) NYT gen 5/26/57 (#9, 2 wk), 5 wk; PW nf 6/3/57 (#8, 1 wk); tot 6 wk.

Hitchcock, Alfred
Alfred Hitchcock's Haunted Houseful [ed.] (Random) NYT ch bst 5/13/62 (#9), pk 11/11/62 (#1, 26 wk), 45 wk.

Hite, Shere
The Hite Report: A Nationwide Study of Female Sexuality (Macmillan) NYT gen 11/28/76 (#9), pk 2/6/77 (#5, 4 wk), 18 wk; PW nf 11/29/76 (#9), pk 12/6/76 (#8, 2 wk), 3 wk; PW hc nf 1/3/77 (#9), pk 1/24/77 (#5, 3 wk), 14 wk; NYT nf 4/3/77 (#7, 1 wk), 4 wk; (Dell) PW mm pb 4/4/77 (#8), pk 5/16/77 (#1, 2 wk), 20 wk; NYT mm pb 4/10/77 (#8), pk 5/15/77 (#2, 2 wk), 19 wk; tot 78 wk.
The Hite Report on Male Sexuality (Knopf) NYT nf 7/26/81 (#8), pk 8/30/81 (#5, 1 wk), 14 wk; PW hc nf 7/31/81 (#10), pk 8/7/81 (#5, 1 wk), 8 wk; tot 22 wk.

Hitler, Adolf
My Battle (Houghton) NYT gen 11/6/38 (#13, 4 wk), 8 wk.
Mein Kampf (Reynal & Hitchcock/Stackpole) PW nf 4/8/39 (#1, 4 wk), 32 wk; NYT gen 4/9/39 (#2, 4 wk), 24 wk; tot 56 wk.
My New Order (Reynal & Hitchcock) PW nf 10/11/41 (#6, 4 wk).

Hitrec, Joseph George
Son of the Moon (Harper) NYT fic 4/4/48 (#12), pk 4/25/48 (#9, 1 wk), 7 wk.

Hix, Charles
Looking Good: A Guide for Men (Hawthorne) NYT nf 10/9/77 (#14), pk 11/13/77 (#10, 1 wk), 3 wk; PW hc nf 10/17/77 (#14, 2 wk); NYT td pb 5/28/78 (#12), pk 7/16/78 (#11, 1 wk), 3 wk; tot 8 wk.
Working Out (Simon & Schuster) PW hc nf 4/8/83 (#13), pk 5/20/83 (#7, 2 wk), 24 wk; NYT nf 4/24/83 (#12), pk 5/29/83 (#7, 2 wk), 21 wk; tot 45 wk.

Hobart, Alice Tisdale
Oil for the Lamps of China (Bobbs Merrill) PW fic 11/11/33 (#8), pk 2/10/34 (#3, 4 wk), 7 wk.
River Supreme (Bobbs Merrill) PW fic 8/11/34 (#9, 8 wk).
Yang and Yin (Bobbs Merrill) PW fic 12/12/36 (#4), pk 2/6/37 (#3, 4 wk), 20 wk; NYT fic 1/31/37 (#4, 8 wk); tot 28 wk.
The Cup and the Sword (Bobbs Merrill) NYT fic 9/27/42 (#10), pk 10/11/42 (#4, 2 wk), 20 wk; PW fic 10/3/42 (#4, 2 wk), 8 wk; tot 28 wk.
The Peacock Sheds His Tail (Bobbs Merrill) NYT fic 10/7/45 (#10), pk 11/4/45 (#4, 6 wk), 21 wk; PW fic 10/20/45 (#10), 1/5/46 (#3, 1 wk), 14 wk; tot 35 wk.
The Cleft Rock (Bobbs Merrill) NYT fic 9/19/48 (#10), pk 10/3/48 (#8, 1 wk), 17 wk; PW fic 10/16/48 (#9), pk 10/23/48 (#5, 2 wk), 4 wk; tot 21 wk.
The Serpent-Wreathed Staff (Bobbs Merrill) NYT fic 12/23/51 (#14, 1 wk), 2 wk.
Venture Into Darkness (Longmans Green) NYT fic 4/10/55 (#11, 1 wk), 9 wk.

Hobbs, Lisa
I Saw Red China (McGraw) NYT gen 3/
27/66 (#9, 3 wk); PW nf 4/4/66 (#8, 1 wk),
4 wk; tot 7 wk.

Hobson, Laura Keane Zametkin
The Trespassers (Simon & Schuster) NYT
gen 10/24/43 (#8, 1 wk), 4 wk.
Gentleman's Agreement (Simon & Schuster) NYT fic 3/16/47 (#14), pk 4/27/47 (#1,
14 wk), 36 wk; PW fic 4/12/47 (#4), pk 5/10/
47 (#1, 12 wk), 28 wk; tot 64 wk.
The Other Father (Simon & Schuster) NYT
fic 6/4/50 (#11), pk 6/18/50 (#9, 1 wk), 5 wk.
The Celebrity (Simon & Schuster) NYT
fic 11/25/51 (#15, 1 wk).

Hochberg, Ilene
*Dogue: A Parody of the World's Most Famous
Fashion Magazine* (Main Street) PW td pb
11/14/86 (#8), pk 11/21/86 (#7, 1 wk), 4 wk.
Catmopolitan (Pocket) PW td pb 11/20/87
(#9), pk 12/4/87 (#2, 5 wk), 14 wk; NYT msc
pb 11/29/87 (#2, 5 wk), 8 wk; tot 22 wk.

Hochhuth, Rolf
The Deputy (Grove) NYT gen 4/5/64 (#8),
pk 4/12/64 (#6, 3 wk), 9 wk; PW nf 4/6/64
(#8), pk 4/13/64 (#6, 2 wk), 9 wk; tot 18 wk.

Hodges, Margaret
The Kitchen Knight [retold by Hodges,
illus. Trina Schart Hyman] (Holiday House)
PW ch pic 9/28/90 (#7, 4 wk).

Hodgins, Eric
Mr. Blandings Builds His Dream House
(Simon & Schuster) NYT fic 1/26/47 (#11),
pk 3/2/47 (#9, 1 wk), 8 wk.

Hodgson, Godfrey H.
See Lewis L. Chester, et al.
See Charles Raw, et al.

Hofer, J.L.
See Jon M. Leonard, et al.

Hoff, Benjamin
The Tao of Pooh (Penguin) NYT td pb 8/
28/83 (#12), pk 9/8/83 (#8, 2 wk), 10 wk.

Hoff, Syd
Danny and the Dinosaur (Harper) NYT ch
bst 5/10/59 (#15, 19 wk).

Hoffenberg, Mason
See Terry Southern and_____

Hoffenstein, Samuel
Poems in Praise of Practically Nothing (Liveright) PW nf 10/27/28 (#4, 4 wk).

Hoffer, William
See Bill Hayes and_____

Hoffman, Abbie
Soon to Be a Major Motion (Putnam/Peri-

gee) NYT td pb 10/19/80 (#15), pk 10/26/80
(#14, 1 wk), 2 wk.

Hoffman, Alice
At Risk (Putnam) PW hc fic 8/5/88 (#14,
1 wk).
Seventh Heaven (Putnam) NYT fic 8/26/
90 (#15), pk 9/2/90 (#10, 2 wk), 5 wk; PW
hc fic 9/7/90 (#12), pk 9/21/90 (#9, 1 wk), 5
wk; tot 10 wk.

Hoffman, Mable
Crockery Cookery (H.P. Books) NYT td pb
4/27/75 (#3), pk 6/15/75 (#1, 10 wk), 51 wk;
PW td pb 2/2/76 (#2, 1 wk), 12 wk; (Bantam) PW mm pb 2/9/76 (#8, 1 wk); tot 64
wk.
Crepe Cookery (H.P. Books) NYT td pb
5/16/76 (#5), pk 5/30/76 (#1, 2 wk), 12 wk;
PW td pb 5/31/76 (#5), pk 6/28/76 (#4, 1
wk), 5 wk; tot 17 wk.

Hoffman, Malvina
Heads and Tales (Scribners) PW nf 11/14/
36 (#7, 8 wk), 12 wk.

Hoffman, Mark S.
See Anonymous (World Almanac)

Hoffman, Paul G.
Peace Can Be Won (Doubleday) NYT gen
5/13/51 (#8), 6/10/51 (#6, 1 wk), 7 wk; PW
nf 6/9/51 (#9, 1 wk); tot 8 wk.

**Hoffman, Ruth, and Helen Car-
rick**
We Married an Englishman (Carrick &
Evans) NYT gen 10/9/38 (#13, 4 wk).

Hoffmann, E.T.A.
Nutcracker [illus. Maurice Sendak, trans.
Ralph Manheim] (Crown) NYT fic 11/25/84
(#14), pk 1/13/85 (#3, 1 wk), 8 wk; PW hc fic
12/14/84 (#14), pk 1/4/85 (#5, 1 wk), 6 wk;
tot 14 wk.

Hofstadter, Douglas Richard
*Godel, Escher, Bach: An Eternal Golden
Braid* (Vintage) NYT td pb 10/19/80 (#13),
pk 11/2/80 (#6, 2 wk), 22 wk; PW td pb
10/24/80 (#8), pk 10/31/80 (#3, 1 wk), 17 wk;
tot 39 wk.
Metamagical Themas (Basic) NYT nf 5/5/
85 (#13, 1 wk), 3 wk.

Hogan, Ben
Power Golf (Barnes) NYT gen 6/20/48
(#14), pk 8/8/48 (#10, 1 wk), 5 wk.

Hogben, Lancelot Thomas
Mathematics for the Million (Norton) PW
nf 5/8/37 (#7), pk 7/10/37 (#4, 4 wk), 28 wk;
NYT gen 6/6/37 (#6), pk 7/4/37 (#5, 4 wk),
16 wk; tot 44 wk.
Science for the Citizen (Knopf) NYT gen

11/6/38 (#8, 4 wk); PW nf 11/12/38 (#6, 4 wk); tot 8 wk.
The Wonderful World of Mathematics (Garden City) NYT ch bst 11/18/56 (#1, 40 wk).

Hoke, Henry Reed
Black Mail (Readers Book Service) NYT gen 9/10/44 (#15), pk 10/1/44 (#8, 1 wk), 3 wk.
It's a Secret (Reynal & Hitchcock) NYT gen 2/24/46 (#15, 1 wk).

Holbrook, Stewart Hall
The Age of the Moguls (Doubleday) NYT gen 11/1/53 (#12), pk 1/24/54 (#5, 2 wk), 23 wk; PW nf 12/12/53 (#9), pk 2/6/54 (#4, 1 wk), 11 wk; tot 34 wk.
The Columbia (Rinehart) NYT gen 3/4/56 (#16), pk 3/11/56 (#15, 1 wk), 2 wk.
Dreamers of the American Dream (Doubleday) NYT gen 12/1/57 (#16, 1 wk).
The Swamp Fox of the Revolution (Random) NYT ch bst 5/8/60 (#14, 19 wk).

Holden, Edith
The Country Diary of an Edwardian Lady (Holt) PW hc nf 11/7/77 (#15), pk 1/2/78 (#5, 1 wk), 41 wk; NYT nf 11/13/77 (#13), pk 12/18/77 (#7, 3 wk), 49 wk; tot 90 wk.

Holdredge, Helen O'Donnell
Mammy Pleasant (Putnam) NYT gen 1/17/54 (#15, 3 wk).

Holiday, Billie, and William Dufty
Lady Sings the Blues (Doubleday) NYT gen 8/26/56 (#16, 2 wk).

Holland, Marion
A Big Ball of String (Random) NYT ch bst 5/10/59 (#13, 19 wk).

Hollander, Xaviera
The Happy Hooker (Dell) NYT pb gen 4/9/72 (#3), pk 6/11/72 (#2, 8 wk), 48 wk.
Xaviera (Warner) NYT pb gen 4/8/73 (#2, 4 wk), 16 wk.
Xaviera Goes Wild (Warner) NYT mm pb 8/11/74 (#5, 4 wk).

Hollander, Zander
Great American Athletes of the 20th Century [ed.] (Random) NYT ch bst 11/5/67 (#4, 26 wk).

Holmes, Beth
The Whipping Boy (Jove) PW mm pb 5/14/79 (#13, 1 wk).

Holmes, Marjorie
Two from Galilee (Bantam) NYT fic 1/7/73 (#10, 2 wk); NYT mm pb 5/12/74 (#8, 4 wk); tot 6 wk.

Holmes, Paul Allen
The Sheppard Murder Case (McKay) NYT

gen 9/3/61 (#14), pk 9/17/61 (#8, 1 wk), 11 wk; PW nf 9/11/61 (#9, 1 wk), 4 wk; tot 15 wk.
The Candy Murder Case (Bantam) NYT pb gen 4/3/66 (#5, 4 wk).

Holst, Imogen
See Benjamin Britten and_____

Holt, Rackham
George Washington Carver (Doubleday) NYT gen 4/25/43 (#20), pk 5/23/43 (#5, 2 wk), 25 wk; PW nf 5/22/43 (#5, 2 wk), 8 wk; tot 33 wk.

Holt, Robert Lawrence
Good Friday (NAL/Signet) PW mm pb 9/23/88 (#15), pk 9/30/88 (#12, 1 wk), 6 wk; NYT pb fic 10/2/88 (#11, 1 wk), 2 wk; tot 8 wk.

Holt, Victoria
Mistress of Mellyn (Doubleday) NYT fic 9/25/60 (#15), pk 11/6/60 (#5, 5 wk), 23 wk; PW fic 10/10/60 (#7), pk 12/5/60 (#3, 2 wk), 16 wk; tot 39 wk.
Kirkland Revels (Doubleday) PW fic 2/5/62 (#11, 2 wk); NYT fic 2/11/62 (#14), pk 2/18/62 (#12, 2 wk), 9 wk; tot 11 wk.
Bride of Pendorric (Doubleday) NYT fic 9/1/63 (#10, 1 wk).
The Legend of the Seventh Virgin (Doubleday) NYT fic 2/7/65 (#9), pk 3/7/65 (#4, 1 wk), 11 wk; PW fic 2/22/65 (#9), pk 4/5/65 (#6, 1 wk), 11 wk; tot 22 wk.
Menfreya in the Morning (Doubleday) NYT fic 5/22/66 (#9), pk 5/29/66 (#8, 2 wk), 3 wk; PW fic 5/30/66 (#8), pk 6/6/66 (#6, 1 wk), 4 wk; tot 7 wk.
King of the Castle (Doubleday) PW fic 7/17/67 (#8), pk 8/14/67 (#7, 2 wk), 10 wk; NYT fic 7/23/67 (#10), pk 8/6/67 (#8, 1 wk), 6 wk; tot 16 wk.
The Queen's Confession (Doubleday) PW fic 8/12/68 (#6, 1 wk), 3 wk; NYT fic 8/25/68 (#9), pk 9/15/68 (#8, 2 wk), 7 wk; tot 10 wk.
The Shivering Sands (Doubleday) NYT fic 12/21/69 (#9, 3 wk); PW fic 1/19/70 (#9), pk 2/16/70 (#8, 1 wk), 3 wk; tot 6 wk.
The Secret Woman (Doubleday) PW fic 7/20/70 (#9), pk 9/21/70 (#4, 1 wk), 20 wk; NYT fic 7/26/70 (#9), pk 9/20/70 (#4, 3 wk), 24 wk; tot 44 wk.
The Shadow of the Lynx (Doubleday) NYT fic 7/18/71 (#9), pk 9/5/71 (#3, 1 wk), 20 wk; PW fic 8/2/71 (#9), pk 9/20/71 (#4, 2 wk), 19 wk; tot 39 wk.
On the Night of the Seventh Moon (Doubleday) NYT fic 10/1/72 (#10), pk 10/22/72 (#4, 2 wk), 17 wk; PW fic 10/9/72 (#6), pk 10/23/72 (#4, 3 wk), 15 wk; NYT pb fic 10/

14/73 (#3), pk 12/9/73 (#1, 4 wk), 16 wk; tot 48 wk.

The Curse of the Kings (Doubleday) PW fic 7/30/73 (#9), pk 10/22/73 (#6, 1 wk), 12 wk; NYT fic 8/19/73 (#8), pk 9/2/73 (#7, 3 wk), 12 wk; (Fawcett) NYT mm pb 9/8/74 (#4, 4 wk), 8 wk; tot 32 wk.

The House of a Thousand Lanterns (Doubleday) PW fic 8/12/74 (#9), pk 9/2/74 (#6, 3 wk), 10 wk; NYT fic 8/18/74 (#8), pk 9/8/74 (#5, 1 wk), 10 wk; (Fawcett) NYT mm pb 7/20/75 (#9), pk 8/10/75 (#2, 1 wk), 6 wk; tot 26 wk.

The Pride of the Peacock (Doubleday) PW hc fic 9/6/76 (#9), pk 9/13/76 (#7, 1 wk), 4 wk; (Fawcett/Crest) PW mm pb 7/18/77 (#15), pk 8/1/77 (#5, 2 wk), 6 wk; NYT mm pb 7/24/77 (#9), pk 8/7/77 (#3, 1 wk), 9 wk; tot 19 wk.

Lord of the Far Island (Fawcett/Crest) PW mm pb 9/13/76 (#8), pk 9/27/76 (#3, 1 wk), 9 wk; NYT mm pb 9/19/76 (#8), pk 10/3/76 (#6, 2 wk), 6 wk; tot 15 wk.

The Devil on Horseback (Doubleday) PW hc fic 10/10/77 (#14, 2 wk); NYT fic 10/30/77 (#15, 1 wk); (Fawcett/Crest) PW mm pb 11/6/78 (#12, 1 wk); NYT mm pb 11/12/78 (#10), pk 11/19/78 (#9, 1 wk), 6 wk; tot 10 wk.

My Enemy, the Queen (Doubleday) PW hc fic 7/31/78 (#15), pk 8/7/78 (#13, 3 wk), 6 wk; (Fawcett/Crest) PW mm pb 7/30/79 (#13, 1 wk), 3 wk; NYT mm pb 8/26/79 (#12, 2 wk); tot 11 wk.

The Spring of the Tiger (Doubleday) PW hc fic 9/17/79 (#12, 1 wk), 2 wk; (Fawcett/Crest) PW mm pb 5/30/80 (#10), pk 6/6/80 (#5, 1 wk), 10 wk; NYT mm pb 6/1/80 (#11), pk 6/8/80 (#4, 1 wk), 12 wk; tot 24 wk.

The Mask of the Enchantress (Fawcett/Crest) PW mm pb 9/4/81 (#12, 2 wk), 3 wk; NYT mm pb 9/6/81 (#15), pk 10/11/81 (#12, 1 wk), 5 wk; tot 8 wk.

The Judas Kiss (Doubleday) PW hc fic 1/8/82 (#14, 1 wk); (Fawcett/Crest) NYT mm pb 1/30/83 (#6, 1 wk), 6 wk; PW mm pb 2/4/83 (#7, 1 wk), 5 wk; tot 12 wk.

The Time of the Hunter's Moon (Doubleday) PW hc fic 1/6/84 (#15, 1 wk); (Fawcett) NYT pb fic 12/30/84 (#10), pk 1/20/85 (#9, 1 wk), 5 wk; PW mm pb 1/11/85 (#15), pk 1/25/85 (#14, 1 wk), 2 wk; tot 8 wk.

The Demon Lover (Fawcett) NYT pb fic 1/1/84 (#14), pk 1/29/84 (#11, 1 wk), 5 wk.

The Road to Paradise Island (Fawcett/Crest) NYT pb fic 11/30/86 (#13), pk 12/14/86 (#11, 1 wk), 4 wk; PW mm pb 12/19/86 (#15), pk 12/26/86 (#14, 1 wk), 2 wk; tot 6 wk.

The Landowner Legacy (Fawcett/Crest) PW mm pb 2/7/86 (#11), pk 2/14/86 (#9, 1

wk), 3 wk; NYT pb fic 2/16/86 (#12, 1 wk); tot 4 wk.

Secret for a Nightingale (Fawcett/Crest) NYT pb fic 12/6/87 (#8, 1 wk), 4 wk; PW mm pb 12/18/87 (#14, 1 wk), 2 wk; tot 6 wk.

The India Fan (Doubleday) NYT fic 8/7/88 (#15, 2 wk); PW Hc fic 8/12/88 (#15), pk 8/19/88 (#12, 1 wk), 2 wk; (Fawcett/Crest) NYT pb fic 8/27/89 (#8), pk 9/24/89 (#6, 1 wk), 8 wk; PW mm pb 9/1/89 (#13), pk 9/22/89 (#4, 2 wk), 9 wk; tot 21 wk.

The Silk Vendetta (Fawcett/Crest) NYT pb fic 1/1/89 (#10), pk 1/15/89 (#7, 1 wk), 6 wk; PW mm pb 1/6/89 (#7), pk 1/20/89 (#6, 2 wk), 8 wk; tot 14 wk.

The Captive (Doubleday) PW hc fic 10/27/89 (#13, 1 wk); (Fawcett/Crest) NYT pb fic 10/28/90 (#11), pk 11/18/90 (#5, 2 wk), 6 wk; PW mm pb 11/2/90 (#8), pk 11/9/90 (#4, 1 wk), 7 wk; tot 14 wk.

Holtby, Winifred
South Riding (Macmillan) NYT fic 5/3/36 (#8, 4 wk); PW fic 5/9/36 (#6), pk 6/13/36 (#5, 4 wk), 12 wk; tot 16 wk.

Holtz, Lou, with John Heisler
A Fighting Spirit: A Championship Season at Notre Dame (Pocket) NYT nf 10/8/89 (#6, 1 wk), 4 wk; PW hc nf 10/13/89 (#14, 2 wk); tot 6 wk.

Homans, Abigail Adams
Education by Uncles (Houghton) PW nf 11/28/66 (#14, 1 wk).

Homer
The Odyssey of Homer [trans. T.E. Shaw] (Oxford Univ,) PW nf 1/14/33 (#10, 4 wk).

Honeycutt, Ann
See James R. Kinney and_____

Hooper, Alfred
A Mathematics Refresher (Holt) NYT nf 9/27/42 (#15), pk 11/29/42 (#6, 1 wk), 13 wk; PW nf 11/14/42 (#10, 2 wk); tot 15 wk.

Hooton, Barbara, and Patrick Dennis
Guestward Ho! (Vanguard) NYT gen 6/10/56 (#11), pk 7/29/56 (#3, 4 wk), 24 wk; PW nf 7/2/56 (#5), pk 7/30/56 (#1, 2 wk), 16 wk; tot 40 wk.

Hoover, Herbert C.
The Challenge to Liberty (Scribner) PW nf 11/10/34 (#2, 4 wk), 8 wk.

The Memoirs of Herbert Hoover (Macmillan) NYT gen 11/11/51 (#11), pk 1/6/52 (#8, 2 wk), 16 wk; PW nf 12/15/51 (#8, 1 wk), 3 wk; tot 19 wk.

The Memoirs of Herbert Hoover Vol. 2 (Macmillan) NYT gen 5/18/52 (#12), pk

6/22/52 (#7, 1 wk), 13 wk; PW nf 6/14/52 (#7, 1 wk), 4 wk; tot 17 wk.

The Memoirs of Herbert Hoover Vol. 3 (Macmillan) NYT gen 9/21/52 (#15), pk 10/12/52 (#8, 1 wk), 4 wk; PW nf 10/11/52 (#9, 1 wk); tot 5 wk.

The Ordeal of Woodrow Wilson (McGraw) NYT gen 5/18/58 (#11), pk 6/15/58 (#6, 4 wk), 19 wk; PW nf 5/26/58 (#7), pk 6/16/58 (#6, 4 wk), 12 wk; tot 31 wk.

_____, and Hugh Gibson
The Problems of Lasting Peace (Doubleday) PW nf 7/11/42 (#10), pk 8/22/42 (#3, 1 wk), 9 wk; NYT nf 8/9/42 (#4), pk 8/30/42 (#3, 1 wk), 10 wk; tot 19 wk.

Hoover, Ike
Forty-Two Years in the White House (Houghton) PW nf 11/10/32 (#3, 16 wk).

Hoover, J. Edgar
Masters of Deceit (Holt) NYT gen 3/30/58 (#5), pk 5/4/58 (#1, 9 wk), 31 wk; PW nf 3/31/58 (#6), pk 4/14/58 (#1, 8 wk), 30 wk; tot 61 wk.

A Study of Communism (Holt) NYT gen 10/21/62 (#14), pk 11/18/62 (#8, 1 wk), 8 wk; PW nf 11/26/62 (#9, 1 wk), 3 wk; tot 11 wk.

Hope, Bob
I Never Left Home (Simon & Schuster) NYT gen 7/9/44 (#4), pk 7/30/44 (#1, 13 wk), 38 wk; PW nf 7/15/44 (#6), pk 8/5/44 (#1, 8 wk), 30 wk; tot 68 wk.

So This Is Peace (Simon & Schuster) NYT gen 11/17/46 (#16), pk 11/24/46 (#4, 1 wk), 12 wk; PW nf 12/14/46 (#5, 1 wk), 3 wk; tot 15 wk.

Have Tux, Will Travel (Simon & Schuster) NYT gen 2/20/55 (#11), pk 3/13/55 (#9, 2 wk), 10 wk; PW nf 3/12/55 (#6), pk 4/9/55 (#5, 1 wk), 4 wk; tot 14 wk.

I Owe Russia $1,200 (Doubleday) NYT gen 6/2/63 (#9), pk 7/21/63 (#1, 1 wk), 34 wk; PW nf 6/3/63 (#8), pk 8/19/63 (#1, 2 wk), 36 wk; tot 70 wk.

_____, and Dwayne Netland
Confessions of a Hooker (Doubleday) NYT nf 5/19/85 (#15), pk 6/30/85 (#3, 1 wk), 21 wk.

_____, and Melville Shavelson
Don't Shoot, It's Only Me (Putnam) NYT nf 6/10/90 (#14), pk 6/17/90 (#3, 3 wk), 17 wk; PW hc nf 6/22/90 (#4, 3 wk), 8 wk; tot 25 wk.

Hopkins, Budd
Intruders (Ballantine) NYT pb nf 2/7/88 (#7), pk 2/21/88 (#5, 1 wk), 4 wk.

Hopkins, Jerry
Elvis: A Biography (Warner) NYT mm pb

9/18/77 (#4, 1 wk); PW mm pb 9/26/77 (#15, 2 wk); tot 3 wk.

_____, and Daniel Sugarman
No One Here Gets Out Alive (Warner) NYT td pb 6/22/80 (#13), pk 7/27/80 (#1, 1 wk), 36 wk; PW td pb 6/27/80 (#4), pk 7/4/80 (#1, 8 wk), 24 wk; PW mm pb 4/17/81 (#12, 1 wk), 3 wk; NYT mm pb 4/26/81 (#13, 1 wk), 2 wk; tot 65 wk.

Hoppe, Arthur
The Love Everybody Crusade (Doubleday) PW nf 8/12/63 (#8, 1 wk), 4 wk.

Hopper, Hedda
From Under My Hat (Doubleday) NYT gen 9/28/52 (#15), pk 10/26/52 (#10, 1 wk), 7 wk.

_____, and James Brough
The Whole Truth and Nothing But (Doubleday) PW nf 3/11/63 (#4), pk 5/22/63 (#1, 5 wk), 32 wk; NYT gen 4/7/63 (#4), pk 5/19/63 (#1, 7 wk), 27 wk; tot 59 wk.

Horan, James David
Confederate Agent (Crown) NYT gen 5/23/54 (#16, 1 wk).

The Seat of Power (Crown) PW fic 11/29/65 (#11, 3 wk), 5 wk.

Horan, Kenneth
A Bashful Woman (Doubleday) NYT fic 2/4/45 (#14, 1 wk).

Horgan, Paul
The Fault of Angels (Harper) PW fic 10/14/33 (#8, 4 wk).

Main Line West (Farrar) NYT fic 5/3/36 (#4, 4 wk).

A Distant Trumpet (Farrar) NYT fic 5/8/60 (#14), pk 5/15/60 (#8, 1 wk), 12 wk; PW fic 5/9/60 (#8), pk 6/6/60 (#7, 2 wk), 9 wk; tot 21 wk.

Horn, Stanley Fitzgerald
The Decisive Battle of Nashville (Univ. of Tennessee) NYT gen 1/13/57 (#15, 2 wk).

Horowitz, Al
See Richard Jerome Roberts, et al.

Horowitz, David
See Peter Collier and_____

Horton, Chase
See John Steinbeck and_____

Horton, Tom
See Yogi Berra and_____

Horwich, Frances R.
Miss Frances' Ding Dong School Book (Rand McNally) NYT ch bst 11/15/53 (#5, 40 wk).

Hotchner, A.E.
Papa Hemingway: A Personal Memoir

(Random) NYT gen 4/24/66 (#7), pk 6/19/66 (#2, 2 wk), 25 wk; PW nf 4/25/66 (#8), pk 6/13/66 (#2, 5 wk), 30 wk; NYT pb gen 5/7/67 (#4), pk 6/4/67 (#3, 8 wk), 12 wk; tot 67 wk.

Doris Day: Her Own Story (Morrow) PW hc nf 2/2/76 (#7), pk 3/1/76 (#1, 5 wk), 20 wk; NYT fic 2/15/76 (#6), pk 3/14/76 (#1, 5 wk), 21 wk; (Bantam) NYT mm pb 11/14/76 (#9), pk 12/5/76 (#5, 1 wk), 5 wk; PW mm pb 11/15/76 (#14), pk 11/22/76 (#7, 1 wk), 8 wk; tot 54 wk.

Sophia, Living and Loving: Her Own Story (Morrow) PW hc nf 3/12/79 (#14), pk 4/9/79 (#3, 1 wk), 15 wk; NYT nf 3/25/79 (#7), pk 4/1/79 (#3, 3 wk), 13 wk; tot 28 wk.

Hough, Emerson

The Covered Wagon (Appleton) PW fic 7/29/22 (#11), pk 8/26/22 (#10, 4 wk), 8 wk.

North of 36 (Appleton) PW fic 9/15/23 (#8, 4 wk).

Mother of Gold (Appleton) PW fic 4/19/24 (#8, 4 wk).

Hough, Henry Beetle

Country Editor (Doubleday) PW nf 10/12/40 (#8, 4 wk).

House, Boyce

I Give You Texas (Naylor) NYT gen 11/14/43 (#22, 1 wk).

House, Edward Mandell

The Intimate Papers of Colonel House (Houghton) PW nf 4/17/26 (#2, 4 wk), 8 wk.

Household, Geoffrey

Rogue Male (Little Brown) NYT fic 10/8/39 (#7, 4 wk).

Watcher in the Shadows (Little Brown) NYT fic 7/24/60 (#12), pk 8/7/60 (#9, 1 wk), 7 wk.

Houston, James

Ghost Fox (Avon) PW mm pb 3/13/78 (#11, 1 wk), 2 wk.

Hoving, Thomas

Tutankhamun: The Untold Story (Simon & Schuster) PW hc nf 11/13/78 (#15), pk 1/8/79 (#9, 1 wk), 15 wk; NYT nf 12/24/78 (#15), pk 2/4/79 (#8, 1 wk), 15 wk; tot 30 wk.

Howar, Barbara

Laughing All the Way (Stein & Day) NYT gen 5/13/73 (#10), pk 6/10/73 (#2, 3 wk), 22 wk; PW nf 5/14/73 (#7), pk 7/2/73 (#1, 1 wk), 19 wk; (Fawcett) NYT mm pb 5/12/74 (#2, 4 wk), 8 wk; tot 49 wk.

Howard, Elizabeth Metzger

Before the Sun Goes Down (Doubleday) NYT fic 2/10/46 (#14), pk 2/24/46 (#5, 2 wk), 16 wk; PW fic 2/23/46 (#5, 2 wk), 3 wk; tot 19 wk.

Howard, Guy

Walking Preacher of the Ozarks (Grosset & Dunlap) NYT gen 2/18/45 (#25, 1 wk).

Howard, Jane

Families (Simon & Schuster) PW hc nf 8/28/78 (#15), pk 9/11/78 (#11, 1 wk), 3 wk.

Howard, Joseph

Damien: The Omen, Part II (NAL/Signet) PW mm pb 5/29/78 (#14), pk 6/5/78 (#7, 2 wk), 8 wk; NYT mm pb 6/11/78 (#9), pk 7/9/78 (#5, 1 wk), 8 wk; tot 16 wk.

Howard, Katherine

Little Bunny Follows His Nose (Golden) NYT ch bst 5/2/71 (#10, 19 wk).

Howard, Richard

See Albert Camus

Howatch, Susan

Penmarric (Simon & Schuster) NYT fic 5/30/71 (#7), pk 6/20/71 (#5, 2 wk), 16 wk; PW fic 6/7/71 (#5), pk 7/19/71 (#2, 1 wk), 17 wk; tot 33 wk.

Cashelmara (Simon & Schuster) NYT fic 5/26/74 (#8), pk 7/7/74 (#3, 2 wk), 21 wk; PW fic 5/27/74 (#9), pk 7/1/74 (#3, 1 wk), 18 wk; (Fawcett) NYT mm pb 5/18/75 (#9), pk 6/1/75 (#5, 2 wk), 7 wk; tot 46 wk.

The Rich Are Different (Simon & Schuster) PW hc fic 5/2/77 (#9, 6 wk), 11 wk; NYT fic 5/8/77 (#10), pk 7/10/77 (#9, 1 wk), 6 wk; (Fawcett/Crest) PW mm pb 3/27/78 (#5), pk 4/10/78 (#4, 1 wk), 9 wk; NYT mm pb 4/2/78 (#12), pk 4/9/78 (#8, 2 wk), 8 wk; tot 34 wk.

Sins of the Fathers (Simon & Schuster) NYT fic 6/29/80 (#14), pk 8/3/80 (#4, 3 wk), 17 wk; PW hc fic 7/4/80 (#11), pk 7/11/80 (#5, 7 wk), 14 wk; (Fawcett/Crest) PW mm pb 7/31/81 (#8), pk 8/28/81 (#2, 2 wk), 12 wk; NYT mm pb 8/2/81 (#10), pk 8/23/81 (#3, 1 wk), 12 wk; tot 55 wk.

The Wheel of Fortune (Simon & Schuster) NYT fic 6/3/84 (#15), pk 7/15/84 (#8, 1 wk), 12 wk; PW hc fic 6/8/84 (#11), pk 7/13/84 (#6, 1 wk), 13 wk; (Fawcett/Crest) NYT pb fic 5/26/85 (#5), pk 6/2/85 (#1, 1 wk), 11 wk; PW mm pb 5/31/85 (#5), pk 6/7/85 (#1, 1 wk), 11 wk; tot 47 wk.

Glittering Images (Fawcett/Crest) NYT pb fic 10/30/88 (#14), pk 11/27/88 (#4, 1 wk), 8 wk; PW mm pb 11/4/88 (#9), pk 11/25/88 (#4, 1 wk), 8 wk; tot 16 wk.

Glamorous Powers (Fawcett) NYT pb fic 11/12/89 (#15, 1 wk).

Ultimate Prizes (Fawcett) NYT pb fic 9/23/90 (#13, 1 wk).

Howe, George Locke

Call It Treason (Viking) NYT fic 10/2/49 (#14), pk 10/23/49 (#8, 1 wk), 5 wk.

Howe, Helen Huntington
The Whole Heart (Holt) NYT fic 2/21/43 (#19), pk 3/7/43 (#6, 1 wk), 7 wk.
We Happy Few (Simon & Schuster) NYT fic 7/21/46 (#12), pk 9/8/46 (#5, 1 wk), 15 wk; PW fic 8/24/46 (#5), pk 8/31/46 (#4, 1 wk), 5 wk; tot 20 wk.
The Circle of the Day (Simon & Schuster) PW fic 7/15/50 (#8, 1 wk); NYT fic 6/18/50 (#11), pk 6/25/50 (#8, 2 wk), 12 wk; tot 13 wk.
The Success (Simon & Schuster) NYT fic 10/14/56 (#16), pk 11/11/56 (#8, 1 wk), 12 wk.

Howe, Irving, and Kenneth Libo
World of Our Fathers (Harcourt) PW hc nf 2/23/76 (#7), pk 4/12/76 (#1, 2 wk), 33 wk; NYT gen 2/29/76 (#8), pk 4/18/76 (#1, 1 wk), 32 wk; tot 65 wk.

Howe, James
Scared Silly: A Halloween Treat [illus. Leslie Morrill] (Avon/Camelot) PW ch yn rd 10/26/90 (#4, 4 wk).

Howell, Michael, and Peter Ford
The True History of the Elephant Man (Penguin) NYT td pb 11/23/80 (#14, 2 wk).

Hoy, Claire
See Victor Ostrovsky and_____

Hubbard, Bernard
Cradle of the Storms (Dodd) NYT gen 2/18/45 (#19, 1 wk).

Hubbard, Elbert
Elbert Hubbard's Scrap Book (Wise) PW nf 6/25/27 (#7, 4 wk), 16 wk.

Hubbard, L. Ron
Dianetics: The Modern Science of Mental Health (Hermitage House) NYT gen 6/18/50 (#10), pk 8/13/50 (#4, 6 wk), 28 wk; PW nf 8/12/50 (#8), pk 9/16/50 (#4, 3 wk), 7 wk; [revised edition] (Bridge) PW td pb 8/22/86 (#4), pk 3/4/88 (#1, 2 wk), 139 wk; NYT msc pb 9/7/86 (#8), pk 3/20/88 (#1, 1 wk), 72 wk; tot 246 wk.
Battlefield Earth (St. Martin's) NYT fic 6/19/83 (#14, 1 wk), 2 wk; PW hc fic 7/1/83 (#14, 2 wk), 3 wk; (Bridge) NYT pb fic 3/11/84 (#14), pk 4/1/84 (#8, 1 wk), 7 wk; PW mm pb 3/23/84 (#14), pk 4/6/84 (#12, 1 wk), 4 wk; tot 16 wk.
The Invader's Plan (Bridge) NYT fic 12/1/85 (#14), pk 12/8/85 (#13, 1 wk), 2 wk; PW hc fic 12/6/85 (#15), pk 1/3/86 (#11, 3 wk), 6 wk; NYT pb fic 6/5/88 (#15, 2 wk); tot 10 wk.
Black Genesis—Fortress of Evil (Bridge) NYT fic 4/6/86 (#14, 1 wk), 3 wk; PW hc fic 4/11/86 (#13), pk 4/18/86 (#10, 2 wk), 5 wk; tot 8 wk.
The Enemy Within (Bridge) NYT fic 5/25/

86 (#10, 1 wk), 2 wk; PW hc fic 5/30/86 (#9), pk 6/13/86 (#8, 1 wk), 5 wk; tot 7 wk.
An Alien Affair (Bridge) NYT fic 8/17/86 (#13, 1 wk), 2 wk; PW hc fic 8/22/86 (#15), pk 9/5/86 (#10, 1 wk), 8 wk; tot 10 wk.
Fortune of Fear (Bridge) NYT fic 10/26/86 (#12), pk 11/2/86 (#10, 1 wk), 4 wk; PW hc fic 11/7/86 (#10, 1 wk), 7 wk; tot 11 wk.
Death Quest (Bridge) NYT fic 1/25/87 (#15), pk 2/1/87 (#10, 1 wk), 4 wk; PW hc fic 1/30/87 (#11), pk 2/6/87 (#8, 1 wk), 6 wk; tot 10 wk.
Voyage of Vengeance (Bridge) NYT fic 5/24/87 (#13, 1 wk), 2 wk.
Disaster (Bridge) NYT fic 8/16/87 (#17, 1 wk); PW hc fic 8/28/87 (#12, 2 wk); tot 3 wk.
Villainy Victorious (Bridge) NYT fic 10/4/87 (#13, 1 wk); PW hc fic 10/16/87 (#14), pk 10/23/87 (#10, 1 wk), 4 wk; tot 5 wk.
The Doomed Planet (Bridge) NYT fic 11/29/87 (#10, 1 wk); PW hc fic 12/4/87 (#10, 1 wk), 3 wk; tot 4 wk.

Hudson, Jay William
Abbe Pierre (Appleton) PW fic 7/29/22 (#12, 4 wk).

Hudson, Rock, and Sara Davidson
Rock Hudson: His Story (Morrow) NYT nf 6/29/86 (#14), pk 7/13/86 (#3, 5 wk), 14 wk; PW hc nf 7/11/86 (#9), pk 7/25/86 (#3, 2 wk), 13 wk; (Avon) NYT pb nf 4/5/87 (#5), pk 4/19/87 (#3, 2 wk), 6 wk; tot 33 wk.

Hudson, Virginia Cary
O Ye Jigs & Juleps! (Macmillan) NYT gen 5/27/62 (#11), pk 10/7/62 (#2, 2 wk), 45 wk; PW nf 7/16/62 (#7), pk 10/22/62 (#1, 1 wk), 56 wk; tot 101 wk.

Huffington, Arianna Stassinopoulos
Picasso: Creator and Destroyer (Simon & Schuster) NYT nf 6/26/88 (#9), pk 7/17/88 (#6, 1 wk), 10 wk; PW hc nf 7/1/88 (#15), pk 7/22/88 (#11, 1 wk), 8 wk; tot 18 wk.

Hughes, Emmet John
America the Vincible (Doubleday) NYT gen 12/27/59 (#16, 2 wk).
The Ordeal of Power (Atheneum) NYT gen 4/14/63 (#8), pk 6/2/63 (#3, 1 wk), 11 wk; PW nf 4/22/63 (#9), pk 5/13/63 (#3, 2 wk), 14 wk; tot 25 wk.

Hughes, Richard
The Fox in the Attic (Harper) NYT fic 2/25/62 (#11), pk 4/8/62 (#2, 1 wk), 20 wk; PW fic 2/26/62 (#11), pk 4/9/62 (#3, 2 wk), 20 wk; tot 40 wk.

Hughes, Robert
The Fatal Shore: The Epic of Australia's

Founding (Knopf) NYT nf 2/1/5/87 (#3, 4 wk), 27 wk; PW hc nf 2/20/87 (#7), pk 2/27/87 (#6, 3 wk), 16 wk; (Vintage) NYT pb nf 2/28/88 (#4), pk 3/20/88 (#2, 1 wk), 13 wk; PW td pb 3/4/88 (#6), pk 3/18/88 (#4, 3 wk), 10 wk; tot 66 wk.

Huie, William Bradford
Mud on the Stars (Fischer) NYT fic 8/9/42 (#11, 1 wk).

Hulbert, Archer B.
Forty-Niners (Little Brown) PW nf 1/16/32 (#9, 4 wk).

Hull, Cordell
The Memoirs of Cordell Hull (Macmillan) NYT gen 6/13/48 (#7, 2 wk), 9 wk; PW nf 7/17/48 (#10, 1 wk); tot 10 wk.

Hull, Edith M.
The Sheik (Small) PW fic 9/3/21 (#4), pk 4/1/21 (#3, 4 wk), 32 wk.
Shadow of the East (Small) PW fic 9/16/22 (#7, 4 wk).
The Desert Healer (Small) PW fic 9/15/23 (#9, 4 wk).

Hull, Helen Rose
Heat Lightning (Coward McCann) PW fic 6/11/32 (#10, 4 wk).
Frost Flower (Coward McCann) NYT fic 3/5/39 (#5, 4 wk); PW fic 3/11/39 (#10, 4 wk); tot 8 wk.
A Circle in the Water (Coward McCann) NYT fic 2/21/43 (#14, 1 wk), 3 wk.

Hull, Raymond
See Laurence J. Peter and_____

Hulme, Kathryn
The Nun's Story (Little Brown) NYT gen 9/30/56 (#9), pk 10/21/56 (#1, 15 wk), 48 wk; PW nf 10/1/56 (#8), pk 10/22/56 (#1, 18 wk), 41 wk; tot 89 wk.
Annie's Captain (Little Brown) NYT gen 4/16/61 (#12, 1 wk), 3 wk.

Humes, Harold Louis
The Underground City (Random) NYT fic 5/25/58 (#15, 2 wk), 3 wk.

Humphrey, William
Home from the Hill (Knopf) NYT fic 3/2/58 (#14), pk 3/9/58 (#13, 1 wk), 8 wk.
The Ordways (Knopf) NYT fic 3/7/65 (#7, 1 wk), 8 wk; PW fic 3/22/65 (#11), pk 3/29/65 (#6, 2 wk), 7 wk; tot 15 wk.

Huneker, James G.
Steeplejack (Scribner) PW gen lit 1/8/21 (#7, 4 wk).

Hungerford, Edward
Wells Fargo (Random) NYT gen 8/21/49 (#15), pk 9/4/49 (#13, 1 wk), 4 wk.

Hunt, Frazier
The Untold Story of Douglas MacArthur (Devin Adair) NYT gen 11/14/54 (#11, 1 wk), 2 wk.

Hunt, Irene
Up a Road Slowly (Follett) NYT ch bst 5/7/67 (#2), pk 11/5/67 (#1, 26 wk), 45 wk.

Hunt, Sir John
The Conquest of Everest (Dutton) NYT gen 2/7/54 (#14), pk 2/28/54 (#3, 3 wk), 17 wk; PW fic 2/20/54 (#3, 5 wk), 12 wk; tot 29 wk.

Hunter, Evan
Strangers When We Meet (Simon & Schuster) NYT fic 6/22/58 (#9), pk 7/20/58 (#7, 4 wk), 15 wk; PW fic 7/28/58 (#8), pk 8/4/58 (#7, 2 wk), 6 wk; tot 21 wk.
Mothers and Daughters (Simon & Schuster) NYT fic 6/11/61 (#15), pk 8/13/61 (#9, 2 wk), 16 wk; PW fic 6/26/61 (#9), pk 7/31/61 (#8, 2 wk), 5 wk; tot 21 wk.

Hunter, Hall
The Bengal Tiger (Doubleday) NYT fic 6/22/52 (#16, 1 wk).

Hunter, John A.
Hunter (Harper) NYT gen 12/14/52 (#14), pk 1/18/53 (#12, 1 wk), 8 wk.

Hurd, Edith and Clement Hurd
The Cat from Telegraph Hill (Lothrop Lee & Shepard) NYT ch bst 11/13/55 (#14, 40 wk).

Hurnard, Hannah
Hinds' Feet on High Places (Tyndale) PW pb rel 10/5/90 (#7, 4 wk), 8 wk.

Hurok, Solomon, and Ruth Goode
Impresario (Random) NYT gen 6/23/46 (#13), pk 7/21/46 (#12, 1 wk), 5 wk.

Hurst, Fannie
A President Is Born (Doubleday) PW fic 4/28/28 (#5, 4 wk).
Back Street (Cosmopolitan) PW fic 2/21/31 (#9), pk 3/21/31 (#1, 4 wk), 12 wk.
Imitation of Life (Harper) PW fic 3/11/33 (#9, 4 wk).
Great Laughter (Harper) NYT fic 11/8/36 (#4, 4 wk); PW fic 12/12/36 (#7, 4 wk); tot 8 wk.
Hallelujah (Harper) NYT fic 1/30/44 (#7, 2 wk), 6 wk.
God Must Be Sad (Doubleday) NYT fic 1/14/62 (#15, 1 wk).

Hurwitz, Ken
See Vincent Bugliosi and_____

Huston, McCready
The Gates of Brass (Lippincott) NYT fic 9/23/56 (#15, 2 wk).

Hutchinson, A.S.M.
If Winter Comes (Little) PW fic 11/12/21 (#6), pk 1/7/22 (#1, 20 wk), 36 wk.
This Freedom (Little Brown) PW fic 10/14/ 22 (#1, 16 wk), 24 wk.
One Increasing Purpose (Little Brown) PW fic 11/21/25 (#2, 8 wk), 12 wk.
The Uncertain Trumpet (Little Brown) PW fic 11/9/29 (#10, 4 wk).

Hutchinson, Ray Coryton
Elephant and Castle (Rinehart) NYT fic 2/20/49 (#13), pk 3/6/49 (#8, 2 wk), 6 wk.
Shining Scabbard (Farrar) NYT fic 1/31/37 (#7, 4 wk).

Hutson, Harold H.
See Donald Wayne Riddle and_____

Huxley, Aldous Leonard
Point Counter Point (Doubleday) PW fic 2/16/29 (#7, 4 wk), 8 wk.
Eyeless in Gaza (Harper) NYT fic 8/2/36 (#9), pk 9/13/36 (#3, 4 wk), 8 wk; PW fic 8/15/36 (#6), pk 9/12/36 (#2, 4 wk), 16 wk; tot 24 wk.
Ends and Means (Harper) NYT gen 2/6/ 38 (#15, 4 wk).
After Many a Summer Dies the Swan (Harper) PW fic 3/9/40 (#8, 4 wk).
Time Must Have a Stop (Harper) NYT fic 9/17/44 (#8), pk 9/24/44 (#7, 1 wk), 14 wk; PW fic 10/14/44 (#8, 1 wk); tot 15 wk.
Perennial Philosophy (Harper) NYT gen 10/28/45 (#8), pk 12/2/45 (#7, 1 wk), 9 wk.
Ape and Essence (Harper) NYT fic 9/12/48 (#16), pk 9/19/48 (#9, 1 wk), 6 wk.
The Devils of Loudun (Harper) NYT gen 10/26/52 (#16), pk 11/16/52 (#7, 1 wk), 8 wk.
The Genius and the Goddess (Harper) NYT fic 9/18/55 (#13), pk 9/25/55 (#11, 1 wk), 3 wk.
Brave New World Revisited (Harper) NYT gen 1/4/59 (#16), pk 2/1/59 (#11, 1 wk), 4 wk.
Island (Harper) NYT fic 4/15/62 (#16), pk 5/20/62 (#7, 1 wk), 11 wk.

Huxley, Elspeth Joscelin Grant
The Flame Trees of Thika (Morrow) NYT gen 9/20/59 (#13, 1 wk).

Huxley, Julian
The Wonderful World of Life (Garden City) NYT ch bst 11/1/59 (#13, 25 wk).

Huxley, Laura Archera
You Are Not the Target (Farrar) NYT gen 7/21/63 (#10, 1 wk).

Huygen, Wil
Gnomes [illus. Rien Poortvliet] (Abrams) PW hc nf 11/21/77 (#7), pk 12/5/77 (#3, 6 wk), 64 wk; NYT nf 11/27/77 (#9), pk 1/14/

79 (#1, 1 wk), 56 wk; (Bantam) NYT td pb 3/4/79 (#11), pk 3/11/79 (#1, 2 wk), 25 wk; PW td pb 3/5/79 (#4, 4 wk), 15 wk; tot 160 wk.

Hyams, Joe
See Chuck Norris and_____
See Michael Reagan and_____

Hybels, Bill
Honest to God? (Zondervan) PW hc rel 10/5/90 (#11), pk 11/9/90 (#9, 4 wk), 8 wk.

Hyde, Anthony
The Red Fox (Knopf) NYT fic 9/29/85 (#15), pk 10/6/85 (#10, 1 wk), 7 wk; PW hc fic 10/4/85 (#15, 3 wk); (Ballantine) NYT pb fic 9/7/86 (#12), pk 9/28/86 (#2, 4 wk), 11 wk; PW mm pb 9/12/86 (#10), pk 9/26/86 (#1, 2 wk), 10 wk; tot 31 wk.

Hyman, B.D.
My Mother's Keeper (Morrow) NYT nf 5/19/85 (#10), pk 6/2/85 (#4, 4 wk), 11 wk; PW hc nf 5/24/85 (#9), pk 6/7/85 (#3, 1 wk), 8 wk; (Berkley) NYT pb nf 5/4/86 (#2), pk 5/18/86 (#1, 2 wk), 7 wk; PW mm pb 5/16/86 (#12), pk 5/23/86 (#10, 1 wk), 3 wk; tot 29 wk.

Hyman, Mac
No Time for Sergeants (Random) NYT fic 10/24/54 (#12), pk 2/13/55 (#2, 1 wk), 66 wk; PW fic 11/6/54 (#5), pk 2/26/55 (#2, 3 wk), 45 wk; tot 111 wk.

Hyman, Trina Schart
See Margaret Hodges

Hynd, Alan
Passport to Treason (McBride) NYT gen 5/30/43 (#18), pk 6/27/43 (#17, 1 wk), 2 wk.
Betrayal from the East (McBride) NYT gen 12/26/43 (#19), pk 1/23/44 (#13, 1 wk), 5 wk.

Iacocca, Lee, with Sonny Kleinfield
Talking Straight (Bantam) NYT nf 6/19/ 88 (#3), pk 7/3/88 (#1, 3 wk), 31 wk; PW hc nf 6/24/88 (#4), pk 7/1/88 (#1, 2 wk), 25 wk; NYT pb nf 6/25/89 (#7), pk 7/2/89 (#1, 1 wk), 7 wk; PW mm pb 7/7/89 (#14, 1 wk); tot 64 wk.

_____, and William Novak
Iacocca: An Autobiography (Bantam) NYT nf 11/4/84 (#1, 40 wk, 88 wk; PW hc nf 11/9/84 (#3), pk 11/16/84 (#1, 35 wk), 79 wk; NYT pb nf 7/6/86 (#1, 7 wk), 18 wk; PW mm pb 1/10/86 (#8), pk 7/18/86 (#1, 1 wk), 10 wk; tot 195 wk.

Ibanez, Vincente Blasco
Mare Nostrum (Dutton) PW fic 10/25/19 (#7), pk 11/1/19 (#4, 4 wk), 16 wk.

The Four Horsemen of the Apocalypse (Dutton) PW fic 5/3/19 (#1, 16 wk), 40 wk.
Woman Triumphant (Dutton) PW fic 7/3/20 (#4, 4 wk), 12 wk.

Ickes, Harold L.
Autobiography of a Curmudgeon (Reynal & Hitchcock) NYT gen 5/9/43 (#22), pk 5/23/43 (#14, 1 wk), 3 wk.
The Secret Diary of Harold L. Ickes (Simon & Schuster) NYT gen 12/20/53 (#12), pk 1/31/54 (#4, 1 wk), 12 wk; PW nf 1/16/54 (#7), pk 1/30/54 (#5, 1 wk), 5 wk; tot 17 wk.
The Secret Diary of Harold L. Ickes Vol. II (Simon & Schuster) NYT gen 5/30/54 (#16, 2 wk).

Idell, Albert E.
Centennial Summer (Holt) PW fic 8/21/43 (#5, 2 wk), 7 wk; NYT fic 8/22/43 (#7), pk 9/5/43 (#5, 1 wk), 9 wk; tot 16 wk.

Ileana, Princess of Romania
I Live Again (Rinehart) NYT gen 3/30/52 (#16, 1 wk).

Ilg, Frances Lillian
See Arnold Gesell, et al.

_____, and Louise Bates Ames
Child Behavior (Harper) NYT gen 10/16/55 (#16), pk 11/6/55 (#15, 1 wk), 2 wk.

Ilin, M.
New Russia's Primer (Houghton) PW nf 7/18/31 (#5, 8 wk), 20 wk.

Infeld, Leopold
See Albert Einstein and _____

Ing, Dean
The Ran.   f Black Stealth One (Todd/-Tor) NYT pu ilc 4/22/90 (#16, 1 wk).

Ingersoll, Ralph
The Battle Is the Pay-Off (Harcourt) NYT gen 11/14/43 (#14), pk 12/5/43 (#6, 1 wk), 9 wk.
Top Secret (Harcourt) NYT gen 5/5/46 (#16), pk 5/19/46 (#2, 9 wk), 24 wk; PW nf 5/18/46 (#2), pk 6/22/46 (#1, 1 wk), 16 wk; tot 40 wk.
The Great Ones (Harcourt) NYT fic 3/14/48 (#8, 1 wk), 6 wk.

Innes, Hammond
The Wreck of the Mary Deare (Knopf) NYT fic 12/16/56 (#14), pk 12/30/56 (#11, 1 wk), 6 wk.
The Land God Gave to Cain (Knopf) NYT fic 1/4/59 (#15, 1 wk).
The Strode Venturer (Knopf) PW fic 12/6/65 (#10), pk 1/31/66 (#8, 1 wk), 2 wk.

Irvine, E. Eastman
See Anonymous (World Almanac)

Irving, Clifford
Daddy's Girl (Zebra) NYT pb nf 4/1/90 (#4, 3 wk), 7 wk; PW mm pb 4/13/90 (#14, 1 wk); tot 8 wk.

Irving, John
The World According to Garp (Harcourt/Dutton) PW hc fic 5/22/78 (#14), pk 7/17/78 (#4, 1 wk), 32 wk; NYT fic 5/28/78 (#9), pk 7/30/78 (#4, 1 wk), 16 wk; (Pocket) PW mm pb 4/9/79 (#4), pk 4/23/79 (#1, 13 wk), 41 wk; NYT mm pb 4/15/79 (#5), pk 4/29/79 (#1, 4 wk), 40 wk; tot 129 wk.
Hotel New Hampshire (Robbins/Dutton) PW hc fic 9/11/81 (#15), pk 10/2/81 (#1, 6 wk), 43 wk; NYT fic 9/20/81 (#5), pk 9/27/81 (#1, 8 wk), 40 wk; PW mm pb 9/17/82 (#3), pk 9/24/82 (#1, 3 wk), 13 wk; NYT mm pb 9/19/82 (#5), pk 9/26/82 (#1, 2 wk), 16 wk; tot 112 wk.
The Cider House Rules (Morrow) PW hc fic 5/24/85 (#10), pk 6/21/85 (#1, 2 wk), 19 wk; NYT fic 5/26/85 (#11), pk 6/16/85 (#1, 1 wk), 21 wk; (Bantam) pb fic 7/6/86 (#5), pk 7/13/86 (#2, 2 wk), 13 wk; PW mm pb 7/11/86 (#9), pk 7/25/86 (#3, 1 wk), 10 wk; tot 63 wk.
A Prayer for Owen Meany (Morrow) NYT fic 3/26/89 (#6), pk 4/16/89 (#2, 3 wk), 19 wk; PW hc fic 3/31/89 (#6), pk 4/21/89 (#2, 3 wk), 17 wk; (Ballantine) NYT pb fic 5/6/90 (#8), pk 5/13/90 (#2, 1 wk), 14 wk; PW mm pb 5/11/90 (#3, 3 wk), 12 wk; tot 62 wk.

Irwin, Margaret
Young Bess (Harcourt) NYT fic 5/6/45 (#16), pk 5/20/45 (#11, 1 wk), 4 wk.
Elizabeth, Captive Princess (Harcourt) NYT fic 1/23/49 (#22), pk 2/6/49 (#12, 1 wk), 3 wk.

Isaacs, Susan
Compromising Positions (Harcourt/Jove) PW mm pb 1/22/79 (#15), pk 1/29/79 (#6, 1 wk), 10 wk; NYT mm pb 2/4/79 (#14), pk 2/11/79 (#7, 1 wk), 10 wk; tot 20 wk.
Close Relations (Avon) PW mm pb 9/25/81 (#10), pk 10/9/81 (#6, 1 wk), 4 wk; NYT mm pb 10/25/81 (#14, 1 wk); tot 5 wk.
Almost Paradise (Harper) NYT fic 2/12/84 (#7), pk 3/18/84 (#3, 2 wk), 16 wk; PW hc fic 2/17/84 (#13), pk 3/16/84 (#5, 3 wk), 16 wk; (Ballantine) NYT pb fic 2/3/85 (#5), pk 2/10/85 (#1, 4 wk), 15 wk; PW mm pb 2/8/85 (#7), pk 2/15/85 (#1, 4 wk), 16 wk; tot 63 wk.
Shining Through (Harper) PW hc fic 8/19/88 (#13), pk 9/23/88 (#7, 1 wk), 8 wk; NYT fic 8/21/88 (#10), pk 9/25/88 (#9, 2 wk), 8 wk; (Ballantine) NYT pb fic 8/6/89 (#13), pk 8/20/89 (#3, 2 wk), 9 wk; PW mm pb 8/11/89 (#10), pk 8/25/89 (#4, 2 wk), 7 wk; tot 32 wk.

Isherwood, Christopher
Vedanta for the Western World [ed.] (Marcel Rodd) NYT gen 4/21/46 (#16, 1 wk).
The World in the Evening (Random) NYT fic 7/4/54 (#14), pk 7/11/54 (#13, 1 wk), 4 wk.

Ishiguro, Kazuo
Remains of the Day (Vintage) PW td pb 12/21/90 (#8, 1 wk).

Israel, Charles E.
Rizpah (Simon & Schuster) NYT fic 5/7/61 (#15, 1 wk).

Israel, Lee
Kilgallen (Delacorte) NYT nf 2/3/80 (#15, 1 wk).

"J"
The Sensuous Woman (Stuart) NYT gen 4/26/70 (#8), pk 9/27/70 (#1, 10 wk), 48 wk; PW nf 5/4/70 (#7), pk 8/31/70 (#1, 11 wk), 46 wk; NYT pb gen 3/7/71 (#2, 20 wk), 32 wk; tot 126 wk.

J.K. Lasser Tax Institute
J.K. Lasser's What the New Tax Law Means to You (Pocket) NYT msc pb 11/30/86 (#12), pk 12/7/86 (#8, 1 wk), 4 wk.
J.K. Lasser's Your Income Tax [1941] (Simon & Schuster) PW nf 2/8/41 (#6), pk 3/15/41 (#3, 4 wk), 8 wk.
J.K. Lasser's Your Income Tax [1942] (Simon & Schuster) PW nf 12/13/41 (#10), pk 3/14/41 (#5, 4 wk), 12 wk.
J.K. Lasser's Your Income Tax [1943] (Simon & Schuster) PW nf 2/13/43 (#9, 1 wk).
J.K. Lasser's Your Income Tax [1946] (Simon & Schuster) NYT gen 1/27/46 (#12), pk 3/17/46 (#5, 1 wk), 10 wk.
J.K. Lasser's Your Income Tax [1947] (Simon & Schuster) NYT gen 2/9/47 (#11, 1 wk), 3 wk.
J.K. Lasser's Your Income Tax [1948] (Simon & Schuster) NYT gen 2/29/48 (#14), pk 3/14/48 (#12, 1 wk), 3 wk.
J.K. Lasser's Your Income Tax [1974] (Simon & Schuster) NYT td pb 3/10/74 (#5, 8 wk).
J.K. Lasser's Your Income Tax [1975] (Simon & Schuster) NYT td pb 1/26/75 (#4), pk 2/23/75 (#2, 2 wk), 12 wk.
J.K. Lasser's Your Income Tax 1977 (Simon & Schuster) PW td pb 1/31/77 (#3), pk 2/28/77 (#1, 1 wk), 12 wk.
J.K. Lasser's Your Income Tax 1978 (Simon & Schuster) PW td pb 1/30/78 (#4), pk 2/20/78 (#2, 6 wk), 13 wk.
J.K. Lasser's Your Income Tax 1979 (Simon & Schuster) PW td pb 1/29/79 (#9), pk 2/12/79 (#3, 2 wk), 9 wk.
J.K. Lasser's Your Income Tax 1980 (Simon & Schuster) PW td pb 2/8/80 (#9), pk 2/22/80 (#4, 6 wk), 11 wk.

J.K. Lasser's Your Income Tax 1981 (Simon & Schuster) PW td pb 2/27/81 (#9), pk 3/13/81 (#6, 3 wk), 7 wk.
J.K. Lasser's Your Income Tax 1982 (Simon & Schuster) PW td pb 2/19/82 (#7), pk 2/26/82 (#4, 2 wk), 9 wk.
J.K. Lasser's Your Income Tax 1984 (Simon & Schuster) NYT msc pb 1/15/84 (#6), pk 1/29/84 (#1, 2 wk), 16 wk; PW td pb 1/27/84 (#9), pk 2/17/84 (#4, 3 wk), 14 wk; tot 30 wk.
J.K. Lasser's Your Income Tax 1985 (Simon & Schuster) PW td pb 2/1/85 (#9), pk 3/15/85 (#5, 1 wk), 10 wk; NYT msc pb 2/3/85 (#5), pk 2/17/85 (#2, 3 wk), 13 wk; tot 23 wk.
J.K. Lasser's Your Income Tax 1986 (Simon & Schuster) PW td pb 1/31/86 (#9), pk 3/7/86 (#2, 1 wk), 15 wk; NYT msc pb 1/12/86 (#12), pk 1/19/86 (#1, 1 wk), 16 wk; tot 31 wk.
J.K. Lasser's Your Income Tax 1987 (Prentice Hall/Lasser Tax Institute) NYT msc pb 1/18/87 (#5), pk 1/25/87 (#3, 1 wk), 12 wk; PW td pb 1/23/87 (#10), pk 2/13/87 (#1, 1 wk), 13 wk; tot 25 wk.
J.K. Lasser's Your Income Tax 1988 (Prentice Hall/Lasser Tax Institute) PW td pb 2/5/88 (#9), pk 2/19/88 (#3, 1 wk), 8 wk; NYT msc pb 2/21/88 (#2, 1 wk), 3 wk; tot 11 wk.
J.K. Lasser's Your Income Tax 1989 (Prentice Hall/Lasser Tax Institute) PW td pb 2/3/89 (#9), pk 2/24/89 (#7, 1 wk), 5 wk; NYT msc pb 3/5/89 (#6), pk 3/19/89 (#5, 1 wk), 2 wk; tot 7 wk.
J.K. Lasser's Your Income Tax 1990 (Prentice Hall/Lasser Tax Institute) PW td pb 1/26/90 (#10), pk 3/2/90 (#5, 1 wk), 6 wk; NYT msc pb 2/18/90 (#3, 3 wk); tot 9 wk.

Jackson, Bo and Dick Schaap
Bo Knows Bo (Doubleday) PW hc nf 11/16/90 (#15), pk 12/14/90 (#3, 2 wk), 4 wk; NYT nf 11/18/90 (#13), pk 12/9/90 (#2, 1 wk), 7 wk; tot 11 wk.

Jackson, Carole
Color Me Beautiful (Ballantine) NYT td pb 5/24/81 (#6), pk 6/20/82 (#1, 1 wk), 136 wk; PW td pb 5/22/81 (#7), pk 5/28/82 (#2, 15 wk), 176 wk; NYT msc pb 1/1/84 (#10), pk 3/11/84 (#3, 8 wk), 44 wk; tot 356 wk.

Jackson, Charles
The Lost Weekend (Farrar) NYT fic 2/27/44 (#7), 3/19/44 (#6, 3 wk), 19 wk; PW fic 3/11/44 (#5, 2 wk), 4 wk; tot 23 wk.
The Fall of Valor (Rinehart) NYT fic 10/27/46 (#7), pk 11/10/46 (#3, 1 wk), 13 wk; PW fic 11/2/46 (#4, 5 wk), 8 wk; tot 21 wk.
A Second-Hand Life (Macmillan) PW fic 9/4/67 (#11), pk 10/9/67 (#8, 1 wk), 8 wk; NYT fic 9/10/67 (#8), pk 10/1/67 (#6, 2 wk), 8 wk; tot 16 wk.

Jackson, Clarence S.
Picture Maker of the Old West [text by]
(Scribner) NYT gen 11/2/47 (#16, 1 wk).

Jackson, Harold Charles LeBaron
Longs and Shorts (Arnold Powers) NYT nf
11/22/42 (#20), pk 12/6/42 (#12, 1 wk), 7 wk.
Ups and Downs (Arnold Powers) NYT gen
10/24/43 (#10, 1 wk), 2 wk.

Jackson, Joseph Henry
Continent's End [ed.] (Doubleday) NYT
gen 12/10/44 (#13), pk 12/24/44 (#11, 2 wks),
8 wk.
San Francisco Murders [ed.] (Duell Sloan
& Pearce) NYT gen 6/22/47 (#11, 1 wk), 3
wk.
The Christmas Flower (Harcourt) NYT fic
12/30/51 (#14, 1 wk).

Jackson, Josephine A., and Helen M. Salisbury
Outwitting Our Nerves (Century) PW nf
5/13/22 (#5, 4 wk), 8 wk; PW gen lit 6/17/22
(#6), pk 7/29/22 (#4, 4 wk), 20 wk; tot 28
wk.

Jackson, Martin
See Linda Sunshine

Jackson, Michael
Moonwalk (Doubleday) NYT nf 5/8/88
(#2), pk 5/15/88 (#1, 2 wk), 11 wk; PW hc nf
5/13/88 (#4), pk 5/20/88 (#1, 2 wk), 11 wk;
tot 22 wk.

Jackson, Reggie, and Mike Lupica
Reggie (Villard) NYT nf 7/22/84 (#15), pk
8/5/84 (#11, 1 wk), 4 wk.

Jackson, Shirley
Life Among the Savages (Farrar) NYT gen
7/12/53 (#16), pk 8/30/53 (#8, 1 wk), 11 wk.
We Have Always Lived in the Castle (Viking) NYT fic 11/4/62 (#15), pk 11/25/62 (#9,
1 wk), 7 wk; PW fic 11/12/62 (#12), pk 12/10/
62 (#7, 1 wk), 7 wk; tot 14 wk.

Jacobson, Edmund
You Must Relax (Whittlesey) PW nf 7/14/
34 (#5, 12 wk), 16 wk.

Jacoby, Annalee
See Theodore H. White and _____

Jacoby, Oswald
How to Win at Canasta (Doubleday) NYT
gen 9/4/49 (#16), pk 9/18/49 (#11, 1 wk), 2
wk.

Jacques, Brian
Redwall (Avon) PW ch yn ad 12/21/90
(#3, 4 wk).
Mossflower (Avon) PW ch yn ad 12/21/90
(#5, 4 wk).

Jaffe, Dennis T.
See Harold H. Bloomfield, M.D., et al.

Jaffe, Rona
The Best of Everything (Simon & Schuster) NYT fic 9/21/58 (#15), pk 10/26/58 (#6,
6 wk), 20 wk; PW fic 10/6/58 (#8), pk 11/3/
58 (#6, 2 wk), 11 wk; tot 31 wk.
Away from Home (Simon & Schuster)
NYT fic 9/11/60 (#13, 1 wk), 5 wk.
Class Reunion (Delacorte) NYT fic 6/10/
79 (#13), pk 9/9/79 (#4, 1 wk), 21 wk; PW hc
fic 6/25/79 (#15), pk 8/27/79 (#5, 1 wk), 16
wk; (Dell) PW mm pb 6/13/80 (#9), pk 7/11/
80 (#2, 1 wk), 16 wk; NYT mm pb 6/15/80
(#2, 2 wk), 18 wk; tot 71 wk.
Mazes and Monsters (Dell) PW mm pb 8/
13/82 (#12, 2 wk), 5 wk; NYT mm pb 9/5/82
(#14, 2 wk); tot 7 wk.
After the Reunion (Delacorte) PW hc fic
8/30/85 (#15), pk 9/13/85 (#11, 2 wk), 4 wk;
NYT fic 9/22/85 (#14), pk 10/6/85 (#11, 1
wk), 4 wk; (Dell) pb fic 9/7/86 (#11), pk
9/14/86 (#6, 3 wk), 5 wk; PW mm pb 9/12/86
(#9), pk 9/19/86 (#7, 2 wk), 5 wk; tot 18 wk.

Jahr, Cliff
See Cheryl Crane and _____

Jakes, John
The Seekers (Pyramid) NYT mm pb 8/31/
75 (#6), pk 9/7/75 (#4, 1 wk), 7 wk.
The Rebels (Pyramid) NYT mm pb 4/6/75
(#10, 2 wk).
The Titans (Pyramid) PW mm pb 7/5/76
(#8), pk 7/19/76 (#1, 1 wk), 15 wk; NYT mm
pb 7/11/76 (#5), pk 7/18/76 (#1, 3 wk), 14 wk;
tot 29 wk.
The Furies (Pyramid) NYT mm pb 1/18/76
(#3), pk 2/15/76 (#1, 1 wk), 12 wk; PW mm
pb 2/2/76 (#2, 2 wk), 9 wk; tot 21 wk.
The Warriors (Pyramid) PW mm pb 4/11/
77 (#9), pk 4/25/77 (#1, 3 wk), 11 wk; NYT
mm pb 4/17/77 (#5), pk 5/1/77 (#1, 5 wk), 12
wk; tot 23 wk.
The Lawless (Harcourt/Jove) PW mm pb
4/17/78 (#6), pk 4/24/78 (#1, 4 wk), 17 wk;
NYT mm pb 4/23/78 (#1, 6 wk), 17 wk; tot
34 wk.
The Bastard (Harcourt/Jove) NYT mm pb
6/11/78 (#11), pk 6/25/78 (#5, 1 wk), 8 wk;
PW mm pb 6/19/78 (#9, 1 wk), 3 wk; tot 11
wk.
The Americans (Jove) PW mm pb 2/15/80
(#2), pk 2/22/80 (#1, 6 wk), 12 wk; NYT mm
pb 2/17/80 (#1, 5 wk), 16 wk; tot 28 wk.
North and South (Harcourt) PW hc fic 2/5/
82 (#10), pk 3/5/82 (#1, 3 wk), 32 wk; NYT
fic 2/7/82 (#12), pk 2/28/82 (#1, 3 wk), 33
wk; (Dell) PW mm pb 2/11/83 (#14), pk 2/
18/83 (#1, 2 wk), 17 wk; NYT mm pb 2/13/83

(#2), pk 2/20/83 (#1, 1 wk), 8 wk; NYT pb fic 11/17/85 (#14), pk 12/1/85 (#2, 2 wk), 8 wk; tot 98 wk.

Love and War (Harcourt) PW hc fic 10/19/ 84 (#11), pk 11/23/84 (#2, 3 wk), 21 wk; NYT fic 10/21/84 (#5), pk 11/11/84 (#2, 3 wk), 21 wk; (Dell) NYT pb fic 11/3/85 (#8), pk 11/24/ 85 (#1, 4 wk), 14 wk; PW mm pb 11/8/85 (#7), pk 12/6/85 (#1, 5 wk), 14 wk; tot 70 wk.

Heaven and Hell (Harcourt) NYT fic 10/4/ 87 (#8), pk 10/18/87 (#2, 1 wk), 20 wk; PW hc fic 10/9/87 (#15), pk 10/16/87 (#3, 4 wk), 17 wk; (Dell) NYT pb fic 10/9/88 (#9), 10/ 30/88 (#1, 1 wk), 12 wk; PW mm pb 10/14/88 (#6), pk 10/28/88 (#1, 2 wk), 11 wk; tot 60 wk.

California Gold (Random) NYT fic 9/17/ 89 (#12), pk 9/24/89 (#3, 4 wk), 17 wk; PW hc fic 9/22/89 (#6), pk 9/29/89 (#3, 5 wk), 17 wk; (Ballantine) NYT pb fic 10/7/90 (#15), pk 10/21/90 (#3, 1 wk), 7 wk; PW mm pb 10/26/90 (#8), pk 11/2/90 (#4, 1 wk), 5 wk; tot 46 wk.

James, Bill J.
The Bill James Baseball Abstract 1984 (Ballantine) NYT msc pb 5/6/84 (#7, 3 wk), 3 wk; PW td pb 5/11/84 (#7, 1 wk), 2 wk; 5 wk.

The Bill James Baseball Abstract 1985 (Ballantine) NYT msc pb 4/21/85 (#7, 3 wk), 4 wk; PW td pb 4/26/85 (#3, 1 wk), 3 wk; tot 7 wk.

The Bill James Baseball Abstract 1986 (Ballantine) NYT msc pb 4/20/86 (#4), pk 5/4/ 86 (#2, 1 wk), 4 wk; PW td pb 4/25/86 (#7), pk 5/9/86 (#3, 1 wk), 5 wk; tot 9 wk.

The Bill James Baseball Abstract 1987 (Ballantine) NYT msc pb 4/19/87 (#4, 1 wk), 2 wk; PW td pb 4/24/87 (#4), pk 5/1/87 (#3, 1 wk), 4 wk; tot 6 wk.

The Bill James Baseball Abstract 1988 (Ballantine) PW td pb 4/22/88 (#3), pk 4/29/88 (#2, 1 wk), 6 wk.

James, Marquis
The Raven: A Biography of Sam Houston (Blue Ribbon) PW nf 7/12/30 (#8), pk 8/23/ 30 (#7, 4 wk), 12 wk.

Andrew Jackson (Bobbs Merrill) PW nf 5/13/33 (#6), pk 11/13/33 (#5, 8 wk), 28 wk.

The Cherokee Strip (Viking) NYT gen 10/ 14/45 (#8, 6 wk), 16 wk; PW nf 1/12/46 (#10, 1 wk); tot 17 wk.

James, Muriel, and Dorothy Jongeward
Born to Win (Addison Wesley) NYT td pb 3/10/74 (#3, 12 wk), 76 wk; PW td pb 10/17/ 77 (#10, 2 wk); tot 78 wk.

James, P.D.
Death of an Expert Witness (Fawcett/Pop-

ular Library) PW mm pb 11/27/78 (#13), pk 12/11/78 (#11, 1 wk), 3 wk; NYT mm pb 12/ 10/78 (#13, 1 wk); tot 4 wk.

Innocent Blood (Scribner) PW hc fic 5/16/ 80 (#12), pk 6/27/80 (#4, 1 wk), 16 wk; NYT fic 5/25/80 (#10), pk 6/15/80 (#3, 1 wk), 16 wk; (Fawcett/Crest) PW mm pb 4/3/81 (#12), pk 4/10/81 (#7, 1 wk), 8 wk; NYT mm pb 4/12/81 (#10, 2 wk), 6 wk; tot 46 wk.

The Skull Beneath the Skin (Warner) PW mm pb 10/7/83 (#6, 2 wk), 5 wk; NYT mm pb 10/9/83 (#13), pk 10/16/83 (#8, 1 wk), 4 wk; tot 9 wk.

A Taste for Death (Knopf) NYT fic 11/2/86 (#8), pk 11/30/86 (#4, 7 wk), 16 wk; PW hc fic 11/7/86 (#13), pk 12/19/86 (#4, 1 wk), 14 wk; (Warner) NYT pb fic 10/4/87 (#5), pk 10/18/87 (#1, 1 wk), 9 wk; PW mm pb 10/9/ 87 (#5), pk 10/23/87 (#1, 1 wk), 10 wk; tot 49 wk.

Devices and Desires (Knopf) NYT fic 1/28/ 90 (#12), pk 2/18/90 (#1, 3 wk), 16 wk; PW hc fic 2/2/90 (#15), pk 3/9/90 (#1, 2 wk), 15 wk; PW hc nf 2/2/90 (#15, 1 wk); tot 32 wk.

James, Will
Smokey, the Cowhorse (Scribner) PW juv 11/22/30 (#7, 4 wk).

Lone Cowboy (Scribner) PW nf 9/20/30 (#5), pk 10/18/30 (#3, 12 wk), 16 wk.

Sun-Up (Scribner) PW juv 7/18/31 (#3, 4 wk), 16 wk.

Big Enough (Scribner) PW juv 11/14/31 (#6, 4 wk), 12 wk.

Young Cowboy (Scribner) NYT juv 12/1/35 (#4, 4 wk).

Jameson, Storm
Three Kingdoms (Knopf) PW fic 5/15/26 (#8, 4 wk).

The Green Man (Harper) NYT fic 4/5/53 (#16), pk 5/3/53 (#10, 1 wk), 8 wk.

Janeway, Eliot
The Economics of Crisis (Weybright & Talley) NYT gen 2/18/68 (#9), pk 2/25/68 (#7, 1 wk), 4 wk; PW nf 3/4/68 (#7, 1 wk); tot 5 wk.

Janeway, Elizabeth
The Walsh Girls (Doubleday) NYT fic 11/ 28/43 (#12, 3 wk), 5 wk.

Daisy Kenyon (Doubleday) NYT fic 11/25/ 45 (#16, 1 wk).

The Third Choice (Doubleday) NYT fic 6/ 14/59 (#13, 1 wk), 3 wk.

Janney, Russell
The Miracle of the Bells (Prentice Hall) NYT fic 10/6/46 (#9), pk 11/3/46 (#2, 3 wk), 54 wk; PW fic 10/19/46 (#4), pk 10/26/46 (#2, 6 wk), 35 wk; tot 89 wk.

Janos, Leo
See Gen. Chuck Yeager and _____

Janowitz, Tama
Slaves of New York (Crown) NYT fic 8/24/
86 (#15, 2 wk); (Washington Square/Pocket)
PW td pb 7/10/87 (#10, 3 wk); tot 5 wk.

Janson, Klaus
See Frank Miller, et al.

Jardim, Anne
See Margaret Hennig and _____

Jarrel, William Henry Randall
Pictures from an Institution (Knopf) NYT
fic 5/30/54 (#13), pk 7/11/54 (#12, 1 wk), 9
wk.

Jarrell, Randall
The Bat-Poet (Doubleday) NYT ch bst
11/1/64 (#7, 25 wk).
The Animal Family (Pantheon) NYT ch
bst 11/6/66 (#9, 26 wk).
See also Jacob Grimm

Jarvis, D.C.
Folk Medicine (Holt) NYT gen 4/19/59
(#14), pk 12/13/59 (#2, 26 wk), 93 wk; PW
nf 5/18/59 (#7), pk 2/15/60 (#1, 6 wk), 83
wk; tot 176 wk.
Arthritis and Folk Medicine (Holt) NYT
gen 10/23/60 (#16), pk 12/4/60 (#9, 1 wk), 9
wk; PW nf 11/21/60 (#10, 1 wk); tot 10 wk.

Jaworski, Leon
*The Right and the Power: The Prosecution
of Watergate* (Reader's Digest/Gulf/Crowell)
PW hc nf 9/20/76 (#5), pk 10/11/76 (#2, 3
wk), 19 wk; NYT gen 9/26/76 (#8), pk 10/17/
76 (#2, 1 wk), 24 wk; (Pocket) PW mm pb
8/8/77 (#15), pk 8/15/77 (#11, 1 wk), 2 wk;
tot 45 wk.

Jay, Antony
See David Frost and _____

Jaynes, Clare
These Are the Times (World Almanac)
NYT fic 5/21/44 (#10), pk 5/28/44 (#9, 1
wk), 2 wk.

Jeans, Sir James
The Universe Around Us (Macmillan) PW
nf 2/15/30 (#10, 4 wk).

Jeffrey, Adi-Kent Thomas
The Bermuda Triangle (Warner) NYT mm
pb 6/22/75 (#10), pk 8/3/75 (#2, 1 wk), 9 wk.

Jekel, Pamela
Sea Star (Harmony) NYT td pb 6/26/83
(#13, 1 wk); PW td pb 7/8/83 (#8, 1 wk), 3
wk; tot 4 wk.

Jenkins, Dan
Semi-Tough (Atheneum) PW fic 10/9/72

(#9), pk 11/27/72 (#2, 1 wk), 28 wk; NYT fic
10/15/72 (#8), pk 11/12/72 (#3, 8 wk), 29 wk;
NYT pb fic 10/14/73 (#4), pk 11/11/73 (#2, 4
wk), 16 wk; tot 73 wk.
*Life Its Ownself: The Semi-Tougher Adven-
tures of Billy Clyde Puckett* (Simon & Schuster) PW hc fic 11/9/84 (#13), pk 12/14/84 (#4,
1 wk), 16 wk; NYT fic 11/18/84 (#13), pk
2/24/85 (#5, 1 wk), 15 wk; tot 31 wk.

Jenkins, Elizabeth
Elizabeth the Great (Coward McCann)
NYT fic 3/22/59 (#11), pk 5/17/59 (#4, 1 wk),
19 wk; PW nf 3/30/59 (#5), pk 5/11/59 (#4,
1 wk), 15 wk; tot 34 wk.
Elizabeth and Leicester (Coward McCann)
NYT gen 3/11/62 (#16, 1 wk).

Jenkins, Geoffrey
A Twist of Sand (Viking) NYT fic 3/6/60
(#16, 2 wk).

Jenkins, Jerry B.
See Orel Hershiser and _____

Jenkins, Peter
A Walk Across America (Morrow) NYT nf
3/25/79 (#14), pk 4/8/79 (#11, 1 wk), 11 wk;
PW hc nf 4/9/79 (#15, 2 wk); tot 13 wk.
Across China (Morrow) NYT nf 1/4/87
(#10, 1 wk), 8 wk; PW hc nf 1/16/87 (#13, 1
wk), 2 wk; (Fawcett) NYT pb nf 5/1/88 (#3,
1 wk), 4 wk; tot 14 wk.

_____, and Barbara Jenkins
The Walk West: A Walk Across America 2
(Morrow) PW hc nf 12/4/81 (#12), pk 1/8/82
(#7, 2 wk), 15 wk; NYT nf 12/27/81 (#4, 1
wk), 15 wk; (Fawcett/Crest) NYT mm pb 1/
2/83 (#13, 2 wk), 3 wk; PW mm pb 1/14/83
(#10, 1 wk), 3 wk; tot 36 wk.

Jennings, Gary
Aztec (Avon) NYT mm pb 1/10/82 (#7), pk
1/17/82 (#2, 3 wk), 12 wk; PW mm pb 1/15/
82 (#6), pk 2/5/82 (#1, 1 wk), 12 wk; tot 24
wk.
The Journeyer (Atheneum) PW hc fic 2/3/
84 (#15), pk 3/2/84 (#8, 1 wk), 9 wk; NYT
fic 2/5/84 (#14), pk 2/26/84 (#9, 1 wk), 9 wk;
(Avon) NYT pb fic 1/13/85 (#11, 2 wk), 3 wk;
tot 21 wk.

Jennings, John Edward
Next to Valour (Macmillan) NYT fic 7/9/
39 (#2, 4 wk), 8 wk; PW fic 7/15/39 (#4), pk
8/12/39 (#3, 4 wk), 20 wk; tot 28 wk.
Gentleman Ranker (Reynal & Hitchcock)
NYT fic 9/27/42 (#9, 1 wk), 12 wk.
The Salem Frigate (Doubleday) NYT fic 9/
1/46 (#12), pk 10/6/46 (#3, 3 wk), 22 wk; PW
fic 9/21/46 (#4), pk 10/5/46 (#3, 2 wk), 7 wk;
tot 29 wk.

The Sea Eagles (Doubleday) NYT fic 3/12/50 (#12), pk 4/2/50 (#8, 1 wk), 8 wk.
The Pepper Tree (Little Brown) NYT fic 1/14/51 (#13, 1 wk), 3 wk.

Jennison, Keith Warren
The Boys and Their Mother (Viking) NYT gen 4/22/56 (#15, 1 wk).

Jenson, Lt. Oliver USNR
Carrier War (Simon & Schuster) NYT gen 4/29/45 (#17), pk 5/6/45 (#10, 1 wk), 4 wk.

Jerger, Joseph A.
Doctor, Here's Your Hat (Prentice Hall) NYT gen 4/9/39 (#8, 4 wk).

Jessel, George
So Help Me (Random) NYT gen 7/4/43 (#17, 1 wk).

Jessup, Ronald Frederick
The Wonderful World of Archaeology (Garden City) NYT ch bst 11/17/57 (#12, 40 wk).

Jillson, Joyce
Real Women Don't Pump Gas (Pocket) NYT td pb 1/2/83 (#9), pk 1/30/83 (#3, 1 wk), 22 wk; PW td pb 1/7/83 (#8), pk 2/11/83 (#2, 3 wk), 19 wk; tot 41 wk.

John, Evan
Crippled Splendour (Dutton) PW fic 10/15/38 (#7), pk 11/12/38 (#6, 4 wk), 8 wk; NYT fic 11/6/38 (#13, 4 wk); tot 12 wk.

Johnson, Barbara
Stick a Geranium in Your Hat and Be Happy! (Word) PW pb rel 11/9/90 (#6, 4 wk).

Johnson, Barbara Ferry
Delta Blood (Avon) PW mm pb 5/2/77 (#14), pk 5/9/77 (#12, 3 wk), 7 wk; NYT mm pb 5/8/77 (#14), pk 6/12/77 (#9, 1 wk), 9 wk; tot 16 wk.
Tara's Song (Avon) PW mm pb 10/2/78 (#15, 1 wk).

Johnson, Crockett
Barnaby and Mr. O'Malley (Holt) NYT gen 10/15/44 (#17, 1 wk).

Johnson, Gerald White
American Heroes and Hero-Worship (Harper) NYT gen 10/24/43 (#12), pk 10/31/43 (#11, 1 wk), 8 wk.
Woodrow Wilson (Harper) NYT gen 7/30/44 (#12), pk 8/13/44 (#9, 1 wk), 10 wk.
America Grows Up (Morrow) NYT ch bst 11/13/60 (#7, 27 wk).

Johnson, Haynes Bonner
The Bay of Pigs (Norton) NYT gen 7/12/64 (#10, 1 wk).

Johnson, John H., and Lerone Bennett, Jr.
Succeeding Against the Odds (Amistad/Warner) PW hc nf 6/23/89 (#15, 1 wk).

Johnson, Josephine Winslow
Now in November (Simon & Schuster) PW fic 7/13/35 (#6, 4 wk), 8 wk.
Wildwood (Harper) NYT fic 3/3/46 (#16, 1 wk).
The Inland Island (Simon & Schuster) NYT gen 5/11/69 (#10, 1 wk).

Johnson, Lady Bird
A White House Diary (Holt) NYT gen 11/22/70 (#4, 1 wk), 13 wk; PW nf 11/30/70 (#4, 3 wk), 10 wk; tot 23 wk.

Johnson, Lyndon Baines
Quotations from Chairman LBJ (Simon & Schuster) NYT pb gen 4/7/68 (#5, 8 wk).
Vantage Point (Holt) PW nf 11/22/71 (#10), pk 12/6/71 (#6, 1 wk), 5 wk; NYT gen 11/28/71 (#8), pk 12/12/71 (#6, 1 wk), 5 wk; tot 10 wk.

Johnson, Martin
Safari (Putnam) PW nf 4/28/28 (#10), pk 5/26/28 (#8, 8 wk), 12 wk.
Lion (Putnam) PW nf 5/11/29 (#9, 4 wk).

Johnson, Osa
I Married Adventure (Lippincott) PW nf 6/8/40 (#9), pk 8/10/40 (#1, 4 wk), 36 wk.

Johnson, Pamela Hansford
Catherine Carter (Knopf) NYT fic 8/10/52 (#12), pk 9/7/52 (#7, 2 wk), 10 wk; PW fic 9/13/52 (#8, 1 wk); tot 11 wk.

Johnson, Paul
Intellectuals (Harper) NYT nf 4/2/89 (#10), pk 4/23/89 (#9, 1 wk), 6 wk; PW hc nf 4/7/89 (#11, 3 wk), 7 wk; tot 13 wk.

Johnson, Sam Houston
My Brother Lyndon (Cowles) NYT gen 3/8/70 (#9, 1 wk).

Johnson, Spencer
One Minute for Myself (Morrow) PW hc nf 2/21/86 (#13), pk 2/28/86 (#8, 2 wk), 9 wk; NYT msc 3/2/86 (#5, 2 wk); tot 11 wk.
See also Kenneth Blanchard and _____

_____, and Larry Wilson
The One Minute Sales Person (Morrow) PW hc nf 10/12/84 (#10), pk 11/16/84 (#4, 3 wk), 33 wk; NYT msc 10/21/84 (#3), pk 11/4/84 (#2, 5 wk), 22 wk; (Avon) NYT msc pb 9/7/86 (#6), pk 9/28/86 (#4, 1 wk), 7 wk; tot 62 wk.

Johnson, Virginia E.
See William Howard Masters M.D. and _____
See William Howard Masters, et al.

Johnson, Walter
1600 Pennsylvania Avenue (Little Brown)
NYT gen 6/12/60 (#15, 3 wk).

Johnston, Alva
The Legendary Mizners (Farrar) NYT gen
5/3/53 (#16), pk 5/10/53 (#10, 1 wk), 4 wk.

Johnston, Denis
Nine Rivers from Jordan (Little Brown)
NYT gen 9/11/55 (#13, 1 wk), 2 wk.

Johnston, Eric
America Unlimited (Doubleday) NYT gen
5/14/44 (#13), pk 7/23/44 (#4, 1 wk), 18 wk;
PW nf 6/10/44 (#9, 1 wk), 2 wk; tot 20 wk.

Johnston, George
See Charmian Clift and _____

Johnston, James A.
Alcatraz Island Prison (Scribner) NYT gen
9/18/49 (#16), pk 9/25/49 (#15, 1 wk), 2 wk.

Johnston, Joe
Star Wars Sketchbook (Ballantine) PW td
pb 12/12/77 (#6, 1 wk), 3 wk.

_____, and Nilo Rodis-Jamero
Return of the Jedi Sketchbook (Ballantine)
NYT td pb 6/12/83 (#11, 1 wk), 3 wk.

Johnston, Stanley
Queen of the Flat-Tops (Dutton) NYT nf
11/22/42 (#13), pk 12/6/42 (#8, 2 wk), 9 wk.

Jonas, Carl
Jefferson Selleck (Little Brown) NYT fic
2/10/52 (#13), pk 3/30/52 (#8, 1 wk), 11 wk;
PW fic 3/15/52 (#8, 1 wk); tot 12 wk.

Jones, E. Stanley
The Christ of the Indian Road (Abingdon)
PW nf 4/23/27 (#8), pk 6/25/27 (#6, 4 wk),
16 wk.
The Christ of Every Road (Abingdon) PW
nf 5/17/30 (#7, 4 wk).
Abundant Living (Abingdon) NYT nf 3/7/
43 (#17), pk 5/2/43 (#16, 1 wk), 5 wk.

Jones, Ernest
Life and Work of Sigmund Freud, Vol. I
(Basic) NYT gen 11/1/53 (#14), pk 11/8/53
(#12, 2 wk), 3 wk.
Life and Work of Sigmund Freud, Vol. II
(Basic) NYT gen 10/9/55 (#14, 1 wk), 2 wk.

Jones, Idwal
The Vineyard (Duell Sloan & Pearce) NYT
fic 11/22/42 (#19), pk 11/29/42 (#16, 1 wk), 3
wk.
Vermilion (Prentice Hall) NYT fic 6/22/47
(#11), pk 7/13/47 (#10, 2 wk), 8 wk.
Vines in the Sun (Morrow) NYT gen 5/22/
49 (#13, 1 wk), 2 wk.
Ark of Empire (Doubleday) NYT gen 7/8/
51 (#15), pk 7/15/51 (#14, 1 wk), 2 wk.

Jones, James
From Here to Eternity (Scribner) NYT fic
3/11/51 (#12), pk 3/25/51 (#1, 20 wk), 66 wk;
PW fic 3/24/51 (#3), pk 3/31/51 (#1, 22 wk),
40 wk; tot 106 wk.
Some Came Running (Scribner) NYT fic
1/26/58 (#11), pk 2/2/58 (#4, 1 wk), 13 wk;
PW fic 2/3/58 (#5), pk 3/3/58 (#3, 1 wk), 9
wk; tot 22 wk.
The Thin Red Line (Scribner) NYT fic 9/
30/62 (#12), pk 12/16/62 (#5, 1 wk), 12 wk;
PW fic 10/15/62 (#10), pk 11/5/62 (#4, 3 wk),
16 wk; tot 28 wk.
Go to the Widow-Maker (Delacorte) NYT
fic 5/7/67 (#9), pk 6/4/67 (#8, 2 wk), 9 wk;
PW fic 5/22/67 (#11), pk 7/3/67 (#7, 1 wk),
8 wk; NYT pb fic 4/7/68 (#3, 8 wk), 12 wk;
tot 29 wk.
A Touch of Danger (Doubleday) PW fic
6/11/73 (#9, 1 wk).
Whistle (Delacorte) PW hc fic 3/13/78
(#15), pk 4/24/78 (#6, 1 wk), 11 wk; NYT fic
4/2/78 (#5, 1 wk), 11 wk; (Dell) PW mm pb
4/23/79 (#9), pk 4/30/79 (#8, 1 wk), 4 wk;
NYT mm pb 4/29/79 (#14, 1 wk); tot 27 wk.

Jones, Jesse H., and Edward Angly
Fifty Billion Dollars (Macmillan) NYT
gen 11/11/51 (#10), pk 12/2/51 (#4, 1 wk), 12
wk; PW nf 11/24/51 (#5), pk 12/1/51 (#3, 1
wk), 4 wk; tot 16 wk.

Jones, John G.
The Amityville Horror #2 (Warner) PW
mm pb 1/15/82 (#10), pk 1/29/82 (#9, 1 wk),
5 wk; NYT mm pb 1/17/82 (#10, 2 wk), 4
wk; tot 9 wk.

Jones, Rachel
See Trudy Baker and _____

Jones, Thelma
Skinny Angel (Whittlesey/McGraw) NYT
gen 4/21/46 (#15, 1 wk).

Jones, Virgil Carrington
Ranger Mosby (Univ. of North Carolina)
NYT gen 10/22/44 (#14), pk 10/29/44 (#12,
2 wk), 8 wk.

Jong, Erica
Fear of Flying (Holt) PW fic 2/18/74 (#10,
2 wk); (NAL/Signet) NYT mm pb 11/10/74
(#10), pk 1/12/75 (#1, 5 wk), 42 wk; tot 44 wk.
How to Save Your Own Life (Holt) PW hc
fic 3/21/77 (#5, 2 wk), 12 wk; NYT fic 4/3/77
(#6), pk 4/17/77 (#5, 3 wk), 15 wk; (NAL/
Signet) PW mm pb 3/27/78 (#11), pk 4/3/78
(#7, 2 wk), 6 wk; NYT mm pb 4/2/78 (#15),
pk 4/9/78 (#6, 2 wk), 7 wk; tot 40 wk.
*Fanny, Being the True History of the Adven-
tures of Fanny Hackabout-Jones* (NAL) PW
hc fic 9/5/80 (#11), pk 9/19/80 (#4, 3 wk), 12

wk; NYT fic 9/7/80 (#13), pk 9/14/80 (#3, 1 wk), 12 wk; (NAL/Plume) PW td pb 5/1/81 (#6), pk 5/8/81 (#4, 1 wk), 9 wk; NYT td pb 5/3/81 (#10), pk 5/24/81 (#7, 1 wk), 9 wk; NYT mm pb 1/3/82 (#13, 1 wk); tot 43 wk.
Parachutes & Kisses (NAL/Signet) NYT pb fic 11/10/85 (#14, 3 wk), 5 wk; PW mm pb 11/15/85 (#11, 1 wk), 3 wk; tot 8 wk.
Serenissima (Houghton) PW hc fic 5/15/87 (#15), pk 5/22/87 (#14, 1 wk), 2 wk.
Any Woman's Blues (Harper) NYT fic 3/18/90 (#14, 1 wk).

Jongeward, Dorothy
See Muriel James and _____

Jonsen, George
Favorite Tales of Monsters and Trolls (Random) NYT ch pb 11/13/77 (#7, 46 wk).

Jordan, Hamilton
Crisis: The Last Year of the Carter Presidency (Putnam) PW hc nf 10/22/82 (#15), pk 11/5/82 (#12, 1 wk), 3 wk.

Jordan, Mildred
One Red Rose Forever (Knopf) PW fic 10/11/41 (#8), pk 11/15/41 (#6, 4 wk), 8 wk.
Apple in the Attic (Grosset & Dunlap) NYT fic 10/11/42 (#12, 2 wk), 7 wk.
Asylum for the Queen (Knopf) NYT fic 6/20/48 (#15), pk 8/15/48 (#9, 1 wk), 9 wk.

Jordan, Penny
Power Play (Harlequin) NYT pb fic 2/25/90 (#14), pk 3/4/90 (#10, 1 wk), 2 wk.

Joseph, Mark
To Kill the Potemkin (NAL/Onyx) NYT pb fic 7/19/87 (#13), pk 7/26/87 (#11, 1 wk), 4 wk; PW mm pb 7/31/87 (#14, 2 wk); tot 6 wk.

Josephs, Ray
Argentine Diary (Random) NYT gen 8/20/44 (#12, 1 wk), 3 wk.

Josephson, Matthew
The Robber Barons (Harcourt) PW nf 4/14/34 (#6, 4 wk), 12 wk.
Victor Hugo (Doubleday) NYT nf 12/20/42 (#15, 1 wk), 2 wk.

Joslin, Sesyle
There Is a Dragon in My Bed (Harcourt) NYT ch bst 5/14/61 (#16), pk 11/12/61 (#11, 26 wk), 46 wk.

Jowitt, William Allen
The Strange Case of Alger Hiss (Doubleday) NYT gen 8/23/53 (#14, 1 wk).

Joyce, James
Ulysses (Random) PW fic 3/10/34 (#5, 4 wk), 8 wk.

Joyce, William
A Day with Wilbur Robinson (Harper-Collins) PW ch pc 10/26/90 (#8, 4 wk).

Juilliard, Ahrgus
See Mary Wilson, et al.

Juster, Norton
The Phantom Tollbooth (Epstein & Carroll/Random) NYT ch bst 5/13/62 (#6), pk 11/11/62 (#5, 26 wk), 45 wk.

Kafka, Barbara
Microwave Gourmet (Morrow) NYT msc 1/3/88 (#5, 4 wk).

Kahn, Albert
See Michael Sayers and_____

Kahn, Brian J.
See Vladimir Pozner and_____

Kahn, James
Poltergeist (Warner) PW mm pb 7/9/82 (#15, 1 wk).
Return of the Jedi [novelization] (Ballantine/Del Rey) NYT mm pb 6/5/83 (#5), pk 6/12/83 (#1, 5 wk), 11 wk; PW mm pb 6/10/83 (#6), pk 6/24/83 (#1, 2 wk), 10 wk; tot 21 wk.
Return of the Jedi [illustrated edition] (Ballantine/Del Rey) NYT td pb 6/12/83 (#9), pk 7/31/83 (#7, 1 wk), 5 wk.
Indiana Jones and the Temple of Doom (Ballantine) NYT pb fic 6/3/84 (#6), pk 6/17/84 (#2, 1 wk), 7 wk; PW mm pb 6/8/84 (#7), pk 6/15/84 (#2, 1 wk), 5 wk; tot 12 wk.

Kahn, Roger
The Boys of Summer (Harper) PW nf 4/10/72 (#10), pk 6/5/72 (#1, 3 wk), 26 wk; NYT gen 4/23/72 (#10), pk 5/28/72 (#1, 6 wk), 24 wk; tot 50 wk.
A Season in the Sun (Harper) NYT nf 9/25/77 (#14, 1 wk).
See also Pete Rose and_____

Kalb, Marvin, and Ted Koppel
In the National Interest (Simon & Schuster) PW hc fic 12/12/77 (#14, 1 wk), 2 wk; NYT fic 1/15/78 (#13, 1 wk); tot 3 wk.

Kallet, Arthur, and F.J. Schlink
100,000,000 Guinea Pigs (Vanguard) PW nf 3/11/33 (#6), pk 4/14/34 (#3, 4 wk), 19 wk.

Kaltenborn, H.V.
Fifty Fabulous Years (Putnam) NYT gen 12/31/50 (#10, 1 wk), 5 wk; PW nf 1/13/51 (#10, 1 wk); tot 6 wk.

Kamholz, Consuelo
See Margaretta Byers and_____

Kamm, Herbert
See Willard Mullin and_____

Kane, Harnett Thomas
The Bayous of Louisiana (Morrow) NYT gen 10/24/43 (#9), pk 5/7/44 (#8, 1 wk), 28 wk.
Deep Delta Country (Duell Sloan & Pearce) NYT gen 11/19/44 (#9, 1 wk), 19 wk.
New Orleans Woman (Doubleday) NYT fic 12/29/46 (#16), pk 1/19/47 (#13, 1 wk), 7 wk.
Plantation Parade (Morrow) NYT gen 1/13/46 (#13), pk 3/3/46 (#12, 1 wk), 3 wk.
Natchez on the Mississippi (Morrow) NYT gen 3/7/48 (#14, 1 wk).
Queen New Orleans (Morrow) NYT gen 10/23/49 (#15), pk 11/6/49 (#14, 1 wk), 2 wk.
Bride of Fortune (Doubleday) PW fic 1/15/49 (#9, 1 wk).
Pathway to the Stars (Doubleday) NYT fic 11/26/50 (#14), pk 12/24/50 (#9, 1 wk), 10 wk; PW fic 1/13/51 (#10, 1 wk); tot 11 wk.
The Lady of Arlington (Doubleday) NYT fic 10/18/53 (#11), pk 1/24/54 (#4, 1 wk), 28 wk; PW fic 11/14/53 (#8), pk 1/9/54 (#4, 2 wk), 13 wk; tot 41 wk.
The Smiling Rebel (Doubleday) NYT fic 11/6/55 (#13), pk 11/27/55 (#9, 3 wk), 11 wk; PW fic 12/17/55 (#10), pk 1/14/56 (#8, 1 wk), 2 wk; tot 13 wk.
The Gallant Mrs. Stonewall (Doubleday) NYT fic 12/8/57 (#12, 4 wk), 7 wk; PW fic 1/20/58 (#9, 1 wk); tot 8 wk.

_____, and Victor Leclerc
The Scandalous Mrs. Blackford (Messner) NYT fic 6/24/51 (#16), pk 7/22/51 (#10, 1 wk), 12 wk; PW fic 8/11/51 (#10, 1 wk); tot 13 wk.

Kane, Joe
Running the Amazon (Knopf) NYT nf 8/20/89 (#15), pk 9/3/89 (#13, 1 wk), 3 wk.

Kanin, Garson
Tracy and Hepburn (Viking) PW nf 12/6/71 (#8), pk 1/10/72 (#2, 7 wk), 22 wk; NYT gen 12/12/71 (#10), pk 1/23/72 (#2, 7 wk), 24 wk; NYT pb gen 9/10/72 (#1, 4 wk), 12 wk; tot 58 wk.
A Thousand Summers (Doubleday) PW fic 12/3/73 (#10), pk 12/31/73 (#9, 1 wk), 3 wk.
Moviola (Simon & Schuster) NYT fic 1/27/80 (#11, 1 wk), 6 wk; PW hc fic 2/15/80 (#15), pk 2/22/80 (#14, 1 wk), 3 wk; (Pocket) NYT mm pb 5/25/80 (#9), pk 6/8/80 (#7, 1 wk), 5 wk; PW mm pb 5/30/80 (#12), pk 6/6/80 (#11, 2 wk), 4 wk; tot 18 wk.

Kannon, Jackie
The JFK Coloring Book (Kanrom) NYT gen 7/15/62 (#13), pk 8/26/62 (#6, 1 wk), 14 wk; PW nf 8/20/62 (#10, 1 wk), 4 wk; tot 18 wk.

Kantor, MacKinlay
Valedictory (Coward McCann) NYT fic 6/11/39 (#14, 4 wk).
Happy Land (Coward McCann) NYT fic 2/7/43 (#18), pk 3/7/43 (#11, 1 wk), 3 wk.
Long Remember (Coward McCann) PW fic 5/12/34 (#3, 4 wk), 8 wk.
The Voice of Bugle Ann (Coward McCann) NYT fic 10/6/35 (#8, 4 wk); PW fic 10/12/35 (#10, 4 wk); tot 8 wk.
Andersonville (World) NYT fic 11/6/55 (#14), pk 1/1/56 (#1, 12 wk), 52 wk; PW fic 11/26/55 (#5), pk 1/21/56 (#1, 9 wk), 44 wk; tot 96 wk.
Spirit Lake (World) NYT fic 1/22/61 (#14), pk 12/17/61 (#4, 2 wk), 20 wk; PW fic 10/30/61 (#9), pk 11/27/61 (#4, 6 wk), 20 wk; tot 40 wk.

Kaplan, Justin
Walt Whitman (Simon & Schuster) PW hc nf 1/9/81 (#13, 1 wk), 2 wk.

Karig, Cmdr. Walter, USNR
Lower Than Angels (Farrar) NYT fic 4/15/45 (#16, 1 wk).
Battle Report Vol. II (Farrar) NYT gen 3/24/46 (#9, 1 wk).
Caroline Hicks (Rinehart) NYT fic 4/8/51 (#15, 1 wk).

_____, and Lt. Welbourn Kelley, USNR
Battle Report (Farrar) NYT gen 12/31/44 (#12), pk 1/14/45 (#10, 1 wk), 11 wk.

Karmel, Ilona
Stephania (Houghton) NYT fic 4/26/53 (#11, 1 wk), 3 wk.

Karnow, Stanley
Vietnam: A History (Viking) NYT nf 10/23/83 (#12), pk 11/27/83 (#6, 4 wk), 17 wk; PW hc nf 10/28/83 (#10), pk 11/25/83 (#5, 1 wk), 18 wk; tot 35 wk.

Karras, Alex, with Herb Gluck
Even Big Guys Cry (Holt) NYT nf 1/1/78 (#14), pk 1/22/78 (#9, 1 wk), 4 wk; PW hc nf 1/9/78 (#15, 1 wk); tot 5 wk.

Karski, Jan [pseud.]
Story of a Secret State (Houghton) NYT gen 3/4/45 (#21), pk 3/11/45 (#15, 2 wk), 5 wk.

Kasdan, Sara
So It Was Just a Simple Wedding (Vanguard) NYT fic 8/13/61 (#16, 1 wk).

Kasner, Edward, and James Newman
Mathematics and the Imagination (Simon & Schuster) PW nf 8/10/40 (#9, 4 wk).

Kasorla, Dr. Irene Chamie
Nice Girls Do (Stratford/Harper) PW hc nf
1/30/81 (#14), pk 2/20/81 (#3, 6 wk), 24 wk;
NYT nf 2/1/81 (#5), pk 3/15/81 (#3, 3 wk),
22 wk; (Playboy) PW mm pb 3/5/82 (#14),
pk 3/12/82 (#9, 1 wk), 7 wk; NYT mm pb 3/
14/82 (#9), pk 3/28/82 (#7, 1 wk), 7 wk; tot
60 wk.
*Go For It! How to Win at Love, Work and
Play* (Delacorte) PW hc nf 6/8/84 (#11), pk
6/15/84 (#9, 1 wk), 8 wk; NYT msc 6/17/84
(#4, 2 wk), 4 wk; (Dell) NYT msc pb 2/24/
85 (#4), pk 3/3/85 (#3, 1 wk), 8 wk; PW mm
pb 3/1/85 (#13), pk 3/8/85 (#8, 1 wk), 7 wk;
tot 27 wk.

Katahn, Dr. Martin
The Rotation Diet (Norton) PW hc nf
5/23/86 (#12), pk 9/5/86 (#1, 4 wk), 45 wk;
NYT msc 5/25/86 (#4), pk 7/27/86 (#1, 10
wk), 45 wk; (Bantam) NYT msc pb 5/10/87
(#5), pk 5/24/87 (#2, 1 wk), 5 wk; PW mm
pb 5/15/87 (#13), pk 6/5/87 (#6, 1 wk), 7 wk;
tot 102 wk.
The T-Factor Diet (Norton) PW hc nf 5/
12/89 (#12), pk 11/10/89 (#5, 1 wk), 37 wk;
NYT msc 5/21/89 (#2), pk 6/4/89 (#1, 2 wk),
30 wk; (Bantam) NYT msc pb 4/1/90 (#5, 4
wk); PW mm pb 4/20/90 (#15), pk 5/11/90
(#11, 1 wk), 4 wk; tot 75 wk.
See also Jamie Pope-Cordle and_____

Katkov, Norman
Eagle at My Eyes (Doubleday) NYT fic
2/8/48 (#10), pk 2/22/48 (#9, 1 wk), 4 wk.
The Fabulous Fanny (Knopf) NYT gen
3/15/53 (#10, 1 wk), 5 wk.
Blood and Orchids (NAL/Signet) NYT pb
fic 10/7/84 (#6), pk 10/14/84 (#2, 2 wk), 10
wk; PW mm pb 10/12/84 (#6), pk 10/19/84
(#4, 2 wk), 8 wk; tot 18 wk.

Katz, Michael
See Robert Levering, et al.

Katzenbach, John
The Traveler (Ballantine) NYT pb fic 2/
14/88 (#12, 2 wk); PW mm pb 2/19/88 (#11,
2 wk); tot 4 wk.

Katzenbach, Maria
The Grab (Morrow) PW hc fic 3/6/78
(#12, 2 wk), 3 wk.

Katzman, John
See Adam Robinson and_____

_____, and Adam Robinson
*The Princeton Review's Cracking the System:
The S.A.T.* (Villard) PW td pb 10/31/86 (#9,
2 wk), 3 wk.

Kaufman, Beatrice
See Alexander Woollcott, et al.

Kaufman, Bel
Up the Down Staircase (Prentice Hall) PW
fic 3/8/65 (#8), pk 5/10/65 (#1, 8 wk), 64 wk;
NYT fic 3/14/65 (#6), pk 5/16/65 (#1, 8 wk),
59 wk; NYT pb fic 3/6/66 (#1, 20 wk), 32 wk;
tot 155 wk.

**Kaufman, Joel, and the Public Citizen
  Health Research Group**
Over the Counter Pills That Don't Work
(Pantheon) NYT td pb 10/16/83 (#13, 1 wk),
2 wk; PW td pb 10/21/83 (#9, 3 wk), 5 wk;
tot 7 wk.

Kaufman, Myron
Remember Me to God (Lippincott) NYT
fic 9/29/57 (#12), pk 10/20/57 (#6, 2 wk), 28
wk; PW fic 11/4/57 (#8), pk 1/27/58 (#7, 2
wk), 6 wk; tot 34 wk.

Kaus, Gina
Catherine, the Portrait of an Empress (Viking) PW nf 7/13/35 (#3, 8 wk), 16 wk.

Kavanaugh, Father James
*A Modern Priest Looks at His Outdated
Church* (Trident) NYT gen 7/16/67 (#9), pk
8/13/67 (#2, 6 wk), 22 wk; PW nf 7/24/67
(#12), pk 9/4/67 (#1, 2 wk), 20 wk; tot 42 wk.

Kaye, Danny
Danny Kaye's Around the World Storybook
(Random) NYT ch bst 11/12/61 (#12, 26 wk).

Kaye, M.M.
The Far Pavilions (St. Martin's) PW hc fic
9/11/78 (#12), pk 10/9/78 (#4, 1 wk), 24 wk;
NYT fic 11/12/78 (#4), pk 12/17/78 (#3, 1
wk), 19 wk; (Bantam) PW mm pb 8/13/79
(#8), pk 9/10/79 (#2, 1 wk), 19 wk; NYT mm
pb 8/19/79 (#7), pk 8/26/79 (#1, 2 wk), 20
wk; tot 82 wk.
Shadow of the Moon (St. Martin's) NYT fic
9/30/79 (#12), pk 11/11/79 (#3, 1 wk), 15 wk;
PW hc fic 10/8/79 (#14), pk 10/22/79 (#8, 1
wk), 14 wk; (Bantam) PW mm pb 9/12/80
(#12), pk 9/19/80 (#6, 1 wk), 6 wk; NYT mm
pb 9/21/80 (#10), pk 9/28/80 (#3, 1 wk), 7
wk; tot 42 wk.
Trade Winds (St. Martin's) PW hc fic 7/10/
81 (#15), pk 7/24/81 (#10, 2 wk), 10 wk; NYT
fic 7/26/81 (#10), pk 8/16/81 (#7, 3 wk), 9 wk;
(Bantam) PW mm pb 7/16/82 (#10), pk 7/
23/82 (#4, 2 wk), 7 wk; NYT mm pb 7/18/82
(#5), pk 8/1/82 (#4, 1 wk), 8 wk; tot 34 wk.
Death in Zanzibar (St. Martin's) PW hc fic
5/6/83 (#14, 1 wk); NYT pb fic 3/4/84 (#14),
pk 3/25/84 (#8, 1 wk), 6 wk; PW mm pb
3/9/84 (#15), pk 3/30/84 (#14, 1 wk), 2 wk;
tot 9 wk.
Death in Kenya (St. Martin's Press) NYT
pb fic 9/23/84 (#11, 1 wk).

Kaye-Smith, Sheila
Rose Deeprose (Harper) NYT fic 3/7/37 (#8, 4 wk).
The Valiant Woman (Harper) NYT fic 12/4/38 (#14, 4 wk).

Kazan, Elia
The Arrangement (Stein & Day) NYT fic 2/26/67 (#10), pk 3/26/67 (#1, 23 wk), 42 wk; PW fic 3/6/67 (#7), pk 4/3/67 (#1, 15 wk), 41 wk; NYT pb fic 4/7/68 (#1, 8 wk), 28 wk; tot 111 wk.
The Assassins (Stein & Day) PW fic 2/21/72 (#7), pk 4/3/72 (#2, 1 wk), 12 wk; NYT fic 2/27/72 (#8), pk 3/26/72 (#4, 2 wk), 11 wk; pb gen 4/8/73 (#5, 4 wk); tot 27 wk.
The Understudy (Stein & Day) PW fic 2/24/75 (#10), pk 3/10/75 (#9, 1 wk), 4 wk; NYT fic 3/9/75 (#10, 2 wk); (Warner) PW mm pb 2/2/76 (#10), pk 2/9/76 (#5, 1 wk), 4 wk; NYT mm pb 2/8/76 (#7), pk 2/15/76 (#5, 1 wk), 3 wk; tot 13 wk.
Acts of Love (Knopf) NYT fic 8/13/78 (#14, 1 wk); (Warner) mm pb 7/22/79 (#9), pk 7/29/79 (#8, 2 wk), 9 wk; PW mm pb 7/23/79 (#12), pk 8/6/79 (#7, 1 wk), 8 wk; tot 18 wk.

Kazantzakis, Nikos
Zorba the Greek (Simon & Schuster) NYT fic 5/10/53 (#13), pk 6/14/53 (#8, 1 wk), 9 wk.
The Greek Passion [trans. Jonathan Griffin] (Simon & Schuster) NYT fic 2/14/54 (#14, 1 wk).
The Last Temptation of Christ (Touchstone/Simon & Schuster) NYT fic 9/4/60 (#16), pk 10/9/60 (#7, 1 wk), 13 wk; PW td pb 9/16/88 (#6), pk 9/30/88 (#2, 1 wk), 5 wk; tot 18 wk.

Keable, Robert
Simon Called Peter (Dutton) PW fic 5/13/22 (#8), pk 8/26/22 (#4, 4 wk), 44 wk.
Mother of All Living (Dutton) PW gen lit 9/16/22 (#12), pk 10/14/22 (#10, 4 wk), 8 wk.
Recompense (Putnam) PW fic 6/21/24 (#8, 4 wk).

Kearns, Doris
Lyndon Johnson and the American Dream (Harper) NYT gen 7/4/76 (#9), pk 8/1/76 (#6, 2 wk), 13 wk; PW hc nf 7/19/76 (#7), pk 8/16/76 (#4, 1 wk), 9 wk; tot 22 wk.

Keats, Ezra Jack
The Snowy Day (Viking) NYT ch bst 5/12/63 (#10), pk 11/10/63 (#6, 26 wk), 45 wk.

Keats, John
The Crack in the Picture Window (Houghton) NYT gen 3/3/57 (#16, 1 wk).
The Insolent Chariots (Lippincott) NYT gen 10/19/58 (#12), pk 11/9/58 (#8, 1 wk), 6 wk.

The Sheepskin Psychosis (Lippincott) PW nf 6/14/65 (#10, 1 wk).

Keegan, John
The Second World War (Viking) NYT nf 2/18/90 (#10), pk 3/11/90 (#7, 1 wk), 6 wk; PW hc nf 3/16/90 (#11, 1 wk), 2 wk; tot 8 wk.

Keene, Carolyn
The Strange Message in Parchment (Grosset & Dunlap) NYT ch hc 11/13/77 (#2, 46 wk).
Trail of Lies (Pocket/Archway) PW ch yn ad 11/30/90 (#3, 4 wk).
Model Crime (Pocket/Archway) PW ch yn ad 9/28/90 (#5, 4 wk).

Kefauver, Estes
Crime in America (Doubleday) NYT gen 7/29/51 (#13), pk 9/16/51 (#4, 1 wk), 13 wk; PW nf 8/25/51 (#5), pk 9/8/51 (#4, 1 wk), 7 wk; tot 20 wk.

Keillor, Garrison
Happy to Be Here (Atheneum) NYT fic 3/28/82 (#14), pk 4/11/82 (#12, 1 wk), 3 wk; PW hc fic 4/23/82 (#13), pk 4/30/82 (#11, 1 wk), 3 wk; (Penguin) NYT td pb 2/27/83 (#10), pk 3/27/83 (#8, 1 wk), 7 wk; PW td pb 3/4/83 (#7), pk 3/11/83 (#5, 2 wk), 7 wk; tot 20 wk.
Lake Wobegon Days (Viking) NYT fic 9/1/85 (#7), pk 9/15/85 (#1, 6 wk), 48 wk; PW hc fic 9/6/85 (#10), pk 9/20/85 (#1, 6 wk), 47 wk; (Penguin) NYT pb fic 7/27/86 (#3), pk 8/3/86 (#1, 7 wk), 21 wk; PW mm pb 8/1/86 (#8), pk 8/8/86 (#1, 7 wk), 17 wk; tot 133 wk.
Leaving Home: A Collection of Lake Wobegon Stories (Viking) NYT fic 10/4/87 (#4), pk 11/15/87 (#2, 1 wk), 21 wk; PW hc fic 10/9/87 (#7), pk 10/23/87 (#2, 1 wk), 18 wk; (Penguin) NYT pb fic 1/1/89 (#12, 3 wk); PW mm pb 1/6/89 (#12), pk 1/13/89 (#10, 1 wk), 5 wk; tot 47 wk.
We Are Still Married: Stories and Letters (Viking) NYT fic 4/9/89 (#12), pk 4/32/89 (#5, 1 wk), 13 wk; PW hc fic 4/14/89 (#8), pk 5/5/89 (#4, 1 wk), 11 wk; tot 24 wk.
More News from Lake Wobegon (Minnesota Public Radio/Publishers Group West) PW aud fic 12/7/90 (#7, 4 wk).

Keith, Agnes Newton
Land Below the Wind (Little Brown) NYT gen 12/10/39 (#6, 4 wk), 8 wk; PW nf 12/16/39 (#9), pk 3/9/40 (#2, 4 wk), 36 wk; tot 44 wk.
Three Came Home (Little Brown) NYT gen 4/27/47 (#16), pk 6/8/47 (#4, 1 wk), 20 wk; PW nf 5/17/47 (#6), pk 5/31/47 (#5, 3 wk), 7 wk; tot 27 wk.
White Man Returns (Little Brown) NYT

gen 8/26/51 (#10), pk 9/23/51 (#4, 6 wk), 14 wk; PW nf 9/15/51 (#8), pk 9/22/51 (#3, 2 wk), 7 wk; tot 21 wk.

Keith, Harold
Rifles for Watie (Crowell) NYT ch bst 11/2/58 (#6, 40 wk).

Keith, Slim, with Annette Tapert
Slim (Simon & Schuster) NYT nf 8/5/90 (#16, 1 wk).

Keller, James, and Meyer Berger
Men of Maryknoll (Scribner) NYT gen 4/2/44 (#14, 1 wk), 2 wk.

Keller, James Gregory
You Can Change the World (Longmans Green) NYT gen 3/20/49 (#12, 1 wk), 5 wk.

Keller, Werner
The Bible as History (Morrow) NYT gen 12/2/56 (#16), pk 1/27/57 (#8, 1 wk), 24 wk; PW nf 2/25/57 (#8), pk 5/20/57 (#6, 1 wk), 4 wk; tot 28 wk.

Kellerman, Jonathan
When the Bough Breaks (NAL/Signet) PW mm pb 5/23/86 (#13), pk 5/30/86 (#9, 1 wk), 8 wk; NYT pb fic 6/8/86 (#13), pk 6/22/86 (#12, 1 wk), 3 wk; tot 11 wk.
Over the Edge (NAL/Signet) NYT pb fic 3/13/88 (#15), pk 4/10/88 (#2, 1 wk), 13 wk; PW mm pb 3/18/88 (#14), pk 4/1/88 (#2, 2 wk), 13 wk; tot 26 wk.
Silent Partner (Bantam) NYT fic 10/1/89 (#13), pk 10/15/89 (#7, 1 wk), 6 wk; PW hc fic 10/6/89 (#13), pk 10/20/89 (#6, 1 wk), 6 wk; NYT pb fic 8/26/90 (#11), pk 9/16/90 (#2, 2 wk), 7 wk; PW mm pb 9/7/90 (#9), pk 9/21/90 (#2, 2 wk), 7 wk; tot 26 wk.
The Butcher's Theater (Bantam) PW mm pb 2/3/89 (#12), pk 2/24/89 (#6, 1 wk), 5 wk; NYT pb fic 2/5/89 (#17), pk 2/19/89 (#7, 2 wk), 6 wk; tot 11 wk.
Time Bomb (Bantam) PW hc fic 10/5/90 (#14, 3 wk).

Kelley, Kevin W.
The Home Planet [ed.] (Addison Wesley) NYT nf 12/18/88 (#15), pk 1/8/89 (#11, 2 wk), 5 wk; PW hc nf 1/13/89 (#12, 1 wk); tot 6 wk.

Kelley, Kitty
Jackie Oh! (Stuart) PW hc nf 10/16/78 (#11), pk 11/13/78 (#7, 1 wk), 20 wk; NYT nf 11/12/78 (#14), pk 12/3/78 (#8, 1 wk), 13 wk; (Ballantine) PW mm pb 6/4/79 (#15), pk 6/18/79 (#7, 2 wk), 8 wk; NYT mm pb 6/17/79 (#13), pk 6/24/79 (#10, 2 wk), 5 wk; tot 46 wk.
Elizabeth Taylor: The Last Star (Simon & Schuster) PW hc nf 10/23/81 (#13), pk 11/27/81 (#9, 2 wk), 14 wk; NYT nf 11/29/81

(#6, 2 wk), 9 wk; (Dell) NYT mm pb 11/21/82 (#6, 1 wk), 3 wk), tot 26 wk.
His Way: The Unauthorized Biography of Frank Sinatra (Bantam) NYT nf 10/12/86 (#1, 7 wk), 22 wk; PW hc nf 10/17/86 (#1, 7 wk), 20 wk; NYT pb nf 8/30/87 (#1, 6 wk), 10 wk; PW mm pb 9/4/87 (#6, 1 wk), 6 wk; tot 58 wk.

Kelley, Lt. Welbourn
See Cmdr. Walter Karig and_____

Kelley, William
Gemini (Doubleday) NYT fic 11/22/59 (#12, 1 wk), 6 wk.

Kellogg, Marjorie
Tell Me That You Love Me, Junie Moon (Farrar) NYT fic 12/15/68 (#8, 1 wk); PW fic 12/30/68 (#10), pk 1/6/69 (#8, 1 wk), 3 wk; tot 4 wk.

Kelly, Amy
Eleanor of Aquitaine and the Four Kings (Harvard Univ.) NYT gen 6/4/50 (#10, 2 wk), 13 wk; PW nf 8/12/50 (#10, 2 wk); tot 15 wk.

Kelly, Eric Philbrook
The Blacksmith of Vilno (Macmillan) PW juv 12/20/30 (#9, 4 wk).
The Trumpeter of Krakow (Macmillan) PW juv 2/15/30 (#4, 8 wk), 24 wk.

Kelly, Judith
Marriage Is a Private Affair (Harper) PW fic 10/11/41 (#4, 4 wk), 8 wk.

Kelly, Maureen Anne Teresa
See Mary Jane Frances Meara, et al.

Kelly, Walt
I Go Pogo (Simon & Schuster) NYT gen 9/21/52 (#14), pk 10/19/52 (#10, 2 wk), 12 wk; PW nf 10/11/52 (#8), pk 11/15/52 (#4, 1 wk), 3 wk; tot 15 wk.
Uncle Pogo So-So Stories (Simon & Schuster) NYT gen 6/7/53 (#15), pk 6/28/53 (#10, 1 wk), 14 wk; PW nf 9/19/53 (#10, 1 wk); tot 15 wk.
The Incompleat Pogo (Simon & Schuster) NYT gen 11/7/54 (#14, 1 wk).

Kelsey, Vera
Red River Runs North (Harper) NYT gen 4/8/51 (#15, 1 wk).

Kelso, Louis O., and Mortimer J. Adler
The Capitalist Manifesto (Random) NYT gen 2/23/58 (#15), pk 3/2/58 (#13, 1 wk), 3 wk.

Kemelman, Harry
Saturday the Rabbi Went Hungry (Crown) NYT fic 8/21/66 (#10), pk 10/23/66 (#8, 1

wk), 8 wk; PW fic 9/12/66 (#11), pk 10/31/66 (#9, 2 wk), 10 wk; tot 18 wk.

Friday the Rabbi Slept Late (Crown) NYT pb fic 1/2/66 (#5, 1 wk).

Sunday the Rabbi Stayed Home (Putnam) NYT fic 3/30/69 (#6, 2 wk), 9 wk; PW fic 4/14/69 (#9), pk 5/19/69 (#6, 1 wk), 7 wk; tot 16 wk.

Monday the Rabbi Took Off (Putnam) NYT fic 4/9/72 (#9), pk 5/7/72 (#7, 1 wk), 5 wk; PW fic 5/1/72 (#10, 3 wk); tot 8 wk.

Tuesday the Rabbi Saw Red (Fields/Dutton) PW fic 2/4/74 (#9), pk 3/11/74 (#4, 1 wk), 13 wk; NYT fic 3/24/74 (#9), pk 4/7/74 (#6, 1 wk), 6 wk; (Fawcett) NYT mm pb 2/2/75 (#7, 2 wk), 6 wk; tot 25 wk.

Wednesday the Rabbi Got Wet (Morrow) NYT fic 10/24/76 (#10), pk 11/14/76 (#9, 1 wk), 2 wk; (Fawcett/Crest) PW mm pb 9/26/77 (#14), pk 10/3/77 (#8, 1 wk), 3 wk; tot 5 wk.

Thursday the Rabbi Walked Out (Morrow) PW hc fic 9/25/78 (#12, 1 wk), 5 wk; NYT fic 11/12/78 (#12, 2 wk), 6 wk; tot 11 wk.

Kendall, Paul Murray
Richard the Third (Norton) NYT gen 9/16/56 (#16), pk 9/23/56 (#10, 1 wk), 5 wk.

Kendrick, Alexander
Prime Time (Little Brown) NYT gen 10/19/69 (#8), pk 11/6/69 (#5, 1 wk), 13 wk; PW nf 10/27/69 (#8), pk 12/15/69 (#4, 1 wk), 15 wk; NYT pb gen 12/6/70 (#5, 4 wk); tot 32 wk.

Kendrick, Baynard Hardwick
The Flames of Time (Scribner) NYT fic 7/4/48 (#13), pk 8/1/48 (#8, 1 wk), 8 wk.

Kennan, George Frost
American Diplomacy, 1900–1950 (Univ. of Chicago) NYT gen 10/21/51 (#16), pk 11/4/51 (#9, 1 wk), 10 wk.

Realities of American Foreign Policy (Princeton Univ.) NYT gen 10/17/54 (#14, 2 wk).

Russia, the Atom and the West (Harper) NYT gen 4/20/58 (#12, 1 wk).

Russia and the West Under Lenin and Stalin (Atlantic Little Brown) NYT gen 6/4/61 (#9), pk 6/25/61 (#5, 5 wk), 27 wk; PW nf 6/12/61 (#6), pk 6/26/61 (#5, 4 wk), 21 wk; tot 48 wk.

Memoirs, 1925–1950 (Atlantic Little Brown) PW nf 11/27/67 (#8), pk 1/1/68 (#3, 1 wk), 20 wk; NYT gen 12/3/67 (#5), pk 12/10/67 (#3, 1 wk), 16 wk; tot 36 wk.

Sketches from a Life (Pantheon) PW hc nf 6/9/89 (#14), pk 6/16/89 (#12, 1 wk), 4 wk; NYT nf 6/18/89 (#14, 1 wk), 3 wk; tot 7 wk.

Kennedy, Jay Richard
Prince Bart (Farrar) NYT fic 3/29/53 (#8), pk 4/26/53 (#4, 1 wk), 13 wk; PW fic 5/16/53 (#10, 2 wk); tot 15 wk.

Kennedy, John F.
Profiles in Courage (Harper) NYT gen 1/22/56 (#9), pk 12/29/63 (#1, 12 wk), 139 wk; PW nf 2/18/56 (#8), pk 10/8/56 (#1, 11 wk), 86 wk; tot 279 wk; (inaugural edition) PW nf 3/13/61 (#9), pk 3/20/61 (#7, 1 wk), 3 wk; (young reader's edition) NYT ch bst 11/12/61 (#7, 26 wk), 51 wk; tot 279 wk.

The Strategy of Peace (Harper) NYT gen 8/14/60 (#15), pk 9/4/60 (#12, 1 wk), 5 wk.

America the Beautiful (Country Beautiful Foundation) NYT gen 5/17/64 (#10, 1 wk).

The Burden and the Glory [ed. Allan Nevins] (Harper) PW nf 7/6/64 (#6, 1 wk), 5 wk.

Thirteen Days (Norton) NYT gen 2/9/69 (#7), pk 2/23/69 (#5, 3 wk), 10 wk; PW nf 2/10/69 (#6), pk 4/14/69 (#2, 1 wk), 10 wk; tot 20 wk.

Kennedy, Lena
Maggie (Pocket) PW mm pb 5/2/80 (#12, 1 wk), 2 wk.

Kitty (Pocket) NYT mm pb 11/22/81 (#10, 1 wk), 2 wk.

Kennedy, Margaret
The Constant Nymph (Doubleday) PW fic 4/18/25 (#4), pk 6/20/25 (#1, 8 wk), 20 wk.

Red Sky at Morning (Doubleday) PW fic 12/31/27 (#5, 4 wk).

The Feast (Rinehart) NYT fic 4/9/50 (#16), pk 4/30/50 (#5, 1 wk), 10 wk; PW fic 5/13/50 (#10, 1 wk); tot 11 wk.

Lucy Carmichael (Rinehart) NYT fic 8/26/51 (#11), pk 9/2/51 (#9, 2 wk), 6 wk; PW fic 9/15/51 (#9, 1 wk), 2 wk; tot 8 wk.

Act of God (Rinehart) NYT fic 3/6/55 (#16, 1 wk).

The Forgotten Smile (Macmillan) NYT fic 5/6/62 (#16, 2 wk).

Kennedy, Paul
The Rise and Fall of the Great Powers: Economic Change and Military Conflict from 1500 to 2000 (Random) PW hc nf 2/5/88 (#15), pk 3/25/88 (#2, 3 wk), 31 wk; NYT nf 2/7/88 (#11), pk 2/28/88 (#2, 6 wk), 34 wk; (Vintage) NYT pb nf 2/19/89 (#7), pk 2/26/89 (#6, 2 wk), 8 wk; PW td pb 3/3/89 (#10), pk 3/17/89 (#7, 1 wk), 3 wk; tot 76 wk.

Kennedy, Robert F.
The Enemy Within (Harper) NYT gen 3/20/60 (#13), pk 4/24/60 (#3, 5 wk), 25 wk; PW nf 3/28/60 (#7), pk 5/9/60 (#2, 2 wk), 19 wk; tot 44 wk.

To Seek a Newer World (Doubleday) NYT pb gen 7/7/68 (#4, 4 wk).

Thirteen Days (Norton) NYT gen 2/9/69 (#7), pk 2/23/69 (#5, 3 wk), 10 wk; PW nf 2/10/69 (#6), pk 4/14/69 (#2, 1 wk), 10 wk; tot 20 wk.

Robert Kennedy: In His Own Words [ed. Edwin O. Guthman and Jeffrey Shulman] (Bantam) NYT nf 6/19/88 (#15), pk 6/26/88 (#10, 1 wk), 3 wk.

Kennedy, Rose Fitzgerald
Times to Remember (Doubleday) NYT gen 4/7/74 (#8), pk 5/19/74 (#1, 6 wk), 23 wk; PW nf 4/8/74 (#7), pk 6/3/74 (#1, 2 wk), 18 wk; (Bantam) NYT mm pb 3/2/75 (#10), pk 3/16/75 (#7, 1 wk), 5 wk; tot 46 wk.

Kennedy, William
Ironweed (Penguin) PW td pb 6/22/84 (#9), pk 1/18/85 (#5, 2 wk), 10 wk.

Quinn's Book (Viking) NYT fic 6/19/88 (#13, 1 wk), 2 wk.

Kent, Jack
There's No Such Thing as a Dragon (Golden) NYT ch pb 11/13/77 (#10, 46 wk).

Kent, Louise Andrews
Mrs. Appleyard's Year (Houghton) PW fic 1/17/42 (#10, 4 wk).

Kent, Margaret
How to Marry the Man of Your Choice (Warner) PW hc nf 8/7/87 (#12), pk 8/14/87 (#6, 1 wk), 13 wk; NYT msc 8/9/87 (#5), pk 8/16/87 (#2, 2 wk), 16 wk; tot 29 wk.

Kent, Rockwell
N By E (Brewer & Warren) PW nf 2/21/31 (#8, 4 wk).

Salamina (Harcourt) PW nf 12/14/35 (#10, 4 wk).

World Famous Paintings [ed.] (Wise) NYT gen 1/7/40 (#2, 4 wk); PW nf 1/13/40 (#9), pk 2/10/40 (#7, 4 wk), 8 wk; tot 12 wk.

See also Geoffrey Chaucer

Kenyon, F.W.
The Emperor's Lady (Crowell) NYT fic 6/21/53 (#13), pk 7/19/53 (#6, 2 wk), 15 wk; PW fic 7/11/53 (#10), pk 7/25/53 (#6, 4 wk), 7 wk; tot 22 wk.

Kernan, Lt. Col. William F.
Defense Will Not Win the War (Little Brown) PW nf 4/11/42 (#3, 4 wk), 8 wk.

Kerouac, Jack
On the Road (Buccaneer) NYT fic 10/6/57 (#14), pk 10/27/57 (#11, 2 wk), 5 wk.

Kerr, Graham
The Graham Kerr Cookbook (Doubleday) NYT gen 12/21/69 (#10), pk 3/22/70 (#4, 1 wk), 18 wk; PW nf 12/29/69 (#8), pk 3/30/70 (#4, 2 wk), 21 wk; tot 39 wk.

Kerr, Jean
Please Don't Eat the Daisies (Doubleday) NYT gen 12/15/57 (#9), pk 2/2/58 (#1, 13 wk), 50 wk; PW nf 12/30/57 (#4), pk 1/27/58 (#1, 12 wk), 46 wk; tot 96 wk.

The Snake Has All the Lines (Doubleday) NYT gen 11/20/60 (#16), pk 1/22/61 (#3, 1 wk), 22 wk; PW nf 12/12/60 (#7), pk 1/16/61 (#3, 2 wk), 19 wk; tot 41 wk.

Kerr, Walter
The Decline of Pleasure (Simon & Schuster) NYT gen 7/8/62 (#14, 1 wk), 2 wk; PW nf 7/30/62 (#10, 1 wk), 2 wk; tot 4 wk.

Kersh, Gerald
Night and the City (Simon & Schuster) NYT fic 5/12/46 (#11, 2 wk), 5 wk.

Kesey, Ken
One Flew Over the Cuckoo's Nest (NAL/ Signet) NYT mm pb 1/25/76 (#9), pk 3/21/ 76 (#4, 3 wk), 23 wk; PW mm pb 2/2/76 (#8), pk 3/22/76 (#3, 1 wk), 22 wk; tot 45 wk.

Kessel, Joseph
The Lion (Knopf) NYT fic 7/12/59 (#14), pk 7/26/59 (#10, 1 wk), 8 wk.

Ketcham, Hank
Dennis the Menace (Holt) NYT gen 12/28/ 52 (#16, 1 wk).

Ketchum, Richard M.
The American Heritage Book of Great Historic Places [ed.] (Simon & Schuster) NYT gen 10/27/57 (#15), pk 11/17/57 (#13, 1 wk), 2 wk; PW nf 11/18/57 (#10, 1 wk); tot 3 wk.

Will Rogers (American Heritage) PW nf 1/21/74 (#10, 1 wk).

Keteyian Armen
See Alexander Wolff and_____

Kett, Joseph F.
See E.D. Hirsch, Jr., et al.

Keyes, Daniel
The Minds of Billy Milligan (Bantam) NYT mm pb 12/12/82 (#13, 1 wk).

Keyes, Evelyn
Scarlett O'Hara's Younger Sister (Fawcett/ Crest) PW mm pb 10/9/78 (#13, 1 wk), 2 wk.

Keyes, Frances Parkinson
Parts Unknown (Messner) NYT fic 7/3/38 (#2, 4 wk), 8 wk; PW fic 7/9/38 (#9, 4 wk); tot 12 wk.

The Great Tradition (Messner) NYT fic 12/10/39 (#6, 4 wk).

Fielding's Folly (Messner) PW fic 12/14/40 (#9, 4 wk), 8 wk.

Crescent Carnival (Messner) NYT fic 11/29/42 (#6), pk 3/14/43 (#5, 1 wk), 43 wk; PW fic 12/5/42 (#5, 2 wk), 13 wk; tot 56 wk.

All That Glitters (Messner) PW fic 1/17/42 (#9, 4 wk), 8 wk.

Also the Hills (Messner) NYT fic 12/5/43 (#11), pk 3/5/44 (#4, 1 wk), 22 wk; PW fic 1/15/44 (#7), pk 2/26/44 (#5, 1 wk), 4 wk; tot 26 wk.

The River Road (Messner) NYT fic 12/23/45 (#6), pk 1/13/46 (#3, 2 wk), 21 wk; PW fic 1/5/46 (#4), pk 1/19/46 (#3, 1 wk), 10 wk; tot 31 wk.

Came a Cavalier (Messner) NYT fic 11/16/47 (#8), pk 12/14/47 (#3, 8 wk), 29 wk; PW fic 11/29/47 (#3, 9 wk), 17 wk; tot 46 wk.

Dinner at Antoine's (Messner) NYT fic 12/12/48 (#5), pk 1/2/49 (#2, 13 wk), 37 wk; PW fic 12/18/48 (#7), pk 1/1/49 (#2, 15 wk), 26 wk; tot 63 wk.

Joy Street (Messner) NYT fic 12/10/50 (#10), pk 1/4/51 (#1, 8 wk), 34 wk; PW fic 1/6/51 (#1, 12 wk), 22 wk; tot 56 wk.

Steamboat Gothic (Messner) NYT fic 11/30/52 (#5), pk 1/4/53 (#3, 9 wk), 34 wk; PW fic 12/6/52 (#5), pk 1/17/53 (#2, 2 wk), 22 wk; tot 56 wk.

The Royal Box (Messner) NYT fic 6/27/54 (#10), pk 7/18/54 (#3, 1 wk), 26 wk; PW fic 7/10/54 (#2, 1 wk), 18 wk; tot 44 wk.

Blue Camellia (Messner) NYT fic 2/3/57 (#12), pk 4/21/57 (#3, 4 wk), 37 wk; PW fic 3/4/57 (#4), pk 3/11/57 (#2, 3 wk), 25 wk; tot 62 wk.

Victorine (Messner) NYT fic 11/16/58 (#16), pk 1/25/59 (#7, 1 wk), 17 wk; PW fic 12/8/58 (#8), pk 1/19/59 (#6, 1 wk), 10 wk; tot 27 wk.

Station Wagon in Spain (Farrar) NYT fic 10/25/59 (#12), pk 11/8/59 (#9, 1 wk), 10 wk; PW fic 11/16/59 (#6, 1 wk); tot 11 wk.

The Chess Players (Farrar) NYT fic 1/15/61 (#13), pk 2/26/61 (#7, 1 wk), 14 wk.

Madame Castel's Lodger (Farrar) PW fic 2/4/63 (#8), pk 2/11/63 (#5, 1 wk), 2 wk.

The Explorer (McGraw) NYT fic 1/10/65 (#10), pk 2/7/65 (#6, 1 wk), 3 wk; PW fic 2/15/65 (#8, 1 wk); tot 4 wk.

I, The King (McGraw) NYT fic 6/26/66 (#9), pk 7/24/66 (#6, 1 wk), 12 wk; PW fic 7/4/66 (#12), pk 7/18/66 (#9, 3 wk), 9 wk; tot 21 wk.

Keyhoe, Donald E.

Flying Saucers from Outer Space (Holt) NYT gen 11/1/53 (#11), pk 11/29/53 (#8, 1 wk), 13 wk; PW nf 11/28/53 (#6, 1 wk), 2 wk; tot 15 wk.

Keynes, John Maynard

Economic Consequences of the Peace (Har-

court) PW gen 3/27/20 (#7), pk 6/12/20 (#1, 8 wk), 28 wk.

Keys, Margaret

See Ancel Benjamin and_____

Khruschev, Nikita

Khruschev Remembers [trans./ed. Strobe Talbott] (Little Brown) NYT gen 1/10/71 (#10), pk 2/14/71 (#3, 1 wk), 17 wk; PW nf 1/18/71 (#8), pk 3/8/71 (#2, 1 wk), 17 wk; tot 34 wk.

Kidder, Tracy

The Soul of a New Machine (Atlantic Little Brown) PW hc nf 9/25/81 (#11), pk 10/23/81 (#7, 1 wk), 10 wk; NYT nf 10/25/81 (#10), pk 11/1/81 (#8, 1 wk), 9 wk; (Avon) NYT mm pb 8/15/82 (#10, 1 wk), 2 wk; PW mm pb 8/20/82 (#12), pk 8/27/82 (#8, 1 wk), 6 wk; tot 27 wk.

House (Houghton) NYT nf 10/27/85 (#6), pk 11/17/85 (#4, 1 wk), 25 wk; PW hc nf 11/1/85 (#8, 5 wk), 17 wk; (Avon) NYT pb nf 10/5/86 (#5), pk 10/12/86 (#3, 3 wk), 8 wk; tot 50 wk.

Among Schoolchildren (Todd/Houghton) NYT nf 9/3/89 (#15), pk 9/24/89 (#2, 1 wk), 29 wk; PW hc nf 9/22/89 (#10), pk 11/3/89 (#4, 1 wk), 17 wk; (Avon) NYT pb nf 9/9/90 (#9), pk 10/7/90 (#4, 1 wk), 12 wk; tot 58 wk.

Kieran, John

A Natural History of New York City (Houghton) NYT gen 10/25/59 (#14), pk 11/1/59 (#10, 1 wk), 2 wk.

Not Under Oath: Recollections and Reflections (Houghton) PW nf 11/9/64 (#7, 2 wk), 10 wk; NYT gen 12/20/64 (#9, 2 wk); tot 12 wk.

Footnotes on Nature (Doubleday) NYT gen 8/31/47 (#15, 1 wk).

Kiley, Dr. Dan

The Peter Pan Syndrome: Men Who Have Never Grown Up (Dodd) NYT nf 9/25/83 (#14), pk 10/23/83 (#9, 6 wk), 20 wk; PW hc nf 10/21/83 (#11), pk 10/28/83 (#8, 1 wk), 8 wk; (Avon) NYT pb nf 9/9/84 (#3, 5 wk), 11 wk; PW mm pb 9/14/84 (#14), pk 10/12/84 (#3, 1 wk), 8 wk; tot 47 wk.

The Wendy Dilemma (Arbor House) NYT nf 9/30/84 (#13), pk 10/7/84 (#9, 1 wk), 7 wk.

Kilgore, Al

See Jim Fitzgerald, et al.

Kilmer, Joyce

Joyce Kilmer: Poems and Essays (Doran) PW gen 6/7/19 (#3, 4 wk), 8 wk.

Kim, Richard E.

The Martyred (Braziller) NYT fic 3/15/64

(#7), pk 4/12/64 (#5, 3 wk), 16 wk; PW fic 3/23/64 (#6), pk 5/4/64 (#5, 4 wk), 16 wk; tot 32 wk.

Kimball, Marie Goebel
Jefferson: The Road to Glory, 1743–1776 (Coward McCann) NYT gen 5/9/43 (#18), pk 5/23/43 (#15, 1 wk), 3 wk.

Kimbrough, Emily
We Followed Our Hearts to Hollywood (Dodd) NYT gen 12/5/43 (#12), pk 12/19/43 (#4, 1 wk), 10 wk; PW nf 12/11/43 (#4, 2 wk), 4 wk; tot 14 wk.
How Dear to My Heart (Dodd) NYT gen 1/21/45 (#17, 1 wk), 2 wk.
It Gives Me Great Pleasure (Dodd) NYT gen 1/16/49 (#14), pk 1/23/49 (#12, 1 wk), 6 wk.
Through Charley's Door (Harper) NYT gen 3/9/52 (#12), pk 3/16/52 (#9, 1 wk), 11 wk; PW nf 4/12/52 (#9, 1 wk); tot 12 wk.
Forty Plus and Fancy Free (Harper) NYT gen 3/28/54 (#13), pk 5/16/54 (#5, 6 wk), 33 wk; PW nf 4/10/54 (#10), pk 5/22/54 (#3, 5 wk), 17 wk; tot 50 wk.
So Near and Yet So Far (Harper) NYT gen 11/13/55 (#12), pk 11/20/55 (#6, 1 wk), 11 wk; PW nf 12/17/55 (#8, 1 wk), 2 wk; tot 13 wk.
Water, Water Everywhere (Harper) NYT gen 12/16/56 (#15), pk 1/20/57 (#11, 1 wk), 8 wk.
See also Cornelia Otis Skinner and_____

Kimmel, Husband Edward
Admiral Kimmel's Story (Regnery) NYT gen 2/6/55 (#14, 1 wk), 3 wk.

Kinder, Dr. Melvyn
See Dr. Connell Cowan and_____

King, Alexander
Mine Enemy Grows Older (Simon & Schuster) NYT gen 2/15/59 (#16), pk 4/12/59 (#1, 9 wk), 39 wk; PW nf 3/2/59 (#5), pk 4/27/59 (#1, 6 wk), 31 wk; tot 70 wk.
May This House Be Safe from Tigers (Simon & Schuster) NYT gen 1/24/60 (#13), pk 3/13/60 (#1, 21 wk), 43 wk; PW nf 2/1/60 (#9), pk 3/14/60 (#1, 19 wk), 39 wk; tot 82 wk.
I Should Have Kissed Her More (Simon & Schuster) NYT gen 10/22/61 (#15), pk 12/3/61 (#7, 1 wk), 19 wk; PW nf 11/13/61 (#8), pk 11/27/61 (#6, 1 wk), 11 wk; tot 30 wk.
Is There Life After Birth? (Simon & Schuster) PW nf 4/22/63 (#10, 1 wk).

King, Basil
The City of Comrades (Harper) PW fic 6/7/19 (#6, 4 wk).
The Thread of Flame (Harper) PW fic 10/23/20 (#5, 4 wk), 8 wk.

The Abolishing of Death (Cosmopolitan) PW gen 1/3/20 (#4, 4 wk).
Conquest of Fear (Doubleday) PW gen lit 7/29/22 (#11), pk 9/16/22 (#8, 4 wk), 12 wk; PW nf 8/26/22 (#11, 4 wk); tot 16 wk.

King, Elizabeth A.
See Dr. Elliot D. Abravanel and_____

King, Larry, and Peter Occhiogrosso
Tell It to the King (Putnam) NYT nf 5/22/88 (#11), pk 6/12/88 (#10, 1 wk), 3 wk.

King, Larry L.
See Bobby Baker and_____

King, Stephen
'Salem's Lot (NAL/Signet) PW mm pb 8/23/76 (#9), pk 9/6/76 (#2, 3 wk), 17 wk; NYT mm pb 8/29/76 (#6), pk 9/26/76 (#1, 2 wk), 14 wk; tot 31 wk.
Carrie (NAL/Signet) PW mm pb 12/6/76 (#13), pk 1/3/76 (#3, 1 wk), 13 wk; NYT mm pb 12/19/76 (#6), pk 1/16/76 (#3, 2 wk), 12 wk; tot 25 wk.
The Shining (Doubleday) PW hc fic 2/28/77 (#10), pk 3/21/77 (#8, 1 wk), 6 wk; NYT fic 3/27/77 (#8, 1 wk); (NAL/Signet) PW mm pb 1/23/78 (#7), pk 2/13/78 (#2, 2 wk), 22 wk; NYT mm pb 1/29/78 (#7), pk 2/12/78 (#3, 1 wk), 26 wk; tot 55 wk.
The Stand (Doubleday) PW hc fic 11/27/78 (#11), pk 12/4/78 (#7, 1 wk), 8 wk; NYT fic 1/21/79 (#15), pk 2/11/79 (#13, 1 wk), 3 wk; (NAL/Signet) PW mm pb 1/18/80 (#11), pk 2/8/80 (#1, 2 wk), 13 wk; NYT mm pb 1/20/80 (#11), pk 2/3/80 (#1, 1 wk), 17 wk; tot 99 wk.
Night Shift (NAL/Signet) PW mm pb 2/26/79 (#12), pk 3/26/79 (#7, 2 wk), 12 wk; NYT mm pb 3/4/79 (#12), pk 4/1/79 (#7, 1 wk), 13 wk; NYT pb fic 4/22/84 (#15, 1 wk); tot 26 wk.
The Dead Zone (Viking) PW hc fic 8/27/79 (#11), pk 10/1/79 (#2, 2 wk), 36 wk; NYT fic 9/9/79 (#8), pk 10/14/79 (#1, 2 wk), 32 wk; (NAL/Signet) PW mm pb 8/8/80 (#11), pk 8/22/80 (#1, 5 wk), 11 wk; NYT mm pb 8/10/80 (#13), pk 8/24/80 (#1, 3 wk), 14 wk; tot 93 wk.
Firestarter (Viking) PW hc fic 8/22/80 (#8), pk 9/26/80 (#1, 4 wk), 37 wk; NYT fic 8/24/80 (#6), pk 9/28/80 (#1, 3 wk), 35 wk; (NAL) PW mm pb 8/14/81 (#1, 4 wk), 12 wk; NYT mm pb 8/16/81 (#1, 4 wk), 12 wk; tot 96 wk.
Cujo (Viking) PW hc fic 8/14/81 (#6), pk 8/28/81 (#1, 5 wk), 33 wk; NYT fic 8/16/81 (#5), pk 8/23/81 (#1, 5 wk), 34 wk; (NAL) PW mm pb 8/6/82 (#4), pk 8/20/82 (#1, 2

wk), 11 wk; NYT mm pb 8/8/82 (#2), pk 8/15/82 (#1, 3 wk), 9 wk; tot 87 wk.

Danse Macabre (Everest House) PW hc nf 4/24/81 (#15), pk 6/12/81 (#9, 1 wk), 9 wk; NYT nf 5/17/81 (#13), pk 6/7/81 (#14, 1 wk), 5 wk; (Berkley) PW mm pb 12/23/83 (#9, 1 wk), 3 wk; tot 17 wk.

Different Seasons (Viking) PW hc fic 8/6/82 (#12), pk 8/27/82 (#2, 5 wk), 33 wk; NYT fic 8/8/82 (#7), pk 8/15/82 (#1, 3 wk), 32 wk; (NAL/Signet) NYT mm pb 7/31/83 (#2, 5 wk), 13 wk; PW mm pb 8/5/83 (#6), pk 8/26/83 (#2, 2 wk), 11 wk; tot 89 wk.

Pet Sematary (Doubleday) NYT fic 11/6/83 (#4), pk 11/13/83 (#1, 13 wk), 32 wk; PW hc fic 11/11/83 (#8), pk 11/25/83 (#1, 14 wk), 32 wk; (NAL/Signet) NYT pb fic 10/28/84 (#1, 3 wk), 22 wk; PW mm pb 11/2/84 (#3), pk 11/9/84 (#1, 2 wk), 19 wk; tot 105 wk.

Christine (Viking) NYT fic 4/10/83 (#3), pk 4/24/83 (#2, 7 wk), 32 wk; PW hc fic 4/15/83 (#5), pk 4/22/83 (#2, 11 wk), 31 wk; (NAL/Signet) PW mm pb 11/25/83 (#11), pk 12/2/83 (#1, 7 wk), 13 wk; NYT mm pb 11/27/83 (#3), pk 12/4/83 (#1, 4 wk), 5 wk; pb fic 1/1/84 (#1, 3 wk), 9 wk; tot 90 wk.

Thinner [as by Richard Bachman] (NAL) NYT fic 3/3/85 (#8), pk 4/28/85 (#1, 4 wk), 25 wk; PW hc fic 3/8/85 (#9), pk 5/10/85 (#1, 2 wk), 25 wk; (NAL/Signet) NYT pb fic 9/1/85 (#1, 6 wk), 16 wk; PW mm pb 9/6/85 (#2), pk 9/13/85 (#1, 5 wk), 14 wk; tot 80 wk.

Skeleton Crew (Putnam) NYT fic 6/23/85 (#1, 10 wk), 32 wk; PW hc fic 6/28/85 (#5), pk 7/5/85 (#1, 8 wk), 32 wk; (NAL/Signet) NYT pb fic 5/25/86 (#3), pk 6/1/86 (#1, 6 wk), 16 wk; PW mm pb 5/30/86 (#7), pk 6/6/86 (#1, 5 wk), 11 wk; tot 91 wk.

Cycle of the Werewolf (NAL/Signet) NYT pb fic 4/28/85 (#9), pk 5/12/85 (#5, 1 wk), 5 wk; PW td pb 5/3/85 (#3, 3 wk), 8 wk; tot 3 wk.

The Bachman Books (NAL) NYT fic 11/17/85 (#10, 1 wk), 3 wk; pb fic 10/13/85 (#9), pk 10/27/85 (#3, 2 wk), 27 wk; (NAL/Plume) PW td pb 10/18/85 (#4), pk 10/25/85 (#1, 10 wk), 19 wk; (NAL/Signet) mm pb 11/7/86 (#6, 3 wk), 4 wk; tot 53 wk.

It (Viking) PW hc fic 9/12/86 (#13), pk 9/19/86 (#1, 12 wk), 33 wk; NYT fic 9/14/86 (#1, 14 wk), 35 wk; (NAL/Signet) NYT pb fic 8/23/87 (#11), pk 8/30/87 (#1, 7 wk), 28 wk; PW mm pb 8/28/87 (#8), pk 9/4/87 (#1, 7 wk), 24 wk; tot 120 wk.

Misery (Viking) NYT fic 6/7/87 (#1, 7 wk), 30 wk; PW hc fic 6/12/87 (#1, 7 wk), 32 wk; (NAL/Signet) NYT pb fic 5/29/88 (#2), pk 6/19/88 (#1, 2 wk), 19 wk; PW mm pb

6/3/88 (#2), pk 6/17/88 (#1, 2 wk), 14 wk; tot 95 wk.

The Tommyknockers (Putnam) NYT fic 11/29/87 (#1, 8 wk), 23 wk; PW hc fic 12/4/87 (#1, 7 wk), 22 wk; (NAL/Signet) PW mm pb 11/18/88 (#8), pk 12/2/88 (#1, 3 wk), 12 wk; NYT pb fic 11/20/88 (#2), pk 12/4/88 (#1, 1 wk), 14 wk; tot 71 wk.

The Eyes of the Dragon (Viking) NYT fic 2/1/87 (#1, 1 wk), 26 wk; PW hc fic 2/6/87 (#2, 8 wk), 23 wk; (NAL/Signet) NYT pb fic 12/27/87 (#4), pk 1/3/88 (#1, 6 wk), 13 wk; PW mm pb 1/8/88 (#3), pk 1/15/88 (#1, 4 wk), 11 wk; tot 73 wk.

The Dark Tower: The Gunslinger (NAL/Plume) NYT pb fic 9/25/88 (#14), pk 10/2/88 (#1, 4 wk), 17 wk; PW td pb 10/14/88 (#1, 4 wk), 20 wk; (NAL/Signet) NYT pb fic 7/2/89 (#6), pk 7/9/89 (#2, 1 wk), 14 wk; PW mm pb 7/7/89 (#7), pk 8/4/89 (#4, 2 wk), 12 wk; tot 59 wk.

The Dark Half (Viking) NYT fic 11/5/89 (#1, 6 wk), 19 wk; PW hc fic 11/10/89 (#4), pk 11/17/89 (#1, 5 wk), 15 wk; (NAL/Signet) NYT pb fic 9/30/90 (#1, 4 wk), 14 wk; PW mm pb 10/5/90 (#2), pk 10/12/90 (#1, 3 wk), 12 wk; tot 60 wk.

The Dark Tower: The Drawing of the Three (NAL/Signet) NYT pb fic 4/16/89 (#4), pk 4/23/89 (#1, 6 wk), 19 wk; PW td pb 4/28/89 (#1, 2 wk), 23 wk; (NAL/Signet) PW mm pb 1/12/90 (#3), pk 1/19/90 (#2, 3 wk), 7 wk; tot 49 wk.

The Stand: The Complete and Uncut Edition (Doubleday) NYT fic 5/13/90 (#1, 4 wk), 31 wk; PW hc fic 5/18/90 (#5), pk 5/25/90 (#1, 4 wk), 27 wk; tot 58 wk.

Four Past Midnight (Viking) NYT fic 9/16/90 (#1, 5 wk), 16 wk; PW hc fic 9/21/90 (#1, 5 wk), 14 wk; tot 30 wk.

_____, and Peter Straub

The Talisman (Viking) NYT fic 10/28/84 (#1, 12 wk), 23 wk; PW hc fic 11/2/84 (#1, 11 wk), 26 wk; (Berkley) NYT pb fic 10/27/85 (#7), pk 11/10/85 (#1, 2 wk), 14 wk; PW mm pb 11/1/85 (#5), pk 11/15/85 (#1, 3 wk), 13 wk; tot 76 wk.

Kingdon, Frank

"That Man" in the White House (Arco) NYT gen 4/30/44 (#17), pk 5/7/44 (#16, 3 wk), 4 wk.

Kingman, Dong

See Herb Caen

Kingsley, Johanna

Scents (Bantam) NYT pb fic 12/30/84 (#9), pk 2/10/85 (#4, 1 wk), 6 wk; PW mm

Klein, Alexander
Grand Deception (Lippincott) NYT gen 10/2/55 (#13, 1 wk).

Klein, Norma
Sunshine (Avon) NYT mm pb 8/11/74 (#10), pk 10/13/74 (#6, 4 wk), 8 wk.

Klein, T.E.D.
The Ceremonies (Bantam) NYT pb fic 7/21/85 (#13, 1 wk).

Kleinfield, Sonny
See Lee Iacocca and_____

Kliban, B.
Cat (Workman) NYT td pb 9/21/75 (#5, 3 wk), 5 wk.
Whack Your Porcupine and Other Drawings (Workman) NYT td pb 7/24/77 (#5), pk 8/7/77 (#4, 3 wk), 10 wk; PW td pb 8/29/77 (#5, 1 wk), 2 wk; tot 12 wk.
Tiny Footprints and Other Drawings (Workman) PW td pb 6/12/78 (#5), pk 7/3/78 (#3, 1 wk), 7 wk; NYT td pb 7/23/78 (#8, 1 wk), 4 wk; tot 11 wk.

Klipper, Miriam Z.
See Herbert Benson M.D. and_____

Knaak, Richard A.
The Legend of Huma (TSR) NYT pb fic 5/22/88 (#15, 1 wk).

Knebel, Fletcher
The Night of Camp David (Harper) NYT fic 6/13/65 (#10), pk 7/11/65 (#5, 2 wk), 16 wk; PW fic 7/5/65 (#8), pk 7/19/65 (#6, 3 wk), 18 wk; tot 34 wk.
Vanished (Doubleday) NYT fic 1/28/68 (#7), pk 3/31/68 (#1, 1 wk), 32 wk; PW fic 2/5/68 (#13), pk 3/18/68 (#1, 2 wk), 33 wk; NYT pb fic 4/6/69 (#3, 4 wk), 16 wk; tot 81 wk.
Dark Horse (Doubleday) NYT fic 7/16/72 (#9), pk 9/24/72 (#3, 1 wk), 19 wk; PW fic 7/24/72 (#8), pk 9/25/72 (#4, 3 wk), 18 wk; tot 37 wk.
The Bottom Line (Pocket) NYT mm pb 11/16/75 (#9, 2 wk), 3 wk.

_____, and Charles W. Bailey II
Seven Days in May (Harper) NYT fic 9/23/62 (#15), pk 11/18/62 (#1, 4 wk), 34 wk; PW fic 10/1/62 (#11), pk 12/10/62 (#1, 8 wk), 49 wk; tot 83 wk.
Convention (Harper) NYT fic 3/29/64 (#8), pk 5/3/64 (#2, 10 wk), 27 wk; PW fic 4/13/64 (#4), pk 5/4/64 (#2, 8 wk), 28 wk; tot 55 wk.

Knef, Hildegard
The Gift Horse (McGraw) NYT gen 8/1/71 (#6), pk 9/26/71 (#2, 3 wk), 17 wk; PW nf 8/9/71 (#6), pk 9/27/71 (#1, 1 wk), 17 wk; tot 34 wk.

Knight, Eric
This Above All (Harper) PW fic 5/10/41 (#6), pk 7/12/41 (#1, 8 wk), 28 wk.

Knight, Hilary
See Kay Thompson

Knight, Jonathan
See Joseph McIntyre, et al.

Knight, Jordan
See Joseph McIntyre, et al.

Knobler, Peter
See Kareem Abdul-Jabbar and_____
See Thomas Henderson and_____

Knott, Blanche
Truly Tasteless Jokes (Ballantine) PW mm pb 2/25/83 (#13), pk 6/3/83 (#4, 2 wk), 29 wk; NYT mm pb 2/27/83 (#15), pk 6/5/83 (#3, 1 wk), 39 wk; tot 68 wk.
Truly Tasteless Jokes II (Ballantine) NYT mm pb 7/10/83 (#4, 2 wk), 21 wk; PW mm pb 7/15/83 (#9), pk 7/29/83 (#5, 2 wk), 16 wk; tot 37 wk.
Truly Tasteless Jokes III (Ballantine) NYT mm pb 12/4/83 (#14), pk 12/25/83 (#3, 1 wk), 4 wk; PW mm pb 12/16/83 (#6), pk 1/20/84 (#3, 1 wk), 10 wk; NYT msc pb 1/1/84 (#1, 3 wk), 11 wk; tot 25 wk.
Truly Tasteless Jokes IV (Pinnacle) NYT msc pb 12/9/84 (#5), pk 1/27/85 (#4, 1 wk), 11 wk.
Truly Tasteless Jokes V (St. Martin's) NYT msc pb 12/29/85 (#12, 1 wk).
Truly Tasteless Jokes VI (St. Martin's) NYT msc pb 7/6/86 (#7), pk 7/20/86 (#6, 1 wk), 4 wk.

Knowles, Horace
Gentlemen, Scholars and Scoundrels [ed.] (Harper) NYT gen 11/15/59 (#14, 2 wk), 8 wk.

Knowles, John
A Separate Peace (Macmillan) NYT fic 3/27/60 (#16, 2 wk).

Knowles, Katherine, and Walter Muir Whitehill
Boston: Portrait of a City [photos by Knowles, text by Whitehill] (Barre) PW nf 8/24/64 (#7, 1 wk).

Knox, Cleone
The Diary of a Young Lady of Fashion in the Year 1764–1765 (Appleton) PW nf 3/20/26 (#8), pk 4/17/26 (#6, 4 wk), 16 wk.

Kobler, John
Capone (Putnam) NYT gen 6/27/71 (#10), pk 9/12/71 (#7, 1 wk), 10 wk; PW nf 8/16/71 (#6), pk 9/20/71 (#5, 1 wk), 5 wk; tot 15 wk.

Koch, Edward I., with William Rauch
Mayor: An Autobiography (Simon & Schuster) NYT nf 2/19/84 (#8), pk 2/26/84 (#1, 8 wk), 21 wk; PW hc nf 2/24/84 (#10), pk 3/16/84 (#2, 1 wk), 17 wk; (Warner) NYT pb nf 1/20/85 (#3, 1 wk), 5 wk; tot 43 wk.

Koda-Callan, Elizabeth
The Silver Slippers (Workman) PW ch yn rd 8/31/90 (#5), pk 11/30/90 (#4, 4 wk), 12 wk.
The Good Luck Pony (Workman) PW ch yn rd 12/21/90 (#4, 4 wk).

Koen, Karleen
Through a Glass Darkly (Random) PW hc fic 8/29/86 (#12), pk 10/17/86 (#3, 1 wk), 20 wk; NYT fic 9/7/86 (#12), pk 9/28/86 (#4, 2 wk), 21 wk; (Avon) NYT pb fic 8/30/87 (#15), pk 9/20/87 (#3, 1 wk), 10 wk; PW mm pb 9/4/87 (#12), pk 9/18/87 (#3, 1 wk), 9 wk; tot 60 wk.

Koestler, Arthur
Thieves in the Night (Macmillan) NYT fic 11/24/46 (#7), pk 12/8/46 (#5, 2 wk), 16 wk; PW fic 12/28/46 (#5, 1 wk), 3 wk; tot 19 wk.
The Age of Longing (Macmillan) NYT fic 3/18/51 (#8), pk 4/1/51 (#5, 4 wk), 11 wk; PW fic 4/21/51 (#5, 1 wk), 2 wk; tot 13 wk.
The Thirteenth Tribe (Random) NYT gen 10/3/76 (#10, 1 wk).

_____, et al.
The God That Failed [ed. Richard Howard Stafford Crossman] (Bantam) NYT gen 2/5/50 (#14), pk 2/12/50 (#12, 1 wk), 5 wk.

Kogan, Herman, and Lloyd Wendt
Chicago: A Pictorial History (Dutton) NYT gen 12/7/58 (#12), pk 12/14/58 (#8, 2 wk), 8 wk; PW nf 1/5/59 (#8, 1 wk), 2 wk; tot 10 wk.
See also Lloyd Wendt and_____

Komroff, Manuel
Coronet (Coward McCann) PW fic 2/15/30 (#7), pk 3/15/30 (#4, 8 wk), 16 wk.

Konicov, Barrie
Stop Smoking (Potentials Unlimited) PW aud nf 10/5/90 (#3, 4 wk).
Weight Loss (Potentials Unlimited) PW aud nf 10/5/90 (#1, 4 wk), 12 wk.

Konigsburg, E.L.
From the Mixed-Up Files of Mrs. Basil E. Frankweiler (Dell) NYT ch bst 5/5/68 (#4), pk 11/3/68 (#3, 26 wk), 64 wk.

Konvitz, Jeffrey
The Sentinel (Ballantine) PW mm pb 2/2/76 (#6, 2 wk), 9 wk; NYT mm pb 2/8/76 (#6), pk 3/28/76 (#5, 1 wk), 9 wk; tot 18 wk.
The Guardian (Bantam) PW mm pb 3/5/79 (#14, 1 wk).

Koontz, Dean R.
Whispers (Berkley) PW mm pb 4/24/81 (#11), pk 5/8/81 (#9, 1 wk), 6 wk; NYT mm pb 5/10/81 (#15), pk 5/31/81 (#12, 1 wk), 2 wk; tot 8 wk.
Phantoms (Berkley) PW mm pb 11/4/83 (#15, 1 wk).
Darkfall (Berkley) NYT pb fic 10/21/84 (#11), pk 10/28/84 (#10, 1 wk), 5 wk; PW mm pb 11/2/84 (#9, 1 wk), 2 wk; tot 7 wk.
Strangers (Putnam) NYT fic 5/11/86 (#15, 1 wk); PW hc fic 5/23/86 (#14), pk 5/30/86 (#12, 1 wk), 2 wk; (Berkley) NYT pb fic 12/7/86 (#12), pk 12/21/86 (#9, 2 wk), 5 wk; PW mm pb 12/26/86 (#15, 1 wk); tot 9 wk.
Watchers (Putnam) PW hc fic 2/6/87 (#13), pk 2/20/87 (#8, 1 wk), 8 wk; NYT fic 2/15/87 (#14), pk 3/1/87 (#13, 2 wk), 4 wk; (Berkley) NYT pb fic 3/27/88 (#16), pk 4/3/88 (#2, 1 wk), 10 wk; PW mm pb 4/8/88 (#6), pk 4/15/88 (#2, 1 wk), 8 wk; tot 30 wk.
Twilight Eyes (Berkley) NYT pb fic 8/30/87 (#13), pk 9/20/87 (#9, 1 wk), 6 wk; PW mm pb 9/11/87 (#9, 1 wk), 4 wk; tot 10 wk.
The Mask (Berkley) PW mm pb 12/2/88 (#12), pk 12/16/88 (#4, 1 wk), 7 wk; NYT pb fic 12/4/88 (#5, 3 wk), 8 wk; tot 15 wk.
Lightning (Putnam) NYT fic 1/24/88 (#15), pk 2/14/88 (#6, 4 wk), 11 wk; PW hc fic 1/29/88 (#12), pk 3/11/88 (#4, 1 wk), 11 wk; (Berkley) NYT pb fic 4/30/89 (#7), pk 5/14/89 (#2, 3 wk), 9 wk; PW mm pb 5/5/89 (#5), pk 5/12/89 (#1, 1 wk), 9 wk; tot 40 wk.
Midnight (Putnam) NYT fic 1/29/89 (#3), pk 2/5/89 (#1, 3 wk), 12 wk; PW hc fic 2/3/89 (#4), pk 2/10/89 (#1, 3 wk), 14 wk; (Berkley) NYT pb fic 10/29/89 (#12), pk 11/12/89 (#1, 2 wk), 11 wk; PW mm pb 11/3/89 (#15), pk 11/17/89 (#1, 2 wk), 9 wk; tot 46 wk.
The Servants of Twilight (Berkley) NYT pb fic 4/29/90 (#1, 5 wk), 10 wk; PW mm pb 5/4/90 (#5), pk 5/11/90 (#1, 4 wk), 8 wk; tot 18 wk.
The Bad Place (Putnam) NYT fic 1/28/90 (#7), pk 2/4/90 (#1, 2 wk), 15 wk; PW hc fic 2/2/90 (#8), pk 2/9/90 (#1, 4 wk), 14 wk; (Berkley) NYT pb fic 11/25/90 (#8), pk 12/16/90 (#1, 4 wk), 6 wk; PW mm pb 12/7/90 (#2), pk 12/14/90 (#1, 2 wk), 3 wk; tot 38 wk.

Kopay, David, and Perry Deane Young
The David Kopay Story (Arbor House) NYT nf 4/17/77 (#9), pk 4/24/77 (#8, 2 wk), 7 wk; PW hc nf 4/18/77 (#9), pk 4/25/77 (#8, 2 wk), 5 wk; tot 12 wk.

Koppel, Ted
See Marvin Kalb and_____

Korda, Michael
Power! How to Get It, How to Use It (Random) PW nf 10/6/75 (#8), pk 12/1/75 (#2, 1 wk), 17 wk; NYT gen 10/19/75 (#7), pk 11/23/75 (#1, 1 wk), 20 wk; (Ballantine) PW mm pb 11/1/76 (#13, 1 wk), 4 wk; tot 41 wk.
Charmed Lives: A Family Romance (Random) PW hc nf 11/26/79 (#11, 4 wk).
Worldly Goods (Random) PW hc fic 7/2/82 (#15, 3 wk); NYT fic 7/25/82 (#14, 1 wk); tot 4 wk.
Queenie (Linden/Simon & Schuster) NYT fic 4/21/85 (#12), pk 5/5/85 (#8, 1 wk), 10 wk; PW hc fic 4/26/85 (#11), pk 5/3/85 (#9, 3 wk), 9 wk; (Warner) NYT pb fic 4/6/86 (#5), pk 4/20/86 (#3, 1 wk), 11 wk; PW mm pb 4/11/86 (#9), pk 5/30/86 (#1, 1 wk), 12 wk; tot 42 wk.
The Fortune (Summit) PW hc fic 2/24/89 (#13), pk 3/17/89 (#6, 1 wk), 7 wk; NYT fic 2/26/89 (#13), pk 3/12/89 (#7, 2 wk), 10 wk; (Warner) NYT pb fic 2/4/90 (#12), pk 2/11/90 (#3, 3 wk), 9 wk; PW mm pb 2/9/90 (#6), pk 2/16/90 (#4, 3 wk), 9 wk; tot 35 wk.

Kornitzer, Bela
The Great American Heritage (Farrar) NYT gen 8/14/55 (#14), pk 9/11/55 (#11, 1 wk), 3 wk.

Kory, Robert B.
See Harold H. Bloomfield, M.D., et al.

Kosinski, Jerzy N.
Being There (Harcourt) NYT fic 5/30/71 (#8, 1 wk).
Cockpit (Houghton) PW fic 9/8/75 (#10, 4 wk); NYT fic 9/28/75 (#10, 1 wk); tot 5 wk.
Passion Play (St. Martin's) NYT fic 10/7/79 (#5, 1 wk), 7 wk; PW hc fic 10/22/79 (#15), pk 10/29/79 (#13, 1 wk), 4 wk; tot 11 wk.
Pinball (Bantam) PW td pb 3/12/82 (#8, 2 wk), 4 wk; NYT td pb 3/21/82 (#15), pk 3/28/82 (#10, 2 wk), 6 wk; tot 10 wk.

Kossak, Zofia
Blessed Are the Meek (Roy) NYT fic 4/16/44 (#9), pk 5/7/44 (#6, 1 wk), 14 wk; PW fic 5/13/44 (#7), pk 5/13/44 (#7, 1 wk), 2 wk; tot 16 wk.

Kotz, Mary Lynn
See J.B. West and_____

Kotzwinkle, William
The E.T. Storybook (Putnam) PW hc fic 8/27/82 (#15), pk 11/19/82 (#5, 1 wk), 24 wk.
E.T.: The Extra-Terrestrial in His Adventure on Earth (Berkley) PW mm pb 6/25/82 (#12), pk 8/6/82 (#1, 2 wk), 17 wk; NYT mm pb 7/4/82 (#12), pk 8/8/82 (#1, 1 wk), 15 wk; tot 32 wk.

E.T.: The Extra-Terrestrial (Berkley) NYT mm pb 7/4/82 (#12), pk 8/8/82 (#1, 1 wk), 15 wk.
E.T.: The Extra-Terrestrial Storybook (Putnam) NYT fic 8/29/82 (#11), pk 9/26/82 (#2, 1 wk), 32 wk.
E.T.: The Book of the Green Planet (Berkley) NYT pb fic 3/24/85 (#11, 1 wk).

Kovacs, Ernie
Zoomar (Doubleday) NYT fic 12/15/57 (#16, 2 wk).

Kovic, Ron
Born on the Fourth of July (Pocket) NYT pb nf 1/28/90 (#6), pk 2/18/90 (#3, 1 wk), 13 wk; PW mm pb 2/9/90 (#15), pk 2/16/90 (#10, 1 wk), 2 wk; tot 15 wk.

Kowalski, Robert
The 8-Week Cholesterol Cure (Harper) NYT msc 7/12/87 (#4), pk 8/9/87 (#1, 58 wk), 115 wk; PW hc nf 7/17/87 (#8), pk 11/4/88 (#1, 5 wk), 103 wk; tot 218 wk.

Kozol, Jonathan
Death at an Early Age (Houghton) PW nf 10/30/67 (#10), pk 12/11/67 (#9, 1 wk), 3 wk; NYT pb gen 6/2/68 (#5, 12 wk); tot 15 wk.

Kramer, Dale
Ross and the New Yorker (Doubleday) NYT gen 12/2/51 (#15, 1 wk).

Kramer, Jerry
Instant Replay (NAL) NYT gen 11/3/68 (#10), pk 1/5/69 (#2, 12 wk), 29 wk; PW nf 11/18/68 (#8), pk 1/20/69 (#2, 4 wk), 26 wk; NYT pb gen 8/3/69 (#4, 12 wk); tot 67 wk.

Kramer, Nora
See Anna Mary Robertson Moses

Kramer-Rolls, Dana
Home Is the Hunter (Pocket) NYT pb fic 12/16/90 (#12, 1 wk).

Krantz, Judith
Scruples (Crown) PW hc fic 2/27/78 (#15), pk 6/19/78 (#1, 3 wk), 41 wk; NYT fic 3/12/78 (#11), pk 6/18/78 (#1, 4 wk), 30 wk; (Warner) PW mm pb 5/7/79 (#8), pk 7/2/79 (#1, 1 wk), 38 wk; NYT mm pb 5/13/79 (#6), pk 5/20/79 (#1, 8 wk), 33 wk; tot 142 wk.
Princess Daisy (Crown) PW hc fic 2/1/80 (#6), pk 2/8/80 (#2, 15 wk), 35 wk; NYT fic 2/3/80 (#7), pk 2/17/80 (#1, 5 wk), 36 wk; (Bantam) NYT mm pb 2/8/81 (#3), pk 2/15/81 (#1, 7 wk), 19 wk; PW mm pb 2/13/81 (#2), pk 2/20/81 (#1, 6 wk), 12 wk; tot 102 wk.
Mistral's Daughter (Crown) NYT fic 11/14/82 (#15), pk 2/20/83 (#1, 1 wk), 23 wk; PW hc fic 11/19/82 (#9), pk 12/17/82 (#2, 2 wk), 20 wk; (Bantam) NYT mm pb 10/30/83 (#3), pk 11/13/83 (#1, 3 wk), 21 wk; PW mm

pb 11/4/83 (#3), pk 11/11/83 (#1, 3 wk), 18 wk; tot 82 wk.

I'll Take Manhattan (Crown) NYT fic 4/27/86 (#2), pk 6/8/86 (#1, 1 wk), 24 wk; PW hc fic 5/2/86 (#2), pk 5/23/86 (#1, 6 wk), 23 wk; (Bantam) NYT pb fic 2/1/87 (#1, 7 wk), 15 wk; PW mm pb 2/6/87 (#1, 5 wk), 14 wk; tot 76 wk.

Till We Meet Again (Crown) PW hc fic 8/19/88 (#6), pk 8/26/88 (#2, 7 wk), 22 wk; NYT fic 8/21/88 (#3), pk 8/28/88 (#2, 5 wk), 19 wk; (Bantam) NYT pb fic 6/4/89 (#4), pk 6/11/89 (#2, 4 wk), 10 wk; PW mm pb 6/9/89 (#5), pk 6/16/89 (#2, 3 wk), 10 wk; tot 61 wk.

Dazzle (Crown) NYT fic 12/2/90 (#8), pk 12/9/90 (#5, 3 wk), 5 wk; PW hc fic 12/7/90 (#8), pk 12/14/90 (#4, 2 wk), 3 wk; tot 8 wk.

Krantz, Steve
Laurel Canyon (Pocket) NYT mm pb 11/25/79 (#10, 1 wk).

Krantzler, Mel
Creative Divorce (Evans/Lippincott) NYT gen 3/1/7/74 (#10), pk 4/7/74 (#9, 1 wk), 5 wk; PW nf 3/25/74 (#8), pk 4/15/74 (#6, 1 wk), 6 wk; tot 11 wk.

Krasilovsky, Phyllis
The Very Little Girl (Doubleday) NYT ch bst 11/15/53 (#6, 40 wk).

Kratochvil, Laurie
Rolling Stone: The Photographs [ed.] (Simon & Schuster) NYT nf 12/31/89 (#15, 1 wk).

Kraus, Rene
Winston Churchill (Lippincott) PW nf 2/8/41 (#3, 4 wk), 16 wk.
Young Lady Randolph (Putnam) NYT gen 5/23/43 (#19), pk 6/13/43 (#8, 2 wk), 8 wk.

Kraus, Robert
The Bunny's Nutshell Library [4 vols.] (Harper) NYT ch bst 5/9/65 (#8, 19 wk).

Krause, Herbert
The Thresher (Bobbs Merrill) NYT fic 2/9/47 (#16), pk 3/2/47 (#13, 1 wk), 2 wk.

Krauss, Ruth
A Hole Is to Dig (Harper) NYT ch bst 11/16/52 (#6, 40 wk).
I'll Be You and You Be Me (Harper) NYT ch bst 11/13/55 (#11, 40 wk).

Kravchenko, Victor
I Chose Freedom (Scribner) NYT gen 5/19/46 (#8), pk 7/21/46 (#3, 14 wk), 36 wk; PW nf 6/8/46 (#10), pk 12/21/46 (#1, 1 wk), 27 wk; tot 63 wk.

Kreidman, Ellen
Light His Fire: How to Keep Your Man Passionately and Hopelessly in Love with You (Vil-

lard) NYT msc 10/15/89 (#5), pk 11/5/89 (#3, 1 wk), 4 wk; PW hc nf 10/20/89 (#12), pk 10/27/89 (#11, 1 wk), 4 wk; tot 8 wk.

Krementz, Jill
A Very Young Dancer (Knopf) NYT ch hc 11/13/77 (#14, 46 wk).

Krey, Laura
And Tell of Time (Houghton) PW fic 9/10/38 (#10), pk 10/15/38 (#3, 4 wk), 24 wk; NYT fic 10/9/38 (#1, 4 wk), 8 wk; tot 32 wk.

Kriegel, Robert
See W. Timothy Gallwey and_____

Krock, Arthur
Memoirs: Sixty Years on the Firing Line (Funk & Wagnalls) NYT gen 10/20/68 (#3), pk 12/15/68 (#1, 1 wk), 21 wk; PW nf 10/28/68 (#6), pk 11/25/68 (#1, 5 wk), 21 wk; tot 42 wk.

Kroeber, Theodora
Ishi in Two Worlds (Univ. of California) PW nf 2/5/62 (#10, 3 wk), 5 wk; NYT gen 3/4/62 (#13, 1 wk), 2 wk; tot 7 wk.

Kronenberger, Louis
Grand Right and Left (Viking) NYT fic 3/23/52 (#15, 1 wk).
Marlborough's Duchess (Knopf) NYT gen 10/26/58 (#15, 1 wk).

Krueger, Kurt
I Was Hitler's Doctor (Biltmore) NYT gen 6/11/44 (#17, 1 wk).

Krumgold, Joseph
And Now Miguel (Crowell) NYT ch bst 11/14/54 (#10, 40 wk).
Onion John (Crowell) NYT ch bst 5/8/60 (#11), pk 11/13/60 (#6, 27 wk), 46 wk.

Krutch, Joseph Wood
Samuel Johnson (Holt) NYT fic 12/17/44 (#18, 2 wk).
The Twelve Seasons (Sloane) NYT gen 5/22/49 (#15, 1 wk).

Kubey, Craig
Scoring Big at Pac-Man (Warner) NYT mm pb 4/18/82 (#15, 1 wk).

Kubler-Ross, Elisabeth, M.D.
On Death and Dying (Macmillan) NYT td pb 9/8/74 (#6), pk 1/30/77 (#2, 5 wk), 99 wk; PW td pb 3/21/77 (#5), pk 5/2/77 (#4, 1 wk), 3 wk; tot 102 wk.

Kundera, Milan
The Unbearable Lightness of Being (Harper/Perennial) NYT fic 7/15/84 (#16, 1 wk); NYT pb fic 3/27/88 (#13, 3 wk), 5 wk; PW td pb 4/8/88 (#6, 3 wk), 7 wk; tot 13 wk.

Kunetka, James
See Whitley Strieber and_____

Kunhardt, Dorothy
Pat the Bunny (Golden) NYT ch bst 11/5/72 (#5), pk 4/30/78 (#3, 24 wk), 50 wk.

Kunhardt, Philip B., Jr.
Life Smiles Back (Simon & Schuster/Fireside) NYT pb nf 1/1/89 (#9, 2 wk).

Kunstler, William Moses
The Minister and the Choir Singer (Morrow) NYT gen 3/8/64 (#10, 1 wk).

Kuralt, Charles
On the Road with Charles Kuralt (Putnam) NYT nf 10/13/85 (#10), pk 12/29/85 (#4, 3 wk), 28 wk; PW hc nf 10/18/85 (#13), pk 1/10/86 (#5, 1 wk), 19 wk; (Fawcett) NYT pb nf 9/28/86 (#6), pk 10/19/86 (#4, 2 wk), 6 wk; tot 53 wk.
A Life on the Road (Putnam) NYT nf 11/18/90 (#8), pk 12/2/90 (#1, 5 wk), 7 wk; PW hc nf 11/23/90 (#6), pk 12/7/90 (#1, 3 wk), 5 wk; tot 12 wk.

Kurth, Peter
Anastasia: The Riddle of Anna Anderson (Little Brown) PW td pb 1/9/87 (#10, 1 wk).

Kurtz, Katherine
The Quest for Saint Camber (Ballantine/Del Rey) NYT pb fic 9/20/87 (#14, 1 wk).

Kushner, Bill
See Jack Tatum and_____

Kushner, Rabbi Harold S.
When Bad Things Happen to Good People (Schocken) NYT nf 2/14/82 (#15), pk 8/15/82 (#3, 6 wk), 53 wk; PW hc nf 3/12/82 (#9), pk 8/20/82 (#2, 1 wk), 50 wk; (Avon) PW mm pb 2/4/83 (#15), pk 3/25/83 (#3, 2 wk), 24 wk; NYT mm pb 2/6/83 (#7), pk 3/20/83 (#4, 3 wk), 23 wk; tot 150 wk.
When All You've Ever Wanted Isn't Enough (Summit/Simon & Schuster) NYT nf 4/20/86 (#11), pk 5/4/86 (#4, 3 wk), 26 wk; PW hc nf 4/25/86 (#13), pk 5/9/86 (#5, 1 wk), 18 wk; (Pocket) NYT pb nf 5/10/87 (#8), pk 6/21/87 (#3, 1 wk), 26 wk; PW mm pb 5/22/87 (#15), pk 6/5/87 (#11, 1 wk), 3 wk; tot 73 wk.
Who Needs God? (Summit) NYT nf 1/21/90 (#15), 2/25/90 (#12, 1 wk), 8 wk.

Kyne, Peter Bernard
Kindred of the Dust (Cosmopolitan) PW fic 7/3/20 (#8), pk 9/25/20 (#1, 4 wk), 20 wk.
Pride of the Palomar (Cosmopolitan) PW fic 1/7/22 (#2, 4 wk), 8 wk.
Cappy Ricks Retires (Cosmopolitan) PW fic 10/14/22 (#11), pk 1/27/23 (#5, 4 wk), 8 wk.

Never the Twain Shall Meet (Cosmopolitan) PW fic 11/24/23 (#12, 4 wk).
The Understanding Heart (Cosmopolitan) PW fic 10/16/26 (#4, 4 wk), 8 wk.
Golden Dawn (Cosmopolitan) PW fic 5/17/30 (#10, 4 wk).

Lacey, Robert
Majesty: Elizabeth II and the House of Windsor (Harcourt) NYT nf 4/17/77 (#10), pk 6/5/77 (#7, 1 wk), 12 wk; PW hc nf 4/25/77 (#10), pk 6/27/77 (#5, 1 wk), 9 wk; tot 21 wk.
Princess (Times) PW hc nf 7/16/82 (#10), pk 8/6/82 (#6, 3 wk), 15 wk; NYT nf 7/18/82 (#14), pk 8/29/82 (#5, 1 wk), 15 wk; tot 30 wk.
Ford: The Man and the Machine (Little Brown) NYT nf 6/22/86 (#9), pk 7/6/86 (#4, 1 wk), 16 wk; PW hc nf 7/4/86 (#14), pk 7/18/86 (#5, 1 wk), 12 wk; NYT pb fic 6/7/87 (#7, 2 wk), 6 wk; tot 34 wk.

Ladas, Alice Kahn, with Beverly Whipple and John D. Perry
The G-Spot (Holt) NYT nf 9/26/82 (#13), pk 10/10/82 (#6, 3 wk), 10 wk; PW hc nf 10/1/82 (#13), pk 10/29/82 (#6, 1 wk), 10 wk; tot 20 wk.

La Farge, Christopher
The Sudden Guest (Coward McCann) NYT fic 10/6/46 (#8, 2 wk), 9 wk.

La Farge, Oliver
Laughing Boy (Houghton) PW fic 7/12/30 (#3, 4 wk), 12 wk.
Sparks Fly Upward (Houghton) PW fic 12/19/31 (#10, 4 wk).
The Copper Pot (Houghton) NYT fic 8/16/42 (#11, 1 wk), 3 wk.

Lagerkvist, Par
Barabbas [trans. Alan Blair] (Random) NYT fic 1/6/52 (#14, 3 wk), 8 wk.

LaGuardia, Robert
Monty: A Biography of Montgomery Clift (Arbor House) NYT nf 9/25/77 (#13), pk 10/2/77 (#12, 3 wk), 5 wk; PW hc nf 10/10/77 (#13, 1 wk), 3 wk; (Avon) NYT mm pb 7/23/78 (#14, 1 wk); tot 9 wk.

Laing, Ronald David
Knots (Pantheon) NYT gen 2/14/71 (#9), pk 2/28/71 (#8, 1 wk), 3 wk.

Lait, Jack, and Lee Mortimer
Chicago Confidential (Crown) NYT gen 3/19/50 (#13), pk 4/16/50 (#3, 1 wk), 40 wk; PW nf 4/22/50 (#4, 1 wk), 4 wk; tot 44 wk.
Washington Confidential (Crown) NYT gen 3/18/51 (#8), pk 4/1/51 (#1, 13 wk), 41 wk; PW nf 3/31/51 (#4), pk 4/21/51 (#1, 9 wk), 35 wk; tot 76 wk.

U.S.A. Confidential (Crown) NYT gen 3/23/52 (#12), pk 4/27/52 (#1, 1 wk), 26 wk; PW nf 3/29/52 (#3), pk 4/5/52 (#2, 7 wk), 16 wk; tot 42 wk.

Lake, Carlton
See Francoise Gilot and _____

Lamarr, Hedy
Ecstasy and Me (Bartholomew) PW nf 11/7/66 (#8, 1 wk); NYT pb gen 7/2/67 (#5), pk 9/3/67 (#1, 4 wk), 20 wk; tot 21 wk.

Lamb, Dana, and June Cleveland
Enchanted Vagabonds (Harper) NYT gen 7/3/38 (#14, 4 wk).

Lamb, Harold
Alexander of Macedon (Doubleday) NYT gen 6/23/46 (#12), pk 7/28/46 (#8, 1 wk), 6 wk.
Garden to the Eastward (Doubleday) NYT fic 4/13/47 (#13, 1 wk), 2 wk.
The March of Muscovy (Doubleday) NYT gen 4/4/48 (#16, 1 wk).
Suleiman the Magnificent: Sultan of the East (Doubleday) NYT gen 4/15/51 (#13, 1 wk).
Theodora and the Emperor (Doubleday) NYT gen 8/24/52 (#13, 1 wk), 6 wk.

Lambert, Gerard Barnes
All Out of Step (Doubleday) NYT gen 1/20/57 (#13, 1 wk), 3 wk.

Lambert, Janet Snyder
Don't Cry, Little Girl (Dutton) NYT ch bst 11/16/52 (#14, 40 wk).
Rainbow After Rain (Dutton) NYT ch bst 11/15/53 (#14, 40 wk).
Welcome Home, Mrs. Jordan (Dutton) NYT ch bst 11/15/53 (#11, 40 wk).

Lamorisse, Albert
The Red Balloon (Doubleday) NYT ch bst 11/17/57 (#10), pk 11/9/69 (#7, 26 wk), 66 wk.

L'Amour, Louis
Bendigo Shafter (Bantam) NYT mm pb 10/28/79 (#14, 1 wk).
Lonely on the Mountain (Bantam) PW mm pb 11/14/80 (#10), pk 11/21/80 (#8, 1 wk), 8 wk; NYT mm pb 11/16/80 (#10), pk 11/23/80 (#5, 2 wk), 9 wk; tot 17 wk.
Comstock Lode (Bantam) NYT td pb 3/8/81 (#3), pk 3/15/81 (#2, 2 wk), 13 wk; PW td pb 3/13/81 (#3), pk 3/20/81 (#2, 2 wk), 10 wk; tot 23 wk.
Milo Talon (Bantam) PW mm pb 8/7/81 (#14), pk 8/14/81 (#12, 1 wk), 3 wk; NYT mm pb 8/9/81 (#6, 1 wk), 4 wk; tot 7 wk.
Buckskin Run (Bantam) PW mm pb 12/4/81 (#15), pk 12/18/81 (#7, 3 wk), 7 wk; NYT mm pb 12/6/81 (#13), pk 1/3/82 (#6, 2 wk), 8 wk; tot 15 wk.

The Shadow Riders (Bantam) NYT mm pb 10/10/82 (#3, 1 wk), 4 wk; PW mm pb 10/15/82 (#7), pk 10/22/82 (#5, 1 wk), 5 wk; tot 9 wk.
The Cherokee Trail (Bantam) PW mm pb 8/6/82 (#6, 1 wk), 5 wk; NYT mm pb 8/8/82 (#5, 1 wk), 6 wk; tot 11 wk.
The Law of the Desert Born (Bantam) NYT mm pb 8/21/83 (#13, 1 wk), 2 wk.
Bowdrie (Bantam) NYT mm pb 2/20/83 (#11), pk 2/27/83 (#4, 1 wk), 7 wk; PW mm pb 2/25/83 (#12), pk 3/18/83 (#7, 1 wk), 6 wk; tot 13 wk.
The Lonesome Gods (Bantam) NYT fic 4/3/83 (#4, 1 wk), 19 wk; PW hc fic 4/8/83 (#4, 1 wk), 21 wk; NYT pb fic 2/12/84 (#4, 3 wk), 8 wk; PW mm pb 2/17/84 (#7), pk 3/2/84 (#5, 1 wk), 5 wk; tot 53 wk.
Ride the River (Bantam) NYT mm pb 6/26/83 (#5, 3 wk), 7 wk; PW mm pb 7/1/83 (#8), pk 7/8/83 (#6, 2 wk), 9 wk; tot 16 wk.
Bowdrie's Law (Bantam) NYT pb fic 11/25/84 (#7), pk 12/2/84 (#4, 3 wk), 10 wk; PW mm pb 12/7/84 (#8), pk 12/14/84 (#5, 2 wk), 6 wk; tot 16 wk.
The Walking Drum (Bantam) NYT fic 5/27/84 (#6), pk 6/17/84 (#2, 2 wk), 16 wk; PW hc fic 6/1/84 (#5), pk 7/6/84 (#2, 1 wk), 18 wk; NYT pb fic 5/12/85 (#2), pk 5/19/85 (#1, 2 wk), 9 wk; PW mm pb 5/17/85 (#4), pk 5/24/85 (#1, 2 wk), 8 wk; tot 51 wk.
Son of a Wanted Man (Bantam) NYT pb fic 4/22/84 (#7), pk 4/29/84 (#3, 1 wk), 10 wk; PW mm pb 4/27/84 (#7), pk 5/4/84 (#6, 3 wk), 6 wk; tot 16 wk.
Passin' Through (Bantam) NYT pb fic 9/22/85 (#15), pk 10/6/85 (#2, 1 wk), 12 wk; PW mm pb 9/27/85 (#12), pk 10/4/85 (#4, 3 wk), 14 wk; tot 26 wk.
Jubal Sackett (Bantam) NYT fic 5/26/85 (#3), pk 6/2/85 (#1, 1 wk), 19 wk; PW hc fic 5/31/85 (#8), pk 6/14/85 (#2, 3 wk), 20 wk; NYT pb fic 6/1/86 (#2, 2 wk), 10 wk; PW mm pb 6/6/86-4 pk 6/20/86 (#2, 1 wk), 8 wk; tot 57 wk.
The Trail to Crazy Man (Bantam) NYT pb fic 8/31/86 (#4, 1 wk), 5 wk; PW mm pb 9/5/86 (#9), pk 9/12/86 (#7, 1 wk), 6 wk; tot 11 wk.
Last of the Breed (Bantam) NYT fic 6/15/86 (#4), pk 6/22/86 (#1, 4 wk), 26 wk; PW hc fic 6/20/86 (#7), pk 7/4/86 (#1, 4 wk), 30 wk; NYT pb fic 7/5/87 (#2, 3 wk), 13 wk; PW mm pb 7/10/87 (#2, 2 wk), 10 wk; tot 79 wk.
The Rider of the Ruby Hills (Bantam) NYT pb fic 8/31/86 (#6, 1 wk), 6 wk; PW mm pb 9/5/86 (#10), pk 9/12/86 (#6, 1 wk), 6 wk; tot 12 wk.

Riding for the Brand (Bantam) NYT pb fic 3/16/86 (#10), pk 3/23/86 (#8, 1 wk), 5 wk; PW mm pb 3/21/86 (#15), pk 3/28/86 (#8, 1 wk), 5 wk; tot 10 wk.

Night Over the Solomons (Bantam) NYT pb fic 11/23/86 (#13), pk 11/30/86 (#6, 1 wk), 8 wk; PW mm pb 12/5/86 (#14), pk 12/12/86 (#8, 1 wk), 5 wk; tot 13 wk.

Dutchman's Flat (Bantam) NYT pb fic 3/9/86 (#15), pk 3/23/86 (#7, 1 wk), 8 wk; PW mm pb 3/21/86 (#14), pk 3/28/86 (#6, 1 wk), 6 wk; tot 14 wk.

West from Singapore (Bantam) NYT pb fic 4/12/87 (#12), pk 4/19/87 (#9, 2 wk), 5 wk; PW mm pb 4/17/87 (#7, 1 wk), 4 wk; tot 9 wk.

The Haunted Mesa (Bantam) NYT fic 5/17/87 (#2), pk 5/31/87 (#1, 1 wk), 20 wk; PW hc fic 5/22/87 (#4), pk 5/29/87 (#2, 8 wk), 18 wk; NYT pb fic 5/8/88 (#3), pk 5/15/88 (#2, 2 wk), 11 wk; PW mm pb 5/13/88 (#3), pk 5/20/88 (#2, 1 wk), 9 wk; tot 58 wk.

A Trail of Memories: The Quotations of Louis L'Amour [comp. Angelique L'Amour] (Bantam) NYT nf 6/19/88 (#11), pk 7/3/88 (#5, 3 wk), 11 wk; PW hc nf 7/1/88 (#11), pk 7/8/88 (#6, 1 wk), 9 wk; tot 20 wk.

Lonigan (Bantam) NYT pb fic 9/25/88 (#11), pk 10/2/88 (#8, 1 wk), 7 wk; PW mm pb 10/7/88 (#12), pk 11/4/88 (#4, 1 wk), 6 wk; tot 13 wk.

The Sackett Companion (Bantam) NYT nf 11/20/88 (#14), pk 11/27/88 (#13, 1 wk), 2 wk.

Long Ride Home (Bantam) NYT pb fic 9/24/89 (#13), pk 10/29/89 (#6, 1 wk), 7 wk; PW mm pb 9/29/89 (#13), pk 10/6/89 (#6, 1 wk), 7 wk; tot 14 wk.

Education of a Wandering Man: A Memoir (Bantam) NYT nf 11/5/89 (#15), pk 11/19/89 (#4, 2 wk), 15 wk; PW hc nf 11/17/89 (#12), pk 12/8/89 (#5, 1 wk), 11 wk; NYT pb nf 12/9/90 (#9), pk 12/23/90 (#3, 2 wk), 4 wk; tot 30 wk.

The Outlaws of Mesquite (Bantam) PW hc fic 6/1/90 (#13), pk 6/29/90 (#10, 1 wk), 6 wk; NYT fic 6/3/90 (#11), pk 7/1/90 (#8, 1 wk), 6 wk; tot 12 wk.

Lamport, Felicia
Mink on Weekdays, Ermine on Sunday (Houghton) NYT gen 6/11/50 (#16, 1 wk).

La Mure, Pierre
Moulin Rouge (Random) NYT fic 12/24/50 (#13), pk 1/14/50 (#11, 2 wk), 17 wk.

Beyond Desire (Random) NYT fic 1/1/56 (#16), pk 1/8/56 (#13, 1 wk), 3 wk.

Lancaster, Bruce
Guns of Burgoyne (Stokes) NYT fic 5/7/39 (#3, 4 wk).

The Scarlet Patch (Little Brown) NYT fic 6/1/47 (#10, 1 wk), 7 wk.

The Secret Road (Little Brown) NYT fic 8/3/52 (#13, 1 wk).

Lancaster, G.B. [pseud.]
Pageant (Century) PW fic 3/11/33 (#6), pk 4/15/33 (#3, 8 wk), 16 wk.

Promenade (Reynal & Hitchcock) NYT fic 6/5/38 (#7, 4 wk), 8 wk.

Landau, Eli
See Amos Aricha and _____

Landau, Capt. Henry
All's Fair (Putnam) PW nf 10/13/34 (#8, 4 wk).

Landers, Ann
Since You Ask Me (Prentice Hall) NYT gen 10/15/61 (#16, 1 wk).

The Ann Landers Encyclopedia A to Z (Doubleday) NYT nf 11/26/78 (#14), pk 1/28/79 (#8, 1 wk), 11 wk; PW hc nf 12/4/78 (#15), pk 1/8/79 (#11, 1 wk), 12 wk; (Ballantine) NYT td pb 10/14/79 (#9), pk 11/11/79 (#6, 2 wk), 15 wk; PW td pb 10/15/79 (#9), pk 11/12/79 (#7, 1 wk), 8 wk; tot 46 wk.

Landon, Fred
Lake Huron (Bobbs Merrill) NYT gen 4/16/44 (#11), pk 5/7/44 (#10, 3 wk), 9 wk.

Landon, Margaret
Anna and the King of Siam (John Day) NYT gen 7/23/44 (#15), pk 8/20/44 (#4, 12 wk), 25 wk; PW nf 8/26/44 (#5), pk 9/30/44 (#3, 2 wk), 17 wk; tot 42 wk.

Landry, Tom, and Gregg Lewis
Tom Landry: An Autobiography (HarperCollins/Zondervan) PW hc nf 8/24/90 (#14), pk 9/14/90 (#5, 1 wk), 5 wk; NYT msc 8/26/90 (#15), pk 9/16/90 (#3, 1 wk), 5 wk; PW hc rel 10/5/90 (#2, 4 wk), 8 wk; tot 18 wk.

Lane, Arthur Bliss
I Saw Poland Betrayed (Bobbs Merrill) NYT gen 3/7/48 (#11), pk 4/4/48 (#8, 1 wk), 8 wk.

Lane, Franklin K.
Letters of Franklin K. Lane (Houghton) PW gen lit 12/23/22 (#7), pk 1/27/23 (#4, 4 wk), 12 wk.

Lane, Hana Umlauf
See Anonymous (World Almanac)

Lane, Mark
Rush to Judgment (Holt) NYT gen 9/11/66 (#9), pk 11/13/66 (#1, 8 wk), 29 wk; PW nf 9/12/66 (#10), pk 10/31/66 (#1, 7 wk), 26 wk; NYT pb gen 3/5/67 (#2), pk 4/2/67 (#1, 4 wk), 16 wk; tot 71 wk.

Lane, Rose Wilder
Free Land (Longmans Green) NYT fic 6/5/38 (#1, 4 wk), 8 wk; PW fic 6/11/38 (#7, 4 wk); tot 12 wk.

Lange, Oliver
Vandenberg (Stein & Day) NYT fic 5/16/71 (#10, 1 wk).

Langley, Adria Locke
A Lion Is in the Streets (Whittlesey) NYT fic 6/3/45 (#14), pk 7/1/45 (#1, 12 wk), 32 wk; PW fic 6/9/45 (#5), pk 6/23/45 (#1, 11 wk), 23 wk; tot 55 wk.

Langley, Dorothy [pseud.]
Dark Medallion (Simon & Schuster) NYT fic 7/29/45 (#21, 1 wk).

Lanham, Edwin
The Iron Maiden (Harcourt) NYT fic 9/19/54 (#15), pk 10/10/54 (#11, 1 wk), 5 wk.

Lansing, Robert
The Peace Negotiations (Houghton) PW gen lit 4/23/21 (#3), pk 6/11/21 (#1, 4 wk), 12 wk.

Lansky, Vicki
The Taming of the C.A.N.D.Y. Monster (Meadowbrook) NYT td pb 4/30/78 (#1, 1 wk), 13 wk; PW td pb 5/22/78 (#10, 3 wk); tot 16 wk.

Lapierre, Dominique
The City of Joy (Doubleday) NYT nf 2/23/86 (#15, 1 wk).
See also Larry Collins and _____

Lare, James
See Walter Lippmann, et al

Larkin, David
The Fantastic Kingdom [ed.] (Ballantine) NYT td pb 12/8/74 (#9, 4 wk).

Larrimore, Lida
Two Keys to a Cabin (Grosset & Dunlap) NYT fic 11/8/36 (#6, 4 wk).
Tuesday Never Comes (Grosset & Dunlap) NYT fic 1/9/38 (#10, 4 wk).
Uncle Caleb's Niece (Macrae Smith) NYT fic 7/9/39 (#3, 4 wk).

Larsen, Richard W.
Bundy: The Deliberate Stranger (Pocket) NYT pb nf 5/25/86 (#8, 1 wk).

Larson, Arthur
A Republican Looks at His Party (Harper) NYT gen 9/9/56 (#15), pk 9/30/56 (#11, 1 wk), 8 wk.

Larson, Gary
Beyond the Far Side (Andrews McMeel & Parker) NYT td pb 10/30/83 (#14), pk 12/25/83 (#9, 1 wk), 7 wk; PW td pb 12/23/83 (#7),

pk 1/6/84 (#6, 2 wk), 4 wk; NYT msc pb 1/15/84 (#7, 2 wk), 3 wk; tot 14 wk.
In Search of the Far Side (Andrews McMeel & Parker) NYT msc pb 8/26/84 (#5), pk 9/16/84 (#1, 3 wk), 19 wk; PW td pb 9/7/84 (#3), pk 9/21/84 (#1, 1 wk), 21 wk; tot 40 wk.
The Far Side Gallery (Andrews McMeel & Parker) PW td pb 11/30/84 (#6), pk 12/14/84 (#1, 9 wk), 54 wk; NYT msc pb 12/9/84 (#3), pk 1/6/85 (#1, 2 wk), 45 wk; tot 99 wk.
Valley of the Far Side (Andrews McMeel & Parker) NYT msc pb 9/1/85 (#4), pk 9/8/85 (#1, 9 wk), 31 wk; PW td pb 9/13/85 (#1, 7 wk), 37 wk; tot 68 wk.
Bride of the Far Side (Andrews McMeel & Parker) NYT msc pb 5/5/85 (#5), pk 5/19/85 (#1, 1 wk), 31 wk; PW td pb 5/10/85 (#6), pk 6/14/85 (#1, 2 wk), 20 wk; tot 51 wk.
It Came from the Far Side (Andrews McMeel & Parker) NYT msc pb 8/3/86 (#3), pk 8/10/86 (#2, 5 wk), 25 wk; PW td pb 8/8/86 (#4), pk 8/15/86 (#1, 5 wk), 21 wk; tot 46 wk.
The Far Side Gallery 2 (Andrews McMeel & Parker) NYT msc pb 9/28/86 (#3), pk 12/14/86 (#1, 4 wk), 18 wk; PW td pb 1/9/87 (#1, 3 wk), 17 wk; tot 35 wk.
Hound of the Far Side (Andrews McMeel & Parker) NYT msc pb 4/26/87 (#3), pk 5/3/87 (#1, 5 wk), 12 wk; PW td pb 5/1/87 (#1, 2 wk), 25 wk; tot 37 wk.
The Far Side Observer (Andrews McMeel & Parker) NYT msc pb 11/1/87 (#1, 11 wk), 15 wk; PW td pb 11/6/87 (#1, 10 wk), 18 wk; tot 33 wk.
Night of the Crash-Test Dummies (Andrews & McMeel) NYT msc pb 7/31/88 (#1, 8 wk), 16 wk; PW td pb 8/5/88 (#4), pk 8/19/88 (#1, 8 wk), 14 wk; tot 30 wk.
The Far Side Gallery 3 (Andrews McMeel & Parker) NYT msc pb 10/30/88 (#4), pk 11/20/88 (#1, 8 wk), 14 wk; PW td pb 11/4/88 (#5), pk 11/18/88 (#1, 3 wk), 14 wk; tot 28 wk.
Wildlife Preserves: A Far Side Collection (Andrews McMeel & Parker) NYT msc pb 4/30/89 (#2, 5 wk), 11 wk; PW td pb 5/5/89 (#5), pk 5/19/89 (#2, 1 wk), 14 wk; tot 25 wk.
The Prehistory of the Far Side: A Tenth Anniversary Exhibit (Andrews McMeel & Parker) NYT msc pb 10/8/89 (#4), pk 11/19/89 (#1, 8 wk), 17 wk; PW td pb 10/13/89 (#5), pk 11/24/89 (#1, 8 wk), 21 wk; tot 38 wk.
Wiener Dog Art: A Far Side Collection (Andrews McMeel & Parker) NYT msc pb 11/11/90 (#5), pk 11/18/90 (#2, 2 wk), 8 wk; PW td pb 11/16/90 (#7), pk 11/30/90 (#3, 2 wk), 6 wk; tot 14 wk.

Larson, Glen A., and Robert Thurston
Battlestar Galactica (Berkley) PW mm pb 9/25/78 (#14), pk 10/9/78 (#8, 1 wk), 6 wk; NYT mm pb 11/12/78 (#12, 1 wk), 3 wk; tot 9 wk.

Lasch, Christopher
The Culture of Narcissism: American Life in an Age of Diminishing Expectations (Norton) PW nc nf 2/12/79 (#13), pk 4/2/79 (#10, 2 wk), 16 wk; NYT nf 3/25/79 (#12), pk 4/15/79 (#11, 2 wk), 7 wk; tot 23 wk.

Lash, Joseph P.
Eleanor and Franklin: The Story of Their Relationship Based on Eleanor Roosevelt's Papers (Norton) NYT gen 10/31/71 (#7), pk 12/5/71 (#1, 15 wk), 40 wk; PW nf 11/1/71 (#6), pk 11/8/71 (#1, 15 wk), 39 wk; NYT pb gen 2/11/73 (#1, 4 wk), 12 wk; tot 91 wk.
Eleanor: The Years Alone (Norton) NYT gen 8/6/72 (#10), pk 10/15/72 (#3, 3 wk), 21 wk; PW nf 8/7/72 (#7), pk 10/9/72 (#2, 2 wk), 21 wk; tot 42 wk.

Laski, Harold Joseph
The American Democracy (Viking) NYT gen 7/18/48 (#13), pk 8/1/48 (#7, 1 wk), 4 wk.

Laski, Marghanite
Little Boy Lost (Houghton) NYT fic 1/22/50 (#16), pk 2/12/50 (#15, 1 wk), 3 wk.

Lasky, Victor
J.F.K.: The Man and the Myth (Macmillan) NYT gen 9/22/63 (#10), pk 10/6/63 (#1, 8 wk), 27 wk; PW nf 9/30/63 (#5), pk 10/14/63 (#1, 7 wk), 30 wk; tot 57 wk.
It Didn't Start with Watergate (Dial) PW hc nf 5/30/77 (#6), pk 7/18/77 (#4, 1 wk), 22 wk; NYT nf 6/5/77 (#9), pk 7/17/77 (#4, 1 wk), 23 wk; tot 46 wk.
See also Ralph de Toledano and _____

Lasswell, Mary
Suds in Your Eye (Houghton) NYT fic 4/25/43 (#17), pk 9/17/44 (#16, 2 wk), 3 wk.
High Time (Houghton) NYT fic 1/7/45 (#13, 1 wk).
One on the House (Houghton) NYT fic 12/11/49 (#12), pk 1/1/50 (#5, 3 wk), 17 wk; PW fic 12/24/49 (#5, 2 wk), 5 wk; tot 22 wk.
Wait for the Wagon (Houghton) NYT fic 12/9/51 (#14), pk 2/3/52 (#10, 2 wk), 10 wk; PW fic 1/12/52 (#7, 1 wk), 3 wk; tot 13 wk.

Latham, Caroline
Michael Jackson Thrill (Zebra) NYT pb nf 4/15/84 (#9, 2 wk).

Latimer, Jonathan
Red Gardenias (Doubleday) NYT fic 10/8/39 (#12, 4 wk).

Lattimore, Owen
Solution in Asia (Little Brown) NYT fic 3/18/45 (#13), pk 4/15/45 (#7, 2 wk), 11 wk; PW nf 4/7/45 (#8, 1 wk), 2 wk; tot 13 wk.
Ordeal by Slander (Little Brown) NYT gen 8/20/50 (#11, 3 wk), 6 wk.

Lauder, Harry
A Minstrel in France (Hearst) PW gen 5/3/19 (#1, 4 wk).

Laughlin, Clara
So You're Going to Italy! (Houghton) PW gen lit 7/18/25 (#10, 4 wk).
So You're Going to Paris! (Houghton) PW gen lit 7/18/25 (#8, 4 wk).

Laurence, William Leonard
The Hell Bomb (Knopf) NYT gen 1/28/51 (#14), pk 2/11/51 (#12, 1 wk), 3 wk.

Laurie, Joe, Jr.
See Abel Green and _____

Lauterbach, Richard E.
These Are the Russians (Harper) NYT gen 6/24/45 (#18), pk 7/1/45 (#8, 1 wk), 8 wk; PW nf 8/11/45 (#10, 1 wk); tot 9 wk.

Lavendar, William
Chinaberry (Pyramid) PW mm pb 7/5/76 (#14, 2 wk), 4 wk.

Lavin, Mary
The House in Clewe Street (Little Brown) NYT fic 6/17/45 (#20), pk 8/5/45 (#18, 1 wk), 2 wk.

Lawes, Lewis E.
Twenty Thousand Years in Sing Sing (Long & Smith) PW nf 6/11/32 (#9), pk 7/9/32 (#5, 8 wk), 16 wk.

Lawrence, D.H.
Lady Chatterly's Lover (Grove) NYT fic 5/17/59 (#9), pk 7/12/59 (#2, 9 wk), 27 wk; PW fic 5/25/59 (#6), pk 7/27/59 (#2, 9 wk), 23 wk; tot 50 wk.
Sons and Lovers (Penguin) NYT td pb 7/3/83 (#11, 1 wk).

Lawrence, Gertrude
A Star Danced (Doubleday) NYT gen 8/12/45 (#7), pk 9/9/45 (#3, 4 wk), 15 wk; PW nf 8/25/45 (#3), pk 8/25/45 (#3, 5 wk), 8 wk; tot 23 wk.

Lawrence, Greg
See Gelsey Kirkland and _____

Lawrence, Josephine
If I Have Four Apples (Stokes) NYT fic 2/2/36 (#3, 4 wk); PW fic 2/15/36 (#10), pk 3/14/36 (#6, 4 wk), 16 wk; tot 20 wk.
The Sound of Running Feet (Stokes) NYT fic 1/31/37 (#3, 4 wk); PW fic 2/6/37 (#9, 4 wk); tot 8 wk.

(#8), pk 3/9/64 (#1, 30 wk), 56 wk; tot 112 wk.

The Looking Glass War (Coward McCann) NYT fic 7/11/65 (#8), pk 8/15/65 (#5, 6 wk), 12 wk; PW fic 7/19/65 (#10), pk 9/6/65 (#2, 2 wk), 19 wk; NYT pb fic 8/7/66 (#5, 4 wk); tot 35 wk.

A Small Town in Germany (Coward McCann) NYT fic 11/10/68 (#9), pk 12/8/68 (#2, 14 wk), 28 wk; PW fic 11/11/68 (#8), pk 2/3/69 (#1, 1 wk), 29 wk; NYT pb fic 3/1/70 (#3, 4 wk), 8 wk; tot 65 wk.

The Naive and Sentimental Lover (Knopf) NYT fic 2/6/72 (#10, 2 wk).

Tinker, Tailor, Soldier, Spy (Knopf) NYT fic 6/23/74 (#8), pk 8/4/74 (#1, 10 wk), 40 wk; PW fic 7/1/74 (#7), pk 7/29/74 (#1, 10 wk), 36 wk; (Bantam) NYT mm pb 8/10/75 (#3), pk 8/17/75 (#2, 1 wk), 10 wk; tot 86 wk.

The Honourable Schoolboy (Knopf) PW hc fic 10/3/77 (#9), pk 11/7/77 (#2, 2 wk), 31 wk; NYT fic 10/9/77 (#12), pk 10/23/77 (#3, 14 wk), 33 wk; (Bantam) PW mm pb 10/16/78 (#8), pk 10/23/78 (#4, 1 wk), 13 wk; NYT mm pb 11/12/78 (#6, 1 wk), 10 wk; tot 87 wk.

Smiley's People (Knopf) NYT fic 12/23/79 (#8), pk 1/20/80 (#1, 4 wk), 28 wk; PW hc fic 12/24/79 (#3), pk 1/18/80 (#1, 6 wk), 22 wk; (Bantam) PW mm pb 12/12/80 (#5), pk 12/26/80 (#1, 4 wk), 12 wk; NYT mm pb 12/14/80 (#5), pk 12/21/80 (#1, 5 wk), 14 wk; tot 76 wk.

The Little Drummer Girl (Knopf) PW hc fic 3/18/83 (#15), pk 3/25/83 (#1, 18 wk), 36 wk; NYT fic 3/20/83 (#1, 12 wk), 34 wk; (Bantam) NYT pb fic 4/8/84 (#3), pk 4/15/84 (#1, 4 wk), 11 wk; PW mm pb 4/23/84 (#3), pk 4/27/84 (#1, 2 wk), 13 wk; tot 94 wk.

A Perfect Spy (Knopf) NYT fic 4/27/86 (#3), pk 5/4/86 (#1, 6 wk), 24 wk; PW hc fic 5/2/86 (#5), pk 5/9/86 (#1, 2 wk), 17 wk; (Bantam) NYT pb fic 5/10/87 (#1, 5 wk), 11 wk; PW mm pb 5/15/87 (#1, 5 wk), 11 wk; tot 63 wk.

The Russia House (Knopf) NYT fic 6/11/89 (#1, 10 wk), 21 wk; PW hc fic 6/16/89 (#1, 11 wk), 20 wk; (Bantam) NYT pb fic 6/24/90 (#6), pk 7/1/90 (#2, 2 wk), 11 wk; PW mm pb 6/29/90 (#2, 3 wk), 12 wk; tot 64 wk.

Leclerc, Victor
See Harnett Thomas Kane and ____

Lederer, William J.
All the Ships at Sea (Norton) NYT gen 4/2/50 (#15), pk 4/9/50 (#9, 1 wk), 6 wk.
A Nation of Sheep (Norton) NYT gen 4/30/61 (#15), pk 7/16/61 (#2, 16 wk), 51 wk; PW nf 5/15/61 (#8), pk 9/18/61 (#1, 1 wk), 45 wk; tot 96 wk.

____, and Eugene L. Burdick
The Ugly American (Norton) NYT fic 10/26/58 (#15), pk 7/5/59 (#2, 1 wk), 76 wk; PW fic 12/1/58 (#8), pk 4/20/59 (#2, 10 wk), 64 wk; tot 140 wk.
Sarkhan (McGraw) PW fic 1/10/66 (#11, 1 wk).

Lee, Alan
See Brian Froud and ____

Lee, C.Y.
The Flower Drum Song (Farrar) NYT fic 6/30/57 (#16), pk 7/28/57 (#14, 3 wk), 8 wk.
Lover's Point (Farrar) NYT fic 5/18/58 (#13, 3 wk).

Lee, Clark Gould
They Call It Pacific (Viking) NYT gen 4/18/43 (#11), pk 5/30/43 (#8, 1 wk), 10 wk.

Lee, Gentry
See Arthur C. Clarke and ____

Lee, Gypsy Rose
Gypsy (Simon & Schuster) NYT gen 5/26/57 (#16, 5 wk).

Lee, Harper
To Kill a Mockingbird (Lippincott) NYT fic 8/7/60 (#13), pk 4/16/61 (#2, 21 wk), 98 wk; PW fic 9/5/60 (#8), pk 5/29/61 (#2, 19 wk), 89 wk; tot 187 wk.

Lee, Homer
The Valor of Ignorance (Harper) PW nf 5/9/42 (#6, 4 wk), 8 wk.

Lee, Laurie
The Edge of Day (Morrow) NYT gen 5/15/60 (#14, 1 wk).

Leech, Margaret
Reveille in Washington (Harper) PW nf 10/11/41 (#3, 8 wk), 20 wk.

Leekley, John
The Blue and the Gray (Dell) PW mm pb 12/17/82 (#11, 1 wk), 2 wk; NYT mm pb 12/19/82 (#15, 1 wk); tot 3 wk.

Leerhsen, Charles
See Gen. Chuck Yeager and ____
See Donald J. Trump and ____

Leggett, John
Wilder Stone (Harper) NYT fic 1/31/60 (#15), pk 2/7/60 (#13, 1 wk), 3 wk.

Lehman, Ernest
The French Atlantic Affair (Warner) PW mm pb 7/17/78 (#14), pk 7/31/78 (#13, 2 wk), 4 wk; NYT mm pb 7/30/78 (#13, 1 wk); tot 5 wk.

Lehmann, Rosamond
Dusty Answer (Holt) PW fic 11/26/27 (#6), pk 12/31/27 (#4, 4 wk), 8 wk.

A Note in Music (Holt) PW fic 10/18/30 (#9, 4 wk).

Invitation to the Waltz (Holt) PW fic 12/17/32 (#10, 4 wk).

Weather in the Streets (Reynal & Hitchcock) PW fic 6/13/36 (#10), pk 7/11/36 (#4, 4 wk), 12 wk; NYT fic 7/5/36 (#2, 4 wk); tot 16 wk.

The Ballad and the Source (Reynal & Hitchcock) NYT fic 4/22/45 (#12), pk 6/17/45 (#4, 1 wk), 20 wk; PW fic 5/12/45 (#10), pk 6/2/45 (#1, 1 wk), 8 wk; tot 28 wk.

The Echoing Grove (Harcourt) NYT fic 5/31/53 (#9), pk 6/28/53 (#5, 1 wk), 12 wk; PW fic 6/20/53 (#5, 2 wk), 3 wk; tot 15 wk.

Lehr, Elizabeth Drexel
"King Lehr" and the Gilded Age (Lippincott) NYT nf 10/6/35 (#5, 4 wk); PW nf 10/12/35 (#5, 4 wk), 8 wk; tot 12 wk.

Leigh, Richard
See Michael Baigent, et al.

Leighton, Frances Spatz
See William "Fishbait" Miller and _____
See Lillian Rogers Parks with _____

Leighton, Isabel
The Aspirin Age 1919–1941 [ed.] (Simon & Schuster) NYT gen 9/11/49 (#14), pk 9/18/49 (#5, 1 wk), 16 wk; PW nf 10/15/49 (#8, 1 wk), 2 wk; 18 wk.

Leighton, Ralph
See Richard P. Feynman and _____

Lekachman, Robert
Greed Is Not Enough (Pantheon) NYT nf 4/11/82 (#11, 1 wk).

Leman, Kevin, and Randy Carlson
Unlocking the Secrets of Your Childhood Memories (Nelson) PW hc nf 7/21/89 (#14, 1 wk).

LeMay, Alan
The Searchers (Harper) NYT fic 1/16/55 (#16, 1 wk).

Lenard, Alexander
See A.A. Milne

L'Engle, Madeleine
A Wrinkle in Time (Farrar) NYT ch bst 5/12/63 (#9, 19 wk), 38 wk.

An Acceptable Time (Dell/Laurel Leaf) PW ch yn ad 12/21/90 (#1, 4 wk).

Lengyel, Olga
Five Chimneys: The Story of Auschwitz (Ziff Davis) NYT gen 9/7/47 (#13, 1 wk).

Lennon, John
John Lennon in His Own Write (Simon & Schuster) NYT gen 6/7/64 (#10), pk 6/21/64

(#6, 2 wk), 5 wk; PW nf 6/8/64 (#9), pk 7/20/64 (#8, 1 wk), 7 wk; tot 13 wk.

A Spaniard in the Works (Simon & Schuster) NYT gen 8/1/65 (#10, 1 wk).

Leno, Jay
Headlines [comp.] (Warner) PW td pb 12/15/89 (#7), pk 1/5/90 (#4, 1 wk), 5 wk.

Lenzner, Robert
The Great Getty: The Life and Loves of J. Paul Getty (Crown) NYT nf 3/9/86 (#12), pk 4/6/86 (#3, 1 wk), 13 wk; PW hc nf 3/21/86 (#11), pk 4/4/86 (#6, 1 wk), 8 wk; tot 21 wk.

Leodhas, Sorche Nic
Always Room for One More (Holt) NYT ch bst 5/8/66 (#8, 19 wk).

Leokum, Arkady
Tell Me Why (Grosset & Dunlap) NYT ch bst 11/6/66 (#7, 26 wk).

Leonard, Elmore
Glitz (Arbor House) NYT fic 2/10/85 (#15), pk 3/3/85 (#2, 1 wk), 18 wk; PW hc fic 2/22/85 (#8), pk 3/15/85 (#3, 3 wk), 16 wk; (Warner) NYT pb fic 3/9/86 (#6), pk 3/30/86 (#4, 1 wk), 9 wk; PW mm pb 3/14/86 (#6), pk 4/4/86 (#4, 1 wk), 8 wk; tot 51 wk.

Bandits (Arbor House) PW hc fic 1/16/87 (#10), pk 1/30/87 (#4, 1 wk), 10 wk; NYT fic 1/18/87 (#8), pk 1/25/87 (#4, 2 wk), 10 wk; (Warner) pb fic 2/7/88 (#6, 2 wk), 7 wk; PW mm pb 2/12/88 (#8), pk 3/4/88 (#6, 1 wk), 6 wk; tot 33 wk.

Touch (Avon) NYT pb fic 9/18/88 (#14, 1 wk).

Freaky Deaky (Arbor House/Morrow) NYT fic 5/22/88 (#11), pk 6/5/88 (#7, 1 wk), 11 wk; PW hc fic 5/27/88 (#11), pk 6/10/88 (#6, 1 wk), 11 wk; (Warner) PW mm pb 4/7/89 (#15), pk 5/5/89 (#12, 1 wk), 5 wk; NYT pb fic 4/16/89 (#13, 1 wk), 3 wk; tot 30 wk.

Killshot (Arbor House/Morrow) PW hc fic 4/7/89 (#10), pk 5/12/89 (#5, 1 wk), 9 wk; NYT fic 4/16/89 (#11), pk 5/14/89 (#6, 1 wk), 8 wk; (Warner) PW mm pb 4/6/90 (#11), pk 4/27/90 (#8, 1 wk), 4 wk; NYT pb fic 4/15/90 (#14), pk 4/22/90 (#13, 1 wk), 2 wk; tot 23 wk.

Get Shorty (Delacorte) PW hc fic 8/10/90 (#11), pk 8/24/90 (#4, 1 wk), 7 wk; NYT fic 8/12/90 (#11), pk 8/19/90 (#5, 1 wk), 6 wk; tot 13 wk.

Leonard, Jon N., J.L. Hofer and Nathan Pritikin
Live Longer Now (Today/Grosset & Dunlap) PW td pb 4/18/77 (#5), pk 5/16/77 (#3, 1 wk), 13 wk; NYT td pb 5/22/77 (#4), pk 5/29/77 (#3, 2 wk), 30 wk; tot 43 wk.

Leopold, Nathan Freudenthal
Life Plus 99 Years (Doubleday) NYT gen 3/23/58 (#12), pk 4/6/58 (#7, 3 wk), 14 wk.

Lerner, Harriet Goldhor
The Dance of Anger (Harper/Perennial) NYT msc pb 8/7/88 (#5), pk 5/21/89 (#4, 8 wk), 16 wk; PW td pb 9/8/89 (#9), pk 11/17/89 (#6, 1 wk), 8 wk; tot 24 wk.
The Dance of Intimacy (Harper/Perennial) PW td pb 5/11/90 (#10), pk 6/15/90 (#7, 1 wk), 3 wk.

Lerner, Max
America as a Civilization (Simon & Schuster) NYT gen 1/12/58 (#13), pk 1/19/58 (#8, 1 wk), 7 wk.

Leske, Gottfried
I Was a Nazi Flier (Dial) PW nf 9/13/41 (#8, 4 wk).

Lesko, Matthew
Getting Yours (Penguin) NYT td pb 7/25/82 (#15, 1 wk).
Information U.S.A. (Penguin) PW td pb 5/20/83 (#6, 1 wk), 5 wk; NYT td pb 6/5/83 (#13), pk 6/19/83 (#10, 1 wk), 3 wk; tot 8 wk.

Leslie, Anita
The Remarkable Mr. Jerome (Holt) NYT gen 10/17/54 (#13, 2 wk), 4 wk.

Leslie, Desmond, and George Adamski
Flying Saucers Have Landed (British Book Centre) NYT gen 1/10/54 (#16), pk 3/21/54 (#11, 2 wk), 10 wk.

Leslie, Doris
Full Flavour (Macmillan) PW fic 10/13/34 (#6), pk 11/10/34 (#4, 4 wk), 12 wk.
Concord in Jeopardy (Macmillan) NYT fic 7/31/38 (#13, 4 wk).

Lessing, Doris
The Summer Before the Dark (Knopf) PW fic 6/4/73 (#10), pk 8/27/73 (#7, 2 wk), 15 wk; NYT fic 6/10/73 (#10), pk 8/26/73 (#7, 1 wk), 11 wk; tot 26 wk.

Letterman, David, with Steve O'Donnell, et al.
The Late Night with David Letterman Book of Top Ten Lists (Pocket) PW td pb 10/26/90 (#5), pk 11/16/90 (#1, 2 wk), 9 wk; NYT msc pb 10/28/90 (#5), pk 11/11/90 (#2, 1 wk), 10 wk; tot 19 wk.

Levaillant, Maurice
The Passionate Exiles (Farrar) NYT gen 6/22/58 (#16, 1 wk).

Levant, Oscar
A Smattering of Ignorance (Doubleday) PW nf 2/10/40 (#5), pk 3/9/40 (#1, 8 wk), 24 wk.

The Memoirs of an Amnesiac (Putnam) NYT gen 9/12/65 (#8, 2 wk).

Leveille, Dr. Gilbert A.
The Setpoint Diet (Ballantine) NYT msc pb 10/6/85 (#4), pk 10/27/85 (#2, 1 wk), 8 wk; PW mm pb 10/11/85 (#12), pk 11/8/85 (#8, 1 wk), 6 wk; tot 14 wk.

Levenson, Sam
Everything but Money (Simon & Schuster) NYT gen 9/25/66 (#8), pk 1/8/67 (#1, 13 wk), 56 wk; PW nf 10/3/66 (#9), pk 1/9/67 (#1, 8 wk); 56 wk; NYT pb gen 3/3/68 (#3), pk 4/7/68 (#1, 4 wk), 8 wk; tot 120 wk.
In One Era and Out the Other (Simon & Schuster) NYT gen 9/23/73 (#9), pk 11/18/73 (#3, 2 wk), 28 wk; PW nf 9/24/73 (#10), pk 11/19/73 (#2, 1 wk), 26 wk; (Pocket) NYT mm pb 12/8/74 (#9, 4 wk); tot 58 wk.
You Don't Have to Be in Who's Who to Know What's What (Simon & Schuster) NYT nf 7/8/79 (#14, 1 wk).

Leverenz, John
See Anonymous (Rand McNally Road Atlas)

Levering, Robert, Milton Moskowitz and Michael Katz
The 100 Best Companies to Work For in America (Addison Wesley) PW hc nf 5/25/84 (#14), pk 6/15/84 (#10, 1 wk), 4 wk; NYT msc 6/17/84 (#5), pk 7/15/84 (#4, 1 wk), 3 wk; tot 7 wk.

Levi, Carlo
Christ Stopped at Eboli [trans. Frances Frenaye] (Farrar) NYT gen 6/1/47 (#13, 2 wk), 3 wk.
Watch (Farrar) NYT fic 8/19/51 (#16, 1 wk).

Levin, Ira
Rosemary's Baby (Random) NYT fic 5/21/67 (#9), pk 10/8/67 (#3, 1 wk), 43 wk; PW fic 5/22/67 (#7), pk 12/11/67 (#4, 1 wk), 45 wk; NYT pb fic 5/5/68 (#2), pk 6/2/68 (#1, 20 wk), 32 wk; tot 120 wk.
The Boys from Brazil (Random) PW hc fic 3/15/76 (#9), pk 4/26/76 (#4, 1 wk), 14 wk; NYT fic 3/21/76 (#8), pk 5/2/76 (#4, 1 wk), 14 wk; (Dell) PW mm pb 3/14/77 (#9), pk 3/28/77 (#5, 1 wk), 17 wk; NYT mm pb 3/27/77 (#5), pk 4/3/77 (#4, 1 wk), 8 wk; tot 53 wk.

Levin, Meyer
Compulsion (Simon & Schuster) NYT fic 11/18/56 (#10), pk 2/17/57 (#2, 4 wk), 54 wk; PW fic 12/31/56 (#10), pk 2/18/57 (#2, 5 wk), 41 wk; tot 95 wk.
Eva (Simon & Schuster) NYT fic 9/13/59 (#13), pk 10/18/59 (#7, 1 wk), 10 wk.

The Fanatic (Simon & Schuster) NYT fic 3/1/64 (#8, 1 wk), 3 wk; PW fic 3/23/64 (#10), pk 4/6/64 (#9, 1 wk), 3 wk; tot 6 wk.
The Settlers (Simon & Schuster) NYT fic 5/28/72 (#9), pk 6/4/72 (#8, 1 wk), 4 wk; PW fic 6/5/72 (#9), pk 7/10/72 (#7, 1 wk), 5 wk; tot 9 wk.

Levin, Richard
See Peter Ueberroth, et al.

Levin, Robert J.
See William H. Masters, et al.

Levine, Irving R.
Main Street, U.S.S.R. (Doubleday) NYT gen 2/22/59 (#15), pk 4/19/59 (#10, 1 wk), 8 wk.

Levine, Michael
Deep Cover (Delacorte) NYT nf 3/18/90 (#15), pk 4/8/90 (#11, 1 wk), 4 wk; PW hc nf 3/23/90 (#11, 1 wk), 2 wk; tot 6 wk.

Levy, Harriet Lane
920 O'Farrell Street (Doubleday) NYT gen 6/29/47 (#10), pk 7/13/47 (#5, 1 wk), 19 wk.

Levy, Judith
Grandmother Remembers: A Written Heirloom for My Grandchildren (Stewart Tabort & Chang) NYT msc 5/27/84 (#2, 1 wk), 2 wk; PW hc nf 6/1/84 (#15, 1 wk); tot 3 wk.

Lewellen, John Bryan
The Boy Scientist (Simon & Schuster) NYT ch bst 11/18/56 (#10, 40 wk).

Lewin, Roger
See Richard E. Leakey and ____.

Lewinsohn, Richard
Animals, Men and Myths (Harper) NYT gen 7/18/54 (#15), pk 8/1/54 (#13, 1 wk), 4 wk.

Lewis, Arthur H.
The Day They Shook the Plum Tree (Harcourt) NYT gen 6/2/63 (#10), pk 9/15/63 (#4, 1 wk), 18 wk; PW nf 6/10/63 (#6), pk 9/23/63 (#4, 1 wk), 19 wk; tot 37 wk.

Lewis, Clive Staples [all titles as by C.S. Lewis]
Surprised by Joy (Harcourt) NYT gen 3/4/56 (#14, 1 wk), 4 wk.
Mere Christianity (Macmillan) PW pb rel 10/5/90 (#9, 4 wk), 8 wk.

Lewis, Ethelreda
Trader Horn (Simon & Schuster) PW nf 8/27/27 (#5), pk 11/26/27 (#1, 12 wk), 32 wk.

Lewis, Gregg
See Tom Landry and ____.

Lewis, Leonard C.
See Special Study Group

Lewis, Lloyd
Sherman, Fighting Prophet (Harcourt) PW nf 1/14/33 (#9, 4 wk).
Captain Sam Grant (Little Brown) NYT gen 7/2/50 (#12), pk 7/23/50 (#11, 1 wk), 5 wk.

Lewis, Michael M.
Liar's Poker: Rising Through the Wreckage on Wall Street (Norton) NYT nf 11/12/89 (#15), pk 1/28/90 (#1, 1 wk), 42 wk; PW hc nf 11/24/89 (#12), pk 2/9/90 (#1, 1 wk), 35 wk; (Penguin) NYT pb nf 9/30/90 (#10), pk 10/21/90 (#1, 1 wk), 14 wk; PW td pb 10/19/90 (#4, 4 wk), 10 wk; tot 101 wk.

Lewis, Oscar
Silver Kings (Knopf) NYT gen 11/16/47 (#10, 2 wk), 7 wk.
High Sierra Country (Duell Sloan & Pearce) NYT gen 8/21/55 (#14), pk 11/6/55 (#11, 1 wk), 11 wk.
Bay Window Bohemia (Doubleday) NYT gen 5/6/56 (#12), pk 5/20/56 (#11, 2 wk), 16 wk.

Lewis, Sinclair
Main Street (Harcourt) PW fic 1/8/21 (#8), pk 4/23/21 (#1, 16 wk), 36 wk.
Babbitt (Harcourt) PW fic 10/14/22 (#6), pk 11/18/22 (#2, 16 wk), 28 wk.
Arrowsmith (Harcourt) PW fic 4/18/25 (#1, 4 wk), 16 wk.
Mantrap (Harcourt) PW fic 7/17/26 (#6, 8 wk).
Elmer Gantry (Harcourt) PW fic 4/23/27 (#1, 16 wk), 24 wk.
Dodsworth (Harcourt) PW fic 4/13/29 (#3), pk 5/11/29 (#1, 8 wk), 20 wk.
Ann Vickers (Doubleday) PW fic 3/11/33 (#1, 12 wk), 20 wk.
Work of Art (Doubleday) PW fic 3/10/34 (#2, 8 wk), 12 wk.
It Can't Happen Here (Doubleday) PW fic 11/9/35 (#8), pk 12/14/35 (#1, 8 wk), 32 wk; NYT fic 12/1/35 (#1, 8 wk), 12 wk; tot 44 wk.
The Prodigal Parents (Doubleday) PW fic 2/12/38 (#8), pk 3/12/38 (#4, 4 wk), 12 wk; NYT fic 3/6/38 (#1, 4 wk); tot 16 wk.
Bethel Merriday (Doubleday) PW fic 5/11/40 (#7, 4 wk), 4 wk.
Gideon Planish (Random) PW fic 5/8/43 (#5), pk 5/22/43 (#4, 6 wk), 11 wk; NYT fic 5/9/43 (#6), pk 6/6/43 (#3, 1 wk), 15 wk; tot 26 wk.
Cass Timberlane (Random) NYT fic 10/21/45 (#11), pk 10/28/45 (#2, 8 wk), 19 wk; PW fic 10/27/45 (#3), pk 11/3/45 (#2, 5 wk), 13 wk; tot 32 wk.
Kingsblood Royal (Random) NYT fic 6/15/47 (#7), pk 7/6/47 (#1, 2 wk), 20 wk; PW fic

6/28/47 (#2), pk 8/2/47 (#1, 2 wk), 15 wk; tot 35 wk.

The God-Seeker (Random) NYT fic 3/20/49 (#11), pk 3/27/49 (#10, 2 wk), 9 wk; PW fic 4/16/49 (#9, 2 wk); tot 11 wk.

World So Wide (Random) NYT fic 4/15/51 (#16), pk 4/29/51 (#15, 1 wk), 3 wk.

Lewisohn, Ludwig
Up Stream (Boni & Liveright) PW gen lit 4/14/23 (#11, 4 wk).

The Island Within (Harper) PW fic 6/30/28 (#10, 4 wk).

Mid-Channel (Harper) PW nf 6/8/29 (#6, 4 wk).

The Case of Mr. Crump (Farrar) NYT fic 5/4/47 (#14, 1 wk).

Libo, Kenneth
See Irving Howe and _____

Liddy, G. Gordon
Will: The Autobiography of G. Gordon Liddy (St. Martin's) PW hc nf 5/9/80 (#4), pk 5/16/80 (#3, 1 wk), 17 wk; NYT nf 5/11/80 (#5), pk 5/18/80 (#4, 4 wk), 14 wk; tot 31 wk.

Lieb, Frederick George
The St. Louis Cardinals (Putnam) NYT gen 9/24/44 (#12), pk 10/22/44 (#7, 1 wk), 7 wk.

Connie Mack: Grand Old Man of Baseball (Putnam) NYT gen 5/27/45 (#21), pk 6/17/45 (#14, 1 wk), 5 wk.

The Detroit Tigers (Putnam) NYT gen 10/13/46 (#12), pk 10/20/46 (#11, 1 wk), 3 wk.

The Boston Red Sox (Putnam) NYT gen 5/11/47 (#14, 2 wk).

Lieberman, Herbert
Shadow Dancers (St. Martin's) NYT pb fic 5/20/90 (#14, 1 wk).

Liebman, Joshua L.
Peace of Mind (Simon & Schuster) NYT gen 4/14/46 (#12), pk 10/27/46 (#1, 58 wk), 173 wk; PW nf 4/27/46 (#5), pk 8/3/46 (#1, 59 wk), 147 wk; tot 320 wk.

Lief, Philip
The Cat's Revenge [produced by] (Simon & Schuster/Wallaby) NYT td pb 11/29/81 (#11), pk 12/27/81 (#8, 4 wk), 14 wk; PW td pb 12/18/81 (#7), pk 1/1/82 (#5, 1 wk), 4 wk; tot 18 wk.

Lifton, David S.
Best Evidence (Macmillan) PW hc nf 2/13/81 (#13), pk 2/27/81 (#4, 2 wk), 13 wk; NYT nf 2/15/81 (#12), pk 3/15/81 (#4, 1 wk), 12 wk; tot 25 wk.

Lilienthal, David Eli
Big Business (Harper) NYT gen 3/29/53 (#15, 1 wk).

Lillard, Richard G.
Desert Challenge (Knopf) NYT nf 10/18/42 (#20), pk 11/8/42 (#16, 1 wk), 3 wk.

Lilly, John Cunningham
Man and Dolphin (Doubleday) NYT gen 10/8/61 (#15, 1 wk).

Lin, Adet, and Anor Lin
Our Family (Cape) NYT gen 5/7/39 (#9), pk 6/11/39 (#3, 4 wk), 8 wk.

Lincoln, Evelyn
My Twelve Years with John F. Kennedy (McKay) NYT gen 9/19/65 (#10), pk 10/31/65 (#8, 1 wk), 4 wk; PW nf 10/4/65 (#11), pk 10/11/65 (#6, 1 wk), 12 wk; tot 16 wk.

Kennedy and Johnson (Holt) NYT gen 3/31/68 (#9), pk 5/19/68 (#7, 1 wk), 7 wk; PW nf 4/1/68 (#12), pk 4/22/68 (#9, 1 wk), 5 wk; tot 12 wk.

Lincoln, Freeman, and Joseph C. Lincoln
Blair's Attic (Coward McCann) PW fic 12/14/29 (#10), pk 1/11/30 (#6, 4 wk), 12 wk.
See also Joseph C. Lincoln and _____

Lincoln, Henry
See Michael Baigent, et al.

Lincoln, Joseph Crosby
Shavings (Appleton) PW fic 5/3/19 (#10, 4 wk).

The Portygee (Appleton) PW fic 6/12/20 (#5), pk 7/3/20 (#2, 4 wk), 16 wk.

Galusha, the Magnificent (Appleton) PW fic 9/3/21 (#3, 4 wk).

Fair Harbor (Appleton) PW fic 11/18/22 (#9), pk 12/23/22 (#4, 4 wk), 16 wk.

Doctor Nye of North Ostable (Appleton) PW fic 11/24/23 (#5, 4 wk).

Queer Judson (Appleton) PW fic 11/21/25 (#7, 4 wk), 8 wk.

The Big Mogul (Appleton) PW fic 10/16/26 (#6, 4 wk), 8 wk.

The Aristocratic Miss Brewster (Appleton) PW fic 11/26/27 (#8, 4 wk), 8 wk.

Silas Bradford's Boy (Appleton) PW fic 11/24/28 (#7), pk 2/16/29 (#6, 4 wk), 12 wk.

Blowing Clear (Appleton) PW fic 10/18/30 (#6), pk 11/22/30 (#4, 4 wk), 12 wk.

All Alongshore (Coward McCann) PW fic 9/19/31 (#9, 4 wk).

Head Tide (Appleton) PW fic 9/10/32 (#7, 4 wk).

Storm Signals (Appleton) PW fic 9/14/35 (#7, 4 wk).

Great Aunt Lavinia (Appleton) PW fic 12/12/36 (#10, 4 wk).

Storm Girl (Appleton) NYT fic 9/12/37 (#3, 4 wk), 8 wk.

A. Hall & Co. (Appleton) NYT fic 9/4/38 (#8, 4 wk).

Christmas Days (Coward McCann) NYT fic 1/8/39 (#7, 4 wk); PW fic 1/14/39 (#9, 4 wk); tot 8 wk.

The Bradshaws of Harniss (Appleton) NYT fic 12/19/43 (#9, 1 wk), 5 wk.

See also Freeman Lincoln and _____

_____, and Freeman Lincoln
The Ownley Inn (Coward McCann) NYT fic 10/8/39 (#14, 4 wk); PW fic 10/14/39 (#10, 4 wk); tot 8 wk.

Lincoln, Victoria Endicott
February Hill (Farrar) PW fic 3/16/35 (#9, 4 wk), 8 wk.

Celia Amberley (Rinehart) NYT fic 11/13/49 (#15, 1 wk).

Lindbergh, Anne Morrow
North to the Orient (Harcourt) PW nf 9/14/35 (#1, 28 wk), 52 wk; NYT nf 10/6/35 (#1, 12 wk), 16 wk; NYT gen 12/1/35 (#1, 8 wk), 20 wk; tot 88 wk.

Listen! The Wind (Harcourt) PW nf 11/12/38 (#2), pk 12/10/38 (#1, 16 wk), 32 wk; NYT gen 12/4/38 (#1, 4 wk), 12 wk; tot 44 wk.

The Wave of the Future (Harcourt) PW nf 11/16/40 (#2), pk 12/14/40 (#1, 4 wk), 16 wk.

The Steep Ascent (Harcourt) NYT fic 4/16/44 (#15), pk 5/7/44 (#11, 1 wk), 6 wk.

Gift from the Sea (Pantheon) NYT gen 3/27/55 (#12), pk 4/17/55 (#1, 46 wk), 80 wk; PW nf 4/2/55 (#3), pk 4/23/55 (#1, 44 wk), 70 wk; tot 150 wk.

The Unicorn and Other Poems (Pantheon) NYT gen 10/7/56 (#16), pk 10/28/56 (#6, 1 wk), 14 wk; PW nf 10/22/56 (#9), pk 11/19/56 (#4, 1 wk), 8 wk; tot 22 wk.

Dearly Beloved (Harcourt) NYT fic 6/17/62 (#12), pk 8/15/62 (#2, 10 wk), 27 wk; PW fic 6/25/62 (#9), pk 8/20/62 (#2, 9 wk), 31 wk; tot 58 wk.

Bring Me a Unicorn (Harcourt) NYT gen 4/2/72 (#7), pk 4/30/72 (#4, 1 wk), 15 wk; PW nf 4/3/72 (#9), pk 6/12/72 (#5, 2 wk), 14 wk; tot 29 wk.

Hour of Gold, Hour of Lead (Harcourt) PW nf 3/26/73 (#9), pk 5/21/73 (#4, 1 wk), 16 wk; NYT gen 4/1/73 (#7), pk 5/13/73 (#5, 3 wk), 17 wk; tot 33 wk.

The Flower and the Nettle: Diaries and Letters 1936–1939 (Wolff/Harcourt) PW hc nf 3/29/76 (#10, 1 wk).

War Within and Without: Diaries and Letters of Anne Morrow Lindbergh (Wolff/Harcourt) PW hc nf 5/16/80 (#15), pk 7/4/80 (#8, 1 wk), 16 wk; NYT nf 5/25/80 (#12), pk 6/1/80 (#9, 1 wk), 9 wk; tot 25 wk.

Lindbergh, Col. Charles A.
We (Putnam) PW nf 8/27/27 (#10), pk 9/24/27 (#1, 8 wk), 32 wk.

Of Flight and Life (Scribner) NYT gen 9/12/48 (#14), pk 10/10/48 (#5, 4 wk), 15 wk; PW nf 10/16/48 (#6), pk 10/23/48 (#4, 1 wk), 6 wk; tot 21 wk.

The Spirit of St. Louis (Scribner) PW nf 10/10/53 (#6), pk 10/31/53 (#2, 6 wk), 17 wk; NYT gen 10/11/53 (#4), pk 10/25/53 (#2, 7 wk), 23 wk; tot 40 wk.

Linde, Shirley Motter
See Dr. Robert C. Atkins and _____

Linderman, Lawrence
See Beverly Sills and _____

Lindgren, Astrid
Mischievous Meg (Viking) NYT ch bst 11/11/62 (#15, 26 wk).

Lindley, Ernest, and Forrest Davis
How War Came (Simon & Schuster) NYT nf 9/20/42 (#10), pk 10/4/42 (#8, 1 wk), 4 wk.

Lindner, Gladys D.
Marcel Proust (Stanford Univ.) NYT nf 1/24/43 (#21, 1 wk).

Lindsey, David
Mercy (Doubleday) PW hc fic 7/6/90 (#15, 1 wk).

Lindsey, Hal
There's a New World Coming (Vision House) NYT td pb 3/10/74 (#2, 4 wk), 16 wk.

Liberation of Planet Earth (Zondervan) NYT td pb 10/13/74 (#4, 4 wk), 8 wk.

The Late Great Planet Earth (Zondervan) NYT td pb 3/10/74 (#10, 4 wk).

The 1980s: Countdown to Armageddon (Bantam) PW td pb 4/10/81 (#7), pk 4/17/81 (#5, 4 wk), 14 wk; NYT td pb 4/12/81 (#7), pk 4/19/81 (#4, 1 wk), 20 wk; tot 34 wk.

The Rapture (Bantam) NYT td pb 7/31/83 (#14), pk 9/4/83 (#10, 2 wk), 11 wk.

Lindsey, Johanna
Captive Bride (Avon) PW mm pb 8/29/77 (#12), pk 9/5/77 (#7, 3 wk), 7 wk; NYT mm pb 9/4/77 (#12), pk 10/2/77 (#7, 1 wk), 8 wk; tot 15 wk.

A Pirate's Love (Avon) PW mm pb 11/6/78 (#15), pk 11/13/78 (#11, 1 wk), 3 wk; NYT mm pb 11/12/78 (#15, 1 wk); tot 4 wk.

Fires of Winter (Avon) PW mm pb 9/26/80 (#14), pk 10/3/80 (#11, 2 wk), 4 wk; NYT mm pb 9/28/80 (#14, 1 wk); tot 5 wk.

Paradise Wild (Avon) PW mm pb 6/26/81 (#9), pk 7/10/81 (#6, 1 wk), 6 wk; NYT mm pb 7/5/81 (#11, 1 wk), 2 wk; tot 8 wk.

Glorious Angel (Avon) PW mm pb 2/26/82

(#13), pk 3/5/82 (#7, 1 wk), 6 wk; NYT mm pb 2/28/82 (#5, 1 wk), 7 wk; tot 13 wk.

So Speaks the Heart (Avon) PW mm pb 5/6/83 (#14), pk 5/20/83 (#4, 1 wk), 6 wk; NYT mm pb 5/8/83 (#5), pk 5/15/83 (#4, 1 wk), 5 wk; tot 11 wk.

Heart of Thunder (Avon) NYT mm pb 11/6/83 (#6), pk 11/13/83 (#4, 2 wk), 5 wk; PW mm pb 11/11/83 (#11), pk 11/25/83 (#5, 1 wk), 5 wk; tot 10 wk.

Brave the Wild Wind (Avon) NYT pb fic 12/2/84 (#11), pk 12/9/84 (#3, 1 wk), 7 wk; PW mm pb 12/14/84 (#6, 2 wk), 4 wk; tot 11 wk.

Gentle Feuding (Avon) NYT pb fic 5/6/84 (#15), pk 5/13/84 (#1, 2 wk), 8 wk; PW mm pb 5/18/84 (#8), pk 5/25/84 (#2, 1 wk), 5 wk; tot 13 wk.

Love Only Once (Avon) NYT pb fic 12/8/85 (#5, 2 wk), 4 wk; PW mm pb 12/13/85 (#5), pk 12/20/85 (#4, 1 wk), 4 wk; tot 8 wk.

Tender Is the Storm (Avon) NYT pb fic 5/26/85 (#2, 1 wk), 7 wk; PW mm pb 5/31/85 (#3, 1 wk), 7 wk; tot 14 wk.

When Love Awaits (Avon) NYT pb fic 6/8/86 (#4, 1 wk), 5 wk; PW mm pb 6/13/86 (#6, 1 wk), 4 wk; tot 9 wk.

A Heart So Wild (Avon) NYT pb fic 12/7/86 (#5, 1 wk), 5 wk; PW mm pb 12/12/86 (#13), pk 12/19/86 (#10, 1 wk), 3 wk; tot 8 wk.

Secret Fire (Avon) NYT pb fic 12/6/87 (#3, 1 wk), 5 wk; PW mm pb 12/11/87 (#6), pk 12/18/87 (#5, 1 wk), 6 wk; tot 11 wk.

Hearts Aflame (Avon) NYT pb fic 5/31/87 (#7), pk 6/7/87 (#3, 3 wk), 7 wk; PW mm pb 6/12/87 (#3, 2 wk), 5 wk; tot 12 wk.

Tender Rebel (Avon) NYT pb fic 5/29/88 (#9), pk 6/12/88 (#3, 1 wk), 6 wk; PW mm pb 6/10/88 (#9), pk 6/24/88 (#6, 2 wk), 5 wk; tot 11 wk.

Silver Angel (Avon) NYT pb fic 12/4/88 (#6), pk 12/11/88 (#4, 3 wk), 8 wk; PW mm pb 12/9/88 (#6), pk 12/16/88 (#5, 1 wk), 4 wk; tot 12 wk.

Savage Thunder (Avon) NYT pb fic 12/3/89 (#3), pk 12/10/89 (#2, 2 wk), 6 wk; PW mm pb 12/8/89 (#6), pk 12/15/89 (#3, 1 wk), 5 wk; tot 11 wk.

Defy Not the Heart (Avon) NYT pb fic 5/28/89 (#11), pk 6/4/89 (#1, 1 wk), 6 wk; PW mm pb 6/9/89 (#2, 1 wk), 5 wk; tot 11 wk.

Warrior's Woman (Avon) NYT pb fic 6/3/90 (#2, 2 wk), 5 wk; PW mm pb 6/8/90 (#2, 3 wk), 5 wk; tot 10 wk.

Gentle Rogue (Avon) NYT pb fic 12/2/90 (#4), pk 12/16/90 (#2, 1 wk), 5 wk; PW mm pb 12/14/90 (#6, 1 wk), 2 wk; tot 7 wk.

Lindsey, Robert

The Falcon and the Snowman: A True Story of Friendship and Espionage (Pocket) NYT mm pb 11/16/80 (#11, 1 wk), 3 wk; PW mm pb 11/28/80 (#14), pk 3/1/85 (#6, 1 wk), 10 wk; NYT pb nf 2/17/85 (#5), pk 2/24/85 (#4, 2 wk), 6 wk; tot 19 wk.

Link, Henry Charles

The Return to Religion (Macmillan) NYT nf 11/8/36 (#9, 4 wk), 8 wk; PW nf 2/6/37 (#10), pk 5/8/37 (#3, 4 wk), 40 wk; NYT gen 5/9/37 (#4, 12 wk), 28 wk; tot 76 wk.

The Rediscovery of Man (Macmillan) NYT gen 11/6/38 (#5, 4 wk).

Linkletter, Art

Kids Say the Darndest Things! (Prentice Hall) NYT gen 11/24/57 (#9), pk 1/5/58 (#2, 7 wk), 65 wk; PW nf 12/2/57 (#7), pk 1/20/58 (#1, 1 wk), 60 wk; tot 125 wk.

The Secret World of Kids (Geis/Random) NYT gen 1/3/60 (#14), pk 1/17/60 (#12, 1 wk), 2 wk.

Old Age Is Not for Sissies (Viking) PW hc nf 2/19/88 (#13, 1 wk), 2 wk.

Linn, Ed

See Leo Durocher and _____

Linn, Dr. Robert, with Sandra Lee Stuart

The Last Chance Diet (Bantam) PW mm pb 6/20/77 (#14, 2 wk); NYT mm pb 9/11/77 (#11, 1 wk); tot 3 wk.

Linton, Calvin D.

Bicentennial Almanac [ed.] (Nelson) NYT td pb 11/23/75 (#5, 1 wk).

Lippmann, Walter

A Preface to Morals (Macmillan) PW nf 6/8/29 (#4), pk 8/10/29 (#3, 4 wk), 24 wk.

The Good Society (Little Brown) NYT gen 11/7/37 (#7, 4 wk); PW nf 12/11/37 (#10, 4 wk); tot 8 wk.

U.S. Foreign Policy (Little Brown) PW nf 7/3/43 (#4), pk 8/21/43 (#1, 2 wk), 21 wk; NYT gen 7/4/43 (#5), pk 8/29/43 (#1, 1 wk), 25 wk; tot 46 wk.

U.S. War Aims (Little Brown) NYT gen 7/30/44 (#10), pk 9/3/44 (#5, 1 wk), 12 wk; PW nf 8/5/44 (#5), pk 8/19/44 (#4, 2 wk), 7 wk; tot 19 wk.

Essays in the Public Philosophy (Little Brown) NYT gen 3/6/55 (#12), pk 4/24/55 (#5, 1 wk), 18 wk.

The Communist World and Ours (Little Brown) NYT gen 2/22/59 (#16, 2 wk).

The Essential Lippmann [ed. Clinton Rossiter and James Lare] (Random) NYT gen 8/18/63 (#10, 1 wk); PW nf 8/26/63 (#9), pk 9/2/63 (#7, 1 wk), 3 wk; tot 4 wk.

_____, and William O. Scruggs
The United States in World Affairs (Harper)
PW nf 4/23/32 (#9, 4 wk).

Lithgow, John
See Tom Wolfe

Littell, Robert
The Defection of A.J. Lewinton (Houghton)
PW fic 5/7/73 (#10, 1 wk).

Little, Malcolm, with Alex Hailey
The Autobiography of Malcolm X [as by
Malcolm X with Alex Hailey] (Grove) NYT
pb gen 10/6/68 (#4), pk 1/5/69 (#2, 4 wk),
24 wk.

Livingstone, Belle
Belle Out of Order (Holt) NYT gen 8/30/
59 (#16, 1 wk).

Livingstone, Harrison Edward
See Robert J. Groden and _____

Llewellyn, J.J., and Brian Froud
The World of the Dark Crystal (Knopf)
NYT td pb 1/23/83 (#13, 1 wk).

Llewellyn, Morgan
Lion of Ireland (Playboy) PW mm pb 5/8/
81 (#10, 1 wk), 5 wk; NYT mm pb 5/24/81
(#12, 1 wk), 3 wk; tot 8 wk.

Llewellyn, Richard
How Green Was My Valley (Macmillan)
PW fic 3/9/40 (#4), pk 4/13/40 (#1, 24 wk),
40 wk.
None But the Lonely Heart (Macmillan)
NYT fic 10/17/43 (#9), pk 10/31/43 (#5, 2
wk), 14 wk; PW fic 10/23/43 (#5, 2 wk), 7 wk;
tot 21 wk.
Chez Pavan (Doubleday) NYT fic 8/24/58
(#16), pk 9/21/58 (#10, 2 wk), 8 wk.
A Man in a Mirror (Doubleday) NYT fic
9/10/61 (#15), pk 9/17/61 (#11, 1 wk), 5 wk.
The End of the Rug (Doubleday) PW fic
8/26/68 (#8), pk 9/2/68 (#7, 1 wk), 2 wk.

Llosa, Mario Vargas
In Praise of the Stepmother (Farrar) NYT fic
11/11/90 (#14, 1 wk); PW hc fic 11/23/90 (#15,
2 wk); tot 3 wk.

Lloyd, Megan
See Linda Williams

Lobal, Arnold
Frog and Toad All Year (Harper) NYT ch
hc 11/13/77 (#9, 46 wk).

Lo Bello, Nino
The Vatican Empire (Trident) NYT gen
6/22/69 (#9, 1 wk); PW nf 6/30/69 (#9, 1
wk); tot 2 wk.

Lobsenz, Norman
See Hendrie Weisinger and _____

Lochner, Louis
What About Germany? (Dodd) NYT nf
1/10/43 (#19, 1 wk).
See also Joseph Paul Goebbels

Locke, William John
The House of Baltazar (John Lane) PW fic
3/27/20 (#4, 4 wk), 8 wk.
The Mountebank (Lane) PW fic 4/23/21
(#3, 8 wk).
The Lengthened Shadow (Dodd) PW fic
11/24/23 (#9, 4 wk).
The Great Pandolfo (Dodd) PW fic 10/24/
25 (#8, 4 wk).

Lockhart, Robert Hamilton Bruce
British Agent (Putnam) PW nf 3/11/33
(#3), pk 5/13/33 (#1, 4 wk), 32 wk.
Retreat from Glory (Putnam) PW nf 11/10/
34 (#4, 4 wk), 8 wk.

Lockridge, Ross, Jr.
Raintree County (Houghton) NYT fic
1/25/48 (#6), pk 4/25/48 (#1, 4 wk), 29 wk;
PW fic 2/7/48 (#3), pk 2/21/48 (#1, 3 wk),
23 wk; tot 52 wk.

Loder, Kurt
See Tina Turner and _____

Lofting, Hugh
Twilight of Magic (Stokes) PW juv 12/20/
30 (#8, 4 wk).
The Story of Doctor Doolittle (Stokes) NYT
ch bst 5/5/68 (#1, 19 wk), 45 wk.

Lofts, Norah
Silver Nutmeg (Doubleday) NYT fic 9/21/
47 (#14, 1 wk), 2 wk; PW fic 10/18/47 (#10,
1 wk); tot 3 wk.
The Lute Player (Doubleday) NYT fic 12/
30/51 (#16, 1 wk).
Bless This House (Doubleday) NYT fic 4/
11/54 (#8), pk 5/2/54 (#2, 8 wk), 25 wk; PW
fic 4/24/54 (#4), pk 5/15/54 (#2, 6 wk), 17
wk; tot 42 wk.
Afternoon of an Autocrat (Doubleday) NYT
fic 7/29/56 (#14), pk 8/5/56 (#13, 2 wk), 7 wk.
Scent of Cloves (Doubleday) NYT fic 12/8/
57 (#16), pk 12/29/57 (#13, 1 wk), 5 wk.
The Town House (Doubleday) NYT fic
9/27/59 (#12), pk 10/18/59 (#11, 1 wk), 6 wk.
The House at Old Vine (Doubleday) NYT
fic 10/1/61 (#15), pk 10/8/61 (#12, 1 wk), 6 wk.
The House at Sunset (Doubleday) NYT fic
11/25/62 (#16, 2 wk).
The Concubine (Doubleday) PW fic 8/5/63
(#8), pk 9/16/63 (#4, 1 wk), 15 wk; NYT fic
8/11/63 (#7, 3 wk), 12 wk; tot 27 wk.
The Lost Queen (Doubleday) NYT fic 3/9/
69 (#10), pk 4/20/69 (#7, 1 wk), 8 wk; PW
fic 3/31/69 (#10), pk 4/21/69 (#7, 1 wk), 5 wk;
tot 13 wk.

Logan, Bob
Cubs Win! (Contemporary) NYT pb nf 10/21/84 (#8, 1 wk).

Long, William Stuart
The Settlers (Dell) PW mm pb 8/22/80 (#13), pk 9/5/80 (#7, 1 wk), 5 wk.
The Exiles (Dell) NYT mm pb 4/6/80 (#13, 1 wk), 2 wk.
The Traitors (Dell) PW mm pb 5/15/81 (#6, 1 wk), 5 wk; NYT mm pb 5/17/81 (#13), pk 5/24/81 (#8, 1 wk), 3 wk; tot 8 wk.
The Explorers (Dell) PW mm pb 7/30/82 (#7, 1 wk); NYT mm pb 8/1/82 (#14, 1 wk); tot 2 wk.

Longford, Elizabeth
Queen Victoria: Born to Succeed (Harper) NYT gen 2/7/65 (#8), pk 4/4/65 (#2, 9 wk), 31 wk; PW nf 2/15/65 (#9), pk 4/5/65 (#2, 7 wk), 31 wk; NYT pb gen 4/3/66 (#4, 4 wk); tot 66 wk.
Wellington (Harper) PW nf 4/13/70 (#10, 2 wk); NYT gen 4/26/70 (#9, 1 wk); tot 3 wk.

Longstaff, John
Frog Went A-Courtin' (Harcourt) NYT ch bst 11/13/55 (#5, 40 wk).

Longstreet, Stephen
The Sound of an American [as by David Ormsbee] (Dutton) NYT fic 9/27/42 (#12), pk 10/4/42 (#9, 1 wk), 7 wk.
The Pedlocks (Simon & Schuster) NYT fic 6/10/51 (#16, 1 wk).
The Beach House (Holt) NYT fic 7/13/52 (#16, 1 wk).

Longworth, Alice Roosevelt
Crowded Hours (Scribners) PW nf 12/9/33 (#2), pk 1/13/34 (#1, 4 wk), 16 wk.

Longyel, Cornel Adam
Presidents of the United States (Golden) NYT ch bst 11/1/64 (#10, 25 wk).

Looker, Earl
The White House Gang (Revell) PW juv 2/15/30 (#10, 4 wk).

Loomis, Frederic
Consultation Room (Knopf) NYT gen 3/5/39 (#5, 4 wk), 8 wk.

Loomis, Stanley
Du Barry (Lippincott) NYT gen 5/10/59 (#16), pk 5/31/59 (#13, 1 wk), 6 wk.

Loos, Anita
Gentlemen Prefer Blondes (Boni & Liveright) PW fic 3/20/26 (#5), pk 5/15/26 (#1, 16 wk), 32 wk.
A Mouse Is Born (Doubleday) NYT fic 5/27/51 (#16, 1 wk).

Loos, Mary
Belinda (Bantam) PW mm pb 6/21/76 (#12, 1 wk), 2 wk.

Lopez, Barry
Arctic Dreams (Scribner) NYT nf 4/6/86 (#11), pk 4/20/86 (#10, 1 wk), 5 wk; (Bantam) pb nf 5/3/87 (#8, 1 wk), 4 wk; tot 9 wk.
Crow and Weasel [illus. Tom Pohrt] (North Point) NYT fic 11/18/90 (#15), pk 12/9/90 (#12, 1 wk), 3 wk.

Lorayne, Harry, and Jerry Lucas
The Memory Book (Stein & Day) NYT gen 6/30/74 (#10), pk 8/25/74 (#2, 9 wk), 38 wk; PW nf 7/15/74 (#7), pk 9/30/74 (#2, 2 wk), 33 wk; (Ballantine) NYT mm pb 6/8/75 (#10), pk 6/15/75 (#8, 2 wk), 3 wk; tot 74 wk.

Lorber, Robert
See Kenneth Blanchard and _____

Lord, Bette Bao
Spring Moon (Harper) PW hc fic 11/27/81 (#7), pk 1/22/82 (#3, 3 wk), 28 wk; NYT fic 11/29/81 (#4), pk 1/31/82 (#2, 1 wk), 29 wk; (Avon) PW mm pb 9/10/82 (#7), pk 9/17/82 (#1, 1 wk), 12 wk; NYT mm pb 9/12/82 (#10), pk 9/19/82 (#1, 1 wk), 11 wk; tot 80 wk.
Legacies: A Chinese Mosaic (Knopf) NYT nf 5/6/90 (#10), pk 5/27/90 (#9, 1 wk), 9 wk; PW hc nf 5/25/90 (#15, 1 wk); tot 10 wk.

Lord, Isabel E.
The Picture Book of Animals (Macmillan) PW juv 12/19/31 (#6, 8 wk), 12 wk.

Lord, Walter
A Night to Remember (Holt) NYT gen 12/11/55 (#12), pk 2/5/56 (#2, 3 wk), 32 wk; PW nf 1/7/56 (#5), pk 2/25/56 (#1, 1 wk), 25 wk; tot 57 wk.
Day of Infamy (Holt) NYT fic 4/14/57 (#9), pk 5/26/57 (#1, 3 wk), 17 wk; PW nf 4/29/57 (#5), pk 6/3/57 (#2, 3 wk), 14 wk; tot 31 wk.
The Good Years (Harper) NYT gen 7/3/60 (#12), pk 9/4/60 (#6, 1 wk), 19 wk; PW nf 7/11/60 (#7), pk 8/8/60 (#2, 1 wk), 15 wk; tot 34 wk.
Incredible Victory (Harper) NYT gen 9/10/67 (#8), pk 10/15/67 (#5, 2 wk), 21 wk; PW nf 9/11/67 (#6), pk 10/9/67 (#4, 3 wk), 22 wk; tot 43 wk.
The Night Lives On (Morrow) NYT nf 9/7/86 (#13), pk 9/14/86 (#12, 1 wk), 2 wk.

Lord Vansittart
Lessons of My Life (Knopf) NYT gen 2/6/44 (#17, 1 wk).

Lorenz, Konrad
On Aggression (Harcourt) NYT pb gen 10/1/67 (#5), pk 12/3/67 (#4, 4 wk), 8 wk.

Lorenz, Lee
See Bruce Feirstein
See Scott Redman, et al.

Loring, Emilie Baker
Give Me One Summer (Grosset & Dunlap) NYT fic 8/2/36 (#4, 4 wk).
As Long as I Live (Grosset & Dunlap) NYT fic 4/4/37 (#8, 4 wk).
Today Is Yours (Grosset & Dunlap) NYT fic 3/6/38 (#6, 4 wk).
High of Heart (Grosset & Dunlap) NYT fic 12/4/38 (#11, 4 wk).
Across the Years (Little Brown) NYT fic 11/5/39 (#13, 4 wk).
Beyond the Sound of Guns (Little Brown) NYT fic 2/10/46 (#16, 2 wk).

Lorrah, Jean
The Vulcan Academy Murders (Pocket) NYT pb fic 11/11/84 (#12, 1 wk).
The Idic Epidemic (Pocket) NYT pb fic 2/14/88 (#7, 1 wk), 3 wk; PW mm pb 2/19/88 (#7, 1 wk), 2 wk; tot 5 wk.
Metamorphosis (Pocket) NYT pb fic 3/11/90 (#11), pk 3/18/90 (#7, 2 wk), 4 wk; PW mm pb 3/23/90 (#15), pk 3/30/90 (#7, 1 wk), 3 wk; tot 7 wk.

Lorrimer, Claire
Mavreen (Bantam) PW mm pb 1/24/77 (#10), pk 2/14/77 (#5, 2 wk), 10 wk; NYT mm pb 2/6/77 (#10), pk 2/27/77 (#2, 1 wk), 11 wk; tot 21 wk.

Loth, David
See Peter Freuchen and _____

Lottman, Eileen
The Greek Tycoon (Warner) PW mm pb 5/29/78 (#13), pk 6/5/78 (#10, 1 wk), 3 wk.

Lovelace, Linda, and Mike Grady
Ordeal (Stuart/Citadel) PW hc nf 3/21/80 (#12), pk 3/28/80 (#6, 2 wk), 8 wk; NYT nf 3/23/80 (#9), pk 3/30/80 (#6, 2 wk), 6 wk; (Berkley) NYT mm pb 2/22/81 (#11), pk 3/1/81 (#3, 1 wk), 7 wk; PW mm pb 2/27/81 (#7, 1 wk), 5 wk; tot 26 wk.

Lovelace, Maud Hart
Winona's Pony Cart (Crowell) NYT ch bst 11/15/53 (#16, 40 wk).

Lovell, Mary S.
Straight On Till Morning: The Biography of Beryl Markham (St. Martin's) NYT nf 9/13/87 (#7), pk 9/20/87 (#6, 1 wk), 10 wk; PW hc nf 9/18/87 (#8, 1 wk), 10 wk; tot 20 wk.
See also Beryl Markham

Lowe, Pardee
Father and Glorious Descendant (Little Brown) NYT gen 5/2/43 (#17), pk 5/9/43 (#16, 1 wk), 3 wk.

Lowell, Amy
John Keats (Houghton) PW gen lit 4/18/25 (#6, 8 wk), 12 wk.

Lowell, Joan
The Cradle of the Deep (Simon & Schuster) PW nf 4/13/29 (#2), pk 5/11/29 (#1, 4 wk), 20 wk.

Lowell, Juliet
Dear Sir [ed.] (Duell Sloan & Pearce) NYT gen 10/15/44 (#9), pk 10/29/44 (#5, 1 wk), 16 wk; PW nf 11/11/44 (#8, 2 wk), 3 wk; tot 19 wk.

Lowry, Albert J.
How You Can Become Financially Independent by Investing in Real Estate (Simon & Schuster) PW hc nf 8/6/79 (#15), pk 5/2/80 (#6, 1 wk), 39 wk; NYT nf 9/30/79 (#14), pk 3/16/80 (#5, 1 wk), 42 wk; tot 81 wk.

Lowry, Lois
Number the Stars (Houghton) PW ch md rd 8/31/90 (#5), pk 10/26/90 (#2, 4 wk), 16 wk.

Lowry, Malcolm
Under the Volcano (Lippincott) NYT fic 3/23/47 (#14), pk 4/20/47 (#10, 1 wk), 8 wk.

Lubell, Samuel
The Future of American Politics (Harper) NYT gen 5/18/52 (#15, 1 wk).

Lucado, Max
The Applause of Heaven (Word) PW hc rel 10/5/90 (#5), pk 11/9/90 (#2, 4 wk), 8 wk.

Lucas, George
See Donald F. Glut and _____

Lucas, Jerry
See Harry Lorayne and _____

Luciano, Ron, with David Fisher
The Umpire Strikes Back (Bantam) PW hc nf 5/28/82 (#15), pk 7/9/82 (#7, 1 wk), 18 wk; NYT nf 5/30/82 (#14), pk 7/11/82 (#5, 1 wk), 18 wk; tot 36 wk.
Strike Two (Bantam) NYT nf 7/1/84 (#12, 1 wk); PW hc nf 7/6/84 (#15, 1 wk); tot 2 wk.

Ludlum, Robert
The Matlock Paper (Dial) PW fic 4/23/73 (#9), pk 5/28/73 (#4, 3 wk), 21 wk; NYT fic 4/29/73 (#6), pk 5/27/73 (#4, 1 wk), 18 wk; tot 39 wk.
The Rhinemann Exchange (Dial) PW fic 9/30/74 (#8, 1 wk), 9 wk; NYT fic 10/6/74 (#10), pk 11/17/74 (#8, 1 wk), 9 wk; (Dell) NYT mm pb 9/7/75 (#8), pk 9/14/75 (#6, 1 wk), 5 wk; PW mm pb 4/4/77 (#14, 1 wk); tot 24 wk.
The Gemini Contenders (Dial) NYT fic 3/21/76 (#6), pk 5/2/76 (#3, 1 wk), 17 wk;

PW hc fic 3/22/76 (#8), pk 4/26/76 (#3, 3 wk), 16 wk; (Dell) NYT mm pb 4/24/77 (#13), pk 5/22/77 (#5, 1 wk), 11 wk; PW mm pb 4/25/77 (#10), pk 5/2/77 (#5, 4 wk), 12 wk; tot 56 wk.

The Chancellor Manuscript (Dial) NYT fic 3/27/77 (#10), pk 4/24/77 (#5, 3 wk), 23 wk; PW hc fic 3/28/77 (#8), pk 5/2/77 (#3, 1 wk), 22 wk; (Bantam) PW mm pb 2/13/78 (#8), pk 2/27/78 (#5, 2 wk), 13 wk; NYT mm pb 2/26/78 (#9), pk 3/12/78 (#5, 1 wk), 11 wk; tot 69 wk.

The Holcroft Covenant (Marek/Putnam) PW hc fic 3/27/78 (#12), pk 5/29/78 (#1, 4 wk), 28 wk; NYT fic 4/9/78 (#8), pk 7/9/78 (#1, 1 wk), 19 wk; (Bantam) PW mm pb 2/19/79 (#7), pk 2/26/79 (#3, 2 wk), 12 wk; NYT mm pb 2/25/79 (#7), pk 3/4/79 (#2, 3 wk), 13 wk; tot 72 wk.

The Matarese Circle (Marek/Putnam) PW hc fic 3/19/79 (#13), pk 4/16/79 (#1, 15 wk), 40 wk; NYT fic 3/25/79 (#11), pk 4/8/79 (#1, 14 wk), 40 wk; (Bantam) PW mm pb 2/22/80 (#7), pk 2/29/80 (#2, 4 wk), 16 wk; NYT mm pb 2/24/80 (#2), 3/16/80 (#1, 2 wk), 16 wk; tot 112 wk.

The Bourne Identity (Marek/Putnam) PW hc fic 3/7/80 (#4), pk 3/21/80 (#1, 17 wk), 33 wk; NYT fic 3/9/80 (#3), pk 3/23/80 #1, 16 wk), 33 wk; (Bantam) mm pb 4/12/81 (#9), pk 4/19/81 (#1, 5 wk), 15 wk; PW mm pb 4/17/81 (#1, 4 wk), 14 wk; tot 95 wk.

The Road to Gandolfo (Bantam) PW mm pb 5/28/82 (#9), pk 6/11/82 (#1, 7 wk), 18 wk; NYT mm pb 5/30/82 (#6), pk 6/6/82 (#1, 5 wk), 19 wk; tot 37 wk.

The Parsifal Mosaic (Random) PW hc fic 3/19/82 (#2), pk 3/26/82 (#1, 20 wk), 41 wk; NYT fic 3/21/82 (#1, 16 wk), 44 wk; (Bantam) NYT mm pb 3/13/83 (#1, 5 wk), 17 wk; PW mm pb 3/18/83 (#1, 5 wk), 18 wk; tot 120 wk.

The Aquitaine Progression (Random) NYT fic 3/11/84 (#1, 13 wk), 34 wk; PW hc fic 3/16/84 (#3), pk 3/23/84 (#1, 13 wk), 34 wk; (Bantam) NYT pb fic 3/10/85 (#1, 7 wk), 17 wk; PW mm pb 3/15/85 (#1, 8 wk), 15 wk; tot 100 wk.

The Bourne Supremacy (Random) NYT fic 3/9/86 (#1, 8 wk), 32 wk; PW hc fic 3/14/86 (#4), pk 3/21/86 (#1, 7 wk), 34 wk; (Bantam) NYT pb fic 3/8/87 (#2), pk 3/15/87 (#1, 7 wk), 18 wk; PW mm pb 3/13/87 (#1, 9 wk), 13 wk; tot 97 wk.

The Icarus Agenda (Random) NYT fic 3/13/88 (#16), pk 3/20/88 (#1, 8 wk), 27 wk; PW hc fic 3/25/88 (#1, 9 wk), 25 wk; (Bantam) PW mm pb 3/10/89 (#11), pk 3/17/89 (#1, 6 wk), 13 wk; NYT pb fic 3/12/89 (#2), pk 3/19/89 (#1, 5 wk), 11 wk; tot 76 wk.

Trevayne (Bantam) NYT pb fic 9/3/89 (#1, 4 wk), 13 wk; PW mm pb 9/8/89 (#1, 6 wk), 13 wk; tot 26 wk.

The Bourne Ultimatum (Random) NYT fic 3/18/90 (#1, 5 wk), 26 wk; PW hc fic 3/23/90 (#1, 6 wk), 24 wk; [read by Darrin McGavin] (Bantam) aud fic 10/5/90 (#7, 4 wk), 8 wk; tot 58 wk.

Ludwig, Emil
Napoleon (Boni & Liveright) PW nf 3/19/27 (#10), pk 8/27/27 (#2, 4 wk), 60 wk.

Bismarck (Little Brown) PW nf 12/31/27 (#5, 4 wk), 8 wk.

The Son of Man (Liveright) PW nf 10/27/28 (#8, 4 wk), 8 wk.

Goethe (Putnam) PW nf 10/27/28 (#1, 12 wk), 16 wk.

Lincoln (Little Brown) PW nf 3/15/30 (#1, 4 wk), 12 wk.

July '14 (Putnam) PW nf 1/11/30 (#5, 4 wk), 8 wk.

Three Titans (Putnam) PW nf 10/18/30 (#7), pk 11/22/30 (#6, 4 wk), 8 wk.

The Nile (Viking) NYT nf 4/4/37 (#6, 4 wk); PW nf 4/10/37 (#6, 8 wk), 16 wk; tot 20 wk.

Roosevelt (Viking) NYT gen 7/3/38 (#12, 4 wk).

The Mediterranean (Whittlesey/McGraw) NYT nf 2/7/43 (#10, 1 wk), 2 wk.

Lukas, J. Anthony
Common Ground (Knopf) NYT nf 9/29/85 (#10), pk 10/13/85 (#8, 1 wk), 15 wk; PW hc nf 10/18/85 (#15, 1 wk); (Vintage) NYT pb nf 10/19/86 (#7, 1 wk), 2 wk; tot 18 wk.

Lukins, Sheila
See Julee Rosso and _____
See Julee Rosso, et al.

Lund, Doris
Eric (Dell) NYT mm pb 11/30/75 (#7, 2 wk), 3 wk.

Lundberg, Ferdinand
America's 60 Families (Vanguard) NYT gen 2/6/38 (#10), pk 3/6/38 (#2, 4 wk), 16 wk; PW nf 2/12/38 (#6), pk 3/12/38 (#5, 4 wk), 12 wk; tot 28 wk.

The Rich and the Super-Rich (Stuart) PW nf 7/1/68 (#8), pk 9/23/68 (#2, 6 wk), 32 wk; NYT gen 7/14/68 (#10), pk 8/18/68 (#2, 12 wk), 33 wk; NYT pb gen 7/6/69 (#5), pk 9/7/69 (#2, 4 wk), 16 wk; tot 81 wk.

_____, and Marynia L. Foot Farnham
Modern Woman: The Lost Sex (Harper) NYT gen 5/18/47 (#10), pk 6/29/47 (#7, 1 wk), 21 wk.

Lupica, Mike
See Reggie Jackson and _____

Lurie, Alison
The War Between the Tates (Random) PW fic 8/12/74 (#8), pk 10/14/74 (#4, 1 wk), 18 wk; NYT fic 9/1/74 (#8), pk 10/13/74 (#5, 2 wk), 14 wk; (Warner) NYT mm pb 6/29/75 (#5), pk 7/13/75 (#3, 1 wk), 8 wk; tot 40 wk.
Foreign Affairs (Avon) PW mm pb 11/15/85 (#12), pk 12/6/85 (#10, 1 wk), 5 wk.

Lustgarten, Karen
The Complete Guide to Disco Dancing (Warner) PW td pb 11/6/78 (#9), pk 11/20/78 (#8, 2 wk), 4 wk; NYT td pb 1/21/79 (#14), pk 2/11/79 (#10, 2 wk), 10 wk; tot 14 wk.

Lyall, Gavin
Midnight Plus One (Scribner) PW fic 5/3/65 (#11), pk 5/31/65 (#9, 1 wk), 4 wk.

Lyle, John M.
The Dry and Lawless Years (Prentice Hall) NYT gen 1/8/61 (#16), pk 1/15/61 (#10, 1 wk), 5 wk.

Lyle, Sparky, and Peter Golenbock
The Bronx Zoo (Crown) NYT nf 5/15/79 (#15), pk 4/29/79 (#2, 8 wk), 29 wk; PW hc nf 4/16/79 (#11), pk 5/21/79 (#2, 1 wk), 29 wk; (Dell) NYT mm pb 3/23/80 (#14), pk 4/13/80 (#13, 1 wk), 4 wk; PW mm pb 3/28/80 (#13, 1 wk), 2 wk; tot 64 wk.

Lynch, Jennifer
The Secret Diary of Laura Palmer (Pocket) PW td pb 10/5/90 (#3), pk 10/12/90 (#2, 3 wk), 11 wk; NYT pb fic 10/7/90 (#14), pk 10/28/90 (#4, 1 wk), 10 wk; tot 21 wk.

Lynch, Peter, and John Rothchild
One Up on Wall Street (Simon & Schuster) PW hc nf 3/17/89 (#8), pk 4/14/89 (#3, 3 wk), 12 wk; NYT msc 3/19/89 (#5), pk 3/26/89 (#3, 5 wk), 9 wk; (Penguin) PW td pb 4/27/90 (#7, 1 wk); tot 22 wk.

Lynd, Robert S., and Helen M. Lynd
Middletown in Transition (Harcourt) NYT nf 6/6/37 (#8, 4 wk).

Lynde, H.H.
The Slender Reed (Crown) NYT fic 4/24/49 (#16), pk 5/1/49 (#14, 1 wk), 3 wk.

Lyndon, Neil
See Armand Hammer and _____

Lynes, Russell
The Tastemakers (Harper) NYT gen 11/7/54 (#16, 1 wk).

Lynn, Loretta, with George Vecsey
Loretta Lynn: Coal Miner's Daughter (Geis/Regnery) PW hc nf 7/26/76 (#8), pk 9/13/76

(#6, 1 wk), 10 wk; NYT gen 8/1/76 (#10), pk 8/8/76 (#8, 3 wk), 8 wk; (Warner) NYT mm pb 5/15/77 (#11, 3 wk), 6 wk; PW mm pb 5/16/77 (#10, 1 wk), 3 wk; tot 27 wk.

Lyon, Marguerite
And So to Bedlam (Bobbs Merrill) NYT gen 11/28/43 (#13, 1 wk), 2 wk.

Lyons, Eugene
Assignment in Utopia (Harcourt) NYT gen 12/12/37 (#7, 4 wk), 12 wk; PW nf 2/12/38 (#7, 4 wk), 8 wk; tot 20 wk.
Our Unknown Ex-President (Doubleday) NYT gen 7/4/48 (#13), pk 8/22/48 (#6, 2 wk), 17 wk; PW nf 8/14/48 (#8, 1 wk), 2 wk; tot 19 wk.
Herbert Hoover: A Biography (Doubleday) PW nf 9/28/64 (#10, 1 wk).

Lytle, Andrew Nelson
The Velvet Horn (McDowell Oblensky) NYT fic 9/15/57 (#16), pk 9/22/57 (#15, 2 wk), 3 wk.

"M"
The Sensuous Man (Stuart) PW nf 3/1/71 (#5), pk 8/23/71 (#2, 2 wk), 36 wk; NYT gen 3/7/71 (#6), pk 4/18/71 (#2, 12 wk), 36 wk; NYT pb gen 1/9/72 (#3), pk 2/13/72 (#2, 8 wk), 12 wk; tot 84 wk.

Maas, Peter
The Valachi Papers (Putnam) PW nf 4/21/69 (#10, 1 wk); NYT pb gen 11/2/69 (#5), pk 2/1/70 (#4, 4 wk), 16 wk; tot 17 wk.
Serpico (Viking) PW nf 6/4/73 (#10), pk 7/23/73 (#9, 1 wk), 6 wk; NYT gen 7/22/73 (#10, 1 wk); (Bantam) NYT mm pb 3/10/74 (#3, 8 wk), 12 wk; tot 19 wk.
Father and Son (Simon & Schuster) PW hc fic 4/7/89 (#14, 1 wk), 2 wk.

Macardle, Dorothy
The Uninvited (Doubleday) NYT fic 8/9/42 (#15), pk 9/27/42 (#4, 1 wk), 23 wk; PW fic 9/12/42 (#7), pk 9/26/42 (#4, 1 wk), 6 wk; tot 29 wk.

MacArthur, Gen. Douglas
Reminiscences (McGraw) PW nf 10/5/64 (#9), pk 11/2/64 (#1, 8 wk), 36 wk; NYT gen 10/11/64 (#5), pk 10/25/64 (#1, 9 wk), 32 wk; NYT pb gen 12/5/65 (#3, 4 wk), 8 wk; tot 76 wk.

Macartney, William Napier
Fifty Years a Country Doctor (Dutton) NYT gen 6/5/38 (#15, 4 wk).

Macaulay, David
The Way Things Work (Houghton) PW hc nf 12/2/88 (#14), pk 1/5/90 (#5, 1 wk), 29 wk; NYT msc 12/11/88 (#4), pk 12/10/89 (#1, 6

wk), 35 wk; PW ch nf 8/31/90 (#5, 4 wk);
tot 68 wk.

Macaulay, Dame Rose
Told by an Idiot (Boni) PW fic 4/19/24
(#6), pk 6/21/24 (#5, 4 wk), 8 wk.
Potterism (Boni) PW fic 2/26/21 (#7), pk
3/26/21 (#5, 4 wk), 12 wk.
The Towers of Trebizond (Farrar) NYT fic
5/5/57 (#12), pk 5/19/57 (#9, 1 wk), 9 wk.

McBain, Ed
Lullaby (Avon) NYT pb fic 1/21/90 (#14,
1 wk).

McBain, Laurie
The Devil's Desire (Avon) NYT mm pb
4/27/75 (#6, 3 wk), 6 wk.
Moonstruck Madness (Avon) PW mm pb
2/14/77 (#9), pk 3/7/77 (#1, 1 wk), 10 wk;
NYT mm pb 2/27/77 (#3), pk 3/6/77 (#2, 2
wk), 10 wk; tot 20 wk.
Tears of Gold (Avon) NYT mm pb 4/22/79
(#14), pk 4/29/79 (#3, 1 wk), 12 wk; PW mm
pb 4/23/79 (#5), pk 5/7/79 (#3, 1 wk), 8 wk;
tot 20 wk.
Chance the Winds of Fortune (Avon) NYT
mm pb 7/20/80 (#10), pk 8/3/80 (#6, 1 wk),
10 wk; PW mm pb 7/25/80 (#7), pk 8/1/80
(#6, 2 wk), 6 wk; tot 16 wk.
Dark Before the Rising Sun (Avon) NYT
mm pb 5/16/82 (#7), pk 5/23/82 (#3, 2 wk),
8 wk; PW mm pb 5/21/82 (#6), pk 5/28/82
(#5, 1 wk), 7 wk; tot 15 wk.
Wild Bells to the Wild Sky (Avon) NYT td
pb 11/20/83 (#5), pk 11/27/83 (#3, 1 wk), 6
wk; PW td pb 12/2/83 (#3, 2 wk), 5 wk; NYT
pb fic 9/16/84 (#9, 1 wk); tot 12 wk.
When the Splendor Falls (Avon) NYT pb
fic 11/3/85 (#13), pk 11/10/85 (#7, 3 wk), 5
wk; PW mm pb 11/8/85 (#15), pk 11/22/85
(#6, 1 wk), 6 wk; tot 11 wk.

McCaffrey, Anne
The White Dragon (Ballantine/Del Rey)
PW hc fic 8/21/78 (#14, 1 wk), 3 wk; PW mm
pb 5/14/79 (#9), pk 5/21/79 (#7, 1 wk), 6 wk;
NYT mm pb 5/20/79 (#12), pk 5/27/79 (#9,
1 wk), 5 wk; tot 14 wk.
Dragondrums (Bantam) NYT mm pb 2/
24/80 (#15, 2 wk).
Crystal Singer (Ballantine/Del Rey) PW
mm pb 8/20/82 (#14), pk 9/3/82 (#10, 1 wk),
4 wk.
Moreta: Dragonlady of Pern (Ballantine/
Del Rey) NYT fic 11/20/83 (#12), pk 12/18/
83 (#6, 2 wk), 16 wk; PW hc fic 12/2/83 (#8),
pk 12/9/83 (#7, 3 wk), 16 wk; NYT pb fic
10/7/84 (#8), pk 10/14/84 (#3, 1 wk), 8 wk;
PW mm pb 10/12/84 (#8), pk 10/19/84 (#6,
2 wk), 8 wk; tot 48 wk.

Dinosaur Planet Survivors (Ballantine/Del
Rey) NYT pb fic 11/11/84 (#11), pk 11/18/84
(#7, 1 wk), 5 wk; PW mm pb 11/16/84 (#11),
pk 11/23/84 (#10, 1 wk), 3 wk; tot 8 wk.
Nerilka's Story (Ballantine/Del Rey) NYT
fic 4/6/86 (#11), pk 4/20/86 (#9, 1 wk), 7 wk;
PW hc fic 4/18/86 (#8, 2 wk), 6 wk; NYT pb
fic 2/22/87 (#12), pk 3/1/87 (#11, 1 wk), 2 wk;
tot 15 wk.
Dragonsdawn (Ballantine/Del Rey) NYT
fic 11/6/88 (#14), pk 11/20/88 (#10, 1 wk), 7
wk; PW hc fic 11/18/88 (#7, 2 wk), 6 wk;
NYT pb fic 9/3/89 (#12), pk 9/17/89 (#6, 1
wk), 6 wk; PW mm pb 9/8/89 (#14), pk
9/22/89 (#7, 1 wk), 4 wk; tot 23 wk.
The Renegades of Pern (Ballantine/Del
Rey) NYT fic 11/26/89 (#10, 1 wk), 4 wk; PW
hc fic 12/1/89 (#13), pk 12/15/89 (#10, 1 wk),
6 wk; NYT pb fic 9/9/90 (#9, 1 wk), 3 wk;
PW mm pb 9/14/90 (#15), pk 9/28/90 (#10,
1 wk), 3 wk; tot 16 wk.
The Rowan (Putnam/Ace) PW hc fic 9/14/
90 (#14, 1 wk); NYT fic 9/16/90 (#15, 1 wk);
tot 2 wk.

_____, **and Elizabeth Moon**
Sassinak (Baen) PW mm pb 3/30/90 (#14,
1 wk).

McCall, Cheryl
See David Breskin, et al.

McCammon, Robert R.
Swan Song (Pocket) NYT pb fic 6/14/87
(#9), pk 6/21/87 (#8, 1 wk), 4 wk; PW mm
pb 6/26/87 (#15, 1 wk); tot 5 wk.
Stinger (Pocket) NYT pb fic 4/17/88 (#16),
pk 4/24/88 (#14, 1 wk), 2 wk.
The Wolf's Hour (Pocket) NYT pb fic 3/19/
89 (#13, 1 wk), 2 wk.

McCarthy, Joe
See Kenneth P. O'Donnell, et al.
See Fred Allen and_____

McCarthy, Mary
The Groves of Academe (Harcourt) NYT fic
4/13/52 (#14, 1 wk).
A Charmed Life (Harcourt) NYT fic 11/27/
55 (#16), pk 12/4/55 (#9, 3 wk), 10 wk.
The Group (Harcourt) NYT fic 9/8/63
(#9), pk 10/6/63 (#1, 19 wk), 51 wk; PW fic
9/16/63 (#9), pk 10/21/63 (#1, 19 wk), 49 wk;
NYT pb fic 5/1/66 (#5), pk 6/5/66 (#4, 12
wk), 16 wk; tot 116 wk.
Birds of America (Harcourt) NYT fic 6/13/
71 (#8, 1 wk).

McCarthy, Mignon
See Kareem Abdul-Jabbar and_____
See Jane Fonda and_____

McClary, Jane McIlvaine
A Portion for Foxes (Simon & Schuster)
NYT fic 6/11/72 (#8), pk 8/6/72 (#6, 2 wk),
17 wk; PW fic 6/26/72 (#7), pk 7/10/72 (#6,
2 wk), 14 wk; tot 31 wk.

McClintic, Guthrie
Me and Kit (Little Brown) NYT gen 10/30
/55 (#15, 1 wk).

McClintick, David
*Indecent Exposure: A True Story of Holly-
wood and Wall Street* (Morrow) PW hc nf
8/13/82 (#11), pk 9/3/82 (#5, 7 wk), 22 wk;
NYT nf 9/5/82 (#11), pk 9/19/82 (#5, 4 wk),
11 wk; (Dell) PW mm pb 8/19/83 (#14), pk
9/2/83 (#8, 1 wk), 5 wk; NYT mm pb 8/21/
83 (#8, 1 wk), 3 wk; tot 41 wk.

McClintock, Marshall
A Fly Went By (Random) NYT ch bst
5/10/59 (#11, 19 wk).

McCloskey, Robert
One Morning in Maine (Viking) NYT ch
bst 11/16/52 (#4, 40 wk).
Make Way for Ducklings (Viking) NYT ch
bst 11/3/68 (#8), pk 5/4/69 (#7, 19 wk), 66
wk.

Maccoby, Michael
*The Gamesman: The New Corporate Lead-
ers* (Simon & Schuster) NYT gen 3/6/77
(#7), pk 3/27/77 (#4, 7 wk), 18 wk; PW hc
nf 3/7/77 (#7), pk 4/4/77 (#4, 1 wk), 15 wk;
tot 33 wk.

McCormack, Mark H.
*What They Don't Teach You at Harvard
Business School: Notes from a Street-Smart
Executive* (Bantam) PW hc nf 9/21/84 (#10),
pk 10/12/84 (#2, 9 wk), 48 wk; NYT msc
9/23/84 (#4), pk 10/14/84 (#1, 17 wk), 38 wk;
PW td pb 6/27/86 (#10), pk 7/18/86 (#4, 4
wk), 15 wk; NYT msc pb 7/6/86 (#3, 4 wk),
11 wk; tot 112 wk.
*The Terrible Truth About Lawyers: What
Every Business Person Needs to Know* (Mor-
row) PW hc nf 10/16/87 (#15, 1 wk); NYT
Msc 10/18/87 (#4, 1 wk), 4 wk; tot 5 wk.

McCormick, Jay
November Storm (Doubleday) NYT fic 3/
14/43 (#17), pk 5/16/43 (#10, 1 wk), 9 wk.

McCoy, Horace
Kiss Tomorrow Goodbye (Random) NYT
fic 7/4/48 (#15, 1 wk).
Scalpel (Appleton) NYT fic 7/20/52 (#16),
pk 8/31/52 (#10, 1 wk), 9 wk.

McCoy, Iola Fuller
The Shining Trail [as by Iola Fuller] (Duell
Sloan & Pearce) NYT fic 7/25/43 (#13), pk
8/22/43 (#8, 1 wk), 8 wk.

McCrae, John
In Flanders' Fields (Putnam) PW gen 5/3/
19 (#6), pk 7/5/19 (#3, 4 wk), 12 wk.

McCrone, Guy
Red Plush (Farrar) NYT fic 12/28/47 (#12),
pk 1/11/48 (#6, 2 wk), 14 wk; PW fic 2/14/48
(#5, 1 wk), 2 wk; tot 16 wk.
Aunt Bel (Farrar) NYT fic 6/12/49 (#13, 1
wk).

**McCrum, Robert, William Cran and
   Robert MacNeil**
The Story of English (Sifton/Viking) NYT
nf 10/12/86 (#12), pk 10/26/86 (#3, 1 wk), 12
wk; PW hc nf 10/24/86 (#8), pk 11/7/86 (#7,
1 wk), 10 wk; tot 22 wk.

McCullers, Carson
Clock Without Hands (Houghton) NYT fic
9/3/61 (#15), pk 10/22/61 (#7, 3 wk), 22 wk;
PW fic 9/25/61 (#9), pk 11/13/61 (#5, 1 wk),
12 wk; tot 34 wk.

McCullough, Colleen
The Thorn Birds (Harper) PW hc fic 5/9/
77 (#9), pk 6/6/77 (#1, 23 wk), 60 wk; NYT
fic 5/22/77 (#10), pk 6/19/77 (#1, 16 wk), 59
wk; (Avon) PW mm pb 6/12/78 (#3), pk 6/
19/78 (#1, 18 wk), 48 wk; NYT mm pb 6/18/
78 (#1, 12 wk), 35 wk; NYT pb fic 1/27/85
(#7), pk 2/3/85 (#10, 1 wk), 2 wk; tot 204 wk.
An Indecent Obsession (Harper) PW hc fic
10/23/81 (#8), pk 11/13/81 (#1, 15 wk), 34 wk;
NYT fic 10/25/81 (#3), pk 11/15/81 (#1, 14
wk), 33 wk; (Avon) PW mm pb 10/8/82 (#4),
pk 10/15/82 (#1, 6 wk), 15 wk; NYT mm pb
10/10/82 (#1, 7 wk), 16 wk; tot 98 wk.
A Creed for the Third Millenium (Harper)
NYT fic 5/12/85 (#13), pk 6/16/85 (#10, 1
wk), 9 wk; PW hc fic 5/17/85 (#12), pk 5/24/
85 (#11, 1 wk), 7 wk; (Avon) NYT pb fic
4/6/86 (#6), pk 4/27/86 (#3, 2 wk), 9 wk;
PW mm pb 4/11/86 (#10), pk 5/23/86 (#2, 1
wk), 12 wk; tot 37 wk.
The Ladies of Missalonghi (Harper) PW hc
fic 4/10/87 (#12), pk 5/29/87 (#3, 1 wk), 13
wk; NYT fic 4/12/87 (#8), pk 5/10/87 (#3, 1
wk), 12 wk; (Avon) NYT pb fic 4/3/88 (#7),
pk 4/17/88 (#2, 1 wk), 9 wk; PW mm pb
4/8/88 (#8), pk 4/22/88 (#3, 3 wk), 10 wk;
tot 44 wk.
The First Man in Rome (Morrow) PW hc
fic 10/12/90 (#12), pk 10/19/90 (#8, 2 wk), 11
wk; NYT fic 10/21/90 (#7, 3 wk), 8 wk; [read
by David Ogden Stiers] (Simon & Schuster) PW aud fic 12/7/90 (#3, 4 wk); tot 23
wk.

McCullough, David
*The Path Between the Seas: The Creation of
the Panama Canal, 1870–1914* (Simon &

Schuster) PW hc nf 8/1/77 (#9), pk 9/26/77 (#6, 1 wk), 18 wk; NYT nf 8/14/77 (#10), pk 10/2/77 (#8, 3 wk), 14 wk; tot 32 wk.

Mornings on Horseback (Simon & Schuster) NYT nf 8/30/81 (#15), pk 9/13/81 (#14, 1 wk), 3 wk; PW hc nf 9/18/81 (#15), pk 9/25/81 (#13, 3 wk), 5 wk; tot 8 wk.

McCutcheon, John Tinney
Drawn from Memory (Bobbs Merrill) NYT gen 10/1/50 (#16), pk 1/21/51 (#10, 1 wk), 7 wk.

MacDonald, Alexander
Revolt in Paradise (Daye) NYT gen 12/17/44 (#24, 1 wk).

MacDonald, Betty Bard
The Egg and I (Lippincott) NYT gen 10/28/45 (#9), pk 12/30/45 (#1, 42 wk), 98 wk; PW nf 11/24/45 (#3), pk 1/5/46 (#1, 33 wk), 89 wk; tot 187 wk.

The Plague and I (Lippincott) NYT gen 11/7/48 (#9), pk 11/28/48 (#6, 2 wk), 15 wk; PW nf 12/18/48 (#7), pk 1/15/49 (#6, 1 wk), 2 wk; tot 17 wk.

Nancy and Plum (Lippincott) NYT ch bst 11/16/52 (#9, 40 wk).

Mrs. Piggle-Wiggle's Farm (Lippincott) NYT ch bst 11/14/54 (#15, 40 wk).

Onions in the Stew (Lippincott) NYT gen 6/5/55 (#8), pk 7/24/55 (#4, 1 wk), 24 wk; PW nf 6/11/55 (#9), pk 7/2/55 (#5, 3 wk), 17 wk; tot 41 wk.

McDonald, Frank
Provenance (Atlantic Little Brown) NYT fic 12/9/79 (#14, 1 wk), 2 wk; (Avon) PW mm pb 9/26/80 (#13, 1 wk), 2 wk; NYT mm pb 10/5/80 (#12, 1 wk), 2 wk; tot 6 wk.

McDonald, Gregory
Fletch's Fortune (Avon) PW mm pb 8/7/78 (#15, 1 wk).

Fletch and Widow Bradley (Warner) PW mm pb 11/20/81 (#12), pk 12/4/81 (#11, 1 wk), 3 wk.

Fletch's Moxie (Warner) PW mm pb 10/15/82 (#14), pk 10/22/82 (#8, 1 wk), 3 wk.

Fletch and the Man Who (Warner) PW mm pb 8/12/83 (#13, 2 wk), 3 wk; NYT mm pb 8/21/83 (#14, 1 wk); tot 4 wk.

Carioca Fletch (Warner) PW mm pb 4/6/84 (#14), pk 4/20/84 (#12, 1 wk), 3 wk.

Fletch, Too (Warner) NYT pb fic 6/14/87 (#15), pk 6/21/87 (#14, 1 wk), 2 wk.

McDonald, Hugh C., as told to Geoffrey Bocca
Appointment in Dallas (Zebra) NYT mm pb 12/28/75 (#9, 1 wk).

McDonald, James Grover
My Mission in Israel (Simon & Schuster) NYT gen 9/23/51 (#11, 1 wk), 4 wk.

McDonald, John
See Alfred P. Sloan, Jr., et al.

MacDonald, John D.
The Turquoise Lament (Fawcett) NYT mm pb 7/14/74 (#7, 4 wk), 8 wk.

The Dreadful Lemon Sky (Lippincott) PW fic 3/17/75 (#8), pk 5/5/75 (#2, 3 wk), 23 wk; NYT fic 3/23/75 (#10), pk 6/8/75 (#3, 1 wk), 23 wk; (Fawcett) NYT mm pb 9/7/75 (#9), pk 9/14/75 (#4, 2 wk), 7 wk; tot 53 wk.

Condominium (Lippincott) PW hc fic 4/11/77 (#9), pk 7/11/77 (#2, 1 wk), 24 wk; NYT fic 4/24/77 (#9), pk 7/24/77 (#3, 1 wk), 27 wk; (Fawcett/Crest) PW mm pb 4/17/78 (#14), pk 5/8/78 (#3, 2 wk), 13 wk; NYT mm pb 4/30/78 (#7), pk 5/7/78 (#3, 2 wk), 12 wk; tot 76 wk.

The Empty Copper Sea (Lippincott) PW hc fic 9/25/78 (#13), pk 10/30/78 (#6, 2 wk), 16 wk; NYT fic 11/12/78 (#7), pk 11/19/78 (#6, 2 wk), 11 wk; (Fawcett/Gold Medal) PW mm pb 4/30/79 (#14), pk 5/21/79 (#4, 1 wk), 10 wk; NYT mm pb 5/6/79 (#13), pk 5/27/79 (#4, 1 wk), 9 wk; tot 46 wk.

The Green Ripper (Lippincott) PW hc fic 10/1/79 (#11), pk 11/19/79 (#4, 1 wk), 17 wk; NYT fic 10/28/79 (#8), pk 12/9/79 (#4, 1 wk), 14 wk; (Fawcett/Gold Medal) PW mm pb 5/30/80 (#9), pk 6/6/80 (#3, 1 wk), 8 wk; NYT mm pb 6/1/80 (#7), pk 6/8/80 (#3, 1 wk), 7 wk; tot 46 wk.

Free Fall in Crimson (Harper) NYT fic 4/26/81 (#11), pk 5/17/81 (#3, 4 wk), 20 wk; PW hc fic 5/1/81 (#9), pk 5/15/81 (#3, 5 wk), 18 wk; (Fawcett/Gold Medal) PW mm pb 11/27/81 (#14), pk 12/4/81 (#2, 3 wk), 11 wk; NYT mm pb 11/29/81 (#10), pk 12/6/81 (#3, 4 wk), 11 wk; tot 60 wk.

Cinnamon Skin (Harper) PW hc fic 6/25/82 (#13), pk 7/23/82 (#2, 1 wk), 14 wk; NYT fic 7/4/82 (#9), pk 7/25/82 (#3, 2 wk), 13 wk; (Fawcett/Gold Medal) mm pb 6/26/83 (#9), pk 7/17/83 (#1, 1 wk), 10 wk; PW mm pb 7/1/83 (#5), pk 7/22/83 (#2, 2 wk), 10 wk; tot 47 wk.

One More Sunday (Knopf) NYT fic 4/1/84 (#15), PK 4/29/84 (#6, 1 wk), 9 wk; PW hc fic 4/6/84 (#9), pk 4/20/84 (#7, 1 wk), 8 wk; (Fawcett/Crest) PW pb fic 2/24/85 (#9), pk 3/3/85 (#3, 1 wk), 10 wk; PW mm pb 3/1/85 (#7), pk 3/8/85 (#4, 1 wk), 9 wk; tot 36 wk.

The Lonely Silver Rain (Knopf) NYT fic 4/7/85 (#5), pk 4/28/85 (#3, 1 wk), 13 wk; PW hc fic 4/12/85 (#7), pk 5/3/85 (#5, 2 wk),

13 wk; (Fawcett/Gold Medal) NYT pb fic 2/23/86 (#8), pk 3/16/86 (#3, 1 wk), 10 wk; PW mm pb 2/28/86 (#8), pk 3/21/86 (#3, 1 wk), 10 wk; tot 46 wk.

Barrier Island (Knopf) NYT fic 6/22/86 (#13), pk 7/27/86 (#11, 1 wk), 9 wk; PW hc fic 7/4/86 (#14), pk 7/11/86 (#11, 2 wk), 7 wk; (Fawcett/Gold Medal) NYT pb fic 5/24/87 (#6), pk 6/7/87 (#2, 1 wk), 8 wk; PW mm pb 5/29/87 (#11), pk 6/5/87 (#3, 1 wk), 7 wk; tot 31 wk.

Macdonald, Malcolm

The World from Rough Stones (NAL/Signet) PW mm pb 3/22/76 (#7), pk 3/29/76 (#6, 1 wk), 7 wk; NYT mm pb 3/28/76 (#9), pk 4/4/76 (#5, 1 wk), 4 wk; tot 11 wk.

The Rich Are with You Always (NAL/Signet) NYT mm pb 12/4/77 (#15, 1 wk).

MacDonald, Patricia J.

Stranger in the House (Dell) PW mm pb 7/29/83 (#14, 1 wk).

Macdonald, Ross

The Goodbye Look (Knopf) PW fic 6/30/69 (#9), pk 8/4/69 (#6, 2 wk), 14 wk; NYT fic 7/6/69 (#10), pk 8/10/69 (#7, 3 wk), 14 wk; tot 28 wk.

The Underground Man (Knopf) PW fic 3/8/71 (#4), pk 3/15/71 (#2, 3 wk), 20 wk; NYT fic 3/14/71 (#10), pk 4/18/71 (#4, 7 wk), 17 wk; tot 37 wk.

Sleeping Beauty (Knopf) NYT fic 5/27/73 (#10), pk 6/24/73 (#9, 1 wk), 6 wk; PW fic 5/28/73 (#8), pk 6/4/73 (#7, 2 wk), 6 wk; tot 12 wk.

MacDonall, Betty

Anybody Can Do Anything (Lippincott) PW nf 10/14/50 (#4, 1 wk), 3 wk; NYT gen 9/17/50 (#11), pk 10/22/50 (#8, 1 wk), 10 wk; tot 13 wk.

McDougall, Dr. John A., and Mary A. McDougall

The McDougall Plan (New Century) NYT msc pb 5/5/85 (#9, 2 wk); PW td pb 5/31/85 (#10, 1 wk); tot 3 wk.

McDowell, Josh

More Than a Carpenter (Tyndale) PW pb rel 10/5/90 (#8, 4 wk), 8 wk.

MacEachern, Diane

Save Our Planet: 750 Everyday Ways You Can Help Clean Up the Earth (Dell) PW td pb 4/20/90 (#8), pk 5/11/90 (#5, 1 wk), 6 wk.

McFadden, Cyra

The Serial: A Year in the Life of Marin County (Knopf) NYT td pb 8/7/77 (#5), pk 10/16/77 (#1, 1 wk), 21 wk; PW td pb 8/8/77 (#3, 3 wk), 16 wk; tot 37 wk.

McFarland, Dennis

The Music Room (Houghton) NYT fic 6/17/90 (#15, 1 wk).

Macfarlane, Peter Clark

Man's Country (Cosmopolitan) PW fic 3/17/23 (#10, 8 wk).

McFee, William

Harbourmaster (Doubleday) PW fic 2/13/32 (#5, 4 wk), 8 wk.

The Beachcomber (Doubleday) NYT fic 10/6/35 (#9, 4 wk).

McGavin, Darrin

See Robert Ludlum

McGeehan, Bernice

See Lawrence Welk and_____

McGibbon, Robin

New Kids on the Block: The Whole Story (Avon) NYT pb nf 7/22/90 (#10, 1 wk); PW td pb 8/10/90 (#10, 1 wk); tot 2 wk.

McGill, Gordon

The Final Conflict: Omen III (NAL/Signet) PW mm pb 1/23/81 (#9), pk 1/30/81 (#8, 1 wk), 5 wk; NYT mm pb 1/25/81 (#13), pk 2/1/81 (#11, 1 wk), 6 wk; tot 11 wk.

McGinley, Phyllis

The Love Letters of Phyllis McGinley (Viking) NYT gen 10/31/54 (#16), pk 1/16/54 (#15, 1 wk), 3 wk.

Sixpence in Her Shoe (Macmillan) PW nf 11/16/64 (#9), pk 3/15/65 (#5, 1 wk), 36 wk; NYT gen 12/6/64 (#7), pk 4/18/65 (#5, 1 wk), 37 wk; NYT pb fic 12/5/65 (#2), pk 1/2/66 (#1, 8 wk), 16 wk; tot 89 wk.

McGinniss, Joe

The Selling of the President 1968 (Trident) NYT gen 10/26/69 (#7), pk 11/30/69 (#1, 11 wk), 31 wk; PW nf 10/27/69 (#6), pk 12/1/69 (#1, 12 wk), 32 wk; NYT pb gen 11/1/70 (#1, 12 wk), 16 wk; tot 79 wk.

Fatal Vision (Putnam) NYT nf 10/2/83 (#7), pk 10/9/83 (#6, 1 wk), 12 wk; PW hc nf 10/7/83 (#6), pk 10/14/83 (#5, 2 wk), 15 wk; (NAL/Signet) NYT pb nf 8/5/84 (#1, 8 wk), 29 wk; PW mm pb 8/10/84 (#10), pk 12/14/84 (#1, 2 wk), 22 wk; tot 78 wk.

Blind Faith (Putnam) NYT nf 1/29/89 (#8), pk 2/12/89 (#1, 2 wk), 19 wk; PW hc nf 2/3/89 (#6), pk 2/10/89 (#1, 3 wk), 16 wk; (NAL/Signet) NYT pb nf 10/1/89 (#1, 8 wk), 29 wk; PW mm pb 10/6/89 (#5), pk 10/27/89 (#2, 4 wk), 13 wk; tot 77 wk.

McGivern, William P.

Soldiers of '44 (Arbor House) PW hc fic 4/16/79 (#15, 1 wk).

McGrady, Patrick, Jr.
See Nathan Pritikin and_____

MacGregor, Rob
Indiana Jones and the Last Crusade (Ballantine) NYT pb fic 6/11/89 (#15), pk 6/18/89 (#11, 1 wk), 3 wk; PW mm pb 6/23/89 (#13, 1 wk); tot 4 wk.

McGuinness, Doreen
See Ingrid Selberg

McGuire, Christine, and Carla Norton
Perfect Victim (Dell) NYT pb nf 7/30/89 (#4), pk 8/20/89 (#1, 4 wk), 18 wk; PW mm pb 8/18/89 (#8), pk 9/1/89 (#5, 1 wk), 9 wk; tot 27 wk.

McHugh, Vincent
I Am Thinking of My Darling (Simon & Schuster) NYT fic 9/5/43 (#10, 2 wk), 4 wk; PW fic 10/9/43 (#9, 1 wk); tot 5 wk.

McInerney, Jay
Ransom (Vintage) PW td pb 10/11/85 (#8, 2 wk).

MacInnes, Helen
Above Suspicion (Little Brown) PW fic 8/16/41 (#9), pk 9/13/41 (#4, 8 wk), 20 wk.
Assignment in Brittany (Little Brown) PW fic 8/8/42 (#4, 7 wk), 11 wk; NYT fic 8/9/42 (#7), pk 8/16/42 (#4, 8 wk), 13 wk; tot 24 wk.
While Still We Live (Little Brown) NYT fic 4/16/44 (#12), pk 5/21/44 (#9, 1 wk), 7 wk; PW fic 5/13/44 (#10, 1 wk); tot 8 wk.
Friends and Lovers (Harcourt) NYT fic 9/14/47 (#13, 1 wk), 3 wk.
Rest and Be Thankful (Little Brown) NYT fic 9/11/49 (#16), pk 9/25/49 (#11, 2 wk), 7 wk.
Neither Five Nor Three (Harcourt) NYT fic 4/1/51 (#16, 3 wk).
I and My True Love (Harcourt) NYT fic 3/8/53 (#12), pk 3/22/53 (#9, 1 wk), 6 wk; PW fic 4/18/53 (#9, 1 wk); tot 7 wk.
Pray for a Brave Heart (Harcourt) NYT fic 1/30/55 (#14), pk 2/27/55 (#7, 1 wk), 12 wk; PW fic 3/5/55 (#4, 1 wk), 2 wk; tot 14 wk.
North from Rome (Harcourt) NYT fic 3/9/58 (#8), pk 4/13/58 (#4, 4 wk), 23 wk; PW fic 3/31/58 (#5), pk 4/14/58 (#3, 1 wk), 16 wk; tot 39 wk.
Decision at Delphi (Harcourt) NYT fic 11/13/60 (#15), pk 12/18/60 (#5, 2 wk), 26 wk; PW fic 11/28/60 (#8), pk 1/2/61 (#3, 3 wk), 19 wk; tot 45 wk.
The Venetian Affair (Harcourt) NYT fic 10/27/63 (#10), pk 12/29/63 (#2, 4 wk), 31 wk; PW fic 11/4/63 (#8), pk 1/13/64 (#2, 5 wk), 32 wk; tot 63 wk.
The Double Image (Harcourt) NYT fic

1/30/66 (#9), pk 3/13/66 (#2, 3 wk), 33 wk; PW fic 1/31/66 (#10), pk 3/7/66 (#1, 6 wk), 34 wk; tot 67 wk.
The Salzburg Connection (Harcourt) NYT fic 9/22/68 (#10), pk 11/10/68 (#1, 18 wk), 42 wk; PW fic 9/30/68 (#5), pk 11/4/68 (#1, 18 wk), 44 wk; NYT pb fic 12/7/69 (#2), pk 2/1/70 (#1, 4 wk), 16 wk; tot 102 wk.
Message from Malaga (Harcourt) NYT fic 10/3/71 (#9), pk 10/24/71 (#4, 12 wk), 28 wk; PW fic 10/4/71 (#5), pk 11/8/71 (#3, 6 wk), 29 wk; NYT pb fic 10/8/72 (#3, 8 wk), 12 wk; tot 69 wk.
The Snare of the Hunter (Harcourt) NYT fic 3/10/74 (#9), pk 4/14/74 (#2, 2 wk), 24 wk; PW fic 3/11/74 (#10), pk 3/25/74 (#3, 6 wk), 21 wk; (Fawcett) NYT mm pb 3/23/75 (#5), pk 3/30/75 (#4, 2 wk), 9 wk; tot 54 wk.
Agent in Place (Harcourt) PW hc fic 5/10/76 (#10), pk 6/1/76 (#4, 1 wk), 21 wk; NYT fic 5/16/76 (#9), pk 6/13/76 (#4, 4 wk), 21 wk; (Fawcett) PW mm pb 4/18/77 (#7, 3 wk), 8 wk; NYT mm pb 4/24/77 (#9), pk 5/15/77 (#6, 1 wk), 10 wk; tot 60 wk.
Prelude to Terror (Harcourt) PW hc fic 9/11/78 (#14), pk 11/20/78 (#6, 1 wk), 19 wk; NYT fic 11/12/78 (#6, 2 wk), 11 wk; (Fawcett/Crest) PW mm pb 10/29/79 (#13), pk 11/5/79 (#4, 4 wk), 9 wk; NYT mm pb 11/4/79 (#13), pk 11/25/79 (#4, 2 wk), 12 wk; tot 51 wk.
The Hidden Target (Harcourt) PW hc fic 10/17/80 (#10), pk 11/14/80 (#8, 1 wk), 16 wk; NYT fic 11/23/80 (#15), pk 12/21/80 (#7, 2 wk), 15 wk; (Fawcett/Crest) PW mm pb 10/2/81 (#9), pk 10/16/81 (#3, 1 wk), 9 wk; NYT mm pb 10/11/81 (#5, 1 wk), 7 wk; tot 47 wk.
Cloak of Darkness (Harcourt) PW hc fic 9/10/82 (#15), pk 10/8/82 (#10, 2 wk), 8 wk; NYT fic 10/10/82 (#15), pk 10/24/82 (#8, 1 wk), 6 wk; (Fawcett/Crest) PW mm pb 8/28/83 (#7), pk 9/11/83 (#5, 1 wk), 7 wk; PW mm pb 9/2/83 (#9), pk 9/9/83 (#6, 1 wk), 6 wk; tot 27 wk.
Ride a Pale Horse (Harcourt) PW hc fic 11/2/84 (#13), pk 11/16/84 (#9, 1 wk), 7 wk; NYT fic 11/11/84 (#13), pk 11/18/84 (#10, 2 wk), 5 wk; (Fawcett) NYT pb fic 9/29/85 (#6), pk 10/13/85 (#5, 1 wk), 10 wk; PW mm pb 10/4/85 (#6), pk 10/18/85 (#4, 3 wk), 10 wk; tot 32 wk.

McIntyre, Joseph, Jonathan Knight, Donnie Wahlberg, Daniel Wood and Jordan Knight
Our Story: New Kids on the Block (Bantam) PW td pb 6/29/90 (#9), pk 8/10/90 (#5, 1 wk), 8 wk; NYT pb nf 7/1/90 (#6, 4 wk), 7

wk; PW ch nf 8/31/90 (#3, 4 wk); tot 19 wk.

McIntyre, Vonda N.
The Wrath of Kahn (Pocket) PW mm pb 6/25/82 (#11), pk 7/2/82 (#4, 2 wk), 6 wk; NYT mm pb 6/27/82 (#6), pk 7/4/82 (#3, 1 wk), 7 wk; tot 13 wk.
The Search for Spock (Pocket) NYT pb fic 6/17/84 (#5), pk 6/24/84 (#2, 1 wk), 5 wk; PW mm pb 6/22/84 (#5), pk 7/6/84 (#3, 1 wk), 6 wk; tot 11 wk.
The Voyage Home (Pocket) NYT pb fic 12/7/86 (#10), pk 12/14/86 (#3, 1 wk), 8 wk; PW mm pb 12/19/86 (#8), pk 1/9/87 (#7, 1 wk), 5 wk; tot 13 wk.
Enterprise: The First Adventure (Pocket) NYT pb fic 9/14/86 (#4, 1 wk), 5 wk; PW mm pb 9/26/86 (#8), pk 10/17/86 (#7, 1 wk), 6 wk; tot 11 wk.

MacIver, Joyce
The Frog Pond (Braziller) NYT gen 4/2/61 (#16), pk 5/7/61 (#9, 1 wk), 11 wk.
The Exquisite Thing (Putnam) PW fic 8/5/68 (#8, 1 wk).

Mackail, Denis
The Square Circle (Houghton) PW fic 6/20/31 (#9, 4 wk).

McKay, Allis
They Came to a River (Macmillan) PW fic 6/14/41 (#5), pk 7/12/41 (#3, 4 wk), 16 wk.

Mackay, Harvey
Swim with the Sharks Without Being Eaten Alive (Morrow) PW hc nf 4/1/88 (#13), pk 4/22/88 (#2, 1 wk), 42 wk; NYT msc 4/10/88 (#3), pk 4/17/88 (#2, 26 wk), 42 wk; (Ivy) PW mm pb 3/3/89 (#7), pk 3/31/89 (#3, 2 wk), 11 wk; NYT msc pb 3/5/89 (#1, 3 wk), 11 wk; tot 106 wk.
Beware the Naked Man Who Offers You His Shirt (Morrow) NYT msc 2/25/90 (#4), pk 3/11/90 (#1, 2 wk), 22 wk; PW hc nf 3/2/90 (#11), pk 3/16/90 (#3, 1 wk), 18 wk; tot 40 wk.

Mackay, Margaret Mackprang
For All Men Born (John Day) NYT fic 3/21/43 (#15, 1 wk).

Macken, Walter
Rain on the Wind (Macmillan) NYT fic 5/27/51 (#12, 1 wk).

McKenna, Richard
The Sand Pebbles (Harper) PW fic 1/28/63 (#5), pk 3/4/63 (#2, 4 wk), 30 wk; NYT fic 4/7/63 (#3, 2 wk), 18 wk; tot 48 wk.

McKenney, Ruth
My Sister Eileen (Harcourt) NYT gen 9/4/38 (#2, 4 wk), 16 wk; PW fic 9/10/38 (#7, 4 wk), 12 wk; tot 28 wk.

Love Story (Harcourt) NYT gen 3/5/50 (#15, 1 wk).

McKie, Roy
See Henry Beard and_____

McKuen, Rod
Lonesome Cities (Random) NYT gen 11/17/68 (#9), pk 12/1/68 (#2, 4 wk), 16 wk; PW nf 11/18/68 (#10), pk 12/16/68 (#9, 1 wk), 4 wk; tot 20 wk.
In Someone's Shadow (Random) NYT gen 1/11/70 (#6, 2 wk), 12 wk; PW nf 1/19/70 (#10), pk 3/23/70 (#6, 1 wk), 12 wk; tot 24 wk.

MacLachlan, Kyle
See Anonymous (The Twin Peaks Tapes of Agent Cooper)

MacLaine, Shirley
Don't Fall Off the Mountain (Norton) PW nf 12/14/70 (#7, 2 wk), 8 wk; NYT gen 12/27/70 (#10, 2 wk); tot 10 wk.
You Can Get There from Here (Norton) PW nf 5/19/75 (#9, 2 wk); NYT gen 5/25/75 (#7, 1 wk); tot 3 wk.
Out on a Limb (Bantam) PW hc nf 7/8/83 (#13), pk 8/26/83 (#5, 3 wk), 15 wk; NYT nf 7/17/83 (#10), pk 8/21/83 (#5, 3 wk), 15 wk; NYT pb nf 4/15/84 (#6), pk 4/22/84 (#1, 15 wk), 53 wk; PW mm pb 4/20/84 (#10), pk 5/11/84 (#1, 4 wk), 30 wk; tot 113 wk.
Dancing in the Light (Bantam) PW hc nf 9/27/85 (#13), pk 10/18/85 (#1, 1 wk), 25 wk; NYT nf 9/29/85 (#2, 7 wk), 30 wk; NYT pb nf 11/2/86 (#3), pk 11/9/86 (#1, 6 wk), 16 wk; PW mm pb 11/14/86 (#7), pk 2/27/87 (#6, 1 wk), 12 wk; tot 83 wk.
It's All in the Playing (Bantam) NYT nf 9/13/87 (#4), pk 10/4/87 (#2, 1 wk), 10 wk; PW hc nf 9/18/87 (#10), pk 10/9/87 (#2, 1 wk), 8 wk; NYT pb nf 9/11/88 (#5), pk 10/2/88 (#4, 1 wk), 7 wk; PW mm pb 10/7/88 (#13, 1 wk); tot 26 wk.
Going Within: A Guide for Inner Transformation (Bantam) NYT msc 4/30/89 (#1, 5 wk), 8 wk; PW hc nf 5/5/89 (#1, 3 wk), 9 wk; NYT msc pb 3/4/90 (#5), pk 3/18/90 (#3, 1 wk), 2 wk; tot 19 wk.

MacLean, Alistair
H.M.S. Ulysses (Doubleday) NYT fic 1/29/56 (#11), pk 2/12/56 (#8, 3 wk), 17 wk; PW fic 3/24/56 (#9), pk 4/21/56 (#8, 1 wk), 2 wk; tot 19 wk.
The Guns of Navarone (Doubleday) NYT fic 3/24/57 (#13), pk 3/31/57 (#12, 1 wk), 3 wk.
Night Without End (Doubleday) NYT fic 3/20/60 (#16), pk 3/27/60 (#13, 1 wk), 2 wk.
The Golden Rendezvous (Doubleday) NYT

fic 7/1/62 (#14), pk 8/12/62 (#13, 1 wk), 8 wk.

The Satan Bug [as by Ian Stuart] (Scribner) NYT fic 9/23/62 (#16, 1 wk).

Ice Station Zebra (Doubleday) NYT fic 12/29/63 (#10, 1 wk); PW fic 1/6/64 (#10), pk 1/13/64 (#8, 1 wk), 3 wk; tot 4 wk.

Where Eagles Dare (Doubleday) PW fic 11/27/67 (#12), pk 1/15/68 (#9, 2 wk), 11 wk; NYT fic 12/17/67 (#10), pk 1/7/68 (#8, 2 wk), 8 wk; tot 19 wk.

Force 10 from Navarone (Doubleday) PW fic 12/16/68 (#10), pk 2/3/69 (#4, 4 wk), 20 wk; NYT fic 12/22/68 (#8), pk 2/16/69 (#4, 2 wk), 18 wk; NYT pb fic 1/4/70 (#5, 8 wk); tot 46 wk.

Puppet on a Chain (Doubleday) PW fic 12/8/69 (#10), pk 2/16/70 (#4, 1 wk), 13 wk; NYT fic 12/14/69 (#10), pk 1/18/70 (#5, 4 wk), 17 wk; tot 30 wk.

Caravan to Vaccares (Doubleday) PW fic 12/7/70 (#8), pk 2/22/71 (#4, 1 wk), 15 wk; NYT fic 12/20/70 (#9), pk 2/14/71 (#6, 1 wk), 12 wk; NYT pb fic 12/12/71 (#5, 8 wk); tot 35 wk.

Bear Island (Doubleday) NYT fic 11/7/71 (#9), pk 11/28/71 (#5, 1 wk), 14 wk; PW fic 11/22/71 (#9), pk 12/27/71 (#6, 2 wk), 13 wk; NYT pb fic 1/14/73 (#3, 4 wk); tot 31 wk.

The Way to Dusty Death (Doubleday) PW fic 10/8/73 (#9, 1 wk); (Fawcett) NYT mm pb 10/13/74 (#2, 4 wk); tot 5 wk.

Circus (Doubleday) NYT fic 8/31/75 (#9), pk 11/2/75 (#5, 1 wk), 12 wk; PW fic 9/1/75 (#9), pk 10/27/75 (#6, 1 wk), 12 wk; (Fawcett/Crest) PW mm pb 8/16/76 (#7, 1 wk), 6 wk; NYT Mm pb 8/29/76 (#8, 1 wk); tot 31 wk.

The Golden Gate (Doubleday) NYT fic 9/12/76 (#9), pk 9/19/76 (#8, 1 wk), 2 wk; PW hc fic 9/20/76 (#7, 1 wk), 4 wk; (Fawcett/Crest) PW mm pb 5/23/77 (#13), pk 6/13/77 (#2, 1 wk), 7 wk; NYT mm pb 5/29/77 (#5), pk 6/26/77 (#4, 1 wk), 8 wk; tot 21 wk.

Seawitch (Doubleday) NYT fic 9/18/77 (#15, 1 wk); (Fawcett/Crest) PW mm pb 7/24/78 (#11), pk 8/14/78 (#2, 1 wk), 9 wk; NYT mm pb 8/6/78 (#4), pk 8/13/78 (#3, 1 wk), 2 wk; tot 12 wk.

Goodbye California (Doubleday) PW hc fic 4/3/78 (#13), pk 5/15/78 (#12, 1 wk), 10 wk; NYT fic 4/30/78 (#12), pk 5/21/78 (#10, 2 wk), 9 wk; (Fawcett/Crest) NYT mm pb 2/25/79 (#9), pk 3/11/79 (#6, 1 wk), 8 wk; PW mm pb 2/26/79 (#8), pk 3/5/79 (#7, 2 wk), 8 wk; tot 35 wk.

Athabasca (Doubleday) PW hc fic 10/31/80 (#15), pk 11/7/80 (#10, 1 wk), 5 wk; (Fawcett/Crest) PW mm pb 4/2/82 (#8), pk 4/16/

82 (#3, 3 wk), 8 wk; NYT mm pb 4/4/82 (#10), pk 4/25/82 (#3, 3 wk), 9 wk; tot 22 wk.

Santorini (Doubleday) NYT fic 4/5/87 (#13, 1 wk), 2 wk; (Fawcett/Crest) NYT pb fic 2/28/88 (#10), pk 3/20/88 (#6, 1 wk), 7 wk; PW mm pb 3/4/88 (#11), pk 3/25/88 (#6, 1 wk), 7 wk; tot 16 wk.

Maclean, Sir Fitzroy

Escape to Adventure (Little Brown) NYT gen 6/4/50 (#15), pk 6/11/50 (#14, 1 wk), 6 wk.

MacLean, Harry N.

In Broad Daylight (Dell) NYT pb nf 2/4/90 (#3), pk 2/18/90 (#2, 1 wk), 9 wk.

McLean, Kathryn Anderson [all titles as by Kathryn Alen Forbes]

Mama's Bank Account (Harcourt) NYT fic 4/25/43 (#16), pk 5/23/43 (#9, 1 wk), 15 wk.

Transfer Point (Harcourt) NYT fic 12/21/47 (#15, 3 wk).

McLendon, Winzola

Martha (Random) NYT nf 9/2/79 (#11, 1 wk).

MacLennan, Hugh

Two Solitudes (Duell Sloan & Pearce) NYT fic 2/11/45 (#13), pk 2/25/45 (#11, 1 wk), 4 wk.

The Watch That Ends the Night (Scribner) NYT fic 3/15/59 (#13), pk 5/10/59 (#8, 1 wk), 19 wk; PW fic 4/6/59 (#8, 2 wk), 8 wk; tot 27 wk.

McLuhan, Herbert Marshall

Understanding Media (McGraw) NYT pb gen 9/4/66 (#4, 16 wk), 28 wk.

_____, and Quentin Fiore

The Medium Is the Massage (Random) NYT pb gen 4/2/67 (#4), pk 5/7/67 (#1, 12 wk), 24 wk.

McMahon, Jim, and Bob Verdi

McMahon! The Bare Truth About Chicago's Brashest Bear (Warner) NYT nf 9/28/86 (#4), pk 1/4/87 (#3, 1 wk), 21 wk; PW hc nf 10/3/86 (#11), pk 1/23/87 (#3, 1 wk), 20 wk; NYT pb nf 9/6/87 (#8), pk 9/20/87 (#6, 1 wk), 5 wk; tot 46 wk.

McManus, Doyle

See Jane Mayer and_____

McManus, Patrick F.

The Grasshopper Trap (Holt) NYT nf 8/18/85 (#11, 1 wk), 6 wk; PW hc nf 9/6/85 (#15, 2 wk); tot 8 wk.

Rubber Legs and White Tail-Hairs (Holt) NYT fic 11/8/87 (#14), pk 12/20/87 (#12, 1 wk), 9 wk.

The Night the Bear Ate Goombaw (Holt)
NYT nf 5/14/89 (#7, 2 wk), 13 wk.

McMeekin, Clark
Show Me a Land (Appleton) PW fic 4/13/
40 (#7, 4 wk), 8 wk.

Macmillan, A.H.
Faith on the March (Prentice Hall) NYT
gen 6/2/57 (#13), pk 6/9/57 (#10, 1 wk), 10
wk; PW nf 6/17/57 (#10, 1 wk); tot 11 wk.

Macmillan, Harold
The Blast of War 1939–1945 (Harper) PW
nf 1/29/68 (#12), pk 2/5/68 (#8, 1 wk), 4 wk.

MacMurray, Claire
Out on a Limbo (Lippincott) NYT gen 8/
20/44 (#15), pk 9/3/44 (#11, 1 wk), 6 wk.

McMurtry, Larry
Lonesome Dove (Simon & Schuster) PW
hc fic 6/28/85 (#13), pk 8/9/85 (#4, 3 wk),
21 wk; NYT fic 6/30/85 (#13), pk 7/14/85
(#4, 1 wk), 24 wk; (Pocket) PW mm pb 8/15/
86 (#12), pk 3/3/89 (#1, 2 wk), 24 wk; NYT
pb fic 8/17/86 (#2), pk 2/26/89 (#1, 2 wk),
27 wk; tot 96 wk.
Texasville (Simon & Schuster) NYT fic
4/12/87 (#15), pk 5/3/87 (#3, 2 wk), 11 wk;
PW hc fic 4/17/87 (#11), pk 5/8/87 (#3, 3
wk), 12 wk; (Pocket) NYT pb fic 3/13/88
(#6), pk 3/20/88 (#5, 2 wk), 7 wk; PW mm
pb 3/18/88 (#5, 1 wk), 6 wk; tot 36 wk.
Anything for Billy (Simon & Schuster)
NYT fic 10/23/88 (#11), pk 11/13/88 (#3, 1
wk), 18 wk; PW hc fic 10/28/88 (#9), pk
11/18/88 (#3, 1 wk), 14 wk; (Pocket) PW mm
pb 11/10/89 (#13), pk 11/24/89 (#2, 1 wk), 8
wk; NYT pb fic 11/12/89 (#7), pk 12/3/89
(#4, 1 wk), 9 wk; tot 49 wk.
Some Can Whistle (Simon & Schuster) PW
hc fic 10/27/89 (#9), pk 11/3/89 (#5, 1 wk),
10 wk; NYT fic 10/29/89 (#11), pk 11/12/89
(#6, 1 wk), 6 wk; (Pocket) NYT pb fic 9/16/
90 (#10), pk 9/23/90 (#8, 1 wk), 3 wk; PW
mm pb 9/21/90 (#9), pk 9/28/90 (#7, 1 wk),
4 wk; tot 23 wk.
Buffalo Girls (Simon & Schuster) NYT fic
10/21/90 (#13), pk 11/4/90 (#6, 1 wk), 7 wk;
PW hc fic 10/26/90 (#11), pk 11/2/90 (#7, 3
wk), 8 wk; tot 15 wk.

McNamara, Robert S.
The Essence of Security (Harper) NYT gen
9/29/68 (#9, 1 wk); PW nf 10/7/68 (#9, 1 wk);
tot 2 wk.

McNaught, Harry
Animal Babies (Random) NYT ch pb 11/
13/77 (#11), pk 4/30/78 (#9, 24 wk), 70 wk.

McNaught, Judith
Something Wonderful (Pocket) NYT pb fic

4/17/88 (#11, 2 wk), 3 wk; PW mm pb 4/22/
88 (#9, 2 wk), 3 wk; tot 6 wk.
A Kingdom of Dreams (Pocket) NYT pb fic
3/12/89 (#15), pk 3/19/89 (#9, 2 wk), 5 wk;
PW mm pb 3/31/89 (#8, 1 wk), 3 wk; tot 8
wk.
Almost Heaven (Pocket) NYT pb fic 4/8/
90 (#6), pk 4/15/90 (#1, 1 wk), 8 wk; PW mm
pb 4/20/90 (#7), pk 5/4/90 (#4, 1 wk), 5 wk;
tot 13 wk.

MacNeil, Robert
Wordstruck (Viking) NYT nf 4/16/89 (#6,
1 wk), 7 wk; PW hc nf 4/28/89 (#13, 2 wk),
3 wk; tot 10 wk.
See also Robert McCrum, et al.

McNeill, George
Rafaella (Bantam) PW mm pb 11/21/77
(#15), pk 12/5/77 (#14, 1 wk), 3 wk.

McNeill, William Hardy
The Rise of the West (Univ. of Chicago)
NYT gen 12/29/63 (#9, 1 wk).

McPartland, John
No Down Payment (Simon & Schuster)
NYT fic 10/6/57 (#15), pk 11/3/57 (#9, 1 wk),
9 wk; PW fic 11/18/57 (#10, 1 wk); tot 10 wk.

McPhee, John
Coming into the Country (Farrar) PW hc nf
1/2/78 (#10), pk 1/9/78 (#5, 2 wk), 23 wk;
NYT nf 1/15/78 (#13), pk 2/5/78 (#5, 4 wk),
20 wk; (Bantam) PW mm pb 1/15/79 (#15),
pk 2/5/79 (#9, 2 wk), 6 wk; NYT mm pb
1/21/79 (#3, 1 wk), 2 wk; tot 51 wk.
The Control of Nature (Farrar) NYT nf 8/
27/89 (#12), pk 9/17/89 (#8, 3 wk), 11 wk;
PW hc nf 9/29/89 (#13, 1 wk); tot 12 wk.
Looking for a Ship (Farrar) NYT nf 10/14/
90 (#12), pk 10/28/90 (#10, 1 wk), 9 wk.

McPherson, James M.
Battle Cry of Freedom (Oxford Univ.) NYT
nf 3/6/88 (#12), pk 4/3/88 (#6, 2 wk), 16 wk;
PW hc nf 3/18/88 (#12), pk 4/15/88 (#6, 1
wk), 12 wk; (Ballantine) NYT pb nf 2/26/89
(#10), pk 4/30/89 (#7, 2 wk), 12 wk; tot 40
wk.

McQuarrie, Ralph
Return of the Jedi Portfolio (Ballantine)
NYT td pb 6/12/83 (#8, 1 wk), 3 wk.

McShane, Rudolph
See Ann Cutler and_____

McSorley, Edward
Our Own Kind (Harper) NYT fic 7/7/46
(#16), pk 7/28/46 (#12, 1 wk), 5 wk.

**McWhirter, Norris and Ross McWhir-
ter**
Guinness Book of World Records [1966]

Mally, Emma Louise
The Mocking Bird Is Singing (Holt) NYT fic 5/21/44 (#11, 1 wk).

Malm, Frances
World Cruise (Doubleday) NYT fic 5/1/60 (#15, 1 wk).

Malone, Dumas
Jefferson the Virginian (Little Brown) NYT gen 5/2/48 (#14), pk 5/9/48 (#13, 1 wk), 2 wk.

Malone, Nola Langer
See Judith Viorst

Maloney, Tom J.
U.S. Camera 1937 [ed.] (U.S. Camera) NYT gen 12/12/37 (#3, 4 wk).
U.S. Camera 1946: Victory Volume [ed. Maloney, photos selected by Edward Steicher] (U.S. Camera/Duell Sloan & Pearce) NYT gen 1/13/46 (#16, 1 wk).

Malraux, André
Anti-Memoirs (Holt) PW nf 11/11/68 (#7), pk 12/2/68 (#3, 1 wk), 11 wk; NYT gen 11/17/68 (#10), pk 12/22/68 (#5, 1 wk), 9 wk; tot 20 wk.

Maltz, Maxwell
Psycho-Cybernetics (Prentice Hall) NYT pb gen 6/5/66 (#5), pk 2/4/68 (#4, 8 wk), 32 wk.

Manchester, William
The Death of a President (Harper) NYT gen 4/16/67 (#9), pk 4/23/67 (#1, 11 wk), 20 wk; PW nf 4/17/67 (#5), pk 5/15/67 (#1, 6 wk), 20 wk; NYT pb gen 7/7/68 (#3, 4 wk), 8 wk; tot 48 wk.
The Arms of Krupp (Little Brown) NYT gen 12/15/68 (#10), pk 1/26/69 (#3, 8 wk), 29 wk; PW nf 12/30/68 (#9), pk 2/3/69 (#1, 5 wk), 29 wk; NYT pb gen 4/5/70 (#3, 8 wk), 12 wk; tot 70 wk.
The Glory and the Dream (Little Brown) NYT gen 1/19/75 (#7, 1 wk).
American Caesar: Douglas MacArthur, 1880–1964 (Little Brown) PW hc nf 10/2/78 (#7), pk 11/6/78 (#2, 2 wk), 34 wk; NYT nf 11/12/78 (#5), pk 11/19/78 (#3, 6 wk), 28 wk; (Dell) PW mm pb 10/15/79 (#11), pk 10/22/79 (#9, 1 wk), 9 wk; NYT mm pb 10/28/79 (#11), pk 11/4/79 (#7, 1 wk), 8 wk; tot 79 wk.
Goodbye, Darkness: A Memoir of the Pacific War (Little Brown) NYT nf 10/5/80 (#12), pk 12/28/80 (#5, 2 wk), 20 wk; PW hc nf 10/10/80 (#11), pk 12/5/80 (#6, 3 wk), 19 wk; (Dell) NYT mm pb 1/24/82 (#12), pk 2/7/82 (#10, 1 wk), 5 wk; tot 44 wk.
The Last Lion: Winston Spencer Churchill, Visions of Glory, 1874–1932 (Little Brown)
NYT nf 5/29/83 (#13), pk 7/3/83 (#8, 1 wk), 18 wk; PW hc nf 6/3/83 (#12), pk 7/1/83 (#5, 1 wk), 17 wk; tot 35 wk.
One Brief Shining Moment: Remembering Kennedy (Little Brown) PW hc nf 12/16/83 (#14), pk 12/23/83 (#9, 1 wk), 5 wk; NYT nf 12/18/83 (#12), pk 1/8/84 (#9, 1 wk), 5 wk; tot 10 wk.
The Last Lion: Winston Spencer Churchill, Alone, 1932–1940 (Little Brown) NYT nf 10/23/88 (#13), pk 11/20/88 (#1, 2 wk), 26 wk; PW hc nf 10/28/88 (#9), pk 11/25/88 (#2, 2 wk), 22 wk; tot 48 wk.

Mandel, Sally
Change of Heart (Dell) PW mm pb 5/22/81 (#12), pk 6/5/81 (#7, 1 wk), 9 wk; NYT mm pb 5/24/81 (#10), pk 5/31/81 (#8, 1 wk), 10 wk; tot 19 wk.

Mandino, Og
A Better Way to Live (Bantam) NYT msc 2/25/90 (#5, 1 wk).

Mandrell, Barbara, with George Vecsey
Get to the Heart: My Story (Bantam) NYT nf 9/23/90 (#15), pk 9/30/90 (#2, 1 wk), 15 wk; PW hc nf 9/28/90 (#14), pk 11/2/90 (#3, 2 wk), 13 wk; tot 28 wk.

Maney, Richard
Fanfare (Harper) NYT gen 12/8/57 (#16, 1 wk).

Manfred, Frederick Feikema
This Is the Year (Doubleday) NYT fic 4/13/47 (#16), pk 5/18/47 (#15, 1 wk), 5 wk.
Lord Grizzly (McGraw) NYT fic 11/28/54 (#16), pk 12/5/54 (#15, 4 wk), 6 wk.

Mangione, Jerre Gerlando
Mount Allegro (Crown) NYT nf 2/7/43 (#19), pk 2/14/43 (#16, 1 wk), 2 wk.

Manheim, Ralph
See Michael Ende
See E.T.A. Hoffmann

Manion, Clarence
The Key to Peace (Heritage Foundation) NYT gen 3/18/51 (#15, 1 wk).

Mankiewicz, Don M.
Trial (Harper) NYT fic 1/23/55 (#10), pk 2/6/55 (#5, 6 wk), 16 wk; PW fic 2/19/55 (#10), pk 2/26/55 (#5, 4 wk), 9 wk; tot 25 wk.

Manly, Chesley
The Twenty-Year Revolution: From Roosevelt to Eisenhower (Regnery) NYT gen 3/21/54 (#15), pk 4/25/54 (#12, 1 wk), 7 wk.

Mann, Thomas
Joseph and His Brothers (Knopf) PW fic 7/14/34 (#8, 4 wk).

Joseph in Egypt (Knopf) NYT fic 4/3/38 (#3, 4 wk), 8 wk; PW fic 4/9/38 (#8, 4 wk), 8 wk; tot 16 wk.

The Coming Victory of Democracy (Knopf) NYT gen 7/31/38 (#6), pk 9/4/38 (#4, 4 wk), 8 wk; PW nf 8/13/38 (#6, 4 wk), 8 wk; tot 16 wk.

The Beloved Returns (Knopf) PW fic 10/12/40 (#3, 4 wk), 8 wk.

The Transposed Heads (Knopf) PW fic 7/12/41 (#9, 4 wk).

Joseph the Provider (Knopf) NYT fic 7/16/44 (#9), pk 7/23/44 (#8, 1 wk), 6 wk; PW fic 8/12/44 (#8, 1 wk), 2 wk; tot 8 wk.

Doctor Faustus (Knopf) NYT fic 11/21/48 (#13), pk 1/9/48 (#9, 1 wk), 12 wk.

The Holy Sinner (Knopf) NYT fic 9/30/51 (#7), pk 10/7/51 (#6, 1 wk), 12 wk; PW fic 11/17/51 (#10, 1 wk); tot 13 wk.

Confessions of Felix Krull, Confidence Man (Knopf) NYT fic 10/9/55 (#9), pk 10/23/55 (#8, 2 wk), 8 wk.

Mannix, Dan
Step Right Up (Harper) NYT gen 4/8/51 (#14, 1 wk).

Manry, Robert
Tinkerbelle (Harper) NYT gen 7/24/66 (#10, 4 wk); PW nf 8/15/66 (#8, 1 wk), 6 wk; tot 10 wk.

Mantecino, Marcel
The Crosskillers (Pocket) PW mm pb 5/26/89 (#15), pk 6/2/89 (#14, 1 wk), 2 wk.

Mantle, Mickey, with Herb Gluck
The Mick (Doubleday) NYT nf 7/28/85 (#7), pk 8/11/85 (#5, 4 wk), 12 wk; PW hc nf 8/9/85 (#11), pk 8/23/85 (#4, 1 wk), 8 wk; (Jove) NYT pb nf 4/13/86 (#9), pk 4/20/86 (#8, 2 wk), 4 wk; tot 24 wk.

Mantle, Robert Burns
The Best Plays of 1934–35 [ed.] (Dodd) NYT nf 11/3/35 (#7, 4 wk).

The Best Plays of 1935–36 [ed.] (Dodd) NYT nf 11/8/36 (#7, 4 wk).

The Best Plays of 1936–37 [ed.] (Dodd) NYT gen 11/7/37 (#10, 4 wk).

The Best Plays of 1937–38 [ed.] (Dodd) NYT gen 11/6/38 (#14, 4 wk), 8 wk.

The Best Plays of 1938–39 [ed.] (Dodd) NYT gen 12/10/39 (#2, 4 wk).

Maracatta, Lindsay
Everything We Wanted (Pinnacle) PW mm pb 8/30/85 (#14, 1 wk).

Maraini, Fosco
Meeting with Japan (Viking) NYT gen 2/7/60 (#16, 1 wk).

Marasco, Robert
Burnt Offerings (Delacorte) PW fic 3/26/73 (#9), pk 4/2/73 (#8, 1 wk), 3 wk.

March, William
The Bad Seed (Rinehart) NYT fic 5/30/54 (#15), pk 7/4/54 (#13, 1 wk), 7 wk.

Marchetti, Victor, and John D. Marks
The CIA and the Cult of Intelligence (Knopf) PW nf 7/22/74 (#8), pk 8/5/74 (#7, 3 wk), 9 wk; NYT gen 8/11/74 (#9), pk 8/25/74 (#8, 1 wk), 4 wk; (Dell) NYT mm pb 2/23/75 (#9), pk 3/2/75 (#7, 1 wk), 2 wk; tot 15 wk.

Marcus, Stanley
Quest for the Best (Viking) NYT nf 9/23/79 (#9, 1 wk), 4 wk; PW PW hc nf 10/8/79 (#12, 1 wk); tot 5 wk.

Mardikian, George Magar
Dinner at Omar Khyyam's (Viking) NYT gen 12/24/44 (#20), pk 1/7/45 (#14, 1 wk), 5 wk.

Song of America (McGraw) NYT gen 7/1/56 (#15, 3 wk), 4 wk.

Maresca, James V.
My Flag Is Down (Dutton) NYT gen 5/2/48 (#12, 1 wk).

Margulies, Stuart
See Bobby Fischer, et al.

Mariana
See Marian Curtis Foster

Marianoff, Dimitri, and Palma Wayne
Einstein: An Intimate Study of a Great Man (Doubleday) NYT gen 9/3/44 (#15, 1 wk).

Marie, Grand Duchess
Education of a Princess (Viking) PW nf 2/21/31 (#3), pk 3/21/31 (#1, 24 wk), 36 wk.

A Princess in Exile (Viking) PW nf 10/15/32 (#2, 4 wk), 8 wk.

Markandaya, Kamala
Nectar in a Sieve (John Day) NYT fic 6/19/55 (#14, 1 wk).

Markham, Beryl
West with the Night (North Point/Farrar) NYT nf 8/23/42 (#11, 1 wk); NYT pb nf 10/26/86 (#4), pk 12/21/86 (#1, 5 wk), 83 wk; PW td pb 10/31/86 (#5), pk 12/26/86 (#3, 1 wk), 56 wk; tot 140 wk.

The Splendid Outcast: Beryl Markham's African Stories [comp. Mary S. Lovell] (North Point) NYT fic 11/22/87 (#15, 1 wk).

Markham, Ronald, and Dominick Bosco
Alone with the Devil (Bantam) NYT pb nf 4/29/90 (#9, 1 wk).

Markoe, Merrill
Late Night with David Letterman: The Book [ed.] (Villard) NYT msc pb 1/5/86 (#10, 1 wk); PW mm pb 1/10/86 (#8), pk 1/24/86 (#7, 1 wk), 4 wk; tot 5 wk.

Marks, John D.
See Victor Marchetti and_____

Marks, Percy
The Plastic Age (Century) PW fic 4/19/24 (#9), pk 6/21/24 (#3, 4 wk), 8 wk.

Marlowe, Derek
A Dandy in Aspic (Putnam) PW fic 12/5/66 (#6, 1 wk).

Marquand, John Phillips
The Late George Apley: A Novel in the Form of a Memoir (Little Brown) PW fic 2/6/37 (#6), pk 3/13/37 (#3, 8 wk), 16 wk; NYT fic 3/7/37 (#2, 4 wk), 8 wk; tot 24 wk.
Wickford Point (Little Brown) PW fic 4/8/39 (#8), pk 5/13/39 (#2, 12 wk), 20 wk; NYT fic 4/9/39 (#3, 4 wk), 12 wk; tot 32 wk.
H.M. Pulham, Esquire (Little Brown) PW fic 3/15/41 (#7), pk 4/12/41 (#2, 8 wk), 24 wk.
So Little Time (Little Brown) PW fic 9/4/43 (#4), pk 10/9/43 (#1, 10 wk), 31 wk; NYT fic 9/12/43 (#4), pk 10/17/43 (#1, 11 wk), 36 wk; tot 67 wk.
Repent in Haste (Little Brown) NYT fic 12/2/45 (#13, 1 wk), 3 wk.
B.F.'s Daughter (Little Brown) NYT fic 11/24/46 (#6), pk 12/1/46 (#1, 9 wk), 24 wk; PW fic 12/7/46 (#2), pk 12/14/46 (#1, 9 wk), 18 wk; tot 42 wk.
Point of No Return (Little Brown) NYT fic 3/20/49 (#9), pk 4/10/49 (#1, 22 wk), 34 wk; PW fic 4/9/49 (#2), pk 4/23/49 (#1, 17 wk), 26 wk; tot 60 wk.
Melville Goodwin, USA (Little Brown) NYT fic 10/21/51 (#5), pk 10/28/51 (#3, 15 wk), 23 wk; PW fic 10/27/51 (#4), pk 12/1/51 (#2, 4 wk), 16 wk; tot 39 wk.
Thirty Years (Little Brown) NYT gen 12/12/54 (#16, 1 wk).
Sincerely, Willis Wayde (Little Brown) NYT fic 3/13/55 (#6), pk 4/10/55 (#1, 6 wk), 25 wk; PW fic 3/19/55 (#4), pk 4/2/55 (#1, 7 wk), 21 wk; tot 46 wk.
Stopover: Tokyo (Little Brown) NYT fic 2/10/57 (#12), pk 2/24/57 (#8, 2 wk), 12 wk; PW fic 3/11/57 (#8, 3 wk); tot 15 wk.
Life at Happy Knoll (Little Brown) NYT fic 7/7/57 (#13), pk 8/4/57 (#6, 1 wk), 13 wk; PW fic 7/29/57 (#5, 1 wk), 4 wk; tot 17 wk.
Women and Thomas Harrow (Little Brown) NYT fic 10/12/58 (#9), pk 11/2/58 (#4, 7 wk), 17 wk; PW fic 10/27/58 (#4, 7 wk), 15 wk; tot 32 wk.

Márquez, Gabriel García
One Hundred Years of Solitude (Harper) PW fic 4/13/70 (#8, 1 wk); NYT fic 4/19/70 (#9, 1 wk); tot 2 wk.
Autumn of the Patriarch (Harper) NYT fic 1/30/77 (#10, 1 wk).
Love in the Time of Cholera (Knopf) NYT fic 4/24/88 (#6), pk 5/8/88 (#2, 3 wk), 39 wk; PW hc fic 4/29/88 (#9), pk 5/20/88 (#3, 2 wk), 39 wk; (Penguin) NYT pb fic 4/16/89 (#7, 2 wk), 18 wk; PW td pb 4/21/89 (#3, 5 wk), 29 wk; tot 125 wk.
The General in His Labyrinth (Knopf) NYT fic 9/23/90 (#10), pk 10/7/90 (#3, 1 wk), 10 wk; PW hc fic 9/28/90 (#8), pk 10/12/90 (#4, 1 wk), 12 wk; tot 22 wk.

Marsh, Dave
Born to Run: The Bruce Springsteen Story (Doubleday/Dolphin) PW td pb 11/12/79 (#10), pk 11/26/79 (#7, 3 wk), 7 wk; NYT td pb 11/25/79 (#10), pk 2/3/80 (#9, 1 wk), 7 wk; tot 14 wk.
Glory Days: Bruce Springsteen in the 1980s (Pantheon) NYT nf 5/10/87 (#12), pk 5/31/87 (#6, 1 wk), 8 wk; PW hc nf 5/15/87 (#13), pk 6/5/87 (#2, 1 wk), 8 wk; tot 16 wk.

Marsh, Ellen Tanner
Reap the Savage Wind (Ace) NYT td pb 11/7/82 (#6, 1 wk), 2 wk.
Wrap Me in Splendor (Berkley) NYT td pb 9/25/83 (#11, 1 wk), 2 wk; PW td pb 10/7/83 (#10, 1 wk); tot 3 wk.

Marsh, George
Ask No Quarter (Morrow) NYT fic 7/1/45 (#16, 1 wk), 3 wk.

Marsh, Ngaio
Overture to Death (Little Brown) NYT fic 7/9/39 (#8, 4 wk).
Colour Scheme (Little Brown) NYT fic 8/8/43 (#16, 1 wk).
Night at the Vulcan (Little Brown) NYT fic 8/5/51 (#15, 1 wk).
False Scent (Little Brown) NYT fic 1/31/60 (#11, 1 wk), 5 wk.

Marshall, Archibald
Many Junes (Dodd) PW fic 6/12/20 (#9, 8 wk).

Marshall, Bruce
The World, the Flesh and Father Smith (Houghton) NYT fic 7/29/45 (#6), pk 9/16/45 (#3, 1 wk), 26 wk; PW fic 8/4/45 (#5), pk 8/25/45 (#2, 1 wk), 14 wk; tot 40 wk.
Yellow Tapers for Paris (Houghton) NYT fic 10/6/46 (#16, 1 wk).
Vespers in Vienna (Houghton) NYT fic 9/21/47 (#16, 1 wk).

The White Rabbit (Houghton) NYT gen 3/15/53 (#14), pk 4/12/53 (#9, 1 wk), 9 wk.

Marshall, Catherine Wood

A Man Called Peter (McGraw) NYT gen 10/28/51 (#10), pk 9/21/52 (#1, 5 wk), 169 wk; PW nf 11/17/51 (#4), pk 10/11/52 (#1, 3 wk), 110 wk; tot 279 wk.

God Loves You (Whittlesey) NYT ch bst 11/15/53 (#4, 40 wk).

Friends with God (Whittlesey) NYT ch bst 11/18/56 (#15, 40 wk).

To Live Again (McGraw) NYT gen 11/10/57 (#14), pk 12/15/57 (#5, 1 wk), 31 wk; PW nf 12/9/57 (#7), pk 1/20/58 (#5, 4 wk), 18 wk; tot 49 wk.

Christy (McGraw) NYT fic 11/5/67 (#9), pk 1/14/67 (#2, 3 wk), 38 wk; PW fic 11/13/67 (#9), pk 1/8/68 (#3, 6 wk), 36 wk; NYT pb fic 11/3/68 (#5), pk 2/2/69 (#1, 12 wk), 44 wk; tot 118 wk.

Julie (McGraw) NYT fic 12/9/84 (#15, 2 wk); (Avon) NYT pb fic 7/28/85 (#13), pk 8/11/85 (#6, 1 wk), 7 wk; PW mm pb 8/2/85 (#8), pk 8/9/85 (#6, 2 wk), 7 wk; tot 16 wk.

See also Peter Marshall and_____

Marshall, Edison

Great Smith (Farrar) NYT fic 5/9/43 (#14, 1 wk), 3 wk.

The Upstart (Farrar) NYT fic 5/13/45 (#16), pk 7/8/45 (#14, 2 wk), 4 wk.

Gypsy Sixpence (Farrar) NYT fic 11/6/49 (#14), pk 11/20/49 (#11, 1 wk), 9 wk; PW fic 12/17/49 (#10, 1 wk); tot 10 wk.

The Infinite Woman (Farrar) NYT fic 12/31/50 (#16, 1 wk).

Marshall, Gen. George C.

General Marshall's Report (Simon & Schuster) NYT gen 10/28/45 (#11), pk 11/4/45 (#2, 7 wk), 14 wk; PW nf 11/10/45 (#5), pk 11/17/45 (#2, 3 wk), 9 wk; tot 23 wk.

Marshall, Katherine Boyce Tupper Brown

Together (Tupper & Love) NYT gen 2/23/47 (#11), pk 3/23/47 (#6, 1 wk), 32 wk; PW nf 3/15/47 (#7), pk 9/13/47 (#6, 1 wk), 8 wk; tot 40 wk.

Marshall, Peter, and Catherine Wood Marshall

Mr. Jones, Meet the Master (Revell) NYT gen 1/8/50 (#15), pk 4/16/50 (#4, 1 wk), 34 wk; PW nf 5/13/50 (#8, 1 wk); tot 35 wk.

The Prayers of Peter Marshall (McGraw) NYT gen 11/28/54 (#13), pk 1/23/55 (#6, 1 wk), 18 wk; PW nf 1/15/55 (#7, 1 wk), 4 wk; tot 22 wk.

The First Easter (McGraw) NYT gen 4/5/59 (#10), pk 4/12/59 (#8, 1 wk), 3 wk; PW nf

4/6/59 (#9), pk 4/13/59 (#7, 1 wk), 3 wk; tot 6 wk.

Marshall, Rosamond

Duchess Hotspur (Prentice Hall) NYT fic 5/26/46 (#8), pk 6/16/46 (#6, 3 wk), 14 wk; PW fic 6/8/46 (#10), pk 6/15/46 (#4, 1 wk), 6 wk; tot 20 wk.

Marshall, Thomas R.

Recollections (Bobbs Merrill) PW nf 12/19/25 (#7, 4 wk), 8 wk.

Martignoni, Margaret E.

The Illustrated Treasury of Children's Literature (Grosset & Dunlap) NYT ch bst 11/18/56 (#2, 40 wk).

Martin, Ann M.

Jessi's Baby-Sitter (Scholastic) PW ch mid rd 8/31/90 (#3, 4 wk).

Kristy's Mystery Admirer (Scholastic) PW ch md rd 10/26/90 (#1, 4 wk).

Poor Mallory! (Scholastic) PW ch mid rd 11/30/90 (#1, 4 wk).

Karen's Grandmother (Scholastic) PW ch yn rd 8/31/90 (#3, 4 wk).

Dawn and the Older Boy (Scholastic) PW ch mid rd 9/28/90 (#4, 4 wk).

California Girls (Scholastic) PW ch mid rd 12/21/90 (#3, 4 wk).

Baby-Sitters Island Adventure (Scholastic) PW ch mid rd 8/31/90 (#1, 4 wk), 8 wk.

Martin, Bill, Jr., and John Archambault

Chicka Chicka Boom Boom [illus. Lois Ehlert] (Simon & Schuster) PW ch pic 8/31/90 (#7, 4 wk), 8 wk.

Martin, Billy, and Peter Golenbock

Number 1 (Delacorte) PW hc fic 9/12/80 (#14, 1 wk); NYT nf 9/28/80 (#7, 1 wk), 9 wk; (Dell) NYT mm pb 6/21/81 (#15, 1 wk); tot 11 wk.

Martin, John Bartlow

Adlai Stevenson (Harper) NYT gen 10/12/52 (#16, 1 wk).

Adlai Stevenson of Illinois (Doubleday) NYT gen 5/2/76 (#9, 1 wk).

Martin, Joseph William, and Robert J. Donovan

My First Fifty Years in Politics (McGraw) NYT gen 10/16/60 (#15, 1 wk).

Martin, Judith

Miss Manners' Guide to Excruciatingly Correct Behavior (Atheneum) PW hc nf 9/24/82 (#15, 4 wk); NYT nf 9/26/82 (#14, 2 wk), 3 wk; (Warner) NYT td pb 9/11/83 (#15), pk 9/25/83 (#10, 3 wk), 7 wk; PW td pb 9/16/83 (#7, 4 wk), 5 wk; tot 19 wk.

Miss Manners' Guide to Rearing Perfect Children (Atheneum) NYT nf 12/9/84 (#14, 1 wk).

Martin, Malachi
The Final Conclave (Stein & Day) PW hc nf 4/3/78 (#13, 1 wk), 2 wk; NYT nf 4/9/78 (#15), pk 5/21/78 (#9, 1 wk), 13 wk; (Pocket) PW mm pb 9/18/78 (#14, 1 wk); tot 16 wk.
The Jesuits (Linden/Simon & Schuster) NYT nf 4/12/87 (#13, 1 wk).

Martin, Pete
See Bing Crosby and_____

Martin, Ralph G.
Jennie (Prentice Hall) NYT gen 3/23/69 (#9), pk 5/11/69 (#1, 9 wk), 30 wk; PW nf 3/31/69 (#7), pk 6/2/69 (#1, 7 wk), 31 wk; NYT pb gen 9/6/70 (#2, 12 wk), 20 wk; tot 81 wk.
Jennie, Vol. 2 (Prentice Hall) NYT gen 11/28/71 (#6), pk 1/30/72 (#4, 2 wk), 18 wk; PW nf 12/6/71 (#9), pk 12/13/71 (#4, 5 wk), 17 wk; NYT pb gen 11/12/72 (#3), pk 1/14/73 (#2, 4 wk), 16 wk; tot 51 wk.
The Woman He Loved (Simon & Schuster) NYT gen 8/18/74 (#10), pk 9/22/74 (#3, 4 wk), 24 wk; PW nf 8/19/74 (#6), pk 9/16/74 (#2, 3 wk), 21 wk; tot 45 wk.
A Hero for Our Time (Macmillan) PW hc nf 9/30/83 (#13), pk 12/16/83 (#10, 2 wk), 16 wk; NYT nf 10/23/83 (#15), pk 12/11/83 (#10, 1 wk), 8 wk; tot 24 wk.
Charles & Diana (Putnam) NYT nf 11/17/85 (#13), pk 11/24/85 (#8, 1 wk), 8 wk; PW hc nf 11/29/85 (#8), pk 12/6/85 (#7, 1 wk), 5 wk; tot 13 wk.

Martin, Steve
Cruel Shoes (Putnam) PW hc nf 5/28/79 (#11), pk 7/9/79 (#2, 7 wk), 39 wk; NYT nf 6/3/79 (#3), pk 7/22/79 (#1, 1 wk), 42 wk; tot 81 wk.
The Jerk (Warner) PW mm pb 1/11/80 (#14, 1 wk).

Martin, William
Back Bay (Crown) NYT fic 4/27/80 (#11, 2 wk), 8 wk; PW hc fic 5/23/80 (#14, 1 wk); (Pocket) mm pb 3/20/81 (#6, 1 wk), 6 wk; NYT mm pb 3/22/81 (#11), pk 4/19/81 (#4, 1 wk), 7 wk; tot 22 wk.
Nerve Endings (Crown) NYT fic 2/19/84 (#15), pk 3/4/84 (#13, 1 wk), 3 wk; PW hc fic 3/2/84 (#14), pk 3/16/84 (#13, 2 wk), 5 wk; tot 8 wk.

Marx, Groucho
The Groucho Letters (Simon & Schuster) PW nf 6/26/67 (#11, 1 wk), 2 wk.

_____, and Bernard Geis
Groucho and Me (Random) NYT gen 10/4/59 (#15), pk 10/25/59 (#8, 1 wk), 17 wk; PW nf 11/16/59 (#9, 3 wk); tot 20 wk.

Marx, Harpo, and Rowland Barber
Harpo Speaks! (Geis/Random) NYT gen 5/28/61 (#11, 1 wk).

Marzollo, Jean
Pretend You're a Cat [illus. Jerry Pinkney] (Dial) PW ch pic 9/28/90 (#9, 4 wk).

Masefield, John
The Bird of Dawning (Macmillan) PW fic 1/13/34 (#5, 4 wk), 8 wk.
Victorious Troy (Macmillan) PW fic 1/11/36 (#10, 4 wk).

Mason, Alpheus Thomas
Brandeis: A Free Man's Life (Viking) NYT gen 10/20/46 (#4, 1 wk), 18 wk; PW nf 2/15/47 (#9, 1 wk); tot 19 wk.

Mason, Francis Van Wyck
Three Harbours (Lippincott) PW fic 12/10/38 (#9), pk 3/11/39 (#4, 4 wk), 24 wk; NYT fic 1/8/39 (#8), pk 3/5/39 (#6, 4 wk), 12 wk; tot 36 wk.
The Cairo Garter Murders (Doubleday) NYT fic 6/5/38 (#11, 4 wk).
The Singapore Exile Murders (Doubleday) NYT fic 7/9/39 (#11, 4 wk).
Stars on the Sea (Lippincott) PW fic 7/13/40 (#2, 8 wk), 20 wk.
Rivers of Glory (Lippincott) PW fic 12/19/42 (#6), pk 1/23/43 (#3, 1 wk), 11 wk; NYT fic 12/20/42 (#10), pk 1/31/43 (#3, 1 wk), 17 wk; tot 28 wk.
Eagle in the Sky (Lippincott) NYT fic 2/15/48 (#8), pk 3/7/48 (#1, 5 wk), 23 wk; PW fic 2/28/48 (#1, 5 wk), 17 wk; tot 40 wk.
Cutlass Empire (Doubleday) NYT fic 3/27/49 (#13), pk 4/10/49 (#4, 8 wk), 22 wk; PW fic 4/9/49 (#4), pk 5/7/49 (#3, 2 wk), 14 wk; tot 36 wk.
Proud New Flags (Lippincott) NYT fic 5/6/51 (#6), pk 5/20/51 (#3, 4 wk), 22 wk; PW fic 5/12/51 (#5), pk 5/26/51 (#2, 3 wk), 15 wk; tot 37 wk.
Himalayan Assignment (Doubleday) NYT fic 2/24/52 (#12, 1 wk), 4 wk; PW fic 3/15/52 (#10, 2 wk); tot 6 wk.
The Golden Admiral (Doubleday) NYT fic 3/8/53 (#14), pk 4/12/53 (#3, 9 wk), 26 wk; PW fic 3/28/53 (#6), pk 5/23/53 (#2, 2 wk), 15 wk; tot 41 wk.
Blue Hurricane (Lippincott) NYT fic 11/21/54 (#12), pk 12/5/54 (#10, 2 wk), 13 wk; PW fic 12/18/54 (#10, 1 wk); tot 14 wk.
Silver Leopard (Doubleday) NYT fic 11/13/55 (#16, 1 wk).

Our Valiant Few (Little Brown) NYT fic 11/18/56 (#16), pk 12/2/56 (#13, 1 wk), 4 wk.

The Young Titan (Doubleday) NYT fic 7/12/59 (#13), pk 8/16/59 (#11, 1 wk), 12 wk; PW fic 8/10/59 (#10, 4 wk), 12 wk; tot 24 wk.

Sea 'Venture (Doubleday) NYT fic 10/15/61 (#16, 1 wk).

Manila Galleon (Little Brown) NYT fic 3/26/61 (#15), pk 4/16/61 (#10, 2 wk), 12 wk.

Mason, Richard

The World of Suzie Wong (World) NYT fic 8/11/57 (#12), pk 9/8/57 (#4, 4 wk), 29 wk; PW fic 8/26/57 (#4), pk 9/2/57 (#3, 3 wk), 17 wk; tot 46 wk.

Mason, Robert

Chickenhawk (Penguin) NYT pb nf 9/2/84 (#5), pk 9/30/84 (#4, 1 wk), 14 wk; PW td pb 9/14/84 (#6), pk 9/28/84 (#1, 3 wk), 14 wk; tot 28 wk.

Massie, Chris

The Love Letters (Grosset & Dunlap) NYT fic 11/26/44 (#13, 1 wk).

Massie, Robert K.

Nicholas and Alexandra (Atheneum) PW nf 9/11/67 (#9), pk 1/8/68 (#1, 6 wk), 39 wk; NYT gen 9/17/67 (#7), pk 11/5/67 (#2, 14 wk), 42 wk; NYT pb gen 3/2/69 (#1, 8 wk), 16 wk; tot 97 wk.

Peter the Great: His Life and World (Knopf) NYT nf 11/9/80 (#14), pk 12/28/80 (#4, 4 wk), 19 wk; PW hc nf 11/14/80 (#13), pk 1/9/81 (#4, 3 wk), 18 wk; (Ballantine) NYT pb nf 2/16/86 (#8), pk 2/23/86 (#3, 2 wk), 17 wk; PW mm pb 2/28/86 (#7, 1 wk), 3 wk; tot 57 wk.

Massman, Patti

See Pamela Beck and_____

Masterman, Sir John

The Double Cross System in the War of 1939-1945 (Yale Univ.) NYT gen 3/5/72 (#10), pk 4/16/72 (#5, 1 wk), 8 wk; PW nf 3/6/72 (#8), pk 3/20/72 (#4, 1 wk), 7 wk; tot 15 wk.

Masters, Dexter, and Katharine Way

One World or None [eds.] (Whittlesey) NYT gen 4/17/46 (#9), pk 5/5/46 (#4, 1 wk), 10 wk; PW nf 5/4/46 (#4, 1 wk), 2 wk; tot 12 wk.

Masters, John

Nightrunners of Bengal (Viking) NYT fic 2/18/51 (#14), pk 3/11/51 (#10, 1 wk), 3 wk; PW fic 3/17/51 (#10, 1 wk); tot 4 wk.

The Lotus and the Wind (Viking) NYT fic 1/25/53 (#16, 1 wk).

Bhowani Junction (Viking) NYT fic 4/18/54 (#11), pk 5/16/54 (#5, 1 wk), 11 wk; PW fic 5/15/54 (#9), pk 5/22/54 (#5, 1 wk), 3 wk; tot 14 wk.

Coromandel! (Viking) NYT fic 4/17/55 (#15, 3 wk).

Bugles and a Tiger (Viking) NYT gen 2/19/56 (#14, 1 wk).

Far, Far the Mountain Peak (Viking) NYT fic 5/19/57 (#13), pk 6/16/57 (#9, 2 wk), 12 wk; PW fic 7/8/57 (#8, 1 wk); tot 13 wk.

The Venus of Konpara (Harper) NYT fic 6/12/60 (#15, 1 wk).

The Road Past Mandalay (Harper) NYT gen 9/17/61 (#15, 1 wk), 2 wk.

Masters, William Howard, M.D., and Virginia E. Johnson

Human Sexual Response (Little Brown) NYT gen 5/15/66 (#10), pk 7/31/66 (#3, 12 wk), 32 wk; PW nf 5/23/66 (#8), pk 9/19/66 (#2, 2 wk), 32 wk; tot 64 wk.

Human Sexual Inadequacy (Little Brown) NYT gen 5/31/70 (#6), pk 6/14/70 (#5, 5 wk), 20 wk; PW nf 6/1/70 (#7), pk 6/29/70 (#4, 2 wk), 21 wk; tot 41 wk.

_____, and Virginina E. Johnson, with Robert J. Levin

The Pleasure Bond (Little Brown) PW nf 3/3/75 (#9), pk 4/28/75 (#5, 2 wk), 11 wk; NYT gen 3/16/75 (#8, 1 wk), 6 wk; tot 17 wk.

Matera, Dary

See Lucy de Barbin and_____

Mathabane, Mark

Kaffir Boy (NAL/Plume) NYT pb nf 9/6/87 (#7), pk 9/20/87 (#3, 2 wk), 13 wk; PW td pb 9/11/87 (#10), pk 10/9/87 (#4, 1 wk), 10 wk; tot 23 wk.

Kaffir Boy in America: An Encounter with Apartheid (Scribner) NYT nf 8/27/89 (#13, 1 wk), 2 wk; PW hc nf 9/1/89 (#15, 2 wk); tot 4 wk.

Mather, Anne

Wild Concerto (Harlequin) NYT td pb 10/9/83 (#9, 1 wk).

Matthews, Jill

Lives and Loves of the New Kids on the Block (Pocket) NYT pb nf 4/8/90 (#2, 5 wk), 8 wk; PW mm pb 4/20/90 (#9, 2 wk), 5 wk; tot 13 wk.

Matthews, Kathy

See Dr. Robert M. Giller and_____
See Roy E. Vartabedian and_____

Matthews, Patricia

Love, Forever More (Pinnacle) PW mm pb 12/5/77 (#11), pk 12/12/77 (#8, 1 wk), 10 wk; NYT mm pb 12/11/77 (#14), pk 1/1/78 (#8, 1 wk), 9 wk; tot 19 wk.

Love's Avenging Heart (Pinnacle) PW mm pb 1/31/77 (#12), pk 2/14/77 (#7, 3 wk), 7 wk; NYT mm pb 2/20/77 (#8), pk 3/6/77 (#6, 1 wk), 4 wk; tot 11 wk.

Love's Wildest Promise (Pinnacle) PW mm pb 6/13/77 (#10), pk 7/4/77 (#6, 1 wk), 8 wk; NYT mm pb 6/26/77 (#9), pk 7/17/77 (#6, 1 wk), 6 wk; tot 14 wk.

Love's Daring Dream (Pinnacle) PW mm pb 5/22/78 (#15), pk 5/29/78 (#11, 1 wk), 3 wk; NYT mm pb 5/28/78 (#10, 1 wk), 6 wk; tot 9 wk.

Love's Pagan Heart (Pinnacle) NYT mm pb 12/24/78 (#13), pk 12/31/78 (#11, 2 wk), 4 wk.

Love's Golden Destiny (Pinnacle) NYT mm pb 9/30/79 (#15, 1 wk); PW mm pb 10/1/79 (#14, 1 wk), 2 wk; tot 3 wk.

Love's Magic Moment (Pinnacle) PW mm pb 5/14/79 (#10, 1 wk), 3 wk; NYT mm pb 5/27/79 (#11, 2 wk), 3 wk; tot 6 wk.

Love's Raging Tide (Pinnacle) PW mm pb 2/1/80 (#13, 1 wk); NYT mm pb 2/3/80 (#11, 1 wk), 3 wk; tot 4 wk.

Love's Sweet Agony (Pinnacle) NYT mm pb 5/18/80 (#13), pk 5/25/80 (#7, 1 wk), 4 wk; PW mm pb 5/23/80 (#11, 1 wk); tot 5 wk.

Love's Bold Journey (Pinnacle) PW mm pb 10/31/80 (#14, 1 wk); NYT mm pb 11/2/80 (#10, 1 wk); tot 2 wk.

Tides of Love (Bantam) NYT td pb 6/14/81 (#8), pk 6/21/81 (#2, 1 wk), 14 wk; PW td pb 6/26/81 (#4, 1 wk), 7 wk; tot 21 wk.

Embers of Dawn (Bantam) NYT td pb 5/2/82 (#12), pk 5/9/82 (#8, 1 wk), 5 wk; PW td pb 5/7/82 (#9), pk 5/14/82 (#7, 2 wk), 3 wk; tot 8 wk.

Matthews, Roy, and Nancy Burstein
Thirty Days to a Flatter Stomach for Men (Bantam) NYT td pb 3/13/83 (#11, 1 wk), 2 wk.

Matthiessen, Peter
Far Tortuga (Random) NYT fic 6/15/75 (#10, 3 wk); PW fic 6/16/75 (#10), pk 6/23/75 (#9, 2 wk), 3 wk; tot 6 wk.

The Snow Leopard (Viking) PW hc nf 9/11/78 (#15), pk 12/25/78 (#10, 2 wk), 16 wk; NYT nf 11/12/78 (#6, 1 wk), 5 wk; tot 21 wk.

Killing Mister Watson (Random) PW hc fic 7/20/90 (#13), pk 7/27/90 (#11, 3 wk), 6 wk; NYT fic 7/29/90 (#15), pk 8/5/90 (#11, 1 wk), 5 wk; tot 11 wk.

Mattingly, Garrett
The Armada (Houghton) NYT gen 11/8/59 (#9), pk 1/3/60 (#4, 2 wk), 20 wk; PW nf 11/30/59 (#7), pk 1/11/60 (#2, 1 wk), 12 wk; tot 32 wk.

Maugham, William Somerset
The Moon and Sixpence (Doran) PW fic 3/27/20 (#10, 4 wk).

Cakes and Ale (Doubleday) PW fic 11/22/30 (#6), pk 2/21/31 (#1, 4 wk), 16 wk.

The Narrow Corner (Doubleday) PW fic 12/17/32 (#8), pk 1/14/33 (#7, 4 wk), 12 wk.

Don Fernando (Doubleday) PW nf 9/14/35 (#8, 4 wk); NYT nf 10/6/35 (#10, 4 wk); tot 8 wk.

Theatre (Doubleday) NYT fic 4/4/37 (#4), pk 5/9/37 (#2, 4 wk), 8 wk; PW fic 4/10/37 (#4), pk 5/8/37 (#2, 4 wk), 20 wk; tot 28 wk.

Summing Up (Doubleday) NYT gen 5/1/38 (#2, 4 wk), 8 wk; PW nf 5/14/38 (#5, 4 wk), 12 wk; tot 20 wk.

Tellers of Tales [comp.] (Doubleday) NYT fic 8/6/39 (#15, 4 wk).

Christmas Holiday (Doubleday) PW fic 11/11/39 (#9), pk 12/16/39 (#5, 4 wk), 12 wk; NYT fic 12/10/39 (#1, 4 wk), 8 wk; tot 20 wk.

The Mixture as Before (Doubleday) PW fic 9/14/40 (#9, 4 wk).

The Hour Before Dawn (Doubleday) NYT fic 8/9/42 (#8, 1 wk), 3 wk; PW fic 8/15/42 (#8, 1 wk); tot 4 wk.

The Razor's Edge (Doubleday) NYT fic 5/14/44 (#4), pk 7/2/44 (#1, 4 wk), 43 wk; PW fic 5/20/44 (#4), pk 7/1/44 (#1, 6 wk), 28 wk; tot 71 wk.

Then and Now (Doubleday) NYT fic 6/16/46 (#3, 5 wk), 15 wk; PW fic 6/22/46 (#4), pk 7/6/46 (#3, 2 wk), 10 wk; tot 25 wk.

Creatures of Circumstance (Doubleday) NYT fic 8/17/47 (#14), pk 9/21/47 (#7, 1 wk), 8 wk; PW fic 9/13/47 (#10), pk 9/27/47 (#5, 1 wk), 2 wk; tot 10 wk.

Catalina (Doubleday) NYT fic 11/14/48 (#13), pk 12/5/48 (#7, 4 wk), 13 wk; PW fic 12/18/48 (#9, 1 wk); tot 14 wk.

A Writer's Notebook (Doubleday) NYT gen 11/13/49 (#11, 1 wk), 4 wk.

Maughan, A.M.
Harry of Monmouth (Sloane) NYT fic 4/15/56 (#16), pk 5/6/56 (#11, 2 wk), 10 wk; PW fic 5/21/56 (#10, 1 wk); tot 11 wk.

Mauldin, Bill
Up Front (World) NYT gen 7/1/45 (#11), pk 8/5/45 (#1, 20 wk), 42 wk; PW nf 7/7/45 (#5), pk 7/21/45 (#1, 25 wk), 39 wk; tot 81 wk.

Back Home (Sloan) NYT gen 11/23/47 (#16), pk 12/28/47 (#9, 1 wk), 11 wk; PW nf 12/20/47 (#10), pk 1/17/48 (#8, 2 wk), tot 13 wk.

Maupin, Armistead
Sure of You (Harper) NYT fic 11/12/89

(#15, 1 wk); PW hc fic 11/17/89 (#13, 1 wk); tot 2 wk.

Maurois, Andre
Ariel (Appleton) PW nf 6/21/24 (#5, 4 wk), 16 wk; PW gen lit 6/20/25 (#7, 4 wk); tot 20 wk.
Disraeli (Appleton) PW nf 4/28/28 (#1, 8 wk), 28 wk.
Byron (Appleton) PW nf 4/12/30 (#1, 8 wk), 24 wk.
The Edwardian Era (Appleton) PW nf 12/9/33 (#5, 4 wk), 12 wk.
The Miracle of England (Harper) NYT nf 6/6/37 (#5, 4 wk); PW nf 6/12/37 (#7, 8 wk), 16 wk; tot 20 wk.
The Art of Living (Harper) PW nf 5/11/40 (#6, 4 wk), 8 wk.
I Remember, I Remember (Harper) NYT nf 11/22/42 (#11, 1 wk).
Lelia (Harper) NYT gen 9/27/53 (#14), pk 11/22/53 (#3, 2 wk), 23 wk; PW nf 10/17/53 (#7), pk 12/5/53 (#2, 1 wk), 11 wk; tot 34 wk.
Olympio: The Life of Victor Hugo (Harper) NYT gen 5/27/56 (#16), pk 7/1/56 (#8, 1 wk), 14 wk.
The Titans (Harper) NYT gen 3/9/58 (#10, 1 wk), 3 wk.
Prometheus: The Life of Balzac (Harper) NYT gen 7/3/66 (#9, 1 wk).

Maxa, Kathleen
See Roxanne Pulitzer and_____

Maxwell, Elsa
R.S.V.P.: Elsa Maxwell's Own Story (Little Brown) NYT gen 11/14/54 (#10), pk 12/5/54 (#6, 1 wk), 15 wk; PW nf 12/18/54 (#7, 1 wk); tot 16 wk.

Maxwell, Gavin
Ring of Bright Water (Dutton) NYT gen 3/12/61 (#15), pk 4/23/61 (#3, 9 wk), 48 wk; PW nf 3/27/61 (#9), pk 6/12/61 (#2, 4 wk), 40 wk; tot 88 wk.

Maxwell, William
The Chateau (Knopf) NYT fic 4/16/61 (#12), pk 5/21/61 (#7, 1 wk), 14 wk; PW fic 5/1/61 (#7), pk 6/12/61 (#6, 1 wk), 6 wk; tot 20 wk.

May, Rollo
Man's Search for Himself (Norton) NYT gen 2/1/53 (#16), pk 2/15/53 (#14, 1 wk), 2 wk.
Love and Will (Norton) NYT gen 2/8/70 (#10), pk 4/26/70 (#5, 2 wk), 18 wk; PW nf 3/16/70 (#9), pk 4/13/70 (#5, 5 wk), 15 wk; tot 33 wk.

Mayer, Jane, and Doyle McManus
Landslide: The Unmaking of the President 1984–1988 (Houghton) NYT nf 10/9/88 (#5, 1 wk), 6 wk; PW hc nf 10/14/88 (#7), pk 10/21/88 (#6, 1 wk), 5 wk; tot 11 wk.

Mayer, Martin
Madison Avenue, U.S.A. (Harper) NYT gen 3/30/58 (#10), pk 4/27/58 (#4, 1 wk), 21 wk; PW nf 4/7/58 (#9), pk 4/28/58 (#5, 5 wk), 10 wk; tot 31 wk.
The Schools (Harper) NYT gen 5/28/61 (#16), pk 6/18/61 (#11, 1 wk), 4 wk.
The Lawyers (Harper) NYT gen 8/27/67 (#7), pk 9/10/67 (#6, 2 wk), 12 wk; PW nf 8/28/67 (#7), pk 9/4/67(#5, 1 wk), 13 wk; tot 25 wk.
The Bankers (Weybright & Talley) NYT gen 2/9/75 (#9), pk 4/13/75 (#4, 1 wk), 17 wk; PW nf 2/10/75 (#10), pk 4/7/75 (#4, 2 wk), 18 wk; tot 35 wk.

Mayo, Katherine
Mother India (Harcourt) PW nf 9/24/27 (#10), pk 12/31/27 (#2, 12 wk), 36 wk.

Mazel, Judy
The Beverly Hills Diet (Macmillan) PW hc nf 5/15/81 (#9), pk 7/17/81 (#1, 18 wk), 31 wk; NYT nf 5/24/81 (#4), pk 7/12/81 (#1, 16 wk), 30 wk; (Berkley) PW mm pb 4/2/82 (#13, 2 wk); NYT mm pb 4/4/82 (#15), pk 5/2/82 (#13, 1 wk), 3 wk; tot 66 wk.

Mazlish, Elaine
See Adele Faber and_____

Mazo, Earl
Richard Nixon (Harper) NYT gen 7/19/59 (#11), pk 8/16/59 (#6, 2 wk), 15 wk; PW nf 8/3/59 (#6, 1 wk), 7 wk; tot 22 wk.

Mead, E.S.
How to Succeed at Business Without Really Trying (Simon & Schuster) NYT gen 9/14/52 (#14), pk 9/28/52 (#10, 1 wk), 10 wk.

Mead, Margaret
Culture and Commitment (Doubleday) PW nf 3/9/70 (#8, 2 wk); NYT gen 3/22/70 (#9, 1 wk); tot 3 wk.

Means, Gaston B., and May D. Thacker
The Strange Death of President Harding (Guild Pub. Corp.) PW nf 5/17/30 (#3), pk 7/12/30 (#1, 12 wk), 36 wk.

Meara, Mary Jane Frances Cavolina, with Jeffrey Allen Joseph Stone, Maureen Anne Teresa Kelly and Richard Glen Michael Davis
Growing Up Catholic (Doubleday) NYT msc pb 6/2/85 (#8), pk 12/1/85 (#4, 1 wk), 36 wk; (Doubleday/Dolphin) PW td pb

6/21/85 (#8), pk 8/23/85 (#1, 1 wk), 39 wk; tot 75 wk.

Medaris, John B.
Countdown for Decision (Putnam) NYT gen 10/16/60 (#16, 1 wk).

Medearis, Mary
Big Doc's Girl (Lippincott) NYT fic 11/8/42 (#16, 1 wk).

Medved, Michael, and David Wallechinsky
What Really Happened to the Class of '65? (Ballantine) PW mm pb 8/22/77 (#14), pk 8/29/77 (#10, 2 wk), 5 wk; NYT mm pb 8/28/77 (#9), pk 9/4/77 (#6, 1 wk), 4 wk; tot 9 wk.

Meeker, Arthur, Jr.
The Ivory Mischief (Houghton) PW fic 2/14/42 (#6, 4 wk), 8 wk.
Prairie Avenue (Knopf) NYT fic 5/15/49 (#8), pk 5/22/49 (#6, 3 wk), 12 wk; PW fic 6/11/49 (#8, 1 wk); tot 13 wk.
Chicago, with Love (Knopf) NYT gen 11/6/55 (#16, 1 wk).

Meier, Paul
See Dr. Frank Minirth, et al.
See Robert Hemfelt, et al.

Meigs, Cornelia
The Willow Whistle (Macmillan) PW juv 11/14/31 (#7, 4 wk).

Meir, Golda
My Life (Putnam) NYT gen 12/21/75 (#7), pk 2/8/76 (#6, 1 wk), 9 wk; PW nf 12/29/75 (#8, 1 wk), 3 wk; PW hc nf 2/9/76 (#7, 1 wk), 2 wk; tot 14 wk.

Mellen, Joan
Bob Knight (Fine) NYT nf 10/16/88 (#15, 1 wk); PW hc nf 10/21/88 (#13, 1 wk); tot 2 wk.

Melman, Yossi
See Dan Raviv and _____

Mencken, Henry Louis [all titles as by H.L. Mencken]
Happy Days (Knopf) PW nf 3/9/40 (#9, 4 wk).
Heathen Days (Knopf) NYT nf 3/21/43 (#11), pk 4/11/43 (#9, 1 wk), 9 wk.
American Language Supplement (Knopf) NYT gen 9/16/45 (#16), pk 9/23/45 (#12, 1 wk), 6 wk.
American Language: Supplement II (Knopf) NYT gen 4/25/48 (#15, 1 wk).
A Mencken Chrestomathy (Knopf) NYT gen 8/7/49 (#12, 1 wk), 2 wk.
Minority Report (Knopf) NYT gen 6/10/56 (#14), pk 7/15/56 (#4, 1 wk), 14 wk; PW

nf 7/9/56 (#7), pk 7/23/56 (#3, 1 wk), 5 wk; tot 19 wk.

Menen, Salvator Aubrey Clarence
The Backward Bride (Scribners) NYT fic 9/3/50 (#15, 1 wk).
The Duke of Gallodoro (Scribners) NYT fic 3/16/52 (#14), pk 3/30/52 (#12, 1 wk), 5 wk.
The Ramayana [as told by] (Scribner) NYT fic 10/10/54 (#13, 3 wk).
The Abode of Love (Scribner) NYT fic 5/6/56 (#15), pk 5/13/56 (#14, 1 wk), 3 wk.
The Fig Tree (Scribner) NYT fic 4/5/59 (#14, 1 wk), 2 wk.

Menjou, Adolphe, and M.M. Musselman
It Took Nine Tailors (Whittlesey) NYT gen 4/4/48 (#15, 1 wk).

Mercer, Charles E.
Rachel Cade (Putnam) NYT fic 10/28/56 (#14), pk 11/11/56 (#13, 3 wk), 7 wk.
Enough Good Men (Putnam) NYT fic 2/21/60 (#16, 1 wk).

Mercier, Cardinal Desire Felicien Francois Joseph
Cardinal Mercier's Own Story (Doran) PW gen 6/12/20 (#7, 4 wk).

Meredith, Roy
Mr. Lincoln's Camera Man: Mathew B. Brady (Dover) NYT gen 3/10/46 (#9, 1 wk), 2 wk.

Mergendahl, Charles Henry
Don't Wait Up for Spring (Little Brown) NYT fic 12/17/44 (#11, 1 wk), 4 wk.
The Bramble Bush (Putnam) NYT fic 9/21/58 (#16), pk 10/12/58 (#12, 3 wk), 8 wk; PW fic 10/27/58 (#8, 1 wk); tot 9 wk.

Merle, Robert
The Day of the Dolphin (Simon & Schuster) PW fic 8/25/69 (#10, 1 wk).

Merriam, Robert E.
Dark December: The Full Account of the Battle of the Bulge (Ziff Davis) NYT gen 9/14/47 (#14, 1 wk).

Merrick, Elliott
Frost and Fire (Scribner) NYT fic 8/6/39 (#13, 4 wk).

Merrick, Gordon
The Lord Won't Mind (Geis) NYT fic 5/31/70 (#10), pk 7/19/70 (#7, 1 wk), 16 wk.

Merton, Thomas
The Seven Storey Mountain (Harcourt) NYT gen 12/19/48 (#16), pk 3/13/49 (#2, 22 wk), 61 wk; PW nf 1/15/49 (#8), pk 3/26/49 (#1, 5 wk), 48 wk; tot 109 wk.
The Waters of Siloe (Harcourt) NYT gen

10/2/49 (#11), pk 10/23/49 (#2, 4 wk), 18 wk; PW nf 10/15/49 (#6), pk 10/22/49 (#2, 2 wk), 11 wk; tot 29 wk.

Seeds of Contemplation (New Directions) NYT gen 5/15/49 (#14, 1 wk), 2 wk.

The Sign of Jonas (Harcourt) NYT gen 3/1/53 (#11), pk 4/12/53 (#7, 1 wk), 12 wk; PW nf 3/14/53 (#9), pk 3/28/53 (#6, 1 wk), 3 wk; tot 15 wk.

Meryman, Richard
Andrew Wyeth (Houghton) PW nf 11/18/68 (#9, 1 wk).
See also Joan Rivers and _____

Mesta, Perle, and Robert Cahn
Perle—My Story (McGraw) NYT gen 5/15/60 (#15), pk 6/5/60 (#8, 1 wk), 8 wk; PW nf 6/13/60 (#9), pk 6/27/60 (#8, 1 wk), 2 wk; tot 10 wk.

Metalious, Grace
Peyton Place (Messner) NYT fic 9/30/56 (#13), pk 11/25/56 (#1, 29 wk), 76 wk; PW fic 10/22/56 (#4), pk 11/5/56 (#1, 31 wk), 59 wk; tot 135 wk.

Return to Peyton Place (Messner) NYT fic 1/3/60 (#14), pk 1/24/60 (#13, 1 wk), 3 wk.

Meyer, Nicholas
The Seven-Per-Cent Solution [as by John H. Watson M.D., ed. Nicholas Meyer] (Dutton) NYT fic 9/15/74 (#10), pk 1/19/75 (#2, 9 wk), 40 wk; PW fic 9/16/74 (#8), pk 12/30/74 (#2, 11 wk), 39 wk; (Ballantine) NYT mm pb 8/17/75 (#10), pk 8/24/75 (#5, 3 wk), 7 wk; tot 86 wk.

The West End Horror (Dutton) PW hc fic 5/31/76 (#9), pk 6/21/76 (#7, 4 wk), 14 wk; NYT fic 6/13/76 (#10), pk 7/4/76 (#7, 1 wk), 11 wk; (Ballantine) PW mm pb 6/27/77 (#11, 1 wk), 3 wk; NYT mm pb 7/3/77 (#12, 1 wk); tot 29 wk.

Michael, Judith
Deceptions (Poseidon) NYT fic 5/30/82 (#11, 1 wk), 2 wk; (Pocket) PW mm pb 3/18/83 (#15), pk 4/1/83 (#6, 1 wk), 9 wk; NYT mm pb 3/20/83 (#5, 2 wk), 7 wk; tot 18 wk.

Possessions (Poseidon/Simon & Schuster) PW hc fic 6/8/84 (#13), pk 6/22/84 (#11, 2 wk), 10 wk; NYT fic 6/17/84 (#11, 1 wk), 9 wk; (Pocket) NYT pb fic 5/12/85 (#9), pk 5/19/85 (#3, 2 wk), 9 wk; PW mm pb 5/17/85 (#7), pk 5/31/85 (#2, 1 wk), 9 wk; tot 37 wk.

Private Affairs (Poseidon/Simon & Schuster) NYT fic 3/2/86 (#12), pk 3/16/86 (#8, 3 wk), 8 wk; PW hc fic 3/7/86 (#13), pk 3/28/86 (#6, 2 wk), 8 wk; (Pocket) NYT pb fic 3/8/87 (#12), pk 3/22/87 (#3, 3 wk), 13 wk; PW mm pb 3/20/87 (#7), pk 4/10/87 (#3, 2 wk), 9 wk; tot 38 wk.

Inheritance (Poseidon/Simon & Schuster) NYT fic 3/20/88 (#15), pk 4/17/88 (#4, 1 wk), 16 wk; PW hc fic 3/25/88 (#15), pk 4/22/88 (#4, 1 wk), 14 wk; (Pocket) NYT pb fic 2/5/89 (#6), pk 2/12/89 (#2, 2 wk), 11 wk; PW mm pb 2/10/89 (#7), pk 2/17/89 (#2, 2 wk), 10 wk; tot 51 wk.

A Ruling Passion (Simon & Schuster) NYT fic 1/21/90 (#8), pk 2/11/90 (#2, 1 wk), 11 wk; PW hc fic 1/26/90 (#6), pk 2/16/90 (#2, 1 wk), 11 wk; tot 22 wk.

Michaels, Barbara
Search the Shadows (Berkley) NYT pb fic 11/6/88 (#16), pk 11/20/88 (#10, 1 wk), 6 wk; PW mm pb 11/11/88 (#11), pk 11/25/88 (#6, 1 wk), 7 wk; tot 13 wk.

Shattered Silk (Berkley) PW mm pb 2/5/88 (#14, 1 wk), 2 wk; NYT pb fic 2/7/88 (#15, 1 wk); tot 3 wk.

Someone in the House (Berkley) NYT pb fic 6/11/89 (#14, 1 wk), 2 wk.

Smoke and Mirrors (Berkley) NYT pb fic 1/21/90 (#9, 1 wk), 2 wk; PW mm pb 1/26/90 (#13), pk 2/2/90 (#11, 1 wk), 2 wk; tot 4 wk.

Michaels, Fern
Captive Passions (Ballantine) NYT mm pb 7/24/77 (#15), pk 8/14/77 (#10, 1 wk), 3 wk; PW mm pb 8/8/77 (#11), pk 8/15/77 (#10, 1 wk), 2 wk; tot 5 wk.

Captive Embraces (Ballantine) NYT mm pb 5/20/79 (#13), pk 5/27/79 (#12, 1 wk), 3 wk; PW mm pb 5/21/79 (#11, 1 wk), 4 wk; tot 7 wk.

Captive Splendors (Ballantine) PW mm pb 7/18/80 (#15), pk 7/25/80 (#13, 1 wk), 3 wk.

Captive Innocence (Ballantine) PW mm pb 11/13/81 (#14), pk 11/20/81 (#11, 2 wk), 5 wk; NYT mm pb 11/15/81 (#9), pk 11/22/81 (#7, 1 wk), 5 wk; tot 10 wk.

Wild Honey (Pocket) NYT mm pb 11/14/82 (#10), pk 11/21/82 (#5, 1 wk), 7 wk; PW mm pb 11/19/82 (#14), pk 12/3/82 (#6, 1 wk), 4 wk; tot 11 wk.

Tender Warrior (Ballantine) PW mm pb 1/21/83 (#14, 1 wk); NYT mm pb 1/23/83 (#13, 1 wk); tot 2 wk.

Texas Rich (Ballantine) NYT pb fic 4/7/85 (#8), pk 5/5/85 (#3, 1 wk), 8 wk; PW mm pb 4/12/85 (#10), pk 5/3/85 (#3, 3 wk), 10 wk; tot 18 wk.

Texas Heat (Ballantine) NYT pb fic 6/8/86 (#9), pk 6/15/86 (#5, 2 wk), 8 wk; PW mm pb 6/13/86 (#7), pk 6/20/86 (#5, 2 wk), 6 wk; tot 14 wk.

To Taste the Wine (Balance) NYT pb fic 3/8/87 (#15), pk 3/22/87 (#7, 1 wk), 5 wk; PW mm pb 3/20/87 (#11, 1 wk), 3 wk; tot 8 wk.

Texas Fury (Ballantine) NYT pb fic 4/9/89 (#3, 1 wk), 6 wk; PW mm pb 4/14/89 (#4, 1 wk), 5 wk; tot 11 wk.

Sins of Omission (Ballantine) NYT pb fic 11/12/89 (#11), pk 11/19/89 (#10, 2 wk), 4 wk; PW mm pb 12/15/89 (#15, 1 wk); tot 5 wk.

Sins of the Flesh (Ballantine) NYT pb fic 6/10/90 (#8, 2 wk), 4 wk; PW mm pb 6/22/90 (#10, 1 wk); tot 5 wk.

Michaud, Steven G., and Hugh Aynesworth
Ted Bundy: Conversations with a Killer (NAL) NYT pb nf 7/9/89 (#11), pk 7/16/89 (#10, 1 wk), 2 wk.

Michelson, Charles
The Ghost Talks (Putnam) NYT gen 5/28/44 (#9), pk 6/18/44 (#8, 1 wk), 6 wk.

Michener, James A.
Fires of Spring (Random) NYT fic 2/27/49 (#14), pk 3/20/49 (#8, 2 wk), 14 wk.

Return to Paradise (Random) NYT fic 5/6/51 (#15), pk 6/17/51 (#3, 11 wk), 26 wk; PW fic 6/2/51 (#4), pk 6/30/51 (#3, 7 wk), 18 wk; tot 44 wk.

The Bridges at Toko-Ri (Random) NYT fic 8/2/53 (#6), pk 8/9/53 (#5, 2 wk), 12 wk; PW fic 8/8/53 (#5, 4 wk), 7 wk; tot 19 wk.

Sayonara (Random) NYT fic 2/14/54 (#6), pk 3/14/54 (#2, 7 wk), 21 wk; PW fic 2/20/54 (#3), pk 3/27/54 (#2, 6 wk), 17 wk; tot 38 wk.

The Bridge at Andau (Random) NYT gen 3/24/57 (#10), pk 4/14/57 (#3, 1 wk), 11 wk; PW nf 4/1/57 (#4, 3 wk), 9 wk; tot 20 wk.

Hawaii (Random) PW fic 11/30/59 (#9), pk 2/15/60 (#1, 41 wk), 88 wk; NYT fic 11/22/59 (#15), pk 1/17/60 (#1, 49 wk), 94 wk; NYT pb fic 2/5/67 (#4, 8 wk); tot 190 wk.

Caravans (Random) NYT fic 8/11/63 (#10), pk 9/8/63 (#2, 4 wk), 29 wk; PW fic 8/26/63 (#6), pk 9/16/63 (#2, 4 wk), 29 wk; tot 58 wk.

The Source (Random) NYT fic 5/30/65 (#7), pk 7/11/65 (#1, 39 wk), 69 wk; PW fic 6/7/65 (#9), pk 7/12/65 (#1, 35 wk), 73 wk; NYT pb fic 2/5/67 (#1, 12 wk), 40 wk; tot 182 wk.

Iberia (Random) NYT gen 5/26/68 (#6), pk 6/23/68 (#2, 5 wk), 28 wk; PW nf 5/27/68 (#7), pk 7/1/68 (#1, 4 wk), 30 wk; NYT pb gen 11/2/69 (#4), pk 1/4/70 (#2, 4 wk), 16 wk; tot 74 wk.

The Drifters (Random) PW fic 6/14/71 (#10), pk 9/6/71 (#3, 3 wk), 24 wk; NYT fic 6/20/71 (#8), pk 7/25/71 (#4, 3 wk), 22 wk; NYT pb fic 6/11/72 (#2, 8 wk), 16 wk; tot 62 wk.

Centennial (Random) PW fic 8/26/74

(#7), pk 10/7/74 (#1, 28 wk), 60 wk; NYT fic 9/1/74 (#9), pk 10/13/74 (#1, 28 wk), 60 wk; (Fawcett/Crest) NYT mm pb 11/19/75 (#7), pk 12/21/75 (#1, 2 wk), 44 wk; PW mm pb 2/2/76 (#3), pk 2/16/76 (#2, 1 wk), 31 wk; tot 195 wk.

Chesapeake (Random) PW hc fic 7/17/78 (#5), pk 7/24/78 (#1, 18 wk), 59 wk; NYT fic 7/23/78 (#1, 14 wk), 48 wk; (Fawcett/Crest) PW mm pb 8/27/79 (#6), pk 9/3/79 (#1, 5 wk), 18 wk; NYT mm pb 9/2/79 (#7), pk 9/9/79 (#1, 6 wk), 21 wk; tot 146 wk.

The Covenant (Random) PW hc fic 10/24/80 (#8), pk 11/7/80 (#1, 24 wk), 42 wk; NYT fic 10/26/80 (#8), pk 11/2/80 (#1, 25 wk), 41 wk; (Fawcett/Crest) NYT mm pb 2/14/82 (#12), pk 2/28/82 (#1, 3 wk), 13 wk; PW mm pb 2/19/82 (#6), pk 3/5/82 (#1, 2 wk), 12 wk; tot 108 wk.

Space (Random) PW hc fic 10/1/82 (#9), pk 10/15/82 (#1, 20 wk), 34 wk; NYT fic 10/3/82 (#5), pk 10/10/82 (#1, 22 wk), 39 wk; (Fawcett/Crest) NYT mm pb 10/23/83 (#9), pk 10/30/83 (#1, 2 wk), 10 wk; PW mm pb 10/28/83 (#4), pk 11/4/83 (#1, 1 wk), 17 wk; NYT pb fic 1/1/84 (#3), pk 1/8/84 (#2, 1 wk), 10 wk; tot 110 wk.

Poland (Random) NYT fic 9/4/83 (#2), pk 9/11/83 (#1, 12 wk), 38 wk; PW hc fic 9/9/83 (#4), pk 9/16/83 (#1, 12 wk), 38 wk; (Fawcett/Crest) NYT pb fic 10/28/84 (#3), pk 11/4/84 (#2, 1 wk), 14 wk; PW mm pb 11/2/84 (#6), pk 11/9/84 (#2, 1 wk), 13 wk; tot 103 wk.

Texas (Random) NYT fic 10/13/85 (#1, 6 wk), 29 wk; PW hc fic 10/18/85 (#2), pk 10/25/85 (#1, 5 wk), 30 wk; (Fawcett) NYT pb fic 7/26/87 (#8), pk 8/9/87 (#3, 1 wk), 10 wk; PW mm pb 7/31/87 (#7), pk 8/14/87 (#3, 1 wk), 10 wk; tot 79 wk.

Legacy (Random) NYT fic 9/6/87 (#6), pk 9/27/87 (#3, 1 wk), 18 wk; PW hc fic 9/11/87 (#5), pk 9/25/87 (#3, 1 wk), 18 wk; (Fawcett/Crest) NYT pb fic 8/28/88 (#16), pk 10/2/88 (#7, 1 wk), 4 wk; PW mm pb 9/23/88 (#13, 1 wk); tot 41 wk.

Alaska (Random) NYT fic 7/3/88 (#1, 5 wk), 33 wk; PW hc fic 7/8/88 (#1, 5 wk), 32 wk; (Fawcett Crest) NYT pb fic 6/25/89 (#10), pk 7/2/89 (#3, 1 wk), 11 wk; PW mm pb 6/30/89 (#8), pk 7/21/89 (#3, 1 wk), 8 wk; tot 84 wk.

Journey (Random) PW hc fic 7/28/89 (#13), pk 8/18/89 (#7, 1 wk), 9 wk; NYT fic 7/30/89 (#13), pk 8/6/89 (#6, 1 wk), 10 wk; tot 19 wk.

Caribbean (Random) NYT fic 11/19/89 (#4), pk 1/28/90 (#2, 1 wk), 22 wk; PW hc fic 11/24/89 (#4), pk 12/8/89 (#3, 5 wk), 18 wk; tot 40 wk.

_____, and Arthur G. Day
Rascals in Paradise (Random) NYT gen 7/7/57 (#13), pk 8/11/57 (#6, 3 wk), 17 wk; PW nf 7/29/57 (#7), pk 8/12/57 (#6, 3 wk), 9 wk; tot 26 wk.

Michie, Allan
Retreat to Victory (Alliance) NYT nf 9/6/42 (#14, 1 wk).

Mickler, Ernest Matthew
White Trash Cooking (Ten Speed) PW td pb 1/16/87 (#8, 1 wk).

Midler, Bette
A View from a Broad (Simon & Schuster) NYT nf 4/27/80 (#14, 1 wk), 3 wk; PW hc nf 6/20/80 (#11, 1 wk), 2 wk; tot 5 wk.
The Saga of Baby Divine [illus. Todd Schorr] (Crown) NYT fic 10/23/83 (#9), pk 11/27/83 (#5, 4 wk), 14 wk; PW hc fic 11/4/83 (#10), pk 12/16/83 (#3, 1 wk), 14 wk; tot 28 wk.

Miers, Earl Schenck
The General Who Marched to Hell (Collier) NYT gen 7/15/51 (#15, 1 wk).
America and Its Presidents (Grosset & Dunlap) NYT ch bst 11/13/60 (#16, 27 wk).

_____, and Richard Brown
Gettysburg (Rutgers Univ.) NYT gen 7/11/48 (#13), pk 8/22/48 (#8, 1 wk), 7 wk.

Milford, Nancy
Zelda (Harper) NYT gen 6/28/70 (#9), pk 8/2/70 (#3, 6 wk), 22 wk; PW nf 6/29/70 (#5), pk 8/10/70 (#2, 1 wk), 25 wk; NYT pb gen 8/8/71 (#3, 8 wk), 12 wk; tot 59 wk.

Millar, George Reid
Isabel and the Sea (Doubleday) NYT gen 8/15/48 (#15, 1 wk).

Millay, Edna St. Vincent
The Buck in the Snow (Harper) PW nf 11/24/28 (#3, 8 wk), 16 wk.
Fatal Interview (Harper) PW nf 5/16/31 (#5), pk 6/20/31 (#3, 8 wk), 20 wk.
Wine from These Grapes (Harper) PW nf 12/15/34 (#4), pk 1/12/35 (#2, 8 wk), 16 wk.
Conversation at Midnight (Harper) PW nf 8/14/37 (#8), pk 9/11/37 (#3, 4 wk), 16 wk; NYT gen 9/12/37 (#2, 4 wk), 8 wk; tot 24 wk.
Huntsman, What Quarry? (Harper) PW nf 6/10/39 (#6, 8 wk), 12 wk; NYT gen 7/9/39 (#1, 4 wk), 8 wk; tot 20 wk.
See also Charles Baudelaire

Miller, Alice Duer
The White Cliffs (Coward McCann) PW nf 12/14/40 (#10), pk 7/12/41 (#1, 1 wk), 13 wk.
I Have Loved England (Putnam) PW nf 8/16/41 (#5, 8 wk).

Miller, Arthur
Focus (Reynal & Hitchcock) NYT fic 2/3/46 (#15, 1 wk).
Death of a Salesman (Viking) NYT gen 6/5/49 (#7, 1 wk), 5 wk.

Miller, Caroline Pafford
Lamb in His Bosom (Harper) PW fic 6/9/34 (#3), pk 7/14/34 (#1, 12 wk), 32 wk.
Lebanon (Blakiston) NYT fic 8/13/44 (#10), pk 8/27/44 (#8, 1 wk), 6 wk.

Miller, Chuck
See Tim Underwood and _____

Miller, Douglas
You Can't Do Business with Hitler (Little Brown) PW nf 8/16/41 (#3), pk 9/13/41 (#2, 8 wk), 16 wk.

Miller, Francis Trevelyn
The World's Great Adventure (Winston) PW juv 7/12/30 (#7, 4 wk), 12 wk.
History of World War II (Universal) NYT gen 12/2/45 (#13), pk 12/16/45 (#6, 1 wk), 4 wk.

Miller, Frank, with Klaus Janson and Lynn Barley
Batman: The Dark Knight Returns (Warner) PW td pb 7/28/89 (#9, 1 wk).

Miller, Helen Topping
Storm Over Eden (Grosset & Dunlap) NYT fic 9/12/37 (#10, 4 wk).
Never Another Moon (Appleton) NYT fic 9/4/38 (#12, 4 wk).

Miller, Henry
Tropic of Cancer (Grove) NYT fic 7/2/61 (#10), pk 7/23/61 (#5, 1 wk), 25 wk; PW fic 7/10/61 (#12), pk 8/21/61 (#6, 2 wk), 21 wk; tot 46 wk.

Miller, Jonathan
The Human Body (Viking) NYT nf 12/18/83 (#9, 3 wk); PW hc nf 12/23/83 (#13, 2 wk), 4 wk; NYT msc 1/8/84 (#1, 1 wk), 4 wk; tot 11 wk.

Miller, Lee G.
The Story of Ernie Pyle (Viking) NYT gen 9/17/50 (#13), pk 9/24/50 (#7, 2 wk), 9 wk; PW nf 9/30/50 (#5, 3 wk); tot 12 wk.

Miller, Merle
That Winter (Sloane) NYT fic 2/8/48 (#16), pk 3/7/48 (#7, 2 wk), 9 wk.
Reunion (Viking) NYT fic 11/7/54 (#15), pk 11/21/54 (#11, 2 wk), 7 wk.
Plain Speaking (Putnam) NYT gen 1/27/74 (#9), pk 2/24/74 (#1, 11 wk), 38 wk; PW nf 1/28/74 (#4), pk 2/11/74 (#1, 11 wk), 30 wk; (Berkley) NYT mm pb 11/10/74 (#3), pk 1/12/75 (#2, 4 wk), 20 wk; tot 88 wk.

Lyndon: An Oral Biography (Putnam) PW hc nf 9/5/80 (#12), pk 10/10/80 (#7, 1 wk), 9 wk; NYT nf 9/28/80 (#11), pk 10/5/80 (#9, 1 wk), 5 wk; tot 14 wk.

Miller, Sue
The Good Mother (Harper) NYT fic 5/18/ 86 (#9), pk 6/8/86 (#4, 1 wk), 24 wk; PW hc fic 5/23/86 (#10), 5/30/86 (#6, 2 wk), 16 wk; (Dell) NYT pb fic 5/3/87 (#2, 5 wk), 12 wk; PW mm pb 5/8/87 (#9), pk 5/15/87 (#2, 4 wk), 11 wk; tot 63 wk.
Family Pictures (Harper) NYT fic 5/13/90 (#15), pk 5/27/90 (#8, 1 wk), 9 wk; PW hc fic 5/18/90 (#9, 2 wk), 7 wk; tot 16 wk.

Miller, William "Fishbait," as told to Frances Spatz Leighton
Fishbait: The Memoirs of the Congressional Doorkeeper (Prentice Hall) PW hc nf 5/23/77 (#8), pk 6/13/77 (#6, 1 wk), 8 wk; NYT nf 5/29/77 (#10), pk 7/24/77 (#8, 1 wk), 12 wk; tot 20 wk.

Millett, Kate
Sexual Politics (Doubleday) NYT gen 9/ 13/70 (#10), pk 10/4/70 (#7, 2 wk), 8 wk; PW nf 9/28/70 (#7), pk 11/2/70 (#6, 1 wk), 9 wk; tot 17 wk.

Milligan, Maurice M.
The Inside Story of the Pendergast Machine (Scribner) NYT gen 4/25/48 (#9), pk 5/2/48 (#8, 2 wk), 8 wk.

Millis, Walter
Road to War (Houghton) PW nf 6/15/35 (#4, 8 wk), 12 wk.
Why Europe Fights (Morrow) PW nf 8/10/ 40 (#7, 4 wk).
See also James Forrestal, et al.

Mills, Charles (11-)
The Choice (Macmillan) NYT fic 5/2/43 (#7, 1 wk), 4 wk.
The Alexandrians (Putnam) NYT fic 6/22/ 52 (#15), pk 7/27/52 (#9, 1 wk), 12 wk.

Mills, Charles Wright (11-)
The Power Elite (Oxford Univ.) NYT gen 7/29/56 (#15, 1 wk).

Mills, James
Report to the Commissioner (Farrar) PW fic 8/14/72 (#10), pk 9/4/72 (#6, 2 wk), 8 wk; NYT fic 8/20/72 (#10), pk 9/24/72 (#7, 1 wk), 7 wk; tot 15 wk.
The Underground Empire: Where Crime and Governments Embrace (Doubleday) PW hc nf 7/18/86 (#15), pk 7/25/86 (#14, 1 wk), 3 wk; NYT nf 7/20/86 (#12), pk 8/3/86 (#9, 1 wk), 9 wk; tot 12 wk.

Milne, Alan Alexander [all titles as by A.A. Milne]
When We Were Very Young (Dutton) PW gen lit 4/18/25 (#5), pk 6/20/25 (#2, 8 wk), 16 wk; PW nf 10/24/25 (#2, 4 wk), 20 wk; tot 36 wk.
Winnie-The-Pooh (Dutton) PW nf 12/18/ 26 (#10, 4 wk); NYT ch bst 5/14/61 (#11), pk 5/8/66 (#1, 19 wk), 378 wk; [trans. Alexander Lenard] *Winnie Ille Pu* (Dutton) NYT fic 2/19/61 (#16), pk 3/19/61 (#7, 5 wk), 20 wk; PW fic 3/13/61 (#9), 3/20/61 (#4, 3 wk), 13 wk; tot 415 wk.
Now We Are Six (Dutton) PW nf 12/31/27 (#9, 4 wk).
The Christopher Robin Story Book (Dutton) PW juv 2/15/30 (#3, 8 wk), 28 wk.
The Christopher Robin Birthday Book (Dutton) PW juv 5/16/31 (#10, 4 wk).
Two People (Dutton) PW fic 1/16/32 (#9, 4 wk).
Autobiography (Dutton) NYT gen 11/5/39 (#13, 4 wk).
Chloe Marr (Dutton) NYT fic 9/22/46 (#16, 1 wk).
The World of Pooh (Dutton) NYT ch bst 11/2/58 (#1, 40 wk), 78 wk.
The World of Christopher Robin (Dutton) NYT ch bst 11/1/59 (#12, 25 wk).
Once on a Time (New York Graphic Society) NYT ch bst 5/13/62 (#16, 19 wk).

Milton, George Fort
The Use of Presidential Power 1789–1943 (Little Brown) NYT gen 6/4/44 (#14, 1 wk).

Minarik, Else Holmelund
Little Bear (Harper) NYT ch bst 11/17/57 (#3, 40 wk).
Little Bear's Friend (Harper) NYT ch bst 11/13/60 (#10, 27 wk).

Mindell, Earl
Earl Mindell's Vitamin Bible (Warner) PW mm pb 2/27/81 (#13), pk 3/13/81 (#9, 2 wk), 13 wk; NYT mm pb 3/15/81 (#15), pk 4/19/81 (#12, 1 wk), 5 wk; tot 18 wk.

Minirth, Dr. Frank, with Paul Meier, Robert Hemfelt and Sharon Sneed
Love Hunger (Nelson) PW hc nf 3/30/90 (#13, 1 wk); PW hc rel 10/5/90 (#3, 4 wk), 8 wk; tot 9 wk.
See also Robert Hemfelt, et al.

Mintz, Morton, and Jerry S. Cohen
America, Inc. (Dial) NYT gen 7/4/71 (#9), pk 9/19/71 (#2, 1 wk), 17 wk; PW nf 7/5/71 (#6), pk 8/2/71 (#3, 6 wk), 16 wk; tot 33 wk.

Mishima, Yukio
The Sound of Waves (Knopf) NYT fic 10/7/ 56 (#13, 1 wk).

Miss Piggy
See Henry Beard

"Miss Read"
See Dora Jessie Saint

Mr. Fresh and the Supreme Rockers
Breakdancing (Avon) NYT msc pb 5/20/ 84 (#8), pk 6/17/84 (#1, 3 wk), 13 wk; PW td pb 5/25/84 (#5), pk 6/22/84 (#2, 5 wk), 14 wk; tot 27 wk.

Mitchell, Margaret
Gone with the Wind (Macmillan) NYT fic 8/2/36 (#1, 40 wk), 80 wk; PW fic 8/15/36 (#1, 44 wk), 64 wk; NYT pb fic 12/3/67 (#5, 4 wk); (Macmillan/50th Anniversary Facsimile Edition) NYT fic 6/22/86 (#10), pk 7/13/86 (#9, 1 wk), 5 wk; PW hc fic 6/27/86 (#11), pk 7/18/86 (#9, 1 wk), 7 wk; tot 160 wk.

Mitchell, Steve
How to Speak Southern [illus. Scrawls] (Bantam) PW mm pb 2/7/77 (#12, 1 wk).

Mitchell, V.E.
Enemy Unseen (Pocket) NYT pb fic 10/ 14/90 (#9, 1 wk), 3 wk.

Mitford, Jessica
Daughters and Rebels (Houghton) NYT gen 8/21/60 (#16), pk 9/4/60 (#14, 1 wk), 4 wk.
The American Way of Death (Simon & Schuster) NYT gen 9/15/63 (#10), pk 12/8/ 63 (#1, 3 wk), 23 wk; PW nf 9/23/63 (#6), pk 10/21/63 (#1, 3 wk), 24 wk; tot 47 wk.

Mitford, Nancy
The Pursuit of Love (Random) NYT fic 7/7/46 (#8, 1 wk), 8 wk.
Love in a Cold Climate (Random) NYT fic 7/31/49 (#12), pk 8/7/49 (#11, 1 wk), 5 wk.
The Blessing (Random) NYT fic 10/28/51 (#9), pk 11/11/51 (#8, 2 wk), 14 wk.
Madame de Pompadour (Random) NYT gen 6/27/54 (#16), pk 8/15/54 (#7, 2 wk), 17 wk; PW nf 8/14/54 (#8), pk 8/21/54 (#7, 2 wk), 4 wk; tot 21 wk.
Noblesse Oblige (Harper) NYT gen 8/19/56 (#10, 1 wk), 7 wk.
Voltaire in Love (Harper) NYT gen 3/16/ 58 (#16), pk 3/30/58 (#12, 2 wk), 9 wk.
Don't Tell Alfred (Harper) NYT fic 4/16/61 (#15), pk 6/11/61 (#6, 1 wk), 13 wk; PW fic 5/8/61 (#6, 1 wk), 5 wk; tot 18 wk.

Mizener, Arthur
The Far Side of Paradise (Houghton) NYT

gen 2/11/51 (#9), pk 3/11/51 (#2, 2 wk), 16 wk; PW nf 3/3/51 (#5), pk 3/31/51 (#2, 1 wk), 9 wk; tot 25 wk.

Moats, Alice-Leone
No Nice Girl Swears (Knopf) PW nf 8/12/ 33 (#8, 4 wk).
Blind Date with Mars (Doubleday) NYT nf 3/21/43 (#21), pk 3/28/43 (#18, 1 wk), 2 wk.

Moll, Elick
Seidman and Son (Putnam) NYT fic 6/15/ 58 (#12), pk 8/3/58 (#6, 1 wk), 15 wk; PW fic 6/30/58 (#7), pk 7/14/58 (#6, 2 wk), 8 wk; tot 23 wk.

Molloy, John T.
The Woman's Dress for Success Book (Follett) PW hc nf 11/14/77 (#11), pk 11/28/77 (#7, 2 wk), 19 wk; NYT nf 11/20/77 (#13), pk 2/5/ 78 (#7, 2 wk), 18 wk; (Warner) PW td pb 9/25/78 (#9), pk 10/9/78 (#2, 4 wk), 15 wk; NYT td pb 11/12/78 (#7), pk 11/19/78 (#6, 1 wk), 42 wk; tot 94 wk.

Molloy, Paul
A Pennant for the Kremlin (Doubleday) NYT fic 11/8/64 (#10, 1 wk); PW fic 2/1/65 (#12, 1 wk); tot 2 wk.

Molloy, Robert
Pride's Way (Macmillan) NYT fic 6/10/45 (#14), pk 6/17/45 (#8, 2 wk), 7 wk.

Monaghan, Jay
See Ramon F. Adams

Monahan, James
Before I Sleep (Farrar) NYT gen 1/7/62 (#16), pk 2/18/62 (#9, 1 wk), 17 wk; PW nf 3/12/62 (#13, 1 wk); tot 18 wk.

Monsarrat, Nicholas
Leave Cancelled (Knopf) NYT fic 10/21/45 (#16), pk 11/11/45 (#13, 1 wk), 4 wk.
The Cruel Sea (Knopf) NYT fic 8/19/51 (#14), pk 9/30/51 (#2, 22 wk), 61 wk; PW fic 9/1/51 (#3), pk 9/22/51 (#2, 18 wk), 43 wk; tot 104 wk.
The Story of Esther Costello (Knopf) NYT fic 10/11/53 (#12, 1 wk).
The Tribe That Lost Its Head (Sloane) PW fic 11/26/56 (#4), pk 12/3/56 (#3, 5 wk), 14 wk; NYT fic 11/11/56 (#16), pk 12/9/56 (#3, 7 wk), 20 wk; tot 34 wk.
The Nylon Pirates (Sloane) NYT fic 11/6/ 60 (#15), pk 12/18/60 (#10, 1 wk), 15 wk; PW fic 12/19/60 (#10, 1 wk); tot 16 wk.
The White Rajah (Sloane) NYT fic 10/22/ 61 (#10), pk 11/5/61 (#9, 1 wk), 8 wk.

Montagne, Prosper
Larousse Gastronomique (Crown) NYT gen 11/19/61 (#16), pk 1/7/62 (#11, 1 wk), 9 wk.

Montagu, Ashley
The Cultured Man (World) NYT gen 8/24/58 (#14, 2 wk), 5 wk.

Montagu, E.E.
The Man Who Never Was (Lippincott) NYT gen 2/21/54 (#10), pk 2/28/54 (#5, 2 wk), 18 wk; PW nf 3/6/54 (#5, 3 wk), 6 wk; tot 24 wk.

Montapert, William David
The Omega Strategy: How You Can Retire Rich by 1986 (Warner) PW hc nf 3/23/84 (#11, 1 wk).

Montgomery, Bernard Law
The Memoirs of Field-Marshal The Viscount Montgomery of Alamein [as by Viscount Montgomery of Alamein] (World) NYT gen 11/2/58 (#14), pk 1/4/59 (#3, 2 wk), 18 wk; PW nf 11/24/58 (#7), pk 12/29/58 (#3, 1 wk), 14 wk; tot 32 wk.

Montgomery, Ruth
A Gift of Prophecy (Morrow) NYT gen 8/29/65 (#8), pk 11/28/65 (#2, 3 wk), 33 wk; PW nf 9/13/65 (#7), pk 11/22/65 (#2, 2 wk), 36 wk; NYT pb gen 7/3/66 (#1, 12 wk), 32 wk; tot 101 wk.
A World Beyond (Coward McCann) NYT gen 4/16/72 (#7, 1 wk), 5 wk; PW nf 5/8/72 (#10), pk 5/15/72 (#6, 2 wk), 12 wk; tot 17 wk.

Moody, Ralph
Little Britches (Norton) NYT gen 1/21/51 (#12), pk 2/11/51 (#11, 1 wk), 4 wk; PW nf 2/17/51 (#9, 1 wk); tot 5 wk.

Moody, Dr. Raymond A., Jr.
Life After Life (Mockingbird) NYT td pb 8/22/76 (#5), pk 10/10/76 (#1, 5 wk), 18 wk; PW td pb 9/6/76 (#2), pk 10/4/76 (#1, 4 wk), 11 wk; (Bantam) PW mm pb 11/22/76 (#5), pk 1/24/77 (#2, 2 wk), 37 wk; NYT mm pb 1/2/77 (#8), pk 1/23/77 (#2, 2 wk), 35 wk; tot 101 wk.
Reflections on Life After Life (Mockingbird/Bantam) NYT td pb 9/11/77 (#10, 1 wk), 7 wk.

Moon, Elizabeth
See Anne McCaffrey and _____

Moon, Lorna
Dark Star (Bobbs Merrill) PW fic 5/11/29 (#7, 4 wk), 8 wk.

Moon, William Least Heat
Blue Highways (Atlantic Little Brown) NYT nf 2/20/83 (#7), pk 2/27/83 (#5, 11 wk), 41 wk; PW hc nf 2/25/83 (#7), pk 3/18/83 (#5, 8 wk), 36 wk; (Fawcett/Crest) NYT pb nf 1/29/84 (#1, 1 wk), 35 wk; PW mm pb 2/3/84 (#4), pk 3/2/84 (#3, 1 wk), 15 wk; tot 127 wk.

Moore, Frederick
With Japan's Leaders (Scribner) NYT nf 8/16/42 (#15, 1 wk).

Moore, Grace
You're Only Human Once (Doubleday) NYT gen 4/16/44 (#9, 1 wk), 6 wk; PW nf 5/13/44 (#9, 1 wk); tot 7 wk.

Moore, John Cecil
The Waters Under the Earth (Lippincott) NYT fic 12/5/65 (#10, 1 wk).

Moore, Kelly, and Dan Reed
Deadly Medicine (St. Martin's) NYT pb nf 10/1/89 (#8), pk 10/22/89 (#6, 2 wk), 7 wk.

Moore, Robin
The Green Berets (Crown) PW fic 6/28/65 (#9), pk 8/2/65 (#2, 7 wk), 30 wk; NYT fic 7/4/65 (#7), pk 10/24/65 (#2, 1 wk), 26 wk; NYT pb fic 12/5/65 (#2), pk 1/2/66 (#1, 8 wk), 32 wk; tot 88 wk.

Moore, Ruth
Spoonhandle (Morrow) NYT fic 7/14/46 (#8), pk 8/11/46 (#6, 2 wk), 15 wk; PW fic 9/14/46 (#9, 1 wk), 2 wk; tot 17 wk.
The Fire Balloon (Morrow) NYT fic 1/2/49 (#16, 1 wk).

Moore, Ruth Ellen
Man, Time and Fossils (Knopf) NYT gen 11/29/53 (#16), pk 12/6/53 (#13, 2 wk), 6 wk.

Moorehead, Alan
The Russian Revolution (Harper) NYT gen 9/14/58 (#13), pk 9/21/58 (#10, 1 wk), 8 wk.
No Room in the Ark (Harper) NYT gen 2/21/60 (#10, 1 wk), 6 wk.
The White Nile (Harper) NYT gen 1/29/61 (#11), pk 3/19/61 (#4, 1 wk), 15 wk; PW nf 2/6/61 (#9), pk 3/6/61 (#4, 1 wk), 8 wk; tot 23 wk.
The Blue Nile (Harper) NYT gen 9/2/62 (#16), pk 10/7/62 (#6, 2 wk), 16 wk; PW nf 9/3/62 (#11), pk 11/5/62 (#4, 1 wk), 15 wk; tot 31 wk.
The Fatal Impact: The Invasion of the South Pacific (Harper) PW nf 5/9/66 (#9, 1 wk).

Moorehouse, Ward
American Reveille (Putnam) NYT fic 8/16/42 (#10, 1 wk), 2 wk.

Moran, Charles McMoran Wilson
Churchill: The Struggle for Survival 1940–1965 (Houghton Mifflin) PW nf 6/6/66 (#10), pk 7/4/66 (#9, 2 wk), 9 wk; NYT gen 6/26/66 (#8), pk 7/3/66 (#7, 1 wk), 3 wk; tot 12 wk.

Moravia, Alberto
The Woman of Rome (Farrar) NYT fic 11/27/49 (#14), pk 12/11/49 (#5, 2 wk), 14 wk;

PW fic 12/31/49 (#5, 3 wk), 4 wk; tot 18 wk.

Two Adolescents (Farrar) NYT fic 8/13/50 (#9), pk 9/3/50 (#6, 2 wk), 11 wk; PW fic 9/9/50 (#5, 1 wk), 2 wk; tot 13 wk.

The Fancy Dress Party (Farrar) NYT fic 8/31/52 (#16), pk 9/7/52 (#15, 1 wk), 2 pk.

Two Women (Farrar) NYT fic 6/22/58 (#15, 2 wk), 3 wk.

Morehouse, Laurence E., and Leonard Gross

Total Fitness in 30 Minutes a Week (Simon & Schuster) PW nf 4/28/75 (#10), pk 6/23/75 (#2, 2 wk), 33 wk; NYT gen 5/4/75 (#6), pk 6/22/75 (#2, 6 wk), 32 wk; (Pocket) NYT mm pb 2/22/76 (#10), pk 3/7/76 (#9, 2 wk), 4 wk; PW mm pb 2/23/76 (#10), pk 3/8/76 (#6, 1 wk), 8 wk; tot 77 wk.

Morgan, Al

The Great Man (Dutton) NYT fic 9/11/55 (#14), pk 10/9/55 (#10, 2 wk), 6 wk.

Morgan, Alice B.

Investors' Road Map (Simon & Schuster) NYT gen 2/10/57 (#15), pk 3/24/57 (#7, 1 wk), 11 wk; PW nf 3/18/57 (#7), pk 4/22/57 (#5, 1 wk), 5 wk; tot 16 wk.

Morgan, Charles

The Fountain (Knopf) PW fic 7/9/32 (#1, 16 wk), 32 wk.

Sparkenbroke (Macmillan) NYT fic 5/3/36 (#2, 4 wk), 12 wk; PW fic 5/9/36 (#4), pk 6/13/36 (#1, 8 wk), 20 wk; tot 32 wk.

Morgan, Charles

The Voyage (Macmillan) PW fic 12/14/40 (#7, 4 wk), 12 wk.

Challenge to Venus (Macmillan) NYT fic 4/21/57 (#16, 1 wk).

Morgan, Elaine

The Descent of Woman (Stein & Day) NYT gen 6/25/72 (#7, 1 wk).

Morgan, Marabel

The Total Woman (Revell) NYT gen 11/3/74 (#10), pk 6/8/75 (#8, 1 wk), 7 wk; PW nf 11/4/74 (#10), pk 5/26/75 (#6, 1 wk), 17 wk; (Pocket) NYT mm pb 11/16/75 (#4), pk 11/23/75 (#3, 2 wk), 14 wk; PW mm pb 3/29/76 (#8, 1 wk), 3 wk; tot 41 wk.

Morgan-Witts, Max

See Gordon Thomas and _____

Morgenstern, George

Pearl Harbor (Devin Adair) NYT gen 2/16/47 (#14), pk 3/2/47 (#6, 3 wk), 9 wk; PW nf 3/15/47 (#10, 1 wk); tot 10 wk.

Morgenstern, Michael

How to Make Love to a Woman (Potter)

PW hc nf 7/2/82 (#12), pk 9/3/82 (#9, 1 wk), 16 wk; NYT nf 7/18/82 (#12), pk 10/3/82 (#10, 1 wk), 13 wk; tot 29 wk.

Morgenthau, Henry

Germany Is Our Problem (Harper) NYT gen 11/4/45 (#12, 1 wk), 2 wk.

Morison, Samuel Eliot

Operations in North African Waters (Little Brown) NYT gen 3/23/47 (#15), pk 4/6/47 (#13, 1 wk), 4 wk.

The Atlantic Battle Won (Little Brown) NYT gen 3/25/56 (#15, 1 wk).

The Liberation of the Philippines (Little Brown) NYT gen 12/13/59 (#15), pk 12/20/59 (#13, 1 wk), 2 wk.

John Paul Jones (Little Brown) NYT gen 10/4/59 (#11, 2 wk), 7 wk.

The Oxford History of the American People (Oxford Univ.) NYT gen 5/16/65 (#6), pk 6/6/65 (#2, 7 wk), 20 wk; PW nf 5/24/65 (#6), pk 6/14/65 (#2, 5 wk), 24 wk; tot 44 wk.

Spring Tides (Houghton) PW nf 8/23/65 (#11, 1 wk).

The European Discovery of America (Oxford Univ.) PW nf 5/3/71 (#7), pk 7/5/71 (#5, 2 wk), 14 wk; NYT gen 5/9/71 (#9), pk 6/27/71 (#7, 2 wk), 11 wk; tot 25 wk.

Morley, Christopher

Mince Pie (Doran) PW gen 6/12/20 (#9, 4 wk), 8 wk.

Pipefuls (Doran) PW gen lit 2/26/21 (#7, 4 wk).

Thunder on the Left (Doubleday) PW fic 3/20/26 (#1, 4 wk), 8 wk.

Kitty Foyle (Lippincott) NYT fic 12/10/39 (#2, 4 wk), 8 wk; PW fic 12/16/39 (#3), pk 2/10/40 (#1, 8 wk), 40 wk; tot 48 wk.

Thorofare (Harcourt) NYT fic 12/13/42 (#9), pk 12/20/42 (#5, 1 wk), 11 wk; PW fic 1/16/43 (#8, 1 wk), 2 wk; tot 13 wk.

The Man Who Made Friends with Himself (Doubleday) NYT fic 7/3/49 (#15), pk 7/24/49 (#10, 1 wk), 4 wk.

Morley, Patrick

The Man in the Mirror (Wolgemuth & Hyatt) PW hc rel 11/9/90 (#10, 4 wk).

Morrell, David

Rambo: First Blood Part II (Jove) PW mm pb 5/10/85 (#12), pk 7/5/85 (#9, 1 wk), 11 wk; NYT pb fic 6/2/85 (#11, 3 wk), 6 wk; tot 17 wk.

The Brotherhood of the Rose (Fawcett/Crest) PW mm pb 2/1/85 (#12), pk 2/22/85 (#5, 2 wk), 7 wk; NYT pb fic 2/3/85 (#11), pk 2/10/85 (#3, 2 wk), 6 wk; tot 13 wk.

The Fraternity of the Stone (Fawcett/Crest)

NYT pb fic 9/28/86 (#12), pk 10/5/86 (#11, 1 wk), 4 wk; PW mm pb 10/10/86 (#12, 1 wk), 3 wk; tot 7 wk.

The League of Night and Fog (Fawcett/ Crest) NYT pb fic 7/31/88 (#10, 1 wk), 3 wk; PW mm pb 8/5/88 (#15), pk 8/19/88 (#14, 1 wk), 2 wk; tot 5 wk.

Morrill, Leslie
See James Howe

Morris, Desmond
The Naked Ape (McGraw) NYT gen 2/11/ 68 (#7), pk 3/3/68 (#1, 11 wk), 32 wk; PW nf 2/12/68 (#8), pk 3/11/68 (#1, 12 wk), 34 wk; NYT pb gen 4/6/69 (#4), pk 6/1/69 (#1, 4 wk), 16 wk; tot 82 wk.

Morris, Edita
My Darling from the Lions (Viking) NYT fic 9/12/43 (#15, 1 wk).

Morris, Edmund
The Rise of Theodore Roosevelt (Coward McCann) PW hc nf 6/4/79 (#13), pk 6/11/79 (#11, 1 wk), 3 wk.

Morris, Frank T.
Pick Out the Biggest (Houghton) NYT gen 9/19/43 (#16, 1 wk).

Morris, Hilda
The Main Stream (Putnam) NYT fic 6/11/ 39 (#13, 4 wk).

Morris, Ira Victor
The Chicago Story (Doubleday) NYT fic 4/20/52 (#16, 2 wk).

Morris, Jean
Brian Piccolo: A Short Season (Rand McNally) NYT gen 1/2/72 (#10), pk 2/13/72 (#7, 1 wk), 12 wk; PW nf 1/31/72 (#10), pk 3/27/72 (#7, 1 wk), 8 wk; NYT pb gen 8/13/ 72 (#3, 4 wk), 8 wk; tot 28 wk.

Morris, Joe Alex
See Arthur Hendrick Vandenberg, Jr., and
_____

Morris, Lloyd R.
Incredible New York (Random) NYT gen 12/16/51 (#9, 1 wk), 3 wk.

Morris, Richard Brandon
Encyclopedia of American History (Harper) NYT gen 5/17/53 (#14, 1 wk).

Morris, William
The American Heritage Dictionary of the English Language [editor in chief] (Hermitage House) NYT gen 10/12/69 (#9), pk 1/11/70 (#3, 1 wk), 38 wk; PW nf 10/20/69 (#10), pk 1/12/70 (#3, 1 wk), 36 wk; tot 74 wk.

The American Heritage Dictionary of the English Language, Abridged Version [editor in

chief] (Dell) NYT pb gen 10/4/70 (#3), pk 12/6/70 (#2, 8 wk), 16 wk.

Morrison, Alex J.
A New Way to Better Golf (Simon & Schuster) PW nf 7/9/32 (#8), pk 9/10/32 (#4, 4 wk), 12 wk.

Morrison, Jim
Wilderness (Villard) NYT fic 1/22/89 (#13, 1 wk).

Morrison, Theodore
The Stones of the House (Viking) NYT fic 3/22/53 (#15), pk 4/5/53 (#11, 1 wk), 5 wk.

Morrison, Toni
Song of Solomon (Knopf) PW hc fic 2/6/78 (#12), pk 2/20/78 (#11, 1 wk), 4 wk; (NAL/ Signet) PW mm pb 11/27/78 (#14), pk 12/11/78 (#10, 1 wk), 6 wk; tot 10 wk.

Tar Baby (Knopf) PW hc fic 4/17/81 (#4, 3 wk), 18 wk; NYT fic 4/19/81 (#7), pk 6/21/ 81 (#5, 1 wk), 17 wk; tot 35 wk.

Beloved (Knopf) NYT fic 9/20/87 (#12), pk 10/4/87 (#3, 1 wk), 31 wk; PW hc fic 9/25/ 87 (#11), pk 10/9/87 (#3, 1 wk), 30 wk; (NAL/ Plume) NYT pb fic 10/16/88 (#15), pk 11/13/ 88 (#5, 1 wk), 19 wk; PW td pb 10/21/88 (#5), pk 2/24/89 (#2, 1 wk), 27 wk; tot 107 wk.

Morrow, Elizabeth Cutter
The Painted Pig (Knopf) PW juv 10/18/30 (#10), pk 11/22/30 (#2, 8 wk), 24 wk.

Morrow, Skip
The Official I Hate Cats Book (Holt) NYT td pb 1/4/81 (#13), pk 2/8/81 (#5, 1 wk), 38 wk; PW td pb 1/16/81 (#6, 1 wk), 3 wk; tot 41 wk.

The Second Official I Hate Cats Book (Owl/ Holt) PW td pb 9/25/81 (#10), pk 10/30/81 (#6, 1 wk), 9 wk; NYT td pb 10/25/81 (#13), pk 1/10/81 (#10, 2 wk), 14 wk; tot 23 wk.

Morse, Melvin, and Paul Perry
Closer to the Light (Villard) NYT nf 10/7/ 90 (#16), pk 11/11/90 (#9, 1 wk), 8 wk; PW hc nf 10/12/90 (#12, 1 wk), 6 wk; tot 14 wk.

Mortimer, John
Paradise Postponed (Viking) NYT fic 4/20/ 86 (#15), pk 5/11/86 (#11, 1 wk), 2 wk.

Mortimer, Lee
Around the World Confidential (Putnam) NYT gen 4/15/56 (#13, 1 wk), 2 wk.
See also Jack Lait and _____

Mortman, Doris
Circles (Bantam) NYT pb fic 5/27/84 (#13), pk 6/10/84 (#5, 1 wk), 7 wk; PW mm pb 6/1/84 (#14), pk 6/29/84 (#6, 1 wk), 6 wk; tot 13 wk.

First Born (Bantam) PW hc fic 7/31/87

(#15), pk 8/21/87 (#13, 1 wk), 4 wk; NYT fic 8/16/87 (#14, 1 wk); NYT pb fic 6/5/88 (#9), pk 6/19/88 (#3, 1 wk), 9 wk; PW mm pb 6/17/88 (#14), pk 6/24/88 (#3, 1 wk), 7 wk; tot 21 wk.

Rightfully Mine (Bantam) PW hc fic 7/14/89 (#14), pk 7/21/89 (#12, 2 wk), 6 wk; NYT fic 7/16/89 (#12), pk 7/30/89 (#11, 1 wk), 5 wk; NYT pb fic 7/22/90 (#12), pk 9/2/90 (#4, 1 wk), 9 wk; PW mm pb 7/27/90 (#15), pk 8/31/90 (#5, 1 wk), 9 wk; tot 29 wk.

Morton, Anthony
See John Creasey

Morton, Charles W.
See Francis Wellington Dahl and _____

Morton, Frederic
The Rothschilds (Atheneum) NYT gen 3/11/62 (#13), pk 6/24/62 (#1, 17 wk), 41 wk; PW nf 3/26/62 (#5), pk 6/4/62 (#1, 19 wk), 43 wk; tot 84 wk.

Morton, Henry Vollam
In the Steps of the Master (Dodd) NYT nf 1/31/37 (#9, 4 wk).

Morwood, Peter
Rules of Engagement (Pocket) NYT pb fic 2/4/90 (#13), pk 2/18/90 (#8, 1 wk), 4 wk; PW mm pb 2/23/90 (#11, 1 wk), 2 wk; tot 6 wk.
See also Diane Duane and _____

Moscovitz, Judy
The Rice Diet Report (Putnam) PW hc nf 4/4/86 (#15), pk 5/2/86 (#6, 1 wk), 19 wk; NYT msc 4/6/86 (#5), pk 6/29/86 (#3, 1 wk), 13 wk; tot 32 wk.

Moscow, Alvin
Collision Course (Putnam) NYT gen 4/5/59 (#8), pk 4/12/59 (#6, 4 wk), 15 wk; PW nf 4/6/59 (#7), pk 5/4/59 (#4, 1 wk), 9 wk; tot 24 wk.

Moscow, Lonna
See Jim Everroad and _____

Moseley, Roy
See Charles Higham and _____

Mosenfelder, Donn
See Bobby Fischer, et al.

Moses, Anna Mary Robertson
The Grandma Moses Storybook [as by Grandma Moses; ed. Nora Kramer] (Random) NYT ch bst 11/11/62 (#11, 26 wk).

Moskowitz, Milton
See Robert Levering, et al.

Moss, Robert
Death Beam (Crown) NYT fic 12/6/81

(#15, 1 wk); (Berkley) PW mm pb 12/24/82 (#10), pk 1/7/83 (#7, 1 wk), 3 wk; NYT mm pb 12/26/82 (#13, 1 wk); tot 5 wk.

Moscow Rules (Villard) NYT fic 2/10/85 (#12), pk 2/17/85 (#6, 1 wk), 6 wk; PW hc fic 2/15/85 (#11), pk 3/1/85 (#7, 2 wk), 6 wk; (Pocket) PW mm pb 12/20/85 (#11, 1 wk), 4 wk; NYT pb fic 12/22/85 (#15, 1 wk); tot 17 wk.

See also Arnaud de Borchgrave and _____

_____, and Arnaud de Borchgrave
Monimbo (Simon & Schuster) PW hc fic 9/16/83 (#14), pk 10/7/83 (#7, 3 wk), 15 wk; NYT fic 9/18/83 (#14), pk 10/2/83 (#9, 4 wk), 12 wk; (Pocket) PW mm pb 9/14/84 (#12), pk 9/28/84 (#10, 1 wk), 4 wk; NYT pb fic 9/16/84 (#8), pk 9/23/84 (#7, 2 wk), 4 wk; tot 35 wk.

Mossiker, Frances
The Queen's Necklace (Simon & Schuster) NYT gen 3/5/61 (#15, 1 wk).

Mostert, Noel
Supership (Knopf) PW nf 12/16/74 (#9), pk 1/13/75 (#7, 4 wk), 10 wk; NYT gen 12/29/74 (#10), pk 1/12/75 (#9, 2 wk), 3 wk; tot 13 wk.

Motley, Willard
Knock on Any Door (Appleton) NYT fic 6/1/47 (#12), pk 7/6/47 (#5, 9 wk), 41 wk; PW fic 8/2/47 (#4, 2 wk), 5 wk; tot 46 wk.
We Fished All Night (Appleton) NYT fic 12/9/51 (#15), pk 1/13/52 (#9, 4 wk), 10 wk.
Let No Man Write My Epitaph (Random) NYT fic 9/7/58 (#16, 1 wk).

Mott, Michael
The Seven Mountains of Thomas Merton (Houghton) NYT nf 2/17/85 (#13), pk 3/24/85 (#8, 1 wk), 9 wk; PW hc nf 3/29/85 (#15, 2 wk); tot 11 wk.

Mowat, Farley
The Dog Who Wouldn't Be (Little Brown) NYT gen 9/15/57 (#16), pk 11/10/57 (#11, 1 wk), 11 wk; PW nf 10/21/57 (#9, 2 wk); tot 13 wk.

Moyers, Bill
Listening to America (Harper's Magazine) NYT gen 4/18/71 (#10, 2 wk); PW nf 5/24/71 (#10, 1 wk); tot 3 wk.
A World of Ideas: Conversations with the Men and Women Whose Ideas Are Shaping America's Future (Doubleday) NYT pb nf 6/4/89 (#4, 3 wk), 8 wk; PW td pb 7/14/89 (#10), pk 7/21/89 (#6, 1 wk), 3 wk; tot 11 wk.
See also Joseph Campbell and _____

Mullin, Willard, and Herbert Kamm
The Junior Illustrated Encyclopedia of Sports (Bobbs Merrill) NYT ch bst 11/13/60 (#15, 27 wk).

Multiple Sclerosis Foundation
Free to Be You and Me (McGraw) NYT td pb 4/14/74 (#6, 12 wk), 16 wk.

Mumford, Lewis
The Culture of Cities (Harcourt) PW nf 6/11/38 (#9, 4 wk).

Munk, Frank
The Legacy of Nazism (Macmillan) NYT gen 10/3/43 (#12, 1 wk), 2 wk.

Munthe, Axel Martin Fredrik
Memories and Vagaries (Dutton) PW nf 12/20/30 (#8, 4 wk).
The Story of San Michele (Dutton) PW nf 7/12/30 (#7), pk 10/18/30 (#1, 16 wk), 60 wk.

Muntz, Hope
The Golden Warrior (Scribner) NYT fic 4/3/49 (#16), pk 4/10/49 (#15, 2 wk), 4 wk.

Muolo, Paul
See Stephen Pizzo, et al.

Murchie, Guy
Song of the Sky (Riverside) NYT gen 1/2/55 (#12, 1 wk), 4 wk.
Music of the Spheres (Houghton) NYT gen 7/2/61 (#16), pk 7/9/61 (#15, 1 wk), 3 wk.

Murdoch, Iris
The Nice and the Good (Viking) PW fic 2/5/68 (#7, 1 wk), 5 wk.

Murkoff, Heidi E.
See Arlene Eisenberg, et al.

Murphy, Alison
Every Which Way in Ireland (Putnam) PW juv 5/17/30 (#10, 4 wk).

Murphy, Audie
To Hell and Back (Holt) NYT gen 3/27/49 (#10), pk 4/10/49 (#8, 2 wk), 14 wk; PW nf 4/16/49 (#9), pk 5/14/49 (#8, 1 wk), 3 wk; tot 17 wk.

Murphy, Charles J.V.
See J. Bryan III and _____

Murphy, Clyde F.
The Glittering Hill (Dutton) NYT fic 12/10/44 (#14, 1 wk).

Murphy, Dennis
The Sergeant (Viking) NYT fic 4/6/58 (#13), pk 5/11/58 (#6, 3 wk), 12 wk; PW fic 5/12/58 (#5, 1 wk), 3 wk; tot 15 wk.

Murphy, Edward Francis
Scarlet Lily (Grosset & Dunlap) NYT gen 12/17/44 (#20), pk 1/28/45 (#12, 1 wk), 3 wk.

Pere Antoine (Doubleday) NYT fic 4/27/47 (#14, 1 wk).

Murphy, Robert Daniel
Diplomat Among Warriors (Doubleday) NYT gen 3/15/64 (#10), pk 5/17/64 (#2, 1 wk), 30 wk; PW nf 3/23/64 (#10), pk 7/13/64 (#2, 1 wk), 31 wk; tot 61 wk.

Murphy, Robert William
The Pond (Dutton) NYT ch bst 11/1/64 (#8, 25 wk).

Murphy, Walter F.
The Vicar of Christ (Macmillan) NYT fic 5/20/79 (#14), pk 5/27/79 (#8, 2 wk), 13 wk; PW hc fic 5/21/79 (#12), pk 7/2/79 (#10, 1 wk), 12 wk; (Ballantine) PW mm pb 4/18/80 (#13), pk 5/2/80 (#7, 1 wk), 5 wk; NYT mm pb 4/27/80 (#11), pk 5/4/80 (#9, 1 wk), 3 wk; tot 33 wk.

Murphy, Warren, and Molly Cochran
Grandmaster (Pinnacle) NYT pb fic 9/30/84 (#8), pk 10/7/84 (#3, 1 wk), 7 wk; PW mm pb 10/12/84 (#13), pk 10/26/84 (#10, 1 wk), 5 wk; tot 12 wk.

Murrow, Edward R.
This I Believe [ed.] (Simon & Schuster) NYT gen 12/14/52 (#15), pk 2/22/53 (#3, 3 wk), 37 wk; PW nf 1/17/53 (#8), pk 2/14/53 (#2, 3 wk), 18 wk; tot 55 wk.

_____, and Raymond Swing
This I Believe, 2 [eds.] (Simon & Schuster) NYT gen 11/14/54 (#13, 1 wk), 5 wk; PW nf 1/15/55 (#9, 1 wk); tot 6 wk.

Musgrove, Margaret
Ashanti to Zulu (Dial) NYT ch hc 11/13/77 (#8, 46 wk).

Music, Lorenzo
See Jim Davis and _____

Musselman, M.M.
See Adolphe Menjou and _____

Musser, Joe
See Joni Eareckson and _____

Mussolini, Benito
My Autobiography (Scribner) PW nf 12/22/28 (#9, 4 wk).

Mydans, Carl
More Than Meets the Eye (Harper) NYT gen 10/11/59 (#15, 1 wk).

Mydans, Shelley Smith
The Open City (Doubleday) NYT fic 3/25/45 (#12, 1 wk).
Thomas (Doubleday) PW fic 10/4/65 (#9), pk 1/31/66 (#5, 1 wk), 21 wk; NYT fic 10/31/

65 (#10), pk 12/12/65 (#6, 4 wk), 16 wk; tot 37 wk.

Myerson, Bess, and Bill Adler

The I Love New York Diet (Morrow) PW hc nf 2/12/82 (#7), pk 3/12/82 (#6, 1 wk), 22 wk; NYT nf 2/14/82 (#8), pk 3/28/82 (#6, 3 wk), 17 wk; tot 39 wk.

Mykel, Agnar

Lasso Round the Moon (Dutton) NYT fic 5/29/60 (#14, 1 wk).

Myrer, Anton

Once an Eagle (Berkley) NYT mm pb 12/26/76 (#6), pk 1/30/77 (#1, 1 wk), 10 wk; PW mm pb 12/27/76 (#8), pk 1/17/76 (#1, 2 wk), 9 wk; tot 19 wk.

The Last Convertible (Putnam) PW hc fic 4/24/78 (#10), pk 5/15/78 (#6, 2 wk), 22 wk; NYT fic 5/14/78 (#12), pk 6/25/78 (#7, 4 wk), 11 wk; (Berkley) PW mm pb 3/12/79 (#10), pk 4/2/79 (#5, 1 wk), 9 wk; NYT mm pb 3/18/79 (#8), pk 4/8/79 (#6, 1 wk), 14 wk; tot 56 wk.

A Green Desire (Putnam) PW hc fic 2/5/82 (#11), pk 3/12/82 (#4, 1 wk), 11 wk; NYT fic 2/7/82 (#15), pk 3/21/82 (#3, 3 wk), 15 wk; (Avon) NYT mm pb 2/6/83 (#8), pk 2/20/83 (#4, 1 wk), 7 wk; PW mm pb 2/11/83 (#7), pk 3/4/83 (#6, 1 wk), 8 wk; tot 41 wk.

Mytinger, Caroline

Headhunting in the Solomon Islands (Macmillan) NYT nf 1/31/43 (#14, 1 wk), 8 wk; PW nf 2/13/43 (#10, 1 wk); tot 9 wk.

Nabokov, Vladimir

Lolita (Putnam) NYT fic 8/31/58 (#12), pk 9/28/58 (#1, 7 wk), 54 wk; PW fic 9/8/58 (#7), pk 10/6/58 (#1, 6 wk), 49 wk; tot 103 wk.

Pale Fire (Putnam) NYT fic 7/8/62 (#15), pk 7/15/62 (#14, 2 wk), 3 wk.

King, Queen, Knave (McGraw) PW fic 6/10/68 (#9, 1 wk).

Ada, or Ardor: A Family Chronicle (McGraw) NYT fic 5/25/69 (#7), pk 6/1/69 (#4, 9 wk), 20 wk; PW fic 6/2/69 (#2, 1 wk), 21 wk; NYT pb fic 7/5/70 (#3, 4 wk); tot 45 wk.

Nader, Ralph

Unsafe at Any Speed (Grossman) NYT gen 4/24/66 (#9), pk 6/12/66 (#7, 2 wk), 14 wk; PW nf 5/16/66 (#10), pk 6/20/66 (#5, 1 wk), 11 wk; tot 25 wk.

Naifeh, Steven, and Gregory White Smith

The Mormon Murders (NAL/Signet) NYT pb nf 6/11/89 (#7), pk 6/18/89 (#3, 2 wk), 10 wk; PW mm pb 6/30/89 (#11), pk 7/14/89 (#10, 1 wk), 4 wk; tot 14 wk.

Naipaul, V.S.

A Bend in the River (Vintage) NYT td pb 7/27/80 (#10, 2 wk), 5 wk; PW td pb 8/1/80 (#7, 1 wk); tot 6 wk.

The Enigma of Arrival (Knopf) NYT fic 4/26/87 (#15), pk 5/3/87 (#13, 2 wk), 3 wk.

Naisbitt, John

Megatrends: Ten New Directions Transforming Our Lives (Warner) PW hc nf 11/5/82 (#14), pk 1/28/83 (#1, 12 wk), 65 wk; NYT nf 11/14/82 (#14), pk 2/27/83 (#1, 8 wk), 66 wk; NYT pb nf 1/29/84 (#2), pk 2/5/84 (#1, 6 wk), 41 wk; PW mm pb 2/3/84 (#5), pk 2/10/84 (#1, 5 wk), 25 wk; tot 197 wk.

_____, and Patricia Aburdene

Re-Inventing the Corporation (Warner) NYT nf 9/22/85 (#14), pk 10/13/85 (#7, 1 wk), 10 wk; PW hc nf 10/11/85 (#10, 1 wk), 3 wk; tot 13 wk.

Megatrends 2000 (Morrow) NYT nf 1/28/90 (#5), pk 2/4/90 (#1, 9 wk), 35 wk; PW hc nf 2/2/90 (#12), pk 2/16/90 (#1, 6 wk), 33 wk; tot 68 wk.

Nash, N. Richard

East Wind, Rain (Atheneum) PW hc fic 5/2/77 (#10, 6 wk); NYT fic 5/15/77 (#10), pk 5/22/77 (#8, 1 wk), 5 wk; tot 11 wk.

The Last Magic (Atheneum) PW hc fic 10/23/78 (#15, 1 wk).

Nash, Ogden

Hard Lines (Simon & Schuster) PW nf 3/21/31 (#4, 4 wk), 8 wk.

I'm a Stranger Here Myself (Little Brown) NYT gen 7/3/38 (#10), pk 12/4/38 (#5, 4 wk), 32 wk; PW nf 9/10/38 (#7), pk 10/15/38 (#5, 4 wk), 28 wk; tot 60 wk.

Good Intentions (Little Brown) NYT nf 1/3/43 (#21), pk 1/17/43 (#10, 1 wk), 5 wk.

The Private Dining Room (Little Brown) NYT gen 5/24/53 (#16, 2 wk).

Nason, Leonard

Chevrons (Doran) PW fic 3/19/27 (#10, 4 wk).

Nathan, Robert

One More Spring (Knopf) PW fic 5/13/33 (#8, 8 wk), 12 wk.

Road of Ages (Knopf) PW fic 3/16/35 (#7, 4 wk).

The Enchanted Voyage (Knopf) NYT fic 10/4/36 (#10, 4 wk); PW fic 10/10/36 (#7, 4 wk); tot 8 wk.

Winter in April (Knopf) NYT fic 2/6/38 (#4, 4 wk), 8 wk; PW fic 2/12/38 (#7, 4 wk), 8 wk; tot 16 wk.

Journey of Tapiola (Knopf) PW fic 12/10/38 (#10, 4 wk).

Portrait of Jennie (Knopf) PW fic 2/10/40 (#6), pk 3/9/40 (#5, 4 wk), 12 wk.

The Sea-Gull Cry (Knopf) NYT fic 8/9/42 (#9, 1 wk), 2 wk; PW fic 8/15/42 (#9, 1 wk); tot 3 wk.

Journal for Josephine (Knopf) NYT gen 4/4/43 (#22, 1 wk).

Mr. Whittle and the Morning Star (Knopf) NYT fic 4/27/47 (#15, 1 wk).

A Star in the Wind (Knopf) NYT fic 2/25/62 (#14), pk 3/18/62 (#13, 1 wk), 3 wk.

Nathanson, E.M.
The Dirty Dozen (Random) NYT pb fic 7/3/66 (#5, 4 wk).

National Advisory Commission on Civil Disorders
Rights in Conflict: The Report of the National Advisory Commission on Civil Disorders [Sam Ervin, Chairman] (Government Printing Office) NYT pb gen 4/7/68 (#2), pk 5/5/68 (#1, 16 wk), 32 wk.

Navratilova, Martina, and George Vecsey
Martina (Knopf) NYT nf 7/21/85 (#5, 3 wk), 10 wk; PW hc nf 7/26/85 (#15), pk 8/16/85 (#5, 1 wk), 8 wk; tot 18 wk.

Naylor, Gloria
The Women of Brewster Place (Penguin) PW mm pb 4/7/89 (#10, 1 wk), 2 wk; NYT pb fic 4/9/89 (#13, 1 wk); tot 3 wk.

Nef, Joan Ulric
War and Human Progress (Norton) NYT gen 1/21/51 (#15, 1 wk).

Nelson, George, and Henry M. Wright
Tomorrow's House (Simon & Schuster) NYT gen 11/11/45 (#14), pk 11/25/45 (#9, 1 wk), 4 wk; PW nf 3/9/46 (#8, 1 wk); tot 5 wk.

Nelson, Willie, and Bud Shrake
Willie (Simon & Schuster) NYT nf 12/11/88 (#15, 1 wk).

Nesbit, Victoria Henrietta Kugler
White House Diary (Doubleday) NYT gen 8/22/48 (#9, 1 wk), 9 wk.

Ness, Evaline
Sam, Bangs & Moonshine (Holt) NYT ch bst 5/7/67 (#4), pk 11/5/67 (#2, 26 wk), 45 wk.

Netland, Dwayne
See Bob Hope and _____

Nettles, Craig, and Peter Golenbock
Balls (Putnam) NYT nf 5/6/84 (#7), pk 7/1/84 (#3, 1 wk), 15 wk; PW hc nf 5/25/84 (#15), pk 6/8/84 (#6, 1 wk), 6 wk; (Pocket)

NYT pb nf 5/19/85 (#5, 1 wk), 2 wk; tot 23 wk.

Neuharth, Al
Confessions of an S.O.B. (Doubleday) NYT nf 10/22/89 (#8), pk 11/5/89 (#5, 1 wk), 7 wk; PW hc nf 10/27/89 (#13), pk 11/17/89 (#5, 1 wk), 7 wk; tot 14 wk.

Neumann, Alfred
Another Caesar (Knopf) PW fic 3/16/35 (#10, 4 wk).

Neumann, Daisy
Now That April's Here (Consolidated) NYT fic 6/24/45 (#17, 1 wk), 2 wk.

Neustadt, Richard E.
Presidential Power (Wiley) NYT gen 2/5/61 (#15), pk 2/12/61 (#13, 1 wk), 3 wk.

Neville, Emily Cheney
It's Like This, Cat (Harper) NYT ch bst 5/10/64 (#7, 19 wk).

Nevin, David
Dream West (Putnam) NYT fic 3/4/84 (#14, 1 wk), 2 wk; (NAL/Signet) NYT pb fic 1/13/85 (#15), pk 1/20/85 (#14, 1 wk), 2 wk; PW mm pb 5/2/86 (#14), pk 5/9/86 (#9, 1 wk), 3 wk; tot 7 wk.

Nevins, Allan
See John F. Kennedy

New, Christopher
Shanghai (Bantam) NYT pb fic 6/8/86 (#8), pk 6/22/86 (#7, 1 wk), 5 wk; PW mm pb 6/13/86 (#9), pk 7/4/86 (#6, 1 wk), 5 wk; tot 10 wk.

New York Herald Tribune Home Institute
America's Cook Book (New York Herald Tribune) NYT gen 12/12/37 (#8, 4 wk).

Newberry, Julia
Julia Newberry's Diary (Norton) PW nf 8/12/33 (#9, 4 wk), 8 wk.

Newby, Percy Howard
The Picnic at Sakkara (Knopf) NYT fic 9/25/55 (#16, 1 wk).

Newcomb, Richard F.
Abandon Ship! (Holt) NYT gen 10/5/58 (#16), pk 11/16/58 (#7, 1 wk), 12 wk; PW nf 11/10/58 (#7, 1 wk), 5 wk; tot 17 wk.

Iwo Jima (Holt) NYT gen 3/28/65 (#10, 1 wk); PW nf 4/19/65 (#10, 1 wk); tot 2 wk.

Newman, Edwin
Strictly Speaking (Bobbs Merrill) NYT gen 12/1/74 (#8), pk 12/29/74 (#3, 8 wk), 26 wk; PW nf 12/1/74 (#8), pk 1/27/75 (#1, 3 wk), 24 wk; (Warner) NYT mm pb 10/12/75 (#10), pk 11/2/75 (#9, 1 wk), 4 wk; tot 54

wk.

A Civil Tongue (Bobbs Merrill) PW hc nf 12/27/76 (#9), pk 1/24/76 (#7, 1 wk), 6 wk; NYT gen 2/6/77 (#9, 1 wk), 2 wk; tot 8 wk.

Newman, James
See Edward Kasner and _____

Newman, Mildred, and Bernard Berkowitz
How to Take Charge of Your Own Life (Harcourt) NYT nf 9/11/77 (#13), pk 9/25/77 (#12, 2 wk), 7 wk.

Newman, Mildred, and Bernard Berkowitz with Jean Owen
How to Be Your Own Best Friend (Random) PW nf 7/23/73 (#6), pk 9/24/73 (#1, 5 wk), 46 wk; NYT gen 7/29/73 (#9), pk 10/14/73 (#1, 5 wk), 48 wk; (Ballantine) NYT mm pb 11/10/74 (#1, 4 wk), 14 wk; tot 108 wk.

Newton, A. Edward
The Greatest Book in the World (Little Brown) PW nf 10/24/25 (#7, 4 wk), 12 wk.

Newton, Joseph Fort
River of Years (Lippincott) NYT gen 4/28/46 (#10), pk 5/5/46 (#7, 1 wk), 8 wk.

Ney, Richard
The Wall Street Jungle (Grove) NYT gen 7/5/70 (#10), pk 11/8/70 (#4, 1 wk), 19 wk; PW nf 7/20/70 (#10), pk 9/7/70 (#6, 3 wk), 17 wk; NYT pb gen 3/7/71 (#4, 4 wk), 12 wk; tot 48 wk.
The Wall Street Gang (Praeger) NYT gen 7/14/74 (#10), pk 8/25/74 (#7, 2 wk), 9 wk; PW nf 8/5/74 (#9), pk 8/12/74 (#8, 1 wk), 3 wk; tot 12 wk.

Nichols, Jerry
See Greg Hildebrandt, et al.

Nicholson, Meredith
Black Sheep! Black Sheep! (Scribners) PW fic 8/14/20 (#8, 4 wk).

Nickerson, William
How I Turned $1,000 into a Million in Real Estate (Simon & Schuster) NYT gen 4/5/59 (#16), pk 6/28/59 (#3, 1 wk), 43 wk; PW nf 5/4/59 (#8), pk 7/6/59 (#3, 3 wk), 34 wk; tot 77 wk.

Nicolson, Sir Harold George
Journey to Java (Doubleday) NYT gen 6/1/58 (#14, 1 wk).
Harold Nicolson's Diaries and Letters, 1930–1939 [ed. Nigel Nicolson] (Atheneum) PW nf 2/13/67 (#11, 1 wk).
Harold Nicolson: The War Years 1939–1945 [ed. Nigel Nicolson] (Atheneum) NYT gen 7/2/67 (#9), pk 7/9/67 (#7, 1 wk), 2 wk; PW nf 7/10/67 (#11), pk 7/31/67 (#9, 2 wk), 5 wk;

tot 7 wk.
The Later Years 1945–1962 (Atheneum) PW nf 9/16/68 (#10, 1 wk).

Nicolson, Nigel
Portrait of a Marriage (Atheneum) NYT gen 11/4/73 (#9), pk 12/23/73 (#4, 2 wk), 19 wk; PW nf 11/5/73 (#6), pk 12/31/73 (#4, 2 wk), 17 wk; tot 36 wk.

Nidetch, Jean
The Weight Watcher's Cook Book (Hearthside) PW nf 7/15/68 (#8, 1 wk), 3 wk.
Weight Watcher's Food Plan Diet Cookbook (NAL) NYT nf 10/3/82 (#15), pk 3/27/83 (#11, 1 wk), 11 wk; PW hc nf 10/29/82 (#12, 1 wk); tot 12 wk.
Weight Watcher's Program Cookbook (Hearthside) PW nf 5/14/73 (#8), pk 7/16/73 (#3, 3 wk), 27 wk; NYT gen 5/27/73 (#10), pk 7/29/73 (#5, 2 wk), 24 wk; tot 51 wk.
Weight Watcher's Quick Start Program Cookbook (NAL) NYT msc 1/20/85 (#4), pk 3/10/85 (#1, 4 wk), 22 wk; PW hc nf 2/1/85 (#10), pk 3/29/85 (#3, 2 wk), 23 wk; tot 45 wk.

Niering, William A., and Nancy C. Olmstead
The Audubon Society Field Guide to North American Wildflowers: Eastern Region (Knopf) NYT td pb 9/2/79 (#15), pk 9/16/79 (#13, 1 wk), 3 wk.

Niesewand, Peter
Fallback (NAL/Signet) NYT mm pb 2/20/83 (#13, 1 wk); PW mm pb 3/4/83 (#14), pk 3/11/83 (#13, 1 wk), 2 wk; tot 3 wk.

Nijinsky, Romola
Nijinsky (Simon & Schuster) PW nf 5/12/34 (#4), pk 7/14/34 (#2, 4 wk), 36 wk.

Nin, Anais
Delta of Venus (Harcourt) PW hc fic 8/1/77 (#6), pk 8/29/77 (#4, 3 wk), 32 wk; NYT fic 8/7/77 (#10), pk 8/14/77 (#4, 5 wk), 36 wk; (Bantam) PW mm pb 6/5/78 (#11), pk 6/26/78 (#4, 3 wk), 12 wk; NYT mm pb 6/18/78 (#10), pk 7/30/78 (#7, 1 wk), 9 wk; tot 89 wk.
Henry and June (Harvest House/Harcourt) NYT pb nf 11/18/90 (#7, 2 wk), 3 wk.

Nitti, Francesco F.
Escape (Putnam) PW nf 3/15/30 (#9, 4 wk), 8 wk.

Niven, David
The Moon's a Balloon (Putnam) PW nf 2/21/72 (#7), pk 3/13/72 (#5, 3 wk), 10 wk; NYT gen 2/27/72 (#7), pk 3/19/72 (#5, 3 wk), 13 wk; tot 23 wk.
Bring on the Empty Horses (Putnam) PW nf 10/20/75 (#10), pk 1/5/76 (#1, 2 wk), 14 wk; NYT gen 10/26/75 (#9), pk 11/30/75 (#1,

12 wk), 28 wk; PW hc nf 2/2/76 (#1, 2 wk), 14 wk; (Dell) mm pb 10/18/76 (#9), pk 11/1/76 (#5, 1 wk), 10 wk; NYT mm pb 10/31/76 (#7), pk 11/7/76 (#6, 1 wk), 7 wk; tot 73 wk.

Go Slowly, Come Back Quickly (Doubleday) PW hc fic 12/4/81 (#12), pk 12/18/81 (#9, 1 wk), 10 wk; NYT fic 12/27/81 (#14), pk 1/17/82 (#9, 3 wk), 11 wk; (Dell) PW mm pb 1/21/83 (#15), pk 1/28/83 (#12, 1 wk), 2 wk; NYT mm pb 1/30/83 (#12, 1 wk); tot 24 wk.

Niven, Larry

The Ringworld Engineers (Ballantine/Del Rey) PW mm pb 3/20/81 (#12), pk 3/20/81 (#12, 1 wk), 4 wk.

The Integral Trees (Ballantine/Del Rey) NYT pb fic 2/17/85 (#13, 1 wk), 2 wk; PW mm pb 3/8/85 (#13, 1 wk); tot 3 wk.

_____, and Jerry Pournelle

Lucifer's Hammer (Fawcett/Crest) PW mm pb 7/31/78 (#5), pk 8/7/78 (#2, 1 wk), 14 wk; NYT mm pb 8/6/78 (#7), pk 8/13/78 (#6, 1 wk), 2 wk; tot 16 wk.

Footfall (Ballantine/Del Rey) NYT fic 6/23/85 (#15), pk 7/7/85 (#14, 1 wk), 3 wk; PW hc fic 6/28/85 (#11), pk 7/19/85 (#10, 4 wk), 9 wk; NYT pb fic 5/4/86 (#12), pk 5/18/86 (#1, 1 wk), 9 wk; PW mm pb 5/9/86 (#10), pk 5/16/86 (#2, 3 wk), 9 wk; tot 30 wk.

Nixon, Raymond B.

Henry W. Grady: Spokesman of the New South (Knopf) NYT gen 12/5/43 (#13, 1 wk), 6 wk.

Nixon, Richard M.

Six Crises (Doubleday) NYT gen 4/8/62 (#14), pk 5/6/62 (#4, 2 wk), 20 wk; PW nf 4/23/62 (#5), pk 5/7/62 (#4, 2 wk), 16 wk; tot 36 wk.

The Memoirs of Richard Nixon (Grosset & Dunlap) PW hc nf 5/29/78 (#14), pk 6/5/78 (#5, 5 wk), 14 wk; NYT nf 6/4/78 (#4), pk 6/11/78 (#2, 1 wk), 11 wk; tot 25 wk.

The Real War (Warner) PW hc nf 5/16/80 (#14), pk 7/4/80 (#3, 4 wk), 19 wk; NYT nf 6/1/80 (#13), pk 7/6/80 (#3, 3 wk), 17 wk; tot 36 wk.

No More Vietnams (Arbor House) NYT nf 5/12/85 (#15, 2 wk).

1999: The Global Challenges We Face in the Next Decade (Simon & Schuster) NYT nf 5/1/88 (#16), pk 5/29/88 (#6, 1 wk), 11 wk; PW hc nf 5/13/88 (#9), pk 5/20/88 (#7, 2 wk), 6 wk; tot 17 wk.

In the Arena: A Memoir of Victory, Defeat and Renewal (Simon & Schuster) NYT nf 4/29/90 (#11), pk 5/20/90 (#4, 2 wk), 11 wk; PW hc nf 5/4/90 (#10), pk 6/1/90 (#2, 2 wk),

12 wk; tot 23 wk.

Nizer, Louis

My Life in Court (Doubleday) PW nf 11/27/61 (#11), pk 1/15/62 (#1, 9 wk), 68 wk; NYT gen 12/3/61 (#13), pk 1/21/62 (#1, 9 wk), 57 wk; tot 125 wk.

The Jury Returns (Doubleday) NYT gen 12/11/66 (#7), pk 1/22/67 (#3, 1 wk), 22 wk; PW nf 1/2/67 (#5), pk 1/30/67 (#3, 5 wk), 19 wk; tot 41 wk.

The Implosion Conspiracy (Doubleday) PW nf 3/5/73 (#9), pk 5/7/73 (#2, 1 wk), 20 wk; NYT gen 3/11/73 (#7), pk 5/20/73 (#3, 1 wk), 20 wk; tot 40 wk.

Noble, Hollister

Woman with a Sword (Doubleday) NYT fic 8/15/48 (#12), pk 9/5/48 (#7, 1 wk), 10 wk; PW fic 9/18/48 (#9, 1 wk); tot 11 wk.

Noble, John W., and Bernard Averbach

Never Plead Guilty (Farrar) NYT gen 9/11/55 (#12), pk 9/25/55 (#7, 3 wk), 11 wk; PW nf 10/15/55 (#10), pk 11/19/55 (#8, 1 wk), 2 wk; tot 13 wk.

Noguchi, Dr. Thomas T., with Joseph DiMona

Coroner (Simon & Schuster) NYT nf 1/22/84 (#14), pk 2/19/84 (#9, 1 wk), 7 wk; PW hc nf 2/10/84 (#13), pk 2/17/84 (#8, 1 wk), 3 wk; (Pocket) NYT pb nf 11/11/84 (#2, 2 wk), 6 wk; PW mm pb 11/16/84 (#12), pk 11/30/84 (#6, 1 wk), 7 wk; tot 23 wk.

Nolan, Christopher

Under the Eye of the Clock (St. Martin's) NYT nf 4/17/88 (#14), pk 5/1/88 (#13, 1 wk), 3 wk; PW hc nf 5/6/88 (#13, 1 wk), 2 wk; tot 5 wk.

Nolen, William A.

The Making of a Surgeon (Random) NYT gen 2/21/71 (#10), pk 3/28/71 (#7, 1 wk), 5 wk; PW nf 3/1/71 (#6, 1 wk), 5 wk; NYT pb gen 3/12/72 (#5, 12 wk); tot 22 wk.

Noonan, Peggy

What I Saw at the Revolution: A Political Life in the Reagan Era (Random) NYT nf 2/25/90 (#13), pk 3/11/90 (#4, 3 wk), 18 wk; PW hc nf 3/2/90 (#12), pk 3/16/90 (#6, 3 wk), 11 wk; tot 29 wk.

Noorbergen, Rene

See Jeane Dixon and _____

Nordhoff, Charles B., and James Norman Hall

Mutiny on the Bounty (Little Brown) PW fic 1/14/33 (#6, 8 wk), 16 wk; NYT fic 2/2/36 (#9, 4 wk); tot 20 wk.

Pitcairn's Island (Little Brown) PW fic

12/15/34 (#6, 8 wk).
Men Against the Sea (Little Brown) PW fic 2/10/34 (#4, 4 wk), 12 wk.
The Hurricane (Little Brown) PW fic 3/14/36 (#2, 8 wk), 16 wk; NYT fic 4/5/36 (#3, 4 wk); tot 20 wk.
The Bounty Trilogy (Little Brown) PW fic 1/16/37 (#8, 4 wk).
The Dark River (Little Brown) NYT fic 7/31/38 (#1, 4 wk), 8 wk; PW fic 8/13/38 (#5, 4 wk), 8 wk; tot 16 wk.
Botany Bay (Little Brown) PW fic 12/13/41 (#6, 8 wk), 12 wk.

Norman, Elizabeth
Castle Cloud (Avon) NYT mm pb 7/17/77 (#14), pk 7/24/77 (#12, 1 wk), 2 wk.

Norman, Hilary
In Love and Friendship (Dell) NYT pb fic 2/7/88 (#11), pk 2/14/88 (#10, 1 wk), 5 wk; PW mm pb 2/12/88 (#13, 3 wk), 5 wk; tot 10 wk.

Norman, Philip
Shout! (Simon & Schuster/Fireside) NYT td pb 7/26/81 (#15, 1 wk).

Norris, Charles Gilman
Brass (Dutton) PW fic 4/1/22 (#6, 4 wk), 8 wk.
Bread (Dutton) PW fic 11/24/23 (#8, 4 wk).
Pig Iron (Dutton) PW fic 4/17/26 (#5, 8 wk), 16 wk.
Zelda Marsh (Dutton) PW fic 10/22/27 (#9, 4 wk).
Seed (Doubleday) PW fic 9/20/30 (#8), pk 10/18/30 (#2, 4 wk), 16 wk.
Zest (Doubleday) PW fic 6/10/33 (#4), pk 7/15/33 (#2, 4 wk), 12 wk.
Hands (Farrar) NYT fic 12/1/35 (#3, 4 wk).
Bricks Without Straw (Doubleday) NYT fic 10/9/38 (#4, 4 wk), 8 wk.
Flint (Doubleday) NYT fic 2/13/44 (#11, 1 wk), 2 wk.

Norris, Chuck, and Joe Hyams
The Secret of Inner Strength: My Story (Little Brown) NYT nf 2/28/88 (#15, 1 wk); PW hc nf 3/4/88 (#12, 1 wk); tot 2 wk.

Norris, Frank
Tower in the West (Harper) NYT fic 1/27/57 (#9, 2 wk), 8 wk.

Norris, George William
Fighting Liberal (Macmillan) NYT gen 6/10/45 (#11, 1 wk), 4 wk.

Norris, Kathleen Thompson
Harriet and the Piper (Doubleday) PW fic 9/25/20 (#2, 8 wk), 16 wk.
Sisters (Doubleday) PW fic 1/3/20 (#8, 4 wk).

Lucretia Lombard (Doubleday) PW fic 5/13/22 (#11), pk 6/17/22 (#9, 4 wk), 12 wk.
Certain People of Importance (Doubleday) PW fic 10/14/22 (#7), pk 11/18/22 (#5, 4 wk), 20 wk.
Little Ships (Doubleday) PW fic 11/21/25 (#10, 8 wk).
Hildegarde (Doubleday) PW fic 12/18/26 (#8, 4 wk).
The Black Flemings (Doubleday) PW fic 4/17/26 (#8), pk 5/15/26 (#6, 4 wk), 12 wk.
The Sea Gull (Doubleday) PW fic 5/21/27 (#7, 4 wk).
Barberry Bush (Doubleday) PW fic 9/24/27 (#6, 8 wk), 12 wk.
The Foolish Virgin (Doubleday) PW fic 10/27/28 (#8, 4 wk).
Beauty and the Beast (Doubleday) PW fic 5/26/28 (#6, 8 wk).
Storm House (Doubleday) PW fic 5/11/29 (#5), pk 6/8/29 (#3, 4 wk), 8 wk.
Passion Flower (Doubleday) PW fic 3/15/30 (#6, 4 wk), 8 wk.
Margaret Yorke (Doubleday) PW fic 8/23/30 (#10, 4 wk).
Belle-Mere (Doubleday) PW fic 10/17/31 (#8, 4 wk), 8 wk.
Second Hand Wife (Doubleday) PW fic 5/14/32 (#5, 4 wk).
Younger Sister (Doubleday) PW fic 8/13/32 (#9, 4 wk).
Walls of Gold (Doubleday) PW fic 4/15/33 (#10), pk 5/13/33 (#4, 4 wk), 8 wk.
Shining Windows (Doubleday) NYT fic 11/3/35 (#2, 4 wk).
Secret Marriage (Collier) NYT fic 4/5/36 (#2, 4 wk).
The American Flaggs (Collier) NYT fic 10/4/36 (#3, 4 wk).
You Can't Have Everything (Doubleday) NYT fic 10/10/37 (#4, 4 wk).
Bread into Roses (Doubleday) NYT fic 4/4/37 (#3, 4 wk).
Heartbroken Melody (Coward McCann) NYT fic 7/31/38 (#3, 4 wk).
The Runaway (Doubleday) NYT fic 5/7/39 (#4, 4 wk).
Lost Sunrise (Doubleday) NYT fic 11/5/39 (#4, 4 wk).

North, Oliver L.
Taking the Stand; The Testimony of Lieutenant Colonel Oliver L. North [intro. by Daniel Schorr] (Pocket) NYT pb nf 8/9/87 (#1, 1 wk), 3 wk; PW mm pb 8/14/87 (#7), pk 8/21/87 (#6, 1 wk), 3 wk; tot 6 wk.

North, Sterling

Rascal: A Memoir of a Better Era (Dutton) NYT gen 8/25/63 (#10), pk 11/24/63 (#3, 4 wk), 28 wk; PW nf 9/16/63 (#8), 1/13/64 (#2, 1 wk), 27 wk; NYT ch bst 11/10/63 (#5, 26 wk); tot 81 wk.
Little Rascal (Dutton) NYT ch bst 11/7/65 (#10, 26 wk).

Northrop, Filmer Stuart Cuckow
The Meeting of East and West (Collier) NYT fic 9/1/46 (#15, 1 wk).

Norton, Carla
See Christine McGuire and _____

Norton, Howard, and Bob Slosser
The Miracle of Jimmy Carter (Logos International) NYT td pb 8/15/76 (#5, 1 wk).

Norton, Mary
The Borrowers (Harcourt) NYT ch bst 11/15/53 (#7), pk 11/14/54 (#2, 40 wk), 80 wk.
The Borrowers Afield (Harcourt) NYT ch bst 11/18/56 (#5, 40 wk).
The Borrowers Afloat (Harcourt) NYT ch bst 5/10/59 (#14, 19 wk).

Norway, Nevil Shute [all titles as by Nevil Shute]
Kindling (Morrow) NYT fic 7/3/38 (#6, 4 wk).
Ordeal (Morrow) NYT fic 5/7/39 (#11, 4 wk).
Pied Piper (Morrow) PW fic 3/14/42 (#8), pk 4/11/42 (#7, 4 wk), 12 wk.
Pastoral (Morrow) NYT fic 9/17/44 (#15), pk 10/22/44 (#7, 2 wk), 15 wk; PW fic 10/14/44 (#10, 1 wk); tot 16 wk.
Most Secret (Morrow) NYT fic 11/18/45 (#16), pk 12/30/45 (#9, 1 wk), 8 wk.
The Chequer Board (Morrow) NYT fic 4/20/47 (#8), pk 4/27/47 (#6, 3 wk), 15 wk; PW fic 5/10/47 (#5, 3 wk), 3 wk; tot 18 wk.
No Highway (Morrow) NYT fic 10/10/48 (#10, 1 wk), 2 wk.
The Legacy (Morrow) NYT fic 7/2/50 (#12), pk 8/27/50 (#4, 4 wk), 18 wk; PW fic 7/29/50 (#3, 3 wk), 9 wk; tot 27 wk.
Round the Bend (Morrow) NYT fic 3/25/51 (#11), pk 4/1/51 (#9, 2 wk), 10 wk; PW fic 4/14/51 (#5, 1 wk); tot 11 wk.
The Far Country (Morrow) NYT fic 9/28/52 (#11), pk 10/5/52 (#10, 4 wk), 10 wk; PW fic 11/15/52 (#9, 1 wk); tot 11 wk.
In the Wet (Morrow) NYT fic 5/24/53 (#13), pk 7/26/53 (#10, 1 wk), 14 wk.
The Breaking Wave (Morrow) NYT fic 5/1/55 (#10), pk 5/22/55 (#8, 2 wk), 13 wk; PW fic 5/14/55 (#8, 3 wk), 5 wk; tot 18 wk.
On the Beach (Morrow) NYT fic 8/11/57 (#14), pk 9/1/57 (#2, 8 wk), 29 wk; PW fic 8/26/57 (#8), pk 9/9/57 (#1, 1 wk), 24 wk; tot 53 wk.
Beyond the Black Stump (Morrow) NYT fic 9/9/56 (#14), pk 10/14/56 (#10, 1 wk), 5 wk; PW fic 10/22/56 (#10, 1 wk); tot 6 wk.
The Rainbow and the Rose (Morrow) NYT fic 11/16/58 (#10, 1 wk), 9 wk.
Trustee from the Toolroom (Morrow) NYT fic 4/10/60 (#14), pk 6/19/60 (#5, 1 wk), 21 wk; PW fic 4/25/60 (#9), pk 6/27/60 (#4, 1 wk), 14 wk; tot 35 wk.

Norwood, Robin
Women Who Love Too Much (Tarcher/St. Martin's) PW hc nf 8/2/85 (#12), pk 5/9/86 (#4, 1 wk), 37 wk; NYT msc 8/18/85 (#2, 5 wk), 36 wk; (Pocket) NYT msc pb 6/8/86 (#2), pk 6/15/86 (#1, 43 wk), 82 wk; PW mm pb 6/20/86 (#6), pk 10/10/86 (#1, 5 wk), 64 wk; tot 219 wk.

Nostradamus
The Prophecies of Nostradamus [ed. & trans. by Erika Cheetham] (Putnam) NYT td pb 4/4/82 (#11), pk 5/9/82 (#6, 2 wk), 23 wk; (Perigee) PW td pb 5/21/82 (#6, 1 wk), 5 wk; tot 28 wk.

Nourse, James G.
The Simple Solution to Rubik's Cube (Bantam) PW mm pb 7/10/81 (#15), pk 10/30/81 (#1, 13 wk), 37 wk; NYT mm pb 8/2/81 (#12), pk 11/8/81 (#1, 14 wk), 35 wk; tot 72 wk.
The Simple Solutions to Cube Puzzles (Bantam) NYT mm pb 1/3/82 (#15), pk 1/24/82 (#6, 1 wk), 4 wk; PW mm pb 1/22/82 (#12, 1 wk); tot 5 wk.

Novak, William
See Lee Iacocca and _____
See Sydney Biddle Barrows and _____
See Nancy Reagan and _____

Novello, Don
See Lazlo Toth and _____

Nowell, Elizabeth
Thomas Wolfe (Doubleday) NYT gen 7/31/60 (#13), pk 8/21/60 (#12, 2 wk), 10 wk.

Nute, Grace Lee
Lake Superior (Bobbs Merrill) NYT gen 8/20/44 (#17), pk 9/17/44 (#12, 1 wk), 3 wk.

Oates, Joyce Carol
Wonderland (Vanguard) NYT pb fic 2/11/73 (#5, 4 wk).
Bellefleur (Dutton) PW hc fic 8/22/80 (#10), pk 9/19/80 (#9, 1 wk), 8 wk; NYT fic 8/24/80 (#13), pk 8/31/80 (#11, 4 wk), 7 wk; (Warner) PW mm pb 9/18/81 (#15), pk 10/16/81 (#8, 1 wk), 7 wk; NYT mm pb 9/20/81 (#11), pk 10/11/81 (#8, 1 wk), 5 wk; tot 27 wk.

O'Brian, Patrick

See Simone de Beauvoir

O'Brien, Darcy
Murder in Little Egypt (NAL/Onyx) NYT pb nf 2/18/90 (#4, 3 wk), 7 wk; PW mm pb 2/23/90 (#8, 1 wk), 2 wk; tot 9 wk.

O'Brien, Frederick
White Shadows in the South Seas (Century) PW gen 6/12/20 (#8), pk 9/25/20 (#2, 12 wk), 24 wk; PW gen lit 1/8/21 (#2, 8 wk), 20 wk; tot 44 wk.
Mystic Isles of the South Seas (Century) PW gen lit 6/11/21 (#3), pk 8/6/21 (#1, 4 wk), 12 wk.

O'Brien, Howard Vincent
So Long, Son (Putnam) NYT gen 10/15/44 (#11, 1 wk), 3 wk.
All Things Considered (Chicago Daily News) NYT gen 6/6/48 (#11, 3 wk), 13 wk.

O'Brien, P.J.
Will Rogers (Winston) NYT gen 12/1/35 (#9), pk 2/2/36 (#2, 4 wk), 12 wk; PW nf 1/11/36 (#10), pk 2/15/36 (#9, 4 wk), 12 wk; tot 24 wk.

O'Brien, Pat
The Wind at My Back (Doubleday) NYT gen 1/10/65 (#8, 1 wk).

O'Brien, Robert
California Called Them (McGraw) NYT gen 1/6/52 (#15, 1 wk).

Occhiogrosso, Peter
See Larry King and_____

O'Connell, Charles
The Other Side of the Record (Knopf) NYT gen 11/16/47 (#14), pk 11/23/47 (#11, 1 wk), 3 wk.

O'Connor, Betty
Better Homes and Gardens Second Storybook [ed.] (Meredith) NYT ch bst 11/16/52 (#3, 40 wk).

O'Connor, Edwin
The Last Hurrah (Little Brown) PW fic 2/25/56 (#8), pk 3/31/56 (#1, 20 wk), 50 wk; NYT fic 2/26/56 (#7), pk 3/25/56 (#1, 21 wk), 53 wk; tot 103 wk.
The Edge of Sadness (Atlantic Little Brown) NYT fic 6/25/61 (#6), pk 7/2/61 (#3, 1 wk), 28 wk; PW fic 6/26/61 (#8), pk 8/7/61 (#2, 1 wk), 23 wk; tot 51 wk.
I Was Dancing (Little Brown) PW fic 5/11/64 (#10, 2 wk), 5 wk; NYT fic 5/31/64 (#10, 1 wk); tot 6 wk.
All in the Family (Little Atlantic) NYT fic 10/23/66 (#9), pk 11/13/66 (#5, 2 wk), 25 wk; PW fic 10/31/66 (#7), pk 1/9/67 (#4, 1 wk),

25 wk; tot 50 wk.

O'Connor, Frank
The Stories of Frank O'Connor (Knopf) NYT fic 9/7/52 (#13, 1 wk), 5 wk.

O'Connor, Philip
Memoirs of a Public Baby (Norton) NYT gen 6/22/58 (#14, 1 wk).

O'Dell, Scott
Hill of the Hawk (Bobbs Merrill) NYT fic 11/2/47 (#15, 2 wk), 4 wk.
Island of Blue Dolphins (Houghton) NYT ch bst 5/14/61 (#7, 20 wk), 39 wk.
The King's Fifth (Dell) NYT ch bst 11/5/67 (#7, 26 wk).

O'Donnell, Kenneth P., and David F. Powers with Joe McCarthy
"Johnny, We Hardly Knew Ye"; Memories of John Fitzgerald Kennedy (Little Brown) NYT gen 12/10/72 (#9), pk 1/21/73 (#5, 5 wk), 19 wk; PW nf 1/1/73 (#9), pk 1/8/73 (#5, 4 wk), 15 wk; NYT pb gen 11/11/73 (#4, 8 wk); tot 42 wk.

O'Donnell, Mary Paula King
Those Other People (Houghton) NYT fic 2/17/46 (#15), pk 3/3/46 (#14, 1 wk), 2 wk.

O'Donnell, Steve
See David Letterman, et al.

Oechsner, Frederick
This Is the Enemy (Little Brown) NYT nf 11/29/42 (#16, 1 wk).

Oemler, Marie
The Purple Heights (Century) PW fic 1/8/21 (#7, 4 wk).

Ogburn, Charlton, Jr.
The Marauders (Harper) NYT gen 5/17/59 (#15, 1 wk).
The Winter Beach (Morrow) PW nf 12/5/66 (#8, 1 wk).

Ogilvy, David
Confessions of an Advertising Man (Atheneum) NYT gen 11/24/63 (#8), pk 2/23/64 (#4, 1 wk), 18 wk; PW nf 12/2/63 (#9), pk 2/17/64 (#5, 2 wk), 14 wk; tot 32 wk.

O'Hara, John
Appointment in Samarra (Harcourt) PW fic 11/10/34 (#10, 4 wk).
Butterfield 8 (Harcourt) PW fic 11/9/35 (#9, 8 wk); NYT fic 12/1/35 (#10, 4 wk); tot 12 wk.
Hope on Heaven (Harcourt) NYT fic 5/1/38 (#2, 4 wk).
Pipe Night (Duell Sloan & Pearce) NYT fic 4/22/45 (#13, 1 wk), 2 wk.
A Rage to Live (Random) NYT fic 9/4/49 (#6), pk 9/18/49 (#1, 6 wk), 32 wk; PW fic

9/10/49 (#5), pk 9/24/49 (#1, 4 wk), 24 wk; tot 56 wk.

The Farmer's Hotel (Random) NYT fic 12/2/51 (#13), pk 12/9/51 (#12, 1 wk), 3 wk.

Ten North Frederick (Random) NYT fic 12/11/55 (#11), pk 3/4/56 (#2, 9 wk), 32 wk; PW fic 1/14/56 (#4), pk 3/24/56 (#1, 1 wk), 22 wk; tot 54 wk.

A Family Party (Random) NYT fic 9/2/56 (#14, 1 wk).

From the Terrace (Random) NYT fic 12/7/58 (#10), pk 1/4/59 (#3, 5 wk), 27 wk; PW fic 12/29/58 (#7), pk 1/26/59 (#3, 3 wk), 24 wk; tot 51 wk.

Sermons and Soda-Water (Random) NYT fic 12/18/60 (#11), pk 1/22/61 (#4, 2 wk), 19 wk; PW fic 1/2/61 (#7), pk 1/16/61 (#4, 3 wk), 12 wk; tot 31 wk.

Ourselves to Know (Random) NYT fic 2/28/60 (#11), pk 3/27/60 (#4, 7 wk), 19 wk; PW fic 3/14/60 (#8), pk 4/4/60 (#4, 5 wk), 14 wk; tot 33 wk.

Assembly (Modern Library) NYT fic 1/14/62 (#16, 1 wk).

The Cape Cod Lighter (Random) NYT fic 12/16/62 (#11, 1 wk); PW fic 1/14/63 (#7), pk 2/4/63 (#5, 1 wk), 7 wk; tot 8 wk.

The Big Laugh (Random) NYT fic 6/3/62 (#9), pk 6/24/62 (#7, 2 wk), 14 wk; PW fic 6/11/62 (#8), pk 6/25/62 (#6, 1 wk), 8 wk; tot 22 wk.

The Hat on the Bed (Random) NYT fic 12/8/63 (#9), pk 1/26/64 (#3, 1 wk), 19 wk; PW fic 1/6/64 (#8), pk 1/27/64 (#4, 7 wk), 15 wk; tot 34 wk.

Elizabeth Appleton (Random) NYT fic 6/9/63 (#8), pk 6/30/63 (#2, 10 wk), 21 wk; PW fic 6/10/63 (#11), pk 7/15/63 (#2, 11 wk), 21 wk; tot 42 wk.

The Horse Knows the Way (Random) NYT fic 12/20/64 (#9), pk 2/7/65 (#4, 2 wk), 11 wk; PW fic 1/11/65 (#10), pk 2/8/65 (#4, 2 wk), 11 wk; tot 22 wk.

The Lockwood Concern (Random) PW fic 12/13/65 (#10), pk 1/24/66 (#3, 3 wk), 19 wk; NYT fic 12/19/65 (#9), pk 1/23/66 (#4, 3 wk), 15 wk; NYT pb fic 12/4/66 (#5), pk 1/1/67 (#4, 4 wk), 8 wk; tot 42 wk.

Waiting for Winter (Random) PW fic 1/2/67 (#10, 3 wk), 7 wk; NYT fic 1/15/67 (#10), pk 2/12/67 (#9, 2 wk), 9 wk; tot 16 wk.

The Instrument (Random) NYT fic 12/17/67 (#8), pk 2/4/68 (#4, 1 wk), 12 wk; PW fic 1/1/68 (#5), pk 1/22/68 (#3, 2 wk), 12 wk; tot 24 wk.

And Other Stories (Random House) NYT fic 12/22/68 (#10), pk 2/9/69 (#7, 1 wk), 6 wk; PW fic 1/27/69 (#9), pk 2/3/69 (#8, 1

wk), 5 wk; tot 11 wk.

O'Hara, Mary
My Friend Flicka (Lippincott) PW fic 11/15/41 (#9, 4 wk), 8 wk.

Thunderhead (Lippincott) NYT fic 10/10/43 (#8), pk 1/2/44 (#6, 3 wk), 18 wk; PW fic 11/13/43 (#7), pk 12/18/43 (#5, 2 wk), 8 wk; tot 26 wk.

Green Grass of Wyoming (Lippincott) NYT fic 12/1/46 (#7), pk 12/22/46 (#4, 1 wk), 14 wk; PW fic 12/14/46 (#5), pk 1/11/47 (#3, 1 wk), 11 wk; tot 25 wk.

The Son of Adam Wyngate (McKay) NYT fic 4/27/52 (#9), pk 6/8/52 (#8, 1 wk), 8 wk; PW fic 5/17/52 (#9, 1 wk); tot 9 wk.

O'Higgins, Patrick
Madame (Viking) PW nf 8/30/71 (#8), pk 9/6/71 (#7, 3 wk), 6 wk; NYT gen 9/19/71 (#10), pk 10/10/71 (#7, 1 wk), 3 wk; tot 9 wk.

Oke, Janette
Julia's Last Hope (Bethany) PW pb rel 11/9/90 (#4, 4 wk).

The Calling of Emily Evans (Bethany) PW pb rel 10/5/90 (#4, 4 wk), 8 wk.

O'Keeffe, Georgia
Georgia O'Keeffe (Penguin) PW td pb 11/28/77 (#8), pk 12/26/77 (#6, 1 wk), 2 wk; NYT td pb 12/4/77 (#13), pk 12/18/77 (#7, 1 wk), 7 wk; tot 9 wk.

Oldenbourg, Zoe
The World Is Not Enough (Pantheon) NYT fic 6/27/48 (#14), pk 7/25/48 (#7, 1 wk), 7 wk.

Cornerstone [trans. Edward Hyams] (Pantheon) NYT fic 1/23/55 (#14), pk 3/6/55 (#10, 1 wk), 10 wk.

Catherine the Great (Pantheon) NYT gen 3/14/65 (#10), pk 4/18/65 (#6, 2 wk), 10 wk; PW nf 3/22/65 (#10), pk 5/3/65 (#6, 1 wk), 9 wk; tot 19 wk.

The Crusades [trans. Anne Carter] (Pantheon) NYT gen 8/7/66 (#8, 1 wk), 2 wk.

Oliver, Edith
Dwarf's Blood (Viking) PW fic 8/15/31 (#9, 4 wk).

Olivier, Laurence
Confessions of an Actor: An Autobiography (Simon & Schuster) PW hc nf 1/28/83 (#15, 2 wk).

Olmstead, Nancy C.
See William A. Niering and_____

Olsen, Jack
Son: A Psychopath and His Victims (Dell) NYT pb nf 5/19/85 (#7), pk 6/2/85 (#2, 1 wk), 9 wk; PW mm pb 6/7/85 (#14, 1 wk);

tot 10 wk.

Doc; The Rape of the Town of Lovell (Dell) NYT pb nf 4/29/90 (#7), pk 5/13/90 (#3, 2 wk), 7 wk; PW mm pb 5/18/90 (#13, 2 wk); tot 9 wk.

Olson, Sigurd F.

The Singing Wilderness (Knopf) NYT gen 5/20/56 (#16, 1 wk).

O'Malley, Mary Dolling Sanders [all titles as by Ann Bridge]

Peking Picnic (Little Brown) PW fic 10/15/32 (#3, 4 wk), 16 wk.

The Ginger Griffin (Little Brown) PW fic 7/14/34 (#6, 4 wk).

Illyrian Spring (Little Brown) PW fic 9/14/35 (#4, 4 wk), 8 wk.

Enchanter's Nightshade (Little Brown) PW fic 12/11/37 (#8), pk 2/12/38 (#6, 4 wk), 16 wk; NYT fic 12/12/37 (#2, 4 wk); tot 20 wk.

Four-Part Setting (Little Brown) NYT fic 12/10/39 (#8, 4 wk).

Frontier Passage (Little Brown) NYT fic 11/1/42 (#17, 1 wk).

Singing Waters (Macmillan) NYT fic 7/14/46 (#15), pk 7/28/46 (#6, 2 wk), 11 wk.

The Dark Moment (Macmillan) NYT fic 1/27/52 (#11), pk 2/10/52 (#8, 1 wk), 5 wk.

The Portugese Escape (Macmillan) NYT fic 8/10/58 (#16), pk 9/21/58 (#9, 1 wk), 7 wk; PW fic 9/22/58 (#10, 1 wk); tot 8 wk.

The Numbered Account (McGraw) NYT fic 8/28/60 (#16, 1 wk).

O'Meara, Walter

The Grand Portage (Bobbs Merrill) NYT fic 5/13/51 (#16), pk 5/20/51 (#14, 1 wk), 2 wk.

O'Neill, Eugene

Mourning Becomes Electra (Liveright) PW nf 12/19/31 (#5, 12 wk), 16 wk.

Strange Interlude (Liveright) PW nf 4/28/28 (#7), pk 10/27/28 (#3, 4 wk), 24 wk.

O'Neill, George, and Nena O'Neill

Open Marriage (Evans) NYT gen 3/12/72 (#10), pk 4/16/72 (#3, 3 wk), 42 wk; PW nf 4/3/72 (#8), pk 10/16/72 (#2, 1 wk), 37 wk; NYT pb gen 5/13/73 (#2), pk 6/10/73 (#1, 8 wk), 24 wk; tot 103 wk.

O'Neill, Olivia

Indigo Nights (Berkley) PW mm pb 10/17/77 (#14, 1 wk).

O'Neill, Tip, with William Novak

Man of the House: The Life and Political Memoirs of Speaker Tip O'Neill (Random) NYT nf 9/13/87 (#15), pk 10/11/87 (#2, 1 wk), 21 wk; PW hc nf 9/18/87 (#9), pk 10/9/87 (#3, 2 wk), 19 wk; (St Martin's) PW mm pb

9/2/88 (#12, 1 wk), 3 wk; NYT pb nf 9/4/88 (#9), pk 9/18/88 (#3, 1 wk), 6 wk; tot 49 wk.

Onstott, Kyle

Mandingo (Denlinger) NYT fic 4/21/57 (#15, 4 wk).

Opie, Iona

The Oxford Nursery Rhyme Book (Oxford Univ.) NYT ch bst 11/18/56 (#14, 40 wk).

Oppenheim, E. Phillips

The Wicked Marquis (Little Brown) PW fic 7/5/19 (#9), pk 8/2/19 (#7, 4 wk), 12 wk.

The Devil's Paw (Little Brown) PW fic 10/23/20 (#7, 4 wk), 8 wk.

The Great Impersonation (Little Brown) PW fic 3/27/20 (#2, 8 wk), 16 wk.

The Profiteers (Little Brown) PW fic 8/6/21 (#6, 4 wk).

Jacob's Ladder (Little Brown) PW fic 3/26/21 (#8, 8 wk).

The Great Prince Shan (Little Brown) PW fic 5/13/22 (#4, 4 wk), 8 wk.

The Mystery Road (Little Brown) PW fic 7/21/23 (#9, 4 wk), 8 wk.

Stolen Idols (Little Brown) PW fic 6/20/25 (#8, 4 wk).

The Treasure House of Martin Hews (Little Brown) PW fic 3/9/29 (#6, 4 wk), 8 wk.

The Million Pound Deposit (Little Brown) PW fic 3/15/30 (#9, 4 wk).

The Lion and the Lamb (Little Brown) PW fic 9/20/30 (#9, 4 wk).

Up the Ladder of Gold (Little Brown) PW fic 2/21/31 (#2, 4 wk), 12 wk.

The Man from Sing Sing (Little Brown) PW fic 2/13/32 (#10, 4 wk).

The Spy Paramount (Little Brown) PW fic 2/9/35 (#7, 4 wk).

The Magnificent Hoax (Trident) NYT fic 9/13/36 (#4, 4 wk).

Floating Peril (Collier) NYT fic 2/2/36 (#6, 4 wk).

The Dumb Gods Speak (Little Brown) NYT fic 1/31/37 (#8, 4 wk).

Envoy Extraordinary (Little Brown) NYT fic 8/8/37 (#9, 4 wk).

Ask Miss Mott (Little Brown) NYT fic 7/4/37 (#4, 4 wk).

Curious Happenings to the Rooke Legatees (Little Brown) NYT fic 5/1/38 (#14, 4 wk).

The Colossus of Arcadia (Little Brown) NYT fic 7/31/38 (#8, 4 wk).

Sir Adam Disappeared (Little Brown) NYT fic 6/11/39 (#11, 4 wk).

Ormsbee, David

See Stephen Longstreet

Ornish, Dr. Dean

Dr. Dean Ornish's Program for Reversing Heart Disease (Random) NYT msc 10/21/90 (#5), pk 11/4/90 (#3, 3 wk), 5 wk; PW hc nf 10/26/90 (#11), pk 11/23/90 (#8, 1 wk), 5 wk; tot 10 wk.

O'Rourke, P.J., et al.
National Lampoon Sunday Newspaper Parody (21st Century Communications/Two Continents) PW td pb 9/4/78 (#7), pk 10/9/78 (#3, 1 wk), 8 wk; NYT td pb 11/19/78 (#12, 1 wk); tot 9 wk.

Orsborne, George Black
Master of the Girl Pat (Doubleday) NYT gen 2/27/49 (#16, 2 wk).

Orwell, George
Animal Farm (Harcourt) NYT gen 9/15/46 (#12), pk 9/29/46 (#7, 1 wk), 8 wk.
Nineteen Eighty-Four (Harcourt) NYT fic 7/3/49 (#13), pk 7/24/49 (#3, 5 wk), 20 wk; PW fic 7/30/49 (#5), pk 8/6/49 (#4, 2 wk), 6 wk; (NAL/Signet) NYT pb fic 1/15/84 (#11), pk 1/22/84 (#1, 7 wk), 14 wk; PW mm pb 1/20/84 (#7), pk 1/27/84 (#1, 2 wk), 11 wk; tot 51 wk.
Keep the Aspidistra Flying (Harcourt) NYT fic 1/29/56 (#15, 1 wk).

Osborn, Vera Maynard
There Were Two of Us (Whittlesey/McGraw) NYT fic 10/15/44 (#12, 1 wk).

Osgood, Phillips E.
Say I to Myself (Harvard Univ.) NYT gen 4/2/44 (#12, 1 wk).

Ossendowski, Ferdinand
Beasts, Men and Gods (Dutton) PW gen lit 4/14/23 (#4, 4 wk), 28 wk.
Man and Mystery in Asia (Dutton) PW gen lit 4/19/24 (#6, 4 wk).

Ostenso, Martha
Wild Geese (Dodd) PW fic 11/21/25 (#9), pk 12/19/25 (#3, 4 wk), 16 wk.
The Dark Dawn (Dodd) PW fic 12/18/26 (#7, 4 wk).

Ostrop, Cyril
Solving the Cube (Price Stern Sloan) NYT td pb 1/24/82 (#9), pk 2/28/82 (#5, 2 wk), 9 wk.

Ostrovsky, Victor, and Claire Hoy
By Way of Deception (St. Martin's) NYT nf 9/30/90 (#12), pk 10/7/90 (#1, 5 wk), 12 wk; PW hc nf 10/5/90 (#13), pk 10/12/90 (#1, 5 wk), 12 wk; tot 24 wk.

O'Sullivan, Maurice
Twenty Years A-Growing (Viking) PW nf 9/16/33 (#8), pk 10/14/33 (#6, 4 wk), 12 wk.

Ottley, Roi

New World A'Comin' (Arno) NYT gen 9/12/43 (#14), pk 9/19/43 (#10, 1 wk), 4 wk.

Ouchi, William G.
Theory Z: How American Business Can Meet the Japanese Challenge (Addison Wesley) PW hc nf 6/5/81 (#14), pk 7/24/81 (#6, 2 wk), 25 wk; NYT nf 6/28/81 (#11), pk 8/23/81 (#6, 2 wk), 22 wk; (Avon) PW mm pb 1/29/82 (#13), pk 2/5/82 (#7, 1 wk), 3 wk; NYT mm pb 3/7/82 (#12, 1 wk); tot 51 wk.

Oursler, Fulton
The Greatest Story Ever Told (Doubleday) NYT gen 3/6/49 (#14), pk 5/1/49 (#1, 3 wk), 47 wk; PW nf 4/2/49 (#4), pk 5/7/49 (#1, 1 wk), 22 wk; tot 69 wk.
The Greatest Book Ever Written (Doubleday) NYT gen 12/16/51 (#13), pk 2/3/52 (#4, 6 wk), 27 wk; PW nf 1/12/52 (#5), pk 3/15/52 (#3, 1 wk), 10 wk; tot 37 wk.
The Greatest Faith Ever Known (Doubleday) NYT gen 11/8/53 (#14), pk 1/31/54 (#12, 1 wk), 9 wk.

Overstreet, Harry Allen
The Mature Mind (Norton) NYT gen 8/28/49 (#14), pk 3/5/50 (#1, 9 wk), 72 wk; PW nf 10/1/49 (#5), pk 2/18/50 (#1, 15 wk), 49 wk; tot 121 wk.
The Great Enterprise (Norton) NYT gen 8/31/52 (#11), pk 11/16/52 (#6, 1 wk), 20 wk; PW nf 10/4/52 (#5, 3 wk), 11 wk; tot 31 wk.

_____, and Bonaro Overstreet
The Mind Alive (Norton) NYT gen 3/7/54 (#14), pk 5/23/54 (#3, 9 wk), 36 wk; PW nf 4/10/54 (#9), pk 7/31/54 (#2, 1 wk), 28 wk; tot 64 wk.
The Mind Goes Forth (Norton) NYT gen 8/5/56 (#12), pk 10/14/56 (#6, 1 wk), 17 wk; PW nf 9/17/56 (#6, 2 wk), 5 wk; tot 22 wk.
What We Must Know About Communism (Norton) NYT gen 2/15/59 (#9), pk 4/12/59 (#3, 7 wk), 25 wk; PW nf 3/9/59 (#8), pk 3/30/59 (#2, 1 wk), 15 wk; tot 40 wk.
The War Called Peace (Norton) NYT gen 5/21/61 (#15, 1 wk).
The Strange Tactics of Extremism (Norton) NYT gen 11/1/64 (#9, 1 wk), 3 wk; PW nf 12/28/64 (#9, 1 wk); tot 4 wk.

Owen, Jean
See Mildred Newman, et al.

Owen, Mark, and Delia Owen
Cry of the Kalahari (Houghton) NYT nf 3/17/85 (#13), pk 3/24/85 (#11, 1 wk), 4 wk.

Oxenbury, Helen
See Michael Rosen

Paar, Jack

My Sabre Is Bent (Simon & Schuster) NYT gen 12/31/61 (#16), pk 2/25/62 (#5, 1 wk), 16 wk; PW nf 1/15/62 (#10), pk 3/12/62 (#5, 1 wk), 11 wk; tot 27 wk.

_____, with John Reddy
I Kid You Not (Little Brown) NYT gen 4/24/60 (#11), pk 7/10/60 (#2, 2 wk), 27 wk; PW nf 5/2/60 (#6), pk 6/27/60 (#2, 1 wk), 20 wk; tot 47 wk.

Pack, Robert
See Larry Speakes and _____

Packard, Vance
The Hidden Persuaders (McKay) NYT gen 6/2/57 (#15), pk 8/4/57 (#1, 6 wk), 50 wk; PW nf 7/1/57 (#6), pk 7/29/57 (#1, 5 wk), 37 wk; tot 87 wk.
The Status Seekers (McKay) NYT gen 5/17/59 (#14), pk 6/14/59 (#1, 18 wk), 51 wk; PW nf 5/25/59 (#3), pk 6/8/59 (#1, 18 wk), 45 wk; tot 96 wk.
The Waste Makers (McKay) NYT gen 10/2/60 (#15), pk 11/6/60 (#1, 4 wk), 31 wk; PW nf 10/17/60 (#7), pk 10/31/60 (#1, 5 wk), 27 wk; tot 58 wk.
The Pyramid Climbers (McGraw) NYT gen 11/18/62 (#15), pk 12/9/62 (#10, 2 wk), 5 wk; PW nf 12/3/62 (#11), pk 1/7/63 (#8, 1 wk), 6 wk; tot 11 wk.
The Naked Society (McKay) NYT gen 4/12/64 (#9), pk 4/26/64 (#5, 10 wk), 23 wk; PW nf 4/13/64 (#10), pk 5/25/64 (#2, 2 wk), 23 wk; tot 46 wk.
A Nation of Strangers (McKay) NYT gen 10/1/72 (#10), pk 11/26/72 (#6, 1 wk), 8 wk; PW nf 10/23/72 (#9), pk 11/20/72 (#7, 2 wk), 7 wk; tot 15 wk.

Packer, Lady Joy Petersen
Valley of the Vines (Lippincott) NYT fic 2/12/56 (#15, 1 wk), 2 wk.

Paderewski, Ignace Jan, and Mary Lawton
The Paderewski Memoirs (Scribner) PW nf 12/10/38 (#10, 4 wk).

Page, Bruce P.
See Lewis L. Chester, et al.
See Charles Raw, et al.

Page, Elizabeth
The Tree of Liberty (Farrar) PW fic 4/8/39 (#4, 4 wk), 24 wk; NYT fic 4/9/39 (#2, 4 wk), 8 wk; tot 32 wk.

Page, Marco
Fast Company (Dodd) NYT fic 5/1/38 (#11, 4 wk).

Palffy, Eleanor

The Lady and the Painter (Coward Mc-Cann) NYT fic 12/23/51 (#15, 5 wk).

Pallone, Dave, with Alan Steinberg
Behind the Mask: My Double Life in Baseball (Viking) NYT nf 7/15/90 (#15), pk 7/29/90 (#8, 2 wk), 5 wk; PW hc nf 7/20/90 (#12), pk 8/10/90 (#6, 1 wk), 7 wk; tot 12 wk.

Palmer, Michael Stephen
The Sisterhood (Bantam) PW mm pb 9/17/82 (#11), pk 10/1/82 (#10, 1 wk), 4 wk; NYT mm pb 9/19/82 (#10, 1 wk), 5 wk; tot 9 wk.
Side Effects (Bantam) NYT pb fic 4/14/85 (#9, 1 wk), 4 wk; PW mm pb 4/19/85 (#12, 2 wk), 3 wk; tot 7 wk.
Flashback (Bantam) NYT pb fic 9/11/88 (#15, 1 wk); PW mm pb 9/16/88 (#12, 1 wk); tot 2 wk.

Paone, Marion
See James Coco and _____

Papashvily, George, and Helen Papashvily
Anything Can Happen (Harper) NYT gen 1/28/45 (#7), pk 3/4/45 (#2, 7 wk), 34 wk; PW nf 2/10/45 (#9), pk 3/17/45 (#1, 4 wk), 21 wk; tot 55 wk.

Papini, Giovanni
Life of Christ (Harcourt) PW gen lit 5/26/23 (#1, 24 wk), 32 wk; PW nf 11/24/23 (#1, 8 wk), 12 wk; tot 44 wk.

Paretsky, Sara
Burn Marks (Delacorte) NYT fic 4/8/90 (#14, 1 wk); PW hc fic 4/20/90 (#14, 1 wk), 3 wk; tot 4 wk.

Parker, Bertha Morris
The Golden Book of Science (Simon & Schuster) NYT ch bst 11/18/56 (#3, 40 wk).

Parker, Cornelia Stratton
An American Idyll (Atlantic) PW gen 1/31/20 (#3, 4 wk), 24 wk.

Parker, Dorothy
Laments for the Living (Viking) PW fic 8/23/30 (#7), pk 9/20/30 (#6, 4 wk), 12 wk.
Death and Taxes (Viking) PW nf 8/15/31 (#8, 4 wk).
After Such Pleasures (Viking) PW fic 12/9/33 (#7), pk 1/13/33 (#6, 4 wk), 8 wk.
Not So Deep as a Well (Viking) NYT gen 1/31/37 (#2, 4 wk).
Here Lies: The Collected Stories of Dorothy Parker (Viking) NYT fic 6/11/39 (#2, 4 wk), 8 wk; PW fic 7/15/39 (#10, 4 wk); tot 12 wk.

Parker, Gilbert

Wild Youth and Another (Lippincott) PW fic 5/3/19 (#9, 4 wk).

No Defence (Lippincott) PW fic 1/8/21 (#9, 8 wk).

Parker, Robert B.
Valediction (Delacorte) NYT fic 5/20/84 (#14, 1 wk), 2 wk.

A Catskill Eagle (Delacorte) PW hc fic 6/14/85 (#12, 4 wk), 7 wk; NYT fic 6/16/85 (#14), pk 7/7/85 (#6, 1 wk), 9 wk; (Dell) NYT pb fic 6/1/86 (#10), pk 6/29/86 (#5, 1 wk), 8 wk; PW mm pb 6/6/86 (#7), pk 6/13/86 (#5, 1 wk), 8 wk; tot 32 wk.

Taming a Sea-Horse (Lawrence/Delacorte) NYT fic 6/15/86 (#8), pk 6/22/86 (#7, 2 wk), 8 wk; PW hc fic 6/20/86 (#11), pk 7/4/86 (#6, 1 wk), 8 wk; (Dell) NYT pb fic 6/7/87 (#6, 1 wk), 5 wk; PW mm pb 6/12/87 (#7, 1 wk), 5 wk; tot 26 wk.

Pale Kings and Princes (Delacorte) PW hc fic 6/12/87 (#11), pk 6/19/87 (#6, 2 wk), 9 wk; NYT fic 6/14/87 (#6), pk 6/21/87 (#3, 1 wk), 10 wk; (Dell) NYT pb fic 7/10/88 (#11), pk 7/17/88 (#7, 1 wk), 5 wk; PW mm pb 7/15/88 (#8, 1 wk), 5 wk; tot 29 wk.

Crimson Joy (Delacorte) PW hc fic 6/3/88 (#12), pk 7/1/88 (#6, 1 wk), 11 wk; NYT fic 6/5/88 (#14), pk 6/19/88 (#6, 3 wk), 11 wk; (Dell) PW mm pb 5/12/89 (#13), pk 5/26/89 (#5, 1 wk), 6 wk; NYT pb fic 5/14/89 (#9), pk 5/21/89 (#7, 1 wk), 4 wk; tot 32 wk.

Playmates (Putnam) NYT fic 5/21/89 (#7), pk 6/4/89 (#5, 1 wk), 8 wk; PW hc fic 5/26/89 (#8), pk 6/9/89 (#5, 1 wk), 8 wk; (Berkley) NYT pb fic 3/4/90 (#8), pk 3/18/90 (#5, 1 wk), 6 wk; PW mm pb 3/9/90 (#9), pk 3/16/90 (#7, 1 wk), 5 wk; tot 27 wk.

Stardust (Putnam) NYT fic 7/29/90 (#12), pk 8/5/90 (#6, 1 wk), 7 wk; PW hc fic 8/3/90 (#7), pk 8/17/90 (#4, 1 wk), 7 wk; tot 14 wk.

See also Raymond Chandler and _____

Parker, Tom
See Dave Winfield and _____

Parkinson, Cyril Northcote
Parkinson's Law (Houghton) NYT gen 11/17/57 (#16), pk 1/5/58 (#9, 1 wk), 20 wk; PW nf 2/17/58 (#10, 2 wk); tot 22 wk.

The Law and the Profits (Houghton) NYT gen 3/20/60 (#11), pk 4/24/60 (#4, 4 wk), 22 wk; PW nf 4/4/60 (#7), pk 5/9/60 (#3, 3 wk), 16 wk; tot 38 wk.

In-Laws and Outlaws (Houghton) NYT gen 9/16/62 (#15), pk 10/28/62 (#11, 1 wk), 8 wk; PW nf 10/8/62 (#14, 1 wk); tot 9 wk.

Parks, Lillian Rogers, with Frances Spatz Leighton
My Thirty Years Backstairs at the White House (Fleet) NYT gen 3/19/61 (#16), pk 5/14/61 (#4, 1 wk), 25 wk; PW nf 4/24/61 (#8), pk 7/3/61 (#3, 1 wk), 19 wk; tot 44 wk.

Parrish, Anne
The Perennial Bachelor (Harper) PW fic 10/24/25 (#6), pk 11/21/25 (#1, 8 wk), 20 wk.

Tomorrow Morning (Harper) PW fic 2/19/27 (#3), pk 3/19/27 (#2, 4 wk), 16 wk.

All Kneeling (Harper) PW fic 10/27/28 (#2, 4 wk), 12 wk.

Loads of Love (Harper) PW fic 3/19/32 (#2, 4 wk), 12 wk.

Sea Level (Harper) PW fic 2/10/34 (#6, 4 wk).

Mr. Despondency's Daughter (Harper) NYT fic 10/9/38 (#5, 4 wk).

Parrott, Ursula
Ex-Wife (Cape & Smith) PW fic 12/14/29 (#7, 4 wk).

Parsons, Louella O.
Gay Illiterate (Doubleday) NYT gen 2/6/44 (#13), pk 2/20/44 (#8, 3 wk), 10 wk.

Parsons, Robert P.
Trail to Light (Bobbs Merrill) NYT gen 8/8/43 (#15, 1 wk).

Parton, Margaret
Laughter on the Hill (Whittlesey) NYT gen 7/1/45 (#18), pk 7/15/45 (#10, 1 wk), 9 wk.

Partridge, Bellamy
Country Lawyer (Whittlesey) PW nf 9/16/39 (#7), pk 11/11/39 (#1, 16 wk), 32 wk; NYT gen 10/8/39 (#1, 12 wk), 16 wk; tot 48 wk.

Big Family (Whittlesey) PW nf 11/15/41 (#4, 4 wk), 16 wk.

Excuse My Dust (McGraw) NYT gen 10/24/43 (#15, 1 wk), 2 wk.

January Thaw (McGraw) NYT fic 9/30/45 (#11, 1 wk), 5 wk.

Pascal, Francine
The Love Bet (Bantam) PW ch yn ad 9/28/90 (#2, 4 wk).

The Parent Plot (Bantam) PW ch pc 8/31/90 (#4, 4 wk).

Friend Against Friend (Bantam) PW ch yn ad 10/26/90 (#3, 4 wk).

Ms. Quarterback (Bantam) PW ch yn ad 11/30/90 (#4, 4 wk).

_____, and Kate William
Perfect Summer [created by Pascal, written by William] (Bantam) NYT pb fic 8/25/85 (#14, 1 wk).

Pascale, Richard Tanner, and Anthony G.

Athos
   The Art of Japanese Management (Simon &
Schuster) NYT nf 7/26/81 (#13), pk 8/16/81
(#11, 1 wk), 3 wk.

Passell, Peter and Leonard Ross
   The Best (Farrar) PW nf 8/12/74 (#9), pk
8/26/74 (#7, 1 wk), 6 wk; NYT gen 9/1/74
(#9, 1 wk); tot 7 wk.

Pasternak, Boris
   Doctor Zhivago (Pantheon) NYT fic 9/28/
58 (#6), pk 11/16/58 (#1, 24 wk), 57 wk; PW
fic 9/29/58 (#7), pk 11/24/58 (#1, 27 wk), 54
wk; NYT pb fic 3/6/66 (#5), pk 7/3/66 (#2,
4 wk), 36 wk; tot 147 wk.
   I Remember: Sketch for an Autobiography
(Pantheon) NYT gen 4/26/59 (#16), pk 5/17/
59 (#10, 1 wk), 7 wk.

Paterson, Isabel
   Never Ask the End (Morrow) PW fic 2/11/
33 (#9, 4 wk).

Patman, Wright
   *Our American Government: What Is It?
How Does It Function?* (Government Print-
ing Office) NYT gen 3/28/48 (#15, 1 wk).

Paton, Alan
   Cry, The Beloved Country (Scribner) NYT
fic 2/29/48 (#15), pk 3/28/48 (#11, 1 wk), 24
wk; PW fic 3/19/49 (#10, 1 wk); tot 25 wk.
   Too Late the Phalarope (Scribner) NYT fic
9/6/53 (#10), pk 10/18/53 (#2, 1 wk), 22 wk;
PW fic 9/26/53 (#3), pk 10/17/53 (#1, 1 wk),
14 wk; tot 36 wk.
   Tales from a Troubled Land (Scribner)
NYT fic 5/21/61 (#16, 1 wk).

Patrick, Vincent
   The Pope of Greenwich Village (Pocket)
NYT mm pb 8/24/80 (#15, 4 wk); PW mm
pb 8/29/80 (#11, 2 wk); tot 6 wk.

Patterson, Harry
   The Valhalla Exchange (Stein & Day) PW
hc fic 3/7/77 (#10), pk 4/4/77 (#8, 4 wk), 9
wk; NYT fic 3/20/77 (#10), pk 4/3/77 (#7, 2
wk), 7 wk; (Fawcett/Crest) PW mm pb 3/6/
78 (#12, 1 wk); NYT mm pb 3/12/78 (#13),
pk 3/19/78 (#3, 1 wk), 3 wk; tot 20 wk.
   To Catch a King (Stein & Day) PW hc fic
8/20/79 (#15, 2 wk); NYT fic 9/23/79 (#13,
1 wk), 4 wk; tot 6 wk.

Patton, Frances Gray
   Good Morning, Miss Dove (Dodd) NYT fic
11/28/54 (#13), pk 1/23/55 (#7, 1 wk), 19 wk;
PW fic 12/18/54 (#9), pk 1/29/55 (#6, 1 wk),
7 wk; tot 26 wk.

Patton, Gen. George S.
   War as I Knew It (Houghton) NYT gen
11/30/47 (#7), pk 12/14/47 (#6, 4 wk), 16 wk;

PW nf 12/13/47 (#5, 1 wk), 4 wk; tot 20 wk.

Paul, Barbara
   The Three-Minute Universe (Pocket) NYT
pb fic 8/14/88 (#12), pk 8/21/88 (#10, 1 wk),
3 wk.

Paul, Elliot Harold
   The Life and Death of a Spanish Town
(Random) NYT gen 9/12/37 (#5, 4 wk).
   The Last Time I Saw Paris (Random) PW
nf 5/9/42 (#7), pk 7/11/42 (#1, 4 wk), 23 wk;
NYT nf 8/9/42 (#1, 1 wk), 16 wk; tot 39 wk.
   Linden on the Saugus Branch (Random)
NYT gen 8/10/47 (#12), pk 9/7/47 (#5, 2
wk), 14 wk; PW nf 8/23/47 (#5, 6 wk); tot
20 wk.
   A Ghost Town on the Yellowstone (Random)
NYT gen 8/8/48 (#14), pk 8/15/48 (#9, 1
wk), 6 wk.
   Springtime in Paris (Random) NYT gen
9/3/50 (#13), pk 9/10/50 (#12, 2 wk), 6 wk.

Pauling, Linus
   How to Live Longer and Feel Better (Freeman) NYT msc pb 4/6/86 (#6, 1 wk).

Paulos, John Allen
   *Innumeracy: Mathematical Illiteracy and Its
Consequences* (Farrar/Hill & Wang) NYT nf
2/26/89 (#15), pk 3/26/89 (#5, 3 wk), 18 wk;
PW hc nf 3/3/89 (#15), pk 3/31/89 (#11, 1
wk), 9 wk; tot 27 wk.

Paulsen, Gary
   Hatchet (Puffin) PW ch yn ad 8/31/90 (#2,
4 wk), 12 wk.

**Pavarotti, Luciano, and William
   Wright**
   Pavarotti: My Own Story (Doubleday) PW
hc nf 4/17/81 (#12), pk 6/12/81 (#6, 1 wk), 12
wk; NYT nf 4/26/81 (#8), pk 5/31/81 (#5, 2
wk), 10 wk; tot 22 wk.

Payne, Pierre Stephen Robert
   Forever China (Dodd) NYT gen 10/28/45
(#16), pk 12/16/45 (#6, 1 wk), 2 wk.
   The Life and Death of Adolf Hitler (Praeger)
PW nf 5/7/73 (#7, 2 wk), 4 wk; NYT gen
5/20/73 (#9), pk 5/27/73 (#8, 1 wk), 2 wk;
tot 6 wk.

Peabody, Marian Lawrence
   To Be Young Was Very Heaven (Houghton)
PW nf 7/3/67 (#11), pk 7/10/67 (#8, 1 wk),
3 wk.

Peacock, Jere
   Valhalla (Putnam) NYT fic 2/26/61 (#12,
1 wk), 3 wk.

Peale, Norman Vincent
   The Power of Positive Thinking (Prentice
Hall) NYT gen 11/9/52 (#12), pk 5/17/53 (#1,

97 wk), 186 wk; PW nf 11/29/52 (#5), pk 2/14/53 (#1, 90 wk), 167 wk; tot 353 wk.

The Amazing Results of Positive Thinking (Prentice Hall) NYT gen 12/6/59 (#16), pk 1/10/60 (#13, 1 wk), 3 wk.

Stay Alive All Your Life (Prentice Hall) NYT gen 4/7/57 (#9), pk 4/28/57 (#4, 6 wk), 37 wk; PW nf 5/6/57 (#6), pk 5/20/57 (#3, 4 wk), 25 wk; tot 62 wk.

_____, and Smiley Blanton
A Guide to Confident Living (Prentice Hall) NYT gen 4/11/48 (#14), pk 8/21/49 (#5, 6 wk), 80 wk; PW hc nf 6/19/48 (#8), pk 9/10/48 (#5, 1 wk), 18 wk; tot 98 wk.

The Art of Real Happiness (Prentice Hall) NYT gen 4/2/50 (#14), pk 5/14/50 (#6, 2 wk), 15 wk; PW nf 4/15/50 (#8), pk 4/29/50 (#5, 1 wk), 5 wk; tot 20 wk.

Pearce, Mary E.
Apple Tree Lean Down (Ballantine) PW mm pb 8/29/77 (#11, 1 wk), 2 wk.

Pearsall, Paul
Super Marital Sex: Loving for Life (Doubleday) NYT msc 11/8/87 (#2, 5 wk), 10 wk; PW hc nf 11/13/87 (#9), pk 1/29/88 (#5, 1 wk), 9 wk; tot 19 wk.

Superimmunity: Master Your Emotions and Improve Your Health (McGraw) PW hc nf 4/10/87 (#14, 1 wk), 2 wk; NYT msc 5/3/87 (#5), pk 5/10/87 (#4, 1 wk), 2 wk; tot 4 wk.

The Power of the Family: Strength, Comfort and Healing (Doubleday) NYT msc 3/25/90 (#5, 2 wk); PW hc nf 3/30/90 (#10, 1 wk), 3 wk; tot 5 wk.

Pearson, Diane
Csardas (Fawcett/Crest) PW mm pb 7/19/76 (#14), pk 8/9/76 (#8, 1 wk), 8 wk; NYT mm pb 8/15/76 (#10), pk 8/22/76 (#8, 1 wk), 2 wk; tot 10 wk.

Pearson, Drew
The Senator (Doubleday) NYT fic 9/15/68 (#10), pk 11/3/68 (#4, 1 wk), 17 wk; PW fic 9/30/68 (#8), pk 11/11/68 (#4, 1 wk), 15 wk; tot 32 wk.

_____, and Robert S. Allen
Washington Merry-Go-Round (Liveright) PW nf 9/19/31 (#1, 16 wk), 32 wk; (Blue Ribbon) PW nf 9/10/32 (#9, 4 wk); tot 36 wk.

More Merry-Go-Round (Liveright) PW nf 10/15/32 (#1, 4 wk), 12 wk.

The Nine Old Men (Doubleday) PW nf 12/12/36 (#10), pk 4/10/37 (#3, 4 wk), 16 wk; NYT nf 3/7/37 (#5), pk 4/4/37 (#4, 4 wk), 8 wk; tot 24 wk.

_____, and Jack Anderson

U.S.A.—Second-Class Power? (Simon & Schuster) NYT gen 11/9/58 (#14, 1 wk).

The Case Against Congress (Simon & Schuster) NYT gen 9/8/68 (#10), pk 9/29/68 (#6, 1 wk), 9 wk; PW nf 10/7/68 (#10), pk 10/28/68 (#8, 1 wk), 5 wk; tot 14 wk.

_____, and Constantine Brown
The American Diplomatic Game (Doubleday) PW nf 3/16/35 (#7, 4 wk).

Pearson, Durk, and Sandy Shaw
Life Extension: Adding Years to Your Life and Life to Your Years—A Practical Scientific Approach (Warner) PW hc nf 7/30/82 (#10), pk 9/10/82 (#1, 9 wk), 35 wk; NYT nf 8/1/82 (#13), pk 8/8/82 (#1, 7 wk), 36 wk; PW td pb 6/3/83 (#8), pk 7/8/83 (#1, 2 wk), 20 wk; NYT td pb 6/5/83 (#6), pk 7/3/83 (#1, 2 wk), 25 wk; tot 116 wk.

The Life Extension Companion (Warner) PW hc nf 4/20/84 (#15, 3 wk); NYT msc 4/22/84 (#5), pk 4/29/84 (#4, 3 wk), 7 wk; tot 10 wk.

The Life Extension Weight Loss Program (Doubleday) PW hc nf 5/16/86 (#14, 1 wk).

Pearson, Hesketh
Oscar Wilde (Harper) NYT gen 8/4/46 (#13), pk 9/29/46 (#5, 1 wk), 13 wk; PW nf 9/14/46 (#10), pk 9/28/46 (#5, 1 wk), 4 wk; tot 17 wk.

Dickens (Methuen) NYT gen 6/26/49 (#8, 1 wk), 3 wk.

Dizzy (Harper) NYT gen 9/9/51 (#16), pk 10/14/51 (#5, 1 wk), 13 wk; PW nf 10/13/51 (#5), pk 11/3/51 (#3, 1 wk), 7 wk; tot 20 wk.

Pearson, T. Gilbert
Birds of America [ed.] (Garden City) PW nf 6/13/36 (#10), pk 7/11/36 (#9, 4 wk), 8 wk.

Pearson, William
A Fever in the Blood (St. Martin's) NYT fic 12/6/59 (#16), pk 12/27/59 (#14, 1 wk), 3 wk.

Pease, Howard
Secret Cargo (Doubleday) PW juv 6/20/31 (#8), pk 7/18/31 (#7, 4 wk), 8 wk.

Peattie, Donald Culross
Green Laurels (Simon & Schuster) PW nf 9/12/36 (#10, 4 wk).

A Prairie Grove (Literary Guild) NYT gen 5/1/38 (#15, 4 wk).

Audubon's America [ed.] (Houghton) PW nf 11/16/40 (#9, 4 wk), 8 wk.

Journey Into America (Houghton) NYT gen 10/24/43 (#14), pk 3/5/44 (#11, 1 wk), 4 wk.

The Rainbow Book of Nature (World) NYT ch bst 11/17/57 (#15, 40 wk).

Peck, Joseph H.

All About Men (Prentice Hall) NYT gen 7/6/58 (#10), pk 7/27/58 (#8, 3 wk), 14 wk; PW nf 7/28/58 (#8, 1 wk), 6 wk; tot 20 wk.
   Life with Women—And How to Survive It (Prentice Hall) NYT gen 6/11/61 (#14), pk 7/9/61 (#8, 7 wk), 16 wk; PW nf 7/3/61 (#8), pk 7/17/61 (#7, 2 wk), 11 wk; tot 27 wk.

Peck, M. Scott, M.D.
   The Road Less Traveled (Simon & Schuster/Touchstone) NYT td pb 10/16/83 (#12), pk 11/6/83 (#10, 2 wk), 11 wk; NYT pb nf 1/22/84 (#4), pk 6/2/85 (#1, 30 wk), 363 wk; PW td pb 6/29/84 (#9), pk 8/30/85 (#1, 12 wk), 286 wk; tot 660 wk.
   People of the Lie (Simon & Schuster/Touchstone) NYT nf 2/12/84 (#13), pk 3/4/84 (#9, 1 wk), 15 wk; NYT pb nf 8/18/85 (#5, 2 wk); tot 17 wk.
   The Different Drum: Community Making and Peace (Simon & Schuster) NYT nf 6/7/87 (#10), pk 6/21/87 (#6, 1 wk), 17 wk; PW hc nf 6/12/87 (#14), pk 6/26/87 (#10, 1 wk), 8 wk; tot 25 wk.
   A Bed by the Window (Bantam) PW hc fic 9/14/90 (#9, 2 wk), 5 wk; NYT fic 9/16/90 (#14), pk 9/23/90 (#13, 2 wk), 4 wk; tot 9 wk.

Pedler, Margaret Bass
   The Moon Out of Reach (Doran) PW fic 7/29/22 (#8, 8 wk).
   The Vision of Desire (Doran) PW fic 5/26/23 (#8, 4 wk).
   Red Ashes (Doran) PW fic 9/26/25 (#7, 4 wk), 8 wk.
   To-Morrow's Tangle (Doran) PW fic 8/14/26 (#8, 4 wk).
   Flame in the Wind (Doubleday) NYT fic 5/9/37 (#5, 4 wk).

Peel, Kathy, and Joy Mahaffey
   A Mother's Manual for Schoolday Survival (Focus/Word) PW pb rel 10/5/90 (#5, 4 wk), 8 wk.

Peeples, Edwin A.
   Swing Low (Houghton) NYT fic 5/6/45 (#17), pk 5/20/45 (#12, 1 wk), 2 wk.

Pella, Judith
   See Michael Phillips and _____

Pendleton, Don
   Mack Bolan: Death Games (Worldwide) NYT pb fic 7/28/85 (#15, 1 wk).

Penkovskiy, Oleg
   The Penkovskiy Papers (Doubleday) NYT gen 12/26/65 (#9), pk 1/16/66 (#7, 3 wk), 12 wk; PW nf 1/3/66 (#9), pk 1/24/66 (#6, 2 wk), 12 wk; tot 24 wk.

Pennell, Joseph Stanley

The History of Rome Hanks (Scribners) NYT fic 8/6/44 (#8), pk 9/3/44 (#4, 4 wk), 15 wk; PW fic 8/12/44 (#9), pk 9/16/44 (#2, 1 wk), 12 wk; tot 27 wk.

Penney, Alexandra
   How to Make Love to a Man (Potter) PW hc nf 7/3/81 (#14), pk 11/13/81 (#2, 2 wk), 42 wk; NYT nf 8/23/81 (#9), pk 9/13/81 (#4, 3 wk), 34 wk; (Dell) PW mm pb 5/14/82 (#12), pk 6/4/82 (#4, 2 wk), 15 wk; NYT mm pb 5/23/82 (#14), pk 7/11/82 (#6, 1 wk), 15 wk; tot 106 wk.
   How to Make Love to Each Other (Putnam) NYT nf 3/20/83 (#12, 1 wk); PW hc nf 3/25/83 (#12, 1 wk), 2 wk; tot 3 wk.
   Great Sex (Putnam) PW hc nf 6/7/85 (#15), pk 6/14/85 (#11, 2 wk), 3 wk.

Penrose, Roger
   The Emperor's New Mind (Oxford Univ.) NYT nf 1/21/90 (#12), pk 2/11/90 (#7, 3 wk), 13 wk; PW hc nf 2/16/90 (#13, 2 wk), 4 wk; tot 17 wk.

Pentecost, Hugh
   See Judson Pentecost Phillips

Pepper, George Wharton
   Philadelphia Lawyer (Lippincott) NYT gen 11/26/44 (#9), pk 1/7/45 (#8, 1 wk), 15 wk.

Percy, Walker
   Love in the Ruins (Farrar) NYT fic 6/6/71 (#9), pk 7/4/71 (#8, 1 wk), 7 wk; PW fic 6/14/71 (#8, 1 wk), 3 wk; tot 10 wk.
   The Second Coming (Farrar) PW hc fic 7/25/80 (#13), pk 8/15/80 (#8, 1 wk), 9 wk; NYT fic 7/27/80 (#10, 4 wk), 7 wk; tot 16 wk.
   The Thanatos Syndrome (Farrar) NYT fic 4/12/87 (#11), pk 5/3/87 (#7, 1 wk), 9 wk; PW hc fic 4/24/87 (#13), pk 5/1/87 (#8, 1 wk), 8 wk; (Ivy) NYT pb fic 5/1/88 (#7, 1 wk), 4 wk; PW td pb 5/6/88 (#11), pk 5/27/88 (#9, 1 wk), 5 wk; tot 26 wk.

Percy, William Alexander
   Lanterns on the Levee (Knopf) PW nf 6/14/41 (#9, 4 wk), 12 wk.

Perelman, Sidney Joseph
   Acres and Pains (Reynal & Hitchcock) NYT gen 9/14/47 (#13), pk 10/12/47 (#8, 1 wk), 3 wk.
   Westward Ha! (Simon & Schuster) NYT gen 8/29/48 (#9), pk 10/3/48 (#4, 1 wk), 19 wk; PW nf 9/18/48 (#8), pk 10/2/48 (#3, 1 wk), 5 wk; tot 24 wk.
   The Road to Miltown (Simon & Schuster) NYT gen 2/10/57 (#12), pk 3/24/57 (#4, 2 wk), 19 wk; PW nf 3/4/57 (#7), pk 4/15/57

(#3, 1 wk), 10 wk; tot 29 wk.

Peretti, Frank
   This Present Darkness (Crossway) PW pb
rel 10/5/90 (#1, 8 wk).
   Piercing the Darkness (Crossway) PW pb
rel 10/5/90 (#2, 8 wk).

Perkins, Frances
   The Roosevelt I Knew (Viking) NYT gen
11/24/46 (#10), pk 1/5/47 (#2, 1 wk), 24 wk;
PW nf 12/14/46 (#4), pk 12/28/46 (#2, 2 wk),
16 wk; tot 40 wk.

Perkins, Lucy Fitch
   The Indian Twins (Houghton) PW juv 2/
21/31 (#6, 4 wk), 16 wk.
   The Chinese Twins (Houghton) NYT juv
12/1/35 (#5, 4 wk).

Perkins, Marlin
   Marlin Perkins' Zooparade (Rand McNally)
NYT ch bst 11/13/55 (#7, 40 wk).

Perry, Bliss
   And Gladly Teach (Houghton) PW hc fic
11/9/35 (#9, 4 wk).

Perry, George Sessions
   Texas: A World in Itself (Whittlesey/
McGraw) NYT nf 11/1/42 (#12), pk 1/31/43
(#8, 1 wk), 20 wk; NYT gen 4/11/43 (#15, 1
wk); tot 21 wk.
   Round-Up Time (McGraw) NYT gen 10/
31/43 (#17), pk 12/26/43 (#15, 1 wk), 3 wk.
   Hackberry Cavalier (Viking) NYT fic 3/5/
44 (#12, 1 wk).
   Where Away (Whittlesey/McGraw) NYT
gen 12/10/44 (#15), pk 1/7/45 (#12, 2 wk), 14
wk.
   Walls Rise Up (Whittlesey) NYT fic 4/22/
45 (#11, 1 wk), 4 wk.

Perry, John D.
   See Alice Kahn Ladas, et al.

Perry, Paul
   See Melvin Morse and _____

Pershing, Gen. John J.
   My Experiences in the World War (Stokes)
PW nf 6/20/31 (#5, 4 wk).

Peter, John
   McCall's Giant Golden Make-It Book [de-
signed and arranged] (Golden) NYT ch bst
11/14/54 (#5, 40 wk).

Peter, Laurence J.
   The Peter Prescription (Morrow) NYT gen
8/13/72 (#8), pk 9/24/72 (#2, 9 wk), 26 wk;
PW nf 8/14/72 (#8), pk 10/2/72 (#2, 3 wk),
26 wk; tot 52 wk.

_____, **and Raymond Hull**
   The Peter Principle (Morrow) NYT gen
5/18/69 (#7), pk 7/20/69 (#1, 21 wk), 48 wk;

PW nf 5/26/69 (#8), pk 8/18/69 (#1, 15 wk),
49 wk; NYT pb gen 3/1/70 (#1, 32 wk), 48
wk; tot 145 wk.

Peterkin, Julia
   Scarlet Sister Mary (Bobbs Merrill) PW fic
6/8/29 (#6), pk 8/10/29 (#3, 4 wk), 12 wk.
   Bright Skin (Bobbs Merrill) PW fic 5/14/
32 (#3, 4 wk), 12 wk.

Peters, Arthur Anderson
   Finistere (Farrar) NYT fic 3/25/51 (#16),
pk 4/1/51 (#15, 1 wk), 2 wk.

Peters, Harry T.
   Currier & Ives (Doubleday) NYT nf 1/10/
43 (#20, 1 wk).

Peters, Lulu Hunt
   Diet and Health (Reilly) NYT nf 5/13/22
(#2), pk 9/26/25 (#1, 8 wk), 72 wk; PW gen
lit 6/17/22 (#3), pk 6/20/25 (#1, 4 wk), 68
wk; tot 140 wk.

Peters, Natasha
   Savage Surrender (Ace) PW mm pb 9/26/
77 (#9), pk 10/3/77 (#7, 2 wk), 9 wk; NYT
mm pb 10/9/77 (#11), pk 11/6/77 (#8, 1 wk),
10 wk; tot 19 wk.
   Dangerous Obsession (Ace) PW mm pb
9/25/78 (#15), pk 10/2/78 (#14, 1 wk), 3 wk.

Peters, Ralph
   Red Army (Pocket) PW hc fic 6/16/89
(#14), pk 7/7/89 (#13, 1 wk), 2 wk; NYT pb
fic 3/18/90 (#10, 1 wk), 3 wk; PW mm pb
3/23/90 (#13, 2 wk); tot 7 wk.

Peters, Thomas J.
   *Thriving on Chaos: A Handbook for a Man-
agement Revolution* (Knopf) NYT nf 10/25/
87 (#14), pk 2/7/88 (#2, 2 wk), 47 wk; PW
hc nf 11/6/87 (#9), pk 2/12/88 (#2, 1 wk), 42
wk; (Harper/Perennial) NYT pb nf 1/22/89
(#10), pk 4/9/89 (#7, 1 wk), 14 wk; tot 103 wk.

_____, **and Nancy K. Austin**
   *A Passion for Excellence: The Leadership
Difference* (Random) NYT nf 5/12/85 (#10),
pk 6/9/85 (#1, 1 wk), 41 wk; PW hc nf 5/17/
85 (#12), pk 6/28/85 (#1, 1 wk), 31 wk; (Warner) NYT pb nf 9/7/86 (#6, 1 wk); tot 73 wk.

_____, **and Robert H. Waterman,
   Jr.**
   *In Search of Excellence: Lessons from Amer-
ica's Best-Run Companies* (Harper) PW hc nf
1/7/83 (#11), pk 3/25/83 (#1, 36 wk), 66 wk;
NYT nf 1/16/83 (#8), pk 4/24/83 (#1, 30 wk),
67 wk; (Warner) NYT pb nf 2/26/84 (#3),
pk 3/18/84 (#1, 9 wk), 96 wk; PW td pb
3/2/84 (#3), pk 3/9/84 (#1, 30 wk), 93 wk;
tot 322 wk.

Petersham, Maud

Miki (Doubleday) PW juv 2/15/30 (#5, 4 wk), 8 wk.

_____, and Miska Petersham
The Ark of Father Noah and Mother Noah (Doubleday) PW juv 12/20/30 (#7, 4 wk). *The Christ Child* (Doubleday) PW juv 12/19/31 (#2, 12 wk), 16 wk.

Peterson, Marcelene
See Deems Taylor, et al.

Peterson, Roger Tory
A Field Guide to the Birds of Eastern and Central North America (Houghton) NYT td pb 11/2/80 (#15), pk 11/30/80 (#3, 1 wk), 37 wk; NYT nf 11/23/80 (#9), pk 11/30/80 (#7, 1 wk), 12 wk; PW td pb 12/5/80 (#9), pk 12/26/80 (#6, 1 wk), 7 wk; PW hc nf 12/19/80 (#15), pk 12/26/80 (#14, 2 wk), 4 wk; tot 59 wk.

_____, and James Fisher
Wild America (Houghton) NYT gen 12/18/55 (#15, 1 wk).

Peterson, Virgilia
A Matter of Life and Death (Atheneum) NYT gen 10/8/61 (#13), pk 10/22/61 (#11, 1 wk), 6 wk; PW nf 10/23/61 (#9, 1 wk); tot 7 wk.

Petrakis, Harry Mark
A Dream of Kings (McKay) NYT fic 10/30/66 (#10), pk 1/8/67 (#8, 1 wk), 12 wk; PW fic 11/7/66 (#10), pk 12/5/66 (#9, 6 wk), 9 wk; tot 21 wk.
The Waves of Night (McKay) NYT fic 6/29/69 (#7, 1 wk), 2 wk.

Petre, Peter
See Thomas J. Watson, Jr., and _____

Petry, Ann Lane
The Street (Houghton) NYT fic 3/3/46 (#12, 1 wk), 5 wk.

Pettingill, Samuel B.
Smoke Screen (America's Future) PW nf 10/12/40 (#10, 8 wk).

Peyser, Joan
Bernstein (Beech Tree Books/Morrow) NYT nf 6/7/87 (#14, 1 wk).

Pfloog, Jan P.
Kittens Are Like That (Random) NYT ch pb 11/13/77 (#12, 46 wk), 70 wk.

Phelan, James
Howard Hughes: The Hidden Years (Random) PW hc nf 2/7/77 (#8), pk 2/14/77 (#7, 3 wk), 9 wk; NYT gen 2/27/77 (#7, 1 wk), 5 wk; tot 14 wk.

Phelps, Robert
See Sidonie Gabrielle Claudine Colette

Phelps, William Lyon
Autobiography with Letters (Oxford Univ.) NYT gen 5/7/39 (#5), pk 6/11/39 (#2, 4 wk), 24 wk; PW nf 5/13/39 (#5), pk 6/10/39 (#2, 4 wk), 28 wk; tot 52 wk.

Philbrick, Herbert A.
I Led 3 Lives (McGraw) NYT gen 3/2/52 (#7), pk 3/9/52 (#5, 3 wk), 11 wk; PW nf 3/8/52 (#3, 1 wk), 5 wk; tot 16 wk.

Phillips, Harlan B.
See Felix Frankfurter and _____

Phillips, J.B.
The New Testament in Modern English [trans.] (Macmillan) NYT gen 10/12/58 (#14), pk 11/23/58 (#8, 1 wk), 16 wk; PW nf 11/3/58 (#8), pk 12/15/58 (#5, 1 wk), 10 wk; tot 26 wk.

Phillips, Jayne Anne
Machine Dreams (Lawrence/Dutton) NYT fic 7/29/84 (#14), pk 8/12/84 (#13, 1 wk), 3 wk; PW hc fic 8/3/84 (#11), pk 8/24/84 (#10, 1 wk), 5 wk; (Pocket) NYT pb fic 4/21/85 (#15), pk 4/28/85 (#13, 1 wk), 2 wk; tot 10 wk.

Phillips, John
The Second Happiest Day (Harper) NYT fic 2/15/53 (#14), pk 3/8/53 (#5, 3 wk), 12 wk; PW fic 3/14/53 (#7), pk 3/28/53 (#4, 1 wk), 4 wk; tot 16 wk.

Phillips, Judson Pentecost
Cancelled in Red [as by Hugh Pentecost] (Dodd) NYT fic 7/9/39 (#10, 4 wk).

Phillips, Kevin
The Politics of Rich and Poor (Random) PW hc nf 8/3/90 (#10), pk 9/7/90 (#3, 1 wk), 13 wk; NYT nf 8/5/90 (#6), pk 8/12/90 (#2, 3 wk), 13 wk; tot 26 wk.

Phillips, M.C.
Skin Deep (Vanguard) PW nf 2/9/35 (#6), pk 3/16/35 (#4, 4 wk), 16 wk.

Phillips, Michael, and Judith Pella
A Daughter of Grace (Bethany) PW pb rel 11/9/90 (#9, 4 wk).
My Father's World (Bethany) PW pb rel 11/9/90 (#16, 4 wk).

Phillips, Shine
Big Spring (Prentice Hall) NYT nf 10/18/42 (#13), pk 11/15/42 (#12, 1 wk), 9 wk.

Phillips, Susan Elizabeth
Fancy Pants (Pocket) NYT pb fic 10/22/89 (#15, 1 wk); PW mm pb 10/27/89 (#15, 1 wk); tot 2 wk.

Pickens, T. Boone, Jr.
Boone (Houghton) NYT nf 3/22/87 (#14),
pk 4/5/87 (#3, 1 wk), 11 wk; PW hc nf 3/27/
87 (#11), pk 4/24/87 (#4, 2 wk), 10 wk; tot 21
wk.

Pickford, Mary
My Rendezvous with Life (Kinsey) NYT
nf 11/3/35 (#6, 4 wk).
Why Not Try God? (Kinsey) PW nf 1/12/35
(#8), pk 2/9/35 (#5, 8 wk), 16 wk; NYT nf
10/6/35 (#7, 4 wk); tot 20 wk.
Sunshine and Shadow (Doubleday) NYT
gen 6/19/55 (#15, 1 wk), 2 wk.

Pielmeier, John
See Leonore Fleischer and _____

Pierce, Ovid Williams
The Plantation (Doubleday) NYT fic 3/
22/53 (#16, 2 wk).

Piercy, Marge
Gone to Soldiers (Fawcett/Crest) NYT pb
fic 5/29/88 (#13), pk 6/19/88 (#11, 1 wk), 5
wk; PW mm pb 6/3/88 (#11), pk 6/24/88 (#5,
1 wk), 5 wk; tot 10 wk.

Pierre, Dominique
See Larry Collins and _____

**Piersall, James A., and Al Hirsh-
berg**
Fear Strikes Out (Little Brown) NYT gen
9/18/55 (#13, 1 wk).

Pierson, Louise Randall
Roughly Speaking (Simon & Schuster)
NYT gen 8/8/43 (#7), pk 10/3/43 (#5, 1 wk),
10 wk; PW nf 9/11/43 (#7), pk 9/25/43 (#5,
1 wk), 3 wk; tot 13 wk.

Pierson, Ransdell
The Queen of Mean (Bantam) NYT pb nf
10/15/89 (#8), pk 11/5/89 (#5, 1 wk), 5 wk.

Pike, Christopher
Witch (Pocket/Archway) PW ch yn ad
12/21/90 (#4, 4 wk).
See You Later (Pocket/Archway) PW ch yn
ad 8/31/90 (#1, 12 wk).
Fall Into Darkness (Pocket/Archway) PW
ch yn ad 8/31/90 (#3, 4 wk).
The Boyfriend (Pocket/Archway) PW ch
yn ad 10/26/90 (#2), pk 11/30/90 (#1, 4 wk),
8 wk.

Pilcher, Rosamunde
The Shell Seekers (St. Martin's) NYT fic
2/21/88 (#15), pk 4/3/88 (#6, 2 wk), 47 wk;
PW hc fic 3/4/88 (#14), pk 4/15/88 (#7, 1
wk), 32 wk; (Dell) NYT pb fic 2/5/89 (#2),
pk 2/12/89 (#1, 3 wk), 73 wk; PW mm pb
2/10/89 (#4), pk 2/17/89 (#1, 2 wk), 54 wk;

[read by Lynn Redgrave] (Bantam) PW aud
fic 12/7/90 (#8, 4 wk); tot 210 wk.
The Blue Bedroom (St. Martin's) NYT pb
fic 6/17/90 (#14, 2 wk).
September (St. Martin's) NYT fic 4/22/90
(#1, 4 wk), 26 wk; PW hc fic 4/27/90 (#2),
pk 5/4/90 (#1, 3 wk), 22 wk; [read by Lynn
Redgrave] (Bantam) PW aud fic 10/5/90 (#8,
4 wk); tot 52 wk.

Pileggi, Nicholas
Wiseguy: The Rise and Fall of a Mobster
(Simon & Schuster) NYT nf 2/16/86 (#10),
pk 3/23/86 (#3, 1 wk), 13 wk; PW hc nf
2/21/86 (#10), pk 4/11/86 (#6, 1 wk), 11 wk;
(Pocket) NYT pb nf 2/15/87 (#4), pk 3/8/87
(#1, 1 wk), 8 wk; PW mm pb 2/20/87 (#14),
pk 3/6/87 (#8, 1 wk), 5 wk; tot 37 wk.

Pilgrim, David
So Great a Man (Harper) NYT fic 11/7/37
(#8, 4 wk); PW fic 11/13/37 (#7, 4 wk); tot 8
wk.

Piller, Emanuel A.
Time Bomb (Arco) NYT gen 8/19/45 (#11,
1 wk), 2 wk.

Pinchon, Edgcumb
*Dan Sickles: Hero of Gettysburg and Yankee
King of Spain* (Doubleday) NYT gen 7/8/45
(#18), pk 7/22/45 (#14, 1 wk), 4 wk.

Pinckney, Callan, and Sallie Batson
Callanetics: 10 Years Younger in 10 Hours
(Morrow) NYT msc 11/3/85 (#4), pk 2/16/86
(#2, 16 wk), 44 wk; PW hc nf 11/22/85 (#11),
pk 2/21/86 (#2, 5 wk), 44 wk; (Avon) PW td
pb 5/8/87 (#10), pk 7/3/87 (#6, 1 wk), 10 wk;
tot 98 wk,

Pinckney, Josephine
Three O'Clock Dinner (Viking) NYT fic
10/14/45 (#10), pk 11/18/45 (#5, 2 wk), 13
wk; PW fic 11/10/45 (#7, 1 wk), 2 wk; tot 15
wk.

Pineau, Roger
See Edwin T. Layton, et al.

Pinkerton, Kathrene
Three's a Crew (Carrick & Evans) PW nf
4/13/40 (#10, 4 wk).

Pinkham, Mary Ellen
Mary Ellen's Best of Helpful Kitchen Hints
(Warner) NYT td pb 9/21/80 (#13), pk
10/26/80 (#2, 3 wk), 27 wk; PW td pb 9/26/
80 (#9), pk 10/17/80 (#2, 4 wk), 18 wk; tot
45 wk.
Mary Ellen's Best of Helpful Hints Book II
(Warner) NYT td pb 12/27/81 (#12, 3 wk),
5 wk.
*Mary Ellen's Help Yourself Diet Plan: The
One That Worked for Me* (Marek/St. Martin's)

NYT nf 2/20/83 (#14), pk 3/27/83 (#7, 7 wk), 16 wk; PW hc nf 3/11/83 (#9), pk 3/18/83 (#7, 7 wk), 15 wk; tot 31 wk.

Mary Ellen's 1000 New Helpful Hints (Doubleday) NYT td pb 12/18/83 (#14), pk 12/25/83 (#13, 1 wk), 2 wk.

_____, and Pearl Higginbotham

Mary Ellen's Best of Helpful Hints (Lansky/Warner) PW td pb 6/4/79 (#4), pk 6/11/79 (#1, 24 wk), 88 wk; NYT td pb 6/17/79 (#6), pk 7/29/79 (#1, 36 wk), 103 wk; tot 191 wk.

Pinkney, Jerry

See Jean Marzollo

Piper, Watty

The Little Engine That Could (Platt & Munk/Grosset & Dunlap) NYT ch hc 4/30/78 (#9, 24 wk); [new edition illus. George Hauman and Doris Hauman] (Platt & Munk) PW ch pic 10/26/90 (#6, 4 wk); tot 28 wk.

Pistone, Joseph D., with Richard Woodley

Donnie Brasco: My Undercover Life in the Mafia (NAL) NYT nf 2/14/88 (#15), pk 3/13/88 (#11, 1 wk), 5 wk; PW hc nf 3/11/88 (#10, 1 wk), 2 wk; NYT pb nf 1/29/89 (#8), pk 2/5/89 (#2, 1 wk), 7 wk; tot 14 wk.

Pitkin, Walter B.

More Power to You! (Simon & Schuster) PW nf 11/11/33 (#4), pk 12/9/33 (#3, 4 wk), 24 wk.

Life Begins at Forty (Whittlesey) PW nf 2/11/33 (#8), pk 11/11/33 (#1, 20 wk), 88 wk.

New Careers for Youth (Simon & Schuster) PW nf 8/11/34 (#7), pk 9/15/34 (#6, 4 wk), 8 wk.

Careers After Forty (Whittlesey/McGraw) NYT nf 5/9/37 (#5, 4 wk).

Making Good Before Forty (McBride) NYT gen 7/9/39 (#8, 4 wk).

Pizzo, Stephen, with Mary Fricker and Paul Muolo

Inside Job (McGraw) NYT nf 8/19/90 (#8, 2 wk), 6 wk.

Plain, Belva

Evergreen (Delacorte) PW hc fic 6/5/78 (#10), pk 8/28/78 (#3, 3 wk), 49 wk; NYT fic 7/2/78 (#13), pk 11/19/78 (#5, 2 wk), 35 wk; (Dell) PW mm pb 7/16/79 (#4), pk 7/30/79 (#1, 5 wk), 27 wk; NYT mm pb 7/22/79 (#2), pk 7/29/79 (#1, 4 wk), 26 wk; NYT pb fic 3/17/85 (#8, 1 wk), 2 wk; tot 139 wk.

Random Winds (Delacorte) PW hc fic 5/9/80 (#13), pk 6/13/80 (#1, 1 wk), 25 wk; NYT fic 5/11/80 (#14), pk 6/29/80 (#2, 6 wk), 28 wk; (Dell) PW mm pb 5/8/81 (#3), pk

5/15/81 (#1, 2 wk), 15 wk; NYT mm pb 5/10/81 (#2, 2 wk), 15 wk; tot 83 wk.

Eden Burning (Delacorte) PW hc fic 6/11/82 (#11), pk 6/18/82 (#4, 2 wk), 13 wk; NYT fic 6/13/82 (#5), pk 7/4/82 (#4, 4 wk), 16 wk; (Dell) NYT mm pb 6/12/83 (#4), pk 6/19/83 (#3, 2 wk), 10 wk; PW mm pb 6/17/83 (#4, 4 wk), 8 wk; tot 47 wk.

Crescent City (Delacorte) NYT fic 9/16/84 (#11), pk 9/23/84 (#5, 1 wk), 10 wk; PW hc fic 9/21/84 (#12), pk 10/5/84 (#5, 3 wk), 12 wk; (Dell) NYT pb fic 9/1/85 (#6), pk 9/8/85 (#2, 2 wk), 12 wk; PW mm pb 9/6/85 (#6), pk 9/13/85 (#2, 1 wk), 10 wk; tot 44 wk.

The Golden Cup (Delacorte) NYT fic 10/12/86 (#9), pk 11/2/86 (#6, 1 wk), 15 wk; PW hc fic 10/17/86 (#9), pk 10/24/86 (#6, 3 wk), 12 wk; (Dell) NYT pb fic 10/11/87 (#8), 10/25/87 (#1, 2 wk), 8 wk; PW mm pb 10/16/87 (#5), pk 10/30/87 (#1, 1 wk), 9 wk; tot 44 wk.

Tapestry (Delacorte) PW hc fic 5/13/88 (#11), pk 5/27/88 (#7, 2 wk), 12 wk; NYT fic 5/15/88 (#15), pk 5/22/88 (#8, 1 wk), 11 wk; (Dell) NYT pb fic 4/9/89 (#7), pk 4/30/89 (#1, 1 wk), 8 wk; PW mm pb 4/14/89 (#3), pk 4/28/89 (#1, 2 wk), 7 wk; tot 38 wk.

Blessings (Delacorte) NYT fic 8/6/89 (#13), pk 8/27/89 (#3, 1 wk), 11 wk; PW hc fic 8/11/89 (#6), pk 8/25/89 (#4, 4 wk), 9 wk; (Dell) NYT pb fic 7/8/90 (#8), pk 7/22/90 (#4, 1 wk), 9 wk; PW mm pb 7/20/90 (#4, 1 wk), 5 wk; tot 34 wk.

Harvest (Delacorte) PW hc fic 9/21/90 (#14, 1 wk).

Plath, Sylvia

The Bell Jar (Harper) NYT fic 5/9/71 (#10), pk 6/20/71 (#4, 3 wk), 24 wk; PW fic 5/17/71 (#6), pk 6/7/71 (#3, 4 wk), 24 wk; NYT pb fic 5/14/72 (#3, 4 wk), 8 wk; tot 56 wk.

Platt, Rutherford Hayes

Walt Disney's Worlds of Nature (Simon & Schuster) NYT ch bst 11/2/58 (#5, 40 wk).

Platt, Samuel C.

Second Sing-A-Song Player Book [as by Sam See] (McLoughlin) NYT gen 2/5/39 (#1, 4 wk), 20 wk.

Pleasants, Henry

A Doctor in the House (Lippincott) NYT gen 8/31/47 (#11), pk 10/12/31 (#7, 1 wk), 12 wk.

Plimpton, George

Paper Lion (Harper) NYT gen 1/1/67 (#8), pk 2/5/67 (#2, 3 wk), 24 wk; PW nf 1/9/67 (#9), pk 1/16/67 (#1, 1 wk), 26 wk; NYT pb gen 12/3/67 (#3, 12 wk); tot 62 wk.

The Bogey Man (Harper) NYT gen 12/8/

68 (#9, 4 wk); PW nf 1/6/69 (#8), pk 1/20/69 (#7, 1 wk), 5 wk; tot 9 wk.
See also Diana Vreeland, et al.
See also Jean Stein and _____

Pogrebin, Letty Cottin
See Marlo Thomas, et al.

Pohrt, Tom
See Barry Lopez

Polish Ministry of Information
The Black Book of Poland (Putnam) NYT nf 10/11/42 (#16), pk 10/25/42 (#15, 1 wk), 3 wk.

Pond, Mimi
The Valley Girls' Guide to Life (Dell) NYT td pb 11/21/82 (#14), pk 12/5/82 (#10, 1 wk), 10 wk; PW td pb 12/3/82 (#10, 2 wk); tot 12 wk.

Ponsot, Marie
The Fairy Tale Book (Golden) NYT ch bst 11/1/59 (#2, 25 wk).

Poole, Ernest
Giants Gone: Men Who Made Chicago (Mc-Graw) NYT nf 3/7/43 (#19), pk 4/4/43 (#14, 1 wk), 8 wk.
The Great White Hills of New Hampshire (Doubleday) NYT gen 8/11/46 (#15), pk 9/1/46 (#13, 1 wk), 2 wk.

Poortvliet, Rien
See Wil Huygen and _____

Pope, Antoinette
The Antoinette Pope School Cook Book (Macmillan) NYT gen 9/30/51 (#13, 1 wk), 2 wk.

Pope-Cordle, Jamie, and Martin Katahn
The T-Factor Fat Gram Counter (Norton) PW td pb 2/9/90 (#2, 4 wk), 45 wk; NYT msc pb 4/1/90 (#6), pk 9/9/90 (#3, 2 wk), 26 wk; tot 71 wk.

Pope-Hennessy, James
Queen Mary, 1867–1953 (Knopf) NYT gen 3/6/60 (#8), pk 3/13/60 (#6, 1 wk), 9 wk; PW nf 3/14/60 (#7, 1 wk), 5 wk; tot 14 wk.

Pope John XXIII
Journal of a Soul (McGraw) NYT gen 5/2/65 (#5), pk 5/30/65 (#3, 1 wk), 18 wk; PW nf 5/3/65 (#8), pk 6/14/65 (#3, 1 wk), 20 wk; tot 38 wk.

Porter, Alyene
Papa Was a Preacher (Abingdon Cokesbury) NYT gen 10/1/44 (#12), pk 11/19/44 (#10, 2 wk), 20 wk.

Porter, Donald Clayton
War Chief (Bantam) NYT mm pb 11/16/80

(#12, 1 wk), 2 wk; PW mm pb 11/21/80 (#11), pk 11/28/80 (#8, 1 wk), 3 wk; tot 5 wk.
The Sachem (Bantam) PW mm pb 4/3/81 (#15), pk 4/10/81 (#10, 1 wk), 3 wk; NYT mm pb 4/5/81 (#11, 1 wk), 3 wk; tot 6 wk.
Renno (Bantam) NYT mm pb 11/8/81 (#15), pk 11/15/81 (#14, 1 wk), 3 wk; PW mm pb 11/27/81 (#15, 1 wk); tot 4 wk.
Tomahawk (Bantam) PW mm pb 6/4/82 (#10), pk 6/11/82 (#9, 1 wk), 2 wk; NYT mm pb 6/6/82 (#10, 1 wk), 3 wk; tot 5 wk.
War Cry (Bantam) NYT mm pb 1/30/83 (#13, 1 wk).
Cherokee (Bantam) NYT pb fic 11/4/84 (#15), pk 11/18/84 (#10, 1 wk), 3 wk.
Choctaw (Bantam) PW mm pb 7/12/85 (#14, 1 wk).

Porter, Eleanor H.
Dawn (Houghton) PW fic 6/7/19 (#4), pk 7/5/19 (#3, 4 wk), 16 wk.
Mary Marie (Houghton) PW fic 7/3/20 (#3), pk 8/14/20 (#1, 4 wk), 16 wk.
Sister Sue (Houghton) PW fic 6/11/21 (#6, 4 wk).

Porter, Gene Stratton
The Keeper of the Bees (Doubleday) PW fic 9/26/25 (#1, 8 wk), 20 wk.

Porter, Katherine Anne
Ship of Fools (Atlantic Little Brown) NYT fic 4/15/62 (#11), pk 4/29/62 (#1, 26 wk), 36 wk; PW fic 4/23/62 (#7), pk 5/7/62 (#1, 26 wk), 43 wk; tot 79 wk.

Porter, Sylvia Field
Sylvia Porter's Money Book (Doubleday) NYT gen 7/13/75 (#8), pk 9/7/75 (#1, 12 wk), 36 wk; PW nf 7/14/75 (#6), pk 9/8/75 (#1, 14 wk), 36 wk; (Avon) PW td pb 10/25/76 (#5), pk 11/1/76 (#1, 17 wk), 26 wk; NYT td pb 10/31/76 (#3), pk 11/7/76 (#1, 14 wk), 35 wk; tot 133 wk.
Sylvia Porter's New Money Book for the 80's (Doubleday) NYT nf 12/23/79 (#13), pk 1/13/80 (#9, 1 wk), 6 wk; (Avon) NYT td pb 1/4/81 (#15), pk 3/1/81 (#3, 1 wk), 13 wk; PW td pb 3/13/81 (#10, 1 wk); tot 20 wk.

Porter, Sylvia Townsend
T.H. White (Viking) PW nf 5/6/68 (#7, 1 wk).

Porterfield, Christopher
See Dick Cavett and _____

Portis, Charles
True Grit (Simon & Schuster) NYT fic 7/21/68 (#9), pk 9/29/68 (#3, 1 wk), 22 wk; PW fic 7/29/68 (#8), pk 9/30/68 (#2, 1 wk), 17 wk; NYT pb fic 3/2/69 (#3, 4 wk); tot 43 wk.

Portola Institute
See Stewart Brand

Post, Emily
Etiquette (Funk & Wagnalls) PW nf 11/24/23 (#2, 4 wk), 20 wk; PW gen lit 12/23/22 (#12), pk 4/14/23 (#1, 4 wk), 40 wk; tot 60 wk.
The Emily Post Cook Book (Funk & Wagnalls) NYT gen 9/2/51 (#13, 1 wk).

Potok, Chaim
The Chosen (Simon & Schuster) NYT fic 5/28/67 (#6), pk 10/1/67 (#1, 3 wk), 39 wk; PW fic 6/5/67 (#7), pk 9/25/67 (#1, 1 wk), 42 wk; NYT pb fic 7/7/68 (#2, 4 wk), 12 wk; tot 93 wk.
The Promise (Knopf) NYT fic 10/5/69 (#7, 3 wk), 11 wk; PW fic 10/13/69 (#7), pk 11/3/69 (#5, 1 wk), 12 wk; tot 23 wk.
My Name Is Asher Lev (Knopf) PW fic 5/8/72 (#5), pk 7/10/72 (#2, 2 wk), 27 wk; NYT fic 5/14/72 (#5), pk 9/3/72 (#3, 1 wk), 26 wk; NYT pb fic 5/13/73 (#3, 4 wk), 8 wk; tot 61 wk.
In the Beginning (Knopf) NYT fic 11/23/75 (#10), pk 11/30/75 (#5, 12 wk), 20 wk; PW fic 11/24/75 (#10), pk 12/29/75 (#5, 4 wk), 9 wk; PW hc fic 2/2/76 (#5, 2 wk), 7 wk; (Fawcett/Crest) PW mm pb 10/18/76 (#13), pk 10/25/76 (#9, 1 wk), 4 wk; NYT mm pb 11/14/76 (#7, 1 wk), 2 wk; tot 42 wk.
Wanderings: Chaim Potok's Story of the Jews (Knopf) PW hc nf 1/8/79 (#14, 1 wk), 2 wk; NYT nf 1/21/79 (#14), pk 1/28/79 (#10, 1 wk), 5 wk; tot 7 wk.
The Book of Lights (Knopf) PW hc fic 11/20/81 (#14), pk 1/1/82 (#13, 1 wk), 8 wk; NYT fic 11/29/81 (#15), pk 12/20/81 (#13, 1 wk), 3 wk; (Fawcett/Crest) PW mm pb 11/5/82 (#13), pk 11/12/82 (#10, 1 wk), 5 wk; NYT mm pb 11/7/82 (#13, 2 wk), 3 wk; tot 19 wk.

Potter, Beatrix
The Tale of Little Pig Robinson (McKay) PW juv 2/21/31 (#9, 4 wk).
The Tale of Peter Rabbit (Warne) NYT ch bst 11/7/71 (#10), pk 5/7/72 (#8, 19 wk), 69 wk.

Potter, Stephen
Lifemanship (Holt) NYT gen 7/29/51 (#14), pk 9/9/51 (#11, 1 wk), 8 wk.

Pottle, Frederick A.
See James Boswell

Pound, Arthur
Lake Ontario (Bobbs Merrill) NYT gen 6/24/45 (#20), pk 7/15/45 (#18, 2 wk), 3 wk.

Pouns, Brauna E.
Amerika (Pocket) NYT pb fic 2/22/87 (#10), pk 3/8/87 (#9, 1 wk), 3 wk.

Pournelle, Jerry
See Larry Niven and _____

Powell, Anthony
A Dance to the Music of Time (Little Brown) NYT fic 2/18/62 (#16, 2 wk).

Powell, Dawn
The Wicked Pavilion (Houghton) NYT fic 10/17/54 (#16, 1 wk).

Powell, J.J.
Why Am I Afraid to Tell You Who I Am (Argus Communications) NYT td pb 10/13/74 (#9), pk 11/10/74 (#6, 4 wk), 8 wk.

Powell, Lyman P.
Mary Baker Eddy (Macmillan) PW nf 12/20/30 (#10, 4 wk).

Powell, Richard
The Philadelphian (Scribner) NYT fic 1/20/57 (#14), pk 3/3/57 (#3, 2 wk), 26 wk; PW fic 2/11/57 (#6), pk 3/4/57 (#3, 3 wk), 16 wk; tot 42 wk.
Pioneer, Go Home! (Scribner) NYT fic 3/15/59 (#15), pk 5/3/59 (#11, 1 wk), 6 wk; PW fic 5/18/59 (#10, 1 wk); tot 7 wk.
I Take This Land (Scribner) PW fic 3/11/63 (#8, 1 wk).

Power, Gen. Thomas S., with Albert A. Arnhym
Design for Survival (Coward McCann) NYT gen 4/18/65 (#10), pk 5/9/65 (#6, 1 wk), 5 wk; PW nf 5/3/65 (#10, 1 wk); tot 6 wk.

Powers, David F.
See Kenneth P. O'Donnell, et al.

Powers, Francis Gary
Operation Overflight (Holt) NYT gen 6/21/70 (#9, 1 wk).

Powers, Tim
Virgin with Butterflies (Bobbs Merrill) NYT fic 5/27/45 (#14, 1 wk).

Powys, John C.
The Art of Happiness (Simon & Schuster) NYT nf 10/6/35 (#8, 4 wk).

Pozner, Vladimir, and Brian J. Kahn
Parting with Illusions (Atlantic Monthly) NYT nf 3/11/90 (#10), pk 4/1/90 (#7, 3 wk), 12 wk; PW hc nf 3/23/90 (#9, 2 wk), 10 wk; tot 22 wk.

Prange, Gordon W.
At Dawn We Slept: The Untold Story of Pearl Harbor (McGraw) PW hc nf 1/1/82 (#14), pk 2/26/82 (#4, 2 wk), 21 wk; NYT nf 1/24/82 (#13), pk 2/21/82 (#4, 2 wk), 19 wk; (Penguin) NYT td pb 12/5/82 (#12), pk 1/2/83 (#5, 1 wk), 15 wk; PW td pb 12/17/82

(#8), pk 1/14/83 (#5, 1 wk), 12 wk; tot 67 wk.

_____, with Donald M. Goldstein and Katherine V. Dillon
Miracle at Midway (McGraw) NYT nf 12/12/82 (#15), pk 1/9/83 (#12, 1 wk), 4 wk; PW hc nf 1/14/83 (#15, 1 wk); tot 5 wk.

Prather, Hugh
Notes to Myself: My Struggle to Become a Person (Real People) NYT td pb 7/14/74 (#6, 4 wk), 24 wk.
Notes on Love & Courage (Doubleday/Dolphin) NYT td pb 2/5/78 (#12), pk 2/26/78 (#10, 2 wk), 20 wk.

Prelutsky, Jack
Something Big Has Been Here [illus. James Stevenson] (Greenwillow) PW ch nf 9/28/90 (#2), pk 10/26/90 (#1, 8 wk), 16 wk.

Prescott, Hilda Frances Margaret
The Man on a Donkey (Macmillan) NYT fic 10/26/52 (#11, 2 wk), 12 wk.

Presley, Priscilla Beaulieu, with Sandra Harmon
Elvis and Me (Putnam) NYT nf 9/22/85 (#3), pk 9/29/85 (#1, 9 wk), 25 wk; PW hc nf 9/27/85 (#4), pk 10/4/85 (#1, 5 wk), 22 wk; (Berkley) NYT pb nf 8/3/86 (#2), pk 8/24/86 (#1, 3 wk), 15 wk; PW mm pb 8/15/86 (#6), pk 9/5/86 (#4, 2 wk), 10 wk; tot 72 wk.

Preston, Robert
How to Prepare for the Coming Crash (Hawkes) NYT td pb 5/12/74 (#9, 4 wk).

Price, Eugenia
New Moon Rising (Lippincott) NYT fic 7/20/69 (#10), pk 8/17/69 (#9, 1 wk), 7 wk; PW fic 8/11/69 (#10), pk 9/8/69 (#9, 1 wk), 2 wk; tot 9 wk.
Savannah (Doubleday) NYT fic 3/20/83 (#14, 1 wk); (Berkley) NYT pb fic 8/12/84 (#15), pk 9/9/84 (#5, 1 wk), 11 wk; PW mm pb 8/24/84 (#8), pk 10/5/84 (#5, 1 wk), 8 wk; tot 20 wk.
To See Your Face Again (Berkley) NYT pb fic 10/5/86 (#13), pk 10/26/86 (#11, 1 wk), 4 wk.
Stranger in Savannah (Doubleday) NYT fic 5/14/89 (#15), pk 5/28/89 (#7, 1 wk), 8 wk; PW hc fic 5/19/89 (#10), pk 6/2/89 (#8, 1 wk), 9 wk; (Jove) NYT pb fic 4/8/90 (#13), pk 4/22/90 (#7, 1 wk), 5 wk; PW mm pb 4/20/90 (#8, 1 wk), 3 wk; tot 25 wk.

Price, Irving
Buying Country Property: Pitfalls and Pleasures (Harper) NYT gen 3/26/72 (#10, 2 wk).

Price, Leontyne
Aida [retold by Leontyne, illus. Leo Dillon and Diane Dillon] (Gulliver/Harcourt) PW ch pic 11/30/90 (#9, 4 wk).

Price, Lucien
See Alfred North Whitehead

Price, Reynolds
A Long and Happy Life (Atheneum) NYT fic 5/6/62 (#15), pk 5/13/62 (#14, 2 wk), 4 wk.
A Generous Man (Atheneum) PW fic 5/2/66 (#9, 1 wk).
Kate Vaiden (Atheneum) NYT fic 8/3/86 (#15, 1 wk).

Priestley, John Boynton [all titles as by J.B. Priestley]
Angel Pavement (Harper) PW fic 10/18/30 (#1, 4 wk), 16 wk.
Faraway (Harper) PW fic 9/10/32 (#4, 4 wk), 8 wk.
English Journey (Harper) PW nf 9/15/34 (#7), pk 10/13/34 (#3, 4 wk), 12 wk.
They Walk in the City (Harper) NYT fic 9/13/36 (#10), pk 10/4/36 (#4, 4 wk), 8 wk; PW fic 10/10/36 (#9, 4 wk); tot 12 wk.
Midnight on the Desert (Harper) NYT nf 5/9/37 (#6, 4 wk).
The Doomsday Men (Harper) NYT fic 9/4/38 (#4, 4 wk).
Let the People Sing (Harper) PW fic 2/10/40 (#8, 4 wk).
Black-Out in Gretley (Harper) PW fic 2/27/43 (#5), pk 3/6/43 (#4, 1 wk), 7 wk; NYT fic 2/28/43 (#12), pk 3/14/43 (#4, 1 wk), 10 wk; tot 17 wk.
Festival (Harper) NYT fic 4/22/51 (#7), pk 5/6/51 (#5, 1 wk), 16 wk; PW fic 5/5/51 (#5), pk 5/12/51 (#4, 3 wk), 6 wk; tot 22 wk.

Principal, Victoria
The Body Principal (Simon & Schuster) NYT nf 10/9/83 (#9), pk 10/30/83 (#3, 2 wk), 12 wk; PW hc nf 10/14/83 (#8), pk 11/4/83 (#4, 1 wk), 17 wk; NYT msc 1/1/84 (#1, 4 wk), 6 wk; tot 35 wk.
The Diet Principal (Simon & Schuster) NYT msc 6/7/87 (#2, 1 wk), 4 wk; PW hc nf 6/12/87 (#8), pk 6/26/87 (#4, 1 wk), 4 wk; tot 8 wk.

Pritikin, Nathan
The Pritikin Permanent Weight-Loss Manual (Grosset & Dunlap) NYT nf 6/7/81 (#10), pk 6/28/81 (#6, 1 wk), 9 wk; PW hc nf 6/19/81 (#10), pk 6/26/81 (#7, 1 wk), 8 wk; tot 17 wk.
The Pritikin Promise: 28 Days to a Longer, Healthier Life (Simon & Schuster) NYT msc 1/29/84 (#4), pk 2/5/84 (#2, 2 wk), 4 wk; PW

hc nf 2/10/84 (#14), pk 2/17/84 (#12, 1 wk),
2 wk; tot 6 wk.
See also Jon M. Leonard, et al.

_____, **and Patrick McGrady, Jr.**
The Pritikin Program for Diet and Exercise
(Grosset & Dunlap) PW hc nf 5/7/79 (#13),
pk 6/4/79 (#2, 8 wk), 53 wk; NYT nf 5/13/79
(#9), pk 6/24/79 (#3, 9 wk), 52 wk; (Bantam) PW mm pb 6/20/80 (#14, 2 wk); NYT
mm pb 6/29/80 (#10, 1 wk), 4 wk; tot 111 wk.

Pritikin, Robert
The New Pritikin Program (Simon &
Schuster) PW hc nf 2/16/90 (#12, 1 wk).

Prochnow, Herbert Victor
Great Stories from Great Lives [ed.] (Books
for Libraries) NYT gen 6/25/44 (#19, 1 wk).

Producers of Sesame Street
See Children's Television Workshop

Prokosch, Frederic
The Seven Who Fled (Harper) PW fic 10/9/
37 (#5, 4 wk), 8 wk; NYT fic 10/10/37 (#6,
4 wk); tot 12 wk.
The Conspirators (Harper) NYT fic 2/14/
43 (#13), pk 4/25/43 (#9, 1 wk), 7 wk.
A Tale for Midnight (Little Brown) NYT
fic 8/14/55 (#16, 2 wk).

Prouty, Olive Higgins
Stella Dallas (Houghton) PW fic 7/21/23
(#6, 4 wk).
White Fawn (Houghton) PW fic 5/16/31
(#5, 4 wk), 12 wk.
Lisa Vale (Houghton) NYT fic 6/5/38 (#2,
4 wk), 8 wk; PW fic 6/11/38 (#9, 4 wk); tot
12 wk.

Provensen, Alice
The Buck Stops Here (HarperCollins) PW
ch pic 10/26/90 (#5, 4 wk); ch nf 12/21/90
(#3, 4 wk); tot 8 wk.

Prudhomme, Paul
Chef Paul Prudhomme's Louisiana Kitchen
(Morrow) NYT msc 7/1/84 (#5), pk 1/13/85
(#3, 1 wk), 13 wk; PW hc fic 7/20/84 (#13),
pk 8/3/84 (#9, 1 wk), 12 wk; tot 25 wk.

Public Citizen Health Research
 Group
See Sidney M. Wolfe, M.D., et al.

Pugsley, John
The Alpha Strategy (Stratford Press/Har-
per) PW hc nf 6/26/81 (#12), pk 7/17/81 (#5,
1 wk), 8 wk; NYT nf 6/28/81 (#13), pk 7/12/
81 (#7, 2 wk), 7 wk; tot 15 wk.

Pulitzer, Roxanne, with Kathleen
 Maxa
The Prize Pulitzer (Villard) NYT nf 2/14/
88 (#10), pk 2/21/88 (#2, 1 wk), 12 wk; PW

hc nf 2/19/88 (#15), pk 2/26/88 (#3, 3 wk),
10 wk; (Ballantine) NYT pb nf 3/12/89 (#1,
5 wk), 14 wk; tot 36 wk.

Putnam, George Palmer
Soaring Wings (Harcourt) NYT gen 10/8/
39 (#15, 4 wk).

Puzo, Mario
The Godfather (Putnam) NYT fic 3/30/69
(#7), pk 9/21/69 (#1, 21 wk), 67 wk; PW fic
3/31/69 (#8), pk 8/25/69 (#1, 22 wk), 67 wk;
NYT pb fic 4/5/70 (#1, 44 wk), 80 wk; tot
214 wk.
Fools Die (Putnam) PW hc fic 9/18/78
(#5), pk 9/25/78 (#2, 4 wk), 25 wk; NYT fic
11/12/78 (#3, 6 wk), 19 wk; (NAL/Signet)
PW mm pb 10/15/79 (#4), pk 10/22/79 (#1,
3 wk), 12 wk; NYT mm pb 10/21/79 (#3), pk
10/28/79 (#1, 5 wk), 15 wk; tot 71 wk.
The Sicilian (Linden/Simon & Schuster)
NYT fic 11/18/84 (#8), pk 1/20/85 (#1, 2 wk),
23 wk; PW hc fic 11/23/84 (#9), pk 1/25/85
(#1, 2 wk), 24 wk; (Bantam) NYT pb fic
12/8/85 (#7), pk 12/22/85 (#1, 2 wk), 10 wk;
PW mm pb 12/13/85 (#6), pk 12/20/85 (#2,
2 wk), 9 wk; tot 66 wk.

Pyle, Ernie
Here Is Your War (Holt) PW nf 11/20/43
(#4), pk 12/25/43 (#1, 2 wk), 39 wk; NYT
gen 11/21/43 (#11), pk 12/12/43 (#2, 9 wk), 61
wk; tot 100 wk.
Brave Men (Holt) NYT gen 12/10/44 (#4),
pk 12/17/44 (#1, 34 wk), 64 wk; PW nf
12/16/44 (#6), pk 12/23/44 (#1, 25 wk), 61
wk; tot 125 wk.
Last Chapter (Holt) NYT gen 6/23/46
(#7), pk 6/30/46 (#5, 10 wk), 17 wk; PW nf
6/29/46 (#4), pk 8/3/46 (#3, 2 wk), 16 wk;
tot 33 wk.
Home Country (Sloan) NYT gen 6/22/47
(#13), pk 9/14/47 (#5, 1 wk), 34 wk; PW nf
7/19/47 (#6, 2 wk), 6 wk; tot 40 wk.

Pym, Barbara
A Very Private Eye (Dutton) NYT nf 8/19/
84 (#14), pk 8/26/84 (#13, 2 wk), 4 wk.

Pynchon, Thomas
Gravity's Rainbow (Viking) NYT pb fic
4/8/73 (#4, 4 wk); NYT gen 4/22/73 (#9),
pk 5/13/73 (#8, 2 wk), 4 wk; PW fic 4/30/73
(#10, 1 wk); tot 9 wk.
Vineland (Little Brown) NYT fic 1/21/90
(#5), pk 2/4/90 (#2, 1 wk), 13 wk; PW hc fic
1/26/90 (#10), pk 2/23/90 (#5, 1 wk), 12 wk;
tot 25 wk.

Quaife, Milo M.
Lake Michigan (Bobbs Merrill) NYT gen
8/20/44 (#19), pk 9/17/44 (#6, 1 wk), 12 wk.

Queen, Ellery
Halfway House (Stokes) NYT fic 8/2/36 (#6, 4 wk).
The Devil to Pay (Lippincott) NYT fic 4/3/38 (#6, 4 wk).
The Dragon's Teeth (Blakiston) NYT fic 11/5/39 (#10, 4 wk).

Queeny, Edgar Monsanto
The Spirit of Enterprise (Scribner) NYT gen 8/1/43 (#9), pk 8/29/43 (#8, 1 wk), 8 wk.

Quet, Pierre
See Pierre Accoce and _____

Quick, Amanda
Surrender (Bantam) PW mm pb 9/28/90 (#13, 1 wk); NYT pb fic 9/30/90 (#12, 1 wk); tot 2 wk.

Quick, Herbert
The Hawkeye (Bobbs Merrill) PW fic 9/15/23 (#6, 4 wk).

Quiller-Couch, Sir Arthur Thomas, and Daphne du Maurier
Castle Dor (Doubleday) NYT fic 3/25/62 (#15, 2 wk).

Quine, Judith Balaban
The Bridesmaids (Weidenfeld & Nicolson) NYT nf 7/9/89 (#14), pk 7/30/89 (#7, 1 wk), 7 wk; (Pocket) pb nf 8/12/90 (#8), pk 8/19/90 (#7, 2 wk), 8 wk; tot 15 wk.

Quinlan, Sterling
The Merger (Doubleday) NYT fic 11/9/58 (#14, 1 wk).

Quinn, Amy
See Peter Ueberroth, et al.

Quinn, Sally
Regrets Only (Simon & Schuster) PW hc fic 8/22/86 (#12), pk 9/5/86 (#5, 2 wk), 11 wk; NYT fic 8/24/86 (#14), pk 8/31/86 (#5, 1 wk), 9 wk; (Ballantine) NYT pb fic 9/6/87 (#12), pk 9/27/87 (#3, 2 wk), 9 wk; PW mm pb 9/11/87 (#10), pk 10/9/87 (#2, 1 wk), 9 wk; tot 38 wk.

Radin, Edward D.
Lizzie Borden (Simon & Schuster) NYT gen 7/9/61 (#10, 1 wk), 6 wk.

Radnor, Gilda
It's Always Something (Simon & Schuster) NYT nf 6/11/89 (#15), pk 7/16/89 (#1, 5 wk), 23 wk; PW hc nf 6/16/89 (#15), pk 7/21/89 (#1, 7 wk), 22 wk; (Avon) NYT pb nf 7/1/90 (#5), pk 7/22/90 (#1, 4 wk), 16 wk; PW mm pb 7/27/90 (#7), pk 8/3/90 (#4, 2 wk), 9 wk; (Simon & Schuster) PW aud nf 10/5/90 (#7, 4 wk); tot 74 wk.

Rainer, Iris
The Boys in the Mailroom (Warner) NYT

mm pb 1/25/81 (#9, 1 wk), 4 wk; PW mm pb 1/30/81 (#15), pk 2/13/81 (#13, 2 wk), 3 wk; tot 7 wk.

Rainier, Maj. Peter William
Pipeline to Battle (Random) NYT gen 3/12/44 (#16, 1 wk).

Rame, David
Wine of Good Hope (Macmillan) NYT fic 5/7/39 (#7, 4 wk); PW fic 5/13/39 (#8, 4 wk), 8 wk; tot 12 wk.

Rampersand, Arnold
See Richard Wright and _____

Rand, Ayn
The Fountainhead (Blakiston) NYT fic 7/4/43 (#10), pk 8/15/45 (#4, 1 wk), 69 wk; PW fic 7/14/45 (#10), pk 8/11/45 (#7, 1 wk), 5 wk; tot 74 wk.
Atlas Shrugged (Random) NYT fic 10/13/57 (#13), pk 12/1/57 (#3, 1 wk), 22 wk; PW fic 10/28/57 (#7), pk 11/11/57 (#2, 2 wk), 18 wk; tot 40 wk.

Randall, Clarence Belden
A Creed for Free Enterprise (Little Brown) NYT gen 7/20/52 (#16, 1 wk).

Randall, James Garfield
Lincoln, the President (Dodd) NYT gen 12/23/45 (#15, 1 wk), 2 wk.

Randall, Ruth
Mary Lincoln (Little Brown) NYT gen 3/1/53 (#16), pk 3/8/53 (#14, 1 wk), 4 wk.

Rankin, Arthur, Jr.
See J.R.R. Tolkien

Ransome, Arthur
Swallows and Amazons (Lippincott) PW juv 6/20/31 (#9, 4 wk).

Raphaelson, Samson
Skylark (Knopf) NYT fic 8/6/39 (#9, 4 wk).

Rapoport, Judith L.
The Boy Who Couldn't Stop Washing (Dutton) NYT nf 2/19/89 (#14), pk 4/9/89 (#10, 1 wk), 9 wk.

Rapp, Joe, and Lynn Rapp
Mother Earth Hassle Free Indoor Plant Book (Hawthorne) NYT td pb 5/12/74 (#10), pk 6/19/74 (#8, 4 wk), 8 wk.

Rascoe, Burton
Titans of Literature (Putnam) PW nf 12/17/32 (#10, 4 wk).
Before I Forget (Doubleday) NYT gen 7/4/37 (#10, 4 wk).

Rascovich, Mark
The Bedford Incident (Atheneum) NYT fic 5/19/63 (#9), pk 6/16/63 (#8, 4 wk), 13 wk;

PW fic 5/27/63 (#11), pk 6/10/63 (#7, 3 wk), 13 wk; tot 26 wk.

Raskin, Barbara
Hot Flashes (St. Martin's) PW hc fic 9/18/87 (#9), pk 10/16/87 (#7, 1 wk), 12 wk; NYT fic 9/20/87 (#13), pk 10/18/87 (#8, 4 wk), 11 wk; PW mm pb 7/29/88 (#13), pk 9/9/88 (#4, 2 wk), 13 wk; NYT pb fic 7/31/88 (#8), pk 9/4/88 (#3, 2 wk), 11 wk; tot 47 wk.

Raso, Anne M.
New Kids on the Block (Modern) NYT pb nf 3/18/90 (#7, 1 wk).

Rather, Dan, and Gary Paul Gates
The Palace Guard (Harper) NYT gen 11/24/74 (#9), pk 2/16/75 (#1, 1 wk), 24 wk; PW nf 12/2/74 (#9), pk 2/10/75 (#1, 1 wk), 19 wk; (Warner) NYT mm pb 7/13/75 (#9), pk 7/27/75 (#4, 1 wk), 5 wk; tot 48 wk.

_____, with Mickey Herskowitz
The Camera Never Blinks: Adventures of a TV Journalist (Morrow) PW hc nf 6/27/77 (#10), pk 10/17/77 (#4, 1 wk), 27 wk; NYT nf 7/31/77 (#7), pk 9/4/77 (#5, 3 wk), 25 wk; (Ballantine) PW mm pb 5/1/78 (#11, 1 wk), 3 wk; tot 55 wk.

Rau, Santha Rama
Home to India (Harper) NYT gen 6/24/45 (#23), pk 9/2/45 (#11, 1 wk), 5 wk.
Remember the House (Harper) NYT fic 5/13/56 (#9, 3 wk), 9 wk.
Gifts of Passage (Harper) NYT gen 6/25/61 (#16), pk 7/23/61 (#14, 1 wk), 4 wk.

Rauch, William
See Edward I. Koch and _____

Raucher, Herman
Summer of '42 (Putnam) NYT fic 4/11/71 (#10), pk 5/23/71 (#7, 1 wk), 10 wk; PW fic 5/17/71 (#9, 2 wk), 4 wk; NYT pb fic 10/10/71 (#4), pk 12/12/71 (#2, 8 wk), 20 wk; tot 34 wk.

Rauschning, Hermann
The Revolution of Nihilism (Alliance) NYT gen 10/8/39 (#3, 4 wk), 16 wk; PW nf 10/14/39 (#7), pk 11/11/39 (#6, 8 wk), 12 wk; tot 28 wk.

Raverat, Gwen
Period Piece (Norton) NYT gen 9/6/53 (#13), pk 11/1/53 (#6, 1 wk), 24 wk; PW nf 11/14/53 (#8, 1 wk), 2 wk; tot 26 wk.

Raviv, Dan, and Yossi Melman
Every Spy a Prince (Houghton) PW hc nf 8/3/90 (#13), pk 9/7/90 (#6, 2 wk), 12 wk; NYT nf 8/12/90 (#15), pk 9/9/90 (#5, 2 wk), 12 wk; tot 24 wk.

Raw, Charles, with Bruce Page and Godfrey Hodgson
Do You Sincerely Want to Be Rich? (Viking) NYT gen 9/5/71 (#9), pk 9/26/71 (#5, 1 wk), 7 wk; PW nf 9/6/71 (#9), pk 9/27/71 (#5, 2 wk), 12 wk; tot 19 wk.

Rawlings, Marjorie Kinnan
South Moon Under (Scribner) PW fic 5/13/33 (#5, 4 wk).
Golden Apples (Scribner) NYT fic 11/3/35 (#7, 4 wk).
The Yearling (Scribner) NYT fic 5/1/38 (#1, 12 wk), 44 wk; PW fic 5/14/38 (#5), pk 7/9/38 (#1, 12 wk), 64 wk; tot 108 wk.
Cross Creek (Scribner) PW nf 4/11/42 (#6), pk 5/9/42 (#1, 8 wk), 19 wk; NYT nf 8/9/42 (#9), pk 8/30/42 (#7, 1 wk), 7 wk; tot 26 wk.
The Sojourner (Scribner) NYT fic 1/18/53 (#14), pk 2/8/53 (#5, 1 wk), 16 wk; PW fic 2/14/53 (#9), pk 2/21/53 (#4, 1 wk), 6 wk; tot 22 wk.

Rawson, Clayton
The Footprints on the Ceiling (Putnam) NYT fic 7/9/39 (#7, 4 wk).

Ray, Elizabeth
The Washington Fringe Benefit (Dell) PW mm pb 6/28/76 (#14), pk 7/12/76 (#8, 2 wk), 7 wk; NYT mm pb 7/4/76 (#6, 1 wk), 4 wk; tot 11 wk.

Ray, Dr. Randolph
Marriage Is a Serious Business (McGraw) NYT gen 3/26/44 (#10, 1 wk), 2 wk.

Raymond, Charles
See Alex Comfort

Raymond, Dalton S.
Earthbound (Ziff Davis) NYT fic 3/7/48 (#13), pk 4/11/48 (#9, 2 wk), 8 wk; PW fic 4/17/48 (#10, 1 wk); tot 9 wk.

Raynolds, Robert
Brothers in the West (Harper) PW fic 10/17/31 (#7, 4 wk).
The Sinner of Saint Ambrose (Bobbs Merrill) NYT fic 8/31/52 (#11), pk 9/28/52 (#10, 1 wk), 9 wk; PW fic 9/13/52 (#10, 1 wk); tot 10 wk.

Razzi, James
Star Trek Puzzle Manual (Bantam) NYT td pb 12/12/76 (#4, 1 wk).

Rea, Lorna
Six Mrs. Greenes (Harper) PW fic 8/10/29 (#10, 4 wk).

Read, Piers Paul
Alive (Lippincott) PW nf 4/29/74 (#5), pk 5/20/74 (#1, 2 wk), 31 wk; (Avon) NYT mm

pb 5/18/75 (#5), pk 5/25/75 (#1, 4 wk), 17 wk; tot 48 wk.

Reagan, Michael, and Joe Hyams
On the Outside Looking In (Zebra) NYT nf 4/10/88 (#11, 1 wk), 3 wk.

Reagan, Nancy, and William Novak
My Turn: The Memoirs of Nancy Reagan (Random) NYT nf 11/5/89 (#8), pk 11/26/89 (#1, 4 wk), 14 wk; PW hc nf 11/10/89 (#7), pk 11/17/89 (#1, 6 wk), 13 wk; (Dell) NYT pb nf 11/18/90 (#9, 1 wk); tot 28 wk.

Reagan, Ronald
An American Life (Simon & Schuster) NYT nf 11/25/90 (#8), pk 12/9/90 (#5, 2 wk), 6 wk; PW hc nf 11/30/90 (#11), pk 12/21/90 (#6, 1 wk), 4 wk; tot 10 wk.

Rebeta-Burditt, Joyce
The Cracker Factory (Macmillan) NYT td pb 9/11/77 (#15), pk 10/23/77 (#11, 1 wk), 5 wk; (Bantam) NYT mm pb 4/30/78 (#13, 1 wk), 2 wk; PW mm pb 5/8/78 (#15, 1 wk); tot 8 wk.
Triplets (Dell) NYT mm pb 10/24/82 (#14, 1 wk); PW mm pb 11/5/82 (#12, 2 wk); tot 3 wk.

Rechy, John
City of Night (Grove) NYT fic 7/7/63 (#7), pk 8/11/63 (#3, 2 wk), 24 wk; PW fic 7/15/63 (#10), pk 8/5/63 (#4, 7 wk), 23 wk; tot 47 wk.

Red Fox, Chief William, and Cash Asher
The Memoirs of Chief Red Fox (McGraw) NYT gen 7/4/71 (#10), pk 7/25/71 (#9, 3 wk), 5 wk; PW nf 8/23/71 (#7, 1 wk), 2 wk; tot 7 wk.

Reddy, John
See Jack Paar and _____

Redgrave, Lynn
See Barbara Taylor Bradford
See Rosamunde Pilcher

Redman, Scott, and Bruce Feirstein
Real Men Don't Cook Quiche [ed. Redman and Feirstein, illus. Lee Lorenz] (Pocket) NYT td pb 12/19/82 (#13), pk 1/9/83 (#12, 1 wk), 5 wk; PW td pb 12/24/82 (#10), pk 1/14/83 (#8, 1 wk), 3 wk; tot 8 wk.

Reed, Dan
See Kelly Moore and _____

Reed, W. Maxwell
The Earth for Sam (Harcourt) PW juv 3/15/30 (#9, 8 wk).

Reedy, Jerry
See Theodore M. Hesburgh and _____

Reeves, Rosser
Reality in Advertising (Knopf) NYT gen 5/7/61 (#14), pk 6/11/61 (#9, 1 wk), 9 wk; PW nf 6/19/61 (#9, 1 wk); tot 10 wk.

Reeves-Stevens, Garfield, and Judith Reeves-Stevens
Memory Prime (Pocket) NYT pb fic 10/16/88 (#10, 1 wk), 4 wk; PW mm pb 10/21/88 (#15), pk 10/28/88 (#10, 1 wk), 4 wk; tot 8 wk.

Reeves-Stevens, Judith, and Garfield Reeves-Stevens
The Prime Directive (Pocket) NYT fic 9/16/90 (#10, 1 wk), 5 wk; PW hc fic 9/28/90 (#15), pk 10/5/90 (#10, 1 wk), 3 wk; [read by James Doohan] (Simon & Schuster) PW aud fic 10/5/90 (#6), pk 11/2/90 (#3, 4 wk), 12 wk; tot 20 wk.

Regan, Donald T.
For the Record: From Wall Street to Washington (Harcourt) PW hc nf 5/27/88 (#11), pk 6/3/88 (#1, 4 wk), 12 wk; NYT nf 5/29/88 (#1, 4 wk), 11 wk; tot 23 wk.

Reich, Charles
The Greening of America (Random) NYT gen 11/29/70 (#10), pk 12/27/70 (#1, 20 wk), 36 wk; PW nf 11/30/70 (#5), pk 1/18/71 (#1, 18 wk), 35 wk; NYT pb gen 7/11/71 (#1, 12 wk), 36 wk; tot 107 wk.

Reich, Robert B.
The Next American Frontier (Times) PW hc nf 6/24/83 (#13, 1 wk).

Reid, Ed, and Ovid Demaris
The Green Felt Jungle (Trident) NYT gen 2/2/64 (#8), pk 2/9/64 (#6, 6 wk), 24 wk; PW nf 2/17/64 (#8), pk 3/16/64 (#3, 2 wk), 25 wk; tot 49 wk.

Reid, Patrick R.
The Colditz Story (Lippincott) NYT gen 4/5/53 (#15), pk 4/19/53 (#14, 1 wk), 3 wk.

Reilly, Helen
Crimefile No. 2: File on Rufus Ray (Morrow) NYT fic 6/6/37 (#4, 4 wk).
All Concerned Notified (Sundial/Doubleday) NYT fic 8/6/39 (#10, 4 wk).

Reilly, Michael Francis, as told to William J. Slocum
Reilly of the White House (Simon & Schuster) NYT gen 10/5/47 (#16), pk 10/12/47 (#9, 1 wk), 2 wk.

Reilly, Rich
See Brian Bosworth and _____

Reinisch, June M., with Ruth Beasley
The Kinsey Institute New Report on Sex (St. Martin's) PW hc nf 10/19/90 (#15, 1 wk).

Reisner, Robert George
Captions Courageous (Abelard Schuman) NYT gen 3/29/59 (#15, 1 wk).

Remarque, Erich Maria
All Quiet on the Western Front (Little Brown) PW fic 8/10/29 (#1, 28 wk), 32 wk.
The Road Back (Little Brown) PW fic 6/20/31 (#1, 8 wk), 12 wk.
Three Comrades (Little Brown) NYT fic 6/6/37 (#5, 4 wk); PW fic 6/12/37 (#9, 4 wk), 8 wk; tot 12 wk.
Flotsam (Little Brown) PW fic 6/14/41 (#7, 4 wk).
Arch of Triumph (Appleton) PW fic 2/9/46 (#10), pk 3/16/46 (#1, 5 wk), 23 wk; NYT fic 2/10/46 (#4), pk 3/10/46 (#1, 8 wk), 27 wk; tot 50 wk.
Spark of Life (Appleton) NYT fic 2/17/52 (#6), pk 3/2/52 (#4, 6 wk), 14 wk; PW fic 3/1/52 (#3, 1 wk), 9 wk; tot 23 wk.
A Time to Love and a Time to Die (Harcourt) NYT fic 6/13/54 (#12), pk 6/20/54 (#6, 2 wk), 17 wk; PW fic 7/17/54 (#9), pk 7/24/54 (#6, 1 wk), 4 wk; tot 21 wk.
The Black Obelisk (Harcourt) NYT fic 4/28/57 (#11), pk 5/5/57 (#8, 1 wk), 9 wk; PW fic 5/13/57 (#8), pk 5/27/57 (#6, 1 wk), 2 wk; tot 11 wk.
Heaven Has No Favorites [trans. Richard Winston and Clara Winston] (Harcourt) NYT fic 4/30/61 (#15, 2 wk).
A Night in Lisbon (Harcourt) NYT fic 4/19/64 (#8), pk 6/7/64 (#3, 1 wk), 20 wk; PW fic 4/27/64 (#9), pk 5/11/64 (#3, 4 wk), 18 wk; tot 38 wk.

Renault, Mary
The Last of the Wine (Pantheon) NYT fic 12/30/56 (#16), pk 1/27/57 (#11, 1 wk), 9 wk.
The King Must Die (Pantheon) NYT fic 7/27/58 (#15), pk 8/17/58 (#3, 3 wk), 27 wk; PW fic 8/11/58 (#7), pk 8/25/58 (#3, 2 wk), 14 wk; tot 41 wk.
The Charioteer (Pantheon) NYT fic 6/7/59 (#13, 1 wk).
The Bull from the Sea (Pantheon) NYT fic 3/4/62 (#12), pk 4/15/62 (#2, 3 wk), 25 wk; PW fic 3/12/62 (#10), pk 4/2/62 (#1, 1 wk), 17 wk; tot 42 wk.
The Mask of Apollo (Pantheon) NYT fic 11/20/66 (#7), pk 2/19/67 (#4, 1 wk), 22 wk; PW fic 11/28/66 (#8), pk 1/16/67 (#3, 2 wk), 20 wk; tot 42 wk.
Fire from Heaven (Pantheon) NYT fic 12/21/69 (#10), pk 1/25/70 (#5, 1 wk), 14 wk;

PW fic 12/29/69 (#9), pk 2/9/70 (#3, 1 wk), 14 wk; tot 28 wk.
The Persian Boy (Pantheon) NYT fic 11/19/72 (#10), pk 2/11/73 (#4, 1 wk), 23 wk; PW fic 11/27/72 (#6), pk 3/26/73 (#3, 1 wk), 22 wk; tot 45 wk.
The Praise Singer (Pantheon) NYT fic 1/7/79 (#15), pk 2/4/79 (#12, 1 wk), 5 wk.
Funeral Games (Pantheon) PW hc fic 1/8/82 (#13, 1 wk).

Renner, Thomas C.
See Antoinette Giancana and _____
See Vincent Teresa with _____

Renoir, Jean
Renoir, My Father (Little Brown) NYT gen 12/9/62 (#14, 2 wk); PW nf 12/10/62 (#12), pk 1/14/63 (#4, 1 wk), 10 wk; tot 12 wk.

Reshevsky, Samuel
See Richard Jerome Roberts, et al.

Restak, Richard M., M.D.
The Brain (Bantam) NYT nf 12/16/84 (#13), pk 1/20/85 (#8, 1 wk), 10 wk; PW hc nf 1/11/85 (#14, 1 wk); tot 11 wk.

Reston, James B.
Prelude to Victory (Knopf) NYT nf 8/9/42 (#14), pk 8/16/42 (#13, 1 wk), 3 wk.

Reuben, Dr. David
Everything You Always Wanted to Know About Sex (McKay) NYT gen 1/25/70 (#10), pk 3/1/70 (#1, 27 wk), 64 wk; PW nf 2/16/70 (#7), pk 3/16/70 (#1, 23 wk), 58 wk; NYT pb gen 2/7/71 (#1, 20 wk), 24 wk; tot 146 wk.
Any Woman Can! (McKay) NYT gen 10/3/71 (#5), pk 11/21/71 (#1, 1 wk), 14 wk; PW fic 10/4/71 (#5), pk 11/22/71 (#1, 1 wk), 15 wk; NYT pb gen 12/10/72 (#5, 4 wk); tot 33 wk.
The Save Your Life Diet (Random) PW nf 7/7/75 (#9), pk 7/14/75 (#5, 3 wk), 22 wk; NYT gen 8/3/75 (#9), pk 9/14/75 (#6, 3 wk), 20 wk; (Ballantine) PW mm pb 5/10/76 (#13), pk 6/7/76 (#11, 1 wk), 5 wk; tot 47 wk.

Revel, Jean-Francois
Without Marx Or Jesus (Doubleday) PW nf 10/11/71 (#7), pk 11/1/71 (#2, 1 wk), 12 wk; NYT gen 10/17/71 (#4), pk 11/7/71 (#3, 1 wk), 8 wk; tot 20 wk.

Revell, Nellie
Right Off the Chest (Doran) PW gen lit 4/19/24 (#7, 4 wk).

Reves, Emery
The Anatomy of Peace (Harper) NYT gen 12/30/45 (#13), pk 3/10/46 (#2, 3 wk), 24 wk; PW nf 2/2/46 (#4), pk 2/16/46 (#2, 7 wk), 14 wk; tot 38 wk.

Reynolds, Quentin James
The Wounded Don't Cry (Dutton) PW nf 3/15/41 (#6), pk 4/12/41 (#4, 4 wk), 8 wk.
Only the Stars Are Neutral (Random) PW nf 7/11/42 (#9), pk 8/8/42 (#5, 3 wk), 10 wk; NYT nf 8/9/42 (#5, 5 wk), 11 wk; tot 21 wk.
Dress Rehearsal (Random) NYT nf 3/21/43 (#12), pk 4/4/43 (#4, 1 wk), 11 wk; PW nf 3/27/43 (#5, 2 wk), 5 wk; tot 16 wk.
The Curtain Rises (Random) NYT gen 3/26/44 (#9), pk 5/7/44 (#2, 4 wk), 27 wk; PW nf 4/1/44 (#3), pk 6/3/44 (#1, 1 wk), 16 wk; tot 43 wk.
Officially Dead (Random) NYT gen 12/16/45 (#14, 3 wk), 4 wk.
70,000 to One (Random) NYT gen 8/18/46 (#8, 1 wk), 2 wk.
Courtroom (Farrar) NYT gen 6/18/50 (#16), pk 8/27/50 (#1, 4 wk), 41 wk; PW nf 7/8/50 (#5), pk 8/26/50 (#1, 3 wk), 19 wk; tot 60 wk.
The Amazing Mr. Doolittle (Appleton) NYT gen 5/24/53 (#13, 1 wk).
They Fought for the Sky (Rinehart) NYT gen 7/7/57 (#15), pk 8/18/57 (#14, 1 wk), 6 wk.

Rhine, J.B.
New Frontiers of the Mind (Farrar) PW nf 12/11/37 (#9, 4 wk).

Rice, Alice Hegan
The Buffer (Century) PW fic 6/8/29 (#10, 4 wk).

Rice, Anne
Interview with the Vampire (Ballantine) PW mm pb 5/16/77 (#12), pk 6/6/77 (#4, 1 wk), 7 wk; NYT mm pb 5/22/77 (#9), pk 6/12/77 (#4, 1 wk), 9 wk; tot 16 wk.
The Vampire Lestat (Knopf) NYT fic 11/17/85 (#9, 1 wk), 7 wk; PW hc fic 11/22/85 (#12), pk 12/6/85 (#11, 1 wk), 6 wk; (Ballantine) NYT pb fic 10/12/86 (#10), pk 11/2/86 (#6, 1 wk), 8 wk; PW mm pb 10/17/86 (#10), pk 10/24/86 (#8, 3 wk), 8 wk; tot 29 wk.
The Queen of the Damned (Knopf) NYT fic 10/23/88 (#2), pk 10/30/88 (#1, 3 wk), 17 wk; PW hc fic 10/28/88 (#2), pk 11/4/88 (#1, 3 wk), 16 wk; (Ballantine) NYT pb fic 10/1/89 (#15), pk 10/8/89 (#5, 4 wk), 8 wk; PW mm pb 10/6/89 (#7), pk 10/13/89 (#5, 4 wk), 7 wk; tot 48 wk.
The Mummy, Or Ramses the Damned (Ballantine) NYT pb fic 5/21/89 (#13), pk 6/4/89 (#8, 2 wk), 10 wk; PW td pb 5/26/89 (#8), pk 6/2/89 (#2, 3 wk), 16 wk; tot 26 wk.
The Witching Hour (Knopf) NYT fic 11/11/90 (#2, 4 wk), 8 wk; PW hc fic 11/16/90 (#4), pk 11/23/90 (#2, 5 wk), 6 wk; [read by Lind-say Crouse] (Random) PW aud fic 12/7/90 (#5, 4 wk); tot 18 wk.

Rice, Edward
Captain Sir Richard Frances Burton (Scribners) NYT nf 7/8/90 (#9), pk 7/15/90 (#7, 2 wk), 10 wk; PW hc nf 7/13/90 (#14), pk 7/27/90 (#8, 3 wk), 9 wk; tot 19 wk.

Rice, Elmer
Imperial City (Coward McCann) NYT fic 12/12/37 (#7, 4 wk), 8 wk; PW fic 1/15/38 (#10, 4 wk); tot 12 wk.

Rice, Grantland
The Tumult and the Shouting (Barnes) NYT gen 11/21/54 (#5), pk 12/19/54 (#2, 9 wk), 26 wk; PW nf 11/27/54 (#4), pk 1/8/55 (#1, 1 wk), 20 wk; tot 46 wk.

Rich, Louise Dickinson
We Took to the Woods (Lippincott) NYT nf 12/20/42 (#8), pk 3/21/43 (#6, 1 wk), 18 wk; PW nf 1/16/43 (#9), pk 2/13/43 (#6, 1 wk), 5 wk; tot 23 wk.
Happy the Land (Lippincott) NYT gen 12/15/46 (#15), pk 12/29/46 (#8, 1 wk), 9 wk.
The Coast of Maine (Crowell) NYT gen 7/29/56 (#16, 1 wk).

Richards, William C.
The Last Billionaire (Scribner) NYT gen 3/14/48 (#14), pk 3/28/48 (#8, 2 wk), 14 wk.

Richardson, Henry Handel
Myself When Young (Norton) NYT gen 8/15/48 (#16, 1 wk).

Richardson, Sullivan Calvin
Adventure South (Arnold Powers) NYT nf 12/6/42 (#11, 1 wk).

Richardson, Wyman
The House on Nauset Marsh (Norton) NYT gen 8/7/55 (#14), pk 8/21/55 (#9, 3 wk), 13 wk; PW nf 9/17/55 (#10), pk 10/1/55 (#7, 1 wk), 2 wk; tot 15 wk.

Richmond, Grace Louise Smith
Red and Black (Doubleday) PW fic 1/31/20 (#8, 4 wk).
Foursquare (Doubleday) PW fic 11/18/22 (#11, 4 wk).
Cherry Square (Doubleday) PW fic 2/19/27 (#10, 4 wk).
The Listening Post (Doubleday) PW fic 9/14/29 (#8, 4 wk).
High Fences (Doubleday) PW fic 9/20/30 (#10, 4 wk).
Red Pepper Returns (Doubleday) PW fic 8/15/31 (#4, 4 wk), 8 wk.

Richter, Conrad
Tacey Cromwell (Knopf) NYT fic 11/15/42 (#20, 1 wk).

The Free Man (Knopf) NYT fic 9/5/43 (#15, 1 wk).

The Town (Knopf) NYT fic 6/11/50 (#12, 1 wk), 2 wk.

The Lady (Knopf) NYT fic 6/16/57 (#15), pk 6/30/57 (#9, 2 wk), 12 wk.

Richter, Lin
See Fred Belliveau and _____

Rickenbacker, Capt. Eddie
Seven Came Through (Doubleday) NYT gen 4/11/43 (#13), pk 5/16/43 (#5, 1 wk), 15 wk; PW nf 4/17/43 (#8), pk 5/8/43 (#5, 1 wk), 4 wk; tot 19 wk.

Rickenbacker (Prentice Hall) PW nf 11/13/67 (#9), pk 12/25/67 (#3, 7 wk), 21 wk; NYT gen 11/19/67 (#10), pk 1/7/68 (#1, 1 wk), 23 wk; tot 44 wk.

Riddle, Donald Wayne, and Harold H. Hutson
New Testament Life and Literature (Univ. of Chicago) NYT gen 7/21/46 (#16, 1 wk).

Riding, Alan
Distant Neighbors: Portrait of the Mexicans (Knopf) NYT nf 3/24/85 (#13), pk 4/28/85 (#12, 1 wk), 6 wk; PW hc nf 5/3/85 (#13, 1 wk); tot 7 wk.

Riefe, Barbara
This Ravaged Heart (Playboy) NYT mm pb 7/24/77 (#13, 1 wk).

Riegle, Donald, and Trevor Armbrister
O Congress (Doubleday) NYT gen 8/20/72 (#10), pk 9/10/72 (#9, 2 wk), 5 wk; PW nf 9/25/72 (#10, 1 wk); tot 6 wk.

Riker, Tim, and Harvey Rottenberg
The Gardener's Catalogue (Morrow) NYT td pb 12/8/74 (#8), pk 2/23/75 (#4, 2 wk), 11 wk.

Riley, Pat
Show Time: Inside the Lakers Breakthrough Season (Warner) NYT nf 6/12/88 (#13), pk 7/17/88 (#8, 1 wk), 6 wk; PW hc nf 6/17/88 (#13), pk 7/1/88 (#7, 1 wk), 9 wk; tot 15 wk.

Rimington, Critchell
Fighting Fleets (Dodd) NYT nf 8/9/42 (#15, 1 wk).

Rinehart, Mary Roberts
Love Stories (Doran) PW fic 8/2/19 (#8, 4 wk).

Dangerous Days (Doran) PW fic 9/6/19 (#1, 8 wk), 20 wk.

A Poor Wise Man (Doran) PW fic 11/27/20 (#3), pk 1/8/21 (#2, 4 wk), 16 wk.

Affinities (Doran) PW fic 8/14/20 (#10, 4 wk).

The Breaking Point (Doran) PW fic 9/16/22 (#4), pk 10/14/22 (#2, 4 wk), 28 wk.

The Red Lamp (Doran) PW fic 9/26/25 (#6), pk 10/24/25 (#4, 4 wk), 8 wk.

Lost Ecstasy (Doran) PW fic 7/30/27 (#5), pk 8/27/27 (#1, 4 wk), 16 wk.

This Strange Adventure (Doubleday) PW fic 4/13/29 (#6), pk 5/11/29 (#4, 8 wk), 12 wk.

The Door (Farrar) PW fic 5/17/30 (#2, 4 wk), 8 wk.

Miss Pinkerton (Farrar) PW fic 3/19/32 (#4), pk 4/23/32 (#3, 4 wk), 12 wk.

The Album (Farrar) PW fic 7/15/33 (#3, 4 wk), 8 wk.

The State Versus Elinor Norton (Farrar) PW fic 3/10/34 (#8, 4 wk), 8 wk.

The Doctor (Farrar) NYT fic 7/5/36 (#1, 4 wk), 8 wk; PW fic 7/11/36 (#3, 8 wk), 16 wk; tot 24 wk.

The Wall (Farrar) NYT fic 7/31/38 (#6), pk 9/4/38 (#3, 4 wk), 8 wk; PW fic 8/13/38 (#6), pk 9/10/38 (#5, 4 wk), 12 wk; tot 20 wk.

Tish Marches On (Farrar) NYT fic 1/9/38 (#8, 4 wk).

A Light in the Window (Rinehart) NYT fic 2/1/48 (#15), pk 2/22/48 (#5, 1 wk), 12 wk; PW fic 3/6/48 (#5, 1 wk), 3 wk; tot 15 wk.

The Swimming Pool (Rinehart) NYT fic 2/10/52 (#14), pk 3/30/52 (#5, 5 wk), 24 wk; PW fic 3/8/52 (#5), pk 4/12/52 (#4, 1 wk), 10 wk; tot 34 wk.

Ringer, Robert J.
Winning Through Intimidation (Funk & Wagnalls) PW nf 9/1/75 (#8), pk 10/20/75 (#2, 7 wk), 33 wk; NYT gen 9/7/75 (#8), pk 3/7/76 (#1, 1 wk), 35 wk; (Fawcett) PW mm pb 5/10/76 (#11), pk 5/24/76 (#4, 4 wk), 15 wk; NYT mm pb 5/16/76 (#9), pk 6/20/76 (#3, 1 wk), 12 wk; tot 95 wk.

Looking Out for #1 (Funk & Wagnalls) PW hc nf 6/27/77 (#8), pk 9/12/77 (#1, 1 wk), 46 wk; NYT nf 7/10/77 (#8), pk 8/21/77 (#1, 1 wk), 47 wk; (Fawcett/Crest) PW mm pb 6/26/78 (#7), pk 7/31/78 (#2, 1 wk), 13 wk; NYT mm pb 7/2/78 (#4), pk 8/6/78 (#2, 2 wk), 7 wk; tot 113 wk.

Restoring the American Dream (Harper/QED) PW hc nf 9/10/79 (#5), pk 10/8/79 (#2, 2 wk), 18 wk; NYT nf 9/16/79 (#4), pk 9/23/79 (#3, 3 wk), 18 wk; NYT mm pb 8/24/80 (#13, 1 wk); tot 37 wk.

Ripley, Alexandra
Charleston (Avon) PW mm pb 4/9/82 (#11, 1 wk), 2 wk.

On Leaving Charleston (Dell) NYT pb fic 3/17/85 (#10), pk 3/24/85 (#9, 1 wk), 3 wk;

PW mm pb 3/22/85 (#14), pk 3/29/85 (#12, 1 wk), 2 wk; tot 5 wk.
New Orleans Legacy (Warner) NYT pb fic 6/5/88 (#13), pk 7/10/88 (#9, 1 wk), 8 wk.

Ripley, Robert L.
Believe It Or Not (Simon & Schuster) PW nf 4/13/29 (#5, 12 wk), 24 wk.

Rivers, Gayle
The Specialist (Charter) NYT pb nf 5/18/86 (#9), pk 6/15/86 (#8, 1 wk), 2 wk.

Rivers, Joan
The Life and Hard Times of Heidi Abromowitz (Delacorte) NYT fic 11/18/84 (#9), pk 1/6/85 (#4, 3 wk), 18 wk; PW hc fic 11/23/84 (#13), pk 3/8/85 (#2, 1 wk), 19 wk; tot 37 wk.

_____, with Richard Meryman
Enter Talking (Delacorte) NYT nf 5/11/86 (#16), pk 5/25/86 (#4, 3 wk), 12 wk; PW hc nf 5/23/86 (#11), pk 6/6/86 (#4, 3 wk), 7 wk; tot 19 wk.

Rivette, Mark
The Incident (World Almanac) NYT fic 12/22/57 (#15, 1 wk), 2 wk.

Roark, Garland
Wake of the Red Witch (Little Brown) NYT fic 4/21/46 (#15), pk 5/5/46 (#6, 6 wk), 11 wk; PW fic 5/11/46 (#10), pk 6/1/46 (#4, 1 wk), 3 wk; tot 14 wk.
Rainbow in the Royals (Doubleday) NYT fic 12/3/50 (#16, 1 wk).

Robards, Karen
Tiger's Eye (Avon) PW mm pb 5/19/89 (#15, 1 wk).

Robbins, Anthony
Unlimited Power (Simon & Schuster) PW hc nf 8/22/86 (#14), pk 10/3/86 (#6, 1 wk), 10 wk; NYT msc 9/28/86 (#5, 4 wk); PW aud nf 11/2/90 (#8, 4 wk); tot 18 wk.

Robbins, Harold
Never Love a Stranger (Simon & Schuster) NYT fic 5/16/48 (#16, 1 wk).
The Dream Merchants (Knopf) NYT fic 11/13/49 (#13), pk 11/27/49 (#10, 1 wk), 10 wk.
A Stone for Danny Fisher (Knopf) NYT fic 4/6/52 (#15), pk 5/4/52 (#12, 1 wk), 7 wk.
79 Park Avenue (Simon & Schuster) NYT fic 8/14/55 (#15), pk 10/23/55 (#12, 1 wk), 9 wk; (Pocket) PW mm pb 10/31/77 (#11), pk 11/7/77 (#6, 1 wk), 5 wk; NYT mm pb 11/6/77 (#15), pk 11/13/77 (#8, 1 wk), 6 wk; tot 20 wk.
The Carpetbaggers (Simon & Schuster) NYT fic 6/25/61 (#9), pk 9/17/61 (#3, 2 wk), 41 wk; PW fic 7/3/61 (#8), pk 8/28/61 (#3, 1 wk), 31 wk; tot 72 wk.

Where Love Has Gone (Simon & Schuster) NYT fic 11/4/62 (#7), pk 12/1/62 (#4, 3 wk), 7 wk; PW fic 11/19/62 (#10), pk 12/10/62 (#6, 1 wk), 8 wk; tot 15 wk.
The Adventurers (Trident) NYT fic 4/3/66 (#10), pk 5/15/66 (#2, 21 wk), 41 wk; PW fic 4/11/66 (#10), pk 5/30/66 (#2, 9 wk), 40 wk; NYT pb fic 2/5/67 (#3), pk 5/7/67 (#1, 4 wk), 32 wk; tot 113 wk.
The Inheritors (Trident) NYT fic 11/30/69 (#6), pk 12/21/69 (#4, 8 wk), 21 wk; PW fic 12/1/69 (#6), pk 1/26/70 (#3, 2 wk), 20 wk; NYT pb fic 3/7/71 (#4), pk 4/4/71 (#3, 4 wk), 8 wk; tot 49 wk.
The Betsy (Trident) NYT fic 12/12/71 (#8), pk 8/13/72 (#2, 2 wk), 26 wk; PW fic 12/27/71 (#7), pk 2/14/72 (#5, 2 wk), 18 wk; (Pocket) PW mm pb 2/27/78 (#13), pk 3/6/78 (#7, 1 wk), 7 wk; NYT mm pb 3/5/78 (#11), pk 3/12/78 (#4, 1 wk), 8 wk; tot 59 wk.
The Pirate (Simon & Schuster) PW fic 10/14/74 (#8), pk 11/18/74 (#3, 2 wk), 22 wk; NYT fic 10/20/74 (#8), pk 11/24/74 (#3, 3 wk), 26 wk; (Pocket) NYT mm pb 6/1/75 (#7), pk 6/15/75 (#1, 2 wk), 13 wk; tot 61 wk.
The Lonely Lady (Simon & Schuster) NYT fic 6/6/76 (#9), pk 8/15/76 (#2, 1 wk), 24 wk; PW hc fic 6/14/76 (#6), pk 8/2/76 (#2, 1 wk), 22 wk; (Pocket) PW mm pb 3/14/77 (#7), pk 3/21/77 (#1, 5 wk), 19 wk; NYT mm pb 3/20/77 (#2), pk 3/27/77 (#1, 5 wk), 18 wk; tot 83 wk.
Dreams Die First (Putnam) PW hc fic 10/24/77 (#11), pk 11/21/77 (#5, 3 wk), 20 wk; NYT fic 10/30/77 (#14), pk 12/4/77 (#6, 3 wk), 25 wk; (Pocket) PW mm pb 8/28/78 (#4), pk 9/4/78 (#2, 3 wk), 12 wk; NYT mm pb 11/12/78 (#9, 1 wk), 5 wk; tot 62 wk.
Memories of Another Day (Simon & Schuster) PW hc fic 11/12/79 (#8), pk 1/18/80 (#4, 3 wk), 22 wk; NYT fic 11/18/79 (#10), pk 12/23/79 (#4, 3 wk), 24 wk; (Pocket) PW mm pb 9/12/80 (#5), pk 9/26/80 (#1, 1 wk), 11 wk; NYT mm pb 9/14/80 (#4), pk 9/21/80 (#1, 2 wk), 15 wk; tot 72 wk.
Goodbye, Janette (Simon & Schuster) PW hc fic 6/12/81 (#11), pk 7/10/81 (#4, 7 wk), 23 wk; NYT fic 6/14/81 (#14), pk 7/5/81 (#3, 3 wk), 21 wk; (Pocket) PW mm pb 2/12/82 (#6), pk 2/19/82 (#1, 2 wk), 13 wk; NYT mm pb 2/14/82 (#4), pk 2/28/82 (#2, 3 wk), 14 wk; tot 71 wk.
Spellbinder (Simon & Schuster) PW hc fic 9/24/82 (#11), pk 10/22/82 (#8, 2 wk), 11 wk; NYT fic 10/17/82 (#10), pk 10/31/82 (#9, 1 wk), 4 wk; (Pocket) NYT mm pb 8/7/83 (#9), pk 8/14/83 (#3, 3 wk), 10 wk; PW mm pb 8/12/83 (#8), pk 9/2/83 (#3, 3 wk), 9 wk; tot 34 wk.

Descent from Xanadu (Simon & Schuster)
NYT fic 4/29/84 (#12), pk 5/20/84 (#6, 1
wk), 8 wk; PW hc fic 5/4/84 (#10), pk 5/11/84
(#7, 4 wk), 13 wk; (Pocket) NYT pb fic 1/6/
85 (#10), pk 1/20/85 (#1, 3 wk), 11 wk; PW
mm pb 1/18/85 (#3), pk 2/1/85 (#1, 2 wk), 8
wk; tot 40 wk.
  The Storyteller (Simon & Schuster) NYT
fic 1/12/86 (#15), pk 2/2/86 (#8, 2 wk), 9 wk;
PW hc fic 1/24/86 (#9), pk 2/14/86 (#7, 1
wk), 7 wk; (Pocket) NYT pb fic 1/11/87 (#7),
pk 1/18/87 (#3, 4 wk), 11 wk; PW mm pb 1/16/
87 (#9), pk 1/30/87 (#2, 1 wk), 8 wk; tot 35 wk.

Robbins, Tom
  Even Cowgirls Get the Blues (Houghton)
PW td pb 8/30/76 (#5, 2 wk); (Bantam) PW
mm pb 4/18/77 (#12, 2 wk), 4 wk; tot 6 wk.
  Still Life with Woodpecker (Bantam) NYT
td pb 9/14/80 (#11), pk 9/21/80 (#1, 9 wk), 28
wk; PW td pb 9/19/80 (#2), pk 9/26/80 (#1,
9 wk), 22 wk; tot 50 wk.
  Jitterbug Perfume (Bantam) NYT fic 12/16/
84 (#15), pk 1/20/85 (#7, 1 wk), 11 wk; PW
hc fic 12/21/84 (#15), pk 1/18/85 (#10, 2 wk),
10 wk; PW mm pb 11/1/85 (#11, 1 wk), 2 wk;
tot 23 wk.
  Skinny Legs and All (Bantam) NYT fic
4/22/90 (#10), pk 4/29/90 (#4, 2 wk), 15 wk;
PW hc fic 4/27/90 (#11), pk 5/11/90 (#4, 2
wk), 11 wk; tot 26 wk.

Roberts, Ann Victoria
  Louisa Elliott (Avon) NYT pb fic 8/19/90
(#14), pk 8/26/90 (#13, 1 wk), 2 wk; PW mm
pb 8/31/90 (#14, 2 wk); tot 4 wk.

Roberts, Cecil
  Victoria 4:30 (Macmillan) PW fic 9/11/37
(#10), pk 10/9/37 (#9, 4 wk), 8 wk.
  They Wanted to Live (Macmillan) NYT fic
5/7/39 (#13, 4 wk).
  One Small Candle (Macmillan) NYT fic
8/30/42 (#11, 1 wk).
  The Labyrinth (Doubleday) NYT fic 6/11/
44 (#12, 1 wk), 2 wk.

Roberts, Elizabeth Madox
  The Great Meadow (Viking) PW fic 4/12/
30 (#5, 8 wk).

Roberts, Howard
  The Chicago Bears (Putnam) NYT gen 9/
21/47 (#6, 2 wk), 4 wk.

Roberts, Janet Louise
  Island of Desire (Ballantine) PW mm pb
10/24/77 (#10, 1 wk); NYT mm pb 10/30/77
(#14, 2 wk); tot 3 wk.

Roberts, Kenneth Lewis
  Rabble in Arms (Doubleday) PW fic 1/13/
34 (#10, 4 wk).

Northwest Passage (Doubleday) NYT fic
8/8/37 (#1, 4 wk), 36 wk; PW fic 8/14/37 (#1,
12 wk), 60 wk; tot 96 wk.
  Trending Into Maine (Little Brown) NYT
gen 7/31/38 (#2, 4 wk), 8 wk; PW nf 8/13/38
(#4, 8 wk); tot 16 wk.
  Oliver Wiswell (Doubleday) PW fic 12/14/
40 (#3), pk 1/11/41 (#1, 4 wk), 32 wk.
  Lydia Bailey (Doubleday) NYT fic 1/19/47
(#14), pk 2/2/47 (#1, 12 wk), 29 wk; PW fic
2/1/47 (#5), pk 2/15/47 (#1, 10 wk), 21 wk;
tot 50 wk.
  I Wanted to Write (Doubleday) NYT gen
5/15/49 (#12), pk 5/22/49 (#8, 1 wk), 5 wk.
  Henry Gross and His Dowsing Rod (Doubleday) NYT gen 2/11/51 (#15), pk 2/18/51
(#10, 2 wk), 9 wk.
  Boon Island (Doubleday) NYT fic 1/22/56
(#9), pk 2/12/56 (#5, 1 wk), 16 wk; PW fic
2/4/56 (#6, 3 wk), 7 wk; tot 23 wk.

**Roberts, Kenneth, and Anna M.
  Roberts**
  See Moreau de St. Mery

**Roberts, Richard Jerome, with Harold C.
  Schonberg, Al Horowitz and Samuel
  Reshevsky**
  *Fischer-Spassky: The New York Times Report
on the Chess Match of the Century* (Quadran-
gle) NYT pb gen 10/8/72 (#4, 4 wk).

Roberts, Thomas Sadler
  Bird Portraits in Color (Univ. of Minnesota) NYT gen 1/22/61 (#15, 1 wk).

Roberts, Walter Adolphe
  Royal Street (Bobbs Merrill) NYT fic 10/
29/44 (#16), pk 11/5/44 (#15, 1 wk), 2 wk.

Roberts, Wess
  Leadership Secrets of Attila the Hun (Warner) PW hc nf 4/14/89 (#9), pk 5/19/89 (#4,
1 wk), 17 wk; NYT msc 4/16/89 (#5), pk 6/
25/89 (#2, 1 wk), 6 wk; PW td pb 3/2/90
(#9), pk 3/9/90 (#8, 1 wk), 3 wk; tot 26 wk.

Robertson, Eileen Arbuthnot
  The Signpost [as by E. Arnot Robertson]
(Macmillan) NYT fic 1/30/44 (#11), pk 2/27/
44 (#8, 1 wk), 11 wk.

Robertson, Pat
  *The Secret Kingdom: A Promise of Hope and
Freedom in a World of Turmoil* (Nelson) PW
hc nf 2/11/83 (#11), pk 2/18/83 (#10, 1 wk), 8
wk.

Robertson, Robert Blackwood
  Of Whales and Men (Knopf) NYT gen
7/4/54 (#14), pk 8/29/54 (#12, 1 wk), 10 wk.

Robertson, Willard
  Oasis (Lippincott) NYT fic 10/1/44 (#13,
1 wk).

Robinson, Adam
　　See John Katzman and _____
_____, **and John Katzman**
　　Cracking the System (Villard) NYT msc pb
　　11/2/86 (#9, 1 wk).

Robinson, Armin L.
　　The Ten Commandments [ed.] (Simon &
　　Schuster) NYT fic 1/9/44 (#14), pk 1/23/44
　　(#7, 1 wk), 4 wk.

Robinson, Corinne Roosevelt
　　My Brother Theodore Roosevelt (Scribner)
　　PW gen lit 2/4/22 (#6, 4 wk).

Robinson, Edwin Arlington
　　Tristram (Macmillan) PW nf 6/25/27
　　(#9), pk 8/27/27 (#6, 4 wk), 28 wk.
　　Cavender's House (Macmillan) PW nf 6/8/
　　29 (#10, 4 wk).

Robinson, Frank M.
　　See Thomas N. Scortia and _____

Robinson, Henry Morton
　　The Cardinal (Simon & Schuster) NYT fic
　　4/9/50 (#6), pk 4/30/50 (#1, 24 wk), 56 wk;
　　PW fic 4/15/50 (#10), pk 4/29/50 (#1, 25 wk),
　　46 wk; tot 102 wk.
　　Water of Life (Simon & Schuster) NYT fic
　　7/3/60 (#14), pk 7/31/60 (#5, 5 wk), 19 wk;
　　PW fic 8/1/60 (#9), pk 8/22/60 (#5, 1 wk),
　　12 wk; tot 31 wk.

Robinson, James Harvey
　　The Mind in the Making (Harper) PW nf
　　5/13/22 (#7), pk 8/26/22 (#5, 4 wk), 12 wk;
　　PW gen lit 6/17/22 (#7), pk 3/3/23 (#3, 8
　　wk), 56 wk; tot 68 wk.
　　See also James H. Breasted and _____

Robsjohn-Gibbings, Terence
　　Harold
　　Goodbye Mr. Chippendale (Knopf) NYT
　　gen 4/9/44 (#17), pk 5/14/44 (#11, 1 wk), 3
　　wk.
　　Homes of the Brave (Knopf) NYT gen 3/
　　21/54 (#14, 1 wk).

Robson, Lucia St. Clair
　　Ride the Wind (Ballantine) NYT td pb 8/
　　22/82 (#14), pk 9/5/82 (#11, 1 wk), 4 wk.

Rock, Phillip
　　The Passing Bells (Seaview/Simon & Schus-
　　ter) PW hc fic 4/30/79 (#14, 3 wk), 4 wk;
　　(Dell) PW mm pb 3/14/80 (#12), pk 3/28/80
　　(#8, 1 wk), 6 wk; NYT mm pb 3/16/80 (#13),
　　pk 4/6/80 (#11, 1 wk), 4 wk; tot 14 wk.

Roddenberry, Gene
　　Star Trek: The Novel (Pocket) PW mm pb
　　12/3/79 (#10), pk 12/24/79 (#2, 2 wk), 8 wk;
　　NYT mm pb 12/9/79 (#9), pk 12/30/79 (#1,
　　3 wk), 8 wk; tot 16 wk.

Rodgers, Dorothy
　　My Favorite Things (Atheneum) PW nf
　　11/23/64 (#14), pk 1/11/65 (#8, 1 wk), 5 wk;
　　NYT gen 12/20/64 (#10), pk 1/3/65 (#8, 1
　　wk), 4 wk; tot 9 wk.

Rodis-Jamero, Nilo
　　See Joe Johnston and _____

Rodmer, Frederick
　　The Loom of Language (Norton) NYT gen
　　4/30/44 (#11), pk 5/14/44 (#9, 1 wk), 7 wk;
　　PW nf 5/13/44 (#10), pk 6/10/44 (#6, 1 wk),
　　2 wk; tot 9 wk.

Rodocanachi, Konstantinos P.
　　Forever Ulysses (Viking) NYT fic 2/6/38
　　(#8, 4 wk).

Roeder, Ralph
　　The Man of the Renaissance (Viking) PW
　　nf 1/13/34 (#5, 4 wk), 12 wk.

Roehrig, Catherine
　　Fun with Hieroglyphs (Metropolitan Mu-
　　seum of Art/Viking) PW ch nf 12/21/90 (#2,
　　4 wk).

Rogers, Agnes
　　Women Are Here to Stay (Harper) NYT gen
　　9/25/49 (#12), pk 10/16/49 (#11, 1 wk), 6 wk.
　　_____, **and Frederick Lewis Allen**
　　The American Procession (Harper) PW nf
　　12/9/33 (#8), pk 1/13/34 (#4, 4 wk), 8 wk.
　　I Remember Distinctly (Harper) NYT gen
　　9/28/47 (#5), pk 11/30/47 (#3, 1 wk), 24 wk;
　　PW nf 10/11/47 (#5), pk 11/1/47 (#2, 1 wk),
　　12 wk; tot 36 wk.

Rogers, Dale E.
　　Angel Unaware (Revell) NYT gen 4/12/53
　　(#11), pk 5/17/53 (#9, 2 wk), 27 wk; PW nf
　　5/16/53 (#10), pk 7/11/53 (#5, 1 wk), 8 wk;
　　tot 35 wk.

Rogers, Rosemary
　　The Wildest Heart (Avon) NYT mm pb
　　11/10/74 (#4, 4 wk), 10 wk.
　　Dark Fires (Avon) NYT mm pb 8/17/75
　　(#5), pk 9/14/75 (#1, 1 wk), 11 wk.
　　Wicked Loving Lies (Avon) PW mm pb
　　10/11/76 (#5), pk 10/25/76 (#1, 5 wk), 17 wk;
　　NYT mm pb 10/24/76 (#2), pk 11/7/76 (#1,
　　2 wk), 14 wk; tot 31 wk.
　　The Crowd Pleasers (Avon) PW td pb 9/
　　18/78 (#2), pk 9/25/78 (#1, 10 wk), 28 wk;
　　NYT td pb 11/12/78 (#1, 4 wk), 37 wk; tot
　　65 wk.
　　The Insiders (Avon) PW mm pb 1/15/79
　　(#5), pk 1/22/79 (#3, 4 wk), 13 wk; NYT mm
　　pb 1/21/79 (#11), pk 2/11/79 (#1, 1 wk), 18 wk;
　　tot 31 wk.
　　Lost Love, Last Love (Avon) PW mm pb

11/21/80 (#1, 5 wk), 13 wk; NYT mm pb 11/23/80 (#1, 4 wk), 14 wk; tot 27 wk.

Love Play (Avon) PW mm pb 9/11/81 (#6), pk 9/25/81 (#1, 3 wk), 13 wk; NYT td pb 9/13/81 (#3), pk 9/20/81 (#1, 4 wk), 14 wk; NYT mm pb 12/19/82 (#13, 1 wk); tot 28 wk.

Surrender to Love (Avon) PW mm pb 7/16/82 (#4), pk 7/30/82 (#1, 1 wk), 10 wk; NYT mm pb 7/18/82 (#1, 3 wk), 12 wk; tot 22 wk.

The Wanton (Avon) NYT pb fic 4/7/85 (#7), pk 4/14/85 (#1, 3 wk), 8 wk; PW mm pb 4/12/85 (#6), pk 5/3/85 (#1, 2 wk), 7 wk; tot 15 wk.

Bound by Desire (Avon) NYT pb fic 2/28/88 (#11), pk 3/6/88 (#2, 3 wk), 7 wk; PW mm pb 3/4/88 (#10), pk 3/18/88 (#2, 1 wk), 7 wk; tot 14 wk.

Rogers, Samuel
Dusk at the Grove (Little Brown) PW fic 10/13/34 (#3, 4 wk), 8 wk.

Rogers, Will
Illiterate Digest (Boni) PW gen lit 4/18/25 (#9, 4 wk).

The Autobiography of Will Rogers [ed. Donald Day] (Houghton) NYT gen 10/30/49 (#10), pk 12/18/49 (#4, 1 wk), 17 wk; PW nf 11/12/49 (#9), pk 12/17/49 (#3, 1 wk), 12 wk; tot 29 wk.

Rolland, Romain
Beethoven the Creator (Harper) PW nf 10/12/29 (#10), pk 11/9/29 (#9, 4 wk), 8 wk.

Rollin, Betty
Last Wish (Linden/Simon & Schuster) NYT nf 9/29/85 (#6), pk 10/6/85 (#5, 3 wk), 7 wk; PW hc nf 10/4/85 (#7), pk 10/18/85 (#6, 1 wk), 6 wk; tot 13 wk.

Rolo, Charles James
Wingate's Raiders (Viking) NYT gen 4/2/44 (#17, 1 wk).

Rolvag, Ole E.
Giants in the Earth (Harper) PW fic 8/27/27 (#6), pk 9/24/27 (#5, 4 wk), 8 wk.

Peder Victorious (Harper) PW fic 2/16/29 (#1, 8 wk), 16 wk.

Pure Gold (Harper) PW fic 3/15/30 (#7, 4 wk), 8 wk.

Romains, Jules
Verdun (Knopf) PW fic 2/10/40 (#10, 4 wk).

Romanowski, Patricia
See Mary Wilson, et al.
See Vanna White and _____

Rombauer, Irma S.
The Joy of Cooking (Bobbs Merrill) NYT gen 6/27/43 (#9, 2 wk), 36 wk.

_____, and Marion Becker
The New Joy of Cooking (Bobbs Merrill) NYT gen 8/5/51 (#16), pk 8/19/51 (#11, 2 wk), 12 wk; PW nf 9/15/51 (#9, 1 wk); tot 13 wk; .

Rommel, Erwin
The Rommel Papers [ed. B.H. Hart and Liddell Hart] (Harcourt) PW nf 7/4/53 (#5, 1 wk), 4 wk; NYT gen 6/7/53 (#11), pk 6/28/53 (#6, 1 wk), 16 wk; tot 20 wk.

Romulo, Col. Carlos Pena
Mother America (Doubleday) NYT gen 12/12/43 (#24, 1 wk).

I Saw the Fall of the Philippines (Doubleday) NYT nf 2/14/43 (#8), pk 2/21/43 (#5, 3 wk), 17 wk; PW nf 2/27/43 (#5, 5 wk); tot 22 wk.

Ronsard, Nicole
Cellulite (Bantam) NYT td pb 2/9/75 (#1, 8 wk), 14 wk.

Rooke, Daphne
Mittee (Houghton) NYT fic 2/24/52 (#14), pk 4/13/52 (#9, 1 wk), 9 wk; PW fic 4/12/52 (#8, 1 wk); tot 10 wk.

Rooney, Andrew A.
A Few Minutes with Andy Rooney (Atheneum) PW hc nf 11/27/81 (#15), pk 1/29/82 (#1, 5 wk), 47 wk; NYT nf 12/13/81 (#12), pk 3/7/82 (#1, 1 wk), 46 wk; (Warner) NYT mm pb 12/5/82 (#5), pk 12/12/82 (#1, 6 wk), 14 wk; PW mm pb 12/17/82 (#1, 6 wk), 11 wk; tot 118 wk.

And More by Andy Rooney (Atheneum) NYT nf 10/24/82 (#14), pk 11/21/82 (#1, 9 wk), 27 wk; PW hc nf 10/29/82 (#11), pk 11/19/82 (#1, 8 wk), 27 wk; (Warner) mm pb 11/11/83 (#8, 3 wk), 10 wk; NYT mm pb 11/13/83 (#8), pk 1/1/84 (#1, 2 wk), 11 wk; tot 75 wk.

Pieces of My Mind (Atheneum) NYT nf 9/16/84 (#3), pk 9/30/84 (#2, 5 wk), 26 wk; PW hc nf 9/21/84 (#11), pk 12/14/84 (#2, 2 wk), 24 wk; (Avon) NYT pb nf 9/29/85 (#7), pk 10/27/85 (#3, 1 wk), 4 wk; PW mm pb 10/4/85 (#14, 2 wk); tot 56 wk.

Word for Word (Putnam) NYT nf 11/23/86 (#15), pk 1/11/87 (#3, 2 wk), 12 wk; PW hc nf 12/5/86 (#15), pk 1/16/87 (#3, 1 wk), 10 wk; (Berkley) NYT pb nf 11/8/87 (#10), pk 11/22/87 (#5, 1 wk), 11 wk; tot 33 wk.

Not That You Asked... (Random) NYT nf 5/21/89 (#14), pk 7/2/89 (#12, 1 wk), 3 wk.

Roosevelt, Eleanor
This Is My Story (Harper) NYT gen 12/12/37 (#10), pk 1/9/38 (#6, 4 wk), 12 wk; PW nf 1/15/38 (#7, 4 wk), 8 wk; tot 20 wk.

This I Remember (Harper) NYT gen

11/27/49 (#6), pk 1/15/50 (#1, 7 wk), 23 wk;
PW nf 12/3/49 (#3), pk 1/21/50 (#1, 3 wk),
20 wk; tot 43 wk.
India and the Awakening East (Harper)
NYT gen 8/16/53 (#16), pk 8/23/53 (#9, 1
wk), 10 wk.
On My Own (Harper) NYT gen 10/5/58
(#13), pk 11/16/58 (#4, 2 wk), 15 wk; PW nf
10/27/58 (#7), pk 11/24/58 (#5, 2 wk), 11 wk;
tot 26 wk.

Roosevelt, Elliott
As He Saw It (Duell, Sloan & Pearce)
NYT gen 10/20/46 (#8), pk 11/17/46 (#2, 1
wk), 21 wk; PW nf 11/2/46 (#3), pk 11/9/46
(#2, 1 wk), 14 wk; tot 35 wk.

_____, **and James Brough**
*The Untold Story: The Roosevelts of Hyde
Park* (Putnam) NYT gen 5/6/73 (#10), pk
5/13/73 (#8, 1 wk), 4 wk; PW nf 5/7/73 (#8,
1 wk), 2 wk; tot 6 wk.

Roosevelt, Franklin D.
Looking Forward (John Day) PW nf 4/15/
33 (#6), pk 5/13/33 (#2, 8 wk), 20 wk.
On Our Way (John Day) PW nf 5/12/34
(#3, 4 wk), 8 wk.
Nothing to Fear [ed. Benjamin David Zevin]
(Houghton) NYT gen 10/20/46 (#10, 2 wk),
4 wk.

**Roosevelt, James R., and Sidney S.
Shalett**
Affectionately, F.D.R. (Harcourt) NYT gen
11/1/59 (#14), pk 11/22/59 (#10, 1 wk), 6 wk.

Roosevelt, Nicholas
A New Birth of Freedom (Scribner) NYT
gen 10/9/38 (#12, 4 wk).

Roosevelt, Theodore
Theodore Roosevelt's Letters to His Children
[ed. Joseph Bucklin Bishop] (Scribner) PW
gen 11/1/19 (#4), pk 1/3/20 (#1, 12 wk), 28
wk; PW gen lit 9/25/20 (#5, 4 wk); tot 32
wk.
*Theodore Roosevelt and His Time, shown in
His Letters, 2 Vols.* [ed. Joseph Bucklin Bis-
hop] (Scribner) PW gen lit 11/27/20 (#3, 8
wk), 16 wk.

_____, **et al.**
The Reader's Digest Reader [eds.] (Doubleday) PW nf 3/15/41 (#10, 4 wk).

Roosevelt, Mrs. Theodore, Jr.
Day Before Yesterday (Doubleday) NYT
gen 7/12/59 (#14, 1 wk), 2 wk.

Rorick, Isabel Scott
Mr. and Mrs. Cugat (Houghton) PW fic
3/15/41 (#8), pk 9/13/41 (#5, 4 wk), 36 wk.

Rorty, James, and Moshe Decter
McCarthy and the Communists (Beacon)
NYT gen 9/26/54 (#10), pk 10/24/54 (#8, 1
wk), 6 wk.

Rorvik, David M.
In His Image: The Cloning of a Man (Lippincott) PW hc nf 4/17/78 (#12), pk 5/1/78
(#8, 1 wk), 9 wk; NYT nf 5/7/78 (#12), pk
5/28/78 (#10, 1 wk), 6 wk; tot 15 wk.

Rose, Billy
Wine, Women and Words (Simon & Schuster) NYT gen 11/14/48 (#15), pk 12/26/48
(#5, 1 wk), 14 wk; PW nf 1/8/49 (#5, 1 wk);
tot 15 wk.

Rose, Marcia
All for the Love of Daddy (Ballantine) NYT
pb fic 11/8/87 (#14), pk 11/22/87 (#12, 1 wk),
3 wk; PW mm pb 11/13/87 (#15, 1 wk); tot 4
wk.

Rose, Pete, and Roger Kahn
Pete Rose: My Story (Macmillan) NYT nf
11/26/89 (#14, 1 wk), 2 wk.

Rosebrook, Jeb
See Alan Dean Foster

Rosen, Michael
We're Going on a Bear Hunt [illus. Helen
Oxenbury] (McElderry) PW ch pic 8/31/90
(#8), pk 10/26/90 (#7, 4 wk), 12 wk.

Rosenberg, David
See Harold Bloom

Rosenfeld, Isadore, M.D.
Second Opinion: Your Medical Alternatives
(Linden/Simon & Schuster) NYT nf 4/3/
81 (#15), pk 4/10/81 (#12, 1 wk), 4 wk; NYT
nf 4/5/81 (#9, 1 wk), 2 wk; tot 6 wk.
Modern Prevention: The New Medicine (Lin-
den/Simon & Schuster) PW hc nf 7/25/86
(#13), pk 8/1/86 (#9, 2 wk), 4 wk; NYT msc
8/3/86 (#4, 1 wk); tot 5 wk.
Symptoms (Simon & Schuster) NYT msc
7/2/89 (#2, 2 wk), 8 wk; PW hc nf 7/7/89
(#7, 2 wk), 9 wk; tot 17 wk.

Rosenman, Ray H.
See Meyer Friedman and _____

Rosenman, Samuel Irving
Working with Roosevelt (Harper) NYT gen
6/22/52 (#13), pk 7/6/52 (#12, 1 wk), 5 wk.

Rosman, Alice Grant
Visitors to Hugo (Minton Balch) PW fic
8/10/29 (#5, 4 wk), 8 wk.
The Young and Secret (Minton Balch) PW
fic 8/23/30 (#3), pk 9/20/30 (#2, 4 wk), 8
wk.
The Sixth Journey (Minton Balch) PW fic
8/15/31 (#2, 4 wk), 8 wk.

Jock the Scot (Minton Balch) PW juv 2/21/
31 (#10, 4 wk).
Benefits Received (Minton Balch) PW fic
8/13/32 (#3, 4 wk), 8 wk.
Protecting Margot (Minton Balch) PW fic
8/12/33 (#4, 4 wk), 8 wk.
Somebody Must (Minton Balch) PW fic
8/11/34 (#10, 4 wk).
Mother of the Bride (Grosset & Dunlap)
NYT fic 8/2/36 (#3, 4 wk).
Truth to Tell (Putnam) NYT fic 8/8/37
(#2, 4 wk).
Unfamiliar Faces (Putnam) NYT fic 7/31/
38 (#7, 4 wk).
William's Room (Putnam) NYT fic 8/6/39
(#6, 4 wk).

Ross, Clarissa
China Shadow (Avon) NYT mm pb 1/12/
75 (#9, 1 wk).

Ross, Dana Fuller
Wyoming! (Bantam) NYT mm pb 12/16/
79 (#15), pk 1/6/80 (#8, 1 wk), 9 wk; PW mm
pb 12/24/79 (#5), pk 1/11/80 (#4, 1 wk), 9 wk;
tot 18 wk.
Texas! (Bantam) NYT mm pb 9/14/80
(#7), pk 10/5/80 (#4, 1 wk), 7 wk; PW mm
pb 9/19/80 (#9), pk 10/3/80 (#5, 1 wk), 4 wk;
tot 11 wk.
Oregon! (Bantam) PW mm pb 4/11/80
(#8), pk 4/18/80 (#4, 1 wk), 7 wk; NYT mm
pb 4/13/80 (#4), 4/20/80 (#2, 2 wk), 7 wk;
tot 14 wk.
Colorado! (Bantam) PW mm pb 8/28/81
(#15), pk 9/25/81 (#5, 1 wk), 6 wk; NYT mm
pb 9/6/81 (#7), pk 9/27/81 (#5, 1 wk), 6 wk;
tot 12 wk.
Nevada! (Bantam) NYT mm pb 12/27/81
(#8), pk 1/3/82 (#3, 2 wk), 8 wk; PW mm pb
1/1/82 (#11), 1/15/82 (#4, 1 wk), 6 wk; tot
14 wk.
California! (Bantam) NYT mm pb 3/1/81
(#11), pk 3/29/81 (#4, 1 wk), 10 wk; PW mm
pb 3/6/81 (#10), pk 3/13/81 (#4, 2 wk), 7 wk;
tot 17 wk.
Washington! (Bantam) PW mm pb 8/27/
82 (#10), pk 9/17/82 (#5, 1 wk), 7 wk; NYT
mm pb 8/29/82 (#9), pk 9/5/82 (#1, 1 wk), 6
wk; tot 13 wk.
Utah! (Bantam) NYT mm pb 12/25/83
(#8), pk 1/1/84 (#4, 2 wk), 8 wk; PW mm pb
1/6/84 (#6, 2 wk), 6 wk; tot 14 wk.
Montana! (Bantam) NYT mm pb 3/27/83
(#3, 1 wk), 6 wk; PW mm pb 4/1/83 (#7), pk
4/8/83 (#6, 1 wk), 6 wk; tot 12 wk.
Dakota! (Bantam) NYT mm pb 7/24/83
(#12), pk 7/31/83 (#8, 3 wk), 7 wk; PW mm
pb 8/5/83 (#13), pk 8/12/83 (#9, 1 wk), 5 wk;
tot 12 wk.

Missouri! (Bantam) NYT pb fic 12/23/84
(#8), pk 12/30/84 (#4, 1 wk), 8 wk; PW mm
pb 1/11/85 (#5, 2 wk), 5 wk; tot 13 wk.
Idaho! (Bantam) NYT pb fic 7/22/84
(#12), pk 7/29/84 (#5, 2 wk), 8 wk; PW mm
pb 8/3/84 (#8), pk 8/17/84 (#6, 1 wk), 6 wk;
tot 14 wk.
Louisiana! (Bantam) NYT pb fic 12/22/85
(#10), pk 1/5/86 (#6, 1 wk), 7 wk; PW mm
pb 1/3/86 (#7), pk 1/10/86 (#5, 1 wk), 6 wk;
tot 13 wk.
Mississippi! (Bantam) NYT pb fic 5/26/85
(#14), pk 6/2/85 (#5, 2 wk), 7 wk; PW mm
pb 5/31/85 (#10), pk 6/14/85 (#5, 1 wk), 6
wk; tot 13 wk.
Tennessee! (Bantam) NYT pb fic 4/20/86
(#15), pk 5/11/86 (#6, 1 wk), 7 wk; PW mm
pb 5/2/86 (#8, 4 wk), 5 wk; tot 12 wk.
Illinois! (Bantam) NYT pb fic 9/28/86
(#8), pk 10/5/86 (#6, 1 wk), 4 wk; PW mm
pb 10/3/86 (#9), pk 10/17/86 (#8, 1 wk), 5
wk; tot 9 wk.
Wisconsin! (Bantam) NYT pb fic 5/3/87
(#7), pk 5/17/87 (#4, 1 wk), 6 wk; PW mm
pb 5/8/87 (#8), pk 5/15/87 (#3, 2 wk), 6 wk;
tot 12 wk.
Kentucky! (Bantam) NYT pb fic 11/1/87
(#8), pk 11/8/87 (#6, 1 wk), 5 wk; PW mm
pb 11/13/87 (#13), pk 11/27/87 (#10, 1 wk), 4
wk; tot 9 wk.
New Mexico! (Bantam) PW mm pb 8/26/
88 (#11, 1 wk); NYT pb fic 8/28/88 (#12), pk
9/11/88 (#9, 1 wk), 4 wk; tot 5 wk.
Arizona! (Bantam) NYT pb fic 2/21/88
(#10), pk 2/28/88 (#8, 1 wk), 7 wk; PW mm
pb 3/4/88 (#15), pk 3/25/88 (#13, 2 wk), 4
wk; tot 11 wk.
Oregon Legacy (Bantam) PW mm pb 11/
24/89 (#10, 1 wk), 2 wk; NYT pb fic 12/3/89
(#16, 1 wk); tot 3 wk.
Celebration! (Bantam) NYT pb fic 10/8/89
(#13), pk 10/22/89 (#6, 1 wk), 5 wk; PW mm
pb 10/13/89 (#10), pk 11/3/89 (#7, 1 wk), 5
wk; tot 10 wk.
Oklahoma! (Bantam) NYT pb fic 4/30/89
(#10, 1 wk), 3 wk; PW mm pb 5/5/89 (#10),
pk 5/12/89 (#8, 1 wk), 4 wk; tot 7 wk.
Oklahoma Pride (Bantam) NYT pb fic
4/29/90 (#13, 2 wk), 3 wk.

Ross, Ishbel
Proud Kate: Portrait of an Ambitious Woman
(Harper) NYT gen 2/15/53 (#13, 1 wk).
Silhouette in Diamonds (Harper) NYT gen
1/15/61 (#14), pk 1/22/61 (#13, 1 wk), 2 wk.

Ross, Katharine
Teenage Mutant Ninja Turtles (Random)
NYT pb fic 5/13/90 (#15, 1 wk); PW ch yn
rd 8/31/90 (#2, 8 wk); tot 9 wk.

Ross, Leonard Q.
The Education of Hyman Kaplan (Harcourt) NYT fic 2/6/38 (#13, 4 wk).
See also Peter Passell and _____

Ross, Lillian Bos
The Stranger (Morrow) NYT fic 11/8/42 (#18), pk 11/15/42 (#17, 1 wk), 3 wk.

Ross, Nancy Wilson
The Left Hand Is the Dreamer (Sloane) NYT fic 3/9/47 (#10), pk 4/13/47 (#8, 2 wk), 16 wk.
I, My Ancestor (Random) NYT fic 2/19/50 (#14), pk 2/26/50 (#9, 1 wk), 6 wk.
The Return of Lady Brace (Random) NYT fic 11/24/57 (#14, 1 wk).

Ross, Thomas B.
See David Wise and _____

Rossiter, Clinton
See Walter Lippmann, et al.

Rossner, Judith
Looking for Mr. Goodbar (Simon & Schuster) NYT fic 6/22/75 (#10), pk 8/3/75 (#1, 3 wk), 36 wk; PW fic 6/23/75 (#7), pk 7/21/75 (#1, 3 wk), 35 wk; (Pocket) PW mm pb 4/5/76 (#9), pk 4/12/76 (#2, 9 wk), 34 wk; NYT mm pb 4/11/76 (#10), pk 6/13/76 (#1, 1 wk), 35 wk; tot 140 wk.
Attachments (Simon & Schuster) NYT fic 11/6/77 (#15), pk 11/13/77 (#14, 1 wk), 2 wk; PW hc fic 11/7/77 (#15, 2 wk); (Pocket) mm pb 8/14/78 (#13), pk 9/4/78 (#5, 1 wk), 7 wk; tot 11 wk.
Emmeline (Pocket) NYT mm pb 9/27/81 (#10, 1 wk), 3 wk.
August (Houghton) PW hc fic 8/12/83 (#15), pk 9/2/83 (#2, 2 wk), 19 wk; NYT fic 8/14/83 (#3, 5 wk), 19 wk; (Warner) pb fic 8/5/84 (#4), pk 8/19/84 (#1, 5 wk), 12 wk; PW mm pb 8/10/84 (#5), pk 8/17/84 (#1, 4 wk), 12 wk; tot 62 wk.

Rosso, Julee, and Sheila Lukins
The New Basics Cookbook (Workman) PW td pb 12/22/89 (#7), pk 1/12/90 (#4, 1 wk), 6 wk; NYT msc pb 1/14/90 (#4, 1 wk); tot 7 wk.

_____**, with Sheila Lukins and Sarah Leah Chase**
The Silver Palate Good Times Cookbook (Workman) PW td pb 6/7/85 (#9), pk 8/2/85 (#5, 1 wk), 13 wk; NYT msc pb 6/16/85 (#4), pk 7/28/85 (#2, 2 wk), 16 wk; tot 29 wk.

Rosten, Leo Calvin
*The Return of H*y*m*a*n K*a*p*l*a*n* (Harper) NYT fic 11/8/59 (#14), pk 1/17/60 (#13, 1 wk), 4 wk.
Captain Newman, M.D. (Harper) NYT fic 1/28/62 (#14), pk 4/15/62 (#7, 1 wk), 23 wk;

PW fic 2/5/62 (#10), pk 3/26/62 (#7, 2 wk), 14 wk; tot 37 wk.
The Joys of Yiddish (McGraw) NYT gen 12/8/68 (#8), pk 2/9/69 (#6, 2 wk), 20 wk; PW nf 1/13/69 (#10), pk 2/3/69 (#5, 1 wk), 28 wk; tot 48 wk.

Rotchstein, Janice
See Alan Ebert and _____

Roth, Lillian
I'll Cry Tomorrow (Fell) NYT gen 6/13/54 (#15), pk 8/8/54 (#2, 14 wk), 44 wk; PW nf 7/10/54 (#6), pk 7/25/54 (#1, 1 wk), 27 wk; tot 71 wk.

Roth, Philip
Letting Go (Random) NYT fic 7/8/62 (#12), pk 9/9/62 (#9, 1 wk), 11 wk; PW fic 7/30/62 (#11), pk 9/3/62 (#9, 1 wk), 7 wk; tot 18 wk.
When She Was Good (Random) PW fic 7/3/67 (#11), pk 7/31/67 (#8, 2 wk), 10 wk; NYT fic 7/30/67 (#8, 1 wk), 4 wk; tot 14 wk.
Portnoy's Complaint (Random) NYT fic 2/23/69 (#9), pk 3/16/69 (#1, 14 wk), 40 wk; PW fic 2/24/69 (#9), pk 3/24/69 (#1, 16 wk), 40 wk; NYT pb fic 3/1/70 (#1, 4 wk), 20 wk; tot 100 wk.
Goodbye Columbus (Houghton) NYT pb fic 6/1/69 (#3), pk 9/7/69 (#2, 12 wk), 32 wk.
Our Gang (Random) NYT fic 11/21/71 (#10), pk 11/28/71 (#6, 1 wk), 18 wk; PW fic 11/22/71 (#6), pk 12/13/71 (#4, 1 wk), 18 wk; tot 36 wk.
My Life as a Man (Holt) PW fic 6/24/74 (#10), pk 7/8/74 (#8, 1 wk), 7 wk.
The Professor of Desire (Farrar) NYT fic 11/20/77 (#15, 3 wk).
The Ghost Writer (Farrar) PW hc fic 10/8/79 (#13, 2 wk), 5 wk; NYT fic 11/4/79 (#15), pk 11/11/79 (#11, 1 wk), 3 wk; tot 8 wk.
Zuckerman Unbound (Farrar) NYT fic 7/5/81 (#15, 1 wk).
The Counterlife (Farrar) NYT fic 1/25/87 (#12, 2 wk), 5 wk; PW hc fic 1/30/87 (#14), pk 2/27/87 (#11, 1 wk), 6 wk; tot 11 wk.
Deceptions (Simon & Schuster) NYT fic 4/1/90 (#15), pk 4/22/90 (#13, 1 wk), 3 wk; PW hc fic 4/6/90 (#14), pk 4/13/90 (#11, 2 wk), 4 wk; tot 7 wk.

Rothchild, John
See Peter Lynch and _____

Rothstein, Larry
See Joan Borysenko and _____

Rottenberg, Harvey
See Tim Riker and _____

Roulston, Marjorie Hillis
New York—Fair Or No Fair (Bobbs Merrill) NYT gen 7/9/39 (#7, 4 wk).

Rounds, Frank, Jr.
A Window on Red Square (Houghton) NYT
gen 6/7/53 (#13, 1 wk).

Rourke, Constance
Audubon (Harcourt) PW nf 12/12/36 (#5),
pk 1/16/37 (#4, 1 wk), 3 wk.

Rovere, Richard Halworth
How & Hummel (Farrar) NYT gen 9/7/47
(#15), pk 9/21/47 (#12, 2 wk), 3 wk.
Senator Joe McCarthy (Harcourt) NYT gen
7/12/59 (#16), pk 8/16/59 (#7, 2 wk), 13 wk.

Rowans, Virginia
The Loving Couple (Crowell) NYT fic 9/
30/56 (#12), pk 11/11/56 (#7, 2 wk), 17 wk;
PW fic 10/22/56 (#8), pk 11/19/56 (#6, 2 wk),
9 wk; tot 26 wk.

Rowe, Guy
See Houston Harte

Rowse, Alfred Leslie
The Churchills: The Story of a Family (Harper) NYT gen 6/29/58 (#16, 1 wk).
William Shakespeare: A Biography (Harper)
NYT gen 1/26/64 (#8), pk 2/2/64 (#7, 2 wk),
6 wk; PW nf 2/3/64 (#7, 2 wk), 6 wk; tot 12
wk.

Roy, Gabrielle
The Tin Flute (Reynal & Hitchcock) NYT
fic 5/25/47 (#15), pk 6/8/47 (#14, 1 wk), 4
wk.

Royko, Mike
Boss (Dutton) NYT gen 4/4/71 (#6), pk
5/23/71 (#4, 6 wk), 26 wk; PW nf 5/3/71
(#10), pk 7/26/71 (#4, 1 wk), 22 wk; NYT pb
gen 11/14/71 (#4, 8 wk); tot 56 wk.

Ruark, Robert Chester
Grenadine Etching (Doubleday) NYT fic
10/19/47 (#16), pk 11/23/47 (#13, 2 wk), 8 wk.
I Didn't Know It Was Loaded (Doubleday)
NYT gen 10/24/48 (#15), pk 11/28/48 (#14,
1 wk), 4 wk.
Horn of the Hunter (Doubleday) NYT gen
9/6/53 (#12, 1 wk), 5 wk.
Something of Value (Doubleday) NYT fic
5/8/55 (#7), pk 7/3/55 (#1, 2 wk), 42 wk; PW
fic 5/14/55 (#9), pk 6/11/55 (#1, 4 wk), 30 wk;
tot 72 wk.
Poor No More (Holt) NYT fic 11/15/59
(#11), pk 12/6/59 (#3, 5 wk), 26 wk; PW fic
11/23/59 (#8), pk 12/14/59 (#3, 3 wk), 19 wk;
tot 45 wk.
Uhuru (McGraw) NYT fic 6/24/62 (#9),
pk 7/29/62 (#4, 1 wk), 24 wk; PW fic 7/16/62
(#10), pk 8/13/62 (#4, 2 wk), 19 wk; tot 43
wk.
The Honey Badger (McGraw) NYT fic 10/
31/65 (#8), pk 12/5/65 (#6, 2 wk), 16 wk; PW

fic 11/8/65 (#10), pk 1/3/66 (#5, 2 wk), 16 wk;
NYT pb fic 10/2/66 (#4), pk 11/6/66 (#3, 12
wk), 20 wk; tot 52 wk.

Rubin, Jerry
Do It!: Scenarios of the Revolution (Simon
& Schuster) NYT pb gen 7/5/70 (#4), pk
8/2/70 (#3, 4 wk), 12 wk.

Rubin, Theodore Isaac
*Reconciliations: Inner Peace in an Age of
Anxiety* (Viking) PW hc nf 10/17/80 (#13, 1
wk); NYT nf 10/26/80 (#14, 1 wk); tot 2 wk.
One to One (Viking) PW hc nf 4/15/83
(#15), pk 4/29/83 (#7, 2 wk), 9 wk; NYT nf
4/17/83 (#9), pk 4/24/83 (#8, 1 wk), 6 wk; tot
15 wk.

Rubinstein, Arthur
My Young Years (Knopf) PW nf 6/11/73
(#9), pk 7/9/73 (#4, 1 wk), 16 wk; NYT gen
6/17/73 (#10), pk 7/15/73 (#6, 1 wk), 15 wk;
tot 31 wk.
My Many Years (Knopf) PW hc nf 3/7/80
(#14, 1 wk); NYT nf 4/6/80 (#14, 2 wk), 3 wk;
tot 4 wk.

Rudkin, Margaret
*The Margaret Rudkin Pepperidge Farm
Cookbook* (Atheneum) NYT gen 11/3/63
(#10), pk 11/10/63 (#9, 1 wk), 2 wk; PW nf
12/16/63 (#8, 1 wk); tot 3 wk.

Ruff, Howard J.
*How to Prosper During the Coming Bad
Years* (Times) PW hc nf 2/12/79 (#12), pk
4/23/79 (#2, 2 wk), 47 wk; NYT nf 3/4/79
(#12), pk 10/14/79 (#2, 1 wk), 46 wk; (Warner) NYT mm pb 1/13/80 (#9), pk 1/20/80
(#1, 1 wk), 21 wk; PW mm pb 1/25/80 (#2, 1
wk), 20 wk; tot 134 wk.
*Survive and Win in the Inflationary Eight-
ies* (Times) PW hc nf 7/10/81 (#14), pk 7/17/
81 (#13, 1 wk), 2 wk.

Ruggles, Eleanor
Prince of Players (Norton) NYT gen 3/22/
53 (#14), pk 4/5/53 (#8, 1 wk), 10 wk; PW nf
4/18/53 (#9), pk 5/16/53 (#8, 1 wk), 2 wk; tot
12 wk.

Rukeyser, Louis
*What's Ahead for the Economy: The Chal-
lenge and the Chance* (Simon & Schuster) PW
hc nf 1/20/84 (#13, 1 wk).

Rule, Ann
The Want-Ad Killer (NAL/Signet) NYT
pb nf 11/20/88 (#11, 1 wk).
*Small Sacrifices: A True Story of Passion and
Murder* (NAL/Signet) NYT pb nf 7/10/88
(#5), pk 7/24/88 (#1, 4 wk), 34 wk; PW mm
pb 7/22/88 (#7), pk 10/28/88 (#4, 1 wk), 22
wk; tot 56 wk.

The Stranger Beside Me (NAL/Signet) NYT pb nf 3/5/89 (#9), pk 3/19/89 (#8, 1 wk), 3 wk.

Runbeck, Margaret Lee
Time for Each Other (Appleton) NYT fic 9/3/44 (#12, 1 wk).
The Great Answer (Houghton) NYT gen 3/4/45 (#16, 1 wk).

Rushdie, Salman
The Satanic Verses (Viking) PW hc fic 3/3/89 (#13), pk 3/31/89 (#1, 9 wk), 25 wk; NYT fic 3/5/89 (#2), pk 3/26/89 (#1, 9 wk), 24 wk; tot 49 wk.

Russ, Martin
The Last Parallel (Rinehart) NYT gen 2/3/57 (#8, 1 wk), 8 wk.

Russell, A.J.
God Calling (Revell/Barbour) PW pb rel 11/9/90 (#15, 4 wk).

Russell, Bertrand
Marriage and Morals (Liveright) PW nf 12/14/29 (#10, 4 wk).
The Conquest of Happiness (Liveright) PW nf 12/20/30 (#9, 4 wk).
A History of Western Philosophy (Simon & Schuster) NYT gen 11/25/45 (#16), pk 1/13/46 (#14, 2 wk), 4 wk.
Unpopular Essays (Simon & Schuster) NYT gen 3/18/51 (#13), pk 4/1/51 (#11, 2 wk), 8 wk.
Satan in the Suburbs (Simon & Schuster) NYT fic 8/23/53 (#16), pk 8/30/53 (#14, 2 wk), 5 wk.
The Autobiography of Bertrand Russell 1872–1914 (Little Atlantic) PW nf 5/1/67 (#8), pk 6/12/67 (#1, 2 wk), 22 wk; NYT gen 5/7/67 (#6), pk 7/2/67 (#2, 2 wk), 17 wk; tot 39 wk.

Russell, Bill, and Taylor Branch
Second Wind (Random) NYT nf 11/25/79 (#13), pk 12/16/79 (#12, 1 wk), 6 wk.

Russell, Mary Annette Beauchamp
Christopher and Columbus [as by The Author of "Elizabeth and her Germnan Garden"] (Doubleday) PW fic 7/5/19 (#10), pk 8/2/19 (#3, 4 wk), 16 wk.
The Enchanted April [as by Elizabeth] (Doubleday) PW fic 3/3/23 (#12), pk 5/26/23 (#2, 4 wk), 24 wk.
Expiation [as by Elizabeth] (Doubleday) PW fic 3/9/29 (#7, 4 wk), 8 wk.
Father [as by Elizabeth] (Doubleday) PW fic 7/18/31 (#3, 8 wk), 12 wk.
Mr. Skeffington [as by Elizabeth] (Doubleday) PW fic 5/11/40 (#5), pk 6/8/40 (#2, 4 wk), 16 wk.

Russell, Phillips
Benjamin Franklin (Bretano) PW nf 2/19/27 (#9, 4 wk).

Russell, Rosalind, and Chris Chase
Life Is a Banquet (Random) NYT nf 12/4/77 (#12), pk 12/11/77 (#11, 1 wk), 3 wk; PW hc nf 1/16/78 (#13, 1 wk); tot 4 wk.

Russianoff, Penelope
Why Do I Think I Am Nothing Without a Man? (Bantam) PW hc nf 6/25/82 (#15, 1 wk).

Rust, Zad
Teddy Bare (Western Islands) NYT td pb 8/11/74 (#4), pk 10/13/74 (#3, 3 wk), 5 wk.

Ruth, Babe and Bob Considine
The Babe Ruth Story (Dutton) NYT gen 5/30/48 (#14, 1 wk), 3 wk.

Rutherfurd, Edward
Sarum (Crown) NYT fic 8/23/87 (#12), pk 9/20/87 (#3, 1 wk), 24 wk; PW hc fic 8/28/87 (#15), pk 10/2/87 (#3, 1 wk), 22 wk; (Ballantine/Ivy) NYT pb fic 7/24/88 (#12), pk 8/7/88 (#5, 1 wk), 11 wk; PW mm pb 7/29/88 (#8), pk 8/5/88 (#5, 1 wk), 11 wk; tot 68 wk.

Ryan, Bob
See Larry Bird and _____

Ryan, Cornelius
The Longest Day (Simon & Schuster) NYT gen 12/13/59 (#10), pk 1/24/60 (#4, 2 wk), 22 wk; PW nf 1/4/60 (#7), pk 2/1/60 (#3, 3 wk), 14 wk; tot 36 wk.
The Last Battle (Simon & Schuster) NYT gen 3/27/66 (#8), pk 5/8/66 (#1, 9 wk), 30 wk; PW nf 4/4/66 (#6), pk 5/9/66 (#1, 9 wk), 30 wk; tot 60 wk.
A Bridge Too Far (Simon & Schuster) PW nf 9/30/74 (#7), pk 11/11/74 (#2, 1 wk), 18 wk; NYT gen 10/6/74 (#9), pk 11/17/74 (#2, 5 wk), 22 wk; tot 40 wk.

Rybakov, Anatoli
Children of the Arbat (Little Brown) PW hc fic 6/17/88 (#14), pk 6/24/88 (#13, 1 wk), 4 wk.

Rybczynski, Witold
The Most Beautiful House in the World (Viking) NYT nf 8/13/89 (#15, 1 wk).

Rylands, Leanne
See Don Taylor and _____

Rylee, Robert
Deep Dark River (Farrar) PW fic 8/10/35 (#7, 4 wk), 8 wk.

Saarinen, Aline Bernstein
The Proud Possessors (Random) NYT gen 11/30/58 (#15), pk 1/18/59 (#9, 3 wk), 15 wk.

Sabatini, Rafael
Captain Blood (Houghton) PW fic 10/14/22 (#8), pk 11/18/22 (#6, 4 wk), 12 wk.
The Sea-Hawk (Houghton) PW fic 5/26/23 (#3, 8 wk), 16 wk.
Fortune's Fool (Houghton) PW fic 11/24/23 (#7, 4 wk).
Mistress Wilding (Houghton) PW fic 4/19/24 (#4, 4 wk), 8 wk.
Bardley the Magnificent (Houghton) PW fic 6/21/24 (#4, 4 wk).
The Carolinian (Houghton) PW fic 4/18/25 (#2, 4 wk), 8 wk.
Bellarion (Houghton) PW fic 10/16/26 (#5, 4 wk), 8 wk.
The Hounds of God (Houghton) PW fic 12/22/28 (#6, 4 wk).
The Romantic Prince (Houghton) PW fic 8/10/29 (#8, 4 wk).
The King's Minion (Houghton) PW fic 11/22/30 (#10, 4 wk).
The Black Swan (Houghton) PW fic 7/9/32 (#5, 4 wk).
The Stalking Horse (Houghton) PW fic 6/10/33 (#10, 4 wk).
Venetian Masque (Houghton) PW fic 10/13/34 (#10, 4 wk).
The Sword of Islam (Houghton) NYT fic 2/5/39 (#15, 4 wk).
The Birth of Mischief (Houghton) NYT fic 9/23/45 (#15, 1 wk), 2 wk.

Sachar, Louis
Wayside School Is Falling Down (Avon/Camelot) PW ch mid rd 8/31/90 (#4, 8 wk), 12 wk.

Sachs, Marilyn
See Ann Durrell and_____

Sacks, Oliver
The Man Who Mistook His Wife for a Hat and Other Clinical Tales (Summit/Simon & Schuster) NYT nf 4/6/86 (#9), pk 4/20/86 (#3, 2 wk), 26 wk; PW hc nf 5/2/86 (#14), pk 5/16/86 (#9, 1 wk), 8 wk; (Harper/Perennial) NYT pb nf 1/4/87 (#4), pk 1/25/87 (#1, 2 wk), 26 wk; PW td pb 2/6/87 (#6), pk 3/6/87 (#5, 1 wk), 11 wk; tot 71 wk.

Sackville-West, Victoria
The Edwardians (Doubleday) PW fic 12/20/30 (#10, 4 wk).
All Passion Spent (Doubleday) PW fic 10/17/31 (#10, 4 wk).
Daughter of France (Doubleday) NYT gen 9/6/59 (#16, 1 wk).
No Signposts in the Sea (Doubleday) NYT fic 5/28/61 (#16, 1 wk).

Sadat, Jehan
A Woman of Egypt (Simon & Schuster)

PW hc nf 9/11/87 (#10, 1 wk), 3 wk; NYT nf 9/20/87 (#13, 2 wk); tot 5 wk.

Sadleir, Michael
Fanny by Gaslight (Appleton) PW fic 4/12/41 (#10, 4 wk).

Safer, Morley
Flashbacks: On Returning to Vietnam (Morrow) NYT nf 5/6/90 (#15), pk 5/20/90 (#9, 1 wk), 6 wk; PW hc nf 5/11/90 (#7, 1 wk), 4 wk; tot 10 wk.

Safire, William
Full Disclosure (Doubleday) NYT fic 7/17/77 (#10), pk 9/11/77 (#4, 1 wk), 14 wk; PW hc fic 7/18/77 (#9), pk 8/8/77 (#4, 4 wk), 12 wk; (Ballantine) PW mm pb 7/17/78 (#12), pk 7/24/78 (#8, 1 wk), 5 wk; NYT mm pb 7/23/78 (#6), pk 7/30/78 (#4, 1 wk), 4 wk; tot 35 wk.
On Language (Times) PW hc nf 1/16/81 (#11, 1 wk), 3 wk.
Freedom (Doubleday) NYT fic 9/13/87 (#13), pk 9/27/87 (#6, 1 wk), 10 wk; PW hc fic 9/18/87 (#8), pk 9/25/87 (#7, 1 wk), 7 wk; tot 17 wk.

Sagan, Carl
The Dragons of Eden: Speculations on the Evolution of Human Intelligence (Random) NYT nf 6/19/77 (#5), pk 7/10/77 (#3, 6 wk), 33 wk; PW hc nf 6/20/77 (#4), pk 8/1/77 (#2, 2 wk), 31 wk; (Ballantine) PW mm pb 5/15/78 (#8), pk 5/29/78 (#4, 1 wk), 17 wk; NYT mm pb 5/21/78 (#13), pk 6/4/78 (#4, 3 wk), 13 wk; tot 94 wk.
Broca's Brain (Random) PW hc nf 6/11/79 (#13), pk 8/20/79 (#5, 3 wk), 23 wk; NYT nf 6/24/79 (#12), pk 8/26/79 (#5, 3 wk), 23 wk; tot 46 wk.
Cosmos (Random) PW hc nf 11/7/80 (#4), pk 11/14/80 (#1, 17 wk), 66 wk; NYT nf 11/9/80 (#1, 16 wk), 70 wk; tot 136 wk.
Contact (Simon & Schuster) PW hc fic 10/11/85 (#11), pk 10/25/85 (#3, 3 wk), 23 wk; NYT fic 10/13/85 (#7), pk 10/20/85 (#3, 2 wk), 24 wk; (Pocket) NYT pb fic 10/12/86 (#12), pk 10/26/86 (#2, 1 wk), 8 wk; PW mm pb 10/17/86 (#13), pk 11/7/86 (#4, 1 wk), 7 wk; tot 62 wk.

_____, **and Ann Druyan**
Comet (Random) NYT nf 1/5/86 (#15), pk 1/12/86 (#8, 5 wk), 8 wk; PW hc nf 1/17/86 (#10, 1 wk), 3 wk; tot 11 wk.

Sagan, Francoise
Bonjour Tristesse (Dutton) NYT fic 3/20/55 (#13), pk 5/22/55 (#1, 12 wk), 38 wk; PW fic 4/2/55 (#5), pk 5/28/55 (#1, 10 wk), 31 wk; tot 69 wk.
A Certain Smile (Dutton) NYT fic 8/19/56

(#14), pk 9/23/56 (#2, 5 wk), 19 wk; PW fic 9/3/56 (#7), pk 9/24/56 (#2, 4 wk), 15 wk; tot 34 wk.
Those Without Shadows (Dutton) NYT fic 11/24/57 (#16), pk 12/1/57 (#12, 1 wk), 3 wk.
Aimez-vous Brahms (Dutton) NYT fic 4/17/60 (#14, 1 wk).

Sagoff, Maurice
Shrinklits (Workman) NYT td pb 8/3/80 (#15, 2 wk).

Sailor, Charles
The Second Son (Avon) NYT mm pb 11/18/79 (#14), pk 12/16/79 (#9, 1 wk), 8 wk.

Saint, Dora Jessie
Storm in the Village [as by Miss Read] (Houghton) NYT fic 3/29/59 (#14, 1 wk).
Thrush Green [as by Miss Read] (Houghton) NYT fic 1/24/60 (#15), pk 1/31/60 (#13, 1 wk), 3 wk.

St. George, Cpl. Thomas R.
C/O Postmaster (Crowell) NYT gen 10/31/43 (#15), pk 12/26/43 (#4, 1 wk), 16 wk; PW nf 11/13/43 (#8), pk 12/4/43 (#4, 3 wk), 10 wk; tot 26 wk.

St. John, Robert
From the Land of Silent People (Doubleday) PW nf 3/14/42 (#8), pk 4/11/42 (#7, 4 wk), 12 wk.
Shalom Means Peace (Doubleday) NYT gen 3/27/49 (#14), pk 4/24/49 (#11, 1 wk), 4 wk.

St. Johns, Adela Rogers
Final Verdict (Doubleday) NYT gen 9/16/62 (#16), pk 4/7/62 (#5, 3 wk), 25 wk; PW nf 10/1/62 (#11), pk 2/18/63 (#3, 1 wk), 39 wk; tot 64 wk.
Tell No Man (Doubleday) NYT fic 3/20/66 (#10), pk 7/10/66 (#4, 1 wk), 29 wk; PW fic 4/4/66 (#9), pk 6/6/66 (#5, 6 wk), 29 wk; tot 58 wk.
The Honeycomb (Doubleday) NYT gen 10/26/69 (#10), pk 11/9/69 (#9, 1 wk), 2 wk.

St. Laurent, Cecil
Caroline Che Rie [trans. Lawrence G. Blochman] (Prentice Hall) NYT fic 5/25/52 (#15, 1 wk).

Salamanca, J.R.
Lilith (Simon & Schuster) NYT fic 9/17/61 (#12, 1 wk).

Sale, Chic
The Specialist (Specialist Pub. Co.) PW nf 8/10/29 (#7), pk 10/12/29 (#1, 12 wk), 36 wk.

Salinger, Jerome David [all titles as by J. D. Salinger]
Catcher in the Rye (Little Brown) NYT fic

7/29/51 (#14), pk 8/19/51 (#4, 10 wk), 29 wk; PW fic 8/25/51 (#5), pk 9/8/51 (#4, 5 wk), 14 wk; tot 43 wk.
Nine Stories (Little Brown) NYT fic 4/26/53 (#10), pk 5/3/53 (#9, 1 wk), 15 wk.
Franny and Zooey (Little Brown) NYT fic 9/24/61 (#10), pk 10/29/61 (#1, 26 wk), 54 wk; PW fic 9/25/61 (#8), pk 10/30/61 (#1, 23 wk), 53 wk; tot 107 wk.
Raise High the Roof Beam, Carpenters (Little Brown) NYT fic 4/7/63 (#1, 6 wk), 21 wk.
Raise High the Roof Beam, Carpenters and Seymour—An Introduction (Little Brown) PW fic 2/18/63 (#10), pk 3/4/63 (#1, 10 wk), 29 wk.

Salinger, Pierre
With Kennedy (Doubleday) NYT gen 10/9/66 (#6), pk 11/20/66 (#5, 2 wk), 15 wk; PW nf 10/17/66 (#10), pk 12/5/66 (#4, 2 wk), 17 wk; NYT pb gen 1/1/67 (#2, 4 wk), 8 wk; tot 40 wk.
On Instructions of My Government (Doubleday) NYT fic 7/11/71 (#9), pk 8/1/71 (#5, 2 wk), 9 wk; PW fic 8/2/71 (#6), pk 8/9/71 (#4, 1 wk), 10 wk; tot 19 wk.

_____, and Sander Vanocur
A Tribute to John F. Kennedy [eds.] (Encyclopedia Britannica) NYT gen 6/28/64 (#7), pk 7/19/64 (#3, 1 wk), 21 wk; PW nf 7/6/64 (#9), pk 8/3/64 (#4, 7 wk), 22 wk; tot 43 wk.

Salisbury, Albert and Jane Salisbury
Here Rolled the Covered Wagons (Bonanza) NYT gen 8/8/48 (#15, 1 wk).

Salisbury, Harrison Evans
American in Russia (Harper) NYT gen 3/13/55 (#13, 2 wk), 3 wk.
The 900 Days (Harper) NYT gen 2/23/69 (#8), pk 5/4/69 (#1, 2 wk), 25 wk; PW nf 2/24/69 (#7), pk 3/24/69 (#1, 9 wk), 30 wk; tot 55 wk.

Salisbury, Helen M.
See Josephine A. Jackson and_____

Salk, Lee
What Every Child Would Like His Parents to Know (McKay) NYT gen 8/6/72 (#8, 1 wk).

Salminen, Sally
Katrina (Farrar) NYT fic 11/7/37 (#4, 4 wk), 8 wk; PW fic 11/13/37 (#6, 4 wk), 8 wk; tot 16 wk.

Salomonson, Finn S.
See Peter F. Freuchen and_____

Salten, Felix
Bambi's Children (Bobbs Merrill) NYT fic 1/7/40 (#12, 4 wk).

Salter, Sir Arthur
Recovery (Century) PW nf 5/14/32 (#8), pk 7/9/32 (#4, 4 wk), 20 wk.

Salvato, Sharon
Bitter Eden (Dell) PW mm pb 12/24/79 (#11, 1 wk).

Salvatore, R.A.
The Halfling's Gem (TSR) NYT pb fic 3/4/90 (#12, 1 wk), 2 wk.

Sam See
See Samuel C. Platt

Sampson, Anthony
The Sovereign State of ITT (Stein & Day) PW nf 8/6/73 (#5, 2 wk), 6 wk; NYT gen 8/12/73 (#10), pk 9/16/73 (#8, 1 wk), 5 wk; tot 11 wk.

Samson, Joan
The Auctioneer (Simon & Schuster) PW hc fic 3/1/76 (#10), pk 3/8/76 (#9, 2 wk), 3 wk; (Avon) mm pb 1/24/77 (#7), pk 2/7/77 (#2, 2 wk), 13 wk; NYT mm pb 1/30/77 (#6), pk 2/20/77 (#2, 1 wk), 14 wk; tot 30 wk.

Samuel, Maurice
Web of Lucifer (Knopf) NYT fic 3/23/47 (#15), pk 3/30/47 (#9, 1 wk), 9 wk.

Sanchez, Tony
Up and Down with the Rolling Stones (Morrow/Quill) NYT td pb 9/23/79 (#14, 4 wk), 5 wk.

Sandburg, Carl
Abraham Lincoln: The Prairie Years (Harcourt) PW nf 3/20/26 (#4, 8 wk), 16 wk.
Abraham Lincoln: The War Years (Harcourt) NYT gen 1/7/40 (#12, 1 wk); PW nf 1/13/40 (#6, 4 wk), 8 wk; tot 9 wk.
Storm Over the Land (Harcourt) NYT nf 11/22/42 (#14), pk 11/29/42 (#10, 1 wk), 3 wk.
Remembrance Rock (Harcourt) NYT fic 10/24/48 (#9), pk 11/14/48 (#3, 4 wk), 21 wk; PW fic 11/13/48 (#4), pk 11/20/48 (#3, 4 wk), 13 wk; tot 34 wk.
Complete Poems (Harcourt) NYT gen 1/21/51 (#16), pk 1/28/51 (#15, 1 wk), 2 wk.
Always the Young Strangers (Harcourt) NYT gen 1/25/53 (#7), pk 2/8/53 (#3, 2 wk), 15 wk; PW nf 2/7/53 (#5), pk 2/28/53 (#2, 2 wk), 8 wk; tot 23 wk.
Abraham Lincoln (Harcourt) NYT gen 10/17/54 (#11), pk 11/21/54 (#2, 4 wk), 25 wk; PW nf 10/30/54 (#3), pk 11/27/54 (#2, 4 wk), 20 wk; tot 45 wk.
The Wedding Procession of the Rag Doll and the Broom Handle and Who Was Was in It (Harcourt) NYT ch bst 11/5/67 (#5, 26 wk).

Sanders, Lawrence
The Anderson Tapes (Putnam) PW fic 3/30/70 (#7, 2 wk), 7 wk.
The First Deadly Sin (Putnam) NYT fic 10/28/73 (#10), pk 2/3/74 (#4, 2 wk), 24 wk; PW fic 10/29/73 (#6), pk 11/5/73 (#2, 1 wk), 24 wk; (Berkley) NYT mm pb 8/11/74 (#6, 8 wk), 12 wk; tot 60 wk.
The Tomorrow File (Berkley) PW mm pb 9/27/76 (#9), pk 10/4/76 (#8, 1 wk), 5 wk.
The Second Deadly Sin (Putnam) NYT fic 9/18/77 (#11), pk 11/13/77 (#6, 2 wk), 24 wk; PW hc fic 9/26/77 (#9), pk 10/24/77 (#8, 2 wk), 19 wk; (Berkley) PW mm pb 8/14/78 (#5), pk 8/21/78 (#4, 1 wk), 9 wk; tot 52 wk.
The Sixth Commandment (Putnam) PW hc fic 1/22/79 (#12), pk 3/5/79 (#6, 1 wk), 11 wk; NYT fic 1/28/79 (#15), pk 3/18/79 (#4, 1 wk), 11 wk; (Berkley) PW mm pb 1/18/80 (#8), pk 1/25/80 (#6, 1 wk), 8 wk; NYT mm pb 1/20/80 (#10), pk 1/27/80 (#6, 1 wk), 10 wk; tot 40 wk.
The Tenth Commandment (Putnam) PW hc fic 9/19/80 (#15), pk 10/10/80 (#5, 4 wk), 18 wk; NYT fic 9/21/80 (#15), pk 10/19/80 (#5, 1 wk), 16 wk; (Berkley) PW mm pb 8/14/81 (#10), pk 8/28/81 (#3, 3 wk), 10 wk; NYT mm pb 8/16/81 (#13), pk 8/23/81 (#2, 2 wk), 9 wk; tot 53 wk.
The Third Deadly Sin (Putnam) PW hc fic 7/24/81 (#14), pk 9/4/81 (#2, 2 wk), 25 wk; NYT fic 8/2/81 (#6), pk 9/6/81 (#2, 1 wk), 24 wk; (Berkley) PW mm pb 8/13/82 (#10), pk 9/3/82 (#1, 2 wk), 13 wk; NYT mm pb 8/15/82 (#15), pk 8/22/82 (#2, 3 wk), 14 wk; tot 76 wk.
The Case of Lucy Bending (Putnam) PW hc fic 7/23/82 (#11), pk 8/13/82 (#4, 3 wk), 13 wk; NYT fic 7/25/82 (#13), pk 9/5/82 (#3, 1 wk), 2 wk; (Berkley) NYT mm pb 7/17/83 (#5), pk 7/24/83 (#1, 1 wk), 12 wk; PW mm pb 7/22/83 (#4), pk 7/29/83 (#1, 2 wk), 10 wk; tot 37 wk.
The Seduction of Peter S. (Putnam) PW hc fic 7/22/83 (#11), pk 8/19/83 (#2, 1 wk), 14 wk; NYT fic 7/24/83 (#9), pk 8/7/83 (#5, 3 wk), 14 wk; (Berkley) NYT pb fic 7/8/84 (#13), pk 7/22/84 (#3, 3 wk), 13 wk; PW mm pb 7/13/84 (#7), pk 7/27/84 (#3, 3 wk), 12 wk; tot 53 wk.
The Passion of Molly T. (Putnam) PW hc fic 9/14/84 (#13), pk 9/28/84 (#10, 1 wk), 5 wk; (Berkley) PW mm pb 7/12/85 (#13), pk 7/26/85 (#1, 1 wk), 10 wk; NYT pb fic 7/14/85 (#3), pk 7/21/85 (#1, 3 wk), 12 wk; tot 27 wk.
The Fourth Deadly Sin (Putnam) PW hc fic 7/19/85 (#12), pk 8/30/85 (#1, 1 wk), 15 wk; NYT fic 7/21/85 (#4), pk 7/28/85 (#2, 5

wk), 15 wk; (Berkley) NYT pb fic 6/29/86
(#7), pk 7/6/86 (#2, 2 wk), 11 wk; PW mm
pb 7/4/86 (#7), pk 7/11/86 (#1, 1 wk), 12 wk;
tot 53 wk.
   Tales of the Wolf (Avon) NYT pb fic 10/5/
86 (#9), pk 10/19/86 (#3, 1 wk), 6 wk; PW
mm pb 10/10/86 (#11), pk 10/31/86 (#3, 1 wk),
6 wk; tot 12 wk.
   The Loves of Harry Dancer (Berkley) NYT
pb fic 1/5/86 (#13), pk 1/19/86 (#6, 3 wk), 8
wk; PW mm pb 1/17/86 (#10), pk 1/24/86
(#7, 3 wk), 6 wk; tot 14 wk.
   The Eighth Commandment (Putnam) NYT
fic 6/8/86 (#8), pk 6/22/86 (#4, 2 wk), 14 wk;
PW hc fic 6/13/86 (#7), pk 7/4/86 (#3, 1 wk),
15 wk; (Berkley) NYT pb fic 6/28/87 (#3, 3
wk), 11 wk; PW mm pb 7/3/87 (#3, 4 wk), 9
wk; tot 49 wk.
   The Dream Lover (Berkley) NYT pb fic
1/4/87 (#10, 5 wk), 6 wk; PW mm pb 1/16/87
(#12), pk 1/30/87 (#4, 1 wk), 5 wk; tot 11 wk.
   Caper (Berkley) NYT pb fic 12/6/87 (#5),
pk 12/20/87 (#4, 1 wk), 12 wk; PW mm pb
12/11/87 (#5), pk 12/18/87 (#3, 2 wk), 11 wk;
tot 23 wk.
   The Timothy Files (Putnam) PW hc fic
6/12/87 (#12), pk 7/10/87 (#4, 1 wk), 13 wk;
NYT fic 6/14/87 (#12), pk 6/28/87 (#5, 2
wk), 12 wk; (Berkley) NYT pb fic 6/19/88
(#12), pk 7/3/88 (#1, 1 wk), 12 wk; PW mm
pb 7/1/88 (#3), pk 7/8/88 (#2, 1 wk), 9 wk;
tot 46 wk.
   Timothy's Game (Putnam) NYT fic 7/17/
88 (#9), pk 8/7/88 (#6, 1 wk), 8 wk; PW hc
fic 7/22/88 (#8), pk 8/5/88 (#6, 1 wk), 7 wk;
(Berkley) NYT pb fic 6/11/89 (#13), pk 6/18/
89 (#4, 2 wk), 9 wk; PW mm pb 6/23/89
(#6), pk 6/30/89 (#4, 1 wk), 7 wk; tot 31 wk.
   Stolen Blessings (Berkley) NYT pb fic 12/
3/89 (#9), pk 12/17/89 (#3, 3 wk), 9 wk; PW
mm pb 12/8/89 (#10), pk 12/22/89 (#3, 2
wk), 8 wk; tot 17 wk.
   Capital Crimes (Putnam) NYT fic 6/4/89
(#15), pk 6/18/89 (#5, 2 wk), 11 wk; PW hc
fic 6/9/89 (#12), pk 7/7/89 (#4, 2 wk), 11 wk;
(Berkley) NYT pb fic 7/1/90 (#4, 1 wk), 7
wk; PW mm pb 7/6/90 (#5, 2 wk), 6 wk; tot
35 wk.
   Love Songs (Berkley) NYT pb fic 1/1/89
(#14), pk 1/29/89 (#4, 1 wk), 8 wk; PW mm
pb 1/6/89 (#14), pk 1/27/89 (#6, 1 wk), 6 wk;
tot 14 wk.
   Sullivan's Sting (Putnam) PW hc fic 6/22/
90 (#14), pk 7/20/90 (#6, 1 wk), 9 wk; NYT
fic 6/24/90 (#13), pk 7/8/90 (#9, 2 wk), 8 wk;
tot 17 wk.

Sandford, John
   Rules of Prey (Berkley) NYT pb fic 4/1/90

(#4, 2 wk), 6 wk; PW mm pb 4/6/90 (#6),
pk 4/13/90 (#5, 2 wk), 6 wk; tot 12 wk.

Sandoz, Mari
   Old Jules (Little Brown) NYT gen 12/1/35
(#4, 4 wk); PW nf 12/14/35 (#6, 4 wk); tot 8
wk.
   Slogum House (Atlantic) NYT fic 1/9/38
(#6, 4 wk).
   Capital City (Little Brown) NYT fic 1/7/
40 (#6, 4 wk).
   *The Cattlemen from the Rio Grande Across
the Far Marias* (Hastings) NYT gen 6/22/58
(#13), pk 6/29/58 (#12, 3 wk), 13 wk.

Sands, Bill
   My Shadow Ran Fast (Prentice Hall) NYT
gen 2/28/65 (#6), pk 4/18/65 (#3, 5 wk), 25
wk; PW nf 3/8/65 (#8), pk 4/19/65 (#2, 3
wk), 29 wk; NYT pb gen 3/6/66 (#5), pk
4/3/66 (#1, 12 wk), 20 wk; tot 74 wk.

Sanford, John
   Shadow Prey (Putnam) PW hc fic 7/20/90
(#14, 1 wk), 2 wk.

Santayana, George
   The Last Puritan (Scribner) PW fic 3/14/
36 (#1, 12 wk), 28 wk; NYT fic 4/5/36 (#1, 8
wk), 12 wk; tot 40 wk.
   Persons and Places (Scribner) NYT gen
1/23/44 (#17), pk 3/26/44 (#3, 1 wk), 16 wk;
PW nf 2/12/44 (#9), pk 2/19/44 (#3, 2 wk),
7 wk; tot 23 wk.
   The Middle Span (Scribner) NYT gen 5/
13/45 (#18, 1 wk), 4 wk.
   Dominations and Powers (Scribner) NYT
gen 5/27/51 (#14), pk 6/10/51 (#10, 1 wk), 6
wk.
   My Host the World (Scribner) NYT gen
4/5/53 (#16), pk 4/19/53 (#15, 2 wk), 3 wk.

Santmyer, Helen Hoover
   And Ladies of the Club (Putnam) NYT fic
6/17/84 (#14), pk 7/8/84 (#1, 7 wk), 37 wk;
PW hc fic 6/22/84 (#10), pk 7/13/84 (#1, 6
wk), 38 wk; (Berkley) NYT pb fic 6/2/85
(#3), pk 6/9/85 (#1, 4 wk), 21 wk; PW mm
pb 6/7/85 (#2), pk 6/14/85 (#1, 7 wk), 20 wk;
tot 116 wk.
   Herbs and Apples (St. Martin's) NYT pb
fic 4/19/87 (#14), pk 5/3/87 (#10, 1 wk), 3 wk;
PW mm pb 4/24/87 (#15), pk 5/8/87 (#14, 1
wk), 3 wk; tot 6 wk.

Santoli, Al
   Everything We Had [ed.] (Random) NYT
nf 7/5/81 (#15, 1 wk); PW hc nf 7/24/81 (#13,
1 wk), 3 wk; tot 4 wk.

Saperstein, David
   Cocoon (Jove) NYT pb fic 7/14/85 (#13, 1

wk), 2 wk; PW mm pb 7/19/85 (#14, 2 wk); tot 4 wk.

Saroyan, William
The Human Comedy (Harcourt) PW fic 3/20/43 (#4), pk 4/3/43 (#2, 14 wk), 28 wk; NYT fic 3/21/43 (#6), pk 4/11/43 (#2, 12 wk), 32 wk; tot 60 wk.
The Adventures of Wesley Jackson (Harcourt) NYT fic 7/7/46 (#12), pk 7/14/46 (#10, 1 wk), 2 wk.

Sarton, May
A Shower of Summer Days (Norton) NYT fic 12/14/52 (#16, 1 wk).
The Small Room (Norton) NYT fic 10/1/61 (#14), pk 10/15/61 (#13, 1 wk), 3 wk.
At Seventy: A Journal (Norton) NYT nf 7/29/84 (#15), pk 8/26/84 (#12, 1 wk), 4 wk.

Sartre, Jean-Paul
The Age of Reason (Knopf) NYT fic 8/17/47 (#16), pk 8/31/47 (#15, 1 wk), 3 wk.
Troubled Sleep (Knopf) NYT fic 3/4/51 (#16, 1 wk).
The Words (Braziller) PW nf 11/16/64 (#10), pk 2/15/65 (#3, 1 wk), 17 wk; NYT gen 11/22/64 (#9), pk 12/13/64 (#7, 6 wk), 16 wk; tot 33 wk.

Sasek, Miroslav
This Is Paris (Macmillan) NYT ch bst 11/1/59 (#11, 25 wk).
This Is New York (Macmillan) NYT ch bst 11/12/61 (#13, 26 wk).
This Is San Francisco (Macmillan) NYT ch bst 11/11/62 (#12, 26 wk).

Sassoon, Vidal, Beverly Sassoon and Camille Duhe
A Year of Beauty and Health (Simon & Schuster) NYT gen 4/18/76 (#10), pk 7/11/76 (#4, 1 wk), 28 wk; PW hc nf 4/12/76 (#6), pk 5/10/76 (#3, 3 wk), 33 wk; (Simon & Schuster/Fireside) NYT td pb 2/25/79 (#15), pk 3/11/79 (#13, 1 wk), 7 wk; tot 68 wk.

Satterlee, Hugh, and I.H. Sher
Your Income Tax: How to Keep It Down (Simon & Schuster) NYT nf 4/5/36 (#7, 4 wk).

Saul, John
Suffer the Children (Dell) PW mm pb 7/11/77 (#12, 2 wk), 3 wk; NYT mm pb 7/24/77 (#10, 1 wk), 3 wk; tot 6 wk.
Punish the Sinners (Dell) PW mm pb 7/3/78 (#15), pk 7/17/78 (#10, 1 wk), 4 wk; NYT mm pb 7/30/78 (#15, 2 wk); tot 6 wk.
Cry for the Strangers (Dell) PW mm pb 6/18/79 (#14), pk 7/2/79 (#5, 1 wk), 6 wk; NYT mm pb 6/24/79 (#6, 1 wk), 6 wk; tot 12 wk.

Comes the Blind Fury (Dell) PW mm pb 6/27/80 (#10, 1 wk), 4 wk; NYT mm pb 6/29/80 (#15, 2 wk); tot 6 wk.
When the Wind Blows (Dell) PW mm pb 8/14/81 (#11, 3 wk), 4 wk; NYT mm pb 8/16/81 (#8, 1 wk), 4 wk; tot 8 wk.
The God Project (Bantam) NYT mm pb 6/12/83 (#12), pk 6/19/83 (#8, 2 wk), 7 wk; PW mm pb 6/17/83 (#11), pk 6/24/83 (#7, 2 wk), 6 wk; tot 13 wk.
Nathaniel (Bantam) PW mm pb 7/13/84 (#10), pk 8/3/84 (#6, 1 wk), 8 wk; NYT pb fic 7/15/84 (#5, 2 wk), 9 wk; tot 17 wk.
Brainchild (Bantam) NYT pb fic 8/11/85 (#14), pk 8/18/85 (#2, 2 wk), 8 wk; PW mm pb 8/16/85 (#11), pk 8/30/85 (#3, 1 wk), 7 wk; tot 15 wk.
Hellfire (Bantam) PW mm pb 8/15/86 (#14), pk 8/29/86 (#7, 1 wk), 5 wk; NYT pb fic 8/17/86 (#6, 2 wk), 6 wk; tot 11 wk.
The Unwanted (Bantam) NYT pb fic 8/2/87 (#11), pk 8/16/87 (#5, 2 wk), 7 wk; PW mm pb 8/14/87 (#6), pk 8/28/87 (#5, 1 wk), 5 wk; tot 12 wk.
The Unloved (Bantam) NYT pb fic 7/3/88 (#12), pk 7/10/88 (#7, 2 wk), 6 wk; PW mm pb 7/8/88 (#7, 2 wk), 5 wk; tot 11 wk.
Second Child (Bantam) NYT fic 7/1/90 (#13, 1 wk), 3 wk; PW hc fic 7/13/90 (#14, 3 wk); tot 6 wk.
Sleepwalk (Bantam) NYT pb fic 12/23/90 (#12), pk 12/30/90 (#7, 1 wk), 2 wk.
Creature (Bantam) NYT pb fic 6/3/90 (#9), pk 6/17/90 (#2, 2 wk), 7 wk; PW mm pb 6/15/90 (#3, 2 wk), 6 wk; tot 13 wk.

Saunders, Hilary St. George
Combined Operations (Macmillan) NYT gen 6/13/43 (#11), pk 6/20/43 (#5, 2 wk), 8 wk; PW nf 6/19/43 (#5, 2 wk), 6 wk; tot 14 wk.

Savage, Christina
Love's Wildest Fires (Dell) NYT mm pb 8/21/77 (#8), pk 8/28/77 (#3, 1 wk), 11 wk; PW mm pb 8/22/77 (#6), pk 8/29/77 (#5, 1 wk), 8 wk; tot 19 wk.
Dawn Wind (Dell) PW mm pb 4/25/80 (#14, 1 wk).

Saxon, Lyle
Fabulous New Orleans (Appleton) NYT gen 11/19/44 (#12, 1 wk), 4 wk.

Sayers, Dorothy L.
Gaudy Night (Harcourt) NYT fic 4/5/36 (#4, 4 wk); PW fic 4/11/36 (#6, 4 wk); tot 8 wk.
Busman's Honeymoon (Harcourt) NYT fic 4/4/37 (#6, 4 wk); PW fic 4/10/37 (#10, 4 wk); tot 8 wk.

Sayers, Gale, and Al Silverman
I Am Third (Viking) PW nf 2/28/72 (#10, 1 wk).

Sayers, Michael, and Albert Kahn
Sabotage! (Harper) NYT nf 10/4/42 (#9), pk 10/25/42 (#2, 1 wk), 16 wk; PW nf 10/17/42 (#2, 1 wk), 6 wk; tot 22 wk.

Scammon, Richard M., and Ben J. Wattenberg
The Real Majority (Coward McCann) NYT gen 11/15/70 (#10, 1 wk).

Scanlon, William T.
God Have Mercy on Us (Century) PW fic 1/11/30 (#10, 4 wk).

Scarf, Maggie
Unfinished Business: Pressure Points in the Lives of Women (Doubleday) PW hc nf 9/19/80 (#14), pk 10/10/80 (#10, 2 wk), 9 wk; NYT nf 10/26/80 (#11), pk 11/23/80 (#10, 1 wk), 3 wk; tot 12 wk.
Intimate Partners: Patterns in Love and Marriage (Random) NYT nf 3/8/87 (#9), pk 3/22/87 (#8, 2 wk), 15 wk; PW hc nf 3/13/87 (#11, 2 wk), 11 wk; (Ballantine) NYT pb nf 5/8/88 (#4, 1 wk), 7 wk; tot 33 wk.

Scarfone, Jay
See John Fricke, et al.

Scarry, Richard
Richard Scarry's Best Word Book Ever (Golden) NYT ch bst 5/9/65 (#19), pk 5/7/72 (#1, 64 wk), 378 wk.
Busy, Busy World (Golden) NYT ch bst 11/6/66 (#5, 26 wk).
Richard Scarry's Storybook Dictionary (Golden) NYT ch bst 11/5/67 (#10, 26 wk).
Richard Scarry's Best Make-It Book Ever (Random) NYT ch pb 4/30/78 (#14, 24 wk).

Schaap, Dick
See Bo Jackson and_____

Schachner, Nathan
Alexander Hamilton (Appleton) NYT gen 7/7/46 (#16, 1 wk).

Schaef, Anne Wilson
When Society Becomes an Addict (Harper) NYT nf 5/17/87 (#16, 1 wk).

Schaeffer, Susan Fromberg
Anya (Avon) PW mm pb 2/9/76 (#7, 1 wk), 2 wk; NYT mm pb 2/15/76 (#8, 1 wk); tot 3 wk.
The Madness of a Seduced Woman (Bantam) NYT pb fic 8/12/84 (#11), pk 8/26/84 (#5, 1 wk), 7 wk; PW mm pb 8/17/84 (#15), pk 8/31/84 (#13, 1 wk), 6 wk; tot 13 wk.

Schama, Simon
Citizens: A Chronicle of the French Revolu-
tion (Knopf) NYT nf 4/16/89 (#16), pk 4/30/89 (#5, 2 wk), 19 wk; PW hc nf 4/21/89 (#13), pk 8/4/89 (#9, 1 wk), 13 wk; tot 32 wk.

Scheim, David E.
Contract on America (Zebra) NYT mm pb 4/16/89 (#8), pk 4/23/89 (#6, 1 wk), 8 wk.

Scheinfeld, Amram
You and Heredity (Stokes) NYT gen 10/8/39 (#12, 4 wk).

Schell, Jonathan
The Fate of the Earth (Knopf) PW hc nf 5/7/82 (#4), pk 5/14/82 (#3, 1 wk), 17 wk; NYT nf 5/9/82 (#7), pk 5/16/82 (#3, 4 wk), 18 wk; tot 35 wk.

Schellenberg, Walter
The Labyrinth (Harper) NYT gen 7/7/57 (#14, 1 wk).

Schembechler, Bo, and Mitch Albom
Bo (Warner) NYT nf 9/24/89 (#14), pk 10/8/89 (#10, 2 wk), 8 wk; PW hc nf 9/29/89 (#12), pk 10/13/89 (#11, 1 wk), 4 wk; tot 12 wk.

Scherman, David E.
The Best of Life [ed.] (Time Life) PW nf 11/26/73 (#9), pk 1/21/74 (#2, 1 wk), 16 wk; NYT gen 12/16/73 (#10), pk 1/20/74 (#4, 1 wk), 15 wk; (Avon/Flare) mm pb 4/6/75 (#5), pk 4/20/75 (#2, 3 wk), 21 wk; tot 52 wk.
Life Goes to the Movies [ed.] (Time Life) PW nf 12/29/75 (#10, 1 wk).

Schiddel, Edmund
The Devil in Bucks County (Simon & Schuster) NYT fic 2/22/59 (#10), pk 5/17/59 (#7, 1 wk), 16 wk.

Schiff, Pearl
Scollay Square (Rinehart) NYT fic 10/5/52 (#15), pk 10/26/52 (#12, 1 wk), 3 wk.

Schindler, John A.
How to Live 365 Days a Year (Prentice Hall) NYT gen 3/27/55 (#14), pk 5/22/55 (#3, 7 wk), 90 wk; PW nf 4/9/55 (#9), pk 6/4/55 (#3, 12 wk), 54 wk; tot 144 wk.

Schlesinger, Arthur M., Jr.
The Age of Jackson (Little Brown) NYT gen 10/21/45 (#13) pk 1/13/46 (#5, 1 wk), 26 wk; PW nf 1/5/46 (#3, 1 wk), 4 wk; tot 30 wk.
The Vital Center (Houghton) NYT gen 10/2/49 (#15), pk 10/9/49 (#12, 1 wk), 4 wk.
The Crisis of the Old Order (Houghton) NYT gen 3/24/57 (#11), pk 4/7/57 (#7, 2 wk), 11 wk; PW nf 4/29/57 (#6, 1 wk), 3 wk; tot 14 wk.

The Coming of the New Deal (Houghton) NYT gen 1/25/59 (#7), pk 3/8/59 (#4, 1 wk), 12 wk; PW nf 2/2/59 (#6), pk 2/9/59 (#5, 2 wk), 8 wk; tot 20 wk.

The Politics of Upheaval (Houghton) NYT gen 10/2/60 (#13), pk 11/27/60 (#4, 2 wk), 22 wk; PW nf 10/10/60 (#6), pk 12/5/60 (#4, 1 wk), 17 wk; tot 39 wk.

Kennedy or Nixon: Does It Matter? (Macmillan) NYT gen 10/23/60 (#13), pk 11/13/60 (#2, 1 wk), 8 wk; PW nf 10/31/60 (#4), pk 11/7/60 (#3, 3 wk), 7 wk; tot 15 wk.

A Thousand Days: John F. Kennedy in the White House (Houghton) NYT gen 12/5/65 (#10), pk 1/9/66 (#1, 4 wk), 26 wk; PW nf 12/6/65 (#9), pk 1/10/66 (#1, 5 wk), 25 wk; tot 51 wk.

The Bitter Heritage (Houghton) NYT gen 3/19/67 (#8, 1 wk); PW nf 3/27/67 (#8, 1 wk); tot 2 wk.

Robert Kennedy and His Times (Houghton) PW hc nf 9/4/78 (#9), pk 9/25/78 (#4, 1 wk), 17 wk; NYT nf 11/12/78 (#10, 2 wk), 9 wk; tot 26 wk.

Schlink, Frederick John
Eat, Drink and Be Wary (Covici Friede) NYT gen 12/1/35 (#8, 4 wk).
See also Arthur Kallet and_____
See also Stuart Chase and_____

Schmidt-Gorg, Joseph, and Hans Schmidt
Ludwig Van Beethoven [eds.] (Praeger) NYT gen 5/3/70 (#10, 1 wk).

Schmitt, Gladys
David the King (Dial) NYT fic 3/17/46 (#11), pk 4/7/46 (#3, 4 wk), 18 wk; PW fic 3/30/46 (#3), pk 4/13/46 (#1, 2 wk), 12 wk; tot 30 wk.

Confessions of the Name (Dial) NYT fic 11/16/52 (#14), pk 11/23/52 (#11, 1 wk), 4 wk.

Rembrandt (Random) NYT fic 7/23/61 (#9), pk 7/30/61 (#8, 8 wk), 17 wk; PW fic 8/7/61 (#9), pk 8/14/61 (#8, 5 wk), 10 wk; tot 27 wk.

Schnaubelt, Franz Joseph
Star Trek Star Fleet Technical Manual (Ballantine) NYT td pb 12/21/75 (#4), pk 1/4/76 (#1, 7 wk), 13 wk; PW td pb 2/2/76 (#3, 2 wk), 6 wk; tot 19 wk.

Schoenbrun, David
As France Goes (Harper) NYT gen 4/28/57 (#14), pk 5/5/57 (#13, 1 wk), 3 wk.

Schoenstein, Ralph
The I-Hate-Preppies Handbook (Wallaby/Pocket) PW td pb 10/2/81 (#10, 1 wk); NYT td pb 10/25/81 (#14, 1 wk), 3 wk; tot 4 wk.

Schonberg, Harold C.
See Richard Jerome Roberts, et al.

Schonfield, Hugh J.
The Passover Plot (Geis) NYT gen 10/16/66 (#9), pk 11/6/66 (#7, 3 wk), 8 wk; PW nf 10/31/66 (#13), pk 11/7/66 (#7, 2 wk), 11 wk; NYT pb gen 10/1/67 (#4), pk 11/5/67 (#2, 8 wk), 24 wk; tot 43 wk.

Schoonover, Lawrence L.
The Burnished Blade (Macmillan) NYT fic 10/31/48 (#12), pk 11/14/48 (#10, 1 wk), 6 wk.

The Spider King (Macmillan) NYT fic 4/18/54 (#13), pk 5/16/54 (#8, 2 wk), 11 wk.

Schorer, Mark
Sinclair Lewis: An American Life (McGraw) NYT gen 10/29/61 (#13, 2 wk), 10 wk.

Schorr, Daniel
See Oliver L. North

Schorr, Todd
See Bette Midler

Schreiber, Flora Rheta
Sybil (Regnery) NYT gen 6/3/73 (#10), pk 7/22/73 (#3, 5 wk), 23 wk; PW nf 6/11/73 (#8), pk 8/13/73 (#2, 2 wk), 20 wk; (Warner) NYT mm pb 6/9/74 (#3), pk 7/14/74 (#2, 7 wk), 34 wk; PW mm pb 11/22/76 (#14), pk 1/3/77 (#1, 1 wk), 10 wk; tot 87 wk.

The Shoemaker (NAL/Signet) NYT pb nf 4/15/84 (#5), pk 4/22/84 (#4, 3 wk), 10 wk; PW mm pb 4/27/84 (#13), pk 5/4/84 (#9, 1 wk), 4 wk; tot 14 wk.

Schulberg, Budd
What Makes Sammy Run? (Random) PW fic 9/13/41 (#10, 4 wk).

The Harder They Fall (Random) NYT fic 8/31/47 (#16), pk 9/21/47 (#9, 3 wk), 8 wk.

The Disenchanted (Random) NYT fic 11/5/50 (#16), pk 12/3/50 (#1, 8 wk), 35 wk; PW fic 11/25/50 (#4), pk 12/9/50 (#1, 3 wk), 25 wk; tot 60 wk.

Schuller, Robert H.
Tough Times Never Last, But Tough People Do (Nelson) NYT nf 9/11/83 (#5), pk 2/19/84 (#3, 2 wk), 31 wk; PW hc nf 9/23/83 (#13), pk 5/4/84 (#3, 1 wk), 33 wk; (Bantam) NYT pb nf 5/27/84 (#3, 8 wk), 14 wk; PW mm pb 6/1/84 (#11), pk 6/8/84 (#6, 2 wk), 6 wk; tot 84 wk.

Tough-Minded Faith for Tenderhearted People (Nelson) NYT nf 2/19/84 (#15), pk 5/6/84 (#6, 1 wk), 15 wk; PW hc nf 2/24/84 (#15), pk 3/16/84 (#14, 2 wk), 4 wk; tot 19 wk.

The Be (Happy) Attitudes (Word) NYT msc 11/10/85 (#3), pk 12/22/85 (#1, 3 wk), 32 wk; PW hc nf 11/15/85 (#14), pk 2/7/86 (#3, 1 wk), 33 wk; tot 65 wk.

Be Happy—You Are Loved! (Nelson) NYT msc 10/26/86 (#4), pk 12/28/86 (#3, 1 wk), 11 wk; PW hc nf 11/7/86 (#11, 1 wk), 7 wk; tot 18 wk.
Believe in the God Who Believes in You (Nelson) PW hc nf 11/10/89 (#12), pk 11/24/89 (#9, 1 wk), 3 wk.

Schulz, Charles M.
Good Ol' Charlie Brown (Holt) NYT gen 11/3/57 (#16, 1 wk).
Snoopy (Holt) NYT gen 9/28/58 (#14, 1 wk), 2 wk.
Happiness Is a Warm Puppy (Determined Productions) NYT gen 12/2/62 (#15), pk 4/7/63 (#2, 2 wk), 30 wk; PW nf 12/3/62 (#10), pk 2/18/63 (#2, 8 wk), 47 wk; NYT ch bst 5/12/63 (#2, 19 wk), 45 wk; tot 122 wk.
Security Is a Thumb and a Blanket (Determined Productions) NYT gen 10/6/63 (#8), pk 10/27/63 (#6, 5 wk), 17 wk; PW nf 10/21/63 (#8), pk 11/18/63 (#3, 1 wk), 15 wk; NYT ch bst 11/10/63 (#7, 26 wk); tot 58 wk.
Peanuts Jubilee (Ballantine) NYT td pb 11/7/76 (#5, 2 wk).
The Charlie Brown Dictionary (Scholastic) NYT ch pb 11/13/77 (#6), pk 4/30/78 (#3, 24 wk), 70 wk.
Charlie Brown's Super Book of Questions and Answers (Random) NYT ch hc 11/13/77 (#1, 46 wk), 70 wk.

Schumacher, E.F.
Small Is Beautiful (Harper/Torchbooks) NYT td pb 7/18/76 (#5, 1 wk).

Schumann, Mary
Strife Before Dawn (Dial) NYT fic 11/5/39 (#15, 4 wk).

Schumer, Fran
See Mary Cunningham and_____

Schuster, M. Lincoln
A Treasury of the World's Great Letters [ed.] (Simon & Schuster) PW nf 12/14/40 (#2), pk 1/11/41 (#1, 8 wk), 16 wk.

Schutz, William Carl
Joy; Expanding Human Awareness (Grove) NYT pb gen 9/7/69 (#5, 4 wk).

Schwager, Jack D.
Market Wizards: Interviews with Top Traders (New York Institute of Finance/Simon & Schuster) PW hc nf 9/22/89 (#11, 1 wk).

Schwartz, Bob
Diets Don't Work (Breakthru Publishers/Publishers Group West) NYT msc pb 3/24/85 (#7), pk 9/1/85 (#3, 2 wk), 13 wk; PW td pb 4/5/85 (#6), pk 9/13/85 (#3, 1 wk), 10 wk; tot 23 wk.

Schwartz, Tony
See Donald J. Trump and_____

Schwarz, Ted
See John Z. DeLorean and_____

Schwarz-Bart, Andre
The Last of the Just (Atheneum) NYT fic 11/20/60 (#14), pk 3/26/61 (#1, 4 wk), 44 wk; PW fic 12/5/60 (#9), pk 3/27/61 (#1, 2 wk), 31 wk; tot 75 wk.

Schwarzenegger, Arnold, and Douglas Kent Hall
Arnold: The Education of a Bodybuilder (Simon & Schuster) PW hc nf 12/5/77 (#14), pk 4/10/78 (#8, 1 wk), 11 wk; NYT nf 1/29/78 (#14), pk 3/19/78 (#10, 1 wk), 11 wk; (Wallaby) PW td pb 10/23/78 (#10, 1 wk); NYT td pb 11/12/78 (#15), pk 11/19/78 (#13, 3 wk), 8 wk; tot 31 wk.
Arnold's Bodyshaping for Women (Simon & Schuster) NYT nf 2/24/80 (#15, 1 wk).

Schweitzer, Albert
Out of My Life and Thought (Holt) NYT gen 8/14/49 (#13), pk 8/28/49 (#9, 1 wk), 4 wk.

Scieszka, Jon
The True Story of the Three Little Pigs [illus. Lane Smith] (Viking) PW ch pic 8/31/90 (#3), pk 9/28/90 (#2, 8 wk), 20 wk.

Scoggin, M.C.
Battle Stations! Your Navy in Action (Knopf) NYT gen 6/16/46 (#11), pk 6/30/46 (#10, 1 wk), 4 wk.

Scortia, Thomas N., and Frank M. Robinson
The Glass Inferno (Doubleday) NYT mm pb 1/26/75 (#3, 1 wk), 3 wk.
The Prometheus Crisis (Bantam) PW mm pb 9/13/76 (#15, 2 wk).

Scott, Alice Howard
Giant Picture Dictionary for Boys and Girls (Doubleday) NYT ch bst 11/2/58 (#12, 40 wk).

Scott, Edgar
How to Lay a Nest Egg (Winston) NYT gen 11/19/50 (#14, 1 wk), 3 wk.

Scott, Lynne W.
See Michael E. DeBakey, et al.

Scott, Natalie Anderson
The Story of Mrs. Murphy (Dutton) NYT fic 7/20/47 (#11), pk 8/3/47 (#5, 1 wk), 11 wk; PW fic 8/2/47 (#5, 1 wk), 4 wk; tot 15 wk.

Scott, Paul
The Jewel in the Crown (Avon) PW mm pb 1/25/85 (#13), pk 2/22/85 (#8, 1 wk), 12

wk; NYT pb fic 2/17/85 (#14), pk 3/31/85 (#12, 2 wk), 8 wk; tot 20 wk.

Scott, Col. Robert L., Jr.
God Is My Co-Pilot (Scribner) NYT gen 8/29/43 (#7), pk 11/21/43 (#3, 1 wk), 33 wk; PW nf 9/11/43 (#9), pk 12/25/43 (#4, 2 wk), 14 wk; tot 47 wk.

Scovell, Jane
See Kitty Dukakis and_____

Scrawls
See Steve Mitchell

Scruggs, William O.
See Walter Lippmann and_____

Scully, Frank
Behind the Flying Saucers (Holt) NYT gen 10/8/50 (#9), pk 11/5/50 (#4, 1 wk), 15 wk; PW nf 10/14/50 (#9), pk 11/4/50 (#5, 4 wk), 6 wk; tot 21 wk.

Seabrook, William Beuhler
The Magic Island (Harcourt) PW nf 2/16/29 (#4), pk 3/9/29 (#3, 4 wk), 16 wk.
Jungle Ways (Harcourt) PW nf 5/16/31 (#6, 8 wk), 12 wk.
Asylum (Harcourt) PW nf 9/14/35 (#6), pk 10/12/35 (#4, 4 wk), 16 wk; NYT nf 10/6/35 (#3, 4 wk), 8 wk; tot 24 wk.

Seager, Alan
Equinox (Simon & Schuster) NYT fic 9/19/43 (#13), pk 10/3/43 (#8, 1 wk), 2 wk.

Seagrave, Gordon S., M.D.
Burma Surgeon (Norton) NYT gen 8/29/43 (#11), pk 10/24/43 (#2, 8 wk), 40 wk; PW nf 9/25/43 (#4), pk 1/1/44 (#1, 1 wk), 27 wk; tot 67 wk.
Burma Surgeon Returns (Norton) NYT gen 3/31/46 (#6), pk 4/7/46 (#5, 1 wk), 13 wk; PW nf 4/6/46 (#9), pk 4/27/46 (#4, 1 wk), 7 wk; tot 20 wk.

Seagrave, Sterling
The Soong Dynasty (Harper) NYT nf 4/21/85 (#11), pk 5/5/85 (#6, 1 wk), 14 wk; PW hc nf 5/10/85 (#12), pk 5/31/85 (#11, 1 wk), 5 wk; tot 19 wk.

Searls, Hank
Jaws 2 (Bantam) PW mm pb 5/8/78 (#7), pk 5/22/78 (#1, 4 wk), 17 wk; NYT mm pb 5/14/78 (#9), pk 6/4/78 (#1, 2 wk), 14 wk; tot 31 wk.
Jaws: The Revenge (Berkley) NYT pb fic 7/26/87 (#13), pk 8/2/87 (#9, 1 wk), 4 wk; PW mm pb 8/7/87 (#12, 1 wk); tot 5 wk.

Sedges, John [pseud.]
The Townsman (John Day) NYT fic 7/15/45 (#11, 1 wk).

The Long Love (John Day) NYT fic 11/27/49 (#15, 1 wk), 2 wk.

Sedgwick, Anne Douglas
The Little French Girl (Houghton) PW fic 4/18/25 (#3, 4 wk).
The Old Countess (Houghton) PW fic 5/21/27 (#2, 8 wk), 16 wk.
Dark Hester (Houghton) PW fic 5/11/29 (#2, 8 wk), 12 wk.
Philippa (Houghton) PW fic 12/20/30 (#1, 4 wk), 8 wk.

Sedgwick, Ellery
The Happy Profession (Little Brown) NYT gen 10/27/46 (#5, 3 wk), 16 wk; PW nf 11/16/46 (#7, 1 wk); tot 17 wk.
Atlantic Harvest [ed.] (Little Brown) NYT gen 11/9/47 (#14, 1 wk).

Sedgwick, Ruth Woodbury
See Katharine Cornell and_____

See, Sam
See Samuel C. Platt

Seeley, Mabel
Woman of Property (Doubleday) NYT fic 10/12/47 (#16), pk 11/2/47 (#12, 1 wk), 6 wk.
The Beckoning Door (Doubleday) NYT fic 3/5/50 (#16, 1 wk).

Segal, Erich
Love Story (Harper) NYT fic 3/1/70 (#8), pk 5/10/70 (#1, 41 wk), 62 wk; PW fic 3/16/70 (#9), pk 4/27/70 (#1, 38 wk), 61 wk; NYT pb fic 12/6/70 (#5), pk 1/3/71 (#1, 24 wk), 32 wk; tot 155 wk.
Oliver's Story (Harper) PW hc fic 3/7/77 (#5), pk 3/28/77 (#1, 5 wk), 25 wk; NYT fic 3/13/77 (#10), pk 4/10/77 (#1, 7 wk), 31 wk; (Avon) PW mm pb 3/27/78 (#4), pk 4/17/78 (#1, 1 wk), 10 wk; NYT mm pb 4/2/78 (#6), pk 4/16/78 (#1, 1 wk), 14 wk; tot 80 wk.
Man, Woman and Child (Harper) PW hc fic 5/9/80 (#14), pk 6/27/80 (#9, 1 wk), 10 wk; NYT fic 6/29/80 (#10, 1 wk), 5 wk; (Ballantine) PW mm pb 6/12/81 (#11), pk 7/3/81 (#6, 2 wk), 10 wk; NYT mm pb 6/14/81 (#13), pk 7/12/81 (#5, 1 wk), 10 wk; tot 35 wk.
The Class (Bantam) NYT fic 4/28/85 (#10), pk 2/23/86 (#3, 1 wk), 28 wk; PW hc fic 5/3/85 (#13), pk 5/17/85 (#8, 1 wk), 12 wk; PW mm pb 2/14/86 (#10), pk 2/28/86 (#2, 1 wk), 12 wk; tot 52 wk.
Doctors (Bantam) PW hc fic 7/29/88 (#11), pk 9/9/88 (#4, 2 wk), 13 wk; NYT fic 7/31/88 (#12), pk 8/14/88 (#4, 3 wk), 12 wk; NYT pb fic 8/6/89 (#5), pk 8/27/89 (#1, 1 wk), 13 wk; PW mm pb 8/11/89 (#4), pk 8/18/89 (#2, 3 wk), 11 wk; tot 49 wk.

Seghers, Anna
The Seventh Cross (Little Brown) NYT fic 10/18/42 (#14), pk 11/8/42 (#3, 1 wk), 17 wk; PW fic 10/24/42 (#3), pk 10/31/42 (#2, 1 wk), 7 wk; tot 24 wk.

Seifert, Elizabeth
Young Doctor Galahad (Aeonian) NYT fic 12/4/38 (#7, 4 wk).
A Great Day (Aeonian) NYT fic 11/5/39 (#11, 4 wk).

Seifert, Shirley
Those Who Go Against the Current (Lippincott) NYT fic 11/7/43 (#9, 1 wk), 3 wk.
Captain Grant (Lippincott) NYT fic 5/19/46 (#15, 2 wk), 3 wk.

Selberg, Ingrid
Secrets of the Deep [illus. Doreen McGuinness] (Dial) PW ch nf 8/31/90 (#2, 4 wk).

Selby, John
The Days Dividing (Putnam) NYT fic 6/22/58 (#13, 1 wk), 2 wk.

Selden, George
See George Selden Thompson

Seldes, George Henry
You Can't Print That: The Truth Behind the News (Payson & Clarke) PW nf 4/13/29 (#8), pk 5/11/29 (#7, 4 wk), 8 wk.
The Great Thoughts [comp.] (Ballantine) NYT pb nf 7/7/85 (#4, 1 wk).
Witness to a Century: Encounters with the Noted, the Notorious & the Three SOBs (Ballantine) NYT nf 8/16/87 (#7, 1 wk), 4 wk; PW hc nf 8/21/87 (#9, 2 wk), 5 wk; tot 9 wk.

Seletz, Jeanette
Hope Deferred (Macmillan) NYT fic 7/18/43 (#17, 1 wk).

Selinko, Annemarie
Desiree (Morrow) NYT fic 2/1/53 (#10), pk 3/8/53 (#1, 32 wk), 54 wk; PW fic 2/14/53 (#7), pk 3/14/53 (#1, 27 wk), 46 wk; tot 100 wk.

Sellier, Charles E., Jr.
See David Balsiger and_____

Seltzer, David
The Omen (NAL/Signet) PW mm pb 7/5/76 (#7), pk 8/9/76 (#1, 3 wk), 18 wk; NYT mm pb 7/11/76 (#7), pk 8/8/76 (#1, 6 wk), 19 wk; tot 37 wk.
Prophecy (Ballantine) PW mm pb 2/19/79 (#8, 1 wk), 5 wk.

Sendak, Maurice
Nutshell Library (Harper) NYT ch bst 5/12/63 (#4), pk 11/10/63 (#3, 26 wk), 45 wk.
Where the Wild Things Are (Harper) NYT ch bst 5/10/64 (#1, 19 wk), 94 wk.

Higglety Pigglety Pop! Or There Must Be More to Life (Harper) NYT ch bst 5/5/68 (#3, 19 wk).
In the Night Kitchen (Harper) NYT ch bst 5/2/71 (#7, 19 wk).
See also Wilhelm Grimm
See also E.T.A. Hoffmann

Seredy, Kate
Philomena (Viking) NYT ch bst 11/18/56 (#16, 40 wk).

Serling, Robert J.
The President's Plane Is Missing (Doubleday) NYT fic 11/26/67 (#10), pk 2/18/68 (#6, 3 wk), 23 wk; PW fic 12/11/67 (#11), pk 3/18/68 (#5, 1 wk), 22 wk; tot 45 wk.

Servan-Schreiber, Jean-Jacques
The American Challenge (Atheneum) NYT gen 8/4/68 (#9), pk 9/29/68 (#4, 2 wk), 18 wk; PW nf 8/12/68 (#8), pk 9/30/68 (#3, 4 wk), 17 wk; tot 35 wk.

Service, Robert W.
Ballads of a Bohemian (Barse) PW gen lit 8/6/21 (#3, 4 wk), 8 wk.

Seton, Anya
Dragonwyck (Houghton) NYT fic 3/5/44 (#13), pk 3/26/44 (#6, 1 wk), 8 wk; PW fic 3/18/44 (#10), pk 3/25/44 (#5, 1 wk), 3 wk; tot 11 wk.
The Turquoise (Houghton) NYT fic 2/24/46 (#11), pk 3/17/46 (#7, 3 wk), 10 wk; PW fic 3/9/46 (#10), pk 4/6/46 (#8, 1 wk), 2 wk; tot 12 wk.
The Hearth and the Eagle (Houghton) NYT fic 12/26/48 (#14), pk 1/30/49 (#7, 2 wk), 14 wk; PW fic 1/15/49 (#10), pk 2/12/49 (#8, 1 wk), 3 wk; tot 17 wk.
Foxfire (Houghton) NYT fic 1/21/51 (#15), pk 3/11/51 (#6, 1 wk), 13 wk; PW fic 2/17/51 (#7), pk 3/3/51 (#5, 1 wk), 4 wk; tot 17 wk.
Katherine (Houghton) NYT fic 10/17/54 (#11), pk 11/21/54 (#2, 2 wk), 29 wk; PW fic 10/30/54 (#4), pk 11/27/54 (#2, 4 wk), 22 wk; tot 51 wk.
The Winthrop Woman (Houghton) NYT fic 3/9/58 (#7), pk 3/30/58 (#2, 12 wk), 31 wk; PW fic 3/10/58 (#7), pk 4/7/58 (#2, 12 wk), 30 wk; tot 61 wk.
Devil Water (Houghton) NYT fic 3/18/62 (#12), pk 6/3/62 (#4, 1 wk), 25 wk; PW fic 3/19/62 (#10), pk 6/18/62 (#3, 1 wk), 22 wk; tot 47 wk.
Green Darkness (Houghton) NYT fic 12/17/72 (#10), pk 3/11/73 (#3, 7 wk), 25 wk; PW fic 1/8/73 (#8), pk 3/19/73 (#3, 2 wk), 21 wk; (Fawcett) NYT mm pb 3/10/74 (#7, 4 wk); tot 50 wk.

Seuss, Dr.
See Theodor Geisel

Sevareid, Eric
Not So Wild a Dream (Knopf) NYT gen
11/3/46 (#9), pk 11/24/46 (#5, 2 wk), 20 wk;
PW nf 12/7/46 (#4, 2 wk), 7 wk; tot 27 wk.
In One Ear (Knopf) NYT gen 8/10/52
(#14), pk 9/7/52 (#12, 1 wk), 7 wk.
Candidates 1960 (Basic) NYT gen 11/8/59
(#16), pk 11/15/59 (#13, 3 wk), 12 wk.

Seymour, Janette
Purity's Passion (Pocket) PW mm pb 12/5/
77 (#10, 1 wk).

**Shabad, Theodore, and Peter M.
 Stern**
The Golden Geographic Encyclopedia (Gol-
den) NYT ch bst 11/1/59 (#10, 25 wk).

Shagan, Steve
The Formula (Morrow) PW hc fic 10/15/79
(#15), pk 11/12/79 (#13, 2 wk), 8 wk; NYT fic
10/28/79 (#13), pk 12/2/79 (#11, 1 wk), 8 wk;
(Bantam) PW mm pb 8/15/80 (#11), pk 8/22/
80 (#8, 1 wk), 5 wk; NYT mm pb 8/24/80
(#6, 1 wk), 7 wk; tot 28 wk.
The Circle (Morrow) PW hc fic 8/20/82
(#14), pk 8/27/82 (#13, 1 wk), 2 wk; NYT
mm pb 5/15/83 (#12), pk 5/22/83 (#5, 1 wk),
4 wk; PW mm pb 5/20/83 (#14), pk 6/10/83
(#13, 1 wk), 3 wk; tot 9 wk.
Vendetta (Bantam) NYT pb fic 6/14/87
(#11), pk 6/21/87 (#10, 1 wk), 3 wk; PW mm
pb 6/19/87 (#15, 1 wk); tot 4 wk.

Shahan, Lynn
Living Alone & Liking It! (Stratford) PW
hc nf 7/24/81 (#12), pk 8/14/81 (#5, 3 wk),
16 wk; NYT nf 8/9/81 (#12), pk 9/6/81 (#5,
2 wk), 15 wk; tot 31 wk.

Shain, Merle
When Lovers Are Friends (Bantam) NYT
td pb 3/2/80 (#15), pk 3/9/80 (#13, 1 wk), 3
wk.

Shainess, Natalie
Sweet Suffering (Bobbs Merrill) NYT nf
6/24/84 (#14, 1 wk).

Shalett, Sidney S.
Old Nameless (Appleton) NYT gen 7/11/43
(#18), pk 7/18/43 (#13, 3 wk), 6 wk.
See also James R. Roosevelt and_____

Shannon, Elaine
Desperados (Penguin) NYT pb nf 1/28/90
(#3, 1 wk), 2 wk.

Shapiro, Irwin
The Golden Book of America [adapted by]
(Golden) NYT ch bst 11/2/58 (#3, 40 wk).

Shapiro, Lionel
The Sixth of June (Doubleday) NYT fic
8/28/55 (#14), pk 10/9/55 (#7, 1 wk), 12 wk;
PW fic 9/17/55 (#9), pk 10/15/55 (#8, 1 wk),
3 wk; tot 15 wk.

Shapley, Harlow
A Treasury of Science [ed.] (Harper) NYT
gen 11/21/43 (#22), pk 1/9/44 (#19, 1 wk), 2
wk.

Sharee, Keith
Gulliver's Fugitives (Pocket) NYT pb fic
5/13/90 (#12), pk 5/20/90 (#10, 1 wk), 2 wk;
PW mm pb 5/25/90 (#14, 1 wk); tot 3 wk.

Sharp, Margery
The Nutmeg Tree (Little Brown) PW fic
10/9/37 (#7), pk 11/13/37 (#4, 4 wk), 32 wk;
NYT fic 10/10/37 (#5, 4 wk), 12 wk; tot 44
wk.
Harlequin House (Little Brown) NYT fic
5/7/39 (#2, 4 wk), 8 wk; PW fic 6/10/39 (#8,
4 wk); tot 12 wk.
The Stone of Chastity (Little Brown) PW
fic 11/16/40 (#8, 4 wk).
Cluny Brown (Little Brown) NYT fic 9/
17/44 (#9), pk 10/1/44 (#7, 2 wk), 13 wk; PW
fic 10/14/44 (#7), pk 10/21/44 (#4, 1 wk), 3
wk; tot 16 wk.
Brittania Mews (Little Brown) NYT fic
7/21/46 (#5), pk 8/11/46 (#2, 1 wk), 17 wk;
PW fic 7/27/46 (#3), pk 8/31/46 (#2, 1 wk),
12 wk; tot 29 wk.
The Foolish Gentlewoman (Little Brown)
NYT fic 6/20/48 (#11), pk 7/11/48 (#5, 1 wk),
11 wk; PW fic 7/10/48 (#3, 1 wk), 3 wk; tot
14 wk.
The Gipsy in the Parlour (Little Brown)
NYT fic 5/9/54 (#11), pk 6/13/54 (#8, 2 wk),
10 wk; PW fic 5/22/54 (#6, 1 wk), 2 wk; tot
12 wk.
The Eye of Love (Little Brown) NYT fic
3/24/57 (#15), pk 3/31/57 (#13, 2 wk), 3 wk.
The Rescuers (Little Brown) NYT fic 1/3/
60 (#16), pk 1/17/60 (#11, 1 wk), 2 wk; (Walt
Disney Productions/Random) NYT ch hc
11/13/77 (#4, 46 wk); tot 48 wk.
Something Light (Little Brown) NYT fic
4/9/61 (#14, 1 wk), 3 wk.

Sharp, Roland Hall
*South America: Uncensored Jungles of Fas-
cism* (Longmans Green) NYT gen 8/5/45
(#16, 1 wk).

Shavelson, Melville
See Bob Hope and_____

Shaw, Charles G.
The Road to Culture (Funk & Wagnalls)
PW nf 4/18/31 (#4, 4 wk), 8 wk.

Shaw, George Bernard
Heartbreak House (Bretano) PW gen 1/31/20 (#5, 4 wk).
Back to Methuselah (Bretano) PW gen lit 8/6/21 (#4, 4 wk), 8 wk.
Intelligent Woman's Guide to Socialism and Capitalism (Bretano/Dodd) PW nf 10/27/28 (#5, 4 wk).
The Adventures of the Black Girl in Her Search for God (Dodd) PW fic 4/15/33 (#6, 4 wk), 8 wk.
Sixteen Self Sketches (Dodd) NYT gen 4/17/49 (#8, 1 wk), 6 wk.

Shaw, Irwin
The Young Lions (Random) NYT fic 10/24/48 (#5), pk 11/7/48 (#1, 4 wk), 34 wk; PW fic 11/6/48 (#4), pk 11/20/48 (#1, 4 wk), 23 wk; tot 57 wk.
The Troubled Air (Random) NYT fic 6/24/51 (#14), pk 8/12/51 (#5, 1 wk), 16 wk; PW fic 7/14/51 (#8), pk 8/11/51 (#6, 1 wk), 5 wk; tot 21 wk.
Lucy Crown (Random) NYT fic 4/8/56 (#12), pk 5/13/56 (#3, 2 wk), 18 wk; PW fic 4/28/56 (#7), pk 5/28/56 (#3, 1 wk), 11 wk; tot 29 wk.
Two Weeks in Another Town (Random) NYT fic 2/7/60 (#15), pk 3/6/60 (#3, 2 wk), 17 wk; PW fic 2/22/60 (#4, 4 wk), 12 wk; tot 29 wk.
Rich Man, Poor Man (Delacorte) NYT fic 10/11/70 (#9), pk 3/7/71 (#3, 1 wk), 33 wk; PW fic 10/26/70 (#7), pk 3/8/71 (#2, 1 wk), 33 wk; NYT pb fic 10/10/71 (#3), pk 11/14/71 (#2, 1 wk), 4 wk; (Dell) PW mm pb 2/23/76 (#7), pk 3/15/76 (#1, 5 wk), 17 wk; NYT mm pb 2/29/76 (#9), pk 3/21/76 (#1, 5 wk), 16 wk; tot 103 wk.
Evening in Byzantium (Delacorte) PW fic 4/23/73 (#8), pk 5/28/73 (#2, 1 wk), 13 wk; NYT fic 4/29/73 (#7), pk 5/27/73 (#5, 3 wk), 13 wk; (Dell) NYT mm pb 7/14/74 (#8, 4 wk); tot 30 wk.
Nightwork (Delacorte) NYT fic 11/30/75 (#10), pk 2/29/76 (#7, 3 wk), 14 wk; PW fic 12/15/75 (#10), pk 1/19/76 (#8, 1 wk), 6 wk; PW hc fic 2/2/76 (#10), pk 2/23/76 (#6, 2 wk), 7 wk; (Dell) PW mm pb 8/16/76 (#12), pk 8/30/76 (#1, 4 wk), 13 wk; NYT mm pb 8/29/76 (#9), pk 9/19/76 (#1, 1 wk), 11 wk; tot 51 wk.
Beggarman, Thief (Delacorte) PW hc fic 10/17/77 (#12), pk 11/21/77 (#6, 3 wk), 21 wk; NYT fic 10/23/77 (#12), pk 12/11/77 (#4, 3 wk), 23 wk; (Dell) PW mm pb 8/14/78 (#7), pk 8/21/78 (#3, 2 wk), 11 wk; tot 55 wk.
The Top of the Hill (Delacorte) PW hc fic 12/10/79 (#15), pk 2/22/80 (#10, 1 wk), 14 wk;

NYT fic 12/16/79 (#13), pk 2/17/80 (#7, 3 wk), 17 wk; (Dell) PW mm pb 10/24/80 (#15), pk 11/7/80 (#9, 1 wk), 4 wk; NYT mm pb 11/23/80 (#10, 1 wk), 3 wk; tot 38 wk.
Bread Upon the Waters (Delacorte) PW hc fic 9/4/81 (#13), 10/16/81 (#10, 2 wk), 13 wk; NYT fic 9/27/81 (#6, 1 wk), 13 wk; (Dell) PW mm pb 8/6/82 (#7), pk 8/13/82 (#3, 3 wk), 16 wk; NYT mm pb 8/8/82 (#6), pk 8/29/82 (#4, 4 wk), 15 wk; tot 57 wk.
Acceptable Losses (Avon) PW mm pb 9/9/83 (#12), pk 9/23/83 (#3, 2 wk), 8 wk; NYT mm pb 9/11/83 (#6), pk 9/8/83 (#3, 4 wk), 9 wk; tot 17 wk.

Shaw, Lau
Rickshaw Boy (Reynal & Hitchcock) NYT fic 8/19/45 (#14), pk 9/9/45 (#5, 1 wk), 13 wk; PW fic 9/15/45 (#9), pk 10/20/45 (#8, 1 wk), 2 wk; tot 15 wk.

Shaw, Sandy
See Durk Pearson and_____

Shaw, Thomas Edward
See Thomas Edward Lawrence

Shaw, Wilbur
Gentlemen, Start Your Engines (Coward McCann) NYT gen 7/24/55 (#15), pk 8/14/55 (#12, 1 wk), 3 wk.

Shawcross, William
Sideshow: Kissinger, Nixon and the Destruction of Cambodia (Simon & Schuster) PW hc nf 6/25/79 (#13), pk 7/2/79 (#12, 1 wk), 4 wk.

Shecter, Leonard
See Jim Bouton and_____

Sheean, Vincent
Personal History (Doubleday) PW nf 3/16/35 (#3), pk 7/13/35 (#1, 8 wk), 36 wk.
Sanfelice (Doubleday) PW fic 7/11/36 (#9), pk 8/15/36 (#5, 4 wk), 16 wk; NYT fic 8/2/36 (#2, 4 wk); tot 20 wk.
A Day of Battle (Literary Guild of America) NYT fic 9/4/38 (#5, 4 wk).
Not Peace but a Sword (Doubleday) PW nf 9/16/39 (#2, 8 wk), 16 wk; NYT gen 10/8/39 (#4, 4 wk), 12 wk; tot 28 wk.
Between the Thunder and the Sun (Random) NYT gen 4/11/43 (#12), pk 5/2/43 (#2, 3 wk), 24 wk; PW nf 4/17/43 (#3), pk 5/1/43 (#2, 1 wk), 17 wk; tot 41 wk.
This House Against This House (Random) NYT gen 4/28/46 (#13), pk 5/5/46 (#11, 1 wk), 3 wk.
Lead, Kindly Light (Random) NYT gen 7/31/49 (#10), pk 8/28/49 (#5, 1 wk), 14 wk; PW nf 8/13/49 (#9), pk 8/27/49 (#4, 1 wk), 5 wk; tot 19 wk.

Dorothy and Red (Houghton) PW nf 12/30/63 (#9), pk 1/6/64 (#7, 1 wk), 4 wk; NYT gen 1/12/64 (#8), pk 1/26/64 (#7, 1 wk), 3 wk; tot 7 wk.

Sheehan, Dr. George A.
Running and Being (Simon & Schuster) PW hc nf 5/1/78 (#14), pk 6/19/78 (#5, 1 wk), 20 wk; NYT nf 5/28/78 (#7), pk 7/16/78 (#4, 1 wk), 12 wk; tot 32 wk.

Sheehan, Neil
A Bright Shining Lie: John Paul Vann and America in Vietnam (Random) PW hc nf 10/28/88 (#15), pk 11/18/88 (#5, 1 wk), 19 wk; NYT nf 10/30/88 (#5), pk 11/13/88 (#3, 1 wk), 24 wk; tot 43 wk.

_____, et al.
The Pentagon Papers (Quadrangle) NYT pb gen 8/8/71 (#4), pk 9/12/71 (#3, 4 wk), 12 wk.

Sheehy, Gail
Passages: The Predictable Crises of Adult Life (Dutton) NYT gen 6/20/76 (#10), pk 8/29/76 (#1, 14 wk), 57 wk; PW hc nf 6/28/76 (#7), pk 8/16/76 (#1, 24 wk), 55 wk; (Bantam) NYT mm pb 6/26/77 (#10), pk 7/24/77 (#1, 5 wk), 47 wk; PW mm pb 6/27/77 (#3), pk 7/18/77 (#1, 11 wk), 45 wk; tot 204 wk.

Pathfinders (Morrow) PW hc nf 10/23/81 (#14), pk 11/27/81 (#2, 2 wk), 22 wk; NYT nf 11/8/81 (#5), pk 2/7/82 (#3, 1 wk), 21 wk; (Bantam) NYT mm pb 12/12/82 (#6, 2 wk), 6 wk; PW mm pb 12/17/82 (#4, 1 wk), 4 wk; tot 53 wk.

Sheen, Fulton John
Communism and the Conscience of the West (Bobbs Merrill) NYT gen 4/11/48 (#13, 1 wk), 2 wk.

Peace of Soul (Whittlesey) NYT gen 4/24/49 (#10), pk 7/3/49 (#2, 1 wk), 44 wk; PW nf 5/7/49 (#5), pk 10/29/49 (#2, 1 wk), 32 wk; tot 76 wk.

Lift Up Your Heart (McGraw) NYT gen 10/29/50 (#16), pk 11/26/50 (#14, 2 wk), 5 wk.

Life Is Worth Living (McGraw) NYT gen 11/8/53 (#9), pk 12/27/53 (#2, 9 wk), 32 wk; PW nf 11/28/53 (#4), pk 1/16/54 (#1, 1 wk), 27 wk; [second series] (Garden City) NYT gen 2/20/55 (#14, 1 wk); tot 64 wk.

Sheldon, Sidney
The Other Side of Midnight (Morrow) NYT fic 5/12/74 (#10), pk 6/16/74 (#9, 2 wk), 6 wk; PW fic 5/20/74 (#9), pk 6/10/74 (#6, 1 wk), 8 wk; (Dell) NYT mm pb 2/23/75 (#6), pk 8/7/77 (#2, 1 wk), 60 wk; PW mm pb 7/4/77 (#14), pk 8/15/77 (#4, 3 wk), 12 wk; tot 86 wk.

A Stranger in the Mirror (Morrow) PW hc fic 4/26/76 (#10), pk 5/17/76 (#3, 4 wk), 21 wk; NYT fic 5/2/76 (#10), pk 5/23/76 (#3, 4 wk), 21 wk; (Warner) PW mm pb 2/28/77 (#8), pk 3/14/77 (#1, 1 wk), 12 wk; NYT mm pb 3/13/77 (#4), pk 3/20/77 (#1, 1 wk), 12 wk; tot 66 wk.

Bloodline (Morrow) PW hc fic 2/6/78 (#8), pk 3/27/78 (#1, 7 wk), 38 wk; NYT fic 2/12/78 (#5), pk 3/12/78 (#1, 13 wk), 27 wk; (Warner) PW mm pb 2/5/79 (#6), pk 2/19/79 (#1, 7 wk), 31 wk; NYT mm pb 2/11/79 (#4), pk 2/25/79 (#1, 8 wk), 35 wk; tot 131 wk.

Rage of Angels (Morrow) PW hc fic 6/27/80 (#11), pk 7/25/80 (#1, 9 wk), 42 wk; NYT fic 6/29/80 (#13), pk 7/13/80 (#1, 11 wk), 42 wk; (Warner) PW mm pb 5/22/81 (#5), pk 5/29/81 (#1, 4 wk), 21 wk; NYT mm pb 5/24/81 (#1, 4 wk), 22 wk; tot 127 wk.

Master of the Game (Morrow) NYT fic 9/5/82 (#9), pk 9/12/82 (#1, 4 wk), 38 wk; PW hc fic 1/7/83 (#3), pk 3/18/83 (#2, 2 wk), 39 wk; (Warner) NYT mm pb 7/31/83 (#1, 6 wk), 27 wk; PW mm pb 8/5/83 (#2), pk 8/12/83 (#1, 6 wk), 27 wk; tot 131 wk.

If Tomorrow Comes (Morrow) NYT fic 1/27/85 (#7), pk 2/3/85 (#1, 9 wk), 36 wk; PW hc fic 2/1/85 (#9), pk 2/8/85 (#1, 11 wk), 37 wk; (Warner) NYT pb fic 12/29/85 (#3), pk 1/5/86 (#1, 2 wk), 21 wk; PW mm pb 1/10/86 (#6), pk 1/17/86 (#1, 2 wk), 18 wk; tot 112 wk.

Windmills of the Gods (Morrow) NYT fic 2/8/87 (#1, 7 wk), 32 wk; PW hc fic 2/13/87 (#1, 7 wk), 33 wk; (Warner) NYT pb fic 11/15/87 (#2), pk 11/29/87 (#1, 5 wk), 19 wk; PW mm pb 11/20/87 (#4), pk 11/27/87 (#1, 2 wk), 18 wk; tot 102 wk.

The Sands of Time (Morrow) NYT fic 11/20/88 (#1, 11 wk), 23 wk; PW hc fic 11/25/88 (#1, 10 wk), 22 wk; (Warner) NYT pb fic 11/19/89 (#2), pk 11/26/89 (#1, 6 wk), 15 wk; PW mm pb 11/24/89 (#3), pk 12/1/89 (#1, 3 wk), 13 wk; tot 73 wk.

Memories of Midnight (Morrow) NYT fic 8/26/90 (#3), pk 9/2/90 (#1, 2 wk), 19 wk; PW hc fic 8/31/90 (#2), pk 9/14/90 (#1, 1 wk), 17 wk; [read by Jenny Agutter] (Dove) PW aud fic 11/2/90 (#5, 4 wk), 8 wk; tot 44 wk.

Shellabarger, Samuel
Captain from Castile (Little Brown) NYT fic 1/28/45 (#9), pk 5/13/45 (#1, 7 wk), 51 wk; PW fic 2/10/45 (#10), pk 4/21/45 (#1, 8 wk), 35 wk; tot 86 wk.

Prince of Foxes (Little Brown) NYT fic 8/3/47 (#6), pk 8/17/47 (#2, 9 wk), 26 wk;

PW fic 8/9/47 (#5), pk 8/23/47 (#2, 9 wk), 18 wk; tot 44 wk.

The King's Cavalier (Little Brown) NYT fic 1/22/50 (#12), pk 3/5/50 (#2, 1 wk), 19 wk; PW fic 2/11/50 (#5), pk 2/25/50 (#2, 5 wk), 12 wk; tot 31 wk.

Lord Vanity (Little Brown) NYT fic 11/8/53 (#12), pk 11/29/53 (#1, 10 wk), 30 wk; PW fic 11/21/53 (#5), pk 12/12/53 (#1, 9 wk), 25 wk; tot 55 wk.

Tolbecken (Little Brown) NYT fic 9/23/56 (#13), pk 10/14/56 (#9, 1 wk), 9 wk.

Shelton, Frederick
See W.M. Kiplinger and_____

Shenkman, Richard
Legends, Lies, and Cherished Myths of American History (Morrow) PW hc nf 2/3/89 (#13, 3 wk), 4 wk; NYT nf 2/5/89 (#10), pk 4/9/89 (#6, 1 wk), 15 wk; tot 19 wk.

Shepard, Odell, and Willard Shepard
Holdfast Gaines (Macmillan) NYT fic 12/8/46 (#12), pk 1/12/47 (#5, 1 wk), 15 wk; PW fic 1/18/47 (#9), pk 1/25/47 (#5, 1 wk), 4 wk; tot 19 wk.

Jenkin's Ear (Macmillan) NYT fic 4/29/51 (#16, 1 wk).

Shepherd, Jack
The Adams Chronicles: Four Generations of Greatness (Little Brown) PW hc nf 3/1/76 (#10), pk 3/29/76 (#7, 2 wk), 7 wk; NYT gen 3/7/76 (#9), pk 3/14/76 (#8, 2 wk), 7 wk; tot 14 wk.
See also Bob Glover and_____

Shepley, James R., and Clay Blair
The Hydrogen Bomb (McKay) NYT gen 10/31/54 (#15, 1 wk).

Sher, I.H.
See Hugh Satterlee and_____

Sherman, Julie
See David R. Hackworth and_____

Sherman, Richard
The Bright Promise (Little Brown) NYT fic 9/28/47 (#13), pk 10/5/47 (#10, 1 wk), 3 wk.

Sherrod, Robert
Tarawa (Duell Sloan & Pearce) NYT gen 3/26/44 (#18), pk 4/16/44 (#5, 3 wk), 17 wk; PW nf 4/15/44 (#10), pk 5/13/44 (#5, 2 wk), 4 wk; tot 21 wk.

Sherwood, Robert Emmet
Abe Lincoln in Illinois (Scribner's) NYT gen 3/5/39 (#9, 4 wk), 8 wk.

Roosevelt and Hopkins (Harper) NYT gen 11/7/48 (#8), pk 12/19/48 (#1, 1 wk), 39 wk;

PW nf 11/27/48 (#2), pk 12/4/48 (#1, 2 wk), 21 wk; tot 60 wk.

Sherwood, Valerie
These Golden Pleasures (Warner) NYT mm pb 12/18/77 (#15), pk 12/25/77 (#13, 2 wk), 5 wk; PW mm pb 12/26/77 (#7), pk 1/16/78 (#6, 1 wk), 4 wk; tot 9 wk.

This Loving Torment (Warner) NYT mm pb 7/31/77 (#14), pk 8/21/77 (#4, 2 wk), 11 wk; PW mm pb 8/1/77 (#10), pk 8/8/77 (#7, 2 wk), 9 wk; tot 20 wk.

This Towering Passion (Warner) NYT mm pb 11/26/78 (#14), pk 1/7/79 (#13, 1 wk), 4 wk.

Her Shining Splendor (Warner) NYT mm pb 8/31/80 (#13, 2 wk).

Bold Breathless Love (Warner) NYT mm pb 8/9/81 (#15, 2 wk).

Wild, Willful Love (Warner) NYT mm pb 11/7/82 (#7), pk 11/14/82 (#6, 1 wk), 6 wk; PW mm pb 11/12/82 (#6), pk 11/19/82 (#4, 1 wk), 4 wk; tot 10 wk.

Rash Reckless Love (Warner) PW mm pb 6/11/82 (#10, 1 wk), 5 wk; NYT mm pb 6/13/82 (#8), pk 6/27/82 (#5, 1 wk), 6 wk; tot 11 wk.

Rich Radiant Love (Warner) NYT mm pb 5/29/83 (#15), pk 6/5/83 (#8, 2 wk), 7 wk; PW mm pb 6/10/83 (#8, 2 wk), 6 wk; tot 13 wk.

Lovely Lying Lips (Warner) NYT mm pb 12/4/83 (#12), pk 12/11/83 (#7, 2 wk), 5 wk; PW mm pb 12/9/83 (#10, 1 wk), 3 wk; tot 8 wk.

Born to Love (Warner) NYT pb fic 7/1/84 (#12), pk 7/22/84 (#9, 2 wk), 6 wk; PW mm pb 7/20/84 (#14, 1 wk); tot 7 wk.

Lovesong (Pocket) NYT pb fic 9/15/85 (#14), pk 9/22/85 (#8, 1 wk), 6 wk; PW mm pb 9/20/85 (#13), pk 10/4/85 (#8, 1 wk), 3 wk; tot 9 wk.

Windsong (Pocket) NYT pb fic 3/23/86 (#9, 1 wk).

Shevchenko, Arkady N.
Breaking with Moscow (Knopf) NYT nf 3/3/85 (#5), pk 3/10/85 (#2, 9 wk), 24 wk; PW hc nf 3/8/85 (#9), pk 3/29/85 (#2, 6 wk), 22 wk; (Ballantine) NYT pb nf 1/12/86 (#3, 1 wk), 6 wk; PW mm pb 1/17/86 (#12, 1 wk), 2 wk; tot 54 wk.

Shiber, Etta
Paris Underground (Scribner) NYT gen 10/10/43 (#12), pk 11/7/43 (#3, 3 wk), 20 wk; PW nf 10/23/43 (#5), pk 10/30/43 (#2, 1 wk), 11 wk; tot 31 wk.

Shilts, Randy
And the Band Played On: Politics, People and

the AIDS Epidemic (St. Martin's) PW hc nf
11/6/87 (#14), pk 11/20/87 (#9, 1 wk), 7 wk;
NYT nf 11/15/87 (#12), pk 11/22/87 (#10, 1
wk), 5 wk; tot 12 wk.

Shipler, David K.
  Russia: Broken Idols, Solemn Dreams (Times)
NYT nf 2/12/84 (#14), pk 3/4/84 (#13, 1 wk),
5 wk.

Shipp, Cameron
  See Lionel Barrymore and_____
  See Billie Burke and_____

Shirer, William Lawrence
  Berlin Diary (Knopf) PW nf 7/12/41 (#4),
pk 8/16/41 (#1, 5 wk), 11 wk.
  End of a Berlin Diary (Knopf) NYT gen
10/19/47 (#6), pk 11/2/47 (#5, 1 wk), 8 wk;
PW nf 11/15/47 (#7, 1 wk); tot 9 wk.
  Midcentury Journey (Farrar) NYT gen
10/12/52 (#15, 1 wk).
  The Rise and Fall of the Third Reich (Simon
& Schuster) NYT gen 11/6/60 (#13), pk
12/4/60 (#1, 39 wk), 80 wk; PW nf 11/7/60
(#5), pk 11/28/60 (#1, 39 wk), 78 wk; tot 158
wk.
  *The Collapse of the Third Republic: An
Inquiry into the Fall of France in 1940* (Simon
& Schuster) NYT gen 11/30/69 (#9), pk
12/14/69 (#4, 1 wk), 13 wk; PW nf 12/1/69
(#9), pk 1/19/70 (#5, 1 wk), 13 wk; tot 26 wk.
  The Nightmare Years: 1930–1940 (Little
Brown) NYT nf 6/10/84 (#14), pk 7/1/84
(#2, 1 wk), 19 wk; PW hc nf 6/15/84 (#14),
pk 7/6/84 (#4, 3 wk), 21 wk; tot 40 wk.

Shobin, David
  The Unborn (Bantam) NYT mm pb 12/20/
81 (#14), pk 12/27/81 (#13, 1 wk), 3 wk; PW
mm pb 1/1/82 (#10), pk 1/8/82 (#9, 1 wk), 2
wk; tot 5 wk.

Shortall, Leonard
  See Child Study Association of America

Shrake, Bud
  See Barry Switzer and_____
  See Willie Nelson and_____

Shriftgiesser, Karl
  *The Gentleman from Massachusetts: Henry
Cabot Lodge* (Little Brown) NYT gen 10/15/
44 (#15, 1 wk).

Shubin, Seymour
  Anyone's My Name (Simon & Schuster)
NYT fic 9/20/53 (#16, 1 wk).

Shuler, Linda Lay
  She Who Remembers (NAL/Signet) NYT
pb fic 8/20/89 (#11), pk 9/17/89 (#8, 2 wk),
12 wk; PW mm pb 8/25/89 (#11), pk 9/29/89
(#6, 1 wk), 12 wk; tot 24 wk.

Shulman, Irving
  Harlow (Geis) NYT gen 7/19/64 (#7), pk
9/27/64 (#2, 5 wk), 22 wk; PW nf 7/27/64
(#8), pk 9/28/64 (#1, 4 wk), 23 wk; tot 45
wk.

Shulman, Jeffrey
  See Robert Kennedy

Shulman, Max
  The Zebra Derby (Doubleday) NYT fic
2/3/46 (#11), pk 3/17/46 (#8, 1 wk), 11 wk.
  Sleep Till Noon (Doubleday) NYT fic 4/
30/50 (#13), pk 5/28/50 (#7, 1 wk), 19 wk;
PW fic 6/3/50 (#5, 1 wk), 3 wk; tot 22 wk.
  Rally Round the Flag, Boys! (Doubleday)
NYT fic 9/1/57 (#13), pk 11/10/57 (#2, 16
wk), 51 wk; PW fic 9/9/57 (#4), pk 10/28/57
(#2, 7 wk), 36 wk; tot 87 wk.
  I Was a Teen-Age Dwarf (Geis/Random)
NYT fic 9/20/59 (#16, 1 wk).
  Anyone Got a Match? (Harper) PW fic 11/
30/64 (#11), pk 2/1/65 (#9, 1 wk), 6 wk.

Shulman, Morton
  Anyone Can Make a Million (McGraw)
NYT pb gen 4/7/68 (#3, 8 wk), 12 wk; PW
nf 5/29/67 (#13), pk 8/21/67 (#1, 1 wk), 33
wk; NYT gen 6/18/67 (#7), pk 7/16/67 (#4,
7 wk), 30 wk; tot 75 wk.
  *How to Invest Your Money and Profit from
Inflation* (Random) NYT nf 5/4/80 (#14, 1
wk).

Shute, Nevil
  See Nevil Shute Norway

Siddons, Anne Rivers
  The House Next Door (Ballantine) PW mm
pb 11/26/79 (#9), pk 12/3/79 (#7, 1 wk), 4
wk; NYT mm pb 12/23/79 (#14), pk 12/30/
79 (#13, 1 wk), 2 wk; tot 6 wk.
  Peachtree Road (Harper) NYT fic 11/6/88
(#15), pk 11/27/88 (#14, 1 wk), 3 wk; (Ballantine) NYT pb fic 12/17/89 (#12, 1 wk), 2
wk; PW mm pb 12/22/89 (#10, 2 wk), 4 wk;
tot 9 wk.

Sidney, Hugh
  John F. Kennedy (Atheneum) NYT gen
12/22/63 (#8, 1 wk), 2 wk.

Siegel, Bernie S.
  Love, Medicine & Miracles (Harper) NYT
nf 4/5/87 (#12), pk 5/17/87 (#1, 5 wk), 56
wk; PW hc nf 5/8/87 (#14), pk 4/29/88 (#1,
3 wk), 53 wk; (Perennial) NYT pb nf 5/29/
88 (#2), pk 6/5/88 (#1, 11 wk), 117 wk; PW
td pb 6/3/88 (#4), pk 6/17/88 (#1, 9 wk), 51
wk; tot 277 wk.
  *Peace, Love and Healing: The Bodymind and
the Path to Self-Healing* (Harper) NYT msc
6/18/89 (#2), pk 7/9/89 (#1, 5 wk), 14 wk;

PW hc nf 6/23/89 (#13), pk 7/14/89 (#6, 2 wk), 15 wk; tot 29 wk.

Silberman, Charles E.
Crisis in Black and White (Random) NYT gen 7/26/64 (#10), pk 8/16/64 (#8, 3 wk), 10 wk; PW nf 8/31/64 (#8, 2 wk), 6 wk; tot 16 wk.
Crisis in the Classroom (Random) NYT gen 1/31/71 (#9, 1 wk), 2 wk.

Sills, Beverly
Bubbles: A Self-Portrait (Bobbs Merrill) PW hc nf 2/14/77 (#8, 4 wk), 9 wk; NYT gen 2/20/77 (#9, 2 wk), 5 wk; tot 14 wk.

_____, **and Lawrence Linderman**
Beverly Sills (Bantam) NYT nf 5/24/87 (#16), pk 6/14/87 (#13, 1 wk), 3 wk.

Silone, Ignazio
Bread and Wine (Harper) NYT fic 5/9/37 (#10, 4 wk).
The Seed Beneath the Snow (Atheneum) NYT fic 10/4/42 (#14, 1 wk).

Silver, James W.
Mississippi: The Closed Society (Harcourt) NYT gen 7/26/64 (#9), pk 8/16/64 (#6, 2 wk), 14 wk; PW nf 8/31/64 (#7, 2 wk), 6 wk; tot 20 wk.

Silverman, Al
See Gale Sayers and_____

Silverstein, Shel
The Giving Tree (Harper) NYT ch bst 11/7/71 (#9), pk 4/30/78 (#2, 24 wk), 140 wk.
The Missing Piece (Harper) NYT ch hc 11/13/77 (#5, 46 wk).
Where the Sidewalk Ends (Harper) NYT ch hc 4/30/78 (#4, 24 wk).
A Light in the Attic (Harper) NYT nf 11/8/81 (#2), pk 11/29/81 (#1, 14 wk), 182 wk; PW hc nf 11/20/81 (#6), pk 12/4/81 (#1, 7 wk), 45 wk; tot 227 wk.

Simkin, Colin
Currier and Ives' America [ed.] (Crown) NYT gen 11/23/52 (#15, 1 wk).

Simmons, Mary Kay
A Fire in the Blood (Pocket) NYT mm pb 6/19/77 (#11, 1 wk), 5 wk; PW mm pb 7/4/77 (#12, 2 wk), 4 wk; tot 9 wk.

Simmons, Richard
Never-Say-Diet Book (Warner) PW hc nf 1/30/81 (#15), pk 3/6/81 (#1, 8 wk), 69 wk; NYT nf 2/8/81 (#9), pk 3/8/81 (#1, 11 wk), 55 wk; PW td pb 2/5/82 (#5), pk 2/12/82 (#1, 6 wk), 29 wk; NYT td pb 2/7/82 (#6), pk 2/14/82 (#1, 5 wk), 34 wk; tot 187 wk.
Never-Say-Diet Cookbook (Warner) NYT nf 6/20/82 (#3, 3 wk), 16 wk.

Simon, Edith
The Golden Hand (Putnam) NYT fic 5/18/52 (#15), pk 6/8/52 (#7, 4 wk), 15 wk; PW fic 6/14/52 (#7, 1 wk), 3 wk; tot 18 wk.

Simon, William E.
A Time for Truth (Reader's Digest/McGraw) PW hc nf 5/22/78 (#10), pk 8/21/78 (#4, 2 wk), 33 wk; NYT nf 7/2/78 (#15), pk 8/13/78 (#3, 1 wk), 16 wk; (Berkley) PW mm pb 4/30/79 (#15, 1 wk); tot 50 wk.

Simonds, William A.
Henry Ford: His Life, His Work, His Genius (Bobbs Merrill) NYT nf 3/14/43 (#23), pk 4/11/43 (#18, 1 wk), 7 wk.

Simonov, Konstantin Mikhailovich
Days and Nights (Simon & Schuster) NYT fic 11/18/45 (#15), pk 1/6/46 (#9, 1 wk), 11 wk.

Simonson, Walt, and Archie Goodwin
Alien: The Illustrated Story (Heavy Metal Communications/Simon & Schuster) PW td pb 7/16/79 (#10), pk 7/30/79 (#9, 1 wk), 3 wk; NYT td pb 7/29/79 (#10), pk 8/5/79 (#7, 1 wk), 7 wk; tot 10 wk.

Simpson, George E., and Neal R. Burger
Ghostboat (Dell) PW mm pb 4/5/76 (#10, 1 wk), 5 wk.

Simpson, Mona
Anywhere but Here (Knopf) NYT fic 3/8/87 (#16), pk 3/29/87 (#12, 1 wk), 3 wk; PW hc fic 4/17/87 (#15, 1 wk); tot 4 wk.

Sims, Marian
Call It Freedom (Lipincott) NYT fic 7/4/37 (#7, 4 wk).
Beyond Surrender (Lippincott) NYT fic 12/27/42 (#18, 1 wk).

Sims, P. Hal
Money Contract (Simon & Schuster) PW nf 3/11/33 (#9, 4 wk).

Sinclair, Harold
The Horse Soldiers (Harper) NYT fic 4/1/56 (#15), pk 4/8/56 (#14, 1 wk), 2 wk.

Sinclair, Jo
Wasteland (Harper) NYT fic 3/10/46 (#7), pk 3/17/46 (#5, 4 wk), 14 wk; PW fic 3/23/46 (#5), pk 4/20/46 (#4, 1 wk), 4 wk; tot 18 wk.

Sinclair, May
Mary Olivier (Macmillan) PW fic 11/1/19 (#9, 4 wk).

Sinclair, Upton
Oil (Boni) PW fic 8/27/27 (#10, 4 wk).
World's End (Viking) PW fic 8/10/40 (#6, 8 wk), 12 wk.

Between Two Worlds (Viking) PW fic 5/10/41 (#10, 4 wk).

Dragon's Teeth (Viking) PW fic 3/14/42 (#10, 4 wk).

Wide Is the Gate (Viking) NYT fic 1/31/43 (#10), pk 2/7/43 (#5, 2 wk), 15 wk; PW fic 3/13/43 (#8), pk 3/20/43 (#6, 1 wk), 3 wk; tot 18 wk.

Presidential Agent (Viking) NYT fic 6/25/44 (#6, 4 wk), 13 wk; PW fic 7/15/44 (#9), pk 7/29/44 (#5, 1 wk), 4 wk; tot 17 wk.

Dragon Harvest (Viking) NYT fic 7/1/45 (#8), pk 7/22/45 (#3, 5 wk), 19 wk; PW fic 7/7/45 (#4), pk 7/21/45 (#2, 3 wk), 10 wk; tot 29 wk.

A World to Win (Viking) NYT fic 6/16/46 (#12), pk 6/23/46 (#5, 3 wk), 10 wk; PW fic 7/6/46 (#5, 1 wk), 3 wk; tot 13 wk.

Presidential Mission (Viking) NYT fic 6/8/47 (#12), pk 7/6/47 (#7, 1 wk), 10 wk; PW fic 7/19/47 (#9), pk 7/26/47 (#5, 1 wk), 2 wk; tot 12 wk.

One Clear Call (Viking) NYT fic 9/19/48 (#16), pk 10/10/48 (#6, 1 wk), 7 wk.

O Shepherd, Speak! (Viking) NYT fic 8/14/49 (#10), pk 8/21/49 (#8, 1 wk), 6 wk.

Sineno, John

The Firefighter's Cookbook (Vintage) NYT msc pb 11/16/86 (#6, 2 wk), 6 wk; PW td pb 12/12/86 (#6, 1 wk), 2 wk; tot 8 wk.

Singer, Isaac Bashevis

Zlateh the Goat (Harper) NYT ch bst 11/5/67 (#6, 26 wk).

Shosha (Farrar) PW hc fic 10/30/78 (#12, 1 wk), 5 wk; PW mm pb 6/4/79 (#14), pk 6/11/79 (#11, 1 wk), 8 wk; tot 13 wk.

Old Love (Farrar) NYT fic 1/27/80 (#15, 4 wk).

Singer, June Flaum

Debutantes (Avon) PW mm pb 8/5/83 (#14, 1 wk).

Singer, Mark

Funny Money (Knopf) NYT nf 8/4/85 (#10), pk 9/8/85 (#9, 1 wk), 8 wk.

Siple, Paul

A Boy Scout with Byrd (Putnam) PW juv 3/21/31 (#1, 16 wk), 32 wk.

Sirica, John J.

To Set the Record Straight (Norton) PW hc nf 4/23/79 (#10), pk 5/14/79 (#5, 1 wk), 18 wk; NYT nf 5/6/79 (#15), pk 5/20/79 (#6, 2 wk), 17 wk; tot 35 wk.

Sitwell, Dame Edith

Fanfare for Elizabeth (Macmillan) NYT gen 8/18/46 (#12), pk 9/8/46 (#8, 1 wk), 4 wk.

The Queens and the Hive (Atlantic Little Brown) PW nf 3/11/63 (#9, 1 wk).

Taken Care Of: The Autobiography of Edith Sitwell (Atheneum) PW nf 5/31/65 (#8, 2 wk), 8 wk; NYT gen 6/13/65 (#10), pk 6/27/65 (#8, 1 wk), 3 wk; tot 11 wk.

Sitwell, Sir Osbert Bart

Left Hand, Right Hand (Little Brown) NYT gen 7/9/44 (#14, 1 wk).

The Scarlet Tree (Little Brown) NYT gen 7/14/46 (#13), pk 8/4/46 (#6, 1 wk), 11 wk.

Laughter in the Next Room (Little Brown) NYT gen 10/31/48 (#12, 1 wk), 4 wk.

Siwoff, Seymour, Steve Hirdt and Peter Hirdt

The 1988 Elias Baseball Analyst (Collier) PW td pb 4/29/88 (#8), pk 5/6/88 (#7, 1 wk), 3 wk.

Skinner, B.F.

Beyond Freedom and Dignity (Knopf) NYT gen 10/17/71 (#6), pk 10/31/71 (#3, 2 wk), 18 wk; PW nf 11/1/71 (#4), pk 11/8/71 (#2, 1 wk), 15 wk; NYT pb gen 10/8/72 (#1, 4 wk), 8 wk; tot 41 wk.

Skinner, Cornelia Otis

Excuse It, Please! (Dodd) NYT nf 1/31/37 (#10, 4 wk).

Dithers and Jitters (Dodd) NYT gen 12/4/38 (#10), pk 1/8/39 (#9, 4 wk), 8 wk; PW nf 12/10/38 (#8, 4 wk), 8 wk; tot 16 wk.

Soap Behind the Ears (Dodd) PW nf 12/13/41 (#9, 4 wk).

Family Circle (Houghton) NYT gen 9/26/48 (#12), pk 10/31/48 (#2, 1 wk), 23 wk; PW nf 10/9/48 (#5), pk 11/6/48 (#2, 2 wk), 14 wk; tot 37 wk.

Nuts in May (Dodd) NYT gen 10/22/50 (#12), pk 11/26/50 (#4, 1 wk), 17 wk; PW nf 11/4/50 (#3, 2 wk), 9 wk; tot 26 wk.

Bottoms Up! (Dodd) NYT gen 4/17/55 (#14), pk 5/22/55 (#10, 2 wk), 13 wk; PW nf 5/14/55 (#8, 3 wk); tot 16 wk.

The Ape in Me (Houghton) NYT gen 10/18/59 (#12), pk 12/13/59 (#8, 2 wk), 15 wk; PW nf 11/16/59 (#10), pk 12/28/59 (#9, 1 wk), 3 wk; 18 wk.

The Elegant Wits and Grand Horizontals (Houghton) NYT gen 11/18/62 (#13), pk 11/25/62 (#11, 1 wk), 5 wk; PW nf 2/11/63 (#8, 1 wk); tot 6 wk.

Madame Sarah (Houghton) NYT gen 1/29/67 (#9), pk 3/12/67 (#1, 4 wk), 26 wk; PW nf 2/6/67 (#9), pk 2/27/67 (#1, 11 wk), 27 wk; tot 53 wk.

_____, and Emily Kimbrough

Our Hearts Were Young and Gay (Dodd) NYT nf 12/6/42 (#13), pk 1/17/43 (#1, 5 wk),

28 wk; PW nf 12/12/42 (#7), pk 1/23/43 (#1, 5 wk), 23 wk; tot 51 wk.

Slansky, Paul
The Clothes Have No Emperor (Simon & Schuster/Fireside) NYT pb nf 1/7/90 (#8, 1 wk), 2 wk.

Slaughter, Frank Gill
In a Dark Garden (Doubleday) NYT fic 11/10/46 (#15, 3 wk).
The Golden Isle (Doubleday) NYT fic 12/7/47 (#14, 1 wk), 2 wk.
Sangaree (Doubleday) NYT fic 10/31/48 (#15), pk 11/21/48 (#14, 2 wk), 5 wk.
The Stubborn Heart (Doubleday) NYT fic 6/25/50 (#13), pk 7/23/50 (#9, 1 wk), 12 wk; PW fic 8/12/50 (#9, 1 wk); tot 13 wk.
The Road to Bithynia (Doubleday) NYT fic 9/16/51 (#16), pk 10/7/51 (#10, 1 wk), 8 wk; PW fic 10/13/51 (#8, 1 wk); tot 9 wk.
Fort Everglades (Doubleday) NYT fic 4/15/51 (#13, 1 wk).
East Side General (Doubleday) NYT fic 5/11/52 (#16), pk 6/1/52 (#13, 1 wk), 5 wk.
The Galileans (Doubleday) NYT fic 2/1/53 (#13), pk 3/1/53 (#10, 3 wk), 12 wk; PW fic 3/14/53 (#10), pk 5/16/53 (#8, 1 wk), 2 wk; tot 14 wk.
The Song of Ruth (Doubleday) NYT fic 5/9/54 (#12), pk 6/13/54 (#5, 1 wk), 22 wk; PW fic 6/12/54 (#4, 1 wk), 6 wk; tot 28 wk.
The Healer (Doubleday) NYT fic 2/20/55 (#15), pk 4/3/55 (#6, 1 wk), 16 wk; PW fic 3/12/55 (#7, 2 wk), 5 wk; tot 21 wk.
The Scarlet Cord (Doubleday) NYT fic 3/4/56 (#16, 1 wk).
The Thorn of Arimathea (Doubleday) NYT fic 3/22/59 (#16), pk 4/12/59 (#13, 1 wk), 2 wk.
Lorena (Doubleday) NYT fic 8/30/59 (#16), pk 9/20/59 (#11, 1 wk), 4 wk.
The Crown and the Cross (World) NYT gen 4/19/59 (#16, 1 wk).

Slayden, Ellen Maury
Washington Wife (Harper) NYT gen 4/28/63 (#9, 1 wk), 2 wk; PW nf 5/6/63 (#9, 1 wk); tot 3 wk.

Slezak, Walter
What Time's the Next Swan? (Doubleday) NYT gen 12/9/62 (#16, 2 wk).

Slifer, Rosejeanne, and Louise Crittenden
The Giant Quiz Book (Crown) NYT gen 5/1/38 (#5, 4 wk), 20 wk.
The Second Giant Quiz Book (Blakiston) NYT gen 12/10/39 (#10, 4 wk).

Sloan, Alfred P., Jr.
My Ten Years with General Motors [ed.

John McDonald with Catherine Stevens] (Doubleday) PW nf 2/10/64 (#8), pk 4/27/64 (#5, 2 wk), 24 wk; NYT gen 2/16/64 (#7), pk 3/8/64 (#4, 2 wk), 22 wk; tot 46 wk.

Sloan, Wilson
The Man in the Gray Flannel Suit (Simon & Schuster) NYT fic 7/31/55 (#14), pk 9/18/55 (#3, 8 wk), 48 wk; PW fic 8/27/55 (#4), pk 9/24/55 (#1, 1 wk), 26 wk; tot 74 wk.

Slocum, William J.
See Jack Dempsey, et al.
See Michael Francis Reilly and_____

Slosser, Bob
See Howard Norton and_____

Slung, Michele
Momilies: As My Mother Used to Say... (Ballantine) NYT msc pb 5/26/85 (#8), pk 5/25/86 (#2, 1 wk), 2 wk; PW mm pb 5/31/85 (#11, 1 wk), 2 wk; tot 4 wk.
More Momilies (Ballantine) NYT msc pb 5/25/86 (#6, 1 wk).

Small, Bertrice
Skye O'Malley (Ballantine) NYT td pb 10/26/80 (#3), pk 11/2/80 (#2, 1 wk), 11 wk; PW td pb 10/31/80 (#6), pk 11/21/80 (#3, 2 wk), 6 wk; tot 17 wk.
Unconquered (Ballantine) PW td pb 1/22/82 (#8), pk 2/5/82 (#4, 1 wk), 6 wk; NYT td pb 1/24/82 (#10), pk 1/31/82 (#8, 1 wk), 9 wk; tot 15 wk.
Beloved (Ballantine) NYT td pb 7/3/83 (#9), pk 7/10/83 (#6, 1 wk), 8 wk; PW td pb 7/15/83 (#7, 3 wk), 6 wk; tot 14 wk.
All the Sweet Tomorrows (Ballantine) PW td pb 5/4/84 (#6, 1 wk), 4 wk.
This Heart of Mine (Ballantine) PW td pb 9/27/85 (#9), pk 10/11/85 (#6, 1 wk), 3 wk.
A Love for All Times (NAL/Signet) PW td pb 8/1/86 (#3, 1 wk), 2 wk.
The Spitfire (Ballantine) PW td pb 8/31/90 (#4, 1 wk), 3 wk.

Smalley, Gary, and John Trent
Love Is a Decision (Word) PW hc rel 10/5/90 (#9, 4 wk), 8 wk.
The Blessing (Pocket) PW pb rel 10/5/90 (#6), pk 11/9/90 (#3, 4 wk), 8 wk.

Smart, Charles Allen
R.F.D. (Norton) NYT nf 4/3/38 (#3, 4 wk), 8 wk; PW nf 4/9/38 (#7, 8 wk); tot 16 wk.

Smith, A.C.H.
The Dark Crystal (Holt/Owl Books) NYT td pb 1/30/83 (#13, 1 wk).

Smith, A. Merriman
Thank You, Mr. President (Harper) NYT gen 10/6/46 (#14), pk 10/13/46 (#9, 1 wk), 5 wk.

Smith, Adam

The Money Game (Random) NYT gen 6/23/68 (#5), pk 7/7/68 (#1, 42 wk), 63 wk; PW nf 6/24/68 (#7), pk 7/29/68 (#1, 24 wk), 66 wk; NYT pb gen 10/5/69 (#2), pk 11/2/69 (#1, 12 wk), 24 wk; tot 153 wk.

Supermoney (Random) NYT gen 10/15/72 (#10), pk 11/26/72 (#2, 3 wk), 22 wk; PW nf 10/23/72 (#7), pk 11/27/72 (#1, 3 wk), 21 wk; tot 43 wk.

Paper Money (Summit) PW hc nf 3/20/81 (#11), pk 4/17/81 (#4, 3 wk), 13 wk; NYT nf 3/22/81 (#13), pk 4/26/81 (#3, 2 wk), 12 wk; tot 25 wk.

Smith, Betty

A Tree Grows in Brooklyn (Harper) NYT fic 9/12/43 (#6), pk 1/2/44 (#1, 22 wk), 59 wk; PW fic 9/18/43 (#4), pk 12/11/43 (#1, 21 wk), 47 wk; tot 106 wk.

Tomorrow Will Be Better (Harper) NYT fic 9/5/48 (#11), pk 10/10/48 (#2, 4 wk), 20 wk; PW fic 9/18/48 (#8), pk 9/25/48 (#1, 5 wk), 13 wk; tot 33 wk.

Maggie-Now (Harper) NYT fic 3/2/58 (#15), pk 3/30/58 (#7, 3 wk), 15 wk; PW fic 3/31/58 (#7), pk 4/7/58 (#6, 1 wk), 5 wk; tot 20 wk.

Joy in the Morning (Harper) NYT fic 9/1/63 (#5, 3 wk), 10 wk; PW fic 9/9/63 (#8), pk 10/21/63 (#6, 1 wk), 11 wk; tot 21 wk.

Smith, Dennis

Report from Engine Co. 82 (Saturday Review) NYT gen 4/16/72 (#10), pk 5/21/72 (#4, 2 wk), 15 wk; PW nf 5/15/72 (#8), pk 6/12/72 (#4, 1 wk), 14 wk; NYT pb gen 3/11/73 (#5, 8 wk); tot 37 wk.

Firefighters (Doubleday) NYT nf 8/21/88 (#11, 2 wk), 3 wk.

Smith, Dodie

I Capture the Castle (Little Brown) NYT fic 11/14/48 (#15), pk 12/26/48 (#7, 2 wk), 20 wk; PW fic 12/18/48 (#10), pk 1/15/49 (#7, 1 wk), 3 wk; tot 24 wk.

Walt Disney's 101 Dalmatians (Golden) NYT ch bst 5/14/61 (#6, 20 wk).

Smith, Lady Eleanor

Flamenco (Bobbs Merrill) PW fic 5/16/31 (#4, 4 wk), 12 wk.

Smith, Gene

When the Cheering Stopped: The Last Years of Woodrow Wilson (Morrow) NYT gen 3/29/64 (#9), pk 4/5/64 (#7, 3 wk), 15 wk; PW nf 4/13/64 (#8), pk 6/15/64 (#7, 2 wk), 13 wk; tot 28 wk.

Smith, Gregory White

See Steven Naifeh and_____

Smith, H. Allen

Low Man on a Totem Pole (Doubleday) PW nf 9/13/41 (#4, 4 wk), 12 wk.

Life in a Putty Knife Factory (Doubleday) NYT gen 4/4/43 (#20), pk 5/23/43 (#7, 1 wk), 15 wk; PW nf 4/10/43 (#10), pk 5/15/43 (#6, 2 wk), 6 wk; tot 21 wk.

Lost in the Horse Latitudes (Doubleday) NYT gen 11/5/44 (#17), pk 11/12/44 (#8, 3 wk), 17 wk; PW nf 11/11/44 (#7, 1 wk), 3 wk; tot 20 wk.

The Desert Island Decameron [comp.] (Doubleday) NYT gen 7/22/45 (#17), pk 8/5/45 (#8, 1 wk), 12 wk; PW nf 9/15/45 (#9), pk 11/10/45 (#8, 1 wk), 3 wk; tot 15 wk.

Rhubarb (Doubleday) NYT fic 8/25/46 (#10), pk 9/1/46 (#4, 3 wk), 13 wk; PW fic 9/14/46 (#6), pk 9/21/46 (#5, 4 wk), 6 wk; tot 19 wk.

Waikiki Beachnik (Little Brown) NYT gen 4/3/60 (#12, 4 wk), 7 wk; PW nf 5/2/60 (#10, 1 wk); tot 8 wk.

See also Ira L. Smith and_____

Smith, Hedrick

The Russians (New York Times/Quadrangle) PW hc nf 2/16/76 (#7), pk 4/5/76 (#1, 1 wk), 29 wk; NYT gen 2/22/76 (#7), pk 5/2/76 (#2, 1 wk), 27 wk; (Ballantine) NYT mm pb 1/16/77 (#9), pk 2/6/77 (#7, 1 wk), 4 wk; PW mm pb 1/17/77 (#13), pk 2/7/77 (#3, 1 wk), 9 wk; tot 69 wk.

The Power Game: How Washington Really Works (Random) PW hc nf 4/15/88 (#14), pk 5/6/88 (#6, 1 wk), 9 wk; NYT nf 4/17/88 (#7, 1 wk), 10 wk; (Ballantine) PW mm pb 6/9/89 (#15), pk 6/16/89 (#14, 1 wk), 2 wk; NYT pb nf 7/9/89 (#12), pk 7/23/89 (#10, 1 wk), 2 wk; tot 23 wk.

Smith, Holland McTyeire, and Percy Finch

Coral and Brass (Scribners) NYT gen 2/20/49 (#14, 1 wk).

Smith, Howard K.

Last Train from Berlin (Knopf) PW nf 9/26/42 (#3, 2 wk), 17 wk; NYT nf 9/27/42 (#16), pk 10/11/42 (#2, 1 wk), 21 wk; tot 38 wk.

Smith, Ira L., and H. Allen Smith

Low and Inside (Doubleday) NYT gen 6/12/49 (#14), pk 7/3/49 (#11, 1 wk), 7 wk.

Smith, Jack

Spend All Your Kisses, Mr. Smith (McGraw) NYT nf 1/7/79 (#15, 1 wk).

Smith, Jeff

The Frugal Gourmet (Morrow) PW hc nf 9/14/84 (#13), pk 5/24/85 (#5, 6 wk), 61 wk; NYT msc 3/31/85 (#5), pk 5/26/85 (#1, 1 wk), 58 wk; (Ballantine) NYT msc pb 2/8/87 (#9), pk 2/22/87 (#3, 4 wk), 9 wk; PW mm pb 2/27/87 (#11, 1 wk), 5 wk; tot 133 wk.

The Frugal Gourmet Cooks American (Morrow) NYT msc 11/29/87 (#5), pk 12/13/87 (#1, 7 wk), 27 wk; PW hc nf 12/18/87 (#10), pk 1/22/88 (#4, 1 wk), 10 wk; tot 37 wk.

The Frugal Gourmet Cooks Three Ancient Cuisines: China, Greece and Rome (Morrow) NYT msc 9/10/89 (#5), pk 1/7/90 (#2, 1 wk), 17 wk; PW hc nf 9/15/89 (#11), pk 10/6/89 (#9, 1 wk), 7 wk; tot 24 wk.

The Frugal Gourmet Cooks with Wine (Morrow) PW hc nf 10/17/86 (#14), pk 2/6/87 (#3, 7 wk), 31 wk; NYT msc 11/2/86 (#5), pk 12/7/86 (#1, 13 wk), 39 wk; tot 70 wk.

The Frugal Gourmet Cooks Your Immigrant Heritage (Morrow) NYT msc 11/25/90 (#5), pk 12/2/90 (#3, 2 wk), 6 wk.

The Frugal Gourmet on Our Immigrant Ancestors (Morrow) PW hc nf 12/7/90 (#6), pk 12/14/90 (#5, 2 wk), 3 wk.

Smith, Jerome F.
The Coming Currency Collapse and What to Do About It (Books in Focus) PW hc nf 11/21/80 (#9), pk 12/26/80 (#3, 2 wk), 17 wk; NYT nf 12/14/80 (#13), pk 2/1/81 (#3, 1 wk), 15 wk; tot 32 wk.

Smith, Julia Cleaver
Morning Glory (Pocket) NYT mm pb 2/26/84 (#14, 1 wk); PW mm pb 3/2/84 (#15, 1 wk); tot 2 wk.

Smith, Lane
See Jon Scieszka

Smith, Lendon, M.D.
Feed Your Kids Right: Dr. Smith's Program for Your Child's Health (McGraw) PW hc nf 7/23/79 (#15), pk 2/22/79 (#12, 1 wk), 11 wk; NYT nf 7/29/79 (#10), pk 2/3/80 (#8, 1 wk), 15 wk; (Dell/Delta) PW td pb 5/16/80 (#8), pk 10/10/80 (#7, 1 wk), 16 wk; NYT td pb 5/25/80 (#5), pk 6/1/80 (#3, 4 wk), 29 wk; tot 71 wk.

Smith, Lillian Eugenia
Strange Fruit (Reynal & Hitchcock) NYT fic 3/19/44 (#12), pk 5/14/44 (#1, 15 wk), 62 wk; PW fic 4/8/44 (#3), pk 5/27/44 (#1, 11 wk), 34 wk; tot 96 wk.

Killers of the Dream (Norton) NYT gen 11/13/49 (#16), pk 11/20/49 (#12, 1 wk), 3 wk.

The Journey (World Almanac) NYT gen 5/16/54 (#15), pk 6/13/54 (#14, 3 wk), 6 wk.

Smith, Liz
The Mother Book (Doubleday) PW hc nf 5/29/78 (#12, 1 wk), 2 wk.

Smith, Logan Pearsall
Unforgotten Years (Little Brown) NYT gen 2/5/39 (#13, 4 wk).

Smith, Manuel J., Ph.D.
When I Say No, I Feel Guilty (Dial) NYT gen 4/20/75 (#9), pk 5/11/75 (#7, 1 wk), 4 wk; PW nf 5/5/75 (#9, 1 wk); (Bantam) NYT mm pb 1/11/76 (#10, 1 wk); tot 6 wk.

Smith, Mark
The Death of a Detective (Avon) NYT mm pb 1/18/76 (#9, 1 wk), 2 wk.

Smith, Martin Cruz
Nightwing (Harcourt/Jove) PW mm pb 6/26/78 (#15), pk 7/3/78 (#14, 1 wk), 3 wk; NYT mm pb 7/23/78 (#7, 1 wk); tot 4 wk.

Gorky Park (Random) NYT fic 4/12/81 (#11), pk 4/26/81 (#1, 2 wk), 45 wk; PW hc fic 4/17/81 (#9), pk 5/1/81 (#1, 2 wk), 42 wk; (Ballantine) PW mm pb 3/12/82 (#5), pk 3/19/82 (#1, 6 wk), 30 wk; NYT mm pb 3/14/82 (#5), pk 3/21/82 (#1, 5 wk), 27 wk; tot 144 wk.

Stallion Gate (Ballantine) NYT fic 6/8/86 (#14, 1 wk); NYT pb fic 7/12/87 (#13), pk 7/19/87 (#12, 1 wk), 3 wk; tot 4 wk.

Polar Star (Random) NYT fic 7/9/89 (#11), pk 8/6/89 (#1, 2 wk), 15 wk; PW hc fic 7/14/89 (#13), pk 9/1/89 (#1, 1 wk), 16 wk; (Ballantine) NYT pb fic 7/8/90 (#6), pk 7/22/90 (#5, 1 wk), 9 wk; PW mm pb 7/13/90 (#8), pk 7/27/90 (#4, 1 wk), 9 wk; tot 49 wk.

Smith, Richard
The Dieter's Guide to Weight Loss During Sex (Workman) NYT td pb 6/11/78 (#10), pk 7/30/78 (#1, 3 wk), 99 wk; PW td pb 6/12/78 (#6), pk 3/26/79 (#1, 1 wk), 54 wk; tot 153 wk.

The Dieter's Guide to Weight Loss After Sex (Workman) NYT td pb 6/29/80 (#12), pk 7/6/80 (#8, 1 wk), 5 wk.

Smith, Robert Kimmel
Jane's House (Pocket) NYT pb fic 1/15/84 (#15), pk 1/29/84 (#4, 1 wk), 8 wk; PW mm pb 1/27/84 (#11), pk 2/10/84 (#7, 1 wk), 6 wk; tot 14 wk.

Smith, Robert Paul
"Where Did You Go?" "Out." "What Did You Do?" "Nothing." (Norton) NYT gen 8/18/57 (#13), pk 12/15/57 (#2, 3 wk), 53 wk; PW nf 9/2/57 (#9), pk 1/6/58 (#1, 1 wk), 42 wk; tot 95 wk.

How to Do Nothing with Nobody All Alone by Yourself (Norton) NYT gen 6/8/58 (#14), pk 6/22/58 (#11, 2 wk), 6 wk; PW nf 8/18/58 (#10, 1 wk); tot 7 wk.

Smith, Sally Bedell
In All His Glory (Simon & Schuster) PW
hc nf 12/21/90 (#11, 1 wk).

Smith, Thorne
Rain in the Doorway (Doubleday) PW fic
5/13/33 (#7, 4 wk), 8 wk.
Skin and Bones (Doubleday) PW fic 2/10/
34 (#10, 4 wk).

Smith, Walter Bedell
My Three Years in Moscow (Lippincott)
NYT gen 1/22/50 (#7), pk 2/5/50 (#5, 4 wk),
10 wk; PW nf 1/28/50 (#5), pk 2/18/50 (#4,
1 wk), 4 wk; tot 14 wk.

Smith, Wilbur
Hungry as the Sea (Doubleday) PW hc fic
3/21/80 (#14), pk 4/18/80 (#10, 1 wk), 7 wk;
NYT fic 3/23/80 (#13), pk 3/30/80 (#7, 1
wk), 10 wk; (NAL/Signet) PW mm pb 2/27/
81 (#14, 2 wk); tot 19 wk.
Delta Decision (Doubleday) PW hc fic 3/6/
81 (#15), pk 3/27/81 (#11, 1 wk), 6 wk; NYT
fic 3/29/81 (#9), pk 4/12/81 (#7, 1 wk), 6 wk;
(NAL/Signet) PW mm pb 2/19/82 (#7), pk
3/5/82 (#5, 1 wk), 11 wk; NYT mm pb
2/21/82 (#8, 1 wk), 9 wk; tot 32 wk.
Flight of the Falcon (Doubleday) PW hc fic
3/12/82 (#14, 1 wk); (Fawcett/Crest) NYT
mm pb 5/29/83 (#14, 1 wk); PW mm pb
6/3/83 (#11, 1 wk), 3 wk; tot 5 wk.

Smolan, Rick, and David Cohen
A Day in the Life of America [project direc-
tors] (Harper/Collins) NYT nf 11/9/86 (#9),
pk 11/30/86 (#1, 3 wk), 54 wk; PW hc nf
11/14/86 (#10), pk 12/5/86 (#1, 3 wk), 43 wk;
tot 97 wk.
A Day in the Life of the Soviet Union [proj-
ect directors] (Collins) NYT nf 11/15/87
(#13), pk 12/13/87 (#7, 2 wk), 10 wk; PW hc
nf 11/27/87 (#10), pk 12/18/87 (#9, 2 wk), 8
wk; tot 18 wk.

Smyth, Henry D.
Atomic Energy for Military Purposes (Princeton Univ.) PW nf 11/3/45 (#5), pk 11/17/45
(#4, 1 wk), 4 wk; NYT gen 10/14/45 (#16),
pk 11/11/45 (#5, 3 wk), 14 wk; tot 18 wk.

Sneed, Sharon
See Dr. Frank Minirth, et al.

Snell, Roy Judson
The Arrow of Fire (Reilly & Lee) PW juv
7/12/30 (#10, 4 wk).
The Gray Shadow (Reilly & Lee) PW juv
7/18/31 (#9, 4 wk), 8 wk.

Snepp, Frank
Decent Interval (Random) PW hc nf 12/12/
77 (#13, 5 wk), 6 wk.

Snider, Duke, with Bill Gilbert
The Duke of Flatbush (Zebra) NYT nf
7/17/88 (#14, 1 wk), 2 wk.

Snodgrass, Melinda
The Tears of the Singers (Pocket) NYT pb
fic 9/16/84 (#15, 1 wk).

**Snow, Charles Percy [all titles as by C.P.
Snow]**
The Affair (Scribner's) NYT fic 5/29/60
(#10), pk 7/17/60 (#5, 2 wk), 23 wk; PW fic
6/6/60 (#9), pk 7/11/60 (#4, 1 wk), 16 wk; tot
39 wk.
Science and Government (Harvard Univ.)
NYT gen 5/21/61 (#16, 1 wk).
Variety of Men (Scribner) PW nf 5/22/67
(#6, 1 wk), 4 wk; NYT gen 6/11/67 (#10), pk
6/18/67 (#8, 1 wk), 3 wk; tot 7 wk.
The Sleep of Reason (Scribner) PW fic 2/17/
69 (#10, 1 wk).

Snow, Edgar
Red Star Over China (Random) NYT gen
2/6/38 (#12), pk 3/6/38 (#5, 4 wk), 8 wk; PW
nf 2/12/38 (#9), pk 3/12/38 (#6, 4 wk), 12
wk; tot 20 wk.
People on Our Side (Random) NYT gen 10/
1/44 (#19), pk 10/22/44 (#6, 1 wk), 26 wk;
PW nf 11/11/44 (#6, 1 wk), 4 wk; tot 30 wk.
The Pattern of Soviet Power (Random)
NYT gen 7/29/45 (#9), pk 8/26/45 (#5, 2
wk), 14 wk; PW nf 9/15/45 (#8, 1 wk), 2 wk;
tot 16 wk.

Snow, Edward Rowe
Famous Lighthouses of New England (Dodd)
NYT gen 1/27/46 (#16, 1 wk).
*Mysteries and Adventures Along the Atlantic
Coast* (Books for Libraries) NYT gen 1/23/
49 (#14, 1 wk).

Sobol, Donald J.
Two Flags Flying (Platt & Munk) NYT
ch bst 11/13/60 (#13, 47 wk).

Sohmer, Steve
Favorite Son (Bantam) NYT pb fic 10/30/
88 (#8), pk 11/20/88 (#4, 1 wk), 6 wk; PW
mm pb 11/18/88 (#10), pk 11/25/88 (#7, 2
wk), 4 wk; tot 10 wk.

Sokol, Julia
See Steven Carter and_____

Soldati, Mario
The Capri Letters (Knopf) NYT fic 3/4/56
(#15), pk 3/11/56 (#14, 2 wk), 5 wk.

Soles, John
See Alvin Toffler

Solomon, Neil
The Truth About Weight Control (Stein &
Day) PW nf 4/24/72 (#8), pk 5/1/72 (#7, 2

wk), 3 wk; NYT gen 6/11/72 (#9, 1 wk); tot
4 wk.

Solomon, Ruth Freeman
   The Candlesticks and the Cross (Putnam)
PW fic 6/5/67 (#10), pk 7/3/67 (#9, 3 wk),
13 wk.

Solotaroff, Theodore
   New American Review [ed.] (Bantam)
NYT pb gen 11/5/67 (#4, 4 wk), 8 wk.

Solzhenitsyn, Alexander
   One Day in the Life of Ivan Denisovich
(Dutton) PW fic 3/4/63 (#7, 1 wk), 4 wk.
   The First Circle (Harper) PW fic 9/30/68
(#10), pk 2/10/69 (#4, 1 wk), 23 wk; NYT fic
10/13/68 (#9), pk 2/9/69 (#4, 1 wk), 22 wk;
tot 45 wk.
   The Cancer Ward (Farrar) NYT pb fic 4/6/
69 (#5), pk 6/1/69 (#4, 4 wk), 12 wk.
   August 1914 (Farrar) NYT fic 9/24/72
(#5), pk 10/8/72 (#2, 8 wk), 29 wk; PW fic
9/25/72 (#6), pk 10/9/72 (#2, 6 wk), 27 wk;
(Bantam) NYT mm pb 4/14/74 (#6, 4 wk),
8 wk; tot 64 wk.
   The Gulag Archipelago (Harper) PW nf
6/24/74 (#2), pk 7/8/74 (#1, 3 wk), 15 wk;
NYT gen 6/30/74 (#6), pk 7/7/74 (#2, 8 wk),
18 wk; NYT td pb 7/14/74 (#1, 12 wk), 25 wk;
tot 58 wk.
   The Gulag Archipelago: Vol. II (Harper)
NYT td pb 2/29/76 (#5, 2 wk).

Somers, Suzanne
   Keeping Secrets: An Autobiography (Warner)
NYT nf 2/21/88 (#10), pk 3/6/88 (#6, 4 wk),
8 wk; PW hc nf 2/26/88 (#6, 2 wk), 7 wk;
NYT pb nf 10/9/88 (#9), pk 10/23/88 (#5, 1
wk), 7 wk; tot 22 wk.

Sondern, Frederick, Jr.
   Brotherhood of Evil (Farrar) NYT gen 3/
22/59 (#14), pk 4/19/59 (#6, 1 wk), 15 wk;
PW nf 4/20/59 (#10), pk 4/27/59 (#7, 2 wk),
5 wk; tot 20 wk.

Sonnichsen, Charles Leland
   Roy Bean: Law West of the Pecos (Devin
Adair) NYT nf 3/28/43 (#23, 1 wk).

Sontag, Susan
   On Photography (Farrar) NYT nf 3/5/78
(#11, 1 wk), 5 wk; PW hc nf 3/6/78 (#14), pk
3/27/78 (#10, 1 wk), 5 wk; tot 10 wk.

Sorensen, Theodore C.
   Kennedy (Harper) PW nf 10/25/65 (#8),
pk 11/15/65 (#1, 7 wk), 26 wk; NYT gen 10/
31/65 (#1, 10 wk), 24 wk; NYT pb gen
10/2/66 (#2, 12 wk); tot 62 wk.

Sorensen, Virginia Eggerston
   The Neighbors (Reynal & Hitchcock) NYT
fic 9/7/47 (#15, 2 wk), 3 wk.

Soubiran, Andre
   The Healing Oath (Putnam) NYT fic 8/22/
54 (#12), pk 9/19/54 (#10, 2 wk), 10 wk; PW
fic 10/16/54 (#10, 1 wk); tot 11 wk.
   The Doctors (Putnam) NYT fic 12/6/53
(#13), pk 1/17/54 (#8, 3 wk), 17 wk; PW fic
1/23/54 (#4, 2 wk), 3 wk; tot 20 wk.

Soukhanov, Anne H.
   *Webster's II: New Riverside University Dic-
tionary* [ed.] (Houghton) NYT msc 8/26/84
(#5), pk 9/16/84 (#2, 2 wk), 10 wk.

**Southern, Terry, and Mason Hoffen-
berg**
   Candy (Putnam) PW fic 6/1/64 (#10), pk
6/29/64 (#2, 4 wk), 35 wk; NYT fic 5/31/64
(#9), pk 9/13/64 (#2, 4 wk), 35 wk; tot 70
wk.

Spada, James
   Grace: The Secret Lives of a Princess (Dou-
bleday/Dolphin) NYT nf 5/24/87 (#13), pk
6/7/87 (#9, 1 wk), 9 wk; PW hc nf 5/29/87
(#12), pk 6/26/87 (#9, 1 wk), 8 wk; (Dell)
NYT pb nf 5/8/88 (#10), pk 5/22/88 (#2, 1
wk), 4 wk; PW mm pb 5/20/88 (#15, 1 wk);
tot 22 wk.

Spafford, Julian, and Lucien Esty
   Ask Me Another (Viking) PW nf 3/19/27
(#6), pk 5/21/27 (#1, 4 wk), 24 wk.

Spargo, John
   Bolshevism (Harper) PW gen 7/5/19 (#4,
4 wk), 12 wk.

Spark, Muriel
   The Mandelbaum Gate (Knopf) PW fic
12/6/65 (#12, 1 wk).

**Spaulding, Charles F., and Otis
Carney**
   Love at First Flight (Houghton) NYT gen
10/17/43 (#16, 1 wk), 2 wk.

Speakes, Larry, and Robert Pack
   *Speaking Out: The Reagan Presidency from
Inside the White House* (Scribner) NYT nf
5/1/88 (#15), pk 5/22/88 (#6, 2 wk), 7 wk;
PW hc nf 5/6/88 (#10), pk 6/10/88 (#8, 1
wk), 8 wk; tot 15 wk.

Speare, Elizabeth George
   The Witch of Blackbird Pond (Houghton)
NYT ch bst 5/10/59 (#8), pk 11/1/59 (#7, 25
wk), 63 wk.
   The Bronze Bow (Houghton) NYT ch bst
5/13/62 (#4), pk 11/11/62 (#2, 26 wk), 45 wk.

Special Study Group
   *Report from Iron Mountain on the Possibil-
ity and Desirability of Peace* [intro. by Leonard
C. Lewis] (Dial) PW nf 12/4/67 (#10), pk

2/12/68 (#9, 2 wk), 6 wk; NYT gen 12/24/67 (#6, 2 wk), 7 wk; tot 13 wk.

Spectorsky, Auguste C.
The Exurbanites (Lippincott) NYT gen 11/20/55 (#13), pk 12/11/55 (#11, 1 wk), 12 wk.
The Book of the Sea (Grosset & Dunlap) NYT gen 1/9/55 (#14, 1 wk).

Speer, Albert
Inside the Third Reich (Macmillan) NYT gen 8/23/70 (#8), pk 9/20/70 (#3, 14 wk), 31 wk; PW nf 8/31/70 (#6), pk 1/4/71 (#1, 1 wk), 33 wk; NYT pb gen 11/14/71 (#3, 8 wk), 16 wk; tot 80 wk.
Spandau: The Secret Diaries (Macmillan) NYT gen 3/14/76 (#9), pk 4/18/76 (#3, 1 wk), 15 wk; PW hc nf 3/15/76 (#9), pk 5/3/76 (#3, 1 wk), 15 wk; tot 30 wk.

Spellenberg, Richard
The Audubon Society Field Guide to North American Wildflowers: Western Region (Knopf) NYT td pb 9/2/79 (#14, 1 wk).

Spellman, Cardinal Francis Joseph
The Foundling (Scribner) NYT fic 6/10/51 (#13), pk 7/8/51 (#5, 2 wk), 17 wk; PW fic 7/14/51 (#6), pk 7/28/51 (#3, 1 wk), 9 wk; tot 26 wk.

Spellman, Cathy Cash
So Many Partings (Dell) PW mm pb 6/22/84 (#12), pk 7/20/84 (#9, 1 wk), 7 wk; NYT pb fic 6/24/84 (#11), pk 7/1/84 (#9, 1 wk), 6 wk; tot 13 wk.

Spence, Hartzell
One Foot in Heaven (Whittlesey) PW nf 3/15/41 (#9, 4 wk).
Get Thee Behind Me (Whittlesey) NYT nf 10/11/42 (#18), pk 10/25/42 (#14, 3 wk), 8 wk; PW nf 11/14/42 (#6, 1 wk), 3 wk; tot 11 wk.

Spence, Jonathan D.
The Search for Modern China (Norton) NYT nf 6/17/90 (#12, 1 wk), 3 wk.

Spencer, Elizabeth
The Voice at the Back Door (McGraw) NYT fic 2/3/57 (#16, 1 wk).
The Light in the Piazza (McGraw) NYT fic 1/15/61 (#16), pk 1/29/61 (#14, 1 wk), 3 wk); PW fic 2/6/61 (#5, 1 wk); tot 4 wk.

Spencer, John Wallace
Limbo of the Lost (Bantam) NYT pb gen 11/11/73 (#5, 4 wk).

Spencer, LaVyrle
The Gamble (Jove) NYT pb fic 3/15/87 (#8, 1 wk), 4 wk; PW mm pb 3/27/87 (#11), pk 4/3/87 (#8, 1 wk), 3 wk; tot 7 wk.
Vows (Jove) NYT pb fic 4/3/88 (#9), pk 4/10/88 (#6, 1 wk), 7 wk; PW mm pb 4/15/88

(#8), pk 4/22/88 (#5, 1 wk), 6 wk; tot 13 wk.
Spring Fancy (Jove) NYT pb fic 9/10/89 (#12, 1 wk), 3 wk; PW mm pb 9/22/89 (#10, 1 wk), 2 wk; tot 5 wk.
Morning Glory (Putnam) PW hc fic 3/24/89 (#12, 2 wk), 7 wk; NYT fic 3/26/89 (#13), pk 4/16/89 (#12, 1 wk), 5 wk; (Jove) NYT pb fic 3/11/90 (#3, 3 wk), 8 wk; PW mm pb 3/16/90 (#13), pk 4/6/90 (#4, 1 wk), 7 wk; tot 27 wk.
The Hellion (Jove) NYT pb fic 3/12/89 (#11), pk 4/2/89 (#8, 1 wk), 4 wk; PW mm pb 3/17/89 (#11, 2 wk), 4 wk; tot 8 wk.
The Endearment (Jove) NYT pb fic 8/12/90 (#8), pk 8/19/90 (#4, 2 wk), 7 wk; PW mm pb 8/17/90 (#8), pk 8/24/90 (#5, 1 wk), 7 wk; tot 14 wk.
Bittersweet (Putnam) NYT fic 3/4/90 (#12), pk 4/1/90 (#5, 1 wk), 10 wk; PW hc fic 3/9/90 (#10), pk 3/16/90 (#5, 1 wk), 10 wk; tot 20 wk.

Spencer, Scott
Endless Love (Avon) PW mm pb 11/7/80 (#15), pk 9/4/81 (#5, 1 wk), 12 wk; NYT mm pb 8/9/81 (#10), pk 8/23/81 (#4, 2 wk), 9 wk; tot 21 wk.

Sperber, A.M.
Murrow: His Life and Times (Freundlich Kampmann) NYT nf 7/20/86 (#13), pk 8/24/86 (#9, 1 wk), 10 wk; PW hc nf 9/19/86 (#15, 2 wk); tot 12 wk.

Spicer, Bart
Act of Anger (Atheneum) NYT fic 9/2/62 (#10), pk 9/30/62 (#9, 2 wk), 16 wk; PW fic 9/3/62 (#10), pk 9/10/62 (#8, 3 wk), 13 wk; tot 29 wk.

Spielberg, Steven
Close Encounters of the Third Kind (Dell) PW mm pb 12/12/77 (#10), pk 1/16/78 (#1, 1 wk), 13 wk; NYT mm pb 12/25/77 (#6), pk 1/8/78 (#1, 1 wk), 16 wk; tot 29 wk.

Spier, Peter
Noah's Ark (Doubleday) NYT ch hc 4/30/78 (#15, 24 wk).

Spillane, Mickey
Kiss Me, Deadly (Dutton) NYT fic 11/9/52 (#12), pk 11/16/52 (#11, 1 wk), 7 wk.

Spink, John George Taylor
Judge Landis and 25 Years of Baseball (Crowell) NYT gen 8/3/47 (#16), pk 8/10/47 (#15, 5 wk), 6 wk.

Spodnik, Jean Perry, and Barbara Gibbons
The 35-Plus Diet for Women (Harper) PW hc nf 8/14/87 (#12), pk 9/4/87 (#9, 1 wk), 5

wk; NYT msc 8/30/87 (#5), pk 9/6/87 (#3, 1 wk), 6 wk; tot 11 wk.

Spring, Howard
My Son, My Son! (Viking) NYT fic 7/3/38 (#3), pk 9/4/38 (#2, 8 wk), 32 wk; PW fic 7/9/38 (#5), pk 10/15/38 (#1, 8 wk), 36 wk; tot 68 wk.
Fame Is the Spur (Viking) PW fic 1/11/41 (#6, 4 wk), 12 wk.
Dunkerley's (Harper) NYT fic 2/23/47 (#13, 1 wk).
There Is No Armour (Harper) NYT fic 4/3/49 (#14, 1 wk).
The Houses in Between (Harper) NYT fic 5/18/52 (#8), pk 7/20/52 (#2, 3 wk), 37 wk; PW fic 6/7/52 (#5), pk 8/9/52 (#2, 2 wk), 23 wk; tot 60 wk.
A Sunset Touch (Harper) NYT fic 11/1/53 (#16, 1 wk).
These Lovers Fled Away (Harper) NYT fic 10/30/55 (#13), pk 11/6/55 (#9, 2 wk), 11 wk.
Time and the Hour (Harper) NYT fic 3/16/58 (#10), pk 4/6/58 (#8, 1 wk), 7 wk; PW fic 4/21/58 (#10, 1 wk); tot 8 wk.
All the Day Long (Harper) NYT fic 3/20/60 (#11, 4 wk), 10 wk; PW fic 4/18/60 (#10, 1 wk); tot 11 wk.
I Met a Lady (Harper) NYT fic 12/17/61 (#11, 1 wk), 7 wk.

Spyri, Johanna
See Charles Tritten

Stabler, Ken, and Berry Stainback
Snake: The Candid Autobiography of Football's Most Outrageous Renegade (Doubleday) NYT nf 9/28/86 (#10), pk 10/5/86 (#4, 1 wk), 8 wk; PW hc nf 10/3/86 (#13), pk 10/17/86 (#9, 1 wk), 6 wk; (Charter) NYT pb nf 11/15/87 (#7, 1 wk); tot 15 wk.

Staff of the New York Times
The End of a Presidency (Bantam) NYT mm pb 9/8/74 (#7, 4 wk).

Stafford, Jean
Boston Adventure (Harcourt) NYT fic 10/22/44 (#15, 1 wk), 2 wk.
The Catherine Wheel (Harcourt) NYT fic 2/3/52 (#13, 1 wk), 2 wk.

Stafford, Tim
See Dave Dravecky and_____

Staffs of the Longview (Washington) Daily News and the Bellevue (Washington) Journal American
Volcano (Madrona) NYT td pb 8/31/80 (#8, 3 wk), 6 wk.

Stainback, Berry
See Ken Stabler and_____

Stallings, Laurence
The First World War [ed.] (Simon & Schuster) PW nf 9/16/33 (#7), pk 10/14/33 (#4, 4 wk), 20 wk.

Stallone, Sylvester
The Official "Rocky" Scrapbook (Grosset & Dunlap/Today) NYT td pb 7/31/77 (#5), pk 8/14/77 (#3, 1 wk), 2 wk.

Standish, Robert
See Digby George Gerahty

Stanford, Sally
The Lady of the House (Putnam) NYT gen 3/27/66 (#10), pk 4/10/66 (#8, 1 wk), 2 wk; PW nf 4/4/66 (#9), pk 4/11/66 (#7, 1 wk), 6 wk; tot 8 wk.

Stanger, Margaret
That Quail, Robert (Lippincott) NYT gen 12/25/66 (#10, 4 wk); PW nf 12/26/66 (#10), pk 2/20/67 (#8, 1 wk), 7 wk; tot 11 wk.

Stanwell-Fletcher, Theodora Cope
Driftwood Valley (Little Brown) NYT gen 9/22/46 (#13), pk 11/10/46 (#11, 1 wk), 9 wk.

Stanwood, Brooks
The Glow (Fawcett/Crest) PW mm pb 9/5/80 (#12, 1 wk).

Stark, George W.
City of Destiny: The Story of Detroit (Arnold Powers) NYT gen 12/12/43 (#22), pk 1/16/44 (#11, 3 wk), 8 wk.

Starling, Col. Edmund, and Thomas Sugrue
Starling of the White House (Simon & Schuster) NYT gen 3/17/46 (#4), pk 3/24/46 (#2, 7 wk), 19 wk; PW nf 3/23/46 (#3), pk 4/13/46 (#1, 1 wk), 15 wk; tot 34 wk.

Starr, John
The Dark Side of the Dream (Warner) NYT mm pb 7/3/83 (#15), pk 7/31/83 (#13, 1 wk), 4 wk; PW mm pb 7/8/83 (#11, 2 wk), 4 wk; tot 8 wk.

Stassen, Harold
Where I Stand (Doubleday) NYT gen 12/14/47 (#16), pk 4/18/48 (#11, 1 wk), 2 wk.

Stassinopoulos, Arianna
Maria Callas: The Woman Behind the Legend (Simon & Schuster) PW hc nf 3/27/81 (#12), pk 4/10/81 (#6, 3 wk), 13 wk; NYT nf 4/5/81 (#10), pk 5/24/81 (#6, 1 wk), 14 wk; (Ballantine) NYT mm pb 2/28/82 (#14, 1 wk); tot 28 wk.

State Department
Peace and War: 1931–1941 (Government Printing Office) NYT nf 2/14/43 (#17, 1 wk).

Statler, Oliver
Japanese Inn (Random) NYT gen 2/19/61 (#15), pk 4/2/61 (#5, 1 wk), 23 wk; PW nf 3/6/61 (#7), pk 4/3/61 (#4, 1 wk), 15 wk; tot 38 wk.

Stearn, Jess
The Sixth Man (Doubleday) NYT gen 4/30/61 (#12), pk 6/18/61 (#8, 1 wk), 13 wk.
Edgar Cayce—The Sleeping Prophet (Doubleday) PW nf 2/27/67 (#9), pk 4/17/67 (#2, 1 wk), 31 wk; NYT gen 3/12/67 (#8), pk 4/16/67 (#3, 2 wk), 30 wk; NYT pb gen 2/4/68 (#2, 8 wk), 24 wk; tot 85 wk.

Steed, Hal
Georgia: An Unfinished State (Ryerson) NYT nf 8/9/42 (#16), pk 2/14/43 (#10, 1 wk), 9 wk.

Steegmuller, Francis
The Grand Mademoiselle (Farrar) NYT gen 2/12/56 (#15, 1 wk).

Steel, Danielle
The Promise (Dell) PW mm pb 5/22/78 (#8), pk 5/29/78 (#5, 1 wk), 19 wk; NYT mm pb 5/28/78 (#5, 2 wk), 12 wk; tot 31 wk.
Summer's End (Dell) PW mm pb 8/13/79 (#13), pk 8/20/79 (#10, 3 wk), 7 wk; NYT mm pb 8/19/79 (#10, 2 wk), 3 wk; tot 10 wk.
To Love Again (Dell) NYT mm pb 1/20/80 (#8, 2 wk), 6 wk; PW mm pb 1/25/80 (#14), pk 2/8/80 (#9, 1 wk), 6 wk; tot 12 wk.
The Ring (Delacorte) NYT fic 11/2/80 (#13), pk 11/16/80 (#11, 1 wk), 6 wk; (Dell) PW mm pb 9/11/81 (#10), pk 10/2/81 (#2, 2 wk), 10 wk; NYT mm pb 9/13/81 (#3), pk 9/20/81 (#2, 4 wk), 10 wk; tot 26 wk.
Loving (Dell) PW mm pb 9/12/80 (#14), pk 10/3/80 (#4, 2 wk), 9 wk; NYT mm pb 9/14/80 (#13), pk 9/21/80 (#7, 1 wk), 10 wk; tot 19 wk.
Remembrance (Delacorte) PW hc fic 10/30/81 (#12), pk 11/27/81 (#6, 1 wk), 21 wk; NYT fic 11/1/81 (#12), pk 12/6/81 (#6, 3 wk), 22 wk; (Dell) NYT mm pb 4/17/83 (#9), pk 5/1/83 (#2, 4 wk), 14 wk; PW mm pb 4/22/83 (#10), pk 5/13/83 (#1, 1 wk), 12 wk; tot 69 wk.
Palomino (Dell) PW td pb 4/17/81 (#4), pk 5/1/81 (#2, 1 wk), 16 wk; NYT td pb 4/19/81 (#7), pk 5/3/81 (#1, 2 wk), 25 wk; NYT mm pb 12/12/82 (#15), pk 1/2/83 (#6, 2 wk), 8 wk; PW mm pb 12/17/82 (#12), pk 12/24/82 (#3, 1 wk), 7 wk; tot 56 wk.
Once in a Lifetime (Dell) PW td pb 4/9/82 (#7), pk 5/21/82 (#1, 2 wk), 20 wk; NYT td pb 4/11/82 (#8), pk 4/18/82 (#1, 1 wk), 23 wk; NYT mm pb 12/4/83 (#15), pk 12/18/83 (#2, 4 wk), 14 wk; PW mm pb 12/9/83 (#14), pk 12/23/83 (#2, 4 wk), 12 wk; tot 69 wk.

A Perfect Stranger (Dell) PW mm pb 2/12/82 (#7), pk 2/19/82 (#2, 3 wk), 14 wk; NYT mm pb 2/14/82 (#1, 1 wk), 15 wk; tot 29 wk.
Crossings (Delacorte) PW hc fic 9/24/82 (#12), pk 10/15/82 (#4, 2 wk), 22 wk; NYT fic 9/26/82 (#10), pk 10/17/82 (#5, 3 wk), 24 wk; (Dell) NYT pb fic 3/11/84 (#2, 5 wk), 27 wk; PW mm pb 3/16/84 (#3), pk 3/23/84 (#2, 5 wk), 21 wk; tot 94 wk.
Thurston House (Dell) NYT td pb 7/10/83 (#2), pk 7/17/83 (#1, 9 wk), 23 wk; PW td pb 7/15/83 (#2), pk 7/22/83 (#1, 13 wk), 22 wk; NYT pb fic 7/8/84 (#15), pk 7/22/84 (#1, 2 wk), 16 wk; PW mm pb 7/13/84 (#3), pk 7/27/84 (#2, 4 wk), 17 wk; tot 78 wk.
Changes (Delacorte) PW hc fic 9/9/83 (#11), pk 9/30/83 (#2, 6 wk), 29 wk; NYT fic 9/11/83 (#6), pk 9/18/83 (#2, 6 wk), 28 wk; (Dell) pb fic 11/4/84 (#3), pk 11/18/84 (#1, 4 wk), 22 wk; PW mm pb 11/9/84 (#3), pk 11/23/84 (#1, 5 wk), 17 wk; tot 96 wk.
Full Circle (Delacorte) PW hc fic 5/25/84 (#14), pk 6/15/84 (#1, 3 wk), 21 wk; NYT fic 5/27/84 (#3), pk 6/3/84 (#1, 4 wk), 20 wk; (Dell) NYT pb fic 6/9/85 (#2), pk 6/23/85 (#1, 3 wk), 21 wk; PW mm pb 6/14/85 (#3), pk 7/12/85 (#1, 2 wk), 18 wk; tot 80 wk.
Secrets (Delacorte) NYT fic 10/27/85 (#4), pk 11/3/85 (#3, 4 wk), 30 wk; PW hc fic 11/1/85 (#5), pk 11/15/85 (#3, 2 wk), 20 wk; (Dell) NYT pb fic 11/2/86 (#1, 2 wk), 9 wk; PW mm pb 11/7/86 (#5), pk 11/14/86 (#1, 2 wk), 14 wk; tot 73 wk.
Family Album (Delacorte) PW hc fic 3/8/85 (#13), pk 4/5/85 (#1, 3 wk), 22 wk; NYT fic 3/10/85 (#2), pk 3/31/85 (#1, 4 wk), 23 wk; (Dell) NYT pb fic 3/2/86 (#3), pk 3/9/86 (#1, 5 wk), 17 wk; PW mm pb 3/7/86 (#5), pk 3/21/86 (#1, 2 wk), 13 wk; tot 75 wk.
Wanderlust (Delacorte) PW hc fic 7/18/86 (#14), pk 8/1/86 (#1, 3 wk), 28 wk; NYT fic 7/20/86 (#1, 4 wk), 28 wk; (Dell) NYT pb fic 7/12/87 (#1, 5 wk), 14 wk; PW mm pb 7/17/87 (#1, 2 wk), 13 wk; tot 83 wk.
Kaleidoscope (Delacorte) NYT fic 10/25/87 (#1, 5 wk), 26 wk; PW hc fic 10/30/87 (#6), pk 11/6/87 (#1, 4 wk), 25 wk; (Dell) NYT pb fic 11/6/88 (#1, 4 wk), 16 wk; PW mm pb 11/11/88 (#1, 3 wk), 13 wk; tot 80 wk.
Fine Things (Delacorte) NYT fic 3/22/87 (#2), pk 3/29/87 (#1, 9 wk), 26 wk; PW hc fic 3/27/87 (#3), pk 4/3/87 (#1, 10 wk), 26 wk; (Dell) NYT pb fic 3/13/88 (#1, 7 wk), 19 wk; PW mm pb 3/18/88 (#1, 6 wk), 17 wk; tot 88 wk.
Zoya (Delacorte) NYT fic 5/15/88 (#1, 7 wk), 23 wk; PW hc fic 5/20/88 (#2), pk 5/27/88 (#1, 6 wk), 23 wk; (Dell) NYT pb fic

7/9/89 (#1, 2 wk), 13 wk; PW mm pb 7/14/89 (#1, 2 wk), 12 wk; tot 71 wk.

Star (Delacorte) NYT fic 2/26/89 (#1, 4 wk), 17 wk; PW hc fic 3/3/89 (#1, 4 wk), 20 wk; (Dell) NYT pb fic 2/25/90 (#1, 4 wk), 12 wk; PW mm pb 3/2/90 (#1, 5 wk), 10 wk; tot 59 wk.

Daddy (Delacorte) NYT fic 11/19/89 (#2), pk 11/26/89 (#1, 7 wk), 22 wk; PW hc fic 11/24/89 (#2), pk 12/1/89 (#1, 6 wk), 19 wk; (Dell) NYT pb fic 10/21/90 (#2), pk 10/28/90 (#1, 2 wk), 11 wk; PW mm pb 10/26/90 (#2), pk 11/2/90 (#1, 2 wk), 9 wk; tot 61 wk.

Message from Nam (Delacorte) NYT fic 6/24/90 (#2, 9 wk), 18 wk; PW hc fic 6/29/90 (#2, 8 wk), 18 wk; tot 36 wk.

Steel, Ronald
Walter Lippmann and the American Century (Atlantic Little Brown) PW hc nf 10/3/80 (#14), pk 10/24/80 (#12, 2 wk), 7 wk; NYT nf 11/2/80 (#15, 1 wk); tot 8 wk.

Steele, Shelby
The Content of Our Character (St. Martin's) NYT nf 11/4/90 (#16, 1 wk).

Steele, Wilbur Daniel
That Girl from Memphis (Doubleday) NYT fic 7/15/45 (#19), pk 7/22/45 (#9, 2 wk), 9 wk; PW fic 8/11/45 (#10, 1 wk); tot 10 wk.

Steen, Marguerite
The Sun Is My Undoing (Viking) NYT fic 8/9/42 (#14), pk 3/14/43 (#9, 1 wk), 11 wk; PW fic 9/13/41 (#6), pk 11/15/41 (#2, 4 wk), 44 wk; tot 55 wk.

Bell Timson (Doubleday) NYT fic 8/25/46 (#7, 2 wk), 7 wk.

Twilight on the Floods (Doubleday) NYT fic 8/21/49 (#7), pk 9/11/49 (#1, 1 wk), 16 wk; PW fic 8/27/49 (#3, 3 wk), 11 wk; tot 27 wk.

The Bulls of Parral (Doubleday) NYT fic 12/12/54 (#16), pk 1/2/55 (#13, 1 wk), 5 wk.

Steffens, Lincoln
The Autobiography of Lincoln Steffens (Harcourt) PW nf 4/23/32 (#10), pk 6/11/32 (#7, 16 wk), 20 wk.

Stegner, Wallace Earl
One Nation (Houghton) NYT gen 1/13/46 (#12, 1 wk).

A Shooting Star (Viking) NYT fic 6/11/61 (#12), pk 7/2/61 (#7, 1 wk), 11 wk; PW fic 7/10/61 (#9), pk 7/17/61 (#8, 1 wk), 5 wk; tot 16 wk.

All the Little Live Things (Viking) NYT fic 9/3/67 (#9, 1 wk); PW fic 9/11/67 (#10, 1 wk); tot 2 wk.

Angle of Repose (Doubleday) NYT fic 5/

23/71 (#8, 1 wk); PW fic 5/24/71 (#9, 1 wk); tot 2 wk.

Collected Stories of Wallace Stegner (Random) NYT fic 4/15/90 (#15), pk 5/20/90 (#14, 1 wk), 3 wk.

Stehling, Wendy
Thin Thighs in 30 Days (Bantam) NYT td pb 6/6/82 (#13), pk 8/22/82 (#1, 5 wk), 70 wk; PW td pb 6/18/82 (#8), pk 10/8/82 (#1, 1 wk), 59 wk; tot 129 wk.

Steichen, Edward
The Family of Man (Simon & Schuster) NYT gen 6/12/55 (#16), pk 8/14/55 (#3, 7 wk), 38 wk; PW nf 7/2/55 (#8), pk 8/27/55 (#3, 1 wk), 21 wk; tot 59 wk.

Steig, William
Sylvester and the Magic Pebble (Simon & Schuster) NYT ch bst 5/24/70 (#4, 21 wk).

The Amazing Bone (Farrar) NYT ch hc 11/13/77 (#15, 46 wk).

Abel's Island (Farrar) NYT ch hc 11/13/77 (#12, 46 wk).

Shrek (Farrar/Di Capua) PW ch pic 11/30/90 (#10, 4 wk).

Stein, Gertrude
The Autobiography of Alice B. Toklas (Harcourt) PW nf 10/14/33 (#10, 4 wk).

Wars I Have Seen (Random) NYT gen 4/22/45 (#13, 1 wk), 2 wk.

Stein, Jean, with George Plimpton
Edie: An American Biography [eds.] (Knopf) PW hc nf 7/23/82 (#13), pk 8/27/82 (#5, 1 wk), 14 wk; NYT nf 8/1/82 (#11), pk 9/5/82 (#5, 2 wk), 12 wk; tot 26 wk.

Stein, Laura
The Bloomingdale's Eat Healthy Diet (St. Martin's) PW hc nf 5/2/86 (#11), pk 5/16/86 (#7, 1 wk), 4 wk.

Steinbeck, John
Of Mice and Men (Covici Friede) NYT fic 4/4/37 (#7), pk 5/9/37 (#3, 4 wk), 20 wk; PW fic 4/10/37 (#7), pk 6/12/37 (#4, 4 wk), 24 wk; tot 44 wk.

The Long Valley (Viking) NYT fic 11/6/38 (#8, 4 wk).

The Grapes of Wrath (Viking) NYT fic 5/7/39 (#1, 16 wk), 32 wk; PW fic 5/13/39 (#4), pk 6/10/39 (#1, 28 wk), 56 wk; tot 88 wk.

The Moon Is Down (Viking) PW fic 4/11/42 (#1, 12 wk), 20 wk; NYT fic 8/9/42 (#4, 1 wk), 14 wk; tot 34 wk.

Cannery Row (Viking) NYT fic 1/21/45 (#9), pk 3/4/45 (#2, 2 wk), 28 wk; PW fic 1/27/45 (#5), pk 2/17/45 (#2, 2 wk), 12 wk; tot 40 wk.

The Wayward Bus (Viking) NYT fic 3/9/47 (#6), pk 3/16/47 (#2, 7 wk), 18 wk; PW fic 3/15/47 (#6), pk 5/3/47 (#1, 2 wk), 14 wk; tot 32 wk.

The Pearl (Viking) NYT fic 12/21/47 (#11, 2 wk), 7 wk.

East of Eden (Viking) NYT fic 10/5/52 (#6), pk 11/2/52 (#1, 11 wk), 39 wk; PW fic 10/11/52 (#5), pk 11/1/52 (#1, 8 wk), 31 wk; (Penguin) PW td pb 3/6/81 (#8), pk 3/20/81 (#3, 5 wk), 11 wk; NYT td pb 3/8/81 (#2, 2 wk), 16 wk; tot 97 wk.

A Russian Journal [photos by Robert Capa] (Vinking) NYT gen 5/9/48 (#9, 1 wk), 5 wk.

Sweet Thursday (Viking) NYT fic 6/27/54 (#8), pk 7/25/54 (#3, 9 wk), 25 wk; PW fic 7/10/54 (#5), pk 8/7/54 (#3, 4 wk), 16 wk; tot 41 wk.

The Short Reign of Pippin IV (Viking) NYT fic 5/5/57 (#9), pk 5/12/57 (#7, 7 wk), 17 wk; PW fic 5/13/57 (#6, 4 wk), 12 wk; tot 29 wk.

The Winter of Our Discontent (Viking) NYT fic 7/9/61 (#6), pk 7/16/61 (#5, 10 wk), 23 wk; PW fic 7/10/61 (#6), pk 8/21/61 (#3, 3 wk), 20 wk; tot 43 wk.

Travels with Charley: In Search of America (Viking) NYT gen 8/12/62 (#15), pk 10/21/62 (#1, 9 wk), 43 wk; PW nf 8/27/62 (#8), pk 10/29/62 (#1, 22 wk), 57 wk; tot 100 wk.

_____, **and Chase Horton**

The Acts of King Arthur and His Noble Knights: From the Winchester Mss. of Thomas Malory and Other Sources (Ballantine/Del Rey) PW td pb 1/23/78 (#6), pk 1/30/78 (#5, 1 wk), 5 wk; NYT td pb 3/5/78 (#11, 2 wk), 6 wk; tot 11 wk.

Steinberg, Alan
See Dave Pallone and_____

Steinem, Gloria
Outrageous Acts and Everyday Rebellions (Holt) PW hc nf 9/30/83 (#12), pk 10/7/83 (#10, 2 wk), 11 wk; NYT nf 10/2/83 (#13), pk 10/30/83 (#10, 2 wk), 11 wk; (NAL/Plume) PW td pb 9/21/84 (#8, 1 wk), 2 wk; tot 24 wk.

Marilyn (Holt) NYT nf 1/18/87 (#15), pk 2/22/87 (#9, 1 wk), 7 wk.

Steiner, Barry
Pay Less Tax Legally, 1981 Edition (NAL) PW td pb 2/27/81 (#10), pk 3/6/81 (#5, 1 wk), 4 wk.

Pay Less Tax Legally [1982] (NAL) PW td pb 2/19/82 (#10), pk 2/26/82 (#7, 3 wk), 6 wk.

Pay Less Tax Legally [1986] (NAL/Signet) PW td pb 2/21/86 (#10), pk 2/28/86 (#6, 1 wk), 6 wk.

Steiner, Jean-Francois
Treblinka (Simon & Schuster) NYT gen 6/18/67 (#10), pk 6/25/67 (#7, 1 wk), 3 wk; PW nf 7/17/67 (#10, 1 wk); tot 4 wk.

Stenso, Martha O.
The Stone Field (Dodd) NYT fic 4/4/37 (#10, 4 wk).

Stern, Gladys Bronwyn
Debonair (Knopf) PW fic 5/26/28 (#7, 4 wk).

The Rueful Mating (Knopf) PW fic 8/13/32 (#7, 4 wk).

The Woman in the Hall (Macmillan) NYT fic 6/11/39 (#5, 4 wk).

The Young Matriarch (Macmillan) NYT fic 1/24/43 (#23, 1 wk).

Stern, Jane and Michael Stern
Elvis World (Knopf) NYT nf 8/30/87 (#15, 1 wk).

Stern, Michael
No Innocence Abroad (Random) NYT gen 6/7/53 (#14, 1 wk).

Stern, Peter M.
See Theodore Shabad and_____

Stern, Philip Maurice
The Great Treasury Raid (Random) NYT gen 3/22/64 (#9, 2 wk), 4 wk.

The Rape of the Taxpayer (Random) PW nf 4/23/73 (#8), pk 4/30/73 (#7, 1 wk), 3 wk.

Stern, Philip Van Doren
The Drums of Morning (Doubleday) NYT fic 9/6/42 (#9), pk 9/27/42 (#5, 1 wk), 16 wk; PW fic 10/10/42 (#9, 1 wk); tot 17 wk.

Stettinius, Edward Reilly, Jr.
Lend-Lease: Weapon for Victory (Macmillan) NYT gen 2/6/44 (#15), pk 3/5/44 (#9, 1 wk), 6 wk.

Roosevelt and the Russians (Doubleday) NYT gen 12/18/49 (#16, 2 wk).

Stevens, Catherine
See Alfred P. Sloan, Jr., et al.

Stevens, Edmund
Russia Is No Riddle (Greenberg) NYT gen 4/15/45 (#20), pk 5/6/45 (#12, 1 wk), 13 wk.

Stevenson, Adlai Ewing
Major Campaign Speeches of Adlai E. Stevenson (Random) NYT gen 12/28/52 (#14), pk 6/28/53 (#3, 1 wk), 20 wk; PW nf 5/16/53 (#9), pk 5/23/53 (#5, 3 wk), 5 wk; tot 25 wk.

Call to Greatness (Harper) NYT gen 9/12/54 (#7), pk 10/3/54 (#3, 6 wk), 19 wk; PW nf 10/16/54 (#3, 1 wk), 7 wk; tot 26 wk.

What I Think (Harper) NYT gen 3/18/56 (#15), pk 4/22/56 (#12, 1 wk), 5 wk.

Friends and Enemies (Harper) NYT gen 4/12/59 (#13), pk 4/26/59 (#10, 3 wk), 5 wk.

Stevenson, James
See Jack Prelutsky

Stevenson, William
Strike Zion! (Bantam) NYT pb gen 8/6/67 (#5, 8 wk).
90 Minutes to Entebbe (Bantam) PW mm pb 8/23/76 (#11), pk 9/6/76 (#8, 1 wk), 7 wk; NYT mm pb 9/5/76 (#10, 1 wk); tot 8 wk.
A Man Called Intrepid: The Secret War (Harcourt) NYT gen 3/28/76 (#10), pk 8/15/76 (#3, 1 wk), 34 wk; PW hc nf 4/5/76 (#10), pk 6/21/76 (#3, 5 wk), 32 wk; (Ballantine) PW mm pb 4/11/77 (#8), pk 4/18/77 (#6, 3 wk), 10 wk; NYT mm pb 4/17/77 (#8), pk 4/24/77 (#6, 2 wk), 10 wk; tot 86 wk.
Intrepid's Last Case (Ballantine) NYT pb nf 10/14/84 (#8), pk 10/21/84 (#3, 1 wk), 5 wk; PW mm pb 11/2/84 (#12, 1 wk), 2 wk; tot 7 wk.

Stewart, Donald Ogden
Parody Outline of History (Doran) PW nf 5/13/22 (#8, 4 wk).
Perfect Behavior (Doran) PW gen lit 1/27/23 (#12), pk 3/17/23 (#5, 4 wk), 20 wk.

Stewart, Edward
Privileged Lives (Dell) NYT pb fic 3/12/89 (#10), pk 3/19/89 (#8, 2 wk), 5 wk; PW mm pb 3/17/89 (#14), pk 3/31/89 (#12, 2 wk), 4 wk; tot 9 wk.

Stewart, Fred Mustard
The Mannings (Bantam) NYT mm pb 9/8/74 (#8, 4 wk).
Century (Morrow) NYT fic 2/22/81 (#10), pk 3/29/81 (#3, 4 wk), 18 wk; PW hc fic 3/13/81 (#13), pk 4/10/81 (#7, 1 wk), 12 wk; (NAL/Signet) NYT mm pb 3/14/82 (#15), pk 3/21/82 (#7, 1 wk), 9 wk; PW mm pb 3/19/82 (#13), pk 3/26/82 (#9, 4 wk), 8 wk; tot 47 wk.
Ellis Island (Morrow) NYT fic 2/20/83 (#10), pk 1/15/84 (#5, 1 wk), 19 wk; PW hc fic 3/4/83 (#14), pk 3/11/83 (#8, 1 wk), 10 wk; (NAL/Signet) PW mm pb 1/13/84 (#13), pk 1/27/84 (#6, 1 wk), 8 wk; tot 37 wk.
The Titan (Pocket) NYT pb fic 2/16/86 (#15), pk 2/23/86 (#14, 1 wk), 2 wk; NYT fic 3/10/85 (#12, 1 wk), 2 wk; tot 4 wk.

Stewart, George Rippey
Storm (Random) PW fic 1/17/42 (#8, 4 wk).
Names on the Land (Random) NYT gen 5/27/45 (#13), pk 7/15/45 (#6, 1 wk), 12 wk.
Fire (Random) NYT fic 4/25/48 (#16), pk 5/23/48 (#8, 1 wk), 11 wk.

Stewart, James B.
The Partners: Inside America's Most Powerful Law Firms (Simon & Schuster) NYT nf 4/3/83 (#14), pk 4/10/83 (#13, 2 wk), 3 wk; PW hc nf 4/22/83 (#14), pk 4/29/83 (#13, 1 wk), 4 wk; tot 7 wk.

Stewart, Jimmy
Jimmy Stewart and His Poems (Crown) NYT fic 9/24/89 (#10), pk 10/15/89 (#3, 2 wk), 17 wk; PW hc fic 9/29/89 (#12), pk 11/3/89 (#3, 1 wk), 16 wk; (Random) PW aud nf 12/7/90 (#8, 4 wk); tot 37 wk.

Stewart, Marjabelle Young, and Ann Buchwald
White Gloves and Party Manners (R.B. Luce) NYT ch bst 11/6/66 (#2, 26 wk).

Stewart, Martha
Martha Stewart's Christmas (Potter) PW hc nf 11/3/89 (#12), pk 12/15/89 (#5, 2 wk), 10 wk; NYT nf 11/5/89 (#4), pk 11/19/89 (#1, 3 wk), 9 wk; tot 19 wk.

Stewart, Mary
Nine Coaches Waiting (Mill Morrow) NYT fic 3/1/59 (#13), pk 7/19/59 (#7, 1 wk), 27 wk; PW fic 5/18/59 (#9), pk 6/1/59 (#8, 3 wk), 7 wk; tot 34 wk.
My Brother Michael (Morrow) NYT fic 4/24/60 (#15), pk 5/8/60 (#10, 1 wk), 9 wk.
The Ivy Tree (Mill Morrow) NYT fic 1/14/62 (#12), pk 3/4/62 (#6, 2 wk), 19 wk; PW fic 1/29/62 (#9), pk 3/12/62 (#6, 2 wk), 15 wk; tot 34 wk.
The Moon-Spinners (Mill) PW fic 1/28/63 (#8), pk 2/18/63 (#5, 5 wk), 20 wk; NYT fic 4/7/63 (#5, 2 wk), 10 wk; tot 30 wk.
This Rough Magic (Mill Morrow) NYT fic 8/23/64 (#9), pk 11/29/64 (#2, 1 wk), 30 wk; PW fic 9/7/64 (#8), pk 11/2/64 (#1, 1 wk), 31 wk; tot 61 wk.
Airs Above the Ground (Mill Morrow) PW fic 10/11/65 (#7), pk 11/29/65 (#2, 1 wk), 23 wk; NYT fic 10/24/65 (#7), pk 10/31/65 (#3, 3 wk), 21 wk; tot 44 wk.
The Gabriel Hounds (Mill Morrow) NYT fic 10/1/67 (#7), pk 10/29/67 (#1, 1 wk), 25 wk; PW fic 10/2/67 (#10), pk 10/30/67 (#1, 2 wk), 26 wk; tot 51 wk.
The Crystal Cave (Morrow) NYT fic 7/5/70 (#7), pk 8/9/70 (#2, 14 wk), 35 wk; PW fic 7/20/70 (#7), pk 8/24/70 (#2, 12 wk), 33 wk; NYT pb fic 8/8/71 (#3), pk 9/12/71 (#1, 4 wk), 16 wk; tot 84 wk.
The Hollow Hills (Morrow) NYT fic 7/15/73 (#10), pk 9/9/73 (#1, 11 wk), 35 wk; PW fic 7/23/73 (#10), pk 9/24/73 (#1, 7 wk), 30 wk; (Fawcett) NYT mm pb 8/11/74 (#2, 4 wk); tot 69 wk.

Touch Not the Cat (Morrow) PW hc fic 8/2/76 (#9), pk 9/6/76 (#2, 2 wk), 22 wk; NYT fic 8/8/76 (#9), pk 10/10/76 (#2, 1 wk), 23 wk; (Fawcett/Crest) PW mm pb 8/15/77 (#15), pk 8/22/77 (#3, 3 wk), 8 wk; NYT mm pb 8/21/77 (#11), pk 9/4/77 (#3, 1 wk), 10 wk; tot 63 wk.

The Last Enchantment (Morrow) PW hc fic 7/30/79 (#12), pk 9/3/79 (#1, 3 wk), 30 wk; NYT fic 8/12/79 (#8), pk 9/9/79 (#1, 4 wk), 30 wk; (Fawcett/Crest) PW mm pb 7/4/80 (#11), pk 7/11/80 (#5, 1 wk), 8 wk; NYT mm pb 7/13/80 (#10), pk 8/10/80 (#6, 1 wk), 10 wk; tot 78 wk.

The Wicked Day (Morrow) PW hc fic 10/28/83 (#15), pk 12/9/83 (#5, 1 wk), 19 wk; NYT fic 11/20/83 (#10), pk 1/1/84 (#5, 2 wk), 16 wk; (Fawcett/Crest) NYT pb fic 8/26/84 (#9), pk 9/9/84 (#2, 4 wk), 9 wk; PW mm pb 8/31/84 (#8), pk 9/28/84 (#4, 1 wk), 8 wk; tot 52 wk.

Thornyhold (Fawcett/Crest) NYT pb fic 12/3/89 (#10), pk 12/17/89 (#6, 2 wk), 7 wk; PW mm pb 12/8/89 (#9), pk 12/15/89 (#8, 1 wk), 5 wk; tot 12 wk.

Stiers, David Ogden
See Tom Clancy
See Colleen McCullough

Stillman, Dr. Irwin Maxwell, and Samm Sinclair Baker
The Doctor's Quick Inches Off Diet (Prentice Hall) NYT gen 10/12/69 (#8, 1 wk).

The Doctor's Quick Weight Loss Diet (Prentice Hall) NYT gen 6/30/68 (#10), pk 7/14/68 (#7, 5 wk), 17 wk; PW nf 7/22/68 (#9), pk 8/19/68 (#7, 1 wk), 11 wk; NYT pb gen 10/6/68 (#2), pk 11/3/68 (#1, 12 wk), 76 wk; tot 104 wk.

Stillman, William
See John Fricke, et al.

Stilwell, Joseph W.
The Stilwell Papers (Sloane) NYT gen 6/13/48 (#14), pk 7/4/48 (#5, 1 wk), 17 wk; PW nf 7/3/48 (#5, 2 wk), 5 wk; tot 22 wk.

Stimpson, George William
A Book About a Thousand Things (Harper) NYT fic 9/1/46 (#14, 1 wk), 3 wk.

Stimson, Henry L., and McGeorge Bundy
On Active Service in Peace and War (Harper) NYT gen 5/9/48 (#14), pk 5/30/48 (#6, 2 wk), 8 wk; PW nf 5/15/48 (#10), pk 6/19/48 (#7, 1 wk), 4 wk; tot 10 wk.

Stine, R.L.
The Stepsister (Pocket/Archway) PW ch yn ad 11/30/90 (#2, 8 wk).

Stinetorf, Louise A.
White Witch Doctor (Westminster) NYT fic 8/13/50 (#12), pk 8/27/50 (#6, 1 wk), 9 wk; PW fic 9/16/50 (#5, 1 wk), 2 wk; tot 11 wk.

Stobaugh, Roger, and Daniel Yergin
Energy Future: The Report of the Harvard Business School Energy Project [eds.] (Random) PW hc nf 8/27/79 (#12), pk 9/17/79 (#8, 3 wk), 16 wk; NYT nf 9/23/79 (#14), pk 11/11/79 (#8, 1 wk), 9 wk; tot 25 wk.

Stock, Gregory
Love & Sex: The Book of Questions (Workman) PW td pb 6/5/87 (#8), pk 6/19/87 (#1, 9 wk), 44 wk; NYT msc pb 6/14/87 (#5), pk 7/5/87 (#1, 8 wk), 25 wk; tot 69 wk.

Stockley, Cynthia
Ponjola (Putnam) PW fic 5/26/23 (#11, 4 wk).

Stockman, David A.
The Triumph of Politics: Why the Reagan Revolution Failed (Harper) NYT nf 5/11/86 (#1, 2 wk), 12 wk; PW hc nf 5/16/86 (#3), pk 5/23/86 (#1, 1 wk), 10 wk; tot 22 wk.

Stockton, J. Roy
The Gashouse Gang (Morrow) NYT gen 5/27/45 (#18), pk 7/15/45 (#15, 1 wk), 3 wk.

Stockwell, John
In Search of Enemies: A CIA Story (Norton) PW hc nf 6/19/78 (#15, 1 wk).

Stoddard, Lothrop
Revolt Against Civilization (Scribner) PW gen lit 10/14/22 (#11, 8 wk), 12 wk.

Stoll, Clifford
The Cuckoo's Egg: Tracking a Spy Through the Maze of Computer Espionage (Doubleday) NYT nf 2/4/90 (#8), pk 3/18/90 (#6, 1 wk), 16 wk; PW hc nf 2/9/90 (#14), pk 3/9/90 (#8, 1 wk), 10 wk; (Pocket) NYT pb nf 12/2/90 (#7), pk 12/9/90 (#4, 2 wk), 5 wk; tot 31 wk.

Stone, I.F.
The Trial of Socrates (Little Brown) NYT nf 4/10/88 (#10, 1 wk), 9 wk.

Stone, Irving
Lust for Life (Longmans Green) PW fic 11/10/34 (#9), pk 12/15/34 (#8, 4 wk), 12 wk.

Sailor on Horseback (Houghton) NYT gen 10/9/38 (#10), pk 11/6/38 (#3, 4 wk), 8 wk; PW nf 10/15/38 (#8), pk 11/12/38 (#7, 4 wk), 12 wk; tot 20 wk.

They Also Ran (Doubleday) NYT gen 6/20/43 (#14), pk 6/27/43 (#8, 3 wk), 9 wk.

Immortal Wife (Doubleday) NYT fic 10/15/44 (#11), pk 1/14/45 (#2, 2 wk), 53 wk;

PW fic 11/11/44 (#7), pk 1/20/45 (#2, 4 wk), 32 wk; tot 85 wk.

Adversary in the House (Doubleday) NYT fic 10/19/47 (#14), pk 10/26/47 (#7, 2 wk), 7 wk; PW fic 11/15/47 (#8, 1 wk); tot 8 wk.

Earl Warren: A Great American Story (Prentice Hall) NYT gen 9/19/48 (#15, 1 wk).

The Passionate Journey (Doubleday) NYT fic 10/16/49 (#16), pk 11/27/49 (#9, 1 wk), 7 wk.

The President's Lady (Doubleday) NYT fic 10/14/51 (#15), pk 1/20/52 (#3, 3 wk), 33 wk; PW fic 11/10/51 (#5), pk 11/17/51 (#3, 3 wk), 15 wk; tot 48 wk.

Love Is Eternal (Doubleday) NYT fic 9/5/54 (#16), pk 10/17/54 (#1, 11 wk), 39 wk; PW fic 9/18/54 (#9), pk 10/23/54 (#1, 13 wk), 33 wk; tot 72 wk.

Men to Match My Mountains (Doubleday) NYT gen 10/21/56 (#13), pk 11/25/56 (#3, 6 wk), 27 wk; PW nf 11/5/56 (#8), pk 11/26/56 (#2, 1 wk), 24 wk; tot 51 wk.

The Agony and the Ecstasy (Doubleday) NYT fic 4/2/61 (#10), pk 4/23/61 (#1, 27 wk), 83 wk; PW fic 4/3/61 (#7), pk 5/1/61 (#1, 28 wk), 78 wk; tot 161 wk.

Those Who Love (Doubleday) NYT fic 10/31/65 (#7), pk 12/5/65 (#2, 14 wk), 39 wk; PW fic 11/1/65 (#8), pk 12/6/65 (#2, 12 wk), 41 wk; tot 80 wk.

The Passions of the Mind (Doubleday) NYT fic 3/28/71 (#7), pk 4/25/71 (#1, 13 wk), 31 wk; PW fic 4/5/71 (#4), pk 5/3/71 (#1, 13 wk), 31 wk; NYT pb fic 6/11/72 (#5, 4 wk); tot 66 wk.

The Greek Treasure (Doubleday) NYT fic 10/26/75 (#10), pk 12/28/75 (#2, 2 wk), 24 wk; PW fic 10/27/75 (#8), pk 11/10/75 (#3, 7 wk), 22 wk; (NAL/Signet) PW mm pb 11/15/76 (#13), pk 12/6/76 (#9, 1 wk), 10 wk; NYT mm pb 11/28/76 (#10), pk 12/19/76 (#8, 1 wk), 2 wk; tot 58 wk.

The Origin: A Biographical Novel of Charles Darwin (Doubleday) PW hc fic 8/22/80 (#13), pk 9/5/80 (#6, 1 wk), 26 wk; NYT fic 8/31/80 (#12), pk 9/28/80 (#4, 1 wk), 24 wk; (NAL/Plume) PW td pb 8/21/81 (#10), pk 9/4/81 (#9, 1 wk), 3 wk; NYT td pb 8/30/81 (#9), pk 9/6/81 (#8, 1 wk), 6 wk; tot 59 wk.

Depths of Glory (Doubleday) PW hc fic 10/11/85 (#14), pk 11/8/85 (#11, 2 wk), 8 wk; NYT fic 10/20/85 (#14), pk 11/3/85 (#11, 1 wk), 4 wk; tot 12 wk.

Stone, Jeffrey Allen Joseph
See Mary Jane Frances Meara, et al.

Stone, Robert
A Flag for Sunrise (Knopf) NYT fic 11/22/81 (#9, 1 wk); PW hc fic 12/4/81 (#14), pk 1/15/82 (#12, 2 wk), 6 wk; (Ballantine) PW mm pb 12/24/82 (#13, 2 wk); tot 9 wk.

Stong, Phillip Duffield
State Fair (Century) PW fic 6/11/32 (#9), pk 8/13/32 (#8, 4 wk), 12 wk.

Stranger's Return (Harcourt) PW fic 8/12/33 (#10, 8 wk).

Buckskin Breeches (Farrar) PW fic 5/8/37 (#10, 4 wk); NYT fic 5/9/37 (#7, 4 wk); tot 8 wk.

Marta of Muscovy (Doubleday) NYT gen 9/2/45 (#15, 1 wk).

Stout, Rex
Too Many Cooks (Farrar) NYT fic 10/9/38 (#13, 4 wk).

The Illustrious Dunderheads [ed.] (Knopf) NYT nf 10/25/42 (#12), pk 11/1/42 (#10, 2 wk), 3 wk.

Stowe, Leland
No Other Road to Freedom (Knopf) PW nf 10/11/41 (#7, 4 wk), 8 wk.

They Shall Not Sleep (Knopf) NYT gen 2/6/44 (#20), pk 4/23/44 (#4, 2 wk), 24 wk; PW nf 3/18/44 (#7), pk 3/25/44 (#4, 1 wk), 6 wk; tot 30 wk.

While Time Remains (Knopf) NYT gen 9/15/46 (#8), pk 10/6/46 (#5, 2 wk), 10 wk; PW nf 10/5/46 (#4, 1 wk), 5 wk; tot 15 wk.

Strachey, Lytton
Queen Victoria (Harcourt) PW gen lit 9/3/21 (#3), pk 11/12/21 (#2, 4 wk), 24 wk; PW nf 4/1/22 (#4, 4 wk), 16 wk; tot 40 wk.

Books and Characters (Harcourt) PW nf 8/26/22 (#8, 4 wk); gen lit 9/16/22 (#9, 4 wk), 8 wk; tot 12 wk.

Elizabeth and Essex (Harcourt) PW nf 2/16/29 (#1, 8 wk), 20 wk.

Strassels, Paul N., with Robert Wool
All You Need to Know About the IRS: A Taxpayer's Guide (Random) PW hc nf 2/29/80 (#12), 4/18/80 (#2, 2 wk), 14 wk; NYT nf 3/9/80 (#10), pk 4/6/80 (#2, 1 wk), 12 wk; tot 26 wk.

All You Need to Know About the IRS: A Taxpayer's Guide, 1981 Edition (Random) PW hc nf 2/27/81 (#15), pk 3/20/81 (#13, 1 wk), 3 wk; NYT nf 3/29/81 (#7, 2 wk), 7 wk; tot 10 wk.

Stratton-Porter, Gene
Her Father's Daughter (Doubleday) PW fic 11/12/21 (#1, 4 wk), 12 wk.

The White Flag (Doubleday) PW fic 9/15/23 (#3, 8 wk).

The Magic Garden (Doubleday) PW fic 4/23/27 (#6), pk 5/21/27 (#5, 4 wk), 12 wk.

Straub, Peter

Ghost Story (Coward McCann) PW hc fic 4/23/79 (#11), pk 5/21/79 (#8, 1 wk), 19 wk; NYT fic 4/29/79 (#12), pk 5/27/79 (#7, 1 wk), 19 wk; (Pocket) PW mm pb 4/11/80 (#4), pk 4/18/80 (#2, 1 wk), 16 wk; NYT mm pb 4/13/80 (#11), pk 5/4/80 (#2, 2 wk), 21 wk; tot 75 wk.

Shadowland (Berkley) PW mm pb 11/13/81 (#8), pk 11/20/81 (#2, 2 wk), 12 wk; NYT mm pb 11/15/81 (#5), pk 11/22/81 (#2, 4 wk), 13 wk; tot 25 wk.

Floating Dragon (Putnam) PW hc fic 2/11/83 (#10), pk 3/11/83 (#5, 2 wk), 12 wk; NYT fic 2/13/83 (#14), pk 2/27/83 (#5, 2 wk), 9 wk; (Berkley) NYT pb fic 3/11/84 (#8), pk 3/25/84 (#5, 2 wk), 8 wk; PW mm pb 3/16/84 (#11), pk 3/23/84 (#10, 2 wk), 5 wk; tot 34 wk.

Koko (Dutton) PW hc fic 9/30/88 (#11), pk 10/14/88 (#6, 2 wk), 9 wk; NYT fic 10/2/88 (#13), pk 10/16/88 (#6, 1 wk), 8 wk; (NAL/Signet) PW mm pb 11/3/89 (#10), pk 11/17/89 (#4, 1 wk), 7 wk; NYT pb fic 11/5/89 (#8), pk 11/26/89 (#4, 1 wk), 7 wk; tot 31 wk.

Mystery (Dutton) PW hc fic 1/12/90 (#15), pk 1/26/90 (#8, 1 wk), 4 wk; NYT fic 1/21/90 (#10, 1 wk), 3 wk; tot 7 wk.

See also Stephen King and_____

Strauss, Lewis L.

Men and Decisions (Doubleday) NYT gen 7/29/62 (#9), pk 8/26/62 (#5, 1 wk), 15 wk; PW nf 8/6/62 (#9), pk 9/3/62 (#6, 2 wk), 7 wk; tot 22 wk.

Street, James Howell

Tap Roots (Dial) NYT fic 8/9/42 (#10), pk 8/30/42 (#8, 3 wk), 22 wk; PW fic 9/12/42 (#9, 1 wk), 2 wk; tot 24 wk.

By Valour and Arms (Dial) NYT fic 10/8/44 (#11), pk 10/29/44 (#9, 1 wk), 6 wk.

The Gauntlet (Doubleday) NYT fic 11/11/45 (#11), pk 12/2/45 (#5, 3 wk), 17 wk; PW fic 12/8/45 (#5, 1 wk), 4 wk; tot 21 wk.

Mingo Dabney (Dial) NYT fic 3/19/50 (#16), pk 4/2/50 (#14, 1 wk), 4 wk.

The High Calling (Doubleday) NYT fic 7/1/51 (#13), pk 9/9/51 (#8, 1 wk), 17 wk; PW fic 8/11/51 (#8, 1 wk), 2 wk; tot 19 wk.

The Velvet Doublet (Doubleday) NYT fic 1/25/53 (#15), pk 2/8/53 (#8, 2 wk), 12 wk; PW fic 2/14/53 (#10), pk 3/14/53 (#9, 1 wk), 2 wk; tot 14 wk.

_____, and James Childers

Tomorrow We Reap (Dial) NYT fic 7/17/49 (#13), pk 8/14/49 (#8, 1 wk), 8 wk; PW fic 9/17/49 (#10, 1 wk); tot 9 wk.

Streeter, Edward

That's Me All Over, Mable (Stokes) PW fic 5/3/19 (#4, 4 wk).

Dere Mable (Stokes) PW fic 5/3/19 (#5, 4 wk).

Daily Except Sunday (Simon & Schuster) NYT nf 1/8/39 (#6, 4 wk).

Father of the Bride (Simon & Schuster) NYT fic 6/5/49 (#12), pk 7/24/49 (#2, 7 wk), 30 wk; PW fic 7/2/49 (#4), pk 8/6/49 (#1, 3 wk), 20 wk; tot 50 wk.

Mr. Hobbs' Vacation (Harper) NYT fic 6/13/54 (#13), pk 8/15/54 (#10, 2 wk), 17 wk; PW fic 8/14/54 (#10, 2 wk); tot 19 wk.

Merry Christmas, Mr. Baxter (Harper) NYT fic 12/2/56 (#12), pk 1/6/57 (#7, 1 wk), 7 wk; PW fic 1/14/57 (#8), pk 1/21/57 (#7, 1 wk), 2 wk; tot 9 wk.

Chairman of the Bored (Harper) NYT fic 10/8/61 (#13), pk 11/26/61 (#6, 5 wk), 39 wk; PW fic 10/30/61 (#7), pk 12/11/61 (#4, 2 wk), 31 wk; tot 70 wk.

Streshinsky, Shirley

Hers the Kingdom (Berkley) PW mm pb 6/24/83 (#14, 1 wk).

Stribling, Thomas Sigismund [all titles as by T.S. Stribling]

The Store (Doubleday) PW fic 9/10/32 (#10), pk 6/10/33 (#7, 4 wk), 12 wk.

Unfinished Cathedral (Doubleday) PW fic 7/14/34 (#4), pk 8/11/34 (#3, 4 wk), 8 wk.

The Sound Wagon (Doubleday) NYT fic 2/2/36 (#7, 4 wk).

Strieber, Whitley

The Wolfen (Bantam) PW mm pb 7/23/79 (#14, 1 wk).

The Hunger (Pocket) NYT mm pb 1/24/82 (#15, 2 wk).

Communion (Beech Tree Books/Morrow) NYT nf 3/1/87 (#12), pk 5/10/87 (#1, 3 wk), 30 wk; PW hc nf 3/13/87 (#9), pk 5/29/87 (#1, 3 wk), 29 wk; (Avon) NYT pb nf 1/31/88 (#1, 14 wk), 19 wk; PW mm pb 2/5/88 (#9), pk 2/12/88 (#1, 3 wk), 13 wk; tot 91 wk.

Transformation: The Breakthrough (Beech Tree/Morrow) NYT nf 9/4/88 (#15), pk 9/25/88 (#7, 3 wk), 8 wk; PW hc nf 9/9/88 (#11), pk 10/7/88 (#9, 1 wk), 7 wk; (Avon) NYT pb nf 8/6/89 (#5), pk 8/20/89 (#3, 1 wk), 9 wk; PW mm pb 8/18/89 (#14, 2 wk); tot 26 wk.

Majestic (Putnam) PW hc fic 10/13/89 (#15, 2 wk); NYT fic 10/15/89 (#14, 1 wk); tot 3 wk.

_____, and James Kunetka

Warday (Holt) PW hc fic 4/27/84 (#11), pk 5/25/84 (#5, 1 wk), 9 wk; NYT fic 4/29/

84 (#15), pk 5/20/84 (#7, 1 wk), 10 wk;
(Warner) NYT pb fic 4/7/85 (#4, 3 wk), 7
wk; PW mm pb 4/12/85 (#7), pk 5/3/85 (#4,
1 wk), 6 wk; tot 32 wk.
  Nature's End (Warner) NYT pb fic 5/17/87
(#14), pk 5/24/87 (#11, 1 wk), 3 wk.

Stringer, Arthur
  The Prairie Mother (Bobbs Merrill) PW
fic 9/25/20 (#7, 4 wk).

Strode, Hudson
  Jefferson Davis (Harcourt) NYT gen 10/2/
55 (#11, 2 wk), 3 wk.

Strong, James
  *The New Strong's Exhaustive Concordance
of the Bible* (Nelson) PW hc rel 10/5/90 (#10,
4 wk), 8 wk.

Stroud, Carsten
  Close Pursuit (Bantam) NYT pb nf 4/10/88
(#3, 1 wk), 5 wk.

Strout, Richard L.
  Maud [ed.] (Macmillan) NYT gen 12/10/
39 (#5, 4 wk), 8 wk.

Strunk, William, Jr.
  The Elements of Style [editorial supervisor
and contributor E.B. White] (Macmillan)
NYT gen 8/2/59 (#14), pk 10/11/59 (#3, 1
wk), 34 wk; PW nf 8/10/59 (#8), pk 9/28/59
(#3, 4 wk), 26 wk; tot 60 wk.

Struther, Jan
  Mrs. Miniver (Harcourt) PW fic 9/14/40
(#2), pk 10/12/40 (#1, 8 wk), 32 wk.

Stryker, Lloyd Paul
  The Art of Advocacy (Simon & Schuster)
NYT gen 4/18/54 (#16, 1 wk).

Stuart, Ian
  See Alistair MacLean

Stuart, Jesse
  Taps for Private Tussie (Dutton) NYT fic
1/9/44 (#10), pk 1/23/44 (#6, 1 wk), 3 wk.

Stuart, Sandra Lee
  See Dr. Robert Linn and_____

Styron, William
  Lie Down in Darkness (Bobbs Merrill)
NYT fic 9/30/51 (#9), pk 10/7/51 (#7, 1 wk),
10 wk; PW fic 10/20/51 (#5, 1 wk); tot 11 wk.
  Set This House on Fire (Random) NYT fic
6/26/60 (#12), pk 7/3/60 (#8, 2 wk), 14 wk;
PW fic 7/11/60 (#8), pk 8/1/60 (#7, 1 wk), 2
wk; tot 16 wk.
  The Confessions of Nat Turner (Random)
NYT fic 10/22/67 (#8), pk 11/5/67 (#1, 21
wk), 44 wk; PW fic 10/23/67 (#7), pk 11/6/67
(#1, 18 wk), 43 wk; NYT pb fic 11/3/68 (#1,
4 wk), 16 wk; tot 103 wk.
  Sophie's Choice (Random) PW hc fic 6/11/

79 (#12), pk 7/23/79 (#1, 8 wk), 40 wk; NYT
fic 6/24/79 (#2), pk 7/22/79 (#1, 6 wk), 47
wk; (Bantam) PW mm pb 7/18/80 (#5), pk
7/25/80 (#1, 5 wk), 29 wk; NYT mm pb
7/20/80 (#3), pk 7/27/80 (#1, 4 wk), 31 wk;
tot 147 wk.
  Darkness Visible: A Memoir of Madness
(Random) NYT nf 9/9/90 (#6), pk 9/16/90
(#1, 1 wk), 12 wk; PW hc nf 9/14/90 (#11), pk
9/21/90 (#2, 1 wk), 12 wk; tot 24 wk.

Suckow, Ruth
  The Folks (Farrar) PW fic 11/10/34 (#8), pk
12/15/34 (#5, 4 wk), 16 wk.

Sues, Ilona Ralf
  Shark's Fins and Millet (Little Brown)
NYT gen 3/5/44 (#16, 1 wk).

Sugarman, Daniel
  See Jerry Hopkins and_____

Sugrue, Thomas
  *A Catholic Speaks His Mind on America's
Religious Conflict* (Harper) NYT gen 5/4/52
(#16, 1 wk).
  See also Col. Edmund Starling and_____

Sulitzer, Paul-Loup
  The Green King (Stuart) PW hc fic 8/10/84
(#15, 1 wk).

Sullivan, Lawrence
  Bureaucracy Runs Amuck (Bobbs Merrill)
NYT gen 3/26/44 (#16), pk 4/23/44 (#12, 1
wk), 2 wk.

Sullivan, Mark
  Our Times, 1909–1914 (Scribner) PW nf
6/19/26 (#5), pk 8/14/26 (#4, 12 wk), 44 wk.
  Our Times, Vol. 2 (Scribner) PW nf 12/31/
27 (#7, 4 wk).
  Pre-War America (Scribner) PW nf 12/20/
30 (#4, 4 wk), 8 wk.
  Over Here (Scribner) PW nf 1/13/34 (#7,
4 wk).
  The Twenties (Scribner) PW nf 12/14/35
(#8, 4 wk).

Sulzberger, C.L.
  A Long Row of Candles (Macmillan) NYT
gen 7/6/69 (#10), pk 7/27/69 (#8, 1 wk), 4
wk; PW nf 7/14/69 (#10, 1 wk); tot 5 wk.

Summers, Anthony
  Goddess: The Secret Lives of Marilyn Monroe (Macmillan) NYT nf 10/6/85 (#16), pk
10/27/85 (#5, 1 wk), 11 wk; PW hc nf 10/11/85
(#15), pk 11/1/85 (#6, 1 wk), 12 wk; (NAL/
Onyx) NYT pb nf 12/21/86 (#4), pk 1/4/87
(#2, 1 wk), 7 wk; PW mm pb 1/9/87 (#11, 1
wk), 3 wk; tot 33 wk.

Summers, F.E.
  Dere Bill (Stokes) PW fic 5/3/19 (#6, 4 wk).

Sunshine, Linda
Plain Jane Works Out [photos by Martin Jackson] (Bantam) NYT td pb 4/24/83 (#11), pk 5/22/83 (#2, 1 wk), 17 wk; PW td pb 4/29/83 (#6), pk 5/20/83 (#3, 2 wk), 12 wk; tot 29 wk.

Surmelian, Leon Z.
I Ask You, Ladies and Gentlemen (Dutton) NYT gen 8/12/45 (#15, 1 wk).

Susann, Jacqueline
Valley of the Dolls (Geis) NYT fic 3/13/66 (#9), pk 5/8/66 (#1, 28 wk), 65 wk; PW fic 3/28/66 (#8), pk 5/9/66 (#1, 22 wk), 65 wk; NYT pb fic 8/6/67 (#1), pk 8/6/67 (#1, 32 wk), 40 wk; tot 170 wk.
The Love Machine (Simon & Schuster) NYT fic 5/25/69 (#8), pk 6/22/69 (#1, 13 wk), 32 wk; PW fic 5/26/69 (#7), pk 6/30/69 (#1, 6 wk), 30 wk; NYT pb fic 8/2/70 (#3), pk 9/6/70 (#2, 4 wk), 20 wk; tot 82 wk.
Once Is Not Enough (Morrow) PW fic 4/2/73 (#9), pk 4/30/73 (#1, 8 wk), 33 wk; NYT fic 4/8/73 (#7), pk 5/6/73 (#1, 8 wk), 36 wk; (Bantam) NYT mm pb 8/11/74 (#1, 12 wk), 14 wk; tot 83 wk.
Dolores (Morrow) PW hc fic 7/12/76 (#8), pk 8/9/76 (#2, 7 wk), 26 wk; NYT fic 7/18/76 (#8), pk 8/22/76 (#2, 7 wk), 25 wk; (Bantam) PW mm pb 5/23/77 (#14), pk 6/13/77 (#1, 1 wk), 10 wk; NYT mm pb 6/5/77 (#5), pk 6/19/77 (#1, 1 wk), 12 wk; tot 73 wk.
Yargo (Bantam) PW mm pb 3/19/79 (#12), pk 3/26/79 (#9, 1 wk), 6 wk; NYT mm pb 3/25/79 (#11), pk 4/1/79 (#9, 3 wk), 7 wk; tot 13 wk.

Suskind, Patrick
Perfume (Knopf) NYT fic 11/2/86 (#14), pk 11/23/86 (#10, 1 wk), 11 wk; PW hc fic 11/28/86 (#15, 3 wk); (Pocket) NYT pb fic 9/13/87 (#11), pk 9/27/87 (#10, 1 wk), 4 wk; PW mm pb 9/18/87 (#13, 2 wk); tot 20 wk.

Sutherland, Halliday
The Arches of the Years (Morrow) PW nf 8/12/33 (#6), pk 10/14/33 (#3, 4 wk), 16 wk.

Sutton, Henry
The Exhibitionist (Geis) PW fic 11/27/67 (#11), pk 1/1/68 (#4, 1 wk), 22 wk; NYT fic 12/3/67 (#4, 1 wk), 20 wk; NYT pb fic 1/5/69 (#5, 4 wk); tot 46 wk.
The Voyeur (Geis) NYT pb fic 2/1/70 (#4, 4 wk); PW fic 3/31/69 (#9, 1 wk); tot 5 wk.

Suyin, Han [pseud.]
A Many-Splendored Thing (Little Brown) NYT gen 12/21/52 (#13), pk 2/1/53 (#10, 1 wk), 12 wk.
The Mountain Is Young (Putnam) NYT fic

11/9/58 (#16), pk 12/7/58 (#11, 1 wk), 12 wk; PW fic 12/15/58 (#10, 1 wk); tot 13 wk.

Swanberg, W.A.
Sickles the Incredible (Scribner) NYT gen 5/20/56 (#14, 2 wk).
Citizen Hearst (Scribner) NYT gen 9/24/61 (#14), pk 11/19/61 (#4, 1 wk), 26 wk; PW nf 9/25/61 (#8), pk 11/13/61 (#3, 1 wk), 21 wk; tot 47 wk.
Luce and His Empire (Scribner) PW nf 10/9/72 (#8), pk 10/30/72 (#6, 1 wk), 4 wk; NYT gen 10/22/72 (#7, 2 wk), 7 wk; tot 11 wk.

Swanson, Gloria
Swanson on Swanson: An Autobiography (Random) PW hc nf 11/21/80 (#14), pk 12/26/80 (#8, 1 wk), 10 wk; NYT nf 12/28/80 (#14), pk 1/25/81 (#11, 1 wk), 7 wk; tot 17 wk.

Swanson, Neil Harmon
The First Rebel (Farrar) NYT gen 9/12/37 (#8, 4 wk).
The Perilous Fight (Farrar) NYT gen 1/20/46 (#16), pk 1/27/46 (#15, 1 wk), 2 wk.
Unconquered (Doubleday) NYT fic 12/21/47 (#14), pk 2/8/48 (#7, 2 wk), 11 wk; PW fic 2/14/48 (#8, 1 wk), 2 wk; tot 13 wk.

Sward, Keith
The Legend of Henry Ford (Rinehart) NYT gen 7/4/48 (#10, 1 wk), 3 wk.

Swarthout, Glendon Fred
They Came to Cordura (Random) NYT fic 3/23/58 (#16), pk 4/20/58 (#15, 2 wk), 3 wk.
Where the Boys Are (Random) NYT fic 2/28/60 (#12, 1 wk), 2 wk.

Sweeny, Col. Charles
Moment of Truth (Scribner) NYT gen 7/11/43 (#15, 1 wk).

Swiggett, Howard
The Durable Fire (Houghton) NYT fic 7/7/57 (#10), pk 7/28/57 (#8, 2 wk), 15 wk; PW fic 7/15/57 (#7), pk 8/5/57 (#5, 1 wk), 4 wk; tot 19 wk.

Swindells, Madge
Summer Harvest (NAL/Signet) NYT pb fic 5/19/85 (#12, 1 wk), 5 wk; PW mm pb 5/24/85 (#8, 1 wk), 3 wk; tot 8 wk.
Song of the Wind (NAL) NYT pb fic 5/18/86 (#13), pk 6/8/86 (#10, 1 wk), 2 wk.

Swindoll, Charles
Stress Fractures (Multnomah) PW pb rel 10/5/90 (#15, 4 wk), 8 wk.
Growing Strong in the Seasons of Life (Multnomah) PW pb rel 10/5/90 (#12, 8 wk).
The Grace Awakening (Word) PW hc rel 10/5/90 (#1, 8 wk).

Swing, Raymond Gram
Preview of History (Doubleday) NYT gen
10/10/43 (#11, 1 wk), 2 wk.
See also Edward R. Murrow and_____

Swinnerton, Frank
September (Doran) PW fic 6/12/20 (#7, 4
wk).

Switzer, Barry, with Bud Shrake
Bootlegger's Boy: My Story (Morrow) NYT
nf 9/16/90 (#2, 2 wk), 9 wk; PW hc nf 9/21/
90 (#4, 2 wk), 9 wk; tot 18 wk.

Sylvester, Harry
Moon Gaffney (Holt) NYT fic 7/13/47
(#16, 2 wk).

Szarkowski, John
The Face of Minnesota (Univ. of Minnesota) NYT gen 6/1/58 (#16), pk 7/13/58
(#13, 1 wk), 8 wk.

Szykitka, Walter
Public Works [ed.] (Links/Quick Fox)
NYT td pb 11/10/74 (#9, 4 wk).

Taber, Gladys Bagg
Especially Father (Macrae Smith) NYT
gen 9/18/49 (#15, 1 wk).

Taft, Sen. Robert A.
A Foreign Policy for Americans (Doubleday)
NYT gen 12/9/51 (#10), pk 12/23/51 (#9, 1
wk), 17 wk; PW nf 3/15/52 (#9, 1 wk); tot 18
wk.

Taintor, Eliot
September Remember (Prentice Hall) NYT
fic 6/10/45 (#17), pk 7/8/45 (#16, 2 wk), 4
wk.

Talbot, Beatrice Bill
And That's No Lie (Houghton) NYT gen
6/30/46 (#16), pk 7/7/46 (#14, 1 wk), 2 wk.

Talbott, Strobe
See Nikita Khruschev

Talese, Gay
The Kingdom and the Power (NAL) NYT
gen 6/29/69 (#8), pk 8/10/69 (#2, 6 wk), 26
wk; PW nf 7/7/69 (#8), pk 8/4/69 (#1, 3 wk),
23 wk; NYT pb gen 7/5/70 (#5, 4 wk); tot
53 wk.
Honor Thy Father (World) PW nf 11/1/71
(#8), pk 11/22/71 (#2, 6 wk), 21 wk; NYT gen
11/7/71 (#4), pk 11/28/71 (#1, 1 wk), 18 wk;
NYT pb gen 11/12/72 (#2), pk 12/10/72 (#1,
8 wk), 16 wk; tot 55 wk.
Thy Neighbor's Wife (Doubleday) PW hc nf
5/9/80 (#8), pk 6/6/80 (#1, 12 wk), 23 wk;
NYT nf 5/11/80 (#12), pk 5/25/80 (#1, 10
wk), 22 wk; (Dell) PW mm pb 6/5/81 (#12),
pk 6/12/81 (#4, 1 wk), 10 wk; NYT mm pb

6/7/81 (#9), pk 6/14/81 (#3, 3 wk), 10 wk; tot
65 wk.

Tallant, Robert
Mrs. Candy Strikes It Rich (Doubleday)
NYT fic 7/18/54 (#16, 1 wk).

Taller, Dr. Herman
Calories Don't Count (Simon & Schuster)
PW nf 11/27/61 (#8), pk 3/19/62 (#1, 11 wk),
39 wk; NYT gen 12/3/61 (#14), pk 3/25/62
(#1, 13 wk), 39 wk; tot 78 wk.

Tamas, Tstv'an
Students of Spalato (Dutton) NYT fic 5/14/
44 (#17, 1 wk).

Tan, Amy
The Joy Luck Club (Putnam) NYT fic
4/9/89 (#15), pk 5/14/89 (#3, 4 wk), 35 wk;
PW hc fic 4/14/89 (#11), pk 6/16/89 (#4, 1
wk), 38 wk; (Ivy) NYT pb fic 5/27/90 (#4),
pk 6/3/90 (#1, 5 wk), 25 wk; PW mm pb
6/1/90 (#3), pk 6/8/90 (#1, 5 wk), 25 wk; tot
123 wk.

Tanizaki, Jun'ichiro
The Key (Knopf) NYT fic 3/19/61 (#15, 1
wk).

Tapert, Annette
See Slim Keith and_____

Taraborrelli, J. Randy
Call Her Miss Ross (Birch Lane/Carol)
NYT nf 11/19/89 (#12, 1 wk), 3 wk; PW hc
nf 12/8/89 (#15, 1 wk); tot 4 wk.

Tarkington, Booth
Ramsey Milholland (Doubleday) PW fic
10/25/19 (#9), pk 11/1/19 (#7, 4 wk), 8 wk.
Alice Adams (Doubleday) PW fic 8/6/21
(#4, 4 wk), 8 wk.
Gentle Julia (Doubleday) PW fic 6/17/22
(#3), pk 7/29/22 (#1, 8 wk), 20 wk.
The Midlander (Doubleday) PW fic 4/19/
24 (#2, 4 wk).
The Plutocrat (Doubleday) PW fic 2/19/27
(#2), pk 3/19/27 (#1, 4 wk), 20 wk.
Claire Ambler (Doubleday) PW fic 4/28/
28 (#4, 4 wk), 8 wk.
Young Mrs. Greeley (Doubleday) PW fic
8/10/29 (#7, 4 wk).
Mary's Neck (Doubleday) PW fic 3/19/32
(#1, 4 wk), 12 wk.
Rumbin Galleries (Doubleday) NYT fic
12/12/37 (#10, 4 wk).
Kate Fennigate (Doubleday) NYT fic 6/13/
43 (#12), pk 8/1/43 (#6, 2 wk), 20 wk; PW
fic 7/10/43 (#10), pk 7/24/43 (#6, 3 wk), 9
wk; tot 29 wk.
Image of Josephine (Doubleday) NYT fic
4/1/45 (#9, 3 wk), 5 wk.

Tarnower, Herman, M.D., and Samm Sinclair Baker
The Complete Scarsdale Medical Diet (Rawson Wade) PW hc nf 1/22/79 (#9), pk 3/26/79 (#1, 35 wk), 50 wk; NYT nf 2/4/79 (#13), pk 4/1/79 (#1, 31 wk), 49 wk; (Bantam) NYT mm pb 1/13/80 (#10), pk 4/6/80 (#1, 4 wk), 80 wk; PW mm pb 1/18/80 (#7), pk 4/4/80 (#1, 7 wk), 75 wk; tot 254 wk.

Tarr, Herbert
Heaven Help Us! (Random) NYT fic 7/7/68 (#10), pk 9/15/68 (#6, 1 wk), 13 wk; PW fic 7/22/68 (#10), pk 11/18/68 (#6, 1 wk), 13 wk; tot 26 wk.

Tasaki, Hanama
Long the Imperial Way (Houghton) NYT fic 9/10/50 (#14, 1 wk).

Tatum, Jack, with Bill Kushner
They Call Me Assassin (Everest House) PW hc nf 3/14/80 (#15), pk 3/21/80 (#10, 1 wk), 7 wk; NYT nf 3/23/80 (#13), pk 3/30/80 (#11, 1 wk), 6 wk; tot 13 wk.

Taves, Isabella
See Margaret Hubbard Ayer and_____

Taylor, Day
The Black Swan (Dell) PW mm pb 7/31/78 (#11), pk 8/7/78 (#8, 2 wk), 6 wk.
Mossrose (Dell) NYT mm pb 7/27/80 (#14, 1 wk).

Taylor, Deems
Of Men and Music (Simon & Schuster) NYT gen 2/6/38 (#13), pk 3/6/38 (#11, 4 wk), 8 wk.
The Well Tempered Listener (Simon & Schuster) PW nf 3/9/40 (#10), pk 4/13/40 (#9, 4 wk), 12 wk.
A Treasury of Gilbert and Sullivan [ed.] (Simon & Schuster) PW nf 11/15/41 (#9), pk 12/13/41 (#4, 8 wk), 12 wk.

_____, Marcelene Peterson and Bryant Hale
A Pictorial History of the Movies (Simon & Schuster) NYT gen 4/2/44 (#20, 1 wk).

Taylor, Don
Mastering Rubik's Cube (Owl/Holt) PW td pb 6/26/81 (#7), pk 11/13/81 (#1, 1 wk), 33 wk; NYT td pb 7/12/81 (#5), pk 10/25/81 (#1, 3 wk), 38 wk; tot 71 wk.

_____, and Leanne Rylands
Cube Games (Holt) NYT td pb 1/24/82 (#12, 1 wk).

Taylor, Edmond
Richer by Asia (Houghton) NYT gen 8/17/47 (#14, 2 wk), 3 wk.
The Fall of the Dynasties (Doubleday) PW

nf 3/4/63 (#6), pk 4/1/63 (#5, 2 wk), 8 wk; NYT gen 4/7/63 (#10), pk 4/14/63 (#5, 1 wk), 5 wk; tot 13 wk.

Taylor, Elizabeth
In a Summer Season (Viking) NYT fic 2/12/61 (#16), pk 3/12/61 (#13, 1 wk), 4 wk.
Elizabeth Takes Off (Putnam) NYT msc 2/7/88 (#2), pk 2/14/88 (#1, 6 wk), 14 wk; PW hc nf 2/12/88 (#4), pk 3/11/88 (#1, 1 wk), 13 wk; tot 27 wk.

Taylor, Frank John
See Neill Compton Wilson and_____

Taylor, Henry Junior
Men in Motion (Doubleday) NYT gen 8/15/43 (#11), pk 8/29/43 (#10, 1 wk), 9 wk.

Taylor, Janelle
First Love, Wild Love (Zebra) NYT pb fic 10/7/84 (#10), pk 10/21/84 (#9, 1 wk), 6 wk; PW mm pb 11/9/84 (#11), pk 11/16/84 (#10, 1 wk), 2 wk; tot 8 wk.
Stolen Ecstasy (Zebra) NYT pb fic 9/8/85 (#15), pk 9/22/85 (#12, 1 wk), 4 wk.
Savage Conquest (Zebra) NYT pb fic 2/3/85 (#13), pk 2/17/85 (#7, 2 wk), 6 wk; PW mm pb 2/22/85 (#11), pk 3/1/85 (#10, 1 wk), 2 wk; tot 8 wk.
Moondust and Madness (Bantam) NYT pb fic 4/27/86 (#16), pk 5/11/86 (#10, 1 wk), 3 wk; PW mm pb 5/16/86 (#13, 1 wk), 2 wk; tot 5 wk.
Whispered Kisses (Zebra) NYT pb fic 3/11/90 (#13, 1 wk), 4 wk.

Taylor, Kressman
Address Unknown (Simon & Schuster) NYT fic 3/5/39 (#10, 4 wk), 8 wk; PW fic 3/11/39 (#7, 4 wk); tot 12 wk.

Taylor, Maxwell Davenport
The Uncertain Trumpet (Harper) NYT gen 1/31/60 (#12), pk 2/14/60 (#10, 1 wk), 7 wk.

Taylor, Peter
A Summons to Memphis (Ballantine) NYT pb fic 9/20/87 (#17), pk 9/27/87 (#13, 1 wk), 2 wk; PW mm pb 9/25/87 (#13), pk 10/2/87 (#11, 1 wk), 2 wk; tot 4 wk.

Taylor, Phoebe Atwood
Spring Harrowing (Norton) NYT fic 6/11/39 (#10, 4 wk).

Taylor, Robert Lewis
W.C. Fields (Doubleday) NYT gen 10/23/49 (#11), pk 11/6/49 (#10, 3 wk), 11 wk; PW nf 12/17/49 (#9, 1 wk); tot 12 wk.
Winston Churchill (Doubleday) NYT gen 6/29/52 (#10), pk 7/13/52 (#9, 1 wk), 9 wk.
The Travels of Jaimie McPheeters (Doubleday) NYT fic 4/27/58 (#12), pk 6/22/58 (#7,

1 wk), 18 wk; PW fic 6/16/58 (#8), pk 6/23/58 (#7, 1 wk), 5 wk; tot 23 wk.

A Journey to Matecumbe (McGraw) NYT fic 5/21/61 (#14), pk 6/18/61 (#8, 1 wk), 22 wk; PW fic 8/28/61 (#9, 1 wk); tot 23 wk.

Taylor, Rosemary
Chicken Every Sunday (McKay) NYT gen 5/2/43 (#18, 1 wk), 4 wk.

Tchernavin, Tatiana
Escape from the Soviets (Dutton) PW nf 7/14/34 (#7), pk 8/11/34 (#6, 4 wk), 12 wk.

Teale, Edwin Way
Autumn Across America (Dodd) NYT gen 11/11/56 (#14), pk 12/16/56 (#7, 1 wk), 14 wk; PW nf 12/10/56 (#8, 4 wk), 6 wk; tot 20 wk.

Tebble, John William
The Inheritors: A Study of America's Great Fortunes and What Happened to Them (Putnam) NYT gen 3/25/62 (#16, 1 wk).

Teichmann, Howard Miles
George S. Kaufman: An Intimate Portrait (Atheneum) NYT gen 7/16/72 (#8), pk 8/20/72 (#5, 1 wk), 13 wk; PW nf 7/24/72 (#7), pk 8/28/72 (#3, 1 wk), 14 wk; tot 27 wk.
See also Henry Fonda and_____

Tennan, Deborah
You Just Don't Understand: Women and Men in Conversation (Morrow) PW hc nf 7/20/90 (#14), pk 10/5/90 (#4, 2 wks), 21 wk; NYT nf 8/5/90 (#11), pk 9/9/90 (#2, 1 wk), 21 wk; tot 42 wk.

Tennenbaum, Silvia
Rachel, The Rabbi's Wife (Morrow) PW hc fic 1/30/78 (#14), pk 3/13/78 (#10, 1 wk), 11 wk; NYT fic 2/19/78 (#15), pk 3/19/78 (#8, 1 wk), 13 wk; tot 23 wk.

Tenzig, Norkey, with James Ramsey Ullman
Tiger of the Snows (Putnam) NYT gen 6/26/55 (#15), pk 7/24/55 (#8, 2 wk), 11 wk; PW nf 8/13/55 (#10, 1 wk); tot 12 wk.

Terasaki, Gwen
Bridge to the Sun (Univ. of North Carolina) NYT gen 10/6/57 (#15), pk 11/3/57 (#14, 1 wk), 4 wk.

Teresa, Vincent, and Thomas Renner
My Life in the Mafia (Doubleday) PW nf 4/30/73 (#9, 1 wk), 2 wk.

Terhune, Albert Payson
A Dog Named Chips (Harper) PW juv 4/18/31 (#7, 4 wk).

Terkel, Studs
Division Street: America (Pantheon) NYT gen 2/19/67 (#9), pk 5/14/67 (#6, 1 wk), 14

wk; PW nf 2/27/67 (#8, 4 wk), 12 wk; tot 26 wk.
Hard Times (Pantheon) NYT gen 5/10/70 (#10), pk 5/17/70 (#6, 6 wk), 15 wk; PW nf 6/1/70 (#6, 1 wk), 15 wk; tot 30 wk.
Working (Pantheon) NYT gen 4/14/74 (#9), pk 5/12/74 (#5, 4 wk), 17 wk; PW nf 4/15/74 (#10), pk 5/6/74 (#5, 3 wk), 17 wk; (Avon) NYT mm pb 3/30/75 (#9), pk 4/6/75 (#7, 1 wk), 3 wk; tot 37 wk.
American Dreams: Lost and Found (Pantheon) PW hc nf 10/24/80 (#10), pk 11/21/80 (#7, 2 wk), 17 wk; NYT nf 10/26/80 (#7), pk 12/7/80 (#6, 3 wk), 18 wk; tot 35 wk.
The Good War: An Oral History of World War II (Pantheon) NYT nf 10/21/84 (#7), pk 11/11/84 (#3, 1 wk), 23 wk; PW hc nf 10/26/84 (#11), pk 1/4/85 (#3, 1 wk), 19 wk; (Ballantine) NYT pb nf 11/10/85 (#4), pk 11/17/85 (#1, 2 wk), 9 wk; PW mm pb 11/15/85 (#13, 1 wk), 4 wk; tot 55 wk.

Terman, Douglas
First Strike (Pocket) PW mm pb 10/31/80 (#15), pk 11/7/80 (#14, 1 wk), 2 wk; NYT mm pb 11/9/80 (#13, 1 wk); tot 3 wk.

Terrell, John Upton
Plume Rouge (Viking) NYT fic 8/23/42 (#14, 1 wk).

Terry, Ellen, and Bernard Bradshaw
Ellen Terry and Bernard Bradshaw: A Correspondence (Putnam) PW nf 11/14/31 (#4, 8 wk), 16 wk.

Thacker, May D.
See Gaston B. Means and_____

Thane, Elswyth
See Elswyth Thane Beebe

Tharp, Louise Hall
The Peabody Sisters of Salem (Little Brown) NYT gen 1/29/50 (#11), pk 4/9/50 (#4, 1 wk), 25 wk; PW nf 2/11/50 (#8), pk 3/11/50 (#3, 4 wk), 19 wk; tot 44 wk.
Three Saints and a Sinner (Little Brown) NYT gen 10/28/56 (#12), pk 12/16/56 (#6, 1 wk), 17 wk; PW nf 12/31/56 (#8, 1 wk), 3 wk; tot 20 wk.
Adventurous Alliance (Little Brown) NYT gen 12/6/59 (#12), pk 1/17/60 (#11, 1 wk), 6 wk.
Mrs. Jack (Little Brown) PW nf 10/4/65 (#6, 1 wk), 14 wk; NYT gen 10/31/65 (#10), pk 11/7/65 (#8, 4 wk), 7 wk; tot 21 wk.

Thayer, Charles Wheeler
Hands Across the Caviar (Lippincott) NYT gen 2/15/53 (#16, 1 wk).
Diplomat (Harper) NYT gen 11/15/59 (#15), pk 12/20/59 (#10, 1 wk), 13 wk.

Thayer, Tiffany

The Old Goat (Random) NYT fic 6/6/37 (#9, 4 wk).

Tiffany Thayer's Three Musketeers (Dial) NYT fic 12/10/39 (#10), pk 1/7/40 (#9, 4 wk), 8 wk.

Thayer, William Roscoe

The Life of Theodore Roosevelt (Houghton) PW gen 1/3/20 (#2, 8 wk), 12 wk.

Theobald, Rear Adm. Robert A.

The Final Secret of Pearl Harbor (Devin Adair) NYT gen 5/16/54 (#13), pk 6/6/54 (#8, 3 wk), 8 wk; PW nf 6/12/54 (#8, 1 wk); tot 9 wk.

Theroux, Paul

The Great Railway Bazaar (Houghton) PW nf 9/22/75 (#9), pk 10/20/75 (#6, 1 wk), 6 wk; NYT gen 10/5/75 (#7, 1 wk), 7 wk; tot 13 wk.

The Old Patagonian Express: By Train Through the Americas (Houghton) PW hc nf 9/10/79 (#15), pk 10/22/79 (#11, 2 wk), 13 wk; NYT nf 10/14/79 (#15), pk 11/11/79 (#9, 1 wk), 9 wk; tot 22 wk.

The Mosquito Coast (Houghton) PW hc fic 3/5/82 (#15), pk 4/9/82 (#5, 1 wk), 10 wk; NYT fic 3/28/82 (#7, 1 wk), 8 wk; (Avon) NYT mm pb 3/13/83 (#14), pk 3/20/83 (#10, 2 wk), 3 wk; PW mm pb 3/18/83 (#10, 2 wk), 5 wk; tot 26 wk.

The Kingdom by the Sea (Houghton) NYT nf 12/25/83 (#15), pk 1/15/84 (#11, 2 wk), 8 wk; PW hc nf 1/27/84 (#13, 2 wk); tot 10 wk.

O-Zone (Ivy/Ballantine) PW mm pb 10/9/87 (#14, 2 wk); NYT pb fic 10/11/87 (#15), pk 10/18/87 (#13, 1 wk), 2 wk; tot 4 wk.

Riding the Iron Rooster (Putnam) PW hc nf 6/10/88 (#13), pk 7/1/88 (#8, 1 wk), 10 wk; NYT nf 6/19/88 (#6), pk 7/24/88 (#4, 1 wk), 16 wk; (Ivy) NYT pb nf 5/7/89 (#7), pk 5/21/89 (#3, 1 wk), 13 wk; tot 39 wk.

My Secret History (Putnam) NYT fic 7/16/89 (#15, 2 wk).

Thirkell, Angela Mackail

The Brandons (Knopf) NYT fic 8/6/39 (#3, 4 wk), 8 wk; PW fic 8/12/39 (#6), pk 9/16/39 (#5, 4 wk), 12 wk; tot 20 wk.

Before Lunch (Knopf) PW fic 8/10/40 (#10, 4 wk).

Peace Breaks Out (Knopf) NYT fic 6/22/47 (#15), pk 7/20/47 (#14, 2 wk), 3 wk.

Private Enterprise (Knopf) NYT fic 2/22/48 (#12, 1 wk), 3 wk.

Love Among the Ruins (Knopf) NYT fic 11/28/48 (#14, 1 wk).

The Old Bank House (Knopf) NYT fic 8/28/49 (#14), pk 9/11/49 (#13, 1 wk), 7 wk.

County Chronicle (Knopf) PW fic 11/18/50 (#10, 1 wk); NYT fic 11/26/50 (#16), pk 12/3/50 (#15, 2 wk), 4 wk; tot 5 wk.

The Duke's Daughter (Knopf) NYT fic 11/11/51 (#13), pk 12/2/51 (#12, 1 wk), 5 wk.

Happy Return (Knopf) NYT fic 10/12/52 (#13, 1 wk), 3 wk.

What Did It Mean? (Knopf) NYT fic 11/7/54 (#16, 2 wk).

Thoene, Bodie

Munich Signature (Bethany) PW pb rel 10/5/90 (#10, 4 wk).

Thoene, Brock, and Bodie Thoene

Riders of the Silver Rim (Bethany) PW pb rel 11/9/90 (#11, 4 wk).

Thom, James Alexander

From Sea to Shining Sea (Ballantine) PW td pb 8/10/84 (#10, 1 wk).

Thomas, Anna

The Vegetarian Epicure, Book Two (Knopf) PW td pb 6/12/78 (#9), pk 6/19/78 (#8, 1 wk), 4 wk.

Thomas, Benjamin

Abraham Lincoln (Knopf) NYT gen 11/30/52 (#9), pk 1/4/53 (#4, 1 wk), 18 wk; PW nf 12/13/52 (#8), pk 1/10/53 (#2, 1 wk), 7 wk; tot 25 wk.

Thomas, Caitlin

Leftover Life to Kill (Little Brown) NYT gen 11/3/57 (#13), pk 11/17/57 (#10, 1 wk), 6 wk.

Thomas, Craig

Firefox (Bantam) PW mm pb 12/11/78 (#15), pk 1/1/79 (#6, 1 wk), 10 wk; NYT mm pb 12/24/78 (#10), pk 1/28/79 (#7, 1 wk), 9 wk; tot 19 wk.

Firefox Down! (Bantam) PW mm pb 10/12/84 (#15), pk 10/19/84 (#11, 2 wk), 3 wk; NYT pb fic 10/14/84 (#7), pk 10/21/84 (#3, 1 wk), 5 wk; tot 8 wk.

Winter Hawk (Morrow) PW hc fic 5/1/87 (#12), pk 5/8/87 (#10, 1 wk), 6 wk; NYT fic 5/3/87 (#16), pk 6/7/87 (#12, 1 wk), 4 wk; (Avon) NYT pb fic 5/8/88 (#7, 2 wk), 5 wk; PW mm pb 5/13/88 (#7, 3 wk), 5 wk; tot 20 wk.

Wildcat (Jove) NYT pb fic 11/19/89 (#16, 1 wk); PW mm pb 11/24/89 (#9, 1 wk), 2 wk; tot 3 wk.

Emerald Decision (Harper) NYT pb fic 7/8/90 (#15), pk 7/15/90 (#14, 1 wk), 2 wk.

Thomas, D.M.

The White Hotel (Viking) PW hc fic 4/10/81 (#14), pk 4/17/81 (#10, 3 wk), 24 wk; NYT fic 4/26/81 (#10), pk 6/21/81 (#6, 1 wk), 19 wk; (Pocket) PW mm pb 3/19/82 (#6), pk

4/2/82 (#2, 3 wk), 13 wk; NYT mm pb 3/21/
82 (#6), pk 3/28/82 (#2, 4 wk), 10 wk; tot 66
wk.

Thomas, Dian
Roughing It Easy (Brigam Young Univ.)
NYT td pb 7/20/75 (#4), pk 8/17/75 (#2, 1
wk), 9 wk.

Thomas, Dylan
Adventures in the Skin Trade (New Directions) NYT fic 6/26/55 (#15, 1 wk), 2 wk.

Thomas, Elizabeth Marshall
Reindeer Moon (Pocket) NYT pb fic 3/27/
88 (#14, 1 wk), 2 wk; PW mm pb 4/1/88
(#15), pk 4/8/88 (#13, 1 wk), 2 wk; tot 4 wk.

**Thomas, Gordon, and Max Morgan-
Witts**
The Day the Bubble Burst (Doubleday)
NYT nf 11/25/79 (#15, 1 wk).

Thomas, Hugh
The Spanish Civil War (Harper) NYT gen
8/6/61 (#16), pk 9/10/61 (#8, 2 wk), 13 wk;
PW nf 9/18/61 (#9, 2 wk), 3 wk; tot 16 wk.

Thomas, Lewis
The Lives of a Cell (Viking) PW nf 9/2/74
(#8), pk 9/9/74 (#7, 1 wk), 9 wk; NYT gen
9/22/74 (#9, 1 wk), 2 wk; tot 11 wk.
The Medusa and the Snail (Viking) PW hc
nf 5/28/79 (#12), pk 6/11/79 (#5, 4 wk), 29
wk; NYT nf 6/3/79 (#13), pk 7/15/79 (#6, 3
wk), 27 wk; tot 56 wk.
*The Youngest Science: Notes of a Medicine
Watcher* (Viking) NYT nf 3/13/83 (#14), pk
4/3/83 (#8, 3 wk), 14 wk; PW hc nf 3/18/83
(#15), pk 4/1/83 (#8, 2 wk), 15 wk; tot 29 wk.
*Late Night Thoughts on Listening to Mah-
ler's Ninth Symphony* (Viking) NYT nf 1/8/84
(#14), pk 2/12/84 (#9, 1 wk), 7 wk.

Thomas, Lowell Jackson
Raiders of the Deep (Doubleday) PW nf
12/22/28 (#10, 4 wk).
Count Luckner the Sea Devil (Doubleday)
PW nf 4/28/28 (#6, 4 wk), 12 wk.
The Hero of Vincennes (Houghton) PW juv
2/15/30 (#9, 4 wk).
Back to Mandalay (Greystone) NYT gen
1/13/52 (#16, 1 wk).
Seven Wonders of the World (Hampver)
NYT gen 12/30/56 (#16, 1 wk).

Thomas, Lowell Jackson, Jr.
Out of This World (Greystone) NYT gen
12/17/50 (#9), pk 1/14/51 (#3, 2 wk), 32 wk;
PW nf 1/6/51 (#5), pk 2/10/51 (#2, 2 wk), 22
wk; tot 54 wk.

**Thomas, Marlo, with Christopher Cerf
and Letty Cottin Pogrebin**
Free to Be ... a Family [eds.] (Bantam)

NYT nf 11/22/87 (#4), pk 11/29/87 (#1, 1 wk),
10 wk; PW hc nf 11/27/87 (#5), pk 12/4/87
(#1, 1 wk), 7 wk; tot 17 wk.

Thomas, Michael M.
Green Monday (Wyndham/Simon & Schuster) PW hc fic 8/1/80 (#12, 3 wk), 4 wk; NYT
fic 8/17/80 (#15), pk 9/14/80 (#13, 1 wk), 6
wk; (Fawcett/Crest) PW mm pb 6/5/81 (#11,
1 wk), 3 wk; NYT mm pb 6/14/81 (#14), pk
6/21/81 (#13, 1 wk), 3 wk; tot 16 wk.

Thomas, Robert B.
See Anonymous (Old Farmer's Almanac)

**Thomason, Col. John W., Jr.,
U.S.M.C.**
And a Few Marines (Scribner) NYT gen
6/13/43 (#12, 1 wk), 2 wk.
Fix Bayonets! (Scribner) PW nf 6/19/26
(#6, 4 wk), 12 wk.

Thompson, Cecil V.R.
I Lost My English Accent (Putnam) NYT
gen 11/5/39 (#12), pk 12/10/39 (#9, 8 wk), 12
wk.

Thompson, Dorothy
Dorothy Thompson's Political Guide (Stackpole) NYT gen 9/4/38 (#14), pk 10/9/38 (#5,
4 wk), 12 wk; PW nf 10/15/38 (#6, 4 wk), 8
wk; tot 20 wk.
Once on Christmas (Oxford Univ.) NYT
gen 2/5/39 (#5, 4 wk).
Let the Record Speak (Houghton) NYT gen
10/8/39 (#2, 4 wk); PW nf 10/14/39 (#8, 4
wk); tot 8 wk.

Thompson, Edward McCray
Leg Man (Dutton) NYT nf 2/21/43 (#15),
pk 2/28/43 (#11, 1 wk), 4 wk.

Thompson, George Selden
The Cricket in Times Square [as by George
Selden] (Farrar) NYT ch bst 5/14/61 (#12),
pk 11/12/61 (#9, 26 wk), 46 wk.

Thompson, Hunter S.
The Great Shark Hunt (Summit/Simon &
Schuster) PW hc nf 8/13/79 (#12), pk 8/27/
79 (#10, 2 wk), 12 wk; NYT nf 9/2/79 (#4, 1
wk), 12 wk; tot 24 wk.
The Curse of Lono (Bantam) NYT td pb
11/27/83 (#13, 1 wk), 2 wk.
*Generation of Swine: Tales of Shame and
Degradation in the '80s: Gonzo Papers Vol. II*
(Summit) NYT nf 7/17/88 (#12), pk 8/7/88
(#3, 4 wk), 17 wk; PW hc nf 7/22/88 (#13),
pk 8/12/88 (#3, 1 wk), 14 wk; (Vintage) NYT
pb nf 8/20/89 (#9), pk 9/24/89 (#5, 1 wk), 11
wk; PW td pb 8/25/89 (#9, 2 wk); tot 44 wk.

Thompson, John Edward
Take Away the Darkness (Murray & Gee)
NYT fic 1/7/45 (#16, 1 wk).

Thompson, Kay

Eloise [illus. Hilary Knight] (Simon & Schuster) NYT gen 1/15/56 (#15), pk 5/6/56 (#6, 1 wk), 26 wk; PW fic 5/7/56 (#8), pk 6/4/56 (#7, 2 wk), 5 wk; tot 31 wk.

Eloise in Paris (Simon & Schuster) NYT gen 12/8/57 (#15), pk 12/29/57 (#8, 4 wk), 10 wk; PW fic 1/6/58 (#6, 2 wk), 4 wk; tot 14 wk.

Thompson, Morton

The Cry and the Covenant (Doubleday) NYT fic 2/5/50 (#13, 1 wk), 3 wk.

Not as a Stranger (Scribner) NYT fic 1/24/54 (#11), pk 2/14/54 (#1, 24 wk), 79 wk; PW fic 2/6/54 (#3), pk 2/20/54 (#1, 23 wk), 58 wk; tot 137 wk.

Thompson, Ruth Plumly

The Yellow Knight of Oz (Reilly & Lee) PW juv 7/12/30 (#6), pk 10/18/30 (#5, 4 wk), 20 wk.

Pirates in Oz (Reilly & Lee) PW juv 7/18/31 (#2, 8 wk), 16 wk.

Thompson, Steven C.

See Walter J. Boyne and_____

Thompson, Sylvia

The Hounds of Spring (Little Brown) PW fic 4/17/26 (#3, 4 wk), 20 wk.

Portrait by Caroline (Little Brown) PW fic 3/21/31 (#7, 4 wk).

Summer's Night (Little Brown) PW fic 3/19/32 (#9, 4 wk).

Unfinished Symphony (Little Brown) PW fic 5/13/33 (#9, 4 wk).

Recapture the Moon (Little Brown) NYT fic 9/12/37 (#4, 4 wk).

The Adventure of Christopher Column (Little Brown) NYT fic 4/9/39 (#10, 4 wk).

Thompson, Thomas

Blood and Money (Doubleday) PW hc nf 10/25/76 (#7, 2 wk), 13 wk; NYT gen 10/31/76 (#9), pk 11/7/76 (#7, 1 wk), 15 wk; (Dell) PW mm pb 10/17/77 (#10, 2 wk), 10 wk; NYT mm pb 10/23/77 (#15), pk 12/18/77 (#9, 1 wk), 12 wk; tot 50 wk.

Serpentine (Doubleday) PW hc nf 10/29/79 (#11), pk 1/11/80 (#7, 3 wk), 17 wk; NYT nf 11/11/79 (#15), pk 12/16/79 (#7, 2 wk), 15 wk; (Dell) PW mm pb 1/16/81 (#4), pk 1/23/81 (#3, 2 wk), 8 wk; NYT mm pb 1/25/81 (#5, 1 wk), 8 wk; tot 48 wk.

Celebrity (Doubleday) PW hc fic 4/23/82 (#5), pk 5/14/82 (#2, 1 wk), 17 wk; NYT fic 4/25/82 (#4), pk 5/16/82 (#2, 1 wk), 18 wk; (Warner) NYT mm pb 4/3/83 (#3, 1 wk), 15 wk; PW mm pb 4/8/83 (#4, 3 wk), 13 wk; tot 63 wk.

Thomson, J. Arthur

The Outline of Science (Putnam) PW gen lit 6/17/22 (#11), pk 12/23/22 (#1, 4 wk), 40 wk; PW nf 8/26/22 (#3, 4 wk); tot 44 wk.

Thorek, Max

A Surgeon's World (Lippincott) NYT gen 12/5/43 (#24, 1 wk).

Thorn, James Alexander

Follow the River (Ballantine) NYT td pb 9/6/81 (#13), pk 9/27/81 (#12, 1 wk), 3 wk.

Thorne, Anthony

Fruit in Season (Random) NYT fic 9/4/38 (#13, 4 wk).

Thorp, Edward O.

Beat the Dealer (Random) NYT gen 4/19/64 (#10, 2 wk); PW nf 5/18/64 (#10, 1 wk); tot 3 wk.

Thorp, Roderick

The Detective (Dial) PW fic 7/4/66 (#9), pk 9/26/66 (#3, 1 wk), 16 wk; NYT fic 7/10/66 (#10), pk 9/4/66 (#4, 1 wk), 15 wk; NYT pb fic 6/4/67 (#3), pk 7/2/67 (#1, 4 wk), 12 wk; tot 43 wk.

Thurber, James

The Last Flower (Harper) NYT gen 1/7/40 (#11, 4 wk).

My World, and Welcome to It (Harcourt) NYT nf 1/3/43 (#17, 1 wk).

Men, Women and Dogs (Dodd) NYT gen 12/26/43 (#20, 1 wk).

The White Deer (Harcourt) NYT fic 10/28/45 (#15), pk 11/4/45 (#12, 1 wk), 2 wk.

The Thurber Carnival (Harper) NYT gen 2/25/45 (#18), pk 3/25/45 (#4, 1 wk), 19 wk; PW fic 3/3/45 (#4), pk 3/24/45 (#2, 2 wk), 11 wk; tot 30 wk.

The Beast in Me and Other Animals (Harcourt) NYT gen 10/31/48 (#11), pk 11/7/48 (#10, 2 wk), 5 wk.

The 13 Clocks (Simon & Schuster) NYT fic 12/24/50 (#15), pk 1/14/51 (#9, 2 wk), 8 wk.

The Thurber Album (Simon & Schuster) NYT gen 6/22/52 (#15), pk 7/20/52 (#5, 3 wk), 16 wk; PW nf 7/12/52 (#9), pk 7/19/52 (#5, 2 wk), 6 wk; tot 22 wk.

Thurber Country (Simon & Schuster) NYT gen 11/29/53 (#13), pk 1/3/54 (#12, 1 wk), 4 wk.

Thurber's Dogs (Simon & Schuster) NYT gen 1/8/56 (#16, 1 wk).

The Wonderful O (Simon & Schuster) NYT fic 6/16/57 (#16), pk 7/28/57 (#10, 2 wk), 13 wk; PW fic 7/22/57 (#6, 2 wk), 3 wk; tot 16 wk.

The Years with Ross (Little Brown) NYT gen 6/14/59 (#10), pk 7/12/59 (#2, 6 wk), 25 wk; PW nf 6/22/59 (#5), pk 7/6/59 (#1, 1 wk), 21 wk; tot 46 wk.

Lanterns and Lances (Harper) NYT gen 6/4/61 (#14, 2 wk), 3 wk.

See also James R. Kinney, et al.

_____, and E.B. White

Is Sex Necessary? (Harper) PW nf 2/15/30 (#8), pk 3/15/30 (#3, 4 wk), 16 wk.

Thurman, Judith

Isak Dinesen: The Life of a Storyteller (St. Martin's) NYT pb nf 1/26/86 (#5), pk 2/2/86 (#3, 3 wk), 16 wk; PW mm pb 2/21/86 (#15), pk 3/21/86 (#9, 1 wk), 6 wk; tot 22 wk.

Thurston, Robert

See Glen A. Larson and_____

Tilling, Thomas

See William E. Donoghue and_____

Tillion, Germaine

Algeria: The Realities (Knopf) NYT gen 8/3/58 (#15, 1 wk).

Tilsley, Frank

Champion Road (Messner) NYT fic 10/22/50 (#14), pk 10/29/50 (#12, 2 wk), 5 wk.

Timerman, Jacobo

Prisoner Without a Name, Cell Without a Number (Knopf) PW hc nf 6/19/81 (#15), pk 7/31/81 (#7, 1 wk), 14 wk; NYT nf 7/26/81 (#6, 1 wk), 4 wk; tot 18 wk.

Titus, Eve

Anatole and the Cat (McGraw) NYT ch bst 11/17/57 (#7, 40 wk).

Tobias, Andrew

Fire and Ice: The Charles Revson/Revlon Story (Morrow) NYT gen 9/5/76 (#10), pk 10/10/76 (#6, 1 wk), 10 wk; PW hc nf 9/20/76 (#10), pk 10/11/76 (#8, 1 wk), 5 wk; tot 15 wk.

The Only Investment Guide You'll Ever Need (Harcourt) PW hc nf 3/20/78 (#10), pk 7/31/78 (#6, 1 wk), 30 wk; NYT nf 4/30/78 (#9), pk 5/7/78 (#4, 1 wk), 17 wk; (Bantam) NYT mm pb 3/4/79 (#11, 1 wk), 3 wk; tot 50 wk.

The Invisible Bankers (Linden/Simon & Schuster) PW hc nf 3/19/82 (#15), pk 6/4/82 (#9, 1 wk), 13 wk; NYT nf 4/25/82 (#15), pk 5/2/82 (#14, 3 wk), 5 wk; tot 18 wk.

Todd, H.L.

See Emily Dickinson, et al.

Toffler, Alvin

Future Shock (Random) NYT gen 10/11/70 (#9), pk 2/7/71 (#2, 10 wk), 46 wk; PW nf 11/2/70 (#10), pk 3/1/71 (#2, 8 wk), 43 wk; NYT pb gen 8/8/71 (#5), pk 10/10/71 (#1, 24 wk), 52 wk; tot 141 wk.

The Third Wave (Morrow) PW hc nf 4/4/

80 (#15), pk 5/2/80 (#2, 5 wk), 26 wk; NYT nf 4/6/80 (#11), pk 4/27/80 (#2, 3 wk), 27 wk; (Bantam) PW mm pb 4/3/81 (#11), pk 4/17/81 (#4, 1 wk), 5 wk; NYT mm pb 4/5/81 (#9), pk 4/26/81 (#6, 1 wk), 9 wk; tot 67 wk.

Powershift (Bantam) PW hc nf 11/2/90 (#14), pk 11/30/90 (#9, 1 wk), 5 wk; NYT nf 11/4/90 (#14), pk 11/25/90 (#6, 1 wk), 8 wk; [read by John Soles] PW aud nf 12/7/90 (#4, 4 wk); tot 17 wk.

Toland, John

But Not in Shame (Random) NYT gen 12/10/61 (#13, 1 wk), 5 wk.

The Last Hundred Days (Random) PW nf 2/28/66 (#10), pk 4/11/66 (#2, 3 wk), 24 wk; NYT gen 3/6/66 (#7), pk 4/3/66 (#3, 3 wk), 19 wk; tot 43 wk.

The Rising Sun (Random) PW nf 2/8/71 (#10), pk 3/15/71 (#9, 1 wk), 3 wk.

Adolf Hitler (Doubleday) NYT gen 10/10/76 (#10), pk 11/7/76 (#5, 2 wk), 20 wk; PW hc nf 10/11/76 (#7), pk 10/18/76 (#6, 7 wk), 16 wk; tot 36 wk.

Infamy: Pearl Harbor and Its Aftermath (Doubleday) PW hc nf 5/14/82 (#13), pk 7/9/82 (#12, 1 wk), 6 wk; NYT nf 5/23/82 (#14), pk 5/30/82 (#8, 1 wk), 7 wk; tot 13 wk.

Tolischus, Otto David

They Wanted War (Reynal & Hitchcock) PW nf 9/14/40 (#6, 4 wk).

Tokyo Record (Reynal & Hitchcock) NYT nf 3/14/43 (#13), pk 3/28/43 (#7, 2 wk), 4 wk.

Tolkien, J.R.R.

The Lord of the Rings (Ballantine) NYT pb fic 9/4/66 (#3), pk 12/4/66 (#1, 8 wk), 48 wk; NYT mm pb 1/12/75 (#10, 1 wk); tot 49 wk.

The Hobbit (Ballantine/Del Rey) PW mm pb 12/5/77 (#15), pk 1/2/78 (#4, 1 wk), 8 wk; NYT mm pb 12/25/77 (#11), pk 2/5/78 (#5, 1 wk), 11 wk; tot 19 wk.

The Hobbit, Or There and Back Again [illus. Arthur Rankin, Jr., and Jules Bass] (Abrams) NYT fic 12/18/77 (#12, 1 wk), 2 wk; PW hc fic 12/26/77 (#11), pk 1/2/78 (#9, 1 wk), 3 wk; NYT td pb 11/19/78 (#11), pk 12/31/78 (#4, 2 wk), 11 wk; PW td pb 12/11/78 (#6), pk 12/25/78 (#3, 1 wk), 5 wk; tot 21 wk.

The Silmarillion [ed. Christopher Tolkien] (Houghton) PW hc fic 9/19/77 (#8), pk 10/3/77 (#1, 18 wk), 60 wk; NYT fic 9/25/77 (#3), pk 10/2/77 (#1, 23 wk), 60 wk; (Ballantine) PW mm pb 3/5/79 (#15), pk 3/19/79 (#5, 1 wk), 9 wk; NYT mm pb 3/11/79 (#12), pk 3/25/79 (#2, 2 wk), 10 wk; tot 139 wk.

Unfinished Tales [ed. Christopher Tolkien] (Houghton) PW hc fic 11/21/80 (#10), pk 12/26/80 (#2, 1 wk), 19 wk; NYT fic 11/23/80

(#10), pk 12/28/80 (#3, 1 wk), 20 wk; tot 39 wk.

Tolstoy, Lyev N.
War and Peace (Simon & Schuster) PW fic 6/13/42 (#8, 4 wk), 9 wk.
Anna Karenina (Penguin) NYT td pb 4/2/78 (#6), pk 4/16/78 (#5, 2 wk), 8 wk.

Tomkins, Calvin
Living Well Is the Best Revenge (Viking) NYT gen 8/22/71 (#9), pk 10/3/71 (#4, 1 wk), 9 wk; PW nf 8/30/71 (#9), pk 9/13/71 (#6, 2 wk), 8 wk; tot 17 wk.

Tomlinson, H.M.
All Our Yesterdays (Harper) PW fic 2/15/30 (#3), pk 3/15/30 (#2, 4 wk), 12 wk.

Tompkins, Peter, and Christopher Bird
Alive: The Story of the Andes Survivors (Harper) NYT gen 4/28/74 (#9), pk 9/15/74 (#2, 1 wk), 30 wk.
The Secret Life of Plants (Harper) PW nf 3/4/74 (#10), pk 3/18/74 (#6, 1 wk), 11 wk; NYT gen 3/24/74 (#7, 2 wk), 6 wk; (Avon) NYT mm pb 11/10/74 (#7, 4 wk); tot 21 wk.

Toole, John Kennedy
A Confederacy of Dunces (Grove) PW td pb 5/15/81 (#2), pk 5/22/81 (#1, 8 wk), 31 wk; NYT td pb 5/17/81 (#4), pk 5/24/81 (#1, 6 wk), 29 wk; tot 60 wk.

Toor, Frances
A Treasury of Mexican Folkways [ed.] (Bonanza/Crown) NYT gen 6/15/47 (#16), pk 7/6/47 (#14, 1 wk), 2 wk.

Torres, Joan
See Dr. Susan Forward and_____

Toth, Lazlo
The Lazlo Letters [ed. Don Novello] (Workman) PW td pb 10/3/77 (#5), pk 10/24/77 (#4, 1 wk), 9 wk; NYT td pb 10/30/77 (#9, 1 wk), 10 wk; tot 19 wk.

Touhy, Roget, and Ray Brennan
The Stolen Years (Pennington) NYT gen 1/31/60 (#14), pk 2/14/60 (#13, 1 wk), 3 wk.

Tower Commission
The Tower Commission Report (Times/Bantam) NYT pb nf 3/22/87 (#1, 4 wk), 5 wk; PW mm pb 3/27/87 (#3), pk 4/3/87 (#2, 1 wk), 4 wk; tot 9 wk.

Townsend, Robert
Up the Organization (Knopf) NYT gen 4/5/70 (#3), pk 5/3/70 (#1, 7 wk), 28 wk; PW nf 4/13/70 (#4), pk 5/11/70 (#1, 8 wk), 29 wk; NYT pb gen 3/7/71 (#3, 8 wk); tot 65 wk.
Further Up the Organization (Knopf)

NYT nf 3/18/84 (#13), pk 4/22/84 (#9, 1 wk), 9 wk.

Towsley, Lena
Peggy and Peter (Farrar) PW juv 11/14/31 (#9, 4 wk).

Toynbee, Arnold Joseph
A Study of History (Oxford Univ.) NYT gen 4/13/47 (#9), pk 6/1/47 (#2, 4 wk), 61 wk; PW nf 5/3/47 (#5), pk 5/24/47 (#2, 11 wk), 44 wk; tot 105 wk.
Civilization on Trial (Oxford Univ.) NYT gen 5/16/48 (#16), pk 6/20/48 (#2, 2 wk), 23 wk; PW nf 5/29/48 (#4), pk 6/5/48 (#1, 4 wk), 13 wk; tot 36 wk.
The World and the West (Oxford Univ.) NYT gen 4/12/53 (#16), pk 4/26/53 (#6, 3 wk), 14 wk; PW nf 5/9/53 (#6), pk 5/30/53 (#5, 1 wk), 8 wk; tot 22 wk.
An Historian's Approach to Religion (Oxford Univ.) NYT gen 10/7/56 (#10), pk 10/28/56 (#9, 2 wk), 11 wk.

Tracy, Don
Crimson Is the Eastern Shore (Dial) NYT fic 5/3/53 (#16, 1 wk).

Tracy, Honor
The Straight and Narrow Path (Random) NYT fic 8/19/56 (#12), pk 9/16/56 (#10, 1 wk), 11 wk.
A Season of Mists (Random) NYT fic 8/27/61 (#14, 1 wk).

Train, Arthur
His Children's Children (Scribners) PW fic 4/14/23 (#6), pk 7/21/23 (#3, 8 wk), 20 wk.

Traprock, Walter E.
See George Shepard Chappell

Traver, Robert
See John Donaldson Voelker

Travers, Pamela L.
Stories from Mary Poppins (Simon & Schuster) NYT ch bst 11/16/52 (#10, 40 wk).

Travis, Neal
Manhattan (Crown) NYT fic 4/1/79 (#11, 2 wk), 6 wk; (Berkley) NYT mm pb 3/2/80 (#14, 1 wk); tot 7 wk.
Castles (Avon) PW mm pb 7/16/82 (#8, 1 wk), 3 wk; NYT mm pb 7/25/82 (#12, 1 wk), 3 wk; tot 6 wk.
Mansions (Avon) NYT pb fic 8/12/84 (#12, 1 wk).

Treanor, Tom
One Damn Thing After Another (Doubleday) NYT gen 8/27/44 (#12), pk 10/15/44 (#6, 1 wk), 17 wk.

Trefil, James
See E.D. Hirsch, Jr., et al.

Tregaskis, Richard
Guadalcanal Diary (Random) PW nf
2/6/43 (#5), pk 2/27/43 (#1, 7 wk), 20 wk;
NYT nf 2/7/43 (#11), pk 3/7/43 (#1, 7 wk),
28 wk; tot 48 wk.
Invasion Diary (Random) NYT gen 9/17/
44 (#7, 3 wk), 6 wk.
John F. Kennedy and PT-109 (Random)
NYT ch bst 5/13/62 (#13, 45 wk).

Trelease, Jim
The Read-Aloud Handbook (Penguin) NYT
td pb 3/13/83 (#8), pk 4/17/83 (#3, 2 wk), 17
wk; PW td pb 3/18/83 (#8), pk 4/8/83 (#4,
2 wk), 12 wk; tot 29 wk.

Trent, John
See Gary Smalley and____

Tressler, Irving D.
How to Lose Friends and Alienate People
(Stackpole) NYT gen 10/10/37 (#9), pk 11/7/
37 (#6, 4 wk), 8 wk.

Trevanian
See Rodney Whitaker

Trevor-Roper, H.R.
The Last Days of Hitler (Macmillan) NYT
gen 9/14/47 (#7), pk 10/12/47 (#6, 1 wk), 8
wk; PW nf 10/18/47 (#8, 1 wk); tot 9 wk.

Trimble, Bjo
The Star Trek Concordance Manual (Ballantine) NYT td pb 1/23/77 (#5, 1 wk).

Tripp, Wallace
Grandfa' Grig Had a Pig (Little Brown)
NYT ch pb 11/13/77 (#9, 46 wk).

Tritten, Charles
Heidi Grows Up [characters originally
developed by Johanna Spyri] (Grosset &
Dunlap) NYT gen 6/5/38 (#7), pk 7/3/38
(#3, 4 wk), 20 wk.

Troupe, Quincy
See Miles Davis and____

Troyat, Henri
Tolstoy (Doubleday) NYT gen 1/7/68 (#9),
pk 2/18/68 (#4, 1 wk), 15 wk; PW nf 1/8/68
(#7), pk 2/5/68 (#3, 1 wk), 20 wk; tot 35 wk.

Trudeau, Garry B.
Guilty, Guilty, Guilty (Holt) NYT td pb
8/11/74 (#8, 4 wk).
The Doonesbury Chronicles (Holt) PW td
pb 2/2/76 (#1, 1 wk), 17 wk; NYT td pb
2/8/76 (#4), pk 4/11/76 (#3, 1 wk), 9 wk; tot
26 wk.
As the Kid Goes for Broke (Holt) NYT td
pb 12/18/77 (#15), pk 12/25/77 (#10, 1 wk), 2
wk.
Doonesbury's Greatest Hits (Holt) PW td
pb 10/9/78 (#8), pk 1/1/79 (#3, 3 wk), 16 wk;

NYT td pb 11/12/78 (#9), pk 12/31/78 (#3, 4
wk), 16 wk; tot 32 wk.
Stalking the Perfect Tan (Holt) PW td pb
5/8/78 (#8, 2 wk), 3 wk; NYT td pb 5/28/78
(#15), pk 7/2/78 (#8, 1 wk), 10 wk; tot 13 wk.
But the Pension Fund Was Just Sitting There
(Holt) PW td pb 6/18/79 (#9, 1 wk); NYT
td pb 7/1/79 (#13), pk 7/8/79 (#10, 1 wk), 6
wk; tot 7 wk.
We're Not Out of the Woods Yet (Holt) NYT
td pb 11/11/79 (#14, 1 wk).
*A Tad Overweight, But Violet Eyes You
Could Die For* (Holt) NYT td pb 5/25/80
(#11, 2 wk), 3 wk.
In Search of Reagan's Brain (Owl/Holt)
PW td pb 10/9/81 (#9), pk 10/16/81 (#7, 1
wk), 3 wk; NYT td pb 10/11/81 (#15), pk
12/20/81 (#12, 1 wk), 3 wk; tot 6 wk.
The People's Doonesbury (Holt) NYT td pb
1/3/82 (#15), pk 1/10/82 (#14, 2 wk), 3 wk.
Doonesbury Dossier: The Reagan Years
(Holt) PW td pb 10/19/84 (#9, 2 wk).
Check Your Egos at the Door (Holt) PW td
pb 11/8/85 (#10, 2 wk).

Trudeau, Margaret
Beyond Reason (Paddington/Grosset &
Dunlap) PW hc nf 5/21/79 (#14, 1 wk); NYT
nf 5/27/79 (#5, 1 wk), 5 wk; tot 6 wk.

Truman, Harry S
Memoirs Vol. I: Year of Decisions (Doubleday) NYT gen 11/20/55 (#10), pk 12/18/55
(#5, 2 wk), 15 wk; PW nf 12/10/55 (#6), pk
12/17/55 (#5, 2 wk), 7 wk; tot 22 wk.
Memoirs Vol. II: Years of Trial and Hope
(Doubleday) NYT gen 3/18/56 (#14), pk
3/25/56 (#8, 1 wk), 8 wk; PW nf 4/21/56
(#10, 1 wk); tot 9 wk.
Mr. Citizen (Geis) NYT gen 7/3/60 (#9),
pk 7/17/60 (#6, 2 wk), 13 wk; PW nf 7/4/60
(#8), pk 7/11/60 (#2, 1 wk), 8 wk; tot 21 wk.

Truman, Margaret
Harry S Truman (Morrow) NYT gen 12/
24/72 (#4), pk 1/14/73 (#1, 3 wk), 20 wk; PW
nf 1/1/73 (#6), pk 2/19/73 (#1, 1 wk), 18 wk;
tot 38 wk.
Murder in the White House (Arbor) NYT
fic 8/3/80 (#9, 1 wk), 4 wk; (Fawcett/Popu-
lar Library) PW mm pb 7/24/81 (#15), pk
7/31/81 (#14, 1 wk), 2 wk; NYT mm pb 7/26/
81 (#15), pk 8/2/81 (#13, 1 wk), 2 wk; tot 8
wk.
Murder on Embassy Row (Fawcett Crest)
NYT pb fic 11/3/85 (#15), pk 11/17/85 (#11,
1 wk), 5 wk; PW mm pb 11/15/85 (#15), pk
11/29/85 (#12, 1 wk), 5 wk; tot 10 wk.
Bess W. Truman (Macmillan) NYT nf 5/4/
86 (#11), pk 5/25/86 (#7, 1 wk), 8 wk; PW hc
nf 5/30/86 (#14, 1 wk); tot 9 wk.

Murder at the FBI (Fawcett/Crest) NYT pb fic 6/29/86 (#10, 2 wk), 6 wk; PW mm pb 7/4/86 (#10, 4 wk), 5 wk; tot 11 wk.

Murder in Georgetown (Fawcett/Crest) NYT pb fic 6/28/87 (#6), pk 7/5/87 (#5, 1 wk), 11 wk; PW mm pb 7/3/87 (#7), pk 7/17/87 (#5, 2 wk), 13 wk; tot 24 wk.

Murder in the CIA (Fawcett/Crest) NYT pb fic 9/25/88 (#15), pk 10/9/88 (#2, 2 wk), 10 wk; PW mm pb 9/30/88 (#9), pk 10/7/88 (#1, 2 wk), 11 wk; tot 21 wk.

Murder at the Kennedy Center (Random) PW hc fic 7/21/89 (#13), pk 8/4/89 (#11, 1 wk), 7 wk; NYT fic 8/6/89 (#9, 2 wk), 7 wk; (Fawcett) NYT pb fic 7/1/90 (#6, 1 wk), 7 wk; PW mm pb 7/6/90 (#4, 2 wk), 6 wk; tot 27 wk.

Trumbull, Robert

The Raft (Holt) NYT nf 9/20/42 (#13), pk 12/13/42 (#10, 1 wk), 11 wk.

Silversides (Holt) NYT gen 9/16/45 (#15, 1 wk).

Trump, Donald J., and Charles Leerhsen

Trump: Surviving at the Top (Random) NYT nf 9/2/90 (#5), pk 9/9/90 (#1, 2 wk), 7 wk; PW hc nf 9/7/90 (#11), pk 9/14/90 (#2, 1 wk), 6 wk; PW aud nf 11/2/90 (#7, 4 wk); tot 17 wk.

_____, with Tony Schwartz

Trump: The Art of the Deal (Random) NYT nf 12/20/87 (#6), pk 1/17/88 (#1, 13 wk), 48 wk; PW hc nf 12/25/87 (#5), pk 1/22/88 (#1, 13 wk), 44 wk; (Warner) NYT pb nf 12/25/88 (#10), pk 1/15/89 (#1, 8 wk), 26 wk; PW mm pb 1/6/89 (#6), pk 2/3/89 (#1, 1 wk), 10 wk; tot 128 wk.

Truscott, Lucian K., III

Dress Gray (Doubleday) PW hc fic 2/5/79 (#9), pk 2/12/79 (#7, 1 wk), 12 wk; NYT fic 2/25/79 (#12), pk 3/4/79 (#5, 2 wk), 13 wk; (Fawcett/Crest) NYT mm pb 1/6/80 (#10), pk 1/27/80 (#8, 2 wk), 7 wk; PW mm pb 1/11/80 (#3, 1 wk), 8 wk; tot 40 wk.

Tryon, Thomas

The Other (Knopf) NYT fic 6/20/71 (#6), pk 8/15/71 (#2, 5 wk), 24 wk; PW fic 6/28/71 (#4), pk 8/30/71 (#2, 4 wk), 24 wk; NYT pb fic 4/9/72 (#2, 8 wk), 40 wk; tot 88 wk.

Harvest Home (Knopf) PW fic 7/9/73 (#6), pk 8/13/73 (#2, 1 wk), 19 wk; NYT fic 7/15/73 (#5), pk 7/29/73 (#4, 3 wk), 18 wk; (Fawcett) NYT mm pb 7/14/74 (#3, 4 wk), 8 wk; tot 45 wk.

Lady (Knopf) NYT fic 12/8/74 (#8), pk 3/23/75 (#3, 2 wk), 24 wk; PW fic 12/16/74 (#9), pk 3/24/75 (#3, 2 wk), 20 wk; (Fawcett)

NYT mm pb 11/9/75 (#6), pk 11/16/75 (#3, 3 wk), 14 wk; tot 58 wk.

Crowned Heads (Knopf) PW hc fic 7/5/76 (#9), pk 8/2/76 (#6, 2 wk), 11 wk; NYT fic 7/11/76 (#7), pk 8/1/76 (#5, 4 wk), 14 wk; (Fawcett/Crest) PW mm pb 6/20/77 (#11), pk 7/18/77 (#4, 1 wk), 9 wk; NYT mm pb 6/26/77 (#7), pk 7/24/77 (#4, 1 wk), 6 wk; tot 40 wk.

All That Glitters (Dell) NYT pb fic 11/15/87 (#15), pk 11/29/87 (#11, 1 wk), 3 wk; PW mm pb 11/27/87 (#15, 1 wk); tot 4 wk.

Tse-Tung, Mao

The Quotations of Mao (Foreign Language Press) NYT gen 5/21/67 (#7, 1 wk), 2 wk.

Tucci, Niccolo

Before My Time (Simon & Schuster) NYT fic 9/16/62 (#14, 1 wk), 3 wk.

Tuchman, Barbara Wertheim

The Guns of August (Macmillan) NYT gen 2/18/62 (#10), pk 4/1/62 (#3, 4 wk), 42 wk; PW nf 2/26/62 (#6), pk 8/6/62 (#2, 1 wk), 37 wk; tot 79 wk.

The Proud Tower (Macmillan) PW nf 1/24/66 (#10), pk 4/4/66 (#2, 2 wk), 28 wk; NYT gen 1/30/66 (#6), pk 3/13/66 (#2, 5 wk), 23 wk; NYT pb gen 3/5/67 (#5, 4 wk); tot 55 wk.

Stilwell and the American Experience in China 1911–1945 (Macmillan) NYT gen 2/28/71 (#10), pk 3/21/71 (#3, 2 wk), 28 wk; PW nf 3/8/71 (#5), pk 3/29/71 (#2, 3 wk), 26 wk; NYT pb gen 3/12/72 (#4, 4 wk); tot 58 wk.

A Distant Mirror: The Calamitous Fourteenth Century (Knopf) PW hc nf 9/25/78 (#8), pk 10/23/78 (#1, 11 wk), 37 wk; NYT nf 11/12/78 (#2, 6 wk), 36 wk; (Ballantine) NYT td pb 10/28/79 (#3, 11 wk), 40 wk; PW td pb 10/29/79 (#3), pk 11/12/79 (#2, 1 wk), 28 wk; tot 141 wk.

The March of Folly: From Troy to Vietnam (Knopf) NYT nf 3/18/84 (#12), pk 4/1/84 (#2, 5 wk), 26 wk; PW hc nf 3/30/84 (#4), pk 4/6/84 (#1, 2 wk), 21 wk; tot 47 wk.

The First Salute: A View of the American Revolution (Knopf) NYT nf 10/16/88 (#14), pk 10/30/88 (#3, 2 wk), 26 wk; PW hc nf 10/21/88 (#12), pk 11/4/88 (#8, 2 wk), 20 wk; tot 46 wk.

Tucker, Augusta

Miss Susie Slagle's (Harper) NYT fic 12/10/39 (#12), pk 1/7/40 (#10, 4 wk), 8 wk.

The Man Miss Susie Loved (Grosset & Dunlap) NYT fic 11/22/42 (#11), pk 1/10/43 (#9, 1 wk), 15 wk.

Tucker, Lael
See Lael Tucker Wertenbaker

Tucker, Louis
Clerical Errors (Harper) NYT gen 8/8/43 (#17, 1 wk).

Tucker, Sophie
Some of These Days (Doubleday) NYT gen 4/22/45 (#20), pk 4/29/45 (#7, 1 wk), 2 wk.

Tudor, Tasha
The Tasha Tudor Book of Fairy Tales (Platt & Munk) NYT ch bst 11/11/62 (#8, 26 wk). *First Delights* (Platt & Munk) NYT ch bst 11/6/66 (#4, 26 wk). *A Time to Keep* (Rand McNally) NYT ch hc 4/30/78 (#12, 24 wk).
See also Anonymous (*First Prayers*)
See also Frances Hodgson Burnett

Tullet, E.V.
See Douglas G. Browne and_____

Tully, Andrew
CIA: The Inside Story (Morrow) NYT gen 2/11/62 (#14), pk 3/25/62 (#5, 1 wk), 16 wk; PW nf 3/5/62 (#10), pk 4/2/62 (#7, 3 wk), 11 wk; tot 27 wk.
Capitol Hill (Simon & Schuster) NYT fic 4/8/62 (#16), pk 4/15/62 (#15, 3 wk), 5 wk.

Turan, Kenneth
See Patty Duke and_____

Turnbull, Agnes Sligh
The Rolling Years (Macmillan) PW fic 4/11/36 (#8), pk 5/9/36 (#7, 4 wk), 12 wk.
Remember the End (Macmillan) NYT fic 1/8/39 (#9, 4 wk).
The Day Must Dawn (Macmillan) NYT fic 11/15/42 (#19), pk 11/29/42 (#11, 1 wk), 10 wk; PW fic 12/12/42 (#10, 1 wk); tot 11 wk.
The Bishop's Mantle (Macmillan) NYT fic 11/23/47 (#14), pk 1/11/48 (#5, 7 wk), 38 wk; PW fic 1/17/48 (#8), pk 4/3/48 (#4, 1 wk), 14 wk; tot 52 wk.
The Gown of Glory (Houghton) NYT fic 4/6/52 (#6), pk 4/20/52 (#3, 11 wk), 37 wk; PW fic 4/12/52 (#6), pk 8/2/52 (#2, 2 wk), 29 wk; tot 66 wk.

Turnbull, Andrew
Scott Fitzgerald (Scribner) NYT gen 4/1/62 (#12), pk 4/29/62 (#7, 3 wk), 16 wk; PW nf 4/23/62 (#10), pk 6/4/62 (#7, 1 wk), 13 wk; tot 29 wk.
Thomas Wolfe (Scribner) NYT gen 2/18/68 (#8), pk 3/3/68 (#7, 1 wk), 4 wk; PW nf 3/4/68 (#9), pk 3/11/68 (#7, 1 wk), 5 wk; tot 9 wk.
See also F. Scott Fitzgerald

Turner, Lana
Lana: The Lady, The Legend, The Truth

(Dutton) PW hc nf 9/17/82 (#11), pk 10/22/82 (#7, 1 wk), 8 wk; NYT nf 10/17/82 (#9, 1 wk), 3 wk; tot 11 wk.

Turner, Nancy Byrd
In the Days of Young Washington (Houghton) PW juv 3/19/32 (#10, 4 wk).

Turner, Tina, with Kurt Loder
I, Tina (Morrow) PW hc nf 9/26/86 (#14), pk 10/31/86 (#8, 1 wk), 7 wk; NYT nf 10/5/86 (#8), pk 10/12/86 (#7, 1 wk), 7 wk; (Avon) NYT pb nf 8/9/87 (#6, 1 wk), 2 wk; tot 16 wk.

Turner, Wallace
Gambler's Money: The New Force in American Life (Houghton) NYT gen 4/11/65 (#9, 1 wk).

Turow, Scott
Presumed Innocent (Farrar) NYT fic 6/28/87 (#10), pk 7/26/87 (#1, 8 wk), 44 wk; PW hc fic 7/3/87 (#9), pk 7/31/87 (#1, 10 wk), 43 wk; (Warner) NYT pb fic 4/24/88 (#2), pk 5/1/88 (#1, 15 wk), 51 wk; PW mm pb 4/29/88 (#1, 17 wk), 50 wk; [read by John Heard] (Simon & Schuster) PW aud fic 10/5/90 (#3, 4 wk), 12 wk; tot 200 wk.
The Burden of Proof (Farrar) NYT fic 6/17/90 (#1, 11 wk), 29 wk; PW hc fic 6/22/90 (#1, 12 wk), 27 wk; [read by Len Cariou] (Simon & Schuster) aud fic 10/5/90 (#1, 4 wk), 12 wk; tot 68 wk.

Tutt, Ephraim
Yankee Lawyer: The Autobiography of Ephraim Tutt (Scribner) NYT gen 9/26/43 (#12), pk 1/9/44 (#4, 1 wk), 20 wk; PW nf 11/13/43 (#10), pk 1/8/44 (#5, 2 wk), 6 wk; tot 26 wk.

Twain, Mark
See Samuel Clemens

Tyler, Anne
Dinner at the Homesick Restaurant (Knopf) NYT fic 4/11/82 (#15), pk 5/23/82 (#8, 2 wk), 17 wk; PW hc fic 4/16/82 (#14), pk 4/30/82 (#7, 2 wk), 17 wk; (Berkley) NYT 3/20/83 (#9, 1 wk), 6 wk; PW mm pb 3/25/83 (#6), pk 4/8/83 (#3, 1 wk), 12 wk; tot 52 wk.
The Accidental Tourist (Knopf) NYT fic 9/22/85 (#10), pk 9/29/85 (#4, 3 wk), 29 wk; PW hc fic 9/27/85 (#14), pk 10/25/85 (#5, 1 wk), 27 wk; (Berkley) NYT pb fic 8/31/86 (#10), pk 9/21/86 (#1, 5 wk), 23 wk; PW mm pb 9/5/86 (#5), pk 9/19/86 (#2, 2 wk), 23 wk; tot 102 wk.
Breathing Lessons (Knopf) NYT fic 9/25/88 (#5), pk 10/2/88 (#2, 3 wk), 33 wk; PW hc fic 9/30/88 (#12), pk 10/14/88 (#2, 2 wk), 29 wk; (Berkley) NYT pb fic 10/1/89 (#11), pk 10/29/89 (#1, 2 wk), 18 wk; PW mm pb

10/6/89 (#4), pk 10/20/89 (#1, 3 wk), 17 wk; tot 97 wk.

Tyler, Tony
See Roy Carr and_____

U.P.I. and American Heritage
Four Days (Simon & Schuster) NYT gen 2/16/64 (#8), pk 3/22/64 (#1, 12 wk), 39 wk; PW nf 2/24/64 (#5), pk 4/6/64 (#1, 11 wk), 40 wk; tot 79 wk.

Udall, Stewart
The Quiet Crisis (Holt) NYT gen 1/5/64 (#10, 5 wk); PW nf 2/3/64 (#10), pk 2/10/64 (#9, 1 wk), 3 wk; tot 8 wk.

Udvardy, Miklos D.F.
The Audubon Society Field Guide to North American Birds: Western Region (Knopf) NYT td pb 12/11/77 (#13), pk 12/25/77 (#9, 2 wk), 15 wk.

Ueberroth, Peter, with Richard Levin and Amy Quinn
Made in America (Morrow) NYT nf 12/8/85 (#14), pk 12/29/85 (#10, 1 wk), 7 wk.

Uhnak, Dorothy
Law and Order (Simon & Schuster) PW fic 5/7/73 (#9), pk 5/14/73 (#6, 2 wk), 10 wk; NYT fic 5/27/73 (#9), pk 6/17/73 (#7, 2 wk), 8 wk; NYT mm pb 5/12/74 (#6, 4 wk); tot 22 wk.
The Investigation (Simon & Schuster) NYT fic 9/4/77 (#9), pk 9/25/77 (#8, 1 wk), 13 wk; PW hc fic 9/5/77 (#10), pk 9/19/77 (#7, 1 wk), 13 wk; (Pocket) PW mm pb 5/15/78 (#7), pk 6/5/78 (#4, 1 wk), 10 wk; NYT mm pb 5/21/78 (#4), pk 5/28/78 (#3, 3 wk), 13 wk; tot 49 wk.
False Witness (Simon & Schuster) PW hc fic 9/4/81 (#15, 1 wk); NYT fic 9/13/81 (#11, 1 wk), 4 wk; (Fawcett/Crest) PW mm pb 8/6/82 (#11, 2 wk), 4 wk; NYT mm pb 8/15/82 (#11), pk 8/29/82 (#10, 1 wk), 5 wk; tot 14 wk.

Ullback, Sylvia
No More Alibis! (McFadden) NYT nf 10/6/35 (#6, 4 wk), 8 wk.

Ullman, James Ramsey
The White Tower (Lippincott) NYT fic 9/16/45 (#11), pk 10/21/45 (#2, 6 wk), 26 wk; PW fic 9/29/45 (#5), pk 10/13/45 (#2, 10 wk), 22 wk; tot 48 wk.
Kingdom of Adventure: Everest [ed.] (Sloane) NYT gen 10/26/47 (#16, 1 wk).
River of the Sun (Lippincott) NYT fic 1/21/51 (#10), pk 2/4/51 (#3, 4 wk), 14 wk; PW fic 2/3/51 (#5), pk 2/10/51 (#3, 5 wk), 11 wk; tot 25 wk.
Windom's Way (Lippincott) NYT fic 6/15/

52 (#13), pk 6/22/52 (#9, 1 wk), 8 wk; PW fic 7/12/52 (#9, 1 wk); tot 9 wk.
The Day on Fire (World) NYT fic 10/12/58 (#16), pk 10/19/58 (#14, 1 wk), 3 wk.
See also Norkey Tenzing and_____

Ullman, Liv
Changing (Knopf) PW hc nf 3/7/77 (#8), pk 3/21/77 (#4, 6 wk), 15 wk; NYT gen 2/27/77 (#9), pk 3/27/77 (#5, 1 wk), 5 wk; nf 4/3/77 (#5), pk 4/24/77 (#4, 1 wk), 13 wk; (Bantam) PW mm pb 1/16/78 (#7), pk 1/13/78 (#4, 1 wk), 6 wk; tot 39 wk.
Choices (Knopf) NYT nf 2/17/85 (#15), pk 2/24/85 (#13, 1 wk), 3 wk.

Underwood, Tim and Chuck Miller
Bare Bones: Conversations on Terror with Stephen King (McGraw) PW hc nf 6/10/88 (#15, 1 wk).

Undset, Sigrid
Gunnar's Daughter [trans. Arthur D. Chater] (Knopf) NYT fic 9/13/36 (#6, 4 wk).
The Faithful Wife (Knopf) NYT fic 11/7/37 (#7, 4 wk).
Images in a Mirror (Knopf) NYT fic 10/9/38 (#11, 4 wk).

Unofficial Observer
The New Dealers (Simon & Schuster) PW nf 5/12/34 (#5, 4 wk), 8 wk.

Untermeyer, Louis
The Golden Treasury of Poetry [ed.] (Golden) NYT ch bst 5/8/60 (#12, 46 wk).

Updike, John
The Poorhouse Fair (Knopf) NYT fic 2/8/59 (#14, 2 wk).
Rabbit, Run (Knopf) NYT fic 11/27/60 (#16), pk 12/25/60 (#14, 1 wk), 10 wk.
Pigeon Feathers and Other Stories (Knopf) NYT fic 4/22/62 (#15), pk 5/20/62 (#13, 2 wk), 7 wk.
The Centaur (Knopf) PW fic 3/18/63 (#9, 2 wk), 6 wk; NYT fic 4/7/63 (#9), pk 5/19/63 (#8, 1 wk), 6 wk; tot 12 wk.
Couples (Knopf) PW fic 4/8/68 (#8), pk 5/6/68 (#2, 21 wk), 36 wk; NYT fic 4/14/68 (#10), pk 6/30/68 (#1, 1 wk), 36 wk; NYT pb fic 5/4/69 (#1, 3 wk), 7 wk; tot 79 wk.
Bech: A Book (Knopf) NYT fic 7/26/70 (#10), pk 8/2/70 (#7, 1 wk), 8 wk; PW fic 8/3/70 (#9, 5 wk), 8 wk; tot 16 wk.
Rabbit Redux (Knopf) NYT fic 12/5/71 (#9), pk 1/16/72 (#4, 2 wk), 17 wk; PW fic 12/13/71 (#5), pk 1/31/72 (#4, 2 wk), 14 wk; NYT pb gen 12/10/72 (#3, 4 wk), 8 wk; tot 39 wk.

Museums and Women (Knopf) NYT gen 11/12/72 (#10, 1 wk).

A Month of Sundays (Knopf) PW fic 3/17/75 (#7), pk 4/7/75 (#5, 1 wk), 13 wk; NYT fic 3/23/75 (#8), pk 5/18/75 (#5, 1 wk), 15 wk; tot 28 wk.

Marry Me (Knopf) NYT fic 11/28/76 (#9), pk 12/26/76 (#7, 1 wk), 6 wk.

The Coup (Knopf) PW hc fic 1/1/79 (#15), pk 1/22/79 (#3, 1 wk), 13 wk; NYT fic 1/7/79 (#11), pk 1/28/79 (#4, 2 wk), 17 wk; (Fawcett/Crest) PW mm pb 2/29/80 (#13, 1 wk), 2 wk; tot 32 wk.

Rabbit Is Rich (Knopf) PW hc fic 10/16/81 (#15), pk 11/6/81 (#7, 2 wk), 20 wk; NYT fic 10/25/81 (#9), pk 1/31/82 (#4, 1 wk), 23 wk; (Fawcett/Crest) PW mm pb 10/1/82 (#13), pk 10/29/82 (#6, 1 wk), 11 wk; NYT mm pb 10/10/82 (#10), pk 10/31/82 (#7, 2 wk), 6 wk; tot 60 wk.

Bech Is Back (Knopf) PW hc fic 11/12/82 (#9), pk 11/19/82 (#8, 1 wk), 3 wk; NYT fic 11/21/82 (#13, 1 wk); tot 4 wk.

The Witches of Eastwick (Knopf) PW hc fic 6/1/84 (#14), pk 6/22/84 (#4, 1 wk), 12 wk; NYT fic 6/3/84 (#7), pk 6/10/84 (#5, 2 wk), 12 wk; (Fawcett/Crest) PW mm pb 6/28/85 (#15), pk 7/26/85 (#5, 1 wk), 18 wk; NYT pb fic 6/30/85 (#8), pk 7/14/85 (#6, 2 wk), 15 wk; tot 57 wk.

Roger's Version (Knopf) NYT fic 9/21/86 (#9), pk 10/5/86 (#4, 1 wk), 15 wk; PW hc fic 9/26/86 (#12), pk 10/10/86 (#6, 2 wk), 10 wk; (Fawcett/Crest) PW mm pb 9/4/87 (#13, 1 wk), 3 wk; tot 28 wk.

S. (Knopf) NYT fic 3/27/88 (#13), pk 4/10/88 (#10, 1 wk), 6 wk; PW hc fic 4/8/88 (#13, 1 wk), 5 wk; tot 11 wk.

Rabbit at Rest (Knopf) NYT fic 10/14/90 (#11), pk 11/4/90 (#8, 1 wk), 7 wk; PW hc fic 10/19/90 (#10), pk 11/30/90 (#7, 1 wk), 10 wk; tot 17 wk.

Uris, Jill, and Leon Uris
Ireland: A Terrible Beauty (Bantam) PW td pb 3/27/78 (#7), pk 4/10/78 (#2, 2 wk), 10 wk; NYT td pb 4/9/78 (#11), pk 4/30/78 (#4, 1 wk), 16 wk; tot 26 wk.

Uris, Leon M.
Battle Cry (Putnam) NYT fic 5/17/53 (#13), pk 6/21/53 (#2, 12 wk), 51 wk; PW fic 6/6/53 (#5), pk 6/20/53 (#2, 9 wk), 29 wk; tot 80 wk.

Exodus (Doubleday) NYT fic 10/12/58 (#13), pk 5/17/59 (#1, 20 wk), 78 wk; PW fic 11/3/58 (#8), pk 5/25/59 (#1, 17 wk), 73 wk; tot 151 wk.

Mila 18 (Doubleday) NYT fic 6/18/61 (#10), pk 8/13/61 (#2, 1 wk), 33 wk; PW fic

6/26/61 (#4), pk 8/14/61 (#2, 1 wk), 26 wk; tot 59 wk.

Armageddon (Doubleday) PW fic 6/29/64 (#8), pk 7/27/64 (#2, 8 wk), 33 wk; NYT fic 6/21/64 (#7), pk 7/12/64 (#2, 8 wk), 34 wk; pb fic 12/5/65 (#4, 8 wk); tot 75 wk.

Topaz (McGraw) PW fic 9/25/67 (#13), pk 3/4/68 (#1, 1 wk), 51 wk; NYT fic 10/1/67 (#9), pk 10/15/67 (#1, 1 wk), 52 wk; NYT pb fic 12/1/68 (#1, 8 wk), 24 wk; tot 127 wk.

QB VII (Doubleday) NYT fic 12/6/70 (#8), pk 2/21/71 (#1, 9 wk), 39 wk; PW fic 12/7/70 (#7), pk 2/8/71 (#1, 11 wk), 39 wk; (Bantam) NYT pb fic 2/13/71 (#1, 12 wk), 16 wk; NYT mm pb 6/9/74 (#7, 4 wk); tot 98 wk.

Trinity (Doubleday) PW hc fic 3/22/76 (#6), pk 6/14/76 (#1, 30 wk), 73 wk; NYT fic 3/28/76 (#6), pk 6/13/76 (#1, 36 wk), 77 wk; (Bantam) PW mm pb 9/5/77 (#3), pk 9/19/77 (#1, 2 wk), 23 wk; NYT mm pb 9/11/77 (#2), pk 9/25/77 (#1, 4 wk), 25 wk; tot 198 wk.

The Haj (Doubleday) NYT fic 4/15/84 (#11), pk 4/29/84 (#2, 5 wk), 24 wk; PW hc fic 4/20/84 (#13), pk 5/4/84 (#2, 5 wk), 21 wk; (Bantam) NYT pb fic 6/9/85 (#9), pk 6/16/85 (#3, 4 wk), 14 wk; PW mm pb 6/14/85 (#9), pk 6/21/85 (#3, 4 wk), 13 wk; tot 72 wk.

Mitla Pass (Doubleday) NYT fic 11/6/88 (#11), pk 11/20/88 (#6, 2 wk), 11 wk; PW hc fic 11/11/88 (#11), pk 12/9/88 (#7, 2 wk), 11 wk; (Bantam) NYT pb fic 11/12/89 (#9), pk 11/19/89 (#5, 2 wk), 6 wk; PW mm pb 11/17/89 (#10), pk 12/1/89 (#5, 1 wk), 5 wk; tot 33 wk.

See also Jill Uris and_____

Ury, William
See Roger Fisher and_____

Ustinov, Peter
Dear Me (Little Brown) NYT nf 11/27/77 (#13, 1 wk); (Penguin) NYT td pb 4/29/79 (#8), pk 5/13/79 (#7, 2 wk), 12 wk; tot 13 wk.

Uston, Ken
Mastering Pac-Man (NAL/Signet) NYT mm pb 2/14/82 (#11), pk 3/28/82 (#9, 2 wk), 8 wk; PW mm pb 2/26/82 (#10), pk 3/5/82 (#9, 1 wk), 7 wk; tot 15 wk.

Utley, Freda
The China Story (Regnery) NYT gen 6/3/51 (#15), pk 6/24/51 (#6, 2 wk), 15 wk; PW nf 8/11/51 (#7, 1 wk); tot 16 wk.

Vailland, Roger
The Law (Knopf) NYT fic 10/19/58 (#15), pk 10/26/58 (#11, 1 wk), 4 wk.

Vale, Eugene
The Thirteenth Apostle (Scribner) NYT fic 9/6/59 (#16), pk 10/25/59 (#6, 2 wk), 22 wk; PW fic 10/12/59 (#8), pk 10/26/59 (#6, 2 wk), 10 wk; tot 32 wk.

Valen, E.G.
The Other Side of the Mountain, Part II (Warner) PW mm pb 4/3/78 (#13, 2 wk).

Valenti, Jack
Speak Up with Confidence: How to Prepare, Learn and Deliver Effective Speeches (Morrow) PW hc nf 8/13/82 (#15, 3 wk).

Valentine, J. Manson
See Charles Berlitz and_____

Vallentin, Antonia
Leonardo da Vinci (Viking) PW nf 1/14/39 (#8, 4 wk).

Valtin, Jan
Out of the Night (Alliance) PW nf 3/15/41 (#1, 12 wk), 28 wk.

Van Allsburg, Chris
The Polar Express [written & illus.] (Houghton) NYT fic 12/22/85 (#6), pk 12/18/88 (#3, 4 wk), 28 wk; PW hc fic 12/9/88 (#13), pk 12/16/88 (#6, 2 wk), 5 wk; tot 33 wk.
Just a Dream (Houghton) PW ch pic 11/30/90 (#1, 4 wk), 8 wk.

Van Buren, Abigail
Dear Abby (Prentice Hall) NYT gen 5/18/58 (#13), pk 6/22/58 (#4, 6 wk), 23 wk; PW nf 5/26/58 (#6), pk 7/28/58 (#4, 2 wk), 21 wk; tot 44 wk.
The Best of Dear Abby (Andrews & McMeel) PW hc nf 11/27/81 (#13), pk 1/1/82 (#9, 2 wk), 7 wk; NYT nf 11/29/81 (#10), pk 12/27/81 (#7, 1 wk), 11 wk; (Pocket) mm pb 10/17/82 (#15), pk 10/24/82 (#13, 1 wk), 2 wk; tot 20 wk.

VanCaspel, Venita
Money Dynamics for the 1980s (Reston/Prentice Hall) NYT nf 2/8/81 (#13), pk 3/15/81 (#11, 1 wk), 10 wk; PW hc nf 3/6/81 (#14, 1 wk); tot 11 wk.
The Power of Money Dynamics (Prentice Hall/Reston) PW hc nf 12/17/82 (#12), pk 1/28/83 (#11, 1 wk), 10 wk.

Vance, Ethel
Escape (Little Brown) NYT fic 11/5/39 (#1, 4 wk), 12 wk; PW fic 11/11/39 (#2, 8 wk), 20 wk; tot 32 wk.
Reprisal (Simon & Schuster) NYT fic 12/13/42 (#8), pk 12/20/42 (#7, 1 wk), 6 wk; PW fic 12/19/42 (#5, 1 wk); tot 7 wk.

Vandenberg, Arthur Hendrick, Jr., with Joe Alex Morris
The Private Papers of Senator Vandenberg (Houghton) NYT gen 5/18/52 (#16, 3 wk).

Vanderbilt, Cornelius, Jr.
Farewell to Fifth Avenue (Simon & Schuster) PW nf 3/16/35 (#10, 8 wk).
The Living Past of America (Crown) NYT gen 7/31/55 (#13), pk 9/11/55 (#9, 1 wk), 8 wk; PW nf 8/13/55 (#9, 1 wk); tot 9 wk.

Vanderbilt, Gloria
Once Upon a Time: A True Story (Knopf) NYT nf 5/5/85 (#8), pk 5/26/85 (#4, 1 wk), 8 wk; PW hc nf 5/10/85 (#13), pk 5/24/85 (#8, 2 wk), 8 wk; (Fawcett) NYT pb nf 5/11/86 (#10, 1 wk); tot 17 wk.

Van der Heide, Dirk
My Sister and I (Harcourt) PW nf 3/15/41 (#4, 4 wk), 20 wk.

Vanderlip, Frank A.
What Happened to Europe (Macmillan) PW gen 9/6/19 (#6), pk 10/25/19 (#5, 4 wk), 12 wk.

Van der Post, Laurens
Venture to the Interior (Morrow) NYT gen 1/20/52 (#15, 1 wk).
Flamingo Feather (Morrow) NYT fic 3/13/55 (#14), pk 4/10/55 (#9, 1 wk), 11 wk; PW fic 4/16/55 (#6, 1 wk); tot 12 wk.

Van Dine, S.S.
The Greene Murder Case (Scribner) PW fic 5/26/28 (#3, 8 wk).
The Bishop Murder Case (Scribner) PW fic 3/9/29 (#4), pk 4/13/29 (#1, 4 wk), 16 wk.
The Scarab Murder Case (Scribner) PW fic 7/12/30 (#2, 4 wk), 8 wk.
The Kennel Murder Case (Scribner) PW fic 2/11/33 (#3, 4 wk), 12 wk.
The Kidnap Murder Case (Grosset & Dunlap) NYT fic 11/8/36 (#7, 4 wk).
The Gracie Allen Murder Case (Grosset & Dunlap) NYT fic 12/4/38 (#10, 4 wk).

Van Doren, Carl
Benjamin Franklin (Viking) NYT gen 11/6/38 (#9), pk 12/4/38 (#7, 4 wk), 16 wk; PW nf 11/12/38 (#5), pk 1/14/39 (#3, 8 wk), 20 wk; tot 36 wk.
The Secret History of the American Revolution (Viking) PW nf 11/15/41 (#7, 8 wk), 12 wk.
The Great Rehearsal (Viking) NYT gen 2/8/48 (#16), pk 3/21/48 (#6, 1 wk), 12 wk; PW nf 2/28/48 (#5, 1 wk), 3 wk; tot 15 wk.

Van Dyke, Henry
The Valley of Vision (Scribner) PW fic 6/7/19 (#7), pk 7/5/19 (#6, 4 wk), 12 wk.

Van Etten, Winifred
I Am the Fox (Little Brown) NYT fic 10/4/36 (#2, 4 wk); PW fic 10/10/36 (#6), pk 11/14/36 (#5, 4 wk), 12 wk; tot 16 wk.

Van Gelder, Robert
Important People (Doubleday) NYT fic 8/15/48 (#16, 1 wk).

Van Hise, Della
Killing Time (Pocket) NYT pb fic 7/14/85 (#14, 1 wk); PW mm pb 7/19/85 (#12, 1 wk), 2 wk; tot 3 wk.

Van Hoesen, Bertha
Petticoat Surgeon (Pelligrini & Cudahy) NYT gen 9/21/47 (#15), pk 10/5/47 (#8, 1 wk), 10 wk.

Van Lawick-Goodall, Jane
In the Shadow of Man (Houghton) NYT gen 1/2/72 (#9, 1 wk); PW nf 1/17/72 (#7, 1 wk), 2 wk; tot 3 wk.

Van Loon, Hendrik Willem
The Story of Mankind (Boni & Liveright) PW nf 4/1/22 (#3), pk 8/26/22 (#2, 4 wk), 12 wk; PW gen lit 5/13/22 (#2), pk 7/29/22 (#1, 4 wk), 40 wk; tot 52 wk.
Story of the Bible (Boni) PW nf 11/24/23 (#10, 4 wk).
Van Loon's Geography (Simon & Schuster) PW nf 10/15/32 (#7), pk 1/4/33 (#1, 8 wk), 32 wk.
Ships (Simon & Schuster) PW nf 4/13/35 (#7, 8 wk), 16 wk.
Around the World with the Alphabet (Simon & Schuster) NYT juv 12/1/35 (#1, 4 wk).
The Arts (Simon & Schuster) NYT gen 11/7/37 (#2, 8 wk), 24 wk; PW nf 11/13/37 (#2), pk 12/11/37 (#1, 8 wk), 24 wk; tot 48 wk.
Our Battle (Simon & Schuster) NYT nf 1/8/39 (#10, 8 wk), 12 wk; PW nf 2/11/39 (#10, 4 wk); tot 16 wk.
Van Loon's Lives (Simon & Schuster) NYT nf 10/11/42 (#20), pk 11/1/42 (#5, 9 wk), 25 wk; PW nf 10/24/42 (#5, 12 wk), 16 wk; tot 41 wk.
_____, **and Grace Castagnetta**
Christmas Carols (Simon & Schuster) NYT gen 1/9/38 (#9, 4 wk).

Van Lustbader, Eric
The Ninja (Evans/Dutton) PW hc fic 5/2/80 (#15), pk 5/16/80 (#6, 5 wk), 24 wk; NYT fic 5/11/80 (#12), pk 6/29/80 (#4, 1 wk), 22 wk; (Fawcett/Crest) PW mm pb 5/1/81 (#4), pk 5/8/81 (#2, 1 wk), 9 wk; NYT mm pb 5/3/81 (#12), pk 5/10/81 (#3, 1 wk), 11 wk; tot 66 wk.
Sirens (Evans) NYT fic 5/24/81 (#15), pk 6/14/81 (#13, 1 wk), 4 wk; (Fawcett/Crest) PW mm pb 6/11/82 (#13), pk 6/18/82 (#12, 1 wk), 2 wk; NYT mm pb 6/13/82 (#13, 2 wk); tot 8 wk.
Black Heart (Evans) PW hc fic 4/1/83 (#15), pk 4/8/83 (#14, 1 wk), 3 wk; (Fawcett/Crest) NYT pb fic 4/29/84 (#7), pk 5/20/84 (#5, 1 wk), 7 wk; PW mm pb 5/4/84 (#7), pk 5/18/84 (#6, 1 wk), 6 wk; tot 16 wk.
The Miko (Villard/Random) PW hc fic 8/24/84 (#13), pk 9/21/84 (#5, 1 wk), 10 wk; NYT fic 8/26/84 (#10), pk 9/16/84 (#8, 3 wk), 9 wk; (Fawcett/Crest) NYT pb fic 7/28/85 (#12), pk 8/4/85 (#5, 2 wk), 8 wk; PW mm pb 8/2/85 (#9), pk 8/23/85 (#4, 1 wk), 8 wk; tot 35 wk.
Jian (Villard/Random) PW hc fic 8/16/85 (#9, 1 wk), 5 wk; NYT fic 9/8/85 (#12, 1 wk); (Fawcett/Crest) NYT pb fic 7/27/86 (#12), pk 8/10/86 (#7, 2 wk), 5 wk; PW mm pb 8/1/86 (#12), pk 8/15/86 (#9, 2 wk), 5 wk; tot 16 wk.
Shan (Random) PW hc fic 1/23/87 (#12, 2 wk), 5 wk; NYT fic 2/8/87 (#16), pk 2/22/87 (#12, 1 wk), 2 wk; (Fawcett/Crest) NYT pb fic 1/3/88 (#14), pk 1/17/88 (#7, 2 wk), 5 wk; PW mm pb 1/8/88 (#15), pk 1/29/88 (#9, 1 wk), 5 wk; tot 17 wk.
Zero (Fawcett/Crest) NYT pb fic 1/29/89 (#9, 2 wk), 6 wk; PW mm pb 2/3/89 (#11), pk 2/17/89 (#9, 2 wk), 5 wk; tot 11 wk.
French Kiss (Fawcett/Columbine) PW hc fic 2/3/89 (#14), pk 2/10/89 (#11, 1 wk), 4 wk; NYT fic 2/19/89 (#11, 1 wk), 2 wk; (Fawcett/Crest) NYT pb fic 2/4/90 (#10), pk 2/18/90 (#6, 1 wk), 4 wk; PW mm pb 2/9/90 (#11, 1 wk), 4 wk; tot 14 wk.
White Ninja (Fawcett/Columbine) NYT fic 2/4/90 (#13), pk 2/25/90 (#12, 1 wk), 4 wk; PW hc fic 2/9/90 (#14), pk 2/23/90 (#10), pk 4 wk; tot 8 wk.

Vanocur, Sander
See Pierre Salinger and_____

Van Paassen, Pierre
Days of Our Years (Hillman Curl) NYT gen 3/5/39 (#4), pk 11/5/39 (#3, 4 wk), 40 wk; PW nf 3/11/39 (#5), pk 5/13/39 (#3, 6 wk), 17 wk; tot 57 wk.
The Time Is Now! (Dial) PW nf 6/14/41 (#5), pk 7/12/41 (#3, 4 wk), 12 wk.
That Day Alone (Dial) PW nf 12/13/41 (#5, 8 wk), 16 wk.
The Forgotten Ally (Dial) NYT gen 11/28/43 (#20), pk 12/26/43 (#9, 1 wk), 8 wk.
Earth Could Be Fair (Dial) NYT gen 5/19/46 (#16), pk 6/2/46 (#8, 3 wk), 19 wk; PW nf 7/13/46 (#10, 1 wk); tot 20 wk.

Vansittart, Robert Gilbert
Lessons of My Life [as by Lord Vansittart] (Knopf) NYT gen 2/6/44 (#17, 1 wk).

Van Slyke, Helen
The Mixed Blessing (Popular Library) PW mm pb 9/6/76 (#11), pk 9/27/76 (#10, 1 wk), 6 wk; NYT mm pb 10/3/76 (#10), pk 10/17/ 76 (#8, 1 wk), 3 wk; tot 9 wk.
The Rich and the Righteous (Popular) PW mm pb 3/14/77 (#14), pk 4/4/77 (#11, 1 wk), 4 wk; NYT mm pb 3/27/77 (#9, 1 wk), 3 wk; tot 7 wk.
The Best Place to Be (Popular Library) PW mm pb 9/12/77 (#14), pk 9/19/77 (#10, 4 wk), 6 wk.
Sisters and Strangers (Doubleday) PW hc fic 9/11/78 (#13, 1 wk), 7 wk; NYT fic 11/19/ 78 (#15, 1 wk); (Fawcett) PW mm pb 8/6/79 (#13), pk 8/20/79 (#8, 5 wk), 10 wk; NYT mm pb 8/12/79 (#13), pk 9/2/79 (#5, 1 wk), 12 wk; tot 30 wk.
Always Is Not Forever (Fawcett/Popular Library) PW mm pb 9/11/78 (#11), pk 9/18/ 78 (#6, 1 wk), 8 wk; NYT mm pb 11/12/78 (#14, 2 wk); tot 10 wk.
A Necessary Woman (Doubleday) PW hc fic 4/30/79 (#15), pk 5/14/79 (#11, 1 wk), 6 wk; NYT fic 5/13/79 (#13), pk 6/10/79 (#8, 1 wk), 11 wk; (Fawcett/Popular Library) PW mm pb 4/18/80 (#8), pk 4/25/80 (#1, 1 wk), 10 wk; NYT mm pb 4/20/80 (#6), pk 4/27/80 (#1, 3 wk), 11 wk; tot 38 wk.
No Love Lost (Lippincott) PW hc fic 4/25/ 80 (#8), pk 5/16/80 (#3, 1 wk), 17 wk; NYT fic 4/27/80 (#8), pk 5/18/80 (#3, 2 wk), 17 wk; (Bantam) PW mm pb 7/17/81 (#4), pk 7/24/81 (#3, 3 wk), 9 wk; NYT mm pb 7/19/ 81 (#3), pk 7/26/81 (#2, 3 wk), 10 wk; tot 53 wk.

_____, **with James Elward**
Public Smiles, Private Tears (Harper) NYT fic 4/25/82 (#10), pk 5/9/82 (#7, 1 wk), 14 wk; PW hc fic 5/14/82 (#10, 2 wk), 5 wk; (Bantam) NYT mm pb 2/13/83 (#13), pk 2/20/83 (#5, 1 wk), 5 wk; PW mm pb 2/18/83 (#9), pk 2/25/83 (#6, 1 wk), 5 wk; tot 29 wk.

Vartabedian, Roy E., and Kathy Matthews
Nutripoints (Harper) PW hc nf 2/9/90 (#15), pk 2/16/90 (#10, 1 wk), 4 wk.

Vartan, Vartanig G.
50 Wall Street (McGraw) PW fic 6/10/68 (#11, 1 wk).

Vassiltchikov, Marie
The Berlin Diaries, 1940–1945 (Knopf) NYT nf 6/28/87 (#17), pk 7/26/87 (#12, 1 wk), 2 wk.

Vecsey, George
See Barbara Mandrell and _____
See Loretta Lynn and _____
See Martina Navratilova and _____

_____, **with Leonore Fleischer**
Sweet Dreams (St. Martin's) NYT pb nf 10/27/85 (#8, 1 wk).

Veeck, Bill
Veeck—As in Wreck (Putnam) NYT gen 7/29/62 (#10), pk 10/7/62 (#8, 1 wk), 15 wk; PW nf 8/13/62 (#10), pk 9/10/62 (#7, 2 wk), 10 wk; tot 25 wk.

Velikovsky, Immanel
Worlds in Collision (Macmillan) NYT gen 4/16/50 (#14), pk 5/7/50 (#1, 11 wk), 31 wk; PW nf 4/29/50 (#3), pk 5/20/50 (#1, 3 wk), 21 wk; tot 52 wk.

Vercel, Roger
Tides of Mont St. Michel (Random) NYT fic 10/9/38 (#12, 4 wk).

Vercours
See Jean Brullers

Verdi, Bob
See Jim McMahon and _____

Verrette, Joyce
Dawn of Desire (Avon) NYT mm pb 6/14/ 76 (#8), pk 6/21/76 (#5, 2 wk), 10 wk; NYT mm pb 6/20/76 (#5), pk 7/4/76 (#4, 2 wk), 10 wk; tot 20 wk.

Verrill, A. Hyatt
Home Radio (Harper) PW gen lit 6/17/22 (#9, 4 wk), 8 wk.

Vidal, Gore
The City and the Pillar (Dutton) NYT fic 2/8/48 (#14), pk 2/29/48 (#7, 1 wk), 8 wk.
Julian (Little Brown) NYT fic 6/14/64 (#10), pk 9/6/64 (#2, 1 wk), 32 wk; PW fic 7/6/64 (#7), pk 8/31/64 (#1, 1 wk), 32 wk; tot 64 wk.
Washington, D.C. (Little Brown) NYT fic 5/21/67 (#7), pk 7/30/67 (#2, 1 wk), 21 wk; PW fic 5/22/67 (#8), pk 7/17/67 (#2, 1 wk), 22 wk; NYT pb fic 6/2/68 (#5, 4 wk); tot 47 wk.
Myra Breckinridge (Little Brown) PW fic 2/26/68 (#11), pk 4/22/68 (#1, 1 wk), 30 wk; NYT fic 3/3/68 (#8), pk 4/21/68 (#2, 2 wk), 30 wk; NYT pb fic 10/6/68 (#2, 4 wk), 20 wk; tot 80 wk.
Burr (Random) PW fic 11/12/73 (#4), pk 12/3/73 (#1, 17 wk), 33 wk; NYT fic 11/18/73 (#4), pk 12/9/73 (#1, 21 wk), 39 wk; (Bantam) mm pb 12/8/74 (#1, 4 wk), 6 wk; tot 78 wk.
1876 (Random) PW hc fic 3/15/76 (#5), pk 3/22/76 (#1, 12 wk), 24 wk; NYT fic 3/21/76 (#5), pk 4/11/76 (#1, 9 wk), 25 wk; (Ballantine)

PW mm pb 3/21/77 (#10), pk 3/28/77 (#4, 1 wk), 5 wk; NYT mm pb 4/3/77 (#10, 1 wk), 3 wk; tot 57 wk.

Kalki (Random) PW hc fic 4/17/78 (#15), pk 5/8/78 (#9, 2 wk), 12 wk; NYT fic 5/28/78 (#7, 1 wk), 9 wk; tot 21 wk.

Creation (Random) PW hc fic 3/27/81 (#13), pk 4/24/81 (#4, 1 wk), 13 wk; NYT fic 4/5/81 (#9), pk 5/3/81 (#2, 1 wk), 16 wk; (Ballantine) PW mm pb 2/19/82 (#11), pk 2/26/82 (#9, 1 wk), 5 wk; tot 34 wk.

Lincoln: A Novel (Random) PW hc fic 6/22/84 (#13), pk 8/24/84 (#1, 1 wk), 35 wk; NYT fic 6/24/84 (#7), pk 7/15/84 (#2, 6 wk), 33 wk; (Ballantine) NYT pb fic 6/9/85 (#6), pk 7/7/85 (#4, 1 wk), 11 wk; PW mm pb 6/14/85 (#4, 2 wk), 10 wk; tot 89 wk.

Empire (Random) NYT fic 6/14/87 (#8), pk 7/5/87 (#3, 1 wk), 13 wk; PW hc fic 6/19/87 (#8), pk 7/3/87 (#3, 2 wk), 10 wk; (Ballantine) NYT pb fic 7/10/88 (#13, 2 wk), 3 wk; PW mm pb 7/15/88 (#11, 1 wk); tot 27 wk.

Hollywood: A Novel of America in the 1920s (Random) PW hc fic 2/16/90 (#14), pk 3/2/90 (#9, 1 wk), 5 wk; NYT fic 2/18/90 (#9, 1 wk), 4 wk; tot 9 wk.

Viertel, Joseph
The Last Temptation (Simon & Schuster) NYT fic 6/26/55 (#16), pk 7/17/55 (#14, 1 wk), 2 wk.

Vinge, Joan D.
Return of the Jedi [illustrated storybook adapted by Vinge] (Random) NYT fic 6/12/83 (#1, 8 wk), 32 wk; PW hc fic 6/17/83 (#13), pk 7/15/83 (#1, 2 wk), 25 wk; tot 57 wk.

Vining, Elizabeth Gray
Windows for the Crown Prince (Lippincott) NYT gen 6/1/52 (#12), pk 6/29/52 (#4, 5 wk), 27 wk; PW nf 6/21/52 (#5), pk 6/28/52 (#3, 5 wk), 17 wk; tot 44 wk.

The Virginia Exiles (Lippincott) NYT fic 5/29/55 (#13, 3 wk), 6 wk.

Return to Japan (Lippincott) NYT gen 5/22/60 (#14, 2 wk), 4 wk.

Take Heed of Loving Me (Lippincott) NYT fic 2/2/64 (#10, 1 wk).

Viorst, Judith
My Mama Says There Aren't Any Zombies, Ghosts, Vampires, Creatures, Demons, Monsters, Fields, Goblins or Things (Atheneum) NYT ch pb 11/13/77 (#14), pk 4/30/78 (#11, 24 wk), 70 wk.

Alexander and the Terrible, Horrible, No Good, Very Bad Day (Atheneum) NYT ch pb 11/13/77 (#3), pk 4/30/78 (#1, 24 wk), 70 wk.

Love & Guilt & the Meaning of Life, Etc. (Simon & Schuster) NYT nf 7/1/79 (#13, 1 wk).

Necessary Losses (Simon & Schuster) NYT nf 4/27/86 (#16), pk 5/4/86 (#3, 12 wk), 35 wk; PW hc nf 5/9/86 (#15), pk 5/23/86 (#8, 1 wk), 25 wk; (Fawcett/Crest) NYT pb nf 3/1/87 (#6), pk 3/15/87 (#1, 3 wk), 70 wk; PW mm pb 3/20/87 (#12), pk 3/27/87 (#10, 2 wk), 15 wk; tot 145 wk.

Forever Fifty: And Other Negotiations (Simon & Schuster) NYT fic 10/22/89 (#10, 1 wk), 6 wk.

Earrings [illus. Nola Langer Malone] (Atheneum) PW ch pic 10/26/90 (#10, 4 wk).

Visson, Andre
The Coming Struggle for Peace (Viking) NYT gen 7/9/44 (#15, 1 wk).

Vivier, Max
Peeps at George Washington (Stokes) PW juv 3/19/32 (#6), pk 4/23/32 (#4, 4 wk), 8 wk.

Voelker, John Donaldson [all titles as by Robert Traver]
Anatomy of a Murder (St. Martin's) NYT fic 1/26/58 (#7), pk 3/9/58 (#1, 29 wk), 59 wk; PW fic 2/3/58 (#8), pk 3/3/58 (#1, 28 wk), 54 wk; tot 113 wk.

Hornstein's Boy (St. Martin's) NYT fic 4/22/62 (#13), pk 5/20/62 (#8, 3 wk), 13 wk; PW fic 5/28/62 (#7, 1 wk), 6 wk; tot 19 wk.

Vogel, Speed [Irving L. Vogel]
See Joseph Heller and_____

Vogel, Steve
Reasonable Doubt (St. Martin's) NYT pb nf 6/3/90 (#8, 1 wk), 4 wk.

Vogt, William
Road to Survival (Sloane) NYT gen 8/29/48 (#15), pk 9/26/48 (#6, 1 wk), 13 wk; PW nf 9/25/48 (#5, 1 wk), 3 wk; tot 16 wk.

Voight, Cynthia
Seventeen Against the Dealer (Fawcett/Juniper) PW ch yn ad 8/31/90 (#5, 4 wk).

Von Daniken, Erich
Chariots of the Gods (Bantam) NYT pb gen 2/11/73 (#2), pk 3/11/73 (#1, 12 wk), 48 wk; mm pb 3/10/74 (#2, 4 wk), 12 wk; tot 60 wk.

The Gold of the Gods [trans. Michael Heron] (Putnam) NYT mm pb 9/8/74 (#5, 4 wk), 8 wk.

von Hoffman, Nicholas
Citizen Cohn: The Life and Times of Roy Cohn (Doubleday) PW hc nf 4/8/88 (#11), pk 4/29/88 (#5, 1 wk), 8 wk; NYT nf 4/10/88 (#5), pk 4/17/88 (#4, 1 wk), 8 wk; tot 16 wk.

von Meck, Barbara and Catherine Drinker Bowen
Beloved Friend (Garden City Publishing) NYT nf 3/7/37 (#9, 4 wk).

Vonnegut, Kurt, Jr.
Slaughterhouse-Five (Lawrence/Delacorte) NYT fic 4/27/69 (#10), pk 5/25/69 (#4, 1 wk), 16 wk; PW fic 5/12/69 (#4), pk 5/26/69 (#3, 1 wk), 16 wk; NYT pb fic 6/7/70 (#4, 4 wk); tot 36 wk.
Breakfast of Champions (Delacorte) NYT fic 5/13/73 (#9), pk 7/1/73 (#1, 10 wk), 28 wk; PW fic 5/14/73 (#7), pk 6/25/73 (#1, 11 wk), 27 wk; (Dell/Delta) NYT td pb 5/12/74 (#2, 8 wk), 28 wk; tot 83 wk.
Wampeters, Foma & Granfalloons (Lawrence/Delacorte) PW nf 7/8/74 (#10, 1 wk).
Slapstick, or Lonesome No More! (Lawrence/Delacorte) NYT fic 9/26/76 (#7), pk 11/7/76 (#4, 10 wk), 24 wk; PW hc fic 10/4/76 (#6), pk 11/1/76 (#3, 1 wk), 20 wk; (Delacorte/Delta) PW td pb 9/26/77 (#5), pk 10/17/77 (#3, 3 wk), 11 wk; NYT Td pb 10/2/77 (#15), pk 10/30/77 (#6, 2 wk), 18 wk; tot 73 wk.
Jailbird (Lawrence/Delacorte) PW hc fic 9/10/79 (#14), pk 10/8/79 (#1, 11 wk), 30 wk; NYT fic 9/23/79 (#6), pk 10/7/79 (#1, 5 wk), 31 wk; (Dell) PW mm pb 11/21/80 (#6), pk 12/5/80 (#2, 1 wk), 9 wk; NYT mm pb 11/30/80 (#13), pk 1/18/81 (#4, 1 wk), 6 wk; tot 76 wk.
Palm Sunday: An Autobiographical Collage (Delacorte) PW hc nf 4/17/81 (#14), pk 4/24/81 (#13, 1 wk), 4 wk.
Deadeye Dick (Lawrence/Delacorte) PW hc fic 11/5/82 (#12), pk 1/14/83 (#10, 1 wk), 13 wk; NYT fic 11/14/82 (#13), pk 12/5/82 (#8, 1 wk), 14 wk; tot 27 wk.
Galapagos (Lawrence/Delacorte) NYT fic 10/20/85 (#12), pk 11/3/85 (#5, 3 wk), 17 wk; PW hc fic 10/25/85 (#10), pk 11/8/85 (#5, 3 wk), 17 wk; (Dell) NYT pb fic 10/12/86 (#11), pk 10/26/86 (#8, 1 wk), 7 wk; PW mm pb 10/17/86 (#12), pk 11/7/86 (#11, 1 wk), 4 wk; tot 45 wk.
Bluebeard (Delacorte) NYT fic 11/1/87 (#14), pk 11/8/87 (#8, 1 wk), 11 wk; PW hc fic 11/6/87 (#11, 1 wk), 7 wk; (Dell) PW mm pb 11/18/88 (#13, 2 wk); tot 20 wk.
Hocus Pocus (Putnam) PW hc fic 9/21/90 (#11), pk 10/5/90 (#4, 1 wk), 8 wk; NYT fic 9/23/90 (#6), pk 9/30/90 (#4, 1 wk), 7 wk; tot 15 wk.

von Schuschnigg, Kurt
Austrian Requiem (Putnam) NYT gen 2/2/47 (#16, 1 wk).

My Austria (Knopf) NYT gen 7/3/38 (#9, 4 wk).

Von Tempski, Armine
Thunder in Heaven (Duell Sloan & Pearce) NYT fic 11/29/42 (#23, 1 wk).

Vornholt, John
Masks (Pocket) NYT pb fic 7/16/89 (#11, 1 wk).

Voynich, Ethel Lillian Boole
Put Off Thy Shoes (Macmillan) NYT fic 7/1/45 (#18, 2 wk).

Vreeland, Diana
D.V. [ed. George Plimpton and Christopher Hemphill] (Knopf) NYT nf 7/22/84 (#11), pk 8/5/84 (#8, 1 wk), 11 wk; PW hc nf 8/3/84 (#13), pk 8/24/84 (#9, 2 wk), 10 wk; tot 21 wk.

Waber, Bernard
The House on East 88th Street (Houghton) NYT ch bst 11/11/62 (#14, 26 wk).

Wachter, Oralee
No More Secrets for Me (Little Brown) NYT msc pb 9/30/84 (#4), pk 11/4/84 (#1, 2 wk), 11 wk; PW td pb 10/5/84 (#8), pk 10/26/84 (#4, 1 wk), 10 wk; tot 21 wk.

Wagenknecht, Edward Charles
The Fireside Book of Christmas Stories [ed.] (Bobbs Merrill) NYT gen 12/16/45 (#13), pk 12/30/45 (#8, 1 wk), 4 wk.

Wagner, Jane
The Search for Signs of Intelligent Life in the Universe (Harper) PW hc nf 12/19/86 (#14), pk 2/27/87 (#9, 1 wk), 10 wk; NYT nf 1/18/87 (#9), pk 1/25/87 (#5, 1 wk), 15 wk; tot 25 wk.

Wagner, Phyllis Cerf
See Bennett Cerf, et al.

Wahlberg, Donnie
See Joseph McIntyre, et al.

Wainwright, Gen. Jonathan Mayhew
General Wainwright's Story [ed. Robert Considine] (Doubleday) NYT gen 5/5/46 (#13, 1 wk).

Waitley, Denis
Seeds of Greatness (Pocket) NYT msc pb 9/30/84 (#6, 1 wk).

Wakeman, Frederic
Shore Leave (Rinehart) NYT fic 11/19/44 (#12, 1 wk).
The Hucksters (Rinehart) NYT fic 6/16/46 (#5), pk 7/14/46 (#1, 19 wk), 32 wk; PW fic 6/22/46 (#3), pk 7/6/46 (#1, 15 wk), 26 wk; tot 58 wk.
The Saxon Charm (Rinehart) NYT fic

11/2/47 (#13), pk 11/16/47 (#10, 1 wk), 3 wk.

Deluxe Tour (Rinehart) NYT fic 11/18/56 (#12, 1 wk), 3 wk.

Waldeck, Rosie Goldschmidt
Lustre in the Sky (Doubleday) NYT fic 6/16/46 (#15, 1 wk).

Walden, Jane B.
Igloo (Putnam) PW juv 12/19/31 (#3), pk 1/16/32 (#1, 12 wk), 20 wk.

Waldo, Anna Lee
Sacajawea (Avon) PW td pb 5/28/79 (#6), pk 6/4/79 (#3, 2 wk), 24 wk; NYT td pb 6/3/79 (#9), pk 7/1/79 (#2, 4 wk), 28 wk; PW mm pb 6/6/80 (#13), pk 7/27/84 (#9), pk 4 wk; tot 56 wk.

Prairie (Berkley) PW td pb 11/28/86 (#5, 1 wk), 5 wk; NYT pb fic 12/28/86 (#14, 1 wk); tot 6 wk.

Walker, Alice
The Color Purple (Harcourt) NYT fic 5/8/83 (#15), pk 5/15/83 (#10, 1 wk), 3 wk; PW hc fic 5/20/83 (#14), pk 6/10/83 (#13, 1 wk), 4 wk; (Pocket/Washington Square) NYT td pb 6/12/83 (#4), pk 6/26/83 (#1, 5 wk), 51 wk; PW td pb 6/17/83 (#6), pk 7/1/83 (#2, 17 wk), 72 wk; NYT pb fic 12/8/85 (#12), pk 1/19/86 (#1, 7 wk), 29 wk; PW mm pb 12/20/85 (#5), pk 1/31/86 (#1, 9 wk), 25 wk; tot 184 wk.

The Temple of My Familiar (Harcourt) NYT fic 5/7/89 (#15), pk 6/4/89 (#3, 2 wk), 21 wk; PW hc fic 5/19/89 (#7), pk 6/2/89 (#4, 2 wk), 20 wk; (Pocket) PW mm pb 5/11/90 (#15), pk 6/15/90 (#4, 1 wk), 8 wk; NYT pb fic 5/13/90 (#9), pk 5/27/90 (#5, 1 wk), 9 wk; tot 58 wk.

Walker, Leslie
Sudden Fury (St. Martin's) NYT pb nf 8/5/90 (#9), pk 8/26/90 (#7, 1 wk), 3 wk.

Walker, Mildred
Dr. Norton's Wife (Harcourt) NYT fic 2/5/39 (#7, 4 wk).

Winter Wheat (Harcourt) NYT fic 3/26/44 (#14, 2 wk).

The Quarry (Harcourt) NYT fic 3/9/47 (#11, 2 wk), 8 wk.

The Southwest Corner (Watts) NYT fic 6/10/51 (#15, 1 wk).

Walker, Stanley
City Editor (Stokes) PW nf 12/15/34 (#8, 4 wk), 12 wk.

Mrs. Astor's Horse (Stokes) NYT gen 12/1/35 (#2, 4 wk), 8 wk; PW nf 12/14/35 (#5, 4 wk), 20 wk; tot 28 wk.

Dewey: An American of This Century

(Whittlesey/McGraw) NYT gen 10/15/44 (#18), pk 10/22/44 (#15, 1 wk), 3 wk.

Wallace, Amy
See David Wallechinsky, et al.
See Irving Wallace, et al.

Wallace, Henry A.
New Frontiers (Reynal & Hitchcock) PW nf 11/10/34 (#5, 4 wk).

Sixty Million Jobs (Simon & Schuster) NYT gen 9/30/45 (#5), pk 10/7/45 (#3, 4 wk), 10 wk; PW nf 10/6/45 (#4), pk 10/13/45 (#3, 3 wk), 6 wk; tot 16 wk.

Wallace, Irving
The Chapman Report (Simon & Schuster) NYT fic 6/5/60 (#15), pk 6/26/60 (#4, 16 wk), 28 wk; PW fic 6/13/60 (#7), pk 7/18/60 (#4, 9 wk), 22 wk; tot 50 wk.

The Twenty-Seventh Wife (Simon & Schuster) NYT gen 8/27/61 (#16, 1 wk).

The Prize (Simon & Schuster) NYT fic 6/24/62 (#14), pk 9/30/62 (#3, 2 wk), 26 wk; PW fic 7/9/62 (#10), pk 7/30/62 (#5, 8 wk), 27 wk; tot 53 wk.

The Three Sirens (Simon & Schuster) NYT fic 10/27/63 (#8), pk 11/24/63 (#7, 1 wk), 12 wk; PW fic 11/18/63 (#9), pk 12/9/63 (#6, 1 wk), 10 wk; tot 22 wk.

The Man (Simon & Schuster) NYT fic 10/4/64 (#9), pk 2/14/65 (#2, 4 wk), 38 wk; PW fic 10/12/64 (#8), pk 12/14/64 (#2, 7 wk), 35 wk; NYT pb fic 12/5/65 (#3, 8 wk), 12 wk; tot 85 wk.

The Plot (Simon & Schuster) NYT fic 6/11/67 (#10), pk 6/25/67 (#5, 11 wk), 16 wk; PW fic 6/26/67 (#7), pk 8/14/67 (#4, 2 wk), 18 wk; NYT pb fic 7/7/68 (#3), pk 8/4/68 (#2, 4 wk), 16 wk; tot 50 wk.

The Seven Minutes (Simon & Schuster) NYT fic 10/26/69 (#6), pk 11/23/69 (#3, 3 wk), 17 wk; PW fic 10/27/69 (#8), pk 12/1/69 (#3, 1 wk), 18 wk; NYT pb fic 10/4/70 (#5), pk 11/1/70 (#2, 8 wk), 20 wk; tot 55 wk.

The Word (Simon & Schuster) NYT fic 3/26/72 (#9), pk 5/14/72 (#1, 2 wk), 31 wk; PW fic 4/3/72 (#5), pk 5/1/72 (#1, 4 wk), 29 wk; NYT pb fic 3/11/73 (#4), pk 4/8/73 (#2, 4 wk), 12 wk; (Pocket) PW mm pb 12/4/78 (#12, 1 wk); NYT mm pb 12/10/78 (#12, 1 wk), 2 wk; tot 75 wk.

The Fan Club (Simon & Schuster) PW fic 4/15/74 (#8), pk 5/13/74 (#3, 6 wk), 19 wk; NYT fic 4/21/74 (#9), pk 6/23/74 (#2, 1 wk), 24 wk; (Bantam) NYT mm pb 4/13/75 (#4), pk 5/4/75 (#2, 1 wk), 12 wk; tot 55 wk.

The R Document (Simon & Schuster) PW hc fic 3/29/76 (#10), pk 5/10/76 (#4, 2 wk), 13 wk; NYT fic 4/11/76 (#9), pk 5/16/76 (#3, 1 wk), 13 wk; (Bantam) PW mm pb 2/28/77

(#12), pk 3/14/77 (#6, 2 wk), 6 wk; NYT mm pb 3/13/77 (#9), pk 3/20/77 (#8, 1 wk), 4 wk; tot 36 wk.

The Pigeon Project (Simon & Schuster) PW hc fic 4/9/79 (#15), pk 4/30/79 (#12, 1 wk), 7 wk; NYT fic 4/29/79 (#15), pk 6/17/79 (#12, 1 wk), 7 wk; (Bantam) PW mm pb 4/18/80 (#14), pk 4/25/80 (#13, 2 wk), 4 wk; NYT mm pb 4/27/80 (#12, 2 wk), 3 wk; tot 21 wk.

The Second Lady (NAL) PW hc fic 10/10/80 (#14), pk 11/14/80 (#10, 1 wk), 11 wk; NYT fic 10/26/80 (#9), pk 11/16/80 (#8, 1 wk), 9 wk; (NAL/Signet) PW mm pb 10/9/81 (#9), pk 10/30/81 (#4, 1 wk), 13 wk; NYT mm pb 10/18/81 (#4), pk 11/1/81 (#3, 2 wk), 10 wk; tot 43 wk.

The Almighty (Doubleday) PW hc fic 12/3/82 (#14, 1 wk); (Dell) NYT pb fic 1/15/84 (#6), pk 1/29/84 (#2, 1 wk), 8 wk; PW mm pb 1/20/84 (#6), pk 1/27/84 (#2, 2 wk), 8 wk; tot 17 wk.

The Miracle (Dutton) PW hc fic 9/14/84 (#15), pk 10/5/84 (#11, 1 wk), 7 wk; (NAL/Signet) NYT pb fic 7/7/85 (#8), pk 7/28/85 (#5, 1 wk), 8 wk; PW mm pb 7/12/85 (#7), pk 8/2/85 (#5, 1 wk), 6 wk; tot 21 wk.

The Seventh Secret (Dutton) PW hc fic 1/24/86 (#14), pk 3/7/86 (#8, 1 wk), 8 wk; NYT fic 2/2/86 (#14), pk 3/2/86 (#11, 1 wk), 6 wk; (NAL/Signet) PW mm pb 11/14/86 (#10), pk 11/28/86 (#4, 1 wk), 8 wk; NYT pb fic 11/9/86 (#8), pk 11/23/86 (#3, 1 wk), 8 wk; tot 30 wk.

The Celestial Bed (Dell) NYT pb fic 1/17/88 (#13), pk 2/7/88 (#10, 1 wk), 4 wk; PW mm pb 1/29/88 (#13, 1 wk); tot 5 wk.

The Golden Room (Dell) NYT pb fic 1/22/89 (#13, 2 wk); PW mm pb 1/27/89 (#13, 1 wk); tot 3 wk.

See also David Wallechinsky and _____
See also David Wallechinsky, et al.

Wallace, Irving, with David Wallech- insky, Amy Wallace and Sylvia Wal- lace
The Book of Lists #2 (Morrow) PW hc nf 3/21/80 (#15), pk 4/25/80 (#10, 1 wk), 10 wk; NYT nf 3/23/80 (#10), pk 4/13/80 (#7, 2 wk), 14 wk; (Bantam) PW mm pb 2/6/81 (#9), pk 2/13/81 (#8, 2 wk), 4 wk; NYT mm pb 2/8/81 (#14), pk 2/15/81 (#10, 2 wk), 6 wk; tot 34 wk.

Wallace, Mike, and Gary Paul Gates
Close Encounters (Morrow) NYT nf 10/7/84 (#15), pk 10/14/84 (#7, 1 wk), 9 wk; PW hc nf 10/12/84 (#14), pk 10/19/84 (#12, 2 wk), 4 wk; tot 13 wk.

Wallace, Sylvia
The Fountain (Bantam) NYT mm pb 5/15/77 (#13, 1 wk).
See also Irving Wallace, et al.

Wallach, Anne Tolstoi
Women's Work (NAL) NYT fic 9/6/81 (#11, 1 wk), 3 wk; PW hc fic 9/18/81 (#15), pk 9/25/81 (#14, 1 wk), 4 wk; (NAL/Signet) NYT mm pb 7/18/82 (#9), pk 8/1/82 (#6, 1 wk), 3 wk; PW mm pb 7/23/82 (#10), pk 7/30/82 (#9, 1 wk), 2 wk; tot 12 wk.

Wallechinsky, David
See Michael Medved and _____

_____, **and Irving Wallace**
The People's Almanac (Doubleday) NYT td pb 12/28/75 (#3), pk 3/7/76 (#1, 12 wk), 42 wk; PW td pb 2/2/76 (#4), pk 2/9/76 (#1, 19 wk), 47 wk; tot 89 wk.

The People's Almanac 2 (Bantam) PW td pb 10/30/78 (#5), pk 12/11/78 (#1, 9 wk), 20 wk; NYT td pb 11/12/78 (#2), pk 12/3/78 (#1, 7 wk), 22 wk; tot 42 wk.

_____, **with Irving Wallace and Amy Wallace**
The Book of Lists (Morrow) PW hc nf 6/6/77 (#8), pk 7/4/77 (#1, 5 wk), 37 wk; NYT nf 6/19/77 (#7), pk 7/24/77 (#1, 3 wk), 35 wk; (Bantam) PW mm pb 2/13/78 (#5), pk 2/27/78 (#2, 5 wk), 16 wk; NYT mm pb 2/19/78 (#9), pk 2/26/78 (#2, 6 wk), 17 wk; tot 105 wk.
See also Irving Wallace, et al.

Waller, George
Kidnap (Dial) NYT gen 9/17/61 (#11), pk 10/15/61 (#8, 1 wk), 11 wk; PW nf 10/2/61 (#10, 4 wk), 6 wk; tot 17 wk.

Waller, Leslie
The Swiss Account (Doubleday) NYT fic 2/29/76 (#10), pk 3/7/76 (#9, 1 wk), 3 wk.

Waller, Mary E.
The Windmill on the Dune (Little Brown) PW fic 7/18/31 (#9), pk 8/15/31 (#8, 4 wk), 12 wk.

Wallerstein, Judith S., and Sandra Blakeslee
Second Chances: Men, Women and Children a Decade After Divorce (Houghton/Ticknor & Fields) NYT nf 3/12/89 (#15), pk 4/2/89 (#9, 2 wk), 6 wk; PW hc nf 3/31/89 (#14, 1 wk), 2 wk; tot 8 wk.

Walling, Robert Alfred John
The Corpse with the Dirty Face (Morrow) NYT fic 8/2/36 (#10, 4 wk).

Waln, Nora
The House of Exile (Little Brown) PW nf

6/10/33 (#5), pk 7/15/33 (#2, 8 wk), 20 wk.

Reaching for the Stars (Little Brown) PW nf 4/8/39 (#2), pk 5/13/39 (#1, 8 wk), 36 wk; NYT gen 4/9/39 (#1, 12 wk), 32 wk; tot 68 wk.

Walpole, Sir Hugh
The Secret City (Doran) PW fic 6/7/19 (#8, 4 wk).

The Captives (Doran) PW fic 2/26/21 (#10, 4 wk).

The Cathedral (Doran) PW fic 1/27/23 (#8), pk 3/3/23 (#5, 12 wk), 20 wk.

Portrait of a Man with Red Hair (Doran) PW fic 12/19/25 (#7, 4 wk).

Harmer John (Doran) PW fic 12/18/26 (#6, 4 wk).

Wintersmoon (Doubleday) PW fic 4/21/28 (#2, 12 wk).

Hans Frost (Doubleday) PW fic 11/9/29 (#7), pk 12/14/29 (#5, 4 wk), 12 wk.

Rogue Herries (Doubleday) PW fic 5/17/30 (#6), pk 7/12/30 (#4, 4 wk), 12 wk.

Judith Paris (Doubleday) PW fic 11/14/31 (#7), pk 12/19/31 (#6, 4 wk), 12 wk.

Above the Dark Tumult (Doubleday) PW fic 5/16/31 (#7, 4 wk).

The Fortress (Doubleday) PW fic 10/15/32 (#4, 4 wk), 8 wk.

Vanessa (Doubleday) PW fic 10/14/33 (#5), pk 11/11/33 (#4, 4 wk), 12 wk.

Captain Nicholas (Doubleday) PW fic 10/13/34 (#7, 4 wk).

The Inquisitor (Doubleday) NYT fic 10/6/35 (#4, 4 wk); PW fic 10/12/35 (#7, 4 wk), 8 wk; tot 12 wk.

John Cornelius: His Life and Adventures (Doubleday) NYT fic 11/7/37 (#6, 4 wk).

A Prayer for My Son (Doubleday) NYT fic 11/8/36 (#9, 4 wk); PW fic 11/14/36 (#10), pk 12/12/36 (#6, 8 wk), 12 wk; tot 16 wk.

Joyful Delaneys: A Novel (Doubleday) NYT fic 11/6/38 (#9, 4 wk).

The Sea Tower (Doubleday) NYT fic 11/5/39 (#5, 4 wk).

The Blind Man's House (Doubleday) PW fic 9/13/41 (#9, 8 wk).

Katherine Christian (Doubleday) NYT fic 7/11/43 (#14), pk 7/18/43 (#9, 1 wk), 6 wk.

Walsh, Edmund A.
Total Empire (Bruce) NYT gen 7/22/51 (#15, 1 wk).

Walsh, Maurice
The Road to Nowhere (Stokes) PW fic 9/15/34 (#7, 4 wk).

The Dark Rose (Stokes) NYT fic 4/3/38 (#12, 4 wk).

Walt Disney Productions
Snow White and the Seven Dwarfs (Walt Disney) NYT gen 5/1/38 (#9, 4 wk).

Waltari, Mika
The Egyptian (Putnam) NYT fic 9/11/49 (#7), pk 10/30/49 (#1, 15 wk), 58 wk; PW fic 9/24/49 (#2), pk 10/22/49 (#1, 17 wk), 41 wk; tot 99 wk.

The Adventurer (Putnam) NYT fic 10/8/50 (#10), pk 10/22/50 (#3, 6 wk), 22 wk; PW fic 10/14/50 (#9), pk 11/11/50 (#1, 2 wk), 16 wk; tot 38 wk.

The Wanderer (Putnam) NYT fic 11/11/51 (#12), pk 12/23/51 (#7, 5 wk), 15 wk; PW fic 12/15/51 (#6), pk 12/29/51 (#5, 1 wk), 5 wk; tot 20 wk.

The Dark Angel (Putnam) NYT fic 6/21/53 (#9), pk 7/5/53 (#3, 6 wk), 17 wk; PW fic 6/27/53 (#6), pk 7/25/53 (#2, 1 wk), 11 wk; tot 28 wk.

The Etruscan (Putnam) NYT fic 1/20/57 (#11), pk 2/3/57 (#7, 3 wk), 10 wk; PW fic 2/4/57 (#7, 3 wk), 5 wk; tot 15 wk.

The Secret of the Kingdom (Putnam) NYT fic 3/12/61 (#15, 1 wk), 2 wk.

Walter, Robert H.
Stacy Tower (Doubleday) NYT fic 6/30/63 (#10, 4 wk).

Walz, Jay and Audrey Walz
The Bizarre Sisters (Duell, Sloan & Pearce) NYT fic 5/28/50 (#11), pk 6/11/50 (#10, 3 wk), 13 wk.

Wambaugh, Joseph
The New Centurions (Atlantic Little Brown) NYT fic 2/7/71 (#10), pk 6/27/71 (#2, 1 wk), 32 wk; PW fic 3/1/71 (#9), pk 4/19/71 (#2, 1 wk), 27 wk; NYT pb fic 3/12/72 (#2, 4 wk), 12 wk; tot 71 wk.

The Blue Knight (Atlantic Little Brown) NYT gen 3/19/72 (#10), pk 4/30/72 (#6, 1 wk), 17 wk; PW fic 3/27/72 (#10), pk 5/1/72 (#4, 2 wk), 21 wk; tot 38 wk.

The Onion Field (Delacorte) NYT gen 9/30/73 (#8), pk 10/21/73 (#4, 4 wk), 14 wk; PW nf 10/8/73 (#4), pk 10/15/73 (#3, 1 wk), 13 (Dell) NYT mm pb 9/8/74 (#2, 4 wk), 8 wk; tot 35 wk.

The Choirboys (Delacorte) PW fic 11/24/75 (#7), pk 1/5/76 (#3, 4 wk), 9 wk; NYT fic 11/30/75 (#7), pk 2/8/76 (#2, 8 wk), 28 wk; PW hc fic 2/2/76 (#2, 6 wk), 17 wk; (Dell) NYT mm pb 9/19/76 (#6), pk 10/10/76 (#1, 3 wk), 14 wk; PW mm pb 9/20/76 (#3), pk 9/27/76 (#1, 3 wk), 19 wk; tot 87 wk.

The Black Marble (Delacorte) PW hc fic 12/12/77 (#15), pk 1/30/78 (#4, 3 wk), 18 wk; NYT fic 1/1/78 (#15), pk 2/5/78 (#3, 2 wk),

18 wk; (Dell) mm pb 1/21/79 (#14), pk 1/28/
79 (#5, 4 wk), 10 wk; PW mm pb 1/22/79
(#5, 5 wk), 8 wk; tot 54 wk.

 The Glitter Dome (Perigord/Morrow) PW
hc fic 6/19/81 (#11), pk 7/17/81 (#2, 4 wk), 23
wk; NYT fic 6/28/81 (#8), pk 7/26/81 (#3, 3
wk), 22 wk; (Bantam) PW mm pb 6/18/82
(#8), pk 6/25/82 (#2, 3 wk), 9 wk; NYT mm
pb 6/20/82 (#4), pk 6/27/82 (#1, 1 wk), 10
wk; tot 64 wk.

 The Delta Star (Perigord/Morrow) PW hc
fic 3/11/83 (#9), pk 4/1/83 (#2, 2 wk), 13 wk;
NYT fic 3/13/83 (#10), pk 3/20/83 (#3, 2
wk), 13 wk; (Bantam) NYT pb fic 1/29/84
(#3), pk 2/5/84 (#2, 2 wk), 11 wk; PW mm
pb 2/3/84 (#3, 4 wk), 9 wk; tot 46 wk.

 Lines and Shadows (Perigord/Morrow)
NYT nf 2/26/84 (#8), pk 3/18/84 (#2, 1 wk),
12 wk; PW hc nf 3/2/84 (#7), pk 3/23/84
(#2, 2 wk), 11 wk; (Perigord/Bantam) NYT
pb nf 12/9/84 (#2), pk 12/23/84 (#1, 7 wk),
15 wk; PW mm pb 12/21/84 (#3), pk 1/4/85
(#2, 1 wk), 8 wk; tot 46 wk.

 The Secrets of Harry Bright (Perigord/Mor-
row) NYT fic 10/6/85 (#15), pk 10/27/85 (#5,
1 wk), 17 wk; PW hc fic 10/11/85 (#8), pk
10/18/85 (#6, 2 wk), 14 wk; (Bantam) NYT
pb fic 10/12/86 (#15), pk 10/26/86 (#1, 1 wk),
8 wk; PW mm pb 10/17/86 (#6), pk 11/7/86
(#3, 1 wk), 8 wk; tot 47 wk.

 Echoes in the Darkness (Morrow) NYT nf
2/15/87 (#15), pk 3/8/87 (#4, 1 wk), 13 wk;
PW hc nf 2/20/87 (#14), pk 3/13/87 (#3, 1
wk), 13 wk; (Bantam) NYT pb nf 10/11/87
(#1, 10 wk), 18 wk; PW mm pb 10/16/87
(#13), pk 11/6/87 (#1, 2 wk), 11 wk; tot 55 wk.

 The Blooding (Morrow/Perigord Press)
PW hc nf 2/17/89 (#13), pk 3/24/89 (#3, 1
wk), 12 wk; NYT nf 2/19/89 (#8), pk 3/5/89
(#3, 5 wk), 13 wk; (Bantam) pb nf 11/26/89
(#3), pk 12/10/89 (#2, 3 wk), 15 wk; PW mm
pb 12/8/89 (#7), pk 12/15/89 (#4, 1 wk), 7
wk; tot 47 wk.

 The Golden Orange (Perigord Press/Mor-
row) NYT fic 5/20/90 (#15), pk 6/3/90 (#5,
2 wk), 11 wk; PW hc fic 5/25/90 (#11), pk
6/15/90 (#5, 2 wk), 10 wk; tot 21 wk.

Warburg, James P.
 Hell Bent for Election (Doubleday) NYT
gen 12/1/35 (#6), pk 4/5/36 (#2, 4 wk), 12
wk; PW nf 2/15/36 (#8), pk 3/14/36 (#5, 4
wk), 16 wk; tot 28 wk.

 Still Hell Bent (Doubleday) NYT gen 7/5/
36 (#8, 4 wk), 8 wk; PW nf 8/15/36 (#9, 4
wk); tot 12 wk.

Ward, Barbara
 The West at Bay (Norton) NYT gen 10/31/
48 (#13, 1 wk), 3 wk.

 Policy for the West (Norton) NYT gen 1/28/
51 (#8, 3 wk), 5 wk.

 The Rich Nations and the Poor Nations
(Norton) NYT gen 4/1/62 (#16), pk 5/13/62
(#11, 1 wk), 5 wk; PW nf 6/4/62 (#10, 1 wk);
tot 6 wk.

**Ward, Geoffrey C., with Ric Burns and
 Ken Burns**
 The Civil War: An Illustrated History
(Knopf) PW hc nf 10/12/90 (#11), pk 11/16/
90 (#1, 3 wk), 11 wk; NYT nf 10/14/90 (#3),
pk 11/11/90 (#1, 3 wk), 12 wk; tot 23 wk.

Ward, Mrs. Humphrey
 Harvest (Dodd) PW fic 6/12/20 (#8, 4
wk).

 Helena (Dodd) PW fic 1/31/20 (#10, 4 wk).

Ward, Maisie
 Gilbert Keith Chesterton (Sheed) NYT gen
11/14/43 (#17, 1 wk).

Ward, Mary Jane
 The Snake Pit (Random) NYT fic 4/28/46
(#13), pk 5/19/46 (#2, 6 wk), 23 wk; PW fic
5/18/46 (#1, 1 wk), 17 wk; tot 40 wk.

Warhol, Andy
 The Andy Warhol Diaries [ed. Pat Hack-
ett] (Warner) NYT nf 5/28/89 (#8), pk 6/11/
89 (#5, 1 wk), 16 wk; PW hc nf 6/2/89 (#8),
pk 6/16/89 (#3, 1 wk), 12 wk; tot 28 wk.

Warren, Charles Marquis
 Only the Valiant (Macmillan) NYT fic
3/28/43 (#10), pk 5/2/43 (#9, 1 wk), 7 wk.

Warren, Lella
 Foundation Stone (Knopf) PW fic 10/12/40
(#5, 12 wk), 20 wk.

Warren, Robert Penn
 All the King's Men (Harcourt) NYT fic
9/15/46 (#6, 3 wk), 9 wk; PW fic 10/12/46
(#8, 1 wk); tot 10 wk.

 World Enough and Time (Random) NYT
fic 7/9/50 (#6), pk 7/30/50 (#2, 8 wk), 18 wk;
PW fic 7/22/50 (#2, 9 wk), 11 wk; tot 29 wk.

 Band of Angels (Random) NYT fic 9/4/55
(#15), pk 9/18/55 (#5, 1 wk), 15 wk; PW fic
10/8/55 (#5, 1 wk), 3 wk; tot 18 wk.

 The Cave (Random) NYT fic 9/13/59 (#9),
pk 10/18/59 (#3, 1 wk), 20 wk; PW fic 9/14/
59 (#8), pk 10/26/59 (#4, 1 wk), 10 wk; tot
30 wk.

 Wilderness (Random) NYT fic 1/7/62 (#16,
1 wk).

Warren Commission
 *The Warren Commission Report on the As-
sassination of John F. Kennedy* [The report was
published by several publishing companies;
the figures reflect combined bestseller list
activity by the Doubleday and McGraw

editions] (Doubleday/McGraw) NYT gen 11/8/64 (#7), pk 11/29/64 (#4, 1 wk), 3 wk; PW nf 11/9/64 (#9), pk 12/7/64 (#5, 1 wk), 5 wk; tot 8 wk.

Warrick, Mrs. Lamar
Yesterday's Children (Crowell) NYT fic 6/13/43 (#14, 1 wk), 2 wk.

Waterman, Robert H., Jr.
The Renewal Factor: How the Best Get and Keep the Competitive Edge (Bantam) NYT nf 10/18/87 (#15), pk 11/8/87 (#12, 1 wk), 3 wk; PW hc nf 11/13/87 (#14, 1 wk); tot 4 wk.
See also Thomas J. Peters and _____

Waters, Ethel and Charles
His Eye Is on the Sparrow (Doubleday) NYT gen 3/25/51 (#9), pk 4/15/51 (#3, 5 wk), 32 wk; PW nf 4/14/51 (#8), pk 4/21/51 (#3, 4 wk), 21 wk; tot 53 wk.

Watling, James
See Linda Hayward

Watson, George
Nutrition and Your Mind (Harper) NYT gen 6/4/72 (#9, 1 wk).

Watson, James D.
The Double Helix (Atheneum) NYT gen 3/24/68 (#10), pk 5/12/68 (#3, 2 wk), 18 wk; PW nf 4/1/68 (#11), pk 5/6/68 (#3, 1 wk), 18 wk; tot 36 wk.

Watson, Jane Werner
The Golden History of the World (Simon & Schuster) NYT fic 12/7/47 (#14, 1 wk), 2 wk.
The Golden Geography (Simon & Schuster) NYT ch bst 11/16/52 (#2, 40 wk).
The Golden Bible for Children: The New Testament (Simon & Schuster) NYT ch bst 11/14/54 (#14, 40 wk).
Walt Disney's Living Desert (Simon & Schuster) NYT ch bst 11/13/55 (#9, 40 wk).
The World of Science (Golden) NYT ch bst 11/2/58 (#15), pk 11/1/59 (#3, 25 wk), 84 wk.
Walt Disney's People and Places (Golden) NYT ch bst 11/13/60 (#11, 27 wk).
Dinosaurs (Golden) NYT ch pb 11/13/77 (#5, 46 wk).
See also Steffi Fletcher and _____

Watson, John H., M.D. [fictional character]
See Nicholas Meyer

Watson, Thomas J., Jr., and Peter Petre
Father, Son & Co.: My Life at IBM and Beyond (Bantam) NYT nf 6/10/90 (#10), pk 7/8/90 (#3, 2 wk), 14 wk; PW hc nf 6/15/90 (#10), pk 7/13/90 (#3, 1 wk), 11 wk; tot 25 wk.

Wattenberg, Ben J.
See Richard M. Scammon and _____

Watterson, Bill
Calvin and Hobbes (Andrews McMeel & Parker) PW td pb 4/10/87 (#10), pk 1/22/87 (#1, 1 wk), 79 wk; NYT msc pb 4/19/87 (#6), pk 5/31/87 (#2, 6 wk), 50 wk; tot 129 wk.
Something Under the Bed Is Drooling: A Calvin and Hobbes Collection (Andrews & McMeel) NYT msc pb 3/27/88 (#1, 18 wk), 27 wk; PW td pb 4/1/88 (#2), pk 4/8/88 (#1, 10 wk), 31 wk; tot 58 wk.
The Essential Calvin and Hobbes (Andrews & McMeel) NYT msc pb 10/2/88 (#2), pk 10/9/88 (#1, 6 wk), 18 wk; PW td pb 10/14/88 (#4), pk 11/4/88 (#1, 3 wk), 28 wk; tot 46 wk.
The Calvin and Hobbes Lazy Sunday Book (Andrews McMeel & Parker) NYT msc pb 10/8/89 (#2), pk 10/15/89 (#1, 6 wk), 17 wk; PW td pb 10/13/89 (#3), pk 11/3/89 (#1, 3 wk), 17 wk; tot 34 wk.
Yukon Ho! (Andrews McMeel & Parker) NYT msc pb 3/26/89 (#1, 15 wk), 27 wk; PW td pb 3/31/89 (#3), pk 4/7/89 (#1, 12 wk), 40 wk; tot 67 wk.
Weirdos from Another Planet! A Calvin and Hobbes Collection (Andrews McMeel & Parker) NYT msc pb 3/25/90 (#2), pk 4/1/90 (#1, 5 wk), 26 wk; PW td pb 3/30/90 (#4), pk 4/6/90 (#1, 7 wk), 29 wk; tot 55 wk.
The Authoritative Calvin and Hobbes (Andrews McMeel & Parker) NYT msc pb 9/30/90 (#5), pk 10/7/90 (#1, 12 wk), 14 wk; PW td pb 10/5/90 (#4), pk 10/12/90 (#1, 6 wk), 12 wk; tot 26 wk.

Waugh, Alec
Island in the Sun (Farrar) NYT fic 1/22/56 (#10), pk 4/8/56 (#5, 1 wk), 20 wk; PW fic 2/11/56 (#7), pk 2/25/56 (#4, 2 wk), 10 wk; tot 30 wk.
Fuel for the Flame (Farrar) NYT fic 1/31/60 (#10, 3 wk), 10 wk; PW fic 3/7/60 (#8, 1 wk); tot 11 wk.

Waugh, Evelyn
Scoop (Little Brown) NYT fic 9/4/38 (#14, 4 wk).
Brideshead Revisited (Little Brown) NYT fic 1/20/46 (#8), pk 1/27/46 (#3, 3 wk), 24 wk; PW fic 1/26/46 (#3, 2 wk), 13 wk; td pb 2/5/82 (#8), pk 3/26/82 (#1, 1 wk), 17 wk; NYT td pb 2/14/82 (#2), pk 3/21/82 (#1, 1 wk), 16 wk; tot 70 wk.
The Loved One (Little Brown) NYT fic 7/18/48 (#6), pk 8/1/48 (#2, 4 wk), 17 wk; PW fic 7/31/48 (#2, 5 wk), 12 wk; tot 29 wk.
Scott-King's Modern Europe (Little Brown) NYT fic 3/20/49 (#15, 1 wk).

Helena (Little Brown) NYT fic 11/5/50 (#14), pk 11/12/50 (#10, 1 wk), 8 wk.

Men at Arms (Little Brown) NYT fic 11/2/52 (#13), pk 11/16/52 (#7, 2 wk), 12 wk.

Officers and Gentlemen (Little Brown) NYT fic 7/24/55 (#16), pk 8/14/55 (#9, 1 wk), 8 wk.

The End of the Battle (Little Brown) NYT fic 2/4/62 (#16), pk 2/25/62 (#15, 1 wk), 2 wk.

Wax, Judith
Starting in the Middle (Holt) NYT nf 8/26/79 (#15, 1 wk).

Way, Katharine
See Dexter Masters and _____

Wayne, Palma
See Dimitri Marianoff and _____

Webb, James
A Country Such as This (Bantam) NYT pb fic 3/31/85 (#14, 1 wk).

Weber, Joe
Defcon One (Jove) NYT pb fic 11/11/90 (#10), pk 12/2/90 (#7, 1 wk), 5 wk; PW mm pb 11/30/90 (#12, 1 wk), 3 wk; tot 8 wk.

Wecter, Dixon
When Johnny Comes Marching Home (Greenwood) NYT gen 10/22/44 (#19), pk 12/24/44 (#12, 1 wk), 2 wk.

Age of the Great Depression, 1929–1941 (Macmillan) NYT gen 8/15/48 (#14), pk 8/29/48 (#13, 1 wk), 2 wk.

Wedemeyer, Gen. Albert C.
Wedemeyer Reports (Holt) NYT gen 12/7/58 (#16), pk 1/18/59 (#3, 5 wk), 18 wk; PW nf 12/29/58 (#5), pk 1/12/59 (#3, 5 wk), 15 wk; tot 33 wk.

Weeks, Edward, and Emily Flint
Jubilee [eds.] (Little Brown) NYT gen 11/24/57 (#15), pk 12/15/57 (#11, 2 wk), 9 wk; PW nf 1/20/58 (#10, 1 wk); tot 10 wk.

Weidman, Jerome
I Can Get It for You Wholesale (Modern Library) NYT fic 7/4/37 (#10, 4 wk).

The Enemy Camp (Random) NYT fic 7/6/58 (#6), pk 7/27/58 (#2, 9 wk), 23 wk; PW fic 7/7/58 (#8), pk 9/15/58 (#1, 1 wk), 18 wk; tot 41 wk.

Before You Go (Random) NYT fic 8/14/60 (#15), pk 8/21/60 (#9, 1 wk), 10 wk; PW fic 8/29/60 (#9, 1 wk); tot 11 wk.

The Sound of Bow Bells (Random) NYT fic 8/19/62 (#13), pk 8/26/62 (#12, 1 wk), 4 wk.

Weil, Joe, as told to J.B. Brannon
"Yellow Kid" Weil (Ziff Davis) NYT gen 8/1/48 (#16), pk 8/22/48 (#14, 1 wk), 2 wk.

Weinberg, Arthur
Attorney for the Damned: Clarence Darrow (Simon & Schuster) PW nf 2/17/58 (#8), pk 3/31/58 (#5, 1 wk), 7 wk; NYT gen 1/12/58 (#15), pk 3/23/58 (#6, 1 wk), 20 wk; tot 27 wk.

Weinstein, Howard
Deep Domain (Pocket) NYT pb fic 4/12/87 (#8, 1 wk), 3 wk; PW mm pb 4/24/87 (#14), pk 5/1/87 (#10, 1 wk), 2 wk; tot 5 wk.

Exiles (Pocket) NYT pb fic 11/11/90 (#9), pk 11/18/90 (#8, 1 wk), 3 wk; PW mm pb 11/23/90 (#15, 1 wk); tot 4 wk.

Weinstock, Matt
My L.A. (Current) NYT gen 11/9/47 (#13), pk 11/16/47 (#11, 1 wk), 5 wk.

Muscatel at Noon (Morrow) NYT gen 2/4/51 (#14, 1 wk), 2 wk.

Weis, Margaret, and Tracy Hickman
War of the Twins (TSR/Random) NYT pb fic 7/6/86 (#12), pk 7/3/86 (#11, 1 wk), 5 wk; PW td pb 7/25/86 (#9), pk 8/1/86 (#5, 2 wk), 8 wk; tot 13 wk.

Dragonlance Legends, Vol. 3: Test of the Twins (TSR/Random) NYT pb fic 10/5/86 (#8), pk 10/12/86 (#4, 1 wk), 5 wk; PW td pb 10/10/86 (#9), pk 10/31/86 (#3, 2 wk), 6 wk; tot 11 wk.

The Magic of Krynn: Dragonlance Tales, Vol. 1 [eds.] (TSR/Random) NYT pb fic 4/26/87 (#10), pk 5/3/87 (#9, 1 wk), 7 wk; PW td pb 5/22/87 (#9), pk 5/29/87 (#7, 1 wk), 4 wk; tot 11 wk.

Kender, Gully Dwarves, and Gnomes [eds.] (TSR) NYT pb fic 9/13/87 (#15), pk 9/20/87 (#12, 1 wk), 4 wk.

Forging the Darksword (Bantam/Spectra) NYT pb fic 12/27/87 (#15), pk 1/17/88 (#14, 1 wk), 2 wk.

Triumph of the Darksword (Bantam/Spectra) NYT pb fic 8/21/88 (#12), pk 8/28/88 (#8, 1 wk), 4 wk; PW mm pb 9/9/88 (#11, 1 wk), 2 wk; tot 6 wk.

Doom of the Darksword (Bantam/Spectra) NYT pb fic 5/1/88 (#9), pk 5/8/88 (#8, 1 wk), 4 wk; PW mm pb 5/13/88 (#9, 1 wk), 4 wk; tot 8 wk.

The Prophet of Akhran (Bantam) NYT pb fic 9/10/89 (#13, 1 wk), 2 wk.

Weisinger, Hendrie, and Norman Lobsenz
Nobody's Perfect (Stratford/Harper) PW hc nf 3/5/82 (#15), pk 4/2/82 (#8, 1 wk), 8 wk; NYT nf 3/21/82 (#15), pk 4/4/82 (#6, 1 wk), 4 wk; tot 12 wk.

(#6, 1 wk), 28 wk; (Warner) NYT pb nf 10/
20/85 (#2, 3 wk), 10 wk; tot 84 wk.

Wendt, Herbert
In Search of Adam (Houghton) NYT gen
9/16/56 (#13, 1 wk).

Wendt, Lloyd, and Herman Kogan
Lords of the Levee (Bobbs Merrill) NYT nf
2/28/43 (#10, 1 wk), 11 wk.
   Give the Lady What She Wants (Rand Mc-
Nally) NYT gen 6/8/52 (#13), pk 7/20/52
(#11, 2 wk), 11 wk.
   See also Herman Kogan and ____

Wentworth, Patricia
Mr. Zero (Lippincott) NYT fic 9/4/38
(#11, 4 wk).

Wenzlick, Roy
The Coming Boom in Real Estate (Simon &
Schuster) NYT gen 7/5/36 (#5, 4 wk).

Werfel, Franz V.
The Forty Days of Musa Dagh (Viking) PW
fic 1/12/35 (#3), pk 2/9/35 (#1, 4 wk), 24 wk.
   Hearken Unto the Voice (Viking) NYT fic
4/3/38 (#8, 4 wk).
   The Song of Bernadette (Viking) PW fic
6/13/42 (#6), pk 8/8/42 (#1, 14 wk), 47 wk;
NYT fic 8/9/42 (#2), pk 8/16/42 (#1, 13 wk),
50 wk; tot 97 wk.
   Star of the Unborn (Viking) NYT fic 3/24/
46 (#12, 2 wk), 3 wk.

Werner, Jane
See Jane Werner Watson

Werner, M.R.
Barnum (Harcourt) PW gen lit 5/26/23
(#11, 8 wk), 12 wk.

Werner, Max
The Great Offensive (Viking) NYT nf 11/8/
42 (#17, 1 wk).

Wertenbaker, Charles
Invasion! (Appleton) NYT gen 9/24/44
(#10), pk 10/1/44 (#9, 1 wk), 4 wk.
   The Death of Kings (Random) NYT fic
3/7/54 (#16), pk 4/4/54 (#12, 1 wk), 6 wk.

Wertenbaker, Lael Tucker
Lament for Four Virgins [as by Lael Tuc-
ker] (Random) NYT fic 8/17/52 (#13, 1 wk),
2 wk.

Wescott, Glenway
The Grandmothers (Harper) PW fic 10/22/
27 (#2, 4 wk), 12 wk.
   Apartment in Athens (Harper) NYT fic
3/25/45 (#11), pk 4/15/45 (#8, 2 wk), 12 wk;
PW fic 5/12/45 (#9, 1 wk); tot 13 wk.

West, Anthony
Heritage (Random) NYT fic 10/23/55
(#16), pk 10/30/55 (#11, 2 wk), 7 wk.

West, J.B., with Mary Lynn Kotz
Upstairs at the White House (Coward Mc-
Cann) PW nf 11/5/73 (#9), pk 1/21/74 (#3, 1
wk), 18 wk; NYT gen 11/11/73 (#10), pk 2/17/
74 (#3, 1 wk), 21 wk; (Warner) NYT mm pb
10/13/74 (#4, 4 wk); tot 43 wk.

West, Jessamyn
The Friendly Persuasion (Harcourt) NYT
fic 1/20/46 (#13), pk 1/27/46 (#12, 1 wk), 3
wk.
   The Witch Diggers (Harcourt) NYT fic
2/4/51 (#12), pk 3/4/51 (#10, 1 wk), 5 wk.
   Cress Delahanty (Harcourt) NYT fic 1/31/
54 (#10), pk 3/14/54 (#8, 1 wk), 11 wk; PW
fic 2/13/54 (#9), pk 3/20/54 (#8, 1 wk), 2 wk;
tot 13 wk.
   Love, Death and the Ladies' Drill Team
(Harcourt) NYT fic 1/8/56 (#16, 1 wk).
   To See the Dream (Harcourt) NYT gen 3/
10/57 (#13, 1 wk), 2 wk.
   South of the Angels (Harcourt) NYT fic
5/15/60 (#14), pk 5/29/60 (#13, 1 wk), 5 wk.
   Except for Me and Thee (Harcourt) NYT
fic 4/20/69 (#10), pk 5/18/69 (#4, 1 wk), 20
wk; PW fic 5/5/69 (#6), pk 6/16/69 (#4, 1
wk), 24 wk; tot 44 wk.
   The Massacre at Fall Creek (Harcourt) PW
fic 5/12/75 (#10), pk 6/2/75 (#6, 3 wk), 13
wk; NYT fic 5/18/75 (#8), pk 6/1/75 (#6, 4
wk), 13 wk; (Fawcett/Crest) PW mm pb 4/
26/76 (#12), pk 5/3/76 (#10, 1 wk), 4 wk; tot
30 wk.

West, Levon
Flight to Everywhere [as by Ivan Dmitri]
(McGraw) NYT gen 2/18/45 (#24, 1 wk).

West, Morris L.
The Devil's Advocate (Morrow) NYT fic
10/4/59 (#14), pk 3/13/60 (#4, 1 wk), 38 wk.
   Daughter of Silence (Morrow) NYT fic 12/
10/61 (#11), pk 2/18/62 (#5, 3 wk), 21 wk; PW
fic 12/25/61 (#8), pk 2/19/62 (#4, 2 wk), 17
wk; tot 38 wk.
   The Shoes of the Fisherman (Morrow) NYT
fic 6/9/63 (#6), pk 6/30/63 (#1, 14 wk), 43
wk; PW fic 6/10/63 (#6), pk 7/1/63 (#1, 16
wk), 44 wk; tot 87 wk.
   The Ambassador (Morrow) PW fic 4/26/65
(#10), pk 6/21/65 (#1, 1 wk), 27 wk; NYT fic
5/2/65 (#7), pk 5/30/65 (#2, 4 wk), 21 wk;
pb fic 2/6/66 (#3, 4 wk), 12 wk; tot 60 wk.
   The Tower of Babel (Morrow) NYT fic
2/25/68 (#9), pk 3/24/68 (#3, 1 wk), 17 wk;
PW fic 3/4/68 (#10), pk 4/1/68 (#2, 1 wk), 19
wk; tot 36 wk.
   Summer of the Red Wolf (Morrow) NYT fic
10/24/71 (#10, 1 wk); PW fic 11/15/71 (#9, 1
wk); tot 2 wk.
   The Salamander (Morrow) NYT fic 9/16/

73 (#9), pk 11/11/73 (#5, 3 wk), 23 wk; PW fic 10/8/73 (#4), pk 11/19/73 (#2, 1 wk), 16 wk; (Pocket) NYT mm pb 11/10/74 (#5, 4 wk), 8 wk; tot 47 wk.

Harlequin (Morrow) NYT fic 10/27/74 (#10), pk 12/1/74 (#7, 10 wk), 20 wk; PW fic 11/4/74 (#10), pk 12/2/74 (#6, 2 wk), 19 wk; tot 39 wk.

The Navigator (Morrow) PW hc fic 10/11/76 (#7, 1 wk), 5 wk; NYT fic 10/17/76 (#10), pk 11/7/76 (#9, 2 wk), 4 wk; tot 9 wk.

Proteus (Morrow) PW hc fic 2/12/79 (#15), pk 3/5/79 (#7, 1 wk), 9 wk; NYT fic 2/25/79 (#11), pk 3/11/79 (#8, 2 wk), 9 wk; (Bantam) PW mm pb 5/9/80 (#13, 1 wk), 3 wk; tot 21 wk.

Clowns of God (Morrow) PW hc fic 6/26/81 (#13), pk 8/7/81 (#7, 1 wk), 15 wk; NYT fic 7/19/81 (#15), pk 8/2/81 (#5, 1 wk), 14 wk; (Bantam) PW mm pb 4/30/82 (#12), pk 5/7/82 (#6, 1 wk), 6 wk; NYT mm pb 5/9/82 (#11), pk 5/23/82 (#9, 1 wk), 7 wk; tot 42 wk.

The World Is Made of Glass (Morrow) NYT fic 7/24/83 (#13, 4 wk).

West, Nathanael
The Complete Works of Nathanael West (Farrar) NYT fic 6/9/57 (#16, 1 wk).

West, Owen
The Funhouse (Jove) PW mm pb 12/12/80 (#15, 2 wk).

West, Patricia Salter
See Ernest Havemann and _____

West, Rebecca
The Thinking Reed (Viking) NYT fic 4/5/36 (#5), pk 5/3/36 (#3, 4 wk), 8 wk; PW fic 4/11/36 (#3), pk 5/9/36 (#2, 4 wk), 20 wk; tot 28 wk.

The Meaning of Treason (Viking) NYT gen 12/28/47 (#13), pk 2/8/48 (#4, 1 wk), 16 wk; PW nf 2/7/48 (#4, 1 wk), 5 wk; tot 21 wk.

A Train of Powder (Viking) NYT gen 4/10/55 (#15), pk 5/15/55 (#13, 1 wk), 7 wk.

The Fountain Overflows (Viking) NYT fic 12/23/56 (#12), pk 1/27/57 (#2, 3 wk), 20 wk; PW fic 1/7/57 (#4), pk 1/28/57 (#2, 4 wk), 12 wk; tot 32 wk.

The Birds Fall Down (Viking) NYT fic 10/30/66 (#8), pk 1/29/66 (#3, 2 wk), 25 wk; PW fic 11/7/66 (#8), pk 12/5/66 (#3, 8 wk), 23 wk; NYT pb fic 11/5/67 (#4, 8 wk), 12 wk; tot 60 wk.

West, Red, with Sonny West and Dave Hebler, as told to Steve Dunleavy
Elvis: What Happened? (Ballantine) PW mm pb 9/5/77 (#9), pk 9/19/77 (#3, 2 wk),

10 wk; NYT mm pb 9/11/77 (#6), pk 9/18/77 (#1, 1 wk), 10 wk; tot 20 wk.

West, Sonny
See Red West, et al.

Westcott, Jan Vlachos
Border Lord (Crown) NYT fic 12/1/46 (#13, 2 wk), 7 wk.

Captain for Elizabeth (Crown) NYT fic 12/5/48 (#16), pk 1/9/49 (#11, 1 wk), 5 wk.

Westheimer, David
Von Ryan's Express (Doubleday) NYT fic 2/23/64 (#10), pk 3/22/64 (#6, 7 wk), 22 wk; PW fic 2/24/64 (#8), pk 3/30/64 (#5, 7 wk), 24 wk; tot 46 wk.

Westmacott, Mary
See Agatha Christie

Weston, Christine
Indigo (Scribner) NYT fic 11/21/43 (#11), pk 2/27/44 (#10, 1 wk), 7 wk; PW fic 2/12/44 (#10, 1 wk); tot 8 wk.

Weygandt, Cornelius
The Plenty of Pennsylvania (Kensey) NYT nf 11/15/42 (#13, 1 wk), 3 wk.

On the Edge of Evening (Putnam) NYT gen 4/14/46 (#8), pk 4/28/46 (#7, 1 wk), 5 wk.

Whalen, Richard
The Founding Father (NAL) NYT gen 1/10/65 (#10), pk 2/28/65 (#2, 5 wk), 28 wk; PW nf 1/25/65 (#4), pk 2/22/65 (#2, 6 wk), 30 wk; NYT pb gen 3/6/66 (#2, 12 wk); tot 70 wk.

Wharton, Edith
The Age of Innocence (Appleton) PW fic 1/8/21 (#3, 12 wk), 16 wk.

Glimpses of the Moon (Appleton) PW fic 9/16/22 (#1, 4 wk), 16 wk.

A Son at the Front (Scribner) PW fic 11/24/23 (#4, 4 wk).

Twilight Sleep (Appleton) PW fic 6/25/27 (#5), pk 7/30/27 (#2, 8 wk), 16 wk.

The Children (Appleton) PW fic 10/27/28 (#4, 4 wk), 12 wk.

The Mother's Recompense (Appleton) PW fic 6/20/25 (#2, 4 wk), 8 wk.

Hudson River Bracketed (Appleton) PW fic 1/11/30 (#3, 4 wk), 8 wk.

The Gods Arrive (Appleton) PW fic 10/15/32 (#9), pk 11/12/32 (#7, 4 wk), 8 wk.

A Backward Glance (Appleton) PW nf 7/14/34 (#6, 4 wk).

The Buccaneers (Viking) NYT fic 11/6/38 (#11, 4 wk).

Wharton, William
Birdy (Avon) NYT mm pb 2/24/80 (#14, 1 wk).

Wheeler, Elmer
The Fat Boy's Book (Avon) NYT gen 4/22/
51 (#12, 1 wk), 4 wk.

Wheeler, Harvey
See Eugene Burdick and _____

Whipple, Beverly
See Alice Kahn Ladas, et al.

Whitaker, John Thompson
We Cannot Escape History (Macmillan)
NYT gen 4/4/43 (#18), pk 5/23/43 (#10, 2
wk), 6 wk.

**Whitaker, Rodney [all titles as by Trevan-
ian]**
The Eiger Sanction (Crown) NYT fic 12/3/
72 (#10), pk 1/28/73 (#8, 2 wk), 9 wk; PW
fic 12/11/72 (#8), pk 1/22/73 (#7, 1 wk), 7 wk;
NYT pb fic 11/11/73 (#4, 4 wk), 8 wk; tot 24
wk.
The Loo Sanction (Crown) PW fic 1/7/74
(#10, 1 wk); (Avon) NYT mm pb 1/12/75 (#4,
1 wk), 3 wk; tot 4 wk.
Shibumi (Crown) NYT fic 5/13/79 (#15),
pk 7/1/79 (#3, 5 wk), 23 wk; PW hc fic
5/14/79 (#12), pk 7/23/79 (#3, 1 wk), 21 wk;
(Ballantine) PW mm pb 6/13/80 (#2), pk 6/
20/80 (#1, 3 wk), 23 wk; NYT mm pb 6/15/
80 (#3, 2 wk), 22 wk; tot 89 wk.
The Summer of Katya (Crown) PW hc fic
5/13/83 (#11), pk 6/10/83 (#4, 6 wk), 18 wk;
NYT fic 5/15/83 (#9), pk 6/5/83 (#5, 2 wk),
19 wk; (Ballantine) NYT pb fic 7/8/84 (#3,
1 wk), 9 wk; PW mm pb 7/13/84 (#4), pk
7/20/84 (#2, 1 wk), 9 wk; tot 55 wk.

White, Anne Hitchcock
*Junket: The Dog Who Liked Everything "Just
So"* (Viking) NYT ch bst 11/13/55 (#10, 40
wk).

White, Anne Terry
The Golden Treasury of Myths and Legends
[adapted by] (Golden) NYT ch bst 11/1/59
(#4, 25 wk).
See also Rachel Carson

White, Burton L.
The First Three Years of Life (Avon) NYT
td pb 7/23/78 (#15), pk 7/30/78 (#8, 1 wk),
4 wk; PW td pb 7/31/78 (#10), pk 8/28/78
(#5, 2 wk), 8 wk; tot 12 wk.

White, Charles William
In the Blazing Light (Duell Sloan &
Pearce) NYT fic 2/3/46 (#16, 1 wk).

White, D. Robert
The Official Lawyer's Handbook (Simon &
Schuster/Wallaby) PW td pb 1/6/84 (#9), pk
1/20/84 (#5, 1 wk), 10 wk.

**White, Elwyn Brooks [all titles as by
E.B. White]**
Wild Flag (Houghton) NYT gen 1/19/47
(#13, 1 wk).
Here Is New York (Harper) NYT gen 1/22/
50 (#12, 1 wk).
Charlotte's Web (Harper) NYT fic 11/9/52
(#13, 1 wk), 3 wk; ch bst 11/16/52 (#7), pk
5/7/67 (#1, 137 wk), 486 wk; tot 489 wk.
The Second Tree from the Corner (Harper)
NYT gen 2/7/54 (#5), pk 2/28/54 (#2, 4 wk),
30 wk; PW nf 2/20/54 (#4), pk 3/13/54 (#1,
1 wk), 16 wk; tot 46 wk.
The Points of My Compass (Harper) NYT
gen 11/18/62 (#10), pk 12/16/62 (#6, 1 wk), 6
wk; PW nf 11/26/62 (#10), pk 1/14/63 (#3, 1
wk), 18 wk; tot 24 wk.
Stuart Little (Harper) NYT ch bst 5/8/66
(#3, 19 wk), 45 wk.
The Trumpet of the Swan (Harper) NYT
ch bst 11/8/70 (#1, 43 wk), 88 wk.
Letters of E.B. White [ed. Dorothy Lobrano
Guth] (Harper) PW hc nf 1/17/77 (#8), pk
2/7/77 (#7, 1 wk), 5 wk; NYT gen 1/30/77
(#8, 1 wk), 3 wk; tot 8 wk.
Essays of E.B. White (Harper) PW hc nf
10/10/77 (#12), pk 11/14/77 (#5, 2 wk), 19 wk;
NYT nf 10/23/77 (#13), pk 11/20/77 (#7, 1
wk), 19 wk; tot 38 wk.
See also James Thurber and _____
See also William Strunk, Jr., and _____

_____, and K.S. White
A Subtreasury of American Humor [eds.]
(Coward McCann) PW nf 1/17/42 (#8, 4
wk).

White, Leslie Turner
Look Away, Look Away (Blakiston) NYT
fic 3/19/44 (#15, 1 wk).

White, Nancy Bean
Meet John F. Kennedy (Random) NYT ch
bst 11/7/65 (#8, 26 wk).

White, Nelia Gardner
No Trumpets Before Him (Westminster)
NYT fic 4/25/48 (#12), pk 5/2/48 (#9, 3 wk),
14 wk; PW fic 5/15/48 (#7, 1 wk); tot 15 wk.
The Pink House (Viking) NYT fic 3/19/50
(#11), pk 4/2/50 (#10, 1 wk), 13 wk; PW fic
4/15/50 (#9, 1 wk); tot 14 wk.
Woman at the Window (Viking) NYT fic
10/28/51 (#16, 1 wk).
The Thorn Tree (Viking) NYT fic 5/22/55
(#15), pk 6/12/55 (#14, 2 wk), 5 wk.

White, Patrick
The Tree of Man (Viking) NYT fic 9/4/55
(#16), pk 9/18/55 (#15, 2 wk), 3 wk.
Eye of the Storm (Viking) PW fic 1/28/74
(#9), pk 2/25/74 (#4, 2 wk), 11 wk; NYT fic

2/3/74 (#8), pk 3/17/74 (#4, 1 wk), 5 wk; (Avon) NYT mm pb 2/9/75 (#10), pk 2/16/75 (#6, 1 wk), 2 wk; tot 18 wk.

White, Robb
Our Virgin Island (Doubleday) NYT gen 8/23/53 (#16, 2 wk).

White, Robin
Elephant Hill (Harper) NYT fic 1/25/59 (#14), pk 3/1/59 (#11, 1 wk), 7 wk.

White, Terence Hanbury [all titles as by T.H. White]
The Sword in the Stone (Putnam) NYT fic 2/5/39 (#10, 4 wk).
Mistress Masham's Repose (Putnam) NYT fic 11/10/46 (#16, 1 wk).
The Once and Future King (Putnam) NYT fic 9/14/58 (#14), pk 10/5/58 (#9, 1 wk), 8 wk; PW fic 9/29/58 (#8, 1 wk); tot 9 wk.
The Book of Merlyn (Univ. of Texas) NYT fic 10/9/77 (#15), pk 11/27/77 (#6, 3 wk), 24 wk; PW hc fic 10/10/77 (#12), pk 1/2/78 (#4, 1 wk), 18 wk; (Berkley) mm pb 9/18/78 (#9), pk 9/25/78 (#7, 1 wk), 5 wk; tot 47 wk.

White, Theodore Harold
Fire in the Ashes (Sloane) NYT gen 12/6/53 (#9), pk 2/7/54 (#4, 1 wk), 22 wk; PW nf 1/16/54 (#10), pk 2/6/54 (#5, 1 wk), 5 wk; tot 27 wk.
The Mountain Road (Sloane) NYT fic 6/1/58 (#15), pk 6/15/58 (#9, 1 wk), 8 wk.
The View from the Fortieth Floor (Sloane) NYT fic 6/12/60 (#13), pk 7/17/60 (#6, 2 wk), 17 wk; PW fic 7/4/60 (#9), pk 7/11/60 (#6, 1 wk), 8 wk; tot 25 wk.
The Making of the President—1960 (Atheneum) NYT gen 7/16/61 (#13), pk 9/10/61 (#1, 19 wk), 56 wk; PW nf 7/24/61 (#7), pk 8/28/61 (#1, 15 wk), 54 wk; tot 110 wk.
The Making of the President—1964 (Atheneum) NYT gen 7/11/65 (#6), pk 8/1/65 (#1, 9 wk), 22 wk; PW nf 7/26/65 (#4), pk 8/2/65 (#1, 14 wk), 26 wk; tot 48 wk.
The Making of the President—1968 (Atheneum) NYT gen 7/27/69 (#6), pk 8/24/69 (#2, 4 wk), 18 wk; PW nf 8/4/69 (#5), pk 10/20/69 (#2, 1 wk), 20 wk; NYT pb gen 8/2/70 (#5), pk 9/6/70 (#4, 4 wk), 8 wk; tot 46 wk.
The Making of the President—1972 (Atheneum) PW nf 8/13/73 (#8), pk 8/27/73 (#2, 1 wk), 13 wk; NYT gen 8/19/73 (#6), pk 9/16/73 (#2, 3 wk), 15 wk; tot 28 wk.
Breach of Faith (Reader's Digest Press/Atheneum) NYT gen 5/25/75 (#10), pk 6/15/75 (#1, 12 wk), 25 wk; PW nf 5/26/75 (#7), pk 6/9/75 (#1, 12 wk), 24 wk; (Dell) mm pb 5/17/76 (#10), pk 6/7/76 (#9, 1 wk),

8 wk; NYT mm pb 6/6/76 (#10), pk 6/27/76 (#9, 1 wk), 3 wk; tot 49 wk.
In Search of History: A Personal Adventure (Harper) PW hc nf 8/14/78 (#8), pk 10/2/78 (#1, 3 wk), 38 wk; NYT nf 11/12/78 (#3, 1 wk), 26 wk; (Warner) PW td pb 8/20/79 (#8), pk 8/27/79 (#2, 6 wk), 24 wk; NYT td pb 8/26/79 (#5), pk 9/2/79 (#2, 6 wk), 34 wk; tot 122 wk.
America in Search of Itself: The Making of the President 1956–1980 (Bessie/Harper) PW hc nf 6/4/82 (#10), pk 7/23/82 (#3, 1 wk), 17 wk; NYT nf 6/6/82 (#13), pk 7/4/82 (#3, 3 wk), 16 wk; tot 33 wk.

_____, and Annalee Jacoby
Thunder Out of China (Sloane) NYT gen 11/24/46 (#6, 1 wk), 13 wk; PW nf 1/18/47 (#7, 1 wk), 2 wk; tot 15 wk.

White, Vanna, and Patricia Romanowski
Vanna Speaks (Warner) NYT nf 5/17/87 (#15), pk 5/24/87 (#14, 1 wk), 2 wk; PW hc nf 5/29/87 (#15, 1 wk); tot 3 wk.

White, Victor Francis
Peter Domanig (Pellegrini & Cudahy) NYT fic 6/18/44 (#8, 1 wk), 2 wk.

White, W.S.
Citadel (Harper) NYT gen 2/3/57 (#10), pk 2/24/57 (#6, 2 wk), 11 wk; PW nf 3/4/57 (#6, 2 wk), 4 wk; tot 15 wk.

White, William
See Ernest Hemingway

White, William Allen
A Puritan in Babylon (Macmillan) PW nf 1/14/39 (#10, 4 wk).
The Autobiography of William Allen White (Macmillan) NYT gen 3/24/46 (#6), pk 3/31/46 (#3, 6 wk), 28 wk; PW nf 3/30/46 (#4), pk 4/13/46 (#2, 2 wk), 14 wk; tot 42 wk.

White, William Lindsay
They Were Expendable [as by W.L. White] (Harcourt) PW nf 10/3/42 (#3), pk 10/24/42 (#2, 4 wk), 23 wk; NYT nf 10/4/42 (#6), pk 10/11/42 (#1, 1 wk), 26 wk; NYT gen 4/4/43 (#11), pk 5/30/43 (#9, 1 wk), 4 wk; tot 53 wk.
Queens Die Proudly (Harcourt) NYT gen 6/20/43 (#11), pk 8/1/43 (#5, 1 wk), 12 wk; PW nf 7/10/43 (#5), pk 7/24/43 (#4, 1 wk), 5 wk; tot 17 wk.
Report on the Russians (Harcourt) NYT gen 4/1/45 (#13), pk 4/29/45 (#4, 1 wk), 19 wk; PW nf 4/7/45 (#6), pk 5/19/45 (#4, 1 wk), 10 wk; tot 29 wk.
Land of Milk and Honey (Harcourt) NYT gen 3/27/49 (#16, 1 wk).

White, William Smith
The Taft Story (Harper) NYT gen 5/2/54
(#15), pk 6/6/54 (#9, 1 wk), 12 wk.

Whitehead, Alfred North
Dialogues of Alfred North Whitehead [recorded by Lucien Price] (Little Brown) NYT
gen 6/13/54 (#16), pk 6/20/54 (#15, 2 wk), 4
wk.

Whitehead, Don
The F.B.I. Story (Random) NYT gen 12/
16/56 (#11), pk 2/3/57 (#1, 17 wk), 38 wk;
PW nf 1/7/57 (#6), pk 2/11/57 (#1, 16 wk),
29 wk; tot 67 wk.

Whitehill, Walter Muir
See Katherine Knowles and _____

Whiteley, Opal
The Story of Opal (Atlantic) PW gen lit
11/27/20 (#6, 4 wk), 12 wk.

Whitlock, Brand
Belgium (Appleton) PW gen 7/5/19 (#2, 8
wk), 24 wk.

Whitney, Courtney
MacArthur: His Rendezvous with History
(Knopf) NYT gen 2/12/56 (#16), pk 3/4/56
(#13, 3 wk), 5 wk.

Whitney, Phyllis A.
Columbella (Doubleday) NYT fic 5/8/66
(#10), pk 6/12/66 (#8, 1 wk), 8 wk; PW fic
6/6/66 (#8, 1 wk), 5 wk; tot 13 wk.
Silverhill (Doubleday) PW fic 6/12/67
(#12, 1 wk).
Snowfire (Fawcett) NYT fic 3/11/73 (#10,
2 wk); NYT mm pb 3/10/74 (#8, 4 wk); tot
6 wk.
A Turquoise Mask (Doubleday) PW fic
4/15/74 (#9), pk 4/22/74 (#8, 1 wk), 2 wk;
NYT fic 4/21/74 (#10, 1 wk); (Fawcett) NYT
mm pb 2/16/75 (#7), pk 2/23/75 (#4, 2 wk),
7 wk; tot 10 wk.
Spindrift (Doubleday) NYT fic 4/27/75
(#10), pk 6/1/75 (#5, 1 wk), 12 wk; PW fic
4/28/75 (#10), pk 6/23/75 (#6, 1 wk), 13 wk;
(Fawcett) NYT mm pb 3/14/76 (#10), pk
4/4/76 (#4, 2 wk), 7 wk; PW mm pb 3/22/76
(#6), pk 3/29/76 (#4, 1 wk), 7 wk; tot 39 wk.
The Golden Unicorn (Fawcett/Crest) NYT
mm pb 3/27/77 (#10), pk 4/10/77 (#4, 1 wk),
7 wk; PW mm pb 3/28/77 (#15), pk 4/4/77
(#5, 1 wk), 7 wk; tot 14 wk.
Stone Bull (Fawcett/Crest) PW mm pb
9/4/78 (#15, 2 wk).
The Glass Flame (Fawcett/Crest) NYT
mm pb 9/23/79 (#15, 1 wk).
Domino (Fawcett/Crest) PW mm pb 12/5/
80 (#8), pk 12/26/80 (#4, 1 wk), 6 wk; NYT

mm pb 12/14/80 (#11), pk 12/28/80 (#5, 1
wk), 5 wk; tot 11 wk.
Poinciana (Fawcett/Crest) PW mm pb 11/
6/81 (#14), pk 11/13/81 (#11, 1 wk), 3 wk; NYT
mm pb 11/8/81 (#13), pk 11/29/81 (#7, 1 wk),
7 wk; tot 10 wk.
Vermilion (Fawcett/Crest) NYT mm pb
11/28/82 (#5, 1 wk), 6 wk; PW mm pb 12/17/
82 (#9, 2 wk), 3 wk; tot 9 wk.
Emerald (Doubleday) PW hc fic 1/28/83
(#15), pk 2/25/83 (#8, 1 wk), 10 wk; NYT fic
2/20/83 (#14), pk 3/13/83 (#12, 1 wk), 5 wk;
(Fawcett/Ballantine) NYT mm pb 12/4/83
(#10, 2 wk), 5 wk; PW mm pb 12/23/83 (#13,
1 wk); tot 21 wk.
Rainsong (Doubleday) PW hc fic 1/27/84
(#14), pk 2/10/84 (#12, 2 wk), 6 wk; NYT fic
2/19/84 (#13, 1 wk), 3 wk; (Fawcett/Crest)
NYT pb fic 11/25/84 (#14), pk 12/2/84 (#7,
1 wk), 6 wk; PW mm pb 12/7/84 (#9, 1 wk),
3 wk; tot 18 wk.
Dream of Orchids (Doubleday) PW hc fic
2/1/85 (#13), pk 2/15/85 (#12, 1 wk), 3 wk;
NYT fic 2/3/85 (#14, 1 wk); (Fawcett/Crest)
NYT pb fic 12/8/85 (#9, 1 wk), 4 wk; PW
mm pb 12/13/85 (#12, 1 wk), 2 wk; tot 10 wk.
Flaming Tree (Fawcett/Ballantine) NYT
pb fic 1/18/87 (#11, 1 wk), 2 wk; PW mm pb
1/23/87 (#13, 1 wk); tot 3 wk.
Silversword (Fawcett) NYT pb fic 1/31/88
(#6, 3 wk), 6 wk; PW mm pb 2/5/88 (#15),
pk 2/12/88 (#6, 2 wk), 4 wk; tot 12 wk.
Feather on the Moon (Doubleday) PW hc
fic 3/18/88 (#15), pk 4/1/88 (#13, 1 wk), 4 wk;
(Fawcett/Crest) NYT pb fic 5/28/89 (#9, 2
wk), 4 wk; PW mm pb 6/2/89 (#9), pk 6/16/
89 (#8, 1 wk), 5 wk; tot 13 wk.
Rainbow in the Mist (Doubleday) PW hc
fic 3/24/89 (#11, 1 wk), 2 wk; NYT fic 4/2/89
(#14, 1 wk); (Fawcett/Crest) NYT pb fic
4/29/90 (#9), pk 5/20/90 (#5, 1 wk), 5 wk;
PW mm pb 5/4/90 (#6, 1 wk), 4 wk; tot 12
wk.
The Singing Stones (Doubleday) PW hc fic
3/30/90 (#15), pk 4/6/90 (#11, 1 wk), 3 wk.

Wholey, Dennis
*The Courage to Change: Hope and Help for
Alcoholics and Their Families* (Houghton)
NYT nf 2/17/85 (#9), pk 4/28/85 (#4, 2 wk),
20 wk; PW hc nf 3/1/85 (#12), pk 5/3/85 (#3,
1 wk), 17 wk; (Warner) NYT pb nf 6/22/86
(#6, 3 wk); tot 40 wk.

Whyte, William H.
The Organization Man (Simon & Schuster) NYT gen 2/10/57 (#13), pk 3/31/57 (#3,
4 wk), 36 wk; PW nf 3/18/57 (#10), pk
4/8/57 (#3, 2 wk), 15 wk; tot 51 wk.

Wickenden, Dan
The Wayfarers (Morrow) NYT fic 7/22/45 (#14), pk 9/2/45 (#7, 1 wk), 7 wk.
Tobias Brandywine (Morrow) NYT fic 6/6/48 (#16), pk 6/13/48 (#11, 1 wk), 2 wk.

Wicker, Tom
Facing the Lions (Viking) NYT fic 6/24/73 (#8), pk 7/8/73 (#3, 6 wk), 18 wk; PW fic 6/25/73 (#7), pk 7/9/73 (#3, 4 wk), 18 wk; (Avon) NYT mm pb 7/14/74 (#9, 4 wk); tot 40 wk.
A Time to Die (Quadrangle/New York Times) PW nf 4/7/75 (#9), pk 4/21/75 (#7, 1 wk), 4 wk; NYT gen 4/13/75 (#10, 1 wk); tot 5 wk.
Unto This Hour (Viking) PW hc fic 3/9/84 (#15), pk 3/30/84 (#9, 1 wk), 6 wk; NYT fic 3/18/84 (#15), pk 3/25/84 (#12, 2 wk), 6 wk; (Berkley) PW mm pb 2/22/85 (#12, 1 wk); tot 13 wk.

Widdemer, Margaret
Eve's Orchard (Farrar) NYT fic 12/1/35 (#6, 4 wk).
Hand on Her Shoulder (Farrar) NYT fic 9/4/38 (#6, 4 wk).
She Knew Three Brothers (Farrar) NYT fic 10/8/39 (#11, 4 wk).

Wiesel, Elie
A Beggar in Jerusalem (Random) PW fic 3/16/70 (#7, 2 wk), 9 wk; NYT fic 3/22/70 (#8, 4 wk), 7 wk; tot 16 wk.
Souls on Fire (Random) NYT gen 4/2/72 (#9, 2 wk).

Wiggam, Albert E.
New Decalogue of Science (Bobbs Merrill) PW nf 6/21/24 (#6, 4 wk).
Fruit of the Family Tree (Bobbs Merrill) PW nf 9/26/25 (#7, 4 wk), 8 wk.

Wigginton, Eliot
The Foxfire Book (Doubleday) NYT pb gen 7/9/72 (#5, 12 wk); NYT td pb 1/12/75 (#4, 1 wk), 3 wk; tot 15 wk.
Foxfire II (Doubleday) NYT td pb 3/10/74 (#8, 4 wk).
Foxfire 3 [ed.] (Doubleday/Anchor) NYT td pb 8/31/75 (#5), pk 9/28/75 (#1, 3 wk), 22 wk.
Foxfire 4: Fiddlemaking, Springhouses, Horse Trading, Sassafras Tea, Berry Buckets, Gardening, and Further Affairs of Plain Living [ed.] (Doubleday/Anchor) PW td pb 11/21/77 (#8), pk 1/9/78 (#2, 2 wk), 18 wk; NYT td pb 12/11/77 (#14), pk 1/1/78 (#1, 4 wk), 21 wk; tot 39 wk.
Foxfire 5: Ironmaking, Blacksmithing, Flintlock Rifles, Bear Hunting and Other Affairs of Plain Living [ed.] (Doubleday/Anchor) PW

td pb 7/2/79 (#8), pk 7/9/79 (#7, 2 wk), 6 wk; NYT td pb 7/29/79 (#9), pk 12/30/79 (#4, 1 wk), 24 wk; tot 30 wk.
Foxfire 6 [ed.] (Doubleday/Anchor) NYT td pb 11/23/80 (#12), pk 12/21/80 (#7, 1 wk), 10 wk; PW td pb 1/9/81 (#10, 1 wk); tot 11 wk.

Wilde, Jennifer
Love's Tender Fury (Warner) PW mm pb 4/19/76 (#7), pk 7/5/76 (#2, 1 wk), 22 wk; NYT mm pb 4/25/76 (#6), pk 6/20/76 (#1, 2 wk), 23 wk; tot 45 wk.
Dare to Love (Warner) PW mm pb 3/27/78 (#8), pk 4/3/78 (#3, 2 wk), 9 wk; NYT mm pb 4/2/78 (#5), pk 4/9/78 (#2, 1 wk), 11 wk; tot 20 wk.
Love Me, Marietta (Warner) NYT mm pb 10/18/81 (#7, 1 wk), 7 wk; PW mm pb 10/23/81 (#12), pk 10/30/81 (#11, 2 wk), 4 wk; tot 11 wk.
Once More, Miranda (Ballantine) NYT mm pb 5/8/83 (#11), pk 5/29/83 (#5, 1 wk), 5 wk; PW mm pb 5/20/83 (#9, 2 wk), 4 wk; tot 9 wk.
When Love Commands (Avon) NYT pb fic 10/7/84 (#14), pk 10/14/84 (#6, 1 wk), 6 wk; PW mm pb 10/12/84 (#14), pk 10/19/84 (#12, 2 wk), 4 wk; tot 10 wk.
Angel in Scarlet (Avon) PW mm pb 8/8/86 (#13), pk 8/15/86 (#11, 2 wk), 4 wk; NYT pb fic 8/3/86 (#12), pk 8/24/86 (#9, 1 wk), 5 wk; tot 9 wk.
The Slipper (Ballantine) NYT pb fic 9/11/88 (#14), pk 9/18/88 (#12, 2 wk), 4 wk.
They Call Her Dana (Ballantine) NYT pb fic 9/10/89 (#15, 1 wk); PW mm pb 9/15/89 (#13, 1 wk); tot 2 wk.

Wilder, Laura Ingalls
Little House in the Big Woods (Harper) NYT ch bst 11/14/54 (#6, 40 wk), 59 wk.
Little House on the Prairie (Harper) NYT ch bst 11/14/54 (#13, 40 wk); NYT ch pb 4/30/78 (#6, 24 wk); tot 64 wk.
The First Four Years (Harper) NYT ch bst 5/2/71 (#19, 19 wk), 45 wk.
The Nine Little House Books, Vols. 1–9 (Harper) NYT td pb 12/8/74 (#5, 5 wk).

Wilder, Robert
Mr. G Strings Along (Putnam) NYT fic 4/30/44 (#12), pk 6/25/44 (#8, 2 wk), 18 wk.
Written on the Wind (Putnam) NYT fic 2/10/46 (#9), pk 3/3/46 (#7, 1 wk), 14 wk; PW fic 3/2/46 (#5, 1 wk), 4 wk; tot 18 wk.
Bright Feather (Putnam) NYT fic 6/13/48 (#13), pk 6/20/48 (#7, 1 wk), 11 wk; PW fic 7/17/48 (#10, 1 wk); tot 12 wk.
Wait for Tomorrow (Putnam) NYT fic 4/16/50 (#15), pk 6/11/50 (#6, 1 wk), 18 wk; PW

fic 5/13/50 (#9), pk 7/15/50 (#6, 1 wk), 3 wk; tot 21 wk.

And Ride a Tiger (Putnam) NYT fic 12/2/51 (#16, 1 wk).

The Wine of Youth (Putnam) NYT fic 7/3/55 (#12), pk 7/31/55 (#9, 1 wk), 16 wk.

The Sun Is My Shadow (Putnam) NYT fic 8/21/60 (#14), pk 9/18/60 (#11, 1 wk), 8 wk.

Wind from the Carolinas (Putnam) NYT fic 3/8/64 (#9, 2 wk), 4 wk; PW fic 5/18/64 (#10, 2 wk), 3 wk; tot 7 wk.

The Sea and the Stars (Putnam) PW fic 7/3/67 (#12, 1 wk).

An Affair of Honor (Putnam) NYT fic 11/16/69 (#9, 1 wk), 3 wk; PW fic 12/15/69 (#6, 1 wk); tot 4 wk.

Wilder, Thornton
The Bridge of San Luis Rey (Boni) PW fic 4/21/28 (#1, 12 wk), 16 wk.

The Woman of Andros (Boni) PW fic 3/15/30 (#10), pk 4/12/30 (#1, 4 wk), 12 wk.

Heaven's My Destination (Harper) PW fic 2/9/35 (#2), pk 3/16/35 (#1, 4 wk), 16 wk.

Our Town (Coward McCann) NYT gen 5/1/38 (#13), pk 6/5/38 (#10, 4 wk), 8 wk.

The Ides of March (Harper) NYT fic 3/7/48 (#16), pk 4/4/48 (#1, 2 wk), 17 wk; PW fic 3/20/48 (#4), pk 5/1/48 (#1, 1 wk), 13 wk; tot 30 wk.

The Eighth Day (Harper) NYT fic 4/16/67 (#8), pk 6/4/67 (#1, 4 wk), 28 wk; PW fic 4/17/67 (#5), pk 6/5/67 (#1, 11 wk), 29 wk; NYT pb fic 5/5/68 (#3, 4 wk), 12 wk; tot 69 wk.

Theophilus North (Harper) PW fic 11/5/73 (#8), pk 11/26/73 (#3, 2 wk), 16 wk; NYT fic 11/11/73 (#9), pk 12/2/73 (#4, 6 wk), 21 wk; (Avon) NYT mm pb 12/8/74 (#6, 4 wk); tot 41 wk.

Wilkin, Eloise
See Esther Burns and _____

Wilkins, Vaughan
And So—Victoria (Macmillan) PW fic 9/11/37 (#1, 4 wk), 24 wk; NYT fic 9/12/37 (#1, 4 wk), 12 wk; tot 36 wk.

Being Met Together (Macmillan) NYT fic 10/1/44 (#12), pk 10/29/44 (#11, 1 wk), 5 wk.

Will, George F.
The Morning After: American Successes and Excesses, 1981–1986 (Free Press/Macmillan) PW hc nf 12/26/86 (#12, 1 wk), 2 wk; NYT nf 2/1/87 (#12, 1 wk), 2 wk; tot 4 wk.

Suddenly (Free Press) PW hc nf 12/7/90 (#12, 1 wk), 2 wk; NYT nf 12/16/90 (#12, 3 wk); tot 5 wk.

Men at Work (Macmillan) PW hc nf 4/13/90 (#12), pk 5/4/90 (#1, 19 wk), 26 wk; NYT

nf 4/15/90 (#15), pk 4/29/90 (#1, 19 wk), 27 wk; tot 53 wk.

William, Kate
See Francine Pascal and _____

Williams, A.L.
All You Can Do Is All You Can Do, but All You Can Do Is Enough! (Nelson) NYT msc 9/11/88 (#2, 3 wk), 14 wk; PW hc nf 9/16/88 (#10), pk 10/28/88 (#4, 2 wk), 12 wk; (Ivy) NYT msc pb 9/17/89 (#4, 1 wk); tot 27 wk.

Williams, Ben Ames
Come Spring (Houghton) PW fic 4/13/40 (#9, 4 wk).

The Strange Woman (Houghton) PW fic 11/15/41 (#5, 4 wk), 8 wk; NYT fic 3/7/43 (#16), pk 9/26/43 (#8, 1 wk), 8 wk; tot 16 wk.

Time of Peace (Houghton) NYT fic 12/13/42 (#6), pk 1/3/43 (#4, 1 wk), 16 wk; PW fic 12/19/42 (#8), pk 1/23/43 (#6, 1 wk), 6 wk; tot 22 wk.

Leave Her to Heaven (Houghton) NYT fic 6/25/44 (#12), pk 10/1/44 (#2, 1 wk), 48 wk; PW fic 7/1/44 (#5), pk 9/23/44 (#2, 6 wk), 27 wk; tot 75 wk.

It's a Free Country (Houghton) NYT fic 8/26/45 (#14, 1 wk).

House Divided (Houghton) NYT fic 9/28/47 (#4), pk 11/9/47 (#1, 15 wk), 40 wk; PW fic 10/11/47 (#3), pk 11/15/47 (#1, 13 wk), 30 wk; tot 70 wk.

Owen Glen (Houghton) NYT fic 9/17/50 (#14), pk 10/22/50 (#6, 1 wk), 13 wk; PW fic 10/7/50 (#5, 1 wk), 4 wk; tot 17 wk.

The Unconquered (Houghton) NYT fic 9/13/53 (#9), pk 10/18/53 (#5, 3 wk), 20 wk; PW fic 10/10/53 (#5), pk 10/24/53 (#4, 2 wk), 7 wk; tot 27 wk.

Williams, Edward Bennett
One Man's Freedom (Atheneum) NYT gen 7/8/62 (#15), pk 9/2/62 (#4, 1 wk), 16 wk; PW nf 8/20/62 (#10), pk 8/27/62 (#9, 2 wk), 6 wk; tot 22 wk.

Williams, Elva
Sacramento Waltz (McGraw) NYT fic 11/3/57 (#16, 1 wk).

Williams, Emlyn
George: An Early Autobiography (Random) NYT gen 5/20/62 (#14, 1 wk), 2 wk.

Williams, Garth
Baby Animals (Golden) NYT ch bst 11/16/52 (#13, 40 wk).

Baby Farm Animals (Golden) NYT ch bst 11/15/53 (#10, 40 wk).

The Rabbit's Wedding (Harper) NYT ch bst 11/2/58 (#9, 40 wk).

Williams, Jay
Everyone Knows What a Dragon Looks Like
(Four Winds) NYT ch hc 11/13/77 (#10, 46
wk).

Williams, Jeanne
The Cave Dreamers (Avon) NYT td pb
7/10/83 (#14, 1 wk).

Williams, Kit
Masquerade (Schocken) NYT fic 1/4/81
(#6), pk 3/8/81 (#2, 6 wk), 43 wk; PW hc fic
1/9/81 (#12), pk 4/17/81 (#2, 2 wk), 36 wk;
tot 79 wk.
A Book Without a Name (Knopf) PW hc fic
6/15/84 (#15), pk 6/22/84 (#9, 1 wk), 9 wk;
NYT fic 6/17/84 (#8), pk 7/8/84 (#2, 3 wk),
10 wk; tot 19 wk.

Williams, Linda
*The Little Old Lady Who Was Not Afraid of
Anything* [illus. Megan Lloyd] (HarperTro-
phy) PW ch pic 10/26/90 (#4, 4 wk).

Williams, Margery
The Velveteen Rabbit (Doubleday) NYT ch
bst 5/4/69 (#19), pk 5/7/72 (#3, 19 wk), 249
wk; (Avon/Camelot) NYT ch pb 4/30/78
(#8, 24 wk); tot 273 wk.

Williams, Tad
Stone of Farewell (DAW) PW hc fic 8/24/
90 (#15, 1 wk).

Williams, Ted
My Turn at Bat (Simon & Schuster) NYT
gen 8/3/69 (#10), pk 8/24/69 (#7, 1 wk), 6
wk.

Williams, Tennessee
. *The Roman Spring of Mrs. Stone* (New
Directions) NYT fic 10/15/50 (#11), pk 10/
22/50 (#10, 2 wk), 4 wk.
Memoirs (Doubleday) NYT gen 12/28/75
(#10), pk 2/1/76 (#7, 1 wk), 9 wk; PW nf
1/26/76 (#10, 1 wk); PW hc nf 2/2/76 (#9),
pk 2/9/76 (#8, 2 wk), 6 wk; tot 16 wk.

Williams, Thomas Harry
Lincoln and His Generals (Knopf) NYT
gen 3/23/52 (#16, 2 wk).
Huey Long (Knopf) NYT pb gen 2/7/71
(#4, 4 wk).

Williams, Walter
*The Mr. Bill Show—Star of Saturday Night
Live* (Running) PW td pb 11/26/79 (#6), pk
3/7/80 (#1, 1 wk), 24 wk; NYT td pb 12/2/79
(#7), pk 1/6/80 (#2, 1 wk), 31 wk; tot 55 wk.

Willison, George F.
Saints and Strangers (Reynal & Hitchcock)
NYT gen 8/26/45 (#15), pk 10/14/45 (#10, 1
wk), 12 wk; PW nf 12/15/45 (#10, 1 wk); tot
13 wk.

Willkie, Wendell
This Is Wendell Willkie (Dodd) PW nf
10/12/40 (#7, 4 wk).
One World (Simon & Schuster) PW fic
4/24/43 (#4), pk 5/1/43 (#1, 17 wk), 24 wk;
NYT gen 5/2/43 (#4), pk 5/9/43 (#1, 17 wk),
28 wk; tot 52 wk.

Willoughby, Charles Andrew
Shanghai Conspiracy (Dutton) NYT gen
3/16/52 (#15, 1 wk).

**Willoughby, Charles Andrew, and John
Chamberlain**
MacArthur—1941–1951 (McGraw) NYT
gen 10/24/54 (#11), pk 11/14/54 (#6, 1 wk), 7
wk.

Wills, Garry
Bare Ruined Choirs (Doubleday) PW nf
12/11/72 (#9, 1 wk).
Reagan's America: Innocents at Home (Doubleday) PW hc nf 2/6/87 (#12), pk 3/20/87
(#10, 1 wk), 8 wk; NYT nf 2/8/87 (#12), pk
3/1/87 (#7, 1 wk), 8 wk; tot 16 wk.

Wills, Royal Barry
Houses for Homemakers (Watts) NYT gen
12/2/45 (#9, 1 wk), 2 wk.

Wilmot, Chester
The Struggle for Europe (Harper) NYT gen
4/20/52 (#12), pk 5/4/52 (#10, 2 wk), 10 wk;
PW nf 5/17/52 (#10, 1 wk); tot 11 wk.

Wilson, Angus
Hemlock and After (Viking) NYT fic 10/19/
52 (#15), pk 11/2/52 (#12, 1 wk), 3 wk.
Anglo-Saxon Attitudes (Viking) NYT fic
10/28/56 (#12), pk 11/4/56 (#11, 2 wk), 13 wk.
The Middle Age of Mrs. Eliot (Viking)
NYT fic 4/19/59 (#11, 1 wk), 7 wk.

Wilson, Carol Green
Gump's Treasure Trade (Crowell) NYT gen
5/22/49 (#14, 1 wk), 2 wk.

Wilson, Colin
The Outsider (Houghton) NYT gen 10/7/
56 (#11), pk 10/21/56 (#5, 5 wk), 20 wk; PW
nf 10/22/56 (#6), pk 10/29/56 (#4, 1 wk), 9
wk; tot 29 wk.

Wilson, Donald Powell
My Six Convicts (Rinehart) NYT gen 2/
18/51 (#11), pk 3/11/51 (#7, 2 wk), 29 wk; PW
nf 3/17/51 (#9), pk 5/12/51 (#6, 1 wk), 5 wk;
tot 34 wk.

Wilson, Dorothy Clarke
Prince of Egypt (Westminster) NYT fic
12/11/49 (#15), pk 1/1/50 (#12, 1 wk), 5 wk;
PW fic 1/14/50 (#9, 1 wk); tot 6 wk.

Wilson, Earl
I Am Gazing Into My 8-Ball (Doubleday)

NYT gen 3/25/45 (#19), pk 5/13/45 (#7, 1 wk), 11 wk; PW nf 5/12/45 (#10, 1 wk); tot 12 wk.

Pike's Peak or Bust (Doubleday) NYT gen 11/10/46 (#12), pk 11/17/46 (#9, 1 wk), 3 wk.

Let 'em Eat Cheesecake (Doubleday) NYT gen 7/10/49 (#13), pk 7/24/49 (#8, 1 wk), 9 wk.

Sinatra (Macmillan) NYT gen 7/18/76 (#10, 4 wk); PW hc nf 8/16/76 (#10, 2 wk); tot 6 wk.

Wilson, Edith Bolling
My Memoir (Bobbs Merrill) NYT gen 4/9/39 (#12, 4 wk), 8 wk; PW nf 5/13/39 (#10, 4 wk); tot 12 wk.

Wilson, Edmund
Memoirs of Hecate County (Nonpareil) NYT fic 4/14/46 (#13), pk 5/26/46 (#7, 1 wk), 15 wk.

The Scrolls from the Dead Sea (Oxford Univ.) NYT gen 11/13/55 (#14), pk 1/29/56 (#5, 8 wk), 34 wk; PW nf 1/21/56 (#8), pk 3/3/56 (#4, 5 wk), 16 wk; tot 50 wk.

Wilson, F. Paul
The Keep (Berkley) NYT mm pb 10/31/82 (#12, 2 wk).

The Tomb (Berkley) NYT pb fic 11/25/84 (#11, 1 wk).

Wilson, Harriet
The Game of Hearts: Harriet Wilson's Memoirs [ed. Lesley Blanch] (Simon & Schuster) NYT gen 7/17/55 (#14), pk 8/14/55 (#9, 1 wk), 8 wk.

Wilson, Larry
See Spencer Johnson and _____

Wilson, Mary, with Patricia Romanowski and Ahrgus Juilliard
Dreamgirl: My Life as a Supreme (St. Martin's) NYT nf 11/2/86 (#8), pk 12/14/86 (#5, 1 wk), 7 wk; PW hc nf 11/7/86 (#8), PK 11/21/86 (#5, 2 wk), 7 wk; NYT pb nf 9/13/87 (#6), pk 9/20/87 (#4, 1 wk), 6 wk; tot 20 wk.

Wilson, Mitchell
The Human Body: What It Is and How It Works (Golden) NYT ch bst 5/8/60 (#19), pk 11/13/60 (#5, 27 wk), 46 wk.

Wilson, Neill Compton, and Frank John Taylor
Southern Pacific (McGraw) NYT gen 3/9/52 (#13, 1 wk).

Wilson, Sloan
A Summer Place (Simon & Schuster) NYT fic 4/27/58 (#11), pk 5/11/58 (#4, 9 wk), 18 wk; PW fic 5/12/58 (#6), pk 5/26/58 (#4, 7 wk), 14 wk; tot 32 wk.

A Sense of Values (Harper) NYT fic 1/15/61 (#14), pk 2/19/61 (#10, 2 wk), 10 wk.

Winant, John Gilbert
Letter from Grosvenor Square (Houghton) NYT gen 12/14/47 (#15), pk 1/25/48 (#9, 2 wk), 12 wk.

Windsor, Duchess of
The Heart Has Its Reasons (McKay) NYT gen 10/21/56 (#12), pk 10/28/56 (#7, 4 wk), 10 wk; PW nf 11/5/56 (#5, 1 wk), 3 wk; tot 13 wk.

Windsor, Duke of (Edward VIII)
A King's Story (Putnam) NYT gen 4/29/51 (#15), pk 5/13/51 (#2, 7 wk), 27 wk; PW nf 5/12/51 (#4), pk 5/19/51 (#2, 8 wk), 20 wk; tot 47 wk.

Winer, Richard
The Devil's Triangle (Bantam) NYT mm pb 2/9/75 (#9), pk 2/16/75 (#5, 1 wk), 11 wk.

Winfield, Dave, and Tom Parker
Winfield: A Player's Life (Norton) NYT nf 4/24/88 (#11), pk 5/8/88 (#8, 2 wk), 6 wk; PW hc nf 5/27/88 (#15, 1 wk); tot 7 wk.

Winkler, John Kennedy
Morgan the Magnificent (Vanguard) PW nf 10/18/30 (#8), pk 11/22/30 (#7, 4 wk), 8 wk.

The Du Pont Dynasty (Reynal & Hitchcock) NYT nf 10/6/35 (#9, 4 wk).

Winn, Dilys
Murder Ink (Workman) PW td pb 12/26/77 (#9), pk 1/16/78 (#6, 1 wk), 4 wk; NYT td pb 1/1/78 (#12), pk 1/8/78 (#8, 2 wk), 5 wk; tot 9 wk.

Winslow, Anne Goodwin
The Springs (Knopf) NYT fic 3/6/49 (#15), pk 3/13/49 (#13, 1 wk), 2 wk.

Winslow, Marjorie
Mud Pies and Other Recipes (Macmillan) NYT ch bst 11/12/61 (#6, 26 wk).

Winsor, Kathleen
Forever Amber (Macmillan) NYT fic 11/5/44 (#3), pk 11/12/44 (#1, 5 wk), 75 wk; PW fic 11/11/44 (#6), pk 12/16/44 (#1, 1 wk), 41 wk; tot 116 wk.

Star Money (Appleton) NYT fic 4/30/50 (#10), pk 5/21/50 (#3, 8 wk), 22 wk; PW fic 5/6/50 (#5), pk 6/24/50 (#2, 1 wk), 15 wk; tot 37 wk.

The Lovers (Appleton) NYT fic 10/5/52 (#16, 1 wk).

Winston, Richard, and Clara Winston
See Willi Heinrich
See Erich Maria Remarque

Winston, Stephanie
Getting Organized (Warner) NYT td pb
11/25/79 (#9), pk 1/27/80 (#8, 1 wk), 25 wk;
PW td pb 2/22/80 (#8, 1 wk); tot 26 wk.

Winterbotham, Frederick W.
The Ultra Secret (Harper) PW nf 1/20/75
(#10), pk 2/10/75 (#5, 1 wk), 10 wk; NYT gen
1/26/75 (#10), pk 3/2/75 (#5, 1 wk), 11 wk;
(Dell) NYT mm pb 1/4/76 (#8), pk 2/1/76
(#4, 1 wk), 5 wk; PW mm pb 2/2/76 (#4, 1
wk), 3 wk; tot 29 wk.

Winters, Jonathan
*Winter's Tales: Stories and Observations for
the Unusual* (Random) PW hc fic 12/25/87
(#14), pk 3/4/88 (#5, 1 wk), 11 wk; NYT fic
12/27/87 (#12), pk 2/21/88 (#4, 1 wk), 14 wk;
tot 25 wk.

Winters, Shelley
Shelley: Also Known as Shirley (Morrow)
PW hc nf 7/18/80 (#14), pk 8/29/80 (#1, 4
wk), 22 wk; NYT nf 7/27/80 (#3), pk 8/3/80
(#1, 7 wk), 21 wk; (Ballantine) PW mm pb
5/8/81 (#5), pk 5/22/81 (#2, 1 wk), 12 wk;
NYT mm pb 5/10/81 (#13), pk 5/24/81 (#2,
3 wk), 14 wk; tot 69 wk.
Shelley II (Simon & Schuster) NYT nf
9/3/89 (#11), pk 9/10/89 (#10, 1 wk), 5 wk;
NYT pb nf 10/7/90 (#11, 1 wk); tot 6 wk.

Winwar, Frances
Poor Splendid Wings (Little Brown) PW nf
11/11/33 (#3, 4 wk), 12 wk.
The Life of the Heart (Harper) NYT gen
11/18/45 (#11), pk 1/27/46 (#5, 1 wk), 16 wk;
PW nf 12/15/45 (#9), pk 1/26/46 (#5, 1 wk),
4 wk; tot 20 wk.

Wise, David, and Thomas B. Ross
The Invisible Government (Random) NYT
gen 7/5/64 (#7), pk 7/26/64 (#2, 9 wk), 22
wk; PW nf 7/13/64 (#4), pk 8/3/64 (#2, 6
wk), 20 wk; tot 42 wk.

Wister, Owen
A Straight Deal or the Ancient Grudge
(Macmillan) PW gen 7/3/20 (#9, 4 wk); PW
gen lit 9/25/20 (#10), pk 10/23/20 (#4, 4 wk),
24 wk; tot 28 wk.
Roosevelt, The Story of a Friendship (Macmillan) PW nf 8/23/30 (#8), pk 9/20/30 (#3,
4 wk), 20 wk.
Owen Wister Out West [ed. Fanny Kemble
Wister] (Univ. of Chicago) NYT gen 5/4/58
(#11, 1 wk), 2 wk.

Wodehouse, P.G.
Heavy Weather (Little Brown) PW fic 9/
16/33 (#8, 4 wk).
Young Men in Spats (Doubleday) PW fic 9/

12/36 (#9, 4 wk); NYT fic 9/13/36 (#7, 4 wk);
tot 8 wk.
The Crime Wave at Blandings (Doubleday)
NYT fic 8/8/37 (#7, 4 wk).

Woititz, Janet Geringer
Adult Children of Alcoholics (Health Communications) NYT msc pb 5/18/86 (#5), pk
6/22/86 (#3, 8 wk), 49 wk; PW td pb 9/26/
86 (#10), pk 4/10/87 (#3, 1 wk), 50 wk; tot
99 wk.

Woiwode, L.
What I'm Going to Do, I Think (Farrar) PW
fic 8/25/69 (#7, 1 wk).

Wojciechowska, Maia
Shadow of a Bull (Atheneum) NYT ch bst
5/9/65 (#10, 19 wk).

Wolcott, Imogene
The Yankee Cook Book [ed.] (Coward Mc-
Cann) NYT gen 8/6/39 (#8, 4 wk).

Wolf, Maritta
Night Shift (Random) NYT fic 12/20/42
(#17, 2 wk), 5 wk.

**Wolfe, Sidney M., M.D., Christopher M.
Coley and the Public Citizen Health
Research Group**
Pills That Don't Work (Farrar) PW td pb
10/23/81 (#8), pk 11/27/81 (#4, 1 wk), 9 wk;
NYT td pb 10/25/81 (#6), pk 11/29/81 (#3, 1
wk), 10 wk; tot 19 wk.

Wolfe, Thomas
Of Time and the River (Scribner) PW fic
4/13/35 (#4), pk 5/11/35 (#2, 8 wk), 28 wk.
The Web and the Rock (Harper) PW fic
7/15/39 (#9), pk 8/12/39 (#2, 4 wk), 16 wk;
NYT fic 8/6/39 (#1, 4 wk); tot 20 wk.
You Can't Go Home Again (Harper) PW fic
10/12/40 (#6), pk 11/16/40 (#2, 4 wk), 12 wk.
The Hills Beyond (Harper) PW fic 12/13/41
(#9, 4 wk).

Wolfe, Tom
*The Kandy-Kolored Tangerine-Flake Stream-
line Baby* (Farrar) PW nf 8/9/65 (#9), pk
9/13/65 (#6, 1 wk), 6 wk; NYT gen 8/22/65
(#10, 2 wk); tot 8 wk.
The Electric Kool-Aid Acid Test (Farrar)
PW nf 9/2/68 (#9), pk 9/30/68 (#6, 4 wk),
10 wk; NYT gen 9/15/68 (#8), pk 9/22/68
(#5, 1 wk), 7 wk; tot 17 wk.
The Right Stuff (Farrar) PW hc nf 10/8/79
(#13), pk 11/5/79 (#4, 2 wk), 24 wk; NYT nf
10/14/79 (#13), pk 11/18/79 (#4, 1 wk), 25 wk;
(Bantam) PW mm pb 11/14/80 (#9), pk 11/
21/80 (#3, 1 wk), 18 wk; NYT mm pb 11/23/
80 (#11), pk 1/1/84 (#3, 1 wk), 18 wk; tot 85
wk.
From Bauhaus to Our House (Farrar) PW

hc nf 10/23/81 (#15), pk 11/27/81 (#6, 1 wk), 16 wk; NYT nf 11/1/81 (#14), pk 11/22/81 (#3, 1 wk), 14 wk; tot 30 wk.

Bonfire of the Vanities (Farrar) NYT fic 11/8/87 (#10), pk 1/24/88 (#1, 8 wk), 56 wk; PW hc fic 11/13/87 (#7), pk 1/29/88 (#1, 8 wk), 55 wk; (Bantam) PW mm pb 12/2/88 (#10), pk 12/16/88 (#1, 6 wk), 40 wk; NYT pb fic 12/4/88 (#3), pk 12/11/88 (#1, 9 wk), 33 wk; [read by John Lithgow] (Random) PW aud fic 11/2/90 (#10, 8 wk); tot 192 wk.

Wolfe, W. Beran
A Woman's Best Years (Emerson) PW nf 9/14/35 (#10), pk 10/12/35 (#9, 4 wk), 8 wk.

Wolfert, Ira
Battle for the Solomons (Houghton) NYT nf 2/14/43 (#19), pk 3/14/43 (#9, 1 wk), 6 wk.

American Guerrilla in the Philippines (Simon & Schuster) NYT gen 5/13/45 (#14), pk 7/29/45 (#10, 1 wk), 8 wk.

An Act of Love (Simon & Schuster) NYT fic 1/23/49 (#13, 2 wk), 5 wk.

Wolff, Alexander, and Armen Keteyian
Raw Recruits (Pocket) PW hc nf 3/30/90 (#12, 1 wk); NYT nf 4/8/90 (#14, 1 wk), 2 wk; tot 3 wk.

Wons, Tony
Tony's Scrap Book (Reilly & Lee) PW nf 6/11/32 (#10), pk 7/9/32 (#9, 4 wk), 8 wk.

Wood, Barbara
Domina (NAL/Signet) NYT pb fic 4/15/84 (#15), pk 4/22/84 (#12, 1 wk), 3 wk; PW mm pb 4/27/84 (#15, 1 wk); tot 4 wk.

Wood, Bari
The Killing Gift (NAL/Signet) PW mm pb 2/21/77 (#13), pk 3/7/77 (#11, 1 wk), 5 wk; NYT mm pb 3/20/77 (#10, 1 wk); tot 6 wk.

The Tribe (NAL) NYT mm pb 11/29/81 (#14), pk 1/3/82 (#8, 1 wk), 6 wk; PW mm pb 12/4/81 (#13, 3 wk), 5 wk; tot 11 wk.

_____, and Jack Geasland
Twins (NAL/Signet) PW mm pb 5/22/78 (#11), pk 6/26/78 (#2, 1 wk), 14 wk; NYT mm pb 5/28/78 (#13), pk 7/23/78 (#4, 1 wk), 12 wk; tot 26 wk.

Wood, Christine
The Dark Wood (Scribner) NYT fic 9/29/46 (#16), pk 10/6/46 (#6, 3 wk), 10 wk; PW fic 10/12/46 (#9), pk 10/19/46 (#5, 1 wk), 3 wk; tot 13 wk.

Wood, Daniel
See Joseph McIntyre, et al.

Wood, Lana
Natalie: A Memoir by Her Sister (Putnam)

NYT nf 5/27/84 (#13), pk 6/17/84 (#10, 2 wk), 5 wk; PW hc nf 6/8/84 (#12), pk 6/15/84 (#5, 1 wk), 3 wk; tot 8 wk.

Wood, Michael
In Search of the Trojan War (Facts on File) NYT nf 7/6/86 (#14), pk 7/27/86 (#10, 1 wk), 9 wk.

Woodbury, George
John Goffe's Mill (Norton) NYT gen 9/19/48 (#13), pk 10/17/48 (#10, 1 wk), 7 wk.

Woodham-Smith, Cecil
Florence Nightingale (McGraw) NYT gen 3/18/51 (#14), pk 4/1/51 (#10, 4 wk), 8 wk; PW nf 4/14/51 (#10, 1 wk); tot 9 wk.

The Reason Why (McGraw) NYT gen 5/23/54 (#14), pk 6/20/54 (#6, 2 wk), 20 wk; PW nf 6/19/54 (#4, 2 wk), 4 wk; tot 24 wk.

The Great Hunger: Ireland, 1845–1849 (Harper) NYT gen 4/21/63 (#10), pk 5/19/63 (#7, 3 wk), 17 wk; PW nf 4/22/63 (#8), pk 6/10/63 (#3, 1 wk), 17 wk; tot 34 wk.

Woodhouse, Barbara
No Bad Dogs: The Woodhouse Way (Summit) PW hc nf 3/26/82 (#11), pk 4/16/82 (#2, 5 wk), 35 wk; NYT nf 4/4/82 (#13), pk 4/25/82 (#2, 4 wk), 34 wk; tot 69 wk.

Woodiwiss, Kathleen E.
The Wolf and the Dove (Avon) NYT mm pb 4/14/74 (#2, 4 wk), 12 wk.

Shanna (Avon) PW td pb 5/9/77 (#1, 27 wk), 33 wk; NYT td pb 5/15/77 (#1, 24 wk), 58 wk; PW td pb 2/20/78 (#9, 1 wk), 2 wk; PW mm pb 8/21/78 (#9, 2 wk), 4 wk; tot 97 wk.

Ashes in the Wind (Avon) PW td pb 10/15/79 (#1, 22 wk), 46 wk; NYT td pb 10/21/79 (#1, 13 wk), 55 wk; PW mm pb 4/24/81 (#15), pk 5/8/81 (#8, 1 wk), 5 wk; NYT mm pb 4/26/81 (#9), pk 5/3/81 (#4, 1 wk), 7 wk; tot 113 wk.

A Rose in Winter (Avon) NYT td pb 11/21/82 (#1, 6 wk), 29 wk; PW td pb 11/26/82 (#3), pk 12/3/82 (#1, 3 wk), 21 wk; PW mm pb 10/14/83 (#15), pk 10/21/83 (#14, 2 wk), 4 wk; NYT mm pb 10/16/83 (#15), pk 10/23/83 (#12, 1 wk), 2 wk; tot 56 wk.

Come Love a Stranger (Avon) NYT pb fic 12/16/84 (#1, 3 wk), 12 wk; PW td pb 12/21/84 (#1, 9 wk), 12 wk; PW mm pb 1/24/86 (#15, 2 wk); NYT pb fic 2/2/86 (#13, 1 wk); tot 27 wk.

So Worthy My Love (Avon) NYT pb fic 10/1/89 (#1, 4 wk), 20 wk; PW td pb 10/6/89 (#1, 4 wk), 13 wk; PW mm pb 10/12/90 (#8), pk 10/19/90 (#4, 1 wk), 8 wk; tot 41 wk.

Woodley, Richard
See Joseph D. Pistone and _____

Woods, Stuart

Deep Lie (Avon) PW mm pb 3/13/87 (#12, 1 wk), 2 wk; NYT pb fic 3/22/87 (#15), pk 3/29/87 (#14, 1 wk), 2 wk; tot 4 wk.

Under the Lake (Avon) NYT pb fic 4/17/88 (#12, 1 wk).

White Cargo (Avon) NYT pb fic 7/9/89 (#11, 3 wk), 4 wk; PW mm pb 7/14/89 (#12), pk 7/28/89 (#11, 1 wk), 3 wk; tot 7 wk.

Woodward, Bob

Wired: The Short Life and Fast Times of John Belushi (Simon & Schuster) NYT nf 6/17/84 (#3), pk 6/24/84 (#1, 4 wk), 17 wk; hc nf 6/22/84 (#2), pk 7/6/84 (#1, 4 wk), 16 wk; (Pocket) NYT pb nf 2/10/85 (#4), pk 2/17/85 (#1, 3 wk), 9 wk; PW mm pb 2/15/85 (#11), pk 2/22/85 (#4, 2 wk), 7 wk; tot 49 wk.

Veil: The Secret Wars of the CIA, 1981-1987 (Simon & Schuster) NYT nf 10/18/87 (#1, 4 wk), 12 wk; PW hc nf 10/23/87 (#1, 4 wk), 10 wk; (Pocket) NYT pb nf 9/11/88 (#7), pk 10/2/88 (#1, 1 wk), 10 wk; PW mm pb 9/23/88 (#11), pk 9/30/88 (#8, 1 wk), 3 wk; tot 35 wk.

See also Carl Bernstein and _____

_____, **and Carl Bernstein**

The Final Days (Simon & Schuster) PW hc nf 4/19/76 (#2), pk 4/26/76 (#1, 16 wk), 28 wk; NYT gen 5/2/76 (#1, 17 wk), 28 wk; (Avon) NYT mm pb 1/30/77 (#5), pk 2/6/77 (#1, 6 wk), 9 wk; PW mm pb 1/31/77 (#1, 5 wk), 11 wk; tot 76 wk.

_____, **and Scott Armstrong**

The Brethren: Inside the Supreme Court (Simon & Schuster) PW hc nf 12/24/79 (#1, 12 wk), 28 wk; NYT nf 12/30/79 (#1, 9 wk), 34 wk; (Avon) PW mm pb 1/23/81 (#5), pk 1/30/81 (#2, 2 wk), 10 wk; NYT mm pb 1/25/81 (#3), pk 2/1/81 (#2, 2 wk), 9 wk; tot 81 wk.

Woodward, Helen

See Richard Boleslavski and _____

Woodward, William E.

Meet General Grant (Liveright) PW nf 2/16/29 (#9), pk 3/9/29 (#8, 4 wk), 8 wk.

The Way Our People Lived (Liveright) NYT gen 6/25/44 (#18), pk 7/23/44 (#16, 1 wk), 2 wk.

Thomas Paine: America's Godfather (Dutton) NYT gen 8/5/45 (#9, 1 wk), 2 wk.

Wool, Robert

See Paul N. Strassels and _____

Woolf, Virginia

Flush (Harcourt) PW nf 11/11/33 (#9, 4 wk).

The Years (Harcourt) PW fic 5/8/37 (#6),

pk 7/10/37 (#1, 4 wk), 20 wk; NYT fic 6/6/37 (#3, 8 wk), 16 wk; tot 36 wk.

Three Guineas (Harcourt) NYT gen 10/9/38 (#14, 4 wk).

A Writer's Diary (Harcourt) NYT gen 4/4/54 (#16, 1 wk).

Woollcott, Alexander

While Rome Burns (Viking) PW nf 4/14/34 (#4), pk 5/12/34 (#1, 44 wk), 76 wk.

The Woollcott Reader [ed.] (Viking) PW nf 1/11/36 (#2, 8 wk), 16 wk; NYT gen 2/2/36 (#3, 4 wk); tot 20 wk.

Woollcott's Second Reader (Viking) PW nf 12/11/37 (#6), pk 1/15/38 (#3, 4 wk), 16 wk; NYT gen 12/12/37 (#5), pk 1/9/38 (#2, 8 wk), 16 wk; tot 32 wk.

Long, Long Ago (Viking) NYT gen 12/5/43 (#23), pk 1/16/44 (#4, 3 wk), 20 wk; PW nf 1/1/44 (#5), pk 1/22/44 (#4, 3 wk), 7 wk; tot 27 wk.

As You Were (Viking) NYT gen 5/2/43 (#7, 1 wk), 6 wk.

The Letters of Alexander Woollcott [ed. Beatrice Kaufman and Joseph Hennessey] (Viking) NYT gen 8/13/44 (#15), pk 8/20/44 (#9, 3 wk), 13 wk; PW nf 9/9/44 (#9, 2 wk); tot 15 wk.

Woollcott, Barbara

None but a Mule (Viking) NYT gen 11/5/44 (#19), pk 11/12/44 (#11, 1 wk), 6 wk.

Wooten, James T.

See Anthony B. Herbert and _____

Word Ministries

Prayers That Avail Much (Harrison) PW pb rel 11/9/90 (#17, 4 wk).

Worden, William L.

See Gen. William Frishe Dean and _____

Work, Milton C.

Auction Methods Up-to-Date (Winston) PW gen lit 3/26/21 (#9, 4 wk), 8 wk.

Auction Bridge of 1924 (Winston) PW gen lit 4/19/24 (#10, 4 wk).

Auction Bridge Complete (Winston) PW nf 5/15/26 (#2, 8 wk), 44 wk.

Contract Bridge for All (Winston) PW nf 8/10/29 (#10), pk 11/9/29 (#7, 4 wk), 16 wk.

Wouk, Herman

Aurora Dawn (Simon & Schuster) NYT fic 5/11/47 (#15), pk 5/25/47 (#8, 1 wk), 4 wk.

The Caine Mutiny (Doubleday) NYT fic 4/22/51 (#12), pk 8/12/51 (#1, 48 wk), 123 wk; PW fic 5/5/51 (#3), pk 9/1/51 (#1, 42 wk), 101 wk; tot 224 wk.

Marjorie Morningstar (Doubleday) NYT fic 9/18/55 (#6), pk 10/2/55 (#1, 13 wk), 37 wk; PW fic 9/24/55 (#4), pk 10/1/55 (#1, 15 wk), 30 wk; tot 67 wk.

This Is My God (Doubleday) NYT gen 10/11/59 (#11), pk 11/29/59 (#2, 6 wk), 29 wk; PW nf 10/26/59 (#7), pk 1/4/60 (#2, 1 wk), 20 wk; tot 49 wk.

Youngblood Hawke (Doubleday) NYT fic 5/27/62 (#10), pk 6/10/62 (#2, 8 wk), 26 wk; PW fic 6/4/62 (#8), pk 6/25/62 (#2, 8 wk), 27 wk; tot 53 wk.

Don't Stop the Carnival (Doubleday) NYT fic 4/4/65 (#7), pk 5/9/65 (#4, 2 wk), 26 wk; PW fic 4/5/65 (#10), pk 5/10/65 (#3, 1 wk), 30 wk; NYT pb fic 5/1/66 (#3, 4 wk), 8 wk; tot 64 wk.

The Winds of War (Little Brown) NYT fic 11/28/71 (#9), pk 1/16/72 (#1, 21 wk), 65 wk; PW fic 11/29/71 (#6), pk 1/31/72 (#1, 20 wk), 62 wk; (Warner) NYT pb fic 7/8/73 (#1, 20 wk), 28 wk; PW mm pb 2/4/83 (#13), pk 3/4/83 (#1, 2 wk), 9 wk; NYT mm pb 2/6/83 (#6), pk 2/27/83 (#1, 2 wk), 8 wk; tot 172 wk.

War and Remembrance (Little Brown) PW hc fic 10/9/78 (#12), pk 11/6/78 (#1, 17 wk), 62 wk; NYT fic 11/12/78 (#1, 9 wk), 61 wk; (Pocket) PW mm pb 5/16/80 (#9), pk 5/30/80 (#1, 2 wk), 31 wk; NYT mm pb 5/18/80 (#7), pk 5/25/80 (#1, 4 wk), 26 wk; NYT pb fic 12/4/88 (#8, 1 wk), 3 wk; tot 183 wk.

Inside, Outside (Little Brown) NYT fic 3/24/85 (#5), pk 4/21/85 (#3, 2 wk), 24 wk; PW hc fic 3/29/85 (#6), pk 4/5/85 (#3, 4 wk), 21 wk; (Avon) PW mm pb 7/4/86 (#13), pk 7/18/86 (#4, 1 wk), 10 wk; NYT pb fic 7/6/86 (#4, 2 wk), 8 wk; tot 63 wk.

Wren, Capt. Percival Christopher
Beau Geste (Stokes) PW fic 7/18/25 (#10), pk 9/18/25 (#9, 4 wk), 8 wk.

Beau Ideal (Stokes) PW fic 10/27/28 (#5, 4 wk).

Beau Sabreur (Stokes) PW fic 9/18/26 (#1, 4 wk), 20 wk.

The Dark Woman (Macrae Smith) NYT fic 3/7/43 (#15), pk 3/14/43 (#13, 1 wk), 2 wk.

Wright, Austin Tappan
Islandia (Farrar) PW fic 5/9/42 (#7), pk 6/13/42 (#3, 4 wk), 12 wk; NYT fic 8/9/42 (#13, 1 wk); tot 13 wk.

Wright, Blanche Fisher
See Anonymous (The Real Mother Goose)

Wright, Dare
The Lonely Doll (Doubleday) NYT ch bst 11/17/57 (#14, 40 wk).

A Holiday for Edith and the Bears (Doubleday) NYT ch bst 11/2/58 (#10, 40 wk).

Wright, H. Norman
Always Daddy's Girl (Regal/Gospel Light) PW hc rel 10/5/90 (#15, 4 wk), 8 wk.

Wright, Harold Bell
The Re-Creation of Brian Kent (Book Supply) PW fic 10/25/19 (#2), pk 11/1/19 (#1, 12 wk), 20 wk.

Helen of the Old House (Appleton) PW fic 11/12/21 (#2, 4 wk), 12 wk.

The Mine with the Iron Door (Appleton) PW fic 8/18/23 (#7), pk 9/15/23 (#1, 8 wk), 12 wk.

A Son of His Father (Appleton) PW fic 9/26/25 (#5, 8 wk), 12 wk.

God and the Groceryman (Appleton) PW fic 9/24/27 (#3, 4 wk), 12 wk.

Exit (Appleton) PW fic 9/20/30 (#5, 4 wk), 8 wk.

Wright, Henry M.
See George Nelson and _____

Wright, J. Patrick
On a Clear Day You Can See General Motors (J. Patrick Wright Associates/Caroline House) PW hc nf 1/11/80 (#13), pk 2/1/80 (#5, 1 wk), 17 wk; NYT nf 2/24/80 (#10, 3 wk), 9 wk; (Avon) PW mm pb 11/28/80 (#13), pk 12/5/80 (#6, 1 wk), 8 wk; tot 34 wk.

Wright, Peter, and Paul Greengrass
Spycatcher: The Candid Autobiography of a Senior Intelligence Officer (Viking) NYT nf 8/2/87 (#4), pk 8/16/87 (#1, 9 wk), 36 wk; PW hc nf 8/7/87 (#6), pk 8/21/87 (#1, 10 wk), 34 wk; (Dell) NYT pb nf 8/7/88 (#3), pk 8/14/88 (#1, 7 wk), 20 wk; PW mm pb 8/12/88 (#9), pk 9/2/88 (#3, 1 wk), 9 wk; tot 99 wk.

Wright, Richard
Native Son (Harper) PW fic 4/13/40 (#5), pk 5/11/40 (#3, 4 wk), 16 wk.

Black Boy (Harper) NYT gen 3/25/45 (#6), pk 4/29/45 (#1, 1 wk), 36 wk; PW nf 3/31/45 (#5), pk 4/28/45 (#1, 1 wk), 31 wk; tot 67 wk.

Wright, Richard
The Outsider [ed. Arnold Rampersand] (Literary Classics/Viking) NYT fic 4/12/53 (#16), pk 5/10/53 (#15, 1 wk), 2 wk.

Wright, S. Fowler
Deluge (Cosmopolitan) PW fic 4/21/28 (#6, 4 wk).

Wright, William
The Big Bonanza [as by Dan De Quille] (Knopf) NYT gen 4/27/47 (#14, 1 wk).
See also Luciano Pavarotti and _____

Wurdemann, Audrey
See Joseph Auslander and _____

Wychoff, Joan
McCall's Golden Do-It Book [adapted by Wychoff, ed. Nan Comstock] (Golden) NYT ch bst 11/12/61 (#16, 26 wk).

Wylie, Max
Trouble in the Flesh (Doubleday) NYT fic 6/28/59 (#15, 1 wk).

Wylie, Philip
A Generation of Vipers (Rinehart) NYT nf 2/14/43 (#11, 1 Wk), 6 wk.
Night Unto Night (Farrar) NYT fic 10/22/44 (#14), pk 11/12/44 (#10, 1 wk), 3 wk.
An Essay on Morals (Rinehart) NYT gen 3/16/47 (#14), pk 3/30/47 (#4, 2 wk), 16 wk; PW nf 4/5/47 (#5), pk 4/26/47 (#4, 1 wk), 5 wk; tot 21 wk.
Opus 21 (Rinehart) NYT fic 6/5/49 (#11), pk 7/17/49 (#7, 2 wk), 16 wk; PW fic 7/16/49 (#7), pk 7/23/49 (#5, 1 wk), 3 wk; tot 19 wk.
The Disappearance (Rinehart) NYT fic 1/21/51 (#13), pk 2/11/51 (#4, 2 wk), 14 wk; PW fic 2/17/51 (#9), pk 2/24/51 (#5, 3 wk), 5 wk; tot 19 wk.
Tomorrow! (Rinehart) NYT fic 2/7/54 (#13), pk 3/7/54 (#5, 3 wk), 17 wk; PW fic 2/20/54 (#5, 5 wk), 7 wk; tot 24 wk.
The Answer (Rinehart) NYT fic 7/8/56 (#15, 1 wk), 3 wk.
The Innocent Ambassadors (Rinehart) NYT gen 5/19/57 (#14), pk 6/16/57 (#2, 6 wk), 27 wk; PW nf 6/3/57 (#7), pk 6/24/57 (#1, 2 wk), 21 wk; tot 48 wk.
Triumph (Doubleday) PW fic 3/11/63 (#10), pk 4/15/63 (#7, 1 wk), 9 wk; NYT fic 4/7/63 (#7, 1 wk), 4 wk; tot 13 wk.

Wyman, David S.
The Abandonment of the Jews (Pantheon) NYT nf 3/17/85 (#14), pk 3/31/85 (#13, 1 wk), 5 wk.

Wyse, Lois
Funny, You Don't Look like a Grandmother (Crown) NYT nf 3/19/89 (#13), pk 5/14/89 (#4, 3 wk), 16 wk; PW hc nf 5/12/89 (#13), pk 6/2/89 (#5, 1 wk), 5 wk; (Avon) NYT pb nf 5/6/90 (#7), pk 5/27/90 (#1, 1 wk), 5 wk; PW td pb 5/18/90 (#10), pk 6/1/90 (#3, 1 wk), 6 wk; tot 32 wk.

Wyss, Johann
Walt Disney's Swiss Family Robinson (Golden) NYT ch bst 5/14/61 (#14, 20 wk).

Yallop, David A.
In God's Name: An Investigation Into the Murder of Pope John Paul I (Bantam) NYT nf 7/8/84 (#5), pk 7/15/84 (#2, 4 wk), 16 wk;

PW hc nf 7/13/84 (#9), pk 8/17/84 (#3, 3 wk), 16 wk; tot 32 wk.

Yalom, Irvin D.
Love's Executioner (Basic) NYT nf 10/1/89 (#15), pk 10/29/89 (#13, 1 wk), 7 wk.

Yancey, Philip
Disappointment with God (Zondervan) PW hc rel 11/9/90 (#20, 4 wk), 8 wk.

Yardley, Herbert O.
The American Black Chamber (Bobbs Merrill) PW nf 8/15/31 (#10, 4 wk).

Yates, Emma Hayden
70 Miles from a Lemon (Houghton) NYT gen 5/4/47 (#16), pk 5/25/47 (#15, 1 wk), 2 wk.

Yeager, Gen. Chuck, and Charles Leerhsen
Press On! Further Adventures in the Good Life (Bantam) NYT nf 10/2/88 (#8), pk 10/23/88 (#3, 1 wk), 10 wk; PW hc nf 10/7/88 (#13), pk 10/21/88 (#11, 1 wk), 4 wk; tot 14 wk.

_____, and Leo Janos
Yeager: An Autobiography (Bantam) NYT nf 7/14/85 (#2), pk 7/21/85 (#1, 18 wk), 51 wk; PW hc nf 7/19/85 (#4), pk 7/26/85 (#1, 14 wk), 42 wk; NYT pb nf 9/7/86 (#3), pk 9/14/86 (#1, 5 wk), 11 wk; PW mm pb 9/19/86 (#5, 1 wk), 4 wk; tot 108 wk.

Yeats-Brown, Maj. Francis
Lives of a Bengal Lancer (Viking) PW nf 12/20/30 (#5), pk 2/21/31 (#4, 4 wk), 16 wk.
Lancer at Large (Viking) NYT nf 3/7/37 (#4, 4 wk).

Yee, Chiang
The Silent Traveller in Boston (Norton) NYT gen 1/10/60 (#11), pk 1/17/60 (#10, 1 wk), 4 wk.
The Silent Traveller in San Francisco (Norton) PW nf 11/23/64 (#13), pk 12/14/64 (#9, 2 wk), 5 wk.

Yerby, Frank Garvin
The Foxes of Harrow (Dial) NYT fic 2/24/46 (#16), pk 3/31/46 (#5, 1 wk), 45 wk; PW fic 4/6/46 (#9), pk 11/16/46 (#3, 1 wk), 10 wk; tot 55 wk.
The Vixens (Dial) NYT fic 5/11/47 (#7), pk 5/25/47 (#2, 4 wk), 29 wk; PW fic 5/24/47 (#5), pk 5/31/47 (#2, 4 wk), 19 wk; tot 48 wk.
The Golden Hawk (Dial) NYT fic 5/9/48 (#8), pk 6/6/48 (#2, 2 wk), 24 wk; PW fic 5/15/48 (#8), pk 5/29/48 (#2, 4 wk), 16 wk; tot 40 wk.
Pride's Castle (Dial) NYT fic 5/22/49 (#10), pk 6/12/49 (#3, 2 wk), 22 wk; PW fic

6/4/49 (#4), pk 7/9/49 (#2, 1 wk), 16 wk; tot 38 wk.

Floodtide (Dial) NYT fic 9/3/50 (#16), pk 10/1/50 (#3, 3 wk), 20 wk; PW fic 9/23/50 (#2), pk 10/7/50 (#1, 1 wk), 10 wk; tot 30 wk.

A Woman Called Fancy (Dial) NYT fic 5/27/51 (#10), pk 7/22/51 (#4, 3 wk), 22 wk; PW fic 6/9/51 (#7), pk 7/7/51 (#3, 1 wk), 13 wk; tot 35 wk.

The Saracen Blade (Dial) NYT fic 4/27/52 (#12), pk 5/18/52 (#4, 4 wk), 22 wk; PW fic 5/17/52 (#6), pk 6/17/52 (#4, 1 wk), 7 wk; tot 29 wk.

The Devil's Laughter (Dial NYT fic 10/18/53 (#10), pk 11/29/53 (#9, 1 wk), 10 wk; PW fic 11/14/53 (#7, 1 wk); tot 11 wk.

Benton's Row (Dial) NYT fic 12/19/54 (#11), pk 1/2/55 (#9, 3 wk), 14 wk; PW fic 1/15/55 (#9, 1 wk); tot 15 wk.

The Treasure of Pleasant Valley (Dial) NYT fic 11/6/55 (#16, 1 wk).

Captain Rebel (Dial) NYT fic 10/14/56 (#14), pk 10/21/56 (#11, 1 wk), 3 wk; PW fic 11/19/56 (#9, 1 wk); tot 4 wk.

Fairoaks (Dial) NYT fic 9/22/57 (#13), pk 10/13/57 (#9, 1 wk), 11 wk; PW fic 10/21/57 (#10), pk 11/18/57 (#9, 1 wk), 2 wk; tot 13 wk.

The Serpent and the Staff (Dial) NYT fic 10/26/58 (#13, 1 wk), 2 wk.

Jarret's Jade (Dial) NYT fic 2/7/60 (#16, 1 wk).

Yergin, Daniel
See Roger Stobaugh and _____

Yolen, Jane
The Devil's Arithmetic (Puffin) PW ch yn ad 11/30/90 (#5, 4 wk).

Yorke, Susan
The Widow (Harcourt) NYT fic 10/22/50 (#16), pk 11/5/50 (#6, 1 wk), 12 wk.

Yorkey, Mike
The Focus on the Family Guide to Growing a Healthy Home [ed.] (Wolgemuth & Hyatt) PW hc rel 11/9/90 (#19, 4 wk).

Young, Agatha
Light in the Sky (Random) NYT fic 8/29/48 (#14, 1 wk).

Young, Arthur, & Co.
The Arthur Young Tax Guide 1985 [ed. Peter W. Bernstein] (Ballantine) NYT msc pb 2/3/85 (#4), pk 3/3/85 (#2, 2 wk), 13 wk; PW td pb 2/8/85 (#4), pk 3/1/85 (#1, 4 wk), 11 wk; tot 24 wk.

The Arthur Young Tax Guide 1986 [ed. Peter W. Bernstein] (Ballantine) NYT msc pb 1/19/86 (#7), pk 2/2/86 (#1, 7 wk), 16 wk; PW td pb 1/31/86 (#8), pk 2/7/86 (#2, 4 wk), 15 wk; tot 31 wk.

The Arthur Young Tax Guide 1987 [ed. Peter W. Bernstein] (Ballantine) NYT msc pb 1/25/87 (#10), pk 2/15/87 (#3, 1 wk), 11 wk; PW td pb 1/30/87 (#3), pk 2/27/87 (#1, 2 wk), 10 wk; tot 21 wk.

The Arthur Young Tax Guide 1988 [ed. Peter W. Bernstein] (Ballantine) PW td pb 1/22/88 (#10), pk 2/19/88 (#1, 2 wk), 12 wk; NYT msc pb 2/7/88 (#1, 6 wk), 7 wk; tot 19 wk.

The Arthur Young Tax Guide 1989 [ed. Peter W. Bernstein] (Ballantine) PW td pb 1/27/89 (#7), pk 2/24/89 (#1, 1 wk), 12 wk; NYT msc pb 2/5/89 (#3), pk 2/12/89 (#2, 3 wk), 6 wk; tot 18 wk.

The Arthur Young Tax Guide 1990 [ed. Peter W. Bernstein] (Ballantine) PW td pb 1/26/90 (#9), pk 3/2/90 (#4, 1 wk), 8 wk; NYT msc pb 2/4/90 (#5, 3 wk); tot 11 wk.

Young, Desmond
Rommel the Desert Fox (Harper) NYT gen 2/4/51 (#6), pk 3/11/51 (#4, 8 wk), 26 wk; PW nf 2/17/51 (#7), pk 3/10/51 (#2, 2 wk), 17 wk; tot 43 wk.

Young, Ed
Lon Po Po (Philomel) PW ch pc 8/31/90 (#6, 4 wk), 8 wk.

Young, Emily Hilda
Celia (Harcourt) NYT fic 4/3/38 (#10, 4 wk).

Young, Francis Brett
Mr. and Mrs. Pennington (Harper) PW fic 2/13/32 (#3, 8 wk), 12 wk.

White Ladies (Harper) NYT fic 10/6/35 (#6, 4 wk), 8 wk.

Far Forest (Reynal & Hitchcock) NYT fic 10/4/36 (#8, 4 wk).

They Seek a Country (Reynal & Hitchcock) PW fic 12/11/37 (#10, 4 wk).

Dr. Bradley Remembers (Reynal & Hitchcock) NYT fic 12/4/38 (#9, 4 wk).

The City of Gold (Reynal & Hitchcock) NYT fic 11/5/39 (#6, 4 wk).

Young, Perry Deane
See David Kopay and _____

Young, Stark
So Red the Rose (Scribner) PW fic 9/15/34 (#2), pk 10/13/34 (#1, 12 wk), 32 wk.

Young, Vash
A Fortune to Share (Bobbs Merrill) PW nf 12/19/31 (#7), pk 4/23/32 (#3, 12 wk), 44 wk.

Let's Start Over Again (Bobbs Merrill) PW nf 10/15/32 (#6, 8 wk), 12 wk.

Yourcenar, Marguerite
Hadrian's Memoirs (Farrar) NYT fic 12/12/

54 (#12), pk 1/30/55 (#6, 5 wk), 20 wk; PW
fic 1/29/55 (#5, 1 wk), 6 wk; tot 26 wk.
   Coup de Grace [trans. Grace Frick] (Farrar) NYT fic 8/11/57 (#16, 1 wk).

Yutang, Lin
   My Country and My People (Reynal &
Hitchcock) NYT nf 11/3/35 (#10, 4 wk);
NYT gen 2/2/36 (#8, 4 wk); PW nf 4/11/36
(#10, 4 wk); tot 12 wk.
   The Importance of Living (Reynal & Hitchcock) NYT gen 1/9/38 (#10), pk 4/3/38 (#1,
16 wk), 56 wk; PW nf 1/15/38 (#6), pk
3/12/38 (#1, 28 wk), 60 wk; tot 116 wk.
   Moment in Peking (John Day) PW fic
12/16/39 (#7), pk 1/13/40 (#3, 4 wk), 20 wk;
NYT fic 1/7/40 (#1, 4 wk); tot 24 wk.
   With Love and Irony (John Day) PW nf
1/11/41 (#8), pk 2/8/41 (#7, 4 wk), 8 wk.
   A Leaf in the Storm (John Day) PW fic
1/17/42 (#7, 8 wk).
   The Wisdom of China and India [ed.] (Random) NYT nf 1/31/43 (#15), pk 2/21/43 (#8,
2 wk), 8 wk; PW nf 3/13/43 (#10, 4 wk); tot
12 wk.
   Between Tears and Laughter (John Day)
NYT gen 8/15/43 (#12), pk 11/7/43 (#5, 1
wk), 24 wk; PW nf 9/11/43 (#6), pk 10/30/43
(#5, 1 wk), 7 wk; tot 31 wk.
   The Vigil of a Nation (John Day) NYT gen
2/18/45 (#8), pk 3/18/45 (#6, 1 wk), 9 wk;
PW nf 4/7/45 (#10, 1 wk); tot 10 wk.
   The Vermilion Gate (John Day) NYT fic
8/9/53 (#15), pk 8/16/53 (#12, 2 wk), 5 wk.

Zacharias, Adm. Ellis M.
   Secret Missions (Putnam) NYT gen 1/26/
47 (#14), pk 3/9/47 (#11, 2 wk), 7 wk.
   Behind Closed Doors (Putnam) NYT gen
8/13/50 (#9, 6 wk), 10 wk; PW nf 9/16/50
(#8), pk 9/30/50 (#4, 1 wk), 3 wk; tot 13 wk.

Zara, Louis
   Against This Rock (Creative Age) NYT fic
11/7/43 (#11, 1 wk).

Zaroulis, Nancy
   The Last Waltz (Zebra) NYT pb fic 5/25/
86 (#10, 1 wk), 4 wk; PW mm pb 6/27/86
(#15, 1 wk); tot 5 wk.

Zelinsky, Paul O.
   The Wheels on the Bus [adapted/illus.]
(Dutton) PW ch pic 11/30/90 (#8, 4 wk), 8 wk.

Zevin, Benjamin David
   See Franklin D. Roosevelt and _____

Ziegel, Vic, and Lewis Grossberger
   The Non-Runner's Book (Macmillan) PW
td pb 12/11/78 (#7), pk 3/12/79 (#5, 1 wk), 15
wk; NYT td pb 12/24/78 (#10), pk 2/4/79
(#5, 1 wk), 21 wk; tot 36 wk.

Ziegler, Philip
   Mountbatten (Knopf) NYT nf 6/2/85
(#15), pk 6/9/85 (#6, 1 wk), 12 wk; PW hc nf
6/28/85 (#14), pk 7/5/85 (#9, 1 wk), 7 wk; tot
19 wk.

Ziff, William Bernard
   The Coming Battle of Germany (Duell
Sloan & Pearce) NYT nf 8/23/42 (#14), pk
9/13/42 (#1, 4 wk), 16 wk; PW nf 8/29/42
(#2), pk 9/19/42 (#1, 3 wk), 9 wk; tot 25 wk.
   The Gentlemen Talk of Peace (Macmillan)
NYT gen 2/11/45 (#15), pk 2/25/45 (#10, 1
wk), 9 wk.

Zigarmi, Patricia
   See Kenneth Blanchard and _____

Ziglar, Zig
   Zig Ziglar's Secrets of Closing the Sale (Revell) PW hc nf 8/17/84 (#9), pk 9/14/84 (#4,
1 wk), 11 wk; NYT msc 8/19/84 (#4, 3 wk),
6 wk; tot 17 wk.

Zilaby, Lajos
   The Dukays (Prentice Hall) NYT fic 2/6/
49 (#14), pk 2/27/49 (#5, 1 wk), 18 wk; PW
fic 3/12/49 (#5, 3 wk), 6 wk; tot 24 wk.

Zimbardo, Philip G.
   Shyness: What It Is, What to Do About It (Addison Wesley) PW td pb 1/16/78 (#8, 8 wk).

Zimmer, Norma
   Norma (Worldwide) NYT td pb 10/30/77
(#8, 1 wk), 3 wk.

Zinsser, Hans
   Rats, Lice and History (Little Brown) PW
nf 3/16/35 (#6), pk 4/13/35 (#3, 4 wk), 24 wk.
   As I Remember Him (Little Brown) PW nf
8/10/40 (#4, 8 wk), 16 wk.

Zolotow, Maurice
   *Stagestruck: The Romance of Alfred Lunt and
Lynn Fontanne* (Harcourt) NYT gen 3/21/65
(#9), pk 4/18/65 (#8, 2 wk), 7 wk; PW nf
3/22/65 (#9, 3 wk), 4 wk; tot 11 wk.

Zweig, Arnold
   The Case of Sergeant Grischa (Viking) PW
fic 2/16/29 (#2, 4 wk), 12 wk.

Zweig, Stefan
   Marie Antoinette (Viking) PW nf 5/13/33
(#4), pk 6/10/33 (#1, 20 wk), 40 wk.
   Mary, Queen of Scotland and the Isles (Viking) NYT nf 10/6/35 (#2, 4 wk), 8 wk; PW
nf 10/12/35 (#2, 4 wk), 12 wk; tot 20 wk.
   Balzac (Viking) NYT gen 12/22/46 (#8),
pk 1/12/47 (#6, 3 wk), 12 wk; PW nf 2/8/47
(#5, 2 wk); tot 14 wk.

Zwick, David R.
   See Mark J. Green, et al.

APPENDIX 1:
AUTHORS WITH 10 OR
MORE LISTED BOOKS
(Numerically Ranked)

L'Amour, Louis 30
Holt, Victoria 28
Caldwell, Taylor 27
Davis, Jim 27
Norris, Kathleen 26
King, Stephen 26
Buck, Pearl S. 25
Ross, Dana Fuller 24
Anthony, Piers 23
MacLean, Alistair 22
Oppenheim, E. Phillips 22
Sanders, Lawrence 22
Steel, Danielle 22
Geisel, Theodor (Dr. Seuss) 21
Lindsey, Johanna 21
Michener, James A. 21
O'Hara, John 21
Wallace, Irving 21
Deeping, Warwick 20
Grey, Zane 20
Lincoln, Joseph C. 20
MacInnes, Helen 20
Walpole, Hugh 20
Keyes, Frances Parkinson 19
Whitney, Phylis A. 19
Bromfield, Louis 18
Gunther, John 18
du Maurier, Daphne 17
Rinehart, Mary Roberts 17

Robbins, Harold 17
Updike, John 17
Christie, Agatha 16
Deighton, Len 16
Lewis, Sinclair 16
Mason, F. van Wyck 16
Shute, Nevil (Nevil Shute Norway) 16
Stone, Irving 16
Costain, Thomas B. 15
Cronin, A.J. 15
Dailey, Janet 15
Deveraux, Jude 15
Goudge, Elizabeth 15
Maugham, W. Somerset 15
Sabatini, Rafael 15
Forester, C.S. 14
Larson, Gary 14
Ludlum, Robert 14
Saul, John 14
Slaughter, Frank G. 14
Steinbeck, John 14
Thurber, James 14
Yerby, Frank 14
Anglund, Joan Walsh 13
Bailey, Temple 13
Chase, Stuart 13
de la Roche, Mazo 13
Gardner, John 13

Hemingway, Ernest 13
Marquand, John P. 13
Stewart, Mary 13
Andrews, V.C. 12
Baldwin, Faith 12
Buckley, William F., Jr. 12
Fast, Howard 12
Ferber, Edna 12
Francis, Dick 12
Gibbs, Philip Hamilton 12
Hubbard, L. Ron 12
Jakes, John 12
Kane, Harnett Thomas 12
Michaels, Fern 12
Matthews, Patricia 12
Sherwood, Valerie 12
Trudeau, Garry B. 12
Wambaugh, Joseph 12
West, Morris 12
White, E.B. 12
Auchincloss, Louis 11
Bemelmans, Ludwig 11
Churchill, Winston S. 11
Culbertson, Ely 11
Douglas, Lloyd Cassel 11
Godden, Rumer 11
Greele, Andrew M. 11
Greeney, Graham 11
Higgins, Jack 11

APPENDIX 2:
BOOKS LISTED FOR
100 WEEKS OR MORE
(Numerically Ranked)

If a book appeared on both the *NYT* and the *PW* lists, the weeks on each list have been added together (example: 6 weeks on *NYT* list + 5 weeks on *PW* list = 11 weeks).

The Joy of Sex (Comfort) 753
The Road Less Traveled (Peck) 660
Charlotte's Web (White) 489
Winnie-The-Pooh (Milne) 415
Richard Scarry's Best Word Book Ever (Scarry) 378
Color Me Beautiful (Jackson) 356
The Power of Positive Thinking (Peale) 353
The One Minute Manager (Blanchard/ Johnson) 344
In Search of Excellence (Peters/Waterman) 322
Peace of Mind (Liebman) 320
All I Really Need to Know I Learned in Kindergarten (Fulghum) 298
Charlie and the Chocolate Factory (Dahl) 296
The Robe (Douglas) 292
The Little Prince (de Saint-Exupery) 291
Profiles in Courage (Kennedy) 279
A Man Called Peter (Marshall) 279
Love, Medicine & Miracles (Siegel) 277
Living, Loving & Learning (Buscaglia) 275
The Velveteen Rabbit (Williams) 273
A Brief History of Time (Hawking) 266

Nothing Down (Allen) 263
Codependent No More (Beattie) 260
The Hunt for Red October (Clancy) 259
The Complete Scarsdale Medical Diet (Tarnower/Baker) 254
Dianetics: The Modern Science of Mental Health (Hubbard) 246
Games People Play (Berne) 240
A Light in the Attic (Silverstein) 227
Your Erroneous Zones (Dyer) 227
The Caine Mutiny (Wouk) 224
Women Who Love Too Much (Norwood) 219
Jane Fonda's Workout Book (Fonda) 218
Garfield at Large (Davis) 215
The Shell Seekers (Pilcher) 210
Our Bodies, Our Selves (Boston Women's Health Collective) 209
Passages: The Predictable Crises of Adult Life (Sheehy) 204
The Thorn Birds (McCullough) 204
Webster's Ninth New Collegiate Dictionary (Anonymous) 202
Presumed Innocent (Turow) 200
Fatherhood (Cosby) 198

APPENDIX 3:
AUTHORS LISTED FOR
100 WEEKS OR MORE
(Numerically Ranked)

If a book appeared on both the *NYT* and the *PW* lists, the weeks on each list have been added together (example: 6 weeks on *NYT* list + 5 weeks on *PW* list = 11 weeks).

King, Stephen 1,731
Michener, James A. 1,652
Geisel, Theodor 1,344
Steel, Danielle 1,295
Caldwell, Taylor 1,172
Davis, Jim 1,029
Ludlum, Robert 981
Uris, Leon 919
Wallace, Irving 892
Wouk, Herman 879
Sheldon, Sidney 872
White, Elwyn Brooks 820
Comfort, Alex 810
Clancy, Tom 806
Robbins, Harold 804
Stone, Irving 749
MacInnes, Helen 742
Sanders, Lawrence 732
Anglund, Joan Walsh 714
Peck, M. Scott, M.D. 711
Le Carré, John 684
Buscaglia, Leo 673
Follett, Ken 653
Herriot, James 652
Hailey, Arthur 650

Gunther, John 643
L'Amour, Louis 630
Douglas, Lloyd Cassel 626
Stewart, Mary 621
Milne, Alan Alexander 618
Wambaugh, Joseph 611
Marshall, Catherine Wood 605
du Maurier, Dame Daphne 600
Bach, Richard 576
Steinbeck, John 575
Bombeck, Erma 575
Larson, Gary 558
Keyes, Frances Parkinson 551
Peale, Norman Vincent 536
Drury, Allen 528
Cronin, A.J. 527
Forsyth, Frederick 515
Vidal, Gore 514
Buck, Pearl S. 513
White, Theodore Harold 511
Costain, Thomas Bertram 509

Peters, Thomas J. 498
Bolles, Richard Nelson 492
Shaw, Irwin 487
Holt, Victoria 478
O'Hara, John 473
Lindbergh, Anne Morrow 472
Krantz, Judith 471
Scarry, Richard 454
Fast, Howard 450
MacDonald, John D. 449
Silverstein, Shel 437
Plain, Belva 430
Auel, Jean M. 430
Jakes, John 429
Dahl, Roald 428
Tuchman, Barbara Wertheim 426
West, Morris L. 423
Susann, Jacqueline 421
Johnson, Spencer 417
Watterson, Bill 415
Updike, John 409
McCullough, Colleen 406
Clavell, James 405

APPENDIX 4:
COMPLETE LIST
OF AUTHORS AND
THEIR TOTAL WEEKS
(Alphabetically Arranged)

If a book appeared on both the *NYT* and the *PW* lists, the weeks on each list have been added together (example: 6 weeks on *NYT* list + 5 weeks on *PW* list = 11 weeks).

Aaron, David 8
Abbe, John 60
Abbe, Patience 64
Abbe, Richard 60
Abbey, Lynn 1
Abbott, Jack Henry 4
Abbott, Jane 12
Abdul-Jabbar, Kareem 11
Abend, Hallett Edward 1
Abingdon, Alexander [pseud.] 48
Abodaher, David 30
Abravanel, Dr. Elliot D. 21
Abt, Isaac A. 4
Aburdene, Patricia 81
Accoce, Pierre 1
Acheson, Dean Gooderham 69
Ackerman, Diane 11
Adamic, Louis 54
Adams, Adrienne 26
Adams, Alice 33
Adams, Ansel Easton 14

Adams, Charles T. 12
Adams, Douglas 223
Adams, Franklin Pierce 1
Adams, Henry 32
Adams, James Truslow 157
Adams, Ramon Frederick 2
Adams, Richard 242
Adams, Samuel Hopkins 70
Adams, Sherman 17
Adamski, George 13
Adamson, Joy 132
Adler, Bill 176
Adler, Mortimer J. 29
Adler, Polly 47
Agar, Herbert 12
Agee, James 16
Agee, Philip 3
Agnew, Spiro T. 12
Agutter, Jenny [reader] 8
Ahlberg, Allan 4
Ahlberg, Janet 4
Aiken, Joan 19
Albert, Dora 1

Albom, Mitch 12
Albrand, Martha 1
Alcott, Carroll 1
Aldington, Richard 8
Aldis, Dorothy 4
Aldrich, Bess Streeter 106
Aldrich, Richard 56
Aldridge, James 20
Aleichem, Sholom [pseud.] 8
Alexander, Dan Dale 77
Alexander, Grand Duke 32
Alexander, Lloyd 19
Alexander, Roy 1
Alexander, Shana 30
Algren, Nelson 37
Alinder, Mary Street 11
Alinsky, Saul David 8
Allee, Marjorie 4
Alleg, Henri 3
Allen, C.M. 4
Allen, Charlotte Vale 2
Allen, Fred 61

352

Allen, Frederick Lewis 132
Allen, George Edward 8
Allen, Hervey 194
Allen, Ida Cogswell Bailey
1
Allen, Robert G. 344
Allen, Col. Robert Sharon
101
Allen, Woody 74
Allende, Isabel 4
Alliluyeva, Svetlana 29
Allison, Linda 46
Alsberg, Henry Garfield 1
Alsop, Joseph W., Jr. 16
Alsop, Stewart 13
Alther, Lisa 68
Alvarez, Alfred 4
Alvin, Julius 20
Amado, Jorge 6
Ambler, Eric 35
Ames, Louise Bates 29
Amis, Martin 5
Amory, Cleveland 228
Andersen, Hans Christian
26
Anderson, Dave 99
Anderson, Erica 7
Anderson, Jack 15
Anderson, Louis 2
Anderson, Peggy 66
Anderson, Sparky 1
Anderson, Cmdr. William
R. 28
Andrews, Bert 1
Andrews, Lynn V. 6
Andrews, M.P. 2
Andrews, Robert Hardy 4
Andrews, Roy Chapman 47
Andrews, V.C. 345
Andrezel, Pierre 7
Angas, Lawrence 4
Angell, Roger 19
Angelou, Maya 16
Anger, Kenneth 5
Angle, Paul M. 21
Anglund, Joan Walsh 714
Angly, Edward 16
Anno, Mitsumasa 46
Anson, Jay 166
Anthony, Katharine 8
Anthony, Piers 145
Arcalli, Franco 8
Arce, Hector 5
Archambault, John 8
Archbold, Rick 14
Archer, Jeffrey 316
Archibald, Norman 4
Arden, Leslie 3
Ardmore, Jane Kesner 25

Ardrey, Robert 10
Aricha, Amos 4
Arkell, Reginald 26
Arkwright, Frank 4
Arlen, Michael 24
Armbrister, Trevor 6
Armer, Laura A. 16
Armitage, Flora 1
Armour, Tommy 40
Armstrong, Hamilton Fish
17
Armstrong, Margaret 36
Armstrong, Scott 81
Arnall, Ellis Gibbs 4
Arnhym, Albert A. 6
Arno, Peter 7
Arnold, Elliott 56
Arnold, Henry Harley 2
Arnold, Thurman W. 24
Arnow, Harriette Louisa
Simpson 54
Aronson, Harvey 45
Arpel, Adrien 68
Arquette, Cliff 23
Arthur Young & Co. 124
Asbell, Bernard 1
Asbury, Herbert 12
Asch, Sholem 264
Ash, Mary Kay 38
Ashe, Penelope 31
Asher, Cash 7
Ashford, Daisy 12
Ashmore, Harry S. 1
Ashton, Helen 1
Ashton-Warner, Sylvia 8
Asimov, Isaac 219
Asprin, Robert Lynn 1
Asquith, Margot 16
Astaire, Fred 2
Astor, Mary 7
Atherton, Gertrude Frank-
lin Horn 62
Athos, Anthony G. 3
Atkins, Dr. Robert C. 137
Atkinson, Oriana Torrey 2
Atkinson, Rick 4
Attenborough, David 24
Atwood, Margaret 118
Auchincloss, Louis 289
Audubon, John James 12
Auel, Jean M. 430
Auletta, Ken 19
Auslander, Joseph 2
Austin, Margot 40
Austin, Nancy K. 73
Ausubel, Nathan 8
Averbuch, Bernard 13
Awlinson, Richard 1
Aydelotte, Dora 4

Ayer, Margaret Hubbard 1
Aynesworth, Hugh 2
Ayres, Ruby Mildred 12

Bacall, Lauren 86
Bach, Richard 576
Bach, Steven 7
Bacheller, Irving 32
Bacher, June Masters 4
Baez, Joan 5
Bagni, Gwen 8
Bagnold, Enid 25
Baigent, Michael 25
Bailey, Charles Waldo, III
138
Bailey, Covert 47
Bailey, F. Lee 51
Bailey, Henry Christopher
4
Bailey, Temple 127
Bainbridge, John 6
Bainton, Roland Herbert 1
Bair, Dierdre 2
Baker, Bobby 4
Baker, Carlos 45
Baker, Dorothy Dodds 15
Baker, Sgt. George 1
Baker, Louise Maxwell 9
Baker, Mark 14
Baker, Ray Stannard 1
Baker, Russell 164
Baker, Samm Sinclair 359
Baker, Trudy 17
Baldrige, Letitia 23
Baldwin, Faith 48
Baldwin, Hanson Weight-
man 11
Baldwin, James 151
Baldwin, Monica 29
Ball, Walter S. 4
Ballantine, Betty [editor] 3
Ballard, J.G. 1
Ballard, Robert D. 14
Balsan, Consuelo Vanderbilt
32
Balsiger, David 21
Bamford, James 6
Bandy, Way 32
Bankhead, Tallulah 45
Banks, Ernest 4
Banks, Lynne Reid 8
Banner, Angela 26
Banning, Margaret Culking
4
Barber, Rowland 1
Barbour, Thomas 2
Bard, Mary 10
Barker, Clive 32
Barker, Shirley 8

TITLE INDEX

383